T0180305

Lecture Notes in Artificial Intelligence 11906

Subseries of Lecture Notes in Computer Science

Ulf Brefeld · Elisa Fromont ·
Andreas Hotho · Arno Knobbe ·
Marloes Maathuis · Céline Robardet (Eds.)

Machine Learning and Knowledge Discovery in Databases

European Conference, ECML PKDD 2019
Würzburg, Germany, September 16–20, 2019
Proceedings, Part I

 Springer

Editors
Ulf Brefeld
Leuphana University
Lüneburg, Germany

Elisa Fromont 🆔
IRISA/Inria
Rennes, France

Andreas Hotho 🆔
University of Würzburg
Würzburg, Germany

Arno Knobbe 🆔
Leiden University
Leiden, the Netherlands

Marloes Maathuis 🆔
ETH Zurich
Zurich, Switzerland

Céline Robardet 🆔
Institut National des Sciences Appliquées
Villeurbanne, France

ISSN 0302-9743   ISSN 1611-3349   (electronic)
Lecture Notes in Artificial Intelligence
ISBN 978-3-030-46149-2   ISBN 978-3-030-46150-8   (eBook)
https://doi.org/10.1007/978-3-030-46150-8

LNCS Sublibrary: SL7 – Artificial Intelligence

This Springer imprint is published by the registered company Springer Nature Switzerland AG
The registered company address is: Gewerbestrasse 11, 6330 Cham, Switzerland

Preface

We are delighted to introduce the proceedings of the 2019 edition of the European Conference on Machine Learning and Principles and Practice of Knowledge Discovery in Databases (ECML PKDD 2019). ECML PKDD is an annual conference that provides an international forum for the latest research in all areas related to machine learning and knowledge discovery in databases, including innovative applications. It is the premier European machine learning and data mining conference and builds upon a very successful series of ECML PKDD conferences.

ECML PKDD 2019 was held in Würzburg, Germany, during September 16–20, 2019. The conference attracted over 830 participants from 48 countries. It also received substantial attention from industry, both through sponsorship and participation at the conference.

The main conference program consisted of presentations and posters of 130 accepted papers and 5 keynote talks by the following distinguished speakers: Sumit Gulwani (Microsoft Research), Aude Billard (EPFL), Indrė Žliobaitė (University of Helsinki), Maria Florina Balcan (Carnegie Mellon University), and Tinne Tuytelaars (KU Leuven). In addition, there were 24 workshops, 8 tutorials, and 4 discovery challenges.

Papers were organized in three different tracks:

- Research Track: research or methodology papers from all areas in machine learning, knowledge discovery, and data mining
- Applied Data Science Track: papers on novel applications of machine learning, data mining, and knowledge discovery to solve real-world use cases, thereby bridging the gap between practice and current theory
- Journal Track: papers that were published in special issues of the journals *Machine Learning* and *Data Mining and Knowledge Discovery*

We received a record number of 733 submissions for the Research and Applied Data Science Tracks combined. We accepted 130 (18%) of these: 102 papers in the Research Track and 28 papers in the Applied Data Science Track. In addition, there were 32 papers from the Journal Track. All in all, the high-quality submissions allowed us to put together a very rich and exciting program.

For 60% of accepted Research Track and Applied Data Science Track papers, accompanying software and/or data were made available. These papers are flagged as Reproducible Research (RR) papers in the proceedings. RR flags, in use since 2016 in the ECML PKDD conference series, underline the importance given to RR in our community.

The Awards Committee selected research papers that were considered to be of exceptional quality and worthy of special recognition:

- Data Mining Best Student Paper Award: "FastPoint: Scalable Deep Point Processes" by Ali Caner Türkmen, Yuyang Wang, and Alexander J. Smola

- Machine Learning Best Student Paper Award: "Agnostic feature selection" by Guillaume Doquet and Michèle Sebag
- Test of Time Award for highest impact paper from ECML PKDD 2009: "Classifier Chains for Multi-label Classification" by Jesse Read, Bernhard Pfahringer, Geoff Holmes, and Eibe Frank

Besides the strong scientific program, ECML PKDD 2019 offered many opportunities to socialize and to get to know Würzburg. We mention the opening ceremony at the Neubau Church, the opening reception at the Residence Palace, the boat trip from Veitshöchheim to Würzburg, the gala dinner at the Congress Center, the poster session at the New University, and the poster session at the Residence Palace Wine Cellar. There were also social events for subgroups of participants, such as the PhD Forum, in which PhD students interacted with their peers and received constructive feedback on their research progress, and the Women in Science Lunch, in which junior and senior women met and discussed challenges and opportunities for women in science and technology.

We would like to thank all participants, authors, reviewers, area chairs, and organizers of workshops and tutorials for their contributions that helped make ECML PKDD 2019 a great success. Special thanks go to the University of Würzburg, especially to Lena Hettinger and the student volunteers, who did an amazing job. We would also like to thank the ECML PKDD Steering Committee and all sponsors. Finally, we thank Springer and Microsoft for their continuous support with the proceedings and the conference software.

February 2020

Ulf Brefeld
Elisa Fromont
Andreas Hotho
Arno Knobbe
Marloes Maathuis
Céline Robardet

Organization

General Chairs

Élisa Fromont   University of Rennes 1, France
Arno Knobbe   Leiden University, the Netherlands

Program Chairs

Ulf Brefeld   Leuphana University of Lüneburg, Germany
Andreas Hotho   University of Würzburg, Germany
Marloes Maathuis   ETH Zürich, Switzerland
Céline Robardet   INSA-Lyon, France

Journal Track Chairs

Karsten Borgwardt   ETH Zürich, Switzerland
Po-Ling Loh   University of Wisconsin, USA
Evimaria Terzi   Boston University, USA
Antti Ukkonen   University of Helsinki, Finland

Local Chairs

Lena Hettinger   University of Würzburg, Germany
Andreas Hotho   University of Würzburg, Germany
Kristof Korwisi   University of Würzburg, Germany
Marc Erich Latoschik   University of Würzburg, Germany

Proceedings Chairs

Xin Du   Technische Universiteit Eindhoven, the Netherlands
Wouter Duivesteijn   Technische Universiteit Eindhoven, the Netherlands
Sibylle Hess   Technische Universiteit Eindhoven, the Netherlands

Discovery Challenge Chairs

Sergio Escalera   University of Barcelona, Spain
Isabelle Guyon   Paris-Sud University, France

Workshop and Tutorial Chairs

Peggy Cellier   INSA Rennes, France
Kurt Driessens   Maastricht University, the Netherlands

Demonstration Chairs

Martin Atzmüller   Tilburg University, the Netherlands
Emilie Morvant   University of Saint-Etienne, France

PhD Forum Chairs

Tassadit Bouadi   University of Rennes 1, France
Tias Guns   Vrije Universiteit Bruxelles, Belgium

Production, Publicity and Public Relations Chairs

Parisa Kordjamshidi   Tulane University and Florida IHMC, USA
Albrecht Zimmermann   Université de Caen Normandie, France

Awards Committee

Katharina Morik   TU Dortmund, Germany
Geoff Webb   Monash University, Australia

Sponsorship Chairs

Albert Bifet   Télécom ParisTech, France
Heike Trautmann   University of Münster, Germany

Web Chairs

Florian Lautenschlager   University of Würzburg, Germany
Vanessa Breitenbach   University of Würzburg, Germany

ECML PKDD Steering Committee

Michele Berlingerio   IBM Research, Ireland
Albert Bifet   Télécom ParisTech, France
Hendrik Blockeel   KU Leuven, Belgium
Francesco Bonchi   ISI Foundation, Italy
Michelangelo Ceci   University of Bari Aldo Moro, Italy
Sašo Džeroski   Jožef Stefan Institute, Slovenia
Paolo Frasconi   University of Florence, Italy
Thomas Gärtner   University of Nottinghem, UK
Jaakko Hollmen   Aalto University, Finland
Neil Hurley   University College Dublin, Ireland
Georgiana Ifrim   University College Dublin, Ireland
Katharina Morik   TU Dortmund, Germany
Siegfried Nijssen   Université catholique de Louvain, Belgium
Andrea Passerini   University of Trento, Italy

Céline Robardet	INSA-Lyon, France
Michèle Sebag	Université Paris Sud, France
Arno Siebes	Utrecht University, the Netherlands
Myra Spiliopoulou	Magdeburg University, Germany
Jilles Vreeken	Saarland University, Germany

Program Committees

Guest Editorial Board, Journal Track

Annalisa Appice	University of Bari Aldo Moro, Italy
Marta Arias	Universitat Politècnica de Catalunya, Spain
Martin Atzmueller	Tilburg University, the Netherlands
Albert Bifet	Télécom ParisTech, France
Hendrik Blockeel	KU Leuven, Belgium
Toon Calders	University of Antwerp, Belgium
Michelangelo Ceci	University of Bari Aldo Moro, Italy
Loïc Cerf	Universidade Federal de Minas Gerais, Brazil
Nicolas Courty	Université Bretagne Sud, IRISA, France
Bruno Cremilleux	Université de Caen Normandie, France
Tijl De Bie	Ghent University, Belgium
Krzysztof Dembczyński	Poznan University of Technology, Poland
Yagoubi Djamel Edine	StarClay, France
Tapio Elomaa	Tampere University of Technology, Finland
Rémi Emonet	Université de Lyon à Saint Étienne, France
Stefano Ferilli	University of Bari, Italy
Joao Gama	University of Porto, Portugal
Tias Guns	VUB Brussels, Belgium
Amaury Habrard	Université Jean Monnet, France
Xiao He	NEC Laboratories Europe, Germany
Jaakko Hollmén	Aalto University, Finland
Szymon Jaroszewicz	Polish Academy of Sciences, Poland
Alipio Jorge	University of Porto, Portugal
Ajin Joseph	University of Alberta, Canada
Samuel Kaski	Aalto University, Finland
Kristian Kersting	TU Darmstadt, Germany
Dragi Kocev	Jožef Stefan Institute, Slovenia
Peer Kröger	Ludwig-Maximilians-Universität Munich, Germany
Ondrej Kuzelka	KU Leuven, Belgium
Mark Last	Ben-Gurion University of the Negev, Israel
Matthijs van Leeuwen	Leiden University, the Netherlands
Limin Li	Xi'an Jiaotong University, China
Jessica Lin	George Mason University, USA
Christoph Lippert	Hasso Plattner Institute, Germany
Brian Mac Namee	University College Dublin, Ireland

Area Chairs, Research and Applied Data Science Tracks

Fabrizio Angiulli	DIMES, University of Calabria, Italy
Roberto Bayardo	Google Research, USA
Michael Berthold	Universität Konstanz, Germany
Albert Bifet	Université Paris-Saclay, France
Hendrik Blockeel	KU Leuven, Belgium
Francesco Bonchi	ISI Foundation, Italy
Toon Calders	Universiteit Antwerpen, Belgium
Michelangelo Ceci	University of Bari, Italy
Nicolas Courty	IRISA, France
Bruno Crémilleux	Université de Caen Normandie, France
Philippe Cudre-Mauroux	Exascale Infolab, Switzerland
Jesse Davis	KU Leuven, Belgium
Tijl De Bie	Ghent University, Belgium
Tapio Elomaa	Tampere University, Finland
Amir-massoud Farahmand	Vector Institute, Canada
Paolo Frasconi	Università degli Studi di Firenze, Italy
Johannes Fürnkranz	TU Darmstadt, Germany
Patrick Gallinari	LIP6, France
Joao Gama	INESC TEC, LIAAD, Portugal
Aristides Gionis	Aalto University, Finland
Thomas Gärtner	University of Nottingham, UK
Allan Hanbury	Vienna University of Technology, Austria
Jaakko Hollmén	Aalto University, Finland
Eyke Hüllermeier	University of Paderborn, Germany
Alipio Jorge	INESC, Portugal
Marius Kloft	University of Southern California, USA
Nick Koudas	University of Toronto, Canada
Stefan Kramer	Johannes Gutenberg University Mainz, Germany
Sébastien Lefèvre	Université de Bretagne Sud, IRISA, France
Jörg Lücke	Universität Oldenburg, Germany
Giuseppe Manco	ICAR-CNR, Italy
Pauli Miettinen	Max-Planck Institute for Informatics, Germany
Anna Monreale	University of Pisa, Italy
Katharina Morik	TU Dortmund, Germany
Siegfried Nijssen	Université Catholique de Louvain, Belgium
Andrea Passerini	University of Trento, Italy
Mykola Pechenizkiy	TU Eindhoven, the Netherlands
Francois Petitjean	Monash University, Australia
Elmar Rueckert	University Luebeck, Germany
Tom Schaul	DeepMind, UK
Thomas Seidl	LMU Munich, Germany
Arno Siebes	Universiteit Utrecht, the Netherlands
Myra Spiliopoulou	Otto-von-Guericke-University Magdeburg, Germany
Einoshin Suzuki	Kyushu University, Japan

Marc Tommasi	Lille University, France
Celine Vens	KU Leuven, Belgium
Christel Vrain	University of Orleans, France
Jilles Vreeken	CISPA Helmholtz Center for Information Security, Germany
Min-Ling Zhang	Southeast University, Bangladesh
Herke van Hoof	University of Amsterdam, the Netherlands

Program Committee Members, Research and Applied Data Science Tracks

Ehsan Abbasnejad	The University of Adelaide, Australia
Leman Akoglu	CMU, USA
Tristan Allard	University of Rennes, France
Aijun An	York University, Canada
Ali Anaissi	The University of Sydney, Australia
Annalisa Appice	University of Bari, Italy
Paul Assendorp	Werum, Germany
Ira Assent	University of Aarhus, Denmark
Martin Atzmüller	Tilburg University, the Netherlands
Alexandre Aussem	Université Lyon 1, France
Suyash Awate	Indian Institute of Technology (IIT) Bombay, India
Antonio Bahamonde	Universidad de Oviedo, Spain
Jaume Baixeries	Universitat Politècnica de Catalunya, Spain
Vineeth N. Balasubramanian	Indian Institute of Technology, India
Jose Balcazar	Universitat Politecnica de Catalunya, Spain
Sambaran Bandyopadhyay	IBM Research, India
Zhifeng Bao	RMIT University, Australia
Mitra Baratchi	Leiden University, the Netherlands
Sylvio Barbon	Universidade Estadual de Londrina, Brazil
Gianni Barlacchi	FBK Trento, Italy
Martin Becker	Stanford University, USA
Srikanta Bedathur	IIT Delhi, India
Edward Beeching	Inria, France
Vaishak Belle	University of Edinburgh, UK
Andras Benczur	Hungarian Academy of Sciences, Hungary
Daniel Bengs	DIPF, Germany
Petr Berka	University of Economics, Prague, Czech Republic
Marenglen Biba	University of New York in Tirana, Albania
Chris Biemann	University of Hamburg, Germany
Battista Biggio	University of Cagliari, Italy
Thomas Bonald	Télécom ParisTech, France
Gianluca Bontempi	Université Libre de Bruxelles, Belgium
Henrik Bostrom	KTH Royal Institute of Technology, Sweden
Tassadit Bouadi	Université de Rennes 1, France
Ahcène Boubekki	Leuphana University of Lüneburg, Germany
Zied Bouraoui	Université d'Artois, France

Paula Branco   Dalhousie University, Canada
Pavel Brazdil   University of Porto, Portugal
Dariusz Brzezinski   Poznan University of Technology, Poland
Sebastian Buschjager   TU Dortmund, Germany
Ricardo Campello   University of Newcastle, Australia
Brais Cancela   University of A. Coruña, Spain
Francisco Casacuberta   Universidad Politecnica de Valencia, Spain
Remy Cazabet   University of Lyon, France
Peggy Cellier   IRISA, France
Loic Cerf   UFMG, Brazil
Tania Cerquitelli   Politecnico di Torino, Italy
Ricardo Cerri   Federal University of São Carlos, Brazil
Tanmoy Chakraborty   Indraprastha Institute of Information Technology Delhi
                            (IIIT-D), India
Edward Chang   HTC Research & Healthcare, USA
Xiaojun Chang   Monash University, Australia
Jeremy Charlier   University of Luxembourg, Luxembourg
Abon Chaudhuri   Walmart Labs, USA
Keke Chen   Wright State University, USA
Giovanni Chierchia   ESIEE Paris, France
Silvia Chiusano   Politecnico di Torino, Italy
Sunav Choudhary   Adobe Research, India
Frans Coenen   The University of Liverpool, UK
Mario Cordeiro   Universidade do Porto, Portugal
Robson Cordeiro   University of São Paulo, Brazil
Roberto Corizzo   University of Bari, Italy
Fabrizio Costa   Exeter University, UK
Vitor Santos Costa   Universidade do Porto, Portugal
Adrien Coulet   Loria, France
Bertrand Cuissart   University of Caen, France
Boris Cule   Universiteit Antwerpen, Belgium
Alfredo Cuzzocrea   University of Trieste and ICAR-CNR, Italy
Alexander Dallmann   University of Würzburg, Germany
Claudia d'Amato   University of Bari, Italy
Maria Damiani   University of Milano, Italy
Martine De Cock   University of Washington Tacoma, USA
Tom Decroos   KU Leuven, Belgium
Juan Jose del Coz   University of Oviedo, Spain
Anne Denton   North Dakota State University, USA
Christian Desrosiers   ETS, Italy
Nicola Di Mauro   University of Bari, Italy
Claudia Diamantini   Università Politecnica delle Marche, Italy
Jilles Dibangoye   INSA-Lyon, France
Tom Diethe   University of Bristol, UK
Wei Ding   University of Massachusetts Boston, USA
Stephan Doerfel   Micromata GmbH, Germany

Carlotta Domeniconi	George Mason University, USA
Madalina Drugan	Eindhoven University of Technology, the Netherlands
Stefan Duffner	University of Lyon, France
Wouter Duivesteijn	TU Eindhoven, the Netherlands
Sebastijan Dumancic	KU Leuven, Belgium
Ines Dutra	INESC TEC, Portugal
Mireille El Gheche	EPFL, Switzerland
Jihane Elyahyioui	Monash University, Australia
Dora Erdos	Boston University, USA
Samuel Fadel	University of Campinas, Brazil
Ad Feelders	Universiteit Utrecht, the Netherlands
Jing Feng	TU Darmstadt, Germany
Stefano Ferilli	University of Bari, Italy
Carlos Ferreira	INESC TEC, Portugal
Cesar Ferri	Universitat Politecnica Valencia, Spain
Matthias Fey	TU Dortmund, Germany
Rémi Flamary	Université côte d'Azur, France
Razvan Florian	Romanian Institute of Science and Technology, Romania
Germain Forestier	University of Haute Alsace, France
Eibe Frank	University of Waikato, New Zealand
Fabio Fumarola	Universita degli Studi di Bari Aldo Moro, Italy
Paulo Gabriel	Universidade Federal de Uberlandia, Brazil
Amita Gajewar	Microsoft Corporation, USA
Esther Galbrun	Aalto University, Finland
Dragan Gamberger	Rudjer Boskovic Institute, Croatia
Byron Gao	Texas State University, USA
Junbin Gao	The University of Sydney, Australia
Paolo Garza	Politecnico di Torino, Italy
Konstantinos Georgatzis	QuantumBlack, Singapore
Pierre Geurts	Montefiore Institute, Belgium
Arnaud Giacometti	University of Tours, France
Rémi Gilleron	Lille University, France
Mike Gimelfarb	University of Toronto, Canada
Uwe Glasser	Simon Fraser University, Canada
Dorota Glowacka	University of Helsinki, Finland
Heitor Gomes	Télécom ParisTech, France
Rafael Gomes Mantovani	Federal Technology University of Parana, Brazil
Vicenç Gomez	Universitat Pompeu Fabra, Spain
Vanessa Gomez-Verdejo	Universidad Carlos III de Madrid, Spain
James Goulding	University of Nottingham, UK
Cédric Gouy-Pailler	CEA, France
Josif Grabocka	Universität Hildesheim, Germany
Michael Granitzer	University of Passau, Germany
Derek Greene	Data Analytics, Ireland
Quanquan Gu	University of California, Los Angeles, USA

Riccardo Guidotti	University of Pisa, Italy
Francesco Gullo	UniCredit R&D, Italy
Tias Guns	Vrije Universiteit Brussel, Belgium
Xueying Guo	University of California, Davis, USA
Deepak Gupta	University of Amsterdam, the Netherlands
Thomas Guyet	IRISA, France
Stephan Günnemann	Technical University of Munich, Germany
Maria Halkidi	University of Pireaus, Greece
Barbara Hammer	CITEC, Switzerland
Jiawei Han	UIUC, USA
Tom Hanika	University of Kassel, Germany
Mohammad Hasan	Indiana University and Purdue University Indianapolis, USA
Xiao He	Alibaba Group, China
Denis Helic	TU Graz, Austria
Andreas Henelius	University of Helsinki, Finland
Daniel Hernandez-Lobato	Universidad Autonoma de Madrid, Spain
Jose Hernandez-Orallo	Polytechnic University of Valencia, Spain
Sibylle Hess	TU Eindhoven, the Netherlands
Thanh Lam Hoang	IBM Research, Ireland
Frank Hoeppner	Ostfalia University of Applied Science, Germany
Arjen Hommersom	University of Nijmegen, the Netherlands
Tamas Horvath	University of Bonn and Fraunhofer IAIS, Germany
Homa Hosseinmardi	USC ISI, USA
Chao Huang	University of Notre Dame, USA
David Tse Jung Huang	The University of Auckland, New Zealand
Yuanhua Huang	European Bioinformatics Institute, UK
Neil Hurley	University College Dublin, Ireland
Dino Ienco	Irstea Institute, France
Angelo Impedovo	University of Bari Aldo Moro, Italy
Iñaki Inza	University of the Basque Country, Spain
Tomoki Ito	The University of Tokyo, Japan
Mahdi Jalili	RMIT University, Australia
Szymon Jaroszewicz	Polish Academy of Sciences, Poland
Giuseppe Jurman	Fondazione Bruno Kessler, Italy
Anup Kalia	IBM Research, USA
Toshihiro Kamishima	National Institute of Advanced Industrial Science and Technology, Japan
Michael Kamp	Fraunhofer IAIS, Germany
Bo Kang	Ghent University, Belgium
Pinar Karagoz	METU, Turkey
Konstantinos Karanasos	Microsoft, UK
Sarvnaz Karimi	DATA61, Australia
George Karypis	University of Minnesota, USA
Mehdi Kaytoue	Infologic, France
Mikaela Keller	University of Lille, France

Latifur Khan	The University of Texas at Dallas, USA
Beomjoon Kim	MIT, USA
Daiki Kimura	IBM Research AI, USA
Frank Klawonn	Helmholtz Centre for Infection Research, Germany
Jiri Klema	Czech Technical University, Czech Republic
Tomas Kliegr	University of Economics, Prague, Czech Republic
Dragi Kocev	Jozef Stefan Institute, Slovenia
Levente Kocsis	Hungarian Academy of Science, Hungary
Yun Sing Koh	The University of Auckland, New Zealand
Effrosyni Kokiopoulou	Google AI, Switzerland
Alek Kolcz	Twitter, USA
Wouter Kool	University of Amsterdam, the Netherlands
Irena Koprinska	The University of Sydney, Australia
Frederic Koriche	Université d'Artois, France
Lars Kotthoff	University of Wyoming, USA
Danai Koutra	University of Michigan, USA
Polychronis Koutsakis	Murdoch University, Australia
Tomas Krilavicius	Vytautas Magnus University, Lithuania
Yamuna Krishnamurthy	NYU, USA, and Royal Holloway University of London, UK
Narayanan C. Krishnan	IIT Ropar, India
Matjaz Kukar	University of Ljubljana, Slovenia
Meelis Kull	University of Tartu, Estonia
Gautam Kunapuli	UT Dallas, USA
Vinod Kurmi	IIT Kanpur, India
Ondrej Kuzelka	University of Leuven, Belgium
Nicolas Lachiche	University of Strasbourg, France
Sofiane Lagraa	University of Luxembourg, Luxembourg
Leo Lahti	University of Turku, Estonia
Christine Largeron	LabHC Lyon University, France
Christine Largouet	IRISA, France
Pedro Larranaga	Universidad Politécnica de Madrid, Spain
Niklas Lavesson	Jonkoping University, Sweden
Binh Le	University College Dublin, Ireland
Florian Lemmerich	RWTH Aachen University, Germany
Marie-Jeanne Lesot	LIP6, France
Dagang Li	Peking University, China
Jian Li	Tsinghua University, China
Jiuyong Li	University of South Australia, Australia
Limin Li	Xi'an Jiaotong University, China
Xiangru Lian	University of Rochester, USA
Jefrey Lijffijt	Ghent University, Belgium
Tony Lindgren	Stockholm University, Sweden
Marco Lippi	University of Modena and Reggio Emilia, Italy
Bing Liu	University of Illinois at Chicago, USA
Corrado Loglisci	Universita degli Studi di Bari Aldo Moro, Italy

Peter Lucas	Leiden University, the Netherlands
Sebastian Mair	Leuphana University, Germany
Arun Maiya	Institute for Defense Analyses, USA
Donato Malerba	University of Bari, Italy
Chaitanya Manapragada	Monash University, Australia
Luca Martino	University of Valencia, Spain
Elio Masciari	ICAR-CNR, Italy
Andres Masegosa	University of Almeria, Spain
Florent Masseglia	Inria, France
Antonis Matakos	Aalto University, Finland
Wannes Meert	KU Leuven, Belgium
Corrado Mencar	University of Bari Aldo Moro, Italy
Saayan Mitra	Adobe, USA
Atsushi Miyamoto	Hitachi America Ltd., USA
Dunja Mladenic	Jozef Stefan Institute, Slovenia
Sandy Moens	Universiteit Antwerpen, Belgium
Miguel Molina-Solana	Imperial College London, UK
Nuno Moniz	University of Porto, Portugal
Hankyu Moon	Samsung SDS Research, USA
Joao Moreira	INESC TEC, Portugal
Luis Moreira-Matias	Kreditech Holding SSL, Germany
Emilie Morvant	Université Jean Monnet, France
Andreas Mueller	Columbia Data Science Institute, USA
Asim Munawar	IBM Research, Japan
Pierre-Alexandre Murena	Télécom ParisTech, France
Mohamed Nadif	LIPADE, Université Paris Descartes, France
Jinseok Nam	Amazon, USA
Mirco Nanni	ISTI-CNR Pisa, Italy
Amedeo Napoli	LORIA, France
Sriraam Natarajan	UT Dallas, USA
Fateme Nateghi	KU Leuven, Belgium
Benjamin Negrevergne	Université Paris Dauphine, France
Benjamin Nguyen	INSA-CVL, France
Xia Ning	OSU, USA
Kjetil Norvag	NTNU, Norway
Eirini Ntoutsi	Leibniz Universität Hannover, Germany
Andreas Nurnberger	Magdeburg University, Germany
Luca Oneto	University of Pisa, Italy
Kok-Leong Ong	La Trobe University, Australia
Francesco Orsini	MDOTM S.r.l., Italy
Martijn van Otterlo	Tilburg University, the Netherlands
Nikunj Oza	NASA Ames, USA
Pance Panov	Jozef Stefan Institute, Slovenia
Apostolos Papadopoulos	Aristotle University of Thessaloniki, Greece
Panagiotis Papapetrou	Stockholm University, Sweden
Youngja Park	IBM, USA

Claudio Sartori	University of Bologna, Italy
Luciano Sbaiz	Google AI, Switzerland
Pierre Schaus	UC Louvain, Belgium
Tobias Scheffer	University of Potsdam, Germany
Ute Schmid	University of Bamberg, Germany
Lars Schmidt-Thieme	University of Hildesheim, Germany
Christoph Schommer	University of Luxembourg, Luxembourg
Matthias Schubert	Ludwig-Maximilians-Universität München, Germany
Rajat Sen	UT Austin and Amazon, USA
Vinay Setty	University of Stavanger, Norway
Mattia Setzu	University of Pisa, Italy
Chao Shang	University of Connecticut, USA
Junming Shao	University of Electronic Science and Technology of China, China
Bernhard Sick	University of Kassel, Germany
Diego Silva	Universidade Federal de São Carlos, Brazil
Jonathan Silva	UFMS, Brazil
Nikola Simidjievski	University of Cambridge, UK
Andrzej Skowron	University of Warsaw, Poland
Dominik Slezak	University of Warsaw, Poland
Daniel V. Smith	DATA61, Australia
Gavin Smith	University of Nottingham, UK
Tomislav Smuc	Institute Ruđer Bošković, Croatia
Arnaud Soulet	University of Tours, France
Mauro Sozio	Institut Mines Télécom, France
Alessandro Sperduti	University of Padova, Italy
Jerzy Stefanowski	Poznan University of Technology, Poland
Bas van Stein	Leiden University, the Netherlands
Giovanni Stilo	University of L'Aquila, Italy
Mahito Sugiyama	National Institute of Informatics, Japan
Mika Sulkava	Natural Resources Institute Finland, Finland
Yizhou Sun	UCLA, USA
Viswanathan Swaminathan	Adobe, USA
Stephen Swift	Brunel University London, UK
Andrea Tagarelli	DIMES - UNICAL, Italy
Domenico Talia	University of Calabria, Italy
Letizia Tanca	Politecnico di Milano, Italy
Jovan Tanevski	Jozef Stefan Institute, Slovenia
Nikolaj Tatti	University of Helsinki, Finland
Maryam Tavakol	TU Dortmund, Germany
Maguelonne Teisseire	Irstea, France
Choon Hui Teo	Amazon, USA
Alexandre Termier	Université Rennes 1, France
Stefano Teso	KU Leuven, Belgium
Ljupco Todorovski	University of Ljubljana, Slovenia
Alexander Tornede	UPB, Germany

Ricardo Torres	IC-Unicamp, Brazil
Volker Tresp	Siemens AG and Ludwig Maximilian University of Munich, Germany
Isaac Triguero	University of Nottingham, UK
Ivor Tsang	University of Technology Sydney, Australia
Vincent Tseng	National Chiao Tung University, Taiwan
Charalampos Tsourakakis	Boston University, USA
Radu Tudoran	Huawei, Germany
Cigdem Turan	TU Darmstadt, Germany
Nikolaos Tziortziotis	Tradelab, France
Theodoros Tzouramanis	University of the Aegean, Greece
Antti Ukkonen	University of Helsinki, Finland
Elia Van Wolputte	KU Leuven, Belgium
Robin Vandaele	Ghent University, Belgium
Iraklis Varlamis	Harokopio University of Athens, Greece
Ranga Vatsavai	North Carolina State University, USA
Julien Velcin	University of Lyon, France
Bruno Veloso	University of Porto, Portugal
Shankar Vembu	University of Toronto, Canada
Deepak Venugopal	University of Memphis, USA
Ricardo Vigario	NOVA University of Lisbon, Portugal
Prashanth Vijayaraghavan	MIT, USA
Herna Viktor	University of Ottawa, Canada
Willem Waegeman	Universiteit Gent, Belgium
Di Wang	Microsoft, USA
Hao Wang	Leiden University, the Netherlands
Jianyong Wang	Tsinghua University, China
Yuyi Wang	ETH Zürich, Switzerland
Jeremy Weiss	Carnegie Mellon University, USA
Marcel Wever	Paderborn University, Germany
Joerg Wicker	The University of Auckland, New Zealand
Marco Wiering	University of Groningen, the Netherlands
Martin Wistuba	IBM Research, Ireland
Christian Wolf	INSA-Lyon, France
Christian Wressnegger	TU Braunschweig, Germany
Gang Wu	Adobe Research, USA
Lina Yao	UNSW, Australia
Philip Yu	University of Illinois at Chicago, USA
Bianca Zadrozny	IBM Research, USA
Gerson Zaverucha	Federal University of Rio de Janeiro, Brazil
Bernard Zenko	Jozef Stefan Institute, Slovenia
Chengkun Zhang	The University of Sydney, Australia
Jianpeng Zhang	TU Eindhoven, the Netherlands
Junping Zhang	Fudan University, China
Shichao Zhang	Guangxi Normal University, China
Yingqian Zhang	Eindhoven University of Technology, the Netherlands

Sichen Zhao	The University of Melbourne, Australia
Ying Zhao	Tsinghua University, China
Shuai Zheng	Hitachi America Ltd., USA
Arthur Zimek	University of Southern Denmark, Denmark
Albrecht Zimmermann	Université de Caen Normandie, France
Indre Zliobaite	University of Helsinki, Finland
Tanja Zseby	TU Wien, Austria

Sponsors

Abstracts of Invited Talks

Programming by Input-Output Examples

Sumit Gulwani

Microsoft Research

Abstract. Programming by examples (PBE) is a new frontier in AI that enables computer users (99% of whom are non-programmers) to create programs from input-output examples. PBE can enable 10-100x productivity increase for data scientists and developers in various task domains like string/datatype transformations (e.g., converting "FirstName LastName" to "lastName, firstName"), table extraction from semi-structured documents (like text-files, webpages, spreadsheets, PDFs), and repetitive editing/refactoring for documents/code. Creating usable PBE systems involves developing efficient search algorithms (to search for programs over an underlying domain-specific programming language), and ambiguity resolution techniques (to select an intended program from among the many that satisfy the examples). Our effective solution builds over interesting combination of logical reasoning and machine learning. Microsoft's PROSE SDK exposes these search and ranking algorithms to aid construction of PBE capabilities for new domains. In this talk, I will describe this new PBE-based programming paradigm: its applications, form factors inside different products (like Excel, PowerBI, Visual Studio, Jupyter Notebooks), and the science behind it.

Bio: Sumit Gulwani is a computer scientist seeking connections: between ideas, between research and practice, and with people with varied roles. He is the inventor of many intent-understanding, programming-by-example, and programming-by-natural-language technologies including the popular Flash Fill feature in Excel used by hundreds of millions of people. He founded and currently leads the PROSE research and engineering team that develops APIs for program synthesis and incorporates them into various products. He has published 120+ peer-reviewed papers in top-tier conferences and journals across multiple computer science areas, delivered 45+ keynotes and invited talks at various forums, and authored 50+ patent applications (granted and pending). He was awarded the ACM SIGPLAN Robin Milner Young Researcher Award in 2014 for his pioneering contributions to end-user programming and intelligent tutoring systems. He obtained his PhD in Computer Science from UC-Berkeley, and was awarded the ACM SIGPLAN Outstanding Doctoral Dissertation Award. He obtained his BTech in Computer Science and Engineering from IIT Kanpur, and was awarded the President's Gold Medal.

Machine Learning for Robust and Fast Control of Manipulation Under Disturbances

Aude Billard

École polytechnique fédérale de Lausanne

Abstract. Dexterous manipulation of objects is robotics' primary goal. It envisions robots capable of manipulating of packing a variety of objects and of chopping vegetables, at high speed. To manipulate these objects cannot be done with traditional control approaches, for lack of accurate models of objects and contact dynamics. Robotics leverages, hence, the immense progress in machine learning to encapsulate models of uncertainty and to support further advances on adaptive and robust control. I will present applications of machine learning for controlling robots to learn non-linear control laws and to model complex deformations of objects. I will show applications of this to have robots peel and grate vegetables, manipulate objects jointly with humans, and catch flying objects.

Bio: Professor Aude Billard is head of the Learning Algorithms and Systems Laboratory (LASA) at the School of Engineering at the EPFL. She received a MSc in Physics from EPFL (1995), a MSc in Knowledge-based Systems (1996) and a PhD in Artificial Intelligence (1998) from the University of Edinburgh. She was the recipient of the Intel Corporation Teaching Award, the Swiss National Science Foundation Career Award in 2002, the Outstanding Young Person in Science and Innovation from the Swiss Chamber of Commerce, and the IEEE-RAS Best Reviewer Award. Aude Billard served as an elected member of the Administrative Committee of the IEEE Robotics and Automation society for two terms (2006–2008 and 2009–2011). She was a plenary speaker at major robotics conferences (ROMAN, ICRA, Humanoids, HRI) and acted on various positions on the Organization Committee of more than 15 International Conferences in Robotics. Her research on human-robot interaction and robot learning from human demonstration is featured regularly in premier venues (BBC, IEEE Spectrum, Wired) and received numerous Best Paper Awards at ICRA, IROS and ROMAN, and the 2015 King-Sun Fu Memorial Award for the best 2014 IEEE Transaction in Robotics paper. Professor Billard is active in a number of research organizations in Switzerland and abroad. She is currently a member of the Swiss Science and Technology Council (SNSF) and a member of the Swiss Academy of Engineering Sciences (SATW).

Palaeontology as a Computational Science

Indrė Žliobaitė

University of Helsinki

Abstract. Palaeontology studies the history of life and evolutionary principles. While biology focuses on how life is, palaeontology is concerned with how life forms change. This is particularly interesting in the context of today's rapidly changing world. The main material for palaeontological studies comes from fossils – remains, traces or impressions of organisms that lived in the past, preserved in rocks. Fossils are found in many places around the world where ancient sediments have been exposed on the surface. Palaeontology has long been a big data discipline; global fossil databases have been around for many decades. Perhaps half of palaeontology research today is computationally-driven, it strongly relies on advanced computational methods, including those of machine learning, for analyzing ancestral relationships, biogeographic patterns of life history, evolutionary processes of life, and its environmental concepts. This talk will discuss what there is to compute in palaeontology, why it matters, and what fundamental questions about the world in the past and today evolutionary palaeontology aims at addressing.

Bio: Indrė Žliobaitė is an Assistant Professor at the University of Helsinki, Finland. Her background is in machine learning with evolving data. In Helsinki she leads a research group called Data Science and Evolution, which focuses on computational analyses of the changing world. For the last five years Indrė has been actively involved in evolutionary palaeontology research studying the mammalian fossil record. Results of this work have been published in Nature, PNAS, Philosophical Transactions of the Royal Society, and other prime venues for natural sciences. By now Indrė is as a palaeontologist as she is a computer scientist. She is a long member of ECMLPKDD community. She has taken chairing roles in several editions of the conference and served as a member of the Steering Committee for ECMLPKDD.

Data Driven Algorithm Design

Maria Florina Balcan

Carnegie Mellon University

Abstract. Data driven algorithm design for combinatorial problems is an important aspect of modern data science and algorithm design. Rather than using off-the-shelf algorithms that only have worst case performance guarantees, practitioners typically optimize over large families of parametrized algorithms and tune the parameters of these algorithms using a training set of problem instances from their domain to determine a configuration with high expected performance over future instances. However, most of this work comes with no performance guarantees. The challenge is that for many combinatorial problems, including partitioning and subset selection problems, a small tweak to the parameters can cause a cascade of changes in the algorithm's behavior, so the algorithm's performance is a discontinuous function of its parameters. In this talk, I will present new work that helps put data driven combinatorial algorithm selection on firm foundations. We provide strong computational and statistical performance guarantees for several subset selection and combinatorial partitioning problems (including various forms of clustering), both for the batch and online scenarios where a collection of typical problem instances from the given application are presented either all at once or in an online fashion, respectively.

Bio: Maria Florina Balcan is an Associate Professor in the School of Computer Science at Carnegie Mellon University. Her main research interests are machine learning, computational aspects in economics and game theory, and algorithms. Her honors include the CMU SCS Distinguished Dissertation Award, an NSF CAREER Award, a Microsoft Faculty Research Fellowship, a Sloan Research Fellowship, and several paper awards. She was a Program Committee co-chair for the Conference on Learning Theory in 2014 and for the International Conference on Machine Learning in 2016. She is currently board member of the International Machine Learning Society (since 2011), a tutorial chair for ICML 2019, and a workshop chair for FOCS 2019.

The Quest for the Perfect Image Representation

Tinne Tuytelaars

KU Leuven

Abstract. Throughout my research career, I've always been looking for the 'optimal' image representation: a representation that captures all relevant information for a given task, including scene composition, 3D information, illumination, and other cues; a representation that can easily generalize and adapt to new tasks; a representation that can be updated over time with new information, without forgetting what was learned before; a representation that is explicit in the sense that it can easily be interpreted or explained; a representation, in short, that supports true understanding of the image content, ultimately allowing the machine to reason and communicate about it in natural language. In this talk, I will describe a few recent efforts in this direction.

Bio: Tinne Tuytelaars is Professor at KU Leuven, Belgium, working on computer vision and, in particular, topics related to image representations, vision and language, incremental learning, image generation, and more. She has been program chair for ECCV 2014, general chair for CVPR 2016, and will again be program chair for CVPR 2021. She also served as associate-editor-in-chief of the IEEE Transactions on Pattern Analysis and Machine Intelligence over the last four years. She was awarded an ERC Starting Grant in 2009 and received the Koenderink Test-of-Time Award at ECCV 2016.

Contents – Part I

Dimensionality Reduction and Feature Selection

Social Networks and Graphs

Decision Trees, Interpretability, and Causality

Strings and Streams

Privacy and Security

Optimization

Contents – Part II

Large-Scale Learning

Deep Learning

Probabilistic Models

Natural Language Processing

Contents – Part III

Ranking

Applied Data Science: Computer Vision and Explanation

Applied Data Science: Healthcare

Applied Data Science: E-commerce, Finance, and Advertising

Applied Data Science: Rich Data

Applied Data Science: Applications

Demo Track

Pattern Mining

DEvIANT: Discovering Significant Exceptional (Dis-)Agreement Within Groups

Adnene Belfodil[1]([✉]), Wouter Duivesteijn[2], Marc Plantevit[3], Sylvie Cazalens[1], and Philippe Lamarre[1]

[1] Univ Lyon, INSA Lyon, CNRS, LIRIS UMR 5205, 69621 Lyon, France
adnene.belfodil@gmail.com
[2] Technische Universiteit Eindhoven, Eindhoven, The Netherlands
[3] Univ Lyon, CNRS, LIRIS UMR 5205, 69622 Lyon, France

Abstract. We strive to find contexts (i.e., subgroups of entities) under which exceptional (dis-)agreement occurs among a group of individuals, in any type of data featuring individuals (e.g., parliamentarians, customers) performing observable actions (e.g., votes, ratings) on entities (e.g., legislative procedures, movies). To this end, we introduce the problem of discovering statistically significant exceptional contextual intra-group agreement patterns. To handle the sparsity inherent to voting and rating data, we use Krippendorff's Alpha measure for assessing the agreement among individuals. We devise a branch-and-bound algorithm, named DEvIANT, to discover such patterns. DEvIANT exploits both closure operators and tight optimistic estimates. We derive analytic approximations for the confidence intervals (CIs) associated with patterns for a computationally efficient significance assessment. We prove that these approximate CIs are nested along specialization of patterns. This allows to incorporate pruning properties in DEvIANT to quickly discard non-significant patterns. Empirical study on several datasets demonstrates the efficiency and the usefulness of DEvIANT.

1 Introduction

Consider data describing voting behavior in the European Parliament (EP). Such a dataset records the votes of each member (MEP) in voting sessions held in the parliament, as well as the information on the parliamentarians (e.g., gender, national party, European party alliance) and the sessions (e.g., topic, date). This dataset offers opportunities to study the agreement or disagreement of coherent subgroups, especially to highlight unexpected behavior. It is to be expected that on the majority of voting sessions, MEPs will vote along the lines of their European party alliance. However, when matters are of interest to a specific

Electronic supplementary material The online version of this chapter (https://doi.org/10.1007/978-3-030-46150-8_1) contains supplementary material, which is available to authorized users.

U. Brefeld et al. (Eds.): ECML PKDD 2019, LNAI 11906, pp. 3–20, 2020.
https://doi.org/10.1007/978-3-030-46150-8_1

nation within Europe, alignments may change and agreements can be formed or dissolved. For instance, when a legislative procedure on fishing rights is put before the MEPs, the island nation of the UK can be expected to agree on a specific course of action regardless of their party alliance, fostering an exceptional agreement where strong polarization exists otherwise.

We aim to discover such exceptional (dis-)agreements. This is not limited to just EP or voting data: members of the US congress also vote on bills, while Amazon-like customers post ratings or reviews of products. A challenge when considering such voting or rating data is to effectively handle the absence of outcomes (sparsity), which is inherently high. For instance, in the European parliament data, MEPs vote on average on only 3/4 of all sessions. These outcomes are not missing at random: special workgroups are often formed of MEPs tasked with studying a specific topic, and members of these workgroups are more likely to vote on their topic of expertise. Hence, present values are likely associated with more pressing votes, which means that missing values need to be treated carefully. This problem becomes much worse when looking at Amazon or Yelp rating data: the vast majority of customers will not have rated the vast majority of products/places.

We introduce the problem of discovering significantly exceptional contextual intra-group agreement patterns, rooted in the Subgroup Discovey (SD) [28]/Exceptional Model Mining (EMM) [6] framework. To tackle the data sparsity issue, we measure the agreement among groups with *Krippendorff's alpha*, a measure developed in the context of content analysis [21] which handles missing outcomes elegantly. We develop a branch-and-bound algorithm to find

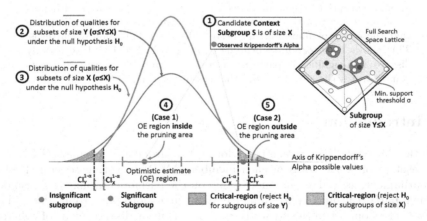

Fig. 1. Main DEvIANT properties for safe sub-search space pruning. A subgroup is reported as significant if its related Krippendorff's Alpha falls in the critical region of the corresponding empirical distribution of random subsets (DFD). When traversing the search space downward (decreasing support size), the approximate confidence intervals are nested. If the optimistic estimates region falls into the confidence interval computed on the related DFD, the sub-search space can be safely pruned.

subgroups featuring statistically significantly exceptional (dis-)agreement among groups. This algorithm enables discarding non-significant subgroups by pruning unpromising branches of the search space (cf. Fig. 1). Suppose that we are interested in subgroups of entities (e.g., voting sessions) whose sizes are greater than a support threshold σ. We gauge the exceptionality of a given subgroup of size $X \geq \sigma$, by its *p-value*: the probability that for a random subset of entities, we observe an intra-agreement at least as extreme as the one observed for the subgroup. Thus we avoid reporting subgroups observing a low/high intra-agreement due to chance only. To achieve this, we estimate the empirical distribution of the intra-agreement of random subsets (DFD: Distribution of False Discoveries, cf. [7,25]) and establish, for a chosen critical value α, a confidence interval $CI_X^{1-\alpha}$ over the corresponding distribution under the null hypothesis. If the subgroup intra-agreement is outside $CI_X^{1-\alpha}$, the subgroup is statistically significant (*p-value* $\leq \alpha$); otherwise the subgroup is a spurious finding. We prove that the analytic approximate confidence intervals are nested: $\sigma \leq Y \leq X \Rightarrow CI_X^{1-\alpha} \subseteq CI_Y^{1-\alpha}$ (i.e., when the support size grows, the confidence interval shrinks). Moreover, we compute a tight optimistic estimate (OE) [15] to define a lower and upper bounds of Krippendorff's Alpha for any specialization of a subgroup having its size greater than σ. Combining these properties, if the OE region falls into the corresponding CI, we can safely prune large parts of the search space that do not contain significant subgroups. In summary, the main contributions are:

(**1**) We introduce the problem of discovering statistically significant exceptional contextual intra-group agreement patterns (Sect. 3).

(**2**) We derive an analytical approximation of the confidence intervals associated with subgroups. This allows a computationally efficient assessment of the statistical significance of the findings. Furthermore, we show that approximate confidence intervals are nested (Sect. 4). Particular attention is also paid to the variability of outcomes among raters (Sect. 5).

(**3**) We devise a branch-and-bound algorithm to discover exceptional contextual intra-group agreement patterns (Sect. 6). It exploits tight optimistic estimates on Krippendorff's alpha and the nesting property of approximate CIs.

2   Background and Related Work

The page limit, combined with the sheer volume of other material in this paper, compels us to restrict this section to one page containing only the most relevant research to this present work.

Measuring Agreement. Several measures of agreement focus on two targets (Pearson's ρ, Spearman's ρ, Kendall's τ, Association); most cannot handle missing values well. As pointed out by Krippendorff [21, p.244], using association and correlation measures to assess agreement leads to particularly misleading conclusions: when all data falls along a line $Y = aX + b$, correlation is perfect, but agreement requires that $Y = X$. Cohen's κ is a seminal measure of agreement between two raters who classify items into a fixed number of mutually exclusive categories. Fleiss' κ extends this notion to multiple raters and requires that each item receives the exact same number of ratings. Krippendorff's alpha generalizes these measures while handling multiple raters, missing outcomes and several metrics [21, p.232].

Discovering Significant Patterns. Statistical assessment of patterns has received attention for a decade [17,27], especially for association rules [16,26]. Some work focused on statistical significance of results in SD/EMM during enumeration [7,25] or a posteriori [8] for statistical validation of the found subgroups.

Voting and Rating Data Analysis. Previous work [2] proposed a method to discover exceptional *inter*-group agreement in voting or rating data. This method does not allow to discover *intra*-group agreement. In rating datasets, groups are uncovered whose members exhibit an agreement or discord [4] or a specific rating distribution [1] (e.g., polarized, homogeneous) given upfront by the end-user. This is done by aggregating the ratings through an arithmetic mean or a rating distribution. However, these methods do not allow to discover exceptional (dis-)agreement within groups. Moreover, they may output misleading hypotheses over the intra-group agreement, since aggregating ratings in a distribution (i) is highly affected by data sparsity (e.g., two reviewers may significantly differ in their number of expressed ratings) and (ii) may conceal the true nature of the underlying intra-group agreement. For instance, a rating distribution computed for a collection of movies may highlight a polarized distribution of ratings (interpreted as a disagreement) while ratings over each movie may describe a consensus between raters (movies are either highly or lowly rated or by the majority of the group). These two issues are addressed by Krippendorff's alpha.

3   Problem Definition

Our data consists of a set of individuals (*e.g., social network users, parliamentarians*) who give outcomes (*e.g., ratings, votes*) on entities (*e.g., movies, ballots*). We call this type of data a *behavioral dataset* (cf. Table 1).

Table 1. Example of behavioral dataset - European Parliament Voting dataset

(a) Entities			(b) Individuals				(c) Outcomes					
ide	themes	date	idi	country	group	age	idi	ide	o(i,e)	idi	ide	o(i,e)
e_1	1.20 Citizen's rights	20/04/16	i_1	France	S&D	26	i_1	e_2	Against	i_3	e_1	For
e_2	5.05 Economic growth	16/05/16					i_1	e_5	For	i_3	e_2	Against
e_3	1.20 Citizen's rights;		i_2	France	PPE	30	i_1	e_6	Against	i_3	e_3	For
	7.30 Judicial Coop	04/06/16					i_2	e_1	For	i_3	e_5	Against
e_4	7 Security and Justice	11/06/16	i_3	Germany	S&D	40	i_2	e_3	Against	i_4	e_1	For
e_5	7.30 Judicial Coop	03/07/16					i_2	e_4	For	i_4	e_4	For
e_6	7.30 Judicial Coop	29/07/16	i_4	Germany	ALDE	45	i_2	e_5	For	i_4	e_6	Against

Definition 1 *(Behavioral Dataset).* *A behavioral dataset* $\mathcal{B} = \langle G_I, G_E, O, o \rangle$ *is defined by (i) a finite collection of Individuals* G_I, *(ii) a finite collection of Entities* G_E, *(iii) a domain of possible Outcomes* O, *and (iv) a function* o : $G_I \times G_E \rightarrow O$ *that gives the outcome of an individual* i *over an entity* e.

The elements from G_I (resp. G_E) are augmented with descriptive attributes $\mathcal{A}_I$ (resp. $\mathcal{A}_E$). Attributes $a \in \mathcal{A}_I$ (resp. $\mathcal{A}_E$) may be Boolean, numerical or categorical, potentially organized in a taxonomy. Subgroups (subsets) of G_I (resp. G_E) are defined using descriptions from $\mathcal{D}_I$ (resp. $\mathcal{D}_E$). These descriptions are formalized by conjunctions of conditions on the values of the attributes. Descriptions of $\mathcal{D}_I$ are called *groups*, denoted g. Descriptions of $\mathcal{D}_E$ are called *contexts*, denoted c. From now on, G (resp. $\mathcal{D}$) denotes both collections G_I (resp. $\mathcal{D}_I$) and G_E (resp. $\mathcal{D}_E$) if no confusion can arise. We denote by G^d the subset of records characterized by the description $d \in \mathcal{D}$. Descriptions from $\mathcal{D}$ are partially ordered by a specialization operator denoted $\sqsubseteq$. A description d_2 is a specialization of d_1, denoted $d_1 \sqsubseteq d_2$, if and only if $d_2 \Rightarrow d_1$ from a logical point of view. It follows that $G^{d_2} \subseteq G^{d_1}$.

3.1 Intra-group Agreement Measure: Krippendorff's Alpha (A)

Krippendorff's Alpha (denoted A) measures the agreement among raters. This measure has several properties that make it attractive in our setting, namely: (i) it is applicable to any number of observers; (ii) it handles various domains of outcomes (ordinal, numerical, categorical, time series); (iii) it handles missing values; (iv) it corrects for the agreement expected by chance. A is defined as:

$$A = 1 - \frac{D_{\text{obs}}}{D_{\text{exp}}} \tag{1}$$

where D_{obs} (resp. D_{exp}) is a measure of the observed (resp. expected) disagreement. Hence, when $A = 1$, the agreement is as large as it can possibly be (given the class prior), and when $A = 0$, the agreement is indistinguishable to agreement by chance. We can also have $A < 0$, where disagreement is larger than expected by chance and which corresponds to systematic disagreement.

Given a behavioral dataset $\mathcal{B}$, we want to measure Krippendorff's alpha for a given context $c \in \mathcal{D}_E$ characterizing a subset of entities $G_E^c \subseteq G_E$, which indicates to what extent the individuals who comprise some selected group are in agreement $g \in \mathcal{D}_I$. From Eq. (1), we have: $A(S) = 1 - \frac{D_{\text{obs}}(S)}{D_{\text{exp}}}$ for any $S \subseteq G_E$. Note that the measure only considers entities having at least two outcomes; we assume the entities not fulfilling this requirement to be removed upfront by a preprocessing phase. We capture observed disagreement by:

$$D_{\text{obs}}(S) = \frac{1}{\sum_{e \in S} m_e} \sum_{o_1 o_2 \in O^2} \delta_{o_1 o_2} \cdot \sum_{e \in S} \frac{m_e^{o_1} \cdot m_e^{o_2}}{m_e - 1} \tag{2}$$

where m_e is the number of expressed outcomes for the entity e and $m_e^{o_1}$ (resp. $m_e^{o_2}$) represents the number of outcomes equal to o_1 (resp. o_2) expressed for the entity e. $\delta_{o_1 o_2}$ is a distance measure between outcomes, which can be defined according to the domain of the outcomes (e.g., $\delta_{o_1 o_2}$ can correspond to the Iverson bracket indicator function $[o_1 \neq o_2]$ for categorical outcomes or distance between ordinal values for ratings. Choices for the distance measure are discussed in [21]). The disagreement expected by chance is captured by:

$$D_{\text{exp}} = \frac{1}{m \cdot (m-1)} \sum_{o_1, o_2 \in O^2} \delta_{o_1 o_2} \cdot m^{o_1} \cdot m^{o_2} \tag{3}$$

where m is the number of all expressed outcomes, m^{o_1} (resp. m^{o_2}) is the number of expressed outcomes equal to o_1 (resp. o_2) observed in the entire behavioral dataset. This corresponds to the disagreement by chance observed on the overall marginal distribution of outcomes.

Example: Table 2 summarizes the behavioral data from Table 1. The disagreement expected by chance equals (given: $m^F = 8$, $m^A = 6$): $D_{\text{exp}} = 48/91$. To evaluate intra-agreement among the four individuals in the global context (considering all entities), first we need to compute the observed disagreement $D_{\text{obs}}(G_E)$. This equals the weighted average of the two last lines by considering the quantities m_e as the weights: $D_{\text{obs}}(G_E) = \frac{4}{14}$. Hence, for the global context, $A(G_E) = 0.46$. Now, consider the context $c = \langle themes \supseteq \{7.30 \text{ Judicial Coop.}\}\rangle$, having as support: $G_E^c = \{e_3, e_5, e_6\}$. The observed disagreement is obtained by computing the weighted average, only considering the entities belonging to the context: $D_{\text{obs}}(G_E^c) = \frac{4}{7}$. Hence, the contextual intra-agreement is: $A(G_E^c) = -0.08$.

Table 2. Summarized Behavioral Data; $D_{\text{obs}}(e) = \sum_{o_1, o_2 \in O^2} \delta_{o_1 o_2} \dfrac{m_e^{o_1} \cdot m_e^{o_2}}{m_e \cdot (m_e - 1)}$

	[F]or			[A]gainst		
	e_1	e_2	e_3	e_4	e_5	e_6
i_1		A			F	A
i_2	F		A	F	F	
i_3	F	A	F		A	
i_4	F			F		A
m_e	3	2	2	2	3	2
$D_{\text{obs}}(e)$	0	0	1	0	$\frac{2}{3}$	0

Comparing $A(G_E^c)$ and $A(G_E)$ leads to the following statement: *"while parliamentarians are slightly in agreement in overall terms, matters of judicial cooperation create systematic disagreement among them"*.

3.2 Mining Significant Patterns with Krippendorff's Alpha

We are interested in finding patterns of the form $(g, c) \in \mathcal{P}$ (with $\mathcal{P} = \mathcal{D}_I \times \mathcal{D}_E$), highlighting an exceptional intra-agreement between members of a group of individuals g over a context c. We formalize this problem using the well-established framework of SD/EMM [6], while giving particular attention to the statistical significance and soundness of the discovered patterns [17].

Given a group of individuals $g \in \mathcal{D}_I$, we strive to find contexts $c \in \mathcal{D}_E$ where the observed intra-agreement, denoted $A^g(G_E^c)$, *significantly* differs from the expected intra-agreement occurring due to chance alone. In the spirit of

[7, 25, 27], we evaluate pattern interestingness by statistical significance of the contextual intra-agreement: we estimate the probability to observe the intra-agreement $A^g(G_E^c)$ or a more extreme value, which corresponds to the *p-value* for some null hypothesis H_0. The pattern is said to be *significant* if the estimated probability is low enough (i.e., under some critical value α). The relevant null hypothesis H_0 is: the observed intra-agreement is generated by the distribution of intra-agreements observed on a bag of i.i.d. random subsets drawn from the entire collection of entities (DFD: Distributions of False Discoveries, cf. [7]).

Problem Statement. (*Discovering Exceptional Contextual Intra-group Agreement Patterns*). Given a behavioral dataset $\mathcal{B} = \langle G_I, G_E, O, o \rangle$, a minimum group support threshold σ_I, a minimum context support threshold σ_E, a significance critical value $\alpha \in]0, 1]$, and the null hypothesis H_0 (the observed intra-agreement is generated by the DFD); find the pattern set $P \subseteq \mathcal{P}$ such that:
$$P = \{(g, c) \in \mathcal{D}_I \times \mathcal{D}_E \ : \ |G_I^g| \geq \sigma_I \text{ and } |G_E^c| \geq \sigma_E \text{ and } p\text{-}value^g(c) \leq \alpha\}$$
where $p\text{-}value^g(c)$ is the probability (under H_0) of obtaining an intra-agreement A at least as extreme as $A^g(G_E^c)$, the one observed over the current context.

---

4 Exceptional Contexts: Evaluation and Pruning

From now on we omit the exponent g if no confusion can arise, while keeping in mind a selected group of individuals $g \in \mathcal{D}_I$ related to a subset $G_I^g \subseteq G_I$.

To evaluate the extent to which our findings are exceptional, we follow the significant pattern mining paradigm[1]: we consider each context c as a hypothesis test which returns a *p-value*. The *p-value* is the probability of obtaining an intra-agreement at least as extreme as the one observed over the current context $A(G_E^c)$, assuming the truth of the null hypothesis H_0. The pattern is accepted if H_0 is rejected. This happens if the *p-value* is under a critical significance value α which amounts to test if the observed intra-agreement $A(G_E^c)$ is outside the confidence interval $\text{CI}^{1-\alpha}$ established using the distribution assumed under H_0.

H_0 corresponds to the baseline finding: the observed contextual intra-agreement is generated by the distribution of random subsets equally likely to occur, a.k.a. *Distribution of False Discoveries* (DFD, cf. [7]). We evaluate the *p-value* of the observed A against the distribution of random subsets of a cardinality equal to the size of the observed subgroup G_E^c. The subsets are issued by uniform sampling without replacement (since the observed subgroup encompasses distinct entities only) from the entity collection. Moreover, drawing samples only from the collection of subsets of size equal to $|G_E^c|$ allows to drive more judicious conclusions: the variability of the statistic A is impacted by the size of the considered subgroups, since smaller subgroups are more likely to observe low/high values of A. The same reasoning was followed in [25].

---

[1] This paradigm naturally raises the question of how to address the *multiple comparisons problem* [19]. This is a non-trivial task in our setting, and solving it requires an extension of the significant pattern mining paradigm as a whole: its scope is bigger than this paper. We provide a brief discussion in Appendix C.

We define $\theta_k : F_k \to \mathbb{R}$ as the random variable corresponding to the observed intra-agreement A of k-sized subsets $S \in G_E$. I.e., for any $k \in [1, n]$ with $n = |G_E|$, we have $\theta_k(S) = A(S)$ and $F_k = \{S \in G_E \ s.t. \ |S| = k\}$. F_k is then the set of possible subsets which are equally likely to occur under the null hypothesis H_0. That is, $\mathbb{P}(S \in F_k) = \binom{n}{k}^{-1}$. We denote by $CI_k^{1-\alpha}$ the $(1 - \alpha)$ confidence interval related to the probability distribution of θ_k under the null hypothesis H_0. To easily manipulate θ_k, we reformulate A using Eqs. (1)–(3):

$$A(S) = \frac{\sum_{e \in S} v_e}{\sum_{e \in S} w_e} \mid w_e = m_e \text{ and } v_e = m_e - \frac{1}{D_{\exp}} \sum_{o_1, o_2 \in O^2} \delta_{o_1 o_2} \cdot \frac{m_e^{o_1} \cdot m_e^{o_2}}{(m_e - 1)}$$

$$(4)$$

Under the null hypothesis H_0 and the assumption that the underlying distribution of intra-agreements is a Normal distribution[2] $\mathcal{N}(\mu_k, \sigma_k^2)$, one can define $CI_k^{1-\alpha}$ by computing $\mu_k = E[\theta_k]$ and $\sigma_k^2 = \text{Var}[\theta_k]$. Doing so requires either empirically calculating estimators of such moments by drawing a large number r of uniformly generated samples from F_k, or analytically deriving the formula of $E[\theta_k]$ and $\text{Var}[\theta_k]$. In the former case, the confidence interval $CI_k^{1-\alpha}$ endpoints are given by [14, p. 9]: $\mu_k \pm t_{1-\frac{\alpha}{2}, r-1} \sigma_k \sqrt{1 + (1/r)}$, with μ_k and σ_k empirically estimated on the r samples, and $t_{1-\frac{\alpha}{2}, r-1}$ the $(1 - \frac{\alpha}{2})$ percentile of Student's t-distribution with $r - 1$ degrees of freedom. In the latter case, (μ_k and σ_k are known/derived analytically), the $(1 - \alpha)$ confidence interval can be computed in its most basic form, that is $CI_k^{1-\alpha} = [\mu_k - z_{(1-\frac{\alpha}{2})} \sigma_k, \mu_k + z_{(1-\frac{\alpha}{2})} \sigma_k]$ with $z_{(1-\frac{\alpha}{2})}$ the $(1 - \frac{\alpha}{2})$ percentile of $\mathcal{N}(0, 1)$.

However, due to the problem setting, empirically establishing the confidence interval is computationally expensive, since it must be calculated for each enumerated context. Even for relatively small behavioral datasets, this quickly becomes intractable. Alternatively, analytically deriving a computationally efficient form of $E[\theta_k]$ is notoriously difficult, given that $E[\theta_k] = \binom{n}{k}^{-1} \sum_{S \in F_k} \frac{\sum_{e \in S} v_e}{\sum_{e \in S} w_e}$ and $\text{Var}[\theta_k] = \binom{n}{k}^{-1} \sum_{S \in F_k} \left(\frac{\sum_{e \in S} v_e}{\sum_{e \in S} w_e} - E[\theta_k] \right)^2$.

Since θ_k can be seen as a weighted arithmetic mean, one can model the random variable θ_k as the ratio $\frac{V_k}{W_k}$, where V_k and W_k are two random variables $V_k : F_k \to \mathbb{R}$ and $W_k : F_k \to \mathbb{R}$ with $V_k(S) = \frac{1}{k} \sum_{e \in S} v_e$ and $W_k(S) = \frac{1}{k} \sum_{e \in S} w_e$. An elegant way to deal with a ratio of two random variables is to approximate its moments using the *Taylor series* following the line of reasoning of [9] and [20, p.351], since no easy analytic expression of $E[\theta_k]$ and $\text{Var}[\theta_k]$ can be derived.

---

[2] In the same line of reasoning of [5], one can assume that the underlying distribution can be derived from what prior beliefs the end-user may have on such distribution. If only the observed expectation μ and variance σ^2 are given as constraints which must hold for the underlying distribution, the maximum entropy distribution (*taking into account no other prior information than the given constraints*) is known to be the Normal distribution $\mathcal{N}(\mu, \sigma^2)$ [3, p.413].

Proposition 1 (An Approximate Confidence Interval $\widehat{CI}_k^{1-\alpha}$ for θ_k).
Given $k \in [1, n]$ and $\alpha \in]0, 1]$ (significance critical value), $\widehat{CI}_k^{1-\alpha}$ is given by:

$$\widehat{CI}_k^{1-\alpha} = \left[\widehat{E}[\theta_k] - z_{1-\frac{\alpha}{2}} \sqrt{\widehat{\text{Var}}[\theta_k]}, \widehat{E}[\theta_k] + z_{1-\frac{\alpha}{2}} \sqrt{\widehat{\text{Var}}[\theta_k]} \right] \quad (5)$$

with $\widehat{E}[\theta_k]$ a Taylor approximation for the expectation $E[\theta_k]$ expanded around (μ_{V_k}, μ_{W_k}), and $\widehat{\text{Var}}[\theta_k]$ a Taylor approximation for $\text{Var}[\theta_k]$ given by:

$$\widehat{E}[\theta_k] = \left(\frac{n}{k} - 1 \right) \frac{\mu_v}{\mu_w} \beta_w + \frac{\mu_v}{\mu_w} \qquad \widehat{\text{Var}}[\theta_k] = \left(\frac{n}{k} - 1 \right) \frac{\mu_v^2}{\mu_w^2} (\beta_v + \beta_w) \quad (6)$$

with:

$$\mu_v = \frac{1}{n} \sum_{e \in G_E} v_e \qquad \mu_w = \frac{1}{n} \sum_{e \in G_E} w_e \qquad n = |G_E|$$

$$\mu_{v^2} = \frac{1}{n} \sum_{e \in G_E} v_e^2 \qquad \mu_{w^2} = \frac{1}{n} \sum_{e \in G_E} w_e^2 \qquad \mu_{vw} = \frac{1}{n} \sum_{e \in G_E} v_e w_e$$

and: $\beta_v = \dfrac{1}{n-1} \left(\dfrac{\mu_{v^2}}{\mu_v^2} - \dfrac{\mu_{vw}}{\mu_v \mu_w} \right) \qquad \beta_w = \dfrac{1}{n-1} \left(\dfrac{\mu_{w^2}}{\mu_w^2} - \dfrac{\mu_{vw}}{\mu_v \mu_w} \right)$

For a proof of these equations, see Appendix A; all appendices are available at https://hal.archives-ouvertes.fr/hal-02161309/document.

Note that the complexity of the computation of the approximate confidence interval $\widehat{CI}_k^{1-\alpha}$ is $\mathcal{O}(n)$, with n the size of entities collection G_E.

4.1 Pruning the Search Space

Optimistic Estimate on Krippendorff's Alpha. To quickly prune unpromising areas of the search space, we define a tight optimistic estimate [15] on Krippendorff's alpha. Eppstein and Hirschberg [11] propose a smart *linear algorithm* `Random-SMWA`[3] to find subsets with maximum weighted average. Recall that A can be seen as a weighted average (cf. Eq. (4)).

In a nutshell, `Random-SMWA` seeks to remove k values to find a subset of S having $|S| - k$ values with maximum weighted average. The authors model the problem as such: given $|S|$ values decreasing linearly with time, find the time at which the $|S| - k$ maximum values add to zero. In the scope of this work, given a user-defined support threshold σ_E on the minimum allowed size of context extents, k is fixed to $|S| - \sigma_E$. The obtained subset corresponds to the smallest allowed subset having support $\geq \sigma_E$ maximizing the weighted average quantity A. The `Random-SMWA` algorithm can be tweaked[4] to retrieve the smallest subset of size $\geq \sigma_E$ having analogously the minimum possible weighted average quantity A. We refer to the algorithm returning the maximum (resp. minimum) possible weighted average by `RandomSMWA`^{max} (resp. `RandomSMWA`^{min}).

---

[3] `Random-SMWA`: Randomized algorithm - Subset with Maximum Weighted Average.
[4] Finding the subset having the minimum weighted average is a dual problem to finding the subset having the maximum weighted average. To solve the former problem using `Random-SMWA`, we modify the values of v_i to $-v_i$ and keep the same weights w_i.

Proposition 2 (Upper and Lower Bounds for A). *Given $S \subseteq G_E$, minimum context support threshold σ_E, and the following functions:*

$$UB(S) = A\left(\texttt{RandomSMWA}^{\max}(S, \sigma_E)\right) \qquad LB(S) = A\left(\texttt{RandomSMWA}^{\min}(S, \sigma_E)\right)$$

we know that LB (resp. UB) is a lower (resp. upper) bound for A, i.e.:

$$\forall c, d \in \mathcal{D}_E \;:\; c \sqsubseteq d \wedge |G_E^c| \geq |G_E^d| \geq \sigma_E \Rightarrow LB(G_E^c) \leq A(G_E^c) \leq UB(G_E^c)$$

Using these results, we define the optimistic estimate for A as an interval bounded by the minimum and the maximum A measure that one can observe from the subsets of a given subset $S \subseteq G_E$, that is: $OE(S, \sigma_E) = [LB(S), UB(S)]$.

Nested Confidence Intervals for A. The desired property between two confidence intervals of the same significance level α related to respectively k_1, k_2 with $k_1 \leq k_2$ is that $CI_{k_1}^{1-\alpha}$ encompasses $CI_{k_2}^{1-\alpha}$. Colloquially speaking, larger samples lead to "narrower" confidence intervals. This property is intuitively plausible, since the dispersion of the observed intra-agreement for smaller samples is likely to be higher than the dispersion for larger samples. Having such a property allows to prune the search subspace related to a context c when traversing the search space downward if $OE(G_E^c, \sigma_E) \subseteq CI_{|G_E^c|}^{1-\alpha}$.

Proving $CI_{k_2}^{1-\alpha} \subseteq CI_{k_1}^{1-\alpha}$ for $k_1 \leq k_2$ for the exact confidence interval is nontrivial, since it requires to analytically derive $E[\theta_k]$ and $\text{Var}[\theta_k]$ for any $1 \leq k \leq n$. Note that the expected value $E[\theta_k]$ varies when k varies. We study such a property for the approximate confidence interval $\widehat{CI}_k^{1-\alpha}$.

Proposition 3 (Minimum Cardinality Constraint for Nested Approximate Confidence Intervals). *Given a context support threshold σ_E and α.*

$$\text{If } \sigma_E \geq C^\alpha = \frac{4n\beta_w^2}{z_{1-\frac{\alpha}{2}}^2(\beta_v + \beta_w) + 4\beta_w^2},$$

$$\text{then } \forall k_1, k_2 \in \mathbb{N} : \sigma_E \leq k_1 \leq k_2 \Rightarrow \widehat{CI}_{k_2}^{1-\alpha} \subseteq \widehat{CI}_{k_1}^{1-\alpha}$$

Combining Propositions 1, 2 and 3, we formalize the pruning region property which answers: *when to prune the sub-search space under a context c?*

Corollary 1 (Pruning Regions). *Given a behavioral dataset $\mathcal{B}$, a context support threshold $\sigma_E \geq C^\alpha$, and a significance critical value $\alpha \in]0,1]$. For any $c, d \in \mathcal{D}_E$ such that $c \sqsubseteq d$ with $|G_E^c| \geq |G_E^d| \geq \sigma_E$, we have:*

$$OE(G_E^c, \sigma_E) \subseteq \widehat{CI}_{|G_E^c|}^{1-\alpha} \Rightarrow A(G_E^d) \in \widehat{CI}_{|G_E^d|}^{1-\alpha} \Rightarrow p\text{-}value(d) > \alpha$$

Proofs. All proofs of propositions and properties can be found in Appendix A.

5   On Handling Variability of Outcomes Among Raters

In Sect. 4, we defined the confidence interval $CI^{1-\alpha}$ established over the DFD. By taking into consideration the variability induced by the selection of a subset of entities, such a confidence interval enables to avoid reporting subgroups indicating an intra-agreement likely (w.r.t. the critical value α) to be observed by a random subset of entities. For more statistically sound results, one should not only take into account the variability induced by the selection of subsets of entities, but also the variability induced by the outcomes of the selected group of individuals. This is well summarized by Hayes and Krippendorff [18]: "The obtained value of A is subject to random sampling variability—specifically variability attributable to the selection of units (i.e., entities) in the reliability data (i.e., behavioral data) and the variability of their judgments". To address these two questions, they recommend to employ a standard Efron & Tibshirani *bootstrapping approach* [10] to empirically generate the sampling distribution of A and produce an empirical confidence interval $CI_{\text{bootstrap}}^{1-\alpha}$.

Recall that we consider here a behavioral dataset $\mathcal{B}$ reduced to the outcomes of a selected group of individuals g. Following the bootstrapping scheme proposed by Krippendorff [18,21], the empirical confidence interval is computed by repeatedly performing the following steps: (1) resample n entities from G_E with replacement; (2) for each sampled entity, draw uniformly $m_e \cdot (m_e - 1)$ pairs of outcomes according to the distribution of the observed pairs of outcomes; (3) compute the observed disagreement and calculate Krippendorff's alpha on the resulting resample. This process, repeated b times, leads to a vector of bootstrap estimates (sorted in ascending order) $\hat{B} = [\hat{A}_1, \ldots, \hat{A}_b]$. Given the empirical distribution $\hat{B}$, the empirical confidence interval $CI_{\text{bootstrap}}^{1-\alpha}$ is defined by the percentiles of $\hat{B}$, i.e., $CI_{\text{bootstrap}}^{1-\alpha} = [\hat{A}_{\lfloor \frac{\alpha}{2} \cdot b \rfloor}, \hat{A}_{\lceil (1-\frac{\alpha}{2}) \cdot b \rceil}]$. We denote by $\text{MCI}^{1-\alpha}$ (Merged CI) the confidence interval that takes into consideration both $CI^{1-\alpha} = [\text{le}_1, \text{re}_1]$ and $CI_{\text{bootstrap}}^{1-\alpha} = [\text{le}_2, \text{re}_2]$. We have $\text{MCI}^{1-\alpha} = [\min(\text{le}_1, \text{le}_2), \max(\text{re}_1, \text{re}_2)]$.

6   A Branch-and-Bound Solution: Algorithm DEvIANT

To detect exceptional contextual intra-group agreement patterns, we need to enumerate candidates $p = (g, c) \in (\mathcal{D}_I, \mathcal{D}_E)$. Both heuristic (e.g., beam search [23]) and exhaustive (e.g., GP-growth [24]) enumeration algorithms exist. We exhaustively enumerate all candidate subgroups while leveraging closure operators [12] (since A computation only depends on the extent of a pattern). This makes it possible to avoid redundancy and to substantially reduce the number of visited patterns. With this aim in mind, and since the data we deal with are of the same format as those handled in the previous work [2], we apply EnumCC to enumerate subgroups g (resp. c) in $\mathcal{D}_I$ (resp. $\mathcal{D}_E$). EnumCC follows the line of algorithm CloseByOne [22]. Given a collection G of records (G_E or G_I), EnumCC traverses the search space depth-first and enumerates only once all closed descriptions fulfilling the minimum support constraint σ. EnumCC follows a yield and wait paradigm (similar to Python's generators) which at each call yield the following candidate and wait for the next call. See Appendix B for details.

DEvIANT implements an efficient branch-and-bound algorithm to **D**iscover statistically significant **E**xceptional **I**ntra-group **A**greement pa**T**terns while leveraging closure, tight optimistic estimates and pruning properties. DEvIANT starts by selecting a group g of individuals. Next, the corresponding behavioral dataset $\mathcal{B}^g$ is established by reducing the original dataset $\mathcal{B}$ to elements concerning solely the individuals comprising G_I^g and entities having at least two outcomes. Subsequently, the bootstrap confidence interval $\mathrm{CI}_{\mathrm{bootstrap}}^{1-\alpha}$ is calculated.

Before searching for exceptional contexts, the minimum context support threshold σ_E is adjusted to $C^\alpha(g)$ (cf. Proposition 3) if it is lower than $C^\alpha(g)$. While in practice $C^\alpha(g) \ll \sigma_E$, we keep this correction for algorithm soundness. Next, contexts are enumerated by EnumCC. For each candidate context c, the optimistic estimate interval $OE(G_E^c)$ is computed (cf. Proposition 2). According to Corollary 1, if $OE(G_E^c, \sigma_E^g) \subseteq \mathrm{MCI}_{|G_E^c|}^{1-\alpha}$, the search subspace under c can be pruned. Otherwise, $A^g(G_E^c)$ is computed and evaluated against $\mathrm{MCI}_{|G_E^c|}^{1-\alpha}$. If $A^g(G_E^c) \notin \mathrm{MCI}_{|G_E^c|}^{1-\alpha}$, then (g, c) is significant and kept in the result set P. To reduce the number of reported patterns, we keep only the most general patterns while ensuring that each significant pattern in $\mathcal{P}$ is represented by a pattern in P. This formally translates to: $\forall p' = (g', c') \in \mathcal{P} \setminus P : p\text{-}value^{g'}(c') \leq \alpha \Rightarrow \exists p = (g, c) \in P$ s.t. $\mathrm{ext}(q) \subseteq \mathrm{ext}(p)$, with $\mathrm{ext}(q = (g', c')) \subseteq \mathrm{ext}(p = (g, c))$ defined by

---

Algorithm 1: DEvIANT$(\mathcal{B}, \sigma_E, \sigma_I, \alpha)$

Inputs : Behavioral dataset $\mathcal{B} = \langle G_I, G_E, O, o \rangle$, minimum support threshold σ_E of a context and σ_I of a group, and critical significance value α.

Output: Set of exceptional intra-group agreement patterns P.

1 $P \leftarrow \{\}$

2 **foreach** $(g, G_I^g, cont_g) \in \mathrm{EnumCC}(G_I, *, \sigma_I, 0, True)$ **do**

3     $G_E(g) = \{e \in E$ s.t. $n_e^g \geq e\}$

4     $\mathcal{B}^g = \langle G_E(g), G_I^g, O, o \rangle$

5     $\mathrm{CI}_{\mathrm{bootstrap}}^{1-\alpha} = [\hat{A}_{\lfloor \frac{\alpha}{2} \cdot b \rfloor}, \hat{A}_{\lceil (1 - \frac{\alpha}{2}) \cdot b \rceil}]$ $\triangleright$ With $\hat{B} = [\hat{A}_1^g, ..., \hat{A}_b^g]$ computed on

6     $\sigma_E^g = \max(C^\alpha(g), \sigma_E)$ respectively b resamples of $\mathcal{B}^g$

7   **foreach** $(c, G_E^c, cont_c) \in \mathrm{EnumCC}(G_E(g), *, \sigma_E^g, 0, True)$ **do**

8        $\mathrm{MCI}_{|G_E^c|}^{1-\alpha} = \mathrm{merge}\left(\widehat{CI}_{|G_E^c|}^{1-\alpha}, \mathrm{CI}_{\mathrm{bootstrap}}^{1-\alpha}\right)$

9   **if** $OE(G_E^c, \sigma_E^g) \subseteq \mathrm{MCI}_{|G_E^c|}^{1-\alpha}$ **then**

10          $cont_c \leftarrow$ False $\triangleright$ Prune the unpromising search subspace under c

11   **else if** $A^g(G_E^c) \notin \mathrm{MCI}_{|G_E^c|}^{1-\alpha}$ **then**

12          $p_{\mathrm{new}} \leftarrow (g, c)$

13   **if** $\nexists p_{\mathrm{old}} \in P$ s.t. $\mathrm{ext}(p_{\mathrm{new}}) \subseteq \mathrm{ext}(p_{\mathrm{old}})$ **then**

14            $P \leftarrow (P \cup p_{\mathrm{new}}) \setminus \{p_{\mathrm{old}} \in P \mid \mathrm{ext}(p_{\mathrm{old}}) \subseteq \mathrm{ext}(p_{\mathrm{new}})\}$

15          $cont_c \leftarrow$ False $\triangleright$ Prune the sub search space (generality concept)

16 **return** P

Table 3. Main characteristics of the behavioral datasets. $C^{0.05}$ represents the minimum context support threshold over which we have nested approximate CI property.

	$|G_E|$	$\mathcal{A}_E$ (Items-Scaling)	$|G_I|$	$\mathcal{A}_I$ (Items-Scaling)	Outcomes	Sparsity	$C^{0.05}$
EPD8[a]	4704	$1H + 1N + 1C$ (437)	848	$3C$ (82)	$3.1M$ (C)	78.6%	$\simeq 10^{-6}$
CHUS[b]	17350	$1H + 2N$ (307)	1373	$2C$ (261)	$3M$ (C)	31.2%	$\simeq 10^{-4}$
Movielens[c]	1681	$1H + 1N$ (161)	943	$3C$ (27)	$100K$ (O)	06.3%	$\simeq 0.065$
Yelp[d]	$127K$	$1H + 1C$ (851)	$1M$	$3C$ (6)	$4.15M$ (O)	0.003%	$\simeq 1.14$

[a]Eighth European Parliament Voting Dataset (04/10/18).
[b]102nd-115th congresses of the US House of Representatives (Period: 1991-2015).
[c]Movie review dataset - https://grouplens.org/datasets/movielens/100k/.
[d]Social network dataset - https://www.yelp.com/dataset/challenge (25/04/17).

$G_I^{g'} \subseteq G_I^g$ and $G_E^{c'} \subseteq G_E^c$. This is based on the following postulate: the end-user is more interested by exceptional (dis-)agreement within larger groups and/or for larger contexts rather than local exceptional (dis-)agreement. Moreover, the end-user can always refine their analysis to obtain more fine-grained results by re-launching the algorithm starting from a specific context or group.

7   Empirical Evaluation

Our experiments aim to answer the following questions: $(\mathbf{Q_1})$ How well does the Taylor-approximated CI approach the empirical CI? $(\mathbf{Q_2})$ How efficient is the Taylor-approximated CI and the pruning properties? $(\mathbf{Q_3})$ Does DEvIANT provide interpretable patterns? Source code and data are available on our companion page: https://github.com/Adnene93/Deviant.

Datasets. Experiments were carried on four real-world behavioral datasets (cf. Table 3): two voting (EPD8 and CHUS) and two rating datasets (Movielens and Yelp). Each dataset features entities and individuals described by attributes that are either categorical (C), numerical (N), or categorical augmented with a taxonomy (H). We also report the equivalent number of items (in an itemset language) corresponding to the descriptive attributes (ordinal scaling [13]).

$\mathbf{Q_1}$. First, we evaluate to what extent the empirically computed confidence interval approximates the confidence interval computed by Taylor approximations. We run 1000 experiments for subset sizes k uniformly randomly distributed in $[1, n = |G_E|]$. For each k, we compute the corresponding Taylor approximation $\widehat{CI}_k^{1-\alpha} = [a^T, b^T]$ and empirical confidence interval $\text{ECI}_k^{1-\alpha} = [a^E, b^E]$. The latter is calculated over 10^4 samples of size k from G_E, on which we compute the observed A which are then used to estimate the moments of the empirical distribution required for establishing $\text{ECI}_k^{1-\alpha}$. Once both CIs are computed, we measure their distance by Jaccard index. Table 4 reports the average μ_{err} and the standard deviation σ_{err} of the observed distances (coverage error) over the 1000 experiments. Note that the difference between the analytic Taylor approximation and the empirical approximation is negligible ($\mu_{err} < 10^{-2}$). Therefore, the CIs

Table 4. Coverage error between empirical CIs and Taylor CIs.

$\mathcal{B}$	μ_{err}	σ_{err}	$\mathcal{B}$	μ_{err}	σ_{err}	$\mathcal{B}$	μ_{err}	σ_{err}	$\mathcal{B}$	μ_{err}	σ_{err}
CHUS	0.007	0.004	EPD8	0.007	0.004	Movielens	0.0075	0.0045	Yelp	0.007	0.004

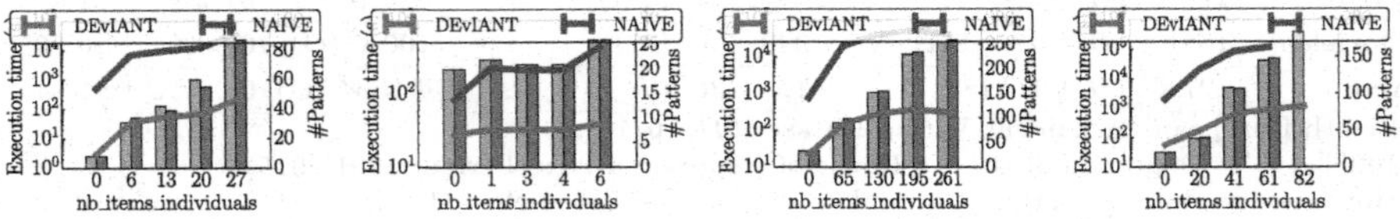

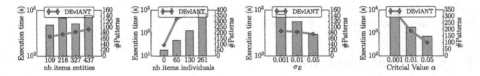

(a) Movielens   (b) Yelp   (c) EPD8   (d) CHUS

Fig. 2. Comparison between DEvIANT and `Naive` when varying the size of the description space $\mathcal{D}_I$. Lines correspond to the execution time and bars correspond to the number of output patterns. Parameters: $\sigma_E = \sigma_I = 1\%$ and $\alpha = 0.05$.

Fig. 3. Effectiveness of DEvIANT on EPD8 when varying sizes of both search spaces $\mathcal{D}_E$ and $\mathcal{D}_I$, minimum context support threshold σ_E and the critical value α. Default parameters: full search spaces $\mathcal{D}_E$ and $\mathcal{D}_I$, $\sigma_E = 0.1\%$, $\sigma_I = 1\%$ and $\alpha = 0.05$.

approximated by the two methods are so close, that it does not matter which method is used. Hence, the choice is guided by the computational efficiency.

Q$_2$. To evaluate the pruning properties' efficiency (**(i)** Taylor-approximated CI, **(ii)** optimistic estimates and **(iii)** nested approximated CIs), we compare DEvIANT with a `Naive` approach where the three aforementioned properties are disabled. For a fair comparison, `Naive` pushes monotonic constraints (minimum support threshold) and employs closure operators while empirically estimating the CI by successive random trials from F_k. In both algorithms we disable the bootstrap $\mathrm{CI}^{1-\alpha}_{\mathrm{bootstrap}}$ computation, since its overhead is equal for both algorithms. We vary the description space size related to groups of individuals $\mathcal{D}_I$ while considering the full entity description space. Figure 2 displays the results: DEvIANT outperforms `Naive` in terms of runtime by nearly two orders of magnitude while outputting the same number of the desired patterns.

Figure 3 reports the performance of DEvIANT in terms of runtime and number of output patterns. When varying the description space size, DEvIANT requires more time to finish. Note that the size of individuals search space $\mathcal{D}_I$ substantially affects the runtime of DEvIANT. This is mainly because larger $\mathcal{D}_I$ leads to more candidate groups of individuals g which require DEvIANT to: (i) generate $\mathrm{CI}^{1-\alpha}_{\mathrm{bootstrap}}$ and (ii) mine for exceptional contexts c concerning

Table 5. All the exceptional consensual/conflictual subjects among **Republican Party** representatives (selected upfront, i.e. G_I restricted over members of Republican party) in the 115th congress of the US House of Representatives. $\alpha = 0.01$.

id	group (g)	context (c)	$A^g(*)$	$A^g(c)$	p-$value$	IA
p_1	Republicans	20.11 Government and Administration issues	0.83	0.32	$< .001$	Conflict
p_2	Republicans	5 Labor	0.83	0.63	$< .01$	Conflict
p_3	Republicans	20.05 Nominations and Appointments	0.83	0.92	$< .001$	Consensus

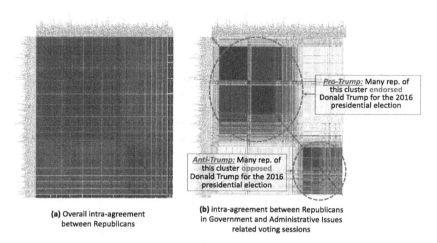

(a) Overall intra-agreement between Republicans

(b) intra-agreement between Republicans in Government and Administrative Issues related voting sessions

Pro-Trump: Many rep. of this cluster endorsed Donald Trump for the 2016 presidential election

Anti-Trump: Many rep. of this cluster opposed Donald Trump for the 2016 presidential election

Fig. 4. Similarity matrix between Republicans, illustrating Pattern p_1 from Table 5. Each cell represents the ratio of voting sessions in which Republicans agreed. Green cells report strong agreement; red cells highlight strong disagreement. (Color figure online)

the candidate group g. Finally, when α decreases, the execution time required for DEvIANT to finish increases while returning more patterns. This may seem counter-intuitive, since fewer patterns are significant when α decreases. It is a consequence of DEvIANT considering only the most general patterns. Hence, when α decreases, DEvIANT goes deeper in the context search space: much more candidate patterns are tested, enlarging the result set. The same conclusions are found on the Yelp, Movielens, and CHUS datasets (cf. Appendix D).

Q₃. Table 5 reports exceptional contexts observed among House Republicans during the 115th Congress. Pattern p_1, illustrated in Fig. 4, highlights a collection of voting sessions addressing Government and Administrative issues where a clear polarization is observed between two clusters of Republicans. A roll call vote in this context featuring significant disagreement between Republicans is "**House Vote 417**" (cf. https://projects.propublica.org/represent/votes/115/house/1/417) which was closely watched by the media (Washington Post: https://wapo.st/2W32I9c; Reuters: https://reut.rs/2TF0dgV).

Table 6 depicts patterns returned by DEvIANT on the Movielens dataset. Pattern p_2 reports that "Middle-aged Men" observe an intra-group agreement

Table 6. Top-3 exceptionally consensual/conflictual genres between Movielens raters, $\alpha = 0.01$. Patterns are ranked by absolute difference between $A^g(c)$ and $A^g(*)$.

id	group (g)	context (c)	$A^g(*)$	$A^g(c)$	p-$value$	IA
p_1	Old	1.Action & 2.Adventure & 6.Crime Movies	−0.06	−0.29	< 0.01	Conflict
p_2	Middle-aged Men	2.Adventure & 12.Musical Movies	0.05	0.21	< 0.01	Consensus
p_3	Old	4.Children & 12.Musical Movies	−0.06	−0.21	< 0.01	Conflict

significantly higher than overall, for movies labeled with both adventure and musical genres (e.g., The Wizard of Oz (1939)).

8 Conclusion and Future Directions

We introduce the task to discover statistically significant exceptional contextual intra-group agreement patterns. To efficiently search for such patterns, we devise DEvIANT, a branch-and-bound algorithm leveraging closure operators, approximate confidence intervals, tight. optimistic estimates on Krippendorff's Alpha measure, and the property of nested CIs. Experiments demonstrate DEvIANT's performance on behavioral datasets in domains ranging from political analysis to rating data analysis. In future work, we plan to (i) investigate how to tackle the multiple comparison problem [17], (ii) investigate intra-group agreement which is exceptional w.r.t. all individuals *over the same context*, and (iii) integrate the option to choose which kind of exceptional consensus the end-user wants: is the exceptional consensus caused by common preference or hatred for the context-related entities? All this is to be done within a comprehensive framework and tool (prototype available at http://contentcheck.liris.cnrs.fr) for behavioral data analysis alongside exceptional inter-group agreement pattern discovery implemented in [2].

Acknowledgments. This work has been partially supported by the project *ContentCheck* **ANR-15-CE23-0025** funded by the French National Research Agency. The authors would like to thank the reviewers for their valuable remarks. They also warmly thank Arno Knobbe, Simon van der Zon, Aimene Belfodil and Gabriela Ciuperca for interesting discussions.

References

1. Amer-Yahia, S., Kleisarchaki, S., Kolloju, N.K., Lakshmanan, L.V., Zamar, R.H..: Exploring rated datasets with rating maps. In: WWW (2017)
2. Belfodil, A., Cazalens, S., Lamarre, P., Plantevit, M.: Flash points: discovering exceptional pairwise behaviors in vote or rating data. In: Ceci, M., Hollmén, J., Todorovski, L., Vens, C., Džeroski, S. (eds.) ECML PKDD 2017. LNCS (LNAI), vol. 10535, pp. 442–458. Springer, Cham (2017). https://doi.org/10.1007/978-3-319-71246-8_27
3. Cover, T., Thomas, J.: Elements of Information Theory. Wiley, Hoboken (2012)

4. Das, M., Amer-Yahia, S., Das, G., Mri, C.Y.: Meaningful interpretations of collaborative ratings. PVLDB **4**(11), 1063–1074 (2011)
5. de Bie, T.: An information theoretic framework for data mining. In: KDD (2011)
6. Duivesteijn, W., Feelders, A.J., Knobbe, A.: Exceptional model mining. Data Min. Knowl. Disc. **30**(1), 47–98 (2016)
7. Duivesteijn, W., Knobbe, A.: Exploiting false discoveries-statistical validation of patterns and quality measures in subgroup discovery. In: ICDM (2011)
8. Duivesteijn, W., Knobbe, A.J., Feelders, A., van Leeuwen, M.: Subgroup discovery meets Bayesian networks - an exceptional model mining approach. In: ICDM (2010)
9. Duris, F., et al.: Mean and variance of ratios of proportions from categories of a multinomial distribution. J. Stat. Distrib. Appl. **5**(1), 1–20 (2018). https://doi.org/10.1186/s40488-018-0083-x
10. Efron, B., Tibshirani, R.J.: An Introduction to the Bootstrap. CRC Press, Boca Raton (1994)
11. Eppstein, D., Hirschberg, D.S.: Choosing subsets with maximum weighted average. J. Algorithms **24**(1), 177–193 (1997)
12. Ganter, B., Kuznetsov, S.O.: Pattern structures and their projections. In: Delugach, H.S., Stumme, G. (eds.) ICCS-ConceptStruct 2001. LNCS (LNAI), vol. 2120, pp. 129–142. Springer, Heidelberg (2001). https://doi.org/10.1007/3-540-44583-8_10
13. Ganter, B., Wille, R.: Formal Concept Analysis - Mathematical Foundations. Springer, Heidelberg (1999). https://doi.org/10.1007/978-3-642-59830-2
14. Geisser, S.: Predictive Inference, vol. 55. CRC Press, Boca Raton (1993)
15. Grosskreutz, H., Rüping, S., Wrobel, S.: Tight optimistic estimates for fast subgroup discovery. In: Daelemans, W., Goethals, B., Morik, K. (eds.) ECML PKDD 2008. LNCS (LNAI), vol. 5211, pp. 440–456. Springer, Heidelberg (2008). https://doi.org/10.1007/978-3-540-87479-9_47
16. Hämäläinen, W.: StatApriori: an efficient algorithm for searching statistically significant association rules. Knowl. Inf. Syst. **23**(3), 373–399 (2010)
17. Hämäläinen, W., Webb, G.I.: A tutorial on statistically sound pattern discovery. Data Min. Knowl. Disc. **33**(2), 325–377 (2018). https://doi.org/10.1007/s10618-018-0590-x
18. Hayes, A.F., Krippendorff, K.: Answering the call for a standard reliability measure for coding data. Commun. Methods Meas. **1**(1), 77–89 (2007)
19. Holm, S.: A simple sequentially rejective multiple test procedure. Scand. J. Stat. 65–70 (1979)
20. Kendall, M., Stuart, A., Ord, J.: Kendall's advanced theory of statistics. v. 1: distribution theory (1994)
21. Krippendorff, K.: Content Analysis, An Introduction to Its Methodology (2004)
22. Kuznetsov, S.O.: Learning of simple conceptual graphs from positive and negative examples. In: Żytkow, J.M., Rauch, J. (eds.) PKDD 1999. LNCS (LNAI), vol. 1704, pp. 384–391. Springer, Heidelberg (1999). https://doi.org/10.1007/978-3-540-48247-5_47
23. van Leeuwen, M., Knobbe, A.J.: Diverse subgroup set discovery. Data Min. Knowl. Discov. **25**(2), 208–242 (2012)
24. Lemmerich, F., Becker, M., Atzmueller, M.: Generic pattern trees for exhaustive exceptional model mining. In: Flach, P.A., De Bie, T., Cristianini, N. (eds.) ECML PKDD 2012. LNCS (LNAI), vol. 7524, pp. 277–292. Springer, Heidelberg (2012). https://doi.org/10.1007/978-3-642-33486-3_18
25. Lemmerich, F., Becker, M., Singer, P., Helic, D., Hotho, A., Strohmaier, M.: Mining subgroups with exceptional transition behavior. In: KDD (2016)

26. Minato, S., Uno, T., Tsuda, K., Terada, A., Sese, J.: A fast method of statistical assessment for combinatorial hypotheses based on frequent itemset enumeration. In: Calders, T., Esposito, F., Hüllermeier, E., Meo, R. (eds.) ECML PKDD 2014. LNCS (LNAI), vol. 8725, pp. 422–436. Springer, Heidelberg (2014). https://doi.org/10.1007/978-3-662-44851-9_27
27. Webb, G.I.: Discov significant patterns. Mach. Learn. **68**(1), 1–33 (2007)
28. Wrobel, S.: An algorithm for multi-relational discovery of subgroups. In: PKDD (1997)

Maximal Closed Set and Half-Space Separations in Finite Closure Systems

Florian Seiffarth[1(✉)], Tamás Horváth[1,2,3], and Stefan Wrobel[1,2,3]

[1] Department of Computer Science, University of Bonn, Bonn, Germany
{seiffarth,horvath,wrobel}@cs.uni-bonn.de
[2] Fraunhofer IAIS, Schloss Birlinghoven, Sankt Augustin, Germany
[3] Fraunhofer Center for Machine Learning, Sankt Augustin, Germany

Abstract. Motivated by various binary classification problems in structured data (e.g., graphs or other relational and algebraic structures), we investigate some algorithmic properties of closed set and half-space separation in abstract closure systems. Assuming that the underlying closure system is finite and given by the corresponding closure operator, we formulate some negative and positive complexity results for these two separation problems. In particular, we prove that deciding half-space separability in abstract closure systems is NP-complete in general. On the other hand, for the relaxed problem of maximal closed set separation we propose a simple greedy algorithm and show that it is efficient and has the best possible lower bound on the number of closure operator calls. As a second direction to overcome the negative result above, we consider Kakutani closure systems and show first that our greedy algorithm provides an algorithmic characterization of this kind of set systems. As one of the major potential application fields, we then focus on Kakutani closure systems over graphs and generalize a fundamental characterization result based on the Pasch axiom to graph structure partitioning of finite sets. Though the primary focus of this work is on the generality of the results obtained, we experimentally demonstrate the practical usefulness of our approach on vertex classification in different graph datasets.

Keywords: Closure systems · Half-space separation · Binary classification

1 Introduction

The theory of binary separation in $\mathbb{R}^d$ by hyperplanes goes back to at least Rosenblatt's pioneer work on perceptron learning in the late fifties [12]. Since then several deep results have been published on this topic including, among others, Vapnik and his co-workers seminal paper on support vector machines [2]. The general problem of binary separation in $\mathbb{R}^d$ by hyperplanes can be regarded as follows: Given two finite sets $R, B \subseteq \mathbb{R}^d$, check whether their convex hulls are disjoint, or not. If not then return the answer "No" indicating that R and B are not separable by a hyperplane. Otherwise, there exists a hyperplane in $\mathbb{R}^d$ such

© Springer Nature Switzerland AG 2020
U. Brefeld et al. (Eds.): ECML PKDD 2019, LNAI 11906, pp. 21–37, 2020.
https://doi.org/10.1007/978-3-030-46150-8_2

that the convex hull of R lies completely in one of the two half-spaces defined by the hyperplane and that of B in the other one. The class of an unseen point in $\mathbb{R}^d$ is then predicted by that of the training examples in the half-space it belongs to. The correctness of this generic method for $\mathbb{R}^d$ is justified by the result of Kakutani [9] that any two disjoint convex sets in $\mathbb{R}^d$ are always separable by a hyperplane.

While hyperplane separation in $\mathbb{R}^d$ is a well-founded field, the adaptation of the above idea to other types of data, such as graphs and other relational and algebraic structures has received less attention by the machine learning community. In contrast, the idea of abstract half-spaces over finite domains has intensively been studied among others in geometry and theoretical computer science (see, e.g., [4,5,10,15]). Using the fact that the set of all convex hulls in $\mathbb{R}^d$ forms a *closure system*, the underlying idea of generalizing hyperplane separation in $\mathbb{R}^d$ to arbitrary finite sets E is to consider some semantically meaningful closure system $\mathcal{C}$ over E (see, e.g., [16] for abstract closure structures). A subset H of E is then considered as an *abstract* half-space, if H and its complement both belong to $\mathcal{C}$. In this field of research there is a special focus on characterization results of special closure systems, called *Kakutani closure systems* (see, e.g., [4,16]). This kind of closure systems satisfy the following property: If the closures of two sets are disjoint then they are half-space separable in the closure system.

Utilizing the results of other research fields, in this work we deal with the *algorithmic* aspects of half-space separation in closure systems over *finite* domains (or ground sets) from the point of view of *binary classification*. In all results presented in this paper we assume that the abstract closure system is given implicitly via the corresponding *closure operator*. This assumption is justified by the fact that the cardinality of a closure system can be exponential in that of the domain. The closure operator is regarded as an *oracle* (or black box) which returns in *unit time* the closure of any subset of the domain. Using these assumptions, we first show that deciding whether two subsets of the ground set are half-space separable in the underlying abstract closure system is NP-complete.

In order to overcome this negative result, we then relax the problem setting of half-space separation to *maximal* closed set[1] separation. That is, to the problem of finding two closed sets in the closure system that are disjoint, contain the two input subsets, and have no supersets in the closure system w.r.t. these two properties. For this relaxed problem we give a simple efficient greedy algorithm and show that it is optimal w.r.t. the number of closure operator calls in the worst-case. As a second way to resolve the negative result mentioned above, we then focus on Kakutani closure systems. We first show that any deterministic algorithm deciding whether a closure system is Kakutani or not requires exponentially many closure operator calls in the worst-case. Despite this negative result, Kakutani closure systems remain highly interesting for our purpose because there are various closure systems which are known to be Kakutani. We also prove that the greedy algorithm mentioned above provides an algorithmic

---

[1] Throughout this work we consistently use the nomenclature "closed sets" by noting that "convex" and "closed" are synonyms by the standard terminology of this field.

characterization of Kakutani closure systems. This implies that for these systems the output is always a partitioning of the domain into two half-spaces containing the closures of the input sets if and only if their closures are disjoint.

Regarding potential applications of maximal closed set and half-space separations, we then turn our attention to graphs.[2] Using the notion of convexity for graphs induced by shortest paths [6], we generalize a fundamental characterization result of Kakutani closure systems based on the Pasch axiom [4] to graph structured partitioning of finite sets. Potential practical applications of this generalization result include e.g. graph clustering and partitioning or mining logical formulas over graphs.

Besides the positive and negative theoretical results, we also present extensive experimental results for binary vertex classification in graphs, by stressing that our generic approach is not restricted to graphs. In the experiments we first consider trees and then arbitrary graphs. Regarding *trees*, the closure systems considered are always Kakutani. Our results clearly demonstrate that a remarkable predictive accuracy can be obtained even for such cases where the two sets of vertices corresponding to the two classes do not form half-spaces in the closure systems. Since the closure systems considered over *arbitrary* graphs are not necessarily Kakutani, the case of vertex classification in arbitrary graphs is reduced to that in trees as follows: Consider a set of random spanning trees of the graph at hand and predict the vertex labels by the majority vote of the predictions in the spanning trees. Our experimental results show that this heuristic results in considerable predictive performance on sparse graphs. We emphasize that we deliberately have *not* exploited any domain specific properties in the experiments, as our primary goal was to study the predictive performance of our *general* purpose algorithm. We therefore also have not compared our results with those of the state-of-the-art domain specific algorithms.

The rest of the paper is organized as follows. In Sect. 2 we collect the necessary notions and fix the notation. Section 3 is concerned with the negative result on the complexity of the half-space separation problem and with the relaxed problem of maximal closed set separation. Section 4 is devoted to Kakutani and Sect. 5 to non-Kakutani closure systems. Finally, in Sect. 6 we conclude and formulate some open problems. Due to space limitations we omit the proofs from this short version.

2 Preliminaries

In this section we collect the necessary notions and notation for set and closure systems (see, e.g., [4, 16] for references on closure systems and separation axioms).

For a set E, 2^E denotes the power set of E. A *set system* over a ground set E is a pair $(E, \mathcal{C})$ with $\mathcal{C} \subseteq 2^E$; $(E, \mathcal{C})$ is a *closure system* if it fulfills the following properties: $\emptyset, E \in \mathcal{C}$ and $X \cap Y \in \mathcal{C}$ holds for all $X, Y \in \mathcal{C}$. The reason

---

[2] An entirely different application to binary classification in *distributive lattices* with applications to inductive logic programming and formal concept analysis is discussed in the long version of this paper.

of requiring $\emptyset \in \mathcal{C}$ is discussed below. Throughout this paper by closure systems we always mean closure systems over *finite* ground sets (i.e., $|E| < \infty$). It is a well-known fact that any closure system can be defined by a *closure operator*, i.e., a function $\rho : 2^E \to 2^E$ satisfying for all $X, Y \subseteq E$: $X \subseteq \rho(X)$ (*extensivity*), $\rho(X) \subseteq \rho(Y)$ whenever $X \subseteq Y$ (*monotonicity*), $\rho(\rho(X)) = \rho(X)$ (*idempotency*).

For a closure operator ρ over E with $\rho(\emptyset) = \emptyset$ the corresponding closure system, denoted $(E, \mathcal{C}_\rho)$, is defined by its fixed points, i.e., $\mathcal{C}_\rho = \{X \subseteq E : \rho(X) = X\}$. Conversely, for a closure system $(E, \mathcal{C}_\rho)$, the corresponding closure operator ρ is defined by $\rho(X) = \bigcap\{C : X \subseteq C \wedge C \in \mathcal{C}\}$ for all $X \subseteq E$. Depending on the context we sometimes omit the underlying closure operator from the notation and denote the closure system at hand by $(E, \mathcal{C})$. The elements of $\mathcal{C}_\rho$ of a closure system $(E, \mathcal{C}_\rho)$ will be referred to as *closed* or *convex* sets.

As an example, for any finite set $E \subset \mathbb{R}^d$, the set system $(E, \mathcal{C})$ with $\mathcal{C} = \{\text{conv}(X) \cap E : X \subseteq E\}$ forms a closure system, where $\text{conv}(X)$ denotes the convex hull of X in $\mathbb{R}^d$. Note that in contrast to convexity in $\mathbb{R}^d$, $\mathcal{C}_\rho$ is not atomic in general, i.e., singletons are not necessarily closed.

We now turn to the generalization of binary separation in $\mathbb{R}^d$ by hyperplanes to that in abstract closure systems by half-spaces (cf. [16] for a detailed introduction into this topic). In the context of machine learning, one of the most relevant questions concerning a closure system $(E, \mathcal{C})$ is whether two subsets of E are separable in $\mathcal{C}$, or not. To state the formal problem definition, we follow the generalization of half-spaces in Euclidean spaces to closure systems from [4]. More precisely, let $(E, \mathcal{C})$ be a closure system. Then $H \subseteq E$ is called a *half-space* in $\mathcal{C}$ if both H and its complement, denoted H^c, are closed (i.e., $H, H^c \in \mathcal{C}$). Note that H^c is also a half-space by definition. Two sets $A, B \subseteq E$ are *half-space separable* if there is a half-space $H \in \mathcal{C}$ such that $A \subseteq H$ and $B \subseteq H^c$; H and H^c together form a *half-space separation* of A and B. Since we are interested in half-space separations, in the definition of closure systems above we require $\emptyset \in \mathcal{C}$, as otherwise there are no half-spaces in $\mathcal{C}$. The following property will be used many times in what follows:

Proposition 1. *Let $(E, \mathcal{C}_\rho)$ be a closure system, $H \in \mathcal{C}$ a half-space, and $A, B \subseteq E$. Then H and H^c are a half-space separation of A and B if and only if they form a half-space separation of $\rho(A)$ and $\rho(B)$.*

Notice that the above generalization does not preserve all natural properties of half-space separability in $\mathbb{R}^d$. For example, for any two *finite* subsets of $\mathbb{R}^d$ it always holds that they are half-space separable if and only if their convex hulls[3] are disjoint. In contrast, this property does not hold for finite closure systems in general. To see this, consider the closure system $(\{1, 2, 3\}, \mathcal{C})$ with $\mathcal{C} = \{\emptyset, \{1\}, \{2\}, \{1, 2\}, \{1, 2, 3\}\}$. Note that $\mathcal{C}$ is non-atomic, as $\{3\} \notin \mathcal{C}$. Although $\{1\}$ and $\{2\}$ are both closed and disjoint, they cannot be separated by a half-space in $\mathcal{C}$ because the only half-space containing $\{1\}$ contains also $\{2\}$.

---

[3] Notice that the function mapping any subset of $\mathbb{R}^d$ to its convex hull is a closure operator.

3   Half-Space and Maximal Closed Set Separation

Our goal in this work is to investigate the algorithmic aspects of half-space and closed set separations in abstract closure systems. That is, given two subsets A, B of the ground set, we require the algorithm to return a half-space separation of A and B in $\mathcal{C}$, if such a half-separation exists; o/w the answer "No". As mentioned above, two finite subsets in $\mathbb{R}^d$ can always be separated by a hyperplane if and only if their convex hulls are disjoint. Thus, to decide if two finite subsets of $\mathbb{R}^d$ are separable by a hyperplane, it suffices to check whether their convex hulls are disjoint, or not. As shown above, the situation is different for abstract closure systems because the disjointness of the closures of A and B does not imply their half-space separability in $\mathcal{C}$. This difference makes, among others, our more general problem setting computationally difficult, as shown in Theorem 3 below. Similarly to the infinite closure system over $\mathbb{R}^d$ defined by the family of all convex hulls in $\mathbb{R}^d$, we also assume that the (abstract) closure system is given implicitly via the closure operator. This is a natural assumption, as the cardinality of the closure system is typically exponential in that of the ground set.

3.1   Half-Space Separation

In this section we formulate some results concerning the computational complexity of the following decision problem:

HALF-SPACE SEPARATION (HSS) PROBLEM: *Given* (i) a closure system $(E, \mathcal{C}_\rho)$ with $|E| < \infty$, where $\mathcal{C}_\rho$ is given by the closure operator ρ which returns in unit time for any $X \subseteq E$ the closure $\rho(X) \in \mathcal{C}_\rho$ and (ii) subsets $A, B \subseteq E$, *decide* whether A and B are half-space separable in $\mathcal{C}_\rho$, or not.

Clearly, the answer is always "No" whenever $\rho(A) \cap \rho(B) \neq \emptyset$, as $\rho(A)$ (resp. $\rho(B)$) are the smallest closed sets in $\mathcal{C}$ containing A (resp. B). The fact that the disjointness of $\rho(A)$ and $\rho(B)$ does not imply the half-space separability of A and B makes the HSS problem computationally intractable. To prove this negative result, we adopt the definition of *convex* vertex sets of a graph defined by shortest paths [6]. More precisely, for an undirected graph $G = (V, E)$ we consider the set system $(V, \mathcal{C}_\gamma)$ with

$$V' \in \mathcal{C}_\gamma \iff \forall u, v \in V', \forall P \in \mathcal{S}_{u,v} : V(P) \subseteq V' \tag{1}$$

for all $V' \subseteq V$, where $\mathcal{S}_{u,v}$ denotes the set of shortest paths connecting u and v in G and $V(P)$ the set of vertices in P. Notice that $(V, \mathcal{C}_\gamma)$ is a closure system; this follows directly from the fact that the intersection of any two convex subsets of V is also convex, by noting that the empty set is also convex by definition. Using the above definition of graph convexity, we consider the following problem definition [1]:

CONVEX 2-PARTITIONING PROBLEM: *Given* an undirected graph $G = (V, E)$, *decide* whether there is a *proper* partitioning of V into two convex sets.

Notice that the condition on properness is necessary, as otherwise $\emptyset$ and V would always form a (trivial) solution. Note also the difference between the HSS and the CONVEX 2-PARTITIONING problems that the latter one is concerned with a property of G (i.e., has no additional input A, B). For the problem above, the following negative result has been shown in [1]:

Theorem 2. *The* CONVEX 2-PARTITIONING *problem is NP-complete.*

Using the above concepts and result, we are ready to state the main negative result for this section, by noting that its proof is based on a reduction from the CONVEX 2-PARTITIONING problem.

Theorem 3. *The* HSS *problem is* NP-*complete.*

Furthermore, we can ask for the input $(E, \mathcal{C}_\rho), A, B$ of the HSS problem if there exist disjoint closed sets $H_1, H_2 \in \mathcal{C}_\rho$ with $A \subseteq H_1$ and $B \subseteq H_2$ of *maximum* combined cardinality (i.e., there are no disjoint closed sets $H_1', H_2' \in \mathcal{C}_\rho$ with $A \subseteq H_1'$ and $B \subseteq H_2'$ such that $|H_1| + |H_2| < |H_1'| + |H_2'|$). More precisely, we are interested in the following problem:

MAXIMUM CLOSED SET SEPARATION PROBLEM: *Given* (i) a closure system $(E, \mathcal{C}_\rho)$ as in the HSS problem definition, (ii) subsets $A, B \subseteq E$, and (iii) an integer $k > 0$, *decide* whether there are disjoint closed sets $H_1, H_2 \in \mathcal{C}_\rho$ with $A \subseteq H_1$, $B \subseteq H_2$ such that $|H_1| + |H_2| \geq k$.

Corollary 4 below is an immediate implication of Theorem 3.

Corollary 4. *The* MAXIMUM CLOSED SET SEPARATION *problem is* NP-*complete.*

The negative results above motivate us to relax below the HSS and the MAXIMUM CLOSED SET SEPARATION problems.

3.2   Maximal Closed Set Separation

One way to overcome the negative results formulated in Theorem 3 and Corollary 4 is to relax the condition on half-space separability in the HSS problem to the problem of *maximal* closed set separation:

MAXIMAL CLOSED SET SEPARATION (MCSS) PROBLEM: *Given* (i) a closure system $(E, \mathcal{C}_\rho)$ as in the HSS problem definition, (ii) subsets $A, B \subseteq E$, *find* two disjoint closed sets $H_1, H_2 \in \mathcal{C}_\rho$ with $A \subseteq H_1$ and $B \subseteq H_2$, such that there are no disjoint sets $H_1', H_2' \in \mathcal{C}_\rho$ with $H_1 \subsetneq H_1'$ and $H_2 \subsetneq H_2'$, or return "NO" if such sets do not exist.

In this section we present Algorithm 1, that solves the MCSS problem and is optimal w.r.t. the worst-case number of closure operator calls. Algorithm 1 takes as input a closure system $(E, \mathcal{C}_\rho)$ over some finite ground set E, where

---

Algorithm 1: MAXIMAL CLOSED SET SEPARATION (MCSS)

Input: finite closure system $(E, \mathcal{C}_\rho)$ given by a closure operator ρ and $A, B \subseteq E$
Output: *maximal* disjoint closed sets $H_1, H_2 \in \mathcal{C}_\rho$ with $A \subseteq H_1$ and $B \subseteq H_2$ if
$\rho(A) \cap \rho(B) = \emptyset$; "No" o/w

1 $H_1 \leftarrow \rho(A)$, $H_2 \leftarrow \rho(B)$
2 **if** $H_1 \cap H_2 \neq \emptyset$ **then**
3 $\quad$ **return** "No"
4 **end**
5 $F \leftarrow E \setminus (H_1 \cup H_2)$
6 **while** $F \neq \emptyset$ **do**
7 $\quad$ choose $e \in F$ and remove it from F
8 $\quad$ **if** $\rho(H_1 \cup \{e\}) \cap H_2 = \emptyset$ **then**
9 $\quad\quad$ $H_1 \leftarrow \rho(H_1 \cup \{e\})$, $F \leftarrow F \setminus H_1$
10 $\quad$ **else if** $\rho(H_2 \cup \{e\}) \cap H_1 = \emptyset$ **then**
11 $\quad\quad$ $H_2 \leftarrow \rho(H_2 \cup \{e\})$, $F \leftarrow F \setminus H_2$
12 $\quad$ **end**
13 **end**
14 **return** H_1, H_2

$\mathcal{C}_\rho$ is given via the closure operator ρ, and subsets A, B of E. If the closures of A and B are not disjoint, then it returns "NO" (cf. Lines 1–3). Otherwise, the algorithm tries to extend one of the largest closed sets $H_1 \supseteq A$ and $H_2 \supseteq B$ found so far consistently by an element $e \in F$, where $F = E \setminus (H_1 \cup H_2)$ is the set of potential generators. By consistency we mean that the closure of the extended set must be disjoint with the (unextended) other one (cf. Lines 8 and 10). Note that each element will be considered at most once for extension (cf. Line 5). If H_1 or H_2 could be extended, then F will be correspondingly updated (cf. Lines 9 and 11), by noting that e will be removed from F even in the case it does not result in an extension (cf. Line 5). The algorithm repeatedly iterates the above steps until F becomes empty; at this stage it returns H_1 and H_2 as a solution. We have the following result for Algorithm 1:

Theorem 5. *Algorithm 1 is correct and solves the MCSS problem by calling the closure operator at most $2|E| - 2$ times.*

To state the optimality of Algorithm 1 w.r.t. the number of closure operator calls in Corollary 7 below, we first state the following result.

Theorem 6. *There exists no deterministic algorithm solving the MCSS problem calling the closure operator less than $2|E| - 2$ times in the worst-case.*

The following corollary is immediate from Theorems 5 and 6.

Corollary 7. *Algorithm 1 is optimal w.r.t. the worst-case number of closure operator calls.*

In Sect. 4 we consider Kakutani closure systems, a special kind of closure systems, for which Algorithm 1 solves the HSS problem correctly and efficiently.

4   Kakutani Closure Systems

A natural way to overcome the negative result stated in Theorem 3 is to consider closure systems in which *any* two disjoint closed sets are half-space separable. More precisely, for a closure operator ρ over a ground set E, the corresponding closure system $(E, \mathcal{C}_\rho)$ is *Kakutani* [4] if it fulfills the S_4 *separation axiom* [5] defined as follows: For all $A, B \subseteq E$, A and B are half-space separable in $(E, \mathcal{C}_\rho)$ if and only if $\rho(A) \cap \rho(B) = \emptyset$. By Proposition 1, any half-space separation of A, B in $\mathcal{C}_\rho$ is a half-space separation of $\rho(A)$ and $\rho(B)$ in $\mathcal{C}_\rho$. We recall that all closure systems $(E, \mathcal{C})$ considered in this work are finite (i.e., $|E| < \infty$). Clearly, the HSS problem can be decided in linear time for Kakutani closure systems: For any $A, B \subseteq E$ just calculate $\rho(A)$ and $\rho(B)$ and check whether they are disjoint, or not.

The following theorem, one of our main results in this paper, claims that Algorithm 1 solving the MCSS problem provides also an *algorithmic characterization* of Kakutani closure systems.

Theorem 8. *Let $(E, \mathcal{C}_\rho)$ be a closure system with corresponding closure operator ρ. Then $(E, \mathcal{C}_\rho)$ is Kakutani if and only if for all $A, B \subseteq E$ with $\rho(A) \cap \rho(B) = \emptyset$, the output of Algorithm 1 is a partitioning of E.*

The characterization result formulated in Theorem 8 cannot, however, be used to decide in time polynomial in $|E|$, whether a closure system $(E, \mathcal{C}_\rho)$ is Kakutani, or not if it is given by ρ. More precisely, in Theorem 9 below we have a negative result for the following problem:

KAKUTANI PROBLEM: *Given* a closure system $(E, \mathcal{C}_\rho)$, where $\mathcal{C}_\rho$ is given intensionally via ρ, *decide* whether $(E, \mathcal{C}_\rho)$ is Kakutani, or not.

Theorem 9. *Any deterministic algorithm solving the Kakutani problem above requires $\Omega\left(2^{|E|/2}\right)$ closure operator calls.*

While the exponential lower bound in Theorem 9 holds for *arbitrary* (finite) closure systems, fortunately there is a broad class of closure systems that are known to be Kakutani. In particular, as a generic application field of Kakutani closure systems, in Sect. 4.1 we focus on graphs. We first present a generalization of a fundamental result [4,5] characterizing Kakutani closure systems over *graphs* by means of the Pasch axiom and mention some potential applications of this generalization result.

---

[4] A similar property was considered by the Japanese mathematician Shizou Kakutani for Euclidean spaces (cf. [9]).

[5] For a good reference on convexity structures satisfying the S_4 separation property, the reader is referred e.g. to [4].

4.1 Kakutani Closure Systems over Graphs

As a generic application field of Kakutani closure systems, in this section we focus our attention on *graphs*. For a graph $G = (V, E)$, we consider the closure system $(V, \mathcal{C}_\gamma)$ defined in (1). The following fundamental result provides a characterization of Kakutani closure systems over graphs.

Theorem 10. *[4, 5] Let $G = (V, E)$ be a graph. Then $(V, \mathcal{C}_\gamma)$ defined in (1) is Kakutani if and only if γ fulfills the Pasch axiom, i.e.,*

$$x \in \gamma(\{u, v\}) \wedge y \in \gamma(\{u, w\}) \quad implies \ \gamma(\{x, w\}) \cap \gamma(\{y, v\}) \neq \emptyset$$

for all $u, v, w, x, y \in V$.

The theorem below is an application of Theorem 10 to trees[6]:

Theorem 11. *Let $G = (V, E)$ be a tree. Then $(V, \mathcal{C}_\gamma)$ defined in (1) is Kakutani.*

Besides the direct application of Theorem 11 to vertex classification in trees, it provides also a natural heuristic for vertex classification in *arbitrary* graphs; we discuss this heuristic together with an empirical evaluation in Sect. 5.

Remark 12. We note that the converse of Theorem 11 does not hold. Indeed, let $G = (V, E)$ be a graph consisting of a single cycle. One can easily check that the corresponding closure system $(V, \mathcal{C}_\gamma)$ defined in (1) is Kakutani, though G is not a tree.

Motivated by potential theoretical and practical applications, in Theorem 13 below we generalize Theorem 10 to a certain type of *structured* set systems. More precisely, a *graph structure partitioning* (GSP) is a triple $\mathfrak{G} = (S, G, \mathcal{P})$, where S is a finite set, $G = (V, E)$ is a graph, and $\mathcal{P} = \{\text{bag}(v) \subseteq S : v \in V\}$ is a partitioning of S into $|V|$ *non-empty* subsets (i.e., $\bigcup_{v \in V} \text{bag}(v) = S$ and $\text{bag}(u) \cap \text{bag}(v) = \emptyset$ for all $u, v \in V$ with $u \neq v$). The set $\text{bag}(v)$ associated with $v \in V$ is referred to as the *bag* of v.

For a GSP $\mathfrak{G} = (S, G, \mathcal{P})$ with $G = (V, E)$, let $\sigma : 2^S \to 2^S$ be defined by

$$\sigma : S' \mapsto \bigcup_{v \in V'} \text{bag}(v) \tag{2}$$

with

$$V' = \gamma(\{v \in V : \text{bag}(v) \cap S' \neq \emptyset\})$$

for all $S' \subseteq S$, where γ is the closure operator corresponding to $(V, \mathcal{C}_\gamma)$ defined in (1). That is, take first the closure $V' \subseteq V$ of the set of vertices of G that are associated with a bag having a non-empty intersection with S' and then the union of the bags for the nodes in V'. We have the following result for σ.

---

[6] The claim holds for outerplanar graphs as well. For the sake of simplicity we formulate it in this short version for trees only, as it suffices for our purpose.

Theorem 13. *Let $\mathfrak{G} = (S, G, \mathcal{P})$ be a GSP with $G = (V, E)$. Then σ defined in (2) is a closure operator on S. Furthermore, the corresponding closure system $(S, \mathcal{C}_\sigma)$ is Kakutani whenever γ corresponding to $(V, \mathcal{C}_\gamma)$ fulfills the Pasch axiom on G.*

Clearly, Theorem 13 generalizes the result formulated in Theorem 10, as any graph $G = (V, E)$ can be regarded as the (trivial) GSP $\mathfrak{G} = (V, G, \mathcal{P})$, where all blocks in $\mathcal{P}$ are singletons with $\text{bag}(v) = \{v\}$ for all $v \in V$. Theorem 13 has several potential applications to graphs with vertices associated with the blocks of a partitioning of some set in a bijective manner. This kind of graphs can be obtained for example from graph clustering (see, e.g., [13]) or graph partitioning (see, e.g., [3]) that play an important role e.g. in community network mining.

Another application of Theorem 13 may arise from *quotient* graphs; a graph $G = (V, E)$ is a quotient graph of a graph $G' = (V', E')$ if V is formed by the equivalence classes of V' with respect to some equivalence relation ρ (i.e., $V = V'/\rho$) and for all $x, y \in V$, $\{x, y\} \in E$ if and only if $x = [u]_\rho, y = [v]_\rho$ for some $u, v \in V'$ with $\{u, v\} \in E'$, where $[u]_\rho$ (resp. $[v]_\rho$) denotes the equivalence class of u (resp. v). Such a quotient graph can be regarded as a GSP $\mathfrak{G} = (V', G, \mathcal{P})$, where $\mathcal{P}$ is the partitioning of V' corresponding to the equivalence relation ρ and for all $v \in V$, $\text{bag}(v) = [v']_\rho$ if $v = [v']_\rho$ for some $v' \in V'$. Quotient graphs play an important role in logic based graph mining[7] (see, e.g., [14]), which, in turn, can be regarded as a subfield of inductive logic programming (ILP). More precisely, regarding a graph $G' = (V', E')$ as a first-order goal clause $C_{G'}$ (see, e.g., [14]), in ILP one may be interested in finding a subgraph G of G', such that $C_{G'}$ logically implies the first-order goal clause C_G representing G and G is of minimum size with respect to this property. In ILP, C_G is referred to as a *reduced* clause (see [11] for further details on clause reduction); in graph theory G is called the *core* of G'. By the characterization result of subsumptions between clauses in [7], logical implication is equivalent to graph *homomorphism* for the case considered. Thus, G can be considered as the quotient graph of G' induced by φ, where all vertices $v \in V$ are associated with the equivalence class $[v] = \{u \in V' : \varphi(u) = v\}$; the vertices of G' in $[v]$ are regarded structurally equivalent with respect to homomorphism. Note that G is a tree structure of G' whenever G' is a tree, allowing for the same heuristic discussed in Sect. 5 for arbitrary GSPs.

4.2 Experimental Results

In this section we empirically demonstrate the potential of Algorithm 1 on predictive problems over Kakutani closure systems. For this purpose we consider the binary vertex classification problem over free trees. We stress that our main goal

---

[7] While in ordinary graph mining the pattern matching is typically defined by subgraph isomorphism, it is the graph homomorphism in logic based graph mining, as subsumption between first-order clauses reduces to homomorphism between graphs (see [8] for a discussion).

with these experiments is to demonstrate that a remarkable predictive performance can be obtained already with the very general version of our algorithm as
described in Algorithm 1 and with its modification for the case that the closures
of the input two sets are not disjoint. The latter case can occur when the sets of
vertices belonging to the same class are not half-spaces. Since we do not utilize
any domain specific features in our experiments (e.g., some strategy for selecting
non-redundant training examples[8]), we do not compare our generic approach to
the state-of-the-art algorithms specific to the vertex classification problem.

We evaluate our algorithm on synthetic tree datasets with binary labeled
vertices (see below for the details). Formally, for a closure system $(E, \mathcal{C}_\rho)$ let
L_r and L_b form a partitioning of E, where the elements of L_r (resp. L_b) will
be referred to as *red* (resp. *blue*) vertices. We consider the following supervised
learning task: *Given* a training set $D = R \cup B$ with $R \subseteq L_r, B \subseteq L_b$ for some
unknown partitioning L_r, L_b of E and an element $e \in E$, *predict* whether $e \in L_r$
or $e \in L_b$. Depending on whether or not L_r (and hence, L_b) forms a half-space
in $(E, \mathcal{C}_\rho)$, we consider the following two cases in our experiments:

(i) If L_r (and hence, L_b) is a half-space, then $\rho(R)$ and $\rho(B)$ are always disjoint
and hence the algorithm returns some half-spaces $H_r, H_b \in (E, \mathcal{C}_\rho)$ with
$R \subseteq H_r$ and $B \subseteq H_b$ because $(E, \mathcal{C}_\rho)$ is Kakutani. The class of e is then
predicted by *blue* if $e \in H_b$; o/w by *red*. Note that H_r and H_b can be different
from L_r and L_b, respectively.

(ii) If L_r (and hence, L_b) is *not* a half-space in $(E, \mathcal{C}_\rho)$ then $\rho(R) \cap \rho(B)$ can be
non-empty. In case of $\rho(R) \cap \rho(B) = \emptyset$, we run Algorithm 1 in its original
form; by the Kakutani property it always returns two half-spaces H_r and
H_b with $R \subseteq H_r$ and $B \subseteq H_b$. The class of e is then predicted in the same
way as described in (i). Otherwise (i.e., $\rho(R) \cap \rho(B) \neq \emptyset$), we greedily select
a maximal subtree T' such that its vertices have not been considered so far
and the closures of the red and blue training examples in T' are disjoint in
the closure system corresponding to T'; note that this is also Kakutani.[9]
We then run Algorithm 1 on this closure system and predict the class of the
unlabeled vertices of T' by the output half-spaces as above. We apply this
algorithm iteratively until all vertices have been processed.

For the empirical evaluation of the predictive performance of Algorithm 1 and
its variant described in (ii) above, we used the following synthetic datasets D1
and D2:

D1 For case (i) we considered random trees of size $100, 200, \ldots, 1000, 2000, \ldots,$
5000 (see the x-axes of Fig. 1). For each tree size we then generated 50 random
trees and partitioned the vertex set (i.e., E) of each tree into L_r and L_b such
that L_r and L_b are half-spaces in $(E, \mathcal{C}_\rho)$ and satisfy $\frac{1}{3} \leq \frac{|L_r|}{|L_b|} \leq 3$.

---

[8] In case of trees, such a non-redundant set could be obtained by considering only
leaves as training examples.

[9] We formulate this heuristic for trees for simplicity. In the long version we show that
this idea can be generalized to any graph satisfying the Pasch axiom.

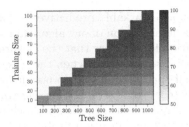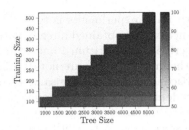

Fig. 1. Accuracy of vertex classifications where labels are half-spaces (cf. dataset D1).

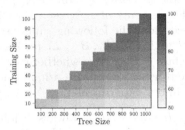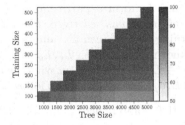

Fig. 2. Accuracy of vertex classification where labels are not half-spaces and partition the tree into around 10 subtrees, each of homogeneous labels (cf. dataset D2).

D2 For case (ii) we proceeded similarly except for the requirement that L_r, L_b are half-spaces. Instead, the labels partition the tree into around 10 maximal subtrees, each of homogeneous labels.

For all trees in D1 and D2 we generated 20 random training sets of different cardinalities (see the y-axes in Fig. 1 and 2). In this way we obtained 1000 learning tasks (50 trees × 20 random training sets) for each tree size (x-axes) and training set cardinality (y-axes).

The results are presented in Fig. 1 for D1 and in Fig. 2 for D2. For each tree size (x-axes) and training set cardinality (y-axes) we plot the average accuracy obtained for the 1000 learning settings considered. The accuracy is calculated in the standard way, i.e., for a partitioning H_r, H_b of E returned by the algorithm it is defined by

$$\frac{|\{e \in E \setminus D : e \text{ is correctly classified}\}|}{|E \setminus D|},$$

where D denotes the training set.

Regarding D1 (Fig. 1) one can observe that a remarkable average accuracy over 80% can be obtained already for 40 training examples even for trees of size 1000. This corresponds to a relative size of 2.5% (see the LHS of Fig. 1). With increasing tree size, the relative size of the training set reduces to 2%, as we obtain a similar average accuracy already for 100 training examples for trees of size 5000 (see the RHS of Fig. 1). The explanation of these surprisingly considerable results raise some interesting theoretical questions for probabilistic combinatorics, as the output half-spaces can be inconsistent with the partitioning formed by L_r, L_b.

Regarding D2 (Fig. 2), we need about 10% training examples to achieve an accuracy of at least 80%, and for trees having at least 600 vertices (see the LHS of Fig. 2). With increasing tree size, the relative amount of training examples decreases to obtain a similar accuracy. In particular, for trees of size 5000, already 150 training examples (i.e., 3%) suffice to achieve 80% accuracy (see the RHS of Fig. 2), indicating that the simple heuristic described in (ii) performs quite well on larger trees. Our further experimental results not presented in this short version suggest that the relative size of the training data depends sublinearly on the number of label homogeneous subtrees.

5   Non-Kakutani Closure Systems

After the discussion of Kakutani closure systems including the negative result on the KAKUTANI problem, in this section we consider non-Kakutani closure systems and show how to extend some of the results of the previous section to this kind of set systems. In particular, we first consider *arbitrary* graphs, which are non-Kakutani, as they do not fulfill the Pasch axiom in general (cf. Theorem 10). As a second type of non-Kakutani closure systems, we then consider finite point configurations in $\mathbb{R}^d$. Although none of these two types of closure systems are Kakutani in general, the experimental results presented in this section show that Algorithm 1, combined with a natural heuristic in case of graphs, can effectively be applied to both cases.

The natural heuristic mentioned above reduces the vertex classification problem in non-Kakutani closure systems over arbitrary graphs to Kakutani closure systems by considering random spanning trees of the underlying graph. More precisely, given a graph $G = (V, E)$ and training sets $R \subseteq L_r$ and $B \subseteq L_b$, where L_r and L_b form an unknown partitioning of V, we proceed as follows:

1. we pick a set of spanning trees, each uniformly at random,
2. apply (ii) from Sect. 4.2 to each spanning tree generated with input R and B, and
3. predict the class of an unlabeled vertex by the majority vote of the vertex classification obtained for the spanning trees.

5.1   Experimental Results

Similarly to Sect. 4.2 on Kakutani closure systems, in this section we empirically demonstrate the potential of Algorithm 1 on predictive problems over non-Kakutani closure systems. We first consider the binary vertex classification problem over arbitrary graphs and then over finite point sets in $\mathbb{R}^d$. Similarly to the case of Kakutani closure systems, we do not utilize any domain specific features, as our focus is on measuring the predictive performance of a general-purpose algorithm. In particular, in case of point configurations in $\mathbb{R}^d$ we use only convex hulls (the underlying closure operator), and no other information (e.g. distances). For the empirical evaluations on graphs and on finite point sets in $\mathbb{R}^d$ we used the following synthetic datasets D3 and D4, respectively:

D3 We generated random connected graphs of size $500, 1000, 1500, 2000$ and edge density (i.e., #edges/#vertices) $1, 1.2, \ldots, 3$. In particular, for each graph size and for each edge density value, 50 random graphs have been picked. We partitioned the vertex set of each graph via that of a random spanning tree into random half-spaces L_r and L_b w.r.t. to the tree's Kakutani closure system. For all labelled graphs generated, the ratio of the vertex labels satisfies $\frac{1}{3} \leq \frac{|L_r|}{|L_b|} \leq 3$.

D4 We considered randomly generated finite point sets in $\mathbb{R}^d$ for $d = 2, 3, 4$ with labels distributing around two centers. For every $d = 2, 3, 4$, we generated 100 different point sets in $\mathbb{R}^d$, each of cardinality 1000.

For all graphs in D3 we generated 20 random training sets with 10% of the size of the graphs. The results are presented in Fig. 3. For each number of random spanning tree generated, edge density, and graph size (x-axes) we plot the average accuracy obtained for the 1000 learning settings considered (i.e., 50 graphs × 20 training datasets). The accuracy is calculated in the same way as above (cf. Sect. 4.2).

In Fig. 3a we first investigate the predictive accuracy depends on the *number of random spanning trees.* One can see that classification via majority vote of around 100 random spanning trees remarkably increases the accuracy over less random spanning trees from 65% to 75%, while considering up to 500 spanning trees has almost no further effect on it. As a trade-off between accuracy and runtime we have therefore fixed the number of spanning trees to (the odd number) 101 for the other experiments.

The results concerning *edge densities* are presented in Fig. 3b. As expected, the edge density has an important effect on the accuracy ranging from 90% for edge density 1 (i.e., trees) to 65% for edge density 3. Notice that for edge density 3, the results are very close to the default value, indicating that our general approach has its remarkable performance on very sparse graphs only. (We recall that except for the closure operator, our algorithm is entirely uninformed regarding the structure.)

Finally, the *graph size* appears to have no significant effect on the predictive performance, as shown in Fig. 3c. For the edge density of 1.2, the accuracy is consistently around 75% for graphs with 500 nodes up to 2000. This is another important positive feature of our algorithm.

For each classification task for finite point sets in $\mathbb{R}^d$ we considered random training sets of different cardinalities for D4 and applied Algorithm 1 with the convex hull operator in $\mathbb{R}^d$ to these training data. The prediction has been made by the algorithm's output consisting of two maximal disjoint closed sets. (Note that they are not necessarily half-spaces because the closure system is not Kakutani in general). Accordingly, some of the points have not been classified. To evaluate our approach, we calculated the precision and recall for each problem

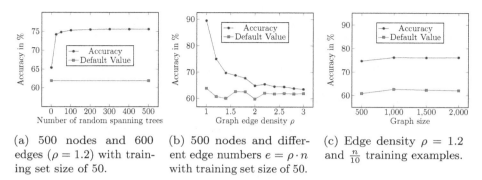

(a) 500 nodes and 600 edges ($\rho = 1.2$) with training set size of 50.

(b) 500 nodes and different edge numbers $e = \rho \cdot n$ with training set size of 50.

(c) Edge density $\rho = 1.2$ and $\frac{n}{10}$ training examples.

Fig. 3. Vertex classification in graphs

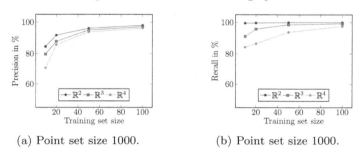

(a) Point set size 1000.

(b) Point set size 1000.

Fig. 4. Classification in finite point sets

setting. The results are reported in Fig. 4. Figure 4a shows that the cardinality of the training set has a significant effect on the accuracy, ranging from 70% to 98% for 10 (i.e., 1%) to 100 (i.e., 10%) training examples, respectively. Note that for small training sets, the precision is very sensitive to the dimension. In particular, the difference is more than 10% for 10 training examples. However, the difference vanishes with increasing training set size. We have carried out experiments with larger datasets as well; the results not presented here for space limitations clearly indicate that the precision remains quite stable w.r.t. the size of the point set. For example, for a training set size of 40, it was consistently around 94% for different cardinalities. Regarding the recall (cf. Fig. 4b), it was at least 90% in most of the cases by noting that it shows a similar sensitivity to the size of the training data as the precision.

In summary, our experimental results reported in this section clearly demonstrate that surprisingly considerable predictive performance can be obtained with Algorithm 1 even for non-Kakutani closure systems.

6   Concluding Remarks

The results of this paper show that despite several theoretical difficulties, impressive predictive accuracy can be obtained by a simple greedy algorithm for binary classification problems over abstract closure systems. This is somewhat surprising because the only information about the "nature" of the data has been encoded in the underlying closure operator.

Our approach raises a number of interesting theoretical, algorithmic, and practical questions. In particular, in this paper we deliberately have not utilized any domain specific knowledge (and accordingly, not compared our results to any state-of-the-art algorithm specific to some structure). It would be interesting to specialize Algorithm 1 to some particular problem by enriching it with additional information and compare only then its predictive performance to some specific method.

For the theoretical and algorithmic issues, we note that it would be interesting to study the relaxed notion of *almost* Kakutani closure systems, i.e., in which the combined size of the output closed sets are close to the cardinality of the ground set. Another interesting problem is to study algorithms solving the HSS and MCSS problems for closure systems, for which an upper bound on the VC-dimension is known in advance. The relevance of the VC-dimension in this context is that for any closed set $C \in \mathcal{C}_\rho$ of a closure system $(E, \mathcal{C}_\rho)$ there exists a set $G \subseteq E$ with $|G| \leq d$ such that $\rho(G) = C$, where d is the VC-dimension of $\mathcal{C}_\rho$ (see, e.g., [8]). It is an interesting question whether the lower bound on the number of closure operator calls can be characterized in terms of the VC-dimension of the underlying closure system.

Acknowledgements. Part of this work has been funded by the Ministry of Education and Research of Germany (BMBF) under project ML2R (grant number 01/S18038C) and by the Deutsche Forschungsgemeinschaft (DFG, German Research Foundation) under Germany's Excellence Strategy – EXC 2070 – 390732324.

References

1. Artigas, D., Dantas, S., Dourado, M., Szwarcfiter, J.: Partitioning a graph into convex sets. Discret. Math. **311**(17), 1968–1977 (2011)
2. Boser, B., Guyon, I., Vapnik, V.: A training algorithm for optimal margin classifiers. In: Proceedings of the 5th Annual ACM Workshop on Computational Learning Theory, pp. 144–152. ACM Press (1992)
3. Buluç, A., Meyerhenke, H., Safro, I., Sanders, P., Schulz, C.: Recent advances in graph partitioning. In: Kliemann, L., Sanders, P. (eds.) Algorithm Engineering. LNCS, vol. 9220, pp. 117–158. Springer, Cham (2016). https://doi.org/10.1007/978-3-319-49487-6_4
4. Chepoi, V.: Separation of two convex sets in convexity structures. J. Geom. **50**(1), 30–51 (1994)
5. Ellis, J.W.: A general set-separation theorem. Duke Math. J. **19**(3), 417–421 (1952)
6. Farber, M., Jamison, R.: Convexity in graphs and hypergraphs. SIAM J. Algebraic Discret. Methods **7**(3), 433–444 (1986)
7. Gottlob, G.: Subsumption and implication. Inform. Process. Lett. **24**(2), 109–111 (1987)
8. Horváth, T., Turán, G.: Learning logic programs with structured background knowledge. Artif. Intell. **128**(1–2), 31–97 (2001)

9. Kakutani, S.: Ein Beweis des Satzes von Edelheit über konvexe Mengen. Proc. Imp. Acad. Tokyo **13**, 93–94 (1937)
10. Kubiś, W.: Separation properties of convexity spaces. J. Geom. **74**(1), 110–119 (2002)
11. Plotkin, G.: A note on inductive generalization. Mach. Intell. **5**, 153–163 (1970)
12. Rosenblatt, F.: The perceptron: a probabilistic model for information storage and organization in the brain. Psychol. Rev. **65**, 386–408 (1958)
13. Schaeffer, S.E.: Survey: graph clustering. Comput. Sci. Rev. **1**(1), 27–64 (2007)
14. Schulz, T.H., Horváth, T., Welke, P., Wrobel, S.: Mining tree patterns with partially injective homomorphisms. In: Berlingerio, M., Bonchi, F., Gärtner, T., Hurley, N., Ifrim, G. (eds.) ECML PKDD 2018, Part II. LNCS (LNAI), vol. 11052, pp. 585–601. Springer, Cham (2019). https://doi.org/10.1007/978-3-030-10928-8_35
15. van de Vel, M.: Binary convexities and distributive lattices. Proc. London Math. Soc. **48**(1), 1–33 (1984)
16. van de Vel, M.: Theory of Convex Structures. North-Holland Mathematical Library, vol. 50. North Holland, Amsterdam (1993)

Sets of Robust Rules, and How to Find Them

Jonas Fischer[1,2(✉)] and Jilles Vreeken[1,2]

[1] Max Planck Institute for Informatics, and Saarland University,
Saarbrücken, Germany
fischer@mpi-inf.mpg.de
[2] CISPA Helmholtz Center for Information Security, Saarbrücken, Germany

Abstract. Association rules are among the most important concepts in data mining. Rules of the form $X \rightarrow Y$ are simple to understand, simple to act upon, yet can model important local dependencies in data. The problem is, however, that there are so many of them. Both traditional and state-of-the-art frameworks typically yield millions of rules, rather than identifying a small set of rules that capture the most important dependencies of the data. In this paper, we define the problem of association rule mining in terms of the Minimum Description Length principle. That is, we identify the best *set of rules* as the one that most succinctly describes the data. We show that the resulting optimization problem does not lend itself for exact search, and hence propose GRAB, a greedy heuristic to efficiently discover good sets of noise-resistant rules directly from data. Through extensive experiments we show that, unlike the state-of-the-art, GRAB does reliably recover the ground truth. On real world data we show it finds reasonable numbers of rules, that upon close inspection give clear insight in the local distribution of the data.

1 Introduction

Association rules are perhaps the most important primitive in data mining. Rules of the form $X \rightarrow Y$ are not only simple to understand, but they are also simple to act upon, and, most importantly, can express important *local* structure in the data. The problem is, however, that there are so many of them, and that telling the interesting from the uninteresting rules has so far proven impossible. Both traditional algorithms based on support and confidence [1], as well as modern approaches based on statistical tests [7] typically discover orders of magnitude more rules than the data has rows – even when the data consists of nothing but noise. In this paper we show how to discover a small, non-redundant set of noise-resistant rules that together describe the data well.

To succinctly express subtly different structures in data, we allow *multiple* items in the consequent of a rule. To illustrate, while rule sets $R_1 = \{A \rightarrow B, A \rightarrow C\}$ and $R_3 = \{A \rightarrow BC\}$ both express that B and C appear frequently in the context of A, the former states they do so independently, while the latter expresses a dependency between B and C. We additionally allow for

© Springer Nature Switzerland AG 2020
U. Brefeld et al. (Eds.): ECML PKDD 2019, LNAI 11906, pp. 38–54, 2020.
https://doi.org/10.1007/978-3-030-46150-8_3

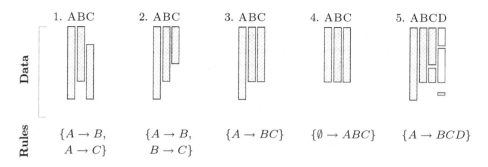

Fig. 1. *Five toy databases with corresponding rule sets.* (1) B and C occur in the context of A but independently of each other, (2) C occurs in the context of B, which in turn occurs in the context of A, (3) B and C show strong joint dependence in the context of A, (4) A, B, C show strong unconditional dependence, and (5) a rule with noise, BCD occuring jointly in the context of A.

patterns, which are simply rules like $R_4 = \{\emptyset \rightarrow ABC\}$ and express uncondi- tional dependencies. Real data is often noisy, and hence we can allow rules to hold *approximately*. That is, for a transaction $t = ABC$, our models may infer that rule $R_5 = \{A \rightarrow BCD\}$ holds, even though item D is not present in t. We call these noise-resistant, or *robust* rules. To determine the quality of a rule set for given data, we rely on information theory.

In particular, we define the rule set mining problem in terms of the Minimum Description Length (MDL) principle [6]. Loosely speaking, this means we identify the best rule set as that one that compresses the data best. This set is naturally non-redundant, and neither under- nor over-fitting, as we have to pay for every additional rule we use, as well as for every error we make. We formally show that the resulting problem is neither submodular, nor monotone, and as the search space is enormous, we propose GRAB, an efficient any-time algorithm to heuristically discover good rule sets directly from data. Starting from a singleton- only model, we iteratively refine our model by considering combinations of rules in the current model. Using efficiently computable tight estimates we minimize the number of candidate evaluations, and as the experiments show, GRAB is both fast in practice, and yields high quality rule sets. On synthetic data, GRAB recovers the ground truth, and on real-world data it recovers succinct models of meaningful rules. In comparison, state of the art methods discover up to several millions of rules for the same data, and are hence hardly useful.

2   Related Work

Pattern mining is arguably one of the most important and well-studied topics in data mining. We aim to give a succinct overview of the work most relevant to ours. The first, and perhaps most relevant proposal is that of association rule mining [1], where in an unsupervised manner the goal is to find all rules of the form $X \rightarrow Y$ from the data that have high frequency and high confidence. As it turns out to be straightforward to distill the high-confidence rules from a given frequent itemset, research attention shifted to discovering frequent itemsets efficiently [8,14,31], and non-redundantly [2,3,17]. Frequency alone is a bad measure of interestingness, however, as it leads to spurious patterns [26]. To alleviate this, statistically sound measures were proposed that can mine patterns with frequencies that deviate significantly from our expectation based on margins [21,29], or richer background knowledge [4,9,24]. Perhaps because it is already difficult enough to determine the interestingness of a pattern, let alone a rule, most proposals restrict themselves to patterns. The key exception is KING-FISHER, which proposes an upper bound for Fisher's exact test that allows to efficiently mine significant dependency rules using the branch-and-bound framework [7]. Notably, however, KINGFISHER can only discover exact rules with a single item consequent. In addition, all these approaches suffer from the problems of multiple test correction, and return all patterns they deem significant, rather than a small non-redundant set.

Less directly related to our problem setting, but still relevant, are supervised methods that discover rules that explain a given target variable Y. Zimmermann and Nijssen [32] give a good general overview. However, unlike Wang et al. [28] and Papaxanthos et al. [19], we are not interested in rules that explain only Y, but rather aim for a set of rules that together explains all of the data well.

Our approach is therewith a clear example of pattern set mining [26]. That is, rather than measuring the quality of individual patterns, we measure quality over a set of patterns [5,27]. Information theoretic approaches, such as MDL and the Maximum Entropy principle, have proven particularly successful for measuring the quality of sets of patterns [13,27]. Most pattern set approaches do not account for noise in the data, with ASSO [15], HYPER+ [30], and PANDA [12] as notable exceptions. However, extending any of the above from patterns to rules turns out to be far from trivial, because rules have different semantics than patterns. PACK [25] uses MDL to mine a small decision tree per item in the data, and while not technically a rule-mining method, we can interpret the paths of these trees as rules. In our experiments we will compare to KINGFISHER as the state-of-the-art rule miner, HYPER+ as a representative of noise resilient pattern miner, and PACK as a pattern miner, which output can be translated into rules.

3   Preliminaries

In this section we discuss preliminaries and introduce notation.

3.1   Notation

We consider binary transaction data D of size n-by-m, with $n = |D|$ transactions over an alphabet $\mathcal{I}$ of $m = |\mathcal{I}|$ items. In general, we denote sets of items as $X \subseteq \mathcal{I}$. A transaction t is an itemset, e.g. the products bought by a customer. We write $\pi_X(D) := \{t \cap X \mid t \in D\}$ for the projection of D on itemset X. The transaction set, or selection, T of itemset X is the multiset of all transactions $t \in D$ that contain X, i.e. $T_X = \{t \in D \mid X \subseteq t\}$. We write $n_X = |T_X|$ to denote the cardinality of a transaction multiset. The *support* of an itemset X is then simply the number of transactions in D that contain X, i.e. $support(X) = |T_X|$.

An association rule $X \rightarrow Y$ consists of two non-intersecting itemsets, the antecedent or head X, and consequent or tail Y. A rule makes a statement about the conditional occurrence of Y in the data where X holds. If $X = \emptyset$, we can interpret a rule as a pattern, as it makes a statement on where in the whole data the consequent holds. Throughout this manuscript, we will use A, B, C to refer to sets of single items and X, Y, Z for itemsets of larger cardinality.

3.2 Minimum Description Length

The Minimum Description Length (MDL) principle [22] is a computable and statistically well-founded approximation of Kolmogorov Complexity [11]. For given data D, MDL identifies the best model M^* in a given model class $\mathcal{M}$ as that model that yields the best lossless compression. In one-part, or, *refined* MDL we consider the length in bits of describing data D using the entire model class, $L(D \mid \mathcal{M})$, which gives strong optimality guarantees [6] but is only feasible for certain model classes. In practice we hence often use two-part, or, *crude* MDL, which is defined as $L(M) + L(D \mid M)$. Here $L(M)$ is the length of the description of the model, and $L(D \mid M)$ the length in bits of the description of the data using M. We will use two-part codes where we have to, and one-part codes where we can. Note that in MDL we are only concerned with code *lengths*, not materialized codes. Also, as we are interested in measuring lengths in bits, all logarithms are to base 2, and we follow the convention $0 \log 0 = 0$.

4 Theory

To use MDL in practice, we first need to define our model class $\mathcal{M}$, how to describe a model M in bits, and how to describe data D using a model M. Before we do so formally, we first give the intuitions.

4.1 The Problem, Informally

Our goal is to find a set of rules that together succinctly describe the given data. Our models M hence correspond to sets R of rules $X \rightarrow Y$. A pattern ABC is simply a rule with an empty head, i.e. $\emptyset \rightarrow ABC$. A rule *applies* to a transaction $t \in D$ if the transaction supports its head, i.e. $X \subseteq t$. For each transaction to which the rule applies, the model specifies whether the rule *holds*, i.e. whether Y is present according to the model. We can either be strict, and require that rules only hold when $Y \subseteq t$, or, be more robust to noise and allow the rule to hold even when not all items of Y are part of t, i.e. $Y \setminus t \neq \emptyset$. In this setting, the model may state that rule $A \rightarrow BCD$ holds for transaction $t = ABC$, even though $D \notin t$ (see Fig. 1(5)). A model M hence needs to specify for every rule

$X \to Y \in R$ a set of transactions ids $T^M_{Y|X}$ where it asserts that Y holds in the context of X, and, implicitly also $T^M_{\bar{Y}|X}$, the set of transactions where it asserts Y does not hold. Last, for both these we have to transmit which items of Y are actually in the data; the fewer errors we make here, the cheaper it will be to transmit. To ensure that we encode any data D over $\mathcal{I}$, we require that a model M contains at least singleton rules, i.e. $\emptyset \to A$ for all $A \in \mathcal{I}$. Cyclic dependencies would prevent us from decoding the data without loss. Any valid model M can hence be represented as a directed acyclic graph (DAG), in which the vertices of the graph correspond to rules in R, where vertex $r = X \to Y$ has incoming edges from all vertices $r' = X' \to Y'$ for which $X \cap Y'$ is non-empty.

We explicitly allow for rules with non-singleton tails, as this allows us to succinctly describe subtly different types of structure. When B happens independently of C in T_A (Fig. 1(1)), rule set $R_1 = \{A \to B, A \to C\}$ is a good description of this phenomenon. In turn, when C occurs often – but not always – in T_B, which in turn happens often in T_A (Fig. 1(2)) rule set $R_2 = \{A \to B, B \to C\}$ is a good description. To succinctly describe that B and C are statistically dependent in T_A (Fig. 1(3)) we need rules with multiple items in its tail, i.e. $R_3 = \{A \to BC\}$. Finally, if A, B, and C frequently occur jointly, but conditionally independent of any other variable, we need patterns to express this, which are just consequents in the context of the whole database $R_4 = \emptyset \to ABC$.

4.2   MDL for Rule Sets

Next, we formalize an MDL score for the above intuition. We start by defining the cost of the data given a model, and then define the cost of a model.

Cost of the Data. We start with the cost of the data described by an individual rule $X \to Y$. For now, assume we know $\pi_X(D)$ and T_X. We transmit the data over Y in the context of X, i.e. $D_{Y|X} = \pi_Y(T_X)$, in three parts. First, we transmit the transaction ids where model M specifies that both X and Y hold, $T^M_{Y|X}$, which implicitly gives $T^M_{\bar{Y}|X} = T_X \setminus T^M_{Y|X}$. We now, in turn transmit that part of $D_{Y|X}$ corresponding to the transactions in $T^M_{Y|X}$, resp. that part corresponding to $T^M_{\bar{Y}|X}$. We do so using optimal data-to-model codes, i.e. indices over canonically ordered enumerations,

$$L(D_{Y|X} \mid M) = \log \binom{|T_X|}{|T^M_{Y|X}|} + \log \binom{|T^M_{Y|X}| \times |Y|}{\mathbb{1}(T^M_{Y|X})} + \log \binom{|T^M_{\bar{Y}|X}| \times |Y|}{\mathbb{1}(T^M_{\bar{Y}|X})},$$

where we write $\mathbb{1}(T^M_{Y|X})$ for the number of 1s in $T^M_{Y|X}$, i.e.

$$\mathbb{1}(T^M_{Y|X}) = \sum_{t \in T^M_{Y|X}} |t \cap Y| \leq |T^M_{Y|X}| \times |Y|.$$

We define $\mathbb{1}(T_{\bar{Y}|X})$ analogue.

When the model makes exact assertions on Y holding when X is present, i.e. when $T_{Y|X}^M = T_{Y|X}$, the second term vanishes, and analogously for the third term when $T_{\bar{Y}|X}^M = T_{\bar{Y}|X}$. Both terms vanish simultaneously only when $D_{Y|X} \in \{\emptyset, Y\}^{|D_X|}$. This is trivially the case when Y is a singleton.

The overall cost of the data given the model simply is the sum of the data costs per rule,

$$L(D \mid M) = \sum_{X \to Y \in M} L(D_{Y|X} \mid M)$$

To decode the data, the recipient will of course need to know each rule $X \to Y$. These are part of the model cost.

Cost of the Model. To encode a rule, we first encode the cardinalities of X and Y using $L_{\mathbb{N}}$, the MDL-optimal code for integers $z \geq 1$, which is defined as $L_{\mathbb{N}}(z) = \log^* z + \log c_0$, where $\log^* z = \log z + \log \log z + ...$, and c_0 is a normalization constant such that $L_{\mathbb{N}}$ satisfies the Krafft-inequality [23]. We can now encode the items of X, resp. Y, one by one using optimal prefix codes, $L(X) = -\sum_{x \in X} \log \frac{s_x}{\sum_{i \in I} s_i}$. Last, but not least we have to encode its parameters, $|T_{Y|X}^M|$, $\mathbb{1}(T_{Y|X}^M)$, and $\mathbb{1}(T_{\bar{Y}|X})$. These we encode using a refined, mini-max optimal MDL code. In particular, we use the regret of the Normalized Maximum Likelihood code length [10] for the class of binomials,

$$L_{pc}(n) = \log \left(\sum_{k=0}^{n} \frac{n!}{(n-k)!k!} \left(\frac{k}{n}\right)^k \left(\frac{n-k}{n}\right)^{n-k} \right),$$

which is also known as the parametric complexity of a model class. Kontkanen and Myllymäki [10] showed that this term can be computed in time $O(n)$ in a recursive manner. We obtain the model cost $L(X \to Y)$ for a rule $X \to Y$ by

$$L(X \to Y) = L_{\mathbb{N}}(|X|) + L(X) + L_{\mathbb{N}}(|Y|) + L(Y) +$$
$$L_{pc}(|T_X|) + L_{pc}(|T_{Y|X}^M| \times |Y|) + L_{pc}(|T_{\bar{Y}|X}^M| \times |Y|).$$

From how we encode the data we can simply ignore the last two terms for rules with $|Y| = 1$. The overall cost of a model M then amounts to

$$L(M) = L_{\mathbb{N}}(|R|) + \sum_{X \to Y \in R} L(X \to Y),$$

where we first send the size of rule set R, and then each of the rules in order defined by the spanning tree of the dependency graph.

4.3   The Problem, Formally

We can now formally define the problem in terms of MDL.

Definition 1 (Minimal Rule Set Problem). *Given data D over items $\mathcal{I}$, find that rule set R and that set of $\mathcal{T}$ of transaction sets $T_{Y|X}^M$ for all $X \to Y \in R$, such that for model $M = (R, \mathcal{T})$ the total description length,*

$$L(D, M) = L(M) + L(D \mid M)$$

is minimal.

Solving this problem involves enumerating all possible models $M \in \mathcal{M}$. There exist $\sum_{i=0}^{|\mathcal{I}|} \left(\binom{|\mathcal{I}|}{i} \times 2^i \right) = 3^{|\mathcal{I}|}$ possible rules – where the second term in the sum describes all possible partitions of i items into head and tail, and the equality is given by the binomial theorem. Assuming that the optimal $T_{Y|X}^M$ are given, there are generally $2^{3^{|\mathcal{I}|}}$ possible models. The search space does not exhibit any evident structure that can be leveraged to guide the search, which is captured by the following two theorems. We postpone the proofs to the online Appendix.[1]

Theorem 1 (Submodularity). *The search space of all possible sets of association rules 2^Ω, when fixing a dataset and using the description length $L(D, M)$ as set function, is not submodular. That is, there exists a data set D s.t. $\exists X \subset Y \subseteq \Omega, z \in \Omega$. $L(D, X \cup \{z\}) - L(D, X) \le L(D, Y \cup \{z\}) - L(D, Y)$.*

Theorem 2 (Monotonicity). *The description length $L(D, M)$ on the space of all possible sets of association rules 2^Ω is not monotonously decreasing. That is, there exists a data set D s.t. $\exists X \subset Y \subseteq \Omega$. $f(X) \le f(Y)$.*

Hence, we resort to heuristics.

5   Algorithm

In this section we introduce GRAB, an efficient heuristic for discovering good solutions to the Minimal Rule Set Problem. GRAB consists of two steps, candidate generation and evaluation, that are executed iteratively until convergence of $L(D, M)$, starting with the singleton-only rule set $R_0 = \{\emptyset \to A \mid A \in \mathcal{I}\}$.

Candidate Generation. From the current rule set R we iteratively discover that refined rule set R' that minimizes the gain $\Delta L = L(D, M') - L(D, M)$. As refinements we consider the combination of two existing rules into a new rule.

We generate candidate refinements by considering all pairs $r_1 = X \to Y, r_2 = X \to Z \in R$, assuming w.l.o.g. $n_{XY} \ge n_{XZ}$, and merging the tails of r_1 and r_2 to obtain candidate rule $r_1' = X \to YZ$, and merging the tail of r_1 with the head to obtain candidate rule $r_2' = XY \to Z$. We now construct refined rule sets R_1' and R_2' by adding rule r_1' resp. r_2'. To reduce redundancy, we remove r_2 from both R_1' and R_2', and r_1 from R_1', taking care not to remove singleton rules. We only evaluate those refined rule sets R' for which the corresponding dependency graph is acyclic, and select the one with minimal gain $\Delta L < 0$. For completeness we give the pseudocode in the online Appendix.

---

[1] http://eda.mmci.uni-saarland.de/grab/.

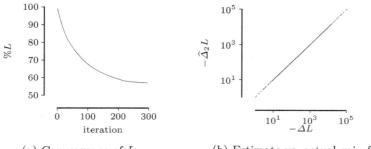

(a) Convergence of L.   (b) Estimate vs. actual gain for L.

Fig. 2. GRAB *searches efficiently and estimates accurately.* For *DNA* we show (left) the convergence of the relative compression of model M at iteration i against the singleton model M_s, $\%L = \frac{L(D,M) \times 100}{L(D,M_s)}$, and (right) the correlation between estimated and actual gain of all evaluated candidates in real data.

Gain Estimation. To avoid naively evaluating the gain ΔL of every candidate, we rely on accurate gain estimations. In particular, we consider two different estimates; the first estimate is very inexpensive to compute, but overly optimistic as it assumes a perfect overlap between the two rules. The second estimate is computationally more costly, as it requires us to compute the intersection of the selections of the two original rules. In practice, however, it is exact (see Fig. 2b).

Depending on how we combine two rules r_1 and r_2, we need different estimate definitions. In the interest of space, we here consider one case in detail: that of combining singleton rules $r_1 = \emptyset \rightarrow A$ and $r_2 = \emptyset \rightarrow B$ into $r = A \rightarrow B$. For the remaining definitions we refer to the online Appendix.

Following the general scheme described above, for the first estimate $\widehat{\Delta}_1$ we assume that $T_B \subseteq T_A$. With singleton tails we do not transmit any errors. Thus, we only subtract the old costs for r_2 and add the estimated cost of sending where the new rule r holds, as well as the estimated regret for the new matrices,

$$\widehat{\Delta}_1(r) = -\log\binom{n}{n_B} + \log\binom{n_A}{n_B} + L_{pc}(n_A) + L_{pc}(n_B) + L_{pc}(n_A - n_B) - L_{pc}(n).$$

For the tighter, second estimate $\widehat{\Delta}_2$ we instead need to retrieve the exact number of usages of the rule by intersecting the transaction sets of merged rules. The change in model costs $L(M)$ by introducing r appearing in $L(M)$ is trivially computable and thus abbreviated by $\hat{L}(M)$. For formerly covered transactions that are not covered by the new rule, we need to send singleton rules with adapted costs, which is estimated through simple set operations on the transaction sets. Additionally, we need to subtract the model costs for r_2, in case B is completely covered by r, ensured by the indicator variable I. We hence have

$$\widehat{\Delta}_2(r) = -\log\binom{n}{n_B} + \log\binom{n_A}{|T_A \cap T_B|} + \log\binom{n}{|T_B \setminus T_A|} + \hat{L}(M) + L_{pc}(n_A)$$
$$+ L_{pc}(|T_A \cap T_B|) + L_{pc}(n_A - |T_A \cap T_B|) - I(T_B \subseteq T_A) \times L_{pc}(n).$$

GRAB first computes the first order estimate $\widehat{\Delta}_1$ per candidate, and only if this shows potential improvement, it computes the second order estimate $\widehat{\Delta}_2$. Out of those, it evaluates all candidates that have the potential to improve over the best refinement found so far. In the next paragraph we describe how to efficiently compute the overall score $L(D, M)$.

Efficiently Computing $L(D, M)$. To get the codelength of a rule set with a new candidate, two steps are carried out, which we summarize in Algorithm 1. First, the data is covered with the new rule to determine where the rule holds and what error matrices to send. Covering the data is straightforward, but to find the error matrices we have—unless we rely on a user-defined threshold—to optimize for the best point to split between additive and destructive noise. We observe that each rule encoding is independent of every other rule (except singletons), that is, changing the error matrices for one rule does not change the matrices for any other rule as we always encode all transactions where the antecedent is fulfilled.

With this in mind, it is clear that we can optimize the split point for each rule $X \rightarrow Y$ separately. Thus, we find a partitioning of T_X into $T_{Y|X}^M$ and $T_{\overline{Y}|X}^M$ that minimizes the contribution of this rule to the overall costs:

$$
\Delta_{T_X, T_{Y|X}^M, T_{\overline{Y}|X}^M, \mathbb{1}(T_{Y|X}^M), \mathbb{1}(T_{\overline{Y}|X}^M)} = L_{pc}(|T_X|) + L_{pc}(|T_{Y|X}^M| \times |Y|)
$$

$$
+ \ L_{pc}(|T_{\overline{Y}|X}^M| \times |Y|) + \log \binom{|T_{Y|X}^M| \times |Y|}{\mathbb{1}(T_{Y|X}^M)} + \log \binom{|T_{\overline{Y}|X}^M| \times |Y|}{\mathbb{1}(T_{\overline{Y}|X}^M)}.
$$

We can also view the problem from a different angle, namely, for each transaction $t \in T_X$ we count how many items of Y are present, which yields a vector of counts B, $B[i] = |\{t \in T_X \mid |t \cap Y| = i\}|$. For fixed split point k, we get the additive and destructive matrix sizes $\mathbb{1}(\cdot)^k$ and transaction set sizes $|\cdot|^k$:

$$
|T_{Y|X}^M|^k := \sum_{i=k}^{|B|+1} B[i] \qquad\qquad |T_{\overline{Y}|X}^M|^k := \sum_{i=1}^{k-1} B[i]
$$

$$
\mathbb{1}(T_{Y|X}^M)^k := \sum_{i=k}^{|B|} B[i] \times i \qquad\qquad \mathbb{1}(T_{\overline{Y}|X}^M)^k := \sum_{i=0}^{k-1} B[i] \times i.
$$

To find the best split k^* we optimize along k using the two equation sets above, which is in time linear in the size of the consequent,

$$
k^* = \arg\min_{k=1...|B|} \left(\Delta_{T_X, T_{Y|X}^M, T_{\overline{Y}|X}^M, \mathbb{1}(T_{Y|X}^M), \mathbb{1}(T_{\overline{Y}|X}^M)} \right). \tag{1}
$$

This yields the best splitpoint k^* for how many items of the consequent are required for a rule to *hold* in terms of our MDL score and thus implicitly gives the error matrices.

Putting everything together, we have GRAB, given in pseudo-code as Algorithm 2.

Algorithm 1: COVER

---

input : Database D, model $M = (R, \mathcal{T})$, refined rule set R'
output : Model $M' = (R', \mathcal{T}')$

1 $T_{Y|X}^{M'} \leftarrow$ according to Equation (1) ;   // Initialize where new rule holds
2 **for** $I \in \mathcal{I}$ **do**   // For each singleton
3 $\quad$ $T_I^{M'} \leftarrow T_I$;   // Reset usage to baseline model
4 $\quad$ **for** $\{X \rightarrow Y \in R' \mid I \in Y\}$ **do**   // For each rule tail containing I
5 $\quad\quad$ $T_I^{M'} \leftarrow T_I^{M'} \setminus T_X$;   // Remove these transactions from list

6 **return** $(R', \{T_I^{M'} \mid I \in \mathcal{I}\} \cup \{T_{U|V}^{M} \in \mathcal{T} \mid U \rightarrow V \in R \cap R'\} \cup \{T_{Y|X}^{M'}\})$;

Algorithm 2: GRAB

---

input : Dataset D
output : Heuristic approximation to M

1 $M \leftarrow \{\emptyset \rightarrow \{A\} \mid A \in \mathcal{I}\}$;   // Initialize model with singletons
2 **do**
3 $\quad$ $C \leftarrow$ GENERATECANDIDATES(D, M);
4 $\quad$ $M^* \leftarrow M$; $\Delta^* \leftarrow 0$;
5 $\quad$ **while** C contains a refinement R with $\widehat{\Delta}_2 < \Delta^*$ **do**
6 $\quad\quad$ $R' \leftarrow$ refinement $R \in C$ with best $\widehat{\Delta}_2$;
7 $\quad\quad$ $M' \leftarrow$ COVER(D, M, R') ;   // Construct model M'
8 $\quad\quad$ $\Delta' \leftarrow L(D, M') - L(D, M)$;   // Compute exact gain
9 $\quad\quad$ **if** $\Delta' < \Delta^*$ **then**
10 $\quad\quad\quad$ $M^* \leftarrow M'$; $\Delta^* \leftarrow \Delta'$;

11 $\quad$ **if** $M^* \neq M$ **then**   // Update best model
12 $\quad\quad$ $M \leftarrow M^*$;

13 **while** $L(D, M) < L(D, M^*)$;
14 **return** M

Complexity. In the worst case we generate all pairs of combinations of rules, and hence at each step GRAB evaluates a number of candidates quadratic in the size of the rule table. Each evaluation of the $O(3^{2^m})$ candidates requires a database cover which costs time $O(n \times m)$, and singleton transaction set update, thus giving an overall time in $O(3^{2^m} \times m \times n)$. However, MDL ensures that the number of rules is small, and hence a more useful statement about runtime is given in the following theorems that are based on the size of the output or in other words the number of mined rules. For the proofs, see the online Appendix.

Theorem 3 (Grab candidate evaluations). *Given that we mine k rules for a given dataset D,* GRAB *evaluates $O((m + k)^3)$ candidates.*

This theorem gives us insight in how many times GRAB calls COVER. For the runtime analysis, we know that in each step i our rule table has size $m + i$

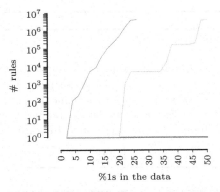 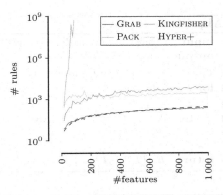

(a) Rules found in pure noise data of different sparsity. GRAB and PACK do not find any rule at all, whereas KINGFISHER and HYPER+ pick up random noise.

(b) Rules found in synthetic data. GRAB closely approximates the ground truth number of planted rules (black, dashed).

Fig. 3. GRAB *recovers ground truth.* Results on random data (left) and synthetic data with planted rules for different data dimensionalities (right).

and GRAB has to compute the cover of the newest rule in time $O(n \times m)$ and update the singleton costs in time $O((m + i) \times m \times n)$.

Theorem 4 (Grab runtime). *Given that we mine k rules for a given dataset D, the overall runtime of* GRAB *is* $O((m + k)^4 \times m \times n)$.

In practice, however, this runtime is never reached both due to our gain estimates and because we only allow to merge rules with the same head.

6   Experiments

In this section we empirically evaluate GRAB quantitatively and qualitatively on both synthetic and real-world data. We implemented GRAB in C++. We make all code and data available for research purposes.[2] All experiments were executed single-threaded on Intel Xeon E5-2643 v3 machines with 256 GB memory running Linux. We report the wall-clock running times.

We compare to state of the art methods for mining statistically significant patterns and association rules. In particular, we compare to HYPER+ [30], which mines noise-resistant patterns, KINGFISHER [7], which is arguably the current state of the art for mining statistically significant rules under the Fisher-exact-test[3], and PACK [25], an MDL-based method that yields a binary tree per item $A \in \mathcal{I}$ of which we can interpret the paths to leafs as rules $X \to A$.

---

[2] http://eda.mmci.uni-saarland.de/grab/.

[3] No relation to the first author.

Synthetic Data. First, we consider data with known ground truth. As a sanity check, we start our experiments on data without any structure. We draw datasets of 10000-by-100 of $d\%$ 1s, and report for each method the average results over 10 independent runs in Fig. 3a. We find that both KINGFISHER and HYPER+ quickly discover up to millions of rules. This is easily explained, as the former relies on statistical significance only, and lacks a notion of support, whereas the latter does have a notion of support, but lacks a notion of significance. PACK and GRAB, however, retrieve the ground truth in all cases.

Next, we consider synthetic data with planted rules. We generate datasets of $n = 20000$ transactions, and vary m from 10 to 1000 items. We generate rules that together cover all features. We sample the cardinality of the heads and tails from a Poisson with $\lambda = 1.5$. To avoid convoluting the ground truth via overlap, or by rules forming chains, we ensure that every item A is used in at most one rule. Per rule, we choose confidence c uniformly at random between 50 and 100%. We then randomly partition the n transactions into as many parts as we have rules, and per part, set the items of the corresponding rule head X to 1, and set Y to 1 for $c\%$ of transactions within the part. Finally, we add noise by flipping 1% of the items in the data – we use this low noise level to allow for a fair comparison to the competitors that do not explicitly model noise.

We provide the results in Fig. 3b. We observe that unlike in the previous experiment, here PACK strongly overestimates the number of rules – it runs out of memory for data of more than 92 features. KINGFISHER and HYPER+ both discover over an order of magnitude more rules than the ground truth. GRAB, on the other hand, is the only one that reliably retrieves the ground truth.

Real-World Data. Second, we verify whether GRAB also yields meaningful results on real data. To this end we consider 8 data sets over a variety of domains. In particular, from the UCI repository we consider *Mushroom, Adult, Covtype,* and *Plants.* In addition we use data of Belgium traffic *Accidents, DNA* amplification [18], *Mammals* [16], and ICDM *Abstracts* [25]. We give basic statistics in Table 1, and provide more detailed information in the online Appendix.

We run each of the methods on each data set, and report the number of discovered non-singleton rules for all methods and the average number of items in head and tail for GRAB in Table 1. We observe that GRAB retrieves much more succinct sets of rules than its competitors, typically in the order of tens, rather than in the order of thousands to millions. The rules that GRAB discovers are also more informative, as it is not constrained to singleton-tail rules. This is also reflected by the number of items in the consequent, where the average tail size is much larger than 1 for e.g. *Mammals* and *Plants,* where we find multiple rules with more than 10 items in the consequent.

To qualitatively evaluate the rules that GRAB discovers, we investigate the results on *Abstracts* and *Mammals* in closer detail. For *Abstracts* we find patterns such as $\emptyset \rightarrow \{naive, bayes\}$, $\emptyset \rightarrow \{nearest, neighbor\}$, $\emptyset \rightarrow \{pattern, frequency\}$, and, notably, $\emptyset \rightarrow \{association, rule\}$. Further, we find meaningful rules, including $\{high\} \rightarrow \{dimension\}$, $\{knowledge\} \rightarrow \{discovery\}$, $\{ensembl\} \rightarrow \{bagging, boosting\}$, and $\{support\} \rightarrow \{vector, machin, SVM\}$. All patterns and rules correspond to well-known concepts in the data mining community.

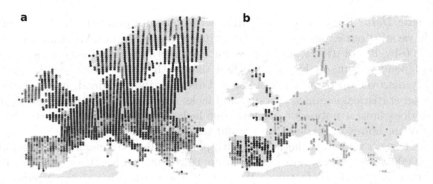

Fig. 4. *Example rules for mammals.* Shown are the inferred presence (green) and absence (red) of **a** pattern $\emptyset \rightarrow \{common\ squirrel,\ deer,\ ermine,\ marten,\ mice^*\}$ and **b** rule $\{Southwest\ European\ cat\} \rightarrow \{Mediterranean\ mice^*,\ Iberian\ rabbit\}$. The intensity of the colour indicates how many items of the tail hold – the ideal result is hence dark green and light red. Yellow dots indicate presence of animals from tail of rule where animals of head of rule were not sighted. (Color figure online)

On *Mammals*, GRAB finds large patterns such as $\emptyset \rightarrow \{red\ deer,\ European\ mole,\ European\ fitch,\ wild\ boar,\ marten,\ mice^*\}$, and $\emptyset \rightarrow \{common\ squirrel,\ deer,\ ermine,\ marten,\ mice^*\}$, that correspond to animals that commonly occur across Europe, with multiple mouse species (items) indicated by mice*. In addition, it also discovers specific patterns, e.g. $\emptyset \rightarrow \{snow\ rabbit,\ elk,\ lynx,\ brown\ bear\}$, which are mammals that appear almost exclusively in northeastern Europe. We visualized the second rule in Fig. 4a to show that the consequent should hold in most of the cases, but not necessarily need to be always present. Moreover, GRAB is able to find meaningful rules in the presence of noise, e.g. $\{Southwest\ European\ cat\} \rightarrow \{Mediterranean\ mice^*,\ Iberian\ rabbit\}$, where the rule should only hold in southwest europe. For the rule that GRAB discovers this is indeed the case, although the data contains (likely spurious) sightings of Iberian rabbits or Mediterranean mice in Norway (see Fig. 4b) and some sightings of mice alone, along the Mediterranean sea.

Runtime and Scalability. Last, but not least, we investigate the runtime of GRAB. We first consider scalability with regard to number of features. For this, in Fig. 5a we give the runtimes for the synthetic datasets we used above. From the figure we see that while GRAB is not as fast as KINGFISHER and HYPER+, it scales favourably with regard to the number of features. Although it considers a much larger search space, GRAB only needs seconds to minutes. On real data GRAB is the fastest method for five of the data sets, and only requires seconds for the other datasets, whereas the other methods take up to hours for particular instances (compare Fig. 5b).

Table 1. For GRAB, the size of the rule set and average size of head $\overline{|X|}$ and tail $\overline{|Y|}$ are given. For the other methods, number of found rules are given, *mem* indicates an aborted run due to memory usage >256 GB.

Dataset	n	m	GRAB			HYPER+	KINGFISHER	PACK
			$\overline{|X|}$	$\overline{|Y|}$	$|R|$	Number of discovered rules		
Abstracts	859	3933	0.9	1.2	29	1508	$42K$	334
Accidents	339898	468	1	1.1	138	$65M$	*mem*	$69M$
Adult	10830	97	1	1.1	27	$26K$	$9K$	$68M$
Covtype	581012	105	1.3	1.1	41	$13K$	$43K$	$286M$
DNA	1316	392	1	1.7	147	49	$140K$	451
Mammals	2183	121	1.5	2	38	*mem*	$\geq 10M$	$2K$
Mushroom	8124	119	1.6	1.5	65	$13K$	$81K$	$7K$
Plants	34781	69	1.2	3.2	20	$6M$	*mem*	910

7   Discussion

The experiments show that GRAB is fast and returns crisp, informative rule sets. On synthetic data it recovers the ground truth, without picking up noise. On real world data, it retrieves concise and easily interpretable rule sets, as opposed to the state of the art that discovers thousands, up to millions of rules.

The results on the *Mammals* data clearly show GRAB recovers known population structures, even in the presence of noise. The results on the ICDM *Abstracts* data are equally good, with rule $\{support\} \rightarrow \{vector, machin, svm\}$ as a notable example. In contrast to machine learning, in data mining "support" is ambiguous. In the ICDM abstracts it means the support of a pattern, as well as support vector machines, and the rule expresses this. To verify this, we additionally ran GRAB on abstracts from the Journal of Machine Learning Research (JMLR), where it instead recovers the pattern $\emptyset \rightarrow \{support, vector, machin, svm\}$.

Thanks to careful implementation and accurate gain estimates, GRAB scales very well in the number of transactions, as well as in the number of features. In practice, GRAB can consider up to several thousand features in reasonable time. Ultimately, we are interested in bioinformatics applications, and are hence interested in rule set search strategies that scale up to millions of features or more. For similar reasons we are interested in extending GRAB towards continuous-valued, and mixed-type data. This we also leave for future work.

Whereas the rules GRAB discovers provide useful insight, they are not necessarily actionable; that is only the case when X causes Y. Currently GRAB can only reward correlation, and we are interested in extending it towards additionally identifying causal rules from observational data [20].

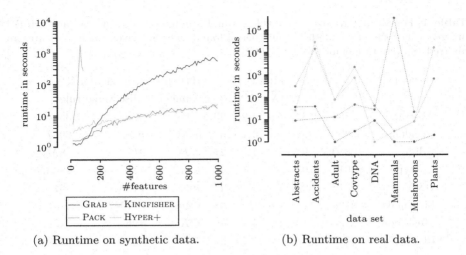

(a) Runtime on synthetic data.   (b) Runtime on real data.

Fig. 5. *Scalability* On the left side, runtimes are visualized on a logarithmic y-axis for synthetic data of varying number of features (x-axis). On the right, runtimes (logarithmic y-axis) are depicted for 8 real world data sets (x-axis). KINGFISHER did not finish on *Accident* and *Plants*, HYPER+ did not finish on *Mammals*.

8   Conclusion

We considered the problem of non-parametrically discovering sets of association rules for a given dataset. We proposed to mine small, non-redundant sets of highly informative noise-resistant rules and patterns, that together succinctly describe the data at hand. To do so, we defined a score based on solid information theoretic grounds, showed the problem does not lend itself for efficient optimization, and proposed GRAB, a highly efficient heuristic that greedily approximates the MDL optimal result. GRAB is unique in that it can discover both patterns and rules, is noise-resistant and allows rules and patterns to hold approximately, and, can discover rules with non-singleton consequents. Through thorough experiments we showed that unlike the state-of-the-art, GRAB is able to recover the ground truth in synthetic data, and discovers small sets of highly meaningful rules from real world data.

References

1. Agrawal, R., Srikant, R.: Fast algorithms for mining association rules. In: VLDB, pp. 487–499 (1994)
2. Bayardo, R.: Efficiently mining long patterns from databases. In: SIGMOD, pp. 85–93 (1998)
3. Calders, T., Goethals, B.: Non-derivable itemset mining. Data Min. Knowl. Disc. **14**(1), 171–206 (2007). https://doi.org/10.1007/s10618-006-0054-6

4. De Bie, T.: Maximum entropy models and subjective interestingness: an application to tiles in binary databases. Data Min. Knowl. Disc. **23**(3), 407–446 (2011). https://doi.org/10.1007/s10618-010-0209-3

5. Fowkes, J., Sutton, C.: A subsequence interleaving model for sequential pattern mining. In: KDD (2016)

6. Grünwald, P.: The Minimum Description Length Principle. MIT Press, Cambridge (2007)

7. Hämäläinen, W.: Kingfisher: an efficient algorithm for searching for both positive and negative dependency rules with statistical significance measures. Knowl. Inf. Syst. **32**(2), 383–414 (2012). https://doi.org/10.1007/s10115-011-0432-2

8. Han, J., Pei, J., Yin, Y.: Mining frequent patterns without candidate generation. In: SIGMOD, pp. 1–12. ACM (2000)

9. Jaroszewicz, S., Simovici, D.A.: Interestingness of frequent itemsets using Bayesian networks as background knowledge. In: KDD, pp. 178–186. ACM (2004)

10. Kontkanen, P., Myllymäki, P.: MDL histogram density estimation. In: AISTATS (2007)

11. Li, M., Vitányi, P.: An Introduction to Kolmogorov Complexity and Its Applications. Springer, New York (1993). https://doi.org/10.1007/978-1-4757-3860-5

12. Lucchese, C., Orlando, S., Perego, R.: Mining top-k patterns from binary datasets in presence of noise. In: SDM, pp. 165–176 (2010)

13. Mampaey, M., Vreeken, J., Tatti, N.: Summarizing data succinctly with the most informative itemsets. ACM TKDD **6**, 1–44 (2012)

14. Mannila, H., Toivonen, H., Verkamo, A.I.: Efficient algorithms for discovering association rules. In: KDD, pp. 181–192 (1994)

15. Miettinen, P., Vreeken, J.: MDL4BMF: minimum description length for Boolean matrix factorization. ACM TKDD **8**(4), A18:1–31 (2014)

16. Mitchell-Jones, T.: Societas Europaea Mammalogica (1999). http://www.euro pean-mammals.org

17. Moerchen, F., Thies, M., Ultsch, A.: Efficient mining of all margin-closed itemsets with applications in temporal knowledge discovery and classification by compression. Knowl. Inf. Syst. **29**(1), 55–80 (2011). https://doi.org/10.1007/s10115-010-0329-5

18. Myllykangas, S., Himberg, J., Böhling, T., Nagy, B., Hollmén, J., Knuutila, S.: DNA copy number amplification profiling of human neoplasms. Oncogene **25**(55), 7324–7332 (2006)

19. Papaxanthos, L., Llinares-López, F., Bodenham, D.A., Borgwardt, K.M.: Finding significant combinations of features in the presence of categorical covariates. In: NIPS, pp. 2271–2279 (2016)

20. Pearl, J.: Causality: Models, Reasoning and Inference, 2nd edn. Cambridge University Press, Cambridge (2009)

21. Pellegrina, L., Vandin, F.: Efficient mining of the most significant patterns with permutation testing. In: KDD, pp. 2070–2079 (2018)

22. Rissanen, J.: Modeling by shortest data description. Automatica **14**(1), 465–471 (1978)

23. Rissanen, J.: A universal prior for integers and estimation by minimum description length. Ann. Stat. **11**(2), 416–431 (1983)

24. Tatti, N.: Maximum entropy based significance of itemsets. Knowl. Inf. Syst. **17**(1), 57–77 (2008)

25. Tatti, N., Vreeken, J.: Finding good itemsets by packing data. In: ICDM, pp. 588–597 (2008)

26. Vreeken, J., Tatti, N.: Interesting patterns. In: Aggarwal, C.C., Han, J. (eds.) Frequent Pattern Mining, pp. 105–134. Springer, Cham (2014). https://doi.org/ 10.1007/978-3-319-07821-2_5
27. Vreeken, J., van Leeuwen, M., Siebes, A.: KRIMP: mining itemsets that compress. Data Min. Knowl. Disc. **23**(1), 169–214 (2011). https://doi.org/10.1007/s10618-010-0202-x
28. Wang, F., Rudin, C.: Falling rule lists. In: AISTATS (2015)
29. Webb, G.I.: Discovering significant patterns. Mach. Learn. **68**(1), 1–33 (2007). https://doi.org/10.1007/s10994-007-5006-x
30. Xiang, Y., Jin, R., Fuhry, D., Dragan, F.F.: Succinct summarization of transactional databases: an overlapped hyperrectangle scheme. In: KDD, pp. 758–766 (2008)
31. Zaki, M.J., Parthasarathy, S., Ogihara, M., Li, W.: New algorithms for fast discovery of association rules. In: KDD, August 1997
32. Zimmermann, A., Nijssen, S.: Supervised pattern mining and applications to classification. In: Aggarwal, C.C., Han, J. (eds.) Frequent Pattern Mining, pp. 425–442. Springer, Cham (2014). https://doi.org/10.1007/978-3-319-07821-2_17

Clustering, Anomaly and Outlier Detection, and Autoencoders

A Framework for Deep Constrained Clustering - Algorithms and Advances

Hongjing Zhang[1(✉)], Sugato Basu[2], and Ian Davidson[1]

[1] Department of Computer Science, University of California, Davis, CA 95616, USA
hjzzhang@ucdavis.edu, davidson@cs.ucdavis.edu
[2] Google Research, Mountain View, CA 94043, USA
sugato@google.com

Abstract. The area of constrained clustering has been extensively explored by researchers and used by practitioners. Constrained clustering formulations exist for popular algorithms such as k-means, mixture models, and spectral clustering but have several limitations. A fundamental strength of deep learning is its flexibility, and here we explore a deep learning framework for constrained clustering and in particular explore how it can extend the field of constrained clustering. We show that our framework can not only handle standard together/apart constraints (without the well documented negative effects reported earlier) generated from labeled side information but more complex constraints generated from new types of side information such as continuous values and high-level domain knowledge. (Source code available at: http://github.com/blueocean92/deep_constrained_clustering)

Keywords: Constrained clustering · Deep learning · Semi-supervised clustering · Reproducible research

1 Introduction

Constrained clustering has a long history in machine learning with many standard algorithms being adapted to be constrained [3] including EM [2], K-Means [25] and spectral methods [26]. The addition of constraints generated from ground truth labels allows a semi-supervised setting to increase accuracy [25] when measured against the ground truth labeling.

However, there are several limitations in these methods and one purpose of this paper is to explore how deep learning can make advances to the field beyond what other methods have. In particular, we find that existing non-deep formulations of constrained clustering have the following limitations:

- *Limited Constraints and Side Information.* Constraints are limited to simple together/apart constraints typically generated from labels. In some domains, experts may more naturally give guidance at the cluster level or generate constraints from continuous side-information.

© Springer Nature Switzerland AG 2020
U. Brefeld et al. (Eds.): ECML PKDD 2019, LNAI 11906, pp. 57–72, 2020.
https://doi.org/10.1007/978-3-030-46150-8_4

- *Negative Effect of Constraints.* For some algorithms though constraints improve performance when *averaged* over many constraint sets, *individual* constraint sets produce results worse than using no constraints [8]. As practitioners typically have one constraint set their use can be "hit or miss".
- *Intractability and Scalability Issues.* Iterative algorithms that directly solve for clustering assignments run into problems of intractability [7]. Relaxed formulations (i.e. spectral methods [17,26]) require solving a full rank eigendecomposition problem which takes $O(n^3)$.
- *Assumption of Good Features.* A core requirement is that good features or similarity function for complex data is already created.

Since deep learning is naturally scalable and able to find useful representations we focus on the first and second challenges but experimentally explore the third and fourth. Though deep clustering with constraints has many potential benefits to overcome these limitations it is not without its challenges. Our major contributions in this paper are summarized as follows:

- We propose a deep constrained clustering formulation that cannot only encode standard together/apart constraints but new triplet constraints (which can be generated from continuous side information), instance difficulty constraints, and cluster level balancing constraints (see Sect. 3).
- Deep constrained clustering overcomes a long term issue we reported in PKDD earlier [8] with constrained clustering of profound practical implications: overcoming the negative effects of individual constraint sets.
- We show how the benefits of deep learning such as scalability and end-to-end learning translate to our deep constrained clustering formulation. We achieve better clustering results than traditional constrained clustering methods (with features generated from an auto-encoder) on challenging datasets (see Table 2).

Our paper is organized as follows. First, we introduce the related work in Sect. 2. We then propose four forms of constraints in Sect. 3 and introduce how to train the clustering network with these constraints in Sect. 4. Then we compare our approach to previous baselines and demonstrate the effectiveness of new types of constraints in Sect. 5. Finally, we discuss future work and conclude in Sect. 6.

2   Related Work

Constrained Clustering. Constrained clustering is an important area and there is a large body of work that shows how *side information* can improve the clustering performance [4,24–26,28]. Here the side information is typically labeled data which is used to generate *pairwise* together/apart constraints used to partially reveal the ground truth clustering to help the clustering algorithm. Such constraints are easy to encode in matrices and enforce in procedural algorithms though not with its challenges. In particular, we showed [8] performance improves with larger constraint sets when **averaged** over many constraint sets generated from the ground truth labeling. However, for a significant fraction (just not the majority) of these constraint sets performance is *worse* than using no constraint set. We recreated some of these results in Table 2.

Moreover, side information can exist in different forms beyond labels (i.e. continuous data), and domain experts can provide guidance beyond pairwise constraints. Some work in the supervised classification setting [10,14,20,21] seek alternatives such as relative/triplet guidance, but to our knowledge, such information has not been explored in the non-hierarchical clustering setting. Complex constraints for hierarchical clustering have been explored [1,5] but these are tightly limited to the hierarchical structure (i.e., x must be joined with y before z) and not directly translated to non-hierarchical (partitional) clustering.

Deep Clustering. Motivated by the success of deep neural networks in supervised learning, unsupervised deep learning approaches are now being explored [11,13,22,27,30]. There are approaches [22,30] which learn an encoding that is suitable for a clustering objective first and then applied an external clustering method. Our work builds upon the most direct setting [11,27] which encodes one self-training objective and finds the clustering allocations for all instances within one neural network.

Deep Clustering with Pairwise Constraints. Most recently, the semi-supervised clustering networks with pairwise constraints have been explored: [12] uses pairwise constraints to enforce small divergence between similar pairs while increasing the divergence between dissimilar pairs assignment probability distributions. However, this approach did not leverage the unlabeled data, hence requires lot's of labeled data to achieve good results. Fogel et al. proposed an unsupervised clustering network [9] by self-generating pairwise constraints from mutual KNN graph and extends it to semi-supervised clustering by using labeled connections queried from the human. However, this method cannot make out-of-sample predictions and requires user-defined parameters for generating constraints from mutual KNN graph.

3   Deep Constrained Clustering Framework

Here we outline our proposed framework for deep constrained clustering. Our method of adding constraints to and training deep learning can be used for most deep clustering method (so long as the network has a k unit output indicating the degree of cluster membership) and here we choose the popular deep embedded clustering method (DEC [27]). We sketch this method first for completeness.

3.1   Deep Embedded Clustering

We choose to apply our constraints formulation to the deep embedded clustering method DEC [27] which starts with pre-training an autoencoder ($x_i = g(f(x_i))$ but then removes the decoder. The remaining encoder ($z_i = f(x_i)$) is then fine-tuned by optimizing an objective which takes first z_i and converts it to a soft allocation vector of length k which we term $q_{i,j}$ indicating the degree of belief instance i belongs to cluster j. Then q is self-trained on to produce p a unimodal "hard" allocation vector which allocates the instance to primarily only one cluster. We now overview each step.

Conversion of z to Soft Cluster Allocation Vector q. Here DEC takes the similarity between an embedded point z_i and the cluster centroid u_j measured by Student's t-distribution [18]. Note that v is a constant as $v = 1$ and q_{ij} is a soft assignment:

$$q_{ij} = \frac{(1 + ||z_i - \mu_j||^2/v)^{-\frac{v+1}{2}}}{\sum_{j'} (1 + ||z_i - \mu_{j'}||^2/v)^{-\frac{v+1}{2}}} \tag{1}$$

Conversion of Q to Hard Cluster Assignments P. The above normalized similarities between embedded points and centroids can be considered as soft cluster assignments Q. However, we desire a target distribution P that better resembles a hard allocation vector, p_{ij} is defined as:

$$p_{ij} = \frac{q_{ij}^2/\sum_i q_{ij}}{\sum_{j'} (q_{ij'}^2/\sum_i q_{ij'})} \tag{2}$$

Loss Function. Then the algorithm's loss function is to minimize the distance between P and Q as follows. Note this is a form of self-training as we are trying to teach the network to produce unimodal cluster allocation vectors.

$$\ell_C = KL(P||Q) = \sum_i \sum_j p_{ij} \log \frac{p_{ij}}{q_{ij}} \tag{3}$$

The DEC method requires the initial centroids given (μ) to calculate Q are "representative". The initial centroids are set using k-means clustering. However, there is no guarantee that the clustering results over an auto-encoders embedding yield a good clustering. We believe that constraints can help overcome this issue which we test later.

3.2 Different Types of Constraints

To enhance the clustering performance and allow for more types of interactions between human and clustering models we propose four types of guidance which are pairwise constraints, instance difficulty constraints, triplet constraints, and cardinality and give examples of each. As traditional constrained clustering methods put constraints on the final clustering assignments, our proposed approach constrains the q vector which is the soft assignment. A core challenge when adding constraints is to allow the resultant loss function to be differentiable so we can derive back propagation updates.

Pairwise Constraints. Pairwise constraints (must-link and cannot-link) are well studied [3] and we showed they are capable of defining any ground truth set partitions [7]. Here we show how these pairwise constraints can be added to a deep learning algorithm. We encode the loss for must-link constraints set ML as:

$$\ell_{ML} = - \sum_{(a,b) \in ML} \log \sum_j q_{aj} * q_{bj} \tag{4}$$

Similarly loss for cannot-link constraints set CL is:

$$\ell_{CL} = - \sum_{(a,b) \in CL} \log \left(1 - \sum_j q_{aj} * q_{bj}\right) \tag{5}$$

Intuitively speaking, the must-link loss prefers instances with same soft assignments and the cannot-link loss prefers the opposite cases.

Instance Difficulty Constraints. A challenge with self-learning in deep learning is that if the initial centroids are incorrect, the self-training can lead to poor results. Here we use constraints to overcome this by allowing the user to specify which instances are easier to cluster (i.e., they belong strongly to only one cluster) and by ignoring difficult instances (i.e., those that belong to multiple clusters strongly).

We encode user supervision with an $n \times 1$ constraint vector M. Let $M_i \in [-1, 1]$ be an instance difficulty indicator, $M_i > 0$ means the instance i is easy to cluster, $M_i = 0$ means no difficulty information is provided and $M_i < 0$ means instance i is hard to cluster. The loss function is formulated as:

$$\ell_I = \sum_{t \in \{M_t < 0\}} M_t \sum_j q_{tj}^2 - \sum_{s \in \{M_s > 0\}} M_s \sum_j q_{sj}^2 \tag{6}$$

The instance difficulty loss function aims to encourage the easier instances to have sparse clustering assignments but prevents the difficult instances having sparse clustering assignments. The absolute value of M_i indicates the degree of confidence in difficulty estimation. This loss will help the model training process converge faster on easier instances and increase our model's robustness towards difficult instances.

Triplet Constraints. Although pairwise constraints are capable of defining any ground truth set partitions from labeled data [7], in many domains no labeled side information exists or strong pairwise guidance is not available. Thus we seek triplet constraints, which are weaker constraints that indicate the relationship within a triple of instances. Given an anchor instance a, positive instance p and negative instance n we say that instance a is more similar to p than to n. The loss function for all triplets $(a, p, n) \in T$ can be represented as:

$$\ell_T = \sum_{(a,p,n) \in T} \max(d(q_a, q_n) - d(q_a, q_p) + \theta, 0) \tag{7}$$

where $d(q_a, q_b) = \sum_j q_{aj} * q_{bj}$ and $\theta > 0$. The larger value of $d(q_a, q_b)$ represents larger similarity between a and b. The variable θ controls the gap distance between positive and negative instances. ℓ_T works by pushing the positive instance's assignment closer to anchor's assignment and preventing negative instance's assignment being closer to anchor's assignment.

Global Size Constraints. Experts may more naturally give guidance at a cluster level. Here we explore clustering size constraints, which means each cluster should be approximately the same size. Denote the total number of clusters as k, total training instances number as n, the global size constraints loss function is:

$$\ell_G = \sum_{c \in \{1,..k\}} (\sum_{i=1}^{n} q_{ic}/n - \frac{1}{k})^2 \tag{8}$$

Our global constraints loss function works by minimizing the distance between the expected cluster size and the actual cluster size. The actual cluster size is calculated by averaging the soft-assignments. To guarantee the effectiveness of global size constraints, we need to assume that during our mini-batch training the batch size should be large enough to calculate the cluster sizes. A similar loss function can be used (see Sect. 3.4) to enforce other cardinality constraints on the cluster composition such as upper and lower bounds on the number of people with a certain property.

3.3 Preventing Trivial Solution

In our framework the proposed must-link constraints we mentioned before can lead to trivial solution that all the instances are mapped to the same cluster. Previous deep clustering method [30] have also met this problem. To mitigate this problem, we combine the reconstruction loss with the must-link loss to learn together. Denote the encoding network as $f(x)$ and decoding network as $g(x)$, the reconstruction loss for instance x_i is:

$$\ell_R = \ell(g(f(x_i)), x_i) \tag{9}$$

where ℓ is the least-square loss: $\ell(x, y) = ||x - y||^2$.

3.4 Extensions to High-Level Domain Knowledge-Based Constraints

Although most of our proposed constraints are generated based on instance labels or comparisons. Our framework can be extended to high-level domain knowledge-based constraints with minor modifications.

Cardinality Constraints. For example, cardinality constraints [6] allow expressing requirements on the number of instances that satisfy some conditions in each cluster. Assume we have n people and want to split them into k dinner party groups. An example cardinality constraint is to enforce each party should have the same number of males and females. We split the n people into two groups as M (males) and F (females) in which $|M|+|F| = n$ and $M \cap N = \emptyset$. Then the cardinality constraints can be formulated as:

$$\ell_{Cardinality} = \sum_{c \in \{1,..k\}} (\sum_{i \in M} q_{ic}/n - \sum_{j \in F} q_{jc}/n)^2 \tag{10}$$

For upper-bound and lower-bound based cardinality constraints [6], we use the same setting as previously described, now the constraint changes as for each party group we need the number of males to range from L to U. Then we can formulate it as:

$$\ell_{CardinalityBound} = \sum_{c \in \{1,..k\}} (\min(0, \sum_{i \in M} q_{ic} - L)^2 + \max(0, \sum_{i \in M} q_{ic} - U)^2) \tag{11}$$

Logical Combinations of Constraints. Apart from cardinality constraints, complex logic constraints can also be used to enhance the expressivity power of representing knowledge. For example, if two instances x_1 and x_2 are in the same cluster then instances x_3 and x_4 must be in different clusters. This can be achieved in our framework as we can dynamically add cannot-link constraint $CL(x_3, x_4)$ once we check the soft assignment q of x_1 and x_2.

Consider a horn form constraint like $r \wedge s \wedge t \rightarrow u$. Denote $r = ML(x_1, x_2)$, $s = ML(x_3, x_4)$, $t = ML(x_5, x_6)$ and $u = CL(x_7, x_8)$. By forward passing the instances within r, s, t to our deep constrained clustering model, we can get the soft assignment values of these instances. By checking the satisfying results based on $r \wedge s \wedge t$, we can decide whether to enforce cannot-link loss $CL(x_7, x_8)$.

4   Putting It All Together - Efficient Training Strategy

Our training strategy consists of two training branches and effectively has two ways of creating mini-batches for training. For instance-difficulty or global-size constraints, we treat their loss functions as addictive losses so that no extra branch needs to be created. For pairwise or triplet constraints we build another output branch for them and train the whole network in an alternative way.

Loss Branch for Instance Constraints. In deep learning it is common to add loss functions defined over the same output units. In the Improved DEC method [11] the clustering loss ℓ_C and reconstruction loss ℓ_R were added together. To this we add the instance difficulty loss ℓ_I. This effectively adds guidance to speed up training convergence by identifying "easy" instances and increase the model's robustness by ignoring "difficult" instances. Similarly we treat the global size constraints loss ℓ_G as an additional additive loss. All instances whether or not they are part of triplet or pairwise constraints are trained through this branch and the mini-batches are created randomly.

Loss Branch for Complex Constraints. Our framework uses more complex loss functions as they define constraints on pairs and even triples of instances.

Thus we create another loss branch that contains pairwise loss ℓ_P or triplet loss ℓ_T to help the network tune the embedding which satisfy these stronger constraints. For each constraint *type* we create a mini-batch consisting of only those instances having that type of constraint. For each *example* of a constraint type, we feed the constrained instances through the network, calculate the loss, calculate the change in weights but do not adjust the weights. We sum the weight adjustments for all constraint examples in the mini-batch and then adjust the weights. Hence our method is an example of batch weight updating as is standard in DL for stability reasons. The whole training procedure is summarized in Algorithm 1.

Algorithm 1. Deep Constrained Clustering Framework

Input: X: data, m: maximum epochs , k: number of clusters, N: total number of batches and N_C: total number of constraints batches.

Output: latent embeddings Z, cluster assignment S.

Train the stacked denosing autoencoder to obtain Z
Initialize centroids μ via k-means on embedding Z.
for *epoch* $= 1$ **to** m **do**
   for *batch* $= 1$ **to** N **do**
      Calculate ℓ_C via Eqn (3), ℓ_R via Eqn (9).
      Calculate ℓ_I via Eqn (6) or ℓ_G via Eqn (8).
      Calculate total loss as $\ell_C + \ell_R + \{\ell_I || \ell_G\}$.
      Update network parameters based on total loss.
   end for
   for *batch* $= 1$ **to** N_C **do**
      Calculate ℓ_P via Eqn (4, 5) or ℓ_T via Eqn (7).
      Update network parameters based on $\{\ell_P || \ell_T\}$.
   end for
end for

---

5   Experiments

All data and code used to perform these experiments are available online (http:// github.com/blueocean92/deep_constrained_clustering) to help with reproducibility. In our experiments we aim to address the following questions:

- How does our end-to-end deep clustering approach using traditional pairwise constraints compare with traditional constrained clustering methods? The latter is given the same auto-encoding representation Z used to initialize our method.
- Are the new types of constraints we create for deep clustering method useful in practice?
- Is our end-to-end deep constrained clustering method more robust to the well known negative effects of constraints we published earlier [8]?

5.1 Datasets

To study the performance and generality of different algorithms, we evaluate the proposed method on two image datasets and one text dataset:

MNIST: Consists of 70000 handwritten digits of 28-by-28 pixel size. The digits are centered and size-normalized in our experiments [15].

FASHION-MNIST: A Zalando's article images-consisting of a training set of 60000 examples and a test set of 10000 examples. Each example is a 28-by-28 grayscale image, associated with a label from 10 classes.

REUTERS-10K: This dataset contains English news stories labeled with a category tree [16]. To be comparable with the previous baselines, we used 4 root categories: `corporate/industrial`, `government/social`, `markets` and `economics` as labels and excluded all documents with multiple labels. We randomly sampled a subset of 10000 examples and computed TF-IDF features on the 2000 most common words.

5.2 Implementation Details

Basic Deep Clustering Implementation. To be comparable with deep clustering baselines, we set the encoder network as a fully connected multilayer perceptron with dimensions $d - 500 - 500 - 2000 - 10$ for all datasets, where d is the dimension of input data (features). The decoder network is a mirror of the encoder. All the internal layers are activated by the ReLU [19] nonlinearity function. For a fair comparison with baseline methods, we used the same greedy layer-wise pre-training strategy to calculate the auto-encoders embedding. To initialize clustering centroids, we run k-means with 20 restarts and select the best solution. We choose Adam optimizer with an initial learning rate of 0.001 for all the experiments. We adopt standard metrics for evaluating clustering performance which measure how close the clustering found is to the ground truth result. Specifically, we employ the following two metrics: normalized mutual information (**NMI**) [23,29] and clustering accuracy (**Acc**) [29]. In our baseline comparisons we use IDEC [11], a non-constrained improved version of DEC published recently.

Pairwise Constraints Experiments. We randomly select pairs of instances and generate the corresponding pairwise constraints between them. To ensure transitivity we calculate the transitive closure over all must-linked instances and then generate entailed constraints from the cannot-link constraints [7]. Since our loss function for must-link constraints is combined with reconstruction loss, we use grid search and set the penalty weight for must-link as 0.1.

Instance Difficulty Constraints Experiments. To simulate human-guided instance difficulty constraints, we use k-means as a base learner and mark all the incorrectly clustered instances as difficult with confidence 0.1, we also mark the correctly classified instances as easy instances with confidence 1. In Fig. 1 we give some example difficulty constraints found using this method.

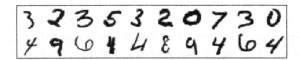

Fig. 1. Example of instance difficulty constraints. Top row shows the "easy" instances and second row shows the "difficult" instances.

Triplet Constraints Experiments. Triplet constraints can state that instance i is more similar to instance j than instance k. To simulate human guidance on triplet constraints, we randomly select n instances as anchors (i), for each anchor we randomly select two instances (j and k) based on the similarity between the anchor. The similarity is calculated as the euclidian distance d between two instances pre-trained embedding. The pre-trained embedding is extracted from our deep clustering network trained with 100000 pairwise constraints. Figure 2 shows the generated triplets constraints. Through grid search we set the triplet loss margin $\theta = 0.1$.

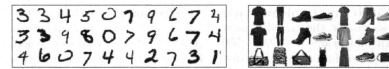

Fig. 2. Examples of the generated triplet constraints for MNIST and Fashion. The three rows for each plot shows the anchor instances, positive instances and negative instances correspondingly.

Global Size Constraints Experiments. We apply global size constraints to MNIST and Fashion datasets since they satisfy the balanced size assumptions. The total number of clusters is set to 10.

5.3 Experimental Results

Experiments on Instance Difficulty. In Table 1, we report the average test performance of deep clustering framework without any constraints in the left. In comparison, we report the average test performance of deep clustering framework with instance difficulty constraints in the right and we find the model learned with instance difficulty constraints outperforms the baseline method in all datasets. This is to be expected as we have given the algorithm more information than the baseline method, but it demonstrates our method can make good use of this extra information. What is unexpected is the effectiveness of speeding up the learning process and will be the focus of future work.

Table 1. Left table shows baseline results for Improved DEC [11] averaged over 20 trials. Right table lists experiments using instance difficulty constraints (mean ± std) averaged over 20 trials.

	MNIST	Fashion	Reuters	MNIST	Fashion	Reuters
Acc (%)	88.29 ± 0.05	58.74 ± 0.08	75.20 ± 0.07	91.02 ± 0.34	62.17 ± 0.06	78.01 ± 0.13
NMI (%)	86.12 ± 0.09	63.27 ± 0.11	54.16 ± 1.73	88.08 ± 0.14	64.95 ± 0.04	56.02 ± 0.21
Epoch	87.60 ± 12.53	77.20 ± 11.28	12.90 ± 2.03	29.70 ± 4.25	47.60 ± 6.98	9.50 ± 1.80

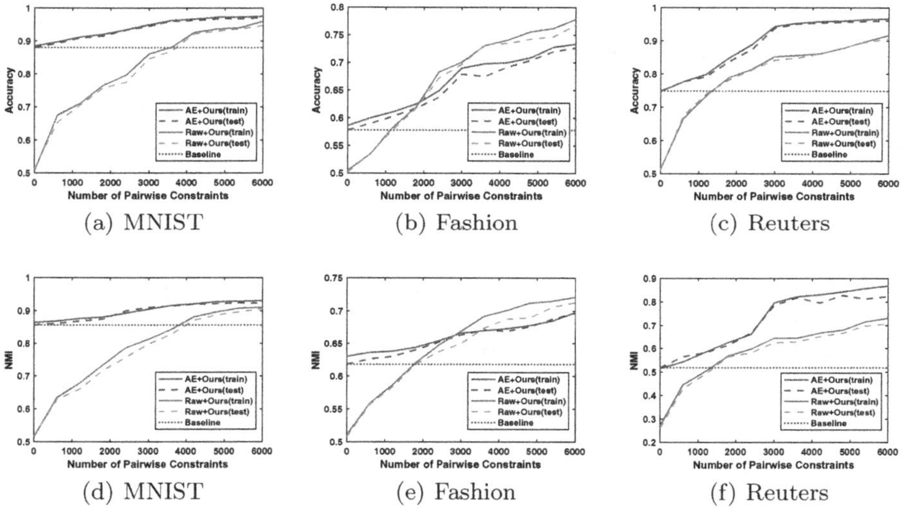

(a) MNIST   (b) Fashion   (c) Reuters

(d) MNIST   (e) Fashion   (f) Reuters

Fig. 3. Clustering accuracy and NMI on training test sets for different number of pairwise constraints. AE means an autoencoder was used to seed our method. The horizontal maroon colored baseline shows the IDEC's [11] test set performance.

Experiments on Pairwise Constraints. We randomly generate 6000 pairs of constraints which are a small fractions of possible pairwise constraints for MNIST (0.0002%), Fashion (0.0002%) and Reuters (0.006%).

Recall the DEC method is initialized with auto-encoder features. To better understand the contribution of pairwise constraints, we have tested our method with both auto-encoders features and raw data. As can be seen from Fig. 3: the clustering performance improves consistently as the number of constraints increases in both settings. Moreover, with just 6000 pairwise constraints the performance on Reuters and MNIST increased significantly especially for the setup with raw data. We also notice that learning with raw data in Fashion achieves a better result than using autoencoder's features. This shows that the autoencoder's features may not always be suitable for DEC's clustering objective. Overall our results show pairwise constraints can help reshape the representation and improve the clustering results.

We also compare the results with recent work [12]: our approach(autoencoders features) outperforms the best clustering accuracy reported for MNIST by a margin of 16.08%, 2.16% and 0.13% respectively for 6, 60 and 600 samples/class. Unfortunately, we can't make a comparison with Fogel's algorithm [9] due to an issue in their code repository.

Table 2. Pairwise constrained clustering performance (mean ± std) averaged over 100 constraints sets. Due to the scalability issues we apply flexible CSP with downsampled data(3000 instances and 180 constraints). Negative ratio is the fraction of times using constraints resulted in poorer results than not using constraints. See Fig. 4 and text for an explanation why our method performs well.

	Flexible CSP*	COP-KMeans	MPCKMeans	Ours
MNIST Acc	0.628 ± 0.07	0.816 ± 0.06	0.846 ± 0.04	**0.963 ± 0.01**
MNIST NMI	0.587 ± 0.06	0.773 ± 0.02	0.808 ± 0.04	**0.918 ± 0.01**
Negative Ratio	19%	45%	11%	**0%**
Fashion Acc	0.417 ± 0.05	0.548 ± 0.04	0.589 ± 0.05	**0.681 ± 0.03**
Fashion NMI	0.462 ± 0.03	0.589 ± 0.02	0.613 ± 0.04	**0.667 ± 0.02**
Negative Ratio	23%	27%	37%	**6%**
Reuters Acc	0.554 ± 0.07	0.712 ± 0.0424	0.763 ± 0.05	**0.950 ± 0.02**
Reuters NMI	0.410 ± 0.05	0.478 ± 0.0346	0.544 ± 0.04	**0.815 ± 0.02**
Negative Ratio	28%	73%	80%	**0%**

Negative Effects of Constraints. Our earlier work [8] showed that for traditional constrained clustering algorithms, that the addition of constraints *on average* helps clustering but many individual constraint sets can hurt performance in that performance is worse than using **no** constraints. Here we recreate these results even when these classic methods use auto-encoded representations. In Table 2, we report the average performance with 3600 randomly generated pairwise constraints. For each dataset, we randomly generated 100 sets of constraints to test the negative effects of constraints [8]. In each run, we fixed the random seed and the initial centroids for k-means based methods, for each method we compare its performance between constrained version to unconstrained version. We calculate the negative ratio which is the fraction of times that unconstrained version produced better results than the constrained version. As can be seen from the table, our proposed method achieves significant improvements than traditional non-deep constrained clustering algorithms [4,25,26].

To understand why our method was robust to variations in constraint sets we visualized the embeddings learnt. Figure 4 shows the embedded representation of a random subset of instances and its corresponding pairwise constraints using t-SNE and the learned embedding z. Based on Fig. 4, we can see the autoencoders embedding is noisy and lot's of constraints are inconsistent based on our earlier definition [8]. Further, we visualize the IDEC's latent embedding and find

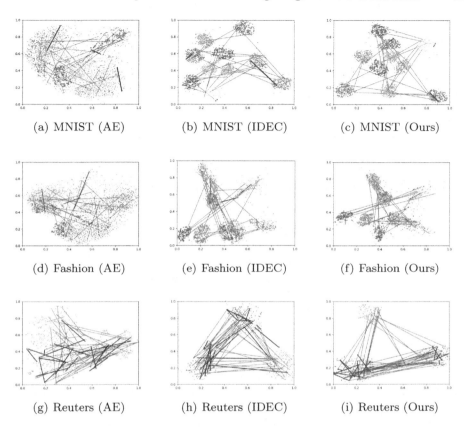

(a) MNIST (AE)   (b) MNIST (IDEC)   (c) MNIST (Ours)

(d) Fashion (AE)   (e) Fashion (IDEC)   (f) Fashion (Ours)

(g) Reuters (AE)   (h) Reuters (IDEC)   (i) Reuters (Ours)

Fig. 4. We visualize (using t-SNE) the latent representation for a subset of instances and pairwise constraints, we visualize the same instances and constraints for each row. The red lines are cannot-links and blue lines are must-links. (Color figure online)

out the clusters are better separated. However, the inconsistent constraints still exist (blue lines across different clusters and redlines within a cluster); these constraints tend to have negative effects on traditional constrained clustering methods. Finally, for our method's results we can see the clusters are well separated, the must-links are well satisfied (blue lines are within the same cluster) and cannot-links are well satisfied (red lines are across different clusters). Hence we can conclude that end-to-end-learning can address these negative effects of constraints by simultaneously learning a representation that is consistent with the constraints and clustering the data. This result has profound practical significance as practitioners typically only have one constraint set to work with.

Experiments on Triplet Constraints. We experimented on MNIST and FASHION datasets. Figure 2 visualizes example triplet constraints (based on embedding similarity), note the positive instances are closer to anchors than

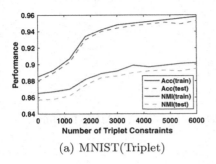 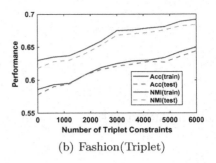

(a) MNIST(Triplet)   (b) Fashion(Triplet)

Fig. 5. Evaluation of the effectiveness of triplet constraints in terms of Acc/NMI.

negative instances. In Fig. 5, we show the clustering Acc/NMI improves consistently as the number of constraints increasing. Comparing with Fig. 3 we can find the pairwise constraints can bring slightly better improvements, that's because our triplets constraints are generated from a continuous domain and there is no exact together/apart information encoded in the constraints. Triplet constraints can be seen as a weaker but more general type of constraints.

Experiments on Global Size Constraints. To test the effectiveness of our proposed global size constraints, we have experimented on MNIST and Fashion training set since they both have balanced cluster sizes (see Fig. 6). Note that the ideal size for each cluster is 6000 (each data set has 10 classes), we can see that blue bars are more evenly distributed and closer to the ideal size.

We also evaluate the clustering performance with global constraints on MNIST (Acc: 0.91, NMI: 0.86) and Fashion (Acc: 0.57, NMI: 0.59). Comparing to the baselines in Table 1, interestingly, we find the performance improved slightly on MNIST but dropped slightly on Fashion.

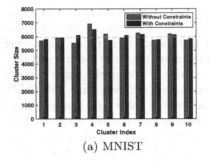 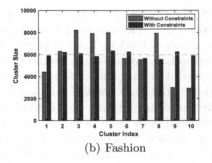

(a) MNIST   (b) Fashion

Fig. 6. Evaluation of the global size constraints. This plot shows each cluster's size before/after adding global size constraints. (Color figure online)

6   Conclusion and Future Work

The area of constrained partitional clustering has a long history and is widely used. Constrained partitional clustering typically is mostly limited to simple pairwise together and apart constraints. In this paper, we show that deep clustering can be extended to a variety of fundamentally different constraint types including instance-level (specifying hardness), cluster level (specifying cluster sizes) and triplet-level.

Our deep learning formulation was shown to advance the general field of constrained clustering in several ways. Firstly, it achieves better experimental performance than well-known k-means, mixture-model and spectral constrained clustering in both an academic setting and a practical setting (see Table 2).

Importantly, our approach does not suffer from the negative effects of constraints [8] as it learns a representation that simultaneously satisfies the constraints and finds a good clustering. This result is quite useful as a practitioner typically has just one constraint set and our method is far more likely to perform better than using no constraints.

Most importantly, we were able to show that our method achieves all of the above but still retains the benefits of deep learning such as scalability, out-of-sample predictions and end-to-end learning. We found that even though standard non-deep learning methods were given the same representations of the data used to initialize our methods the deep constrained clustering was able to adapt these representations even further. Future work will explore new types of constraints, using multiple constraints at once and extensions to the clustering setting.

Acknowledgements. We acknowledge support for this work from a Google Gift entitled: "Combining Symbolic Reasoning and Deep Learning".

References

1. Bade, K., Nürnberger, A.: Creating a cluster hierarchy under constraints of a partially known hierarchy. In: SIAM (2008)
2. Basu, S., Bilenko, M., Mooney, R.J.: A probabilistic framework for semi-supervised clustering. In: KDD (2004)
3. Basu, S., Davidson, I., Wagstaff, K.: Constrained Clustering: Advances in Algorithms, Theory, and Applications. CRC Press, Boca Raton (2008)
4. Bilenko, M., Basu, S., Mooney, R.J.: Integrating constraints and metric learning in semi-supervised clustering. In: ICML (2004)
5. Chatziafratis, V., Niazadeh, R., Charikar, M.: Hierarchical clustering with structural constraints. arXiv preprint arXiv:1805.09476 (2018)
6. Dao, T.B.H., Vrain, C., Duong, K.C., Davidson, I.: A framework for actionable clustering using constraint programming. In: ECAI (2016)
7. Davidson, I., Ravi, S.: Intractability and clustering with constraints. In: ICML (2007)
8. Davidson, I., Wagstaff, K.L., Basu, S.: Measuring constraint-set utility for partitional clustering algorithms. In: Fürnkranz, J., Scheffer, T., Spiliopoulou, M. (eds.) PKDD 2006. LNCS (LNAI), vol. 4213, pp. 115–126. Springer, Heidelberg (2006). https://doi.org/10.1007/11871637_15

9. Fogel, S., Averbuch-Elor, H., Goldberger, J., Cohen-Or, D.: Clustering-driven deep embedding with pairwise constraints. arXiv preprint arXiv:1803.08457 (2018)
10. Gress, A., Davidson, I.: Probabilistic formulations of regression with mixed guidance. In: ICDM (2016)
11. Guo, X., Gao, L., Liu, X., Yin, J.: Improved deep embedded clustering with local structure preservation. In: IJCAI (2017)
12. Hsu, Y.C., Kira, Z.: Neural network-based clustering using pairwise constraints. arXiv preprint arXiv:1511.06321 (2015)
13. Jiang, Z., Zheng, Y., Tan, H., Tang, B., Zhou, H.: Variational deep embedding: An unsupervised and generative approach to clustering. arXiv preprint arXiv:1611.05148 (2016)
14. Joachims, T.: Optimizing search engines using clickthrough data. In: KDD (2002)
15. LeCun, Y., Bottou, L., Bengio, Y., Haffner, P.: Gradient-based learning applied to document recognition. Proc. IEEE 86(11), 2278–2324 (1998)
16. Lewis, D.D., Yang, Y., Rose, T.G., Li, F.: Rcv1: a new benchmark collection for text categorization research. JMLR 5, 361–397 (2004)
17. Lu, Z., Carreira-Perpinan, M.A.: Constrained spectral clustering through affinity propagation. In: CVPR (2008)
18. Maaten, L.V.D., Hinton, G.: Visualizing data using t-SNE. J. Mach. Learn. Res. 9(Nov), 2579–2605 (2008)
19. Nair, V., Hinton, G.E.: Rectified linear units improve restricted Boltzmann machines. In: ICML (2010)
20. Schroff, F., Kalenichenko, D., Philbin, J.: Facenet: a unified embedding for face recognition and clustering. In: CVPR (2015)
21. Schultz, M., Joachims, T.: Learning a distance metric from relative comparisons. In: NIPS (2004)
22. Shaham, U., Stanton, K., Li, H., Nadler, B., Basri, R., Kluger, Y.: Spectralnet: spectral clustering using deep neural networks. arXiv preprint arXiv:1801.01587 (2018)
23. Strehl, A., Ghosh, J., Mooney, R.: Impact of similarity measures on web-page clustering. In: Workshop on Artificial Intelligence for Web Search (AAAI 2000), vol. 58, p. 64 (2000)
24. Wagstaff, K., Cardie, C.: Clustering with instance-level constraints. In: AAAI (2000)
25. Wagstaff, K., Cardie, C., Rogers, S., Schrödl, S., et al.: Constrained k-means clustering with background knowledge. In: ICML (2001)
26. Wang, X., Davidson, I.: Flexible constrained spectral clustering. In: KDD (2010)
27. Xie, J., Girshick, R., Farhadi, A.: Unsupervised deep embedding for clustering analysis. In: ICML (2016)
28. Xing, E.P., Jordan, M.I., Russell, S.J., Ng, A.Y.: Distance metric learning with application to clustering with side-information. In: NIPS (2003)
29. Xu, W., Liu, X., Gong, Y.: Document clustering based on non-negative matrix factorization. In: SIGIR (2003)
30. Yang, B., Fu, X., Sidiropoulos, N.D., Hong, M.: Towards k-means-friendly spaces: simultaneous deep learning and clustering. arXiv preprint arXiv:1610.04794 (2016)

A Framework for Parallelizing
Hierarchical Clustering Methods

Silvio Lattanzi[1], Thomas Lavastida[2(✉)], Kefu Lu[3], and Benjamin Moseley[2]

[1] Google Zürich, Zürich, Switzerland
silviol@google.com
[2] Tepper School of Business, Carnegie Mellon University, Pittsburgh, PA, USA
{tlavasti,moseleyb}@andrew.cmu.edu
[3] Computer Science Department, Washington and Lee University,
Lexington, VA, USA
klu@wlu.edu

Abstract. Hierarchical clustering is a fundamental tool in data mining, machine learning and statistics. Popular hierarchical clustering algorithms include top-down divisive approaches such as bisecting k-means, k-median, and k-center and bottom-up agglomerative approaches such as single-linkage, average-linkage, and centroid-linkage. Unfortunately, only a few scalable hierarchical clustering algorithms are known, mostly based on the single-linkage algorithm. So, as datasets increase in size every day, there is a pressing need to scale other popular methods.

We introduce efficient distributed algorithms for bisecting k-means, k-median, and k-center as well as centroid-linkage. In particular, we first formalize a notion of closeness for a hierarchical clustering algorithm, and then we use this notion to design new scalable distributed methods with strong worst case bounds on the running time and the quality of the solutions. Finally, we show experimentally that the introduced algorithms are efficient and close to their sequential variants in practice.

Keywords: Hierarchical clustering · Parallel and distributed algorithms · Clustering · Unsupervised learning

1 Introduction

Thanks to its ability in explaining nested structures in real world data, hierarchical clustering is a fundamental tool in any machine learning or data mining library. In recent years the method has received a lot of attention [4,6,9,14,21, 22,32,33,35]. But despite these efforts, almost all proposed hierarchical clustering techniques are sequential methods that are difficult to apply on large data sets.

The input to the hierarchical clustering problem is a set of points and a function specifying either their pairwise similarity or their dissimilarity. The output of the problem is a rooted tree representing a hierarchical structure of the input

U. Brefeld et al. (Eds.): ECML PKDD 2019, LNAI 11906, pp. 73–89, 2020.
https://doi.org/10.1007/978-3-030-46150-8_5

data, also known as a dendrogram (Fig. 1). The input points are the leaves of this tree and subtrees induced by non-leaf nodes represent clusters. These clusters should also become more refined when the root of the corresponding subtree is at a lower level in the tree. Hierarchical clustering is useful because the number of clusters does not need to be specified in advance and because the hierarchical structure yields a taxonomy that allows for interesting interpretations of the data set. For an overview of hierarchical clustering methods refer to [16,25,29].

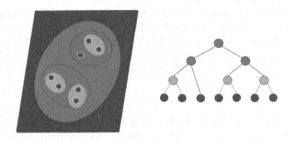

Fig. 1. A Hierarchical Clustering Tree. The grey leaves are the input data points. Internal nodes represent a cluster of the leaves in the subtree rooted at the internal node.

Several algorithms have emerged as popular approaches for hierarchical clustering. Different techniques are used depending on the context because each method has its own advantages and disadvantages. There are various classes of data sets where each method outperforms the others. For example, the centroid-linkage algorithm has been used for biological data such as genes [11], whereas, an alternative method, bisecting k-means, is popular for document comparison [34]. The most commonly used methods can be categorized into two families: agglomerative algorithms and divisive algorithms.

Divisive algorithms are top-down. They partition the data starting from a single cluster and then refine the clusters iteratively layer by layer. The most commonly used techniques to refine clusters are k-means, k-median, or k-center clustering with $k = 2$. These divisive algorithms are known as bisecting k-means (respectfully, median, center) algorithms [20]. Agglomerative algorithms are based on a bottom up approach (see [15] for details). In an agglomerative algorithm, all points begin as their own cluster. Clusters are then merged through some merging strategy. The choice of merging strategy determines the algorithm. Common strategies include single-linkage, average-linkage and centroid-linkage.

Most of these algorithms are inherently sequential; they possess a large number of serial dependencies and do not lend themselves to efficient parallelization. For example, in centroid-linkage one cannot simultaneously perform many merges because the selection of which clusters to merge may depend strongly on prior merges (and their resultant centroids).

Recently, there has been interest in making hierarchical clustering scalable [4,14,21,22,28,31,33,36]. Nevertheless most prior work has focused on scaling the single-linkage algorithm; efficient MapReduce and Spark algorithms are known for this problem [4,21,22,36]. This includes the result of [36] giving strong theoretical guarantees and practical performance for scaling single-linkage clustering. This is unsurprising because single-linkage can be reduced to computing a Minimum-Spanning-Tree [13], and there has been a line of work on efficiently computing minimum spanning trees in parallel and distributed settings [1,2,24,26,30]. Unfortunately this approach does not extend to other hierarchical clustering techniques. In contrast, to the best of our knowledge no efficient distributed algorithm is known for centroid-linkage or divisive clustering methods. Thus, scaling methods such as centroid-linkage and bisecting k-means are open problems and the main focus of this paper.

Our Contribution: In this paper we introduce fast scalable hierarchical clustering algorithms. The main results of the paper are the following:

A Theoretical Framework: This paper develops a theoretical framework for scaling hierarchical clustering methods. We introduce the notion of *closeness* between two hierarchical clustering algorithms. Intuitively, two algorithms are close if they make provably close or similar decisions. This enforces that our scalable algorithms produce similar solutions to their sequential counterpart. Using this framework, the paper formalizes the root question for scaling existing methods.

Provably Scalable Algorithms: We introduce fast scalable algorithms for centroid-linkage and the bisecting k-means, k-median and k-center algorithms. These new algorithms are the main contribution of the paper. The algorithms are proved to be close to their sequential counterparts and efficient in parallel and distributed models. These are the first scalable algorithms for divisive k-clustering as well as centroid-linkage.

Empirical Results: We empirically study the algorithms on three datasets to show that they are efficient. The empirical results demonstrate that the distributed algorithms are closer to their sequential counterparts than the theory suggests. This shows that the new methods produce clusterings remarkably similar to those produced by the sequential methods.

The algorithms can be used for most data sets. The scalable bisecting k-clustering algorithms apply to data belonging to any metric space. For centroid linkage, we assume that the input data points belong to some Euclidean space so that computing the centroid of a finite set of points is well defined. In this case, our techniques generalize to any distance function between points in Euclidean space for which a family of Locality Sensitive Hash (LSH) functions is known, such as distances induced by an ℓ_p-norm for $p \in (0, 2]$ [10].

2   Preliminaries

In this section we formally define the hierarchical clustering problem, describe popular sequential approaches, and provide other necessary background information.

Problem Input: The input is a set S of n data points. The distance between points specifies their dissimilarity. Let $d(u, v) \geq 0$ denote the distance between two points $u, v \in S$. It is assumed that d is a metric.

Problem Output: The output is a rooted tree where all of the *input* points are at the leaves. Internal nodes represent clusters; the leaves of the subtree rooted at a node correspond to the points in that specific cluster.

Computational Model: We analyze our algorithms in the massively parallel model of computation [18,24][1]. Let N be the input size. In this model we have $m = O(N^{1-\delta})$ machines with *local* memory of size $\tilde{O}(N^{\delta})$, for constant $\delta > 0$. The $\tilde{O}$ suppresses logarithmic factors. Notice that the total amount of memory used is near linear. The computation occurs in rounds and during each round each machine runs a sequential polynomial time algorithm on the data assigned to it. No communication between machines is allowed during a round. Between rounds, machines are allowed to communicate as long as each machine receives no more communication than its memory and no computation occurs. Ideally, in this model one would like to design algorithms using a number of rounds that is no more than logarithmic in the input size.

k-Clustering Methods: We recall the definitions of k-{center,median,means} clusterings. Let $C = \{c_1, c_2, \ldots, c_k\}$ be k distinct points of S called centers. For $x \in S$ let $d(x, C) = \min_{c \in C} d(x, c)$ We say that these centers solve the k-{center,median,means} problem if they optimize the following objectives, respectively: k-center: $\min_C \max_{x \in S} d(x, C)$, k-medians: $\min_C \sum_{x \in S} d(x, C)$ and finally k-means: $\min_C \sum_{x \in S} d(x, C)^2$.

The choice of centers induces a clustering of S in the following natural way. For $i = 1, \ldots, k$ let $S_i = \{x \in S \mid d(x, c_i) = d(x, C)\}$, that is we map each point to its closest center and take the clustering that results. In general it is NP-hard to find the optimal set of centers for each of these objectives, but efficient $O(1)$-approximations are known [8,17,23].

Classic Divisive Methods: We can now describe the classical divisive k-clustering algorithms. The pseudocode for this class of methods is given in Algorithm 1. As stated before, these methods begin at the root of the cluster tree corresponding to the entire set S and recursively partition the set until we reach the leaves of the tree. Note that at each node of the tree, we use an optimal 2-clustering of the current set of points to determine the two child subtrees of the current node.

---

[1] This model is widely used to capture the class of algorithms that scale in frameworks such as Spark and MapReduce.

Classic Agglomerative Methods: Recall that agglomerative methods start with each data point as a singleton cluster and iteratively merge clusters to build the tree. The choice of clusters to merge is determined by considering some cost on pairs of clusters and then choosing the pair that minimizes the cost. For example, in average-linkage the cost is the average distance between the clusters, and for centroid-linkage the cost is the distance between the clusters' centroids. In this paper we focus on the centroid-linkage method, and have provided pseudocode for this method in Algorithm 2.

Notation: We present some additional notation and a few technical assumptions. Let X be a finite set of points and x a point in X. We define the ball of radius R around x, with notation $B(x, R)$, as the set of points with distance at most R from x in the point set X, i.e. $B(x, R) = \{y \mid d(x, y) \leq R, y \in X\}$. Let $\Delta(X) = \max_{x,y \in X} d(x, y)$ be the maximum distance between points of X. When X is a subset of Euclidean space, let $\mu(X) = \frac{1}{|X|} \sum_{x \in X} x$ be the centroid of X. Finally, WLOG we assume that all points and pairwise distances are distinct[2] and that the ratio between the maximum and minimum distance between two points is polynomial in n.

---

1 DivisiveClustering(S)
2 **if** $|S| = 1$ **then**
3 | Return a leaf node corresponding to S
4 **else**
5 | Let S_1, S_2 be an optimal 2-clustering of S /* One of the means, median,
          or center objectives is used   */
6 | $T_1 \leftarrow$ DivisiveClustering(S_1)
7 | $T_2 \leftarrow$ DivisiveClustering(S_2)
8 | Return a tree with root node S and children T_1, T_2
9 **end**

Algorithm 1: Standard Divisive Clustering

---

1 CentroidClustering(S)
2 Let T be an empty tree
3 For each $x \in S$ add a leaf node corresponding to the cluster $\{x\}$ to T
4 Let $\mathcal{C}$ be the current set of clusters
5 **while** $|\mathcal{C}| > 1$ **do**
6 | $S_1, S_2 \leftarrow \arg\min_{A, B \in \mathcal{C}} d(\mu(A), \mu(B))$ /* $\mu(A) :=$ centroid of A */
7 | Add a node to T corresponding to $S_1 \cup S_2$ with children S_1 and S_2
8 | $\mathcal{C} \leftarrow \mathcal{C} \setminus \{S_1, S_2\} \cup \{S_1 \cup S_2\}$
9 **end**
10 Return the resulting tree T

Algorithm 2: Centroid Linkage Clustering

---

[2] We can remove this assumption by adding a small perturbation to every point.

3   A Framework for Parallelizing Hierarchical Clustering Algorithms

We now introduce our theoretical framework that we use to design and analyze scalable hierarchical clustering algorithms. Notice that both divisive and agglomerative methods use some cost function on pairs of clusters to guide the decisions of the algorithm. More precisely, in divisive algorithms the current set of points S is partitioned into S_1, and S_2 according to some cost $c(S_1, S_2)$. Similarly, agglomerative algorithms merge clusters S_1 and S_2 by considering some cost $c(S_1, S_2)$. So in both settings the main step consists of determining the two sets S_1 and S_2 using different cost functions. As an example, observe that $c(S_1, S_2)$ is the 2-clustering cost of the sets S_1 and S_2 in the divisive method above and that $c(S_1, S_2) = d(\mu(S_1), \mu(S_2))$ in centroid linkage.

The insistence on choosing S_1, S_2 to minimize the cost S_1, S_2 leads to the large number of serial dependencies that make parallelization of these methods difficult. Thus, the main idea behind this paper is to obtain more scalable algorithms by relaxing this decision making process to make near optimal decisions. This is formalized in the following definitions.

Definition 1 (α-close sets). *Let c be the cost function on pairs of sets and let S_1, S_2 be the two sets that minimize $c(S_1, S_2)$. Then we say that two sets S_1', S_2' are α-close to the optimum sets for cost c if $c(S_1', S_2') \leq \alpha c(S_1, S_2)$, for $\alpha \geq 1$.*

Definition 2 (α-close algorithm). *We say that a hierarchical clustering algorithm is α-close to the optimal algorithm for cost function c if at any step of the algorithm the sets selected by the algorithm are α-close for cost c, for $\alpha \geq 1$.*[3]

A necessary condition for efficiently parallelizing an algorithm is that it must not have long chains of dependencies. Now we formalize the concept of chains of dependencies.

Definition 3 (Chain of dependency). *We say that a hierarchical clustering algorithm has a chain of dependencies of length ℓ, if every decision made by the algorithm depends on a chain of at most ℓ previous decisions.*

We now define the main problem tackled in this paper.

Problem 1. *Is it possible to design hierarchical clustering algorithms that have chain of dependencies of length at most poly($\log n$) and that are α-close, for small α, for the k-means, the k-center, the k-median and centroid linkage cost functions?*

It is not immediately obvious that allowing our algorithms to be α-close will admit algorithms with small chains of dependencies. In Sects. 4.1 and 4.2 we answer this question affirmatively for divisive k-clustering methods and centroid

---

[3] Note that the guarantees is on each single choice made by the algorithm but not on all the choices together.

linkage[4]. Then in Sect. 4.3 we show how to efficiently implement these algorithms in the massively parallel model of computation. Finally, we give experimental results in Sect. 5, demonstrating that our algorithms perform close to the sequential algorithms in practice.

4 Fast Parallel Algorithms for Clustering

4.1 Distributed Divisive k-Clustering

We now present an $O(1)$-close algorithm with dependency chains of length $O(\log(n))$ under the assumption that the ratio of the maximum to the minimum distance between points is polynomial in n.

As discussed in Sects. 2 and 3, the main drawback of Algorithm 1 is that its longest chains of dependencies an be linear in the size of the input[5]. We modify this algorithm to overcome this limitation while remaining $O(1)$-close with respect to the clustering cost objective. In order to accomplish this we maintain the following invariant. Each time we split S into S_1 and S_2, each set either contains a constant factor fewer points than S or the maximum distance between any two points has been decreased by a constant factor compared to the maximum distance in S. This property will ensure that the algorithm has a chain of dependency of logarithmic depth. We present the pseudocode for the new algorithm in Algorithms 3 and 4.

```
1 CloseDivisiveClustering(S)
2 if |S| = 1 then
3  |  Return a leaf node corresponding to S
4 else
5  |  Let S₁, S₂ be an optimal 2-clustering of S /* One of the means, median,
   |     or center objectives is used                                    */
6  |  S₁, S₂ ← Reassign(S₁, S₂, Δ(S)) /* Key step, see Algorithm 4        */
7  |  T₁ ← CloseDivisiveClustering(S₁)
8  |  T₂ ← CloseDivisiveClustering(S₂)
9  |  Return a tree with root S and children T₁, T₂
10 end
```

Algorithm 3: $O(1)$-Close Divisive k-Clustering Algorithm

The goal of this subsection is to show the following theorem guaranteeing that Algorithm 3 is provably close to standard divisive k-clustering algorithms, while having a small chain of serial dependencies.

Theorem 1. *Algorithm 3 is $O(1)$-close for the k-center, k-median, and k-means cost functions and has a chain of dependencies of length at most $O(\log n)$.*

---

[4] In prior work, Yaroslavtsev and Vadapalli [36] give an algorithm for single-linkage clustering with constant-dimensional Euclidean input that fits within our framework.

[5] Consider an example where the optimal 2-clustering separates only 1 point at a time.

The main difference between Algorithm 1 and Algorithm 3 is the reassignment step. This step's purpose is to ensure that the invariant holds at any point during the algorithm as shown in the following lemma. Intuitively, if both S_1 and S_2 are contained within a small ball around their cluster centers, then the invariant is maintained. However, if this is not the case, then there are many points "near the border" of the two clusters, so we move these around to maintain the invariant.

Lemma 1. *After the execution of Reassign(S_1, S_2) in Algorithm 3 either $|S_1| \leq \frac{7}{8}|S|$ or $\Delta(S_1) \leq \frac{1}{2}\Delta(S)$. Similarly, either $|S_2| \leq \frac{7}{8}|S|$ or $\Delta(S_2) \leq \frac{1}{2}\Delta(S)$.*

Proof. Let S_1, S_2 be the resulting clusters and v_1, v_2 be their centers. Consider the sets $B_i = B(v_i, \Delta(S)/8) \cap S$, for $i = 1, 2$. If $S_1 \subseteq B_1$ and $S_2 \subseteq B_2$, then both clusters are contained in a ball of radius $\Delta(S)/8$. By the triangle inequality the maximum distance between any two points in either S_1 or S_2 is at most $\Delta(S)/2$.[6]

```
 1  Reassign(S₁, S₂, Δ)
 2  Let v₁, v₂ be the centers of S₁, S₂, respectively
 3  for i = 1, 2 do
 4  │   Bᵢ ← B(vᵢ, Δ/8) ∩ (S₁ ∪ S₂)
 5  end
 6  if S₁ ⊆ B₁ and S₂ ⊆ B₂ then
 7  │   Return S₁, S₂
 8  else
 9  │   U ← (S₁ \ B₁) ∪ (S₂ \ B₂)
10  │   if |U| ≤ n/c /* c is constant parameter, default is c = 4         */
11  │   then
12  │   │   Assign U to the smaller of B₁ and B₂
13  │   else
14  │   │   Split U evenly between B₁ and B₂
15  │   end
16  │   Return B₁, B₂
17  end
```

Algorithm 4: Reassign Subroutine for Divisive Clustering

Otherwise, consider U, the set of points not assigned to any B_i. We consider $c = 4$ as in the default case. If $|U| \leq |S|/4$, then the algorithm assigns U to the smaller of B_1 and B_2 and the resulting cluster will have size at most $3|S|/4$ since the smaller set has size at most $|S|/2$. Furthermore the other cluster is still contained within a ball of radius $\Delta/8$ and thus the maximum distance between points is at most $\Delta(S)/2$. If $|U| \geq |S|/4$ then the points in U are distributed evenly between S_1 and S_2. Both sets in the recursive calls are guaranteed to have less than $|S| - |U|/2 \leq \frac{7}{8}|S|$ points since U was evenly split. Similar properties can be shown for other values of c.

---

[6] By the generalized triangle inequality this is true for $p = 1, 2$ and it is true for $p = \infty$. So this is true for the cost of k-center, k-means and k-median.

Next we can show that the algorithm is $O(1)$-close by showing that the algorithm is an $O(1)$-approximation for the desired k-clustering objective in each step.

Lemma 2. *Let p be the norm of the clustering objective desired (i.e. $p = 2$ for k-means, $p = \infty$ for k-center or $p = 2$ for k-median). The clustering produced in each iteration is a constant approximation to any desired k-clustering objective with any constant norm $p \in (0, 2]$ or $p = \infty$.*

The proof of Lemma 2 is deferred to the full version of this paper. Combining Lemma 1 and Lemma 2 we obtain Theorem 1 as a corollary.

4.2 Distributed Centroid-Linkage

As discussed in Sects. 2 and 3, Algorithm 2 has a linear chain of dependencies. In this subsection we show how to modify step 4 of Algorithm 2 to overcome this difficulty.

The main intuition is to change Algorithm 2 to merge any pair of clusters A, B whose centroids are within distance $\alpha\delta$, where δ is the current smallest distance between cluster centroids and $\alpha \geq 1$ is a small constant. Our algorithm will find a collection of disjoint pairs of clusters which meet this condition. The algorithm then merges all such pairs and updates the minimum distance before repeating this procedure. This procedure is described in Algorithm 5.

---

1   `CloseCentroidClustering`(S, α)
2   Let T be an empty tree
3   For each $x \in S$ add a leaf node corresponding to $\{x\}$ to T
4   Let $\mathcal{C}$ be the current set of clusters **while** $|\mathcal{C}| > 1$ **do**
5      $\delta \leftarrow \min_{A, B \in \mathcal{C}} d(\mu(A), \mu(B))$
6   **for** $X \in \mathcal{C}$ **do**
7   **if** $\exists Y \in \mathcal{C}$ *such that* $d(\mu(X), \mu(Y)) \leq \alpha\delta$ **then**
8   Add a node corresponding to $X \cup Y$ with children X, Y to T
9            $\mathcal{C} \leftarrow \mathcal{C} \setminus \{X, Y\} \cup \{X \cup Y\}$
10   **end**
11   **end**
12 **end**
13 Return the resulting tree T

Algorithm 5: Idealized Close Centroid Clustering Algorithm

By definition, Algorithm 5 will be α-close to the centroid linkage algorithm. There are two issues that arise when bounding the algorithm's worst-case guarantees. First, it is not clear how to efficiently implement lines 5–10 in the distributed setting. We will address this issue in Sect. 4.3, where we describe the distributed implementations. Intuitively, we apply the popular locality-sensitive-hashing (LSH) technique, allowing us to perform these steps efficiently in the distributed setting.

The second issues is that it is difficult to bound the chain of dependencies for this algorithm since we cannot guarantee that the minimum distance δ increases by a constant factor after each iteration of the while loop.[7] Nevertheless, we find that this formulation of the algorithm works well empirically despite not having a formal bound on the round complexity. See Sect. 5 for these results.

To understand why this algorithm might have small round complexity in practice, we developed an algorithm with strong guarantees on its running time. See the full version of this paper for a proper description of this algorithm. For intuition, the algorithm maintains the following two invariants. First, if two clusters X, Y are merged during the algorithm, then the distance between their centroids is $O(\log^2(n)\delta)$, where δ is the current minimum distance between any two clusters. Second, at the end of the merging step the minimum distance between the centroids of the resulting clusters is at least $(1 + \epsilon)\delta$, for some constant $\epsilon > 0$.[8] These two invariants taken together imply an $O(\log^2(n))$-close algorithm for centroid linkage with $O(\text{poly}(\log n))$ length dependency chains when the ratio of the maximum to the minimum distance in S is bounded by a polynomial in n.

To achieve these invariants our new algorithm carefully merges nodes in two stages. A first where the algorithm recursively merges subsets of points that are close at the beginning of the stage. Then a second where the algorithm merges the leftover points from different merges of the first stage. With this two stage approach, we can formally bound the dependency chains and the closeness of the resulting algorithm. The precise description and analysis of this algorithm is involved and is presented in the full version of this paper. The following theorem characterizes the main theoretical result of this section.

Theorem 2. *There exists an algorithm that is $O(\log^2(n))$-close to the sequential centroid linkage algorithm and it has $O(\text{poly}(\log n))$ length chains of dependencies.*

The main trade-off involved in this result is that in order to ensure a fast running time our algorithm must be willing to make some merges that are an $O(\log^2(n))$-factor worse than the best possible merge available at that time. This is due to considering a worst-case analysis of our algorithm. In practice, we find that the closeness of a variation of Algorithm 5 is much smaller than Theorem 2 would suggest while maintaining a fast running time. See Sect. 5.

4.3 From Bounded Length Dependency Chains to Parallel Algorithms

We now discuss how to adapt our algorithms to run on distributed systems. In particular we show that every iteration between consequent recursive calls of our

---

[7] It is possible to construct worst-cases instances where the minimum distance δ can decrease between iterations of the while loop.

[8] In order to guarantee this second invariant, our algorithm must be allowed to make merges at distance $O(\log^2(n)\delta)$.

algorithms can be implemented using a small number of rounds in the massively parallel model of computation and so we obtain that both algorithms can be simulated in a polylogarithmic number of rounds.

Parallelizing Divisive k-Clustering: We start by observing that there are previously known procedures [3,5,7,12] to compute approximate k-clusterings in the massively parallel model of computation using only a constant number of rounds. Here we use these procedures as a black-box.

Next, the reassignment operation can be performed within a constant number of parallel rounds. Elements can be distributed across machines and the centers v_1 and v_2 can be sent to every machine. In a single round, every element computes the distance to v_1 and v_2 and in the next round the size of B_1, B_2 and U are computed. Finally given the sizes of B_1, B_2 and U the reassignment can be computed in a single parallel round.

So steps 4, 5 and 6 of Algorithm 3 can be implemented in parallel using a constant number of parallel rounds. Furthermore, we established that the algorithm has at most logarithmic chain of dependencies. Thus we obtain the following theorem:

Theorem 3. *There exist $O(\log n)$-round distributed hierarchical clustering algorithms that are $O(1)$-close to bisecting k-means, bisecting k-center or bisecting k-median.*

Parallelizing Centroid-Linkage: Parallelizing our variant of centroid-linkage is more complicated. As stated before, the main challenge is to find an efficient way to implement lines 5–10 of Algorithm 5. The solution to this problem is the use of Locality Sensitive Hashing (LSH). For simplicity of exposition we focus on the Euclidian distances and we use the sketch from [10] for norm $p \in (0, 2]$, nevertheless we note that our techniques can be easily extended to any LSH-able distance function. We refer the interested reader to the full version of this paper for complete technical details. The following Theorem is restated from [10].

Theorem 4. *Fix a domain S of points a parameter $\delta > 0$ and constant parameter $\epsilon > 0$. There exists a class of hash functions $\mathcal{H} = \{h : S \to U\}$ and constants $p_1, p_2 > 0$ with $p_1 > p_2$ such that for any two points u and v in S if $d(u,v) \leq \delta$ then $Pr_{\mathcal{H}}[h(v) = h(u)] \geq p_1$ and if $d(u,v) \geq (1+\epsilon)\delta$ then $Pr_{\mathcal{H}}[h(v) = h(u)] \leq p_2$.*

Intuitively the LSH procedure allows us to group together points that are near each other. Using the previous theorem and the classic amplification technique for LSH presented in [19], it is possible to show the following theorem.

Theorem 5. *Fix a domain S of points, a parameter $\delta > 0$ and a small constant $\epsilon > 0$. Let S' be the set of points where there exists another point within distance δ and S'' be the set of points where there exists another point within distance $(1 + \epsilon)\delta$. With probability $1 - n^{-2}$ for each points $v \in S'$ there is a $O(1)$ round distributed procedure that can identify another point u such that $d(u,v) \leq (1+\epsilon)\delta$. Furthermore the same procedure identifies for some $v \in S''$ another point u such that $d(u,v) \leq (1 + \epsilon)\delta$.*

Using these tools, we now describe a parallelizable variant of Algorithm 5. See Algorithm 6 for the pseudocode. Intuitively, we apply LSH to the centroids of the current set of clusters in order to identify candidate merges that are α-close for centroid-linkage.

We note that LSH can also be applied to the theoretically efficient algorithm alluded to in Theorem 2. This allows us to get a theoretically efficient distributed algorithm that is close to centroid-linkage. The following theorem characterizes this result, however its proof is technical and deferred to the full version of this paper.

Theorem 6. *There exists an algorithm running in $O(\log^2(n)\log\log(n))$ distributed rounds and is $O(\log^2(n))$-close to the sequential centroid-linkage algorithm.*

---

1 **FastCentroid**(S, α)
2 Let T be an empty tree
3 For each $x \in S$ add a leaf node corresponding to $\{x\}$ to T
4 Let $\mathcal{C}$ be the current set of clusters
5 **while** $|\mathcal{C}| > 1$ **do**
6       $\delta \leftarrow \min_{A,B \in \mathcal{C}} d(\mu(A), \mu(B))$
7   Use LSH with distance parameter $\alpha\delta$ on each point $\mu(X)$ for $X \in \mathcal{C}$
8   For each hash value h, let $\mathcal{C}_h$ denote all the clusters hashed to this value
9   For each h place $\mathcal{C}_h$ on a single machine
10   Pair clusters that are within distance $\alpha\delta$ in $\mathcal{C}_h$ until all remaining clusters have no other cluster within distance $\alpha\delta$
11   Merge the paired clusters and add the corresponding nodes to the tree T
12   Update $\mathcal{C}$ appropriately to contain the new clusters but not the old clusters used in each merge.
13 **end**
14 Return the resulting tree T

        Algorithm 6: Fast α-Close Centroid Clustering Algorithm

5   Experimental Results

In this section we empirically evaluate the algorithms in this paper. The algorithms will be referred to as *Div-k-clust.* (for the k-means algorithm) and *CentroidLink* (for the centroid algorithm). The sequential baseline algorithms are *kBase* and *cBase*. These are evaluated on three datasets from the UCI machine learning repository commonly used for clustering experimentation: Shuttle, Covertype, and Skin [27].

Parameters. Both of our algorithms are parameterized with an adjustable parameter. This is c in the divisive algorithm and α in the centroid algorithm. Both parameters were set to 4 in the experiments if not specified.

Evaluation Criteria. The algorithms are evaluated on their efficiency as well as the quality of the solution compared to the sequential algorithms. The closeness is a measure of quality; the number of rounds measures the efficiency. We also examine the effect of varying the parameter on the efficiency of the algorithm.

Quality Evaluation: Here we examine the closeness of the algorithm to their sequential counterparts.

CentroidLink. For the *CentroidLink* algorithm the parameter α specifies the closeness. Recall that the sequential algorithm merges the pair of clusters whose centroids are closest to form a subtree; whereas, the distributed algorithm merges all pairs with distance at most an α factor greater than the smallest distance. The experimenter can freely choose how close the parallel algorithm will adhere to the sequential one with a tradeoff in the number of rounds. We are interested in the closeness of the algorithm's decisions compared to that of the sequential algorithm. We will show this by presenting the ratio of the distance between the pair the algorithm merges compared to the actual distance of the closest pair of nodes.

Div-k-clust. Recall that *Div-k-clust.* differs from *kBase* by having an extra step in which some points are reassigned before the recursion. This step can potentially cause *Div-k-clust.* to deviate from *kBase* by placing points in different subtrees than *kBase* would. The closeness should be a measure of the cost of this difference. We measure closeness as the ratio of the k-means cost before and after the reassignment.

On average, the closeness ratio of the algorithms are small constants for each data set. Tables 1(b) and (a) have a more detailed breakdown of the results. There, we break down the data on closeness by noting the size of the subtree the moment the algorithm makes the decision which might differ from the sequential algorithm. As there are many different sizes for subtrees, we have grouped the subtrees which are close to each other in size and averaged them, for example,

Table 1. Evaluation of the closeness

(a) Closeness of *Div-k-clust.* to *kBase*

Size	Shuttle	Skin	Covertype
$\leq$1000	1.51	1.61	1.51
2000	1.69	1.74	1.58
3000	1.74	1.91	1.22
4000	1.57	2.10	1.74
5000	-	1.19	-
6000	-	2.30	-
8000	1.64	-	2.01
$\geq$10000	1.74	1.84	1.07
Overall	1.52	1.61	1.51

(b) Closeness of *CentroidLink* to *cBase*

Size	Shuttle	Skin	Covertype
$\leq$1000	2.74	2.66	2.38
2000	2.66	2.56	2.70
3000	2.76	2.25	2.72
4000	2.50	2.89	-
5000	-	3.16	1.81
6000	1.84	-	-
7000	2.48	3.40	2.11
8000	2.72	1.16	-
9000	-	-	1.92
$\geq$10000	1	2.84	1
Overall	2.74	2.66	2.38

subtrees of size 0–1000 are averaged together in the first row of the table. The dashes, '-', in the table indicate that there were no resultant subtrees of the corresponding size range. Note that the ratios are small in general for both algorithms.

Efficiency Evaluation: Figure 2 plots the number of rounds used by each algorithm on each dataset. Data points are subsampled and averaged over five trials. We compare our algorithms against the baseline sequential algorithms. However, in theory, the centroid baseline is very sequential; the ith merge must depend on all $i - 1$ previous merges. Therefore, it has a round complexity of $\Omega(n)$. For a more reasonable comparison, we have instead plotted the function $2\ln(n)$ for comparison as we expect our algorithms to scale logarithmically. The sequential algorithm is much worse than this.

Both *Div-k-clust.* and *kBase* perform poorly on the Skin dataset. One explanation is that this 2-class dataset mostly contains data points of one class, therefore, k-means clustering results in tall trees taking requiring rounds to compute. This is an example of a dataset in which the centroid algorithm may be preferred by a practitioner.

In general, the number of rounds are quite low, stable, and below the logarithmic function, especially for the centroid algorithm.

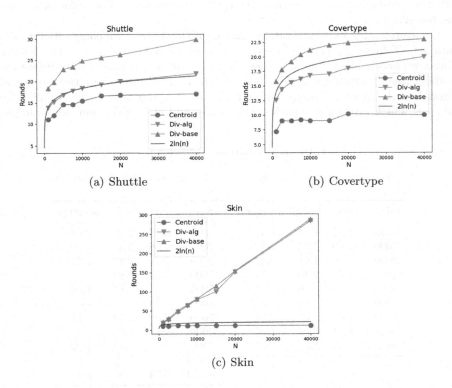

(a) Shuttle   (b) Covertype

(c) Skin

Fig. 2. Evaluation of the number of rounds

Table 2. Effect of c/α on rounds for shuttle

c/α	Div-k-$clust.$	$CentroidLink$
1.5	21.8	13.6
2	19.1	7.6
4	18.5	7.4
8	17.3	5.8

Table 2 presents results from varying the parameter c or α on the number of rounds. These results were computed with $N = 10000$ on the `Shuttle` dataset. In the table, the closer the parameter is to 1, the better the algorithms simulates the sequential variant and this tradeoff with number of rounds.

6   Conclusion and Future Work

In this work we develop scalable hierarchical clustering algorithms that are close to the sequential bisecting k-clustering and centroid-linkage algorithms. The distributed algorithms run in a small number of rounds and give empirical results that support our theory. An interesting open question is how to apply this paper's framework to other popular methods such as average-linkage or Ward's method.

References

1. Andoni, A., Nikolov, A., Onak, K., Yaroslavtsev, G.: Parallel algorithms for geometric graph problems. In: Symposium on Theory of Computing (STOC) (2014)
2. Bader, D.A., Cong, G.: Fast shared-memory algorithms for computing the minimum spanning forest of sparse graphs. J. Parallel Distrib. Comput. **66**(11), 1366–1378 (2006)
3. Balcan, M., Ehrlich, S., Liang, Y.: Distributed k-means and k-median clustering on general communication topologies. In: NIPS, pp. 1995–2003 (2013)
4. Bateni, M., Behnezhad, S., Derakhshan, M., Hajiaghayi, M., Lattanzi, S., Mirrokni, V.: On distributed hierarchical clustering. In: NIPS 2017 (2017)
5. Bateni, M., Bhaskara, A., Lattanzi, S., Mirrokni, V.S.: Distributed balanced clustering via mapping coresets. In: NIPS 2014 (2014)
6. Charikar, M., Chatziafratis, V.: Approximate hierarchical clustering via sparsest cut and spreading metrics. In: SODA 2017 (2017)
7. Charikar, M., Chekuri, C., Feder, T., Motwani, R.: Incremental clustering and dynamic information retrieval. SICOMP **33**(6), 1417–1440 (2004)
8. Charikar, M., Guha, S., Tardos, É., Shmoys, D.B.: A constant-factor approximation algorithm for the k-median problem. J. Comput. Syst. Sci. **65**(1), 129–149 (2002)
9. Dasgupta, S.: A cost function for similarity-based hierarchical clustering. In: STOC 2016, pp. 118–127 (2016)
10. Datar, M., Immorlica, N., Indyk, P., Mirrokni, V.S.: Locality-sensitive hashing scheme based on p-stable distributions. In: SoCG 2004 (2004)

11. Eisen, M.B., Spellman, P.T., Brown, P.O., Botstein, D.: Cluster analysis and display of genome-wide expression patterns. Proc. Natl. Acad. Sci. **95**(25), 14863–14868 (1998)
12. Ene, A., Im, S., Moseley, B.: Fast clustering using MapReduce. In: KDD, pp. 681–689 (2011)
13. Gower, J.C., Ross, G.J.S.: Minimum spanning trees and single linkage cluster analysis. J. Roy. Stat. Soc. Ser. C (Appl. Stat.) **18**(1), 54–64 (1969)
14. Gower, J.C., Ross, G.J.S.: Parallel algorithms for hierarchical clustering. Parallel Comput. **21**(8), 1313–1325 (1995)
15. Hastie, T., Tibshirani, R., Friedman, J.: Unsupervised learning. In: The Elements of Statistical Learning: Data Mining, Inference, and Prediction. SSS, pp. 485–585. Springer, New York (2009). https://doi.org/10.1007/978-0-387-84858-7_14
16. Heller, K.A., Ghahramani, Z.: Bayesian hierarchical clustering. In: ICML 2005, pp. 297–304 (2005)
17. Hochbaum, D.S., Shmoys, D.B.: A unified approach to approximation algorithms for bottleneck problems. J. ACM **33**(3), 533–550 (1986)
18. Im, S., Moseley, B., Sun, X.: Efficient massively parallel methods for dynamic programming. In: STOC 2017 (2017)
19. Indyk, P., Motwani, R.: Approximate nearest neighbors: towards removing the curse of dimensionality. In: STOC 1998, pp. 604–613 (1998)
20. Jain, A.K.: Data clustering: 50 years beyond k-means. Pattern Recogn. Lett. **31**(8), 651–666 (2010)
21. Jin, C., Chen, Z., Hendrix, W., Agrawal, A., Choudhary, A.N.: Incremental, distributed single-linkage hierarchical clustering algorithm using MapReduce. In: HPC 2015, pp. 83–92 (2015)
22. Jin, C., Liu, R., Chen, Z., Hendrix, W., Agrawal, A., Choudhary, A.N.: A scalable hierarchical clustering algorithm using spark. In: BigDataService 2015, pp. 418–426 (2015)
23. Kanungo, T., Mount, D.M., Netanyahu, N.S., Piatko, C.D., Silverman, R., Wu, A.Y.: A local search approximation algorithm for k-means clustering. Comput. Geom. **28**(2–3), 89–112 (2004)
24. Karloff, H.J., Suri, S., Vassilvitskii, S.: A model of computation for MapReduce. In: SODA 2010, pp. 938–948 (2010)
25. Krishnamurthy, A., Balakrishnan, S., Xu, M., Singh, A.: Efficient active algorithms for hierarchical clustering. In: ICML 2012 (2012)
26. Lattanzi, S., Moseley, B., Suri, S., Vassilvitskii, S.: Filtering: a method for solving graph problems in MapReduce. In: SPAA 2011 (Co-located with FCRC 2011), pp. 85–94 (2011)
27. Lichman, M.: UCI machine learning repository (2013). http://archive.ics.uci.edu/ml
28. Mao, Q., Zheng, W., Wang, L., Cai, Y., Mai, V., Sun, Y.: Parallel hierarchical clustering in linearithmic time for large-scale sequence analysis. In: 2015 IEEE International Conference on Data Mining, pp. 310–319, November 2015
29. Murtagh, F., Contreras, P.: Algorithms for hierarchical clustering: an overview. Wiley Interdisc. Rev.: Data Min. Discov. **2**(1), 86–97 (2012)
30. Qin, L., Yu, J.X., Chang, L., Cheng, H., Zhang, C., Lin, X.: Scalable big graph processing in MapReduce. In: Proceedings of the 2014 ACM SIGMOD International Conference on Management of Data. SIGMOD 2014, pp. 827–838 (2014)
31. Rajasekaran, S.: Efficient parallel hierarchical clustering algorithms. IEEE Trans. Parallel Distrib. Syst. **16**(6), 497–502 (2005)

32. Roy, A., Pokutta, S.: Hierarchical clustering via spreading metrics. In: NIPS 2016, pp. 2316–2324 (2016)
33. Spark (2014). https://spark.apache.org/docs/2.1.1/mllib-clustering.html
34. Steinbach, M., Karypis, G., Kumar, V.: A comparison of document clustering techniques. In: KDD Workshop on Text Mining (2000)
35. Wang, J., Moseley, B.: Approximation bounds for hierarchical clustering: average-linkage, bisecting k-means, and local search. In: NIPS (2017)
36. Yaroslavtsev, G., Vadapalli, A.: Massively parallel algorithms and hardness for single-linkage clustering under lp distances. In: ICML 2018, pp. 5596–5605 (2018)

Unsupervised and Active Learning Using Maximin-Based Anomaly Detection

Zahra Ghafoori$^{(\boxtimes)}$, James C. Bezdek, Christopher Leckie, and Shanika Karunasekera

School of Computing and Information Systems, The University of Melbourne, Melbourne, VIC 3010, Australia
{ghafooriz,jbezdek,caleckie,karus}@unimelb.edu.au

Abstract. Unsupervised anomaly detection is commonly performed using a distance or density based technique, such as K-Nearest neighbours, Local Outlier Factor or One-class Support Vector Machines. One-class Support Vector Machines reduce the computational cost of testing new data by providing sparse solutions. However, all these techniques have relatively high computational requirements for training. Moreover, identifying anomalies based solely on density or distance is not sufficient when both point (isolated) and cluster anomalies exist in an unlabelled training set. Finally, these unsupervised anomaly detection techniques are not readily adapted for active learning, where the training algorithm should identify examples for which labelling would make a significant impact on the accuracy of the learned model. In this paper, we propose a novel technique called Maximin-based Anomaly Detection that addresses these challenges by selecting a representative subset of data in combination with a kernel-based model construction. We show that the proposed technique (a) provides a statistically significant improvement in the accuracy as well as the computation time required for training and testing compared to several benchmark unsupervised anomaly detection techniques, and (b) effectively uses active learning with a limited budget.

Keywords: Anomaly detection · Unsupervised learning · Active learning

1 Introduction

Anomaly detection is a key component of many monitoring applications, which aim to detect harmful rare events that can be subsequently controlled [8]. It has been used in a wide range of domains from cybersecurity [7,33] to health and safety applications such as fall detection for elderly people [27,35]. A key challenge for anomaly detection is the abundance of unlabelled data [23]. The high cost of labelling hinders the application of supervised anomaly detection techniques, which require labelled examples of anomalies and normal data [8]. Although one-class classification techniques mitigate this issue by building a

© Springer Nature Switzerland AG 2020
U. Brefeld et al. (Eds.): ECML PKDD 2019, LNAI 11906, pp. 90–106, 2020.
https://doi.org/10.1007/978-3-030-46150-8_6

normal profile given only normal data, they are not sufficiently robust to the presence of unknown anomalies in the training set [3,16,32]. Even if the training set only comprises normal data but is noisy, one-class classification can deliver unsatisfactory results [15,16]. Since one-class classification techniques such as *One-Class Support Vector Machine* (OCSVM) [30] and *Support Vector Data Description* (SVDD) [32] provide sparse solutions and are very fast during the testing phase, they have been enhanced to work in an unsupervised manner [3,15,16]. However, depending on the implementation and the characteristics of the dataset, training may require $O(n^2)$ to $O(n^3)$ operations, where n is the cardinality of the training data. Unsupervised anomaly detection techniques such as *K-Nearest Neighbours* (KNN) and *Local Outlier Factor* (LOF), have high computational requirements for processing new observations in a continuously monitored system. For scroring/labelling a new data point, anomaly scores of all or a subset of existing data points should be recomputed in a fairly large reference dataset. Therefore, these methods have limited scope for real-time anomaly detection. In other words, they do not learn an explicit model a priori, which can be later on used for timely evaluation of future observations [1]. iForest [25] is another unsupervised method that attempts to address these challenges by filtering anomalies through isolating trees that are trained on several subsets of the data. This way, iForest is not based on a density or distance measure and lowers the computational cost by sampling. However, the solution provided by iForest is not sparse like OCSVM and SVDD, and to score a test instance it must scan several trees.

In some applications, it might be possible to obtain expert feedback on whether an instance is normal or anomalous. Having that feedback on a small number of critical examples can make a substantial difference to the accuracy of the final model [23]. This process, known as *Active Learning* (AL), has been widely used in classification [34] and rare class discovery [17,20] using supervised or semi-supervised learning. Using AL in unsupervised anomaly detection is an emerging trend [1,19]. Sharma et al. [31] used active learning to train a two-class classifier for identifying operationally significant anomalies from insignificant ones in a flight trajectory dataset. They used the OCSVM algorithm first to identify top-ranked anomalies in an unsupervised manner. Given their scores, the top-ranked anomalies are then presented to an expert to generate a labelled set of operationally significant and insignificant anomalies. This labelled set is used to train a two-class SVM that distinguishes between interesting and unimportant anomalies. Pelleg and Moore [26] proposed a general framework for the same purpose that runs several loops for data modelling (using Gaussian mixtures) and labelling. The algorithm starts with an unlabelled dataset. After each modelling round, labels of 35 instances are asked from an expert. Three strategies are used to choose these instances: choosing instances with low likelihood under the current model, choosing instances that the model is not certain about them, and a combination of the two strategies. Our work is different as we aim to enhance the ability of the underlying unsupervised anomaly detection, which is used by these techniques to find interesting anomalies or discover rare classes. The ability of an anomaly detection technique to efficiently and effectively use the AL budget is vital for adversarial tasks such as fraud detection, where anomalies can be similar to the normal data due to fraudsters mimicking normal behaviour [1].

In this paper, we present a novel approach called *Maximin-based Anomaly Detection* (MMAD). The contributions of this work are as follows. First, we use random sampling followed by the *Maximin* (MM) sampling technique [22] to select a *representative subset* of the input data, which achieves low constant computational cost for big datasets. Then, we use a *cluster validity index* (CVI) called the Silhouette index [29] on the representative samples that should contribute to defining a kernel-based model, which is subsequently used to score anomalies and normal data in nearly real-time. Second, we incorporate AL into MMAD. We show that with only a few labels, this enhancement of MMAD improves the accuracy of unsupervised anomaly detection. Our numerical experiments on benchmark anomaly detection datasets show that our proposed technique outperforms several state-of-the-art unsupervised anomaly detection techniques in terms of the time-complexity of training a model and testing the future data. Moreover, our technique provides statistically significant improvements in accuracy even when the AL budget is zero.

2   Definitions and Problem Specification

Let the normal data D^* be (an unknown) subset of a given unlabelled training set D, i.e., $D^* \subseteq \mathcal{D} = \{x_1, x_2, ..., x_n\} \subset \mathbb{R}^d$, drawn from an unknown probability distribution P on $\mathbb{R}^d$. The probability distribution P can be approximated by estimating the parameter values θ of P such that:

$$\theta = \underset{\theta \in \Theta}{\arg\min} \sum_x [(1 - P(x; \theta)) \times I(x \in D^*) + P(x; \theta) \times I(x \notin D^*)], \qquad (1)$$

where Θ represents the set of parameter values for the probability distribution, and $I(.)$ is the indicator function. The cardinality and mean value of a set D are respectively shown by $|D|$ and $\bar{D}$, and for the training set $|D| = n$. In the unsupervised case, estimating θ is done without ground truth or a priori knowledge about the data. The estimated probability distribution P can be used to score data instances such that anomalies get low scores.

We assume that a limited budget B for AL is available, i.e., labels of B instances can be queried from an oracle. *However, the training data might not be available after the query. Thus, the model should be updated after gaining a label from the oracle without having to build the model from scratch.*

3   Methodology

An accurate description of a parametric probability distribution $P(x; \theta)$ for real datasets is usually unavailable. Therefore, instead of solving (1), MMAD estimates a non-parametric probability density of the form:

$$P(x; \{w_{1..n}\}) = \sum_{i=1}^{n} w_i k(x, x_i), \text{ subject to } w_i \geq 0, \sum_{i=1}^{n} w_i = 1, \qquad (2)$$

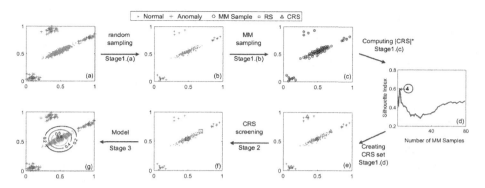

Fig. 1. Demonstration of the three stages of the MMAD Algorithm on the toy example X_{toy}. A candidate set of representative samples CRS is chosen in Stage 1. By removing anomalies from CRS, the final set of representative samples RS is generated in Stage 2. A kernel-based model is learned in Stage 3.

where k represents an arbitrary kernel function and w is the weight vector of the kernel. Our aim is to find a subset $\mathcal{X} \subseteq D$ of $\mathbb{R}^d$ that represents the normal data D^* and divides $\mathbb{R}^d$ into two subsets $\mathcal{X}$ and $\mathbb{R}^d - \mathcal{X}$. Substituting θ with $\{w_{1..n}\}$ in (1), $P(x; \{w_{1..n}\})$ is viewed as a scoring function that assigns high scores to normal data and low scores to anomalies. The computational cost of testing an instance using $P(x; \{w_{1..n}\})$ scales with the number of non-zero w_i ($i = 1..n$), thus a sparse solution that minimises $\sum_{i=1}^{n} w_i$ is desirable.

To learn $P(x; \{w_{1..n}\})$, MMAD assigns the values of each w_i in three stages as shown in Fig. 1 for a toy example X_{toy}, and explained in Algorithm 1. Figure 1(a) draws X_{toy}. The first stage includes the following steps. A subset of X_{toy} is selected at random as set S in Fig. 1(b). MM sampling [22] is performed on S to generate a uniformly selected subsample from S shown in Fig. 1(c). Choosing a large value for $|S|$ and running this extra MM sampling step is necessary, because relying only on random sampling to secure a representative subset of the input data is not sufficient for two reasons. First, it does not guarantee the selection of representative samples from all clusters in the data, especially if there are very small clusters in the data. Second, random sampling does not provide a mechanism to eliminate anomalies from the model, especially when a high fraction of anomalies exists in the training data. After MM sampling, a set called *Candidate Representative Samples* (CRS) is built using representative MM samples. By evaluating each MM sample as a CRS object, in Fig. 1(d) an optimal cardinality $|CRS|^*$ for this set is defined. In this step the first two MM samples are designated as cluster centers, and a crisp 2-partition U_2 of S, i.e., a partition into two mutually exclusive clusters, is built using the *nearest neighbour prototype rule* (NPR). Then, the value of a CVI called the Silhouette index [29] is computed on U_2. After finding the third MM sample and designating it as a new cluster center, U_3 is built and the value of the Silhouette index is computed on it. This procedure stops when a predefined number of MM samples are assigned as

---

Algorithm 1. MMAD

    Input: training set $D = \{x_1, x_2, ..., x_n\}$, sample size $|S|$
        budget B, metric δ
    Output: model M: RSs, W, and γ
    Stage 1.(a):
1: $S = \text{randSample}(D, |S|)$ ▷ random sampling from D
    Stage 1.(b):
2: $[I_{CRS}, \Delta] = \text{Maximin}(S, [0.4 * |S|], \delta)$ ▷ call Algorithm 2
3: **for** $i = 2..|CRS|$ **do**
4:     compute $Silh_i$ using (3) given $C = \{s_{I_{CRS}^{1..i}}\}$
5: **end for**
6: $|CRS|^* = \underset{i}{argmax}\; Silh_i$ ▷ maximising Silhouette index
7: $I_{CRS} = I_{CRS}^{1..|CRS|^*}$
8: **for** $i = 1..|CRS|$ **do**
                        ▷ Substitute CRSs with closet point to their cluster mean
9:     $c_i = \{s\}$, where $I_{CRS}^i == \underset{j}{\arg min}\; \delta(s, s_{I_{CRS}^j})$
10:    $I_{CRS}^i = \underset{j}{\arg min}\delta(\overline{c_i}, s_j \in c_i)$
11: **end for**
    Stage 2:
12: identify *type* of the dataset
13: **if** *type* $== WS$ **then**
14:    $I_{RS} = \text{screen}(I_{CRS})$ ▷ remove anomalous CRSs
15:    set γ using (4)
16: **else**
17:    $I_{RS} = I_{CRS}$
18:    set γ using (5)
19: **end if**
20: **if** $B > 0$ **then**
21:    $I_{RS} = BS(I_{RS}, B, \Delta_{RS})$ ▷ call Algorithm 3
22: **end if**
    Stage 3:
23: $cn_j = count(c_j), j = 1..|RS|$ ▷ count each cluster's members
24: $w_j = \frac{cn_j}{\sum cn_j}, j = 1..|RS|$
25: M $= (s_{I_{RS}}, \gamma, W)$

---

cluster centers and used to generate NPR partitions of S. Then, $|CRS|^*$ is chosen as the number of MM samples that maximises the computed Silhouette index values. The first $|CRS|^*$ MM samples form the set CRS (Fig. 1(e)). Removing anomalous instances from CRS is performed in Fig. 1(f) and the new points are called *Representative Samples* (*RS*). Optionally, if an AL budget is available for securing labels from an oracle, it will be spent. In this figure we assumed that no AL budget is available. Finally in Fig. 1(g), the model is built using RS data. The contour plot of the scores assigned to the data instances in this figure, shows that anomalies have scores close to zero. Next, we explain each of the steps in detail.

Algorithm 2. Maximin

Input: set S, number of objects $|CRS|$, metric δ
Output: Indexes I_{CRS}, pairwise dissimilarities Δ
1: $\Delta = [\delta(s_i, s_j)]$ for all $(i,j) \in 1..|S|$ ▷ Cost $O(|S|^2)$
2: $I^0_{CRS} = \arg\min\limits_{1 \le i \le |S|} \delta(\overline{S}, s_i)$ ▷ Closet point to the mean of S
3: $\Gamma_0 = \Delta_{I^0_{CRS}}$
4: **for** $p = 1..|CRS|$ **do**
5:      $I^p_{CRS} = \arg\max\limits_{1 \le p \le |S|} \Gamma_{p-1}$
6:      $\Gamma_p = [min(\Delta_{I^p_{CRS}}, \Gamma_{p-1})]$
7: **end for**

3.1 Stage 1: CRS Selection

To reduce the time-complexity for processing big data, MMAD first selects a subset S of the training set by shuffling it and randomly selecting $|S|$ instances. The sample S is used as an input to the MM algorithm [22], which is shown in Algorithm 2. Our implementation of MM sampling starts by finding the index of the closest point to the mean of S (line 2 of Algorithm 2). At each iteration of its main loop (lines $4 - 7$ of Algorithm 2), MM adds the index of the point that has maximum dissimilarity to the points already selected. We believe that this sampling technique guarantees that the indexes I_{CRS} of the representative object set CRS have at least one member from each of the unknown clusters in the data (see Proposition 1 in [18] for a theoretical guarantee in certain - but not all - cases). Towards this end, we need to define the optimal cardinality $|CRS|^*$. One way to achieve this is to evaluate the appropriateness of the cluster centers $C = \{c_{1..|CRS|}\}$ that are defined on the CRS objects. CVIs can be used for this purpose [4]. However, the presence of anomalies in a dataset can mislead CVIs. We experimented with several popular indexes including Dunn [12], C-Index [21], Calinski-Harabasz [6], Davies-Bouldin [11], and Silhouette [29], and concluded that the Silhouette index provides the best estimate of $|CRS|^*$ such that *most of the point anomalies are isolated as singleton cluster centers in S.*

Given cluster centers $C = \{c_{1..|C|}\}$, each sample $s_i \in S$ is assigned to the closest cluster center c_p with the NPR, i.e., $\|s_i - c_p\| < \|s_i - c_q\| \; \forall q \in 1..|C|, q \ne p$. The set of points accumulated this way for each cluster center are the $|C|$ crisp clusters in this partition of S. Let δ denote any metric on the input space. For each cluster center c_p, the Silhouette index uses the average within-cluster dissimilarity (cohesion) $In^\delta_i = \frac{1}{|c_p|} \sum_{s_i, s_j \in c_p} \delta(s_i, s_j)$ of s_i to the other members of c_p, which indicates how well s_i matches the other data in c_p. The smallest average between-cluster dissimilarity (separation) $Out^\delta_i = min\{\frac{1}{|c_q|} \sum_{\substack{s_i \in c_p, \\ s_j \in c_q, q \ne p}} \delta(s_i, s_j)\}$ of s_i measures how suitable would be the assignment of s_i to its closest neighbouring cluster c_q. The Silhouette index combines the cohesion (In^δ_i) and separation (Out^δ_i) measures to derive a Silhouette value for each s_i as:

$$Silh_{s_i} = \frac{Out_i^\delta - In_i^\delta}{max(In_i^\delta, Out_i^\delta)}, \tag{3}$$

which is in the range $[-1, 1]$, where a high value indicates that s_i fits well within its own cluster. When $Silh_C = \frac{1}{|S|} \sum_{i=1}^{|S|} Silh_{s_i}$ is close to 1, the corresponding partition is preferred to those with lesser values.

Given that $|CRS|^*$ is not known a priori, we need to examine the value of the Silhouette index by increasing the number of CRS objects selected by MM, and choose $|CRS|^*$ such that the Silhouette index is maximised. Therefore, MMAD first initialises $|CRS| = [0.4 * |S|]$, and chooses $|CRS|$ objects in S by MM sampling (Fig. 1(c)). This value for $|CRS|$ is chosen because it is assumed that majority of the data is normal. Therefore, in the worst case, at least 60% of data is normal. MMAD starts with $Silh_1 = 0$. Then, it picks the first two CRS objects and computes $Silh_2$ considering these objects as cluster centers. From there, MMAD computes $Silh_3$ after adding the third CRS as a new cluster center, and keeps repeating this until the last selected object by MM is added to the cluster centers. Let the Silhouette index be maximised at $Silh_m$. Then, $|CRS|^* = m$, and the size of CRS is reduced such that it comprises the m first CRSs selected by MM sampling (Fig. 1(d)). After this, a further adjustment is performed on CRS as follows (lines 8–11 of Algorithm 1). A crisp m-partition U_m is built by considering each of the m samples in CRS as a cluster center. Each of these m points is then replaced by the closest point to the cluster mean in its partition (Fig. 1(e)). Since the representative samples are chosen using MM sampling, the cluster centers, i.e., CRSs, are expected to be close to the border of their partitions. Therefore, this further adjustment is required to locate them close to the center of the partition.

We identified two types of datasets when using the Silhouette index to estimate $|CRS|^*$: **Not Well-Separated** (NWS) and **Well-Separated** (WS). If the value of the Silhouette index in $[Silh_{1..|CRS|}]$ has an increasing trend peaking at $Silh_{|CRS|}$, then anomalies and normal samples are not well-separated, otherwise anomalies and normal samples are well-separated. Examples of these types of datasets are shown later in Fig. 3. This property is used in subsequent stages.

3.2   Stage 2: CRS Screening

This stage has two steps. First, an unsupervised heuristic approach is used to detect anomalies in the CRS set, which is generated in Stage 1. Removing potential anomalies from CRS results in creating the RS set, i.e., representative samples. Second, if a budget for AL is available, i.e., a small number of labels are allowed to be asked from an oracle, an optional active learning step is used to improve accuracy.

Given that in unsupervised learning anomalies are a minority, it is expected that anomalous clusters in data have fewer members compared to normal clusters. Based on this intuition, if a dataset is classified as type WS (i.e., normal data and anomalies are well-separated according to the Silhouette index values),

---

Algorithm 3. Budget Spending (BS)

    Input: Representative Samples RS, budget B, dissimilarities Δ_{RS}
    Output: I_{RS}
1: $\{y_i^{RS} = 1\}, i = 1..|RS|$
2: **if** $B \geqslant |RS|$ **then**
3:     $y_i^{RS} = l_i, 1 \leq i \leq |RS|$ ▷ get true label per RS_i
4: **else**
5:     $\Pi(I_{RS})$: same order as selected by MM sampling
6:     relocate indexes of clusters with one member to end of $\Pi(I_{RS})$
7:     **for** $i = 1..|B|$ **do**
8:         $y_{\Pi(i)}^{RS} = l_{\Pi(i)}, 1 \leq i \leq |RS|$ ▷ get true label of $RS_{\Pi(i)}$
9:         **if** $y_{\Pi(i)}^{RS} == -1$ **then**   ▷ find indexes of other poor RSs
10:             $NNs = find(e^{-\gamma \times \Delta(\Pi(i),j)} > 0.5)$
11:             $y_{NNs}^{RS} = -1$
12:         **end if**
13:     **end for**
14: **end if**
15: $I_{RS} = \cup_i$ where $y_i^{RS} == 1$

---

the set CRS is used to generate RS as follows. Samples in CRS are sorted in the reverse order of the number of their cluster members. Let π^{CRS} denote the permuted indexes for the ordered set and n_π^i denotes the corresponding number of members in the ith largest cluster indexed by π_i^{CRS} where $i = 1...|CRS|$. The RS set is initially empty. Then, samples from CRS in the order given by π^{CRS} are added to RS until n_π^i is less than a predefined threshold. In this paper, we evaluate values of n_π^i as follows: when $\frac{n_\pi^{i-1}}{n_\pi^i} \geq 2$, we stop adding the remaining samples from CRS to RS. In contrast, if the dataset is classified as type NWS (i.e., differentiating anomalous and normal objects is difficult because they are not well separated by their distance nor by density), we choose $RS = CRS$ because there is insufficient information available to filter anomalies.

Active Learning Sub-stage. In some application contexts, it may be possible to apply AL to assign a label for one or more selected points as either normal or anomalous by asking an oracle for the labels. Given that the budget for asking an oracle for labels is usually restricted to a small number of points, a key challenge is how to select the points that are likely to be most informative in terms of improving the accuracy if a label is given. If a budget B is available via AL, we can ask for a maximum of B labels from the oracle. If $B \geq |RS|$, all the RSs can be validated by the oracle to remove any anomalies that were left from the screening stage. Otherwise, labels are asked for clusters that have more than one member in the order that they were selected by MM sampling. Anomalous RSs are removed accordingly. This stage of removing anomalous RSs are shown in Algorithm 3 and can take place here or at any time after building the model.

3.3   Stage 3: Model Construction

For the choice of the kernel function, in this paper we use the *Radial Basis kernel Function* (RBF), $k(x,y) = e^{-\gamma\|x-y\|^2}$ to localise the influence of RSs in the final model. The γ parameter is the kernel bandwidth and we set it based on the dataset type identified in Stage 1.

If the dataset is classified as type WS, anomalies and normal data are declared separable. The γ parameter in this case is estimated using the technique proposed by Evangelista et al. [13]. The reason is that this technique chooses a value for γ that maximises the dissimilarity of clusters in the data. We use a candidate set $\Gamma = \{2^{-6}, 2^{-5}, ..., 2^6\}$ for γ to extract the kernel matrix $K = [e^{-\gamma \times \Delta}]$, $\Delta = [\delta(s_i, s_j)] \; \forall (i,j) \in 1..|S|$, and select a γ^* such that:

$$\gamma^* = \underset{\gamma}{argmax} \frac{\sigma^2}{\overline{K}_{offDiag} + \varepsilon}, \tag{4}$$

where σ^2 and $\overline{K}_{offDiag}$ are the variance and the mean of the off-diagonal kernel matrix entries, and ε is a small value to avoid division by zero.

If the dataset is classified as type NWS, potential anomalies are close to normal data. Therefore, γ^* is chosen so that the similarities in the feature space created by the RBF kernel are approximately the same as those in the input space:

$$\frac{e^{-\gamma \Delta_{max}^2}}{e^{-\gamma \Delta_{min}^2}} = \frac{\Delta_{min}}{\Delta_{max}} \implies \gamma^* = \frac{-ln(\frac{\Delta_{min}}{\Delta_{max}})}{\Delta_{max}^2 - \Delta_{min}^2}. \tag{5}$$

where the values of Δ are an output of Algorithm 2. To build the final model, values of $\{w_{1..|RS|}\}$ are assigned for $RS = \{s_{I_{RS}^{1..|RS|}}\}$ and the rest of the data is deleted. For the jth RS, its weight is defined as $w_j = \frac{cn_j}{\sum_{t=1..|RS|} cn_t}$, where cn_j denotes the number of cluster members for the corresponding RS. The final model is $M = (RS, \{w_{1..|RS|}\}, \gamma)$ and a test point is evaluated using the following scoring function:

$$P(x; \{w_{1..|RS|}\}) = \sum_{i=1}^{|RS|} w_i \times k(x, RS_i). \tag{6}$$

If AL is used after constructing the model and deleting the training data, RSs labelled as anomalies by the oracle are deleted from the model, and the weight vector for the rest of the RSs is normalised to add up to one again.

4   Experimental Evaluation

We compare our MMAD method[1] to OCSVM [30] and its unsupervised extensions *Robust OCSVM* (ROCSVM) and ηOCSVM [3], and also to iForest [25]. The default settings appearing in the referenced papers were used for each of

---

[1] Implementation of MMAD is available at https://github.com/zghafoori/MMAD.

Table 1. Description of the datasets

Dataset	DSA	HAR	MNIST	Cancer	Credit	Shuttle	NKH	Pen	Satimage2	Forest
#Instances	1,117,521	10,299	70,000	675	283,726	36,752	221,902	6,870	5,801	286,048
#Features	45	561	784	10	30	9	3	16	36	10
#Normal	60,000	1,777	7,877	439	283,253	34,108	221,830	6,714	5,732	214,839
#Anomaly	1,057,521	8,522	62,123	236	473	2,644	72	156	69	2,747

these existing techniques. For iForest the default sample size is 256 and it trains 100 trees. For MMAD, the sample size $|S| = min(200, [|D|/2])$. We repeated our experiments by changing $|S|$ in the range $[100, 500]$, and observed that for $|S| > 200$, the result does not change significantly. Euclidean distance was used as the dissimilarity metric δ, but any other metric can be used when circumstances warrant a departure from this choice. To evaluate accuracy, we used the *Receiver Operating Characteristic* (ROC) curve and the corresponding *Area Under the Curve* (AUC). The reported AUC values were averaged over 100 runs. The experiments were conducted on a machine with an Intel Core i7CPU at 3.40 GHz and 16 GB RAM. The MATLAB LIBSVM toolbox [9] was used to implement OCSVM.

4.1 Datasets

We ran our experiments on four benchmark anomaly detection datasets from the *Outlier Detection DataSets* (ODDS) collection [28], namely *Forest Cover* (Forest), *Pendigits* (Pen), Satimage2, and Shuttle. From the *UCI Machine Learning Repository* [24], we selected the *Breast Cancer Wisconsin* (Cancer), MNIST, *Human Activity Recognition* (HAR), and *Daily and Sports Activities* (DSA) datasets. Table 1 shows that DSA, HAR and MNIST contain many more anomalies than normals. In the experiments we use a random subset of anomalies such that majority of data is normal.

For the Cancer dataset, the aim was to detect malignant breast cytology as anomalies. For the MNIST dataset, following Rayana [28], Bandaragoda et al. [5] and Amarbayasgalan et al. [2], digit zero was considered as the normal concept and instances of digit six were considered as anomalies. The HAR dataset included sensor signals of six different activities by a group of 30 volunteers within the age range [19, 48]. In this dataset, we used the sitting activity as the normal concept and walking in different ways, standing and laying as anomalies. The DSA dataset comprises sensor signals for 19 activities, each of which is performed by four females and four males within the age range [20, 30]. Again, the first activity (sitting) from all the 8 subjects in this dataset is considered as normal and the rest of activities from all subjects are considered as anomalies. This creates clusters of different shapes and cardinalities (Fig. 2(a)) in order to evaluate the effectiveness and robustness of anomaly detection methods. We removed duplicates from normal and anomalous instances, which resulted in generating a dataset with $60,000$ normal and $1,057,521$ anomalous instances for DSA. We also used the *Credit Card Fraud Detection* (Credit) [10] dataset that contains

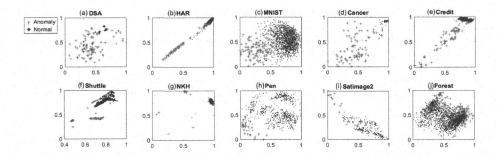

Fig. 2. Visualisation of the datasets

credit card transactions of European cardholders in September 2013. The goal was to detect fraudulent transactions as anomalies. Finally, from the NSL-KDD[2] dataset, we used HTTP data, which we refer to as *NSL-KDD-HTTP* (NKH). Attacks on HTTP services were regarded as anomalies in NKH.

The datasets' descriptions including the number of unique observations and features are summarised in Table 1. Down-sampling on anomalies and normal instances (if required) is used to generate training sets with anomaly fractions chosen from the set $\{0.01, 0.05, 0.1, 0.15, 0.2, 0.25, 0.3\}$. For each fraction of anomalies we randomly selected up to 10,000 instances from each dataset, and repeated the experiment 100 times. All datasets were re-scaled in the range $[0, 1]$ based on maximum and minimum values observed in the training set. Test and training sets were randomly selected with a ratio of 1 to 4.

4.2   Results and Discussion

For each dataset, we took a subset of the data and used a variant of t-SNE called LN-SNE [14] to visualise it in Fig. 2. The labels were used to draw the plots and were not provided to any of the anomaly detection techniques. This figure shows that there are different types of anomalies in the datasets. DSA and MNIST mainly have point anomalies, while shuttle and NKH have clusters of anomalies. Some of the anomalies in HAR and Credit occur inside the normal region. The density and distance similarities for anomalies is similar to the normal samples in Satimage2 and Forest. In the Pen dataset, anomalies have higher density compared to the normal samples and appear very close to them.

To see how the Silhouette index (3) changes by increasing the number of selected representative objects using MM sampling, in Fig. 3, we plotted graphs of the Silhouette values for three datasets, namely DSA, HAR and Pen. The other datasets exhibit a similar trend so we do not present their corresponding plots to save space. The samples size was $|S| = 200$. The fraction of anomalies was increased in the sub-figures from (a) to (g) to test the robustness of the proposed technique to the anomaly ratio in different types of datasets. The fractions of

---

[2] http://nsl.cs.unb.ca/NSL-KDD/.

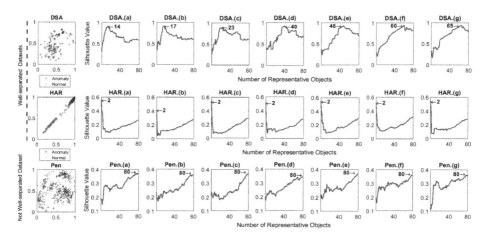

Fig. 3. Silhouette values obtained by increasing the number of objects selected by MM sampling for three representative datasets. For the well-separated datasets DSA and HAR, the the Silhouette value is maximised at an index less than 80, which indicates that separable clusters are identified in the data. However, for the Pen dataset, this index continues to increase to the maximum at 80, which means the data forms a single cluster.

anomalies are (a) 0.01, (b) 0.05, (c) 0.1, (d) 0.15, (e) 0.2, (f) 0.25, (g) 0.3. The index drops for DSA and HAR but reaches its maximum at $|CRS| = 80$ for Pen. Therefore, the DSA and HAR datasets are categorised as type WS (i.e., well-separated) based on the definitions in Sect. 3.1. The difference is that in DSA the normal data comprises several clusters and anomalies are point anomalies; each anomaly is treated as a separate cluster center to maximise the Silhouette index. However, in HAR there are two clusters in the data and one of them is anomalous. The Pen dataset is an example of a type NWS dataset (i.e., not well-separated) because the value of the Silhouette vector is maximised at the end. It can be confirmed via the visualisation given in Fig. 2 that anomalies and normal data in Pen are not well separated via distance or density dissimilarities when no ground truth is available.

Figure 4 depicts the average accuracy over 100 runs of each method for all the datasets for each anomaly fraction. This box-plot shows how the accuracy of the methods changes under different conditions of anomaly type and fraction. Each box-plot shows the variations of AUC for different fractions of anomalies including $\{0.01, 0.05, 0.1, 0.15, 0.2, 0.25, 0.3\}$. Increasing the fraction of anomalies can affect the accuracy of the corresponding technique in a negative manner. For MMAD, the results are reported for different AL budget limits $B = \{0, 1, 5, 10, 15, 20\}$. MMAD-B0 means that no budget was available for AL, while MMAD-B* where $* \neq 0$ means that labels for $*$ number of samples could be asked from the AL oracle. MMAD-B0 and iForest have better results than the different versions of OCSVMs. On average, MMAD-B0 works better than iForest

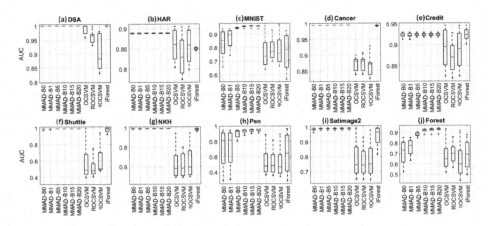

Fig. 4. The average and standard deviation of AUC for MMAD and other techniques.

Table 2. Results of Wilcoxon test for the accuracy of MMAD-B0 vs other methods.

MMAD*-B0 Vs	*-B1	*-B5	*-B10	*-B15	*-B20	OCSVM	ROCSVM	ηOCSVM	iForest
R^+	141	85	84	84	83	2296	2396	2391	1970
R^-	1344	1806	1807	1807	1808	189	89	94	515
p-value	2.23E-07	6.38E-10	6.09E-10	6.09E-10	5.82E-10	7.04E-10	1.47E-11	1.80E-11	2.07E-05

considering all scenarios of the anomaly fraction over all the datasets, especially in HAR, Shuttle and Satimage2. Using an AL budget in the first 7 datasets provides limited advantage because MMAD-B0 effectively screens anomalies in the training phase for these datsets. However, for Pen and Forest, which had the most difficult type of anomalies, access to a limited AL budget $B = 5$ or even $B = 1$ in Forest, increases the accuracy to a great extent.

To assess the statistical significance of the differences in the accuracy shown in Fig. 4 for each method, Table 2 lists the results of a Wilcoxon signed-rank test with a level of significance of $\alpha = 0.05$ on all the pairs of accuracy values per the anomaly fraction. In each comparison, the aim was to investigate to what extent the null hypothesis H_0, which indicates that there is no difference between the first and second methods in terms of their accuracy, can be rejected. For each comparison, the test returns the sum of positive ranks (R^+) and negative ranks (R^-) of the first method, and the p-value. The p-value represents the lowest level of significance of a hypothesis that results in a rejection and if it is less than α, the null hypothesis H_0 can be rejected and the improvement is significant at

Table 3. Training and testing CPU-times for MMAD compared to other methods.

Dataset	Train time (seconds) of				Test time (seconds per sample) of				
	MMAD	OCSVM	ROCSVM	ηOCSVM	iForest	MMAD	OCSVM	ROCSVM	ETAOCSVM	iFOREST
DSA	0.093	26.450	29.323	32.439	0.19	3.15E-07	1.27E-04	1.32E-05	4.85E-06	1.38E-03
HAR	0.116	38.047	39.759	38.141	0.41	9.75E-06	2.70E-04	1.27E-04	1.08E-04	1.37E-03
MNIST	0.127	269.453	281.008	289.487	0.67	3.43E-05	1.76E-03	4.76E-04	2.70E-04	1.47E-03
Cancer	0.060	0.054	0.060	0.114	0.10	1.79E-06	2.15E-05	1.70E-05	1.26E-05	1.37E-03
Credit	0.097	46.705	48.847	46.752	0.15	3.29E-07	9.26E-05	1.30E-05	8.61E-06	1.47E-03
Shuttle	0.090	18.605	19.171	34.718	0.16	7.88E-07	7.04E-05	1.71E-05	1.15E-05	1.36E-03
NKH	0.098	9.272	7.377	16.662	0.11	<1E-12	7.44E-05	1.80E-05	9.42E-06	1.50E-03
Pendig	0.088	11.042	11.911	24.427	0.25	5.66E-06	6.40E-05	2.37E-05	1.58E-05	1.53E-03
Satimage2	0.091	9.588	10.379	10.867	0.20	1.21E-06	5.83E-05	1.74E-05	1.08E-05	1.52E-03
Forest	0.093	28.479	29.537	39.239	0.20	2.36E-06	5.31E-05	9.30E-06	7.48E-06	1.47E-03
Average	0.095	45.770	47.737	53.285	0.24	5.65E-06	2.59E-04	7.32E-05	4.59E-05	1.44E-03

the level α. Table 2 shows that spending even a limited budget $B = 1$ provides a statistically significant improvement and by increasing the budget, a better result can be achieved. This finding shows the importance of using a technique that can incorporate AL into its training. The small p-values for MMAD-B0 against OCSVM, ROCSVM, ηOCSVM, and iForest, MMAD-B0 indicates that MMAD-B0 provides a statistically significant improvement compared to all of the comparison methods.

Table 3 reports the training and test CPU-times of the different techniques. MMAD and iForest have constant time given that they work on a fixed-size sample of the data. Given the size of the sample $|S|$, the training time-complexity for MMAD is $O(d \times |S|^2)$ and for iForest is $O(t \times |S| \times log|S|)$, where t is the number of trees. For testing, the time-complexity of MMAD is $O(d \times |RSs|)$ per instance, whereas it is $O(t \times log|S|)$ for iForest. The table shows that on average, the training time of MMAD is half of that for iForest, mainly because its default sample size is 200, whereas it is 256 for iForest. However, the testing time per sample for MMAD is more than 250 times less than iForest. For the HAR and Credit datasets, testing times per sample for MMAD are more than 4,000 times faster than iForest. Both MMAD and iForest are considerably faster than the OCSVM-based methods. The improvements by MMAD in accuracy and its capability of being used with AL, demonstrates that MMAD outperforms iForest on the examined datasets in this paper. To compare the scalability of MMAD and iForest to the different types of OCSVMs, we chose the DSA dataset with over a million instances, and ran all the methods several times by changing the size of the training set from 10,000 to 50,000 with a step size equal to 10,000. The results are shown in Fig. 5, confirming that MMAD and iForest have constant time regardless of the size of the training set, while the training time of the OCSVM variants depends on the size of the training set. This example shows the superiority of algorithms with constant time in processing big data.

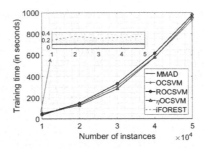

Fig. 5. Scalability of the five methods on DSA.

5 Conclusion

We have proposed a constant time unsupervised anomaly detection technique called MMAD that can be used effectively with active learning to enhance the accuracy of unsupervised anomaly detection when anomalies mimic the behaviour of normal data. MMAD combines a representative subset selection with a cluster validity index and kernel-based model construction in a novel way that results in statistically significant improvement of the accuracy and training time for unsupervised anomaly detection on the examined datasets. In our future work, we will study the use of kernels other than RBF, distance measures other than Euclidean, and CVIs other than the Silhouette index. The information gained via active learning can be used in new ways to further identify the dataset characteristics and improve the accuracy. Finally, this technique can be extended to perform constant time clustering for big datasets that have point or cluster anomalies.

References

1. Abe, N., Zadrozny, B., Langford, J.: Outlier detection by active learning. In: Proceedings ACM SIGKDD International Conference Data Mining Knowledge Discovery, pp. 504–509 (2006)
2. Amarbayasgalan, T., Jargalsaikhan, B., Ryu, K.: Unsupervised novelty detection using deep autoencoders with density based clustering. Appl. Sci. **8**(9), 1468 (2018)
3. Amer, M., Goldstein, M., Abdennadher, S.: Enhancing one-class support vector machines for unsupervised anomaly detection. In: Proceedings ACM SIGKDD Workshop, Outlier Detection Description, pp. 8–15 (2013)
4. Arbelaitz, O., Gurrutxaga, I., Muguerza, J., Pérez, J.M., Perona, I.: An extensive comparative study of cluster validity indices. Pattern Recognit. **46**(1), 243–256 (2013)
5. Bandaragoda, T.R., Ting, K.M., Albrecht, D., Liu, F.T., Wells, J.R.: Efficient anomaly detection by isolation using nearest neighbour ensemble. In: Proceedings of IEEE International Conference Data Mining Workshop, pp. 698–705 (2014)
6. Caliński, T., Harabasz, J.: A dendrite method for cluster analysis. Commun. Stat. Theory Methods **3**(1), 1–27 (1974)

7. Cao, Q., Yang, X., Yu, J., Palow, C.: Uncovering large groups of active malicious accounts in online social networks. In: Proceedings of ACM SIGSAC Conference Computer Communication Security, pp. 477–488 (2014)
8. Chandola, V., Banerjee, A., Kumar, V.: Anomaly detection: a survey. ACM Comput. Surv. **41**(3), 15 (2009)
9. Chang, C.C., Lin, C.J.: Libsvm: a library for support vector machines. ACM Trans. Intell. Syst. Technol. **2**(3), 1–27 (2011)
10. Dal Pozzolo, A., Caelen, O., Johnson, R.A., Bontempi, G.: Calibrating probability with undersampling for unbalanced classification. In: Proceedings IEEE Symposium Series Computer Intelligence, pp. 159–166 (2015)
11. Davies, D.L., Bouldin, D.W.: A cluster separation measure. IEEE Trans. Pattern Anal. Mach. Intell. **2**, 224–227 (1979)
12. Dunn, J.C.: A fuzzy relative of the isodata process and its use in detecting compact well-separated clusters. J. Cybern. **3**(3), 32–57 (1973)
13. Evangelista, P.F., Embrechts, M.J., Szymanski, B.K.: Some properties of the Gaussian kernel for one class learning. In: Proceedings of International Conference Artificial Neural Network, pp. 269–278 (2007)
14. Ghafoori, Z., Erfani, S.M., Bezdek, J.C., Karunasekera, S., Leckie, C.A.: LN-SNE: Log-normal distributed stochastic neighbor embedding for anomaly detection. IEEE Trans. Knowl. Data Eng. **32**(4), 815–820 (2019)
15. Ghafoori, Z., Erfani, S.M., Rajasegarar, S., Bezdek, J.C., Karunasekera, S., Leckie, C.: Efficient unsupervised parameter estimation for one-class support vector machines. IEEE Trans. Neural Netw. Learn. Syst. **29**(10), 5557–5570 (2018)
16. Ghafoori, Z., Rajasegarar, S., Erfani, S.M., Karunasekera, S., Leckie, C.A.: Unsupervised parameter estimation for one-class support vector machines. In: Proceedings Pacific-Asia Conference Knowledge Discovery Data Mining, pp. 183–195 (2016)
17. Görnitz, N., Kloft, M., Brefeld, U.: Active and semi-supervised data domain description. In: Buntine, W., Grobelnik, M., Mladenić, D., Shawe-Taylor, J. (eds.) ECML PKDD 2009. LNCS (LNAI), vol. 5781, pp. 407–422. Springer, Heidelberg (2009). https://doi.org/10.1007/978-3-642-04180-8_44
18. Hathaway, R.J., Bezdek, J.C., Huband, J.M.: Scalable visual assessment of cluster tendency for large data sets. Pattern Recogn. **39**(7), 1315–1324 (2006)
19. He, J., Carbonell, J.G.: Nearest-neighbor-based active learning for rare category detection. In: Proceedings of Advances Neural Information Processing System, pp. 633–640 (2008)
20. Hospedales, T.M., Gong, S., Xiang, T.: Finding rare classes: active learning with generative and discriminative models. IEEE Trans. Knowl. Data Eng. **25**(2), 374–386 (2013)
21. Hubert, L.J., Levin, J.R.: A general statistical framework for assessing categorical clustering in free recall. Psychol. Bull. **83**(6), 1072 (1976)
22. Kennard, R.W., Stone, L.A.: Computer-aided design experiments. Technometrics **11**(1), 137–148 (1969)
23. Krishnakumar, A.: Active learning literature survey. Technical report, University of California, Santa Cruz. 42 (2007)
24. Lichman, M.: UCI machine learning repository (2013). http://archive.ics.uci.edu/ml
25. Liu, F.T., Ting, K.M., Zhou, Z.H.: Isolation forest. In: Proceedings of IEEE International Conference Data Mining, pp. 413–422 (2008)

26. Pelleg, D., Moore, A.W.: Active learning for anomaly and rare-category detection. In: Proceedings of Advances Neural Information Processing System, pp. 1073–1080 (2005)
27. Quellec, G., Lamard, M., Cozic, M., Coatrieux, G., Cazuguel, G.: Multiple-instance learning for anomaly detection in digital mammography. IEEE Trans. Med. Imag. **35**(7), 1604–1614 (2016)
28. Rayana, S.: ODDS library. http://odds.cs.stonybrook.edu
29. Rousseeuw, P.J.: Silhouettes: a graphical aid to the interpretation and validation of cluster analysis. J. Computat. Appl. Math. **20**, 53–65 (1987)
30. Schölkopf, B., Platt, J.C., Shawe-Taylor, J., Smola, A.J., Williamson, R.C.: Estimating the support of a high-dimensional distribution. Neural Comput. **13**(7), 1443–1471 (2001)
31. Sharma, M., Das, K., Bilgic, M., Matthews, B., Nielsen, D., Oza, N.: Active learning with rationales for identifying operationally significant anomalies in aviation. In: Berendt, B., et al. (eds.) ECML PKDD 2016. LNCS (LNAI), vol. 9853, pp. 209–225. Springer, Cham (2016). https://doi.org/10.1007/978-3-319-46131-1_25
32. Tax, D.M., Duin, R.P.: Support vector data description. Mach. Learn. **54**(1), 45–66 (2004)
33. Thottan, M., Ji, C.: Anomaly detection in ip networks. IEEE Trans. Signal Process. **51**(8), 2191–2204 (2003)
34. Tong, S., Koller, D.: Support vector machine active learning with applications to text classification. J. Mach. Learn. Res. **2**(Nov), 45–66 (2001)
35. Wang, Y., Wu, K., Ni, L.M.: Wifall: Device-free fall detection by wireless networks. IEEE Trans. Mobile Comput. **16**(2), 581–594 (2017)

The Elliptical Basis Function Data Descriptor (EBFDD) Network: A One-Class Classification Approach to Anomaly Detection

Mehran Hossein Zadeh Bazargani[✉] and Brian Mac Namee

The Insight Centre for Data Analytics, School of Computer Science,
University College Dublin, Dublin, Ireland
mehran.hosseinzadehbazarga@ucdconnect.ie, brian.macnamee@ucd.ie

Abstract. This paper introduces the Elliptical Basis Function Data Descriptor (EBFDD) network, a one-class classification approach to anomaly detection based on Radial Basis Function (RBF) neural networks. The EBFDD network uses elliptical basis functions, which allows it to learn sophisticated decision boundaries while retaining the advantages of a shallow network. We have proposed a novel cost function, whose minimisation results in a trained anomaly detector that only requires examples of the *normal* class at training time. The paper includes a large benchmark experiment that evaluates the performance of EBFDD network and compares it to state of the art one-class classification algorithms including the One-Class Support Vector Machine and the Isolation Forest. The experiments show that, overall, the EBFDD network outperforms the state of the art approaches.

Keywords: Anomaly detection · Elliptical basis function · Neural networks

1 Introduction

Chandola and Kumar [4] define *anomaly detection* as *"the problem of finding patterns in data that do not conform to expected behavior"*. Although anomaly detection is essentially a binary classification problem (i.e. instances are classified as either *normal* or *anomalous*), in anomaly detection scenarios the classes are highly imbalanced—there is very limited, or sometimes no access to anomalous instances during training, although there is usually an abundance

This work was supported by Science Foundation Ireland under Grant No. 15/CDA/3520 and Grant No. 12/RC/2289.

Electronic supplementary material The online version of this chapter (https://doi.org/10.1007/978-3-030-46150-8_7) contains supplementary material, which is available to authorized users.

U. Brefeld et al. (Eds.): ECML PKDD 2019, LNAI 11906, pp. 107–123, 2020.
https://doi.org/10.1007/978-3-030-46150-8_7

of normal instances. Anomaly detection approaches that do not use anomalous instances during training can be classified as *semi-supervised* machine learning approaches, and are often referred to as *one-class classifiers* [12]. Anomaly detection approaches have been used in a variety of applications including credit scoring [11], intrusion detection [2], forensics [13], medical applications [14], and computer network security [27].

The main contribution of this paper is to adapt the Radial Basis Function (RBF) network [3] for one-class classification through a novel cost function. We have named the resultant one-class neural network the Elliptical Basis Function Data Descriptor (EBFDD) network. Coupled with our novel cost function, the EBFDD network is a semi-supervised one-class classification approach that utilizes elliptical kernels to learn sophisticated decision boundaries, while retaining the advantages of a shallow network, which include: easy retraining, interpretability, reduced data requirements, and shorter training time.

The remainder of the paper is structured as follows: Sect. 2 reviews related work, and briefly explains the motivation behind the EBFDD network approach. In Sect. 3 the EBFDD network approach is explained in detail. Section 4 describes the design of an evaluation experiment that compares the performance of the EBFDD network to state of the art algorithms across a number of benchmark datasets. Section 5 presents the results of the experiment, which then discusses their implications. Finally, Sect. 6 concludes the paper and suggests directions for future work.

2   Related Work

In this section we first describe some of the common approaches to anomaly detection. Then we describe the standard RBF network before explaining how it has been adapted for anomaly detection in the EBFDD network.

2.1   Common Approaches to Anomaly Detection

Semi-supervised machine learning approaches to anomaly detection are dominated by a family of algorithms that are modifications of the Support Vector Machine (SVM) algorithm [24], designed to work with only examples of a single class: One-Class SVM (OCSVM) [23]. In fact Khan and Madden [12] go so far as to say that one-class classification algorithms and methods should be divided into OCSVMs and non-OCSVMs.

The idea underpinning OCSVM is quite similar to the standard SVM method, and the *kernel trick* is still a key part of the OCSVM for the transformation of the input space into a feature space of higher dimensionality. The OCSVM approach finds a hyper-plane that separates all of the normal data points in a training set from the origin, while maximizing the distance between the origin and this hyper-plane. This results in a binary function, whose output is 1 for the regions of the input space belonging to the normal data, and -1 anywhere else. The main disadvantage of the OCSVM is the assumption that the anomalous data instances are concentrated around the origin [12]. Variations of the OCSVM approach include the Support Vector Machine Data Description (SVDD) [26], which uses hyper-spheres rather than hyper-planes to achieve separation. Interestingly, the authors in [22] propose the idea of a deep SVDD, where the SVDD is mixed with deep learning to accomplish anomaly detection.

On the non-OCSVM side, Auto-Encoder networks (AENs) [7], and all their variations have been increasingly used for anomaly detection [29–31]. An AEN does not learn a discriminative model, but rather a generative model of the input data. After transforming the input data into a representation with reduced dimensionality, it learns to reconstruct the original input data from the dimensionally-reduced representation. The error between the input and the reconstruction of the input, referred to as the reconstruction error, can be used as an anomaly detection signal—normal instances should be accurately reproduced leading to low reconstruction error, while anomalous instances should be poorly reproduced leading to large reconstruction errors. The AEN is trained on normal data only and learns features that could best reconstruct the normal data.

Isolation Forest (iForest) [28] is another interesting non-OCSVM approach to anomaly detection. The iForest tries to isolate individual data points in the training set by splitting the space randomly and repeatedly. The intuition behind this approach is that less splits should be required to isolate anomalous instances. An anomaly score can be calculated based on the number of splits required to isolate a data point.

Gaussian Mixture Models (GMMs) [1] are also used for anomaly detection. GMMs assume that normal data is generated by a collection of H Gaussians, which are placed randomly in the input space in the beginning of training. Then using the Expectation Maximization (EM) [1], the means and covariance matrices of the Gaussians are learned such that the likelihood of observing the training data is maximised. During testing, one can measure the likelihood of the test data, and if it is below a certain threshold it could be labeled as anomalous, and normal otherwise.

2.2   Radial Basis Function Networks

A Radial Basis Function (RBF) network [3] is a local-representation learning technique, which divides the input space among local kernels. For every input data point, depending on where in the input space it appears, a fraction of these locally-tuned kernel units get activated. It is as if these local units have divided the input space among themselves and each one takes responsibility for a subspace. The idea of locality, inherently implies the need for a distance function that measures the similarity between a given input data instance X, with dimensionality D, and the center, μ_h, of every kernel unit h. The common choice for this measure is the Euclidean distance, $\|X - \mu_h\|$. The response function for these local units, should have a maximum when $X = \mu_h$, and decrease as X and μ_h get less similar. The most commonly used response function for the RBF units is the Gaussian function. Not only have the RBF networks been used for traditional classification [18] and regression [25] problems, they have also been applied to anomaly detection tasks, which we will explore below.

RBF networks have been applied to anomaly detection in two main ways. First, if examples of both normal and anomalous data are available during training, the standard binary/multi-class classification RBF networks can be used with modifications. For example, in [19], a hybrid optimisation algorithm based on RBF networks, which combines gradient descent with quantum-behaved particle swarm optimisation is used to train the RBF network for anomaly detection. Similarly, in [21], an RBF network is trained for the task of intrusion detection. The model keeps adding hidden units to the architecture until a certain performance goal is met.

In the second approach to using RBF networks for anomaly detection, only examples of the normal class are used at training time. This can be achieved by modifying the dataset or modifying the algorithm. As an example of the first type, in [20] an augmented training set is composed using the instances belonging to the normal class as random proxy anomalous patterns and used to train an anomaly detection model for time series data. As an example of the second type, in [17], the RBF network algorithm is combined with the Support Vector Data Descriptor (SVDD) [26] algorithm, resulting in a hybrid model. The hidden layer of the RBF network is used as a feature extractor and the outputs for the subsequent transformed feature space are then used as inputs to the SVDD algorithm with a linear kernel.

The EBFDD network approach modifies the cost function used to train an RBF network to ensure that it learns a compact set of Gaussian kernels that concentrate around the normal region of the input space, covering all of it, while excluding other regions. During testing, for a given input data, X, the output of the model would be high, if X belongs to the normal region, and low, otherwise.

3   The Elliptical Basis Function Data Descriptor (EBFDD) Network

The EBFDD network is a semi-supervised one-class classifier, which is based on the Radial Basis Function (RBF) network [3]. Figure 1 illustrates the architecture of the EBFDD network. This is a shallow network containing one hidden layer and one output layer with a single node. There are H hidden nodes in the hidden layer, each of which uses a Gaussian activation function. The activation, $p_h(X)$, of the hth Gaussian node is defined as:

$$p_h(X) = exp\left[-\frac{1}{2}(X - \mu_h)^T \Sigma_h^{-1}(X - \mu_h)\right] \tag{1}$$

where X is the input vector of length D; x_d is the value of the dth dimension of X; and the parameters μ_h and Σ_h are the mean vector (which is D-dimensional) and the covariance matrix (which is a $D \times D$ matrix) of the hth Gaussian kernel.

The outputs of the nodes in the hidden layer are connected to a single output node via a weight vector W, where w_h is the weight parameter connecting the

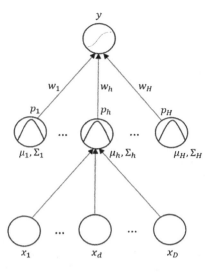

Fig. 1. The Architecture of the EBFDD network.

h^{th} hidden node to the output node. In the output node the modified hyperbolic tangent, $tanh$, activation function proposed in [15] is used as it avoids saturation:

$$y = 1.7159 \times tanh\left(\frac{2z(X)}{3}\right) \tag{2}$$

where $z(X)$ is the weighted sum of the outputs of the hidden layer, when X is the input vector:

$$z(X) = \sum_{h=1}^{H} w_h \times p_h\left(X\right) \tag{3}$$

The intuition behind the EBFDD network is that, it can be trained to learn a compact set of elliptical kernels that gather around the region in the input space where the normal data resides. This means that a trained model will output a high value for any *normal* query data point that falls within this region, and a low value for any *anomalous* query data point that falls outside this region. Thresholding this value will allow accurate anomaly detection.

EBFDD training begins with a pre-training phase that provides an initial set of positions for the H Gaussian kernels at the hidden layer. This phase uses the k-means [1] clustering algorithm, using Euclidean distance, applied to the training dataset. The resulting cluster centres are used to initialise the Gaussian kernel centres, μ_h, and covariance matrices, Σ_h, for each of the H hidden nodes. Initially these kernels are radial and assume equal variance in all directions. The number of hidden nodes in the network, H, (which is also the number of clusters found by k-means) is a hyper-parameter set before training starts.

The parameter values in the network (μ_h, Σ_h, and w_h) for each node in the network are then optimised using mini-batch gradient descent [1] (mini-batch sizes are always set to 32) and the back-propagation of error algorithm [1]. The cost function to be minimised in this process is:

$$E = \frac{1}{2} \left[(1 - y)^2 + \beta R_\Sigma + \lambda R_W \right] \qquad (4)$$

where y is the output of the network; R_Σ and R_W are regularisation terms defined below in Eq. (5) and Eq. (6); and β and λ are hyper-parameters that control the influence of the regularisation terms.

This cost function is a weighted sum of three main terms that ensure the network learns a compact set of Gaussians that cover just the normal training data. The first term in this summation, $(1 - y)^2$ encourages the network training process to learn a model that outputs a value as close as possible to 1 for instances belonging to the normal class.

The second term in the cost function, $R(\Sigma)$, regularises the variances of the Gaussian kernels in the hidden layer of the network. This term introduces the optimisation criterion of having the most compact set of Gaussians possible to represent the normal data. As the size of a Gaussian ellipsoid is dictated by the diagonal elements (i.e., the variances) of its covariance matrix, off-diagonal elements are excluded from the regularisation. R_Σ is defined as:

$$R_\Sigma = \sum_{h=1}^{H} \sum_{d=1}^{D} (\Sigma_h [d, d])^2 \qquad (5)$$

which is the squared L-2 norm [7] of the variances (i.e., the diagonal elements in each of the H Gaussian covariance matrices). Here, D denotes the dimensionality of the input space and $\Sigma_h [d, d]$ refers to the dth diagonal element of the convariance matrix for the hth hidden node.

The third term in the cost function, R_W, is the squared L-2 norm of the weight vector, W, connecting the hidden layer nodes to the output node. This discourages the weights from becoming so large that they would actually ignore the outputs from the hidden nodes. It also makes the EBFDD network robust to outliers in the training set [7]. R_W is defined as:

$$R_W = \sum_{h=1}^{H} w_h^2 \qquad (6)$$

where w_h is the weight connecting the hth hidden node to the output node.

We argue that a gradient descent training process based on the minimisation of the cost function in Eq. (4) will find a compact set of Gaussians, whose collective output is still high for the normal region of the input space and low, anywhere else (i.e., where we believe the anomalies would appear).

Based on the application of the back-propagation of error algorithm using gradient descent, the following update rules for learning the parameters of the EBFDD network have been derived in Eq. (7), Eq. (8) and Eq. (9) (the update rules are described for a single training instance for ease of reading, but are easily expandable to a mini-batch scenario by summing across the instances in the mini-batch). Below, we have derived the learning rules for all 3 learnable parameters of the EBFDD network. The general structure of these learning rules is $a = a - \eta \times \frac{\partial E}{\partial a}$, where a is the learnable parameter, and E is the cost function defined in Eq. (4). Each of the weights, w_h, connecting a hidden unit to the output unit is updated using:

$$
\begin{aligned}
w_h &= w_h - \eta \times \frac{\partial E}{\partial w_h} \\
&= w_h - \eta \left[\frac{\partial \frac{1}{2}(1-y)^2}{\partial w_h} + \frac{\partial \frac{1}{2}\lambda R_W}{\partial w_h} \right] \\
&= w_h - \eta \left[\frac{\partial \frac{1}{2}(1-y)^2}{\partial y} \times \frac{\partial y}{\partial z_h(X)} \times \frac{\partial z_h(X)}{\partial w_h} + \frac{\partial \frac{1}{2}\lambda R_W}{\partial w_h} \right] \\
&= w_h - \eta [(y-1) \times [1.1439(1 - tanh(\frac{2z_h(X)}{3})^2)] \times p_h(X) + \lambda w_h] \quad (7)
\end{aligned}
$$

where η is the learning rate, and $z_h(X)$ is defined as in Eq. 3 (although we omit the summation because only the hth hidden unit is relevant). All other terms are defined as before. Each of the kernel centres, μ_h, is updated using:

$$
\begin{aligned}
\mu_h &= \mu_h - \eta \times \frac{\partial E}{\partial \mu_h} \\
&= \mu_h - \eta \left[\frac{\partial \frac{1}{2}(1-y)^2}{\partial \mu_h} \right] \\
&= \mu_h - \eta \left[\frac{\partial \frac{1}{2}(1-y)^2}{\partial y} \times \frac{\partial y}{\partial z_h(X)} \times \frac{\partial z_h(X)}{\partial p_h(X)} \times \frac{\partial p_h(X)}{\partial \mu_h} \right] \\
&= \mu_h - \eta [(y-1) \times [1.1439(1 - tanh(\frac{2z_h(X)}{3})^2)] \times w_h \\
&\quad \times [p_h(X)\Sigma_h^{-1}(X - \mu_h)]]
\end{aligned} \quad (8)
$$

And for the covariance matrix of the hth Gaussian, Σ_h, the learning rule is:

$$
\begin{aligned}
\Sigma_h &= \Sigma_h - \eta \times \frac{\partial E}{\partial \Sigma_h} \\
&= \Sigma_h - \eta \times \left[\frac{\partial \frac{1}{2}(1-y)^2}{\partial \Sigma_h} + \frac{\partial \frac{1}{2}\beta R_\Sigma}{\partial \Sigma_h} \right] \\
&= \Sigma_h - \eta \times \left[\frac{\partial \frac{1}{2}(1-y)^2}{\partial y} \times \frac{\partial y}{\partial z_h(X)} \times \frac{\partial z_h(X)}{\partial p_h(X)} \times \frac{\partial p_h(X)}{\partial \Sigma_h} + \frac{\partial \frac{1}{2}\beta R_\Sigma}{\partial \Sigma_h} \right] \\
&= \Sigma_h - \eta \times [(y-1) \times [1.1439(1 - tanh(\frac{2z_h(X)}{3})^2)] \times w_h \\
&\quad \times [p_h(X)(-\Sigma_h^{-T}(X - \mu_h)(X - \mu_h)^T \Sigma_h^{-T})] + \beta Diag(\Sigma_h)]
\end{aligned} \quad (9)
$$

where the function $Diag()$ diagonalises the covariance matrix Σ_h by turning all non-diagonal elements to 0.

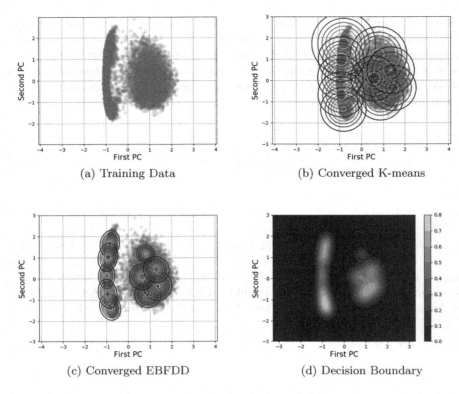

(a) Training Data   (b) Converged K-means

(c) Converged EBFDD   (d) Decision Boundary

Fig. 2. Considering images of digits 0 and 1 from the MNIST dataset as class *normal* instances for training and using the first two principal components, starting from left to right, we have the visualizations of the transformed training data after applying PCA in red circles, the Gaussians after K-means pre-training, trained EBFDD network, and the decision surface of the trained EBFDD network. (Color figure online)

When Eq. 9 is applied, the resulting covariance matrix my not be invertible. This is a problem, as the inverse of the covariance matrices are used in both forward and backward propagation in the network. In such cases, we replace the covariance matrix generated with its closest positive semi-definite matrix found using the method proposed by Higham [8].

As explained earlier, the output of the EBFDD network, y, needs to be thresholded for the anomaly detection to take place. Any of the common thresholding schemes used with other anomaly detection algorithms [4] can be used with EBFDD networks. The thresholding method is not the focus of this paper as we have used the Area Under the Curve (AUC) of the ROC curve as the metric of evaluation. This gives us a good estimate of the performance of the algorithms assuming that we have a method of choosing the best threshold on the outputs for each one of the algorithms used in our experiments.

To illustrate the behaviour of an EBFDD network we present a simple example based on the MNIST dataset of handwritten digits [16], and we have used 10 Gaussians in this illustration. We have also used images of digits 0 and 1 as the normal class. So that the behaviour of the network can be visualised, the dimensionality of the input data is reduced to 2 using Principal Component Analysis (PCA) [1]. Figure 2a shows the training dataset of normal instances (images of digits 0 and 1). Figure 2b shows the output of the k-means algorithm after the pre-training phase, which provides the EBFDD network with an initial set of well positioned Gaussian kernels. Figure 2c shows the compact set of kernels covering the normal region after the EBFDD network is trained. Finally, Fig. 2d shows the decision surface that has been learned, where brighter colors correspond to higher outputs by the EBFDD network.

4   Experimental Method

This section describes the design of an experiment conducted to measure the performance of the EBFDD network and compare it with a number of state of the art anomaly detection approaches. In these experiments, we have trained EBFDD networks with 2 kernel options: (1) Elliptical Gaussian kernels and (2) Radial Gaussian Kernels. In the case of the latter, we are hoping that a less computationally expensive kernel, the radial kernel, would bring us an advantage. The state of the art algorithms in our experiments are the One-Class SVM (OCSVM) models [23], Auto-Encoders (AEN) [7], Gaussian Mixture Models (GMM) [1], and the Isolation Forests (iForest) [28]). These algorithms have performed anomaly detection tasks on a selection of datasets using *only normal* examples during training. The remainder of this section describes the datasets and performance metrics used in the experiments.

4.1   Benchmark Datasets and Anomaly Detection Scenarios

Following Emmott, et al. [5] we use fully labelled classification datasets to simulate anomaly detection scenarios so that performance metrics can be calculated. For each dataset used, where possible, we have considered different anomaly detection scenarios, where we consider different normal and anomalous classes to add more variety into our experiments.

We have chosen a random subset of the datasets used in [5] for our experiments[1]. All of these datasets come from the UCI repository[2]. From these datasets a number of different anomaly detection scenarios can be generated. These scenarios can be divided into two main groups:

---

[1] Since every dataset leads to multiple experiments (One vs All/ All vs One/ difficult scenarios in [5]) we chose a subset of the datasets available to reduce the computation required to run the complete set of experiments.

[2] https://archive.ics.uci.edu/ml/datasets.html.

- Binary Classification Datasets: In this case, the instances in each dataset belong to either of 2 classes. The normal class is selected based on the recommendations in [5], and only examples from this class are used for training.
- Multi-Class Classification Datasets: In this case, we have followed 3 approaches. First, is the one-vs-all approach where we select instances in a particular class as normal and treat all other classes as anomalous. Only normal instances are used during training. This is interesting, because it explores scenarios where anomalous instances might come from a variety of different distributions, but a compact distribution defines the normal class. So, if a dataset has K classes, we define K one-vs-all experiments. The second approach is the all-vs-one approach, where we choose instances of one class as anomalous and the instances of the other classes as normal. Only normal instances are used during training. This method explores scenarios where we might have a variety of definitions of the normal data coming from different distributions but a well-defined compact distribution generating the anomalous instances. Similarly, if a dataset has K classes, we define K all-vs-one experiments. The last type are more difficult scenarios recommended by Emmott, et al. [5] where an analysis is performed to find the most challenging partition of classes, in terms of separability, into normal and anomalous groups for the datasets they use in their experiments. We use these partitions to define the third set of scenarios in our experiments.

Table 1. The datasets used in our experiments

Dataset name	Number of rows	Number of classes	Number of features	Number of generated scenarios
Magic gamma telesacope	19021	2	10	1
Spambase	4602	2	57	1
Skin segmentation	245058	2	3	1
Steel plates faults	1941	7	27	15
Image segmentation	2311	7	18	15
Page blocks classification	5473	5	10	11
Statlog (Landsat satellite)	6436	6	36	13
Waveform database generator (Version 1)	5000	3	21	7

Table 1 summarises the datasets that have been used in our experiments. The number of rows, classes, and features in each one, as well as the number of anomaly detection scenarios extracted are shown. For all datasets feature values have been normalised to $[0, 1]$ using range normalisation.

4.2   Experimental Method and Performance Metrics

For each algorithm, dataset and scenario combination we use an experimental design that is similar to bootstrapping [10]. We extract an 80% sample (with no replacement) from the whole normal portion of a dataset to use to train a model. The remaining 20% is then mixed with all the anomalous data to constitute the test set. This is repeated 10 times and average performance results are reported. For every algorithm a grid search is performed to find the best set of hyper-parameters and the results of the best performing set of hyper-parameters are reported. All of our code and scripts used in our experiments are available on GitHub[3].

The tunable hyper-parameters used to generate these results, for each algorithm across all the datasets and scenarios, are presented in Table 2. It is important to mention that the values for H in the hyper-parameter grid search are determined by the dimensionality of each dataset, and in our experiments they do not exceed the dimensionality of the input. The range tested for H starts with 1 and then increases in steps of 5 all the way up to the dimensionality of the data, D. In the case of the Page Blocks Classification, and Magic Gamma Telescope datasets we reduce the step size to 2, and for the Skin Segmentation dataset the step size of 1, as the dimensionality of these datasets is rather low. As a result, the EBFDD/RBFDD, and AEN always tend to compress the input data in their hidden representation and similarly, the number of Gaussians in the GMM is also bounded by the dimensionality of the input, D. However, in the case of the Isolation Forest, we have chosen the same number of estimators across all the datasets. In the case of OCSVM, ν is the upper bound on the fraction of training errors and a lower bound of the fraction of support vectors, and γ is the kernel coefficient.

The area under the ROC curve [9] has been chosen as the evaluation metric in these experiments. This allows us to avoid defining a specific thresholding function to use with each model, but still measures the ability of a model to distinguish between normal and anomalous classes. The ROC curves are generated from the raw output of each model type.

---

[3] https://github.com/MLDawn/EBFDD.

Table 2. Hyper-parameter ranges for each algorithm

Algorithms	Hyper-parameters	Investigated hyper-parameters
EBFDD	Number of kernels (H)	[1, 5, 10, ..., D]
	η	[0.01, 0.001, 0.0001]
	β	[0.9, 0.5, 0.1, 0.05, 0.01, 0.001, 0.0001]
	λ	[0.9, 0.5, 0.1, 0.05, 0.01, 0.001, 0.0001]
RBFDD	Number of kernels (H)	[1, 5, 10, ..., D]
	η	[0.01, 0.001, 0.0001]
	β	[0.9, 0.5, 0.1, 0.05, 0.01, 0.001, 0.0001]
	λ	[0.9, 0.5, 0.1, 0.05, 0.01, 0.001, 0.0001]
OCSVM	ν	[0.9, 0.5, 0.1, 0.05, 0.01, 0.001, 0.0001]
	γ	[0.9, 0.5, 0.1, 0.05, 0.01, 0.001, 0.0001]
AEN	Number of hidden units (H)	[1, 5, 10, ..., D]
	η	[0.01, 0.001, 0.0001]
	Hidden layer activation functions	[sigmoid, relu]
	Output layer activation functions	[sigmoid, relu, linear]
	Error functions	[mean squared error, cross entropy]
GMM	Number of kernels (H)	[1, 5, 10, ..., D]
Isolation Forest	Number of estimators	[100, 200, 500, 800, 1000]

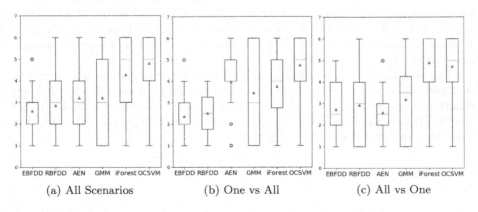

(a) All Scenarios   (b) One vs All   (c) All vs One

Fig. 3. The average rank of the algorithms across the experiments. On each box plot the median ranks are shown via the horizontal orange lines and the mean ranks are shown using green triangles. (Color figure online)

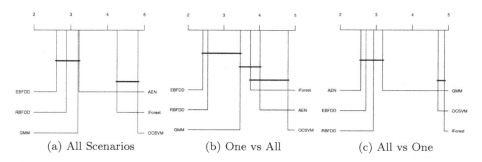

(a) All Scenarios   (b) One vs All   (c) All vs One

Fig. 4. Friedman's aligned test results where the statistical significance is $\alpha = 0.05$

5   Results and Discussion

The performances of each algorithm on each anomaly detection scenario for each dataset were compared and ranked. The distribution of the ranks for each algorithm for all anomaly detection scenarios are shown in Fig. 3a, and the average rank scores are summarised in Table 3[4]. The average ranks in Table 3 show that the EBFDD network has the lowest average rank over all experiments. It is also clear from Fig. 3a that the ranks of EBFDD have low variance indicating its consistent strong performance.

Table 3. Average rank across all experiments

	EBFDD	RBFDD	AEN	GMM	iForest	OCSVM
Average rank	2.59	2.85	3.20	3.20	4.26	4.80

Figure 3 also shows the distribution of ranks of the different approaches on the one-vs-all and all-vs-one scenarios (distributions for the other scenarios are not included as there are too few results to generate meaningful distributions). While the overall pattern is largely the same for these subsets as for the overall results, it is worth noting that there is a marked difference in the performance of the AEN models on the one-vs-all scenarios—performance is relatively poor—and on the all-vs-one scenarios—performance is quite good.

A Friedman test [6] with a significance level of $\alpha = 0.05$ was performed on the rank data. This showed a statistically significant difference in the performance of the different algorithms and so, following the recommendations of [6], a post-hoc Friedman aligned rank test, with $\alpha = 0.05$, was performed to further investigate the pairwise differences between the performance of the algorithms. Figure 4 summarises the results of these tests (tests were performed for all scenarios and independently for the one-vs-all and all-vs-one scenarios)[5].

---

[4] The full tables of results are provided in the supplementary material.
[5] The Win/Loss/Draw tables for the Friedman aligned rank test for $\alpha = 0.1$, 0.05, and 0.01 are provided in the supplementary material.

In all cases the performance of a group of the best performing algorithms cannot be separated in a statistically significant way. This group includes EBFDD, RBFDD, GMM, and (except for the one-vs-all scenario subset) AEN. The poorer performances of the OCSVM and iForest approaches are statistically significantly different to the performance of the other approaches. The poor performance of OCSVM is somewhat surprising, however, it is in line with previous benchmarks, for example [5].

Both the EBFDD and RBFDD algorithms accomplish their training through minimizing our proposed cost function in Eq. (4). We believe that the EBFDD out-performs RBFDD because of the more flexible nature of the decision boundaries that it is able to learn because of the use of elliptical kernels.

It is worth noting, however, that the cost of the good performance of the EBFDD algorithm is the very large number of parameters that must be learned in this model. For an EBFDD network, as the full covariance matrices are learnable, the number of trainable parameters is quite high:

$$(H \times D) + \left(H \times \frac{D(D+1)}{2} \right) + H \tag{10}$$

where H is the number of hidden nodes, and D is the dimensionality of the input. Moreover, if we consider radial kernels for the EBFDD networks, i.e. an RBFDD network, the number of trainable parameters is reduced to:

$$(H \times D) + (H \times D) + H \tag{11}$$

This means that training EBFDD networks can take longer than training equivalently sized RBFDD networks.

There is a minor difference in the number of trainable parameters in a GMM compared to an EBFDD network. As the weights used to combine distributions in a GMM sum to 1, for H Gaussians only $(H - 1)$ weights need to be learned as the last weight can be computed by subtracting the sum of those weights from 1. As a result, the number of trainable parameters in a GMM is equal to:

$$(H \times D) + \left(H \times \frac{D(D+1)}{2} \right) + (H - 1) \tag{12}$$

In addition the number of trainable parameters for the AEN is:

$$(H \times D) + H \tag{13}$$

It is not possible to talk about the number of trainable parameters for the iForest and OCSVM models in a meaningful way and so these are not compared. Moreover, as the implementations of algorithms used in these experiments come from different packages with differing levels of optimisation we do not believe that detailed comparisons of training times are appropriate.

As observed in Table 3, the empirical results show that the added complexity of the EBFDD network has made it a stronger anomaly detector compared to its simpler version that is the RBFDD network. In addition, even though the

EBFDD network and GMM have almost the same number of trainable parameters, it seems that the optimisation of the proposed cost function in the EBFDD network, which utilises gradient descent, allows it to find better solutions than the expectation maximisation approach used in a GMM.

6   Conclusions and Future Work

This paper presents a novel cost function, whose minimisation can adapt the Radial Basis Function (RBF) network into a one-class classifier. We have named the resultant anomaly detector the Elliptical Basis Function Data Descriptor (EBFDD) network. EBFDD utilises elliptical kernels that can elongate and rotate to allow it to learn sophisticated decision surfaces. An evaluation experiment conducted using a large set of datasets compared the EBFDD network with state of the art anomaly detection algorithms. Although statistical significance is not shown in all cases, the empirical results show that the EBFDD network has a better overall performance across all the experiments.

In future work, we plan to add recurrent connections to the EBFDD network architecture to allow contextual anomalies within streams to be identified, as well as the point anomalies identified by the current architecture. Moreover, we would like to investigate the idea of building a deep architecture where the EBFDD network and a deep network would be trained in an end to end fashion, the motivation being that the backpropagation signal for training the EBFDD network might push the deep network into learning better features for the Gaussian kernels of the EBFDD network to work with. An alternative would be to train the deep architecture separately and use the extracted features to train the EBFDD network, and this will also be explored. Finally, we will investigate how EBFDD can be adapted to handle concept drift scenarios in which the characteristics of what constitutes normal change over time.

References

1. Alpaydin, E.: Introduction to Machine Learning. MIT Press, Cambridge (2004)
2. Balupari, R., Tjaden, B., Ostermann, S., Bykova, M., Mitchell, A.: Real-time Network-based Anomaly Intrusion Detection. Nova Science Publishers Inc., New York (2003)
3. Bishop, C.M.: Pattern Recognition and Machine Learning. Springer, Heidelberg (2007)
4. Chandola, V., Banerjee, A., Kumar, V.: Anomaly detection: a survey. ACM Comput. Surv. (CSUR) 41(3), 1–58 (2009)
5. Emmott, A.F., Das, S., Dietterich, T., Fern, A., Wong, W.K.: Systematic construction of anomaly detection benchmarks from real data. In: Proceedings of the ACM SIGKDD workshop on outlier detection and description, pp. 16–21. ACM (2013)

6. Garcia, S., Fernandez, A., Luengo, J., Herrera, F.: Advanced nonparametric tests for multiple comparisons in the design of experiments in computational intelligence and data mining: Experimental analysis of power. Information Sciences **180**(10), 2044–2064 (2010). https://doi.org/10.1016/j.ins.2009.12.010. http://www.sciencedirect.com/science/article/pii/S0020025509005404, special Issue on Intelligent Distributed Information Systems
7. Goodfellow, I., Bengio, Y., Courville, A.: Deep Learning. The MIT Press, Cambridge (2016)
8. Higham, N.J.: Computing a nearest symmetric positive semidefinite matrix. Linear Algebra Appl. **103**, 103–118 (1988). https://doi.org/10.1016/0024-3795(88)90223-6
9. Japkowicz, N., Shah, M.: Evaluating Learning Algorithms: A Classification Perspective. Cambridge University Press, Cambridge (2011)
10. Kelleher, J.D., Mac Namee, B., D'Arcy, A.: Machine Learning for Predictive Data Analytics. MIT Press, Cambridge (2015)
11. Kennedy, K., Namee, B.M., Delany, S.J.: Using semi-supervised classifiers for credit scoring. J. Oper. Res. Soc. **64**(4), 513–529 (2013)
12. Khan, S.S., Madden, M.G.: One-class classification: Taxonomy of study and review of techniques. CoRR abs/1312.0049 (2013). http://arxiv.org/abs/1312.0049
13. Kruegel, C., Vigna, G.: Anomaly detection of web-based attacks. In: Proceedings of the 10th ACM Conference on Computer and Communications Security., CCS '03, pp. 251–261. ACM, New York (2003). https://doi.org/10.1145/948109.948144
14. Laurikkala, J., Juhola, M., Kentala, E., Lavrac, N., Miksch, S., Kavsek, B.: Informal identification of outliers in medical data. In: Fifth International Workshop on Intelligent Data Analysis in Medicine and Pharmacology, vol. 1, pp. 20–24 (2000)
15. LeCun, Y.A., Bottou, L., Orr, G.B., Müller, K.-R.: Efficient BackProp. In: Montavon, G., Orr, G.B., Müller, K.-R. (eds.) Neural Networks: Tricks of the Trade. LNCS, vol. 7700, pp. 9–48. Springer, Heidelberg (2012). https://doi.org/10.1007/978-3-642-35289-8_3
16. LeCun, Y., Cortes, C.: MNIST handwritten digit database (2010). http://yann.lecun.com/exdb/mnist/
17. Li, J., Xiao, Z., Lu, Y.: Adapting radial basis function neural networks for one-class classification. In: IEEE International Joint Conference on Neural Networks, 2008. IJCNN 2008. (IEEE World Congress on Computational Intelligence). IEEE, Hong Kong, September 2008
18. Lin, W.M., Yang, C.D., Lin, J.H., Tsay, M.T.: A fault classification method by RBF neural network with OLS learning procedure. IEEE Trans. Power Deliv. **16**(4), 473–477 (2001). https://doi.org/10.1109/61.956723
19. Ma, R., Liu, Y., Lin, X., Wang, Z.: Network anomaly detection using RBF neural network with hybrid QPSO. In: IEEE International Conference on Networking, Sensing and Control (ICNSC). IEEE, Sanya, April 2008
20. Oliveira, A.L.I., Neto, F.B.L., Meira, S.R.L.: Combining MLP and RBF neural networks for novelty detection in short time series. In: Monroy, R., Arroyo-Figueroa, G., Sucar, L.E., Sossa, H. (eds.) MICAI 2004. LNCS (LNAI), vol. 2972, pp. 844–853. Springer, Heidelberg (2004). https://doi.org/10.1007/978-3-540-24694-7_87
21. Rapaka, A., Novokhodko, A., Wunsch, D.: Intrusion detection using radial basis function network on sequences of system calls. In: Proceedings of the International Joint Conference on Neural Networks. IEEE, August 2003
22. Ruff, L., et al.: Deep one-class classification. In: Dy, J., Krause, A. (eds.) Proceedings of the 35th International Conference on Machine Learning. Proceedings of Machine Learning Research, vol. 80, pp. 4393–4402. PMLR (2018). http://proceedings.mlr.press/v80/ruff18a.html

23. Scholkopf, B., Platt, J.C., Shawe-Taylor, J., Smola, A.J., Williamson, R.C.: Estimating the support of a high-dimensional distribution. Neural Comput. **13**, 1443–1471 (2001)
24. Scholkopf, B., Smola, A.J.: Learning with Kernels: Support Vector Machines, Regularization, Optimization, and Beyond. MIT press, Cambridge (2001)
25. Staiano, A., Tagliaferri, R., Pedrycz, W.: Improving rbf networks performance in regression tasks by means of a supervised fuzzy clustering. Neurocomputing **69**(13–15), 1570–1581 (2006)
26. Tax, D.M.J., Duin, R.P.W.: Support vector data description. Mach. Learn. **54**(1), 45–66 (2004). https://doi.org/10.1023/B:MACH.0000008084.60811.49
27. Thottan, M., Ji, C.: Anomaly detection in ip networks. IEEE Trans. Signal Process. **51**(8), 2191–2204 (2003). https://doi.org/10.1109/TSP.2003.814797
28. Ting, K.M., Liu, F.T., Zhou, Z.: Isolation Forest. In: 2008 Eighth IEEE International Conference on Data Mining (ICDM), vol. 00, pp. 413–422 (2008). https://doi.org/10.1109/ICDM.2008.17
29. Wang, Y., Cai, W., Wei, P.: A deep learning approach for detecting malicious javascript code. Secur. Commun. Netw. **9**(11), 1520–1534 (2016)
30. Xiong, Y., Zuo, R.: Recognition of geochemical anomalies using a deep autoencoder network. Comput. Geosci. **86**, 75–82 (2016). Elsevier
31. Yan, W., Yu, L.: On accurate and reliable anomaly detection for gas turbine combustors: a deep learning approach. In: Annual Conference of Prognostics and Health Management Society (2015)

Heavy-Tailed Kernels Reveal a Finer Cluster Structure in t-SNE Visualisations

Dmitry Kobak[1(✉)], George Linderman[2], Stefan Steinerberger[3], Yuval Kluger[2,4], and Philipp Berens[1]

[1] Institute for Ophthalmic Research, University of Tübingen, Tübingen, Germany
{dmitry.kobak,philipp.berens}@uni-tuebingen.de
[2] Applied Mathematics Program, Yale University, New Haven, USA
[3] Department of Mathematics, Yale University, New Haven, USA
[4] Department of Pathology, Yale School of Medicine, New Haven, USA
{george.linderman,stefan.steinerberger,yuval.kluger}@yale.edu

Abstract. T-distributed stochastic neighbour embedding (t-SNE) is a widely used data visualisation technique. It differs from its predecessor SNE by the low-dimensional similarity kernel: the Gaussian kernel was replaced by the heavy-tailed Cauchy kernel, solving the 'crowding problem' of SNE. Here, we develop an efficient implementation of t-SNE for a t-distribution kernel with an arbitrary degree of freedom ν, with $\nu \to \infty$ corresponding to SNE and $\nu = 1$ corresponding to the standard t-SNE. Using theoretical analysis and toy examples, we show that $\nu < 1$ can further reduce the crowding problem and reveal finer cluster structure that is invisible in standard t-SNE. We further demonstrate the striking effect of heavier-tailed kernels on large real-life data sets such as MNIST, single-cell RNA-sequencing data, and the HathiTrust library. We use domain knowledge to confirm that the revealed clusters are meaningful. Overall, we argue that modifying the tail heaviness of the t-SNE kernel can yield additional insight into the cluster structure of the data.

Keywords: Dimensionality reduction · Data visualisation · t-SNE

1 Introduction

T-distributed stochastic neighbour embedding (t-SNE) [12] and related methods [13,15] are used for data visualisation in many scientific fields dealing with thousands or even millions of high-dimensional samples. They range from single-cell cytometry [1] and transcriptomics [16,19], where samples are cells and features are proteins or genes, to population genetics [4], where samples are people and features are single-nucleotide polymorphisms, to humanities [14], where samples are books and features are words.

The original version of this chapter was revised: The supplementary file and its link has been added. The correction to this chapter is available at https://doi.org/10.1007/978-3-030-46150-8_44

Electronic supplementary material The online version of this chapter (https://doi.org/10.1007/978-3-030-46150-8_8) contains supplementary material, which is available to authorized users.

U. Brefeld et al. (Eds.): ECML PKDD 2019, LNAI 11906, pp. 124–139, 2020.
https://doi.org/10.1007/978-3-030-46150-8_8

T-SNE was developed from an earlier method called SNE [5]. The central idea of SNE was to describe pairwise relationships between high-dimensional points in terms of normalised affinities: close neighbours have high affinity whereas distant samples have near-zero affinity. SNE then positions the points in two dimensions such that the Kullback-Leibler divergence between the high- and low-dimensional affinities is minimised. This worked to some degree but suffered from what was later called the 'crowding problem': distinct high-dimensional clusters tended to overlap in the embedding. The idea of t-SNE was to adjust the kernel transforming pairwise low-dimensional distances into affinities: the Gaussian kernel was replaced by the heavy-tailed Cauchy kernel (t-distribution with one degree of freedom ν), ameliorating the crowding problem.

The choice of the specific heavy-tailed kernel was mostly motivated by mathematical and computational simplicity: a t-distribution with $\nu = 1$ has a density proportional to $1/(1+x^2)$ which is mathematically compact and fast to compute. However, a t-distribution with any finite ν has heavier tails than the Gaussian distribution (which corresponds to $\nu \to \infty$). It is therefore reasonable to explore the whole spectrum of the values of ν from ∞ to 0. Given that t-SNE ($\nu = 1$) outperforms SNE ($\nu = \infty$), it might be that for some data sets $\nu < 1$ would offer additional insights into the structure of the data.

While this seems like a straightforward extension and has already been discussed in the literature [10,18], no efficient implementation of this idea has been available until now. T-SNE is usually optimised via adaptive gradient descent. While it is easy to write down the gradient for an arbitrary value of ν, the exact t-SNE from the original paper requires $\mathcal{O}(n^2)$ time and memory, and cannot be run for sample sizes much larger than $n \approx 10\,000$. Efficient approximations have been developed allowing to run approximate t-SNE for much larger sample sizes [9,11], but until now have only been implemented for $\nu = 1$. As a result, the effect of $\nu \neq 1$ on large real-life datasets has remained unknown.

Here we show that the recent FIt-SNE approximation [9] can be modified to use an arbitrary value of ν and demonstrate that $\nu < 1$ can reveal 'hidden' structure, invisible with standard t-SNE.

2   Results

2.1   t-SNE with Arbitrary Degree of Freedom

SNE defines directional affinity of point $\mathbf{x}_j$ to point $\mathbf{x}_i$ as

$$p_{j|i} = \frac{\exp(-\|\mathbf{x}_i - \mathbf{x}_j\|^2/2\sigma_i^2)}{\sum_{k \neq i} \exp(-\|\mathbf{x}_i - \mathbf{x}_k\|^2/2\sigma_i^2)}.$$

For each i, this forms a probability distribution over all points $j \neq i$ (all $p_{i|i}$ are set to zero). The variance of the Gaussian kernel σ_i^2 is chosen such that the *perplexity* of this probability distribution

$$\exp\left(-\ln(2) \cdot \sum_{j \neq i} p_{j|i} \log_2 p_{j|i}\right)$$

has some pre-specified value. In symmetric SNE (SSNE)[1] and t-SNE the affinities are symmetrised and normalised

$$p_{ij} = \frac{p_{i|j} + p_{j|i}}{2n}$$

to form a probability distribution on the set of all pairs (i, j).

The points are then arranged in a low-dimensional space to minimise the Kullback-Leibler (KL) divergence between p_{ij} and the affinities in the low-dimensional space, q_{ij}:

$$\mathcal{L} = \sum_{i,j} p_{ij} \log \frac{p_{ij}}{q_{ij}},$$

$$q_{ij} = \frac{w_{ij}}{Z}, \quad w_{ij} = k(\|\mathbf{y}_i - \mathbf{y}_j\|), \quad Z = \sum_{k \neq l} w_{kl}.$$

Here $k(d)$ is a kernel that transforms Euclidean distance d between any two points into affinities, and $\mathbf{y}_i$ are low-dimensional coordinates (all q_{ii} are set to 0).

SNE uses the Gaussian kernel $k(d) = \exp(-d^2)$. T-SNE uses the t-distribution with one degree of freedom (also known as Cauchy distribution): $k(d) = 1/(1 + d^2)$. Here we consider a general t-distribution kernel

$$k(d) = \frac{1}{(1 + d^2/\nu)^{(\nu+1)/2}}. \tag{$\star$}$$

As in [18], we use a simplified version defined as

$$k(d) = \frac{1}{(1 + d^2/\alpha)^\alpha}. \tag{$\star\star$}$$

This kernel corresponds to the *scaled* t-distribution with $\nu = 2\alpha - 1$. This means that using $(\star\star)$ instead of $(\star)$ in t-SNE produces an identical output apart from the global scaling by $\sqrt{2\nu/(\nu+1)}$. At the same time, $(\star\star)$ allows to use any $\alpha > 0$, including $\alpha \in (0, 1/2]$ corresponding to negative ν, i.e. it allows kernels with tails heavier than any possible t-distribution.[2] Yang et al. [18] use the same kernel but with α replaced by $1/\alpha$, and call it 'heavy-tailed SNE' (HSSNE).

The gradient of the loss function (see Appendix or [18]) is

$$\frac{\partial \mathcal{L}}{\partial \mathbf{y}_i} = 4 \sum_j (p_{ij} - q_{ij}) w_{ij}^{1/\alpha} (\mathbf{y}_i - \mathbf{y}_j).$$

Any implementation of exact t-SNE can be easily modified to use this expression instead of the $\alpha = 1$ gradient.

---

[1] In the following text we will not make a distinction between the symmetric SNE (SSNE) and the original, asymmetric, SNE.

[2] Equivalently, we could use an even simpler kernel $k(d) = (1 + d^2)^{-\alpha}$ that differs from $(\star\star)$ only by scaling. We prefer $(\star\star)$ because of the explicit Gaussian limit at $\alpha \to \infty$.

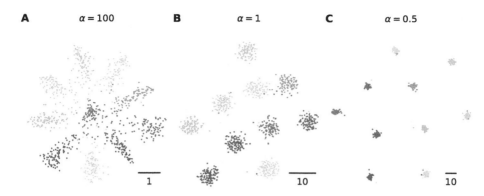

Fig. 1. Toy example with ten Gaussian clusters. (**A**) SNE visualisation of 10 spherical clusters that are all equally far away from each other ($\alpha = 100$). (**B**) Standard t-SNE visualisation of the same data set ($\alpha = 1$). (**C**) t-SNE visualisation with $\alpha = 0.5$. The same random seed was used for initialisation in all panels. Scale bars are shown in the bottom-right of each panel.

Modern t-SNE implementations make two approximations. First, they set most p_{ij} to zero, apart from only a small number of close neighbours [9,11], accelerating the attractive force computations (that can be very efficiently parallelised). This carries over to the $\alpha \neq 1$ case. The repulsive forces are approximated in FIt-SNE by interpolation on a grid, further accelerated with the Fourier transform [9]. This interpolation can be carried out for the $\alpha \neq 1$ case in full analogy to the $\alpha = 1$ case (see Appendix).

Importantly, the runtime of FIt-SNE with $\alpha \neq 1$ is practically the same as with $\alpha = 1$. For example, embedding MNIST ($n = 70\,000$) with perplexity 50 as described below took 90 s with $\alpha = 1$ and 97 s with $\alpha = 0.5$ on a computer with 4 double-threaded cores, 3.4 GHz each.[3]

2.2   Toy Examples

We first applied exact t-SNE with various values of α to a simple toy data set consisting of several well-separated clusters. Specifically, we generated a 10-dimensional data set with 100 data points in each of the 10 classes (1000 points overall). The points in class i were sampled from a Gaussian distribution with covariance $\mathbf{I}_{10}$ and mean $\boldsymbol{\mu}_i = 4\mathbf{e}_i$ where $\mathbf{e}_i$ is the i-th basis vector. We used perplexity 50, and default optimisation parameters (1000 iterations, learning rate 200, early exaggeration 12, length of early exaggeration 250, initial momentum 0.5, switching to 0.8 after 250 iterations).

Figure 1 shows the t-SNE results for $\alpha = 100$, $\alpha = 1$, and $\alpha = 0.1$. A t-distribution with $\nu = 2\alpha - 1 = 199$ degrees of freedom is very close to the

---

[3] The numbers correspond to 1000 gradient descent iterations. The slight speed decrease is due to a more efficient implementation of the interpolation code for the special case of $\alpha = 1$.

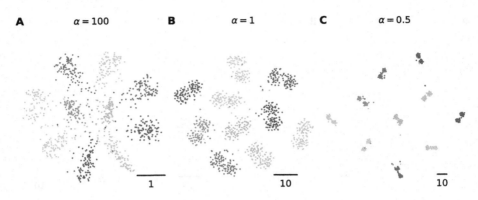

Fig. 2. Toy example with ten 'dumbbell'-shaped clusters. (**A**) SNE visualisation of 10 dumbbell-shaped clusters ($\alpha = 100$). (**B**) Standard t-SNE visualisation ($\alpha = 1$). (**C**) t-SNE visualisation with $\alpha = 0.5$.

Gaussian distribution, so here and below we will refer to the $\alpha = 100$ result as SNE. We see that class separation monotonically increases with decreasing α: t-SNE (Fig. 1B) separates the classes much better than SNE (Fig. 1A), but t-SNE with $\alpha = 0.5$ separates them much better still (Fig. 1C).

In the above toy example, the choice between different values of α is mostly aesthetic. This is not the case in the next toy example. Here we change the dimensionality to 20 and shift 50 points in each class by $2\mathbf{e}_{10+i}$ and the remaining 50 points by $-2\mathbf{e}_{10+i}$ (where i is the class number). The intuition is that now each of the 10 classes has a 'dumbbell' shape. This shape is invisible in SNE (Fig. 2A) and hardly visible in standard t-SNE (Fig. 2B), but becomes apparent with $\alpha = 0.5$ (Fig. 2C). In this case, decreasing α below 1 is necessary to bring out the fine structure of the data.

2.3   Mathematical Analysis

We showed that decreasing α increases cluster separation (Figs. 1 and 2). Why does this happen? An informal argument is that in order to match the between-cluster affinities p_{ij}, the distance between clusters in the t-SNE embedding needs to grow when the kernel becomes progressively more heavy-tailed [12].

To quantify this effect, we consider an example of two standard Gaussian clusters in 10 dimensions ($n = 100$ in each) with the between-centroid distance set to $5\sqrt{2}$; these clusters can be unambiguously separated. We use exact t-SNE (perplexity 50) with various values of α from 0.2 to 3.0 and measure the cluster separation in the embedding. As a scale-invariant measure of separation we used between-centroids distance divided by the root-mean-square within-cluster distance. Indeed, we observed a monotonic decrease of this measure with growing α (Fig. 3).

The informal argument mentioned above can be replaced by the following formal one. Consider two high-dimensional clusters (n points in each) with all

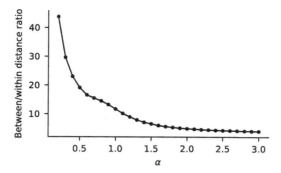

Fig. 3. Separation in the t-SNE visualisation between the two well-separated clusters as a function of α. Separation was measured as the between-centroids distance divided by the root-mean-square within-cluster distance.

pairwise within-cluster distances equal to D_w and all pairwise between-cluster distances equal to $D_b \gg D_w$ (this can be achieved in the space of $2n$ dimensions). In this case, the p_{ij} matrix has only two unique non-zero values: all within-cluster affinities are given by p_w and all between-cluster affinities by p_b,

$$
p_w = \frac{K(D_w)}{n\big[(n-1)K(D_w) + nK(D_b)\big]}
$$
$$
p_b = \frac{K(D_b)}{n\big[(n-1)K(D_w) + nK(D_b)\big]},
$$

where $K(D)$ is the Gaussian kernel corresponding to the chosen perplexity value. Consider an exact t-SNE mapping to the space of the same dimensionality. In this idealised case, t-SNE can achieve zero loss by setting within- and between-cluster distances d_w and d_b in the embedding such that $q_w = p_w$ and $q_b = p_b$. This will happen if

$$
\frac{k(d_b)}{k(d_w)} = \frac{K(D_b)}{K(D_w)}.
$$

Plugging in the expression for $k(d)$ and denoting the constant right-hand side by $c < 1$, we obtain

$$
\sqrt{\frac{\alpha + d_b^2}{\alpha + d_w^2}} = c^{-1/(2\alpha)}.
$$

The left-hand side can be seen as a measure of class separation close to the one used in Fig. 3, and the right-hand side monotonically decreases with increasing α.

In the simulation shown in Fig. 3, the p_{ij} matrix does not have only two unique elements, the target dimensionality is two, and the t-SNE cannot possibly achieve zero loss. Still, qualitatively we observe the same behaviour: approximately power-law decrease of separation with increasing α.

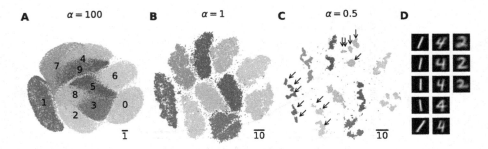

Fig. 4. MNIST data set ($n = 70\,000$). **(A)** SNE visualisation ($\alpha = 100$). **(B)** Standard t-SNE visualisation ($\alpha = 1$). **(C)** t-SNE visualisation with $\alpha = 0.5$. The colours are consistent across panels (A–C), labels are shown in (A). PCA initialisation was used in all three cases. Transparency 0.5 for all dots in all three panels. Arrows mark clusters shown in (D). **(D)** Average images for some individual sub-clusters from (C). The sub-clusters were isolated via DBSCAN with default settings as it is implemented in `scikit-learn`. Up to five subclusters with at least 100 points are shown, ordered from top to bottom by abundance. (Color figure online)

2.4 Real-Life Data Sets

We now demonstrate that these theoretical insights are relevant to practical use cases on large-scale data sets. Here we use approximate t-SNE (FIt-SNE).

MNIST. We applied t-SNE with various values of α to the MNIST data set (Fig. 4), comprising $n = 70\,000$ grayscale 28×28 images of handwritten digits. As a pre-processing step, we used principal component analysis (PCA) to reduce the dimensionality from 784 to 50. We used perplexity 50 and default optimisation parameters apart from learning rate that we increased to $\eta = 1000$.[4] For easier reproducibility, we initialised the t-SNE embedding with the first two PCs (scaled such that PC1 had standard deviation 0.0001).

To the best of our knowledge, Fig. 4A is the first existing SNE ($\alpha = 100$) visualisation of the whole MNIST: we are not aware of any SNE implementation that can handle a dataset of this size. It produces a surprisingly good visualisation but is nevertheless clearly outperformed by standard t-SNE ($\alpha = 1$, Fig. 4B): many digits coalesce together in SNE but get separated into clearly distinct clusters in t-SNE. Remarkably, reducing α to 0.5 makes each digit further split into multiple separate sub-clusters (Fig. 4C), revealing a fine structure within each of the digits.

To demonstrate that these sub-clusters are meaningful, we computed the average MNIST image for some of the sub-clusters (Fig. 4D). In each case, the

---

[4] To get a good t-SNE visualisation of MNIST, it is helpful to increase either the learning rate or the length of the early exaggeration phase. Default optimisation parameters often lead to some of the digits being split into two clusters. In the cytometric context, this phenomenon was described in detail by [2].

shapes appear to be meaningfully distinct: e.g. for the digit "4", the hand-writing is more italic in one sub-cluster, more wide in another, and features a non-trivial homotopy group (i.e. has a loop) in yet another one. Similarly, digit "2" is separated into three sub-clusters, with the most abundant one showing a loop in the bottom-left and the next abundant one having a sharp angle instead. Digit "1" is split according to the stroke angle. Re-running t-SNE using random initialisation with different seeds yielded consistent results. Points that appear as outliers in Fig. 4C mostly correspond to confusingly written digits.

MNIST has been a standard example for t-SNE starting from the original t-SNE paper [12], and it has been often observed that t-SNE preserves meaningful within-digit structure. Indeed, the sub-clusters that we identified in Fig. 4C are usually close together in Fig. 4B.[5] However, standard t-SNE does not separate them into visually isolated sub-clusters, and so does not make this internal structure obvious.

Single-Cell RNA-Sequencing Data. For the second example, we took the transcriptomic dataset from [16], comprising $n = 23\,822$ cells from adult mouse cortex (sequenced with Smart-seq2 protocol). Dimensions are genes, and the data are the integer counts of RNA transcripts of each gene in each cell. Using a custom expert-validated clustering procedure, the authors divided these cells into 133 clusters. In Fig. 5, we used the cluster ids and cluster colours from the original publication.

Figure 5A shows the standard t-SNE ($\alpha = 1$) of this data set, following common transcriptomic pre-processing steps as described in [7]. Briefly, we row-normalised and log-transformed the data, selected 3000 most variable genes and used PCA to further reduce dimensionality to 50. We used perplexity 50 and PCA initialisation. The resulting t-SNE visualisation is in a reasonable agreement with the clustering results, however it lumps many clusters together into contiguous 'islands' or 'continents' and overall suggests many fewer than 133 distinct clusters.

Reducing the number of degrees of freedom to $\alpha = 0.6$ splits many of the contiguous islands into 'archipelagos' of smaller disjoint areas (Fig. 5B). In many cases, this roughly agrees with the clustering results of [16]. Figure 5C shows a zoom-in into the *Vip* clusters (west-southwest part of panel B) that provide one such example: isolated islands correspond well to the individual clusters (or sometimes pairs of clusters). Importantly, the cluster labels in this data set are not ground truth; nevertheless the agreement between cluster labels and t-SNE with $\alpha = 0.6$ provides additional evidence that this data categorisation is meaningful.

HathiTrust Library. For the final example, we used the HathiTrust library data set [14]. The full data set comprises 13.6 million books and can be described

---

[5] This can be clearly seen in an animation that slowly decreases α from 100 to 0.5, see http://github.com/berenslab/finer-tsne.

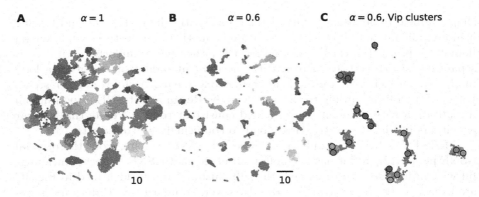

Fig. 5. Tasic et al. data set ($n = 23\,822$). (**A**) Standard t-SNE visualisation ($\alpha = 1$). Cluster ids and cluster colours are taken from the original publication [16]: cold colours for excitatory neurons, warm colours for inhibitory neurons, and grey/brown colours for non-neural cells such as astrocytes or microglia. (**B**) t-SNE visualisation with $\alpha = 0.6$. (**C**) A zoom-in into the left side of panel (B) showing all *Vip* clusters from Tasic et al. Black circles mark cluster centroids (medians). (Color figure online)

with several million features that represent word counts of each word in each book. We used the pre-processed data from [14]: briefly, the word counts were row-normalised, log-transformed, projected to 1280 dimensions using random linear projection with coefficients ± 1, and then reduced to 100 PCs.[6] The available meta-data include author name, book title, publication year, language, and Library of Congress classification (LCC) code. For simplicity, we took a $n = 408\,291$ subset consisting of all books in Russian language. We used perplexity 50 and learning rate $\eta = 10\,000$.

Figure 6A shows the standard t-SNE visualisation ($\alpha = 1$) coloured by the publication year. The most salient feature is that pre-1917 books cluster together (orange/red colours): this is due to the major reform of Russian orthography implemented in 1917, leading to most words changing their spelling. However, not much of a substructure can be seen among the books published after (or before) 1917. In contrast, t-SNE visualisation with $\alpha = 0.5$ fragments the corpus into a large number of islands (Fig. 6B).

We can identify some of the islands by inspecting the available meta-data. For example, mathematical literature (LCC code QA, $n = 6490$ books) is not separated from the rest in standard t-SNE, but occupies the leftmost island in t-SNE with $\alpha = 0.5$ (contour lines in the bottom right in both panels). Several neighbouring islands correspond to the physics literature (LCC code QC, $n = 5104$ books; not shown). In an attempt to capture something radically different from mathematics, we selected all books authored by several famous Russian

---

[6] The $13.6 \cdot 10^6 \times 100$ data set was downloaded from https://zenodo.org/record/1477018.

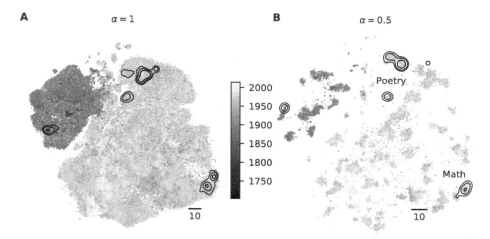

Fig. 6. Russian language part of the HathiTrust library ($n = 408\,291$). (**A**) Standard t-SNE visualisation ($\alpha = 1$). Colour denotes publication year. (**B**) t-SNE visualisation with $\alpha = 0.5$. Black contours in both panels are kernel density estimate contour lines for mathematical literature (lower right) and poetry (upper left), plotted with `seaborn.kdeplot()` with Gaussian bandwidth set to 2.0. Contour levels were manually tuned to enclose the majority of the books). (Color figure online)

poets[7] ($n = 1369$ in total). This is not a curated list: there are non-poetry books authored by these authors, while many other poets were not included (the list of poets was not cherry-picked; we made the list before looking at the data). Nevertheless, when using $\alpha = 0.5$, the poetry books printed after 1917 seemed to occupy two neighbouring islands, and the ones printed before 1917 were reasonably isolated as well (Fig. 6B, top and left). In the standard t-SNE visualisation poetry was not at all separated from the surrounding population of books.

3   Related Work

Yang et al. [18] introduced symmetric SNE with the kernel family

$$k(d) = \frac{1}{(1 + \alpha d^2)^{1/\alpha}},$$

calling it 'heavy-tailed symmetric SNE' (HSSNE). This is exactly the same kernel family as ($\star\star$), but with α replaced by $1/\alpha$. However, Yang et al. did not show any examples of heavier-tailed kernels revealing additional structure compared to $\alpha = 1$ and did not provide an implementation suitable for large sample sizes

---

[7] Anna Akhmatova, Alexander Blok, Joseph Brodsky, Afanasy Fet, Osip Mandelstam, Vladimir Mayakovsky, Alexander Pushkin, and Fyodor Tyutchev.

(i.e. it is not possible to use their implementation for $n \gtrsim 10\,000$). Interestingly, Yang et al. argued that gradient descent is not suitable for HSSNE and suggested an alternative optimisation algorithm; here we demonstrated that the standard t-SNE optimisation works reasonably well in a wide range of α values (but see Discussion).

Van der Maaten [10] discussed the choice of the degree of freedom in the t-distribution kernel in the context of parametric t-SNE. He argued that $\nu > 1$ might be warranted when embedding the data in more than two dimensions. He also implemented a version of parametric t-SNE that optimises over ν. However, similar to [18], [10] did not contain any examples of $\nu < 1$ being actually useful in practice.

UMAP [13] is a promising recent algorithm closely related to an earlier largeVis [15]; both are similar to t-SNE but modify the repulsive forces to make them amenable for a sampling-based stochastic optimisation. UMAP uses the following family of similarity kernels:

$$k(d) = \frac{1}{1 + ad^{2b}},$$

which reduces to Cauchy when $a = b = 1$ and is more heavy-tailed when $0 < b < 1$. UMAP default is $a \approx 1.6$ and $b \approx 0.9$ with both parameters adjusted via the `min_dist` input parameter (default value 0.1). Decreasing `min_dist` all the way to zero corresponds to decreasing b to 0.79. In our experiments, we observed that modifying `min_dist` (or b directly) led to an effect qualitatively similar to modifying α in t-SNE. For some data sets this required manually decreasing b below 0.79. In case of MNIST, $b = 0.3$, but not $b = 0.79$, revealed sub-digit structure (Figure S1)—an effect that has not been described before (cf. [13] where McInnes et al. state that `min_dist` is "an essentially aesthetic parameter"). In other words, the same conclusion seems to apply to UMAP: heavy-tailed kernels reveal a finer cluster structure. A more in-depth study of the relationships between the two algorithms is beyond the scope of this paper.

4   Discussion

We showed that using $\alpha < 1$ in t-SNE can yield insightful visualisations that are qualitatively different compared to the standard choice of $\alpha = 1$. Crucially, the choice of $\alpha = 1$ was made in [12] for the reasons of mathematical convenience, and we are not aware of any *a priori* argument in favour of $\alpha = 1$. As $\alpha \neq 1$ still yields a t-distribution kernel (scaled t-distribution to be precise), we prefer not to use a separate acronym (HSSNE [18]). If needed, one can refer to t-SNE with $\alpha < 1$ as 'heavy-tailed' t-SNE.

We found that lowering α below 1 makes progressively finer structure apparent in the visualisation and brings out smaller clusters, which—at least in the data sets studied here—are often meaningful. In a way, $\alpha < 1$ can be thought of as a 'magnifying glass' for the standard t-SNE representation. We do not think that there is one ideal value of α suitable for all data sets and all situations;

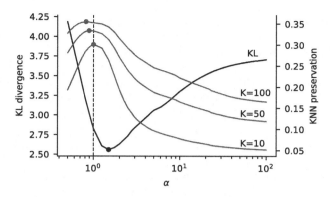

Fig. 7. Quality assessment of the MNIST embedding with $\alpha \in [0.5, 100]$ after 1000 gradient descent iterations with learning rate $\eta = 1000$ (scaled PCA initialisation). The horizontal axis is on the log scale. The α values were sampled on a grid with step 0.01 for $\alpha < 1$, 0.25 for $1 \leq \alpha \leq 5$ and 1 for $\alpha > 5$. The black line shows KL divergence (left axis) with minimum at $\alpha = 1.5$. Running gradient descent with $\alpha = 0.5$ for 10 000 iterations (Figure S3) lowered KL divergence down to 3.6, which was still above the minimum value. Blue lines show neighbourhood preservation (the fraction of k nearest neighbours of each point that remain within k nearest neighbours in the embedding, averaged over all $n = 70\,000$ points) for $k = 10$, $k = 50$, and $k = 100$. (Color figure online)

instead we consider it a useful adjustable parameter of t-SNE, complementary to the perplexity. We observed a non-trivial interaction between α and perplexity: Small vs. large perplexity makes the affinity matrix p_{ij} represent the local vs. global structure of the data [7]. Small vs. large α makes the embedding represent the finer vs. coarser structure of the affinity matrix. In practice, it can make sense to treat it as a two-dimensional parameter space to explore. However, for large data sets ($n \gtrsim 10^6$), it is computationally unfeasible to substantially increase the perplexity from its standard range of 30–100 (as it would prohibitively increase the runtime), and so α becomes the only available parameter to adjust.

One important caveat is to be kept in mind. It is well-known that t-SNE, especially with low perplexity, can find 'clusters' in pure noise, picking up random fluctuations in the density [17]. This can happen with $\alpha = 1$ but gets exacerbated with lower values of α. A related point concerns clustered real-life data where separate clusters (local density peaks) can sometimes be connected by an area of lower but non-zero density: for example, [16] argued that many pairs of their 133 clusters have intermediate cells. Our experiments demonstrate that lowering α can make such clusters more and more isolated in the embedding, creating a potentially misleading appearance of perfect separation (see e.g. Figure 1). In other words, there is a trade-off between bringing out finer cluster structure and preserving continuities between clusters.

Choosing a value of α that yields the most faithful representation of a given data set is challenging because it is difficult to quantify 'faithfulness' of any given embedding [8]. For example, for MNIST, KL divergence is minimised at $\alpha \approx 1.5$ (Fig. 7), but it may not be the ideal metric to quantify the embedding quality [6]. Indeed, we found that k-nearest neighbour (KNN) preservation [8] peaked elsewhere: the peak for $k = 10$ was at $\alpha \approx 1.0$, for $k = 50$ at $\alpha \approx 0.9$, and for $k = 100$ at $\alpha \approx 0.8$ (Fig. 7). We stress that we do not think that KNN preservation is the most appropriate metric here; our point is that different metrics can easily disagree with each other. In general, there may not be a single 'best' embedding of high-dimensional data in a two-dimensional space. Rather, by varying α, one can obtain different complementary 'views' of the data.

Very low values of α correspond to kernels with very wide and very flat tails, leading to vanishing gradients and difficult convergence. We found that $\alpha = 0.5$ was about the smallest value that could be safely used (Figure S2). In fact, it may take more iterations to reach convergence for $0.5 < \alpha < 1$ compared to $\alpha = 1$. As an example, running t-SNE on MNIST with $\alpha = 0.5$ for ten times longer than we did for Fig. 4C, led to the embedding expanding much further (which leads to a slow-down of FIt-SNE interpolation) and, as a result, resolving additional sub-clusters (Figure S3). On a related note, when using only one single MNIST digit as an input for t-SNE with $\alpha = 0.5$, the embedding also fragments into many more clusters (Figure S4), which we hypothesise is due to the points rapidly expanding to occupy a much larger area compared to what happens in the full MNIST embedding (Figure S4). This can be counterbalanced by increasing the strength of the attractive forces (Figure S4). Overall, the effect of the embedding scale on the cluster resolution remains an open research question.

In conclusion, we have shown that adjusting the heaviness of the kernel tails in t-SNE can be a valuable tool for data exploration and visualisation. As a practical recommendation, we suggest to embed any given data set using various values of α, each inducing a different level of clustering, and hence providing insight that cannot be obtained from the standard $\alpha = 1$ choice alone.[8]

5 Appendix

The loss function, up to a constant term $\sum p_{ij} \log p_{ij}$, can be rewritten as follows:

$$\mathcal{L} = -\sum_{i,j} p_{ij} \log q_{ij} = -\sum_{i,j} p_{ij} \log \frac{w_{ij}}{Z}$$
$$= -\sum_{i,j} p_{ij} \log w_{ij} + \log \sum_{i,j} w_{ij}, \qquad (1)$$

where we took into account that $\sum p_{ij} = 1$. The first term in Eq. (1) contributes attractive forces to the gradient while the second term yields repulsive forces.

---

[8] Our code is available at http://github.com/berenslab/finer-tsne. The main FIt-SNE repository at http://github.com/klugerlab/FIt-SNE was updated to support any α (version 1.1.0).

The gradient is

$$\frac{\partial \mathcal{L}}{\partial \mathbf{y}_i} = -2 \sum_j p_{ij} \frac{1}{w_{ij}} \frac{\partial w_{ij}}{\partial \mathbf{y}_i} + 2 \sum_j \frac{1}{Z} \frac{\partial w_{ij}}{\partial \mathbf{y}_i} \tag{2}$$

$$= -2 \sum_j (p_{ij} - q_{ij}) \frac{1}{w_{ij}} \frac{\partial w_{ij}}{\partial \mathbf{y}_i}. \tag{3}$$

The first expression is more convenient for numeric optimisation while the second one can be more convenient for mathematical analysis.

For the kernel

$$k(d) = \frac{1}{(1 + d^2/\alpha)^\alpha}$$

the gradient of $w_{ij} = k(\|\mathbf{y}_i - \mathbf{y}_j\|)$ is

$$\frac{\partial w_{ij}}{\partial \mathbf{y}_i} = -2w^{\frac{\alpha+1}{\alpha}} (\mathbf{y}_i - \mathbf{y}_j). \tag{4}$$

Plugging Eq. 4 into Eq. 3, we obtain the expression for the gradient [18][9]

$$\frac{\partial \mathcal{L}}{\partial \mathbf{y}_i} = 4 \sum_j (p_{ij} - q_{ij}) w_{ij}^{1/\alpha} (\mathbf{y}_i - \mathbf{y}_j).$$

For numeric optimisation it is convenient to split this expression into the attractive and the repulsive terms. Plugging Eq. 4 into Eq. 2, we obtain

$$\frac{\partial \mathcal{L}}{\partial \mathbf{y}_i} = \mathbf{F}_{\text{att}} + \mathbf{F}_{\text{rep}}$$

where

$$\mathbf{F}_{\text{att}} = 4 \sum_j p_{ij} w_{ij}^{1/\alpha} (\mathbf{y}_i - \mathbf{y}_j)$$

$$\mathbf{F}_{\text{rep}} = -4 \sum_j w_{ij}^{\frac{\alpha+1}{\alpha}} / Z (\mathbf{y}_i - \mathbf{y}_j)$$

It is noteworthy that the expression for $\mathbf{F}_{\text{attr}}$ has w_{ij} raised to the $1/\alpha$ power, which cancels out the fractional power in $k(d)$. This makes the runtime of $\mathbf{F}_{\text{attr}}$ computation unaffected by the value of α. In FIt-SNE, the sum over j in $\mathbf{F}_{\text{attr}}$ is approximated by the sum over 3Π approximate nearest neighbours of point i obtained using Annoy [3], where Π is the provided perplexity value. The 3Π heuristic comes from [11]. The remaining p_{ij} values are set to zero.

---

[9] Note that the C++ Barnes-Hut t-SNE implementation [11] absorbed the factor 4 into the learning rate, and the FIt-SNE implementation [9] followed this convention.

The $\mathbf{F}_{\text{rep}}$ can be approximated using the interpolation scheme from [9]. It allows fast approximate computation of the sums of the form

$$\sum_j K(\|\mathbf{y}_i - \mathbf{y}_j\|)$$

and

$$\sum_j K(\|\mathbf{y}_i - \mathbf{y}_j\|)\mathbf{y}_j,$$

where $K(\cdot)$ is any smooth kernel, by using polynomial interpolation of K on a fine grid.[10] All kernels appearing in $\mathbf{F}_{\text{rep}}$ are smooth.

Acknowledgements. This work was supported by the Deutsche Forschungsgemeinschaft (BE5601/4-1, EXC 2064, Project ID 390727645) (PB), the Federal Ministry of Education and Research (FKZ 01GQ1601, 01IS18052C), and the National Institute of Mental Health under award number U19MH114830 (DK and PB), NIH grants F30HG010102 and U.S. NIH MSTP Training Grant T32GM007205 (GCL), NSF grant DMS-1763179 and the Alfred P. Sloan Foundation (SS), and the NIH grant R01HG008383 (YK). The content is solely the responsibility of the authors and does not necessarily represent the official views of the National Institutes of Health.

References

1. Amir, E.A.D., et al.: viSNE enables visualization of high dimensional single-cell data and reveals phenotypic heterogeneity of leukemia. Nat. Biotechnol. **31**(6), 545 (2013)
2. Belkina, A.C., Ciccolella, C.O., Anno, R., Spidlen, J., Halpert, R., Snyder-Cappione, J.: Automated optimized parameters for T-distributed stochastic neighbor embedding improve visualization and analysis of large datasets. Nat. Commun. **10**, 5415 (2019)
3. Bernhardsson, E.: Annoy. https://github.com/spotify/annoy (2013)
4. Diaz-Papkovich, A., Anderson-Trocme, L., Ben-Eghan, C., Gravel, S.: UMAP reveals cryptic population structure and phenotype heterogeneity in large genomic cohorts. PLoS Genet. **15**(11), e1008432 (2019)
5. Hinton, G., Roweis, S.: Stochastic neighbor embedding. In: Advances in Neural Information Processing Systems, pp. 857–864 (2003)
6. Im, D.J., Verma, N., Branson, K.: Stochastic neighbor embedding under f-divergences. arXiv (2018)
7. Kobak, D., Berens, P.: The art of using t-SNE for single-cell transcriptomics. Nat. Commun. **10**, 5416 (2019)
8. Lee, J.A., Verleysen, M.: Quality assessment of dimensionality reduction: rank-based criteria. Neurocomputing **72**(7–9), 1431–1443 (2009)
9. Linderman, G.C., Rachh, M., Hoskins, J.G., Steinerberger, S., Kluger, Y.: Fast interpolation-based t-SNE for improved visualization of single-cell RNA-seq data. Nat. Methods **16**, 243–245 (2019)

---

[10] The accuracy of in the interpolation can somewhat decrease for small values of α. One can increase the accuracy by decreasing the spacing of the interpolation grid (see FIt-SNE documentation). We found that it did not noticeably affect the visualisations.

10. van der Maaten, L.: Learning a parametric embedding by preserving local structure. In: International Conference on Artificial Intelligence and Statistics, pp. 384–391 (2009)
11. van der Maaten, L.: Accelerating t-SNE using tree-based algorithms. J. Mach. Learn. Res. **15**(1), 3221–3245 (2014)
12. van der Maaten, L., Hinton, G.: Visualizing data using t-SNE. J. Mach. Learn. Res. **9**, 2579–2605 (2008)
13. McInnes, L., Healy, J., Melville, J.: UMAP: Uniform manifold approximation and projection for dimension reduction. arXiv (2018)
14. Schmidt, B.: Stable random projection: Lightweight, general-purpose dimensionality reduction for digitized libraries. J. Cult. Anal. (2018)
15. Tang, J., Liu, J., Zhang, M., Mei, Q.: Visualizing large-scale and high-dimensional data. In: Proceedings of the 25th International Conference on World Wide Web, pp. 287–297. International World Wide Web Conferences Steering Committee (2016)
16. Tasic, B., et al.: Shared and distinct transcriptomic cell types across neocortical areas. Nature **563**(7729), 72 (2018)
17. Wattenberg, M., Viégas, F., Johnson, I.: How to use t-SNE effectively. Distill **1**(10), e2 (2016)
18. Yang, Z., King, I., Xu, Z., Oja, E.: Heavy-tailed symmetric stochastic neighbor embedding. In: Advances in Neural Information Processing Systems, pp. 2169–2177 (2009)
19. Zeisel, A., et al.: Molecular architecture of the mouse nervous system. Cell **174**(4), 999–1014 (2018)

Uncovering Hidden Block Structure for Clustering

Luce le Gorrec[1(✉)], Sandrine Mouysset[1], Iain S. Duff[2,3], Philip A. Knight[4], and Daniel Ruiz[1]

[1] Université de Toulouse - IRIT, 2 rue Camichel, Toulouse, France
luce.le-gorrec@strath.ac.uk, {sandrine.mouysset,daniel.ruiz}@enseeiht.fr
[2] R7l, STFC Rutherford Appleton Laboratory, Didcot, OX OX11 0QX, UK
iain.duff@stfc.ac.uk
[3] CERFACS, Toulouse, France
[4] University of Strathclyde, Richmond Street, Glasgow, UK
p.a.knight@strath.ac.uk

Abstract. We present a multistage procedure to cluster directed and undirected weighted graphs by finding the block structure of their adjacency matrices. A central part of the process is to scale the adjacency matrix into a doubly-stochastic form, which permits detection of the whole matrix block structure with minimal spectral information (theoretically a single pair of singular vectors suffices).

We present the different stages of our method, namely the impact of the doubly-stochastic scaling on singular vectors, detection of the block structure by means of these vectors, and details such as cluster refinement and a stopping criterion. Then we test the algorithm's effectiveness by using it on two unsupervised classification tasks: community detection in networks and shape detection in clouds of points in two dimensions. By comparing results of our approach with those of widely used algorithms designed for specific purposes, we observe that our method is competitive (for community detection) if not superior (for shape detection) in comparison with existing methods.

Keywords: Clustering and unsupervised learning · Spectral clustering · Doubly-stochastic scaling · Community detection · Shape detection

1 Introduction

Grouping together similar elements among a set of data is a challenging example of unsupervised learning for which many so-called clustering techniques have been proposed. A classical way to cluster elements consists in finding blocks in matrices used to represent data—such as adjacency matrices, affinity matrices, contingency tables or a graph Laplacian.

The link between spectral and structural properties of matrices is a motivating factor behind many existing clustering algorithms [12,16,28]. To extract multiple clusters, classical spectral algorithms recursively split the nodes in two

© Springer Nature Switzerland AG 2020
U. Brefeld et al. (Eds.): ECML PKDD 2019, LNAI 11906, pp. 140–155, 2020.
https://doi.org/10.1007/978-3-030-46150-8_9

sets by means of the signs of a given singular vector or eigenvector. This can be costly since each partition into two clusters requires a new vector to be computed. Moreover, the returned partition at each iteration may be a poor fit to the natural block structure in the matrix (an example is shown in the right-most plot of Fig. 2, where the red separation line does not match the blocking). Other existing methods [20, 24, 30] rely on spectral embedding with various graph Laplacian matrices. Such methods require a priori knowledge of the number of clusters.

In this paper, we present a novel approach to spectral clustering. Our aim is to be able to find clusters in a strongly connected, directed weighted graph. We work with a matrix $\mathbf{A}$ that represents the weighted adjacency graph.

The main novelty of our method is to use a doubly-stochastic scaling of the matrix $\mathbf{A}$ before extracting spectral components. That is we find two positive diagonal matrices $\mathbf{D}$ and $\mathbf{F}$ so that all the row sums and column sums of the scaled matrix $\mathbf{P} = \mathbf{DAF}$ are equal to one. We show in Sect. 2 that the scaling improves the fidelity of the structural information contained in the leading singular vectors of $\mathbf{P}$. In particular, we only need to compute a few singular vectors to obtain significant information on the underlying structure without any prior information on the number of blocks. Additionally, working with singular vectors of $\mathbf{P}$ makes it feasible to analyse directed graphs, and can provide an accurate clustering when the graph structure is distinctly asymmetric.

The paper is structured as follows. In Sect. 2 we outline the connection between the singular vectors of a doubly-stochastic matrix scaling and its block structure. In Sect. 3 we use tools from signal processing to detect clustering information in the vectors. Section 4 is dedicated to the rearrangement of the blocks: we have to collate information provided by left and right singular vectors and further refinement may be necessary when we iterate our process by analysing several singular vectors in turn. We also present a bespoke measure we have designed to evaluate the quality of the clustering, and to derive a stopping criterion. Empirical results using benchmark data sets are provided in Sect. 5 to indicate the effectiveness of our algorithm and finally we present some concluding remarks in Sect. 6.

2   Doubly-Stochastic Scaling

Scaling a matrix into doubly-stochastic form is always possible if the matrix is *bi-irreducible*, that is there exist no row and column permutations that can rearrange $\mathbf{A}$ into a block triangular form [29]. If $\mathbf{A}$ is the adjacency matrix of a strongly connected directed graph then it is bi-irreducible so long as its diagonal is zero free. If necessary, we can add nonzero terms to the diagonal without affecting the underlying block structure.

The following theorem is a straightforward consequence of the Perron–Frobenius theorem [17, 26].

Theorem 1. *Suppose that* $\mathbf{S} \in \mathbb{R}^{n \times n}$ *is symmetric, irreducible, and doubly-stochastic. The largest eigenvalue of* $\mathbf{S}$ *is* 1, *with multiplicity* 1, *and the associated* *eigenvector is equal to a multiple of* **e**, *the vector of ones. If* **S** *has total support—that is* **S** *can be permuted symmetrically into a block diagonal structure with k irreducible blocks, then the eigenvalue* 1 *has multiplicity k. A basis for the corresponding eigenvectors is*

$$\{\mathbf{v}_1, \mathbf{v}_2, \ldots, \mathbf{v}_k\},$$

where v_{pq} for $p \in \{1, \ldots, k\}$ is given by

$$v_{pq} = \begin{cases} 1, & \text{for all } q \text{ in block } p \\ 0, & \text{otherwise.} \end{cases}$$

If we compute an eigenvector of such a matrix **S** associated with the eigenvalue 1 then it will be of the form

$$\mathbf{x} = a_1\mathbf{v}_1 + a_2\mathbf{v}_2 + \cdots + a_k\mathbf{v}_k.$$

By forcing **x** to lie in the orthogonal complement of the constant vector **e**, it is reasonable to assume that the a_i are distinct. Since these vectors are formed by a disjoint partition of $\{1, \ldots, n\}$ we can identify the precise contribution from each block, and then characterise the partition exactly using the set

$$\{a_1, \ldots, a_k\}.$$

Indeed, reordering **x** according to the block structure puts it in piecewise constant form. Conversely, symmetrically permuting rows and columns of **S** according to the ascending order of entries from **x** reveals the block structure of **S**.

As a corollary of Theorem 1, consider an non-symmetric but still doubly-stochastic matrix **P**. Both $\mathbf{PP}^T$ and $\mathbf{P}^T\mathbf{P}$ are also doubly-stochastic, and the results of Theorem 1 apply. Suppose then that we compute the principal left and right singular vectors of **P**. If either $\mathbf{PP}^T$ or $\mathbf{P}^T\mathbf{P}$ exhibits some block structure, then the dominant singular vectors of **P** have contributions from each of the corresponding basis vectors. Thus we can directly identify the row and/or column block structure of **P** using the same trick as for the matrix **S**.

Our algorithm is designed for matrices that are perturbations of matrices with total support. If the matrix has a structure that is close to block diagonal, the leading singular vectors can be assumed to have a structure similar to the piecewise constant form. The impact of a small perturbation on the scaling of a block diagonal matrix can be found in [11, §2.1]. If we then look for steps in the computed vectors we should be able to reveal some underlying approximate block structure, or at least some row blocks (respectively column blocks) that are weakly correlated with each other. To find a doubly-stochastic scaling we use the Newton method described in [18]. Typically, this is very cheap to do, requiring only matrix–vector products.

To emphasize the power of the doubly-stochastic scaling compared to other spectral clustering techniques, we use a small example in Fig. 1 to illustrate how the spectral information may vary when extracting eigenvectors from either the Laplacian or from the doubly-stochastic matrix. In this example, the graph has three distinct clusters that are loosely linked together. To ensure bi-irreducibility the diagonal of the adjacency matrix of the graph is set to 10^{-8} times the identity matrix, before scaling to doubly-stochastic form. In the lower half of Fig. 1 we see the numerical structure of the eigenvectors used to identify the clusters. The lower graph is a sorted version of the upper. For the Laplacian we have illustrated the eigenvectors of the two smallest positive eigenvalues (the Fiedler vector in blue) and for the stochastic scaling we have used the two subdominant vectors. In the case of the Laplacian matrix, we can see that the eigenvectors cannot easily resolve the clusters (the same is also true for the normalised Laplacian, too). On the other hand, for the doubly-stochastic scaling we can use either of the vectors to resolve the clusters perfectly and unambiguously.

As we said in Sect. 1, it is possible to iterate our process of finding and analysing singular vectors to refine our clustering. Such an iterative process needs to analyse different singular vectors at each step to obtain additional information. In [11, §4], we describe our implementation.

3   Cluster Identification

A key stage in our algorithm is to identify clusters using the largest singular vectors of the doubly-stochastic bi-irreducible matrix $\mathbf{P}$. We note that we are assuming no a priori knowledge regarding the number of clusters nor the row and column permutations that may reveal the underlying block structure.

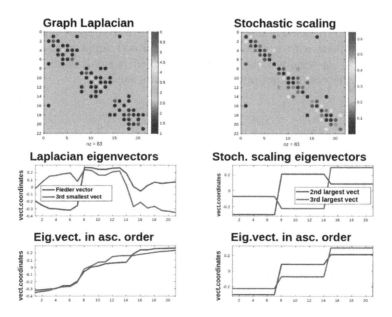

Fig. 1. Two matrix representations of a graph and their corresponding eigenvectors (Color figure online)

Partitioning algorithms that work on vectors analogous to the Fiedler vector divide the matrix in two parts according to the signs of the vector entries. But thanks to our previous doubly-stochastic scaling we are able to see more than two blocks, as explained in Sect. 2. If $\mathbf{PP}^T$ or $\mathbf{P}^T\mathbf{P}$ has an underlying nearly block diagonal structure, its leading eigenvectors are expected to have nearly piecewise constant pattern when reordered according to the size of their entries, as in the right bottom plot of Fig. 1. Our problem is thus to detect steps in the reordered vector, which we choose to view as a signal processing issue. In fact, this vector can be considered as a 1D signal whose steps are to be detected. Hence, we proceed in our cluster detection by applying tools from signal processing, in particular using a convolution product between the current singular vector and a specific filter. The peaks in the convolution product correspond to edges in the signal. These tools have the added bonus of not needing prior knowledge of the number of clusters.

We have chosen to use the Canny filter [4], which is widely used in both signal and image processing for edge detection. To optimise edge detection it combines three performance criteria, namely good detection, good localization, and the constraint that an edge should correspond to a peak in an appropriate convolution. In order to satisfy these criteria the Canny filter uses an operator constructed from the convolution product of the output Signal-to-Noise Ratio (SNR) and a localization function (the filter). The optimal localization function is the first derivative of a Gaussian kernel [4].

Much effort has gone into refining our implementation of edge detection to make it optimal for our particular application. When using the filter for the convolution we can vary a parameter that we call the sliding window size. The window size determines whether the filter has a narrow support and has a steep profile (as happens with a small window) or a broad support and a smoother profile (with a big window), as shown in Fig. 2(a). A small window can create many peaks whereas a larger one will detect fewer edges.

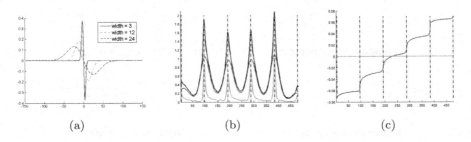

(a)   (b)   (c)

Fig. 2. (a) The filter for different sliding window sizes; (b) Convolution products; (c) Step detection (Color figure online)

To avoid the side effects of the window size on the convolution product the step detection is performed with two window widths of size $n/30$ and $n/150$ respectively where n is the size of the vector. We then sum both convolution

results in order to detect the principal peaks and to make sure that our steps
are both sharp and of a relatively significant height.

Figure 2(b) shows an example of how the sliding window can affect the step
detection using the 480×480 matrix rbsb480 from the SuiteSparse collection [8].
We can see from this figure that the peaks corresponding to steps in the vector
are better identified using this sum. In Fig. 2(c), the associated right singular
vector is plotted indicating the quality of the steps detected by the filters. In
contrast, the horizontal red line in Fig. 2(c) indicates the bipartitioning suggested
by the Fiedler vector. This presumes that there are precisely two clusters and
the separation is not aligned with any of the steps indicated by the singular
vector.

It is possible for the edge detector to identify spurious clusters. In [11, §6]
we give an illustrative example and also describe how to deal with this issue
in general by validating peaks and also by incorporating additional information
provided by other singular vectors to resolve the boundaries between blocks with
high precision.

4   Cluster Improvement

We now explain how to merge the different clusters found for each individually
analysed singular vector, as well as those found on rows and columns once the
iterative process is over. We then present a bespoke measure to evaluate the
quality of our clustering which allows us to amalgamate some small clusters.
Using the measure, we develop a stopping criterion to determine convergence of
the iterative process.

Throughout this section we illustrate our comments with the rbsb480
matrix [8] because of its interesting fine block structure on both rows and
columns. We observe that in Figs. 3 and 4, we are not presenting a clustering in
a formal sense, but simply an overlapping of the independent row and column
partitions.

4.1   Overlapping the Clusterings

Each time our algorithm analyses a right (respectively left) singular vector of
the matrix it may find a row (respectively column) partition of the matrix. Of
course, the resulting partition may be different for every analysed vector and we
need to merge them in an embedded manner. This process is illustrated in Fig. 3,
where the first detection step identifies only 4 row clusters and 5 column clusters,
while the second left and right singular vectors suggest a different picture with
3 row clusters and 4 column clusters. These new clusters are complementary
to the first set and the merged clustering gives 12 row clusters and 20 column
clusters with fairly well separated sub-blocks in the resulting reordered matrix,
as shown in the left-hand plot in Fig. 4.

As we can see from our tests on rbsb480, it may be sensible to analyse
several vectors in turn and merge these results. However, this can be overdone

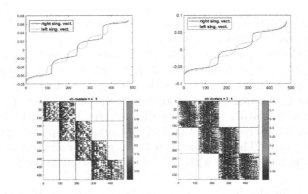

Fig. 3. Cluster identification using different singular vectors

and we may produce a very fine partitioning of the original matrix. This issue is illustrated in the right-hand plot of Fig. 4, where 3 steps have been merged to give a fine grain clustering (with 48 by 100 clusters) and motivates our development of an effective method for amalgamating blocks.

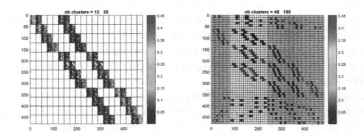

Fig. 4. Recursive cluster identification obtained by analysing several vectors in turn

4.2 Quality Measure

We base our cluster analysis on the modularity measure from [23]. Modularity can be interpreted as the sum over all clusters of the difference between the fraction of links inside each cluster and the expected fraction, by considering a random network with the same degree distribution.

We can evaluate our row clustering using the modularity of our doubly-stochastic matrix $\mathbf{PP}^T$ given by the formula

$$\mathcal{Q}_r = \frac{1}{n} \sum_{k=1}^{r_C} \left(\mathbf{v}_k^T \mathbf{PP}^T \mathbf{v}_k - \frac{1}{n} |\mathcal{J}_k|^2 \right). \tag{1}$$

Here, n is the number of rows in $\mathbf{P}$, r_C is the number of row clusters and $|\mathcal{J}_k|$ is the cardinality of cluster k. The equation is easily derived from the definition of modularity from [1], noticing that $2m = n$ in the doubly-stochastic case. In a similar way, we derive a quality measure $\mathcal{Q}_c$ for the column clustering by considering the matrix $\mathbf{P}^T\mathbf{P}$ and summing over the sets of column clusters.

In [11, §7.1] we prove that the quality measure falls between the bounds

$$0 \leq \mathcal{Q}_r \leq 1 - \frac{1}{r_C} \,, \qquad (2)$$

with the upper bound being reached only when the r_C clusters have the same cardinality.

Despite issues with the so-called resolution limit [13], modularity is still one of the most widely used measures in the field of community detection and we are comfortable in employing it here. Furthermore, in the specific case of k-regular graphs, many measures including the Newman and Girvan modularity behave similarly [6]. Since doubly-stochastic matrices can be considered as adjacency matrices of weighted 1-regular graphs most common quality measures can be expected to give similar results.

To avoid tiny clusters as in the right plot of Fig. 4, we recursively amalgamate the pair of clusters that gives the maximum increase in modularity measure. The algorithm stops naturally when there is no further improvement to be made by amalgamating pairs of clusters together. A proof that this method always provides a local maximum can be found in [11, §7.2] where it is also shown that it is computationally cheap.

The amalgamation process prevents an explosion in the number of clusters and gives some control over the amount of work for testing the $r_C(r_C-1)/2$ possibilities and is applied after overlapping the clusterings obtained independently for each singular vector.

As a stopping criterion, we compare the quality of the clustering updated by the amalgamation process, $\mathcal{Q}_r^{upd}$ with that obtained immediately beforehand, $\mathcal{Q}_r^{ref}$. There are four possibilities to consider.

- If $\mathcal{Q}_r^{upd} < \mathcal{Q}_r^{ref}$ we reject the update.
- If $\mathcal{Q}_r^{upd} > \mathcal{Q}_r^{ref}$ but the number of clusters increases we accept the update only if there is a sizeable jump in modularity taking into account the upper bound in (2). We compare the quality measure increase with its theoretical potential increase using the ratio

$$\rho = \frac{\mathcal{Q}_r^{upd} - \mathcal{Q}_r^{ref}}{\frac{1}{nbClust^{ref}} - \frac{1}{nbClust^{upd}}}\,.$$

The threshold can be tuned to control the number of iterations we take and the granularity of the clustering. In tests, a threshold value between 0.01 and 0.1 seems to be effective.

- If $\mathcal{Q}_r^{upd} > \mathcal{Q}_r^{ref}$ and the number of clusters does not increase, we accept the update.
- If the clusterings are identical up to a permutation then we can terminate the algorithm, which is equivalent to rejecting the update.

5   Applications

We illustrate the performance of our algorithm in community detection in Sect. 5.1 and we test it on shape detection using the `Scikit-learn` package [25] in Sect. 5.2.

5.1   Community Detection

We first test our algorithm on simple networks. To ensure bi-irreducibility with minimal effect on the clusters we set the diagonal to 10^{-8}.

Before the detection phase, we remove dominant entries (>0.55) from the scaled matrix since they give rise to near-canonical eigenvectors that tend to lack well defined steps. From the first iteration, we consider each dominant entry as an already identified block when looking at the projected eigenvector of the matrix, as explained in [11, §3]. These large entries are associated with structures not strongly linked to communities, such as hub or pendant nodes, and we incorporate them during the amalgamation process to optimise modularity once our algorithm has converged.

We have compared our algorithm (US) against four established community detection algorithms from the `igraph` package [7], namely Walktrap (WT) [27], Louvain (ML) [2], Fast and Greedy (FG) [5], and Leading Eigenvector (LE) [22]. WT and ML are specifically designed to work on graph structures directly whereas LE focuses (like ours) on exploiting spectral information. FG is a natural greedy algorithm to optimise the modularity. WT and ML have been shown to be among the three best community detection algorithms in a recent study [31].

We have applied these algorithms to four datasets of 500 node networks generated with the Lancichinetti–Fortunato–Radicchi benchmark (LFR) [19] which is widely used in community detection because its characteristics are close to those of real-world networks. Each dataset corresponds to a different average degree $\overline{k}$. More details are given in Table 1.

Table 1. Parameters for benchmark generation

Parameter	Value	
Number of nodes	500	
Average degree $\overline{k}$	{10,20,40,75}	
Maximum degree	$2 \times \overline{k}$	
Degree distribution exponent	-2	*Exponent of the power law used to generate degree distribution*
Community size distribution exponent	-1	*Exponent of the power law used to generate community size distribution*

We test the behaviour of community detection algorithms using the network mixing parameter, which quantifies the strength of a community structure. Initially, it measures the strength of a node's community membership by computing the ratio between its links outside the community and its degree. The greater the mixing parameter for each node, the weaker the community structure. The network mixing parameter μ is the mean value of the nodal mixing parameters.

We measure the accuracy of the community structures returned by the algorithms by using the Normalised Mutual Information (NMI). This is a measure taken from information theory (see for instance [15]). It measures the deviation between two candidate partitions with no requirement that they have the same number of blocks and is widely used in the community detection field [31]. The NMI takes its values in $[0, 1]$, and is equal to 1 when the two partitions are identical.

The results are shown in Fig. 5. Each plot corresponds to a different value of $\overline{k}$. In each plot, we have generated 50 networks for each μ value and display the mean value of the NMI. We remark that we can pair existing algorithms in terms of performance: ML and WT, where NMI is close to 1 even for large values of μ, and FG and LE where NMI decreases rapidly. Our algorithm falls between the two groups.

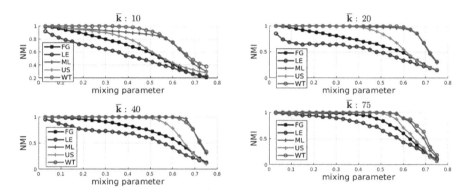

Fig. 5. Curves of NMI for FG, LE, ML, WT, US

We note that the two groups tend to behave similarly in terms of NMI when increasing $\overline{k}$. This can be explained by the constraints on the network that result in larger communities for large $\overline{k}$ values, as shown in Fig. 6. Here, two adjacency networks from our dataset have been plotted with $\mu = 0.3$. The matrix in the left plot has an average degree $\overline{k} = 10$ and 40 communities, whereas for the matrix in the right plot $\overline{k} = 75$ and there are 5 communities. It is known that large communities are more accurately detected by most community detection algorithms. But it seems that it is not the only factor that makes our algorithm work better for large $\overline{k}$, as its NMI curves are more sensitive to $\overline{k}$ than FG and LE.

We have tested whether this behaviour may be due to the fact that, in very sparse networks, leading eigenvectors may be associated with features other than the community structure [14]. Thus, we have compared the accuracy of two

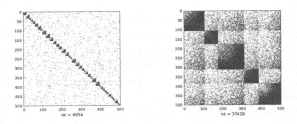

Fig. 6. Adjacency matrices of two networks

versions of our algorithm. In the first we add 10^{-8} to the diagonal entries of **A** (USd). In the second we add a perturbation to the whole matrix (USw): this version works with $\mathbf{A} + \epsilon \mathbf{e}\mathbf{e}^T$ where **A** is the adjacency matrix of the network. We have set ϵ to 0.15 as is often suggested with Google's Pagerank [3]. The results of both algorithms can be viewed in Fig. 7 for two different values of $\overline{k}$. We observe that the two versions behave similarly when $\overline{k} = 75$, whereas USw (blue curve) is much more accurate than USd (pink curve) for $\overline{k} = 20$.

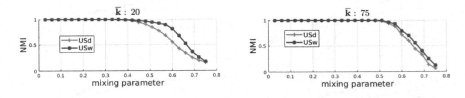

Fig. 7. Curves of NMI for USd and USw (Color figure online)

To complete this study, we have investigated the behaviour of WT, ML, USd and USw with increasing $\overline{k}$. The results are shown in Fig. 8. We see that ML, WT and USw first improve their accuracy, seem to reach a threshold and finally worsen for the largest value of $\overline{k}$. USd also improves its accuracy, but does not worsen when $\overline{k}$ reaches its maximum test value.

Hence, although our algorithm does not beat all existing community detections algorithms on very sparse networks, it is able to correctly detect communities better than some widely-used purpose-built algorithms. Moreover it seems to be a very encouraging alternative when the networks become denser as it retains its accuracy in these circumstances. Indeed, we will see in Sect. 5.2 that it is very good at detecting block structures in affinity matrices, and such matrices are nothing but adjacency matrices of weighted complete graphs.

Finally, our algorithm is not constrained to work with only symmetric matrices and so provides a versatile tool for community detection in directed graphs even when these graphs have unbalanced flows, i.e. an imbalance between links that enter and then leave a subgroup. Moreover, WT and ML, which both symmetrize the matrix by working on $A + A^T$, produce spurious results in this case.

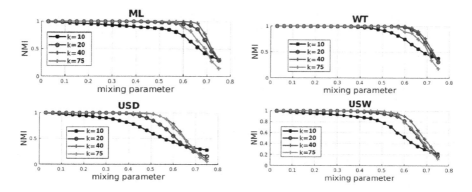

Fig. 8. NMI curves of ML, WT, USd, USw for some $\overline{k}$ values

An example is shown in Fig. 9, where two communities are connected in an asymmetric fashion, and the partitions suggested by the algorithms are shown. Thus by working on the normal equations of the scaled matrix we are able to perfectly detect the community structure of the graph, while both WT and ML fail.

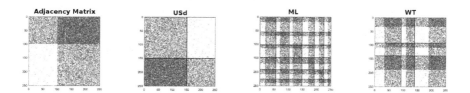

Fig. 9. Detecting asymmetric clusters

5.2 Shape Detection

To show the potential of our algorithm for other clustering tasks, we have tested it on datasets from the `Scikit-learn` package [25]. To enable a quick visual validation, we have used it to detect, through their affinity matrices, coherent clouds of points in two dimensions with 1500 points for each dataset. The affinity matrix [24] of a set of points $\{x_i \in \mathbb{R}^p, i = 1...n\}$ is the symmetric matrix with zeros on the diagonal and

$$\mathbf{A}_{i,j} = \exp\left(-\frac{\|x_i - x_j\|^2}{2\sigma^2}\right),$$

elsewhere. The accuracy of our method strongly depends on the choice of the Gaussian parameter σ. We follow the prescription in [21] to take into account both density and dimension of the dataset. Since the affinity matrix has a zero diagonal we enforce bi-irreducibility as before by adding 10^{-8} to the diagonal.

As for community detection, we preprocess by removing dominant entries in the scaled matrix. In postprocessing we reassign these entries to the cluster that contains their closest neighbour in Euclidean distance.

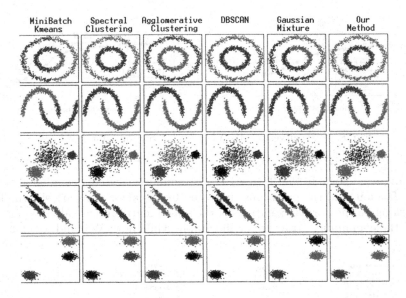

Fig. 10. Comparison between clustering algorithms

As a baseline, we have compared it with the clustering algorithms from the Scikit-learn package. The results for five of these algorithms are provided in Fig. 10. Here each row corresponds to a specific two-dimensional dataset, and each column to an algorithm. The points are coloured with respect to the cluster they have been assigned by the algorithm. The rightmost column gives the results for our method when we stop after the analysis of a single eigenvector. It is clear that this vector provides enough information to roughly separate the data into coherent clusters for all the datasets whatever their shape. The NMI is given in Table 2, following the same order as in Fig. 10 for the datasets. We see that our algorithm always achieves the best score except for two datasets: the fourth for which one element has been misplaced by the postprocessing and the third for which our algorithm still has a NMI larger than 0.9. We also note that, except for DBSCAN, all these algorithms need to know the number of clusters.

Table 2. NMI for the clusterings shown in Fig. 10

MiniBatch Kmeans	Spectral Clust.	Agglo. Clust.	DB SCAN	Gaussian mixture	Our method
2.9×10^{-4}	1	0.993	1	1.3×10^{-6}	1
0.39	1	1	1	0.401	1
0.813	0.915	0.898	0.664	**0.942**	0.902
0.608	0.942	0.534	0.955	1	0.996
1	1	1	1	1	1

6   Conclusions

We have developed a spectral clustering algorithm that is able to partition a matrix by means of only a few singular vectors (sometimes as few as one), mainly thanks to the spectral properties of the doubly-stochastic scaling. Moreover, our method does not need to know the number of clusters in advance and needs no artificial symmetrization of the matrix. We have illustrated the use of our algorithm on standard data analysis problems, where we are competitive with methods specifically designed for these applications. However, it is more versatile than those classical algorithms because it can be applied on matrices from very diverse applications, simply needing adaptive post- and pre-processing to be used on specific applications.

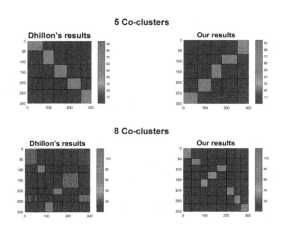

Fig. 11. Detection of co-clusters

In future work we aim to customise our method for co-clustering since it naturally detects rectangular patterns in square matrices. In Fig. 11 we compare our algorithm with the spectral co-clustering algorithm designed by Dhillon in [9]. We observe that Dhillon's algorithm misplaces elements of the 8 cluster matrix whilst our algorithm succeeds in recovering the ground truth structure. While we have to keep in mind that these co-clusterings have to be understood as the overlapping of independent clusterings on the matrix rows and columns, and that it is shown in [10] that the intertwining between row and column clusters is an important factor in co-clustering quality, our preliminary results are most encouraging. A study of the algorithm complexity is ongoing, as well as an efficient implementation. For now, a simple Matlab implementation can be found in the Data Mining section of the webpage http://apo.enseeiht.fr/doku. php?id=software.

References

1. Bagrow, J.P.: Communities and bottlenecks: trees and treelike networks have high modularity. Phys. Rev. E **85**(6), 066118 (2012)
2. Blondel, V.D., Guillaume, J.L., Lambiotte, R., Lefebvre, E.: Fast unfolding of communities in large networks. J. Stat. Mech: Theory Exp. **2008**(10), P10008 (2008)
3. Brin, S., Page, L.: The anatomy of a large-scale hypertextual web search engine. Comput. Netw. ISDN Syst. **30**(1–7), 107–117 (1998)
4. Canny, J.: A computational approach to edge detection. IEEE Trans. Pattern Anal. Mach. Intell. **8**, 679–698 (1986)
5. Clauset, A., Newman, M.E.J., Moore, C.: Finding community structure in very large networks. Phys. Rev. E **70**(6), 066111 (2004)
6. Conde-Cespedes, P.: Modélisation et extension du formalisme de l'analyse relationnelle mathématique à la modularisation des grands graphes. Ph.D thesis, Université Pierre et Marie Curie (2013)
7. Csardi, G., Nepusz, T.: The igraph software package for complex network research. InterJournal Complex Syst. **1695**, 1–9 (2006)
8. Davis, T.A., Hu, Y.: The University of Florida sparse matrix collection. ACM Trans. Math. Softw. **38**(1), 1–14 (2011)
9. Dhillon, I.S.: Co-clustering documents and words using bipartite spectral graph partitioning. In: Proceedings of the Seventh ACM SIGKDD International Conference on Knowledge Discovery and Data Mining, KDD 2001, pp. 269–274. ACM (2001)
10. Dhillon, I.S., Mallela, S., Modha, D.S.: Information-theoretic co-clustering. In: Proceedings of the Ninth ACM SIGKDD International Conference on Knowledge Discovery and Data Mining, KDD 2003, pp. 89–98. ACM (2003)
11. Duff, I., Knight, P., Le Gorrec, L., Mouysset, S., Ruiz, D.: Uncovering hidden block structure. Technical report TR/PA/18/90, CERFACS, August 2018
12. Fortunato, S.: Community detection in graphs. Phys. Rep. **486**(3), 75–174 (2010)
13. Fortunato, S., Barthélemy, M.: Resolution limit in community detection. Proc. Nat. Acad. Sci. **104**(1), 36–41 (2007)
14. Fortunato, S., Hric, D.: Community detection in networks: a user guide. CoRR abs/1608.00163 (2016)
15. Fred, A.L.N., Jain, A.K.: Robust data clustering. In: CVPR, no. 2, pp. 128–136. IEEE Computer Society (2003)
16. Fritzsche, D., Mehrmann, V., Szyld, D.B., Virnik, E.: An SVD approach to identifying metastable states of Markov chains. Electron. Trans. Numer. Anal. **29**, 46–69 (2008)

17. Frobenius, G.: Ueber matrizen aus nicht negativen elementen. Sitzungsber. Königl. Preuss. Akad. Wiss, 456–477 (1912)
18. Knight, P.A., Ruiz, D.: A fast algorithm for matrix balancing. IMA J. Numer. Anal. **33**(3), 1029–1047 (2013)
19. Lancichinetti, A., Fortunato, S., Radicchi, F.: Benchmark graphs for testing community detection algorithms. Phys. Rev. E **78**(4), 046110 (2008)
20. Lei, J., Rinaldo, A., et al.: Consistency of spectral clustering in stochastic block models. Ann. Stat. **43**(1), 215–237 (2015)
21. Mouysset, S., Noailles, J., Ruiz, D.: Using a global parameter for gaussian affinity matrices in spectral clustering. In: Palma, J.M.L.M., Amestoy, P.R., Daydé, M., Mattoso, M., Lopes, J.C. (eds.) VECPAR 2008. LNCS, vol. 5336, pp. 378–390. Springer, Heidelberg (2008). https://doi.org/10.1007/978-3-540-92859-1_34
22. Newman, M.E.J.: Finding community structure in networks using the eigenvectors of matrices. Phys. Rev. E **74**(3), 036104 (2006)
23. Newman, M.: Analysis of weighted networks. Phys. Rev. E **70**, 056131 (2004)
24. Ng, A.Y., Jordan, M.I., Weiss, Y.: On spectral clustering: analysis and an algorithm. In: Proceedings of the 14th International Conference on Neural Information Processing Systems: Natural and Synthetic, NIPS 2001, pp. 849–856. MIT Press (2001)
25. Pedregosa, F., Varoquaux, G., Gramfort, A., Michel, V., Thirion, B., Grisel, O., Blondel, M., Prettenhofer, P., Weiss, R., Dubourg, V., Vanderplas, J., Passos, A., Cournapeau, D., Brucher, M., Perrot, M., Duchesnay, E.: Scikit-learn: machine learning in Python. J. Mach. Learn. Res. **12**, 2825–2830 (2011)
26. Perron, O.: Zur theorie der matrices. Mathematische Annalen **64**(2), 248–263 (1907)
27. Pons, P., Latapy, M.: Computing communities in large networks using random walks (long version). arXiv Physics e-prints, December 2005
28. Schaeffer, S.E.: Graph clustering. Comput. Sci. Rev. **1**(1), 27–64 (2007)
29. Sinkhorn, R., Knopp, P.: Concerning nonnegative matrices and doubly stochastic matrices. Pacific J. Math. **21**, 343–348 (1967)
30. Von Luxburg, U.: A tutorial on spectral clustering. Stat. Comput. **17**(4), 395–416 (2007)
31. Yang, Z., Algesheimer, R., Tessone, C.J.: A comparative analysis of community detection algorithms on artificial networks. Sci. Rep. **6**, 30750 (2016)

CatchCore: Catching Hierarchical Dense Subtensor

Wenjie Feng[1,2(✉)], Shenghua Liu[1,2], and Xueqi Cheng[1,2]

[1] CAS Key Laboratory of Network Data Science and Technology,
Institute of Computing Technology, Chinese Academy of Sciences,
Beijing 100190, China
{fengwenjie,cxq}@ict.ac.cn, liu.shengh@gmail.com
[2] University of Chinese Academy of Sciences (UCAS), Beijing 100049, China

Abstract. Dense subtensor detection gains remarkable success in spotting anomaly and fraudulent behaviors for the multi-aspect data (i.e., tensors), like in social media and event streams. Existing methods detect the densest subtensors flatly and separately, with an underlying assumption that these subtensors are exclusive. However, many real-world scenario usually present hierarchical properties, e.g., the core-periphery structure or dynamic communities in networks. In this paper, we propose CatchCore, a novel framework to effectively find the hierarchical dense subtensors. We first design a unified metric for dense subtensor detection, which can be optimized with gradient-based methods. With the proposed metric, CatchCore detects hierarchical dense subtensors through the hierarchy-wise alternative optimization. Finally, we utilize the minimum description length principle to measure the quality of detection result and select the optimal hierarchical dense subtensors. Extensive experiments on synthetic and real-world datasets demonstrate that CatchCore outperforms the top competitors in accuracy for detecting dense subtensors and anomaly patterns. Additionally, CatchCore identified a hierarchical researcher co-authorship group with intense interactions in DBLP dataset. Also CatchCore scales linearly with all aspects of tensors.

Code of this paper is available at: http://github.com/wenchieh/catchcore.

1 Introduction

Dense subgraph and subtensor detection have been successfully used in a variety of application domains, like detecting the anomaly or fraudulent patterns (e.g., lockstep behavior, boost ratings) in social media or review sites [10,11], identifying malicious attacks in network traffic logs or stream data [20,22], and spotting changing gene-communities in biological networks, etc.

Several algorithms detect the densest subtensors or blocks in a flat manner [11,20–22], i.e., remove-and-redetect one-by-one, with an underlying assumption that these subtensors are exclusive and separate. However, many real-world tensors usually present hierarchical properties, like the core-peripheral structure in networks and dynamic communities in social media. So it will be difficult to identify subtle structures (like multi-layer core) within the dense block

© Springer Nature Switzerland AG 2020
U. Brefeld et al. (Eds.): ECML PKDD 2019, LNAI 11906, pp. 156–172, 2020.
https://doi.org/10.1007/978-3-030-46150-8_10

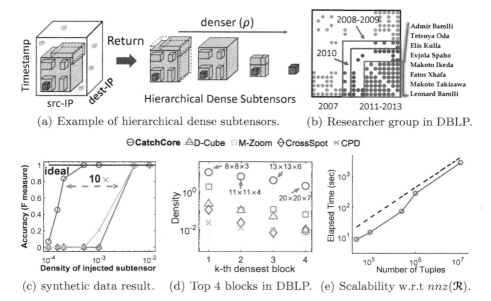

(a) Example of hierarchical dense subtensors.   (b) Researcher group in DBLP.

(c) synthetic data result.   (d) Top 4 blocks in DBLP.   (e) Scalability w.r.t $nnz(\mathcal{R})$.

Fig. 1. Examples and CATCHCORE **Performance Overview.** (a) Example and workflow of hierarchical dense subtensors detection. (b) shows the detected dense co-authorship researcher group (a multi-layer core) of 20 users in DBLP. The densest block (red) last 3 years (2011–2013) containing 8 authors as the list shows, the outer hierarchies (with different colors) include other researchers and exist in various time ranges (text marked). (c) CATCHCORE outperforms competitors for detecting injected blocks in synthetic data, it achieves lower detection bound than others. (d) CATCHCORE detects dense subtensors with higher density compared with baselines for the top four densest blocks in DBLP. These blocks correspond to a hierarchical group as (b) shows. (e) CATCHCORE is linearly scalable w.r.t the number of tuples in tensor. (Color figure online)

and the relations (e.g., overlapping or inclusion) among the different blocks. Meanwhile, other methods for community detection [4, 6, 25] and dense subgraph detection [10, 19, 26] only concentrate on the plain graph.

One challenging problem is how to efficiently detect the hierarchical dense subtensors in the multi-aspect data, and Fig. 1(a) illustrates an example for the TCP dumps scenario. The network intrusion attacks dynamically changed in interacting-intensity at different stages along the time and among various hosts, resulting in a multi-layer and high-density core. So, hierarchical dense subtensor detection can help to understand the process and spot such anomaly patterns.

We propose CATCHCORE, a novel framework to detect hierarchical dense cores in multi-aspect data (i.e. tensors). Our main contributions are as follows:

- **Unified metric and algorithm**: We design a unified metric can be optimized with the gradient methods to detect dense blocks, and propose CATCHCORE for hierarchical dense core detection with theoretical guarantee and MDL based measurement.

- **Accuracy**: CATCHCORE outperforms the state-of-the-art methods in accurately detecting densest blocks and hierarchical dense subtensors in both synthetic and real-world datasets (Fig. 1(c), (d)).
- **Effectiveness**: CATCHCORE successfully spots anomaly patterns, including suspicious friend-connections, periodical network attacks, etc., and found a hierarchical researcher co-authorship group with heavy interactions (Fig. 1(b)).
- **Scalability**: CATCHCORE is scalable, with linear time (Fig. 1(e)) and space complexity with all aspects of tensors (Theorems 7, 8).

Reproducibility: Our open-sourced code and the data we used is available at http://github.com/wenchieh/catchcore (Supplement is also contained).

2   Notions and Concepts

Throughout the paper, vectors are denoted by boldface lowercases (e.g. x), scalars are denoted by lowercase letters (e.g. c), and $\lfloor x \rceil \equiv \{1, \ldots, x\}$ for brevity.

Let $\mathcal{R}(A_1, \ldots, A_N, C)$ be a <u>relation</u> consisting of N dimension attributes denoted by $\{A_1, \ldots, A_N\}$, and the non-negative measure attribute $C \in \mathbb{N}^{\geq 0}$, (see the running example in supplement). We use $\mathcal{R}_n$ to denote the set of distinct values of A_n, whose element is $a_k \in \mathcal{R}_n$. For each entry (tuple) $t \in \mathcal{R}$ and for each $n \in \lfloor N \rceil$, we use $t[A_n]$ and $t[C]$ to denote the values of A_n and C respectively in t, i.e. $t[A_n] = a_n$ and $t[C] = c$. Thus, the relation $\mathcal{R}$ is actually represented as an N-way tensor of size $|\mathcal{R}_1| \times \cdots \times |\mathcal{R}_N|$, and the value of each entry in the tensor is $t[C]$. Let $\mathcal{R}(n, a_n) = \{t \in \mathcal{R}; t[A_n] = a_n\}$ denote all the entries of $\mathcal{R}$ where its attribute A_n is fixed to be a_n. We define the mass of $\mathcal{R}$ as $M_{\mathcal{B}} = \sum_{t \in \mathcal{R}} t[C]$, the volume of $\mathcal{R}$ as $V_{\mathcal{R}} = \prod_{n=1}^{N} |\mathcal{R}_n|$, and the cardinality of $\mathcal{R}$ as $D_{\mathcal{R}} = \sum_{n=1}^{N} |\mathcal{R}_n|$.

For a <u>subtensor</u> $\mathcal{B}$, which is composed of the subset of attributes in $\mathcal{R}$, is defined as $\mathcal{B} = \{t \in \mathcal{R}; t[A_n] \in \mathcal{B}_n, \forall n \in \lfloor N \rceil\}$, i.e. the set of tuples where each attribute A_n has a value in $\mathcal{B}_n$. We use $\mathcal{B} \preccurlyeq \mathcal{R}$ to describe that $\mathcal{B}$ is the subtensor of $\mathcal{R}$. Mathematically, for any $n \in \lfloor N \rceil$, we can use a indicator vector $x \in \{0, 1\}^{|\mathcal{R}_n|}$ to denote whether any $a_n \in \mathcal{R}_n$ belongs to $\mathcal{B}_n$, and $x[a_n] = 1$ iff $\mathcal{B}(n, a_n) \subseteq \mathcal{R}(n, a_n)$. Thus the inclusion relationship between $\mathcal{B}$ and $\mathcal{R}$ can be represented with an indicator vectors collection $\mathbf{X}_{\mathcal{B}} = \{x_n \in \{0, 1\}^{|\mathcal{R}_n|}; \forall n \in \lfloor N \rceil\}$. Specially, $\mathbf{X}_0 = \{\{0\}^{|\mathcal{R}_n|}; \forall n \in \lfloor N \rceil\}$ corresponds to **NULL** tensor ($\emptyset$), and $\mathbf{X}_1 = \{\{1\}^{|\mathcal{R}_n|}; \forall n \in \lfloor N \rceil\}$ corresponds to $\mathcal{R}$.

Given an indicator vector $x \in \{0, 1\}^{|\mathcal{R}_n|}$ for tensor $\mathcal{R}$, the subtensor whose n-th dimension consists of $\{a; x[a] = 1, a \in \mathcal{R}_n\}$ can be denoted as $\mathcal{R} \times_n x$, where "$\times_n$" is the *n-mode product* for a tensor and a vector[1].

3   Framework and Formulation

In this section, we propose a unified metric, which can be optimized with the gradient methods, to detect dense blocks, then we give the formal definition of the hierarchical dense subtensors detection problem.

---

[1] Entrywise, the n-mode product between the tensor $\mathcal{R}$ and vector x can be denoted as: $(\mathcal{R} \times_n x)_{i_1 \ldots i_{n-1} i_{n+1} \ldots i_N} = \sum_{i_n=1}^{|\mathcal{R}_n|} t(i_1, \cdots, i_N, c) x_{i_n}$.

3.1   Densest Subtensor Detection Framework

Let $\mathcal{R}$ is an N-way tensor, and $\mathcal{B}$ is the subtensor of $\mathcal{R}$ defined by the indicator vectors collection $\mathbf{X}_{\mathcal{B}}$. Then the mass $M_{\mathcal{B}}$ can be represented as $M_{\mathcal{B}} = \mathcal{R} \,\bar{\times}\, \mathbf{X}_{\mathcal{B}} = \mathcal{R} \times_1 \boldsymbol{x}_1 \cdots \times_N \boldsymbol{x}_N$, where the *full-mode product* $\bar{\times}$ applies the n-mode tensor-vector product $\times_n$ to indicator vectors along the corresponding dimension[2]. We propose the following unified metric inspired by [24],

Definition 1 (Entry-Plenum). *Assume $\mathbf{X}$ is an indicator vectors collection for some subtensor in $\mathcal{R}$, and $\phi > 0$ is a constant. Given any two strictly increasing functions g and h, the entry-plenum is defined as:*

$$f_\phi(\mathbf{X}) = \begin{cases} 0 & \mathbf{X} = \mathbf{X}_0, \\ g(M_\mathbf{X}) - \phi \cdot h(S_\mathbf{X}) & \text{otherwise.} \end{cases} \tag{1}$$

where $M_\mathbf{X}$ is the mass and $S_\mathbf{X}$ is the size of subtensor defined by $\mathbf{X}$ in $\mathcal{R}$, and $S_\mathbf{X}$ can be $V_\mathbf{X}$, $D_\mathbf{X}$ or other forms.

Most popular existing subtensor density measures [11,20,21] can be subsumed into the above definition as

- Let $g(x) = \log x, h(x) = \log \frac{x}{N}, \phi = 1$ and $S_\mathbf{X} = D_\mathbf{X}$, $f_\phi(\mathcal{B})$ is equal to the *arithmetic average mass* $\rho_{ari}(\mathcal{B}) = M_{\mathcal{B}}/(D_{\mathcal{B}}/N)$.
- Let $g(x) = h(x) = \log x$, $S_\mathbf{X} = V_\mathbf{X}$, if $\phi = 1$, then $f_\phi(\mathcal{B})$ corresponds to *volume density* $\rho_{vol}(\mathcal{B}) = M_{\mathcal{B}}/V_{\mathcal{B}}$; and if set $\phi = \frac{1}{N}$, the $f_\phi(\mathcal{B})$ comes down to the *geometric average mass* $\rho_{geo}(\mathcal{B}) = M_{\mathcal{B}}/V_{\mathcal{B}}^{1/N}$.

In principle, for the entry-plenum definition, the first term $g(M_\mathbf{X})$ favors subtensors with the large mass, whereas the second term $-\phi \cdot h(S_\mathbf{X})$ acts as regularization to penalize large-size block. Thus, detecting the densest subtensor can be rewritten as the following problem under the entry-plenum metric.

Problem 2 (Densest (g, h, ϕ)-entry-plenum Subtensor). Given an N-way tensor $\mathcal{R}$, a constant $\phi > 0$, and a pair of increasing functions g and h, find an indicator vectors collection $\mathbf{X}^*$ such that $f_\phi(\mathbf{X}^*) \geq f_\phi(\mathbf{X})$ for all feasible $\mathbf{X} = \{\boldsymbol{x}_n \in \{0,1\}^{|\mathcal{R}_n|} : \forall n \in \lfloor N \rceil\}$. The subtensor derived from $\mathbf{X}^*$ is referred to be as the **Densest (g, h, ϕ)-entry-plenum Subtensor** of the tensor $\mathcal{R}$.

In general, finding the densest block in terms of some measure is NP-hard [2,20], infeasible for the large dataset. Existing methods [10,20,21] resort to greedy approximation algorithm, which iteratively selects the local optimal subtensor from candidates based on some density measure defined in the ratio form, for scalability. Instead, our framework formulates the densest subtensor detection problem in an optimization perspective as follows, it utilizes the indicator vectors collection $\mathbf{X}$, which can be treated as a block-variable, to make the above problem can be solved through *block-nonlinear Gauss-Seidel (GS) method* [9] with convergence guarantee by introducing relaxation. $M_\mathbf{X}$ and $S_\mathbf{X}$ are derivable to each indicator vector under this condition, and we can use gradient-based optimization strategy for updating as long as the g and h are differentiable. Moreover, this process is linearly scalable as our proposed CATCHCORE does in Sect. 4.5.

---

[2] We use $\bar{\times}_{(-n)}$ to denote conducting full-mode product except the n-th mode.

3.2 Hierarchical Dense Subtensor Detection

In practice, different dense blocks in $\mathcal{R}$ may be overlapping or even inclusive rather than being separate or flat as many dense-block detection methods [11,20,21] assumed, whereas they can be described by the *hierarchical dense subtensors*. We present the following example and definition to manifest the hierarchical structure in multi-aspect data, and Fig. 1(a) gives a pictorial illustration.

Example 3 (Network Intrusion). The DARPA dataset contains 60% records labeled as anomalous belonging to (attacks), which mostly occurred in infrequent bursts, and dominant by 9 types of attacks, like `neptune`, `smurf`, and `satan` etc. These different attacks had various intrusion intensity and burst activities among hosts, leading to discriminative dense patterns at various time ranges.

Given an N-way tensor $\mathcal{R}$, we want to find the dense subtensors, comprising a set of different entries, in several hierarchies. We use $\rho(\mathcal{B})$ to denote the density of subtensor $\mathcal{B}$, and $\mathcal{B}^k$ as the kth-hierarchy dense subtensor in $\mathcal{R}$. In order to find some meaningful patterns and to avoid getting identical subtensors across distinct hierarchies, we have following definition.

Definition 4 (Hierarchical Dense Subtensors (HDS-tensors)). *Given the tensor $\mathcal{B}^0 \leftarrow \mathcal{R}$ and a constant $K \in \mathbb{N}^+$. For any $k \in \lfloor K \rceil$, the $\mathcal{B}^{k-1}$ and $\mathcal{B}^k$ are subtensors in two adjacent hierarchies, it is required that*

(i) **density:** *the densities should be significantly different from each other, that is, for some $\eta > 1$, $\rho(\mathcal{B}^k) \geq \eta\rho(\mathcal{B}^{k-1})$.*
(ii) **structure:** *subtensors in higher hierarchies are more "close-knit" (multi-layer dense core) $\mathcal{B}^k \preccurlyeq \mathcal{B}^{k-1}$, i.e., $\mathcal{B}_n^k \subseteq \mathcal{B}_n^{k-1}, \forall n \in \lfloor N \rceil$.*

*Thus, all subtensors in K hierarchies consist of **Hierarchical Dense Subtensors**.*

Noteworthy is the fact that it is *not feasible* to recursively apply off-the-shelf dense subtensor detection methods to find HDS-tensors since they do not consider the relationship among different blocks, even if possible, it might return trivial results (e.g. identical dense subtensors across distinct hierarchies); and how to design the overall objective function to be optimized by the recursive heuristic is also not clear.

Formally, with the indicator vectors collection $\mathbf{X}^k$ denoting the dense subtensor $\mathcal{B}^k$, the HDS-tensors detection problem is defined as follows.

Problem 5 (HDS-tensors Detection). **Given:** (1) the input N-way tensor $\mathcal{R}$, (2) the expected density ratio between two adjacent hierarchies η^3, (3) the maximum number of hierarchies K. **Find:** the indicator vectors collections $\{\mathbf{X}^1, \ldots, \mathbf{X}^r\}$, $r \leq K$ for hierarchical dense subtensors in the r significant hierarchies.

---

[3] More generally, we can also set different density ratios between hierarchies rather than the fixed one parameter for specific concern.

We require that $\rho(\mathbf{X}^r) \geq \eta \rho(\mathbf{X}^{r-1}) \geq \cdots \geq \eta^{r-1} \rho(\mathbf{X}^1)$, and $\mathbf{X}^r \preccurlyeq \cdots \preccurlyeq \mathbf{X}^1$.

In addition, we define a three-level coordinate (k, n, i) to index the indicator vectors collections, i.e., $\mathbf{X}_{(k,n,i)}$ denotes the i-th scalar element x_i of the n-th indicator vector $\boldsymbol{x}_n$ in $\mathbf{X}^k$. Also, $\mathbf{X}_{(k,\cdot,\cdot)}$ and $\mathbf{X}_{(k,n,\cdot)}$ represent $\mathbf{X}^k$ and indicator vector $\boldsymbol{x}_n$ of $\mathbf{X}^k$ respectively.

4 Proposed Method

In this section, we propose an optimization based algorithm, CATCHCORE, to detect HDS-tensors, and provide analysis for the properties of CATCHCORE.

4.1 Optimization Based Dense Subtensor Detection

Here, we provide an **interpretable instantiation** for the entry-plenum metric based on the volume density. With the indicator vectors collection $\mathbf{X}_{\mathcal{B}}$ of subtensor $\mathcal{B}$, the density is represented as $\rho_{\mathcal{B}} = \frac{M_{\mathcal{B}}}{V_{\mathcal{B}}} = \frac{M_{\mathcal{B}}}{\prod_{x \in \mathbf{X}_{\mathcal{B}}} \|x\|_1}$, where $V_{\mathcal{B}}$ is the product of the size of indicator vector for each mode, i.e, $\prod_{x \in \mathbf{X}_{\mathcal{B}}} \|x\|_1$, which equals to the total number of possible entries (including zeros).

To find the dense subtensor, if we directly maximize the density measure $\rho_{\mathcal{B}}$, however, it leads to some trivial solutions (the entries with maximum measure value, or any single entry in binary-valued tensor); while maximize the vector-based subtensor mass $M_{\mathcal{B}}$ by optimizing $\mathbf{X}_{\mathcal{B}}$ will also engender another trivial result—the $\mathcal{R}$ itself, since no any size or volume limitation is taken into account.

Intuitively, we need to **maximize** the mass of entries while **minimize** the mass of missing entries in the block. So we proposed the optimization goal as

$$\max_{\mathbf{X}} \mathcal{F}(\mathbf{X}) = (1+p)\mathcal{R} \bar{\times} \mathbf{X} - p \prod_{\boldsymbol{x}_n \in \mathbf{X}} \|\boldsymbol{x}_n\|_1 \, ; \text{ s.t.} \boldsymbol{x}_n \in \{0,1\}^{|\mathcal{R}_n|}, \forall n \in \lfloor N \rfloor.$$

(2)

where $p > 0$ is the penalty parameter, and $\mathbf{X} = \{\boldsymbol{x}_1, \ldots, \boldsymbol{x}_N\}$.

The rationale behind above definition is that each existing entry t in the resultant subtensor contributes $t[C]$ as itself to $\mathcal{F}(\mathbf{X})$, while each missing one $\tilde{t}$ is penalized by p (i.e. $\tilde{t}[C] = -p$). In this way, the objective function maximize the total mass in the resultant subtensor while minimizing the total penalty of the missing entries. Moreover, it is also an instantiation of densest (g, h, ϕ)-entry-plenum subtensor by setting $g(x) = h(x) = x, \phi = p/(1+p)$, and $S_{\mathbf{X}} = V_X$.

The optimization of the objective function $\mathcal{F}(\cdot)$ is an *NP-hard* problem due to the combinatorial nature stemming from the binary constraints of $\boldsymbol{x}_n$. So, we relax these constraints from a 0–1 integer programming to a polynomial-time solvable linear programming problem, i.e., $\mathbf{0}^{|\mathcal{R}_n|} \leq \boldsymbol{x}_n \leq \mathbf{1}^{|\mathcal{R}_n|}$, which represents the probability that the slice $\mathcal{R}(n, a_n)$ belonging to the resultant dense block. Finally, only the attribute value with probability exactly 1 will be selected.

4.2   Hierarchical Dense Subtensors Detection

Based on the optimization formulation for finding dense subtensor in one hierarchy, intuitively, we maximize the objective function in Eq. (2) for each hierarchy to detect K hierarchical dense subtensors, i.e. to maximize $\sum_{k=1}^{K} \mathcal{F}(\mathbf{X}^k)$, and also consider aforementioned prerequisites of HDS-tensors. The *density* constraint is represented as $\rho_{\mathbf{X}^{k+1}} \geq \eta \rho_{\mathbf{X}^k}$ for the kth hierarchy with density increase ratio $\eta > 1$; and for the *structure* requirement $(\mathcal{B}^{k+1} \preccurlyeq \mathcal{B}^k \preccurlyeq \mathcal{B}^{k-1})$, we impose additional constraints on indicator vectors to prevent identical results, as $\mathbf{X}_{(k+1,n,\cdot)} \leq \mathbf{X}_{(k,n,\cdot)} \leq \mathbf{X}_{(k-1,n,\cdot)}, \forall n \in \lfloor N \rfloor$. We assume $\mathbf{X}^0 = \mathbf{X_1}, \mathbf{X}^{K+1} = \mathbf{X_0}$.

Consequently, the overall optimization formulation is defined as follows,

$$\max_{\mathbf{X}^1,...,\mathbf{X}^K} \sum_{k=1}^{K} \mathcal{F}(\mathbf{X}^k)$$

$$\text{s.t. } \rho_{\mathbf{X}^{h+1}} \geq \eta \rho_{\mathbf{X}^h}, \ \mathbf{X}_{(h+1,n,\cdot)} \leq \mathbf{X}_{(h,n,\cdot)} \leq \mathbf{X}_{(h-1,n,\cdot)}. \ \forall h \in \lfloor K \rfloor; n \in \lfloor N \rfloor.$$

Obviously, this *bound-constrained multi-variable nonlinear programming (BMV-NLP)* optimization problem is non-convex and numerically intractable to solve. So we take following relaxation for the constraint to make it to be a regularization term in the objective function. Let $d^{k-1} = \eta \rho_{\mathbf{X}^{k-1}}$ which is a constant w.r.t $\mathbf{X}^k$, so the regularization term can be written as (also with entry-plenum form) $\mathcal{G}(\mathbf{X}^k) = \mathcal{R} \bar{\times} \mathbf{X}^k - d^{k-1} \prod_{n=1}^{N} \left\| \mathbf{X}_{(k,n,\cdot)} \right\|_1$. Thus, the resultant objective function with relaxation constraints for HDS-tensors detection is given by

$$\max_{\mathbf{X}^1,...,\mathbf{X}^K} \sum_{k=1}^{K} \mathcal{F}(\mathbf{X}^k) + \lambda \sum_{j=2}^{K} \mathcal{G}(\mathbf{X}^j) \tag{3}$$

$$\text{s.t. } \mathbf{X}_{(h+1,n,\cdot)} \leq \mathbf{X}_{(h,n,\cdot)} \leq \mathbf{X}_{(h-1,n,\cdot)}. \ \forall h \in \lfloor K \rfloor; n \in \lfloor N \rfloor.$$

where the parameter λ controls the importance of the regularization term.

4.3   Optimization Algorithms

In this section, we first explain the optimization techniques, and then present the algorithm CATCHCORE (as Algorithm 1 summarized) to solve the problem.

Using the programming methods to solve the BMV-NLP optimization problem, the objective in Eq. (3) is a non-convex and higher-order bounded function with respect to each indicator vectors collection $\mathbf{X}_{(k,\cdot,\cdot)}$, which allows us to apply the alternative update method where we fix all variables of other hierarchies as constants except the current collections in each iteration; the similar strategy is also used to update each indicator vector $\mathbf{X}_{(k,n,\cdot)}$ alternatively.

Based on the *structure* constraints, for any dimension $n \in \lfloor N \rfloor$, the feasible solution $\mathbf{X}_{(k,n,\cdot)}$ is bounded by the indicator vectors $\mathbf{X}_{(k-1,n,\cdot)}$ and $\mathbf{X}_{(k+1,n,\cdot)}$ of two adjacent hierarchies in the high-dimensional space. We relax these constraints to $\mathbf{0}^{|\mathcal{R}_n|} \leq \mathbf{X}_{(k,n,\cdot)} \leq \mathbf{X}_{(k-1,n,\cdot)}$ for optimizing, thus we can obtain

---

Algorithm 1. CatchCore for HDS-tensors detection

Input: (1) the N-way tensor: $\mathcal{R}$ (2) the maximum number of hierarchies: K
        (3) the penalty value for each missing entry: p
        (4) the density ratio between two adjacent hierarchies: η
        (5) the regularization parameter: λ (6) maximum number of iterations: $t_{\max}$
Output: The dense subtensors indicator vector collections: $\{\mathbf{X}^1, \cdots, \mathbf{X}^r\}$.
 1: initialize $\mathbf{X}^1, \cdots, \mathbf{X}^K$ as $\mathbf{X}_{(k,n,\cdot)}^{\text{init}}$, and $t \leftarrow 1$, $r \leftarrow 1$
 2: **while** $t \leq t_{\max}$ **and** Eq. (5) is not satisfied **do**   ▷ Gauss-Seidel method
 3:    **for** $k \leftarrow 1 \ldots K$ **do**   ▷ for the kth hierarchy
 4:       **for** $n \leftarrow 1 \ldots N$ **do**   ▷ for the nth dimension
 5:          $\boldsymbol{x}_n^k \leftarrow \text{OneWayOpt}(\boldsymbol{x}_n^k)$
 6:       update $\mathbf{X}^k$
 7:    $t \leftarrow t + 1$
 8: **while** $r \leq K$ **do**   ▷ select significant subtensors
 9:    $\mathcal{S} = \{\mathbf{X}_{(r,n,\cdot)}; \max \mathbf{X}_{(r,n,\cdot)} < 1, \forall n \in \lfloor N \rfloor\}$
10:    **if** $\mathcal{S} \neq \varnothing$ **then**
11:       **break**   ▷ no significant subtensors for hierarchies $> r$
12:    **else:**
13:       $r \leftarrow r + 1$
14: **return** the resultant r indicator vector collections $\{\mathbf{X}^1, \cdots, \mathbf{X}^r\}$.

$\mathbf{X}^1, \mathbf{X}^2, \cdots, \mathbf{X}^K$ in order. That is, we first get $\mathbf{X}^1$ with the constraints $\{\mathbf{0}^{|\mathcal{R}_n|} \leq \mathbf{X}_{(1,n,\cdot)} \leq \mathbf{1}^{|\mathcal{R}_n|}, \forall n \in \lfloor N \rfloor\}$ by ignoring the constraints of other variables in other $\mathbf{X}^k$s, then we obtain $\mathbf{X}^2$ based on the result at the first step under the constraints $\{\mathbf{0}^{|\mathcal{R}_n|} \leq \mathbf{X}_{(2,n,\cdot)} \leq \mathbf{X}_{(1,n,\cdot)}, \forall n \in \lfloor N \rfloor\}$ and also ignore other constraints. In this way, we can solve the K dense subtensors detection subproblems hierarchy-by-hierarchy. Technically, we adopt trust-region approach [5] to solve each nonlinear box-constrained programming subproblem. We rewrite the optimization problem in Eq. (3) as,

$$\min_{\mathbf{X}^1, \ldots, \mathbf{X}^K} f(\mathbf{X}^1, \ldots, \mathbf{X}^K) = -(1+p)\mathcal{R} \bar{\times} \mathbf{X}_{(1,\cdot,\cdot)} + p \prod_{n=1}^{N} ||\mathbf{X}_{(1,n,\cdot)}||_1$$

$$- (1+p+\lambda) \sum_{k=2}^{K} \mathcal{R} \bar{\times} \mathbf{X}_{(k,\cdot,\cdot)} + \sum_{k=2}^{K} (p + \lambda d^{k-1}) \prod_{n=1}^{N} ||\mathbf{X}_{(k,n,\cdot)}||_1 \qquad (4)$$

$$\text{s.t. } \mathbf{X}_{(h+1,n,\cdot)} \leq \mathbf{X}_{(h,n,\cdot)} \leq \mathbf{X}_{(h-1,n,\cdot)}. \qquad \forall h \in \lfloor K \rfloor; n \in \lfloor N \rfloor.$$

We use the alternative projected gradient descent [15,16] method that is simple and efficient to solve the optimization problem. For any dimension n, we denote the gradient of subtensor mass $M_{\mathcal{B}}$ w.r.t $\boldsymbol{x}_n$ as $\nabla_{\boldsymbol{x}_n} M_{\mathcal{B}} = \mathcal{R} \bar{\times}_{(-n)} \mathbf{X}_{\mathcal{B}}$, so the gradient of $f(\cdot)$ w.r.t $\boldsymbol{x}_n^1$ ($\mathbf{X}_{(1,n,\cdot)}$) and $\boldsymbol{x}_n^k$ ($\mathbf{X}_{(k,n,\cdot)}, k \geq 2$) are

$$\nabla_{\boldsymbol{x}_n^1} f = -(1+p)\nabla_{\boldsymbol{x}_n^1} M_{\mathbf{X}^1} + p \prod_{\boldsymbol{x}_n \in \mathbf{X}^1/\{\boldsymbol{x}_n^1\}} \|\boldsymbol{x}_n\|_1 \mathbf{1},$$

$$\nabla_{\boldsymbol{x}_n^k} f = -(1+p+\lambda)\nabla_{\boldsymbol{x}_n^k} M_{\mathbf{X}^k} + (p+\lambda d^{k-1}) \prod_{\boldsymbol{x}_n \in \mathbf{X}^k/\{\boldsymbol{x}_n^k\}} \|\boldsymbol{x}_n\|_1 \mathbf{1}$$

where $\mathbf{1}$ is a $|\mathfrak{R}_n|$-dimensional all-ones vector. Let $\boldsymbol{x}_n$ be the current iterator vector of any k^{th} hierarchy in the projected gradient approach, the new iterator is given by $\tilde{\boldsymbol{x}}_n = P(\boldsymbol{x}_n - \alpha\nabla_{\boldsymbol{x}_n} f)$ update rule. Here, the operator $P(\cdot)$ projects the vector back to the bounded feasible region, $-\nabla_{\boldsymbol{x}_n} f$ is the gradient-related search direction and α is a step size computed e.g., by means of an Armijo step size strategy. In the case of an Armijo's rule line search, a good step size α is chosen until $f(\cdot, \mathbf{X}_{\boldsymbol{x}_n \to \tilde{\boldsymbol{x}}_n}^k, \cdot) - f(\cdot, \mathbf{X}^k, \cdot) \leq \sigma(\nabla_{\boldsymbol{x}_n} f)^T(\tilde{\boldsymbol{x}}_n - \boldsymbol{x}_n)$ is satisfied, where $\mathbf{X}_{\boldsymbol{x}_n \to \tilde{\boldsymbol{x}}_n}^k$ means replacing the indicator vector $\boldsymbol{x}_n$ with the updated version $\tilde{\boldsymbol{x}}_n$ in $\mathbf{X}^k$, and a common choice of the parameter σ $(0 < \sigma < 1)$ is 0.01. Thus we can alternatively update each indicator vector $\boldsymbol{x}_n$ for the current k^{th}-hierarchy, and the details are listed in the ONEWAYOPT algorithm in supplement.

We propose CATCHCORE to solve the optimization problem in Eq. (4), First, we initialize the indicator vectors collection with rules that the probabilities of selecting the slices $\mathfrak{R}(n, a_n)$ (i.e. $\mathbf{X}_{(k,n,i)}^{\text{init}}$) are 0.5 in the 1st hierarchy and 0.01 in other hierarchies. In this way, we can fairly avoid some trivial results. To make the solution to be close to the stationary point regarding convergence, we apply the following common condition as a stop criteria for the bounded-constrained optimization method besides the limitation for total iterations $t_{\max}$.

$$\left\| \left\{ \nabla_{\boldsymbol{x}_n^k}^P f; \forall n, k \right\} \right\|_2 \leq \epsilon \left\| \left\{ \nabla_{\mathbf{X}_{(k,n,\cdot)}^{\text{init}}}^P f; \forall n, k \right\} \right\|_2, \tag{5}$$

where $\nabla_{\boldsymbol{x}_n^k}^P f$ is the *elementwise projected gradient* defined as (the i-th element)

$$(\nabla_{\boldsymbol{x}_n^k}^P f)_i = \begin{cases} \min(0, (\nabla_{\boldsymbol{x}_n^k}^P f)_i) & \text{if } \mathbf{X}_{(k,n,i)} = \mathbf{X}_{(k+1,n,i)}, \\ (\nabla_{\boldsymbol{x}_n^k}^P f)_i & \text{if } \mathbf{X}_{(k+1,n,i)} < \mathbf{X}_{(k,n,i)} < \mathbf{X}_{(k-1,n,i)}, \\ \max(0, (\nabla_{\boldsymbol{x}_n^k}^P f)_i) & \text{if } \mathbf{X}_{(k,n,i)} = \mathbf{X}_{(k-1,n,i)}. \end{cases}$$

Then CATCHCORE calls ONEWAYOPT to alternatively update all the indicator vector for each dimension and hierarchy iteratively. In final, we only select these significant subtensors (the top r of K hierarchies) to return (Line 8–13).

4.4   Parameters Evaluation Using MDL

The penalty value p for missing entries controls the resultant lowest density, and the ratio parameter η affects density-diversity and the number of hierarchies in final. Thus, it is a challenging problem to set them appropriately or evaluate the quality of detection result under some parameter configuration, especially in the un-supervised application. We propose to measure the result w.r.t different parameter settings based on the Minimum Description Length (MDL). In the principle manner, we compute the number of bits needed to encode the tensor $\mathcal{R}$ with detected hierarchical dense subtensors for selecting the best model (parameters), achieving the shortest code length. Intuitively, the less missing entries and the more accurate of detecting hierarchies will lead to fewer bits needed to encode $\mathcal{R}$ in a lossless compression employing the characterization.

For the indicator vector $\mathbf{X}_{(k,n,\cdot)}$ ($k \in \lfloor K \rceil$, $n \in \lfloor N \rceil$), we can adopt Huffman or arithmetic coding to encode the binary string, which formally can be viewed as a sequence of realizations of a binomial random variable X. Due to $\mathbf{X}_{(k,n,\cdot)} \le \mathbf{X}_{(k-1,n,\cdot)}$, we only consider the overlapping part $\bar{x}_n^k = \{\mathbf{X}_{(k,n,i)}; \mathbf{X}_{(k-1,n,i)} = 1, \forall i \in \lfloor |\mathcal{R}|_n \rceil\}$ to avoid redundant encoding of 0s. We denote the entropy of indicator vector x as: $H(x) = -\sum_{q \in \{0,1\}} P(X=q) \log P(X=q)$, where $P(X = q) = n_q / \|x\|_1$ and n_q is the number of q in x. The description length of $\mathbf{X}^k$ is defined as $L(\mathbf{X}^k) = \sum_{n=1}^{N} \left(\log^* \left\| \mathbf{X}_{(k,n,\cdot)} \right\|_1 + \left\| \mathbf{X}_{(k-1,n,\cdot)} \right\|_1 \cdot H(\bar{x}_n^k) \right)$.[4]

Assume that $\mathbf{X}^{K+1} = \mathbf{X_0}$, For the dense subtensor $\mathcal{B}^k$ defined by $\mathbf{X}^k$, we only need to encode the entries in $\bar{\mathcal{B}}^k = \mathcal{B}^k - \mathcal{B}^{k+1}$ due to $\mathcal{B}^{k+1} \preccurlyeq \mathcal{B}^k$, based on some probability distribution. For the entry $t \in \bar{\mathcal{B}}^k$, specifically, if $t[C] \in \{0,1\}$, t is sampled from binomial distribution; and if $t[C] \in \mathbb{N}^{\ge 0}$, we instead model the data by using the *Poisson* distribution [11] parameterized by the density of $\bar{\mathcal{B}}^k$, i.e. $\rho_{\bar{\mathcal{B}}^k}$. Therefore the code length for encoding $\bar{\mathcal{B}}^k$ is

$$L(\bar{\mathcal{B}}^k) = - \sum_{q \in \{t[C]; t \in \bar{\mathcal{B}}^k\}} n_q \cdot \log P(X=q) + C_{para},$$

where $P(X = q)$ is the probability of q in the probability distribution function $\mathbf{P}$, and C_{para} is for encoding the parameters of $\mathbf{P}$ (like the mean in Poisson).

As for the residual part $\bar{\mathcal{R}} = \mathcal{R} - \mathcal{B}^1$, we use Huffman coding to encode its entries considering the sparsity and discrete properties, the code length is denoted as L_ϵ.

Putting all together, we can write the total code length for representing the tensor $\mathcal{R}$ with the resultant K hierarchies indicator vectors collections as:

$$L(\mathcal{R}; \mathbf{X}^1, \ldots, \mathbf{X}^K) = \log^* K + \sum_{n=1}^{N} \log^* |\mathcal{R}_n| + \sum_{k=1}^{K} L(\mathbf{X}^k) + L(\bar{\mathcal{B}}^k) + L_\epsilon. \quad (6)$$

To get the optimal parameters, we can heuristically conduct a grid search over possible values and pick the configuration that minimizes MDL. We demonstrate that the parameters according to the MDL principle results in optimal quality of detecting HDS-tensors, and the search space is limited.

4.5 Algorithm Analysis

In this section, we provide the analysis for the convergence, the time and space complexity of CATCHCORE. The details of proofs refer to the supplement.

---

[4] $\log^* x$ is the universal code length for an integer x [18].

Table 1. Summary of real-world datasets.

Name	Size	$D_{\mathcal{R}}$	$nnz(\mathcal{R})$	Category
Android	1.32M × 61.3K × 1.28K × 5	1.38M	2.23M	**Rating**
BeerAdvocate	26.5K × 50.8K × 1,472 × 1	78.7K	1.07M	
StackOverflow	545K × 96.7K × 1,154 × 1	643K	1.30M	
DBLP	1.31M × 1.31M × 72	2.63M	18.9M	**Social network**
Youtube	3.22M × 3.22M × 203	6.45M	18.5M	
DARPA	9.48K × 23.4K × 46.6K	79.5K	522K	**TCP dumps**
AirForce	3 × 70 × 11 × 7.20K × 21.5K × 512 × 512	39.7K	863K	

Lemma 6 states the convergence properties of the gradient method for our CATCHCORE.

Lemma 6. CATCHCORE *algorithm converges to a critical point.*

Theorem 7 states the time complexity of CATCHCORE algorithm, which is linear with K, N, and $nnz(\mathcal{R})$—the number of non-zero entries in $\mathcal{R}$. And the space complexity is given in Theorem 8.

Theorem 7 (Worst-case Time Complexity). *Let t_{als} be the number of iterations for Armoji's line search used in the ONEWAYOPT Algorithm for updating any indicator vector, the worst-case time complexity of the CATCHCORE Algorithm 1 is $O(K \cdot N \cdot t_{\max} \cdot t_{\mathrm{als}} \cdot (nnz(\mathcal{R}) + c \cdot D_{\mathcal{R}}))$.*

Theorem 8 (Memory Requirements). *The amount of memory space required by CATCHCORE is $O(nnz(\mathcal{R}) + 2K \cdot D_{\mathcal{R}})$.*

Parameter Analysis: For the maximum significant hierarchies $K_{\max} = \log_\eta(\frac{\max(\mathcal{R})}{\rho_{\mathcal{R}}})$, where $\max(\mathcal{R})$ is the maximum value of measure attributes of $\mathcal{R}$. In practice, we have following observations to ensure the efficiency of CATCHCORE,

○ $nnz(\mathcal{R}) \gg D_{\mathcal{R}}$, $K \ll K_{\max}$, i.e., there is only few significant hierarchies;
○ $t < t_{\max}$, i.e., early stopping for iterations;
○ a small t_{als}, i.e., few iterations for searching the step size.

and the dimension-update (Line 4) could be solved separately, a situation suitable for parallel environment.

5   Experiments

We design experiments to answer the following questions:

– **Q1. Accuracy**: How accurately does CATCHCORE detect HDS-tensors? Does the MDL evaluation select the optimal parameters?
– **Q2. Pattern and anomaly detection**: What patterns does CATCHCORE detect in real-world data? What is behavior of the detected anomalies?
– **Q3. Scalability**: Does CATCHCORE scale linearly with all aspects of data?

Table 2. Hierarchical subtensors detection results for BeerAdvocate dataset.

K	Injected Density	H1				H2					H3				
		CC	D/M	CS	CPD	CC	D	M	CS	CPD	CC	D	M	CS	CPD
	0.05 + 0.01	1	1	1	0.99	1	0.12	0.04	0	0.08					
	0.2 + 0.1	1	0	0.24	0.24	1	1	1	1	0.99					
2	0.7 + 0.1	1	0	0.33	0.33	1	1	1	1	0.52		–			
	1 + 0.05	1	0	0.78	0.78	1	1	1	1	0.99					
	1 + 0.2	1	0	0.79	0.79	1	1	1	1	0.99					
	0.2 + 0.1 + 0.05	1	0	0.26	0.26	1	0	0	0	0	1	1	1	1	0.98
3	1 + 0.2 + 0.01	1	0	0	0	1	0.99	1.0	1.0	0.22	1	0.44	0.43	0.75	0.85
	1 + 0.7 + 0.2	1	0	0	0	1	0	0	0.98	0.98	1	1	1	1	0.99

* The abbreviations mean that CC: CATCHCORE, D: D-CUBE, M: M-ZOOM, CS: CROSSSPOT.
* The injected shape w.r.t density is: 0.01: $1K \times 800 \times 15$, 0.05: $800 \times 600 \times 10$, 0.1: $500 \times 500 \times 5$, 0.2: $300 \times 300 \times 5$, 0.7: $200 \times 100 \times 2$, 1: $100 \times 80 \times 1$.

5.1 Experimental Settings

Baselines: We selected several state-of-the-art methods for dense-block detection as the baselines, including D-CUBE [21], M-ZOOM [20], CROSSSPOT [11], and CP Decomposition (CPD) [12]. In all experiments, a sparse tensor format was used for efficient memory usage, and the ρ_{ari} and ρ_{geo} were used for D-CUBE and M-ZOOM; we used a variant of CROSSSPOT which maximizes the same density metrics and used the CPD result for seed selection as did in [20].

Data: Table 1 summarizes the real-world datasets in our experiments. In *Rating* category, data are 4-way tensors *(user, item, timestamp, rating)*, where entry values are the number of reviews. In *Social network*, data are 3-way tensors *(user, user, timestamps)*, where entry values are the number of interactions (co-authorship/favorite). *DARPA* is the TCP dumps represented with a 3-way tensor *(source IP, destination IP, timestamps)*, where entry values are the number of connections between two IP addresses (hosts). *AirForce* is also a network intrusion dataset, which is represented as a 7-way tensor *(protocol, service, src_ bytes, dst_ bytes, flag, host_ count, src_ count, #connections)*. Timestamps are in minutes for DARPA, in dates for Ratings and Youtube, and in years for DBLP.

5.2 Q1. Accuracy of CATCHCORE

We compare how accurately each method detects injected dense subtensors in the synthetic and real-world datasets.

We randomly and uniformly generated a $5K \times 5K \times 2K$ 3-way tensor $\mathcal{R}$ with a density of $3 \cdot 10^{-6}$. Into $\mathcal{R}$, one $200 \times 300 \times 100$ block is injected with distinct density, for testing the detection bound of each method. Figure 1(c) demonstrated that CATCHCORE effectively detects block as low as a tenth of the density that the best baselines detect, which means that our method can spot such fraudsters with more adversarial effort.

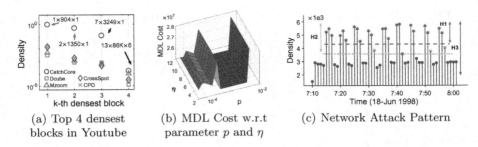

(a) Top 4 densest blocks in Youtube	(b) MDL Cost w.r.t parameter p and η	(c) Network Attack Pattern

Fig. 2. (a) CATCHCORE detects higher-density blocks containing suspicious behaviors. (d) The optimal hierarchies achieve the lowest MDL cost w.r.t p and η. CATCHCORE can obtain optimal hierarchical dense subtensors for a wide parameters range. (c) Detected hierarchical network intrusion attack happened on June 18, 1998 in DARPA dataset.

We then injected K subtensors with different size and density into BeerAdvocate and synthetic tensor in a hierarchical manner. Table 2 lists the result for former (the result for synthetic data is listed in the supplement), where H1 is the densest or the first subtensor detected by methods, and the density (order) decreases (increases) from H1 to H3, and the information of injected blocks is listed at the bottom. CATCHCORE can accurately detect all injected subtensors in various hierarchies, size and density diversity, and consistently outperforms other baselines which fail to accurately detect or even miss at least one block. D-CUBE and M-ZOOM have similar accuracy (except some special cases as highlighted), they can not identify the structure of dense blocks, leading to some of the sparsest or densest injected blocks are missed or overwhelmed by large-volume result. CROSSSPOT and CPD also do not find hierarchical dense subtensors accurately. Similar conclusions can be drawn for the synthetic dataset.

Dense Blocks in Real Data: We apply CATCHCORE for various real-world datasets, and measure the density instead of the mass to avoid the trivial results since that the blocks with higher density contain interesting patterns w.h.p. Figures 1(d) and 2(a) only show the densities of top four densest blocks found by the methods for DBLP and Youtube dataset. CATCHCORE spots denser blocks for each data, where it consistently outperforms the competitors for all blocks.

MDL-based Evaluation. We evaluate the utility of our MDL criterion for measuring the quality of hierarchies returned by CATCHCORE under different parameters. The BeerAdvocate data with 3 hierarchical injected dense blocks (as the $K = 3$ case in Table 2) is used, we computed the MDL cost for the detection result by varying a pair of parameters p and η, the result is shown in Fig. 2. The optimal hierarchies achieve the lowest MDL cost w.r.t p and η. In addition, our model can obtain optimal results for a wide range of parameters.

Table 3. CATCHCORE identifies network attacks from the real-world TCP Dumps dataset with best or comparable performance in F-measure (Left); it spots different hierarchical dense blocks with interesting patterns for DARPA (Right).

	DARPA	AirForce	H	Subtensor Shape	Anomaly Ratio
CPD	0.167	0.785	1	$1 \times 1 \times 96$	100%
CROSSSPOT	0.822	0.785	2	$1 \times 1 \times 100$	100%
M-ZOOM	0.826	0.906	3	$1 \times 1 \times 274$	100%
D-CUBE	0.856	**0.940**	4	$16 \times 5 \times 24.7K$	87.0%
CATCHCORE	**0.877**	0.902	5	$171 \times 15 \times 29.2K$	85.4%

5.3   Q2. Pattern and Anomaly Detection

Anomaly Detection. CATCHCORE detected network intrusion in TCP dumps with high accuracy and identified attack patterns for DARPA and AirForce dataset, where each intrusion connection are labeled. Table 3 compares the accuracy of each method. CATCHCORE outperformed competitors for DARPA data, and also spotted the hierarchical behavior pattern of `Neptune` attack in H1 - H3, which are composed of the connections in different time for a pair of IPs. Figure 2(c) shows the attack pattern snippet occurred during 7am–8am on June 18, 1998. The densities (attack intensity) vary greatly over different hierarchies, i.e. the density in H1 is about 5K, while it is only about 3 K for remain parts in H3. And the intense attacks represented cyclic patterns in 5 min. Although, the hierarchical structure of all subtensors include almost malicious connections (with recall = 98%) with the cost of containing some false positive samples, CATCHCORE achieves comparable performance for AirForce dataset.

CATCHCORE also discerned denser and more anomaly subtensors. For the Youtube in Fig. 2(a), these dense blocks are missed by other competitors. Especially, the block with highest-density (H1) represents one user became friend with 904 users in a day, the other user in H2 also created connections with 475 users at the same time. So, they are more likely fraudulent. The densest block in StackOverflow shows one user marked 257 posts as the favorite in a day, which is too much than the normality. Although some of the densest blocks found may be rank-1 in all but one of the dimensions, CATCHCORE detects holistically optimal multi-layers dense subtensors and the densest one is only part of it rather than our direct target. The volume density tends to non-empty blocks and may result in some locally 1D slices (may not the densest slices within the whole tensor) in the highest-density layer. Other density metrics could eliminate this issue.

Evolving Community Pattern. As the Fig. 1(d), (b) show the evolving co-authorship structure of dense subtensors in the top 4 densest hierarchies for DBLP dataset, corresponding to the interaction between 20 researchers during 2007 to 2013, and Fig. 1(d) also presents their densities. The block in H1 with

the size $8 \times 8 \times 3$, consists of research cooperation between **Leonard Barolli,**
Makoto Takizawa, and **Fatos Xhafa,** etc. during 2011 to 2013 in 'Algorithm
and Distributed System' field and the average connection between them is more
than 10.7 in each year, forming a high-density clique. Also, the subtensors in
other hierarchies are extended with their other common co-authors and years,
and contain relatively less connections than H1, but the density of blocks in
H4 is also more than 2. Therefore, CATCHCORE can cater to detect evolving
community structures at different scales in a hierarchical fashion.

5.4   Q3. Scalability of CATCHCORE

Empirically, we show that CATCHCORE scales (sub-) linearly with every aspect
of input, i.e., the number of tuples, the number of dimension attributes, and the
cardinality of dimension attributes we aim to find. To measure the scalability
with each factor, we started with finding the injected subtensor with two hierarchies, which are $100 \times 100 \times 2$ with density 0.2 and $50 \times 50 \times 1$ with density 1.0,
in a randomly generated tensor $\mathcal{R}$ which contains 1 millions tuples with three
attributes whose total cardinality is 100K. Then, we measured the running time
as we changed one factor at a time. As seen in Fig. 1(e) and result in supplement, CATCHCORE scales linearly with the number of tuples and the number of
attributes, it also scales sub-linearly with the cardinalities of attributes, which
illustrates the complexity of CATCHCORE in Theorem 7 is too pessimistic.

6   Related Work

Dense Subgraph/Subtensor Detection. The detection of dense-subgraph
has been extensively studied [2,7], and many algorithms for the NP-hard problem are applied to detect community structure [3,4,26] and anomaly [1,10],
or extend to multi-aspect data [20–22]. CROSSSPOT [11] finds suspicious dense
blocks by adjusting the seed in a greedy way until converges to a local optimum.
Tensor decomposition such as HOSVD and CP decomposition [12] are also used
to spot dense subtensors. M-ZOOM [20] and D-CUBE [21] adopt greedy approximation algorithm with quality guarantees to detect dense-subtensors for large-
scale tensors. [22] spots dense subtensors for tensor stream with an incremental
algorithm. None of them consider the relationship and structures of different
blocks, and can not trace the evolving of dense subtensors or the hierarchical
patterns.

Hierarchical Patterns Mining. Communities exit ubiquitously in various
graphs [4,14], their evolving behavior and hierarchical structure also have been
explored in different scenes [13,17,25]. [8] proposed a framework for joint learning the overlapping structure and activity period of communities. [23] detected
video event with hierarchical temporal association mining mechanism for multimedia applications. HIDDEN [26] detects hierarchical dense patterns on graph
and also finds financial frauds. [19] uses k-core decomposition to compute the
hierarchy of dense subgraphs given by peeling algorithm. Our method can deal

with multi-aspect data, provide an information-theoretical measurement for the result, and advanced analyze for the performance.

Anomaly and Fraudulent Detection. The survey [1] provides a structured overview and summary for the methods of detection anomaly in graphs. The dense-subgraphs or dense-subtensors usually contain suspicious patterns, such as fraudsters in social network [10,26], port-scanning activities in network analysis [11,21], and lockstep behaviors or vandalism [11,21,22].

7   Conclusions

In this work, we propose CATCHCORE algorithm to detect the hierarchical dense subtensors with gradient optimization strategy, based on an novel and interpretable uniform framework for dense block detection, in large tensor. CATCHCORE accurately detects dense blocks and hierarchical dense subtensors for the synthetic and real data, and outperforms state-of-the-art baseline methods, it can identify anomaly behaviors and interesting patterns, like periodic attack and dynamic researcher group. In addition, CATCHCORE also scales up linearly in term of all aspects of tensor.

Acknowledgments. This material is based upon work supported by the Strategic Priority Research Program of CAS (XDA19020400), NSF of China (61772498, 61425016, 61872206), and the Beijing NSF (4172059).

References

1. Akoglu, L., Tong, H., Koutra, D.: Graph based anomaly detection and description: a survey. In: Data Mining and Knowledge Discovery (2015)
2. Andersen, R., Chellapilla, K.: Finding dense subgraphs with size bounds. WAW
3. Balalau, O.D., Bonchi, F., Chan, T.H.H., Gullo, F., Sozio, M.: Finding subgraphs with maximum total density and limited overlap. In: WSDM 2015 (2015)
4. Chen, J., Saad, Y.: Dense subgraph extraction with application to community detection. IEEE Trans. Knowl. Eng. **24**(7), 1216–1230 (2010)
5. Coleman, T.F., Li, Y.: An interior trust region approach for nonlinear minimization subject to bounds. SIAM J. Optim. **6**(2), 418–445 (1996)
6. Edler, D., Bohlin, L., et al.: Mapping higher-order network flows in memory and multilayer networks with infomap. Algorithms **10**(4), 112 (2017)
7. Gibson, D., Kumar, R., Tomkins, A.: Discovering large dense subgraphs in massive graphs. In: VLDB 2005. VLDB Endowment (2005)
8. Gorovits, A., Gujral, E., Papalexakis, E.E., Bogdanov, P.: LARC: learning activity-regularized overlapping communities across time. In: SIGKDD 2018. ACM (2018)
9. Grippo, L., Sciandrone, M.: On the convergence of the block nonlinear Gauss-Seidel method under convex constraints. Oper. Res. Lett. **26**(3), 127–136 (2000)
10. Hooi, B., Song, H.A., Beutel, A., Shah, N., Shin, K., Faloutsos, C.: FRAUDAR: bounding graph fraud in the face of camouflage. In: SIGKDD 2016, pp. 895–904 (2016)
11. Jiang, M., Beutel, A., Cui, P., Hooi, B., Yang, S., Faloutsos, C.: A general suspiciousness metric for dense blocks in multimodal data. In: ICDM 2015 (2015)

12. Kolda, T.G., Bader, B.W.: Tensor decompositions and applications. In: SIAM (2009)
13. Kumar, R., Novak, J., Tomkins, A.: Structure and evolution of online social networks. In: Link Mining: Models, Algorithms, and Applications (2010)
14. Leskovec, J., Lang, K.J., Dasgupta, A., Mahoney, M.W.: Statistical properties of community structure in large social and information networks. In: WWW (2008)
15. Lin, C.J.: Projected gradient methods for nonnegative matrix factorization. Neural Comput. **19**(10), 2756–2779 (2007)
16. Lin, C.J., Moré, J.J.: Newton's method for large bound-constrained optimization problems. SIAM J. Optim. **9**(4), 1100–1127 (1999)
17. Papadimitriou, S., Sun, J., Faloutsos, C., Yu, P.S.: Hierarchical, parameter-free community discovery. In: Daelemans, W., Goethals, B., Morik, K. (eds.) ECML PKDD 2008. LNCS (LNAI), vol. 5212, pp. 170–187. Springer, Heidelberg (2008). https://doi.org/10.1007/978-3-540-87481-2_12
18. Rissanen, J.: A universal prior for integers and estimation by minimum description length. Ann. Stat. **11**(2), 416–431 (1983)
19. Sariyüce, A.E., Pinar, A.: Fast hierarchy construction for dense subgraphs. VLDB
20. Shin, K., Hooi, B., Faloutsos, C.: M-zoom: fast dense-block detection in tensors with quality guarantees. In: Frasconi, P., Landwehr, N., Manco, G., Vreeken, J. (eds.) ECML PKDD 2016. LNCS (LNAI), vol. 9851, pp. 264–280. Springer, Cham (2016). https://doi.org/10.1007/978-3-319-46128-1_17
21. Shin, K., Hooi, B., Kim, J., Faloutsos, C.: D-cube: Dense-block detection in terabyte-scale tensors. In: WSDM 2017. ACM (2017)
22. Shin, K., Hooi, B., Kim, J., Faloutsos, C.: DenseAlert: incremental dense-subtensor detection in tensor streams (2017)
23. Siddique, B., Akhtar, N.: Temporal hierarchical event detection of timestamped data. In: ICCCA 2017 (2017)
24. Tsourakakis, C., Bonchi, F., Gionis, A., Gullo, F., Tsiarli, M.: Denser than the densest subgraph: extracting optimal quasi-cliques with quality guarantees. In: SIGKDD 2013. ACM (2013)
25. Yang, B., Di, J., Liu, J., Liu, D.: Hierarchical community detection with applications to real-world network analysis. In: DKE (2013)
26. Zhang, S., et al.: Hidden: hierarchical dense subgraph detection with application to financial fraud detection. In: SDM 2017. SIAM (2017)

Fast and Parallelizable Ranking with Outliers from Pairwise Comparisons

Sungjin Im$^{(\boxtimes)}$ and Mahshid Montazer Qaem

EECS, University of California, 5200 N Lake Road, Merced, CA 95343, USA
{sim3,mmontazerqaem}@ucmerced.edu

Abstract. In this paper, we initiate the study of the problem of ordering objects from their pairwise comparison results when allowed to discard up to a certain number of objects as outliers. More specifically, we seek to find an ordering under the popular Kendall tau distance measure, i.e., minimizing the number of pairwise comparison results that are inconsistent with the ordering, with some outliers removed. The presence of outliers challenges the assumption that a global consistent ordering exists and obscures the measure. This problem does not admit a polynomial time algorithm unless NP $\subseteq$ BPP, and therefore, we develop approximation algorithms with provable guarantees for all inputs. Our algorithms have running time and memory usage that are almost linear in the input size. Further, they are readily adaptable to run on massively parallel platforms such as MapReduce or Spark.

Keywords: Rank aggregation · Outliers · Approximation · Distributed algorithms

1 Introduction

Ranking is a fundamental problem arising in various contexts, including web pages ranking, machine learning, data analytics, and social choice. It is of particular importance to order n given objects by aggregating pairwise comparison information which could be inconsistent. For example, if we are given $A \prec B$ (meaning that B is superior to A) and $B \prec C$, it would be natural to deduce a complete ordering, $A \prec B \prec C$. However, there exists no complete ordering creating no inconsistencies, if another pairwise comparison result $C \prec A$ is considered together. As a complete ordering/ranking is sought from partial orderings, this type of problems is called rank aggregation and has been studied extensively, largely in two settings: (i) to find a true ordering (as accurately as possible) that is assumed to exist when some inconsistencies are generated according to a certain distribution; and (ii) to find a ranking that is the closest to an arbitrarily given set of the partial orderings for a certain objective, with no stochastic assumptions.

This paper revisits a central rank aggregation problem in the second domain, with a new angle.

© Springer Nature Switzerland AG 2020
U. Brefeld et al. (Eds.): ECML PKDD 2019, LNAI 11906, pp. 173–188, 2020.
https://doi.org/10.1007/978-3-030-46150-8_11

The Minimum Feedback Arc Set Tournament Problem (FAST). The input is a tournament.[1] The goal is to delete the minimum number of edges in order to make the resulting graph acyclic. This is equivalent to finding a linear ordering of the vertices to incur the fewest 'backward' edges.

The FAST problem is well-studied: it does not admit a polynomial time algorithm unless NP $\subseteq$ BPP [3] and there are several constant approximations known for the problem [3,11,18]. We note that this is a special case of the more general problem (*Minimum Feedback Arc Set;* FAS *for short*) where the input graph is not necessarily complete.

1.1   Necessity of Another Measure for Inconsistencies

The FAST problem measures the quality of an ordering by the number of pairs that are inconsistent with the ordering; this measure was proposed by Kemeny [17] and is also known as the Kendall tau distance. Unfortunately, this measure fails to capture the 'locality' of inconsistencies, namely whether or not the inconsistencies are concentrated around a small number of objects. To see this, consider the two instances in Figs. 1.

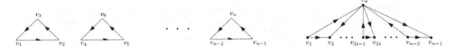

Fig. 1. The left graph consists of $\frac{n}{3}$ disjoint triangles (the rest of the arcs (v_i, v_j) for all $i < j$ are omitted). In the right graph, $v_1, v_2, \cdots, v_{n-1}$ has an ordering with no inconsistencies among them and v_n is a successor of other odd-indexed vertices while being a predecessor of even-indexed vertices.

It is easy to see no matter how we order the vertices in the left instance, we end up with having at least $n/3$ pairs that are inconsistent with the ordering, one from each triangle. Likewise, the number of inconsistent pairs in the right instance is at least $(n - 1)/2$ in any ordering, one from each triangle $\{v_n, v_{2i-1}, v_{2i}\}$. Since the ordering, $v_1, v_2, \cdots, v_n$, creates $O(n)$ inconsistent pairs in both examples, the optimal objective is $\Theta(n)$ for both. However, the two instances have inconsistencies of very different natures. In the first graph, the inconsistent pairs are scattered all over the graph. In contrast, in the second graph, the inconsistent pairs are concentrated on the single vertex v_n – the second input graph becomes acyclic when v_n is removed.

The above two examples raise a question if the Kendall tau distance alone is an effective measure in the presence of outliers. We attempt to order or rank

---

[1] A directed graph $G = (V, E)$ is called a tournament if it is complete and directed. In other words, for any pair $u \neq v \in V$, either $(u, v) \in E$ or $(v, u) \in E$.

objects because we believe that they are comparable to one another, and therefore, there exists an ordering well summarizing the whole set of pairwise comparisons. However, this belief is no longer justified if there are some outliers that do not belong to the 'same' category of comparable objects. In the second input graph, perhaps, we should think of v_n as an outlier, as the input graph has no inconsistencies without it. Counting the number of inconsistent pairs could fail to capture the quality of the output ordering without removing outliers. This is the case particularly because we can only hope for approximate solutions and noises incurred by outliers could render multiplicative approximation guarantees not very interesting.

Motivated by this, we propose a new measure that factors in outlier vertices as well as inconsistent pairs/edges:

The Minimum Feedback Arc Set Tournament with Outliers Problem (FASTO). This is a generalization of FAST. As in FAST, we are given as input a tournament $G = (V, E)$, along with a pair of target numbers, (x^*, y^*). A pair $(V' \subseteq V, E' \subseteq E)$ is a feasible solution if $(V \setminus V', E \setminus E')$ is a DAG – we refer to V' as the outlier set and E' as the backward edge set. Here, E' is a subset of edges between $V \setminus V'$. The solution quality is measured as $(\frac{|V'|}{x^*}, \frac{|E'|}{y^*})$, which are the number of outliers and backward edges incurred, respectively, relative to the target numbers, x^* and y^*. We can assume w.l.o.g. that $x^* > 0$ since otherwise FASTO becomes exactly FAST.

We will say that a solution is (α, β)-approximate if $|V'| \leq \alpha x^*$ and $|E'| \leq \beta y^*$. An algorithm is said to be a (α, β)-approximation if it always produces a (α, β)-approximate solution for all inputs. Here, it is implicitly assumed that there is a feasible solution (V', E') w.r.t. (x^*, y^*), i.e., $|V'| \leq x^*$ and $|E'| \leq y^*$ – if not, the algorithm is allowed to produce any outputs. Equivalently, the problem can be viewed as follows: Given that we can remove up to αx^* vertices as outliers, how many edges do we need to flip their directions so as to make the input graph acyclic. But we assume that we are given a target pair (x^*, y^*), as it makes our presentation cleaner.

1.2 Our Results and Contributions

Throughout this paper, we use n to denote the number of vertices in the input graph and $N = \Theta(n^2)$, which is the asymptotic input size. We use $\tilde{O}$ or $\tilde{\Theta}$ to suppress logarithmic factors. Recall that x^* is the target number of outliers. While we propose several algorithms that are scalable and parallelizable, the following is our main theoretical result with performance guarantees for all inputs; the first case is more interesting but we also study the second case for completeness.

Theorem 1. There is an approximation algorithm for FASTO with $\tilde{O}(N)$ running time and $\tilde{O}(N)$ memory usage that outputs a solution, with probability at least $1/2 - 1/n$, that is

- $(O(1), O(1))$-approximate when $x^* \leq \sqrt{n}$ (Sect. 2); and
- $(O(\log n), O(1))$-approximate when $x^* > \sqrt{n}$ (Omitted from this paper due to space limit).

Further, this algorithm can be adapted to massively parallel computing platforms so that they run in $O(\log n)$ rounds.

We note that the running time of our algorithm, which is almost linear in the input size, is essentially *optimal*. To see this, consider a simple instance that admits an ordering with one backward edge, with $(x^*, y^*) = (1, 0)$. Then, it is unavoidable to actually find the backward edge, which essentially requires to read all edges. While we do not know how to obtain a constant approximation for the case when $x^* > \sqrt{n}$ in the massively parallel computing setting, we can still get a relatively fast algorithm in the single machine setting. More precisely, we can obtain an $(O(1), O(1))$-approximate solution for all instances, with probability at least $1/2 - 1/n$, using $\tilde{O}(\sqrt{N}x^{*2})$ running time and $\tilde{O}(\sqrt{N}x^{*2})$ memory. For the formal model of massively parallel computing platforms, see [6].

Below, we outline our contributions.

Proposing a New Metric for Ranking: Ranking with Some Outliers Removed. Outliers have been extensively studied in various fields, such as statistics, machine learning, and databases. Outliers were considered before together with ranking, but they were mostly focused on the evaluation of outliers themselves, e.g., ranking outliers [22]. Our work is distinguished, as we seek to find a clean ordering which otherwise could be obscured by outliers. Various combinatorial optimization problems have been studied in a spirit similar to ours, particularly for clustering problems [9,10,15,21]. For example, the k-means clustering problem can be extended to minimize the sum of squares of distances to the k centers from all points, except a certain number of outliers [15,16]. We feel that it is a contribution of conceptual importance to study ranking problems in this direction for the first time. We believe this new direction is worth further investigation; see Sect. 4 for future research directions.

Fast and Memory-efficient Algorithms with Provable Guarantees. Our work is inspired by Aboud's work [1] on a closely related clustering problem – in the Correlational Clustering problem, there is an undirected complete graph where each edge is labeled as either '−' or '+'. The goal is to partition the vertices so as to minimize the number of inconsistent pairs where an edge (u, v) labeled '+' (resp., '−') incurs a unit cost if the two vertices u and v are placed into different groups (resp., the same group). This problem is closely related to FAST, and there exist simple and elegant 3-approximate randomized algorithms, called KWIK-SORT, for both problems, which can be seen as a generalization of quicksort: a randomly chosen pivot recursively divide an instance into two subinstances. In the case of FAST, one subproblem contains the predecessors of the pivot and the other the successors of the pivot. Likewise, in the correlational clustering case, the vertices are divided based on their respective affinities to the pivot.

Aboud considered an outlier version of the Correlational Clustering problem and gave an $(O(1), O(1))$-approximation.[2] Not surprisingly, one can adapt

---

[2] More precisely, he considered a slightly more general version where each vertex may have a different cost when removed as an outlier.

his result to obtain a $(O(1), O(1))$-approximation for FASTO. Unfortunately, Aboud's algorithm uses memory and running time that are at least linear in the number of 'bad' triangles, which can be as large as $\Omega(n^3) = \Omega(N^{1.5})$. In our problem, FASTO, a bad triangle v_1, v_2, v_3 is a triangle that does not admit a consistent ranking, i.e., $(v_1, v_2), (v_2, v_3), (v_3, v_1) \in E$ or $(v_2, v_1), (v_3, v_2), (v_1, v_3) \in E$.

To develop a fast and memory-efficient algorithm, we combine sampling with Aboud's algorithm. This combination is not trivial; for example, applying Aboud's algorithm to a reduced-sized input via sampling does not work. At a high-level, Aboud's algorithm uses a primal-dual approach. The approach sets up a linear programming (LP) and solves the LP by increasing the variables of the LP and its dual, where the constructed integer solution to the LP is used to identify outlier vertices. We have to adapt the LP, as we have to carefully handle the sampled points and argue their effects on potential backward edges. After all, we manage to reduce the memory usage and running time to $\tilde{O}(N)$ preserving the approximation factors up to constant factors[3] under the assumption that the number of outliers is small, which we believe to be reasonable in practice.

Algorithms Adaptable to Massively Parallel Platforms. Finally, our algorithm can be easily adapted to run on massively parallel platforms such as MapReduce or Spark. On such platforms, each machine is assumed to have insufficient memory to store the whole input data, and therefore, multiple machines must be used. Aboud's algorithm is not suitable for such platforms, as it uses significantly super-linear memory. In contrast, our algorithm uses sampling appropriately to reduce the input size while minimally sacrificing the approximation guarantees. More precisely, our algorithm for FASTO can be adapted to run in $O(\log n)$ rounds on the parallel platforms – the number of rounds is often one of the most important measures due to the huge communication overhead incurred in each round.

As a byproduct, for the first time we show how to convert KWIK-SORT for FAST to the distributed setting in $O(1)$ rounds (see Sects. 2.1 and 2.4), which is interesting on its own. The algorithm recursively finds a pivot and divides a subset of vertices into two groups, thus obtaining $O(\log n)$ rounds is straightforward. But we observe that as long as the pivot is sampled uniformly at random from each subgroup, the algorithm's performance guarantee continues to hold. Therefore, the algorithm still works even if we consider vertices in a random order as pivots – the sub-instance including the pivot is divided into two. Thus, we construct a decision tree from a prefix of the random vertex ordering, and using this decision tree, we partition the vertex set into multiple groups in a distributed way. This simple yet important observation also plays a key role in breaking bad triangles, thus reducing the memory usage of our algorithm for FASTO.

---

[3] We show that our algorithm is $(180, 180)$-approximate, which can be improved arbitrarily close to $(60, 60)$ if one is willing to accept a lower success probability. In contrast, Aboud's algorithm can be adapted to be $(18, 18)$-approximate for FASTO; however as mentioned above, it uses considerably more memory and run time than ours.

1.3   Other Related Work

The only problem that studies ranking with the possibility of removing certain outlier vertices, to our best knowledge, is the Feedback Vertex Set problem (FVS). The FVS problem asks to remove a minimum subset of vertices to make the remaining graph acyclic. It is an easy observation that FVS is a special case of our problem with $y^* = 0$ if the input graph were an arbitrary directed graph, not just a tournament. The FVS problem is known to be NP-hard and the current best approximation for the problem has an approximation factor of $O(\log n \log \log n)$ [13]. Thus, if we allow the input graph to be an arbitrary directed graph for our problem FASTO, then we cannot hope for a better than $(O(\log n \log \log n), c)$-approximation for any $c > 0$ unless we improve upon the best approximation for FVS. We are not aware of any other literature that considers rank aggregation with the possibility of removing outlier vertices, with the exception of the aforementioned Aboud's work on a closely related clustering problem [1]. Due to the vast literature on the topic, we can only provide an inherently incomplete list of work on ranking without outliers being considered. There exist several approximation algorithms for FAST. As mentioned, Ailon et al. [3] give the randomized KWIK-SORT that is 3-approximate for the problem, which can be derandomized [25]. Also, the algorithm that orders vertices according to their in-degrees is known to be a 5-approximation [11]. Kenyon-Mathieu and Schudy [18] give a PTAS; a PTAS is a $(1 + \epsilon)$-approximate polynomial-time algorithm for any fixed $\epsilon > 0$. The complementary maximization version (maximizing the number of forward edges in the linear ordering) was also studied, and PTASes are known for the objective [7,14]. For partial rankings, see [2] and pointers in the paper. Extension to online and distributed settings are studied in [26] but the performance guarantee is not against the optimal solution, but against a random ordering, which incurs $\Theta(n^2)$ backward edges. For another extensive literature on stochastic inputs, see [4,5,12,19,23,24] and pointers therein.

1.4   Notation and Organization

We interchangeably use $(u, v) \in E$ and $u \prec v$ – we will say that u is v's predecessor, or equivalently, v is u's successor. We use $\tilde{O}$ or $\tilde{\Theta}$ to suppress logarithmic factors in the asymptotic quantities. We use n to denote the number of vertices in the input graph and $N = \Theta(n^2)$ to denote the asymptotic input size. The subgraph of G induced on V' is denoted $G[V']$. Let $[k] := \{1, 2, 3, \ldots, k\}$.

In Sect. 2, we present our algorithm for FASTO when the target number of outliers is small, i.e., $x^* \leq \sqrt{n}$. We omit the other case in this paper due to space limit. In Sect. 3, we evaluate our algorithms and other heuristics we develop via experiments. In Sect. 4, we close with several interesting future research directions. Due to the space constraints, we will defer most analysis to the full version of this paper.

2   When the Target Number of Outliers x^* is Small

Our algorithm when $x^* \leq \sqrt{n}$ consists of three main steps:

Step 1: Partitioning via KWIK-SORT-SEQ on Sample. Each vertex in V is sampled independently with probability $\frac{1}{4x^*}$ and placed into S. Randomly permute S and run KWIK-SORT-SEQ on the ordered set S to construct a decision tree $\tau(S)$. Let $k = |S|$. Partition the other vertices, $V \setminus S$, into $k + 1$ groups, $V_1, V_2, \cdots, V_{k+1}$, using $\tau(S)$.

Step 2: Identifying Outliers via Primal-Dual. Formulate Linear Programming (LP) relaxation and derive its dual. Solve the primal and dual LPs using a primal-dual method, which outputs the set of outliers to be chosen.

Step 3: Final Ordering. Run KWIK-SORT on the non-outlier vertices in each group V_i, $i \in \{1, 2, \ldots k + 1\}$.

In the following, we give a full description of all the steps of our algorithm; the last step is self-explanatory, and thus, is briefly discussed at the end of Sect. 2.2. Following the analysis of the algorithm, the extension to the distributed setting is discussed in the final subsection.

2.1   Step 1: Partitioning via KWIK-SORT-SEQ

We first present a sequential version of the original KWIK-SORT algorithm [3] which was described in a divide-and-conquer manner. As usual, there are multiple ways to serialize a parallel execution. So, as long as we ensure that a pivot is sampled from each subgraph *uniformly at random* for further partitioning, we can simulate the parallel execution keeping the approximation guarantee. Here, we introduce one specific simulation, KWIK-SORT-SEQ, which generates a random ordering of V, takes a pivot one by one from the random ordering, and gradually refines the partitioning. We show that this is indeed a valid way of simulating KWIK-SORT.

Algorithm 1. KWIK-SORT-SEQ $(G = (V, A))$

1: $\pi(V) \leftarrow$ a random permutation of V
2: $\mathcal{V} = \{V\}$
3: For $i = 1$ to $n = |V|$:
4:    $\pi_i(V) \leftarrow$ ith vertex in the ordering $\pi(V)$
5:    Let $V' \in \mathcal{V}$ be such that $\pi_i(V) \in V'$
6:    $V'_L, V'_R \leftarrow \emptyset$
7:    For all vertices $j \in V' \setminus \{\pi_i(V)\}$:
8:       If $(j, i) \in A$, then add j to V'_L; else add j to V'_R
9:    Put $V'_L, \{\pi_i(V)\}, V'_R$ in place of V', in this order
10: Return $\mathcal{V}$ (Order vertices in the same order they appear in $\mathcal{V}$).

Lemma 2. *KWIK-SORT-SEQ is a legitimate way of simulating KWIK-SORT, keeping the approximation guarantee. Therefore, KWIK-SORT-SEQ is a 3-approximation for* FAST.

Due to the space constraints, we defer the proof to the full version of this paper. Note that a fixed random permutation $\pi(V)$ completely determines the final ordering of vertices. Likewise, a fixed length-i prefix of $\pi(V)$ completely determines the intermediate partitioning $\mathcal{V}$ after $\pi_1(V)$, $\pi_2(V)$, ..., $\pi_i(V)$ being applied, and the partitioning only refines as more pivots are applied. Thus, we can view this intermediate partitioning as the classification outcome of $V \setminus S$ via the decision tree $\tau(S)$ generated by KWIK-SORT-SEQ on the ordered set $S = \{\pi_1(V), \pi_2(V), \ldots, \pi_i(V)\}$. See Fig. 2 for illustration.

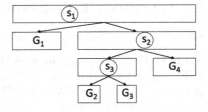

Fig. 2. Illustration of the construction of $\tau(S)$ and partitioning of $V \setminus S$ via $\tau(S)$. In this example, the decision tree $\tau(S)$ is induced by a(n ordered) sample $S = \{s_1, s_2, s_3\}$, where $s_1 \prec s_2$, $s_3 \prec s_2$, and $s_1 \prec s_3$. If a vertex $v \in V \setminus S$ is such that $s_1 \prec v$, $v \prec s_2$, $s_3 \prec v$, then v is placed into G_3.

The first step of our algorithm is essentially identical to what KWIK-SORT-SEQ does, except that our algorithm only needs a prefix of the random permutation, not the entire $\pi(V)$. It is an easy observation that sampling each vertex independently with the same probability and randomly permuting them is a valid way of getting a prefix of a random permutation. We note that we sample each vertex with probability $\frac{1}{4x^*}$, to avoid sampling any outlier (in the optimal solution) with a constant probability.

2.2   Step 2: Identifying Outliers

To set up our linear programming relaxation, we first need some definitions. We consider the ordered sample S and the induced groups $V_1, V_2, \cdots, V_{k+1}$ in the order they appear in the linear ordering produced by KWIK-SORT-SEQ performed in Step 1. For notational convenience, we reindex the sampled points so that they appear in the order of $s_1, s_2, \cdots, s_k$. We classify edges into three categories: Let E_{in} be the edges within the groups, S_{back} the backward edges with both end points in S, and E_{back} the backward edges $e = (u, v)$ such that $u \in V_i$, $v \in V_j$ for $i > j$; or $u = s_i$, $v \in V_j$ for $i \geq j$; or $v = s_i$, $u \in V_j$ for $i \leq j$. See Fig. 3.

Finally, we let T_{in} be the set of bad triangles with all vertices in the same group; recall that a bad triangle is a cycle of length 3. We are now ready to define an integer programming (IP) for a penalty version of FASTO, where a backward edge incurs a unit penalty and each outlier incurs $c := y^*/x^*$ units of penalty:

$$LP_{fasto}^{primal}(G) := \min \sum_{e \in E_{in}} y_e + \sum_{x \in V \setminus S} p_x \cdot c + \sum_{e \in E_{back}} z_e + |S_{back}| \qquad \text{(PRIMAL)}$$

$$s.t. \quad \sum_{e \subset t} y_e + \sum_{x \in t} p_x \geq 1 \qquad \forall t \in T_{in} \tag{1}$$

$$p_u + p_v + z_e \geq 1 \qquad \forall e = (u, v) \in E_{back} : \{u, v\} \cap S = \emptyset \tag{2}$$

$$p_u + z_e \geq 1 \qquad \forall e = (u, v) \in E_{back} : v \in S \wedge u \in V \setminus S \tag{3}$$

$$p_v + z_e \geq 1 \qquad \forall e = (u, v) \in E_{back} : u \in S \wedge v \in V \setminus S, \tag{4}$$

over variables $y_e \geq 0$ for all $e \in E_{in}$, $p_x \geq 0$ for all $x \in V \setminus S$, and $z_e \geq 0$ for all $e \in E_{back}$.

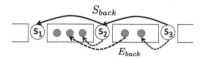

Fig. 3. Classification of edges. The rectangles shown represent groups V_1, V_2, V_3, V_4 from the left. Edges in S_{back} are shown as solid arcs and edges E_{back} as dotted arcs. Edges in E_{in} are those within groups and are omitted.

This IP has the following interpretation: an edge e in E_{in} (E_{back}, resp.) becomes backward if $y_e = 1$ ($z_e = 1$, resp.). Assuming that we will choose no sampled points as outliers, all edges in S_{back} will become backward. And each non-sampled point x incurs penalty c if it is chosen as an outlier when $p_x = 1$. Constraint (1) follows from the fact that for each bad triangle t, at least one edge e of t must become backward unless t is broken; a triangle gets broken when at least one of its vertices is chosen as outlier. The other constraints force each edge in E_{back} to become backward if its neither end point is chosen as outlier. A Linear Programming (LP) relaxation, which will be referred to as LP_{fasto}^{primal}, is obtained by allowing variables to have fractional values. Using the fact that KWIK-SORT is a 3-approximation, assuming that there is a feasible solution w.r.t. the target pair (x^*, y^*), conditioned on the sample being disjoint from the feasible solution's outlier, we can argue that the expected optimal objective of LP_{fasto}^{primal} is at most $4y^*$.

To obtain an approximate integer solution to LP_{fasto}^{primal}, we will use the primal-dual method. Primal-dual is a common technique for designing approximation algorithms [27]. The dual LP is shown below.

$$LP^{dual} = \max \sum_{t \in T_{in}} \alpha_t + \sum_{e \in E_{back}} \beta_e + |S_{back}| \qquad \text{(DUAL)}$$

$$s.t. \quad \sum_{e \subset t} \alpha_t \leq 1 \quad \forall e \in E_{in} \tag{5}$$

$$\sum_{x \in t} \alpha_t + \sum_{x \in e} \beta_e \leq c \quad \forall x \notin S \tag{6}$$

$$\beta_e \leq 1 \quad \forall e \in E_{back} \tag{7}$$

To develop an algorithm based on a primal-dual method, we replace Constraint (6) with two sufficient conditions (8).

$$\sum_{x \in t} \alpha_t \leq \frac{3}{5}c \quad \forall x \in V \setminus S; \text{ and } \quad \sum_{x \in e} \beta_e \leq \frac{2}{5}c \quad \forall x \in V \setminus S \quad (8)$$

Below, we give our algorithm, **Algorithm 3**, that sets the variables of our primal with the help of the above dual. Although the algorithm updates all variables, the only information we need to run the final Step 3 is the outlier set U, as Step 3 runs KWIK-SORT on each group with vertices U removed as outliers. But the other outputs will be useful for the analysis of our algorithm. Note that although the dual variables can have fractional values, the primal variables will only have integer values. Note that E' and E^2 represent the backward edges within the groups and across the groups, respectively; since our algorithm samples no outlier vertices in the optimal solution, all edges in S_{back} become backward and they are counted separately.

Algorithm 2. Primal-Dual Algorithm

1: *Initialization:* $p \leftarrow 0, y \leftarrow 0, z \leftarrow 0, \alpha \leftarrow 0, \beta \leftarrow 0, U \leftarrow \emptyset, E' \leftarrow \emptyset, E^2 \leftarrow \emptyset$.
   Initially, all α_t and β_e variables are active.
2: **while** $\exists$ active dual variables α_t or β_e **do**
3:     Uniformly increase active dual variables until Constraints (5),
       (7), either of the two in (8) become tight.
4:     **for** each $e \in E_{in}$ s.t. $\sum_{e \subset t} \alpha_t = 1$, **do** add e to E'; and inactivate
       α_t for all t s.t. $e \subset t$.
5:     **for** each $x \in V \setminus S$ s.t. $\sum_{x \in t} \alpha_t = \frac{3}{5}c$, **do** add x to U; and inactivate
       α_t for all t s.t. $x \in t$
6:     **for** each $x \in V \setminus S$ s.t. $\sum_{x \in e} \beta_e = \frac{2}{5}c$, **do** add x to U; and inactivate
       β_e for all e s.t. $x \in e$.
7:     **for** each $e \in E_{back}$ s.t. $\beta_e = 1$, **do** add e to E^2; and inactivate β_e.
8: Remove from E' and E^2 all the edges e with $e \cap U \neq \emptyset$.
9: **for** $e \in E'$ **do** $y_e \leftarrow 1$;   **for** $\forall e \in E^2$ **do** $z_e \leftarrow 1$; and   **for** $\forall x \in U$ **do** $p_x \leftarrow 1$
10: return p, y, z, U, E', E^2

2.3 Sketch of the Analysis: Approximation Guarantees, Memory Usage, and Running Time

In this subsection, we only give a sketch of the analysis due to space constraints. In Step 1, we can show that the sample S is disjoint from the optimal solution's outlier set, with a constant probability (at least 3/4). Conditioned on that, as mentioned earlier, the expected optimal objective of LP_{fasto}^{primal} can be shown to be at most $4y^*$. The primal-dual method in Step 2 obtains an integer solution to LP_{fasto}^{primal} that is a constant approximate against the optimal LP objective, which is established by LP duality. Therefore, the outlier set U's contribution to the

LP_{fasto}^{primal}'s objective is $c|U| = (y^*/x^*) \cdot |U|$ and it is upper bounded by $O(1)y^*$. This shows our algorithm chooses at most $O(1)x^*$ outliers. We now turn our attention to upper bounding the number of backward edges. The primal solution to LP_{fasto}^{primal} gives the number of backward edges within groups 'covering' all the unbroken triangles, which upper bounds the minimum number of backward edges achievable within groups [3], and counts the number of other backward edges explicitly by z_e and $|S_{back}|$. Since the latter is determined by the partial ordering produced by Step 1 and U and we run a 3-approximate KWIK-SORT on each group, we can also establish that the final number of backward edges output is $O(1)y^*$.

Now we discuss our algorithm's memory usage and running time. We show that each group size is $\tilde{O}(n/k)$ if $|S| = \Omega(\log n)$. This requires us to prove that a randomly chosen pivot partitions a problem into two subproblems of similar sizes with a constant probability, meaning that there is a large fraction of vertices that have similar numbers of predecessors and successors. Then, the total number of bad triangles within groups is $(\tilde{O}(n/k))^3 \cdot k = \tilde{O}(n^2) = \tilde{O}(N)$ when $k \simeq \frac{n}{x^*} \geq \sqrt{n}$, as desired. Since the number of variables in our algorithm, particularly in Step 2 is dominated by the number of bad triangles in consideration and edges, it immediately follows that the memory usage is $\tilde{O}(N)$. Further, one can increase dual variables by a factor of $(1 + \epsilon)$ in each iteration for an arbitrary constant precision parameter $\epsilon > 0$, starting from $1/n^2$. Using this one can show the number of iterations needed is $O(\log n)$. This immediately leads to the claim that the running time is $\tilde{O}(n^2) = \tilde{O}(N)$ when $x^* \leq \sqrt{n}$.

2.4   Extension to the Distributed Setting

Due to space constraints, in this subsection, we briefly discuss how we can adapt the algorithm to run in a distributed way. For formal theoretical models of the distributed setting we consider, see [6]. We assume that the input graph is stored across machines arbitrarily. Clearly, Step 1 of taking a sample S can be done in parallel. All edges between points in S are sent to a machine to construct the decision tree $\tau(S)$. The decision tree is broadcast to all machines to partition vertices in $k + 1$ groups in a distributed way. If FAST were the problem considered, we would sample each vertex with probability $1/\sqrt{n}$ and move the subgraph induced on each group G_i to a machine and continue to run KWIK-SORT on the subgraph. Then, we can implement KWIK-SORT to run in $O(1)$ rounds assuming that each machine has $\tilde{\Omega}(n)$ memory. If FASTO is the problem considered, we can implement Step 2 in $O(\log n)$ rounds, as discussed in the previous subsection. Step 3, which is the execution of KWIK-SORT on each group, can be run in one round. Again, the only constraint is that each machine has $\tilde{\Omega}(n)$ memory for an arbitrary number of machines.

3   Experiments

In this section, we perform experiments to evaluate our algorithm against synthetic data sets. All experiments were performed on Ubuntu 14.04 LTS with

RAM size 15294 MB and CPU Intel(R) Xeon(R) CPU E5-2670 v2 @ 2.50GHz. We implemented the following four algorithms including ours for comparison. The last two (RSF and IOR) are new heuristics we developed in this paper, but with no approximation guarantees. We assume that all algorithms are given a 'budget' B on the number of outliers, which limits the number of vertices that can be chosen as outliers.

- Primal-Dual with Sampling (PDS): Our algorithm when x^* is small. We run the algorithm for all target pairs (x^*, y^*) of powers of two, where $x^* \in [0, B], y^* \in [0, B']$, and choose the best solution with at most $1.5B$ outliers. Here, B' is the number of back edges output by KWIK-SORT. Note that we allow PDS to choose slightly more outliers although it may end up with choosing less since the only guarantee is that PDS chooses up to $O(x^*)$ outliers. The running time is summed up over all pairs.
- Aboud's algorithm (ABD): The algorithm in [1] for Correlational Clustering is adapted to FASTO. As above, the best solution with at most $1.5B$ outliers is chosen over all the above target pairs. ABD is essentially PDS with $S = \emptyset$ in Step 1. The running time is again summed up over all pairs considered.
- Random Sample Filter (RSF): Take a random Sample S from V (for fair comparison, the same sample size is used as in PDS). Order S using KWIK-SORT and let $\pi(S)$ be the resulting order. For each $v \in V \setminus S$, let $b(v)$ be the minimum number of backward edges with v as one endpoint over all these $|S| + 1$ possible new permutations created by adding v to $\pi(S)$. Outputs B vertices $v \in V \setminus S$ with the highest $b(v)$ values as the outliers and order the remaining vertices by KWIK-SORT.
- Iterative Outlier Removal (IOR): We iteratively remove the vertex without which KWIK-SORT outputs the least back edges. Initially, $U = \emptyset$. In each iteration, for each vertex $v \in V$, run KWIK-SORT on $V \setminus v$, which yields $|V|$ permutations. Among all the achieved permutations, consider the one with minimum number of backward edges. Let $v \in V$ be the missing vertex in this permutation. Add v to U; and $V \leftarrow V \setminus \{v\}$. Stop when $|U| = B$. Then, output U as outliers and run KWIK-SORT on V/U.

We mainly use two natural models to generate synthetic data sets. The first model, which we call the *uniform* model, assumes inconsistencies uniformly scattered over edges, in addition to randomly chosen outlier vertices. More precisely, the uniform model is described by a quadruple $\langle p, q, r, n \rangle$: For a tournament $G = (V, E)$ over n vertices with no inconsistencies, flip each edge with probability p and perturb each vertex v with probability q by flipping each edge incident on v with probability r – all independently. The second model, which essentially follows the *Bradley-Terry-Luce* model [8,20] and therefore we refer to as BTL, assumes that each vertex i has a certain (hidden) score $w_i > 0$. Then, each pair of vertices i and j has edge (i, j) with probability $\frac{w_j}{w_i + w_j}$; or edge (j, i) with the remaining probability. Intuitively, if edge (i, j) is present for every i, j such that $w_i < w_j$, we will have a tournament that is a DAG. However, some edges are flipped stochastically – in particular, edges between vertices with similar scores are more likely to be flipped. Assuming that the underlying vertex scores are a geometric sequence, we can compactly describe a BTL instance by a quadruple $\langle b, q, r, n \rangle$, where the score of the n vertices forms a geometric sequence of ratio b. Then, edges are first generated as described above, and vertices are perturbed using the parameters q and r as are done for the uniform model.

We first confirm that ABD is not very scalable (Table 1).

Table 1. PDS withsample size $1/(2q) = 50$ vs. ABD for the uniform model $\langle p = 0.001, q = 0.01, r = 0.50, n \rangle$ and $B = nq$. Bad $\triangle$s denotes the number of bad triangles in 1000 units.

pts (n)	outliers		back edges		bad $\triangle$s		time (sec)	
	PDS	ABD	PDS	ABD	PDS	ABD	PDS	ABD
250	0	2	269	33	0	18	0.2	3.8
500	6	7	377	152	365	228	4.8	100.0
1000	9	N/A	1597	N/A	441	1032	20.0	600+

Even when $n = 1000$, ABD does not terminate in 600 s while our algorithm PDS does in 20 s. Our algorithm's speed-up is explained by the significantly smaller number of bad triangles. For $n = 500$, PDS outputs factor 2 or 3 more back edges than ABD. But we were not able to compare the two algorithms for larger inputs because of ABD's large run time.

Next, we compare PDS to RSF and IOR for inputs generated under the uniform and BTL models (Tables 2 and 3). Note that RSF and IOR choose exactly the same number of outliers, B.

Table 2. PDS with sample size $1/(2q) = 50$ vs RSF vs IOR for the uniform input $\langle p = 0.001, q = 0.01, r = 0.50, n \rangle$ and $B = nq$.

pts (n)	outliers		back edges (10^3)			time (sec)		
	RSF	PDS	RSF	IOR	PDS	RSF	IOR	PDS
500	5	6	1.1	0.98	0.4	0.1	0.1	4.7
1000	10	9	2.6	1.8	1.6	0.4	0.5	20.3
2000	20	16	7.5	6.1	2.5	1.1	3.8	145.4
4000	40	55	26.2	71.5	11.8	3.8	41.3	1132

Our algorithm PDS outperforms the other two in terms of the number of back edges although it occasionally chooses slightly more outliers. However, PDS is considerably slower than RSF and IOR.

Table 3. PDS with sample size $1/(2q) = 50$ vs RSF vs IOR for the BTL input with $q = 0.01, r = 0.50$, $(b, n) \in \{(4.2, 500), (2.3, 1000), (1.57, 2000), (1.266, 4000)\}$; here $B = nq$.

pts (n)	outliers		back edges (10^3)			time (sec)		
	RSF	PDS	RSF	IOR	PDS	RSF	IOR	PDS
500	5	1	0.3	0.0	0.3	0.1	0.1	1
1000	10	9	0.8	0.3	0.8	0.3	0.5	8.3
2000	20	26	7.9	7.6	1.6	0.9	2.3	73
4000	40	33	8.1	8.0	7.9	3.4	15.9	381.3

Finally, to showcase the major advantage of our algorithm PDS that it has performance guarantees for all inputs, in contrast to the two heuristics RSF and IOR, we consider certain specific instances. First, we observe that RSF significantly underperforms compared to PDS and IOR when the instance is constructed by choosing $\sqrt{n}$ points at random and flipping edges among them. As before, note that RSF and IOR choose the same number of outliers, B, thus we only display RSF for the outliers column.

Table 4. PDS with sample size $\sqrt{n}/2$ vs RSF with sample size $\sqrt{n}/2$ vs IOR. Each vertex is perturbed with probability $1/\sqrt{n}$ – each edge between perturbed vertices is flipped with probability $1/2$. $B = \sqrt{n}$.

pts (n)	outliers		back edges			time (sec)		
	RSF	PDS	RSF	IOR	PDS	RSF	IOR	PDS
1000	31	31	226	0	0	0.2	1.2	6.4
2000	44	44	541	0	0	0.8	7.3	27.2
4000	63	63	1570	0	0	3.3	62.8	130.2
8000	89	89	2887	0	0	13.4	442.0	702.7

As shown in Table 4, when $n = 4000$, all algorithms choose exactly 63 outliers; but RSF produces 1570 back edges while the other two produce no back edges. For all cases when $n = 1000, 2000, 4000$ and 8000, PDS and IOR create no back edges while RSF does a considerable number of back edges. Interestingly, IOR appears not to be very scalable. For $n = 8000$, IOR is only twice faster than PDS.

We continue to observe that IOR also quite underperforms compared to PDS for a certain class of instances. The instance we create is parameterized by t. The instance is constructed by combining $4t$ sub-tournaments, $G_1, G_2, G_3, \cdots, G_{4t}$, which are identical. Each G_i has t vertices and admits a perfect ordering with one vertex removed therein – each edge in G_i incident on the vertex is flipped with probability $1/2$. We connect the sub-tournaments, so that for any $i < j$, all vertices in G_i are predecessors of all vertices in G_j. As shown in Table 5, when $n = 4096$, PDS creates no back edges while IOR creates 313 back edges; both chooses the same number of outliers, 128. Further, PDS is slower than IOR only by a factor of at most 3.

Table 5. PDS with sample size $t/2$ vs IOR

pts (n)	outliers		back edges		time (sec)	
	IOR	PDS	IOR	PDS	IOR	PDS
1024	64	62	87	7	2.4	21.4
2116	92	89	142	79	16.7	203.2
4096	128	128	313	0	129.5	305.5

4 Conclusions

In this paper, we studied how to order objects in the presence of outliers. In particular, we developed approximation algorithms that are nearly optimal in terms of running time and can be adapted to the distributed setting, along with potentially useful heuristics. There are many interesting future research directions. First, our algorithm may choose more than x^* outliers. It would be interesting if one can get an approximation algorithm that finds an ordering resulting in $O(1)y^*$ backward edges with strictly no more than x^* outliers. Second, we currently do not know if it is possible to obtain a $(O(1), O(1))$-approximation algorithm whose running time is almost linear in the input size when $x^* > \sqrt{n}$. Finally, it would be of significant interest to consider arbitrary directed graphs as input.

Acknowledgements. This work was supported in part by NSF grants CCF-1409130 and CCF-1617653.

References

1. Aboud, A.: Correlation clustering with penalties and approximating the reordering buffer management problem. Master's thesis. The Technion Israel Institute of Technology (2008)
2. Ailon, N.: Aggregation of partial rankings, p-ratings and top-m lists. Algorithmica **57**(2), 284–300 (2010)
3. Ailon, N., Charikar, M., Newman, A.: Aggregating inconsistent information: ranking and clustering. J. ACM **55**(5), 23 (2008)
4. Altman, A., Tennenholtz, M.: Ranking systems: the pagerank axioms. In: ACM EC (2005)
5. Ammar, A., Shah, D.: Ranking: Compare, don't score. In: IEEE Allerton (2011)
6. Andoni, A., Nikolov, A., Onak, K., Yaroslavtsev, G.: Parallel algorithms for geometric graph problems. In: ACM STOC, pp. 574–583 (2014)

7. Arora, S., Frieze, A., Kaplan, H.: A new rounding procedure for the assignment problem with applications to dense graph arrangement problems. Math Program. **92**(1), 1–36 (2002)
8. Bradley, R.A., Terry, M.E.: Rank analysis of incomplete block designs: I. the method of paired comparisons. Biometrika **39**(3/4), 324–345 (1952)
9. Charikar, M., Khuller, S., Mount, D.M., Narasimhan, G.: Algorithms for facility location problems with outliers. In: ACM-SIAM SODA (2001)
10. Chen, K.: A constant factor approximation algorithm for k-median clustering with outliers. In: ACM-SIAM SODA (2008)
11. Coppersmith, D., Fleischer, L.K., Rurda, A.: Ordering by weighted number of wins gives a good ranking for weighted tournaments. ACM Trans. Algorithms **6**(3), 55 (2010)
12. Duchi, J.C., Mackey, L.W., Jordan, M.I.: On the consistency of ranking algorithms. In: ICML, pp. 327–334 (2010)
13. Even, G., (Seffi) Naor, J., Schieber, B., Sudan, M.: Approximating minimum feedback sets and multicuts in directed graphs. Algorithmica **20**(2), 151–174 (1998)
14. Frieze, A., Kannan, R.: Quick approximation to matrices and applications. Combinatorica **19**(2), 175–220 (1999)
15. Guha, S., Li, Y., Zhang, Q.: Distributed partial clustering. In: ACM SPAA (2017)
16. Gupta, S., Kumar, R., Lu, K., Moseley, B., Vassilvitskii, S.: Local search methods for k-means with outliers. PVLDB **10**(7), 757–768 (2017)
17. Kemeny, J.G.: Mathematics without numbers. Daedalus **88**(4), 577–591 (1959)
18. Kenyon-Mathieu, C., Schudy, W.: How to rank with few errors. In: ACM STOC (2007)
19. Lu, T., Boutilier, C.: Learning mallows models with pairwise preferences. In: ICML (2011)
20. Luce, R.D.: Individual Choice Behavior a Theoretical Analysis. Wiley, Hoboken (1959)
21. Malkomes, G., Kusner, M.J., Chen, W., Weinberger, K.Q., Moseley, B.: Fast distributed k-center clustering with outliers on massive data. In: NIPS (2015)
22. Muller, E., Sánchez, P.I., Mulle, Y., Bohm, K.: Ranking outlier nodes in subspaces of attributed graphs. In: IEEE ICDEW (2013)
23. Negahban, S., Oh, S., Shah, D.: Rank centrality: ranking from pairwise comparisons. Oper. Res. **65**(1), 266–287 (2016)
24. Rajkumar, A., Agarwal, S.: A statistical convergence perspective of algorithms for rank aggregation from pairwise data. In: ICML (2014)
25. van Zuylen, A., Williamson, D.P.: Deterministic algorithms for rank aggregation and other ranking and clustering problems. In: Kaklamanis, C., Skutella, M. (eds.) WAOA 2007. LNCS, vol. 4927, pp. 260–273. Springer, Heidelberg (2008). https://doi.org/10.1007/978-3-540-77918-6_21
26. Wauthier, F., Jordan, M., Jojic, N.: Efficient ranking from pairwise comparisons. In: ICML (2013)
27. Williamson, D.P., Shmoys, D.B.: The Design of Approximation Algorithms. Cambridge University Press, Cambridge (2011)

Black Box Explanation by Learning Image Exemplars in the Latent Feature Space

Riccardo Guidotti[1]([⊠]), Anna Monreale[2], Stan Matwin[3,4], and Dino Pedreschi[2]

[1] ISTI-CNR, Pisa, Italy
`riccardo.guidotti@isti.cnr.it`
[2] University of Pisa, Pisa, Italy
{`anna.monreale,dino.pedreschi`}`@unipi.it`
[3] Dalhousie University, Halifax, Canada
`stan@cs.dal.ca`
[4] Institute of Computer Science, Polish Academy of Sciences, Warsaw, Poland

Abstract. We present an approach to explain the decisions of black box models for image classification. While using the black box to label images, our explanation method exploits the latent feature space learned through an adversarial autoencoder. The proposed method first generates exemplar images in the latent feature space and learns a decision tree classifier. Then, it selects and decodes exemplars respecting local decision rules. Finally, it visualizes them in a manner that shows to the user how the exemplars can be modified to either stay within their class, or to become counter-factuals by "morphing" into another class. Since we focus on black box decision systems for image classification, the explanation obtained from the exemplars also provides a saliency map highlighting the areas of the image that contribute to its classification, and areas of the image that push it into another class. We present the results of an experimental evaluation on three datasets and two black box models. Besides providing the most useful and interpretable explanations, we show that the proposed method outperforms existing explainers in terms of fidelity, relevance, coherence, and stability.

Keywords: Explainable AI · Adversarial autoencoder · Image exemplars

1 Introduction

Automated decision systems based on machine learning techniques are widely used for classification, recognition and prediction tasks. These systems try to capture the relationships between the input instances and the target to be predicted. Input attributes can be of any type, as long as it is possible to find a convenient representation for them. For instance, we can represent images by matrices of pixels, or by a set of features that correspond to specific areas or patterns of the image. Many automated decision systems are based on very accurate classifiers such as deep neural networks. They are recognized to be

© Springer Nature Switzerland AG 2020
U. Brefeld et al. (Eds.): ECML PKDD 2019, LNAI 11906, pp. 189–205, 2020.
https://doi.org/10.1007/978-3-030-46150-8_12

"black box" models because of their opaque, hidden internal structure, whose complexity makes their comprehension for humans very difficult [5]. Thus, there is an increasing interest in the scientific community in deriving explanations able to describe the behavior of a black box [5,6,13,22], or explainable by design approaches [18,19]. Moreover, the *General Data Protection Regulation*[1] has been approved in May 2018 by the European Parliament. This law gives to individuals the right to request "...meaningful information of the logic involved" when automated decision-making takes place with "legal or similarly relevant effects" on individuals. Without a technology able to explain, in a manner easily understandable to a human, how a black box takes its decision, this right will remain only an utopia, or it will result in prohibiting the use of opaque, but highly effective machine learning methods in socially sensitive domains.

In this paper, we investigate the problem of black box explanation for image classification (Sect. 3). Explaining the reasons for a certain decision can be particularly important. For example, when dealing with medical images for diagnosing, how we can validate that a very accurate image classifier built to recognize cancer actually focuses on the malign areas and not on the background for taking the decisions?

In the literature (Sect. 2), the problem is addressed by producing explanations through different approaches. On the one hand, gradient and perturbation-based attribution methods [25,27] reveal saliency maps highlighting the parts of the image that most contribute to its classification. However, these methods are *model specific* and can be employed only to explain specific deep neural networks. On the other hand, *model agnostic* approaches can explain, yet through a saliency map, the outcome of any black box [12,24]. Agnostic methods may generate a local neighborhood of the instance to explain and mime the behavior of the black box using an interpretable classifier. However, these methods exhibit drawbacks that may negatively impact the reliability of the explanations. First, they do not take into account existing relationships between features (or pixels) during the neighborhood generation. Second, the neighborhood generation does not produce "meaningful" images since, e.g., some areas of the image to explain in [24] are obscured, while in [12] they are replaced with pixels of other images. Finally, transparent-by-design approaches produce prototypes from which it should be clear to the user why a certain decision is taken by the model [18,19]. Nevertheless, these approaches cannot be used to explain a trained black box, but the transparent model has to be directly adopted as a classifier, possibly with limitations on the accuracy achieved.

We propose ABELE, an Adversarial Black box Explainer generating Latent Exemplars (Sect. 5). ABELE is a local, model-agnostic explanation method able to overcome the existing limitations of the local approaches by exploiting the latent feature space, learned through an adversarial autoencoder [20] (Sect. 4), for the neighborhood generation process. Given an image classified by a given black box model, ABELE provides an explanation for the reasons of the proposed classification. The explanation consists of two parts: *(i)* a set of *exemplars*

---

[1] https://ec.europa.eu/justice/smedataprotect/.

and *counter-exemplars* images illustrating, respectively, instances classified with the same label and with a different label than the instance to explain, which may be visually analyzed to understand the reasons for the classification, and *(ii)* a *saliency map* highlighting the areas of the image to explain that contribute to its classification, and areas of the image that push it towards another label.

We present a deep experimentation (Sect. 6) on three datasets of images and two black box models. We empirically prove that ABELE overtakes state of the art methods based on saliency maps or on prototype selection by providing relevant, coherent, stable and faithful explanations. Finally, we summarize our contribution, its limitations, and future research directions (Sect. 7).

2   Related Work

Research on black box explanation methods has recently received much attention [5, 6, 13, 22]. These methods can be characterized as model-specific *vs* model-agnostic, and local *vs* global. The proposed explanation method ABELE is the next step in the line of research on local, model-agnostic methods originated with [24] and extended in different directions by [9] and by [11, 12, 23].

In image classification, typical explanations are the *saliency maps*, i.e., images that show each pixel's positive (or negative) contribution to the black box outcome. Saliency maps are efficiently built by gradient [1, 25, 27, 30] and perturbation-based [7, 33] attribution methods by finding, through backpropagation and differences on the neuron activation, the pixels of the image that maximize an approximation of a linear model of the black box classification outcome. Unfortunately, these approaches are specifically designed for deep neural networks. They cannot be employed for explaining other image classifiers, like tree ensembles or hybrid image classification processes [13]. Model-agnostic explainers, such as LIME [24] and similar [12] can be employed to explain the classification of any image classifier. They are based on the generation of a local neighborhood around the image to explain, and on the training of an interpretable classifier on this neighborhood. Unlike the global distillation methods [17], they do not consider (often non-linear) relationships between features (e.g. pixel proximity), and thus, their neighborhoods do not contain "meaningful" images.

Our proposed method ABELE overcomes the limitations of both saliency-based and local model-agnostic explainers by using AAEs, local distillation, and exemplars. As ABELE includes and extends LORE [11], an innovation w.r.t. state of the art explainers for image classifiers is the usage of counter-factuals. Counter-factuals are generated from "positive" instances by a minimal perturbation that pushes them to be classified with a different label [31]. In line with this approach, ABELE generates counter-factual rules in the latent feature space and exploits them to derive counter-exemplars in the original feature space.

As the explanations returned by ABELE are based on exemplars, we need to clarify the relationship between *exemplars* and *prototypes*. Both are used as a foundation of representation of a category, or a concept [8]. In the prototype view, a concept is the representation of a specific instance of this concept. In the exemplar view, the concept is represented by means of a set of typical examples, or

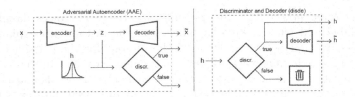

Fig. 1. *Left*: Adversarial Autoencoder architecture: the *encoder* turns the image x into its latent representation z, the *decoder* re-builds an approximation $\tilde{x}$ of x from z, and the *discriminator* identifies if a randomly generated latent instance h can be considered valid or not. *Right*: Discriminator and Decoder (*disde*) module: input is a randomly generated latent instance h and, if it is considered valid by the *discriminator*, it returns it together with its decompressed version $\tilde{h}$.

exemplars. ABELE uses exemplars to represent a concept. In recent works [4, 19], image prototypes are used as the foundation of the concept for interpretability [2]. In [19], an explainable by design method, similarly to ABELE, generates prototypes in the latent feature space learned with an autoencoder. However, it is not aimed at explaining a trained black box model. In [4] a convolutional neural network is adopted to provide features from which the prototypes are selected. ABELE differs from these approaches because is model agnostic and the *adversarial* component ensures the similarity of feature and class distributions.

3   Problem Formulation

In this paper we address the *black box outcome explanation problem* [13]. Given a black box model b and an instance x classified by b, i.e., $b(x) = y$, our aim is to provide an explanation e for the decision $b(x) = y$. More formally:

Definition 1. Let b be a black box, and x an instance whose decision $b(x)$ has to be explained. The *black box outcome explanation problem* consists in finding an explanation $e \in E$ belonging to a human-interpretable domain E.

We focus on the black box outcome explanation problem for image classification, where the instance x is an image mapped by b to a class label y. In the following, we use the notation $b(X) = Y$ as a shorthand for $\{b(x) \mid x \in X\} = Y$. We denote by b a black box image classifier, whose internals are either unknown to the observer or they are known but uninterpretable by humans. Examples are neural networks and ensemble classifiers. We assume that a black box b is a function that can be queried at will.

We tackle the above problem by deriving an explanation from the understanding of the behavior of the black box in the local neighborhood of the instance to explain [13]. To overcome the state of the art limitations, we exploit adversarial autoencoders [20] for generating, encoding and decoding the local neighborhood.

4   Adversarial Autoencoders

An important issue arising in the use of synthetic instances generated when developing black box explanations is the question of maintaining the identity of the distribution of the examples that are generated with the prior distribution of the original examples. We approach this issue by using an Adversarial Autoencoder (AAE) [20], which combines a Generative Adversarial Network (GAN) [10] with the autoencoder representation learning algorithm. Another reason for the use of AAE is that, as demonstrated in [29], the use of autoencoders enhances the robustness of deep neural network classifiers more against malicious examples.

AAEs are probabilistic autoencoders that aim at generating new random items that are highly similar to the training data. They are regularized by matching the aggregated posterior distribution of the latent representation of the input data to an arbitrary prior distribution. The AAE architecture (Fig. 1-left) includes an $encoder : \mathbb{R}^n \rightarrow \mathbb{R}^k$, a $decoder : \mathbb{R}^k \rightarrow \mathbb{R}^n$ and a $discriminator : \mathbb{R}^k \rightarrow [0, 1]$ where n is the number of pixels in an image and k is the number of latent features. Let x be an instance of the training data, we name z the corresponding latent data representation obtained by the $encoder$. We can describe the AAE with the following distributions [20]: the prior distribution $p(z)$ to be imposed on z, the data distribution $p_d(x)$, the model distribution $p(x)$, and the encoding and decoding distributions $q(z|x)$ and $p(x|z)$, respectively. The encoding function $q(z|x)$ defines an aggregated posterior distribution of $q(z)$ on the latent feature space: $q(z) = \int_x q(z|x)p_d(x)dx$. The AAE guarantees that the aggregated posterior distribution $q(z)$ matches the prior distribution $p(z)$, through the latent instances and by minimizing the reconstruction error. The AAE generator corresponds to the encoder $q(z|x)$ and ensures that the aggregated posterior distribution can confuse the $discriminator$ in deciding if the latent instance z comes from the true distribution $p(z)$.

The AAE learning involves two phases: the $reconstruction$ aimed at training the $encoder$ and $decoder$ to minimize the reconstruction loss; the $regularization$ aimed at training the $discriminator$ using training data and encoded values. After the learning, the decoder defines a generative model mapping $p(z)$ to $p_d(x)$.

5   Adversarial Black Box Explainer

ABELE (Adversarial Black box Explainer generating Latent Exemplars) is a local model agnostic explainer for image classifiers solving the outcome explanation problem. Given an image x to explain and a black box b, the explanation provided by ABELE is composed of *(i)* a set of *exemplars* and *counter-exemplars*, *(ii)* a *saliency map*. Exemplars and counter-exemplars shows instances classified with the same and with a different outcome than x. They can be visually analyzed to understand the reasons for the decision. The saliency map highlights the areas of x that contribute to its classification and areas that push it into another class.

The explanation process involves the following steps. First, ABELE generates a neighborhood in the latent feature space exploiting the AAE (Sect. 4). Then,

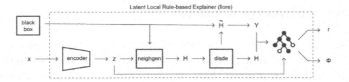

Fig. 2. Latent Local Rules Extractor. It takes as input the image x to explain and the black box b. With the *encoder* trained by the AAE, it turns x into its latent representation z. Then, the *neighgen* module uses z and b to generate the latent local neighborhood H. The valid instances are decoded in $\widetilde{H}$ by the *disde* module. Images in $\widetilde{H}$ are labeled with the black box $Y = b(\widetilde{H})$. H and Y are used to learn a decision tree classifier. At last, a decision rule r and the counter-factual rules Φ for z are returned.

it learns a decision tree on that latent neighborhood providing local decision and counter-factual rules. Finally, ABELE selects and decodes exemplars and counter-exemplars satisfying these rules and extracts from them a saliency map.

Encoding. The image $x \in \mathbb{R}^n$ to be explained is passed as input to the AAE where the *encoder* returns the latent representation $z \in \mathbb{R}^k$ using k latent features with $k \ll n$. The number k is kept low by construction avoiding high dimensionality problems.

Neighborhood Generation. ABELE generates a set H of N instances in the latent feature space, with characteristics close to those of z. Since the goal is to learn a predictor on H able to simulate the local behavior of b, the neighborhood includes instances with both decisions, i.e., $H = H_= \cup H_{\neq}$ where instances $h \in H_=$ are such that $b(\widetilde{h}) = b(x)$, and $h \in H_{\neq}$ are such that $b(\widetilde{h}) \neq b(x)$. We name $\widetilde{h} \in \mathbb{R}^n$ the decoded version of an instance $h \in \mathbb{R}^k$ in the latent feature space. The neighborhood generation of H (*neighgen* module in Fig. 2) may be accomplished using different strategies ranging from pure random strategy using a given distribution to a genetic approach maximizing a fitness function [11]. In our experiments we adopt the last strategy. After the generation process, for any instance $h \in H$, ABELE exploits the *disde* module (Fig. 1-right) for both checking the validity of h by querying the *discriminator*[2] and decoding it into $\widetilde{h}$. Then, ABELE queries the black box b with $\widetilde{h}$ to get the class y, i.e., $b(\widetilde{h}) = y$.

Local Classifier Rule Extraction. Given the local neighborhood H, ABELE builds a decision tree classifier c trained on the instances H labeled with the black box decision $b(\widetilde{H})$. Such a predictor is intended to locally mimic the behavior of b in the neighborhood H. The decision tree extracts the decision rule r and counter-factual rules Φ enabling the generation of *exemplars* and *counter-exemplars*. ABELE considers decision tree classifiers because: *(i)* decision rules can naturally be derived from a root-leaf path in a decision tree; and, *(ii)* counter-factual rules can be extracted by symbolic reasoning over a decision tree.

---

[2] In the experiments we use for the *discriminator* the default validity threshold 0.5 to distinguish between real and fake exemplars. This value can be increased to admit only more reliable exemplars, or decreased to speed-up the generation process.

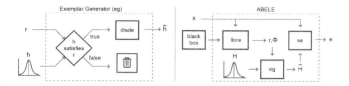

Fig. 3. *Left*: (Counter-)Exemplar Generator: it takes a decision rule r and a randomly generated latent instance h, checks if h satisfies r and applies the *disde* module (Fig. 1-right) to decode it. *Right*: ABELE architecture. It takes as input the image x for which we require an explanation and the black box b. It extracts the decision rule r and the counter-factual rules Φ with the *llore* module. Then, it generates a set of latent instances H which are used as input with r and Φ for the *eg* module (Fig. 3-left) to generate exemplars and counter-exemplars $\widetilde{H}$. Finally, x and $\widetilde{H}$ are used by the *se* module for calculating the saliency maps and returning the final explanation e.

The premise p of a decision rule $r = p \rightarrow y$ is the conjunction of the splitting conditions in the nodes of the path from the root to the leaf that is satisfied by the latent representation z of the instance to explain x, and setting $y = c(z)$. For the counter-factual rules Φ, ABELE selects the closest rules in terms of splitting conditions leading to a label $\hat{y}$ different from y, i.e., the rules $\{q \rightarrow \hat{y}\}$ such that q is the conjunction of splitting conditions for a path from the root to the leaf labeling an instance h_c with $c(h_c) = \hat{y}$ and minimizing the number of splitting conditions falsified w.r.t. the premise p of the rule r. Figure 2 shows the process that, starting from the image to be explained, leads to the decision tree learning, and to the extraction of the decision and counter-factual rules. We name this module *llore*, as a variant of LORE [11] operating in the latent feature space.

Explanation Extraction. Often, e.g. in medical or managerial decision making, people explain their decisions by pointing to exemplars with the same (or different) decision outcome [4,8]. We follow this approach and we model the explanation of an image x returned by ABELE as a triple $e = \langle \widetilde{H}_e, \widetilde{H}_c, s \rangle$ composed by *exemplars* $\widetilde{H}_e$, *counter-exemplars* $\widetilde{H}_c$ and a *saliency map* s. Exemplars and counter-exemplars are images representing instances similar to x, leading to an outcome equal to or different from $b(x)$. Exemplars and counter-exemplars are generated by ABELE exploiting the *eg* module (Fig. 3-left). It first generates a set of latent instances H satisfying the decision rule r (or a set of counter-factual rules Φ), as shown in Fig. 2. Then, it validates and decodes them into exemplars $\widetilde{H}_e$ (or counter-exemplars $\widetilde{H}_c$) using the *disde* module. The saliency map s highlights areas of x that contribute to its outcome and areas that push it into another class. The map is obtained by the saliency extractor *se* module (Fig. 3-right) that first computes the pixel-to-pixel-difference between x and each exemplar in the set $\widetilde{H}_e$, and then, it assigns to each pixel of the saliency map s the median value of all differences calculated for that pixel. Thus, formally for each pixel i of the saliency map s we have: $s[i] = median_{\forall \widetilde{h}_e \in \widetilde{H}_e}(x[i] - \widetilde{h}_e[i])$.

Table 1. Datasets resolution, type of color, train and test dimensions, and black box model accuracy.

Dataset	Resolution	rgb	Train	Test	RF	DNN
mnist	28×28	✗	$60k$	$10k$	.9692	.9922
fashion	28×28	✗	$60k$	$10k$	.8654	.9207
cifar10	32×32	✓	$50k$	$10k$	.4606	.9216

Table 2. AAEs reconstruction error in terms of RMSE.

Dataset	Train	Test
mnist	39.80	43.64
fashion	27.41	30.15
cifar10	20.26	45.12

In summary, ABELE (Fig. 3-right), takes as input the instance to explain x and a black box b, and returns an explanation e according to the following steps. First, it adopts *llore* [11] to extract the decision rule r and the counterfactual rules Φ. These rules, together with a set of latent random instances H are the input of the *eg* module returning *exemplars* and *counter-exemplars*. Lastly, the *se* module extracts the *saliency map* starting from the image x and its exemplars.

6   Experiments

We experimented with the proposed approach on three open source datasets[3] (details in Table 1): the mnist dataset of handwritten digit grayscale images, the fashion mnist dataset is a collection of Zalando's article grayscale images (e.g. shirt, shoes, bag, etc.), and the cifar10 dataset of colored images of airplanes, cars, birds, cats, etc. Each dataset has ten different labels.

We trained and explained away the following black box classifiers. Random Forest [3] (RF) as implemented by the *scikit-learn* Python library, and Deep Neural Networks (DNN) implemented with the keras library[4]. For mnist and fashion we used a three-layer CNN, while for cifar10 we used the *ResNet20 v1* network described in [16]. Classification performance are reported in Table 1.

For mnist and fashion we trained AAEs with sequential three-layer encoder, decoder and discriminator. For cifar10 we adopted a four-layer CNN for the encoder and the decoder, and a sequential discriminator. We used 80% of the test sets for training the adversarial autoencoders[5]. In Table 2 we report the reconstruction error of the AAE in terms of *Root Mean Square Error* (RMSE) between the original and reconstructed images. We employed the remaining 20% for evaluating the quality of the explanations.

We compare ABELE against LIME and a set of saliency-based explainers collected in the DeepExplain package[6]: Saliency (SAL) [27], GradInput (GRAD) [25],

---

[3] Dataset: http://yann.lecun.com/exdb/mnist/, https://www.cs.toronto.edu/~kriz/cifar.html, https://www.kaggle.com/zalando-research/.

[4] Black box: https://scikit-learn.org/, https://keras.io/examples/.

[5] The encoding distribution of AAE is defined as a Gaussian distribution whose mean and variance is predicted by the encoder itself [20]. We adopted the following number of latent features k for the various datasets: mnist $k=4$, fashion $k=8$, cifar10 $k=16$.

[6] Github code links: https://github.com/riccotti/ABELE, https://github.com/marcotcr/lime, https://github.com/marcoancona/DeepExplain.

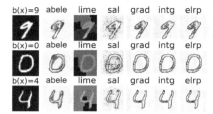

Fig. 4. Explain by saliency map mnist.

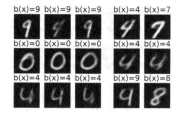

Fig. 5. Exemplars & counter-exemplars. (Color figure online)

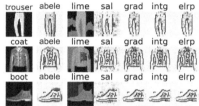

Fig. 6. Explain by saliency map fashion. (Color figure online)

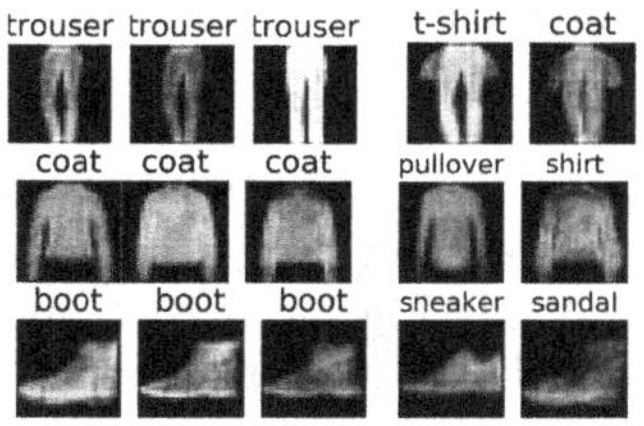

Fig. 7. Exemplars & counter-exemplars.

IntGrad (INTG) [30], ε-lrp (ELRP) [1], and Occlusion (OCC) [33]. We refer to the set of tested DeepExplain methods as DEX. We also compare the exemplars and counter-exemplars generated by ABELE against the prototypes and criticisms[7] selected by the MMD and K-MEDOIDS [18]. MMD exploits the maximum mean discrepancy and a kernel function for selecting the best prototypes and criticisms.

Saliency Map, Exemplars and Counter-Exemplars. Before assessing quantitatively the effectiveness of the compared methods, we visually analyze their outcomes. We report explanations of the DNNs for the mnist and fashion datasets in Fig. 4 and Fig. 6 respectively[8]. The first column contains the image to explain x together with the label provided by the black box b, while the second column contains the saliency maps provided by ABELE. Since they are derived from the difference between the image x and its exemplars, we indicate with yellow color the areas that are common between x and the exemplars $\widetilde{H}_e$, with red color the areas contained only in the exemplars and blue color the areas contained only in x. This means that yellow areas must remain unchanged to obtain the same label $b(x)$, while red and blue areas can change without impacting the black box decision. In particular, with respect to x, an image obtaining the same label can be darker in blue areas and lighter in red areas. In other words, blue and red areas express the boundaries that can be varied, and for

---

[7] Criticisms are images not well-explained by prototypes with a regularized kernel function [18].

[8] Best view in color. Black lines are not part of the explanation, they only highlight borders. We do not report explanations for cifar10 and for RF for the sake of space.

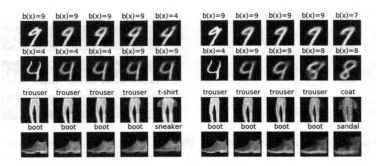

Fig. 8. Interpolation from the image to explain x to one of its counter-exemplars $\widetilde{h}_c$.

which the class remains unchanged. For example, with this type of saliency map we can understand that a *nine* may have a more compact circle, a *zero* may be more inclined (Fig. 4), a *coat* may have no space between the sleeves and the body, and that a *boot* may have a higher neck (Fig. 6). Moreover, we can notice how, besides the background, there are some "essential" yellow areas within the main figure that can not be different from x: e.g. the leg of the *nine*, the crossed lines of the *four*, the space between the two *trousers*.

The rest of the columns in Figs. 4 and 6 contain the explanations of the competitors: red areas contribute positively to the black box outcome, blue areas contribute negatively. For LIME's explanations, nearly all the content of the image is part of the saliency areas[9]. In addition, the areas have either completely positive or completely negative contributions. These aspects can be not very convincing for a LIME user. On the other hand, the DEX methods return scattered red and blue points which can also be very close to each other and are not clustered into areas. It is not clear how a user could understand the black box outcome decision process from this kind of explanation.

Since the ABELE's explanations also provide exemplars and counter-exemplars, they can also be visually analyzed by a user for understanding which are possible similar instances leading to the same outcome or to a different one. For each instance explained in Figs. 4 and 6, we show three exemplars and two counter-exemplars for the `mnist` and `fashion` datasets in Figs. 5 and 7, respectively. Observing these images we can notice how the label *nine* is assigned to images very close to a *four* (Fig. 5, 1st row, 2nd column) but until the upper part of the circle remains connected, it is still classified as a *nine*. On the other hand, looking at counter-exemplars, if the upper part of the circle has a hole or the lower part is not thick enough, then the black box labels them as a *four* and a *seven*, respectively. We highlight similar phenomena for other instances: e.g. a *boot* with a neck not well defined is labeled as a *sneaker* (Fig. 7).

To gain further insights on the counter-exemplars, inspired by [28], we exploit the latent representations to visually understand how the black box labeling changes w.r.t. real images. In Fig. 8 we show, for some instances previously ana-

---

[9] This effect is probably due to the figure segmentation performed by LIME.

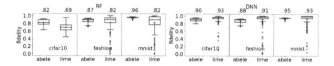

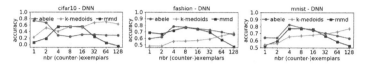

Fig. 9. Box plots of *fidelity*. Numbers on top: mean values (the higher the better).

Fig. 10. 1-NN exemplar classifier accuracy varying the number of (counter-)exemplars.

lyzed, how they can be changed to move from the original label to the counter-factual label. We realize this change in the class through the latent representations z and h_c of the image to explain x and of the counter-exemplar $\widetilde{h}_c$, respectively. Given z and h_c, we generate through linear interpolation in the latent feature space intermediate latent representations $z < h_c^{(i)} < h_c$ respecting the latent decision or counter-factual rules. Finally, using the *decoder*, we obtain the intermediate images $\widetilde{h}_c^{(i)}$. This convincing and useful explanation analysis is achieved thanks to ABELE's ability to deal with both real and latent feature spaces, and to the application of latent rules to real images which are human understandable and also clear exemplar-based explanations.

Lastly, we observe that prototype selector methods, like MMD [18] and K-MEDOIDS cannot be used for the same type of analysis because they lack any link with either the black box or the latent space. In fact, they propose as prototypes (or criticism) existing images of a given dataset. On the other hand, ABELE generates and does not select (counter-)exemplars respecting rules.

Interpretable Classifier Fidelity. We compare ABELE and LIME in terms of *fidelity* [5,11], i.e., the ability of the local interpretable classifier c[10] of mimicking the behavior of a black box b in the local neighborhood H: $fidelity(H, \widetilde{H}) = accuracy(b(\widetilde{H}), c(H))$. We report the fidelity as box plots in Fig. 9. The results show that on all datasets ABELE outperforms LIME with respect to the RF black box classifier. For the DNN the interpretable classifier of LIME is slightly more faithful. However, for both RF and DNN, ABELE has a fidelity variance markedly lower than LIME, i.e., more compact box plots also without any outlier[11]. Since these fidelity results are statistically significant, we observe that the local interpretable classifier of ABELE is more faithful than the one of LIME.

Nearest Exemplar Classifier. The goal of ABELE is to provide useful exemplars and counter-exemplars as explanations. However, since we could not validate them with an experiment involving humans, inspired by [18], we tested

---

[10] A decision tree for ABELE and a linear lasso model for LIME.
[11] These results confirm the experiments reported in [11].

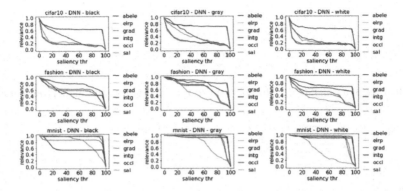

Fig. 11. Relevance analysis varying the percentile threshold τ (the higher the better).

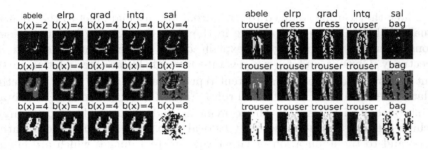

Fig. 12. Images masked with *black*, *gray* and *white* having pixels with saliency for DNN lower than $\tau = 70\%$ for the explanations of *four* and *trouser* in Figs. 4 and 6.

their effectiveness by adopting memory-based machine learning techniques such as the k-nearest neighbor classifier [2] (k-NN). This kind of experiment provides an objective and indirect evaluation of the quality of exemplars and counter-exemplars. In the following experiment we generated n exemplars and counter-exemplars with ABELE, and we selected n prototypes and criticisms using MMD [18] and K-MEDOIDS [2]. Then, we employ a 1-NN model to classify unseen instances using these exemplars and prototypes. The classification accuracy of the 1-NN models trained with exemplars and counter-exemplars generated to explain the DNN reported in Fig. 10 is comparable among the various methods[12]. In particular, we observe that when the number of exemplars is low $(1 \leq n \leq 4)$, ABELE outperforms MMD and K-MEDOIDS. This effect reveals that, on the one hand, just a few exemplars and counter-exemplars *generated* by ABELE are good for recognizing the real label, but if the number increases the 1-NN is getting confused. On the other hand, MMD is more effective when the number of prototypes and criticisms is higher: it *selects* a good set of images for the 1-NN classifier.

---

[12] The ABELE method achieves similar results for RF not reported due to lack of space.

Table 3. Coherence analysis for DNN classifier (the lower the better).

Dataset	ABELE	ELRP	GRAD	INTG	LIME	OCC	SAL
cifar10	$.575 \pm .10$	$.542 \pm .08$	$.542 \pm .08$	$.532 \pm .11$	$1.919 \pm .25$	$1.08 \pm .23$	$.471 \pm .05$
fashion	$.451 \pm .06$	$.492 \pm .10$	$.492 \pm .10$	$.561 \pm .17$	$1.618 \pm .16$	$.904 \pm .23$	$.413 \pm .03$
mnist	$.380 \pm .03$	$.740 \pm .21$	$.740 \pm .21$	$.789 \pm .22$	$1.475 \pm .14$	$.734 \pm .21$	$.391 \pm .03$

Table 4. Stability analysis for DNN classifier (the lower the better).

Dataset	ABELE	ELRP	GRAD	INTG	LIME	OCC	SAL
cifar10	$.575 \pm .10$	$.518 \pm .08$	$.518 \pm .08$	$.561 \pm .10$	$1.898 \pm .29$	$.957 \pm .14$	$.468 \pm .05$
fashion	$.455 \pm .06$	$.490 \pm .09$	$.490 \pm .09$	$.554 \pm .18$	$1.616 \pm .17$	$.908 \pm .23$	$.415 \pm .03$
mnist	$.380 \pm .04$	$.729 \pm .21$	$.729 \pm .21$	$.776 \pm .22$	$1.485 \pm .14$	$.726 \pm .21$	$.393 \pm .03$

Relevance Evaluation. We evaluate the effectiveness of ABELE by partly masking the image to explain x. According to [15], although a part of x is masked, $b(x)$ should remain unchanged as long as relevant parts of x remain unmasked. To quantitatively measure this aspect, we define the *relevance* metric as the ratio of images in X for which the masking of relevant parts does not impact on the black box decision. Let $E=\{e_1, \ldots, e_n\}$ be the set of explanations for the instances $X=\{x_1, \ldots, x_n\}$. We identify with $x_m^{\{e,\tau\}}$ the masked version of x with respect to the explanation e and a threshold mask τ. Then, the explanation *relevance* is defined as: $relevance_\tau(X, E) = |\{x \mid b(x) = b(x_m^{\{e,\tau\}}) \ \forall \langle x, e \rangle \in \langle X, E \rangle\}| \ / \ |X|$. The masking $x_m^{\{e,\tau\}}$ is got by changing the pixels of x having a value in the saliency map $s \in e$ smaller than the τ percentile of the set of values in the saliency map itself. These pixels are substituted with the color *0, 127* or *255*, i.e. *black, gray* or *white*. A low number of black box outcome changes means that the explainer successfully identifies *relevant* parts of the images, i.e., parts having a high relevance. Figure 11 shows the *relevance* for the DNN[13] varying the percentile of the threshold from 0 to 100. The ABELE method is the most resistant to image masking in `cifar10` regardless of the color used. For the other datasets we observe a different behavior depending on the masking color used: ABELE is among the best performer if the masking color is *white* or *gray*, while when the mask color is *black*, ABELE's relevance is in line with those of the competitors for `fashion` and it is not good for `mnist`. This effect depends on the masking color but also on the different definitions of saliency map. Indeed, as previously discussed, depending on the explainer, a saliency map can provide different knowledge. However, we can state that ABELE successfully identifies relevant parts of the image contributing to the classification.

For each method and for each masking color, Fig. 12 shows the effect of the masking on a sample from `mnist` and another from `fashion`. It is interesting to notice how for the SAL approach a large part of the image is quite relevant,

---

[13] The ABELE method achieves similar results for RF not reported due to lack of space.

Table 5. Coherence (left) and stability (right) for RF classifier (the lower the better).

Dataset	ABELE	LIME	Dataset	ABELE	LIME
cifar10	.794 ± .34	1.692 ± .32	cifar10	.520 ± .14	1.460 ± .23
fashion	.821 ± .37	2.534 ± .70	fashion	.453 ± .06	1.464 ± .18
mnist	.568 ± .29	2.593 ± 1.25	mnist	.371 ± .04	1.451 ± .17

causing a different black box outcome (reported on the top of each image). As already observed previously, a peculiarity of ABELE is that the saliency areas are more connected and larger than those of the other methods. Therefore, given a percentile threshold τ, the masking operation tends to mask more contiguous and bigger areas of the image while maintaining the same black box labeling.

Robustness Assessment. For gaining the trust of the user, it is crucial to analyze the stability of interpretable classifiers and explainers [14] since the stability of explanations is an important requirement for interpretability [21]. Let $E = \{e_1, \ldots, e_n\}$ be the set of explanations for $X = \{x_1, \ldots, x_n\}$, and $\{s_1, \ldots, s_n\}$ the corresponding saliency maps. We asses the *robustness* through the local Lipschitz estimation [21]: $robustness(x) = argmax_{x_i \in \mathcal{N}(x)}(\|s_i - s\|_2 / \|x_i - x\|_2)$ with $\mathcal{N}(x) = \{x_j \in X \mid \|x_j - x\|_2 \leq \epsilon\}$. Here x is the image to explain and s is the saliency map of its explanation e. We name *coherence* the explainer's ability to return similar explanations to instances labeled with the same black box outcome, i.e., similar instances. We name *stability*, often called also *sensitivity*, the capacity of an explainer of not varying an explanation in the presence of noise with respect to the explained instance. Therefore, for coherence the set X in the *robustness* formula is formed by real instances, while for stability X is formed by the instances to explain modified with random noise[14].

Tables 3 and 4 report mean and standard deviation of the local Lipschitz estimations of the explainers' *robustness* in terms of *coherence* and *stability*, respectively. As showed in [21], our results confirm that LIME does not provide robust explanations, GRAD and INTG are the best performers, and ABELE performance is comparable to them in terms of both *coherence* and *stability*. This high resilience of ABELE is due to the usage of AAE, which is also adopted for image denoising [32]. Table 5 shows the robustness in terms of coherence and stability for the model agnostic explainers ABELE and LIME with respect to the RF. Again, ABELE presents a more robust behavior than LIME. Figures 13 and 14 compare the saliency maps of a selected image from mnist and fashion labeled with DNN. Numbers on the top represent the ratio in the robustness formula. Although there is no change in the black box outcome, we can see how for some of the other explainers like LIME, ELRP, and GRAD, the saliency maps vary considerably. On the other hand, ABELE's explanations remain coherent and stable. We observe how in both *nines* and *boots* the yellow fundamental area does not change especially within the image's edges. Also the red and blue parts, that can

---

[14] As in [21], in our experiments, we use ϵ=0.1 for $\mathcal{N}$ and we add salt and pepper noise.

be varied without impacting on the classification, are almost identical, e.g. the *boots'* neck and the sole in Fig. 13, or the top left of the *zero* in Fig. 14.

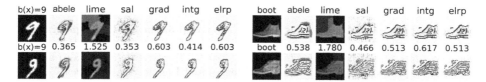

Fig. 13. Saliency maps for `mnist` (left) and `fashion` (right) comparing two images with the same DNN outcome; numbers on the top are the *coherence* (the lower the better)

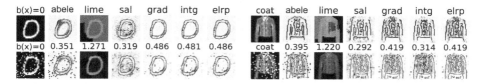

Fig. 14. Saliency maps for `mnist` (left) and `fashion` (right) comparing the original image in the first row and the modified version with salt and pepper noise but with the same DNN outcome; numbers on the top are the *stability* (the lower the better). (Color figure online)

7   Conclusion

We have presented ABELE, a local model-agnostic explainer using the latent feature space learned through an adversarial autoencoder for the neighborhood generation process. The explanation returned by ABELE consists of exemplar and counter-exemplar images, labeled with the class identical to, and different from, the class of the image to explain, and by a a saliency map, highlighting the importance of the areas of the image contributing to its classification. An extensive experimental comparison with state of the art methods shows that ABELE addresses their deficiencies, and outperforms them by returning coherent, stable and faithful explanations.

The method has some limitations: it is constrained to image data and does not enable casual or logical reasoning. Several extensions and future work are possible. First, we would like to investigate the effect on the explanations of changing some aspect of the AAE: *(i)* the latent dimensions k, *(ii)* the rigidity of the *discriminator* in admitting latent instances, *(iii)* the type of autoencoders (e.g. variational autoencoders [26]). Second, we would like to extend ABELE to make it work on tabular data and on text. Third, we would employ ABELE in a case study generating exemplars and counter-exemplars for explaining medical imaging tasks, e.g. radiography and fMRI images. Lastly, we would conduct extrinsic interpretability evaluation of ABELE. Human decision-making in a specific task (e.g. multiple-choice question answering) would be driven by ABELE explanations, and these decisions could be objectively and quantitatively evaluated.

Acknowledgements. This work is partially supported by the EC H2020 programme under the funding schemes: Research Infrastructures G.A. 654024 *SoBigData*, G.A. 78835 *Pro-Res*, G.A. 825619 *AI4EU* and G.A. 780754 *Track&Know*. The third author acknowledges the support of the Natural Sciences and Engineering Research Council of Canada and of the Ocean Frontiers Institute.

References

1. Bach, S., Binder, A., et al.: On pixel-wise explanations for non-linear classifier decisions by layer-wise relevance propagation. PloS One **10**(7), e0130140 (2015)
2. Bien, J., et al.: Prototype selection for interpretable classification. AOAS (2011)
3. Breiman, L.: Random forests. Mach. Learn. **45**(1), 5–32 (2001)
4. Chen, C., Li, O., Barnett, A., Su, J., Rudin, C.: This looks like that: deep learning for interpretable image recognition. arXiv:1806.10574 (2018)
5. Doshi-Velez, F., Kim, B.: Towards a rigorous science of interpretable machine learning. arXiv:1702.08608 (2017)
6. Escalante, H.J., et al. (eds.): Explainable and Interpretable Models in Computer Vision and Machine Learning. TSSCML. Springer, Cham (2018). https://doi.org/10.1007/978-3-319-98131-4
7. Fong, R.C., Vedaldi, A.: Interpretable explanations of black boxes by meaningful perturbation. In: ICCV, pp. 3429–3437 (2017)
8. Frixione, M., et al.: Prototypes vs exemplars in concept representation. In: KEOD (2012)
9. Frosst, N., et al.: Distilling a neural network into a soft decision tree. arXiv:1711.09784 (2017)
10. Goodfellow, I., et al.: Generative adversarial nets. In: NIPS (2014)
11. Guidotti, R., et al.: Local rule-based explanations of black box decision systems. arXiv:1805.10820 (2018)
12. Guidotti, R., Monreale, A., Cariaggi, L.: Investigating neighborhood generation for explanations of image classifiers. In: PAKDD (2019)
13. Guidotti, R., Monreale, A., Ruggieri, S., Turini, F., et al.: A survey of methods for explaining black box models. ACM CSUR **51**(5), 93:1–93:42 (2018)
14. Guidotti, R., Ruggieri, S.: On the stability of interpretable models. In: IJCNN (2019)
15. Hara, S., et al.: Maximally invariant data perturbation as explanation. arXiv:1806.07004 (2018)
16. He, K., et al.: Deep residual learning for image recognition. In: CVPR (2016)
17. Hinton, G., et al.: Distilling the knowledge in a neural network. arXiv:1503.02531 (2015)
18. Kim, B., et al.: Examples are not enough, learn to criticize! In: NIPS (2016)
19. Li, O., Liu, H., Chen, C., Rudin, C.: Deep learning for case-based reasoning through prototypes: a neural network that explains its predictions. In: AAAI (2018)
20. Makhzani, A., Shlens, J., et al.: Adversarial autoencoders. arXiv:1511.05644 (2015)

21. Melis, D.A., Jaakkola, T.: Towards robust interpretability with self-explaining neural networks. In: NIPS (2018)
22. Molnar, C.: Interpretable machine learning. LeanPub (2018)
23. Panigutti, C., Guidotti, R., Monreale, A., Pedreschi, D.: Explaining multi-label black-box classifiers for health applications. In: W3PHIAI (2019)
24. Ribeiro, M.T., Singh, S., Guestrin, C.: Why should i trust you?: Explaining the predictions of any classifier. In: KDD, pp. 1135–1144. ACM (2016)
25. Shrikumar, A., et al.: Not just a black box: learning important features through propagating activation differences. arXiv:1605.01713 (2016)
26. Siddharth, N., Paige, B., Desmaison, A., de Meent, V., et al.: Inducing interpretable representations with variational autoencoders. arXiv:1611.07492 (2016)
27. Simonyan, K., Vedaldi, A., Zisserman, A.: Deep inside convolutional networks: visualising image classification models and saliency maps. arXiv:1312.6034 (2013)
28. Spinner, T., et al.: Towards an interpretable latent space: an intuitive comparison of autoencoders with variational autoencoders. In: IEEE VIS (2018)
29. Sun, K., Zhu, Z., Lin, Z.: Enhancing the robustness of deep neural networks by boundary conditional gan. arXiv:1902.11029 (2019)
30. Sundararajan, M., et al.: Axiomatic attribution for DNN. In ICML, JMLR (2017)
31. van der Waa, J., et al.: Contrastive explanations with local foil trees. arXiv:1806.07470 (2018)
32. Xie, J., et al.: Image denoising with deep neural networks. In: NIPS (2012)
33. Zeiler, M.D., Fergus, R.: Visualizing and understanding convolutional networks. In: Fleet, D., Pajdla, T., Schiele, B., Tuytelaars, T. (eds.) ECCV 2014. LNCS, vol. 8689, pp. 818–833. Springer, Cham (2014). https://doi.org/10.1007/978-3-319-10590-1_53

Robust Anomaly Detection in Images Using Adversarial Autoencoders

Laura Beggel[1,2(✉)], Michael Pfeiffer[1], and Bernd Bischl[2]

[1] Bosch Center for Artificial Intelligence, Renningen, Germany
{laura.beggel,michael.pfeiffer3}@de.bosch.com
[2] Department of Statistics, Ludwig-Maximilians-University Munich,
Munich, Germany
bernd.bischl@stat.uni-muenchen.de

Abstract. Reliably detecting anomalies in a given set of images is a task of high practical relevance for visual quality inspection, surveillance, or medical image analysis. Autoencoder neural networks learn to reconstruct normal images, and hence can classify those images as anomalies, where the reconstruction error exceeds some threshold. Here we analyze a fundamental problem of this approach when the training set is contaminated with a small fraction of outliers. We find that continued training of autoencoders inevitably reduces the reconstruction error of outliers, and hence degrades the anomaly detection performance. In order to counteract this effect, an adversarial autoencoder architecture is adapted, which imposes a prior distribution on the latent representation, typically placing anomalies into low likelihood-regions. Utilizing the likelihood model, potential anomalies can be identified and rejected already during training, which results in an anomaly detector that is significantly more robust to the presence of outliers during training.

Keywords: Anomaly detection · Robust learning · Adversarial autoencoder

1 Introduction

The goal of anomaly detection is to identify observations in a dataset that significantly deviate from the remaining observations [9]. Since anomalies are rare and of diverse nature, it is not feasible to obtain a labeled dataset representative of all possible anomalies. A successful approach for anomaly detection is to learn a model of the normal class, under the assumption that the training data consists entirely of normal observations. If an observation deviates from that learned model, it is classified as an anomaly [5].

Autoencoder neural networks have shown superior performance for detecting anomalies on high dimensional data such as images. Autoencoders consist of an encoder network, which performs nonlinear dimensionality reduction from the input into a lower-dimensional latent representation, followed by a decoder

© Springer Nature Switzerland AG 2020
U. Brefeld et al. (Eds.): ECML PKDD 2019, LNAI 11906, pp. 206–222, 2020.
https://doi.org/10.1007/978-3-030-46150-8_13

network, which reconstructs the original image from this latent representation. Autoencoders do not require label information since the input image also represents the desired output. By learning to extract features and to reconstruct the original images, the network yields a model that generalizes to the reconstruction of images similar to those in the training set. Conversely, images which show significant deviations from those observed during training will lead to reconstruction errors. The reconstruction error of an image can thus be used as an anomaly score.

Although the autoencoder approach performs well on benchmark datasets [22], we identify in this article several major shortcomings for real-world scenarios. First, autoencoder methods for anomaly detection are based on the assumption that the training data consists only of instances that were previously confirmed to be normal. In practice, however, a clean dataset cannot always be guaranteed, e.g., because of annotation errors, or because inspection of large datasets by domain experts is too expensive or too time consuming. It is therefore desirable to learn a model for anomaly detection from completely unlabeled data, thereby risking that the training set is contaminated with a small proportion of anomalies. However, we find that autoencoder-based anomaly detection methods are very sensitive to even slight violations of the clean-dataset assumption. A small number of anomalies contaminating the training might result in the autoencoder learning to reconstruct anomalous observations as well as normal ones. We analyze the underlying causes for this vulnerability of standard autoencoders, and present several key ideas that make anomaly detection with autoencoders more robust to training anomalies, thereby improving the overall anomaly detection performance.

In summary, our contributions are: First, we use adversarial autoencoders [16], which allow to control the distribution of latent representations, thereby defining a prior distribution in the bottleneck layer. While (adversarial) autoencoders have been used for anomaly detection before [15,24], we here propose a novel criterion for detecting anomalies consisting of both reconstruction error and likelihood in latent space. Since anomalies are expected to have a low likelihood under the given prior of the normal data, the combination of likelihood and reconstruction error yields an improved anomaly score and therefore better detection performance. Second, we define an iteration refinement method for training sample rejection. Potential anomalies in the training set are identified in the lower dimensional latent space by a variation of 1-class SVM [18], and by rejecting the least normal observations we can increase robustness to contaminated data. Third, we propose a retraining method to increase separation in both latent and image space. We compare our method to [10,16], which only partially use the techniques combined in our approach, and show that our proposed method results in a significantly more robust anomaly detector against anomalies present during training.

2 Related Work

Autoencoders were originally intended for nonlinear dimensionality reduction and feature extraction [10], but it has been realized early on that their capability to model the training data distribution makes them suitable for anomaly detection [11]. More recent work has proposed probabilistic interpretations of deep autoencoders, which can directly model aspects of the data generating process. Denoising autoencoders [20] learn reconstruction of images from noise corrupted inputs. This form of regularization makes the latent representation focus on a data manifold which encodes the most relevant image features. In [1,2] it was shown that regularized autoencoders implicitly estimate the data generating process, and have established links between reconstruction error and the data generating density. [24] applied these concepts to anomaly detection with deep structured energy based models, showing that a criterion based on an energy score leads to better results than the reconstruction error criterion. Adversarial autoencoders (AAE) [16] learn a generative model of the input data by combining the reconstruction error with an adversarial training criterion [8]. A discriminator network learns to distinguish between samples coming from the encoder and from a desired arbitrary prior distribution, which gives AAEs great flexibility to represent assumptions about the data distribution. AAEs for anomaly detection were first proposed in [15], using a Gaussian mixture model as prior. It was found that a purely unsupervised approach did not separate anomalies and normal images into different clusters, and it was proposed to either condition on class labels, or train an explicit rejection class with random images.

Almost all approaches for anomaly detection with autoencoders require the training data to consist of normal examples only, but this alone is no guarantee for anomalies to have large reconstruction errors. Robust deep autoencoders [25] address this issue by combining denoising autoencoders with robust PCA, thereby isolating noise and outliers from training of the reconstruction. The method achieves significantly better results in the presence of anomalies in the training set on MNIST. [19] proposed using a combination of robust loss function for autoencoder training together with semi-supervised training of a classifier in latent space to overcome the problem of corrupted training data. The method achieves good detection performance, however, their evaluation shows that this increase is mainly due to semi-supervised training. A combination of deep learning and kernel based methods for anomaly detection in high dimensional data was proposed by [6], who combine a Deep Belief Network for feature extraction, and a 1-class SVM for anomaly detection in the compressed latent space. Their method can deal with anomalies in the training data, but does not use this information to refine the training set. In contrast, [17] directly optimized the objective function of a variation of 1-class SVM in the output space during network training. By doing so, anomalies can be detected immediately in the output space but this information is not used during training for sample rejection. When considering detection of potential adversarial examples, [7] have proposed density based measures in a ConvNet to identify data points that lie outside the data manifold. They increase the robustness of their method by adding a Bayesian uncertainty estimate, which handles complementary situations.

3   Autoencoders and Their Limitations

An autoencoder (AE) is a neural network that maps an input image $\mathbf{x} \in \mathcal{X} = \mathbb{R}^n$ to an output image $\mathbf{x}' \in \mathcal{X}$. It consists of an encoder function $f : \mathcal{X} \to \mathcal{Z}$ and a decoder function $g : \mathcal{Z} \to \mathcal{X}$, each implemented as a multi-layer neural network. They jointly compute $\mathbf{x}' = g(f(\mathbf{x}))$. The output of the encoder $\mathbf{z} = f(\mathbf{x}) \in \mathcal{Z} = \mathbb{R}^m$ ($m \ll n$) is a low-dimensional latent representation of $\mathbf{x}$. This bottleneck prevents the AE from learning a trivial identity function. The autoencoder is trained to minimize the reconstruction error $L(\mathbf{x}, \mathbf{x}')$, which is typically the pixelwise mean squared error or the Euclidean distance in the image space $\mathcal{X}$. After training, anomaly detection can be performed by comparing $L(\mathbf{x}, \mathbf{x}')$ to a decision threshold T_{rec}, classifying all images $\mathbf{y}$ with $L(\mathbf{y}, g(f(\mathbf{y}))) > T_{\text{rec}}$ as anomalies. T_{rec} is selected based on the distribution of all reconstruction errors L_{train} on the training set $\mathbf{X}_{\text{train}}$. Typical choices are the maximum reconstruction error $T_{\text{rec}} = \max_{\mathbf{x} \in \mathbf{X}_{\text{train}}} L(\mathbf{x}, \mathbf{x}')$, or a large (e.g., 90%) percentile $T_{rec} = p_{0.9}(L(\mathbf{x}, \mathbf{x}') | \mathbf{x} \in \mathbf{X}_{\text{train}})$, which is more robust. Using autoencoder networks for detecting anomalies with this procedure is based on the assumption that all training examples should be reconstructed well, or in other words that the training set is clean and consists only of normal observations.

3.1   Training with Anomalies

A standard autoencoder learns to reconstruct images from an intrinsic lower dimensional latent representation, and by simultaneously learning a mapping from image into latent space also learns in its weights an implicit model of the data it has seen. For the task of anomaly detection this leads to a trade-off between generating reconstructions of previously unseen normal images with minimal error, while maximizing the reconstruction error of anomalous images. Since no labels are available during training, neither of the criteria can be directly optimized. Instead, the AE is trained to minimize reconstruction errors on the entire training set, which will only directly optimize the first criterion if all training images are normal. During training, the objective rewards exact reconstructions of all training images, including anomalies. Overfitting singular anomalies can be avoided by reducing model capacity or early stopping, such that the AE focuses on reconstructing the majority class. Early stopping, however, may prevent the autoencoder from learning a model which can precisely reconstruct the majority of (normal) training observations, and may thus lead to false detections.

We demonstrate this effect for a conventional autoencoder trained on two classes of images of handwritten digits from MNIST [14]. A detailed description of the architecture can be found in Sect. 5. The digit '0' is arbitrarily defined as the normal class, whereas digit '2' is the anomaly class (different combinations

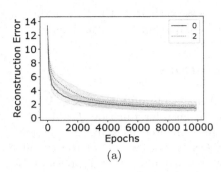 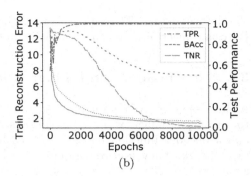

(a)   (b)

Fig. 1. Limitations of conventional autoencoders for anomaly detection. (a) Mean reconstruction error of a conventional AE trained on MNIST, where 95% of the images are from the normal class (digit '0', green, solid line), and 5% are anomalies (digit '2', red, dashed line). The shaded area shows the standard deviation. As training progresses, the AE learns to reconstruct the anomalous as well as the normal images. (b) Detection performance on test data from MNIST, measured by the True Positive Rate (TPR), True Negative Rate (TNR), and Balanced Accuracy (BAcc), where the reconstruction threshold is set to the 90th percentile. The gray lines indicate the mean training reconstruction error as displayed in (a). As training progresses, the AE produces more and more false positives, since the distribution of reconstruction errors between normal and anomalous images increasingly overlap (Color figure online).

of digits lead to similar results). In this experiment the training set includes 5% anomalies. Figure 1(a) shows the reconstruction error for a conventional AE trained over 10000 epochs, which results in a network that reconstructs both classes with very similar error. Using early stopping as proposed in [21,25], e.g., after only 100 or 1000 iterations results in a model that is better at reconstructing normal compared to anomalous images, but it has not yet learned an accurate reconstruction model for the normal class. Convergence is reached only after more than 4000 epochs, but at that time the model reconstructs both normal and anomalous images equally well. This results in poor performance as an anomaly detector, as shown in Fig. 1(b).

We evaluate the True Positive Rate (TPR), True Negative Rate (TNR), and Balanced Accuracy (BAcc) at different epochs (where an anomaly is a positive event). BAcc is defined as $\frac{\text{TPR}+\text{TNR}}{2} \in [0,1]$ and thus balances detection performance [3]. We do not use the F1 score, which is commonly used in anomaly detection, since it neglects the true negative prediction performance. Clearly, the importance of each metric depends on the role that false negatives (i.e., missed anomalies) and false alarms have for the task at hand. But obviously, approaching a TPR of 1 at the cost of a TNR going towards 0 (as is the case for an autoencoder trained until convergence) is not desirable. For the evaluation we use the known labels of images, which are, however, never used during training.

An immediate observation from Fig. 1(b) is that continued training leads to a drop in TNR and thus BAcc, which is due to increasing overlap between the distribution of reconstruction errors of normal and anomalous images. A possible explanation for this behavior lies in the nature of stochastic gradient descent, the method used to train autoencoders. In the initial phase, the AE learns to reconstruct the normal class, which is heavily overrepresented in the training set, and thus leads to more training updates. This effect is visible in Fig. 1(a), where the reconstruction error of the normal class shrinks much faster initially than that of anomalous examples. After a few hundred epochs, the error for normal images continues to shrink slowly, but the error for anomalies falls faster. This is due to the small gradient for normal examples, whereas anomalies with still large errors result in large gradients, and therefore dominate the direction of updates. As a result, the difference in reconstruction quality between normal and anomalous images vanishes at later epochs. One strategy could be to reduce model capacity, with the hope that in a smaller network only the majority class can be accurately reconstructed. However, this strategy also results in lower quality reconstructions for normal images, and therefore in a higher reconstruction threshold, which is again prone to yielding many false negatives. A similar argument explains why early stopping does not solve the issue.

3.2 Adversarial Autoencoders

Adversarial autoencoders (AAE) [16] extend the concept of autoencoders by inducing a prior distribution $p(\mathbf{z})$ in the latent space. A generative model of the data distribution $p_{\text{data}}(\mathbf{x})$ is thus obtained by applying the decoder to samples from the imposed prior in latent space. The main difference to Variational autoencoders [13] is the use of an adversarial training criterion [8]. As a result, AAEs can impose any prior distribution from which samples can be drawn, and have smoothly varying outputs in data space for small changes in corresponding latent space. An example of an AAE structure is displayed in Fig. 2.

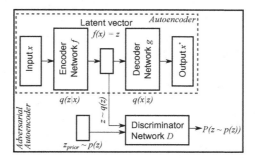

Fig. 2. Schematic structure of conventional autoencoder (blue dashed box) and the extension to an adversarial autoencoder (Color figure online).

From the perspective of anomaly detection AAEs are interesting because apart from the reconstruction error, the latent code provides an additional indication for anomalies [15]. Simply put, we expect anomalies $\mathbf{x}$ (characterized by low $p_{\text{data}}(\mathbf{x})$) to map to latent representations with low density $p(\mathbf{z}|\mathbf{x})$, or otherwise have high reconstruction error $L(\mathbf{x}, \mathbf{x}')$, because high likelihood latent codes should be decoded into normal images (see Fig. 3).

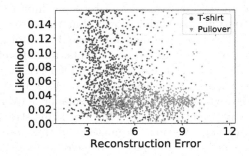

Fig. 3. Reconstruction error and likelihood for an AAE trained on a clean subset of Fashion-MNIST [23] containing only class 'T-shirt' (blue). Test data from the anomaly class 'Pullover' (red) yield lower likelihood values and higher reconstruction errors (Color figure online).

The previous analysis suggests a strategy to improve the robustness of autoencoders for anomaly detection in the presence of anomalies in the training set: If anomalies in the training set can be identified during training, there are ways to prevent a further improvement of their reconstruction quality. The simplest such strategy is to remove them from the training set, but other options are possible. In the following we present a novel mechanism based on AAE, which actively manipulates the training set during training by sample rejection, and thereby focuses AE training on the normal class.

4 Robust Anomaly Detection

If the training set contains anomalies, then the AAE will model them as part of its generative model for p_{data}, leading in principle to the same fundamental problem encountered in conventional AE. However, depending on the imposed prior, we can at least expect a separation in latent space between the normal and anomalous instance encodings, since AAEs have smoothly varying outputs for nearby points in latent space. This feature of AAEs can be explicitly utilized by defining a prior distribution with a dedicated rejection class for anomalies [15], but we have observed the same effect even in the case of unimodal priors such as Gaussians.

Separation between anomalies and normal instances in latent space is particularly useful if a rough estimate of the training anomaly rate α is known. In this case standard outlier detection methods such as 1-class SVM [18] can be employed on the latent representations, searching for a boundary that contains a fraction of $1 - \alpha$ of the whole dataset. Once potential anomalies are identified, they can be excluded for further training, or their contribution to the total loss might be reweighted. Such procedure approximates the case of a clean training set, where the combination of reconstruction error and latent density yields reliable results.

4.1 Likelihood-Based Anomaly Detection

Since AAEs impose a prior distribution $p(\mathbf{z})$ on the latent representations $\mathbf{z}$, the likelihood $p(\hat{\mathbf{z}})$ under the prior of a new code vector $\hat{\mathbf{z}} = f(\hat{\mathbf{x}})$ can be used as an anomaly score [15]. Anomalies are expected to have lower scores than normal examples. However, it is also clear that $p(\hat{\mathbf{z}})$ alone is an imperfect score, because anomalies in local clusters with small support might indeed be assigned higher scores than normal examples in boundary regions. Furthermore, the encoder might not be able to learn a mapping that exactly reproduces the prior. Despite these weaknesses, a likelihood-based criterion is able to identify most anomalies with similar performance as a reconstruction-based approach, and in addition allows a combination of both approaches. A decision threshold T_{prior} is defined by measuring the likelihood $p(f(\mathbf{x}))$ under the imposed prior for all training samples $\mathbf{x}$ and then selecting a specified percentile in the distribution of $p(f(\mathbf{x}))$ depending on the expected anomaly rate α. New examples $\mathbf{y}$ with $p(f(\mathbf{y})) < T_{\mathrm{prior}}$ are then classified as anomalies. Ideally we could set T_{prior} to the α percentile, but in practice the criterion is chosen slightly differently to compensate for approximation errors in the encoder and for biases induced by a finite training set. In our scenarios, $p_{0.1}(f(\mathbf{x}))$ was chosen empirically as it showed most robust behavior throughout all experiments. In the case of a clean dataset one can also fix the threshold, e.g., to a specified number of standard deviations, without optimizing on the training set. Likelihood-based anomaly detection can be easily combined with reconstruction-based methods, and our results have shown that they complement each other well. We choose a simple combination whereby a new example $\mathbf{y}$ is classified as an anomaly if either $L(\mathbf{y}, \mathbf{y}') > T_{\mathrm{rec}}$, or $p(f(\mathbf{y})) < T_{\mathrm{prior}}$. Alternative methods such as a 1-class SVM in the 2-dimensional space of reconstruction errors and likelihoods did not improve our results. Although we focus on these two measures, it is also straightforward to integrate more criteria, such as denoising performance [20], or sensitivity-based measures [4].

To compare the individual performance to a combination of both measures, we trained an AAE on a clean dataset consisting only of 'T-shirt's from Fashion-MNIST [23] (cf. Fig. 3). For new test observations stemming from the normal class and a previously unseen anomaly class ('Pullover'), both the reconstruction error and the likelihood estimate identify anomalies with similar performance (BAcc: 0.72 and 0.73, respectively), and a combination of both criteria increases performance (BAcc: 0.80). The architecture is described in detail in Sect. 5.

4.2 Iterative Training Set Refinement (ITSR)

In order to improve the robustness against contaminated datasets, we propose an iterative refinement of the training set. This method reduces the influence of likely anomalies for further autoencoder training, thus learning a more accurate model of the normal data distribution. If the adversarial autoencoder is trained with an imposed unimodal prior, e.g., a multivariate Gaussian, we expect the normal instances to cluster around the mode of the prior in latent space. This assumption is reasonable whenever instances of the normal class can be expected to be similar, e.g., in quality control. If anomalies are contained in the training set, we observe that the AAE maps them to low-likelihood regions of the prior (see Fig. 3). Anomalies either form their own clusters if they belong to reoccurring patterns (e.g., anomalies from a separate class), or will be represented sparsely and distant from the peak. In order to identify likely anomalies, standard outlier detection methods such as 1-class SVM [18] are applied to the representations of training images in the lower-dimensional latent space. The 1-class SVM receives as a hyperparameter an upper bound on the expected fraction of anomalies via the parameter ν. In our experiments, we use a 1-class SVM with RBF kernel and fix $\nu = 0.02$, since we assume to have no knowledge of the true anomaly rate. If available, however, knowledge of the true anomaly rate can be incorporated here.

The output of the 1-class SVM is a decision boundary, and a list of all normal data points. All other data points can be considered potential anomalies, and can be either completely removed from the training set, or weighted to contribute less to the overall loss than normal points. After modifying the training set the autoencoder is re-trained, yielding representations that better capture the true data manifold of the normal class, and with less incentive to reconstruct outliers accurately. In the following we describe our proposed training procedure in more detail.

First, every training sample $\mathbf{x}_i$ is associated with a weight w_i, which is used to compute a weighted reconstruction loss for the autoencoder:

$$L_{\mathbf{w}} = \sum_{i=1}^{N} w_i L(\mathbf{x}_i, g(f(\mathbf{x}_i))).$$

The autoencoder is trained to minimize the weighted reconstruction loss, where weights can change over time. The same associated sample weight w_i is used in the adversarial training procedure.

To iteratively refine the training set to make the model robust to anomalies present in training, the training procedure is split into three phases:

1. **Pretraining:** the AAE is initialized by training on the complete training set for a fixed number of epochs where all weights are set to the identical value $w_i = 1$. This is the starting point for anomaly detection in latent space with 1-class SVM in the subsequent step.

2. **Detection and Refinement:** a 1-class SVM is trained on the latent representations with a constant expected anomaly rate ν, yielding a set of candidate anomalies denoted $\hat{A}$. All instances within $\hat{A}$ are assigned a new weight $w_i = 0$, thereby removing it from further training. The model is then trained on the reduced training set $\mathbf{X} \setminus \hat{A}$ for a short number of epochs. These two steps are repeated d times where each repetition increases the total number of detected training anomalies. By iteratively excluding candidate anomalies, the model of the normal class is refined.

3. **Re-training:** after detecting anomalies in the training set and refining the model of the normal class, the model is re-trained such that reconstruction errors on detected anomalies increase. This can be achieved by setting $w_i < 0, \mathbf{x}_i \in \hat{A}$, forcing a better separability of the two classes. The method, however, created many false positive detections in the previous refinement phase, which with this strict reweighting, would erroneously be forced to be reconstructed worse. Since refining the model on normal observations still leads to good reconstructions of those false positive observations (they resemble the true normal observations), we define a threshold $T_{\text{retrain}} = p_{retrain}(L(\mathbf{x}, f(g(\mathbf{x})))|\mathbf{x} \in \hat{A})$ which is used as a new decision threshold for reweighting the potential anomalies, i.e., $w_i = w_{anomaly} < 0$ if $L(\mathbf{x}_i, f(g(\mathbf{x}_i))) > T_{\text{retrain}}$, else $w_i = 0, \mathbf{x}_i \in \hat{A}$. This forces the model to learn a higher reconstruction error and lower likelihood for the detected candidate anomalies that exceed the threshold T_{retrain}.

Our proposed ITSR model yields an autoencoder which over time focuses more and more on the reconstruction of normal images and matching their latent-distribution to the expected prior, thereby increasing the robustness for true normal observations in both training and test set. In Fig. 4, results for applying our ITSR model on MNIST with 5% anomalies in training are presented. While during the refinement phase the model is trained to robustly represent the normal class, the model increases separability between normal and anomalous observations during re-training (Fig. 4(a)). Moreover, the expected effect that anomalies represented in high-likelihood regions have a high reconstruction error becomes more distinct (Fig. 4(b)). In Sect. 5, we also discuss how to set the parameters ν for detecting candidate anomalies and the threshold T_{retrain} for re-training in more detail.

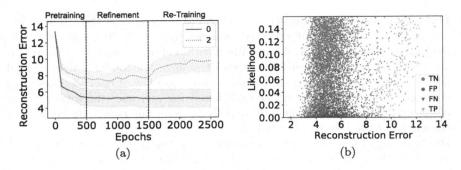

Fig. 4. Increasing the robustness of anomaly detection with iterative training set refinement. (a) Reconstruction error over the three phases of ITSR. We show the mean reconstruction error trained on MNIST, where 95% of the images are from the normal class (digit '0', green, solid line), and 5% are anomalies (digit '2', red, dashed line). The shaded area shows the standard deviation. (b) Reconstruction and likelihood of all points in the training set after ITSR. Colors indicate the final classification result produced by the 1-class SVM in ITSR: true normal (blue), false positive (green), true positive (orange), false negative (red). Iteratively refining and re-training our model increases separability between normal and anomalous observations. Additionally, the expected behavior that anomalies that falsely lie in a high-density region are badly reconstructed becomes even more evident (Color figure online).

5   Experimental Setup and Discussion of Results

Experimental Setup. Anomaly detection is evaluated on the classical MNIST [14] dataset, and the more recent and more complex Fashion-MNIST [23] database containing gray-level images of different pieces of clothing such as T-shirts, boots, or pullovers, which in contrast has more ambiguity between classes. Throughout our experiments, we use the original train-test splits, resulting in 60000 potential training (6000 per class) and 10000 test observations. From the available classes in both datasets, we define one class to be normal and a second class to be anomalous for training. In the case of MNIST, we arbitrarily select digit '0' as normal, and digit '2' as anomaly. For Fashion-MNIST, we conduct two experiments with increasing difficulty: in both cases, the class 'T-shirt' is defined as normal. In the first experiment anomalies are from the class 'Boot', which is easy to distinguish from T-shirts. In the second experiment, anomalies stem from the class 'Pullover', which is visually more similar to T-shirts, except for longer sleeves, and thus harder to detect. The final training data consists of the two previously defined classes, but only $\alpha = \{5\%, 1\%, 0.1\%\}$ of the instances are from the anomalous class. The experiments with an anomaly rate $\alpha = \{1\%, 0.1\%\}$ show that our approach performs also favorable if anomalies occur even less frequently. Since our main focus is to improve AE-based anomaly detection, we thus focus on a comparison to the methods that only partially use the techniques that we combine in our approach. The complete code for our evaluation is available on request from the authors.

Test Set Split. Our proposed model increases robustness to anomalies that are present during training. In order to evaluate whether this also increases robustness to unobserved types of anomalies, we evaluate on an independent test set, and split the anomalies into classes that were observed during training, and those that were not part of training (e.g. new digit classes in MNIST). For the set containing observed anomalies, the test set contains all normal test observations and observations from the class of anomalies that was present during training. The set containing unobserved anomalies consists again of the entire set of normal test instances, and all instances from classes that were never observed during training. For example for MNIST, the test set containing observed anomalies consists of images of digit '0' and digit '2' (1000 observations each). The set with unobserved anomalies contains again all images of digit '0' and all images of anomaly classes '1', '3'-'9' (1000 observations each). This results in a ratio of normal to anomalous observations in the test sets of 1:1 and 1:8, respectively, but does not affect the anomaly rate during training.

Setting of Parameters ν and Re-training Threshold T_{retrain}. For our proposed Iterative Training Set Refinement, the parameters ν, which influences how many candidate anomalies are detected during training, and the threshold for re-training are crucial. In fact, setting the parameters depends on the prior knowledge about the data. If the normal data are expected to be very homogeneous (e.g., in quality inspection), they will lie close in latent space and potential anomalies will most likely lie outside this region, so a smaller ν will suffice. If, on the other hand, the normal class is very heterogeneous (e.g., if different types of anomalies are expected), more normal observations will spread over latent space and more candidate anomalies (i.e., a larger ν) needs to be detected to 'catch' the true anomalies. In practice the true anomaly rate is not known precisely, but our results show that it is not necessary to have a precise estimate for ν (we know the true anomaly rate in the training data but fix $\nu = 0.02$) and that our proposed approach is robust.

For the threshold T_{retrain} for re-training, the relation between data homogeneity and parameter value is reversed: since this threshold defines the corresponding percentile of the reconstruction error, a large value is possible for a homogeneous normal class, whereas a lower value is required for heterogeneous normal data. In more detail, the threshold T_{retrain} for re-training should depend on the upper bound of falsely detected normal observations during refinement phase. In case of perfect detection of all true anomalies the fraction of falsely detected normal observations in $\hat{A}$ is $\frac{\nu \cdot d - \alpha}{\nu \cdot d}$. Since in general we do not know the true anomaly rate α (but show robustness up to $\alpha = 0.05$) and might also miss true anomalies in the refinement process, we additionally expect 5% of false detections. For our chosen parameter $\nu = 0.02$ together with the number of refinement steps $d = 10$ (see next subsection Architecture) this yields a re-training threshold of $T_{\text{retrain}} = p_{0.8}(L(\mathbf{x}, f(g(\mathbf{x})))|\mathbf{x} \in \hat{A})$.

Architecture. Encoder and decoder in the conventional autoencoder both consist of 2 fully-connected layers with 1000 units each. The ReLU activation function is used in all layers, with the exception of the final encoder layer (using linear activation), and the last decoder layer (using sigmoid activation). The latent space is restricted to 32 dimensions. This architecture is used in all experiments, but for AAEs the latent space is reduced to 2 dimensions. On MNIST, training is stopped after 4000 epochs, on Fashion-MNIST after 10000 epochs, using Adam [12] to adapt learning rates. For the AAE, a discriminator network is added, consisting of 2 fully connected layers with 1000 units each, and sigmoid activation in the last layer. Following [16], batch normalization is performed after each layer in the encoder. As latent prior we assume a 2-dimensional Gaussian $p(z) = [N(0, 1)]^2$. Training is stopped after 1000 epochs. Our proposed method ITSR is applied to the same AAE architecture. First, pretraining is performed for 500 epochs, then $d = 10$ repetitions (each 100 epochs) of the detection and refinement phase with $\nu = 0.02$ are computed. Retraining is done for 1000 epochs on MNIST and 500 epochs on Fashion-MNIST with $w_{anomaly} = -0.1$. For the combined likelihood and reconstruction anomaly score that is used as detection criterion for AAE and ITSR, the 90% percentile $T_{rec} = p_{0.90}(L(\mathbf{x}, \mathbf{x}^*)|\mathbf{x} \in \mathbf{X})$ of reconstruction errors, and the 10% percentile of likelihoods $T_{prior} = p_{0.10}(f(\mathbf{x})|\mathbf{x} \in \mathbf{X})$ are used. Conventional AEs use the same reconstruction-based threshold T_{rec}.

Results and Discussion. Figure 5 shows that for all investigated scenarios with $\alpha = 5\%$ anomalies in the training set our ITSR model yields better balanced accuracy than conventional autoencoders and adversarial autoencoders. The AAE without refinement improves the anomaly detection performance on MNIST, but has no beneficial effect for Fashion-MNIST. The results show the desired increased robustness to the presence of anomalies in the training set, in particular for the observed anomalies that stem from the same class that contaminates the training set, and which pose the greatest challenge for standard AEs. ITSR improves the balanced accuracy compared to the conventional AE by more than 30% for the experiment on MNIST (Fig. 5(a)), and by more than 20% over the AAE in general. The performance improvement over the AAE is greatest (30%) for the most difficult case of detecting 'Pullover' anomalies in the Fashion-MNIST dataset, with 'T-shirt's being normal (see Fig. 5(c)). Additional experiments in Table 1 show that even with a decreased anomaly rate $\alpha = \{1\%, 0.1\%\}$ our method still performs favorable.

Comparing the performance on anomaly classes that were observed or unobserved during training, we find that standard AEs and AAEs perform similarly on both types. ITSR results in higher accuracy for anomalies observed during training, which is the desired effect. This observations even holds if the training set only contains 0.1% anomalies, or in other words, when the training data is almost completely normal. Furthermore, our model performs at par or slightly better than the other methods on unobserved anomalies. It is expected that the effect for unobserved anomalies is smaller, since they cannot influence training, and any improvement can only come from a more accurate model for the normal class. We thus conclude that iterative refinement of the training set improves

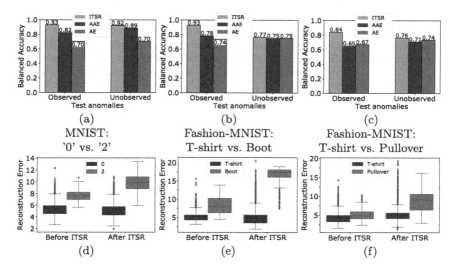

Fig. 5. Anomaly detection performance on an independent test set with an anomaly rate of 5% in training. The images differ in their experimental setup as follows. (a),(d): MNIST data with digit '0' normal class and digit '2' anomaly class. (b)–(c),(e)–(f): Fashion-MNIST data with class 'T-shirt' defined as normal and 'Boot' ((b),(e)) or 'Pullover' ((c),(f)) as anomalous.
(a)–(c): We compare the BAcc of AE, AAE, and ITSR on a test set containing only types of anomalies observed during training (left), and a set with unobserved anomalies (right). The detection of anomalies during training in ITSR increases the robustness against the type of anomalies contaminating the training set, while the performance on novel anomalies is similar or slightly better. (d)—(f): Reconstruction error for ITSR for normal (blue) and anomalous (orange) training observations. The reconstruction error before and after ITSR is shown. Normal images are always accurately reconstructed, but due to ITSR the error for anomalies increases, thus facilitating anomaly detection (Color figure online).

anomaly detection with autoencoders in general, without negatively affecting the detection of novel types of anomalies.

In order to understand the cause for the improved robustness, Fig. 5(d)–(f) show the reconstruction errors on training set before and after ITSR, separately for the normal and anomaly classes. We only visualize the case of $\alpha = 5\%$, even though similar observations can be made for decreased anomaly rates. We observe only minor changes for the normal class, but a strongly increased reconstruction error for anomalies after ITSR. This implies that the ITSR model has learned to robustly represent the normal class in the low-dimensional latent space and reconstruct it to the original space, while becoming insensitive to the anomalies present in training. There is still some overlap between the reconstruction errors of the two classes, but the increased separation results in a higher balanced accuracy.

Table 1. Balanced accuracy results for anomaly detection on an independent test set with anomaly rate $\alpha = \{1\%, 0.1\%\}$ in training. We compare conventional autoencoder (AE) and adversarial autoencoder (AAE) approaches to our proposed Iterative Training Set Refinement method (ITSR). The defined normal and anomaly class are similar to Fig. 5(a)–(c), i.e., MNIST data with digit '0' normal class and digit '2' anomaly class, and Fashion-MNIST data with class 'T-shirt' defined as normal and 'Boot' or 'Pullover' as anomalous. We split evaluation into a test set containing only types of anomalies observed during training (left), and a set with unobserved anomalies (right).

| | Anomaly rate $\alpha = 1\%$ | | | | | |
| | Observed anomaly type | | | Unobserved anomaly type | | |
Dataset	AE	AAE	ITSR	AE	AAE	ITSR
MNIST: '0' vs. '2'	0.69	0.91	**0.94**	0.69	0.91	**0.93**
Fashion-MNIST: T-shirt vs. Boot	0.74	0.89	**0.92**	0.73	0.78	**0.79**
Fashion-MNIST: T-shirt vs. Pull.	0.74	0.70	**0.81**	0.74	0.78	**0.81**
	Anomaly rate $\alpha = 0.1\%$					
Dataset	AE	AAE	ITSR	AE	AAE	ITSR
MNIST: '0' vs. '2'	0.68	0.90	**0.91**	0.68	0.89	**0.90**
Fashion-MNIST: T-shirt vs. Boot	0.74	0.89	**0.90**	0.73	0.77	**0.80**
Fashion-MNIST: T-shirt vs. Pull.	0.73	0.71	**0.80**	0.73	0.79	**0.80**

6   Conclusion

A novel method called Iterative Training Set Refinement (ITSR) for anomaly detection in images is presented, which exploits the capabilities of adversarial autoencoders in order to address the shortcomings of conventional autoencoders in the presence of anomalies in the training set. Our method compares favorably to state-of-the art methods, and its increased robustness reduces the need for a clean training dataset, and thus the need for expert information. In practice this makes the ITSR method very attractive for scenarios where it is known that the anomaly rate is very low, e.g., in quality inspection. Instead of letting experts inspect a potentially very large training set and picking only normal instances, an unprocessed dataset can be used, leaving it to ITSR to exclude potential anomalies from training. ITSR works directly in the latent space of the adversarial autoencoder, and is a general method to focus the learning process on the true manifold of the normal majority class. No label information is necessary for this approach, but obviously our method can be extended to a semi-supervised setting, or an active learning approach, where an interactive query for labels for instances close to the border identified by the 1-class SVM is performed. Although presented only on image data in this article, our approach easily translates to other high-dimensional data types, e.g., spectrograms or time series.

Acknowledgments. This work has been partially supported by the German Federal Ministry of Education and Research (BMBF) under Grant No. 01IS18036A. The authors of this work take full responsibilities for its content.

References

1. Alain, G., Bengio, Y.: What regularized auto-encoders learn from the data-generating distribution. J. Mach. Learn. Res. **15**(1), 3563–3593 (2014)
2. Bengio, Y., Yao, L., Alain, G., Vincent, P.: Generalized denoising auto-encoders as generative models. Adv. Neural Inf. Process. Syst. **1**, 899–907 (2013)
3. Brodersen, K.H., Ong, C.S., Stephan, K.E., Buhmann, J.M.: The balanced accuracy and its posterior distribution. In: International Conference on Pattern Recognition, pp. 3121–3124. IEEE (2010)
4. Chan, P.P., Lin, Z., Hu, X., Tsang, E.C., Yeung, D.S.: Sensitivity based robust learning for stacked autoencoder against evasion attack. Neurocomputing **267**, 572–580 (2017)
5. Chandola, V., Banerjee, A., Kumar, V.: Anomaly detection: a survey. ACM Comput. Surv. (CSUR) **41**(3), 15 (2009)
6. Erfani, S.M., Rajasegarar, S., Karunasekera, S., Leckie, C.: High-dimensional and large-scale anomaly detection using a linear one-class svm with deep learning. Pattern Recogn. **58**, 121–134 (2016)
7. Feinman, R., Curtin, R.R., Shintre, S., Gardner, A.B.: Detecting adversarial samples from artifacts. arXiv preprint arXiv:1703.00410 (2017)
8. Goodfellow, I., et al.: Generative adversarial nets. Adv. Neural Inf. Process. Syst. **2**, 2672–2680 (2014)
9. Hawkins, D.M.: Identification of Outliers, vol. 11. Springer, Dordrecht (1980)
10. Hinton, G.E., Salakhutdinov, R.R.: Reducing the dimensionality of data with neural networks. Science **313**(5786), 504–507 (2006)
11. Japkowicz, N., Myers, C., Gluck, M., et al.: A novelty detection approach to classification. In: Proceedings of the International Joint Conference on Artificial Intelligence, vol. 1, pp. 518–523 (1995)
12. Kingma, D.P., Ba, J.: Adam: a method for stochastic optimization. In: Proceedings of the International Conference on Learning Representations (2015). http://arxiv.org/abs/1412.6980
13. Kingma, D.P., Welling, M.: Auto-encoding variational bayes. In: Proceedings of the International Conference on Learning Representations (2014)
14. LeCun, Y., Bottou, L., Bengio, Y., Haffner, P.: Gradient-based learning applied to document recognition. Proc. IEEE **86**(11), 2278–2324 (1998)
15. Leveau, V., Joly, A.: Adversarial autoencoders for novelty detection. Technical report, Inria - Sophia Antipolis (2017). https://hal.inria.fr/hal-01636617
16. Makhzani, A., Shlens, J., Jaitly, N., Goodfellow, I., Frey, B.: Adversarial autoencoders. arXiv preprint arXiv:1511.05644 (2015)
17. Ruff, L., et al.: Deep one-class classification. In: Proceedings of the International Conference on Machine Learning, pp. 4390–4399 (2018)
18. Schölkopf, B., Platt, J.C., Shawe-Taylor, J., Smola, A.J., Williamson, R.C.: Estimating the support of a high-dimensional distribution. Neural Comput. **13**(7), 1443–1471 (2001)

19. Shah, M.P., Merchant, S., Awate, S.P.: Abnormality detection using deep neural networks with robust quasi-norm autoencoding and semi-supervised learning. In: Proceedings of the 15th International Symposium on Biomedical Imaging, pp. 568–572. IEEE (2018)

20. Vincent, P., Larochelle, H., Bengio, Y., Manzagol, P.: Extracting and composing robust features with denoising autoencoders. In: Proceedings of the International Conference on Machine Learning, pp. 1096–1103. ACM (2008)

21. Vincent, P., Larochelle, H., Lajoie, I., Bengio, Y., Manzagol, P.: Stacked denoising autoencoders: learning useful representations in a deep network with a local denoising criterion. J. Mach. Learn. Res. **11**, 3371–3408 (2010)

22. Williams, G., Baxter, R., He, H., Hawkins, S., Gu, L.: A comparative study of RNN for outlier detection in data mining. In: Proceedings of the 2002 IEEE International Conference on Data Mining, pp. 709–712. IEEE (2002)

23. Xiao, H., Rasul, K., Vollgraf, R.: Fashion-MNIST: a novel image dataset for benchmarking machine learning algorithms. arXiv preprint arXiv:1708.07747 (2017)

24. Zhai, S., Cheng, Y., Lu, W., Zhang, Z.: Deep structured energy based models for anomaly detection. In: Proceedings of the International Conference on Machine Learning, pp. 1100–1109 (2016)

25. Zhou, C., Paffenroth, R.C.: Anomaly detection with robust deep autoencoders. In: Proceedings of the 23rd ACM SIGKDD International Conference on Knowledge Discovery and Data Mining, pp. 665–674. ACM (2017)

Holistic Assessment of Structure Discovery Capabilities of Clustering Algorithms

Frank Höppner[✉] and Maximilian Jahnke

Department of Computer Science,
Ostfalia University of Applied Sciences, 38302 Wolfenbüttel, Germany
f.hoeppner@ostfalia.de

Abstract. Existing cluster validity indices often possess a similar bias as the clustering algorithm they were introduced for, e.g. to determine the optimal number of clusters. We suggest an efficient and holistic assessment of the structure discovery capabilities of clustering algorithms based on three criteria. We determine the robustness or stability of cluster assignments and interpret it as the confidence of the clustering algorithm in its result. This information is then used to label the data and evaluate the consistency of the stability-assessment with the notion of a cluster as an area of dense and separated data. The resulting criteria of stability, structure and consistency provide interpretable means to judge the capabilities of clustering algorithms without the typical biases of prominent indices, including the judgment of a clustering tendency.

1 Introduction

Clustering algorithms are used in various settings of exploratory data analysis, pattern recognition, etc. They are often used as a tool in a longer preprocessing pipeline to support some other goal than just clustering the data for its own sake (e.g. classification, discretization, compression). The *best clustering algorithm* is then simply the one that supports the original goal best, so we may only be in charge of providing an (external) evaluation of the surrounding task.

We exclude such objectives in this paper, but concentrate on those cases where *clustering* itself is the core objective. We thus understand the *clustering task* in a narrow sense as *structure discovery*: Does the dataset itself suggest a partitioning into multiple, separated groups? This would be a valuable result in an explorative analysis of new data, for instance, it would suggest to explore and compare the partitions individually. In the context of, say, customer relationship management we would *not* ask if it is *possible* to subdivide all customers into groups, which seems always possible in one way or another, but whether the data provides evidence that customers naturally decompose in distinctive groups. This is also reflected by widely used definitions of clustering, where clusters are well-separated groups that define a compact or dense area of data.

© Springer Nature Switzerland AG 2020
U. Brefeld et al. (Eds.): ECML PKDD 2019, LNAI 11906, pp. 223–239, 2020.
https://doi.org/10.1007/978-3-030-46150-8_14

From a *structure discovery* perspective, a clustering algorithm claims that it has discovered *structure* in the dataset. So the research question in this paper is how to assess the capabilities of the various existing clustering algorithms in this regard. Although the large number of clustering algorithms is flanked by an impressive number of validity indices, we argue that they are usually not suited for a fair comparison across many different clustering algorithms with respect to their structure discovery capabilities. The main contribution of this paper is a holistic assessment of the structure discovery capabilities of clustering algorithms. We determine the robustness or stability of cluster assignments and interpret it as the confidence of the clustering algorithm in its result. This information is then used to label the data and evaluate its consistency with the notion of a cluster as an area of dense and separated data. This approach allows us to apply methods that are otherwise restricted to supervised learning. The three criteria of stability, discovered structure and consistency provide better means to judge about the capabilities of clustering algorithms without the typical biases of prominent indices, including the judgment of a clustering tendency.

2 Related Work

There is a great variety of clustering algorithms, covered in various textbooks, e.g. [1, 8, 13]. We do not focus on any particular type of clustering algorithm, but will use a spectrum of well-known algorithms (k-means, hierarchical clustering, mean shift, dbscan) as representatives. We assume the reader is familiar with these popular algorithms. They all share – more or less – the same goal, but vary in the computational approach and bias. The review [12] advises to choose an algorithm based on "the manner in which clusters are formed", which clearly demonstrates the dilemma we face if clustering is intended as an explorative technique and not much is known about the data yet.

With so many algorithms at hand, it seems natural to try them all on new data. This leads to the question, which result we should trust most. Some suggest to use external information (class labels), which might be the right approach if classification is the ultimate goal. With explorative structure discovery in mind we agree "that it is an inherent flaw in design of clustering algorithms if the researcher designing the algorithm evaluates it only w.r.t. the class labels of classification datasets" [9], because the class labels do not necessarily respect the typical properties of clusters, such as compactness and separation. But there are also many cluster validity measures that consider *internal information* only (rather than external class labels). Recent extensive studies [2, 4] compare 30 such indices and among the best-performing indices were Silhouette [18], Davies-Bouldin (DB) [5], Calinski-Harabasz (CH) [3], and SDBw [11]. The study [19] uses 10 external and 3 internal measures (Silhouette [18], Dunn [7], DB [5]).

Many internal measures were introduced to overcome a parameter selection problem. The k-means algorithm, for instance, requires the number of clusters to be specified in advance, so the algorithm is run for multiple values and the validity index identifies the best choice. This leads to measures particularly tailored to single clustering algorithms (e.g. [17]). For such a purpose a measure works best, if it adopts the bias of the considered clustering algorithm. But if we intend to compare the results of various clustering algorithms *with different biases*, an evaluation based on such a measure would not be impartial (cf. [16]).

While the literature agrees on the objectives of clustering on an abstract level (compactness and separation), the exact interpretation may vary considerably. K-means was designed with spherical clusters in mind, so the mean distance to the cluster center is an appropriate way of measuring compactness, but arbitrary cluster shapes will not be evaluated adequately. Sixteen out of the 30 cluster validity indices covered in [2], however, include the notion of a cluster centroid, which represents a bias on the cluster shape. Other examples for biases on the shape include the use of a cluster diameter or an average within-cluster-distance.

To identify a natural grouping, clusters need to be separated. But how important is the actual distance between clusters? Some measures use a ratio of intra-cluster and inter-cluster distance. While meaningful for small ratios, above some threshold (e.g. >3) we consider clusters as being well-separated, regardless of the actual ratio. Incorporating the ratio in the measure may overemphasize the separation of clusters. Yet other measures incorporate concepts like the single nearest neighbor (e.g. the Dunn index). They are used, for instance, to measure the gap between two clusters (closest point of a different cluster). As many partitional clustering algorithms exhaustively assign all data points to some cluster, including noise and outliers, such measures are heavily affected by noisy datasets. The measure assumes a noise-free void between the clusters, which also represents a bias. These problems underline that the results of many cluster validity indices for two different algorithms are difficult to interpret, to say the least. A worse validity index cannot be unambiguously attributed to a worse clustering result, it might as well be caused by a bias-mismatch.

Many studies have applied algorithms repeatedly to accumulate evidence of multiple clusterings to find a better partition. In [10] the accumulated evidence was used to compose new similarity data to which yet another clustering algorithm may be applied. Using (only) the stability of the obtained results as a validity measure was proposed in [15]. The stability of k-means clustering was also examined in [14] to pick the correct number of k-means clusters, but there it was observed that the stability correlated well with the accuracy of (ensemble) clustering for some datasets – but poorly with other datasets. In this work we are neither interested in improving partitions nor in parameter selection for a particular clustering algorithm, but to directly compare the performance of *different clustering algorithms*. This includes but is not limited to the stability of the results, as we will demonstrate that stability alone is not sufficient.

3   Threefold Assessment of Structure Discovery

We assume a dataset D of size $n = |D|$ is given. We denote $\mathcal{P} = \{C_1, \ldots, C_c\}$ as a **partition of D of size** c if $\forall 1 \leq i, j \leq c$: $C_i \subseteq D$, $C_i \cap C_j = \emptyset$ and $\bigcup_i C_i \subseteq D$. We use the abbreviation $\bigcup \mathcal{P}$ for $\bigcup_{i=1}^{c} C_i$. Note that we do not require $\bigcup_i C_i = D$: some algorithms (e.g. dbscan) mark data as outliers. We also remove singleton clusters as they also represent outliers.

A clustering algorithm delivers a partition of D of size c, where the c groups are usually called clusters. We use the notation $C_x^{\mathcal{P}}$ for any $x \in D$ to refer to the unique cluster $C_j \in \mathcal{P}$ with $x \in C_j$. For illustrative purposes we use R implementations of hierarchical clustering (single-, complete- and average-linkage), k-means, dbscan and meanshift with varying parameters (e.g. 2–7 clusters). For the hierarchical clustering we obtain the final clusters in a rather naive way by cutting the tree to get the intended number of subtrees (clusters).

3.1 Point Stability

Lacking data from the full population, clustering algorithms are typically executed on a (random) sample, so there is always some uncertainty in the selection of the data involved. We can check an obtained partition to see whether x and y belong to the same cluster, but we actually want to know if x and y would belong to the same cluster *in general*, that is, if the full population was clustered rather than this particular data sample only.

We have only access to a partition $\mathcal{P}$ obtained from our algorithm by applying it to sample D. We would like to know, for any $x \in D$, how likely other objects y, co-clustered with x in $\mathcal{P}$, belong to the same cluster if we had a different sample. Assuming the existence of a *ground truth partition* $\mathcal{T}$ for a moment, we are interested, for a given x, in

$$P(y \in C_x^{\mathcal{T}} | y \in C_x^{\mathcal{P}}) = \frac{|(C_x^{\mathcal{T}} \cap C_x^{\mathcal{P}}) \backslash \{x\}|}{|C_x^{\mathcal{P}} \backslash \{x\}|} = \frac{|C_x^{\mathcal{T}} \cap C_x^{\mathcal{P}}| - 1}{|C_x^{\mathcal{P}}| - 1} \tag{1}$$

This conditional probability characterizes the stability of a single data point as it is perceived by the selected clustering algorithm. A probability of 1 would mean that all *co-grouped data* of x in $\mathcal{P}$ would actually co-group identically in the true partition. As there is no chance of knowing $\mathcal{T}$ and even $\mathcal{P}$ depends on our sample D, we estimate this probability by executing the same algorithm multiple times on different subsets of D: We may then estimate how likely a point y belongs to the same cluster as x (in any other partition), given we observed that x and y co-group in one given partition.

Definition 1 (Point Stability). *Given a dataset D and a clustering algorithm. Let $k, m \in \mathbb{N}$. Just as in k-fold cross-validation, we use a random partition $\mathcal{R} = \{R_1, \ldots, R_k\}$ of D with equal-sized groups and define (training) datasets $D_i = D \backslash R_i$, $1 \leq i \leq k$. This process is repeated m times with shuffled data, such that we obtain a set M of $k \cdot m$ different partitions by applying the clustering algorithm to the resp. D_i. We define the (k,m)-point stability of $x \in D$ as*

$$PS(x) := \frac{1}{|M_x^2|} \sum_{(\mathcal{P}, \mathcal{Q}) \in M_x^2} P(y \in C_x^{\mathcal{Q}} | y \in C_x^{\mathcal{P}}) = \frac{1}{|M_x^2|} \sum_{(\mathcal{P}, \mathcal{Q}) \in M_x^2} \frac{|C_x^{\mathcal{Q}} \cap C_x^{\mathcal{P}}| - 1}{|C_x^{\mathcal{P}}| - 1}$$

where M_x^2 is defined as $M_x^2 := \{(\mathcal{P}, \mathcal{Q}) \mid \mathcal{P} \in M, \mathcal{Q} \in M, \mathcal{P} \neq \mathcal{Q}, x \in \mathcal{P}, x \in \mathcal{Q}\}$.

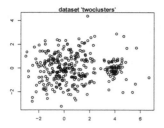 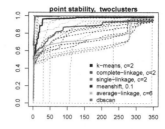

Fig. 1. Simple dataset with two clusters (left) and point stability plot (right) for all considered clustering algorithms (color-coded). Thick lines are discussed in the text. (Color figure online)

Having removed singleton clusters (cf. page 3), we will not face a division by zero. Throughout the paper we use $k = m = 5$, which yields 25 partitions and $25 \cdot 24 = 600$ partition comparisons. The point stability is already an informative tool if all values are sorted and plotted as shown in Fig. 1. For the sample data on the left, each line in the point stability plot on the right corresponds to one algorithm/parameter setting. The color indicates the clustering algorithm, the few thick lines are from top to bottom: single-linkage ($c = 2$), almost identical to mean-shift (threshold 0.1), k-means ($c = 2$), complete-linkage ($c = 2$), and average-linkage ($c = 6$). About 50 data objects receive a point stability close to 1 from many algorithms, which means that they get clustered reliably. They correspond to the small cluster on the right. The remaining objects receive quite different stability values. As the true number of clusters is 2, the large cluster is splitted arbitrarily depending on the chosen subsample for $c > 2$. Thus data pairs get grouped differently from run to run and their stability decreases. But even when the clustering algorithms were asked for 2 clusters, there is still considerable variance in the stability curves. The stability of the highlighted meanshift and single-linkage (top curves) is clearly superior over k-means and average-linkage, which respond more sensitive to changes in the sample.

3.2   Stably Discovered Structure

In Fig. 1 two algorithms achieved consistently high stability values for almost all data objects, but for a completely different reason. As already mentioned, the hierarchical single-linkage algorithm was used in a naive way: the hierarchy was cut off to obtain a certain number of clusters. In the particular case of Fig. 1(left), which contains noisy data points, the first few clusters are typically singleton clusters that correspond to outliers. The second cluster then consists of all remaining data and it is not surprising to achieve high stability values for all of them. In contrast, the results of the meanshift clustering consistently discovered both clusters in Fig. 1. Stability alone is thus not sufficient, we have to measure the amount of actually discovered structure.

Definition 2 (Stable Partition). *We define the largest set $D_S \subseteq D$ of data objects that are robustly clustered by the clustering algorithm (i.e. have a point stability of 1) as the* **stably clustered data.** *From all obtained partitions $\mathcal{P}_i \in M$ we can thus identify a single* **stable partition** *$\mathcal{P}_S$ which (1) consists of all stably clustered data ($\bigcup \mathcal{P}_S = D_S$) and (2) is consistent with all partitions ($\forall \mathcal{P}_i : \forall C \in \mathcal{P}_i : \exists C_s \in \mathcal{P}_S : C \cap D_S = C_s$).*

To identify $\mathcal{P}_S$ we have to keep in mind that, although stability is measured object-wise, an unstable object degrades the stability of *all data objects* in the same cluster. In other words, removing one instable object will increase the stability of all remaining objects in a cluster. Therefore we identify D_S by ordering all objects (increasingly) by their point stability and successively removing objects until all remaining points reach a stability of 1. Each removal increases the stability of all objects in C_x, so D_S is usually much larger than the set of objects that receive values close to 1 in the point stability plots of Fig. 1. We will discuss how to compute D_S efficiently in Sect. 3.5.

So we define the fraction of stable data $|D_S|/|D|$ as the **stability index**, which serves as a first quality indicator. The higher the stability index, the more data was clustered reliably. But we have seen that the number of data objects alone is not sufficient since all stable objects may belong to a single cluster (cf. single-linkage example): Without any (sub)structure being discovered, a high stability is pointless. We may add the number of clusters as a second quality indicator, but this would not take the cluster sizes into account. Instead we use the partition entropy of the stable partition as a **(discovered) structure index**: In an information-theoretic sense, entropy denotes the amount of information in a transmitted message. The message consists of the (reliably) assigned clusters to each data object. The higher the amount of information in the cluster assignments, the more structure has been discovered. Then three clusters receive a higher structure value than two clusters, two equal sized clusters receive a higher value than a 95%:5% cluster constellation (less structured).

Definition 3 (Partition Entropy). *Given a partition $\mathcal{P} = \{C_1, \ldots, C_n\}$, by partition entropy we refer to $PE(\mathcal{P}) = -\sum_{i=1}^{n} p_i \log p_i$ where $p_i = \frac{|C_i|}{|\bigcup \mathcal{P}|}$.*

Figure 2(left) shows which data was recognized as stable for a k-means clustering ($c = 2$) and Fig. 2(middle) for average-linkage clustering ($c = 3$). The stably clustered data is shown as black crosses, the instably clustered data as red circles. For k-means we see that all red points lie half way between both cluster centers, the right cluster contains more data than appropriate (due to k-means' bias towards equal-sized clusters). For the average-linkage example the number of clusters was not ideal ($c = 3$ instead of 2): depending on the current subsample, the surplus middle cluster varied in location and size, leading to a large portion of instably clustered data. Compared to k-means, fewer data was stably clustered and the structure index is similar as the stable partition also consists of two clusters only – despite its initialization with $c = 3$.

All algorithms can be compared in the scatterplot of the stability index and the structure index as shown in Fig. 2(right). A single point corresponds to the

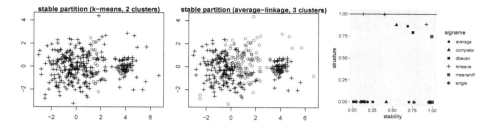

Fig. 2. Stably clustered data (black), instable portion in red for k-means (c = 2) and average-linkage (c = 3). Right: Entropy and size of stable partition for all algorithms. (Color figure online)

evaluation of a clustering algorithm (with fixed parameters). The horizontal line indicates the entropy for 2 equal-sized clusters. All results at the bottom of the Fig. correspond to algorithms, where the *fraction of stable data* consisted of a *single cluster only*: the algorithms did not identify any substructure reliably. Another group of results aligns somewhat below the line 'entropy of 1'. From our background information about the dataset (two unequal cluster sizes) we expect the best result to be near this line but not to reach it, because the clusters are not of the same size. Only the stable partition of the meanshift algorithm covers almost 100% of the data **and** reliably detects both clusters. The second best result comes from k-means, which has a higher structure index but less stably clustered data (lower stability index). From the plot we can read immediately, that the meanshift and k-means runs are superior to all other results wrt. to stability and structure index. The inappropriate assignment of data from the "left true cluster" to the "right k-means cluster" is, however, not yet reflected.

3.3   Compactness and Separation

So far we have evaluated the resulting partitions only, but did not use any distance information. The example of Fig. 2(left) shows that information from the partition alone is not sufficient. K-means claims two clusters of roughly the same size, but cuts off some data from the large cluster and disregards the cluster separation. This will be addressed by a third criterion. We will not make assumptions about the shape of the clusters as this would bias our measure towards clustering algorithms with the same assumption.

We have to clarify our notion of compactness and separation first. Clusters correspond to dense groups of data objects, so cluster members should be identifiable by means of some level of data density. As a simple indicator of density we use the following distance $d_k(x)$ to the kth neighbor:

Definition 4 (k^{th} Nearest Neighbor). *By $d_k(x) = \max_{y \in N_k(x)} \|x - y\|$ we denote the distance to the kth nearest neighbor of x in D, where $N_k(x) \subseteq D$ is the k-neighborhood around x such that $\forall y \in D \backslash N_k(x) : \|x - y\| \geq d_k(x)$ and $|N_k(x)| = k + 1$.*

Table 1. Consistency of 'notion of compactness' (density-based, $d_k \leq \varrho$) and 'well-clustered' (partition-based, pure and stable)

	Stably clustered and pure	Instably clustered or impure
Within cluster: $d_k \leq \varrho$	TP	FP
Outside cluster: $d_k > \varrho$	FN	TN

$$\text{precision} = \frac{TP}{TP+FP}$$

$$\text{recall} = \frac{TP}{TP+FN}$$

We intend to use $d_k(x)$ as a score that indicates the predisposition of x to belong to a cluster. If a data object has k neighbors within some (small) threshold distance, we may speak of a compact, densely packed area, which therefore qualifies for cluster membership. Being part of a cluster, we expect objects in the neighborhood to belong to the same cluster. We do *not* expect data from other clusters in the neighborhood (this would violate the separation). Furthermore, we expect from a good clustering algorithm to stably identify a cluster, that is, x as well as its neighbors (but not any instably clustered data).

For any $x \in D$ we now have two sources of information: (i) Based on the distance, we infer a *clustering tendency* from $d_k(x) \leq \varrho$ for some density threshold ϱ. (ii) From our stability analysis we know whether our clustering algorithm perceives x as part of a stable cluster. For a good clustering, both information about x should be consistent: dense data should be clustered stably. So the third criterion measures how well both views match. Are the objects, that likely belong to clusters, stably clustered and well separated? To measure the degree of consistency we consider a contingency table shown in Table 1: If a data object qualifies for cluster membership ($d_k \leq \varrho$), and the algorithm clustered it stably and with pure neighborhood, the compactness (small d_k distance) and the separation (stable, pure neighborhood) are consistent (true positive). If, however, the object was not clustered stably or the neighborhood is not pure, we recognize a false positive.

The consistency depends on ϱ: For a small threshold, only the dense center of a cluster may meet the condition $d_k \leq \varrho$. Those points are likely to get stably clustered (TP, increases precision), but many other stably-clustered but less dense areas will be missed (FN, low recall). Data towards the border of a cluster may require a larger threshold ϱ to accept them as 'dense enough to be part of a cluster'. With ϱ getting larger, the risk of including data from other clusters in the neighborhood increases. For non-separated clusters, an increasing recall may therefore lead to a drop in precision. The overall consistency of the partition with the data density is thus well-captured by means of a precision-recall graph, cf. Fig. 3(left) for the data set from Fig. 1. We expect a curve of a reasonable run to start in the top left corner. If there is a threshold ϱ that separates all clusters from another, we reach 100% recall with 100% precision (line close to the ideal line $(0,1)$–$(1,1)$). The earlier the curve drops from the ideal line, the worse the

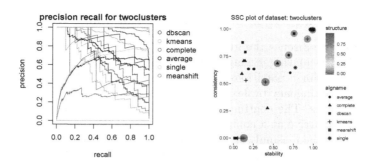

Fig. 3. Precision-recall graph for data set `twoclusters` and its SSC-plot.

consistency of the clusters (not separated or not stably clustered). We may also observe curves starting at $(0, 0)$, which indicates that the clustering algorithm did not even succeed to stably cluster the regions with the highest data density. This may happen if c was chosen too high and multiple prototypes compete for a single true cluster: The true cluster is split into multiple parts and its core data gets assigned to alternate clusters, which renders them instable.

As the optimal curve in such a graph is a constant line of precision 1, the area under the precision-recall graph serves as the third **consistency index**. The final **SSC-plot** (stability, structure, consistency) shows the relative size of the stable dataset on the x-axis, the consistency (area under precision-recall curve) on the y-axis and the structure (entropy of the stable partition) by the dot size and its color, cf. Fig. 3(right). Optimal results lie in the upper right corner (all data stably clustered, highly consistent). Several runs lie in this corner in Fig. 3(right), but only one meanshift result discovered a non-trivial structure. The second best result is still k-means (for 2 clusters), but with lower stability and consistency values, the latter reflects the missing separation in Fig. 2(left).

3.4 Ranking

The SSC-plot offers a holistic view on the algorithms performance. In a particular context there might be a focus on one of the measures stability, structure, or consistency. If considered as a multicriteria problem, there might be no single best solution, so the Pareto front has to be explored. When a unique ranking is needed to select the best algorithm automatically, we suggest to sum how many other runs are dominated by a given run in the three criteria individually. In our running example the two highest scores correspond to the best solutions identified in the discussion: the meanshift run gets a score of 81 and the k-means a score of 77 with an average score of 41.6. (With 34 runs in the experiment the theoretical maximum is 33 for each index, 99 in total for all three indices.)

3.5   Efficient Calculation of a p% Stable Partition

In this section we discuss the identification of a partition with an average stability of p%. Calculating a single point stability $PS(x)$ for data object x is straightforward: For r partitions we carry out $r \cdot (r-1)$ comparisons; for each comparison a contingency table of size $c \times c$ is constructed in $O(n)$, where c is the number of clusters. The contingency tables contain the cluster intersections of definition 1. We arrive at a complexity of $O(r^2 \times n)$. We calculate $PS(x)$ once, order the points increasingly by their point stability, and successively remove objects from the dataset in this order. We stop if the average $PS(x)$ for all remaining x reaches p%. A recalculation of $PS(x)$ after each removal would lead us to $O(r^2 \cdot n^2)$.

A more efficient implementation makes use of the fact that upon removal of the next data object the contingency tables need not be recalculated because they change only in one cell by 1. The partitions associated with the table tell us which cell is affected. Furthermore we want to remove data objects successively until we reach the desired average stability for the remaining data, so we actually do not need to calculate individual stability values $PS(x)$ but only the average stability $PS(x)$ of all remaining x. For the average stability $\overline{PS}$ we have

$$\overline{PS} = \frac{1}{|D|} \sum_{x \in D} PS(x) = \frac{1}{|D|} \sum_{x \in D} \frac{1}{|M_x^2|} \sum_{(\mathcal{P},\mathcal{Q}) \in M_x^2} \frac{|C_x^{\mathcal{Q}} \cap C_x^{\mathcal{P}}| - 1}{|C_x^{\mathcal{P}}| - 1} \quad (2)$$

As the rightmost term in (2) is the same for all data objects in the same cell of the contingency table (and $|M_x^2| = |M|(|M| - 1)$ regardless of x) we arrive at

$$\overline{PS} = \frac{1}{|D||M|(|M| - 1)} \sum_{(\mathcal{P},\mathcal{Q}) \in M^2, \mathcal{P} \neq \mathcal{Q}} \sum_{P \in \mathcal{P}, Q \in \mathcal{Q}} |Q \cap P| \cdot \frac{|Q \cap P| - 1}{|P| - 1}$$

Thus the calculation of $\overline{PS}$ can be done in $O(r^2 \cdot c^2)$ and is independent of the dataset size n. Recalculating $\overline{PS}$ until it reaches a value of 1 has therefore a complexity of $O(r^2 \cdot c^2 \cdot n)$.

4   Empirical Evaluation

We use standard R implementations for the clustering algorithms as well as the validity indices [6]. We report results for a selection of indices, such as SDbw (identified as best index in [16]) or Silhouette (identified as best index in [2]).

4.1   Artificial Datasets

We consider a set of 6 artificially generated, two-dimensional datasets first, shown in Fig. 4. In this setting, a decision about the correct clustering can be done by visual inspection. For a range of clustering algorithms and parameters the same number of $k \cdot m = 25$ runs were evaluated by the validity indices and then

Table 2. Results of popular cluster validity indices for various datasets. Correct result in bold face. If multiple runs achieved the same evaluation, only one is listed.

Dataset	CH	Dunn	Silhouette	DB	SDbw
disc	kmeans, 7	single, 2	kmeans, 3	kmeans, 7	kmeans, 7
triangle	**single, 3**	**single, 3**	**single, 3**	**single, 3**	**single, 3**
ring	kmeans, 7	**single, 2**	dbscan, 0.1	kmeans, 7	kmeans, 7
grid	kmeans, 4	average, 7	dbscan 0.1	kmeans, 4	kmeans, 4
block	kmeans, 7	single, 2	**dbscan 0.1**	kmeans, 7	kmeans, 7
ellipse	kmeans, 6	dbscan, 0.075	kmeans, 4	dbscan, 0.075	dbscan, 0.075

averaged. Among the results, the Table 2 reports one run that achieved the best average value. The correctness of the partition was evaluated by visual inspection and is indicated by bold face in the Table.

No Structure: We start with a dataset that has no structure at all, the `disc` dataset in Fig. 4(top left). In absence of any clusters or focal points, the clusters in different runs do not have much in common. The SSC plot for this dataset is shown in Fig. 5(top left). The runs that have high consistency and high stability (top right corner) do not discover any structure (no coloured circles visible): The single-linkage and dbscan runs group all data in one cluster (and exclude only a few outliers). All other runs have a very poor stability value, almost all of the data was marked as unstable. The SSC plot shows clearly that none of the algorithms did discover anything of interest – which is perfectly right for the disc dataset. In contrast, most validity measures favour kmeans ($c = 7$) – due to a monotonic behavior in c and $c = 7$ was the highest value in our experiments. Most validity indices are not prepared for this case as they compare at least two clusters.

Compact Clusters: Next we consider a clear structure, the `triangle` dataset of Fig. 4(top middle). This is a simple task for many clustering algorithms, but may still cause problems. For instance, even with the correct number of clusters, k-means splits one of the three clusters from time to time (R implementation initializes prototypes with random points). The top right corner of well-performing runs in the SSC plot of Fig. 5(top middle) is populated with various runs (e.g. single linkage, $c = 3$), many of them indicating the stable discovery of 3 equal-sized clusters by means of a structure index of about 1.6. In Fig. 4(top middle) only a single object has been marked as instable by the average-linkage clustering. The validity indices also work well with this dataset, all of the indices prefer the correct number of clusters $c = 3$. But for many indices, the average evaluation of k-means is only slightly worse than that of single-linkage, but the SSC plot tells a different story: Because of the occasional cluster splitting the k-means runs receive lower consistency and stability values, it yields the correct solution less reliable.

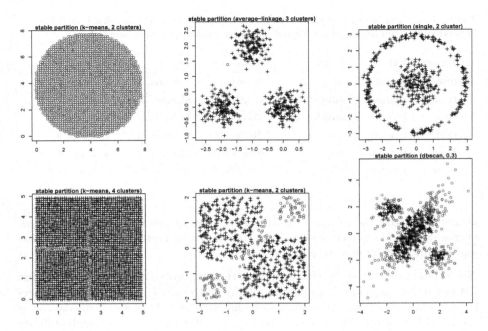

Fig. 4. Datasets from top left to bottom right: disc, triangle, ring, grid, block, ellipse. The red color refers to the stability obtained of some selected clustering algorithm. (Color figure online)

Cluster Shape: The `ring` dataset in Fig. 4(top right) has been used many times in the literature. It has been chosen because many validity indices have a bias towards compact clusters and would not accept the inner cluster and the ring as two clusters. Only the Dunn validity index selects a correct solution, while the other measures prefer k-means again ($c = 7$). The runs with high values of c, however, do not lead to stable partitions, they subdivide the outer ring arbitrarily, these clusters are not reproducible. In contrast to the validity indices, the SSC-plot in Fig. 5(top right) clearly favors the single-linkage ($c = 2$) solution as an optimal solution. (The icon is somewhat difficult to see, because several meanshift results with zero structure lie at approximately the same position). There is a clear gap to other runs in terms of stability and consistency.

A second dataset `ellipse` with varying shapes is shown in Fig. 4(bottom right): two small spherical and one large long-stretched cluster. The SSC plots indicates that only the meanshift algorithm manages to discover these clusters almost perfectly. Other runs in the top-right corner assign all data to a single cluster and thus discover no structure. A k-means run claims to discover more structure, but far less consistent: The visual inspection of the result shows that the long-stretched cluster is broken up into several portions of roughly equal size. Again, the results selected by the cluster validity indices in Table 2 do not correspond to the correct solution. Either many clusters are used to split up the

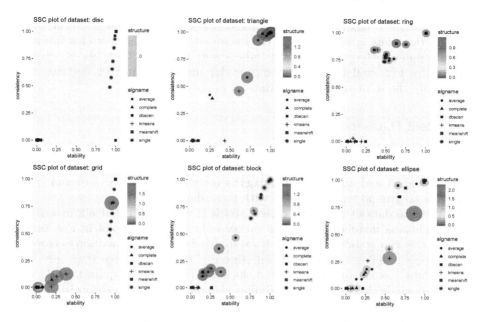

Fig. 5. SSC-plots (top left to bottom right): disc, triangle, ring, block, grid, ellipse.

long-stretched cluster, a single cluster with all data (meanshift, 0.3), or a few tiny clusters with over 90% of the dataset marked as noise (dbscan, 0.075).

Clustering Tendency: The `grid` dataset of Fig. 4(bottom left) is another example for a dataset that carries no internal structure. In contrast to `disc`, most validity indices suggest $c = 4$ instead of $c = 7$ now. This is due to the corners, which were absent in the `disc` dataset. They serve as focal points and stabilize the cluster positions, while at the same time guaranteeing four equal-sized clusters (cf. stable points in Fig. 4). The SSC-plot of Fig. 5(bottom left) looks similar to the `disc` dataset: Most runs have low stability and low consistency (lower left corner) and those runs with higher stability offer no structure. The only exception is the discussed phenomenon with k-means ($c = 4$), where the corner stabilize the cluster positions, which yields a high stability value. However, as we can see from the instable points (marked red) in Fig. 4(bottom left), the clusters and not separated and we achieve a quite low consistency value.

The `grid` dataset is also meant as a counterpart of the `block` dataset, where two of the four corners actually form separated clusters, so we have 3 clusters in total. The SSC plot clearly shows a few runs (dbscan, single-linkage) that deliver optimal results at an entropy close to 0.8 (because we have one very large cluster and two small clusters). On the contrary, the best k-means run suggests two equal-sized clusters that split the large cluster into two (cf. instable portion in Fig. 4(bottom middle)). This leads to a structure index close to 1 (two equal-sized clusters), but the consistency is poor (below 0.75). The SSC-plot reflects the performance again very well, whereas most validity indices favour many clusters (k-means, $c = 7$). None of the measures hints at the correct solution.

In summary, the cluster validity indices were misled by their biases, whereas the SSC-plot (as well as the selection procedure mentioned in Sect. 3.4) managed to identify the most reliable algorithm for every dataset.

4.2   Real Datasets

Next we examine the results on three real dataset from the UCI machine learning repository: `wine` (all attributes except the class), `ecoli` (selected attributes: mcg, gvh, aac, alm1 and alm2), and `pendigits` (attributes #6, #8, #10 and #12). There is no ground truth available with these datasets.

The `wine` dataset has three classes and it is well-known that a k-means run with 3 clusters matches the classes pretty well. In the SSC-plot in Fig. 6(left) exactly this run stands out by the highest structure index (partition entropy of ≈ 1.6, corresponding to 3 equal-sized clusters). But we also see that only 65% of the data was clustered stably and the consistency is also quite low. So it is safe to conclude that we observe a similar phenomenon as with the `grid` dataset: The data distribution provides focal points for three clusters, but we do not have three separated clusters. The k-means run with $c = 2$ has much better stability and consistency values.

A 5D-excerpt of the `ecoli` dataset is shown in Fig. 6(bottom middle). Upon visual inspection some scatterplots offer no structure (aac vs gvh), others seem to suggest two clusters (aac vs alm2), some may even hint at three clusters (gvh vs alm1). The SSC-plot supports this impression we got by visual inspection very well: we see a close-to-optimal meanshift result for two clusters, but also a runner-up with three clusters (86% stability, 92% consistency). Other algorithms reach a similar structure index, but are less stable and less consistent.

Finally we discuss results for a real dataset where the visual inspection is not conclusive: the `pendigits` dataset (handwritten digit recognition). Although we use only 4 attributes from the original dataset, the scatterplot matrix looks very confusing and nothing hints at the existence of separated clusters. From the SSC-plot in Fig. 6(right) we see a very good k-means result with stability and consistency close to 1 – no cluster splitting or lacking separation with k-means for this run. The precision-recall allows to diagnose the results: For instance, for two k-means runs we observe a steep drop in precision followed by an almost constant segment (curves (b)). For these runs, only a few dense points were stably discovered (TP), but most of the surrounding, less dense data was marked instable as it was assigned to alternating clusters. The k-means curve that drops earliest recovers later (curve (c)): This means that one particularly dense area was not stably clustered (FP), possibly a cluster splitting phenomenon, but for the less dense data the algorithm performed much better (more TPs). Several average-linkage curves (d) achieve good results in medium dense areas, but perform extremely poor in the areas of highest and lowest density.

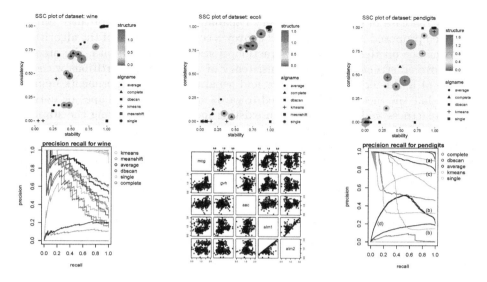

Fig. 6. Real Datasets and SSC-plot from left to right: wine, ecoli, pendigits.

4.3 Sensitivity

The consistency index depends on the parameter k in $d_k(\cdot)$. We have used $k = 16$ throughout all experiments. The size of k influences the degree of separation that is required for clusters: For $k = 0$ all neighborhoods are pure and none for $k = n$. A cluster that does not even consist of k points will not have any pure neighborhoods. The role of k is that of assuring separation at the border of a cluster, where data from the own cluster may lie on one side and data from another cluster on the opposite side. If the gap is large enough such that the k nearest objects all belong to the same cluster as x, we consider x well separated from other clusters. We have calculated consistency values for $k \in \{8, 12, 16, 20, 24\}$ over 27 datasets and obtained a lowest pairwise Pearson correlation of 0.989 ($k = 12$ vs $k = 24$) and a correlation coefficient of 1 for $k = 8$ vs $k = 12$. So the results are robust and not sensitive to the exact choice of k.

5   Summary and Conclusions

We have revisited the problem of evaluating clustering algorithms from a structure discovery perspective. Recent studies list and compare 30 different validity indices to find out the best measure. But all these measures seem to have strong biases, which makes them less suited to directly compare the performance of an arbitrary selection of algorithms on an unknown dataset. This has also been confirmed by our experiments. While it is common to apply a broad range of classifiers to a new dataset to see which method may work best with the unknown data, we seem to have nothing comparable for clustering methods.

For the case of structure discovery capabilities, a collection of three indices has been proposed in this paper that convey a complete picture of the algorithms performance on this dataset: the fraction of stably clustered data, the amount of discovered structure, and the consistency of the resulting partitions with the notion of a cluster being "compact and separated". The experiments demonstrate that the method is less biased towards specific cluster shapes or notions of compactness and separation than existing methods. Addressing the stability of each object and its density separately, allows us to apply methods usually restricted to classification task in the field of unsupervised clustering. The proposal may therefore strike a new path for a systematic and direct comparison of clustering algorithms from different paradigms and with different biases – at least as far as structure discovery capabilities are concerned.

The results are reproducible. The source code, the datasets and all figures are available at https://public.ostfalia.de/~hoeppnef/validity.html.

References

1. Aggarwal, C.C., Reddy, C.K. (eds.): Data Clustering: Algorithms and Applications. Chapman & Hall, London (2013)
2. Arbelaitz, O., Gurrutxaga, I., Muguerza, J., Perez, J.M., Perona, I.: An extensive comparative study of cluster validity indices. Pattern Recogn. **46**, 243–256 (2013)
3. Calinski, T., Harabasz, J.: A dendrite method for cluster analysis. Commun. Stat. - Theory Methods **3**(1), 1–27 (1974)
4. Chouikhi, H., Charrad, M., Ghazzali, N.: A comparison study of clustering validity indices. In: Global Summit on Computer & Information Technology, pp. 1–4 (2015)
5. Davies, D., Bouldin, D.: A cluster separation measure. Trans. Pattern Anal. Mach. Intell. **1**, 224–227 (1979)
6. Desgraupes, B.: Clustering indices. R-package 'clusterCrit' (2017)
7. Dunn, J.: Well separated clusters and optimal fuzzy partitions. J. Cybern. **4**(1), 95–104 (1974)
8. Everitt, B.S., Landau, S.: Cluster Analysis. Wiley, Hoboken (2011)
9. Färber, I., et al.: On using class-labels in evaluation of clustering. In Proceedings of MultiClust 2010 (2010)
10. Fred, A., Jain, A.K.: Combining multiple clusterings using evidence accumulation. IEEE Trans. Pattern Anal. Mach. Intell. **27**(6), 835–850 (2005)
11. Halkidi, M., Vazirgiannis, M.: Clustering validity assessment: finding the optimal partitioning of a data set. In: IEEE International Conference on Data Mining, pp. 187–194 (2001)
12. Jain, A.K., Murty, N.M., Flynn, P.J.: Data clustering: a review. ACM Comput. Surv. **31**(3), 264–323 (1999)
13. Kaufman, L.: Finding Groups in Data: An Introduction to Cluster Analysis. Wiley, Hoboken (2005)
14. Kuncheva, L.I., Vetrov, D.P.: Evaluation of stability of k-means cluster ensembles with respect to random initialization. IEEE Trans. Pattern Anal. Mach. Intell. **28**(11), 1798–1808 (2006)
15. Lange, T., Roth, V., Braun, M.L., Buhmann, J.M.: Stability-based validation of clustering solutions. Neural Comput. **16**(6), 1299–1323 (2004)

16. Liu, Y., Li, Z., Xiong, H., Gao, X., Wu, J.: Understanding of internal clustering validation measures. In: Proceedings of International Conference on Data Mining, pp. 911–916 (2010)
17. Pal, N.R., Bezdek, J.C.: On cluster validity for the fuzzy c-means model. IEEE Trans. Fuzzy Syst. **3**(3), 379–379 (1995)
18. Rousseeuw, P.J.: Silhouettes: a graphical aid to the interpretation and validation of cluster analysis. J. Comput. Appl. Math. **20**, 53–65 (1987)
19. Wiwie, C., Baumbach, J., Röttger, R.: Comparing the performance of biomedical clustering methods. Nat. Methods **12**(11), 1033–1040 (2015)

Pattern-Based Anomaly Detection in Mixed-Type Time Series

Len Feremans[1], Vincent Vercruyssen[2(✉)], Boris Cule[1], Wannes Meert[2], and Bart Goethals[1,3]

[1] Department of Mathematics and Computer Science, University of Antwerp, Antwerp, Belgium
{len.feremans,boris.cule,bart.goethals}@uantwerpen.be
[2] Department of Computer Science, KU Leuven, Leuven, Belgium
{vincent.vercruyssen,wannes.meert}@cs.kuleuven.be
[3] Monash University, Melbourne, Australia

Abstract. The present-day accessibility of technology enables easy logging of both sensor values and event logs over extended periods. In this context, detecting abnormal segments in time series data has become an important data mining task. Existing work on anomaly detection focuses either on continuous time series or discrete event logs and not on the combination. However, in many practical applications, the patterns extracted from the event log can reveal contextual and operational conditions of a device that must be taken into account when predicting anomalies in the continuous time series. This paper proposes an anomaly detection method that can handle mixed-type time series. The method leverages frequent pattern mining techniques to construct an embedding of mixed-type time series on which an isolation forest is trained. Experiments on several real-world univariate and multivariate time series, as well as a synthetic mixed-type time series, show that our anomaly detection algorithm outperforms state-of-the-art anomaly detection techniques such as MATRIXPROFILE, PAV, MIFPOD and FPOF.

Keywords: Anomaly detection · Time series · Distance measure · Pattern-based embedding · Frequent pattern mining

1 Introduction

Anomaly detection in time-series is an important real-world problem, especially as an increasing amount of data of human behaviour and a myriad of devices is collected, with an increasing impact on our everyday lives. We live in an "Internet of Things" world, where a network of devices, vehicles, home appliances and other items embedded with software and electronics are connected and exchanging data [9]. Although many organisations are collecting time series data, automatically analysing them and extracting meaningful knowledge, such

---

L. Feremans and V. Vercruyssen—These authors contributed equally to the work.

© Springer Nature Switzerland AG 2020
U. Brefeld et al. (Eds.): ECML PKDD 2019, LNAI 11906, pp. 240–256, 2020.
https://doi.org/10.1007/978-3-030-46150-8_15

as an understandable model that automatically flags relevant anomalies, remains a difficult problem, even after decades of research.

Exploring different benchmark datasets for time series anomaly detection, we found that these datasets often consist of univariate time series, where anomalies are local or global extrema or *point anomalies* [2]. In contrast, we focus on *collective and contextual anomalies*: a collection of points in the time series is anomalous depending on the surrounding context. For instance, most smartphones log many *continuous* times series from various sensors, such as the accelerometer, gyroscope, internal thermometer, and battery level. In addition, smartphones log *discrete* events in different operating system logs, such as applications starting or stopping, certain hardware components being turned on or off, or application-specific events. Such events are crucial in determining whether the behaviour observed in the continuous time series, e.g., a spike in power usage, is anomalous. We argue that for many real-world applications one needs to extract information from both types of sources to successfully detect anomalies.

In the active research area for anomaly detection in continuous time series, much attention has been given to finding anomalies using continuous *n-grams*, *dynamic time warping* distance, and similarity to the nearest neighbors [15,18], but not to integrating event log data. On the other hand, pattern mining based techniques for detecting anomalies have been developed for discrete event logs, but not for continuous time series. In this paper, we propose how to circumvent the apparent mismatch between discrete patterns and continuous time series data. We introduce a pattern-based anomaly detection method that can detect anomalies in *mixed-type time series*, i.e., time series consisting of both continuous sensor values and discrete event logs.

Given a time series dataset, the method leverages the mature field of *frequent pattern mining* research [19] to find frequent patterns in the data, serving as a template for the frequently occurring normal behaviour. Then, the frequent patterns are used to map the time series data to a feature-vector representation. This newly found pattern-based embedding of the data combines the information in both the continuous time series and the discrete event logs into a single feature vector. Finally, a state-of-the-art anomaly detection algorithm is used to find the anomalies in the embedded space.

The remainder of this paper is organised as follows. In Sect. 2, we introduce the necessary preliminaries. In Sect. 3, we provide a detailed description of our method for pattern mining, feature representation, and anomaly detection. In Sect. 4, we present an experimental evaluation of our method and compare with state-of-the-art methods. We present an overview of related work in Sect. 5 and conclude our work in Sect. 6.

2 Preliminaries

2.1 Time Series Data

A *continuous time series* is defined as a sequence of real-valued measurements $(\langle x_1, t_1 \rangle, \ldots, \langle x_n, t_n \rangle)$, where $x_k \in \mathbb{R}$ and each measurement has a distinct timestamp t_k. Although this is not required, we will assume that the continuous time series are sampled regularly, that is $t_{i+1} - t_i$ is constant, and do not contain missing values. A *discrete event log* is a sequence of discrete events $(\langle e_1, t_1 \rangle, \ldots, \langle e_n, t_n \rangle)$ where $e_k \in \Sigma$, with Σ a finite domain of discrete event types. Unlike continuous time series, we assume that multiple events can co-occur at the same timestamp, i.e. $t_i \leq t_{i+1}$, and that events can occur sparsely.

In this paper, we consider a *mixed-type time series* **S**. This is a collection of N continuous time series and M event logs. Thus, **S** has $M + N$ dimensions. Typical time series representations are special cases of this: when $N = 1$ and $M = 0$ it is a *univariate time series*; and when $N > 1$ and $M = 0$ it is a *multivariate time series*. A single time series in **S** is denoted as S^i and has only one dimension.

A *time series window* $S^i_{t,l}$ is a contiguous subsequence of a time series S^i and contains all measurements for which $\{\langle x_i, t_i \rangle$ or $\langle e_i, t_i \rangle | t \leq t_i < t + l\}$. Additionally, we can define a window over all dimensions of **S** simultaneously and thus use the same values for timestamp t and length l for all series in **S**, regardless of whether they are continuous time series or discrete events. In this work, we use *fixed-sized sliding windows*. This means choosing a fixed l given **S** (e.g., 1 h, 5 min, ...) and iteratively incrementing t with a fixed value.

2.2   Pattern Mining

We provide the following definitions for frequent pattern mining [19], adapted to the context of mixed-type time series.

The first type of pattern we consider is an *itemset*. For an itemset, *no temporal order* between items is required. An itemset X consists of one or more items $x_j \in \Omega$, where Ω is a finite domain of discrete values, that is, $X = \{x_1, \ldots, x_m\} \subseteq 2^{|\Omega|}$. An itemset X *occurs* in, or is covered by, a window $S^i_{t,l}$ if all items in X occur in that window in any order, that is,

$$X \prec S^i_{t,l} \Leftrightarrow \forall x_j \in X : \exists \langle x_j, t_j \rangle \in S^i_{t,l}.$$

Given the set of all windows $\mathcal{S}$ of a time series, we define *cover* and *support* as

$$cover(X, \mathcal{S}) = \{S^i_{t,l} | S^i_{t,l} \in \mathcal{S} \land X \prec S^i_{t,l}\} \text{ and } support(X, \mathcal{S}) = |cover(X, \mathcal{S})|.$$

The second type of pattern we consider is a *sequential pattern*. A sequential pattern X_s consists of an ordered list of one or more items, denoted as $X_s = (x_1, \ldots, x_m)$, where $x_j \in \Omega$. A sequential pattern can contain repeating items, and, unlike n-grams, an occurrence of a sequential pattern allows *gaps* between items. We define that a sequential pattern X_s *occurs* in a window $S^i_{t,l}$ using

$$X_s \prec S^i_{t,l} \Leftrightarrow \exists \langle x_1, t_1 \rangle, \ldots, \langle x_p, t_m \rangle \in S^i_{t,l} : \forall i, j \in \{1, \ldots, p\} : i < j \Rightarrow t_i < t_j.$$

The definitions of cover and support are equivalent to those of itemsets. Finally, an itemset or a sequential pattern is *frequent* if its support is higher than a user-defined threshold on *minimal support* (parameter *min_sup*).

Given a set of windows $\mathcal{S}$ and *discretised* continuous values, we can use existing itemset or sequential pattern mining algorithms [8, 19] to efficiently mine all *frequent* patterns in both continuous and discrete time series. However, even with the restriction that patterns must occur at least *min_sup* times, it remains a challenge to filter out *redundant* patterns. We will focus on algorithms that mine only *closed* or *maximal* patterns. An itemset X is not closed, and thus redundant, if and only if there exists an itemset Z, such that $X \subset Z$ and $support(X, \mathcal{S}) = support(Z, \mathcal{S})$. Likewise, a sequential pattern X_s is not closed if there exists a sequential pattern Z_s, such that $X_s \sqsubset Z_s$ and $support(X_s, \mathcal{S}) = support(Z_s, \mathcal{S})$, where $\sqsubset$ is used to denote the subsequence relation.

3   Pattern-Based Anomaly Detection

3.1   Problem Setting

The problem we are trying to solve can be defined as:

Given: A univariate, multivariate, or mixed-type time series $\mathbf{S}$.
Do: Identify periods of abnormal behaviour in $\mathbf{S}$.

In this section we outline our proposed *pattern-based anomaly detection* method (PBAD) that computes for each time series window of $\mathbf{S}$ an anomaly score. The method has four major steps. First, the time series is preprocessed. Second, frequent itemsets and sequential patterns are mined from the individual time series or event logs $S^i \in \mathbf{S}$. Third, the distance-weighted similarity scores between the frequent patterns and each time series window are computed to construct a pattern-based embedding of time series $\mathbf{S}$. Fourth, the embedding is used to construct an anomaly detection classifier to detect the anomalous periods of $\mathbf{S}$. We use the ISOLATIONFOREST classifier. These steps are illustrated in Fig. 1. In the following paragraphs, we outline each step in more detail.

3.2   Preprocessing

Preprocessing is the first step in PBAD shown in Algorithm 1, line 1–7. First, we *normalise* each continuous time series S^i in $\mathbf{S}$ to values between 0 and 1, because multivariate time series can have widely different amplitudes.

Then, we segment each time series in $\mathbf{S}$ using *fixed-size sliding windows* of length l. Frequent patterns are often limited in length, i.e., a length of 5 is already quite high. Therefore, it can be useful for certain datasets to also reduce the length of each window such that a frequent sequential pattern or itemset covers a large proportion of each window. For example, we can reduce a continuous window of length 100, using a *moving average*, by storing the average value for every 5 consecutive values. The resulting window now has a length of 20 and subsequently any matching sequential pattern or itemset of size 5 will cover a large part of the window.

Frequent pattern mining only works on *discretised* data. For a continuous time series, each window $S_{t,l}^i = (x_1, \ldots, x_l)$ must be discretised using a function h

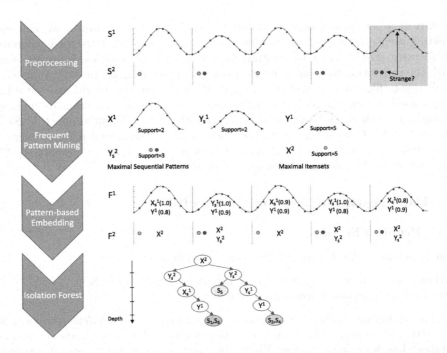

Fig. 1. Illustration of major steps in pattern-based anomaly detection method in mixed-type time series. Note that the 1st and 3th window, and the 2nd and 4th windows match the same set of patterns extracted from both the time series and the event log. The 5th window is anomalous because of the co-occurrence of a peak with a green event. The isolation forest step in PBAD marks it as such since its depth is only 2. (Color figure online)

to yield a discrete representation $h(S^i_{t,l}) = (x_1', \ldots, x_l')$ where $x_j' \in \Omega$. Examples of such functions include equal-width or equal-frequency *binning*, or aggregating windows and computing a symbol using Symbolic Aggregate Approximation [13].

3.3   Extracting Frequent Patterns

After preprocessing, PBAD mines frequent itemsets and sequential patterns from time series **S**. Given the assumption that anomalous behaviour occurs infrequently in the time series, the frequent patterns would characterise the frequently observed, normal behaviour. To extract the frequent patterns, we leverage the mature field of *frequent pattern mining*. This has two main advantages. First, the existing techniques can be extended to mine patterns in different types of time series data. Second, the mined patterns are easily interpretable and can later be presented to the user to give intuitions as to why the classifier labeled a segment as normal or anomalous.

Extracting Frequent Itemsets and Sequential Patterns. After preprocessing, we have created a set of windows for each series. These can trivially be

---

Algorithm 1: PBAD($\mathbf{S}$, l, min_sup, $is\_maximal$, max_sim) Anomaly detection using late integration

---

Input: A time series $\mathbf{S}$, window length l, support threshold min_sup, $is\_maximal$ is either **maximal** or **closed**, threshold on max Jaccard similarity max_sim

Result: Anomaly scores for each window $S_{t,l}$

    // 1. Preprocessing: create windows and discretise

1 $\mathcal{S} \leftarrow \varnothing$

2 **foreach** $S^i \in \mathbf{S}$ **do**

3   **if** S^i *is continuous* **then**

4        $\mid$ $T^i \leftarrow$ CREATE_WINDOWS(DISCRETISE(NORMALISE(S^i)), l)

5   **else**

6        $\mid$ $T^i \leftarrow$ CREATE_WINDOWS(S^i, l)

7     $\mathcal{S} \leftarrow \mathcal{S} \cup T^i$

    // 2. Mine maximal/closed frequent itemsets and sequential patterns

8 $\mathcal{P} \leftarrow \varnothing$

9 **foreach** $T^i \in \mathcal{S}$ **do**

10    $\mathcal{P}^i \leftarrow$ MINE_FREQUENT_ITEMSETS(T^i, min_sup, $is\_maximal$)

11    $\mathcal{P}^i \leftarrow \mathcal{P}^i \cup$ MINE_FREQUENT_SEQUENTIAL_PATTERNS(T^i, min_sup, $is\_maximal$)

       // Remove redundant patterns using Jaccard

12    $\mathcal{P}^i \leftarrow$ SORT $\mathcal{P}^i$ on descending support

13   **for** $1 \leqslant i < |\mathcal{P}^i|$ **do**

14   **for** $i + 1 \leqslant j \leqslant |\mathcal{P}^i|$ **do**

15   **if** $J(X_i, X_j) \geqslant max\_sim$ **then**

16            $\mid$ $\mathcal{P}^i \leftarrow \mathcal{P}^i \backslash X_j$

17    $\mathcal{P} \leftarrow \mathcal{P} \cup \mathcal{P}^i$

    // 3. Compute pattern based embedding

18 $\mathbf{F} \leftarrow$ matrix of 0.0 values with $|\mathcal{P}|$ columns and $|\mathcal{S}|$ rows for each window $S_{t,l}$

19 **for** $1 \leqslant i \leq |\mathbf{S}|$ **do**

20   **for** $1 \leqslant j \leqslant |\mathcal{P}^i|$ **do**

21       $idx \leftarrow$ global index of X_j^i in $\mathcal{P}$

22   **for** $1 \leqslant t \leqslant |\mathcal{S}|$ **do**

          // Weighted similarity between pattern X_j^i and window $S_{t,l}^i$ in dimension i for time series

23          $\mathbf{F}_{k,idx} \leftarrow 1.0 - \dfrac{\text{EXACTMINDIST}(X_j^i, S_{t,l}^i)}{|X_j^i|}$

    // 4. Compute anomalies using Isolation Forest

24 $scores \leftarrow$ ISOLATION_FOREST($\mathcal{S}$, $\mathbf{F}$)

25 $scores \leftarrow$ SORT $scores$ descending

---

transformed to a transaction (or sequence) database, required by existing frequent pattern mining algorithms [19]. Said algorithms generate candidate patterns with growing length. Since support decreases with the length of either the itemset or sequential pattern, it is relatively straightforward for these algorithms to only enumerate patterns that are frequent by pruning the candidate patterns on *min_sup*. We always mine both itemsets and sequential patterns, but filter either on *closed* or *maximal* patterns depending on the status of the parameter *is_maximal* (line 9–11). The implementation of both closed and maximal itemsets and sequential pattern mining algorithms is available in the SPMF library [8].

Removing Overlapping Patterns. Frequent pattern mining algorithms can generate too many redundant patterns. To further reduce the set of patterns, we employ *Jaccard similarity* to remove itemsets and sequential patterns that co-occur in a large percentage of windows. Formally, we use a parameter *max_sim*, and remove all patterns with a high enough Jaccard similarity:

$$J(X_1, X_2) = \frac{|cover(X_1) \cap cover(X_2)|}{support(X_1) + support(X_2) - |cover(X_1) \cap cover(X_2)|}$$

If $J(X_1, X_2) \geq max\_sim$, we remove the pattern with the lowest support. We created a straightforward routine that compares all pattern pairs (line 12–17).

Dealing with Multivariate and Mixed-Type Time Series. For multivariate and mixed-type time series, we consider two strategies for pattern extraction: *early* and *late integration*. Under the *early integration* strategy, the items of all preprocessed series in **S** are combined into a single event sequence. The frequent patterns are then mined over this new event sequence, resulting in patterns containing values from multiple dimensions. For example, the windows $S_{1,4}^1 = (1, 2, 3, 4)$ and $S_{1,4}^2 = (10, 10, 11, 11)$ spanning the same period in two time series S^1 and S^2, can be combined into a single event sequence $E_{1,4} = (\{1^1, 10^2\}, \{2^1, 10^2\}, \{3^1, 11^2\}, \{4^1, 11^2\})$. Frequent patterns can now be mined in this single event sequence, yielding candidate patterns such as the sequential pattern $X_s = (1^1, 2^1, 11^2, 11^2)$, meaning that value 1 followed by 2 in series S^1 is followed by 2 occurrences of 11 in series S^2.

In contrast, the *late integration* strategy mines patterns in each time series of **S** separately and takes the union of the resulting set of patterns. Now, each pattern is associated with exactly one time series. While it would be tempting to conclude that early integration is better since it can uncover patterns containing events from different dimensions as well as any order between these events, we prefer *late integration* in our experiments for two reasons. First, in practice, early integration leads to an exponential increase in the search space of possible patterns, i.e., *pattern explosion*, since the pattern mining algorithms consider every possible combination of values in each of the time series. Second, the anomaly detection classifier in PBAD is constructed on the union of pattern-based embeddings of each time series in **S**. As such, it learns the structure between patterns from the separate time series.

3.4   Constructing the Pattern-Based Embedding

Having obtained a set of patterns for the time series in **S**, PBAD maps **S** to a pattern-based embedding in two steps. First, it computes a similarity score between each window $S_{t,l}^i$ and each pattern X^i mined from the corresponding time series S^i in **S**. If S^i is continuous, PBAD computes a *distance-weighted similarity score*. If S^i is an event log, PBAD computes the exact match, i.e. 1 if $X^i < S_{t,l}^i$ and 0 otherwise. Second, it concatenates the similarity scores over all dimensions, yielding the feature-vector representation of the window of **S**. Since this process is repeated for each window in **S**, we end up with a pattern-based embedding of the full time series (line 18–23). We argue that normal time series windows are more frequent than the anomalous windows and as such normal windows match the set of patterns better. As a result, they will be clustered together in the embedded space whereas the less frequent anomalous windows will have lower similarity scores and will be more scattered in the embedded space.

Computing the Distance-Weighted Similarity Score. The intuition behind a weighted similarity score can be illustrated with a simple example. For instance, the sequential pattern $X^1 = (0.1, 0.5)$ clearly matches time series window $S_{1,3}^1 = (0.1, 0.55, 1.0)$ better than window $S_{4,3}^1 = (0.8, 0.9, 1.0)$. Thus, the similarity between a sequential pattern X^i of length m and a time series window $S_{t,l}^i$ of length l depends on the *minimal* Euclidean distance between the pattern and the window:

$$weighted\_dist(X^i, S_{t,l}^i) = \min_{E \subset S_{t,l}^i} \sqrt{\sum_{j=1}^{m} (E_j - X_j^i)^2} \tag{1}$$

where E is a subsequence of m elements from window $S_{t,l}^i$. The optimisation yields the minimal distance by only observing the best matching elements in the pattern and the window. Given the weighted distance between the sequential pattern and a window, the similarity score is computed as follows:

$$sim(X^i, S_{t,l}^i) = 1.0 - weighted\_dist(X^i, S_{t,l}^i)/|X^i|$$

If the distance between the pattern and the time series window is small, the similarity increases. Since the patterns can have different lengths, the distance is normalised for the length of the pattern. Going back to the simple example, the similarity with window $S_{1,3}^1$ is $1.0 - \sqrt{(0.1 - 0.1)^2 + (0.55 - 0.5)^2}/2 = 0.975$ while the similarity with window $S_{4,3}^1$ is only $1.0 - \sqrt{(0.8 - 0.1)^2 + (0.9 - 0.5)^2}/2 = 0.597$.

Because a sequential pattern imposes a total order on its items, Eq. 1 cannot be solved trivially. We design an exact algorithm for computing Eq. 1 with the added ordering constraint. Our exact algorithm matches every element in the pattern with exactly one unique element in the window such that the sum of the distances between the matched elements is minimal. The approach is based on the *Smith-Waterman* algorithm for local sequence alignment. However, in contrast, our algorithm ensures that every element in the window and pattern can only be matched once and enforces a match for every element in the pattern. Furthermore, it imposes no gap penalty for skipping elements. Finally, it returns an exact distance between the pattern and the window. Since it is a *dynamic programming algorithm*, it is guaranteed to find the optimal alignment of the pattern and the segment that minimises the distance. For the sake of brevity, we include the full EXACTMINDIST algorithm in Appendix A.1.[1]

Dealing with Itemsets. PBAD also computes the similarity between itemsets and windows. In contrast to a sequential pattern, an itemset does not impose an order on its elements. We can simply sort the elements of the both the itemset and window before using the EXACTMINDIST algorithm to obtain the correct weighted distance and compute the similarity score.

Constructing the Embedding Under the Early Integration Strategy. In case of the early integration strategy, we must deal with patterns with mixed items from different continuous time series and event logs when computing the similarity score. For itemsets, we adapt Eq. 1 and compute the minimal distance in each dimension separately and then sum all distances over all dimensions. The distance is computed either weighted, i.e., between an item and a continuous time series value, or binary, i.e., between an item and a discrete event log value. For sequential patterns, we consider the subsequence in each dimension separately and sum all distances. However, in this case we have to satisfy the total order constraint within each time series and between different time series. A brute-force way to compute this, is to generate all possible subsequences (with gaps) over each dimension that satisfy the local and global order constraints, induced by each sequential pattern, and take the subsequence that has the smallest distance. In practice, this is feasible since the length of the time series and patterns is limited to small numbers.

Time Complexity. The time complexity of constructing the pattern-based embedding of $\mathbf{S}$ is $\mathcal{O}(|\mathcal{P}| \cdot |\mathcal{S}| \cdot o)$ where $o = \mathcal{O}(l \cdot m)$ is required by the EXACT-MINDIST algorithm, $|\mathcal{P}|$ the number of frequent patterns found, and $|\mathcal{S}|$ the number of windows in the time series. Under the late integration strategy, this complexity increases linearly with the number of dimensions of $\mathbf{S}$.

3.5 Constructing the Anomaly Classifier

The final step of PBAD is to construct the anomaly detection classifier (lines 24–25 in Algorithm 1). Given the pattern-based embedding of $\mathbf{S}$, any state-of-the-art anomaly detector can be used to compute an anomaly score for each window of $\mathbf{S}$. PBAD uses the ISOLATIONFOREST classifier [16] since it has been empirically shown to be the state-of-the-art in unsupervised anomaly detection [7]. An isolation forest is an ensemble of decision trees. Each tree finds anomalies by recursively making random partitions of the instance space. Anomalies are isolated quickly from the data, resulting in shorter path lengths in the tree, as illustrated in Fig. 1. Usually, the anomaly score is used to rank the segments from most to least anomalous such that the user can easily inspect the most anomalous parts of the data. To generate discrete alarms, one can threshold the score to a specific percentile of the distribution of all scores.

---

[1] http://adrem.uantwerpen.be/bibrem/pubs/pbad.pdf.

4 Experiments

In this section, we address the following research questions:

Q1: How does PBAD perform compared to the state-of-the-art pattern based anomaly detection algorithms?
Q2: Can PBAD handle different types of time series data?

We evaluate PBAD on three types of time series: real-world univariate time series, real-world multivariate time series, and synthetic mixed-type time series. Before discussing the results, we lay out the experimental setup.

4.1 Experimental Setup

We compare PBAD with following state-of-the-art pattern based anomaly detection methods:

- *Matrix profile* (MP) is an anomaly detection technique based on all-pairs-similarity-search for time series data [18]. The anomalies are the time series discords.
- *Pattern anomaly value* (PAV) is a multi-scale anomaly detection algorithm based on infrequent patterns, specifically bi-grams, for univariate time series [3].
- *Minimal infrequent pattern based outlier factor* (MIFPOD) is an anomaly detection method for event logs [11]. Their outlier factor is based on minimal infrequent, or *rare*, itemsets.
- *Frequent pattern based outlier factor* (FPOF) computes an outlier factor based on the number of frequent itemsets that exactly match the current transaction for transactional databases [10]. We adapt FPOF and compute the outlier factor based on closed itemsets and reduce itemsets further using Jaccard similarity as in PBAD.

Experimental Setup. The experimental setup corresponds to the standard setup in time series anomaly detection [11]. Given a time series **S** with a number of labelled timestamps: (i) divide the time series into fixed-sized, sliding windows; (ii) each window that contains a labelled timestamp takes its label; (iii) construct the anomaly detection model on the full time series data; (iv) use the model to predict an anomaly score for each window in the time series; (v) evaluate the predictions on the labelled windows by computing the *area under the receiver operating characteristic* (AUROC) and *average precision* (AP).

Parametrisation of Methods. Each method has the same preprocessing steps which includes setting an appropriate window size and increment to create the fixed-sized, sliding windows. Continuous variables are discretised using equal-width binning.[2] PAV has no parameters. MATRIXPROFILE has a single parameter, the window size. The parameters of FPOF and MIFPOD are chosen by an

---

[2] See Table 4 in Appendix A.2 for details on setting preprocessing parameters.

oracle that knows the optimal settings for each dataset. For PBAD, as a rule of thumb, we set minimal support relatively high, that is $min\_sup = 0.01$. The Jaccard threshold is set to 0.9. Intuitively, if two patterns cover almost the same windows, e.g., 90 out of 100 windows, using both patterns is both unnecessary and less efficient. For mining *closed itemsets* we use CHARM, and for mining *maximal itemsets* we use CHARM-MFI. For mining *closed* and *maximal sequential patterns* we use CM-CLASP and MAXSP respectively. CHARM and CM-CLASP are based on a vertical representation. MAXSP is inspired by PRE-FIXSPAN which only generates candidates that have at least one occurrence in the database [8,19]. The sequential patterns should have a minimal length of 2, and by default we set pattern pruning to *closed*. We use the ISOLATIONFOREST classifier implemented in SCIKIT-LEARN with 500 trees in the ensemble. The implementation, datasets and experimental scripts for PBAD are publicly available.[3] We do not report detailed runtime results, however, on the selected datasets PBAD requires less than 30 min on a standard PC.

4.2   Anomaly Detection in Univariate Time Series

For the univariate test case, we use 9 real-world datasets. Three datasets are from the Numenta time series anomaly detection benchmark [1]. Temp tracks the ambient temperature in an office during 302 days where the goal is to detect periods of abnormal temperature. Latency monitors CPU usage for 13 days in a data center with the goal of detecting abnormal CPU usage. Finally, Taxi logs the number of NYC taxi passengers for 215 days in order to detect periods of abnormal traffic. The 6 remaining datasets are not publicly available. Each tracks on average 2.5 years of water consumption in a different store of a large retail company. The company wants to detect periods of abnormal water consumption possibly caused by leaks or rare operational conditions. Domain experts have labelled between 547 and 2 391 h in each store.

Results and Discussion. Table 1 shows the AUROC and AP obtained by each method on each of the 9 univariate time series datasets as well as the ranking of each method. PBAD outperforms the existing baselines for detecting anomalies in univariate time series data in 5 of the 9 datasets.

In the experiments, MP sometimes performs close to random. Because MP detects anomalous windows as those with the highest distance to its nearest neighbour window in the time series, its performance degrades if the data contain two or more similar anomalies. This is, for instance, the case for the water consumption data where each type of leak corresponds to a specific time series pattern. A more detailed discussion of the univariate datasets, parameter settings and results is included in Appendix A.2.

We compared the impact of computing the distance-weighted similarity between a pattern and time series window, versus computing an exact match, on the univariate datasets. In this case, using distance-weighted similarity, results

---

[3] Implementation of PBAD: https://bitbucket.org/len_feremans/pbad/.

Table 1. The table shows the AUROC and AP obtained by each method on 9 univariate time series. PBAD outperforms the baselines in 5 of the 9 datasets.

Dataset	AUROC					AP				
	MP	Pav	Mifpod	Fpof	Pbad	MP	Pav	Mifpod	Fpof	Pbad
Temp	0.240	0.590	0.997	**0.999**	0.998	0.014	0.040	0.917	**0.957**	0.917
Taxi	0.861	0.281	0.846	0.877	**0.879**	0.214	0.057	0.300	0.403	**0.453**
Latency	0.599	**0.608**	0.467	0.493	0.553	0.515	0.361	0.255	0.296	**0.382**
Water 1	0.656	0.482	0.514	0.825	**0.884**	0.499	0.301	0.328	0.812	**0.821**
Water 2	0.600	0.520	0.513	0.857	**0.945**	0.353	0.127	0.094	0.688	**0.862**
Water 3	0.536	0.457	0.544	**0.671**	0.605	0.126	0.121	0.079	**0.350**	0.233
Water 4	0.675	0.579	0.548	0.613	**0.721**	0.774	0.687	0.700	**0.817**	0.808
Water 5	0.444	0.581	0.455	0.790	**0.960**	0.199	0.243	0.111	0.671	**0.906**
Water 6	0.682	0.609	0.500	**0.874**	0.752	0.578	0.431	0.228	**0.692**	0.551
Average	0.588	0.523	0.598	0.778	**0.811**	0.364	0.263	0.335	0.632	**0.659**
Ranking	3.333	3.889	4.167	2	**1.611**	3.111	4.111	4.278	1.778	**1.722**

in a higher AUROC and AP on 8 of the 9 datasets. Using the combination of both frequent itemsets and frequent sequential patterns instead of only itemsets or only sequential patterns results in higher AUROC on 6 of the 9 datasets.

4.3 Anomaly Detection in Multivariate Time Series

For the multivariate test case, we use an indoor exercise monitoring dataset [5]. The data contain recordings of 10 people each executing 60 repetitions of three types of exercises: squats (`Sq`), lunges (`Lu`), and side-lunges (`Si`). The (x, y, z) positions of 25 sensors attached to each person were tracked during execution, resulting in a multivariate time series **S** of dimension 75.

We construct 4 multivariate time series datasets containing anomalies by randomly combining around 90 repetitions of one exercise type with 8–12 repetitions of a different type. Then, the goal is to accurately detect the minority exercise. Before applying the algorithms, we use the methodology outlined in [5] to preprocess the raw data and further reduce the number of dimensions of **S** to 3. Note that the baseline algorithms are not naturally equipped to deal with multivariate time series. The straightforward solution is to compute an anomaly score for each time series separately and add the scores.

Results and Discussion. Table 2 shows the AUROC and AP obtained by each method on the 4 multivariate time series datasets as well as the ranking of each method. PBAD and FPOF outperform the other methods, with PBAD improving the AUROC and AP over FPOF with $1.3 \pm 2.7\%$ and $23.8 \pm 33.2\%$ respectively.

Table 2. The table shows the AUROC and AP obtained by each method on 4 multivariate time series. Each dataset contains tracking of movement during indoor exercises where the normal exercise is listed first, and the anomalous exercise second. For instance, `Lu/Sq` contains 90 repetitions of the *lunge* exercise and 8 repetitions of the *squat* exercise.

Dataset	AUROC					AP				
	MP	PAV	MIFPOD	FPOF	PBAD	MP	PAV	MIFPOD	FPOF	PBAD
Lu+Si/Sq	0.472	0.571	0.819	0.966	**0.983**	0.283	0.255	0.430	0.862	**0.888**
Lu/Sq	0.604	0.671	0.775	**0.966**	0.940	0.082	0.110	0.131	0.662	**0.737**
Si/Lu	0.471	0.425	0.804	0.864	**0.907**	0.128	0.115	0.444	0.572	**0.573**
Sq/Si	0.484	0.504	0.482	0.903	**0.914**	0.094	0.092	0.087	0.391	**0.707**
Average	0.508	0.542	0.720	0.925	**0.936**	0.147	0.143	0.273	0.622	**0.726**
Ranking	4.5	4	3.5	1.75	**1.25**	4	4.5	3.5	2	**1**

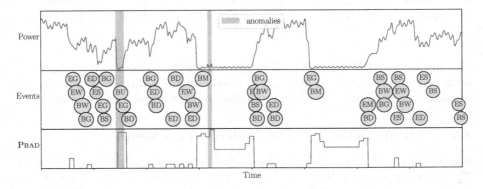

Fig. 2. The figure shows 5 days of synthetic power grid data. The top plot shows continuous power output of the grid. The middle plot shows the discrete events, B and E indicate begin and end respectively, while W, S, D, G, M, and U refer to wind, solar, diesel, gas, maintenance, and shutdown respectively. The bottom plot shows the anomaly score of PBAD. The first anomaly corresponds to a discrete event (BU) that did not generate the expected power response.

4.4   Anomaly Detection in Mixed-Type Time Series

Due to the lack of publicly-available, labelled mixed-type time series datasets, we construct a realistic synthetic data generator. The generator simulates the electricity production in a microgrid consisting of 4 energy resources: a small wind turbine, a solar panel, a diesel generator, and a microturbine. Each resource has a distinct behaviour. The operator controlling the grid can take 12 discrete actions: turning on and off each of the energy resources, shutting down and starting up the grid, and starting and stopping grid maintenance. Then, a full year of data is generated in three steps. First, a control strategy determines every 5 min which actions to take and logs them. It is also possible to take no action. Second, the actions determine the power output of the grid at each time step, forming the continuous time series. Finally, 90 control failures are introduced in the system. These are actions not having the desired effect, e.g., starting the wind turbine does not lead to an increase in electricity production, actions without effect, and effects that are not logged. Using the generator, we generate 45 variations of mixed-type time series, each with different anomalies, and report averaged results. The full details of the generator can be found in Appendix A.3.

Results and Discussion. We only ran PBAD on the mixed-type data to detect the control failures. MP and PAV cannot handle event logs, while MIFPOD and FPOF do not naturally handle mixed-type time series. However, we run PBAD three times: only on the continuous component of the synthetic data (AUROC $= 0.81 \pm 0.13$), only on the event logs (AUROC $= 0.63 \pm 0.07$), and on the full mixed-type series (AUROC $= 0.85 \pm 0.08$). This indicates that PBAD successfully leverages the information in the combined series to detect the anomalous data points. Figure 2 shows 7 days of the power generated by the microgrid and the corresponding event log. The anomaly score generated by PBAD is plotted underneath the data, illustrating that it can accurately detect the anomalies in this case.

5   Related Work

In this section we place our work into the wider context of time series anomaly detection. Existing pattern-based anomaly detection methods each differ in how they define patterns, support, anomaly scores, and what type of input they are applicable to. The original FPOF method [10] mines frequent itemsets for detecting anomalous transactions in a transaction database, using the traditional definition of support. Their outlier factor is defined as the number of itemsets that match the current transaction versus the total number of frequent itemsets. The more recent MIFPOD method [11] mines minimal infrequent, or rare, itemsets for detecting outliers in data streams. Rare itemsets are not frequent, i.e., they do not satisfy the minimal support threshold, but have only subsets that are frequent. They define support as usual, but based on the most recent period, and not necessarily the entire event log. Finally, they compute the outlier factor as the number of rare itemsets that match the current transaction versus the total number of rare itemsets, similar to FPOF, but weighted by the sum of deviation in support of matching rare itemsets. Finally, the PAV method [3] uses linear patterns, i.e., two consecutive continuous values in a univariate time series. The final outlier factor is computed as the relative support of this single pattern in sliding windows of size 2. In contrast to these methods, PBAD considers extensions specific to multivariate and mixed-type time series: it uses a distance-weighted similarity to bridge the gap between a discrete pattern and a continuous signal, employs a late integration scheme to avoid pattern explosion, removes redundant patterns using a threshold on Jaccard similarity, and derives an anomaly score using the ISOLATIONFOREST classifier and the pattern-based embedding of the time series.

The MATRIXPROFILE technique [18] is the state-of-the-art anomaly detection technique for continuous time series. This technique computes for each time series segment an anomaly score by computing the Euclidean distance to its nearest neighbour segment. In contrast, PBAD can also handle the combination of event logs and continuous time series. A host of *time series representation methods* and *similarity measures* have been developed [6] for time series classification. Time series *shapelets* are subsequences from a continuous time series and are used in combination with the dynamic time warping distance to classify time series segments [17]. Sequential patterns used by PBAD are different from shapelets, because we use non-continuous subsequences with missing elements, or gaps. Itemsets are even more different, because the order of values is discarded. Another key difference is that the enumeration process for shapelets is usually reduced by only considering subsequences of a specific length [12], while we make use of the anti-monotonic property of support to enumerate patterns of varying length without constraints. Finally, itemsets and sequential patterns can also be extracted from discrete event logs.

Another approach, related to classification, is to employ a *minimal redundancy, maximal relevance* strategy to select *discriminative* patterns [4]. Currently, we employ an unsupervised technique, but for future work we could adopt a strategy for selecting patterns that are the most discriminative towards anomalies. Finally, deep learning techniques are becoming a popular choice for time series anomaly detection [14]. For instance, autoencoders could be used to learn an embedding of a mixed-type time series. A key difference with PBAD is that, unlike deep learning techniques, frequent patterns are easily interpretable.

6   Conclusions and Future Work

Research on anomaly detection in time series so far has prioritised either continuous time series or event logs, but not the combination of both, so-called mixed-type time series. In this paper, we present PBAD, a pattern-based anomaly detection method for mixed-type time series. The method leverages frequent pattern mining techniques to transform the time series into a pattern-based embedding that serves as input for anomaly detection using an isolation forest. An experimental study on univariate and multivariate time series found PBAD to outperform state-of-the-art time series anomaly detection techniques, such as MATRIXPROFILE, PAV, MIFPOD and FPOF. Furthermore, unlike existing techniques, PBAD is able to handle mixed-type time series.

For future research, we see our method as a promising general framework for time series anomaly detection, where certain variations might be more effective in different applications. These include variations on mining a non-redundant and relevant pattern set, on distance measures to match pattern occurrences, and on anomaly detection classification techniques. A useful addition would be an efficient algorithm for computing the similarity between a pattern and window under the early integration strategy. Because the patterns characterise the behaviour of the time series, they can serve as the basis for an anomaly detection classifier that makes explainable predictions. Another possible direction is to adapt the algorithm to work efficiently within a streaming context.

Acknowledgements. The authors would like to thank the VLAIO SBO HYMOP project for funding this research.

References

1. Ahmad, S., Lavin, A., Purdy, S., Agha, Z.: Unsupervised real-time anomaly detection for streaming data. Neurocomputing **262**, 134–147 (2017)
2. Chandola, V., Banerjee, A., Kumar, V.: Anomaly detection: a survey. ACM Comput. Surv. (CSUR) **41**(3), 15 (2009)
3. Chen, X.Y., Zhan, Y.Y.: Multi-scale anomaly detection algorithm based on infrequent pattern of time series. J. Comput. Appl. Math. **214**(1), 227–237 (2008)
4. Cheng, H., Yan, X., Han, J., Hsu, C.W.: Discriminative frequent pattern analysis for effective classification. In: IEEE 23rd International Conference on Data Engineering, ICDE 2007, pp. 716–725. IEEE (2007)
5. Decroos, T., Schütte, K., De Beéck, T.O., Vanwanseele, B., Davis, J.: AMIE: automatic monitoring of indoor exercises. In: Brefeld, U., et al. (eds.) ECML PKDD 2018, Part III. LNCS (LNAI), vol. 11053, pp. 424–439. Springer, Cham (2019). https://doi.org/10.1007/978-3-030-10997-4_26
6. Ding, H., Trajcevski, G., Scheuermann, P., Wang, X., Keogh, E.: Querying and mining of time series data: experimental comparison of representations and distance measures. Proc. VLDB Endow. **1**(2), 1542–1552 (2008)
7. Domingues, R., Filippone, M., Michiardi, P., Zouaoui, J.: A comparative evaluation of outlier detection algorithms: experiments and analyses. Pattern Recogn. **74**, 406–421 (2018)
8. Fournier-Viger, P., et al.: The SPMF open-source data mining library version 2. In: Berendt, B., et al. (eds.) ECML PKDD 2016, Part III. LNCS (LNAI), vol. 9853, pp. 36–40. Springer, Cham (2016). https://doi.org/10.1007/978-3-319-46131-1_8
9. Gershenfeld, N., Krikorian, R., Cohen, D.: The internet of things. Sci. Am. **291**(4), 76–81 (2004)
10. He, Z., Xu, X., Huang, Z.J., Deng, S.: FP-outlier: frequent pattern based outlier detection. Comput. Scie. Inf. Syst. **2**(1), 103–118 (2005)
11. Hemalatha, C.S., Vaidehi, V., Lakshmi, R.: Minimal infrequent pattern based approach for mining outliers in data streams. Expert Syst. Appl. **42**(4), 1998–2012 (2015)
12. Karlsson, I., Papapetrou, P., Boström, H.: Generalized random shapelet forests. Data Min. Knowl. Disc. **30**(5), 1053–1085 (2016). https://doi.org/10.1007/s10618-016-0473-y
13. Lin, J., Keogh, E., Lonardi, S., Chiu, B.: A symbolic representation of time series, with implications for streaming algorithms. In: Proceedings of the 8th ACM SIGMOD Workshop on Research Issues in Data Mining and Knowledge Discovery, pp. 2–11. ACM (2003)
14. Malhotra, P., Vig, L., Shroff, G., Agarwal, P.: Long short term memory networks for anomaly detection in time series. In: 23rd European Symposium on Artificial Neural Networks, Computational Intelligence and Machine Learning. ESANN (2015)

15. Mueen, A., Keogh, E., Zhu, Q., Cash, S., Westover, B.: Exact discovery of time series motifs. In: Proceedings of the 2009 SIAM International Conference on Data Mining, pp. 473–484. SIAM (2009)
16. Ting, K.M., Liu, F.T., Zhou, Z.: Isolation forest. In: 2008 Eighth IEEE International Conference on Data Mining (ICDM), pp. 413–422. IEEE, December 2008
17. Ye, L., Keogh, E.: Time series shapelets: a new primitive for data mining. In: Proceedings of the 15th ACM SIGKDD International Conference on Knowledge Discovery and Data Mining, pp. 947–956. ACM (2009)
18. Yeh, C.C.M., et al.: Matrix profile i: all pairs similarity joins for time series: a unifying view that includes motifs, discords and shapelets. In: 2016 IEEE 16th International Conference on Data Mining (ICDM), pp. 1317–1322. IEEE (2016)
19. Zaki, M.J., Meira, W.: Data Mining and Analysis: Fundamental Concepts and Algorithms. Cambridge University Press, Cambridge (2014)

k Is the Magic Number—Inferring the Number of Clusters Through Nonparametric Concentration Inequalities

Sibylle Hess$^{(\boxtimes)}$ and Wouter Duivesteijn

Data Mining Group, Technische Universiteit Eindhoven, Eindhoven, The Netherlands
{s.c.hess,w.duivesteijn}@tue.nl

Abstract. Most convex and nonconvex clustering algorithms come with one crucial parameter: the k in k-means. To this day, there is not one generally accepted way to accurately determine this parameter. Popular methods are simple yet theoretically unfounded, such as searching for an elbow in the curve of a given cost measure. In contrast, statistically founded methods often make strict assumptions over the data distribution or come with their own optimization scheme for the clustering objective. This limits either the set of applicable datasets or clustering algorithms. In this paper, we strive to determine the number of clusters by answering a simple question: given two clusters, is it likely that they jointly stem from a single distribution? To this end, we propose a bound on the probability that two clusters originate from the distribution of the unified cluster, specified only by the sample mean and variance. Our method is applicable as a simple wrapper to the result of any clustering method minimizing the objective of k-means, which includes Gaussian mixtures and Spectral Clustering. We focus in our experimental evaluation on an application for nonconvex clustering and demonstrate the suitability of our theoretical results. Our SPECIALK clustering algorithm automatically determines the appropriate value for k, without requiring any data transformation or projection, and without assumptions on the data distribution. Additionally, it is capable to decide that the data consists of only a single cluster, which many existing algorithms cannot.

Keywords: k-means · Concentration inequalities · Spectral clustering · Model selection · One-cluster clustering · Nonparametric statistics

1 Introduction

When creating a solution to the task of clustering—finding a natural partitioning of the records of a dataset into k groups—the holy grail is to automatically

Electronic supplementary material The online version of this chapter (https://doi.org/10.1007/978-3-030-46150-8_16) contains supplementary material, which is available to authorized users.

© Springer Nature Switzerland AG 2020
U. Brefeld et al. (Eds.): ECML PKDD 2019, LNAI 11906, pp. 257–273, 2020.
https://doi.org/10.1007/978-3-030-46150-8_16

determine k. The current state of the art in clustering research has not yet achieved this holy grail to a satisfactory degree. Since many papers on parameter-free clustering exist, this statement might sound unnecessarily polemic without further elaboration. Hence, we must describe what constitutes "satisfactory", which we will do by describing unsatisfactory aspects of otherwise perfectly fine (and often actually quite interesting) clustering solutions. Some solutions can only handle convex cluster shapes [17], while most real-life phenomena are not necessarily convex. Some solutions manage to avoid determining k, at the cost of having to specify another parameter that effectively controls k [1]. Some solutions define a cluster criterion and an algorithm to iteratively mine the data: the best single cluster is found, after which the algorithm is run again on the data minus that cluster, etcetera [11]; this runs the risk of finding a local optimum. We, by contrast, introduce a clustering algorithm that can handle nonconvex shapes, is devoid of parameters that demand the user to directly or indirectly set k, and finds the global optimum for its optimization criterion.

We propose a probability bound on the operator norm of centered, symmetric decompositions based on the matrix Bernstein concentration inequality. We apply this bound to assess whether two given clusters are likely to stem from the distribution of the unified cluster. Our bound provides a statistically founded decision criterion over the minimum similarity within one cluster and the maximum similarity between two clusters: this entails judgment on whether two clusters should be separate or unified. Our method is easy to implement and statistically nonparametric. Applied on spectral clustering methods, to the best of the authors' knowledge, providing a statistically founded way to automatically determine k is entirely new.

We incorporate our bound in an algorithm called SPECIALK, since it provides a method for SPEctral Clustering to Infer the Appropriate Level k. On synthetic datasets, SPECIALK outperforms some competitors, while performing roughly on par with another competitor. However, when unleashed on a synthetic dataset consisting of just random noise, all competitors detect all kinds of clusters, while only SPECIALK correctly determines the value of k to be one. If you need an algorithm that can correctly identify a sea of noise, SPECIALK is the only choice. On four real-life datasets with class labels associated to the data points, we illustrate how all available algorithms, including SPECIALK, often cannot correctly determine the value of k corresponding to the number of classes available in the dataset. We argue that this is an artefact of a methodological mismatch: the class labels indicate one specific natural grouping of the points in the dataset, but the task of clustering is to retrieve *any* natural grouping of the points in the dataset, not necessarily the one encoded in the class label. Hence, such an evaluation is fundamentally unfit to assess the performance of clustering methods.

2   Three Sides of a Coin: k-means, Gaussian Mixtures and Spectral Clustering

To embed our work in already existing related work, and to describe the preliminary building blocks required as foundation on which to build our work, we must first introduce some notation. We write $\mathbf{1}$ for a constant vector of ones, whose dimension can be derived from context unless otherwise specified. We denote with $\mathbb{1}^{m \times k}$ the set of all binary matrices which indicate a partition of m elements into k sets. Such a partition is computed by k-means clustering; every element belongs to exactly one cluster. Let $D \in \mathbb{R}^{m \times n}$ be a data matrix, collecting m points $D_{j\cdot}$, which we identify with their index j. The objective of k-means is equivalent to solving the following matrix factorization problem:

$$\min_{Y,X} \left\| D - YX^\top \right\|^2 \quad \text{s.t.} \quad Y \in \mathbb{1}^{m \times k}, X \in \mathbb{R}^{n \times k}. \tag{1}$$

The matrix Y indicates the cluster assignments; point j is in cluster c if $Y_{jc} = 1$. The matrix X represents the cluster centers, which are given in matrix notation as $X = D^\top Y \left(Y^\top Y \right)^{-1}$. The well-known optimization scheme of k-means, *Lloyd's algorithm* [17], employs the convexity of the k-means problem if one of the matrices X or Y is fixed. The algorithm performs an alternating minimization, updating Y to assign each point to the cluster with the nearest center, and updating $X_{\cdot c}$ as the mean of all points assigned to cluster c.

2.1 Gaussian Mixtures

The updates of Lloyd's algorithm correspond to the expectation and maximization steps of the EM-algorithm [2,3]. In this probabilistic view, we assume that every data point $D_{j\cdot}$ is independently sampled by first selecting cluster c with probability π_c, and then sampling point $D_{j\cdot}$ from the Gaussian distribution:

$$p(\xi|c) = \frac{1}{\sqrt{2\pi\epsilon}} \exp\left(-\frac{1}{2\epsilon} \left\| \xi - X_{\cdot c} \right\|^2 \right) \sim \mathcal{N}(\xi | X_{\cdot c}, \epsilon I).$$

This assumes that the covariance matrix of the Gaussian distribution is equal for all clusters: $\Sigma_c = \epsilon I$. From this sampling procedure, we compute the log-likelihood for the data and cluster assignments:

$$\log p(D, Y | X, \epsilon I, \pi) = \log \left(\prod_{j=1}^{m} \prod_{c=1}^{k} \left(\frac{\pi_c}{\sqrt{2\pi\epsilon}} \exp\left(-\frac{1}{2\epsilon} \left\| D_{j\cdot} - X_{\cdot c}^\top \right\|^2 \right) \right)^{Y_{jc}} \right)$$

$$= \sum_{j=1}^{m} \sum_{c=1}^{k} Y_{jc} \left(\ln\left(\frac{\pi_c}{\sqrt{2\pi\epsilon}} \right) - \frac{1}{2\epsilon} \left\| D_{j\cdot} - X_{\cdot c}^\top \right\|^2 \right)$$

$$= -\frac{1}{2\epsilon} \left\| D - YX^\top \right\|^2 - \frac{m}{2} \ln(2\pi\epsilon) + \sum_{c=1}^{k} |Y_{\cdot c}| \ln(\pi_c).$$

Hence, if $\epsilon > 0$ is small enough, maximizing the log-likelihood of the Gaussian mixture model is equivalent to solving the k-means problem.

2.2   Maximum Similarity Versus Minimum Cut

There are multiple alternative formulations of the k-means problem. Altering the Frobenius norm in Eq. (1) with the identity $\|A\|^2 = \mathrm{tr}(AA^\top)$ begets:

$$
\begin{aligned}
\left\|D - YX^\top\right\|^2 &= \|D\|^2 - 2\,\mathrm{tr}\left(D^\top Y X^\top\right) + \mathrm{tr}\left(XY^\top Y X^\top\right) \\
&= \|D\|^2 - \mathrm{tr}\left(Y^\top DD^\top Y \left(Y^\top Y\right)^{-1}\right),
\end{aligned}
$$

where the last equality derives from inserting the optimal X, given Y. Thus, we transform the k-means objective, defined in terms of distances to cluster centers, to an objective defined solely on similarity of data points. The matrix $DD^\top$ represents similarity between points, measured via the inner product $sim(j, l) = D_{j\cdot} D_{l\cdot}^\top$. The k-means objective in Eq. (1) is thus equivalent to the *maximum similarity problem* for a similarity matrix $W = DD^\top$:

$$
\max_{Y \in \mathbb{1}^{m \times k}} Sim(W, Y) = \sum_c R(W, Y_{\cdot c}), \quad R(W, y) = \frac{y^\top W y}{|y|}. \tag{2}
$$

Here, we introduce the function $R(W, y)$, which is known as the *Rayleigh coefficient* [10], returning the ratio similarity of points within cluster y.

An alternative to maximizing the *similarity within* a cluster, is to minimize the *similarity between* clusters. This is known as the *ratio cut* problem, stated for a symmetric similarity matrix W as:

$$
\min_{Y \in \mathbb{1}^{m \times k}} Cut(W, Y) = \sum_s C(W, Y), \quad C(W, y) = \frac{y^\top W \bar{y}}{|y|}.
$$

The function $C(W, y)$ sums the similarities between points indicated by cluster y and the remaining points indicated by $\bar{y} = \mathbf{1} - y$. Imagining the similarity matrix W as a weighted adjacency matrix of a graph, the function $C(W, y)$ sums the weights of the edges which would be cut if we *cut out* the cluster y from the graph. Defining the matrix $L = \mathrm{diag}(W\mathbf{1}) - W$, also known as the *difference graph Laplacian* [5], we have $C(W, y) = R(L, y)$. As a result, the maximum similarity problem with respect to the similarity matrix $-L$ is equivalent to the minimum cut problem with similarity matrix W.

2.3   Spectral Clustering

If similarities are defined via the inner product, then the similarity in Eq. (2) is maximized when *every* point in a cluster is similar to *every other* point in that cluster. As a result, the obtained clusters by k-means have convex shapes. If we expect nonconvex cluster shapes, then our similarities should only locally be compared. This is possible, e.g., by defining the similarity matrix as the adjacency matrix to the kNN graph or the ϵ-neighborhood graph. Clustering methods employing such similarities are known as *spectral clustering* [20].

It is related to minimizing the cut for the graph Laplacian of a given similarity matrix. Spectral clustering computes a truncated eigendecomposition of $W = -L \approx V^{(k+1)}\Lambda^{(k+1)}V^{(k+1)^\top}$, where $\Lambda^{(k+1)}$ is a diagonal matrix having the $(k+1)$ largest eigenvalues on its diagonal $\Lambda_{11} \geq \ldots \geq \Lambda_{k+1k+1}$, and $V^{(k+1)}$ represents the corresponding eigenvectors. Graph Laplacian theory says that the eigenvectors to the largest eigenvalue indicate the connected components of the graph, while in practical clustering application the entire graph is assumed to be connected. To honor this assumption, the first eigenvector is omitted from the matrix $V^{(k+1)}$, which is subsequently discretized by k-means clustering [18]. Considering the relation between the minimum cut objective and k-means clustering, the objective to minimize the $Cut(L, Y)$ is actually equivalent to solving k-means clustering for a data matrix D such that $W = DD^\top$. This relation was recently examined [9], with the disillusioning result that k-means clustering on the decomposition matrix D usually returns a local optimum, whose objective value is close to the global minimum but whose clustering is unfavorable. Consequently, the authors propose the algorithm SPECTACL, approximating the similarity matrix by a matrix product of projected eigenvectors, such that:

$$W \approx DD^\top, \quad D_{ji} = \left|V_{ji}^{(n)}\right|\left|\Lambda_{ii}^{(n)}\right|^{-(1/2)} \tag{3}$$

for a large enough dimensionality $n > k$. Although this increases the rank of the factorization from k in traditional spectral clustering to $n > k$, the search space, which is spanned by the vectors $D_{\cdot i}$, is reduced in SPECTACL. The projection of the orthogonal eigenvectors $V_{\cdot i}$ to the positive orthant introduces linear dependencies among the projections $D_{\cdot i}$.

2.4 Estimating *k*

Depending on the view on k-means clustering—as a matrix factorization, a Gaussian mixture model, or a graph-cut algorithm—we might define various strategies to derive the correct k. The *elbow* strategy is arguably the most general approach. Plotting the value of the objective function for every model when increasing k, a kink in the curve is supposed to indicate the correct number of clusters. With regard to spectral clustering, the elbow method is usually deployed on the largest eigenvalues of the Laplacian, called *eigengap heuristic* [18]. Depending on the application, the elbow may not be easy to spot, and the selection of k boils down to a subjective trade-off between data approximation and model complexity.

To manage this trade-off in a less subjective manner, one can define a cost measure beforehand. Popular approaches employ Minimum Description Length (MDL) [4,14] or the Bayesian Information Criterion (BIC) [21]. The nonconvex clustering method Self-Tuning Spectral Clustering (STSC) [24] defines such a cost measure on the basis of spectral properties of the graph Laplacian. The k-means discretization step is replaced by the minimization of this cost measure, resulting in a rotated eigenvector matrix which approximates the form of partitioning matrices, having only one nonzero entry in every row. The definition of the cost measure derives from the observation that a suitable rotation of the eigenvectors also defines a transformation of the graph Laplacian into a block-diagonal form. In this form, the connected components in the graph represent the clustering structure. STSC then chooses the largest number k obtaining minimal costs, from a set of considered numbers of clusters.

The definition of a cost measure may also rely on statistical properties of the dataset. Tibshirani et al. deliver the statistical foundations for the elbow method with the gap statistic [22]. Given a reference distribution, the gap statistic chooses the value of k for which the gap between the approximation error and its expected value is the largest. The expected value is estimated by sampling the data of the reference distribution, and computing a clustering for every sampled dataset and every setting of k.

The score-based methods cannot deliver a guarantee over the quality of the gained model. This is where statistical methods come into play, whose decisions over the number of clusters are based on statistical tests. GMEANS [7] performs statistical tests for the hypothesis that the points in one cluster are Gaussian distributed. PGMEANS [6] improves over GMEANS, by applying the Kolmogorov-Smirnov test for the goodness of fit between one-dimensional random projections of the data and the Gaussian mixture model. They empirically show that this approach is also suitable for non-Gaussian data. An alternative to the Normality assumption is to assume that every cluster follows a unimodal distribution in a suitable space, which can be validated by the dip test. DIPMEANS provides a wrapper for k-means-related algorithms, testing for individual data points whether the distances to other points follow a unimodal distribution [12]. Maurus and Plant argue that this approach is sensitive to noise and propose the algorithm SKINNYDIP, focusing on scenarios with high background noise [19]. Here, the authors assume that a basis transformation exists such that the clusters form a unimodal shape in all coordinate directions. All these approaches require a data transformation or projection, in order to apply the one-dimensional tests.

3   A Nonparametric Bound

We propose a bound on the probability that a specific pair of clusters is generated by a single cluster distribution. Our bound relies on concentration inequalities, which have as input the mean and variance of the unified cluster distribution, which are easy to estimate. No assumptions on the distribution shape (e.g., Gaussian) must be made, and no projection is required. The core concentration inequality which we employ is the matrix Bernstein inequality.

Theorem 1 (Matrix Bernstein [23, Theorem 1.4]). *Consider a sequence of independent, random, symmetric matrices $A_i \in \mathbb{R}^{m \times m}$ for $1 \leq i \leq n$. Assume that each random matrix satisfies:*

$$\mathbb{E}[A_i] = \mathbf{0} \qquad and \qquad \|A_i\|_{op} \leq \nu \ almost \ surely,$$

and set $\sigma^2 = \left\| \sum_i \mathbb{E}[A_i^2] \right\|_{op}$. *Then, for all* $t \geq 0$:

$$\mathbb{P}\left(\left\| \sum_i A_i \right\|_{op} \geq t \right) \leq m \exp\left(-\frac{1}{2} \frac{t^2}{\sigma^2 + \nu t/3} \right).$$

The matrix Bernstein bound employs the operator norm. For real-valued, symmetric matrices this equals the maximum eigenvalue in magnitude:

$$\|A\|_{op} = \sup_{\|x\|=1} \|Ax\| = \max_{1 \leq j \leq m} |\lambda_j(A)| = \max_{x \in \mathbb{R}^m} R(A, x). \tag{4}$$

The relationship to the Rayleigh coefficient is important. This relationship is easy to derive by substituting A with its eigendecomposition. We derive the following central result for the product matrix of centered random matrices.

Theorem 2 (*ZZ* Top Bound). *Let* $Z_{\cdot i} \in \mathbb{R}^m$ *be independent samples of a random vector with mean zero, such that* $\|Z_{\cdot i}\| \leq 1$ *for* $1 \leq i \leq n$. *Further, assume that* $\mathbb{E}[Z_{ji}Z_{li}] = 0$ *for* $j \neq l$ *and* $\mathbb{E}[Z_{ji}^2] = \sigma^2$ *for* $0 < \sigma^2 < 1$ *and* $1 \leq j \leq m$. *Then, for* $t > 0$:

$$\mathbb{P}\left(\left\| ZZ^\top - n\sigma^2 I \right\|_{op} \geq t \right) \leq m \exp\left(-\frac{1}{2} \cdot \frac{t^2}{n\sigma^2 + t/3} \right).$$

Proof. We apply the matrix Bernstein inequality (Theorem 1) to the sum of random matrices:
$$ZZ^\top - n\sigma^2 I = \sum_i \left(Z_{\cdot i} Z_{\cdot i}^\top - \sigma^2 I \right).$$

Assuming that the expected values satisfy $\mathbb{E}[Z_{ji}Z_{li}] = 0$ for $j \neq l$ and $\mathbb{E}[Z_{ji}Z_{ji}] = \sigma^2$, yields that the random matrix $A_i = Z_{\cdot i} Z_{\cdot i}^\top - \sigma^2$ has mean zero:

$$\mathbb{E}[A_i] = \mathbb{E}\left[Z_{\cdot i} Z_{\cdot i}^\top - \sigma^2 I \right] = \left(\mathbb{E}[Z_{ji}Z_{li}] \right)_{jl} - \sigma^2 I = 0.$$

The operator norm of the random matrices A_i is bounded by one:

$$\|A_i\|_{op} = \left\| Z_{\cdot i} Z_{\cdot i}^\top - \sigma^2 I \right\|_{op} = \sup_{\|x\|=1} x^\top \left(Z_{\cdot i} Z_{\cdot i}^\top - \sigma^2 I \right) x = \sup_{\|x\|=1} \left(Z_{\cdot i}^\top x \right)^2 - \sigma^2$$
$$\leq 1 - \sigma^2 \leq 1.$$

The expected value of A_i^2 is:

$$\mathbb{E}\left[\left(Z_{\cdot i} Z_{\cdot i}^\top - \sigma^2 I \right) \left(Z_{\cdot i} Z_{\cdot i}^\top - \sigma^2 I \right) \right] \leq \mathbb{E}\left[Z_{\cdot i} Z_{\cdot i}^\top - 2\sigma^2 Z_{\cdot i} Z_{\cdot i}^\top + \sigma^4 I \right] = \sigma^2 I.$$

Thus, the norm of the total variance is:

$$\left\| \sum_i \mathbb{E}[A_i A_i] \right\|_{op} = \left\| n\sigma^2 I \right\|_{op} = n\sigma^2.$$

The matrix Bernstein inequality then yields the result. $\qquad\square$

Applying Eq. (4) to Theorem 2 yields the following corollary.

Corollary 1. *Let $Z_{\cdot i} \in \mathbb{R}^m$ be independent samples of a random vector with mean zero, such that $\|Z_{\cdot i}\| \leq 1$ for $1 \leq i \leq n$. Further assume that $\mathbb{E}[Z_{\cdot i} Z_{\cdot i}^\top] = \sigma^2 I$ for $0 < \sigma^2 < 1$ and $1 \leq i \leq n$. Let $y \in \{0,1\}^m$ be an indicator vector of a cluster candidate, and denote:*

$$t = R\left(ZZ^\top, y\right) - n\sigma^2. \tag{5}$$

Then, the probability that an indicator vector $y^* \in \{0,1\}^m$ exists with a Rayleigh coefficient such that $R(ZZ^\top, y) \leq R(ZZ^\top, y^*)$, is bounded as follows:

$$\mathbb{P}\left(\max_{y^* \in \{0,1\}^m} R\left(ZZ^\top, y^*\right) - n\sigma^2 \geq t\right) \leq m \exp\left(-\frac{1}{2} \cdot \frac{t^2}{n\sigma^2 + t/3}\right).$$

In practice, we must estimate the mean and variance of a candidate cluster. In this case, the relationship between the Rayleigh coefficient for the centered random matrix Z and the original data matrix is specified as follows (assuming the data matrix D is reduced to the observations belonging to a single cluster).

Remark 1. Assume we want to bound the probability that two clusters indicated by $y, \bar{y} \in \{0,1\}^m$ are parts of one unified cluster represented by $D \in \mathbb{R}^{m \times n}$. We denote with $\mu = \frac{1}{m} D^\top \mathbf{1}$ the vector of sample means over the columns of D. The Rayleigh coefficient of y with respect to the columnwise centered matrix $Z = D - \mathbf{1}\mu^\top$ is equal to (see supplementary material [8] for full derivation):

$$R\left(ZZ^\top, y\right) = \frac{|\bar{y}|}{m}\left(\frac{|\bar{y}|}{m} R\left(DD^\top, y\right) - \frac{|y|}{m} Cut\left(DD^\top, [y\ \bar{y}]\right) + \frac{|y|}{m} R\left(DD^\top, \bar{y}\right)\right)$$

The higher $R\left(ZZ^\top, y\right)$ is, the higher t is in Eq. (5), and the lower the probability is that y indicates a subset of the cluster represented by D. Remark 1 shows that the probability of y indicating a subset of the larger cluster D, is determined by three things: the similarity within each of the candidate clusters ($R(DD^\top, y)$ and $R(DD^\top, \bar{y})$), the rational cut between these clusters ($Cut\left(DD^\top, [y\ \bar{y}]\right)$), and the ratio of points belonging to the one versus the other cluster ($|y|$ versus $|\bar{y}|$). As a result, the ZZ Top Bound provides a natural balance of the within- and between-cluster similarity governing acceptance or rejection of a given clustering.

3.1   A Strategy to Find a Suitable Number of Clusters

Remark 1 and Corollary 1 provide a method to bound the probability that two clusters are generated by the same distribution. Let us go through an example to discuss how we can employ the proposed bounds in a practical setting. Imagine two clusterings, the one employing a larger cluster covering the records denoted by the index set $\mathcal{J} \subset \{1, \ldots, m\}$, having center $\mu \in \mathbb{R}^n$; the other containing a subset of $\mathcal{J}$, indicated by y. Assume the following.

Assumption 1. *If the indices $\mathcal{J}$ form a* true *cluster, then the columns $D_{\mathcal{J}i}$ are independent samples of a random vector with mean $\mu_i \mathbf{1} \in \mathbb{R}^{|\mathcal{J}|}$, for $\mu_i \in \mathbb{R}$.*

Algorithm 1. SPECIALK(W, n, α)

1: $W \approx V^{(n)} \Lambda^{(n)} V^{(n)\top}$ ▷ Compute truncated eigendecomposition
2: $D_{ji} = \left|V_{ji}^{(n)}\right| |\Lambda_{ii}|^{1/2}$ ▷ For all $1 \leq j \leq m$, $1 \leq i \leq n$
3: **for** $k = 1, \ldots$ **do**
4:     $Y^{(k)} \leftarrow \text{K-MEANS}(D, k)$
5:     **for** $c_1, c_2 \in \{1, \ldots, k\}, c_1 > c_2$ **do**
6:        $\mathcal{J} \leftarrow \left\{j \Big| Y_{jc_1}^{(k)} + Y_{jc_2}^{(k)} > 0\right\}$
7:        $Z_{\cdot i} \leftarrow \dfrac{1}{\|D_{\mathcal{J}i}\|} \left(D_{\mathcal{J}i} - \dfrac{|D_{\mathcal{J}i}|}{|\mathcal{J}|}\mathbf{1}\right)$ ▷ For all $j \in \mathcal{J}$
8:        $\sigma^2 \leftarrow \frac{1}{n|\mathcal{J}|} \sum_{j,i} Z_{ji}^2$ ▷ Sample variance
9:        $t \leftarrow \max\left\{R(ZZ^\top, Y_{\mathcal{J}c}) - n\sigma^2 \big| c \in \{c_1, c_2\}\right\}$
10:        **if** $|\mathcal{J}| \exp\left(-\dfrac{1}{2} \cdot \dfrac{t^2}{n\sigma^2 + t/3}\right) > \alpha$ **then**
11:           **return** $Y^{(k-1)}$

We then define the $|\mathcal{J}|$-dimensional scaled and centered sample vectors:

$$Z_{\cdot i} = \frac{1}{\|D_{\mathcal{J}i}\|}(D_{\mathcal{J}i} - \mu_i \mathbf{1}) \quad \text{for all } 1 \leq i \leq n.$$

Now, if one were to assume that $y \in \{0, 1\}^m$ satisfies:

$$R(ZZ^\top, y) \geq \sqrt{2n\sigma^2 \ln\left(\frac{m}{\alpha}\right) + \frac{1}{9}\ln\left(\frac{m}{\alpha}\right)^2} + n\sigma^2 + \frac{1}{3}\ln\left(\frac{m}{\alpha}\right), \quad (6)$$

then Corollary 1 implies that the probability of $\mathcal{J}$ being a true cluster and Eq. (6) holding is at most α. Hence, if α is small enough, then we conclude that $\mathcal{J}$ is not a true cluster; this conclusion is wrong only with the small probability α (which functions as a user-set significance level of a hypothesis test).

Assumption 1 may not hold for all datasets. In particular, the assumption that the column vectors of the data matrix (comprising points from only one cluster) are sampled with the same variance parameter and a mean vector which is reducible to a scaled constant one vector, is not generally valid. Especially if the features of the dataset come from varying domains, the cluster assumptions may not hold. In this paper, we evaluate the ZZ Top Bound in the scope of spectral clustering, where the feature domains are comparable; every feature corresponds to one eigenvector. In particular, we consider a decomposition of the similarity matrix as shown in Eq. (3). The rank of this decomposition is independent from the expected number of k, unlike in traditional spectral clustering algorithms. Hence, a factor matrix D as computed in Eq. (3) can be treated like ordinary k-means input data.

We propose Algorithm 1, called SPECIALK, since it provides a method for SPEctral Clustering to Infer the Appropriate Level k. Its input is a similarity matrix W, the feature dimensionality of the computed embedding, and the significance level $\alpha > 0$. In the first two steps, the symmetric decomposition

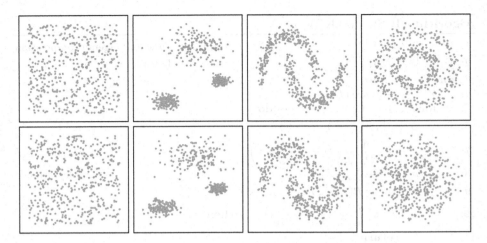

Fig. 1. Visualization of the datasets (from left to right: random, three blobs, two moons, and two circles) with noise parameters equal to 0.1 (top row) and 0.15 (bottom row).

$W \approx DD^\top$ is computed. For an increasing number of clusters, we compute a k-means clustering. For every pair of clusters, we compute the probability that both clusters are actually subsets of the unified cluster. If this probability is larger than the significance level α, then we conclude that the current clustering splits an actual cluster into two and we return the previous model.

4   Experiments

In comparative experiments, our state-of-the-art competitors are Self-Tuning Spectral Clustering (STSC) [24] and PGMEANS [6], whose implementations have been kindly provided by the authors. Since we strive for applicability on nonconvex cluster shapes, we apply PGMEANS to the projected eigenvectors (as computed in Line 2 in Algorithm 1) of a given similarity matrix. We set for PGMEANS the significance level for every test of 12 random projections to $\alpha = 0.01/12$. We also included SKINNYDIP [19] in our evaluation. However, applying this algorithm on the decomposition matrix results in a vast number of returned clusters ($\hat{k} \approx 50$ while the actual value is $k \leq 3$) where most of the data points are attributed to noise. Since this result is clearly wrong, we eschew further comparison with this algorithm.

We consider two variants of similarity matrices: W_R and W_C. The former employs the ϵ-neighborhood adjacency matrix, where ϵ is set such that 99% of the data points have at least ten neighbors; the latter employs the symmetrically normalized adjacency matrix of the kNN graph. STSC computes its own similarity matrix for a given set of points. To do so, it requires a number of considered neighbors, which we set to the default value of 15. Note that the result of STSC comes with its own quality measurement for the computed models;

higher is better. We provide a Python implementation of SPECIALK[1]. In this implementation, we do not assess for all possible pairs of clusters if they emerge from one distribution, but only for the ten cluster pairs having the highest cut.

4.1   Synthetic Experiments

We generate benchmark datasets, using the scikit library for Python. Figure 1 provides examples of the generated datasets, which come in four types of seeded cluster shape (random, blobs, moons, and circles), and a noise parameter (set to 0.1 and 0.15, respectively, in the figure). For each shape and noise specification, we generate $m = 1500$ data points. The noise is Gaussian, as provided by the scikit noise parameter (cf. http://scikit-learn.org). This parameter takes a numeric value, for which we investigate ten settings: we traverse the range $[0, 0.225]$ by increments of size 0.025. For every shape and noise setting, we generate five datasets. Unless otherwise specified, we employ a dimensionality of $n = 200$ as parameter for SPECIALK. However, we use a different rank of $n = 50$ for PGMEANS, whose results benefit from this setting. We set SPE-CIALK's significance level to $\alpha = 0.01$. For all algorithms, we consider only values of $k \in \{1, \ldots, 5\}$; Fig. 1 illustrates that higher values are clearly nonsense.

In Fig. 2, we plot every method's estimated number of clusters for the four datasets (rows) and two similarity matrices (columns) W_R and W_C (since STSC employs its own similarity matrix, the plot with respect to STSC does not vary for these settings: STSC behaves exactly the same in left-column and right-column subplots on the same dataset). In every subplot, the x-axis denotes the setting for the noise parameter. On the y-axis we aggregate the number of clusters detected by each of the three competitors; the correct number of clusters (3 for blobs, 2 for moons and circles, and 1 for random) for each subplot is highlighted by a pink band. Every column in every subplot corresponds to a single setting of shape and noise; recall that we generated five version of the dataset for such a setting. The column now gathers for each of the three competitors (marked in various shapes; see the legend of the figure) which setting of k it determines to be true how often out of the five times. This frequency is represented by mark size: for instance, if PGMEANS determines five distinct values of k for the five datasets, we get five small squares in the column, but if it determines the same value of k for all five datasets, we get one big square in the column. An algorithm performs well if many of its big marks fall in the highlighted band.

Figure 2 illustrates that PGMEANS is all over the place. For the moons and circles datasets, it correctly identifies the number of clusters at low noise levels, but from a certain noise level onwards, it substantially overestimates k. On the moons dataset under W_R this behavior is subtle; under W_C and on the circles dataset the jump from 2 to 5 clusters is jarring. On the blobs dataset, which really isn't that difficult a task, PGMEANS systematically underestimates k. STSC, on the other hand, does quite well. It doesn't make a single mistake on the blobs dataset. STSC generally has the right idea on the circles and moons

---

[1] https://github.com/Sibylse/SpecialK.

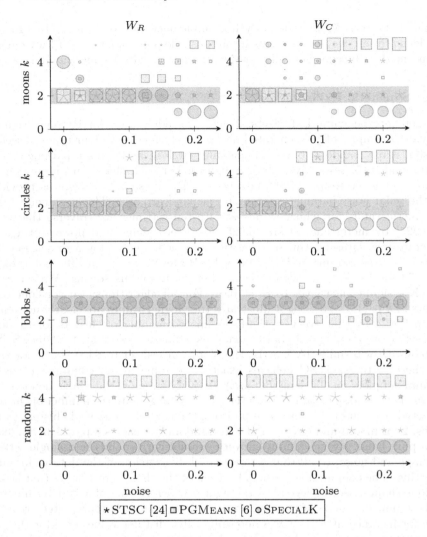

Fig. 2. Variation of noise, comparison of the derived number of clusters for the two moons, two circles, three blobs, and random datasets.

datasets: at low noise levels, it correctly determines k, and at higher noise levels, it alternates between the correct number of clusters and an overestimation. Conversely, SPECIALK has a tendency to err on the other side, if at all. On the circles dataset, it correctly identifies the number of clusters at low noise levels, and packs all observations into a single cluster at high noise levels, which, visually, looks about right (cf. Fig. 1, lower right). On the blobs dataset, SPECIALK generally finds the right level of k, only making incidental mistakes. Performance seems more erratic on the two moons dataset, especially with the W_C similarity

Table 1. Experimental results on real-world datasets. The left half contains metadata on the employed datasets: names, numbers of rows (m) and columns (d), and the real number of classes in the data (Actual k). The right half contains the results of the experiments: the number of classes k determined by the algorithms STSC and SPECIALK, the latter parameterized with similarity matrices W_R and W_C.

Dataset	m	d	Actual k	Determined k		
				STSC	SPECIALK	
					W_R	W_C
Pulsar	17898	9	2	2	2	2
Sloan	10000	16	3	4	4	2
MNIST	60000	784	10	2	2	3
HMNIST	5000	4096	8	3	4	4

matrix. Similarity matrices to this dataset exhibit unusual effects, which are due to the symmetry of the two clusters [9]. To counter these effects, we discard all eigenvectors which are extremely correlated, which we define as having an absolute Spearman rank correlation $|\rho| > 0.95$. Subsequently, the rank is correctly estimated until the noise makes the two clusters appear as one.

The bottom row of Fig. 2 is quite revealing. It illustrates how both STSC and PGMEANS are prone to overfitting. On data that is pure noise, both these methods tend to find several clusters anyway, despite there being no natural grouping in the dataset: it really rather is one monolithic whole. SPECIALK is the only algorithm capable of identifying this, and it does so without a single mistake. Oddly, STSC seems to favor an even number of clusters in random data. PGMEANS tends to favor defining as many clusters as possible on random data.

Empirical results on the sensitivity to the input parameter n (the employed number of eigenvectors) are given in the supplementary material [8].

4.2 Real-World Data Experiments

Experiments on synthetic datasets provide ample evidence that PGMEANS cannot compete with STSC and SPECIALK. Hence, we conduct experiments with only those latter two algorithms on selected real-world datasets, whose characteristics are summarized in the left half of Table 1. The Pulsar dataset[2] contains samples of Pulsar candidates, where the positive class of real Pulsar examples poses a minority against noise effects. The Sloan dataset[3] comprises measurements of the Sloan Digital Sky Survey, where every observation belongs either to a star, a galaxy, or a quasar. The MNIST dataset [16] is a well-known collection of handwritten numbers: the ten classes are the ten digits from zero to nine. The HMNIST dataset [13] comprises histology tiles from patients with colorectal cancer. The classes correspond to eight types of tissue. For these real-world

---

[2] https://www.kaggle.com/pavanraj159/predicting-pulsar-star-in-the-universe.
[3] https://www.kaggle.com/lucidlenn/sloan-digital-sky-survey.

Table 2. NMI scores, probability bounds (p) and costs for the MNIST dataset. The selected rank and the corresponding NMI score is highlighted for every method.

k	SPECIALK				STSC [24]	
	W_C		W_R		NMI	Quality
	NMI	p	NMI	p		
2	0.317	10^{-6}	**0.195**	10^{-23}	0.306	**0.987**
3	**0.518**	10^{-4}	0.207	1.000	0.290	0.978
4	0.668	0.019	0.244	1.000	0.282	0.969
5	0.687	0.011	0.281	1.000	0.274	0.970
6	0.759	0.004	0.294	1.000	0.271	0.970
7	0.760	1.000	0.311	1.000	0.287	0.948
8	0.759	1.000	0.333	1.000	0.279	0.954
9	0.757	1.000	0.347	1.000	0.277	0.956
10	0.756	1.000	0.350	1.000	0.297	0.942
11	0.747	1.000	0.348	1.000	0.362	0.957

datasets, we increase SPECIALK's parameter to $n = 1000$, since the real-world datasets have at least three times as many examples as the synthetic datasets.

Results of the procedure when we let k simply increase up to eleven are given in Table 2. By p we denote the maximum of the probability bounds SPECIALK computes, as outlined in line 10 of Algorithm 1 and mirrored at the end of Corollary 1. For STSC, we output the quality values on which the algorithm bases its decisions (higher is better). Additionally, we give the Normalized Mutual Information (NMI) scores between the constructed clustering and the actual class labels, matched via the Hungarian algorithm [15]; typically, higher is better.

STSC returns the k for which the quality column contains the highest value. By Algorithm 1, SPECIALK returns the lowest k for which its p-value is below α, while the p-value for $k + 1$ is above α. The selected values are highlighted in Table 2, and the determined values for k are entered in the right half of Table 1.

Across all datasets, the right half of Table 1 gives the determined values for k. All methods reconstruct the actual k well on the Pulsar dataset, but none of the determined values for k are equal to the actual value for k on the other three datasets. On Sloan, both methods are in the correct ballpark. On HMNIST, SPECIALK is closer to the right answer than STSC. On MNIST, the true value of k is 10, but both methods determine a substantially lower number of clusters as appropriate. One can get more information on the behavior of the algorithms by taking a closer look at Table 2; similar tables for the other datasets can be found in the supplementary material [8].

For STSC, the highest NMI value is actually obtained for $k = 11$, which is a too high number of clusters, but quite close to the actual k. However, the computed quality does not mirror this finding. Also, the NMI value for the actual $k = 10$ is substantially lower than the NMI for $k = 11$, and the NMI for $k = 10$

is lower than the NMI value for the selected $k = 2$. Hence, NMI cannot just replace the quality in STSC. For SPECIALK, p-value behavior is unambiguous under W_R. Notice that NMI peaks at the right spot.

Under W_C, things get more interesting. While the p-value for $k = 4$ indeed surpasses the threshold α, a slightly less restrictive setting (in many corners of science, $\alpha = 5\%$ is considered acceptable) would have changed the outcome to $k = 6$. At that stage, the p-value suddenly unambiguously shoots to 1; more than 6 clusters is definitely not acceptable. We see this behavior persist through the other datasets as well: there is always a specific value of k, such that the p-values for all $k' > k$ are drastically higher than the p-values for all $k'' \leq k$. While Algorithm 1 makes an automated decision (and this is a desirable property of an algorithm; no post-hoc subjective decision is necessary), if an end-user wants to invest the time to look at the table and select the correct number of clusters themselves, the p-values give a clear and unambiguous direction to that decision.

The entire last paragraph glosses over the fact that the actual k for MNIST is not 6, but 10. In fact, at first sight, the right half of Table 1 paints an unpleasant picture when compared to the Actual k column in the left half. However, the correct conclusion is that column label is misleading. We have some real-world datasets with a given class label, providing a natural grouping of the data into k clusters. The task of clustering is also to find a natural grouping in the dataset. Clustering, however, is not necessarily built to *reconstruct any given* natural grouping: this task is unsupervised! Hence, if an algorithm finds a natural group on the MNIST dataset of relatively bulbous digits, this is a rousing success in terms of the clustering task. However, this group encompasses the digits 6, 8, and 9 (and perhaps others), which reduces the cardinality of the resulting clustering when compared to the clustering that partitions all digits. Therefore, no hard conclusions can be drawn from the determined k not matching the actual k. This is a cautionary tale (also pointed out in [9]), warning against a form of evaluation that is pervasive in clustering, but does not measure the level of success it ought to measure in a solution to the clustering task.

5   Conclusions

We propose a probability bound, that enables to make a hard, statistically founded decision on the question whether two clusters should be fused together or kept apart. Given a significance level α (with the usual connotation and canonical value settings), this results in an algorithm for spectral clustering, automatically determining the appropriate number of clusters k. Since it provides a method for SPEctral Clustering to Infer the Appropriate Level k, the algorithm is dubbed SPECIALK. Automatically determining k in a statistically nonparametric manner for clusters with nonconvex shapes is, to the best of our knowledge, a novel contribution to data mining research. Also, unlike existing algorithms, SPECIALK can decide that the data encompasses only one cluster.

SPECIALK is built to automatically make a decision on which k to select, which it does by comparing subsequent p-values provided by the probability bound, and checking whether they undercut the significance level α. As a consequence, the user can elect to simply be satisfied with whatever k SPECIALK provides. In the experiments on the MNIST dataset, we have seen that the perfect setting of k is in the eye of the beholder: several people can have several contrasting opinions of what constitutes a natural grouping of the data in a real-world setting. In such a case, one can extract more meaningful information out of the results SPECIALK provides, by looking into the table of NMI scores and p-values for a range of settings of k. Eliciting meaning from this table is a subjective task. However, in all such tables for all datasets we have seen so far, there is a clear watershed moment where k gets too big, and relatively low p-values are followed by dramatically high p-values for any higher k. Turning this soft observation into a hard procedure would be interesting future work.

References

1. Alamgir, M., von Luxburg, U.: Multi-agent random walks for local clustering on graphs. In: Proceedings ICDM, pp. 18–27 (2010)
2. Bauckhage, C., Drachen, A., Sifa, R.: Clustering game behavior data. IEEE Trans. Comput. Intell. AI Games **7**(3), 266–278 (2015)
3. Bishop, C.M.: Pattern Recognition and Machine Learning. Springer, New York (2006)
4. Böhm, C., Faloutsos, C., Pan, J.Y., Plant, C.: RIC: parameter-free noise-robust clustering. Trans. Knowl. Discov. Data **1**(3), 10 (2007)
5. Chung, F.R.K.: Spectral Graph Theory. American Mathematical Society, Providence (1997)
6. Feng, Y., Hamerly, G.: PG-means: learning the number of clusters in data. In: Advances in Neural Information Processing Systems, pp. 393–400 (2007)
7. Hamerly, G., Elkan, C.: Learning the k in k-means. In: Advances in Neural Information Processing Systems, pp. 281–288 (2004)
8. Hess, S., Duivesteijn, W.: k is the magic number—supplementary material. arXiv (2019, to appear)
9. Hess, S., Duivesteijn, W., Honysz, P., Morik, K.: The SpectACl of nonconvex clustering: a spectral approach to density-based clustering. In: Proceedings of the AAAI (2019)
10. Horn, R.A., Johnson, C.A.: Matrix Analysis. Cambridge University Press, Cambridge (1985)
11. Hou, J., Sha, C., Chi, L., Xia, Q., Qi, N.: Merging dominant sets and DBSCAN for robust clustering and image segmentation. In: Proceedings of the ICIP, pp. 4422–4426 (2014)
12. Kalogeratos, A., Likas, A.: Dip-means: an incremental clustering method for estimating the number of clusters. In: Advances in Neural Information Processing Systems, pp. 2393–2401 (2012)
13. Kather, J.N., et al.: Multi-class texture analysis in colorectal cancer histology. Sci. Rep. **6**, 27988 (2016)
14. Kontkanen, P., Myllymäki, P., Buntine, W., Rissanen, J., Tirri, H.: An MDL framework for data clustering. In: Advances in Minimum Description Length Theory and Applications. Neural Information Processing Series, pp. 323–353 (2005)
15. Kuhn, H.W.: The Hungarian method for the assignment problem. Nav. Res. Logist. Q. **2**(1–2), 83–97 (1955)

16. LeCun, Y., Bottou, L., Bengio, Y., Haffner, P.: Gradient-based learning applied to document recognition. Proc. IEEE **86**(11), 2278–2324 (1998)
17. Lloyd, S.P.: Least square quantization in PCM. IEEE Trans. Inf. Theory **28**(2), 129–137 (1982)
18. von Luxburg, U.: A tutorial on spectral clustering. Stat. Comput. **17**(4), 395–416 (2007)
19. Maurus, S., Plant, C.: Skinny-dip: clustering in a sea of noise. In: Proceedings of the KDD, pp. 1055–1064 (2016)
20. Ng, A.Y., Jordan, M.I., Weiss, Y.: On spectral clustering: analysis and an algorithm. In: Proceedings of the NIPS, pp. 849–856 (2001)
21. Pelleg, D., Moore, A.W.: X-means: extending k-means with efficient estimation of the number of clusters. In: Proceedings of the ICML, pp. 727–734 (2000)
22. Tibshirani, R., Walther, G., Hastie, T.: Estimating the number of clusters in a data set via the gap statistic. J. R. Stat. Soc.: Ser. B (Stat. Methodol.) **63**(2), 411–423 (2001)
23. Tropp, J.A.: User-friendly tail bounds for sums of random matrices. Found. Comput. Math. **12**(4), 389–434 (2012)
24. Zelnik-Manor, L., Perona, P.: Self-tuning spectral clustering. In: Proceedings NIPS, pp. 1601–1608 (2005)

From Abstract Items to Latent Spaces to Observed Data and Back: Compositional Variational Auto-Encoder

Victor Berger[✉] and Michèle Sebag

TAU, CNRS, INRIA, LRI, Univ. Paris-Saclay, 91405 Orsay, France
victor.berger@inria.fr

Abstract. Conditional Generative Models are now acknowledged an essential tool in Machine Learning. This paper focuses on their control. While many approaches aim at disentangling the data through the coordinate-wise control of their latent representations, another direction is explored in this paper. The proposed COMPVAE handles data with a natural multi-ensemblist structure (*i.e.* that can naturally be decomposed into elements). Derived from Bayesian variational principles, COMPVAE learns a latent representation leveraging both observational and symbolic information. A first contribution of the approach is that this latent representation supports a compositional generative model, amenable to multi-ensemblist operations (addition or subtraction of elements in the composition). This compositional ability is enabled by the invariance and generality of the whole framework w.r.t. respectively, the order and number of the elements. The second contribution of the paper is a proof of concept on synthetic 1D and 2D problems, demonstrating the efficiency of the proposed approach.

Keywords: Generative model · Semi-structured representation · Neural nets

1 Introduction

Representation learning is at the core of machine learning, and even more so since the inception of deep learning [2]. As shown by e.g., [3,12], the latent representations built to handle high-dimensional data can effectively support desirable functionalities. One such functionality is the ability to directly control the observed data through the so-called representation disentanglement, especially in the context of computer vision and image processing [20,26] (more in Sect. 2).

This paper extends the notion of representation disentanglement from a latent coordinate-wise perspective to a semi-structured setting. Specifically, we tackle the ensemblist setting where a datapoint can naturally be interpreted as the combination of multiple parts. The contribution of the paper is a generative model built on the Variational Auto-Encoder principles [17,28], *controlling*

© Springer Nature Switzerland AG 2020
U. Brefeld et al. (Eds.): ECML PKDD 2019, LNAI 11906, pp. 274–289, 2020.
https://doi.org/10.1007/978-3-030-46150-8_17

the data generation from a description of its parts and supporting ensemblist operations such as the addition or removal of any number of parts.

The applicative motivation for the presented approach, referred to as *Compositional Variational AutoEncoder* (COMPVAE), is the following. In the domain of Energy Management, a key issue is to simulate the consumption behavior of an ensemble of consumers, where each household consumption is viewed as an independent random variable following a distribution law defined from the household characteristics, and the household consumptions are possibly correlated through external factors such as the weather, or a football match on TV (attracting members of some but not all households). Our long term goal is to infer a simulator, taking as input the household profiles and their amounts: it should be able to simulate their overall energy consumption and account for their correlations. The data-driven inference of such a programmable simulator is a quite desirable alternative to the current approaches, based on Monte-Carlo processes and requiring either to explicitly model the correlations of the elementary random variables, or to proceed by rejection.

Formally, given the description of datapoints and their parts, the goal of COMPVAE is to learn the distribution laws of the parts (here, the households) and to sample the overall distribution defined from a varying number of parts (the set of households), while accounting for the fact that the parts are not independent, and the sought overall distribution depends on shared external factors: *the whole is not the sum of its parts.*

The paper is organized as follows. Section 2 briefly reviews related work in the domain of generative models and latent space construction, replacing our contribution in context. Section 3 gives an overview of COMPVAE, extending the VAE framework to multi-ensemblist settings. Section 4 presents the experimental setting retained to establish a proof of concept of the approach on two synthetic problems, and Sect. 5 reports on the results. Finally Sect. 6 discusses some perspectives for further work and applications to larger problems.

2   Related Work

Generative models, including VAEs [17,28] and GANs [9], rely on an embedding from the so-called latent space Z onto the dataspace X. In the following, data space and observed space are used interchangeably. It has long been observed that continuous or discrete operations in the latent space could be used to produce interesting patterns in the data space. For instance, the linear interpolation between two latent points z and z' can be used to generate a morphing between their images [27], or the flip of a boolean coordinate of z can be used to add or remove an elementary pattern (the presence of glasses or moustache) in the associated image [7].

The general question then is to control the flow of information from the latent to the observed space and to make it actionable. Several approaches, either based on information theory or on supervised learning have been proposed to do so. Losses inspired from the Information Bottleneck [1,30,32] and enforcing the independence of the latent and the observed variables, conditionally to the relevant content of information, have been proposed: enforcing the decorrelation of the latent coordinates in β-VAE [12]; aligning the covariances of latent and observed data in [19]; decomposing the latent information into pure content and pure noise in InfoGAN [3]. Independently, explicit losses have been used to yield conditional distributions in conditional GANs [23], or to enforce the scope of a latent coordinate in [18,33], (e.g. modelling the light orientation or the camera angle).

The structure of the observed space can be mimicked in the latent space, to afford expressive yet trainable model spaces; in Ladder-VAE [31], a sequence of dependent latent variables are encoded and reversely decoded to produce complex observed objects. Auxiliary losses are added in [22] in the spirit of semi-supervised learning. In [16], the overall generative model involves a classifier, trained both in a supervised way with labelled examples and in an unsupervised way in conjunction with a generative model.

An important case study is that of sequential structures: [5] considers fixed-length sequences and loosely mimicks an HMM process, where latent variable z_i controls the observed variable x_i and the next latent z_{i+1}. In [13], a linear relation among latent variables z_i and z_{i+1} is enforced; in [6], a recurrent neural net is used to produce the latent variable encoding the current situation. In a more general context, [34] provides a generic method for designing an appropriate inference network that can be associated with a given Bayesian network representing a generative model to train.

The injection of explicit information at the latent level can be used to support "information surgery" via loss-driven information parsimony. For instance in the domain of signal generation [4], the neutrality of the latent representation w.r.t. the locutor identity is enforced by directly providing the identity at the latent level: as z does not need to encode the locutor information, the information parsimony pressure ensures z independence wrt the locutor. Likewise, *fair* generative processes can be enforced by directly providing the sensitive information at the latent level [35]. In [21], an adversarial mechanism based on Maximum Mean Discrepancy [10] is used to enforce the neutrality of the latent. In [24], the minimization of the mutual information is used in lieu of an adversary.

Discussion. All above approaches (with the except of sequential settings [5,13], see below) handle the generation of a datapoint as a whole naturally involving diverse facets; but not composed of inter-related parts. Our goal is instead to tackle the proper parts-and-whole structure of a datapoint, where the *whole is not necessarily the simple sum of its parts* and the parts of the whole are interdependent. In sequential settings [5,13], the dependency of the elements in the sequence are handled through parametric restrictions (respectively considering fixed sequence-size or linear temporal dependency) to enforce the proper match of the observed and latent spaces. A key contribution of the proposed COMPVAE is to tackle the parts-to-whole structure with no such restrictions, and specifically accommodating a varying number of parts − possibly different between the training and the generation phases.

3   Overview of CompVAE

This section describes the CompVAE model, building upon the VAE principles [17] with the following difference: CompVAE aims at building a *programmable generative model* p_θ, taking as input the ensemble of the parts of a whole observed datapoint. A key question concerns the latent structure most appropriate to reflect the ensemblist nature of the observed data. The proposed structure (Sect. 3.1) involves a latent variable associated to each part of the whole. The aggregation of the part is achieved through an order-invariant operation, and the interactions among the parts are modelled at an upper layer of the latent representation.

In encoding mode, the structure is trained from the pairs formed by a whole, and an abstract description of its parts; the latent variables are extracted along an iterative non-recurrent process, oblivious of the order and number of the parts (Sect. 3.2) and defining the encoder model q_ϕ.

In generative mode, the generative model is supplied with a set of parts, and accordingly generates a consistent whole, where variational effects operate jointly at the part and at the whole levels.

Notations. A datapoint x is associated with an ensemble of parts noted $\{\ell_i\}$. Each ℓ_i belongs to a finite set of categories Λ. Elements and parts are used interchangeably in the following. In our illustrating example, a consumption curve x involves a number of households; the i-th household is associated with its consumer profile ℓ_i, with ℓ_i ranging in a finite set of profiles. Each profile in Λ thus occurs 0, 1 or several times. The generative model relies on a learned distribution $p_\theta(x|\{\ell_i\})$, that is decomposed into latent variables: a latent variable named w_i associated to each part ℓ_i, and a common latent variable z.

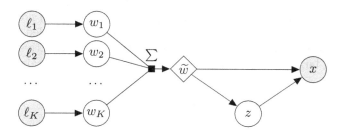

Fig. 1. Bayesian network representation of the CompVAE generative model.

3.1   CompVAE: Bayesian Architecture

The architecture proposed for CompVAE is depicted as a graphical model on Fig. 1. As said, the i-th part belongs to category ℓ_i and is associated with a latent variable w_i (different parts with same category are associated with different latent variables). The ensemble of the w_is is aggregated into an intermediate latent variable $\widetilde{w}$. A key requirement is for $\widetilde{w}$ to be *invariant* w.r.t. the order of elements in x. In the following $\widetilde{w}$ is set to the sum of the w_i, $\widetilde{w} = \sum_i w_i$. Considering other order-invariant aggregations is left for further work.

The intermediate latent variable $\widetilde{w}$ is used to condition the z latent variable; both $\widetilde{w}$ and z condition the observed datapoint x. This scheme corresponds to the following factorization of the generative model p_θ:

$$p_\theta(x, z, \{w_i\}|\{\ell_i\}) = p_\theta(x|z, \widetilde{w})p_\theta(z|\widetilde{w}) \prod_i p_\theta(w_i|\ell_i) \tag{1}$$

In summary, the distribution of x is conditioned on the ensemble $\{\ell_i\}$ as follows: The i-th part of x is associated with a latent variable w_i modeling the generic distribution of the underlying category ℓ_i together with its specifics. Variable $\widetilde{w}$ is deterministically computed to model the aggregation of the w_i, and finally z models the specifics of the aggregation.

Notably, each w_i is linked to a single ℓ_i element, while z is global, being conditioned from the global auxiliary $\widetilde{w}$. The rationale for introducing z is to enable a more complex though still learnable distribution at the x level − compared with the alternative of conditioning x only on $\widetilde{w}$. It is conjectured that an information-effective distribution would store in w_i (respectively in z) the *local information* related to the i-th part (resp. the *global information* describing the interdependencies between all parts, e.g. the fact that the households face the same weather, vacation schedules, and so on). Along this line, it is conjectured that the extra information stored in z is limited compared to that stored in the w_is; we shall return to this point in Sect. 4.1.

The property of invariance of the distribution w.r.t. the order of the ℓ_i is satisfied by design. A second desirable property regards the robustness of the distribution w.r.t. the varying number of parts in x. More precisely, two requirements are defined. The former one, referred to as *size-flexibility property*, is that the number K of parts of an x is neither constant, nor bounded *a priori*. The latter one, referred to as *size-generality property* is the generative model p_θ to accommodate larger numbers of parts than those seen in the training set.

3.2   Posterior Inference and Loss

Letting $p_D(x|\{\ell_i\})$ denote the empirical data distribution, the learning criterion to optimize is the data likelihood according to the sought generative model p_θ: $\mathbb{E}_{p_D} \log p_\theta(x|\{\ell_i\})$.

The (intractable) posterior inference of the model is approximated using the Evidence Lower Bound (ELBO) [14], following the Variational AutoEncoder approach [17,28]. Accordingly, we proceed by optimizing a lower bound of the log-likelihood of the data given p_θ, which is equivalent to minimizing an upper bound of the Kullback-Leibler divergence between the two distributions:

$$D_{KL}(p_D \| p_\theta) \le H(p_D) + \mathop{\mathbb{E}}_{x \sim p_D} \mathcal{L}_{ELBO}(x) \tag{2}$$

The learning criterion is, with $q_\phi(z, \{w_i\}|x, \{\ell_i\})$ the inference distribution:

$$
\begin{aligned}
\mathcal{L}_{ELBO}(x) = {}& \underset{z, \{w_i\} \sim q_\phi}{\mathbb{E}} \log \frac{q_\phi(z, \{w_i\}|x, \{\ell_i\})}{p_\theta(z|\widetilde{w}) \prod_i p_\theta(w_i|\ell_i)} \\
& - \underset{z, \{w_i\} \sim q_\phi}{\mathbb{E}} \log p_\theta(x|z, \widetilde{w})
\end{aligned}
\tag{3}
$$

The inference distribution is further factorized as $q_\phi(\{w_i\}|z, x, \{\ell_i\}) q_\phi(z|x)$, yielding the final training loss:

$$
\begin{aligned}
\mathcal{L}_{ELBO}(x) = {}& \underset{z, \{w_i\} \sim q_\phi}{\mathbb{E}} \log \frac{q_\phi(\{w_i\}|x, z, \{\ell_i\})}{\prod_i p_\theta(w_i|\ell_i)} \\
& + \underset{z, \{w_i\} \sim q_\phi}{\mathbb{E}} \log \frac{q_\phi(z|x)}{p_\theta(z|\widetilde{w})} \\
& - \underset{z, \{w_i\} \sim q_\phi}{\mathbb{E}} \log p_\theta(x|z, \widetilde{w})
\end{aligned}
\tag{4}
$$

The training of the generative and encoder model distributions is described in Algorithm 1.

$\theta, \phi \leftarrow$ Random initialization;
while *Not converged* **do**
    $x, \{\ell_i\} \leftarrow$ Sample minibatch;
    $z \leftarrow$ Sample from $q_\phi(z|x)$;
    $\{w_i\} \leftarrow$ Sample from $q_\phi(\{w_i\}|x, z, \{\ell_i\})$;
    $\mathcal{L}_w \leftarrow D_{KL}(q_\phi(\{w_i\}|x, z, \{\ell_i\}) \| \Pi_i p_\theta(w_i|\ell_i))$;
    $\mathcal{L}_z \leftarrow \log \frac{q_\phi(z|x)}{p_\theta(z|\widetilde{w})}$;
    $\mathcal{L}_x \leftarrow -\log p_\theta(x|z, \widetilde{w})$;
    $\mathcal{L}_{ELBO} \leftarrow \mathcal{L}_w + \mathcal{L}_z + \mathcal{L}_x$;
    $\theta \leftarrow$ Update$(\theta, \nabla_\theta \mathcal{L}_{ELBO})$;
    $\phi \leftarrow$ Update$(\phi, \nabla_\phi \mathcal{L}_{ELBO})$;
end

Algorithm 1. COMPVAE Training Procedure.

3.3   Discussion

In COMPVAE, the sought distributions are structured as a Bayesian graph (see p_θ in Fig. 1), where each node is associated with a neural network and a probability distribution family, like for VAEs. This neural network takes as input the parent variables in the Bayesian graph, and outputs the parameters of a distribution in the chosen family, e.g., the mean and variance of a Gaussian distribution. The reparametrization trick [17] is used to back-propagate gradients through the sampling.

A concern regards the training of latent variables when considering Gaussian distributions. A potential source of instability in COMPVAE comes from the fact that the Kullback-Leibler divergence between q_ϕ and p_θ (Eq. (4)) becomes very large when the variance of some variables in p_θ becomes very small[1]. To limit this risk, some care is exercized in parameterizing the variances of the normal distributions in p_θ to making them lower-bounded.

Modelling of $q_\phi(\{w_i\}|x, z, \{\ell_i\})$. The latent distributions $p_\theta(z|\tilde{w})$, $p_\theta(w_i|\ell_i)$ and $q_\phi(z|x)$ are modelled using diagonal normal distributions as usual. Regarding the model $q_\phi(\{w_i\}|z, x, \{\ell_i\})$, in order to be able to faithfully reflect the generative model p_θ, it is necessary to introduce the correlation between the w_is in $q_\phi(\{w_i\}|z, x, \{\ell_i\})$ [34].

As the aggregation of the w_i is handled by considering their sum, it is natural to handle their correlations through a multivariate normal distribution over the w_i. The proposed parametrization of such a multivariate is as follows. Firstly, correlations operate in a coordinate-wise fashion, that is, $w_{i,j}$ and $w_{i',j'}$ are only correlated if $j = j'$. The parametrization of the w_is ensures that: (i) the variance of the sum of the $w_{i,j}$ can be controlled and made arbitrarily small in order to ensure an accurate VAE reconstruction; (ii) the Kullback-Leibler divergence between $q_\phi(\{w_i\}|x, z, \{\ell_i\})$ and $\prod_i p_\theta(w_i|\ell_i)$ can be defined in closed form.

The learning of $q_\phi(\{w_i\}|x, z, \{\ell_i\})$ is done using a fully-connected graph neural network [29] leveraging graph interactions akin message-passing [8]. The graph has one node for each element ℓ_i, and every node is connected to all other nodes. The state of the i-th node is initialized to $(pre_\phi(x), z, e_\phi(\ell_i) + \epsilon_i)$, where $pre_\phi(x)$ is some learned function of x noted, $e_\phi(\ell_i)$ is a learned embedding of ℓ_i, and ϵ_i is a random noise used to ensure the differentiation of the w_is. The state of each node of the graph at the k-th layer is then defined by its $k-1$-th layer state and the aggregation of the state of all other nodes:

$$\begin{cases} h_i^{(0)} = (pre_\phi(x), z, e_\phi(\ell_i) + \epsilon_i) \\ h_i^{(k)} = f_\phi^{(k)}\left(h_i^{(k-1)}, \sum_{j \neq i} g_\phi^{(k)}(h_j^{(k-1)})\right) \end{cases} \tag{5}$$

where $f_\phi^{(k)}$ and $g_\phi^{(k)}$ are learned neural networks: $g_\phi^{(k)}$ is meant to embed the current state of each node for an aggregate summation, and $f_\phi^{(k)}$ is meant to "fine-tune" the i-th node conditionally to all other nodes, such that they altogether account for $\tilde{w}$.

4   Experimental Setting

This section presents the goals of experiments and describes the experimental setting used to empirically validate COMPVAE.

---

[1] Single-latent variable VAEs do not face such problems as the prior distribution $p_\theta(z)$ is fixed, it is not learned.

4.1 Goals of Experiments

As said, COMPVAE is meant to achieve a programmable generative model. From a set of latent values w_i, either derived from $p_\theta(w_i|\ell_i)$ in a generative context, or recovered from some data x, it should be able to generate values $\hat{x}$ matching any chosen subset of the w_i. This property is what we name the "ensemblist disentanglement" capacity, and the first goal of these experiments is to investigate whether COMPVAE does have this capacity.

A second goal of these experiments is to examine whether the desired properties (Sect. 3.1) hold. The order-invariant property is enforced by design. The size-flexibility property will be assessed by inspecting the sensitivity of the extraction and generative processes to the variability of the number of parts. The size-generality property will be assessed by inspecting the quality of the generative model when the number of parts increases significantly beyond the size range used during training.

A last goal is to understand how COMPVAE manages to store the information of the model in respectively the w_is and z. The conjecture done (Sect. 3.1) was that the latent w_is would take in charge the information of the parts, while the latent z would model the interactions among the parts. The use of synthetic problems where the quantity of information required to encode the parts can be quantitatively assessed will permit to test this conjecture. A related question is whether the generative model is able to capture the fact that the whole is not the sum of its parts. This question is investigated using non-linear perturbations, possibly operating at the whole and at the parts levels, and comparing the whole perturbed x obtained from the ℓ_is, and the aggregation of the perturbed x_is generated from the ℓ_i parts. The existence of a difference, if any, will establish the value of the COMPVAE generative model compared to a simple Monte-Carlo simulator, independently sampling parts and thereafter aggregating them.

4.2 1D and 2D Proofs of Concept

Two synthetic problems have been considered to empirically answer the above questions.[2]

In the 1D synthetic problem, the set Λ of categories is a finite set of frequencies $\lambda_1 \ldots \lambda_{10}$. A given "part" (here, curve) is a sine wave defined by its frequency ℓ_i in Λ and its intrinsic features, that is, its amplitude a_i and phase κ_i. The whole x associated to $\{\ell_1, \ldots \ell_K\}$ is a finite sequence of size T, deterministically defined from the non-linear combination of the curves:

$$x(t) = K \tanh\left(\frac{C}{K} \sum_{i=0}^{K} a_i \cos\left(\frac{2\pi\ell_i}{T} t + \kappa_i \right) \right)$$

with K the number of sine waves in x, C a parameter controlling the non-linearity of the aggregation of the curves in x, and T a global parameter controlling the

---

[2] These problems are publicly available at https://github.com/vberger/compvae.

sampling frequency. For each part (sine wave), a_i is sampled from $\mathcal{N}(1; 0.3)$, and κ_i is sampled from $\mathcal{N}\left(0; \frac{\pi}{2}\right)$.

The part-to-whole aggregation is illustrated on Fig. 2, plotting the non-linear transformation of the sum of 4 sine waves, compared to the sum of non-linear transformations of the same sine waves. C is set to 3 in the experiments.

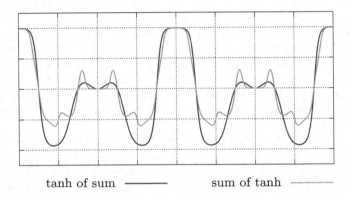

tanh of sum ———   sum of tanh ———

Fig. 2. Non-linear part-to-whole aggregation (purple) compared to the sum of non-linear perturbations of the parts (green). Better seen in color. Both curves involve a non-linear transform factor $C = 3$. (Color figure online)

This 1D synthetic problem features several aspects relevant to the empirical assessment of COMPVAE. Firstly, the impact of adding or removing one part can be visually assessed as it changes the whole curve: the general magnitude of the whole curve is roughly proportional to its number of parts. Secondly, each part involves, besides its category ℓ_i, some intrinsic variations of its amplitude and phase. Lastly, the whole x is not the sum of its parts (Fig. 2).

The generative model $p_\theta(x|z, \sum_i w_i)$ is defined as a Gaussian distribution $\mathcal{N}(\mu; \Delta(\sigma))$, the vector parameters μ and σ of which are produced by the neural network.

In the 2D synthetic problem, each category in Λ is composed of one out of five colors ($\{red, green, blue, white, black\}$) associated with a location (x, y) in $[0, 1] \times [0, 1]$. Each ℓ_i thus is a colored site, and its internal variability is its intensity. The whole x associated to a set of ℓ_is is an image, where each pixel is colored depending on its distance to the sites and their intensity (Fig. 3). Likewise, the observation model $p_\theta(x|z, \sum_i w_i)$ is a Gaussian distribution $\mathcal{N}(\mu; \Delta(\sigma))$, the parameters μ and σ of which are produced by the neural network. The observation variance is shared for all three channel values (red, green, blue) of any given pixel.

The 2D problem shares with the 1D problem the fact that each part is defined from its category ℓ_i (resp. a frequency, or a color and location) on the one hand, and its specifics on the other hand (resp, its amplitude and frequency, or

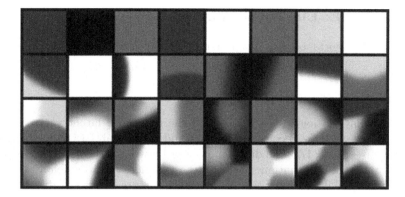

Fig. 3. 2D visual synthetic examples, including 1 to 4 sites (top to bottom). Note that when neighbor sites have same color, the image might appear to have been generated with less sites than it actually has. (Color figure online)

its intensity); additionally, the whole is made of a set of parts in interaction. However, the 2D problem is significantly more complex than the 1D, as will be discussed in Sect. 5.2.

4.3   Experimental Setting

COMPVAE is trained as a mainstream VAE, except for an additional factor of difficulty: the varying number of latent variables (reflecting the varying number of parts) results in a potentially large number of latent variables. This large size and the model noise in the early training phase can adversely affect the training procedure, and lead it to diverge. The training divergence is prevented using a batch size set to 256. The neural training hyperparameters are dynamically tuned using the Adam optimizer [15] with $\alpha = 10^{-4}$, $\beta_1 = 0.5$ and $\beta_2 = 0.9$, which empirically provide a good compromise between training speed, network stability and good convergence. On the top of Adam, the annealing of the learning rate α is achieved, dividing its value by 2 every 20,000 iterations, until it reaches 10^{-6}.

For both problems, the data is generated on the fly during the training, preventing the risk of overfitting. The overall number of iterations (batches) is up to[3] 500,000. The computational time on a GPU GTX1080 is 1 day for the 1D problem, and 2 days for the 2D problem.

Empirically, the training is facilitated by gradually increasing the number K of parts in the datapoints. Specifically, the number of parts is uniformly sampled in $[[1, K]]$ at each iteration, with $K = 2$ at the initialization and K incremented by 1 every 3,000 iterations, up to 16 parts in the 1D problem and 8 in the 2D problem.

---

[3] Experimentally, networks most often converge much earlier.

5   CompVAE: Empirical Validation

This section reports on the proposed proofs of concept of the CompVAE approach.

5.1   1D Proof of Concept

Figure 4 displays in log-scale the losses of the w_is and z latent variables along time, together with the reconstruction loss and the overall ELBO loss summing the other three (Eq. (4)). The division of labor between the w_is and the z is seen as the quantity of information stored by the w_is increases to reach a plateau at circa 100 bits, while the quantity of information stored by z steadily decreases to around 10 bits. As conjectured (Sect. 3.1), z carries little information.

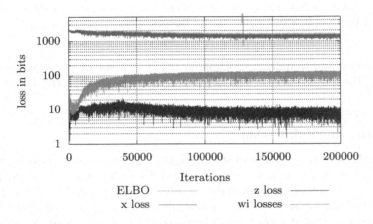

Fig. 4. CompVAE, 1D problem: Losses of the latent variables respectively associated to the parts (w_i, green), to the whole (z, blue), and the reconstruction loss of x (yellow), in log scale. Better seen in color. (Color figure online)

Note that the x reconstruction loss remains high, with a high ELBO even at convergence time, although the generated curves "look good". This fact is explained from the high entropy of the data: on the top of the specifics of each part (its amplitude and phase), x is described as a T-length sequence: the temporal discretization of the signal increases the variance of x and thus causes a high entropy, which is itself a lower bound for the ELBO. Note that a large fraction of this entropy is accurately captured by CompVAE through the variance of the generative model $p_\theta(x|z, \widetilde{w})$.

The ability of "ensemblist disentanglement" is visually demonstrated on Fig. 5: considering a set of ℓ_i, the individual parts w_i are generated (Fig. 5, left) and gradually integrated to form a whole x (Fig. 5, right) in a coherent manner.

The size-generality property is satisfactorily assessed as the model could be effectively used with a number of parts K ranging up to 30 (as opposed to 16

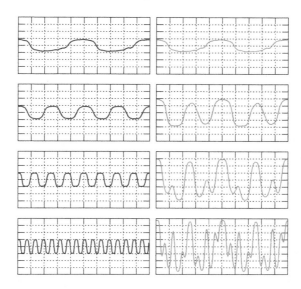

Fig. 5. CompVAE, 1D problem: Ensemblist recomposition of the whole (right column) from the parts (left column). On each row is given the part (left) and the whole (right) made of this part and all above parts.

during the training) without requiring any re-training or other modification of the model (results omitted for brevity).

5.2   2D Proof of Concept

As shown in Fig. 6, the 2D problem is more complex. On the one hand, a 2D part only has a local impact on x (affecting a subset of pixels) while a 1D part has a global impact on the whole x sequence. On the other hand, the number of parts has a global impact on the range of x in the 1D problem, whereas each pixel value ranges in the same interval in the 2D problem. Finally and most importantly, x is of dimension 200 in the 1D problem, compared to dimension $3,072$ ($3 \times 32 \times 32$) in the 2D problem. For these reasons, the latent variables here need to store more information, and the separation between the w_i (converging toward circa 200–300 bits of information) and z (circa 40–60 bits) is less clear.

Likewise, x reconstruction loss remains high, although the generated images "look good", due to the fact that the loss precisely captures the discrepancies in the pixel values that the eye does not perceive.

Finally, the ability of "ensemblist disentanglement" is inspected by incrementally generating the whole x from a set of colored sites (Fig. 7). The top row displays the colors of $\ell_1 \dots \ell_5$ from left to right. On the second row, the i-th square shows an image composed from $\ell_1 \dots \ell_i$ by the ground truth generator, and rows 3 to 6 show images generated by the model from the same $\ell_1 \dots \ell_i$. While the generated x generally reflects the associated set of parts, some advents

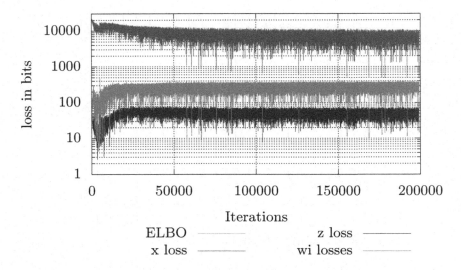

Fig. 6. COMPVAE, 2D problem: Losses of the latent variables respectively associated to the parts (w_i, green), to the whole (z, blue), and the reconstruction loss of x (yellow), in log scale. Better seen in color. (Color figure online)

of black and white glitches are also observed (for instance on the third column, rows 3 and 5). These glitches are blamed on the saturation of the network (as black and white respectively are represented as $(0, 0, 0)$ and $(1, 1, 1)$ in RGB), since non linear combinations of colors are used for a good visual rendering[4].

6   Discussion and Perspectives

The main contribution of the paper is the generative framework COMPVAE, to our best knowledge the first generative framework able to support the generation of data based on a multi-ensemble $\{\ell_i\}$. Built on the top of the celebrated VAE, COMPVAE learns to optimize the conditional distribution $p_\theta(x|\{\ell_i\})$ in a theoretically sound way, through introducing latent variables (one for each part ℓ_i), enforcing their order-invariant aggregation and learning another latent variable to model the interaction of the parts. Two proofs of concepts for the approach, respectively concerning a 1D and a 2D problem, have been established with respectively very satisfactory and satisfactory results.

This work opens several perspectives for further research. A first direction in the domain of computer vision consists of combining COMPVAE with more advanced image generation models such as PixelCNN [25] in a way similar to PixelVAE [11], in order to generate realistic images involving a predefined set of elements along a consistent layout.

---

[4] Color blending in the data generation is done taking into account gamma-correction.

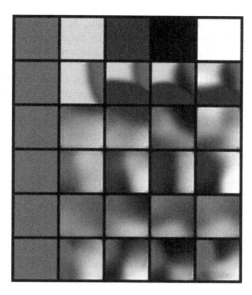

Fig. 7. COMPVAE, 2D problem. First row: parts $\ell_1 \ldots \ell_5$. Second row: the i-th square depicts the x defined from ℓ_1 to ℓ_i as generated by the ground truth. Rows 3–6: different realizations of the same combination by the trained COMPVAE - see text. Best viewed in colors. (Color figure online)

A second perspective is to make one step further toward the training of fully programmable generative models. The idea is to incorporate explicit biases on the top of the distribution learned from unbiased data, to be able to sample the desired sub-spaces of the data space. In the motivating application domain of electric consumption for instance, one would like to sample the global consumption curves associated with high consumption peaks, that is, to bias the generation process toward the top quantiles of the overall distribution.

Acknowledgments. This work was funded by the ADEME #1782C0034 project *NEXT* (https://www.ademe.fr/next).

The authors would like to thank Balthazar Donon and Corentin Tallec for the many useful and inspiring discussions.

References

1. Achille, A., Soatto, S.: Emergence of invariance and disentanglement in deep representations. J. Mach. Learn. Res. **19**(1), 1947–1980 (2018)
2. Bengio, Y., Courville, A., Vincent, P.: Representation learning: a review and new perspectives. IEEE Trans. Pattern Anal. Mach. Intell. **35**(8), 1798–1828 (2013). https://doi.org/10.1109/TPAMI.2013.50

3. Chen, X., Duan, Y., Houthooft, R., Schulman, J., Sutskever, I., Abbeel, P.: Info-GAN: interpretable representation learning by information maximizing generative adversarial nets. In: Advances in Neural Information Processing Systems, pp. 2172–2180 (2016)
4. Chorowski, J., Weiss, R.J., Bengio, S., van den Oord, A.: Unsupervised speech representation learning using WaveNet autoencoders (2019). http://arxiv.org/abs/1901.08810
5. Chung, J., Kastner, K., Dinh, L., Goel, K., Courville, A.C., Bengio, Y.: A recurrent latent variable model for sequential data. In: Cortes, C., Lawrence, N.D., Lee, D.D., Sugiyama, M., Garnett, R. (eds.) Advances in Neural Information Processing Systems 28, pp. 2980–2988 (2015)
6. Co-Reyes, J.D., Liu, Y., Gupta, A., Eysenbach, B., Abbeel, P., Levine, S.: Self-consistent trajectory autoencoder: hierarchical reinforcement learning with trajectory embeddings. In: International Conference on Machine Learning (2018)
7. Dumoulin, V., et al.: Adversarially learned inference. In: International Conference on Learning Representations (2017)
8. Gilmer, J., Schoenholz, S.S., Riley, P.F., Vinyals, O., Dahl, G.E.: Neural message passing for quantum chemistry. In: International Conference on Machine Learning, pp. 1263–1272 (2017)
9. Goodfellow, I., et al.: Generative adversarial nets. In: Advances in Neural Information Processing Systems 27, pp. 2672–2680. Curran Associates, Inc. (2014)
10. Gretton, A., Borgwardt, K.M., Rasch, M.J., Schölkopf, B., Smola, A.: A kernel two-sample test. J. Mach. Learn. Res. **13**, 723–773 (2012)
11. Gulrajani, I., et al.: PixelVAE: a latent variable model for natural images. In: International Conference on Learning Representations (2017)
12. Higgins, I., et al.: beta-VAE: learning basic visual concepts with a constrained variational framework. In: International Conference on Learning Representations (2017)
13. Hsu, W.N., Zhang, Y., Glass, J.: Unsupervised learning of disentangled and interpretable representations from sequential data. In: Advances in Neural Information Processing Systems 30, pp. 1878–1889. Curran Associates, Inc. (2017)
14. Jordan, M.I., Ghahramani, Z., Jaakkola, T.S., Saul, L.K.: An introduction to variational methods for graphical models. Mach. Learn. **37**(2), 183–233 (1999). https://doi.org/10.1023/A:1007665907178
15. Kingma, D.P., Ba, J.: Adam: a method for stochastic optimization. In: International Conference on Learning Representations (2014)
16. Kingma, D.P., Rezende, D.J., Mohamed, S., Welling, M.: Semi-supervised learning with deep generative models. In: Neural Information Processing Systems (2014)
17. Kingma, D.P., Welling, M.: Auto-encoding variational Bayes. In: International Conference on Learning Representations (2013)
18. Kulkarni, T.D., Whitney, W.F., Kohli, P., Tenenbaum, J.: Deep convolutional inverse graphics network. In: Advances in Neural Information Processing Systems 28, pp. 2539–2547. Curran Associates, Inc. (2015)
19. Kumar, A., Sattigeri, P., Balakrishnan, A.: Variational inference of disentangled latent concepts from unlabeled observations. In: International Conference on Learning Representations (2017)
20. Liu, L., et al.: Deep learning for generic object detection: a survey (2018). http://arxiv.org/abs/1809.02165
21. Louizos, C., Swersky, K., Li, Y., Welling, M., Zemel, R.: The variational fair autoencoder (2015). http://arxiv.org/abs/1511.00830

22. Maaløe, L., Sønderby, C.K., Sønderby, S.K., Winther, O.: Auxiliary deep generative models. In: International Conference on Machine Learning, pp. 1445–1453 (2016)
23. Mirza, M., Osindero, S.: Conditional generative adversarial nets (2014). http://arxiv.org/abs/1411.1784
24. Moyer, D., Gao, S., Brekelmans, R., Galstyan, A., Ver Steeg, G.: Invariant representations without adversarial training. In: Advances in Neural Information Processing Systems, pp. 9084–9093 (2018)
25. van den Oord, A., Kalchbrenner, N., Espeholt, L., Kavukcuoglu, K., Vinyals, O., Graves, A.: Conditional image generation with PixelCNN decoders. In: Advances in Neural Information Processing Systems 29, pp. 4790–4798. Curran Associates, Inc. (2016)
26. Prasad, D.K.: Survey of the problem of object detection in real images. Int. J. Image Process. (IJIP) **6**(6), 441 (2012)
27. Radford, A., Metz, L., Chintala, S.: Unsupervised representation learning with deep convolutional generative adversarial networks. In: International Conference on Learning Representations (2015)
28. Rezende, D.J., Mohamed, S., Wierstra, D.: Stochastic backpropagation and approximate inference in deep generative models. In: International Conference on Machine Learning, pp. 1278–1286 (2014)
29. Scarselli, F., Gori, M., Tsoi, A.C.; Hagenbuchner, M., Monfardini, G.: The graph neural network model. IEEE Trans. Neural Netw. **20**(1), 61–80 (2009). https://doi.org/10.1109/TNN.2008.2005605
30. Shwartz-Ziv, R., Tishby, N.: Opening the black box of deep neural networks via information (2017). http://arxiv.org/abs/1703.00810
31. Sønderby, C.K., Raiko, T., Maaløe, L., Sønderby, S.K., Winther, O.: Ladder variational autoencoders. In: Advances in Neural Information Processing Systems, pp. 3738–3746 (2016)
32. Tishby, N., Pereira, F.C., Bialek, W.: The information bottleneck method. CoRR physics/0004057 (2000)
33. Tran, L., Yin, X., Liu, X.: Disentangled representation learning GAN for pose-invariant face recognition. In: Proceedings of the IEEE Conference on Computer Vision and Pattern Recognition, pp. 1415–1424 (2017)
34. Webb, S., et al.: Faithful inversion of generative models for effective amortized inference. In: Advances in Neural Information Processing Systems, pp. 3070–3080 (2018)
35. Zemel, R., Wu, Y., Swersky, K., Pitassi, T., Dwork, C.: Learning fair representations. In: International Conference on Machine Learning, pp. 325–333 (2013)

Dimensionality Reduction and Feature Selection

Joint Multi-source Reduction

Lei Zhang[1]([✉]) [iD], Shupeng Wang[1]([✉]), Xin Jin[2]([✉]), and Siyu Jia[1]([✉])

[1] Institute of Information Engineering, Chinese Academy of Sciences,
Beijing 100093, China
{zhanglei1,wangshupeng,jiasiyu}@iie.ac.cn
[2] National Computer Network Emergency Response Technical Team/Coordination
Center of China, Beijing 100029, China
13911191965@139.com

Abstract. The redundant sources problem in multi-source learning always exists in various real-world applications such as multimedia analysis, information retrieval, and medical diagnosis, in which the heterogeneous representations from different sources always have three-way redundancies. More seriously, the redundancies will cost a lot of storage space, cause high computational time, and degrade the performance of learner. This paper is an attempt to jointly reduce redundant sources. Specifically, a novel Heterogeneous Manifold Smoothness Learning (HMSL) model is proposed to linearly map multi-source data to a low-dimensional feature-isomorphic space, in which the information-correlated representations are close along manifold while the semantic-complementary instances are close in Euclidean distance. Furthermore, to eliminate three-way redundancies, we present a new Correlation-based Multi-source Redundancy Reduction (CMRR) method with 2,1-norm equation and generalized elementary transformation constraints to reduce redundant sources in the learned feature-isomorphic space. Comprehensive empirical investigations are presented that confirm the promise of our proposed framework.

Keywords: Multi-source · Redundant · Heterogeneous · Manifold measure · Dimension reduction · Sample selection

1 Introduction

Generally, due to incorrect data storage manner and the like, not all instances are a concise and effective reflection of objective reality, inevitably leading to the redundant sources of multi-source data. Note that different from duplicated data, multi-source heterogeneous redundant data are those which could seriously affect the performance of the learner. Rather, as shown in Fig. 1, there is a distinct difference between the redundant sources problem in multi-source learning and mono-source scenario, because multi-source heterogeneous redundant data contain the following three-way redundancies:

© Springer Nature Switzerland AG 2020
U. Brefeld et al. (Eds.): ECML PKDD 2019, LNAI 11906, pp. 293–309, 2020.
https://doi.org/10.1007/978-3-030-46150-8_18

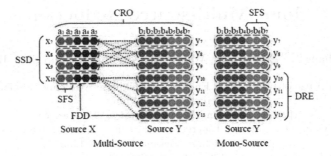

Fig. 1. Multi- and Mono-Source Redundant Data. The x_7, x_8, x_9, and x_{10} denote the redundant representations from Source S_x. Similarly, the y_7, y_8, y_9, y_{10}, y_{11}, y_{12}, and y_{13} are the redundant representations from Source S_y. The a_1, a_2, a_3, a_4, and a_5 represents the features in the representations from Source S_x. The features in the representations from Source S_y are composed of the b_1, b_2, b_3, b_4, b_5, b_6, and b_7. The three-way redundancies are DRE, SFS, and CRO, respectively. The double-level heterogeneities consist of FDD and SSD.

- **Data Representations Excessiveness (DRE).** The existing of multiple unduplicated representations of the same object in the same source leads to taking up too much storage space.
- **Sample Features Superabundance (SFS).** Superabundance caused by curse of dimensionality [4] refers to a high-dimensional space embedding some related or randomized dimensions, resulting in high computational time.
- **Complementary Relationships Overplus (CRO).** One representation from one source has corresponding relationships with multiple heterogeneous descriptions from another source. This overplus will bring about a significant decline in the performances of multi-source representations.

Consequently, due to the existing of three-way redundancies, the redundant sources problem owns double-level heterogeneities, i.e., Feature Dimension Dissimilarity (FDD) and Sample Size Difference (SSD) (see Fig. 1). First, different sources use different dimensions and different attributes to represent the same object [10,14,29]; besides, there are different number of instances in each source. Even more serious is that these redundancies severely impact the performances of multi-source data, resulting in false analysis, clustering, classification, and retrieval [12,24,25]. Therefore, it is extremely necessary to develop an effective reducing method for multi-source heterogeneous redundant data.

For the past few years, to deal with redundancies problem, various machine learning methods have been investigated to reduce computational cost and improve learning accuracy. Up to now, the existing methods involve dimension reduction techniques [13,17,18,24] and sample selection approaches [5,21,22,25].

Dimension Reduction Techniques. In [18], Huan et al. investigated a feature extraction approach, called Knowledge Transfer with Low-Quality Data (KTLQD), to leverage the available auxiliary data sources to aid in knowledge discovery. Nie et al. [17] proposed an Efficient and Robust Feature Selection via Joint $\ell_{2,1}$-Norms Minimization (ERFSJNM) method, which used $\ell_{2,1}$-norm regularization to extract meaningful features and eliminate noisy ones across all data points with joint sparsity. Wang et al. [24] studied a feature selection framework, called Feature Selection via Global Redundancy Minimization (FSGRM), to globally minimize the feature redundancy with maximizing the given feature ranking scores. An unsupervised feature selection scheme, namely, Nonnegative Spectral Analysis with Constrained Redundancy (NSACR), was developed by Li et al. [13] through jointly leveraging nonnegative spectral clustering and redundancy analysis.

Sample Selection Approaches. Wang et al. [25] proposed a sample selection mechanism based on the principle of maximal classification ambiguity, i.e., Maximum Ambiguity-based Sample Selection in Fuzzy Decision Tree Induction (MASSFDTI), to select a number of representative samples from a large database. In [5], a Sample Pair Selection with Rough Set (SPSRS) framework was proposed in order to compress the discernibility function of a decision table so that only minimal elements in the discernibility matrix were employed to find reducts. Shahrian and Rajan [21] designed a content-based sample selection method, called Weighted Color and Texture Sample Selection for Image Matting (WCTSSIM), in which color information was leveraged by color sampling-based matting methods to find the best known samples for foreground and background color of unknown pixels. Su et al. [22] developed an Active Correction Propagation (ACP) method using a sample selection criterion for active query of informative samples by minimizing the expected prediction error.

Generally, these existing methods can eliminate only one kind of redundancy, not three kinds of redundancy. Moreover, these methods were designed for single-source data like many other conventional data mining methods. Accordingly, it is impossible for them to eliminate the double-level heterogeneities among different redundant sources. To address the limitations of existing methods, we attempt to explore a multi-source reducing framework to jointly eliminate three-way redundancies and double-level heterogeneities at the same time.

1.1   Organization

The remainder of this paper is organized as follows: A general framework for jointly reducing the redundant sources of multi-source data is proposed in Sect. 2. Furthermore, the efficient algorithms are provided to solve the proposed framework in Sect. 3. Section 4 evaluates and analyzes the proposed framework on three multi-source datasets. Finally, our conclusions are presented in Sect. 5.

1.2   Notations

In Table 1, we describe the notations needed to understand our proposed algorithm.

Table 1. Notations

Notation	Description
S_x	Source X
S_y	Source Y
$X_N \in \mathbb{R}^{n_1 \times d_x}$	Non-redundant samples in S_x
$Y_N \in \mathbb{R}^{n_1 \times d_y}$	Non-redundant samples in S_y
$L_N \in \mathbb{R}^{n_1 \times m}$	Label indicator matrix
$x_i \in \mathbb{R}^{d_x}$	The i-th sample from S_x
$y_i \in \mathbb{R}^{d_y}$	The i-th sample from S_y
n_1	Number of non-redundant samples
d_x	Dimensionality of S_x
d_y	Dimensionality of S_y
m	Number of labels
(x_i, y_i)	The i-th multi-source datum
$X_R \in \mathbb{R}^{n_2 \times d_x}$	Redundant representations in S_x
$Y_R \in \mathbb{R}^{n_3 \times d_y}$	Redundant representations in S_y
n_2	Number of redundant samples in S_x
n_3	Number of redundant samples in S_y
$\|\cdot\|_F$	Frobenius norm
$\|\cdot\|_*$	Trace norm
$\mathbb{S}_+^{k \times k}$	Positive semi-definite matrices
$\nabla f(\cdot)$	Gradient of smooth function $f(\cdot)$
$|\cdot|$	Absolute value
$I_k \in \mathbb{R}^{k \times k}$	Identity matrix

2   Reducing Multi-source Heterogeneous Redundant Data

A general simplifying framework is proposed in this section to jointly reduce the redundant sources of multi-source data. Figure 2 presents an overview of the proposed framework. In this example, a set of multi-source data consists of Source X and Source Y. There are a certain amount of multi-source non-redundant data such as X_N and Y_N. However, some multi-source data X_R and Y_R have three-way redundancies and double-level heterogeneities. For instance, the CRO among different sources brings about that the sample x_7 in Source X is correlated with multiple instances y_7, y_8, and y_9 in Source Y; additionally, there are multiple representations y_{11}, y_{12}, and y_{13} similar to y_{10} due to the DRE in Source Y; furthermore, the representations in the sources are too much superabundant because of the SFS. As a result, the feature dimensions are heterogeneous and there are different number of samples in these sources, i.e., FDD and SSD.

To jointly reduce the redundant sources of multi-source data, HMSL model learns a low-dimensional feature homogeneous subspace, in which

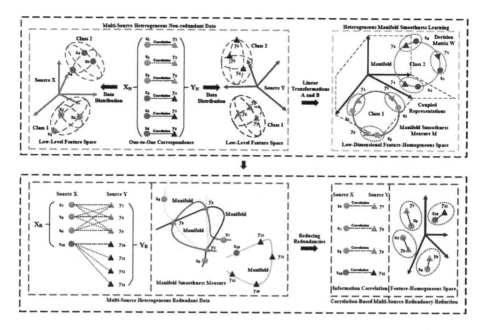

Fig. 2. Framework for joint multi-source reduction.

the information-correlated representations are close along manifold while the semantic-complementary instances are close in Euclidean distance at the same time. Then, CMRR model removes the three-way redundancies and double-level heterogeneities existing in the multi-source heterogeneous redundant data X_R and Y_R from the feature-homogeneous space under the learned complementarity, correlation, and distributivity restraints.

The following subsections present more details.

2.1   The Proposed HMSL Model

This subsection presents a new HMSL model, which has pseudo-metric constraints, manifold regularization, and leave-one-out validation to correlate different sources. In HMSL model, the existing non-redundant heterogeneous representations X_N and Y_N are utilized to learn two heterogeneous linear transformations A and B, a decision matrix W, and a manifold smoothness measure M to mine the semantic complementarity, information correlation, and distributional similarity among different sources. As a consequence, the heterogeneous representations from different sources are linearly mapped into a low-dimensional feature-homogeneous space, in which the information-correlated samples are close along manifold while the semantic-complementary instances are close in Euclidean distance.

Specifically, the proposed method can be formulated as follows:

$$\min_{\Psi_1:A,B,W,M} f_S(A,B,W) + \alpha g_M(A,B,M) - \beta h_D(A,B) \tag{1}$$
$$s.t. \ A^T A = I, \quad B^T B = I, \quad and \quad M \succeq 0,$$

where $A \in \mathbb{R}^{d_x \times k}$, $B \in \mathbb{R}^{d_y \times k}$, $k \leq min(d_x, d_y)$, and α and β are two trade-off parameters. The orthogonal constraints $A^T A = I$ and $B^T B = I$ can effectively eliminate the correlation among different features in the same source. The positive semidefinite restraint $M \in \mathbb{S}_+^{k \times k} \succeq 0$ can be used to obtain a well-defined pseudo-metric.

The objective function in Eq. (1) consists of the semantic, correlation, and distributional subfunctions. The semantic subfunction $f_S(A,B,W)$:

$$f_S(A,B,W) = \left\| \begin{bmatrix} X_N A \\ Y_N B \end{bmatrix} W - \begin{bmatrix} L_N \\ L_N \end{bmatrix} \right\|_F^2, \tag{2}$$

is based on multivariant linear regression to capture the semantic complementarity between different sources.

The first term in the objective function is multivariate linear regression based on the semantic function, which is used to capture the semantic complementarity between different sources.

Moreover, we define the new distance metrics as follow to obtain a Mahalanobis distance:

$$\mathcal{D}_{M_X}(x_i, x_j) = (x_i - x_j)^T M_X (x_i - x_j), \tag{3}$$

$$\mathcal{D}_{M_Y}(y_i, y_j) = (y_i - y_j)^T M_Y (y_i - y_j), \tag{4}$$

where $M_X = A^T A$ and $M_Y = B^T B$. Therefore, each pair of co-occurring heterogeneous representations (x_i, y_i) can be embedded by the linear transformations A and B into a feature-homogeneous space.

Accordingly, the motivation of introducing the correlation function $g_M(A, B, M)$:

$$g_M(A,B,M) = \| X_N A M B^T Y_N^T \|_F^2, \tag{5}$$

is to measure the smoothness between A and B to extract the information correlation among heterogeneous representations.

Additionally, $\mathcal{C}_X^t$ and $\mathcal{C}_Y^t$ denote respectively the sample sets of t-th class from the sources V_x and V_y. We assume that each sample x_i selects another sample y_j from another source as its neighbor with the probability p_{ij}. Similarly, q_{ij} refers to the probability that y_i is the neighbor of x_j.

We apply the softmax under the Euclidean distance in the feature-homogeneous space to define p_{ij} and q_{ij} as follows:

$$p_{ij} = \frac{exp(- \| Ax_i - By_j \|^2)}{\sum_k exp(- \| Ax_i - By_k \|^2)}, \tag{6}$$

$$q_{ij} = \frac{exp(- \| By_i - Ax_j \|^2)}{\sum_k exp(- \| By_i - Ax_k \|^2)}. \tag{7}$$

Accordingly, the probabilities p_i and q_i:

$$p_i = \sum_{x_i \in \mathcal{C}_X^t \ \& \ y_j \in \mathcal{C}_Y^t} p_{ij}, \tag{8}$$

$$q_i = \sum_{y_i \in \mathcal{C}_Y^t \ \& \ x_j \in \mathcal{C}_X^t} q_{ij}, \tag{9}$$

represents the odds which the sample i will be correctly classified. Consequently, the distributional similarity subfunction $h_D(A, B)$ based on Mahalanobis distance:

$$h_D(A, B) = \sum p_i + \sum q_i, \tag{10}$$

is a leave-one-out validation, which is used to capture the distributional similarity between different sources.

Section 3.1 presents an efficient algorithm to solve Ψ_1.

2.2   The Proposed CMRR Model

Furthermore, to reduce the three-way redundancies and remove double-level heterogeneities, we propose a new CMRR model with GET constraints and GEC criterion to recover one-to-one complementary relationship between the heterogeneous representations from redundant sources in the learned feature-homogeneous space.

Specifically, assuming (A^*, B^*, W^*, M^*) be the optimal solutions of Ψ_1. Then the proposed approach can be formulated:

$$\Omega_1: \quad \begin{array}{c} \min_{P,Q} \|P^T H W^* - Q^T R W^*\|_F^2 + \gamma \|P^T H M^* R^T Q\|_F^2 + \\ \tau \| \left(P^T H + Q^T R\right)/2 \|_* \\ s.t. \ P \in \Sigma_{n_2 \times n_4}, Q \in \Sigma_{n_3 \times n_4}, \|P\|_{2,1} = \|Q\|_{2,1} = n_4, \end{array} \tag{11}$$

where γ and τ are two regularization parameters, P and Q are two GET matrices, $H = X_R A^*$ and $R = Y_R B^*$ are the redundant matrices in S_x and S_y, $\Sigma_{n_2 \times n_4} \in \mathbb{R}^{n_2 \times n_4}$ and $\Sigma_{n_3 \times n_4} \in \mathbb{R}^{n_3 \times n_4}$ are two set of GET matrices, and $n_4 = min(n_2, n_3)$.

The first term in the objective function uses A^*, B^*, and W^* to build one-to-one complementary relationship between the heterogeneous representations of the same object while removing CRO and eliminating SFS. The second term in the objective function is used to clear DRE in the same source by M^* in order to extract the correlated information between heterogeneous representations. The low-rank regularization based on trace norm (the third term in the objective function) is used to make the complex representations as linearly-separable as possible. As shown in Fig. 3, to switch the rows in H and R, the GET constraints are imposed on P and Q to establish one-to-one complementary relationship while removing CRO. The motivation of introducing the 2,1-norm equality restraint is to clear DRE in H and R through favoring a number of zero rows in P and Q. Note that if there is but only 2,1-norm equality restraint, the P and Q may become a matrix containing only one non-zero row [1]. Thus,

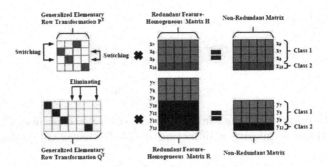

Fig. 3. Correlation-based Multi-source Redundancy Reduction. To establish one-to-one complementary relationship while removing CRO, CMRR model imposes the GET constraints on P and Q to switch the rows in H and R.

it is essential for selecting complementary representations to add the GET constraints on P and Q in Ω_1.

Based on the gradient energy measure [20], the GEC criterion [28] can be used to build a GET matrix effectively. Specifically, every internal element G_{ij} is connected to its four neighbors $G_{i-1,j}$, $G_{i+1,j}$, $G_{i,j-1}$, and $G_{i,j+1}$ in a gradient matrix G obtained by gradient descent method. We can obtain the between-sample energy E_{bs} of G_{ij} according to the ℓ_1-norm gradient magnitude energy [20]:

$$E_{bs} = \frac{\partial}{\partial x}G = \mid G(i+1,j) - G(i,j) \mid + \mid G(i,j) - G(i-1,j) \mid, \qquad (12)$$

and the within-sample energy E_{ws} as

$$E_{ws} = \frac{\partial}{\partial y}G = \mid G(i,j+1) - G(i,j) \mid + \mid G(i,j) - G(i,j-1) \mid. \qquad (13)$$

We can calculate the global energy of G_{ij} by E_{bs} and E_{ws}:

$$E_{globe} = \delta * E_{bs} + (1 - \delta) * E_{ws}, \qquad (14)$$

where δ is a trade-off parameter.

The global energy of every element in G can be computed by Eq. (14), and then we can obtain an energy matrix E. As a result, we can compare he global energies of every element. It can be seen that the winner with maximum energy will be set to 1, and the remaining elements in the same row and column will be set to 0. We can repeat the cycle until a GET matrix Q is built.

Section 3.2 presents an efficient algorithm to solve Ω_1.

3   Optimization Technique

In this section, we present an optimization technique to solve the proposed framework.

3.1 An Efficient Solver for Ψ_1

The optimization problem Ψ_1 (see Eq. (1)) can be simplified as follows:

$$\min_{Z \in \mathcal{C}} \quad F(Z), \tag{15}$$

where $F(\cdot) = f_S(\cdot) + \alpha g_M(\cdot) - \beta h_D(\cdot)$ is a smooth function, $Z = [A_Z \quad B_Z \quad W_Z \quad M_Z]$ symbolizes the optimization variables, and the set $\mathcal{C}$ is closed for each variable:

$$\mathcal{C} = \{Z | A_Z^T A_Z = I, B_Z^T B_Z = I, M_Z \succeq 0\}. \tag{16}$$

Because $F(\cdot)$ is continuously differentiable for each variable with Lipschitz continuous gradient L [16], it is appropriate to solve Eq. (15) by Accelerated Projection Gradient (APG) [16] method.

The first-order gradient algorithm APG can accelerate each gradient step and minimize the smooth function, so as to obtain the optimal solution. A solution sequence $\{Z_i\}$ is updated from a search point sequence $\{S_i\}$ in the method.

Due to orthogonal constraints, it is exceedingly difficult for us to optimize the non-convex optimization problem in Eq. (15). However, if Gradient Descent Method with Curvilinear Search (GDMCS) [27] satisfies Armijo-Wolfe conditio,

---

Algorithm 1: Heterogeneous Manifold Smoothness Learning (**HMSL**)

Input: $Z_0 = [A_{Z_0} B_{Z_0} W_{Z_0} M_{Z_0}]$, $F(\cdot)$, $f_S(\cdot)$, $g_M(\cdot)$, $h_D(\cdot)$, X_N, Y_N, $\gamma_1 > 0$, $t_0 = 1$, τ_1, $0 < \rho_1 < \rho_2 < 1$, and $maxIter$.

Output: Z^*.

1: Define $F_{\gamma,S}(Z) = F(S) + \langle \nabla F(S), Z - S \rangle + \gamma \|Z - S\|_F^2 / 2$
2: Calculate $[A_{Z_0}] = \boldsymbol{Schmidt}(A_{Z_0})$.
3: Calculate $[B_{Z_0}] = \boldsymbol{Schmidt}(B_{Z_0})$.
4: Set $A_{Z_1} = A_{Z_0}$, $B_{Z_1} = B_{Z_0}$, $W_{Z_1} = W_{Z_0}$, and $M_{Z_1} = M_{Z_0}$.
5: **for** $i = 1, 2, \cdots, maxIter$ **do**
6:     Set $a_i = (t_{i-1} - 1)/t_{i-1}$.
7:     Calculate $A_{S_i} = (1 + \alpha_i)A_{Z_i} - \alpha_i A_{Z_{i-1}}$.
8:     Calculate $B_{S_i} = (1 + \alpha_i)B_{Z_i} - \alpha_i B_{Z_{i-1}}$.
9:     Calculate $W_{S_i} = (1 + \alpha_i)W_{Z_i} - \alpha_i W_{Z_{i-1}}$.
10:     Calculate $M_{S_i} = (1 + \alpha_i)M_{Z_i} - \alpha_i M_{Z_{i-1}}$.
11:     Set $S_i = [A_{S_i} \quad B_{S_i} \quad W_{S_i} \quad M_{S_i}]$.
12:     Calculate $\nabla_{A_S} F(A_{S_i})$, $\nabla_{B_S} F(B_{S_i})$, $\nabla_{W_S} F(W_{S_i})$, and $\nabla_{M_S} F(M_{S_i})$.
13:     Define $F_A(A_{Z_i}, B)$ and $F_B(A, B_{Z_i})$.
14:     **while** (true)
15:         Calculate $\widehat{A_S} = A_{S_i} - \nabla_{A_S} F(A_{S_i})/\gamma_i$.
16:         Calculate $[\widehat{A_S}] = \boldsymbol{Schmidt}(\widehat{A_S})$.
17:         Calculate $\widehat{B_S} = B_{S_i} - \nabla_{B_S} F(B_{S_i})/\gamma_i$.
18:         Calculate $[\widehat{B_S}] = \boldsymbol{Schmidt}(\widehat{B_S})$.
19:         Set $[A_{Z_{i+1}}, B_{Z_{i+1}}] = \boldsymbol{GDMCS}(F(\cdot), \widehat{A_S}, \widehat{B_S}, \tau_1, \rho_1, \rho_2)$.
20:         Calculate $W_{Z_{i+1}} = W_{S_i} - \nabla_{W_S} Q(W_{S_i})/\gamma_i$.

21:        Calculate $\widehat{M_S} = M_{S_i} - \nabla_{M_S} Q(M_{S_i})/\gamma_i$.
22:        Calculate $[M_{Z_{i+1}}] = \boldsymbol{PSP}(\widehat{M_S})$.
23:        Set $Z_{i+1} = [A_{Z_{i+1}} \quad B_{Z_{i+1}} \quad W_{Z_{i+1}} \quad M_{Z_{i+1}}]$.
24:        if $F(Z_{i+1}) \le F_{\gamma_i, S_i}(Z_{i+1})$, then break;
25:        else Update $\gamma_i = \gamma_i \times 2$.
26:        endIf
27:    endWhile
28:    Update $t_i = \left(1 + \sqrt{1 + 4t_{i-1}^2}\right)/2$, $\gamma_{i+1} = \gamma_i$.
29: endFor
30: Set $Z^* = Z_{i+1}$.

---

it has been proved by Guo and Xiao in [9] that GDMCS can effectively solve the non-convex problem. We can use the method in [9] to prove that the proposed HMSL algorithm met the using conditions of GDMCS algorithm.

APG projects a given point s onto set $\mathcal{C}$ in the following way:

$$proj_{\mathcal{C}}(s) = arg \min_{z \in \mathcal{C}} \|z - s\|_F^2/2. \tag{17}$$

Positive Semi-definite Projection (PSP) proposed by Weinberger et al. in [26] can remain positive semi-definite constraints, when it minimize a smooth function. It will project optimal variables into a cone of all positive semi-definite matrices after each gradient step. The projection is computed from the diagonalization of optimal variables, which effectively truncates any negative eigenvalues from the gradient step, setting them to zero. PSP can be utilized to solve the problem in Eq. (17).

Finally, when applying APG for solving Eq. (15), a given point S can be projected into the set $\mathcal{C}$ as follows:

$$proj_{\mathcal{C}}(S) = arg \min_{Z \in \mathcal{C}} \|Z - S\|_F^2/2. \tag{18}$$

The problem in Eq. (18) can be solved by the combination of APG, PSP, and GDMCS. The details are given in Algorithm 1, in which the function $\boldsymbol{Schmidt}(\cdot)$ [15] denotes the GramSchmidt process.

3.2   An Efficient Solver for Ω_1

To solve the model Ω_1 (See Sect. 2.2), an efficient algorithm is given in this subsection. Similarly, the problem in Eq. (11) can be simplified as:

$$\min_{\Theta \in \mathcal{Q}} \quad H(\Theta) = w(\Theta) + \tau t(\Theta), \tag{19}$$

where $w(\cdot) = \|\cdot\|_F^2 + \gamma\|\cdot\|_F^2$ is a smooth subfunction, $t(\cdot) = \|\cdot\|_*$ is an undifferentiable subfunction, $\Theta = [P_\Theta \quad Q_\Theta]$ symbolizes the optimization variables, and set $\mathcal{Q}$ is closed for each variable:

$$\mathcal{Q} = \{\Theta | P_\Theta \in \Sigma_{n_2 \times n_4}, Q_\Theta \in \Sigma_{n_3 \times n_4}, \|P_\Theta\|_{2,1} = \|Q_\Theta\|_{2,1} = n_4\}. \tag{20}$$

Because $w(\cdot)$ is continuously differentiable for each variable with Lipschitz continuous gradient L [16], it is also appropriate to solve Eq. (19) by APG [16] method.

Similarly, APG projects a given point s onto set $\mathcal{Q}$ in the following way:

$$proj_{\mathcal{Q}}(s) = arg\ \min_{\theta \in \mathcal{Q}} \|\theta - s\|_F^2/2, \tag{21}$$

The GEC criterion (See Sect. 2.2) can be used to map the approximate solution of Eq. (21) into the generalized elementary transformation constraint $\mathcal{Q}$. Zhang et al. [28] have successfully used the functions $Energy(\cdot)$ and $Competition(\cdot)$ to implement the GEC criterion according to Eq. (12, 13, 14).

Algorithm 2: Correlation-based Multi-source Redundancy Reduction (**CMRR**)

Input: $H(\cdot)$, $w(\cdot)$, $t(\cdot)$, $P_{Z_0} = I_{n_2 \times n_4}$, $Q_{Z_0} = I_{n_3 \times n_4}$, $Z_0 = [P_{Z_0}\ Q_{Z_0}]$, X_R, Y_R, δ, $\varepsilon_1 > 0$, $t_0 = 1$, and $maxIter$.

Output: Z^*.

1: Define $H_{\varepsilon,S}(Z) = w(S) + \langle \nabla w(S), Z - S \rangle + \varepsilon \|Z - S\|_F^2/2 + \tau t(Z)$.
2: Set $P_{Z_1} = P_{Z_0}$ and $Q_{Z_1} = Q_{Z_0}$.
3: for $i = 1,2,\cdots,maxIter$ do
4:     Set $a_i = (t_{i-1} - 1)/t_{i-1}$.
5:     Calculate $P_{S_i} = (1 + \alpha_i)P_{Z_i} - \alpha_i P_{Z_{i-1}}$.
6:     Calculate $Q_{S_i} = (1 + \alpha_i)Q_{Z_i} - \alpha_i Q_{Z_{i-1}}$.
7:     Set $S_i = [P_{S_i}\quad Q_{S_i}]$.
8:     Derive $\nabla_{P_S} w(P_{S_i})$ and $\nabla_{Q_S} w(Q_{S_i})$.
9:     while (true)
10:         Calculate $\widehat{P_S} = -\nabla_{P_S} w(P_{S_i})/\varepsilon_i$.
11:         Calculate $[\widehat{P_{Z_{i+1}}}] = \boldsymbol{Energy}(\widehat{P_S}, \delta)$.
12:         Calculate $[P_{Z_{i+1}}] = \boldsymbol{Competition}(\widehat{P_{Z_{i+1}}})$.
13:         Calculate $\widehat{Q_S} = -\nabla_{Q_S} w(Q_{S_i})/\varepsilon_i$.
14:         Calculate $[\widehat{Q_{Z_{i+1}}}] = \boldsymbol{Energy}(\widehat{Q_S}, \delta)$.
15:         Calculate $[Q_{Z_{i+1}}] = \boldsymbol{Competition}(\widehat{Q_{Z_{i+1}}})$.
16:         Set $Z_{i+1} = [P_{Z_{i+1}}\quad Q_{Z_{i+1}}]$.
17:         if $H(Z_{i+1}) \leq H_{\varepsilon_i,S_i}(Z_{i+1})$, then break;
18:         else Update $\varepsilon_i = \varepsilon_i \times 2$.
19:         endIf
20:     endWhile
21:     Update $t_i = \left(1 + \sqrt{1 + 4t_{i-1}^2}\right)/2$, $\varepsilon_{i+1} = \varepsilon_i$.
22: endFor
23: Set $Z^* = Z_{i+1}$.

By combining APG, the function $Energy(\cdot)$, and the function $Competition(\cdot)$, the problem in Eq. (19) can be solved. The Algorithm 2 provides the details.

4   Experimental Results and Analyses

4.1   Datasets and Settings

The three benchmark multi-source datasets, i.e., Wikipedia [19], Corel 5K [8], and MIR Flickr [11], are used to evaluate the proposed framework. The statistics of the datasets are given in Table 2, and brief descriptions of the chosen feature sets in the above-mentioned datasets are listed in Table 3.

These three datasets are divided into train and test subsets. We randomly select 10% of multi-source data in the train and test sets, respectively. Then the heterogeneous representations of these multi-source data are rearranged in random order and we manually generated 10% of the redundant representations from Source S_y in the data. We use the 5-fold cross-validation to tune some important parameters in all the methods. Additionally, all the experiments take the LIBSVM classifier as the benchmark for classification tasks.

Table 2. Statistics of the multi-source datasets

Dataset	Total attributes	Total classes	Total samples
Wikipedia	258	10	2866
Corel 5K	200	260	4999
MIR Flickr	5857	38	25000

Table 3. Brief descriptions of the feature sets

Dataset	Feature set	Total attributes	Total labels	Total instances
Wikipedia	Image (S_x)	128	10	2866
	Text (S_y)	130	10	2866
Corel 5K	DenseHue (S_x)	100	260	4999
	HarrisHue (S_y)	100	260	4999
MIR Flickr	Image (S_x)	3857	38	25000
	Text (S_y)	2000	38	25000

4.2   Analysis of Manifold Learning Algorithms

To verify the manifold smoothness measure learned by the proposed HMSL method, HMSL is compared in classification performance with other four state-of-the-art manifold learning algorithms such as ESRM [6], EMR [7], MKPLS [2], and DDGR [3]. The MIR FLICKR dataset is used in the experiment, and the best performance is reported. The data in training set are randomly sampled in the ratio $\{25\%, 50\%, 75\%, 100\%\}$, and the size of the test set is fixed. Unlike our framework, before comparing ESRM, EMR, MKPLS and DDGR, we first implement CCA [23] to construct feature-homogeneous space between different sources. We select $min(d_x, d_y)$ as the dimensionality k of the feature-homogeneous space. The setting of parameters in ESRM, EMR, MKPLS, and DDGR is the same as the original works [2, 3, 6, 7].

In essence, the proposed HMSL model is also a manifold learning method based on manifold regularization. However, there are significant differences between HMSL and the above-mentioned other four methods. The main difference between HMSL and ESRM is that ESRM is a mono-source learning algorithm without the ability of handling multi-source problem. Moreover, though MKPLS also use manifold regularization to exploit the correlation among heterogeneous representations, the distributional similarity among different sources is not utilized fully. Additionally, different from EMR and DDGR, HMSL takes full account of the semantic complementarity between different sources.

Table 4. Classification performance of manifold learning methods in terms of AUC.

Method	Sampling ratio			
	25%	50%	75%	100%
DDGR	0.5374	0.5963	0.6245	0.6756
MKPLS	0.5481	0.6040	0.6372	0.6824
EMR	0.5171	0.5744	0.6268	0.6654
ESRM	0.5445	0.5978	0.6554	0.6813
HMSL	**0.5991**	**0.6596**	**0.7053**	**0.7494**

From Table 4, we can clearly observe that HMSL greatly outperforms other manifold learning methods in classification performance. The results present that HMSL can capture information correlation between different sources more effectively than the comparative methods. In addition, as the number of training samples increases, the performance of HMSL will also be improved. Accordingly, a certain number of existing nonredundant samples is essential for HMSL to learn an excellent manifold smoothness measure.

4.3 Evaluation of Dimension Reduction Techniques

In order to evaluate the possibility of eliminating SFS in the proposed CMRR model, we further compare the effect of dimension reduction among different state-of-the-art methods, such as KTLQD [18], ERFSJNM [17], FSGRM [24], and NSACR [13]. The generalized identity matrices are taken as the initial values of P and Q in Algorithm 2. The regularization parameters γ and τ are tuned among the set $\{10^i | i = -2, -1, 0, 1, 2\}$. The parameter δ in Eq. (14) is set to 0.1. For KTLQD, ERFSJNM, FSGRM, and NSACR, the experimental setups follow the original ones [13, 17, 18, 24], respectively.

In machine learning, the eliminating of sample features superabundance can be divided into feature selection and dimension reduction. It is a key component in building robust machine learning models for analysis, classification, clustering, and retrieval to avoid high computational time. To achieve this goal, CMRR reduces the superabundance of sample features by using the learned multiple heterogeneous linear transformations. Therefore, after eliminating SFS, the multi-source heterogeneous redundant data is more likely to be separated linearly.

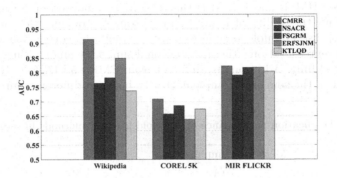

Fig. 4. Comparison of classification performance of dimension reduction algorithms.

We can observe from Fig. 4 that CMRR has better classification performance than KTLQD, ERFSJNM, FSGRM, and NSACR. This observation further justifies that CMRR can effectively eliminate SFS.

4.4 Comparison of Sample Selection Approaches

To test the performance of the proposed CMRR in different redundancy rates, we further compare the classification performances of CMRR with other sample selection methods such as MASSFDTI [25], SPSRS [5], WCTSSIM [21], and ACP [22] in the larger MIR Flickr dataset. We tune the redundancy rates on the set $\{10\%, 15\%, 20\%, 25\%\}$.

From the view of the function, the proposed CMRR model is also essentially a sample selection method such as MASSFDTI, SPSRS, WCTSSIM, and ACP. However, there are some significant differences between CMRR and other methods. CMRR is based on the correlation among sample representations from different sources. So it will be more favorable to clear DRE and remove CRO for reestablishing the one-to-one complementary relationship among heterogeneous representations.

Just to pursue such a purpose, we first use HMSL to project the multi-source data into a feature-homogeneous space and then apply MASSFDTI, SPSRS, WCTSSIM, ACP, and CMRR to reduce redundant samples. The setting of the parameters in MASSFDTI, SPSRS, WCTSSIM, and ACP is the same as the original works [5,21,22,25].

It can be seen in Fig. 5 that CMRR is superior to the other models in the classification performance. This observation further confirms that CMRR has an obvious advantage over other methods in removing FDD and SSD and rebuilding the one-to-one complementary relationship among heterogeneous representations. Nevertheless, with the increasing of redundancy rate, the performance of CMRR will degrade. Thus, CMRR also has some limitations that it needs a certain number of existing nonredundant samples to reduce redundant source.

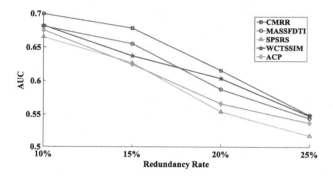

Fig. 5. Comparison of classification performance of sample selection approaches in different redundancy rates.

5 Conclusion

This paper investigates the redundant sources problem in multi-source learning. We developed a general simplifying framework to reduce redundant sources of multi-source data. Within this framework, a feature-homogeneous space is learned by the proposed HMSL model to capture the semantic complementarity, information correlation, and distributional similarity among different sources. Meanwhile, we proposed a CMRR method with GET constraints based on GEC criterion to remove the three-way redundancies and double-level heterogeneities in the learned feature-homogeneous space. Finally, we evaluated and verified the effectiveness of the proposed framework on five benchmark multi-source heterogeneous datasets.

Acknowledgment. This work was supported in part by National Natural Science Foundation of China (No. 61601458).

References

1. Argyriou, A., Evgeniou, T., Pontil, M.: Convex multi-task feature learning. Mach. Learn. **73**(3), 243–272 (2008)

2. Bakry, A., Elgammal, A.: MKPLS: manifold kernel partial least squares for lipreadingand speaker identification. In: Proceedings of the IEEE Computer Vision and Pattern Recognition, pp. 684–691 (2013)
3. Belkin, M., Niyogi, P., Sindhwani, V.: Manifold regularization: a geometric framework for learning from labeled and unlabeled examples. J. Mach. Learn. Res. **7**, 2399–2434 (2006)
4. Bellman, R.: Dynamic programming and lagrange multipliers. Proc. Natl. Acad. Sci. U.S.A. **42**(10), 767 (1956)
5. Chen, D., Zhao, S., Zhang, L., Yang, Y., Zhang, X.: Sample pair selection for attribute reduction with rough set. IEEE Trans. Knowl. Data Eng. **24**(11), 2080–2093 (2012)
6. Freedman, D.: Efficient simplicial reconstructions of manifolds from their samples. IEEE Trans. Pattern Anal. Mach. Intell. **24**(10), 1349–1357 (2002)
7. Geng, B., Tao, D., Xu, C., Yang, L., Hua, X.: Ensemble manifold regularization. IEEE Trans. Pattern Anal. Mach. Intell. **34**(6), 1227–1233 (2012)
8. Guillaumin, M., Verbeek, J., Schmid, C.: Multimodal semi-supervised learning for image classification. In: Proceedings of the IEEE Computer Vision and Pattern Recognition, pp. 902–909 (2010)
9. Guo, Y., Xiao, M.: Cross language text classification via subspace co-regularized multi-view learning. In: Proceedings of the ACM International Conference on Machine Learning, pp. 915–922 (2012)
10. He, X., Li, L., Roqueiro, D., Borgwardt, K.: Multi-view spectral clustering on conflicting views. In: Ceci, M., Hollmén, J., Todorovski, L., Vens, C., Džeroski, S. (eds.) ECML PKDD 2017, Part II. LNCS (LNAI), vol. 10535, pp. 826–842. Springer, Cham (2017). https://doi.org/10.1007/978-3-319-71246-8_50
11. Huiskes, M.J., Lew, M.S.: The MIR Flickr retrieval evaluation. In: Proceedings of the ACM International Conference on Multimedia Information Retrieval, pp. 39–43 (2008)
12. Lan, C., Huan, J.: Reducing the unlabeled sample complexity of semi-supervised multi-view learning. In: Proceedings of the ACM SIGKDD International Conference on Knowledge Discovery and Data Mining, pp. 627–634 (2015)
13. Li, Z., Tang, J.: Unsupervised feature selection via nonnegative spectral analysis and redundancy control. IEEE Trans. Image Process. **24**(12), 5343–5355 (2015)
14. Luo, P., Peng, J., Guan, Z., Fan, J.: Multi-view semantic learning for data representation. In: Appice, A., Rodrigues, P.P., Santos Costa, V., Soares, C., Gama, J., Jorge, A. (eds.) ECML PKDD 2015, Part I. LNCS (LNAI), vol. 9284, pp. 367–382. Springer, Cham (2015). https://doi.org/10.1007/978-3-319-23528-8_23
15. Meyer, C.D.: Matrix Analysis and Applied Linear Algebra. SIAM, Philadelphia (2000)
16. Nesterov, Y.: Introductory Lectures on Convex Optimization, vol. 87. Springer, New York (2004). https://doi.org/10.1007/978-1-4419-8853-9
17. Nie, F., Huang, H., Cai, X., Ding, C.H.: Efficient and robust feature selection via joint $\ell_{2,1}$-norms minimization. In: Proceedings of the Advances in Neural Information Processing Systems, pp. 1813–1821 (2010)
18. Quanz, B., Huan, J., Mishra, M.: Knowledge transfer with low-quality data: a feature extraction issue. IEEE Trans. Knowl. Data Eng. **24**(10), 1789–1802 (2012)
19. Rasiwasia, N., et al.: A new approach to cross-modal multimedia retrieval. In: Proceedings of the ACM International Conference on Multimedia, pp. 251–260 (2010)
20. Rubinstein, M., Shamir, A., Avidan, S.: Improved seam carving for video retargeting. ACM Trans. Graph. **27**(3), 16 (2008)

21. Shahrian, E., Rajan, D.: Weighted color and texture sample selection for image matting. In: Proceedings of the IEEE Computer Vision and Pattern Recognition, pp. 718–725 (2012)
22. Su, H., Yin, Z., Kanade, T., Huh, S.: Active sample selection and correction propagation on a gradually-augmented graph. In: Proceedings of the IEEE Computer Vision and Pattern Recognition, pp. 1975–1983 (2015)
23. Sun, L., Ji, S., Ye, J.: Canonical correlation analysis for multilabel classification: a least-squares formulation, extensions, and analysis. IEEE Trans. Pattern Anal. Mach. Intell. **33**(1), 194–200 (2011)
24. Wang, D., Nie, F., Huang, H.: Feature selection via global redundancy minimization. IEEE Trans. Knowl. Data Eng. **27**(10), 2743–2755 (2015)
25. Wang, X., Dong, L., Yan, J.: Maximum ambiguity-based sample selection in fuzzy decision tree induction. IEEE Trans. Knowl. Data Eng. **24**(8), 1491–1505 (2012)
26. Weinberger, K.Q., Saul, L.K.: Distance metric learning for large margin nearest neighbor classification. J. Mach. Learn. Res. **10**, 207–244 (2009)
27. Wen, Z., Yin, W.: A feasible method for optimization with orthogonality constraints. Math. Program. **142**(1), 397–434 (2012). https://doi.org/10.1007/s10107-012-0584-1
28. Zhang, L., et al.: Collaborative multi-view denoising. In: Proceedings of the ACM SIGKDD International Conference on Knowledge Discovery and Data Mining, pp. 2045–2054 (2016)
29. Zhuang, Y., Yang, Y., Wu, F., Pan, Y.: Manifold learning based cross-media retrieval: a solution to media object complementary nature. J. VLSI Signal Process. **46**(2–3), 153–164 (2007)

Interpretable Discriminative Dimensionality Reduction and Feature Selection on the Manifold

Babak Hosseini$^{(\boxtimes)}$ (iD) and Barbara Hammer

CITEC Centre of Excellence, Bielefeld University, Bielefeld, Germany
{bhosseini,bhammer}@techfak.uni-bielefeld.de

Abstract. Dimensionality reduction (DR) on the manifold includes effective methods which project the data from an implicit relational space onto a vectorial space. Regardless of the achievements in this area, these algorithms suffer from the lack of interpretation of the projection dimensions. Therefore, it is often difficult to explain the physical meaning behind the embedding dimensions. In this research, we propose the interpretable kernel DR algorithm (I-KDR) as a new algorithm which maps the data from the feature space to a lower dimensional space where the classes are more condensed with less overlapping. Besides, the algorithm creates the dimensions upon local contributions of the data samples, which makes it easier to interpret them by class labels. Additionally, we efficiently fuse the DR with feature selection task to select the most relevant features of the original space to the discriminative objective. Based on the empirical evidence, I-KDR provides better interpretations for embedding dimensions as well as higher discriminative performance in the embedded space compared to the state-of-the-art and popular DR algorithms.

Keywords: Dimensionality reduction · Interpretability · Supervised

1 Introduction

Dimensionality reduction (DR) is an essential preprocessing phase in the application of many algorithms in machine learning and data analytics. The general goal in any DR approach is to obtain an embedding to transfer the data from the original high-dimensional (HD) space to a low-dimension (LD) space, such that this projection preserves the vital information about the data distribution [23]. It is common to split the dimensionality reduction methods into two groups of unsupervised and supervised algorithms. The first group includes methods such as Principal Component Analysis (PCA) [13] which finds a new embedding space in which the dimensions are sorted based on the maximum data variation they can achieve, or locally linear embedding (LLE) [23] that focuses on preserving the relational structure of data points in the local neighborhoods of the space throughout an embedding.

© Springer Nature Switzerland AG 2020
U. Brefeld et al. (Eds.): ECML PKDD 2019, LNAI 11906, pp. 310–326, 2020.
https://doi.org/10.1007/978-3-030-46150-8_19

The second group of algorithms, known as supervised (discriminative) DR methods, assume that data classes can obtain the same or even better separations in an intrinsic LD space. As a popular supervised algorithm, Linear Discriminant Analysis (LDA) [19] tries to find a mapping which increases the distance between the class centroids while preserving the intra-class variations. Its subsequent algorithms such as LLDA [14] and CPM [29] tried to relax the constraints on within-class variations to project the sub-clusters to the LD space more efficiently.

It is possible to consider an implicit mapping of data to a high-dimensional reproducing kernel Hilbert space (RKHS) primarily to obtain a relational representation of the non-vectorial or structured data distributions. Consequently, a branch of DR algorithms (kernel-DR) is focused on kernel-based data representations to transfer the data from the original RKHS to a vectorial space. This projection can become significant especially when it makes the application of many vectorial algorithms possible on LD embedding of such data. The most famous kernel-DR algorithms are Kernelized PCA (K-PCA) and K-FDA [19] which are the kernelized versions of PCA and LDA algorithms respectively. In these methods and many other kernel-DR algorithms, it is common to construct the embedding dimensions upon different weighted combinations of data points in the original RKHS. Other notable examples of kernel-based methods include algorithms such as KDR [8], KEDR [1], and LDR [24].

Additionally, by assuming a set of non-linear mappings to different sub-spaces in the feature space, it is possible to obtain one specific kernel representation for each dimension of the data [6,10]. Consequently, a specific group of methods tried to apply DR frameworks also to feature selection tasks on manifolds [12,16].

One of the important practical concerns regarding dimensionality reduction is the interpretation of new dimensions. It is common to observe in many DR methods that the embedding dimensions are constructed upon arbitrary combinations of many uncorrelated physical dimensions [4,25]. Such occasions can make the interpretation of these dimensions difficult or impossible. Such condition becomes even more severe for kernel-DR methods where the embedding dimensions are an implicit combination of data points in RKHS. For instance methods similar to K-PCA, the embedding vectors almost use weighted combination of all data points from all the classes. Hence, it would be difficult to relate any of the dimensions to any class of data (Fig. 1(a)). Furthermore, a high correlation between embedding directions can be found when considering the class-contributions in them (Fig. 1(b)).

As an improvement, sparse K-PCA [27] applies an l_1-norm sparsity objective to form embedding vectors from sparse combinations of training samples. However, these samples still belong to different classes which makes the resulting embeddings weak according to the class-based interpretation (Fig. 1).

1.1 Motivation

As discussed in the previous paragraphs, one crucial challenge for kernel-DR algorithms is the interpretation of their projection dimensions. Based on the

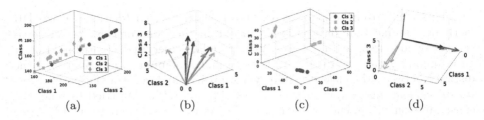

Fig. 1. When embedding vectors use all data points: (a) its projection on class-labels is coupled and (b) the embedding vectors are highly correlated in the label space. A class-based interpretable embedding: (c) provides a more distinct projection on class labels and (d) its dimensions can be distinguished and explained based on class labels.

relation of these dimensions to the selection of data points, it is logical to focus on having each selection linked to mostly one class of data. This strategy can lead to the class-based interpretation as in Fig. 1(c), (d).

Besides, current kernel-DR methods cannot efficiently embed the multi-cluster data classes to an LD space such that the clusters could still be separated from each other. In particular, they suffer from considering the local distributions inside the classes.

Based on the current state-of-the-art, the research in kernel-DR is always distinct from feature selection on the manifold. Although in some research, these concerns are employed in a single framework [12,16], the DR aspect of the problem was not well investigated. Nevertheless, in particular for discriminative tasks, these two aspects should act as each other's complements in a single framework.

1.2   Contributions

In this work, we propose a novel discriminative dimensionality reduction method which projects the data from an implicit RKHS space to a low-dimension vectorial space. Besides, it can join this embedding with feature selection in case of having multiple representations for the data on the manifolds. We can summarize our contributions as follows:

- We introduce the class-based interpretation concern for the kernel-DR frameworks through which the embedding dimensions can be explained according to the classes they most represent.
- We show that focusing on the within-class local similarities and between-class dissimilarities can provide a more discriminative embedding.
- We fuse feature selection with our kernel-DR framework which leads to a more discriminative feature selection compared to the state-of-the-art.

In the rest of this paper, we provide preliminaries in Sect. 2 and discuss our discriminative kernel-DR framework in Sect. 3. The optimization steps and the experimental results are discussed in Sect. 3.5 and Sect. 4 respectively. We summarize our findings in the conclusion section.

2 Preliminaries

2.1 Notations

We denote the matrix of training data by $\mathbf{X} = [\boldsymbol{x}_1, ..., \boldsymbol{x}_N] \in \mathbb{R}^{d \times N}$, and the corresponding class label matrix is given as $\mathbf{H} = [\boldsymbol{h}_1, ..., \boldsymbol{h}_N] \in \{0, 1\}^{c \times N}$. Each $\boldsymbol{h}_i$ is a zero vector except in its q-th entry where $h_{qi} = 1$ if $\boldsymbol{x}_i$ belongs to class q in a c-class setting. In general, for a given matrix $\mathbf{A}$, $\boldsymbol{a}_i$ denotes its i-th column, $\mathbf{A}(j, :)$ denotes its j-th row, and a_{ji} refers to the j-th entry in $\boldsymbol{a}_i$.

2.2 Kernel-Based Dimensionality Reduction

Assume there exists an implicit non-linear mapping $\Phi(\mathbf{X})$ corresponding to the mapping of $\mathbf{X}$ into an RKHS, which corresponds to a kernel matrix $\mathcal{K}(\mathbf{X}, \mathbf{X}) = \Phi^\top(\mathbf{X})\Phi(\mathbf{X})$. Generally, a kernel-DR algorithm tries to obtain an embedding $\boldsymbol{\gamma} = \mathbf{U}^\top \Phi(\boldsymbol{x})$ as a mapping from the features space to an LD space. Since the dimensions of $\Phi(\boldsymbol{x})$ are not directly accessible in the feature space, it is common to assume embedding dimensions are constructed as

$$\mathbf{U} = \Phi(\mathbf{X})\mathbf{A}, \tag{1}$$

where $\mathbf{A} \in \mathbb{R}^{N \times k}$. Hence, the matrix $\mathbf{A}$ projects the data from the HD feature space to a k-dimensional space, where each embedding vector $\boldsymbol{a}_i$ is a combination of the training samples in RKHS.

Regarding the above, the K-PCA method preserves the variance of the reconstruction and to obtain embedding dimensions which are orthogonal and sorted based on their maximum variations. To that aim, K-PCA uses the following optimization:

$$\begin{aligned} &\min_{\mathbf{A}} \|\Phi(\mathbf{X}) - \Phi(\mathbf{X})\mathbf{A}\mathbf{A}^\top \Phi(\mathbf{X})^\top \Phi(\mathbf{X})\|_F^2 \\ &\text{s.t. } \mathbf{A}^\top \Phi(\mathbf{X})^\top \Phi(\mathbf{X})\mathbf{A} = \mathbf{I}, \end{aligned} \tag{2}$$

Although K-PCA is a powerful preprocessing algorithm to eliminate the low-variate dimensions, it does not have any direct focus on the discrimination of the embedded data classes. Also, each embedding vectors ν_i consists of both positive and negative contributions from all training samples which makes their interpretation difficult.

On the other hand, the K-FDA algorithm tries to obtain an embedding $\mathbf{W}$ which increases the between-class covariance matrix $\mathbf{S}_\mathbf{B}^\phi$ while preserving the total within-class covariance matrix $\mathbf{S}_\mathbf{W}^\phi$ in RKHS [19]. It uses the following optimization framework:

$$\max_{\mathbf{W}} \text{Tr}(\mathbf{W}^\top \mathbf{S}_\mathbf{B} \mathbf{W}) \qquad \text{s.t.} \mathbf{W}^\top \mathbf{S}_\mathbf{W} \mathbf{W} = \mathbf{I}, \tag{3}$$

where $\mathbf{W}$ has a structure analogous to Eq. (1). Regardless of its supervised performance, the constraint on intra-class variances can become a critical weakness when there are sub-clusters in each data class. In such cases, the constraint in Eq. (3) cause considerable overlapping between different classes.

Our proposed framework improves the state-of-the-art in both discriminative kernel-DR and class-based interpretation of embedding dimensions.

3   Interpretable Discriminative Dimensionality Reduction

We want to obtain the embedding

$$\gamma = \mathbf{A}^\top \Phi(\mathbf{X})^\top \Phi(\boldsymbol{x}) \qquad \mathbf{\Gamma} \in \mathbb{R}^k \tag{4}$$

as a projection from the original implicit RKHS to a k-dimensional explicit space which also preserves the essential characteristics of $\mathbf{X}$ in the original space.

Definition 1. *The embedding vector $\Phi(\mathbf{X})\boldsymbol{a}_i$ is class-based interpretable if we have $\frac{\mathbf{H}(q|h_{qi}=1,:)\boldsymbol{a}_i}{\|\mathbf{H}\boldsymbol{a}_i\|_1} \approx 1$, and it acts as the projection of data points on class q.*

In other words, $\Phi(\mathbf{X})\boldsymbol{a}_i$ can be interpreted as a projection to class q if it is constructed only from that class of data. Although Definition 1 considers an ideal situation regarding the interpretability of an embedding dimension, we consider the value of

$$\mathbf{H}(q|h_{qi} = 1,:)\boldsymbol{a}_i/\|\mathbf{H}\boldsymbol{a}_i\|_1 \tag{5}$$

as a measure of class-based interpretation as well. To be more specific regarding our framework, we aim for the following objectives:

O1: Increasing the class-based interpretation of embedding dimensions.
O2: The embedding should make the classes more separated in the LD space.
O3: The classes should be locally more condensed in the embedded space.
O4: The DR framework should also support the feature selection objective if a multiple kernel representation is provided.

Therefore, we formulate the following optimization scheme w.r.t. all the above objectives:

$$\min_{\mathbf{A},\beta} \mathcal{J}_{Sim} + \lambda \mathcal{J}_{Dis} + \mu \mathcal{J}_{Ip}$$
$$\text{s.t.} \ \sum_{m=1}^{d}\beta_m = 1, \ \sum_{j=1}^{N} a_{ji} = 1, \forall i \tag{6}$$
$$a_{ij}, \beta_i \in \mathbb{R}^+, \ \forall ij.$$

In Eq. (6), the cost functions $\mathcal{J}_{Dis}$, $\mathcal{J}_{Ip}$, and $\mathcal{J}_{Sim}$ and the constraints on the optimization variables are designed to fulfill our research objectives **O1–O4**. In the following sub-sections, we explain each specific term in our framework in detail and provide the rationales behind their definitions.

3.1   Interpretability of the Dimensions

In Eq. (4), each dimension $\boldsymbol{a}_i$ of the embedding is composed of a weighted selection of data points in RKHS. In K-PCA, typically all $a_{ji}, \forall j = 1,\ldots,N$ have non-zero values. More specifically, for each $\boldsymbol{a}_i$, a wide range of training data from different classes are selected with large weights which weaken the interpretation of $\boldsymbol{a}_i$ regarding the class to which it could be related.

To make each $\boldsymbol{a}_i$ more interpretable in our framework, we propose the cost function $\mathcal{J}_{Ip}$ that its minimization enforces $\boldsymbol{a}_i$ to be constructed using similar samples in the RKHS:

$$\mathcal{J}_{Ip}(\mathbf{X}, \mathbf{A}) = \frac{1}{2}\sum_{i=1}^{k}\sum_{s,t=1}^{N} a_{si}a_{ti}\|\Phi(\boldsymbol{x}_s) - \Phi(\boldsymbol{x}_t)\|_2^2, \tag{7}$$

where we restrict $a_{ij} \geq 0, \forall ij$. We call $\mathcal{J}_{Ip}$ as the interpretability term (Ip-term) which is an unsupervised function and independent from the value of $\mathbf{H}$. The Ip-term enforces each embedding dimension $\boldsymbol{a}_i$ to use samples in $\Phi(\mathbf{X})$ that are located in a local neighborhood of each other in RKHS (Fig. 2) by introducing a penalty term $a_{si}a_{ti}\|\Phi(\boldsymbol{x}_s)-\Phi(\boldsymbol{x}_t)\|_2^2$ on its entries. Resulting from this term along with the non-negativity constraint on $\mathbf{A}$, non-zero entries of $\boldsymbol{a}_i$ correspond to the neighboring points such as (s,t) where their pairwise distance $\|\Phi(\boldsymbol{x}_s) - \Phi(\boldsymbol{x}_t)\|_2^2$ is small. Furthermore, although Ip-term does not employ the label information, by assuming a smooth labeling for the data, this regularization term constructs each $\boldsymbol{a}_i$ by contributions from more likely one particular class. Therefore, as a solution to our first research objective (**O1**), using Ip-term improves the class-based interpretation of $\boldsymbol{a}_i$ to relate it a sub-group of data points mostly belonging to one specific class of data (Eq. (5)).

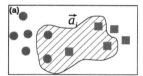 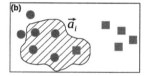

Fig. 2. Effect of using $\mathcal{J}_{Ip}$ on the formation of an embedding vector $\boldsymbol{a}_i$ as the weighted combination of selected data points (inside the hatched area) in the RKHS. (a): Without using $\mathcal{J}_{Ip}$, the learned $\boldsymbol{a}_i$ cannot be assigned to either of $\{circle, square\}$ classes. (b): After employing $\mathcal{J}_{Ip}$, the formed $\boldsymbol{a}_i$ can almost be interpreted by the *circle* class.

3.2   Inter-class Dissimilarity

Regarding our second objective (**O2**), we focus on increasing the inter-class dissimilarities in the LD space which makes the embedded classes more distinct. To that aim, we define the loss term $\mathcal{J}_{Dis}$ as

$$\begin{aligned}\mathcal{J}_{Dis}&(\mathbf{X}, \mathbf{H}, \mathbf{A})\\&= \text{Tr}(\overline{\mathbf{H}}^\top \mathbf{H}\Phi(\mathbf{X})^\top\Phi(\mathbf{X})\mathbf{A}\mathbf{A}^\top\Phi(\mathbf{X})^\top\Phi(\mathbf{X})),\end{aligned} \tag{8}$$

where $\overline{\mathbf{H}}$ is the logical complement of $\mathbf{H}$. Throughout simple algebraic operations, we can show that Eq. (8) is the reformulation of

$$\sum_{i}\sum_{j|h_j\neq h_i}\langle\mathbf{A}^\top\Phi(\mathbf{X})^\top\Phi(\boldsymbol{x}_i), \mathbf{A}^\top\Phi(\mathbf{X})^\top\Phi(\boldsymbol{x}_j)\rangle. \tag{9}$$

Hence, minimizing $\mathcal{J}_{Dis}$ motivates the global separation of the classes in the embedded space by reducing the similarity between their projected vectors $\mathbf{A}^\top \Phi(\mathbf{X})^\top \Phi(\boldsymbol{x})$.

3.3   Intra-class Similarities

Even though the introduced cost term $\mathcal{J}_{Dis}$ helps the embedded classes to obtain more distance from each other, it still does not consider the intra-class similarities which concerns our third objective (**O3**). It is important to note that we want to make the projected vectors $\boldsymbol{\gamma}_i$ of each class more similar to each other, while still preserving the local structure of the class respecting the possible sub-classes. This characteristic works against the drawback of K-FDA when facing distinct sub-classes as pointed out by [17].

To address the above concern, we proposed the following cost function

$$\mathcal{J}_{Sim} = \sum_{i=1}^{N} (\mathbf{H}(q|h_{qi} = 1, :)\mathbf{A}\mathbf{A}^\top \Phi(\mathbf{X})^\top \Phi(\boldsymbol{x}_i) - 1)^2, \tag{10}$$

in which q is the class to which $\boldsymbol{x}_i$ belongs. Furthermore, based on Eq. (6), we apply an affine constraint on columns of $\mathbf{A}$ as $\|\boldsymbol{a}_s\|_1 = 1, \forall s = 1, \ldots, N$. By combining Eq. (10) with $\boldsymbol{\gamma}_i$ from Eq. (4) we have

$$\mathcal{J}_{Sim} = \sum_{i=1}^{N} (\mathbf{H}(q|h_{qi} = 1, :)\mathbf{A}\boldsymbol{\gamma}_i - 1)^2, \tag{11}$$

which applies constraints on columns of $\mathbf{A}$ corresponding to large entries of $\boldsymbol{\gamma}_i$. Specifically, those constraints aim the entries which are related to the data points which have the same label as $\boldsymbol{x}_i$. For instance, if γ_{si} has a relatively large value, minimizing $\mathcal{J}_{Sim}$ optimizes the entries a_{js} where $\boldsymbol{h}_j = \boldsymbol{h}_i$. Besides, the applied l_1-norm sparsity constraint $\|\boldsymbol{a}_s\|_1 = 1$ enforces some entries in $\boldsymbol{a}_s$ to shrink near to zero. Therefore, it is simple to conclude that these entries would mostly include a_{js} where $\boldsymbol{h}_j \neq \boldsymbol{h}_i$.

On the other hand, $\gamma_{si} = \sum_{t=1}^{N} a_{ts}\Phi(\boldsymbol{x}_t)^\top \Phi(\boldsymbol{x}_i)$. Hence, Having the l_1-norm of $\boldsymbol{a}_s$ restricted along with its non-negativity constraint naturally motivates the optimization process to assign large values to entries a_{ts} corresponding to data points $\boldsymbol{x}_t$ with large $\Phi(\boldsymbol{x}_t)^\top \Phi(\boldsymbol{x}_i)$. In other words, $\boldsymbol{a}_s$ selects the nearby data points of $\boldsymbol{x}_i$ as its most similar neighbors. Combining this finding with our first conclusion about the effect of Eq. (10), along with the localization role of $\mathcal{J}_{Ip}$, minimizing $\mathcal{J}_{Sim}$ helps each data point $\boldsymbol{x}_i$ to be encoded in particular by its nearby embedding vectors $\boldsymbol{a}_s$, which are also constructed mostly by the same-class of samples in the vicinity of $\boldsymbol{x}_i$ (**O1**). Consequently, the data points from each local sub-class are embedded by similar sets of columns in $\mathbf{A}$ and are mapped into a local neighborhood in the LD space. In other words, This embedding increases the intra-class similarities for the projected columns in $\boldsymbol{\Gamma} = [\boldsymbol{\gamma}_1, \ldots, \boldsymbol{\gamma}_N]$.

3.4 Feature Selection on the Manifold

It is a feasible assumption for any structured and non-structure $\mathbf{X}$ to have d different kernel representations available [2], such that each $\mathcal{K}_m(\mathbf{X}, \mathbf{X}), \forall m = 1, \ldots, d$, maps the m-th dimension of the original data into an RKHS or is derived from the m-th descriptor (e.g., for images). Given the above, we can assume

$$\Phi(\boldsymbol{x}) = [\phi_1^\top(\boldsymbol{x}), \ldots, \phi_d^\top(\boldsymbol{x})]^\top, \tag{12}$$

where each $\phi_m : \mathbb{R} \to \mathbb{R}^{f_m}, \forall m = 1, \ldots, d$ represents an implicit mapping from the original space to a subspace of the RKHS, such that $\mathcal{K}_m(\boldsymbol{x}_t, \boldsymbol{x}_s) = \phi_m^\top(\boldsymbol{x}_t)\phi_m(\boldsymbol{x}_s)$. Therefore, we can consider a diagonal matrix $\mathbf{B} \in \mathbb{R}^{d \times d}$ which provides scaling of the RKHS by

$$\hat{\Phi}(\boldsymbol{x}) = \mathbf{B}\Phi(\mathbf{X}) = [\sqrt{\beta_1}\phi_1^\top(\boldsymbol{x}), \cdots, \sqrt{\beta_d}\phi_d^\top(\boldsymbol{x})]^\top, \tag{13}$$

where $\boldsymbol{\beta}$ is the vector of combination weights derived from diagonal entries of $\mathbf{B}$. We can compute the weighted kernel matrix $\hat{\mathcal{K}}$ corresponding to $\hat{\Phi}(\mathbf{X})$ as

$$\hat{\mathcal{K}}(\boldsymbol{x}_t, \boldsymbol{x}_s) = \sum_{m=1}^d \beta_m \mathcal{K}_m(\boldsymbol{x}_t, \boldsymbol{x}_s). \tag{14}$$

Additionally, we apply a non-negativity constraint on entries of $\boldsymbol{\beta}$ as $\beta_i \geq 0$ to make the resulted kernel weights interpreted as the relative importance of each kernel in the weighted representation $\hat{\Phi}(\mathbf{X})$ [10]. Consequently, we can obtain a feature selection profile by sorting entries of $\boldsymbol{\beta}$ based on their magnitude. For the ease of reading, in the rest of the paper, we denote $\hat{\mathcal{K}}(\mathbf{X}, \mathbf{X})$ and $\mathcal{K}_i(\mathbf{X}, \mathbf{X})$ by $\hat{\mathcal{K}}$ and $\mathcal{K}_i$ respectively.

Substituting $\Phi(\mathbf{X})$ by $\hat{\Phi}(\mathbf{X})$ in the definitions of $\mathcal{J}_{Dis}$, $\mathcal{J}_{Ip}$, and $\mathcal{J}_{Sim}$ reformulates them also as a function of $\mathbf{B}$. Therefore, minimizing those terms also optimizes the value of $\mathbf{B}$ regarding their specific purposes. Furthermore, we apply an l_1-norm restriction on the value of $\mathbf{B}$ as the affine constraint $\sum_{m=1}^d \beta_m = 1$. This constraint prevents $\boldsymbol{\beta}$ from becoming a vector of zeros as the trivial solution and additionally results in a sparse feature selection to reduce the redundancies between different kernel representations [22]. We can claim that by using $\hat{\Phi}(\mathbf{X})$ in each of the defined terms, the resulted feature selection also complies with those specific characteristics. In the next section, we discuss the optimization scheme of Eq. (6).

3.5 Optimization Scheme

The cost function $\mathcal{J}_{Sim}$ is non-convex which makes the objective function of Eq. (6) non-convex as well. Hence, we define a variable matrix $\mathbf{S}$ and relax Eq. (6) to the following optimization problem

$$\begin{aligned}
\min_{\mathbf{A}, \beta, \mathbf{S}, \boldsymbol{\Gamma}} \quad & \sum_{i=1}^N (\mathbf{H}(q|h_{qi} = 1, :)\boldsymbol{s}_i - 1)^2 \\
& + \lambda \mathrm{Tr}(\mathbf{A}^\top \hat{\mathcal{K}} \overline{\mathbf{H}}^\top \mathbf{H} \hat{\mathcal{K}} \mathbf{A}) + \mu \mathrm{Tr}(\mathbf{A}^\top \tilde{\mathcal{K}} \mathbf{A}) \\
& + \tau \|\mathbf{S} - \mathbf{A}\boldsymbol{\Gamma}\|_F^2 + \zeta \|\boldsymbol{\Gamma} - \mathbf{A}^\top \mathcal{K}\|_F^2 \\
\text{s.t.} \quad & \sum_{m=1}^d \beta_m = 1, \quad \sum_{j=1}^N a_{ji} = 1, \forall i \\
& a_{ij}, \beta_i \in \mathbb{R}^+, \quad \forall ij,
\end{aligned} \tag{15}$$

in which $\tilde{\mathcal{K}} = diag(\hat{\mathcal{K}}\mathbf{1}) - \hat{\mathcal{K}}$, and the operator $diag(.)$ creates a diagonal matrix from its vector argument. The constants λ, μ are the control parameters for the role of introduced loss terms in the optimization scheme, and the constants τ, ζ should be large enough to make sure the slack variables $\mathbf{S}, \mathbf{\Gamma}$ have appropriate values. The second and third parts of the objective in Eq. (15) are reformulations of $\mathcal{J}_{Dis}$ and $\mathcal{J}_{Ip}$, which can be obtained by using the *kernel trick* and the Laplacian matrix [26]. We initialize the embedding matrix $\mathbf{A}$ using random entries and adjust its columns to have unit l_1-norm. Then, we optimize $\mathbf{\Gamma}, \mathbf{S}, \mathbf{A}$, and β alternatively based on the following steps.

(1) Fix $\mathbf{S}, \mathbf{A}$, and β and update $\mathbf{\Gamma}$ as:

$$\mathbf{\Gamma}^* = \mathbf{A}^\top \hat{\mathcal{K}}. \tag{16}$$

(2) Fix $\mathbf{\Gamma}, \mathbf{A}$, and β and update $\mathbf{S}$:

$$\boldsymbol{s_i}^* = \arg\min_{\boldsymbol{s_i}} \boldsymbol{s_i}^\top (\boldsymbol{u_i}^\top \boldsymbol{u_i} + \mathbf{I})\boldsymbol{s_i} - 2(\boldsymbol{u_i} + \boldsymbol{\gamma_i}^\top \mathbf{A}^\top)\boldsymbol{s_i}, \tag{17}$$

where $\boldsymbol{u_i} = \mathbf{H}(q|h_{qi} = 1, :)$. This unconstrained quadratic programming has the closed-form solution

$$\boldsymbol{s_i}^* = (\boldsymbol{u_i}^\top \boldsymbol{u_i} + \mathbf{I})^{-1}(\boldsymbol{u_i} + \boldsymbol{\gamma_i}^\top \mathbf{A}^\top)^\top. \tag{18}$$

(3) Fix $\mathbf{\Gamma}, \mathbf{S}$, and β and update $\mathbf{A}$ as:

$$\begin{aligned} \mathbf{A}^* = \arg\min_{\mathbf{A}} \ &\lambda \mathrm{Tr}(\mathbf{A}^\top \hat{\mathcal{K}}\overline{\mathbf{H}}^\top \mathbf{H}\hat{\mathcal{K}}\mathbf{A}) + \mu \mathrm{Tr}(\mathbf{A}^\top \tilde{\mathcal{K}}\mathbf{A}) \\ &+ \tau\|\mathbf{S} - \mathbf{A}\mathbf{\Gamma}\|_F^2 + \zeta\|\mathbf{\Gamma} - \mathbf{A}^\top \mathcal{K}\|_F^2 \\ \text{s.t.} \quad &\mathbf{A}^\top \mathbf{1} = \mathbf{1}, \ a_{ij} \in \mathbb{R}^+, \forall ij. \end{aligned} \tag{19}$$

Calling the objective of Eq. (19) $\mathcal{J}_\mathbf{A}$, it is possible to show that $\mathcal{J}_\mathbf{A}$ consists of convex parts and its gradient w.r.t. $\mathbf{A}$ can be computed as:

$$\nabla_\mathbf{A} \mathcal{J}_\mathbf{A} = \Omega \mathbf{A} + \Psi, \tag{20}$$

where (Ω, Ψ) can be obtained by simple algebraic operations. Therefore, we use the direction method of multipliers (ADMM) [3] by defining the Lagrangian formulation for Eq. (19):

$$\begin{aligned} \mathcal{L}_\rho(&\mathbf{A}, \mathbf{A}_+, \Delta, \delta) \\ &= \mathcal{J}_A + \tfrac{\rho}{2}\|\mathbf{A} - \mathbf{A}_+\|_2^2 + \tfrac{\rho}{2}\|\mathbf{A}^\top \mathbf{1} - \mathbf{1}\|_2^2 \\ &+ tr(\Delta^\top(\mathbf{A} - \mathbf{A}_+)) + \delta^\top(\mathbf{A}^\top \mathbf{1} - \mathbf{1}), \end{aligned} \tag{21}$$

and following these steps:

$$\begin{cases} \mathbf{A}^{(t+1)} = \arg\min_{\mathbf{A}} \mathcal{L}_\rho(\mathbf{A}, \mathbf{A}_+, \Delta, \delta), \\ \mathbf{A}_+^{(t+1)} = \max(\mathbf{A}^{(t+1)} + \tfrac{1}{\rho}\Delta^{(t)}, 0), \\ \Delta^{(t+1)} = \Delta^{(t)} + \rho(\mathbf{A}^{(t+1)}\mathbf{1} - \mathbf{1}), \\ \delta^{(t+1)} = \delta^{(t)} + \rho(\mathbf{A}^{(t+1)} - \mathbf{A}_+^{(t+1)}), \end{cases} \tag{22}$$

In Eq. (22), $\mathbf{A}_+$ is an axillary matrix related to the non-negativity constraint, $\Delta \in \mathbb{R}^{N \times N}$ and $\boldsymbol{\delta} \in \mathbb{R}^N$ are the Lagrangian multipliers, and $\rho \in \mathbb{R}^+$ is the penalty parameter. We update the matrix $\mathbf{A}^{(t+1)}$ based on its closed-form solution derived from having $\nabla_{\mathbf{A}} \mathcal{L}_\rho = 0$.

(4) Fix $\boldsymbol{\Gamma}, \mathbf{S}$ and $\mathbf{A}$ and update $\boldsymbol{\beta}$: By combining Eq. (14) and Eq. (15) and removing the constant terms, $\boldsymbol{\beta}$ can be updated by the following quadratic programming (QP)

$$\boldsymbol{\beta}^* = \arg\min_{\boldsymbol{\beta}} \tfrac{1}{2} \boldsymbol{\beta}^\top \mathbf{Q} \boldsymbol{\beta} + \boldsymbol{v}^\top \boldsymbol{\beta},$$
$$\text{s.t.} \qquad \boldsymbol{\beta}^\top \mathbf{1} = 1, \ \beta_i \in \mathbb{R}^+, \forall i. \tag{23}$$

In this formulation, $\forall ij = 1, \ldots, d$:

$$\mathbf{Q}_{ij} = \lambda \mathrm{Tr}(\mathbf{A}^\top \hat{\mathcal{K}}_i \overline{\mathbf{H}}^\top \mathbf{H} \hat{\mathcal{K}}_j \mathbf{A}) + \zeta \mathrm{Tr}(\hat{\mathcal{K}}_i \mathbf{A}^\top \mathbf{A} \hat{\mathcal{K}}_j), \tag{24}$$

and

$$v_i = \mu \mathrm{Tr}(\mathbf{A}^\top \tilde{\mathcal{K}}_i \mathbf{A}) - 2\mathrm{Tr}(\boldsymbol{\Gamma}^\top \mathbf{A}^\top \hat{\mathcal{K}}_i). \tag{25}$$

The optimization problem of Eq. (23) is an instance of constraint quadratic programming and can be efficiently solved by QP solvers such as CGAL [9] or MOSEK [20].

As a result, in each iteration of the main optimization loop, we compute the closed-form solution of $\boldsymbol{\Gamma}, \mathbf{S}$ and update $\mathbf{A}, \boldsymbol{\beta}$ rapidly using the ADMM and QP solvers respectively. The precise implementation of our kernel-DR framework is available on the online repository[1].

3.6   Time Complexity of the Algorithm

In the training phase, we update $\mathbf{A}, \mathbf{S}, \boldsymbol{\Gamma}$, and $\boldsymbol{\beta}$ alternatively. For each iteration of the algorithm, the variables $\{\mathbf{A}, \mathbf{S}, \boldsymbol{\Gamma}, \boldsymbol{\beta}\}$ are updated with the time complexities of $\mathcal{O}(\mathbf{M}(k^3 + k^2 N + kN^2))$, $\mathcal{O}(N(N^3 + N))$, $\mathcal{O}(kN)$, and $\mathcal{O}(d^2(kc + kN + k^2) + d(k^2 + kN) + d^2 L)$ respectively, where $\mathbf{M}$ is the number of iterations which takes for the ADMM algorithm to update $\mathbf{A}$, and $\mathcal{O}(d^2 L)$ is the time complexity of the QP for updating $\boldsymbol{\beta}$. In practice, values of k, c, and d are much smaller than N. Hence, the computationally expensive part of the algorithm is due to computing the inverse of $(\boldsymbol{u}_i^\top \boldsymbol{u}_i + \mathbf{I})^{-1}$ to update each column of $\mathbf{S}$. However, this particular computation is independent of update rules in the iterations, and we conduct it only once in the initialization phase of the algorithm, which considerably accelerates the convergence speed.

4   Experiments

In this section, we implement our proposed I-KDR algorithm on real-world datasets to analyze its DR and feature selection performance. For all the datasets

---

[1] https://github.com/bab-git/.

Table 1. Selected datasets. {**Dim**: #dimensions, **Cls**: #classes, **Num**: #data samples}.

Dataset	Num	Dim	Cls	Dataset	Num	Dim	Cls
Yale	165	1024	15	Gli85	85	22283	2
Sonar	208	60	2	CNS	60	7129	2
Colon	62	2000	2	Dbwork	64	4702	2
20NG	4852	28299	4	XM2VTS50	1180	1024	20

we compute the kernels based on the Gaussian kernel function

$$\mathcal{K}(\boldsymbol{x}_i, \boldsymbol{x}_j) = exp(-\|\boldsymbol{x}_i - \boldsymbol{x}_j\|_2^2/\delta), \tag{26}$$

in which δ denotes the average of $\|\boldsymbol{x}_i - \boldsymbol{x}_j\|_2$ for all training samples.

4.1 Datasets

We implement our DR algorithm on real-world benchmark datasets including Yale face recognition[2], {Sonar, Dbworld} from the UCI repository[3], XM2VTS50 image dataset [18], the text datasets 20newsgroups7[4], and {Colon, Gli85, Central-Nervous-System (CNS)} from the feature selection repository[5]. For the 20newsgroups7 dataset, we choose the large topic *comp*, and for Colon and Gli35 datasets we use the first two classes. The characteristics of the datasets are reported in Table 1.

We evaluate the performance of the algorithms based on the average classification accuracy with 10-fold cross-validation (CV), and we use the 1-nearest neighbor method (1-NN) to predict the label of test data based on $\boldsymbol{\Gamma}$ of the training set. Moreover, the parameters λ and μ are tuned based on conducting CV on the training sets. The same policy is applied to the selected baseline algorithms.

4.2 Dimensionality Reduction

In this section, we only evaluate the dimensionality reduction performance of our I-KDR in a single-kernel scenario, meaning that we use $\mathcal{K}$ in Eq. (15) instead of $\hat{\mathcal{K}}$, and $\boldsymbol{\beta}$ is not involved in the framework. As baseline kernel-DR methods, we choose the supervised algorithm K-FDA, LDR [24], SDR [21], KDR [7], and unsupervised DR algorithms JSE [15], SKPCA [5], and KEDR [1]. The classification results are reported in Table 2.

We can observe that I-KDR obtains better performance than baselines on almost all selected datasets. For the Colon dataset, I-KDR obtained 8.26% higher

---

[2] http://cvc.yale.edu/projects/yalefaces/yalefaces.html.
[3] http://archive.ics.uci.edu/ml/datasets.html.
[4] http://qwone.com/~jason/20Newsgroups/.
[5] http://featureselection.asu.edu/datasets.php.

accuracy than the best approach. We can conclude that our designed elements of
Eq. (6) results in better discriminative projections than other baselines. Regarding other algorithm, the supervised methods (e.g., LDR and SDR) generally
outperform the unsupervised ones which is due to their advantage of using the
supervised information in the trainings. For Sonar and Dbwork datasets, LDR
almost achieved a performance comparative to I-KDR.

Table 2. Classification accuracies (%) on the selected datasets.

Dataset	I-KDR	LDR	SDR	KDR	K-FDA	JSE	KEDR	SKPCA
Yale	**79.43**	72.80	71.13	69.50	67.88	66.23	64.61	60.75
Sonar	87.01	86.79	84.59	85.92	83.45	81.11	82.44	71.26
Colon	**83.37**	75.09	74.03	73.19	72.05	70.81	70.00	68.12
20NG	**85.74**	80.76	79.62	80.18	78.99	77.82	76.82	72.73
Gli85	**76.45**	72.15	70.66	69.26	67.50	65.79	66.68	61.38
CNS	**72.96**	68.77	67.09	65.84	64.61	63.21	63.96	58.93
Dbwork	88.24	87.67	86.28	84.90	83.27	81.74	80.40	77.32
XM2VTS50	**95.51**	92.67	91.62	92.17	90.88	89.52	88.55	84.86

The best result (**bold**) is according to a two-valued t-test at a 5% significance
level.

In Fig. 3, we compare the classification accuracy of the baselines for different
numbers of selected dimensions. Based on the accuracy curves, I-KDR shows a

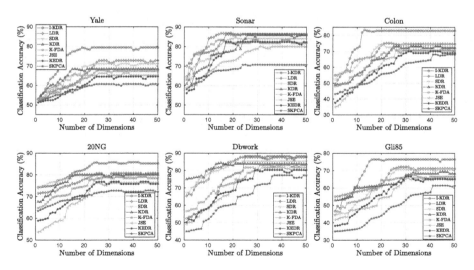

Fig. 3. Classification accuracy (%) of the baselines respect to the number of selected
dimensions for the datasets Yale, Sonar, Colon, 20NG, Dbwork, and Gli85.

distinct performance compared to other methods for the datasets Yale, Colon, and Gli85. Especially for the high-dimensional datasets Colon and Gli85, our DR algorithm achieves the peak of its performance for a smaller number of selected dimensions in comparison. For Sonar and Dbwork, I-KDR algorithm shows a competitive performance to the best baseline (LDR algorithm). Considering the classification accuracies for Yale dataset in Fig. 3, I-KDR's curve reaches the peak accuracy of each baseline while selecting fewer dimensions for the embeddings. Regarding the baseline DR algorithms, the supervised methods generally outperform the unsupervised algorithms in both the accuracy and number of selected dimension. This finding also complies with the reported information in Table 2. Therefore, applying constraints regarding the interpretability of the DR model in I-KDR does not sacrifice its discriminative performance.

4.3 Interpretation of the Embedding Dimension

To evaluate the effect of $\mathcal{J}_{Ip}$ in Eq. (6), we use the Ip measure defined as $Ip = \frac{1}{k}\sum_{i=1}^{k}(\max_q \mathbf{H}(q,:)\boldsymbol{a}_i)/\|\mathbf{H}\boldsymbol{a}_i\|_1$. The Ip value considers the interpretability of each $\boldsymbol{a}_i$ based on the data points from which it is constructed. Assuming there exists considerable similarities between the class members in RKHS, a highly interpretable embedding dimension would be formed by contributions taken from mostly one class of data. In such a case, the value of Ip should grow towards 1. Table 3 reports the value of this measure for those experiments in Table 2 where computing Ip is possible. Based on the results, I-KDR obtained the most interpretable embeddings among other baselines, K-FDA has the weakest Ip performance while SKPCA and KDR are jointly the runner up methods in this Table. Regardless of the interpretation-effective sparsity term of SKPCA, its unsupervised model allows cross-class contributions to happen in the formation of the columns of $\mathbf{A}$. From another point of view, for Yale and CNS datasets, I-KDR has smaller Ip values compared to XM2VTS and 20NG datasets for instance. This difference happened due to substantial overlapping of the classes in the first group of datasets.

Additionally, to visualize the interpretation of the embeddings, we project the embedding dimensions on the label-space by computing $\mathbf{D} = \mathbf{H}\mathbf{A} \in \mathbb{R}^{c\times k}$. Each column of $\mathbf{D}$ is a c-dimensional vector that its q-th entry explains how strong is the relation of this dimension to the class q. Figure 4 visualizes the columns of $\mathbf{D}$ for I-KDR, K-FDA, SKPCA, and KDR according to their implementations on the Sonar dataset. Each embedding was done for 10 target dimensions. Based on the results, I-KDR's embedding dimensions are almost separated into two distinct groups each of which mostly related to one class in the data. Although for SKPCA and KDR the vectors almost belong to two separate groups, they cannot be assigned to any of the classes confidently. For K-FDA, almost none of the above can be observed.

Table 3. Comparison of the Ip measure between the baselines.

Dataset	I-KDR	SKPCA	KDR	SDR	K-FDA
Yale	**0.80**	0.64	0.61	0.58	0.55
Sonar	**0.88**	0.64	0.66	0.63	0.57
Colon	**0.91**	0.72	0.69	0.66	0.63
20NG	**0.94**	0.75	0.77	0.73	0.64
Gli85	**0.84**	0.69	0.64	0.59	0.57
CNS	**0.83**	0.66	0.67	0.66	0.63
Dbwork	**0.86**	0.73	0.77	0.70	0.61
XM2VTS50	**0.96**	0.82	0.86	0.79	0.60

The best result (**bold**) is according to a two-valued
t-test at a 5% significance level.

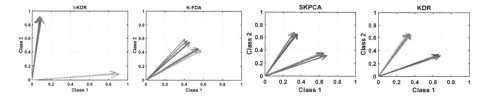

Fig. 4. Projecting the embedding dimensions on the label-space for the Sonar dataset.

4.4   Feature Selection

In order to evaluate the feature selection performance of our I-KDR algorithm,
we compute Eq. (26) for each dimension of the data individually which results in
a set of kernels $\{\mathcal{K}_i\}_{i=1}^{d}$ for each dataset. We feed these kernels to the optimization framework of Eq. (15) to optimize their corresponding weights in β. Besides
the classification accuracy, we also measure $\|\beta\|_0$ to evaluate the feature selection
performance of the algorithms. Accordingly, we choose the following relevant set
of baselines: MKL-TR [12], MKL-DR [16], KNMF-MKL [11], and DMKL [28].
Based on Table 4, by optimizing the value of β in Eq. (6), I-KDR achieves better
discriminations in the embedded space. Consequently, as a general trend among
the datasets, I-KDR's accuracies are improved after we optimized it in the multiple kernel framework (Compared to Table 2). Regarding the number of selected
features, I-KDR, MKL-TR, and DMKL obtained similar results. Even more, for
some of the datasets, the baselines obtained sparser feature selections than I-
KDR. Nevertheless, I-KDR demonstrates that its number of selected features
are more efficient than others due to its supremacy in classification accuracies.
Therefore, we can claim that I-KDA performed more efficient than others in
discriminative feature selection scenarios. For CNS and Sonar dataset, I-KDR
obtains competitive accuracy and feature selection performance compared to
MKL-TR and DMKL, while for the Colon dataset, it outperforms the next best
method (MKL-TR) with 7.73% accuracy margin. As an explanation regarding

the relatively high values of $\|\beta\|_0$ for KNMF-MKL, this algorithm uses a DR model, but it does not have a discriminative objective in its optimization.

Table 4. Comparison of classification accuracies (%) and $\|\beta\|_0$ (in parenthesis).

Dataset	I-KDR	DMKL	MKL-TR	MKL-DR	KNMF-MKL
Yale	**83.22 (20)**	78.25 (39)	79.88 (34)	70.34 (93)	68.43 (543)
Sonar	87.91 (37)	**87.53(34)**	87.94 (41)	70.34 (93)	68.43 (543)
Colon	**89.29** (25)	80.32**(21)**	81.56 (34)	80.67 (67)	78.43 (1321)
20NG	**88.41** (73)	85.01 (57)	84.42**(55)**	86.24 (384)	83.11 (14483)
Gli85	**79.65 (33)**	73.13 (54)	74.46 (50)	72.83 (79)	71.78 (10764)
CNS	76.53 (47)	76.37**(32)**	75.84 (25)	74.23 (109)	72.43 (4872)
Dbwork	**91.98 (29)**	87.23 (41)	86.53 (46)	85.14 (85)	85.34 (1049)
XM2VTS50	**97.74 (17)**	92.76 (31)	93.84 (29)	92.88 (55)	90.89 (389)

The best result (**bold**) is according to a two-valued t-test at a 5% significance level.

5   Conclusion

In this paper, we proposed a novel algorithm to perform discriminative dimensionality reduction on the manifold. Our I-KDR method constructs its embedding dimensions by selecting data points from local neighborhoods in the RKHS. This strategy results in embeddings with better class-based interpretations for their bases. Besides, by focusing on within-class local similarities and between-class dissimilarities, our method improves the separation of the classes in the projected space. The I-KDR algorithm has a bi-convex optimization problem, and we use the alternating optimization framework to solve it efficiently. Furthermore, our approach can fuse the feature selection and dimensionality reduction for RKHS. Our empirical results show that I-KDR outperforms other relevant baselines in both DR and feature selection scenarios.

References

1. Álvarez-Meza, A.M., Lee, J.A., Verleysen, M., Castellanos-Dominguez, G.: Kernel-based dimensionality reduction using Renyi's α-entropy measures of similarity. Neurocomputing **222**, 36–46 (2017)
2. Bach, F.R., Lanckriet, G.R., Jordan, M.I.: Multiple kernel learning, conic duality, and the SMO algorithm. In: ICML 2004 (2004)
3. Boyd, S., Parikh, N., Chu, E., Peleato, B., Eckstein, J., et al.: Distributed optimization and statistical learning via the alternating direction method of multipliers. Found. Trends® Mach. Learn. **3**(1), 1–122 (2011)
4. Chipman, H.A., Gu, H.: Interpretable dimension reduction. J. Appl. Stat. **32**(9), 969–987 (2005)

5. Das, R., Golatkar, A., Awate, S.: Sparse kernel PCA for outlier detection. arXiv preprint arXiv:1809.02497 (2018)
6. Dileep, A.D., Sekhar, C.C.: Representation and feature selection using multiple kernel learning. In: IJCNN 2009, pp. 717–722. IEEE (2009)
7. Fukumizu, K., Bach, F.R., Jordan, M.I.: Dimensionality reduction for supervised learning with reproducing kernel Hilbert spaces. J. Mach. Learn. Res. 5(Jan), 73–99 (2004)
8. Fukumizu, K., Bach, F.R., Jordan, M.I.: Kernel dimensionality reduction for supervised learning. In: Advances in Neural Information Processing Systems, pp. 81–88 (2004)
9. Gärtner, B., Schönherr, S.: An efficient, exact, and generic quadratic programming solver for geometric optimization. In: Proceedings of the Sixteenth Annual Symposium on Computational Geometry, pp. 110–118. ACM (2000)
10. Gönen, M., Alpaydın, E.: Multiple kernel learning algorithms. JMLR 12(Jul), 2211–2268 (2011)
11. Gu, Y., Wang, Q., Wang, H., You, D., Zhang, Y.: Multiple kernel learning via low-rank nonnegative matrix factorization for classification of hyperspectral imagery. IEEE J-STARS 8(6), 2739–2751 (2015)
12. Jiang, W., Chung, F.L.: A trace ratio maximization approach to multiple kernel-based dimensionality reduction. Neural Netw. 49, 96–106 (2014)
13. Jolliffe, I.: Principal component analysis. In: International Encyclopedia of Statistical Science, pp. 1094–1096. Springer (2011)
14. Kim, T.K., Kittler, J.: Locally linear discriminant analysis for multimodally distributed classes for face recognition with a single model image. IEEE Trans. Pattern Anal. Mach. Intell. 27(3), 318–327 (2005)
15. Lee, J.A., Renard, E., Bernard, G., Dupont, P., Verleysen, M.: Type 1 and 2 mixtures of Kullback-Leibler divergences as cost functions in dimensionality reduction based on similarity preservation. Neurocomput. 112, 92–108 (2013)
16. Lin, Y.Y., Liu, T.L., Fuh, C.S.: Multiple kernel learning for dimensionality reduction. IEEE Trans. Pattern Anal. Mach. Intell. 33(6), 1147–1160 (2011)
17. Liu, X., Wang, Z., Feng, Z., Tang, J.: A pairwise covariance-preserving projection method for dimension reduction. In: 2007 Seventh IEEE International Conference on Data Mining (ICDM 2007), pp. 223–231. IEEE (2007)
18. Messer, K., Matas, J., Kittler, J., Luettin, J., Maitre, G.: XM2VTSDB: The extended M2VTS database. In: Second International Conference on Audio and Video-Based Biometric Person Authentication, vol. 964, pp. 965–966 (1999)
19. Mika, S., Ratsch, G., Weston, J., Scholkopf, B., Mullers, K.R.: Fisher discriminant analysis with kernels. In: Proceedings of the 1999 IEEE Signal Processing Society Workshop on Neural Networks for Signal Processing IX, pp. 41–48. IEEE (1999)
20. Mosek, A.: The MOSEK optimization toolbox for MATLAB manual (2015)
21. Orlitsky, A., et al.: Supervised dimensionality reduction using mixture models. In: Proceedings of the 22nd International Conference on Machine Learning, pp. 768–775. ACM (2005)
22. Rakotomamonjy, A., Bach, F.R., Canu, S., Grandvalet, Y.: SimpleMKL. J. Mach. Learn. Res. 9(Nov), 2491–2521 (2008)
23. Roweis, S.T., Saul, L.K.: Nonlinear dimensionality reduction by locally linear embedding. Science 290(5500), 2323–2326 (2000)
24. Suzuki, T., Sugiyama, M.: Sufficient dimension reduction via squared-loss mutual information estimation. Neural Comput. 25(3), 725–758 (2013)
25. Tian, T.S., James, G.M.: Interpretable dimension reduction for classifying functional data. Comput. Stat. Data Anal. 57(1), 282–296 (2013)

26. Von Luxburg, U.: A tutorial on spectral clustering. Stat. Comput. **17**(4), 395–416 (2007). https://doi.org/10.1007/s11222-007-9033-z
27. Wang, D., Tanaka, T.: Sparse kernel principal component analysis based on elastic net regularization. In: 2016 International Joint Conference on Neural Networks (IJCNN), pp. 3703–3708. IEEE (2016)
28. Wang, Q., Gu, Y., Tuia, D.: Discriminative multiple kernel learning for hyperspectral image classification. IEEE Trans. Geosci. Remote Sens. **54**(7), 3912–3927 (2016)
29. Ye, J., Xiong, T., Janardan, R.: CPM: a covariance-preserving projection method. In: Proceedings of the 2006 SIAM International Conference on Data Mining, pp. 24–34. SIAM (2006)

On the Stability of Feature Selection in the Presence of Feature Correlations

Konstantinos Sechidis[1], Konstantinos Papangelou[1], Sarah Nogueira[2],
James Weatherall[3], and Gavin Brown[1(✉)]

[1] School of Computer Science, University of Manchester,
Manchester M13 9PL, UK
{konstantinos.sechidis,konstantinos.papangelou,
gavin.brown}@manchester.ac.uk
[2] Criteo, Paris, France
s.nogueira@criteo.com
[3] Advanced Analytics Centre, Global Medicines Development, AstraZeneca,
Cambridge SG8 6EE, UK
James.Weatherall@astrazeneca.com

Abstract. Feature selection is central to modern data science. The 'stability' of a feature selection algorithm refers to the sensitivity of its choices to small changes in training data. This is, in effect, the *robustness* of the chosen features. This paper considers the estimation of stability when we expect strong pairwise correlations, otherwise known as feature *redundancy*. We demonstrate that existing measures are inappropriate here, as they systematically *underestimate* the true stability, giving an overly pessimistic view of a feature set. We propose a new statistical measure which overcomes this issue, and generalises previous work.

Keywords: Feature selection · Stability · Bioinformatics

1 Introduction

Feature Selection (FS) is central to modern data science—from exploratory data analysis, to predictive model building. The overall question we address with this paper is *"how can we quantify the reliability of a feature selection algorithm?"*. The answer to this has two components—first, how *useful* are the selected features when used in a predictive model; and second, how *sensitive* are the selected features, to small changes in the training data. The latter is known as *stability* [9]. If the selected set varies wildly, with only small data changes, perhaps the algorithm is not picking up on generalisable patterns, and is responding to noise. From this perspective, we can see an alternative (and equivalent) phrasing, in that we ask *"how reliable is the set of chosen features?"*—i.e. how likely are we

Electronic supplementary material The online version of this chapter (https://doi.org/10.1007/978-3-030-46150-8_20) contains supplementary material, which is available to authorized users.

© Springer Nature Switzerland AG 2020
U. Brefeld et al. (Eds.): ECML PKDD 2019, LNAI 11906, pp. 327–342, 2020.
https://doi.org/10.1007/978-3-030-46150-8_20

to get a different recommended feature set, with a tiny change to training data. This is particularity important in domains like bioinformatics, where the chosen features are effectively hypotheses on the underlying biological mechanisms.

There are many measures of stability proposed in the literature, with a recent study [14] providing a good summary of the advantages and disadvantages of each. The particular contribution of this paper is on how to estimate stability in the presence of *correlated features*, also known as feature *redundancy*. We will demonstrate that any stability measure not taking such redundancy into account necessarily gives a *systematic under-estimate* of the stability, thus giving an overly pessimistic view of a given FS algorithm. This systematic under-estimation of stability can have a variety of consequences, depending on the application domain. In biomedical scenarios, it is common to use data-driven methods to generate candidate biomarker sets, that predict disease progression [16]. If we are comparing two biomarker sets, we might estimate their stability, judge one to be unstable, and discard it. However, if there are background feature correlations, and thus we are overly conservative on the stability, we might miss an opportunity.

We provide a solution to this problem, with a novel stability measure that takes feature redundancy into account. The measure generalises a recent work [14] with a correction factor that counteracts the systematic under-estimation of stability. Since the selection of a FS algorithm can be seen as a multi-objective optimisation problem we show how the choice of a stability measure changes the Pareto-optimal solution. Additionally, we demonstrate the utility of the measure in the context of biomarker selection in medical trials, where strong correlations and necessary robustness of the choices are an unavoidable part of the domain[1].

2   Background

We assume a dataset $\mathcal{D} = \{\mathbf{x}_n, y_n\}_{n=1}^N$, with a d-dimensional input $\mathbf{x}$. The task of feature selection is to choose a subset of the dimensions, of size $k \ll d$, subject to some constraints; typically we would like to select the smallest subset that contains all the relevant information to predict y.

2.1   Estimating the Stability of Feature Selection

Let us assume we take $\mathcal{D}$ and run some feature selection algorithm, such as L1 regularization where we take non-zero coefficients to be the 'selected' features, or ranking features by their mutual information with the target [3]. When using all N datapoints, we get a subset of features: $s_{\mathcal{D}}$. We would like to know the *reliability* of the chosen feature set under small perturbations of the data. If the algorithm changes preferences drastically, with only small changes in the training data, we might prefer not to trust the set $s_{\mathcal{D}}$, and judge it as an 'unstable' set.

To quantify this, we repeat the same selection procedure M times, but each time leaving out a small random fraction δ of the original data. From this we

---

obtain a sequence $S = \{s_1, s_2, \ldots, s_M\}$, where each subset came from applying a FS algorithm to a different random perturbation of the training data. At this point it turns out to be more notationally and mathematically convenient to abandon the set-theoretic notation, and use instead a matrix notation. We can treat the sequence S as an $M \times d$ binary matrix, where the d columns represent whether or not (1/0) each feature was chosen on each of the M repeats. For example, selecting from a pool of $d = 6$ features, and $M = 4$ runs:

$$
\mathcal{Z} = \begin{matrix} Z_1\ Z_2\ Z_3\ Z_4\ Z_5\ Z_6 \\ \begin{pmatrix} 1 & 0 & 1 & 0 & 0 & 0 \\ 0 & 1 & 1 & 0 & 0 & 0 \\ 1 & 0 & 0 & 1 & 0 & 0 \\ 0 & 1 & 0 & 1 & 0 & 0 \end{pmatrix} \end{matrix} \begin{matrix} \ldots\mathbf{z}_1, \quad \text{selections on 1st run} \\ \ldots\mathbf{z}_2, \quad \text{selections on 2nd run} \\ \ldots \end{matrix} \tag{1}
$$

We then choose some measure $\phi(a, b)$ of similarity between the resulting feature sets from two runs, and evaluate the stability from $\mathcal{Z}$, as an average over all possible pairs:

$$
\hat{\Phi}(\mathcal{Z}) = \frac{1}{M(M-1)} \sum_i \sum_{j \neq i} \phi(\mathbf{z}_i, \mathbf{z}_j) \tag{2}
$$

Let us take for example $\phi(\mathbf{z}_i, \mathbf{z}_j)$ to be a dot-product of the two binary strings. For a single pair, this would correspond to the number of selected features that are common between the two – or the *size of the subset intersection*. Over the M runs, this would correspond to the average subset intersection—so on average, if the feature subsets have large pairwise intersection, the algorithm is returning similar subsets despite the data variations. This of course has the disadvantage that the computation expands quadratically with M, and large M is necessary to get more reliable estimates. Computation constraints aside, if the result indicated sufficiently high stability (high average subset intersection) we might decide we can trust s_D and take it forward to the next stage of the analysis.

A significant body of research, e.g. [5,9,10,17], suggested different similarity measures ϕ that could be used, and studied properties. Kuncheva [11] conducted an umbrella study, demonstrating several undesirable behaviours of existing measures, and proposing an axiomatic framework to understand them. Nogueira et al. [14] extended this, finding further issues and avoiding the pairwise, set-theoretic, definition of ϕ entirely—presenting a measure in closed form, allowing computation in $O(Md)$ instead of $O(M^2d)$. From the matrix $\mathcal{Z}$, we can estimate various stochastic quantities, such as the average number of features selected across M runs, denoted as $\bar{k}$ and the probability that the feature X_f was selected, denoted as $p_f = \mathbb{E}[Z_f = 1]$. Using these, their recommended stability measure is,

$$
\hat{\Phi}(\mathcal{Z}) = 1 - \frac{\sum_f \frac{M}{M-1} \hat{p}_f(1 - \hat{p}_f)}{\bar{k}(1 - \frac{\bar{k}}{d})} \tag{3}
$$

The measure also generalises several previous works (e.g. [11]), and was shown to have numerous desirable statistical properties. For details we refer the reader to [14], but the intuition is that the numerator measures the average sample variance, treating the columns of $\mathcal{Z}$ as Bernoulli variables; the denominator is a normalizing term that ensures $\hat{\Phi}(\mathcal{Z}) \in [0, 1]$, as $M \to \infty$.

In the following section we illustrate how stability becomes much more complex to understand and measure, when there are either observed feature correlations, or background domain knowledge on the dependencies between features.

2.2   The Problem: Estimating Stability Under Feature Correlations

The example in Eq. (1) can serve to illustrate an important point. On each run (each row of $\mathcal{Z}$) the algorithm seems to change its mind about which are the important features—first 1&3, then 2&3, then 1&4, and finally 2&4. Various measures in the literature, e.g. [14] will identify this to be *unstable* as it changes its feature preferences substantially on every run. However, suppose we examine the original data, and discover that features X_1 and X_2 are very *strongly correlated*, as are X_3 and X_4. For the purposes of building a predictive model these are interchangeable, redundant features. What should we now conclude about stability? Since the algorithm always selects one feature from each strongly correlated pair, it always ends up with *effectively the same information* with which to make predictions—thus we should say that it *is in fact perfectly stable*. This sort of scenario is common to (but not limited to) the biomedical domain, where genes and other biomarkers can exhibit extremely strong pairwise correlations. A further complication also arises in this area, in relation to the *semantics* of the features. Certain features may or may not have strong observable *statistical* correlations, but for the purpose of interpretability they hold very similar *semantics* – e.g. if the algorithm alternates between two genes, which are not strongly correlated, but are both part of the renal metabolic pathway, then we can determine that the kidney is playing a stable role in the hypotheses that the algorithm is switching between.

To the best of our knowledge there are only two published stability measures which take correlations/redundancy between features into account, however both have significant limitations. The measure of Yu et al. [19] requires the estimation of a mutual information quantity between features, and the solution of a constrained optimisation problem (bipartite matching), making it quite highly parameterised, expensive, and stochastic in behaviour. The other is nPOGR [20] which can be shown to have several pathological properties [14]. In particular, the measure is not lower-bounded which makes interpretation of the estimated value very challenging – we cannot judge how "stable" a FS algorithm is without a reference point. The nPOGR measure is also very computationally demanding, requiring generation of random pairs of input vectors, and computable in $O(M^2 d)$. To estimate stability in large scale data, computational efficiency is a critical factor.

In the next section, we describe our approach for estimating stability under strong feature correlations, which also allows incorporation of background knowledge, often found in biomedical domains.

3   Measuring Stability in the Presence of Correlations

As discussed in the previous section, a simple stability measure can be derived if we define $\Phi(\cdot, \cdot)$ as the *size of the intersection* between two subsets of feature, and apply Eq. (2). The more co-occurring features between repeated runs, the more stable we regard the algorithm to be. It turns out that, to understand stability in the presence of correlated features, we need to revise our concept of subset *intersection*, to one of *effective subset intersection*.

3.1   Subset Intersection and *Effective* Subset Intersection

We take again the example from Eq. (1). We have $\mathbf{z}_1 = [1, 0, 1, 0, 0, 0]$, and $\mathbf{z}_2 = [0, 1, 1, 0, 0, 0]$. The subset intersection, given by the inner product is $\mathbf{z}_1 \, \mathbf{z}_2^T = 1$, due to the selection of the third feature. But, as mentioned, perhaps we learn that in the original data, X_1 and X_2 are strongly correlated, effectively *interchangeable* for the purposes of building a predictive model. When comparing the two subsets, X_1 and X_2 should be treated similarly, thus increasing the size of the intersection to 2. Hence, we do not have a simple subset intersection, but instead an *effective* subset intersection, based not on the *indices* of the features (i.e. X_1 vs X_2) but instead on the *utility* or *semantics* of the features.

We observed that the intersection between two subsets s_i and s_j, i.e. the two rows $\mathbf{z}_i$ and $\mathbf{z}_j$ of the binary matrix $\mathcal{Z}$, can be written as an inner product: $r_{i,j} = |s_i \cap s_j| = \mathbf{z}_i \, \mathbb{I}_d \, \mathbf{z}_j^T$ where $\mathbb{I}_d$ is the $d \times d$ identity matrix. We can extend this with a *generalised* inner product, where the inner product matrix will capture the feature relationships.

Definition 1 (Effective subset intersection). *The "effective" subset intersection with correlated features is given by the generalised inner product:*

$$r_{i,j}^{\mathbb{C}} = |s_i \cap s_j|_{\mathbb{C}} = \mathbf{z}_i \, \mathbb{C} \, \mathbf{z}_j^T$$

The inner product matrix $\mathbb{C}$ has diagonal elements set to 1, while the off-diagonals capture the relationships between pairs of features, i.e.

$$\mathbb{C} = \begin{bmatrix} 1 & c_{1,2} & \dots & c_{1,d} \\ c_{2,1} & 1 & \dots & c_{2,d} \\ \vdots & \vdots & \vdots & \vdots \\ c_{d,1} & c_{d,2} & \dots & 1 \end{bmatrix} \tag{4}$$

with $c_{f,f'} = c_{f',f} > 0 \ \forall \ f \neq f'$.

The entries of the matrix $\mathbb{C}$ *could* be absolute correlation coefficients $c_{f,f'} = |\rho_{X_f, X_{f'}}|$ thus capturing redundancy as explained by the data. But in general we emphasise that entries of $\mathbb{C}$ are not necessarily statistical correlations between features. For example, $\mathbb{C}$ could be a binary matrix, where $c_{f,f'} = \delta(|\rho_{X_f, X_{f'}}| > \theta)$, or constructed based on domain knowledge, thus capturing redundancy as explained by domain experts (e.g. two biomarkers appearing in the same metabolic pathway). The following theorem shows why we are guaranteed to underestimate the stability, if feature redundancy is not taken into account.

Theorem 2. *The effective intersection is greater than or equal to intersection,*

$$|s_i \cap s_j|_{\mathbb{C}} \geq |s_i \cap s_j|$$

The proof of this can be seen by relating the "traditional" intersection $|s_i \cap s_j|$ and the "effective" intersection as follows:

Lemma 3. *The effective intersection can be written,*

$$|s_i \cap s_j|_{\mathbb{C}} = |s_i \cap s_j| + \sum_{f=1}^{d} \sum_{\substack{f'=1 \\ f' \neq f}}^{d} c_{f,f'} z_{i,f} z_{j,f'}$$

If all entries in $\mathbb{C}$ are non-negative, we have $r_{i,j}^{\mathbb{C}} \geq r_{i,j}$—without this correction, we will systematically under-estimate the true stability.

The set-theoretic interpretation of stability is to be contrasted with the binary matrix representation $\mathcal{Z} \in \{0,1\}^{M \times d}$. Nogueira et al. [14] proved the following result, bridging these two conceptual approaches to stability. The average subset intersection among M feature sets can be written,

$$\frac{1}{M(M-1)} \sum_{i=1}^{M} \sum_{\substack{j=1 \\ j \neq i}}^{M} |s_i \cap s_j| = \overline{k} - \sum_{f=1}^{d} \widehat{\text{var}}(Z_f)$$

where $\overline{k}$ is the average number of features selected over M rows, and $\widehat{\text{var}}(Z_f) = \frac{M}{M-1}\hat{p}_f(1-\hat{p}_f)$, i.e. the unbiased estimator of the variance of the Bernoulli random feature Z_f. Then a stability measure defined as an increasing function of the intersection can be equivalently phrased as a decreasing function of the variance of the columns of the selection matrix, thus bridging the set-theoretic view with a probabilistic view. This property is also known as monotonicity [11,14] and is a defining element of a stability measure. In the presence of redundancy we instead would like our measure to be an increasing function of the effective intersection. The following theorem bridges our set-theoretic view with the statistical properties of the selection matrix in the presence of feature redundancy captured in the matrix $\mathbb{C}$.

Theorem 4. *The effective average pairwise intersection among the M subsets can be written:*

$$\frac{1}{M(M-1)} \sum_{i=1}^{M} \sum_{\substack{j=1 \\ j \neq i}}^{M} |s_i \cap s_j|_{\mathbb{C}} = \overline{k}_{\mathbb{C}} - \text{tr}(\mathbb{C}\mathbf{S})$$

where $\overline{k}_{\mathbb{C}} = \sum_{f=1}^{d}\sum_{f'=1}^{d} c_{f,f'}\overline{z}_{f,f'}$ the effective average number of features selected over M runs. The unbiased estimator of the covariance between Z_f and $Z_{f'}$ is $\widehat{\mathrm{cov}}(Z_f, Z_{f'}) = \frac{M}{M-1}(\hat{p}_{f,f'} - \hat{p}_f\hat{p}_{f'})$, $\forall\ f, f'\ \in\ \{1...d\}$, while $\mathbf{S}$ is an unbiased estimator of the variance-covariance matrix of $\mathcal{Z}$.

Proof: Provided in Supplementary material Section A.

We are now in position to introduce our new measure, which based on the above theorem should be a decreasing function of $\mathrm{tr}(\mathbb{C}\mathbf{S})$. There is a final element that needs to be taken into account—we need to normalise our estimation to bound it so that it can be interpretable and comparable between different FS approaches, developed in the next section.

3.2   A Stability Measure for Correlated Features

Based on the previous sections, we can propose the following stability measure.

Definition 5 (Effective Stability). *Given a matrix of feature relationships* $\mathbb{C}$, *the effective stability is*

$$\hat{\Phi}_{\mathbb{C}}\left(\mathcal{Z}\right) = 1 - \frac{\mathrm{tr}(\mathbb{C}\mathbf{S})}{\mathrm{tr}(\mathbb{C}\mathbf{\Sigma^0})},$$

where $\mathbf{S}$ *is an unbiased estimator of the variance-covariance matrix of* $\mathcal{Z}$, *i.e.* $\mathbf{S}_{f,f'} = \widehat{\mathrm{Cov}}(Z_f, Z_{f'}) = \frac{M}{M-1}(\hat{p}_{f,f'} - \hat{p}_f\hat{p}_{f'})$, $\forall\ f, f'\ \in\ \{1...d\}$, *while* $\mathbf{\Sigma^0}$ *is the matrix which normalises the measure.*

To derive a normaliser, we need to estimate the variance/covariance under the *Null Model* of feature selection [14, Definition 3]. The Null Model expresses the situation where there is *no preference* toward any particular subset, and all subsets of size k have the same probability of occurrence, thus accounting for the event of a completely random selection procedure. For a detailed treatment of this subject we refer the reader to the definition of this, by Nogueira et al. [14].

Theorem 6. *Under the Null Model, the covariance matrix of* $\mathcal{Z}$ *is given by:*

$$\mathbf{\Sigma^0} = \begin{bmatrix} \mathrm{var}\left(Z_1 \big| H_0\right) & \cdots & \mathrm{cov}\left(Z_1, Z_d \big| H_0\right) \\ \vdots & \ddots & \vdots \\ \mathrm{cov}\left(Z_d, Z_1 \big| H_0\right) & \cdots & \mathrm{var}\left(Z_d \big| H_0\right) \end{bmatrix},$$

where the main diagonal elements are given by: $\mathrm{var}\left(Z_f \big| H_0\right) = \frac{\overline{k}}{d}\left(1 - \frac{\overline{k}}{d}\right)$ *and the off-diagonal elements,* $f \neq f'$, *are:* $\mathrm{cov}\left(Z_f, Z_{f'} \big| H_0\right) = \frac{\overline{k^2}-\overline{k}}{d^2-d} - \frac{\overline{k}^2}{d^2}$

Proof: Provided in Supplementary material Section B.

It can immediately be seen that the proposed measure is a generalisation of Nogueira et al. [14], as it reduces to Eq. (3) when $\mathbb{C}$ is the identity, in which case

---

Algorithm 1: Recommended protocol for estimating FS stability.

Input   : A dataset $\mathcal{D} = \{\mathbf{x}_i, y_i\}_{i=1}^N$, where $\mathbf{x}$ is d-dimensional.
A procedure $f(\mathcal{D})$ returning a subset of features $s_\mathcal{D}$, of size $k < d$.
A matrix $\mathbb{C}$, specifying known feature redundancies.

Output: Stability estimate $\hat{\varPhi}$, for feature set $s_\mathcal{D}$.

Define $\mathcal{Z}$, an empty matrix of size $M \times d$.
for $j := 1$ *to* M **do**
   | Generate $\mathcal{D}_j$, a random sample from $\mathcal{D}$ (e.g. leave out 5% rows, or
   | bootstrap)
   | Set $s_j \leftarrow f(\mathcal{D}_j)$
   | Set the jth row of $\mathcal{Z}$ as the binary string corresponding to selections s_j.

Return stability estimate $\hat{\varPhi}(\mathcal{Z})$ using Definition 2.

$\mathrm{tr}(\mathbb{C}S) = \sum_i \mathrm{var}(z_i)$. At this point we can observe that when $\mathbb{C} = \mathbb{I}_d$ we implicitly assume the columns of the selection matrix to be independent variables hence considering only their variance. In contrast, our measure accounts additionally for all pairwise covariances weighted by the coefficients of the matrix $\mathbb{C}$. As we already discussed these coefficients can be seen as our confidence on the correlation between the columns of the selection matrix as explained by the data (using for example Spearman's correlation coefficient) or by domain experts.

Finally, we can summarise the protocol for estimating the stability of a FS procedure in a simple algorithm shown in Algorithm 1. We also compare the computational time of our measure against nPOGR, as the dimensionality of the feature set increases—shown in Fig. 1—we observe that our measure is as expected, orders of magnitude faster to compute.

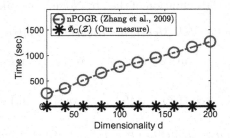

Fig. 1. Computational cost of nPOGR versus our measure as the number of features grow. We generated randomly selection matrices $\mathcal{Z}$ of dimension $M \times d$, with $M = 50$ and various values of d. The proposed measure remains largely unaffected by the dimensionality (taking milliseconds).

In the next section, we demonstrate several cases where incorporating prior knowledge and using our proposed stability measure, we may arrive to completely different conclusions on the reliability of one FS algorthm versus another, hence potentially altering strategic decisions in a data science pipeline.

4 Experiments

Our experimental study is split in two sections. Firstly we will show how our measure can be used for choosing between different feature selection criteria in real-world datasets. We will apply the protocol described in the previous section to estimate the stability which along with the predictive performance of the resulting feature set can give the full picture on the performance of a FS procedure. Secondly, we will show how we can use stability in clinical trials data to identify robust groups of biomarkers.

4.1 Pareto-Optimality Using Effective Stability

In many applications, given a dataset we might wish to apply several feature selection algorithms, which we evaluate and compare. The problem of deciding which FS algorithm we should trust can be seen as a multi-objective optimisation combining two criteria: (1) the features result in high accuracy, and (2) we want algorithms that generate *stable subsets*, i.e. stable hypotheses on the underlying mechanisms. In this context, we define the Pareto-optimal set as the set of points for which no other point has both higher accuracy and higher stability, thus the members of the Pareto-optimal set are said to be non-dominated [7]. In this section we will explore whether using the proposed stability measure, $\hat{\Phi}_C(\mathcal{Z})$, can result in different optimal solutions in comparison with the original measure, $\hat{\Phi}(\mathcal{Z})$, that ignores feature redundancy.

We used ten UCI datasets and created $M = 50$ versions of each one of them by removing 5% of the examples at random. We applied several feature selection algorithms and evaluated the predictive power of the selected feature sets using a simple nearest neighbour classifier (3-nn). By using this classifier we make few assumptions about the data and avoid additional variance from hyperparameter tuning. For each dataset, we estimated the accuracy on the hold-out data (5%). To ensure a fair comparison of the feature selection methods, all algorithms are tuned to return the top-k features for a given dataset. We chose k to be the 25% of the number of features d of each dataset. Here we provide a short description of the feature selection methods we used and implementation details.

- **Penalized linear model (LASSO):** with the regularisation parameter λ tuned such that we get k non-zero coefficients—these are the selected features.
- **Tree-based methods (RF/GBM):** We used Random Forest (RF) [2] and Gradient Boosted Machines (GBM) with decision stumps [8] to choose the top-k features with highest importance scores. For both algorithms we used 100 trees.

- **Information theoretic methods (MIM/mRMR/JMI/CMIM):** We used various information theoretic feature selection methods, each one of them making different assumptions (for a complete description of the assumptions made by each method we refer the reader to [3]). For example MIM quantifies only the relevancy, mRMR the relevancy and redundancy [15], while the JMI [18] and CMIM [6] the relevancy, the redundancy and the complementarity. To estimate mutual and conditional mutual information terms, continuous features were discretized into 5 bins using an equal-width strategy.

The UCI datasets do not contain information about correlated features. In order to take into account possible redundancies we used Spearman's ρ correlation coefficient to assess non-linear relationships between each pair of features. For estimating the effective stability, we incorporate these redundancies in the $\mathbb{C}$ matrix using the rule: $c_{f,f'} = \delta(|\rho_{X_f,X_{f'}}| > \theta)$. Following Cohen [4], two features X_f and $X_{f'}$ are assumed to be strongly correlated, when the co-efficient is greater than $\theta = 0.5$.

Figure 2 shows the Pareto-optimal set for two selected datasets. The criteria on the top-right dominate the ones on the bottom left and they are the ones that should be selected. We observe that by incorporating prior knowledge (r.h.s. in Fig. 2a and Fig. 2b) we change our view about the best-performing algorithms in terms of the accuracy/stability trade-off. Notice that mRMR, a criterion that penalizes the selection of redundant features, becomes much more stable using our proposed measure, $\hat{\Phi}_{\mathbb{C}}(\mathcal{Z})$. A summary of the Pareto-optimal solutions for all datasets is given in Table 1, where we can observe that similar changes occur in most cases.

Table 1. Pareto-optimal solutions for 10 UCI datasets. We observe that in most cases incorporating prior knowledge about possible feature redundancies changes the optimal solutions.

Dataset	Pareto-optimal set (accuracy vs stability)	Pareto-optimal set (accuracy vs *effective* stability)	Change ?
breast	LASSO, MIM	MIM	✓
ionosphere	LASSO, GBM, MIM	LASSO, GBM, MIM mRMR	✓
landsat	mRMR	JMI	✓
musk2	LASSO, MIM	LASSO	✓
parkinsons	LASSO, MIM	MIM, mRMR, JMI	✓
semeion	GBM, MIM, mRMR, JMI	GBM, mRMR, JMI, CMIM	✓
sonar	MIM, JMI	MIM, mRMR, JMI	✓
spect	MIM	MIM	
waveform	GBM, mRMR	GBM, mRMR	
wine	MIM, CMIM	MIM, CMIM	

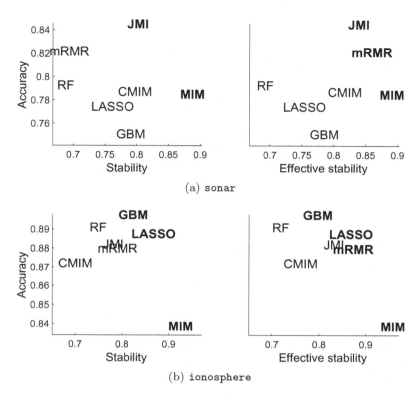

Fig. 2. Accuracy/stability trade-off between different feature selection algorithms for two UCI datasets. The methods on top right corner are the Pareto-optimal solutions.

Furthermore, Table 2 shows the non-dominated rank of the different criteria across all datasets. This is computed per data set as the number of other criteria which dominate a given criterion, in the Pareto-optimal sense, and then averaged over the 10 datasets. Similarly to our earlier observations (Fig. 2), the average rank of mRMR increases dramatically. Similarly JMI increases its average position, as opposed to MIM that captures only the relevancy.

In the next section, we describe how incorporating prior knowledge about the *semantics* of biomarkers may incur changes on the stability of feature selection in clinical trials.

4.2   Stability of Biomarker Selection in Clinical Trials

The use of highly specific biomarkers is central to personalised medicine, in both clinical and research scenarios. Discovering new biomarkers that carry prognostic information is crucial for general patient care and for clinical trial planning, i.e. prognostic markers can be considered as covariates for stratification. A prognostic biomarker is a biological characteristic or a clinical measurement that

Table 2. Column 1: Non-dominated rank of different criteria for the trade-off of accuracy/stability estimated by $\Phi(\mathcal{Z})$. Criteria with a higher rank (closer to 1.0) provide a better tradeoff than those with a lowerrank. Column 2: As column 1 but using our measure $\Phi_C(\mathcal{Z})$ for estimating effective stability.

Accuracy/stability	Accuracy/effective stability
MIM (1.6)	mRMR (1.7)
GBM (1.8)	MIM (2)
JMI (2.6)	JMI (2.4)
LASSO (2.7)	GBM (2.4)
mRMR (2.9)	CMIM (2.9)
CMIM (2.9)	LASSO (3.1)
RF (3.1)	RF (3.1)

provides information on the likely outcome of the patient irrespective of the applied treatment [16]. For this task, any supervised feature selection algorithm can be used to identify and rank the biomarkers with respect to the outcome Y. Having *stable* biomarker discovery algorithms, i.e. identifying biomarkers that can be reproduced across studies, is of great importance in clinical trials. In this section we will present a case study on how to evaluate the stability of different algorithms, and how we can incorporate prior knowledge over groups of biomarkers with semantic similarities.

We focus on the IPASS study [13], which evaluated the efficacy of the drug *gefitinib* (Iressa, AstraZeneca) versus first-line chemotherapy with *carboplatin* (Paraplatin, Bristol-Myers Squibb) plus *paclitaxel* (Taxol, Bristol-Myers Squibb) in an Asian population of 1217 light- or non-smokers with advanced non-small cell lung cancer. A detailed description of the trial and the biomarkers used in the IPASS study are given in the Appendix A.

In this section we will focus on two commonly used algorithms: Gradient Boosted Machines [8] and conditional mutual information maximisation (CMIM) [6]. GBM sequentially builds a weighted voting ensemble of decision stumps based on single features, while CMIM is an information theoretic measure based on maximising conditional mutual information. These two methods are quite different in nature: for example GBM builds decision trees, while CMIM estimates two-way feature interactions. As a result, they often return different biomarker subsets and choosing which one to take forward in a phased clinical study is an important problem.

Table 3 presents the top-4 prognostic biomarkers derived by each method. We observe that the two methods return significantly different biomarker sets; Which one should we trust? To answer this question we estimate their stability with respect to data variations using $M = 50$ and 5% leave-out. This could simulate the scenario where for some patients we do not know the outcome e.g. they dropped out from the trial. In Table 4 we see that when using $\widehat{\Phi}(\mathcal{Z})$, in agreement with data science folklore, GBM is judged a stable method, more so than CMIM.

Table 3. Top-4 prognostic biomarkers in IPASS for each competing method. The results can be interpreted by domain experts (e.g. clinicians) on their biological plausibility. However, to answer in what extend these sets are reproducible and how they can be affected by small changes in the data (such as patient dropouts) we need to evaluate their stability.

Rank	GBM	CMIM
1	EGFR expression (X_4)	EGFR mutation (X_2)
2	Disease stage (X_{10})	Serum ALP(X_{13})
3	WHO perform. status (X_1)	Blood leukocytes (X_{21})
4	Serum ALT(X_{12})	Serum ALT (X_{12})

But, with a closer study of the biomarkers considered in IPASS, there are in fact groups of them which are biologically related: **(Group A)** those that describe the receptor protein EGFR, X_2, X_3, X_4, **(Group B)** those which are measures of liver function, X_{12}, X_{13}, X_{14}, and **(Group C)** those which are counts of blood cells, $X_{20}, X_{21}, X_{22}, X_{23}$. There are also sub-groupings at play here. For instance, given that neutrophils are in fact a type of leukocyte (white blood cell), one may expect X_{21} and X_{22} to exhibit a stronger pairwise correlation than any other pair of cell count biomarkers.

We can take these groupings and redundancies into account by setting to 1, all of the elements in $\mathbb{C}$ matrix that represent pairs of features that belong the same group. Table 4 compares the effective stability of the two algorithms using our novel measure $\widehat{\Phi}_{\mathbb{C}}(\mathcal{Z})$, which takes into account the groups A, B and C. This time, CMIM is substantially *more stable* than GBM—leading to the conjecture that the instability in GBM is generated by variations *between groups*, while CMIM is caused by *within-group variations*.

Table 4. Stability and effective stability of GBM and CMIM in IPASS. The instability of CMIM is caused by variations within groups of semantically related biomarkers. When this is taken into account using $\widehat{\Phi}_{\mathbb{C}}(\mathcal{Z})$ the method is deemed more stable than GBM.

	GBM		CMIM
Stability $\widehat{\Phi}(\mathcal{Z})$	**0.87**	>	0.68
- within **Group A**	0.96		0.45
- within **Group B**	0.82		0.80
- within **Group C**	0.14		0.43
Effective stability $\widehat{\Phi}_{\mathbb{C}}(\mathcal{Z})$	0.87	<	**0.91**

To validate this conjecture, we calculate the stability within each group using $\widehat{\Phi}(\mathcal{Z})$. In Table 4 we observe that CMIM has small stability, especially within the groups A and C. The algorithm alternates between selecting biomarkers that are biologically related, hence when we incorporate domain knowledge the effective stability of CMIM increases significantly. Thus, based on our prior knowledge on feature relationships, CMIM is the more desirable prospect to take forward.

5   Conclusions

We presented a study on the estimation of stability of feature selection in the presence of feature redundancy. This is an important topic, as it gives an indication of how reliable a selected subset may be, given correlations in the data or domain knowledge. We showed that existing measures are unsuitable and potentially misleading, also proving that many will systematically under-estimate the stability. As a solution to this, we presented a novel measure which allows us to incorporate information about correlated and/or semantically related features. An empirical study across 10 datasets and 7 distinct feature selection methods confirmed the utility, while a case study on real clinical trial data highlighted how critical decisions might be altered as a result of the new measure.

Acknowledgements. KS was funded by the AstraZeneca Data Science Fellowship at the University of Manchester. KP was supported by the EPSRC through the Centre for Doctoral Training Grant [EP/1038099/1]. GB was supported by the EPSRC LAMBDA project [EP/N035127/1].

A   IPASS description

The IPASS study [13] was a Phase III, multi-center, randomised, open-label, parallel-group study comparing gefitinib (Iressa, AstraZeneca) with carboplatin (Paraplatin, Bristol-Myers Squibb) plus paclitaxel (Taxol, Bristol-Myers Squibb) as first-line treatment in clinically selected patients in East Asia who had NSCLC. 1217 patients were balanced randomised (1:1) between the treatment arms, and the primary end point was progression-free survival (PFS); for full details of the trial see [13]. For the purpose of our work we model PFS as a Bernoulli endpoint, neglecting its time-to-event nature. We analysed the data at 78% maturity, when 950 subjects have had progression events.

The covariates used in the IPASS study are shown in Table 5. The following covariates have missing observations (as shown in parentheses): X_5 (0.4%), X_{12} (0.2%), X_{13} (0.7%), X_{14} (0.7%), X_{16} (2%), X_{17} (0.3%), X_{18} (1%), X_{19} (1%), X_{20} (0.3%), X_{21} (0.3%), X_{22} (0.3%), X_{23} (0.3%). Following Lipkovich et al. [12], for the patients with missing values in biomarker X, we create an additional category, a procedure known as the *missing indicator method* [1].

Table 5. Covariates used in the IPASS clinical trial.

Biomarker	Description	Values
X_1	WHO perform. status	0 or 1, 2
X_2	EGFR mutation status	Negative, Positive, Unknown
X_3	EGFR FISH status	Negative, Positive, Unknown
X_4	EGFR expression status	Negative, Positive, Unknown
X_5	Weight	(0, 50], (50, 60], (60, 70], (70, 80], (80, $+\infty$)
X_6	Race	Oriental, Other
X_7	Ethnicity	Chinese, Japanese, Other Asian, Other not Asian
X_8	Sex	Female, Male
X_9	Smoking status	Ex-Smoker, Smoker
X_{10}	Disease stage	Locally Advanced, Metastatic
X_{11}	Age	(0, 44], [45, 64], [65, 74], [75, $+\infty$)
X_{12}	Serum ALT	Low, Medium, High
X_{13}	Serum ALP	Low, Medium, High
X_{14}	Serum AST	Low, Medium, High
X_{15}	Bilirubin	Low, Medium, High
X_{16}	Calcium	Low, Medium, High
X_{17}	Creatinine	Low, Medium, High
X_{18}	Potassium	Low, Medium, High
X_{19}	Sodium	Low, Medium, High
X_{20}	Blood hemoglobin	Low, Medium, High
X_{21}	Blood leukocytes	Low, Medium, High
X_{22}	Blood neutrophils	Low, Medium, High
X_{23}	Blood platelets	Low, Medium, High

References

1. Allison, P.D.: Missing Data. Sage University Papers Series on Quantitative Applications in the Social Sciences, pp. 07–136. Sage, Thousand Oaks (2001)
2. Breiman, L.: Random forests. Mach. Learn. **45**(1), 5–32 (2001). https://doi.org/10.1023/A:1010933404324
3. Brown, G., Pocock, A., Zhao, M.J., Luján, M.: Conditional likelihood maximisation: a unifying framework for information theoretic feature selection. J. Mach. Learn. Res. **13**(1), 27–66 (2012)
4. Cohen, J.: Statistical Power Analysis for the Behavioral Sciences, 2nd edn. Routledge Academic, Abingdon (1988)
5. Dunne, K., Cunningham, P., Azuaje, F.: Solutions to instability problems with sequential wrapper-based approaches to feature selection. Technical report, TCD-CS-2002-28, Trinity College Dublin, School of Computer Science (2002)
6. Fleuret, F.: Fast binary feature selection with conditional mutual information. J. Mach. Learn. Res. (JMLR) **5**, 1531–1555 (2004)

7. Fonseca, C.M., Fleming, P.J.: On the performance assessment and comparison of stochastic multiobjective optimizers. In: Voigt, H.-M., Ebeling, W., Rechenberg, I., Schwefel, H.-P. (eds.) PPSN 1996. LNCS, vol. 1141, pp. 584–593. Springer, Heidelberg (1996). https://doi.org/10.1007/3-540-61723-X_1022

8. Friedman, J.H.: Greedy function approximation: a gradient boosting machine. Ann. Stat. **29**(5), 1189–1232 (2001)

9. Kalousis, A., Prados, J., Hilario, M.: Stability of feature selection algorithms. In: IEEE International Conference on Data Mining, pp. 218–255 (2005)

10. Kalousis, A., Prados, J., Hilario, M.: Stability of feature selection algorithms: a study on high-dimensional spaces. Knowl. Inf. Syst. **12**, 95–116 (2007). https://doi.org/10.1007/s10115-006-0040-8

11. Kuncheva, L.I.: A stability index for feature selection. In: Artificial Intelligence and Applications (2007)

12. Lipkovich, I., Dmitrienko, A., D'Agostino Sr., R.B.: Tutorial in biostatistics: data-driven subgroup identification and analysis in clinical trials. Stat. Med. **36**(1), 136–196 (2017)

13. Mok, T.S., et al.: Gefitinib or carboplatin/paclitaxel in pulmonary adenocarcinoma. N. Engl. J. Med. **361**(10), 947–957 (2009)

14. Nogueira, S., Sechidis, K., Brown, G.: On the stability of feature selection algorithms. J. Mach. Learn. Res. **18**(174), 1–54 (2018)

15. Peng, H., Long, F., Ding, C.: Feature selection based on mutual information criteria of max-dependency, max-relevance, and min-redundancy. IEEE Trans. Pattern Anal. Mach. Intell. (PAMI) **27**(8), 1226–1238 (2005)

16. Sechidis, K., Papangelou, K., Metcalfe, P., Svensson, D., Weatherall, J., Brown, G.: Distinguishing prognostic and predictive biomarkers: an information theoretic approach. Bioinformatics **34**(19), 3365–3376 (2018)

17. Shi, L., Reid, L.H., Jones, W.D., et al.: The MicroArray Quality Control (MAQC) project shows inter-and intraplatform reproducibility of gene expression measurements. Nat. Biotechnol. **24**(9), 1151–61 (2006)

18. Yang, H.H., Moody, J.: Data visualization and feature selection: new algorithms for non-gaussian data. In: Neural Information Processing Systems, pp. 687–693 (1999)

19. Yu, L., Ding, C., Loscalzo, S.: Stable feature selection via dense feature groups. In: Proceedings of the 14th ACM SIGKDD International Conference on Knowledge Discovery and Data Mining, pp. 803–811. ACM (2008)

20. Zhang, M., et al.: Evaluating reproducibility of differential expression discoveries in microarray studies by considering correlated molecular changes. Bioinformatics **25**(13), 1662–1668 (2009)

Agnostic Feature Selection

Guillaume Doquet$^{(\boxtimes)}$ and Michèle Sebag

TAU, CNRS – INRIA – LRI – Université Paris-Saclay, Paris, France
{doquet,sebag}@lri.fr

Abstract. Unsupervised feature selection is mostly assessed along a supervised learning setting, depending on whether the selected features efficiently permit to predict the (unknown) target variable. Another setting is proposed in this paper: the selected features aim to efficiently recover the whole dataset. The proposed algorithm, called AGNOS, combines an AutoEncoder with structural regularizations to sidestep the combinatorial optimization problem at the core of feature selection. The extensive experimental validation of AGNOS on the scikit-feature benchmark suite demonstrates its ability compared to the state of the art, both in terms of supervised learning and data compression.

Keywords: Clustering and unsupervised learning · Feature selection · Interpretable models

1 Introduction

With the advent of big data, high-dimensional datasets are increasingly common, with potentially negative consequences on the deployment of machine learning algorithms in terms of (i) computational cost; (ii) accuracy (due to overfitting or lack of robustness related to e.g. adversarial examples (Goodfellow et al. 2015)); and (iii) poor interpretability of the learned models.

The first two issues can be handled through dimensionality reduction, based on feature selection (Nie et al. 2016; Chen et al. 2017; Li et al. 2018) or feature construction (Tenenbaum et al. 2000; Saul and Roweis 2003; Wiatowski and Bölcskei 2018). The interpretability of the learned models, an increasingly required property for ensuring *Fair, Accountable* and *Transparent* AI (Doshi-Velez and Kim 2017), however is hardly compatible with feature construction, and feature selection (FS) thus becomes a key ingredient of the machine learning pipeline.

This paper focuses on *unsupervised feature selection*. Most FS approaches tackle supervised FS (Chen et al. 2017), aimed to select features supporting a (nearly optimal) classifier. Quite the contrary, unsupervised feature selection is not endowed with a natural learning criterion. Basically, unsupervised FS approaches tend to define pseudo-labels, e.g. based on clusters, and falling back on supervised FS strategies, aim to select features conducive to identify the pseudo labels (more in Sect. 3). Eventually, unsupervised FS approaches are assessed within a supervised learning setting.

© Springer Nature Switzerland AG 2020
U. Brefeld et al. (Eds.): ECML PKDD 2019, LNAI 11906, pp. 343–358, 2020.
https://doi.org/10.1007/978-3-030-46150-8_21

Following LeCun's claim (LeCun 2016) that unsupervised learning constitutes the bulk of machine learning, and that any feature can in principle define a learning goal, this paper tackles *Agnostic Feature Selection* with the goal of *leaving no feature behind.* Specifically, an unsupervised FS criterion aimed to select a subset of features supporting the prediction of *every* initial feature, is proposed. The proposed AGNOS approach combines AutoEncoders with structural regularizations, and delegates the combinatorial optimization problem at the core of feature selection to a regularized data compression scheme (Sect. 2).

The contribution of the paper is threefold. Firstly, three regularization schemes are proposed and compared to handle the redundancy of the initial data representation. Informally, if the feature set includes duplicated features, the probability of selecting *one* copy of this feature should increase; but the probability of selecting several copies of any feature should be very low at all times. Several types of regularizations are proposed and compared to efficiently handle feature redundancy: regularization based on slack variables (AGNOS-S); L_2-L_1 regularization based on the AutoEncoder weights (AGNOS-W); and L_2-L_1 regularization based on the AutoEncoder gradients (AGNOS-G).

A second contribution is to show on the scikit-feature benchmark (Li et al. 2018) that AGNOS favorably compares with the state of the art (He et al. 2005; Zhao and Liu 2007; Cai et al. 2010; Li et al. 2012) considering the standard assessment procedure. A third contribution is to experimentally show the brittleness of this standard assessment procedure, demonstrating that it does not allow one to reliably compare unsupervised FS approaches (Sect. 5). The paper concludes with a discussion and some perspectives for further research.

Notations. In the following, the dataset is denoted $X \in \mathbb{R}^{n \times D}$, with n the number of samples and D the number of features. x_i (respectively f_j) denotes the i-th sample (resp. the j-th feature). The feature set is noted $F = (f_1, ..., f_D)$. $f_i(x_k)$ denotes the value taken by the i-th feature on the k-th sample.

2   AGNOS

The proposed approach relies on feature construction, specifically on AutoEncoders, to find a compressed description of the data. As said, feature construction does not comply with the requirement of interpretability. Therefore, AGNOS will use an enhanced learning criterion to retrieve the initial features most essential to approximate *all features*, in line with the goal of *leaving no feature behind.*

This section is organized as follows. For the sake of self-containedness, the basics of AutoEncoders are summarized in Sect. 2.1. A key AutoEncoder hyperparameter is the dimension of the latent representation (number of neurons in the hidden layer), which should be set according to the intrinsic dimension (ID) of the data for the sake of information preserving. Section 2.2 thus briefly introduces the state of the art in ID estimation.

In order to delegate the feature selection task to the AutoEncoder, the learning criterion is regularized to be robust w.r.t. redundant feature sets. A first option considers weight-based regularization along the lines of LASSO (Tibshirani 1996) and Group-LASSO (Yuan and Lin 2007) (Sect. 2.4). A second option uses a regularization defined on the gradients of the encoder ϕ (Sect. 2.4). A third option uses slack variables, inspired from (Leray and Gallinari 1999; Goudet et al. 2018) (Sect. 2.5).

2.1 AutoEncoders

AutoEncoders (AE) are a class of neural networks designed to perform data compression via feature construction. The encoder ϕ and the decoder ψ are trained to approximate identity, i.e. such that for each training point x

$$\psi \circ \phi(x) \approx x$$

in the sense of the Euclidean distance, where the dimension d of the hidden layer is chosen to avoid the trivial solution of $\phi = \psi = Id$. Formally,

$$\phi, \psi = \arg\min \sum_{i=1}^{n} \|x_i - \psi \circ \phi(x_i)\|_2^2$$

Letting f_i denote the i-th initial feature and $\hat{f}_i$ its reconstructed version, the mean square error (MSE) loss above can be rewritten as:

$$L(F) = \sum_{i=1}^{D} \|\hat{f}_i - f_i\|_2^2 \tag{1}$$

The use of AE to support feature selection raises two difficulties. The first one concerns the setting of the dimension d of the hidden layer (more below). The second one is the fact that the MSE loss (Eq. 1) is vulnerable to the redundancy of the initial description of the domain: typically when considering duplicated features, the effort devoted by the AE to the reconstruction of this feature increases with its number of duplicates. In other words, the dimensionality reduction criterion is biased to favor redundant features.

2.2 Intrinsic Dimension

The *intrinsic dimension* (ID) of a dataset is informally defined as *the minimal number of features necessary to represent the data without losing information.* Therefore, a necessary (though not sufficient) condition for the auto-encoder to preserve the information in the data is that the hidden layer is at least as large as the ID of the dataset. Many different mathematical formalizations of the concept of ID were proposed over the years, e.g. Hausdorff dimension (Gneiting et al. 2012) or box counting dimension (Falconer 2004). Both the ML and statistical physics communities thoroughly studied the problem of estimating the ID of a dataset empirically (Levina and Bickel 2005; Camastra and Staiano 2016; Facco et al. 2017), notably in relation with data visualization (Maaten and Hinton 2008; McInnes et al. 2018).

The best known linear ID estimation relies on Principal Component Analysis, considering the eigenvalues λ_i (with $\lambda_i > \lambda_{i+1}$) of the data covariance matrix and computing d such that the top-d eigenvalues retain a sufficient fraction τ of the data inertia ($\sum_{i=1}^{d} \lambda_i^2 = \tau \sum_{i=1}^{D} \lambda_i^2$). Another approach is based on the minimization of the stress (Cox and Cox 2000), that is, the bias between the distance of any two points in the initial representation, and their distance along a linear projection in dimension d. Non-linear approaches such as Isomap (Tenenbaum et al. 2000) or Locally Linear Embedding (Saul and Roweis 2003), respectively aim at finding a mapping on $\mathbb{R}^d$ such that it preserves the geodesic distance among points or the local barycentric description of the data.

The approach used in the following relies instead on the Poisson model of the number of points in the hyper-sphere in dimension d $\mathcal{B}(0, r)$, increasing like r^d (Levina and Bickel 2005; Facco et al. 2017). Considering for each point x its nearest neighbor x' and its 2nd nearest neighbor x'', defining the ratio $\mu(x) = \|x - x'\| / \|x - x''\|$ and averaging μ over all points in the dataset, it comes (Facco et al. 2017):

$$d = \frac{\log(1 - H(\mu))}{\log(\mu)} \tag{2}$$

with $log(1 - H(\mu))$ the linear function associating to $log(\mu_i)$ its normalized rank among the $\mu_1, \ldots \mu_n$ in ascending order.[1]

2.3 AGNOS

AGNOS proceeds like a standard AutoEncoder, with every feature being preliminarily normalized and centered. As the dimension of the latent representation is no less than the intrinsic dimension of the data by construction, and further assuming that the neural architecture of the AutoEncoder is complex enough, the AE defines a latent representation capturing the information of the data to the best possible extent (Eq. 1).

The key issue in AGNOS is twofold. The first question is to extract the initial features best explaining the latent features; if the latent features capture all the data information, the initial features best explaining the latent features will be sufficient to recover *all* features. The second question is to address the feature redundancy and prevent the AE to be biased in favor of the most redundant features.

Two approaches have been considered to address both goals. The former one is inspired from the well-known LASSO (Tibshirani 1996) and Group-LASSO

---

[1] That is, assuming with no loss of generality that

$$\mu_i < \mu_{i+1}$$

one approximates the curve $(log(1 - i/n), log(\mu_i))$ with a linear function, the slope of which is taken as approximation of d.

(Yuan and Lin 2007). These approaches are extended to the case of neural nets (below). The latter approach is based on a particular neural architecture, involving slack variables (Sect. 2.5). In all three cases, the encoder weight vector W is normalized to 1 after each training epoch ($\|W\|_2 = 1$), to ensure that the LASSO and slack penalizations are effective.

2.4 AGNOS with LASSO Regularization

This section first provides a summary of the basics of LASSO and group-LASSO. Their extension within the AutoEncoder framework to support feature selection is thereafter described.

LASSO and Group-LASSO. Considering a standard linear regression setting on the dataset $\{(x_i, y_i), x_i \in \mathbb{R}^D, y_i \in \mathbb{R}, i = 1 \ldots n\}$, the goal of finding the best weight vector $\beta \in \mathbb{R}^D$ minimizing $\sum_i \|y_i - \langle x_i, \beta \rangle\|^2$ is prone to overfitting in the large D, small n regime. To combat the overfitting issue, Tibshirani (1996) introduced the *LASSO* technique, which adds a L_1 penalization term to the optimization problem, parameter $\lambda > 0$ governing the severity of the penalization:

$$\beta^* = \arg\min_{\beta} \|\mathbf{y} - X\beta\|_2^2 + \lambda \|\beta\|_1 \tag{3}$$

Compared to the mainstream L_2 penalization (which also combats overfitting), the L_1 penalization acts as a sparsity constraint: every i-th feature with corresponding weight $\beta_i = 0$ can be omitted, and the L_1 penalization effectively draws the weight of many features to 0. Note that in counterpart the solution is no longer rotationally invariant (Ng 2004).

The *group LASSO* (Yuan and Lin 2007) and its many variants (Meier et al. 2008; Simon et al. 2013; Ivanoff et al. 2016) have been proposed to retain the sparsity property while preserving the desired invariances among the features. Let us consider a partition of the features in groups $G_1, \ldots, G_k$, the L_2-L_1 penalized regression setting reads:

$$\beta^* = \arg\min_{\beta} \|y - X\beta\|_2^2 + \lambda \sum_{i=1}^{k} \frac{1}{|G_i|} \sqrt{\sum_{j \in G_i} \beta_j^2} \tag{4}$$

where the L_1 part enforces the sparsity at the group level (as many groups are inactive as possible) while preserving the rotational invariance within each group.

AGNOS-**W: with L_2-L_1 Weight Regularization.** Under the assumption that all latent variables are needed to reconstruct the initial features (Sect. 2.2), denoting $\phi(F) = (\phi_1 \ldots, \phi_d)$ the encoder function, with $\phi_k = \sigma(\sum_{\ell=1}^{D} W_{\ell,k} f_\ell + W_{0,k})$ and $W_{i,j}$ the encoder weights, the impact of the i-th feature on the latent variables is visible through the weight vector $W_{i,\cdot}$. It thus naturally comes to define the L_2-L_1 penalization within the encoder as:

$$L(W) = \sum_{i=1}^{D} \sqrt{\sum_{k=1}^{d} W_{i,k}^2} = \sum_{i=1}^{D} \|W_{i,\cdot}\|_2$$

and the learning criterion of AGNOS-W (Algorithm 1) is accordingly defined as:

$$L(F) = \sum_{i=1}^{D} \|\hat{f}_i - f_i\|_2^2 + \lambda L(W) \tag{5}$$

with λ the penalization weight. The sparsity pressure exerted through penalty $L(W)$ will result in setting $W_{i,\cdot}$ to 0 whenever the contribution of the i-th initial variable is not necessary to reconstruct the initial variables, that is, when the i-th initial variable can be reconstructed from the other variables.

This learning criterion thus expectedly supports the selection of the most important initial variables. Formally, the score of the i-th feature is the maximum absolute value of $W_{i,j}$ for j varying in $1, \ldots D$:

$$Score_W(f_i) = \|W_{i,\cdot}\|_\infty \tag{6}$$

The rationale for considering the infinity norm of $W_{i,\cdot}$ (as opposed to its L_1 or L_2 norm) is based on the local informativeness of the feature (see also *MCFS* (Cai et al. 2010), Sect. 3): the i-th feature matters as long as it has a strong impact on at least one of the latent variables.

The above argument relies on the assumption that all latent variables are needed, which holds by construction.[2]

Input   : Feature set $F = \{f_1, ..., f_D\}$
Parameter: λ
Output   : Ranking of features in F
Normalize each feature to zero mean and unit variance.
Estimate intrinsic dimension $\widehat{ID}$ of F.
Initialize neural network with $d = \widehat{ID}$ neurons in the hidden layer.
Repeat
Backpropagate $L(F) = \sum_{i=1}^{D} \|\hat{f}_i - f_i\|_2^2 + \lambda \sum_{i=1}^{D} \|W_{i,\cdot}\|_2$
until convergence
Rank features by decreasing scores with $Score_W(f_i) = \|W_{i,\cdot}\|_\infty$.
          Algorithm 1: AGNOS-W

AGNOS-G: with L_2-L_1 **Gradient Regularization.** In order to take into account the overall flow of information from the initial variables f_i through the auto-encoder, another option is to consider the gradient of the encoder

---

[2] A question however is whether all latent variables are equally important. It might be that some latent variables are more important than others, and if an initial variable f_i matters a lot for an unimportant latent variable, the f_i relevance might be low. Addressing this concern is left for further work.

$\phi = (\phi_1 \ldots \phi_d)$. Varga et al. (2017), Alemu et al. (2018), Sadeghyan (2018) have recently highlighted the benefits of hidden layer gradient regularization for improving the robustness of the latent representation.

Along this line, another L_2-L_1 regularization term is considered:

$$L(\phi) = \sum_{i=1}^{D} \sqrt{\sum_{k=1}^{n} \sum_{j=1}^{d} \left(\frac{\partial \phi_j}{\partial f_i}(x_k) \right)^2}$$

and the learning criterion is likewise defined as:

$$L(F) = \sum_{i=1}^{D} ||\hat{f}_i - f_i||_2^2 + \lambda L(\phi) \tag{7}$$

The sparsity constraint now pushes toward cancelling all gradients of the ϕ_j w.r.t. an initial variable f_i. The sensitivity score derived from the trained auto-encoder, defined as:

$$\text{Score}_G(f_i) = \max_{1 \le j \le d} \sum_{k=1}^{n} \left(\frac{\partial \phi_j}{\partial f_i}(x_k) \right)^2 \tag{8}$$

is used to rank the features by decreasing score. The rationale for using the max instead of the average is same as for Score_W. Note that in the case of an encoder with a single hidden layer with *tanh* activation, one has:

$$\text{Score}_G(f_i) = \max_{1 \le j \le d} \sum_{k=1}^{n} \left(W_{i,j}(1 - \phi_j(x_k)^2) \right)^2 \tag{9}$$

Input   : Feature set $F = \{f_1, ..., f_D\}$
Parameter: λ
Output   : Ranking of features in F
Normalize each feature to zero mean and unit variance.
Estimate intrinsic dimension $\widehat{ID}$ of F.
Initialize neural network with $d = \widehat{ID}$ neurons in the hidden layer.
Repeat

Backpropagate $L(F) = \sum_{i=1}^{D} ||\hat{f}_i - f_i||_2^2 + \lambda \sum_{i=1}^{D} \sqrt{\sum_{k=1}^{n} \sum_{j=1}^{d} \left(\frac{\partial \phi_j}{\partial f_i}(x_k) \right)^2}$

until convergence
Rank features by decreasing scores with
$Score_G(f_i) = \max\limits_{j \in [1,...,d]} \sum\limits_{k=1}^{n} \left(\frac{\partial \phi_j}{\partial f_i}(x_k) \right)^2$.

Algorithm 2: AGNOS-G

2.5   AGNOS-S: With Slack Variables

A third version of AGNOS is considered, called AGNOS-S and inspired from Leray and Gallinari (1999); Goudet et al. (2018). The idea is to augment the neural

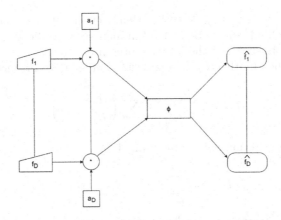

Fig. 1. Structure of the neural network used in AGNOS-S

architecture of the auto-encoder with a first layer made of *slack variables*. Formally, to each feature f_i is associated a (learned) coefficient a_i in $[0,1]$, and the encoder is fed with the vector $(a_i f_i)$ (Fig. 1). The learning criterion here is the reconstruction loss augmented with an L_1 penalization on the slack variables:

$$L(F) = \sum_{i=1}^{D} ||\hat{f}_i - f_i||_2^2 + \lambda \sum_{i=1}^{D} |a_i| \qquad (10)$$

Like in LASSO, the L_1 penalization pushes the slack variables toward a sparse vector. Eventually, the score of the i-th feature is set to $|a_i|$. This single valued coefficient reflects the contribution of f_i to the latent representation, and its importance to reconstruct the whole feature set.

Input   : Feature set $F = \{f_1, ..., f_D\}$
Parameter: λ
Output   : Ranking of features in F
Normalize each feature to zero mean and unit variance.
Estimate intrinsic dimension $\widehat{ID}$ of F.
Initialize neural network with $(a_1, ..., a_D) = \mathbf{1_D}$ and $d = \widehat{ID}$ neurons in the hidden layer.
Repeat
Backpropagate $L(F) = \sum_{i=1}^{D} ||\hat{f}_i - f_i||_2^2 + \lambda \sum_{i=1}^{D} |a_i|$
until convergence
Rank features by decreasing scores with $Score_S(f_i) = |a_i|$.
Algorithm 3: AGNOS-S

3   Related Work

This section briefly presents related work in unsupervised feature selection. We then discuss the position of the proposed AGNOS.

Most unsupervised FS algorithms rely on *spectral clustering theory* (Luxburg 2007). Let *sim* and M respectively denote a similarity metric on the instance space, e.g. $sim(x_i, x_j) = exp\{-\|x_i - x_j\|_2^2\}$ and M the $n \times n$ matrix with $M_{i,j} = sim(x_i, x_j)$. Let Δ be the diagonal degree matrix associated with M, i.e. $\Delta_{ii} = \sum_{k=1}^{n} M_{ik}$, and $L = \Delta^{-\frac{1}{2}}(\Delta - M)\Delta^{-\frac{1}{2}}$ the normalized Laplacian matrix associated with M.

Spectral clustering relies on the diagonalization of L, with λ_i (resp. ξ_i) the eigenvalues (resp. eigenvectors) of L, with $\lambda_i \leq \lambda_{i+1}$. Informally, the ξ_i are used to define soft cluster indicators (i.e. the degree to which x_k belongs to the i-the cluster being proportional to $\langle x_k, \xi_j \rangle$), with λ_k measuring the inter-cluster similarity (the smaller the better).

The general unsupervised clustering scheme proceeds by clustering the samples and falling back on supervised feature selection by considering the clusters as if they were classes; more precisely, the features are assessed depending on how well they separate clusters. Early unsupervised clustering approaches, such as the *Laplacian score* (He et al. 2005) and *SPEC* (Zhao and Liu 2007), score each feature depending on its average alignment with the dominant eigenvectors ($\langle f_i, \xi_k \rangle$).

A finer-grained approach is *MCFS* (Cai et al. 2010), that pays attention to the local informativeness of features and evaluates features on a per-cluster basis. Each feature is scored by its maximum alignment over the set of eigenvectors ($max_k \langle f_i, \xi_k \rangle$).

Letting A denote the feature importance matrix, with $A_{i,k}$ the relevance score of f_i for the k-th cluster, *NDFS* (Li et al. 2012) aims to actually reduce the number of features. The cluster indicator matrix Ξ (initialized from eigenvectors $\xi_1, \ldots, \xi_n$) is optimized jointly with the feature importance matrix A, with a sparsity constraint on the rows of A (few features should be relevant).

SOGFS (Nie et al. 2016) goes one step further and also learns the similarity matrix. After each learning iteration on Ξ and A, M is recomputed where the distance/similarity among the samples is biased to consider only the most important features according to A.

Discussion. A first difference between the previous approaches and the proposed AGNOS, is that the spectral clustering approaches (with the except of Nie et al. (2016)) rely on the Euclidean distance between points in $\mathbb{R}^D$. Due to the curse of dimensionality however, the Euclidean distance in high dimensional spaces is notoriously poorly informative, with all samples being far from each other (Duda et al. 2012). Quite the contrary, AGNOS builds upon a non-linear dimensionality reduction approach, mapping the data onto a low-dimensional space.

Another difference regards the robustness of the approaches w.r.t. the redundancy of the initial representation of the data. Redundant features can indeed distort the distance among points, and thus bias spectral clustering methods, with the except of Li et al. (2012); Nie et al. (2016). In practice, highly correlated features tend to get similar scores according to *Laplacian score*, *SPEC* and

MCFS. Furthermore, the higher the redundancy, the higher their score, and the more likely they will *all* be selected. This weakness is addressed by *NDFS* and *SOGFS* via the sparsity constraint on the rows of A, making it more likely that only one out of a cluster of redundant features be selected.

Finally, a main difference between the cited approaches and ours is the ultimate goal of feature selection, and the assessment of the methods. As said, unsupervised feature selection methods are assessed along a supervised setting: considering a target feature f^* (not in the feature set), the FS performance is measured from the accuracy of a classifier trained from the selected features. This assessment procedure thus critically depends on the relation between f^* and the features in the feature set. Quite the contrary, the proposed approach aims to data compression; it does not ambition to predict some target feature, but rather to approximate *every* feature in the feature set.

4   Experimental Setting

4.1   Goal of Experiments

Our experimental objective is threefold: we aim to compare the three versions of AGNOS to unsupervised FS baselines w.r.t. (i) supervised evaluation; and (ii) data compression. Thirdly, these experiments will serve to confirm or infirm our claim that the typical supervised evaluation scheme is unreliable.

4.2   Experimental Setup

Experiments are carried on eight datasets taken from the scikit-feature database (Li et al. 2018), an increasingly popular benchmark for feature selection (Chen et al. 2017). These datasets include face image, sound processing and medical data. In all datasets but one (Isolet), the number of samples is small w.r.t. the number of features D. Dataset size, dimensionality, number of classes, estimated intrinsic dimension[3] and data type are summarized in Table 1. The fact that the estimated ID is small compared to the original dimensionality for every dataset highlights the potential of feature selection for data compression.

AGNOS-W, AGNOS-G and AGNOS-S are compared to four unsupervised FS baselines: the *Laplacian score* (He et al. 2005), *SPEC* (Zhao and Liu 2007), *MCFS* (Cai et al. 2010) and *NDFS* (Li et al. 2012). All implementations have also been taken from the scikit-feature database, and all their hyperparameters have been set to their default values. In all experiments, the three variants of AGNOS are ran using a single hidden layer, *tanh* activation for both encoder and decoder, *Adam* (Kingma and Ba 2015) adjustment of the learning rate, initialized to 10^{-2}. Dimension d of the hidden layer is set for each dataset to its estimated intrinsic dimension $\widehat{ID}$. Conditionally to $d = \widehat{ID}$, preliminary

---

[3] The estimator from Facco et al. (2017) was used as this estimator is empirically less computationally expensive, requires less datapoints to be accurate, and is more resilient to high-dimensional noise than other ID estimators (Sect. 2.2).

Table 1. Summary of benchmark datasets

	# samples	# features	# classes	Estimated ID	Data type
arcene	200	10000	2	40	Medical
Isolet	1560	617	26	9	Sound processing
ORL	400	1024	40	6	Face image
pixraw10P	100	10000	10	4	Face image
ProstateGE	102	5966	2	23	Medical
TOX171	171	5748	4	15	Medical
warpPie10P	130	2400	10	3	Face image
Yale	165	1024	15	10	Face image

experiments have shown a low sensitivity of results w.r.t. penalization weight λ in the range $[10^{-1}, ..., 10^{1}]$, and degraded performance for values of λ far outside this range in either direction. Therefore, the value of λ is set to 1. The AE weights are initialized after Glorot and Bengio (2010). Each performance indicator is averaged on 10 runs with same setting; the std deviation is negligible (Doquet 2019).

For a given benchmark dataset, unsupervised FS is first performed with the four baseline methods and the three AGNOS variants, each algorithm producing a ranking S of the original features. Two performance indicators, one *supervised* and one *unsupervised*, are then computed to assess and compare the different rankings.

Following the typical supervised evaluation scheme, the first indicator is the K-means *clustering accuracy (ACC)* (He et al. 2005; Cai et al. 2010) for predicting the ground truth target f^*. In the following, clustering is performed considering the top $k = 100$ ranked features w.r.t. S, with $K = c$ clusters, with c the number of classes in f^*.

The second indicator corresponds to the unsupervised FS goal of recovering *every* initial feature f. For each $f \in F$, a 5-NearestNeighbor regressor is trained to fit f, where the neighbors of each point x are computed considering the Euclidean distance based on the top $k = 100$ ranked features w.r.t. S. The goodness-of-fit is measured via the R^2 score (a.k.a. *coefficient of determination*) $R^2(f, S) \in] - \infty, 1]$. The unsupervised performance of S is the individual R^2 score averaged over the *whole* feature set F (the higher the better):

$$Score(S) = \frac{1}{D} \sum_{j=1}^{D} R^2(f_j, S)$$

5   Experimental Results and Discussion

Supervised FS Assessment. Table 2 reports the ACC score for each selection method and dataset. On all datasets but *TOX171*, the highest ACC is achieved by one of the three AGNOS variants, showing the robustness of AGNOS compared with the baselines. On average, AGNOS-S outperforms AGNOS-W and AGNOS-G.

Table 2. Clustering ACC score on the ground truth labels, using the top 100 ranked features. Statistically significantly (according to a t-test with a p-value of 0.05) better results in boldface

	Arcene	Isolet	ORL	pixraw10P	ProstateGE	TOX171	warpPIE10P	Yale
AgnoS-S	**0.665**	0.536	**0.570**	**0.812**	**0.608**	0.404	0.271	0.509
AgnoS-W	0.615	**0.583**	0.548	0.640	0.588	0.292	0.358	0.382
AgnoS-G	0.630	0.410	0.528	0.776	0.569	0.357	**0.419**	**0.533**
Laplacian	0.660	0.482	0.550	0.801	0.578	0.450	0.295	0.442
MCFS	0.550	0.410	0.562	0.754	0.588	**0.480**	0.362	0.400
NDFS	0.510	0.562	0.538	0.783	0.569	0.456	0.286	0.442
SPEC	0.655	0.565	0.468	0.482	0.588	0.474	0.333	0.400

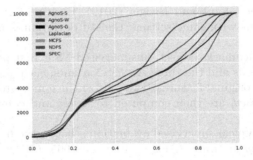

Fig. 2. Cumulative distribution functions of the R^2 scores of a 5-NearestNeighbors regressor using the top 100 ranked features on *Arcene*. If a point has coordinates (x, y), then the goodness-of-fit of the regressor is $\leq x$ or y initial features

Data Compression FS Assessment. Figure 2 depicts the respective cumulative distribution of the R^2 scores for all selection methods on the *Arcene* dataset. A first observation is that every FS algorithm leads to accurate fitting (R^2 score >0.8) for *some* features and poor fitting (R^2 score <0.2) on *some* other features. This empirical evidence suggests that the prediction based on the selected features is very sensitive w.r.t. the variable to predict, supporting our claim that supervised assessment of unsupervised FS (dealing with a *single* target) is unreliable.

Another observation is that FS algorithms differ in the number of poorly fitted features. R^2 scores <0.2 are achieved for less than 20% of features using any declination of AGNOS and more than 35% of features using MCFS, showing that AGNOS retains information about more features than MCFS on the *Arcene* dataset.

Table 3. Average of R^2 score of 5-NearestNeighbors regressor fitting *any* feature, using the top 100 ranked features. Statistically significantly (according to a t-test with a p-value of 0.05) better results in boldface

	Arcene	Isolet	ORL	pixraw10P	ProstateGE	TOX171	warpPIE10P	Yale
AgnoS-S	**0.610**	**0.763**	**0.800**	**0.855**	**0.662**	**0.581**	**0.910**	**0.703**
AgnoS-W	0.460	0.762	0.795	0.782	0.620	0.580	0.897	0.696
AgnoS-G	0.560	0.701	0.780	0.832	0.606	0.528	0.901	0.671
Laplacian	0.576	0.680	0.789	0.840	0.655	0.563	0.903	0.601
MCFS	0.275	0.720	0.763	0.785	0.634	0.549	0.870	0.652
NDFS	0.490	0.747	0.796	0.835	0.614	0.520	0.904	0.677
SPEC	0.548	0.733	0.769	0.761	0.646	0.559	0.895	0.659

Table 3 reports the average R^2 score of a 5-NearestNeighbors regressor on the whole feature set, for each FS algorithm and dataset. AGNOS-S is shown to achieve a higher mean R^2 score than AGNOS-W, AGNOS-G and all baselines on all datasets. These results empirically demonstrate that the selection subsets induced by AGNOS-S retain more information about the features *on average* than the baselines.

Notably, AGNOS-S generally outperforms AGNOS-W and AGNOS-G in a very significant manner, while AGNOS-W and AGNOS-G happen to be outperformed by the baselines. A tentative interpretation for this difference of performance among the three AGNOS variants is based on the key difference between the LASSO regularization and the slack variables. On one hand, the encoder weights in AGNOS-W (resp. the encoder gradients in AGNOS-G) are simultaneously responsible for producing the compressed data representation and enforcing sparsity among the original features. On the other hand, the slack variables in AGNOS-S are only subject to the sparsity pressure exerted by the L_1 penalty and have no other functional role. It is thus conjectured that the optimization of the slack variables can enforce sparse feature selection more efficiently than in AGNOS-W and AGNOS-G.

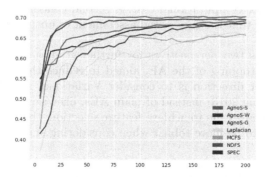

Fig. 3. Average R^2 score on *Yale* w.r.t. the number k of top ranked features considered

Sensitivity w.r.t. the Number of Selected Features. Figure 3 reports the R^2 score (averaged on the whole feature set) achieved by a 5-NearestNeighbors regressor on the *Yale* dataset for a number k of selected features in $[5, 10, \ldots, 200]$. AGNOS-S is shown to reliably outperform the baselines for every value of k (with the exception of $k \in \{5, 10\}$ where it is tied with NDFS).

Additionally, the *unsupervised* ranking of the considered FS algorithms appears to be stable w.r.t. k. This stability property does not hold using the ACC score, for which additional experiments have shown that the *supervised* ranking of FS algorithms is sensitive w.r.t. k (Doquet 2019), confirming again the brittleness of the mainstream supervised assessment of feature selection methods.

Table 4. Empirical runtimes on a single Nvidia Geforce GTX 1060 GPU, in seconds

	arcene	Isolet	ORL	pixraw10P	ProstateGE	TOX171	warpPie10P	Yale
AgnoS	265	25	29	242	145	143	31	14
Laplacian	<1	<1	<1	<1	<1	<1	<1	<1
SPEC	3	9	<1	2	1	2	1	<1
MCFS	<1	2	<1	<1	<1	<1	<1	<1
NDFS	130	16	17	193	80	76	18	7

A main limitation of the proposed approach is its computational time. Table 4 reports the empirical runtimes of the baselines and AGNOS. AGNOS is shown to be between 25% and 100% slower than NDFS, and several orders of magnitude slower than Laplacian score, SPEC and NDFS.

6   Conclusion and Perspectives

In this paper, we have introduced a novel unsupervised FS algorithm based on data compression. A main merit of the proposed AGNOS-S is to better recover the whole feature set (and the target feature) compared to the baselines, in counterpart for its higher computational cost. A second contribution of the paper is to empirically show that the supervised assessment of unsupervised FS methods is hardly reliable.

This work opens two perspectives for further studies. The first one is concerned with early stopping of the AE, aimed to reduce the computational cost of AGNOS. Another direction is to consider Variational AutoEncoders (VAE) (Kingma and Welling 2013) instead of plain AEs, likewise augmenting the VAE loss with an L_1 penalization to achieve feature selection; the expected advantage of VAEs would be to be more robust when considering small datasets.

Acknowledgments. We wish to thank Diviyan Kalainathan for many enjoyable discussions. We also thank the anonymous reviewers, whose comments helped to improve the experimental setting and the assessment of the method.

References

Alemu, H., Wu, W., Zhao, J.: Feedforward neural networks with a hidden layer regularization method. Symmetry **10**(10), 525 (2018)

Cai, D., Zhang, C., He, X.: Unsupervised feature selection for multi-cluster data. In: International Conference on Knowledge Discovery and Data Mining, pp. 333–342 (2010)

Camastra, F., Staiano, A.: Intrinsic dimension estimation: advances and open problems. Inf. Sci. **328**, 26–41 (2016)

Chen, J., Stern, M., Wainwright, M.J., Jordan, M.I.: Kernel feature selection via conditional covariance minimization. In: Advances in Neural Information Processing Systems, pp. 6946–6955 (2017)

Cox, T.F., Cox, M.A.: Multidimensional Scaling. Chapman and Hall/CRC, Boca Raton (2000)

Doquet, G.: Unsupervised feature selection. Ph.D. thesis, Université Paris-Sud (2019, to appear)

Doshi-Velez, F., Kim, B.: Towards a rigorous science of interpretable machine learning. arXiv:1702.08608 (2017)

Duda, R.O., Hart, P.E., Stork, D.G.: Pattern Classification. Wiley, Hoboken (2012)

Facco, E., d'Errico, M., Rodriguez, A., Laio, A.: Estimating the intrinsic dimension of datasets by a minimal neighborhood information. Nature **7**(1), 1–8 (2017)

Falconer, K.: Fractal Geometry: Mathematical Foundations and Applications. Wiley, Hoboken (2004)

Glorot, X., Bengio, Y.: Understanding the difficulty of training deep feedforward neural networks. In: International Conference on Artificial Intelligence and Statistics, pp. 249–256 (2010)

Gneiting, T., Ševčíková, H., Percival, D.B.: Estimators of fractal dimension: assessing the roughness of time series and spatial data. Stat. Sci. **27**, 247–277 (2012)

Goodfellow, I.J., Shlens, J., Szegedy, C.: Explaining and harnessing adversarial examples. In: International Conference on Learning Representations (2015)

Goudet, O., Kalainathan, D., Caillou, P., Guyon, I., Lopez-Paz, D., Sebag, M.: Learning functional causal models with generative neural networks. In: Escalante, H.J., et al. (eds.) Explainable and Interpretable Models in Computer Vision and Machine Learning. TSSCML, pp. 39–80. Springer, Cham (2018). https://doi.org/10.1007/978-3-319-98131-4_3

He, X., Cai, D., Niyogi, P.: Laplacian score for feature selection. In: Advances in Neural Information Processing Systems, pp. 507–514 (2005)

Ivanoff, S., Picard, F., Rivoirard, V.: Adaptive Lasso and group-lasso for functional poisson regression. J. Mach. Learn. Res. **17**(1), 1903–1948 (2016)

Kingma, D.P., Ba, J.: Adam: a method for stochastic optimization. In: International Conference on Learning Representations (2015)

Kingma, D.P., Welling, M.: Auto-encoding variational bayes. arXiv:1312.6114 (2013)

LeCun, Y.: The next frontier in AI: unsupervised learning. https://www.youtube.com/watch?v=IbjF5VjniVE (2016)

Leray, P., Gallinari, P.: Feature selection with neural networks. Behaviormetrika **26**(1), 145–166 (1999). https://doi.org/10.2333/bhmk.26.145

Levina, E., Bickel, P.J.: Maximum likelihood estimation of intrinsic dimension. In: Advances in Neural Information Processing Systems, pp. 777–784 (2005)

Li, J., et al.: Feature selection: a data perspective. ACM Comput. Surv. (CSUR) **50**(6), 1–45 (2018)

Li, Z., Yang, Y., Liu, Y., Zhou, X. Lu,, H.: Unsupervised feature selection using non-negative spectral analysis. In: AAAI (2012)

Von Luxburg, U.: A tutorial on spectral clustering. Stat. Comput. **17**(4), 395–416 (2007)

Maaten, L.V.D., Hinton, G.: Visualizing data using t-SNE. J. Mach. Learn. Res. **9**(Nov), 2579–2605 (2008)

McInnes, L., Healy, J., Melville, J.: UMAP: uniform manifold approximation and projection for dimension reduction. arXiv:1802.03426 (2018)

Meier, L., Van De Geer, S., Bühlmann, P.: The group Lasso for logistic regression. J. R. Stat.Soc.: Ser. B (Stat. Methodol.) **70**(1), 53–71 (2008)

Ng, A.Y.: Feature selection, l_1 vs. l_2 regularization, and rotational invariance. In: International Conference on Machine Learning (2004)

Nie, F., Zhu, W., Li, X.: Unsupervised feature selection with structured graph optimization. In: AAAI, pp. 1302–1308 (2016)

Sadeghyan, S.: A new robust feature selection method using variance-based sensitivity analysis. arXiv:1804.05092 (2018)

Saul, L.K., Roweis, S.T.: Think globally, fit locally: unsupervised learning of low dimensional manifolds. J. Mach. Learn. Res. **4**(Jun), 119–155 (2003)

Simon, N., Friedman, J., Hastie, T., Tibshirani, R.: A sparse-group Lasso. J. Comput. Graph. Stat. **22**(2), 231–245 (2013)

Tenenbaum, J.B., De Silva, V., Langford, J.C.: A global geometric framework for nonlinear dimensionality reduction. Science **290**(5500), 2319–2323 (2000)

Tibshirani, R.: Regression shrinkage and selection via the Lasso. J. R. Stat. Soc. Ser. B (Methodol.) **58**, 267–288 (1996)

Varga, D., Csiszárik, A., Zombori, Z.: Gradient regularization improves accuracy of discriminative models. arXiv:1712.09936 (2017)

Wiatowski, T., Bölcskei, H.: A mathematical theory of deep convolutional neural networks for feature extraction. IEEE Trans. Inf. Theory **64**(3), 1845–1866 (2018)

Yuan, M., Lin, Y.: Model selection and estimation in regression with grouped variables. J. R. Stat. Soc.: Ser. B (Stat. Methodol.) **68**(1), 49–67 (2007)

Zhao, Z., Liu, H.: Spectral feature selection for supervised and unsupervised learning. In: International Conference on Machine Learning (2007)

Social Networks and Graphs

User-Guided Clustering in Heterogeneous Information Networks via Motif-Based Comprehensive Transcription

Yu Shi[✉], Xinwei He, Naijing Zhang, Carl Yang, and Jiawei Han

University of Illinois at Urbana-Champaign, Urbana, IL, USA
{yushi2,xhe17,nzhang31,jiyang3,hanj}@illinois.edu

Abstract. Heterogeneous information networks (HINs) with rich semantics are ubiquitous in real-world applications. For a given HIN, many reasonable clustering results with distinct semantic meaning can simultaneously exist. User-guided clustering is hence of great practical value for HINs where users provide labels to a small portion of nodes. To cater to a broad spectrum of user guidance evidenced by different expected clustering results, carefully exploiting the signals residing in the data is potentially useful. Meanwhile, as one type of complex networks, HINs often encapsulate higher-order interactions that reflect the interlocked nature among nodes and edges. Network motifs, sometimes referred to as meta-graphs, have been used as tools to capture such higher-order interactions and reveal the many different semantics. We therefore approach the problem of user-guided clustering in HINs with network motifs. In this process, we identify the utility and importance of directly modeling higher-order interactions without collapsing them to pairwise interactions. To achieve this, we comprehensively transcribe the higher-order interaction signals to a series of tensors via motifs and propose the MoCHIN model based on joint non-negative tensor factorization. This approach applies to arbitrarily many, arbitrary forms of HIN motifs. An inference algorithm with speed-up methods is also proposed to tackle the challenge that tensor size grows exponentially as the number of nodes in a motif increases. We validate the effectiveness of the proposed method on two real-world datasets and three tasks, and MoCHIN outperforms all baselines in three evaluation tasks under three different metrics. Additional experiments demonstrated the utility of motifs and the benefit of directly modeling higher-order information especially when user guidance is limited. (The code and the data are available at https://github.com/NoSegfault/MoCHIN.)

Y. Shi, X. He, and N. Zhang—These authors contributed equally to this work.

Electronic supplementary material The online version of this chapter (https://doi.org/10.1007/978-3-030-46150-8_22) contains supplementary material, which is available to authorized users.

© Springer Nature Switzerland AG 2020
U. Brefeld et al. (Eds.): ECML PKDD 2019, LNAI 11906, pp. 361–377, 2020.
https://doi.org/10.1007/978-3-030-46150-8_22

Keywords: Heterogeneous information networks · User-guided clustering · Higher-order interactions · Network motifs · Non-negative tensor factorization

1   Introduction

Heterogeneous information network (HIN) has been shown to be a powerful approach to model linked objects with informative type information [21,23,24,28]. Meanwhile, the formation of complex networks is often partially attributed to the higher-order interactions among objects in real-world scenarios [2,18,35], where the "players" in the interactions are nodes in the network. To reveal such higher-order interactions, researchers have since been using network motifs. Leveraging motifs is shown to be useful in tasks such as clustering [2,36], ranking [37] and representation learning [20].[1]

Clustering is a traditional and fundamental task in network mining [7]. In the context of an HIN with rich semantics, reasonable clustering results with distinct semantic meaning can simultaneously exist. In this case, personalized clustering with user guidance can be of great practical value [6,10,17,21,29]. Carefully exploiting the fine-grained semantics in HINs via modeling higher-order interaction is a promising direction for such user-guided clustering since it could potentially generate a richer pool of subtle signals to better fit different users' guidance, especially when users cannot provide too much guidance and the supervision is hence weak.

However, it is non-trivial to develop a principled HIN clustering method that exploits signals revealed by motifs as comprehensively as possible. This is because most network clustering algorithms are based on signals derived from the relatedness between each pair of nodes [7]. While a body of research has shown that it is beneficial for clustering methods to derive features for each node pair using motifs [5,8,10,16,38], this approach essentially collapses a higher-order interaction into pairwise interactions, which is an irreversible process. Such irreversible process is not always desirable as it could cause information loss. For example, consider a motif instance involving three nodes – A, B, and C. After collapsing the higher-order interaction among A, B, and C into pairwise interactions, we are still able to sense the tie between A and C, but such a tie would no longer depend on B – a potentially critical semantic facet of the relationship between A and C. Such subtle information could be critical to distinguishing different user guidance. We will further discuss this point by real-world example in Sect. 4 and experiments in Sect. 7. Furthermore, although it is relatively easy to find semantically meaningful HIN motifs [5,8], motifs in HINs can have more complex topology compared to motifs in homogeneous networks do [2,36]. In order

---

[1] Higher-order interaction is sometimes used interchangeably with high-order interaction in the literature, and clustering using signals from higher-order interactions is referred to as higher-order clustering [2,36]. Motifs in the context of HINs are sometimes called the meta-graphs, and we opt for motifs primarily because meta-graphs have been used under a different definition in the study of clustering [27].

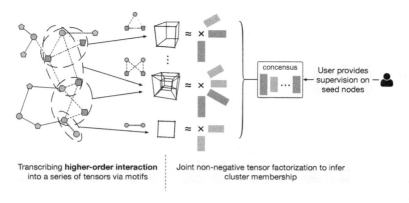

Transcribing **higher-order interaction**   Joint non-negative tensor factorization to infer
into a series of tensors via motifs   cluster membership

Fig. 1. Overview of the proposed method MoCHIN that directly models all nodes in higher-order interactions where each type of nodes in the HIN corresponds to a color and a shape in the figure.

to fully unleash the power of HIN motifs and exploit the signals extracted by them, we are motivated to propose a method that applies to arbitrary forms of HIN motifs.

To avoid such information loss with a method applicable to arbitrary forms of motifs, we propose to directly model the higher-order interactions by comprehensively transcribing them into a series of tensors. As such, the complete information of higher-order interactions is preserved. Based on this intuition, we propose the MoCHIN model, short for **Mo**tif-based **C**lustering in **HIN**s, with an overview in Fig. 1. MoCHIN first transcribes information revealed by motifs into a series of tensors and then performs clustering by joint non-negative tensor decomposition with an additional mechanism to reflect user guidance.

In this direction, an additional challenge arises from inducing tensor via corresponding motif – the size of the tensor grows exponentially as the number of nodes involved in the motif increases. Fortunately, motif instances are often sparse in real-world networks just as the number of edges is usually significantly smaller than the number of node pairs in a large real-world network. This fact is to be corroborated in Sect. 3 of the supplementary file. We hence develop an inference algorithm taking advantage of the sparsity of the tensors and the structure of the proposed MoCHIN model.

Lastly, we summarize our contributions as follows: (i) we identify the utility of modeling higher-order interaction without collapsing it into pairwise interactions to avoid losing the rich and subtle information captured by motifs; (ii) we propose the MoCHIN model that captures higher-order interaction via motif-based comprehensive transcription; (iii) we develop an inference algorithm and speed-up methods for MoCHIN; (iv) experiments on two real-world HINs and three tasks demonstrated the effectiveness of the proposed method as well as the utility of the tensor-based modeling approach in user-guided HIN clustering.

2   Related Work

Network Motifs and Motifs in HINs. Network motifs, or graphlets, are usually used to identify higher-order interactions [2, 18, 35, 36]. One popular research direction on network motifs has centered on efficiently counting motif instances such as triangles and more complex motifs [1, 26]. Applications of motifs have also been found in tasks such as network partition and clustering [2, 12, 36, 39] as well as ranking [37].

In the context of HINs, network motifs are sometimes referred to as meta-graphs or meta-structures and have been studied recently [5, 8, 10, 15, 16, 20, 33, 38]. Many of these works study pairwise relationship such as relevance or similarity [5, 8, 15, 16, 38], and some other address the problem of representation learning [20, 33] and graph classification [34]. Some of these prior works define meta-graphs or meta-structures to be directed acyclic graphs [8, 38], whereas we do not enforce this restriction on the definition of HIN motifs.

Clustering in Heterogeneous Information Networks. As a fundamental data mining problem, clustering has been studied for HINs [13, 21, 22, 28–30]. One line of HIN clustering study leverages the synergetic effect of simultaneously tackling ranking and clustering [22, 30]. Clustering on specific types of HINs such as those with additional attributes has also been studied [13]. Wu et al. [32] resort to tensor for HIN clustering. Their solution employs one tensor for one HIN and does not model different semantics implied by different structural patterns.

User guidance brings significantly more potentials to HIN clustering by providing a small portion of seeds [21, 29], which enables users to inject intention of clustering. To reveal the different semantics in an HIN, pioneering works exploit the meta-path, a special case of the motif, and reflect user-guidance by using the corresponding meta-paths [17, 29].

To the best of our knowledge, a recent preprint [3] is the only paper that tackles HIN clustering and applies to arbitrary forms of HIN motifs, which is not specifically designed for the scenario with user guidance. Given an HIN and a motif (*i.e.*, typed-graphlet), this method filter the original adjacent matrix to derive the typed-graphlet adjacency matrix and then perform spectral clustering on the latter matrix. While being able to filter out information irrelevant to the given motif, this method essentially exploits the edge-level pairwise information in the adjacent matrix rather than directly modeling each occurrence of higher-order interaction. Other related works include a meta-graph–guided random walk algorithm [10], which is shown to outperform using only meta-paths. Note that this method cannot distinguish motif AP4TPA from meta-path APTPA, which are to be introduced in Sect. 4. Sankar et al. [20] propose a convolutional neural network method based on motifs which can potentially be used for user-guided HIN clustering. This approach restricts the motifs of interest to those with a target node, a context node, and auxiliary nodes. Gujral et al. [6] propose a

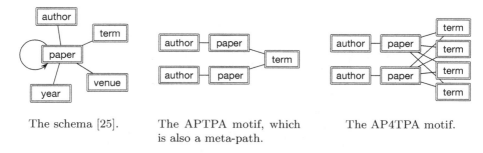

The schema [25].   The APTPA motif, which   The AP4TPA motif.
                          is also a meta-path.

Fig. 2. Examples of schema and motif in the DBLP network.

method based on tensor constructed from stacking a set of adjacency matrices, which can successfully reflect user guidance and different semantic aspects. This method essentially leverages features derived for node pairs.

We additionally review the related work on matrix and tensor factorization for clustering in the supplementary file for this paper. These studies are relevant but cannot be directly applied to the scenario of higher-order HIN clustering.

3   Preliminaries

In this section, we define related concepts and notations.

Definition 1 (Heterogeneous information network and schema [28]). *An information network is a directed graph $G = (\mathcal{V}, \mathcal{E})$ with a node type mapping $\varphi : \mathcal{V} \to \mathcal{T}$ and an edge type mapping $\psi : \mathcal{E} \to \mathcal{R}$. When $|\mathcal{T}| > 1$ or $|\mathcal{R}| > 1$, the network is referred to as a **heterogeneous information network (HIN)**. The **schema** of an HIN is an abstraction of the meta-information of the node types and edge types of the given HIN.*

As an example, Fig. 2a illustrates the schema of the DBLP network to be used in Sect. 7. We denote all nodes with the same type $t \in \mathcal{T}$ by $\mathcal{V}_t$.

Definition 2 (HIN motif and HIN motif instance). *In an HIN $G = (\mathcal{V}, \mathcal{E})$, an **HIN motif** is a structural pattern defined by a graph on the type level with its node being a node type of the original HIN and an edge being an edge type of the given HIN. Additional constraints can be optionally added such as two nodes in the motif cannot be simultaneously matched to the same node instance in the given HIN. Further given an HIN motif, an **HIN motif instance** under this motif is a subnetwork of the HIN that matches this pattern.*

Figure 2c gives an example of a motif in the DBLP network with four distinct terms referred to as $AP4TPA$. If a motif is a path graph, it is also called a meta-path [29]. The motif, $APTPA$, in Fig. 2b is one such example.

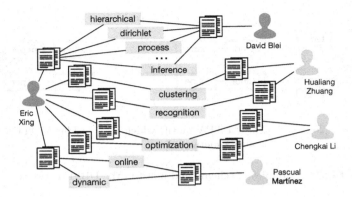

Fig. 3. A subnetwork of DBLP. According to the ground truth data, *Eric Xing* and *David Blei* were graduated from the same research group.

Definition 3 (Tensor, k-mode product, mode-k matricization [19]). *A **tensor** is a multidimensional array. For an N-th-order tensor $\mathcal{X} \in \mathbb{R}^{d_1 \times \dots \times d_N}$, we denote its $(j_1, \dots, j_N)$ entry by $\mathcal{X}_{j_1, \dots, j_N}$. The k-**mode product** of $\mathcal{X}$ and a matrix $\mathbf{A} \in \mathbb{R}^{d_k \times d}$ is denoted by $\mathcal{Y} = \mathcal{X} \times_k \mathbf{A}$, where $\mathcal{Y} \in \mathbb{R}^{d_1 \times \dots \times d_{k-1} \times d \times d_{k+1} \times \dots \times d_N}$, and $\mathcal{Y}_{\dots, j_{k-1}, j, j_{k+1}, \dots} = \sum_{s=1}^{d_k} \mathcal{X}_{\dots, j_{k-1}, s, j_{k+1}, \dots} \mathbf{A}_{s,j}$. We denote matrix $\mathcal{X}_{(k)} \in \mathbb{R}^{(d_1 \cdot \dots \cdot d_{k-1} \cdot d_{k+1} \cdot \dots \cdot d_N) \times d_k}$ the mode-k **matricization**, i.e., mode-k unfolding, of the tensor $\mathcal{X}$, where the i-th column of $\mathcal{X}_{(k)}$ is obtained by vectorizing the $(n-1)$-th order tensor $\mathcal{X}_{\dots, :, j, :, \dots}$ with j on the k-th index.*

For simplicity, we denote $\mathcal{X} \times_{i=1}^{N} \mathbf{A}_i := \mathcal{X} \times_1 \mathbf{A}_1 \times_2 \dots \times_N \mathbf{A}_N$. Additionally, we define $[\otimes_{i=1}^{N \setminus k} \mathbf{A}_i] := \mathbf{A}_1 \otimes \dots \otimes \mathbf{A}_{k-1} \otimes \mathbf{A}_{k+1} \otimes \dots \otimes \mathbf{A}_N$, where $\otimes$ is the Kronecker product [19].

Lastly, we introduce a useful lemma that converts the norm of the difference between two tensors to that between two matrices.

Lemma 4 ([4]). *For all $k \in \{1, 2, \dots, N\}$,*

$$\left\| \mathcal{X} - \mathcal{Y} \times_{i=1}^{N} \mathbf{A}_i \right\|_F = \left\| \mathcal{X}_{(k)} - \mathbf{A}_k \mathcal{Y}_{(k)} [\otimes_{i=1}^{N \setminus k} \mathbf{A}_i]^\top \right\|_F,$$

where $\|\cdot\|_F$ is the Frobenius norm.

4   Higher-Order Interaction in Real-World Dataset

In this section, we use a real-world example to motivate the design of our method that aims to comprehensively model higher-order interactions revealed by motifs.

DBLP is a bibliographical network in the computer science domain [31] that contains nodes with type author, paper, term, *etc.* In Fig. 3, we plot out a subnetwork involving five authors: *Eric Xing, David Blei, Hualiang Zhuang, Chengkai Li,* and *Pascual Martinez.* According to the ground truth labels, *Xing* and *Blei* graduated from the same research group, while the other three authors graduated from other groups. Under meta-path $APTPA$, one would be able to find many path instances from $Xing$ to authors from different groups. However, if we use motif $AP4TPA$, motif instances can only be found over $Xing$ and $Blei$, but not between $Xing$ and authors from other groups. This implies motifs can provide more subtle information than meta-paths do, and if a user wishes to cluster authors by research groups, motif $AP4TPA$ can be informative.

More importantly, if we look into the $AP4TPA$ motif instances that are matched to $Xing$ and $Blei$, the involved terms such as $dirichlet$ are very specific to their group's research interest. In other words, $dirichlet$ represents an important semantic facet of the relationship between $Xing$ and $Blei$. Modeling the higher-order interaction among $dirichlet$ and other nodes can therefore kick in more information. If one only used motifs to generate pairwise or edge-level signals, such information would be lost. In Sect. 7, we will further quantitatively validate the utility of comprehensively modeling higher-order interactions.

5   The MoCHIN Model

In this section, we describe the proposed model with an emphasis on its intention to comprehensively model higher-order interaction while availing user guidance.

Revisit on Clustering by Non-negative Matrix Factorization. Non-negative matrix factorization (NMF) has been a popular method clustering [11,14]. Usually with additional constraints or regularization, the basic NMF-based algorithm solves the following optimization problem for given adjacency matrix M

$$\min_{\mathbf{V}_1, \mathbf{V}_2 \geq 0} \left\| \mathbf{M} - \mathbf{V}_1^\top \mathbf{V}_2 \right\|_F^2, \tag{1}$$

where $\|\cdot\|_F$ is the Frobenius norm, $\mathbf{A} \geq 0$ denotes matrix $\mathbf{A}$ is non-negative, and $\mathbf{V}_1$, $\mathbf{V}_2$ are two $C \times |\mathcal{V}|$ matrices with C being the number of clusters. In this model, the j-th column of $\mathbf{V}_1$ or that of $\mathbf{V}_2$ gives the inferred cluster membership of the j-th node in the network.

Single-Motif–Based Clustering in HINs. Recall that an edge essentially characterizes the pairwise interaction between two nodes. To model higher-order interaction without collapsing it into pairwise interactions, a natural solution to clustering is using the inferred cluster membership of all involved nodes to reconstruct the existence of each motif instance. This solution can be formulated by non-negative tensor factorization (NTF), and studies on NTF per se and clustering via factorizing a single tensor can be found in the literature [19].

Specifically, given a single motif m with N nodes having node type $t_1, \ldots, t_N$ of the HIN, we transcribe the higher-order interaction revealed by this motif to a N-th–order tensor $\mathcal{X}$ with dimension $|\mathcal{V}_{t_1}| \times \ldots \times |\mathcal{V}_{t_N}|$. We set the $(j_1, \ldots, j_N)$ entry of $\mathcal{X}$ to 1 if a motif instance exists over the following n nodes: j_1-th of $\mathcal{V}_{t_1}$, $\ldots$, j_N-th of $\mathcal{V}_{t_N}$; and set it to 0 otherwise. By extending Eq. (1), whose

Table 1. Summary of symbols

Symbol	Definition	Symbol	Definition
$\mathcal{V}, \mathcal{E}$	The set of nodes and the set of edges	$\mathcal{X}^{(m)}$	The tensor constructed from motif m
φ, ψ	The node and the edge type mapping	$\mathbf{M}^{(t)}$	The seed mask matrix for node type t
$\mathcal{T}, \mathcal{R}, \mathcal{M}$	The set of node types, edge types, and candidate motifs	$\mathbf{V}_i^{(m)}$	The cluster membership matrix for the i-th node in motif m
$\mathcal{V}_t$	The set of all nodes with type t	$\mathbf{V}_t^*$	The consensus matrix for node type t
$o(m)$	The number of nodes in motif $m \in \mathcal{M}$	$\boldsymbol{\mu}$	The vector $(\mu_1, \ldots, \mu_{|\mathcal{M}|})$ of motif weights
C	The number of clusters	$\times_k$	The mode-k product of a tensor and a matrix
λ, θ, ρ	The hyperparameters	$\otimes$	The Kronecker product of two matrices

objective is equivalent to $\left\| \mathbf{M} - \mathbf{V}_1^\top \mathbf{I} \mathbf{V}_2 \right\|_F^2$ with $\mathbf{I}$ being the identity matrix, we can approach the clustering problem by solving

$$\min_{\mathbf{V}_1, \mathbf{V}_2 \geq 0} \left\| \mathcal{X} - \mathcal{I} \times_{i=1}^N \mathbf{V}_i \right\|_F^2 + \lambda \sum_{i=1}^N \|\mathbf{V}_i\|_1 , \tag{2}$$

where $\mathcal{I}$ is the N-th order identity tensor with dimension $C \times \ldots \times C$, $\|\cdot\|_1$ is the entry-wise l-1 norm introduced as regularization to avoid trivial solution, and λ is the regularization coefficient. We also note that this formulation is essentially the CP decomposition [19] with additional l-1 regularization and non-negative constraints. We write this formula in a way different from its most common form for notation convenience in the inference section (Sect. 6) considering the presence of regularization and constraints.

Proposed Model for Motif-Based Clustering in HINs. Real-world HINs often contain rich and diverse semantic facets due to its heterogeneity [25,28,29]. To reflect the different semantic facets of an HIN, a set $\mathcal{M}$ of more than one candidate motifs are usually necessary for the task of user-guided clustering. With additional clustering seeds provided by users, the MoCHIN model selects the motifs that are both meaningful and pertinent to the seeds.

To this end, we assign motif-specific weights $\boldsymbol{\mu} = (\mu_1, \ldots, \mu_{|\mathcal{M}|})$, such that $\sum_{m \in \mathcal{M}} \mu_m = 1$ and $\mu_m \geq 0$ for all $m \in \mathcal{M}$. Denote $\mathcal{X}^{(m)}$ the tensor for motif m, $\mathbf{V}_i^{(m)}$ the cluster membership matrix for the i-th node in motif m, $o(m)$ the number of nodes in motif m, and $\varphi(m, i)$ the node type of the i-th node in motif m. For each node type $t \in \mathcal{T}$, we put together cluster membership matrices concerning this type and motif weights to construct the consensus matrix

$$\mathbf{V}_t^* := \sum_{\varphi(m,i)=t} \frac{\mu_m \mathbf{V}_i^{(m)}}{\sum_{i'=1}^{o(m)} \mathbb{1}_{[\varphi(m,i')=\varphi(m,i)]}}, \text{ where } \mathbb{1}_{[P]} \text{ equals to 1 if } P \text{ is true and 0}$$

otherwise. With this notation, $\sum_{i'=1}^{o(m)} \mathbb{1}_{[\varphi(m,i')=\varphi(m,i)]}$ is simply the number of nodes in motif m that are of type t.

Furthermore, we intend to let (i) each cluster membership $\mathbf{V}_i^{(m)}$ be close to its corresponding consensus matrix $\mathbf{V}_{\varphi(m,i)}^*$ and (ii) the consensus matrices not assign seed nodes to the wrong cluster. We hence propose the following objective with the third and the fourth term modeling the aforementioned two intentions

$$\mathcal{O} = \sum_{m \in \mathcal{M}} \left\| \mathcal{X}^{(m)} - \mathcal{I}^{(m)} \times_{i=1}^{o(m)} \mathbf{V}_i^{(m)} \right\|_F^2 + \lambda \sum_{m \in \mathcal{M}} \sum_{i=1}^{o(m)} \left\| \mathbf{V}_i^{(m)} \right\|_1$$
$$+ \theta \sum_{m \in \mathcal{M}} \sum_{i=1}^{o(m)} \left\| \mathbf{V}_i^{(m)} - \mathbf{V}_{\varphi(m,i)}^* \right\|_F^2 + \rho \sum_{t \in \mathcal{T}} \left\| \mathbf{M}^{(t)} \circ \mathbf{V}_t^* \right\|_F^2, \tag{3}$$

where $\circ$ is the Hadamard product and $\mathbf{M}^{(t)}$ is the seed mask matrix for node type t. Its (i,c) entry $\mathbf{M}_{i,c}^{(t)} = 1$ if the i-th node of type t is a seed node and it should not be assigned to cluster c, and $\mathbf{M}_{i,c}^{(t)} = 0$ otherwise.

Finally, solving the problem of HIN clustering by modeling higher-order interaction and automatically selecting motifs is converted to solving the following optimization problem with Δ being the standard simplex

$$\min_{\{\mathbf{V}_i^{(m)} \geq 0\}, \mu \in \Delta} \mathcal{O}. \tag{4}$$

6   The Inference Algorithm

In this section, we first describe the algorithm for solving the optimization problem as in Eq. (4). Then, a series of speed-up tricks are introduced to circumvent the curse of dimensionality, so that the complexity is governed no longer by the dimension of the tensors but by the number of motif instances in the network.

Update $\mathbf{V}_k^{(l)}$ and μ. Each clustering membership matrix $\mathbf{V}_k^{(l)}$ with non-negative constraints is involved in all terms of the objective function (Eq. (3)), where $l \in \mathcal{M}$ and $k \in \{1, \ldots, o(l)\}$. We hence develop multiplicative update rules for $\mathbf{V}_k^{(l)}$ that guarantees monotonic decrease at each step, accompanied by projected gradient descent (PGD) to find global optimal of $\mu = [\mu_1, \ldots, \mu_{|\mathcal{M}|}]^\top$. Overall, we solve the optimization problem by alternating between $\{\mathbf{V}_k^{(l)}\}$ and μ.

To update $\mathbf{V}_k^{(l)}$ when $\{\mathbf{V}_i^{(m)}\}_{(m,i)\neq(l,k)}$ and μ are fixed under non-negative constraints, we derive the following theorem. For notation convenience, we further denote $\mathbf{V}_t^* = \sum_{\varphi(m,i)=t} \eta_i^m \mathbf{V}_i^{(m)}$, where $\eta_i^m := \frac{\mu_m}{\sum_{i'=1}^{o(m)} \mathbb{1}_{[\varphi(m,i')=\varphi(m,i)]}}$.

Algorithm 1: The MoCHIN inference algorithm

    Input : $\{\mathcal{X}^{(m)}\}$, supervision $\mathbf{M}^{(t)}$, the number of clusters C, hyperparameters
              θ, ρ, and λ
    Output: the cluster membership matrices $\{\mathbf{V}_t^*\}$

1 **begin**
2   **while** *not converged* **do**
3   **for** $m \in \mathcal{M}$ **do**
4   **while** *not converged* **do**
5   **for** $i \in \{1, \ldots, o(m)\}$ **do**
6   Find local optimum of $\mathbf{V}_i^{(m)}$ by Eq. (5).

7   Find global optimum of $\boldsymbol{\mu}$ by PGD.

Theorem 5. *The following update rule for* $\mathbf{V}_k^{(l)}$ *monotonically decreases the objective function.*

$$
\mathbf{V}_k^{(l)} \leftarrow \mathbf{V}_k^{(l)} \circ \left[\frac{\mathcal{X}_{(k)}^{(l)}[\otimes_{i=1}^{o(l)\backslash k}\mathbf{V}_i^{(l)}]\mathcal{I}_{(k)}^{(l)\top} + \theta(1-\eta_k^l)(\mathbf{V}_{\varphi(l,k)}^* - \eta_k^l\mathbf{V}_k^{(l)})}{\mathbf{V}_k^{(l)}\mathcal{I}_{(k)}^{(l)}[\otimes_{i=1}^{o(l)\backslash k}\mathbf{V}_i^{(l)}]^\top[\otimes_{i=1}^{o(l)\backslash k}\mathbf{V}_i^{(l)}]\mathcal{I}_{(k)}^{(l)\top} + \rho\eta_k^l\mathbf{M}^{\varphi(l,k)}\circ\mathbf{V}_{\varphi(l,k)}^*}\right.
$$
$$
\left. \frac{+\theta\eta_k^l\sum_{\varphi(m,i)=\varphi(l,k)}^{(m,i)\neq(l,k)}[\mathbf{V}_i^{(m)} - \mathbf{V}_{\varphi(l,k)}^* + \eta_k^l\mathbf{V}_k^{(l)}]^+}{+\theta\eta_k^l\sum_{\varphi(m,i)=\varphi(l,k)}^{(m,i)\neq(l,k)}([\mathbf{V}_i^{(m)} - \mathbf{V}_{\varphi(l,k)}^* + \eta_k^l\mathbf{V}_k^{(l)}]^- + \eta_k^l\mathbf{V}_k^{(l)}) + \theta(1-\eta_k^l)^2\mathbf{V}_k^{(l)} + \lambda}\right]^{\frac{1}{2}},
$$
$$
\tag{5}
$$

where for any matrix $\mathbf{A}$, $[\mathbf{A}]^+ := \frac{|\mathbf{A}|+\mathbf{A}}{2}$, $[\mathbf{A}]^- := \frac{|\mathbf{A}|-\mathbf{A}}{2}$.

We refer the proof of this theorem to Sect. 1 of the supplementary file. For fixed $\{\mathbf{V}_i^{(m)}\}$, the objective function Eq. (3) is convex with respect to $\boldsymbol{\mu}$. We therefore use PGD to update $\boldsymbol{\mu}$, where the gradient can be analytically derived with straightforward calculation.

Computational Speed-Up. Unlike the scenario where researchers solve the NTF problem with tensors of order independent of the applied dataset, our problem is specifically challenging because the tensor size grows exponentially with the tensor order. For instance, the AP4TPA motif discussed in Sect. 4 is one real-world example involving 8 nodes, which leads to an 8-th order tensor.

In the proposed inference algorithm, the direct computation of three terms entails complexity subject to the size of the tensor: (i) the first term in the numerator of Eq. (5), $\mathcal{X}_{(k)}^{(l)}[\otimes_{i=1}^{o(l)\backslash k}\mathbf{V}_i^{(l)}]\mathcal{I}_{(k)}^{(l)\top}$, (ii) the first term in the denominator of Eq. (5), $\mathbf{V}_k^{(l)}\mathcal{I}_{(k)}^{(l)}[\otimes_{i=1}^{o(l)\backslash k}\mathbf{V}_i^{(l)}]^\top [\otimes_{i=1}^{o(l)\backslash k}\mathbf{V}_i^{(l)}]\mathcal{I}_{(k)}^{(l)\top}$, and (iii) the first term of the objective function Eq. (3), $\left\|\mathcal{X}^{(m)} - \mathcal{I}^{(m)}\times_{i=1}^{o(m)}\mathbf{V}_i^{(m)}\right\|_F^2$. Fortunately, all these terms can be significantly simplified by exploiting the composition of dense matrix $[\otimes_{i=1}^{o(l)\backslash k}\mathbf{V}_i^{(l)}]\mathcal{I}_{(k)}^{(l)\top}$ and the sparsity of tensor $\mathcal{X}^{(l)}$ ($\mathcal{X}^{(m)}$).

Consider the example that motif $l \in \mathcal{M}$ involves 5 nodes, each node type has 10,000 node instances, and the nodes are to be clustered into 10 clusters. Then the induced dense matrix $[\otimes_{i=1}^{o(l)\backslash k}\mathbf{V}_i^{(l)}]\mathcal{I}_{(k)}^{(l)\top}$ would have $\prod_{\substack{i=1\\i\neq k}}^{o(l)}|\mathcal{V}_{\varphi(l,i)}|\cdot C^{o(l)-1}=$ 10^{20} entries. As a result, computing term (i), $\mathcal{X}_{(k)}^{(l)}[\otimes_{i=1}^{o(l)\backslash k}\mathbf{V}_i^{(l)}]\mathcal{I}_{(k)}^{(l)\top}$, would involve matrix multiplication of a dense 10^{20} entry matrix. However, given the sparsity of $\mathcal{X}^{(l)}$, one may denote the set of indices of the non-zero entries in tensor $\mathcal{X}$ by $\mathrm{nz}(\mathcal{X}) := \{J = (j_1,\ldots,j_N)\mid \mathcal{X}_{j_1,\ldots,j_N}\neq 0\}$ and derive the following equivalency

$$\mathcal{X}_{(k)}^{(l)}[\otimes_{i=1}^{o(l)\backslash k}\mathbf{V}_i^{(l)}]\mathcal{I}_{(k)}^{(l)\top} = \sum_{J\in\,\mathrm{nz}(\mathcal{X}^{(l)})}\mathcal{X}_{j_1,\ldots,j_{o(l)}}^{(l)}\mathbf{h}(j_k)\prod_{\substack{i=1\\i\neq k}}^{o(l)}(\mathbf{V}_i^{(l)})_{j_i,:},$$

where $\prod$ is Hadamard product of a sequence and $\mathbf{h}(j_k)$ is one-hot column vector of size $|\mathcal{V}_{\varphi(l,k)}|$ that has entry 1 at index j_k. Computing the right-hand side of this equivalency involves the summation over Hadamard product of a small sequence of small vectors, which has a complexity of $O(\mathrm{nnz}(\mathcal{X}^{(l)})\cdot(o(l)-1)\cdot C)$ with $\mathrm{nnz}(\cdot)$ being the number of non-zero entries. In other words, if the previous example comes with $1,000,000$ motif instances, the complexity would decrease from manipulating a 10^{20}-entry dense matrix to a magnitude of 4×10^7.

Similarly, by leveraging the sparsity of tensors and composition of dense matrices, one can simplify the computation of term (ii) from multiplication of matrix with 10^{20} entries to that with 10^5 entries; and reduce the calculation of term (iii) from a magnitude of 10^{20} to a magnitude of 10^8. We provide detailed derivation and formulas in the supplementary file.

Finally, we remark that the above computation can be highly parallelized, which has further promoted the efficiency in our implementation. An empirical efficiency study is available in Sect. 3 of the supplementary file. We summarize the algorithm in Algorithm 1.

7 Experiments

We present the quantitative evaluation results on two real-world datasets through multiple tasks and conduct case studies under various circumstances.

7.1 Datasets and Evaluation Tasks

In this section, we briefly describe (i) the datasets, (ii) the evaluation tasks, and (iii) the metrics used in the experiments. All of their detailed descriptions are provided in Sect. 4 of the supplementary file.

Datasets. We use two real-world HINs for experiments. **DBLP** is a heterogeneous information network that serves as a bibliography of research in computer science area [31]. The network consists of 5 types of node: author (A), paper (P), key term (T), venue (V) and year (Y). In DBLP, we select two candidate motifs for all applicable methods, including $AP4TPA$ and $APPA$. **YAGO** is a knowledge graph constructed by merging Wikipedia, GeoNames and WordNet. YAGO dataset consists of 7 types of nodes: person (P), organization (O), location (L), prize (R), work (W), position (S) and event (E). In YAGO, the candidate motifs used by all compared methods include $P^6O^{23}L$, $P^7O^{23}L$, $P^8O^{23}L$, $2P2W$, $3PW$.

Evaluation Tasks. In order to evaluate models' capability in reflecting different user guidance, we use two sets of labels on authors to conduct two tasks in DBLP similar to previous study [29]. Additionally, we design another task on YAGO with labels on persons. **DBLP-group** – Clustering authors to 5 research groups where they graduated. 5% of the 250 authors with labels are randomly selected as seeds from user guidance. **DBLP-area** – Clustering authors to 14 research areas. 1% of the 7, 165 authors with labels are randomly selected as seeds from user guidance. **YAGO** – Clustering people to 10 popular countries in the YAGO dataset. 1% of the 11, 368 people are randomly selected as seeds from user guidance.

Evaluation Metrics. We use three metrics to evaluate the quality of the clustering results generated by each model: Accuracy (Micro-F1), Macro-F1, and NMI. Note that in multi-class classification tasks, accuracy is always identical to Micro-F1. For all these metrics, higher values indicate better performance.

7.2   Baselines and Experiment Setups

Baselines. We use five different baselines to obtain insight on different aspects of the performance of MoCHIN. **KNN** is a classification algorithm that assigns the label of each object in the test set is according to its nearest neighbors. In our scenario, the distance between two nodes is defined as the length of the shortest path between them. **KNN+Motifs** uses signals generated by motifs, but does not directly model all players in higher-order interactions. To extract information from motifs, we construct a motif-based network for each candidate motif, where an edge is constructed if two nodes are matched to a motif instance in the original HIN. KNN is then applied to each motif-based network. Finally, a linear combination is applied to the outcome probability matrices generated by KNN from the motif-based networks and the original HIN with weights tuned to the best. **GNetMine** [9] is a graph-based regularization framework to address the transductive classification problem in HINs. This method only leverages edge-level information without considering structural patterns such as meta-paths or motifs. **PathSelClus** [29] is a probabilistic graphical model that performs clustering tasks on HINs by integrating meta-path selection with user-guided clustering. For this baseline, we additionally add $APVPA$, $APTPA$, APT, APA, and, $APAPA$ into the set of candidate meta-paths for both DBLP tasks as suggested by the original paper [29] and add $P^{14}O^{14}P$, $P^{15}O^{15}P$, and $P^{16}O^{16}P$ for YAGO task. **TGS** [3] leverages motifs but does not directly model each occurrence of higher-order interaction. It is hence another direct comparison to MoCHIN, besides KNN+Motifs, which is used to analyze the utility of comprehensively transcribing motif instances into tensors. As the authors did not discuss how to inject user guidance into their basic bipartitioning clustering algorithm, we apply multi-class logistic regression on the accompanied typed-graphlet spectral

Table 2. Quantitative evaluation on clustering results in three tasks.

Task	DBLP-group			DBLP-area			YAGO		
Metric	Acc./ Micro-F1	Macro-F1	NMI	Acc./ Micro-F1	Macro-F1	NMI	Acc./ Micro-F1	Macro-F1	NMI
KNN	0.4249	0.2566	0.1254	0.4107	0.4167	0.2537	0.3268	0.0921	0.0810
KNN+Motifs	0.4549	0.2769	0.1527	0.4811	0.4905	0.3296	0.3951	0.1885	0.1660
GNetMine [9]	0.5880	0.6122	0.3325	0.4847	0.4881	0.3469	0.3832	0.2879	0.1772
PathSelClus [29]	0.5622	0.5535	0.3246	0.4361	0.4520	0.3967	0.3856	0.3405	0.2864
TGS [3]	0.6609	0.6513	0.3958	0.4391	0.4365	0.2790	0.6058	0.3564	0.4406
MoCHIN	**0.7382**	**0.7387**	**0.5797**	**0.5318**	**0.5464**	**0.4396**	**0.6134**	**0.5563**	**0.4607**

embedding algorithm proposed in the same paper. The typed-graphlet adjacency matrices of multiple motifs are summed together to derive the input for the algorithm as the author suggested in the paper.

Experiment Setups. For MoCHIN, we set hyperparameters $\theta = 1$, $\rho = 100$ and $\lambda = 0.0001$ across all tasks in our experiments. For each model involving motifs, edge-level motifs corresponding to the edge types are included into the set of candidate motifs. For each baseline in each task, we always tune its hyperparameters to achieve the best performance.

7.3 Quantitative Evaluation Result

We report the main quantitative results in Table 2. Overall, MoCHIN uniformly outperformed all baselines in all three tasks under all metrics. Note that these three metrics measure different aspects of the model performance. For instance, in the DBLP-area task, PathSelClus outperforms GNetMine under Macro-F1 and NMI, while GNetMine outperforms PathSelClus under Acc./Micro-F1. Achieving superior performance uniformly under all metrics is hence strong evidence that MoCHIN with higher-order interaction directly modeled is armed with greater modeling capability in the task of user-guided HIN clustering.

MoCHIN Prevails in User-Guided Clustering by Exploiting Signals from Motifs more Comprehensively. Recall that KNN+Motifs, TGS, and MoCHIN all exploit signals from motifs. However, the two baselines do not directly model each occurrence of motif instances and only preserve pairwise or edge-level information. In our experiments, even though TGS can generally outperform other baselines, it alongside KNN+Motifs still cannot generate results as good as MoCHIN, which demonstrates the utility of more comprehensively exploiting signals from motifs as MoCHIN does. We interpret this result as when user guidance is limited, a fine-grained understanding of the rich semantics of an HIN is instrumental in dissecting users' intention and generating desirable results.

Impact of Candidate Motif Choice. In this section, we study how the choice of candidate motifs impacts MoCHIN and additionally use the concrete example

Table 3. Ablation study of the MoCHIN model on the DBLP-group task with the non–edge-level motifs, $APPA$ and $AP4TPA$, optionally removing from the full model.

Metric	Acc./Micro-F1	Macro-F1	NMI	Result for Eric Xing
W/o both	0.6567	0.6411	0.5157	✗
W/ APPA	0.7039	0.7062	0.5166	✗
W/ AP4TPA	0.6781	0.6589	0.5502	✓
Full model	**0.7382**	**0.7387**	**0.5797**	✓

The APPA motif. The AP4TPA motif.

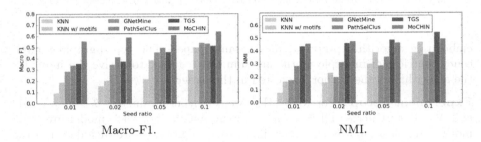

Macro-F1.   NMI.

Fig. 4. Quantitative evaluation on the YAGO task under varied seed ratio.

in Fig. 3 to understand the model outputs. Particularly, we conducted an ablation study by taking out either or both of the two non–edge-level motifs, $APPA$ and $AP4TPA$, in the DBLP-group task and reported the result in Table 3. The full MoCHIN model outperformed all partial models, demonstrating the utility of these motifs in clustering.

Moreover, we scrutinized the concrete example in Fig. 3 and checked how each model assigned cluster membership for Eric Xing. The result is also included in Table 3, which shows only the model variants with $AP4TPA$ made the correct assignment on Eric Xing. In Sect. 2 of the supplementary file, a visualization of this ablation study is provided to further corroborate our observation.

7.4   Varied Seed Ratio

In addition to using 1% people as seeds for the YAGO task reported in Table 2, we experiment under varied seed ratio 2%, 5%, and 10%. The results are reported in Fig. 4. We omit Accuracy (Micro-F1), which has a similar trend with NMI.

For all methods, the performance increased as the seed ratio increased. Notably, MoCHIN outperformed most baselines, especially when seed ratio is small. This suggests MoCHIN is particularly useful when users provide less guidance for being able to better exploit subtle information from limited data. Note that higher seed ratio is uncommon in practice since it is demanding for users to provide more than a few seeds.

Lastly, an efficiency study that empirically evaluates the proposed algorithm is provided in Sect. 3 of the supplementary file.

8 Discussion, Conclusion and Future Work

One limitation of MoCHIN is that it may not be easily applied to very large datasets even with speed-up methods due to the complexity of the model itself. However, MoCHIN would stand out in the scenario where fine-grained understanding of the network semantics is needed. In the experiment, we have shown that MoCHIN can scale to HINs with tens of thousands of nodes. We note that for user-guided clustering, it is possible the users are mostly interested in the data instances most relevant to their intention, which could be a subset of a larger dataset. For instance, if a data mining researcher wanted to cluster DBLP authors by research group, it is possible they would not care about the nodes not relevant to data mining research. As such the majority of the millions of nodes in DBLP can be filtered out in preprocessing, and this user-guided clustering problem would become not only manageable to MoCHIN but also favorable due to MoCHIN's capability in handling fine-grained semantics. Moreover, in the case where the network is inevitably large, one may trade the performance of MoCHIN for efficiency by using only relatively simple motifs. It is also worth noting that incremental learning is possible for MoCHIN – when new nodes are available, one do not have to retrain the model from scratch.

In conclusion, we studied the problem of user-guided clustering in HINs with the intention to model higher-order interactions. We identified the importance of modeling higher-order interactions without collapsing them into pairwise interactions and proposed the MoCHIN algorithm. Experiments validated the effectiveness of the proposed model and the utility of comprehensively modeling higher-order interactions. Future works include exploring further methodologies to join signals from multiple motifs, which is currently realized by a simple linear combination in the MoCHIN model. Furthermore, as the current model takes user guidance by injecting labels of the seeds, it is also of interest to extend MoCHIN to the scenario where guidance is made available by must-link and cannot-link constraints on node pairs.

Acknowledgments. This work was sponsored in part by U.S. Army Research Lab. under Cooperative Agreement No. W911NF-09-2-0053 (NSCTA), DARPA under Agreement No. W911NF-17-C-0099, National Science Foundation IIS 16-18481, IIS 17-04532, and IIS-17-41317, DTRA HDTRA11810026, and grant 1U54GM114838 awarded by NIGMS through funds provided by the trans-NIH Big Data to Knowledge (BD2K) initiative (www.bd2k.nih.gov). Any opinions, findings, and conclusions or recommendations expressed in this document are those of the author(s) and should not be interpreted as the views of any U.S. Government. The U.S. Government is authorized to reproduce and distribute reprints for Government purposes notwithstanding any copyright notation hereon.

References

1. Ahmed, N.K., Neville, J., Rossi, R.A., Duffield, N.: Efficient graphlet counting for large networks. In: ICDM (2015)
2. Benson, A.R., Gleich, D.F., Leskovec, J.: Higher-order organization of complex networks. Science **353**(6295), 163–166 (2016)
3. Carranza, A.G., Rossi, R.A., Rao, A., Koh, E.: Higher-order spectral clustering for heterogeneous graphs. arXiv preprint arXiv:1810.02959 (2018)
4. De Lathauwer, L., De Moor, B., Vandewalle, J.: A multilinear singular value decomposition. SIMAX **21**(4), 1253–1278 (2000)
5. Fang, Y., Lin, W., Zheng, V.W., Wu, M., Chang, K.C.C., Li, X.L.: Semantic proximity search on graphs with metagraph-based learning. In: ICDE. IEEE (2016)
6. Gujral, E., Papalexakis, E.E.: SMACD: semi-supervised multi-aspect community detection. In: ICDM (2018)
7. Han, J., Pei, J., Kamber, M.: Data Mining: Concepts and Techniques. Elsevier, Amsterdam (2011)
8. Huang, Z., Zheng, Y., Cheng, R., Sun, Y., Mamoulis, N., Li, X.: Meta structure: computing relevance in large heterogeneous information networks. In: KDD. ACM (2016)
9. Ji, M., Sun, Y., Danilevsky, M., Han, J., Gao, J.: Graph regularized transductive classification on heterogeneous information networks. In: Balcázar, J.L., Bonchi, F., Gionis, A., Sebag, M. (eds.) ECML PKDD 2010. LNCS (LNAI), vol. 6321, pp. 570–586. Springer, Heidelberg (2010). https://doi.org/10.1007/978-3-642-15880-3_42
10. Jiang, H., Song, Y., Wang, C., Zhang, M., Sun, Y.: Semi-supervised learning over heterogeneous information networks by ensemble of meta-graph guided random walks. In: AAAI (2017)
11. Lee, D.D., Seung, H.S.: Algorithms for non-negative matrix factorization. In: Advances in Neural Information Processing Systems, pp. 556–562 (2001)
12. Li, P., Milenkovic, O.: Inhomogeneous hypergraph clustering with applications. In: NIPS (2017)
13. Li, X., Wu, Y., Ester, M., Kao, B., Wang, X., Zheng, Y.: Semi-supervised clustering in attributed heterogeneous information networks. In: WWW (2017)
14. Liu, J., Wang, C., Gao, J., Han, J.: Multi-view clustering via joint nonnegative matrix factorization. In: SDM, vol. 13, pp. 252–260. SIAM (2013)
15. Liu, Z., Zheng, V.W., Zhao, Z., Li, Z., Yang, H., Wu, M., Ying, J.: Interactive paths embedding for semantic proximity search on heterogeneous graphs. In: KDD (2018)
16. Liu, Z., Zheng, V.W., Zhao, Z., Zhu, F., Chang, K.C.C., Wu, M., Ying, J.: Distance-aware DAG embedding for proximity search on heterogeneous graphs. AAAI (2018)
17. Luo, C., Pang, W., Wang, Z.: Semi-supervised clustering on heterogeneous information networks. In: Tseng, V.S., Ho, T.B., Zhou, Z.-H., Chen, A.L.P., Kao, H.-Y. (eds.) PAKDD 2014. LNCS (LNAI), vol. 8444, pp. 548–559. Springer, Cham (2014). https://doi.org/10.1007/978-3-319-06605-9_45
18. Milo, R., Shen-Orr, S., Itzkovitz, S., Kashtan, N., Chklovskii, D., Alon, U.: Network motifs: simple building blocks of complex networks. Science **298**(5594), 824–827 (2002)
19. Papalexakis, E.E., Faloutsos, C., Sidiropoulos, N.D.: Tensors for data mining and data fusion: models, applications, and scalable algorithms. TIST **8**(2), 16 (2017)

20. Sankar, A., Zhang, X., Chang, K.C.C.: Motif-based convolutional neural network on graphs. arXiv preprint arXiv:1711.05697 (2017)
21. Shi, C., Li, Y., Zhang, J., Sun, Y., Philip, S.Y.: A survey of heterogeneous information network analysis. TKDE **29**(1), 17–37 (2017)
22. Shi, C., Wang, R., Li, Y., Yu, P.S., Wu, B.: Ranking-based clustering on general heterogeneous information networks by network projection. In: CIKM (2014)
23. Shi, Y., Chan, P.W., Zhuang, H., Gui, H., Han, J.: PReP: path-based relevance from a probabilistic perspective in heterogeneous information networks. In: KDD (2017)
24. Shi, Y., Gui, H., Zhu, Q., Kaplan, L., Han, J.: AspEm: embedding learning by aspects in heterogeneous information networks. In: SDM (2018)
25. Shi, Y., Zhu, Q., Guo, F., Zhang, C., Han, J.: Easing embedding learning by comprehensive transcription of heterogeneous information networks. In: KDD (2018)
26. Stefani, L.D., Epasto, A., Riondato, M., Upfal, E.: Triest: counting local and global triangles in fully dynamic streams with fixed memory size. TKDD **11**(4), 43 (2017)
27. Strehl, A., Ghosh, J.: Cluster ensembles-a knowledge reuse framework for combining multiple partitions. JMLR **3**(Dec), 583–617 (2002)
28. Sun, Y., Han, J.: Mining heterogeneous information networks: a structural analysis approach. SIGKDD Explor. **14**(2), 20–28 (2013)
29. Sun, Y., Norick, B., Han, J., Yan, X., Yu, P.S., Yu, X.: Integrating meta-path selection with user-guided object clustering in heterogeneous information networks. In: KDD (2012)
30. Sun, Y., Yu, Y., Han, J.: Ranking-based clustering of heterogeneous information networks with star network schema. In: KDD, pp. 797–806. ACM (2009)
31. Tang, J., Zhang, J., Yao, L., Li, J., Zhang, L., Su, Z.: ArnetMiner: extraction and mining of academic social networks. In: KDD (2008)
32. Wu, J., Wang, Z., Wu, Y., Liu, L., Deng, S., Huang, H.: A tensor CP decomposition method for clustering heterogeneous information networks via stochastic gradient descent algorithms. Sci. Program. **2017**, 1–13 (2017)
33. Yang, C., Feng, Y., Li, P., Shi, Y., Han, J.: Meta-graph based HIN spectral embedding: methods, analyses, and insights. In: ICDM (2018)
34. Yang, C., Liu, M., Zheng, V.W., Han, J.: Node, motif and subgraph: leveraging network functional blocks through structural convolution. In: ASONAM (2018)
35. Yaveroğlu, Ö.N., et al.: Revealing the hidden language of complex networks. Sci. Rep. **4**, 4547 (2014)
36. Yin, H., Benson, A.R., Leskovec, J., Gleich, D.F.: Local higher-order graph clustering. In: KDD (2017)
37. Zhao, H., Xu, X., Song, Y., Lee, D.L., Chen, Z., Gao, H.: Ranking users in social networks with higher-order structures. In: AAAI (2018)
38. Zhao, H., Yao, Q., Li, J., Song, Y., Lee, D.L.: Meta-graph based recommendation fusion over heterogeneous information networks. In: KDD (2017)
39. Zhou, D., et al.: A local algorithm for structure-preserving graph cut. In: KDD (2017)

Novel Dense Subgraph Discovery Primitives: Risk Aversion and Exclusion Queries

Charalampos E. Tsourakakis[1(✉)], Tianyi Chen[1], Naonori Kakimura[2], and Jakub Pachocki[3]

[1] Boston University, Boston, MA, USA
ctsourak@bu.edu
[2] Keio University, Tokyo, Japan
[3] OpenAI, San Francisco, USA

Abstract. In the densest subgraph problem, given an undirected graph $G(V, E, w)$ with non-negative edge weights we are asked to find a set of nodes $S \subseteq V$ that maximizes the degree density $w(S)/|S|$, where $w(S)$ is the sum of the weights of the edges in the graph induced by S. This problem is solvable in polynomial time, and in general is well studied. But what happens when the edge weights are negative? Is the problem still solvable in polynomial time? Also, why should we care about the densest subgraph problem in the presence of negative weights?

In this work we answer the aforementioned questions. Specifically, we provide two novel graph mining primitives that are applicable to a wide variety of applications. Our primitives can be used to answer questions such as "how can we find a dense subgraph in Twitter with lots of replies and mentions but no follows?", "how do we extract a dense subgraph with high expected reward and low risk from an uncertain graph"? We formulate both problems mathematically as special instances of dense subgraph discovery in graphs with negative weights. We study the hardness of the problem, and we prove that the problem in general is **NP**-hard, but we also provide sufficient conditions under which it is poly-time solvable. We design an efficient approximation algorithm that works best in the presence of small negative weights, and an effective heuristic for the more general case. Finally, we perform experiments on various real-world datasets that verify the value of the proposed primitives, and the effectiveness of our proposed algorithms.

The code and the data are available at https://github.com/negativedsd.

1 Introduction

Dense subgraph discovery (abbreviated as *DSD* henceforth) is a major and active topic of research in the fields of graph algorithms and graph mining. A wide range of real-world, data mining applications rely on DSD including correlation mining, fraud detection, electronic commerce, bioinformatics, mining Twitter

© Springer Nature Switzerland AG 2020
U. Brefeld et al. (Eds.): ECML PKDD 2019, LNAI 11906, pp. 378–394, 2020.
https://doi.org/10.1007/978-3-030-46150-8_23

data, efficient algorithm design for fast distance queries in massive networks, and graph compression [15].

In this work we introduce two novel primitives for DSD. These two primitives are strongly motivated by real-world applications that we discuss in greater detail in Sect. 3.1. The first question that our work addresses is related to uncertain graphs. Uncertain graphs appear in a wide variety of applications that we survey in Sect. 2. We define the uncertain graph model we use formally in Sect. 3.1, but intuitively, uncertain graphs model probabilistically real-world scenarios where each edge may exist or not in a graph (e.g., failure of a link). Problem 1 aims to find a *risk-averse* dense subgraph. A similar formulation was suggested recently by Tsourakakis et al. for graph matchings [31].

> *Problem 1 (Risk-averse DSD).* Given an uncertain graph $\mathcal{G}$, how do we find a set of nodes S that induces a dense subgraph in expectation, and the probability of not being dense in a realization/sample of $\mathcal{G}$ is low?

Our second problem focuses on multigraphs whose edges are associated with different types. Such graphs appear naturally in numerous applications, and are also known as multilayer multigraphs, e.g., [11]. For example, similarity between two videos can be defined based on different criteria, e.g., audio, visual, and how frequently these videos are being co-watched on Youtube. Similarity between time series can be defined using a variety of measures including Euclidean distance, Fourier coefficients, dynamic time wraping, edit distance among others [28]. Emails between people can be classified based on the nature of the interaction (e.g., business, family). Twitter users may interact in various ways, including *follow, reply, mention, retweet, like,* and *quote.* We formulate Problem 2, whose goal is to detect efficiently dense subgraphs that exclude certain types of edges. Later, we will define two variations, soft- and hard-exclusion queries.

> *Problem 2 (DSD-Exclusion-Queries).* Given a multigraph $G(V, E, \ell)$, where $\ell : E \rightarrow \{1, \ldots, L\} = [L]$ is the labeling function, and L is the number of types of interactions, and an input set $\mathcal{I} \subseteq [L]$ of interactions, how do we find a set of nodes S that induces a dense subgraph but does not induce any edge e such that $\ell(e) \in \mathcal{I}$?

Contributions. Our contributions are summarized as follows.

- We introduce two novel problems, (i) risk averse DSD, and (ii) DSD in large-scale multilayer networks with exclusion queries. We show in Sect. 3.1 that these two problems are special cases of DSD in undirected graphs with negative weights. To the best of our knowledge, this is the first work that introduces these algorithmic primitives.
- We prove that DSD in the presence of negative weights is **NP**-hard in general by reducing MAX-CUT to our problem (Sect. 3.2), but we also provide sufficient conditions under which it is exactly solvable in polynomial time.

- We design a space-, and time-efficient approximation algorithm that performs best in the presence of small negative weights. In the case of existence of large negative weights, we design a well-performing heuristic.
- We deploy our developed primitives on the two real-world applications we introduce. We extract subgraphs from uncertain graphs with high expected induced weight and low risk. Finally, we mine Twitter data by finding dense subgraphs that exclude certain types of interactions. A non-trivial experimental contribution is the creation of an uncertain graph from the TMDB database and Twitter graphs from the Greek Twitter-verse, that we will make available to the community. Our tools provide insights, and we are confident that will find numerous applications in graph mining, and anomaly detection.

In the following sections we use the notation summarized in Table 1.

Table 1. Notation

Notation	Description
$deg^+(u)$ $(deg^-(u))$	Positive (negative) degree of node u. $deg^+(u) > 0$, $deg^-(u) > 0$
$d(u)$	Total degree of u. $d(u) = deg^+(u) - deg^-(u)$
$w^+(e)(w^-(e))$	Positive (negative) weight of edge e. $w^+(e) > 0$, $w^-(e) > 0$
$deg_S^+(u)$ $(deg_S^-(u))$	Positive (negative) degree of node u within node set $S \subseteq V$. $deg_S^+(u) = \sum_{v \in S} w^+(u,v)$, $deg_S^-(u) = \sum_{v \in S} w^-(u,v)$
$w^+(S)$ $(w^-(S))$	Total positive (negative) induced weight by S. $w^+(S) = \sum_{e \in E(S)} w^+(e)$, $w^-(S) = \sum_{e \in E(S)} w^-(e)$
$d_S(u)$	Total degree of node u within S. $d_S(u) = deg_S^+(u) - deg_S^-(u)$

2   Related Work

Uncertain graphs model naturally a wide variety of datasets and applications including protein-protein interactions [21], kidney exchanges [27], and influence maximization [19] While a lot of research work has focused on designing graph mining algorithms for uncertain graphs, e.g., [6,22,24], there is less work on designing efficient risk-averse optimization algorithms, and even lesser with solid theoretical guarantees.

Risk-aversion has been implicitly discussed by Lin et al. in their work on reliable clustering [22], where the authors show that interpreting probabilities as weights does not result in good clusterings. Repetitive sampling from a large-scale uncertain graph in order to reduce the risk is inefficient. Motivated by this observation, Parchas et al. have proposed a heuristic to extract a good possible world in order to combine risk-aversion with efficiency [24]. However, their work comes with no guarantees. Jin et al. provide a risk-averse algorithm for distance queries on uncertain graphs [18]. He and Kempe propose robust algorithms for the influence maximization problem [17]. Closest to our work lies the recent work by Tsourakakis et al. who studied the problem of finding efficiently risk averse graph and hypergraph matching algorithms [31].

Dense subgraph discovery (DSD) is a major graph mining topic, with numerous diverse applications, ranging from fraud detection to bioinformatics, see [15,30] for a detailed account of such applications. The *densest subgraph problem* (DSP) a popular DSD objective, that is solvable in polynomial time [13,16]. The DSP for undirected, weighted graphs $G(V, E, w), w : E \rightarrow \mathbb{R}^+$ maximizes the degree density $\rho(S) = \frac{w(S)}{|S|}$ over all possible subgraphs $S \subseteq V$, where $w(S) = \sum_{e \in e[S]} w(e)$ is the total induced weight by subgraph. In addition to the exact algorithm that is based on maximum flow computation, Charikar [8] proved that a greedy peeling algorithm produces a $\frac{1}{2}$-approximation of the densest subgraph in linear time, see also [20]. Galimberti et al. studied core decompositions – a concept intimately connected to DSD – on multilayer graphs [12]. Finally, Cadena et al. first studied DSD with negative weights [7], but their work focuses on anomaly detection, and the streaming nature of their input.

DSD on uncertain graphs is a less well studied topic. Zou was the first who discussed the DSP on uncertain graphs. His work shows –as expected– that the DSP in expectation can be solved in polynomial time [32]. The closest work related to our formulation is the recent work by Miyauchi and Takeda [23]. While their original motivation is also DSD on uncertain graphs, the modeling assumptions, and the mathematical objective differ significantly from ours. To the best of our knowledge, there is no work on risk-averse DSD under general probabilistic assumptions as ours.

3   Proposed Method

3.1   Why Negative Weights?

Risk-Averse Dense Subgraph Discovery. Uncertain graphs model the inherent uncertainty associated with graphs in a variety of applications. Here, we adopt the general model for uncertain graphs introduced by Tsourakakis et al. [31]. For completeness we present it in the following.

Model: Let $\mathcal{G}([n], E, \{g_e(\theta_e)\}_{e \in E})$ be an uncertain complete graph on n nodes, with the complete edge set $E = \binom{[n]}{2}$. The weight $w(e)$ (reward) of each edge $e \in E$ is drawn according to some probability distribution g_e with parameters θ_e, i.e., $w(e) \sim g_e(x; \theta_e)$. We assume that the weight of each edge is drawn independently from the rest; each probability distribution is assumed to have finite mean, and finite variance. Given this model, we define the probability of a given graph G with weights $w(e)$ on the edges as:

$$\mathbf{Pr}\left[G; \{w(e)\}_{e \in E}\right] = \prod_{e \in E} g_e(w(e); \theta_e). \tag{1}$$

This model includes the standard Bernoulli model that is used extensively in the existing literature as a special case. Specifically, in the standard binomial uncertain graph model an uncertain graph is modeled by the triple $\mathcal{G} = (V, E, p)$ where $p : E \rightarrow (0, 1]$ is the function that assigns a probability of success to each edge independently from the other edges. According to the possible-world semantics [5,10] that interprets $\mathcal{G}$ as a set $\{G : (V, E_G)\}_{E_G \subseteq E}$ of $2^{|E|}$ possible deterministic graphs (worlds), each defined by a subset of E. The probability of observing any possible world $G(V, E_G) \in 2^E$ is

$$\mathbf{Pr}\,[G] = \prod_{e \in E_G} p(e) \prod_{e \in E \setminus E_G} (1 - p(e)).$$

A key property of these models to keep in mind, is that each edge e in the uncertain graph is independently distributed from the rest, and is associated with an expected reward μ_e (expectation) and a risk σ_e^2 (variance). Finally, observe that without any loss of generality in our general model described by Eq. (1) we have assumed that the edge set is $\binom{[n]}{2}$; non-edges can be modeled as edges with probability of existence zero.

Problem Formulation. Intuitively, our goal is to find a subgraph $G[S]$ induced by $S \subseteq V$ such that its average reward $\frac{\sum_{e \in E(S)} w_e}{|S|}$ is large and the average associated risk is low $\frac{\sum_{e \in E(S)} \sigma_e^2}{|S|}$. To achieve this purpose we model the problem as a densest subgraph discovery problem in a graph with positive (reward) and negative (risk) edge weights. Specifically, for every edge $e = (u, v) \in E(G)$ we create two edges, a positive edge with weight equal to the expected reward, i.e., $w^+(e) = \mu_e$ and a negative edge with weight equal to the opposite of the risk of the edge, i.e., $w^-(e) = \sigma_e^2$. We wish to find a subgraph $S \subseteq V$ that has large positive average degree $\frac{w^+(S)}{|S|}$, and small negative average degree $\frac{w^-(S)}{|S|}$. We combine the two objectives into one objective $f : 2^V \rightarrow \mathbb{R}$ that we wish to maximize:

$$f(S) = \frac{w^+(S) + \lambda_1|S|}{w^-(S) + \lambda_2|S|}.$$

The parameters $\lambda_1, \lambda_2 \geq 0$ are positive reals. First, observe that this dense subgraph discovery formulation is applicable to any graph with positive and negative weights. Parameters λ_1, λ_2 allow us to control the size of the output as follows. Let us reparameterize the two parameters as $\lambda_1 = \rho\lambda, \lambda_2 = \lambda$. Then $f(S) = \frac{w^+(S) + \rho\lambda|S|}{w^-(S) + \lambda|S|}$, so if the ratio $\rho \geq 1$, then the objective favors larger node sets, whereas when $\rho < 1$ we favor smaller node sets.

We show how to solve the problem $\max_{S \subseteq V} f(S)$ by reducing it to standard dense subgraph discovery [16]. We perform binary search on $f(S)$ by answering queries of the following form:

Does there exist a subset of nodes $S \subseteq V$ such that $f(S) \geq q$, where q is a query value?

Assuming an efficient algorithm for answering this query, and that the weights are polynomial functions of n, then using $O(\log n)$ queries we can find the optimal value for our objective $f : V \to \mathbb{R}$. By analyzing what each query corresponds to, we find:

$$\frac{w^+(S) + \lambda_1|S|}{w^-(S) + \lambda_2|S|} \geq q \to w^+(S) + \lambda_1|S| \geq q(w^-(S) + \lambda_2|S|) \to \quad (2)$$

$$\sum_{e \in E(S)} \underbrace{\left(w^+(e) - qw^-(e) \right)}_{\tilde{w}(e)} \geq |S| \underbrace{(q\lambda_2 - \lambda_1)}_{q'} \to \sum_{e \in E(S)} \frac{\tilde{w}(e)}{|S|} \geq q'.$$

The latter inequality suggests that our original problem corresponds to querying in $\tilde{G}$, a modified version of G where the edge weight of any edge e becomes $w^+(e) - qw^-(e)$, whether there exists a subgraph S with density greater than q', where $q' = q\lambda_2 - \lambda_1$. However, this does not imply that our problem is poly-time solvable. The densest subgraph problem is poly-time solvable using a maximum flow formulation when the weights are positive rationals [16]. As we will prove in the next section, the densest subgraph problem when there exist negative weights is **NP**-hard in general. However, our analysis above leads to a straight-forward corollary that is worth stating. Intuitively, when for *each edge* e the ratio $\frac{w^+(e)}{w^-(e)}$ is large enough, then our problem is solvable in polynomial time.

Corollary 1. *Assume that $w^+(e) \geq q_{max}w^-(e)$ for all $e \in E^+ \cup E^-$, where q_{max} is the maximum possible query value. Then, the densest subgraph problem is solvable in polynomial time.*

Proof. If $w^+(e) \geq q_{max}w^-(e)$ for each $e \in E$, we obtain $\tilde{w}(e) \geq 0$ for each $e \in E$ in inequality (2) is equivalent to solving the densest subgraph problem in an undirected graph with non-negative weights, see [16,29].

Observe that a trivial upper bound of q_{max} can be obtained by setting $w^+(S) = \sum_{e \in E(G)} w^+(e), w^-(S) = 0$, and since $\lambda_1|S| \leq \lambda_1 n, \lambda_2|S| \geq \lambda_2$ for all $S \neq \emptyset$, we see that $q_{max} \leq \frac{\sum_{e \in E(G)} w^+(e) + \lambda_1 n}{\lambda_2}$. For polynomially bounded weights, this is a polynomial function of n, hence the number of binary search iterations is logarithmic.

Controlling the Risk in Practice. There exist real-world scenarios where the practitioner wants to control the trade-off between reward and risk, see [31]. An effective way to change the risk tolerance is as follows by multiplying the negative induced weight $w^-(S)$ by $B \in (0, +\infty)$. Namely, our objective $f : 2^V \to \mathbb{R}$ is $f(S) = \frac{w^+(S) + \lambda_1|S|}{Bw^-(S) + \lambda_2|S|}$. An interesting open problem is to develop a formal (bi-criteria) approximation for risk averse DSD along the lines of [26,31].

Soft and Hard Exclusion Dense Subgraph Queries. Given the Twitter network, where user accounts may interact in more than one ways (e.g., *follow,* *retweet, mention, quote, reply*), can we find a dense subgraph that does not contain any *follow* but contains many *reply* interactions? We ask this question in a more general form.

> *Problem 3.* Given a large-scale multilayer network, how do we find a dense subgraph that *excludes* certain types of edges?

We consider two types of such queries, the *soft* and *hard* queries. In the former case we want to find subgraphs with perhaps few edges of certain types, in the latter case we want to exclude fully such edges. An algorithmic primitive that can answer efficiently these queries can be used to understand the structure of large-scale multilayer networks, and find anomalies and interesting patterns. In principle, we set the edge weight of an excluded type to $-W$ where $W > 0$ is an input parameter. If we set $W = +\infty$, subgraphs that do not induce any edge of any excluded type will have positive weight, whereas subgraphs that induce even one edge of a forbidden type will have $-\infty$ weight. If we set W to a small value, then there may be some undesired edges in the output subgraph. The pseudo-code in Algorithm 1 describes this approach.

Algorithm 1: Exclusion-Queries

Input: $G(V, E), \{\text{labels}\}, W > 0$
for $e \in E(G)$ **do**
    for $c \in labels$ **do**
        if *If type(e) = c* **then**
            | $w(e) \leftarrow -W$ (else $w(e)$ remains 1)
        end
    end
end
return $S \subseteq V$ *that achieves maximum average degree in* $G(V, E, w)$.

3.2 Hardness

We prove that solving the densest subgraph problem on graphs with negative weights is **NP**-hard. We formally define our problem NEG-DSD.

> *Problem 4 (Neg-DSD).* Given a graph G with loops and possibly negative weights, find the subset A of V that maximizes $\frac{w(A)}{|A|}$.

We prove that NEG-DSD is **NP**-hard. Our reduction is based on the proposed strategy by Peter Shor for showing that the max-cut problem on graphs with possibly negative edges is **NP**-hard [1]. This is stated as the Theorem 1. For convenience, we also define the decision version of the maximum cut problem [1].

Theorem 1. NEG-DSD is **NP**-hard.

Problem 5 (Max-Cut). Given a graph $G(V, E)$ and a constant c, find a partition (V_1, V_2) of V such that $cut(V_1, V_2) = \sum_{u \in V_1, v \in V_2} w(u, v) > c$.

Our proof strategy is inspired by Peter Shor's proof that max-cut with negative weight edges is **NP**-hard [1]. We provide a detailed proof sketch.

Proof. First, we define the POSITIVE-CUT problem, and show that it is **NP**-hard by reducing the MAX-CUT problem to it.

Problem 6 (Positive-Cut). Given a graph G with possibly negative weights, find a partition (V_1, V_2) of V such that $cut(V_1, V_2) > 0$.

We choose two nodes u, v that lie on opposite sides of an optimal max cut (V_1^*, V_2^*). Despite the fact we do not know the max cut, we can perform this step in polynomial time by repeating the following procedure for all possible pairs of nodes; if we cannot find a positive cut for any of the pairs, then the answer to the MAX-CUT is negative. With a vary large value d (e.g. $d = 1 + \max_{e \in E}(w^+(e))$), we construct a graph G' by adding negative weight equal to $-d$ from u and v to all other vertices, and an edge of weight $(n-2)d - c$ between u, v. All cuts that place u, v on the same side will be negative in G' provided d is sufficiently large. All other cuts will be positive if and only if the corresponding cut in G is greater than c. Therefore, POSITIVE-CUT is **NP**-hard.

Finally we prove that NEG-DSD is **NP**-hard using a reduction from POSITIVE-CUT. We construct a graph G' by negating every weight in G putting a loop on every vertex so that its weighted degree is zero. Therefore, the sum of the degrees of any set A in G' is equal to $\sum_{v \in A} 0 = 2w(A) + cut(A, V \backslash A)$. Finally, observe that a cut (V_1, V_2) has positive weight in G if and only if V_1 has positive average degree.

3.3 Algorithms and Heuristics

A popular algorithm for the densest subgraph problem is Charikar's algorithm [8]. We study the performance of this algorithm in the presence of negative weights. The pseudocode is given as Algorithm 2. The algorithm iteratively removes from the graph the node of the smallest degree $d(v) = deg^+(v) - deg^-(v)$, and among the sequence of n produced graphs, outputs the one that achieves the highest degree density. Our main theoretical result for the performance of Algorithm 2 is stated as Theorem 2.

Theorem 2. Let $G(V, E, w)$, $w : E \to \mathbb{R}$ be an undirected weighted graph with possibly negative weights. Let S^* be the optimal densest subgraph in G with average density $\frac{w(S^*)}{|S^*|} = \rho^*$. If the negative degree $deg^-(u)$ of any node u is upper bounded by Δ, then Algorithm 2 outputs a set whose density is at least $\frac{\rho^*}{2} - \frac{\Delta}{2}$.

Algorithm 2: Peeling

Input: G
$n \leftarrow |V|, H_n \leftarrow G$;
for $i \leftarrow n$ **to** 2 **do**
  Let v be the vertex of G_i of minimum degree, i.e.,
  $d(v) = deg^+(v) - deg^-(v)$ (break ties arbitrarily);
  $H_{i-1} \leftarrow H_i \backslash v$;
end
return H_j *that achieves maximum average degree among* $H_i s$, $i = 1, \ldots, n$.

Proof. By the optimality of S^* we obtain that $d_{S^*}(v) \geq \rho^*$, and then trivially $deg^+(v) \geq \rho^*$. Consider the execution of Algorithm 2, and let $u \in S^*$ be the first vertex from S^* removed during the peeling. Let S be the set of nodes at that iteration, including u. By the peeling process, we have $d_S(v) \geq d_S(u)$ for all $v \in S$. Furthermore,

$$d_S(u) = deg_S^+(u) - deg_S^-(u) \geq deg_S^+(u) - \Delta,$$

since by our assumption $deg_S^-(u) \leq deg^-(u) \leq \Delta$. This implies that

$$2w(S) = \sum_{v \in S} d_S(v) \geq \sum_{v \in S} deg_S^+(v) - |S|\Delta \geq |S|(\rho^* - \Delta) \rightarrow \frac{w(S)}{|S|} \geq \frac{\rho^*}{2} - \frac{\Delta}{2}.$$

This yields that the output of Algorithm 2 outputs a set of nodes $\bar{S}$ with density at least $\frac{\rho^*}{2} - \frac{\Delta}{2}$.

When the additive error term in the approximation is small compared to the term $\frac{\rho^*}{2}$, then the peeling algorithm performs effectively with strong guarantee. In practice, Algorithm 2 performs well on large-scale graphs where the negative weights are small. In the presence of very large negative weights, the approximation guarantees become meaningless.

Claim. In the presence of large negative weights, Algorithm 2 may perform arbitrarily bad.

This is illustrated in Fig. 1(a) that provides an instance of a graph with large negative weights. Intuitively, in bad instances when there exist large negative degrees, nodes that should not be removed early on by the peeling process, are actually removed. Specifically, consider when $W = \frac{n-4}{3}$, then $3W - n < -3$. The degrees of nodes are

$$\underbrace{3W - n}_{\text{one node}} < \underbrace{-3}_{n-2 \text{ nodes}} < \underbrace{-2}_{\text{two nodes}} < 0 < \underbrace{2\epsilon + W}_{\text{three nodes}}.$$

Therefore, the center node is removed first, and the peeling algorithm will output as the densest subgraph the triangle of density ϵ. The optimal densest subgraph

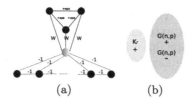

Fig. 1. Bad peeling instances. For details, see Sect. 3.

has $\frac{3W+3\epsilon}{4}$. By allowing ϵ to be arbitrarily small, we observe that the approximation ratio becomes arbitrarily bad. To tackle such scenarios, i.e., where nodes from the densest subgraph are peeled earlier than when they should, we propose an effective heuristic which is outlined in Algorithm 3. The algorithm again peels the nodes but scores every node u according to $Cdeg^+(u) - deg^-(u)$, where $C > 0$ is a parameter that is part of the input.

Remark About C in Algorithm 3. While Fig. 1(a) suggests the use of $C \geq 1$, it could be the case that C has to be set to a value less than 1 to obtain good results. We provide an example where using $C < 1$ can help in providing a better peeling permutation of the nodes. Consider a graph whose weights are either $+1$ or -1, that consists of two connected components. The first component is a positive clique on r nodes. The second component is the union of two random binomial graphs $G(n, p)$ where $p = \frac{1}{2}$. This is illustrated in Fig. 1(b). The degree of any node u in the first component is $deg(u) = deg^+(u) - deg^-(u) = (r-1) - 0$. The expected degree of any node in the second component is 0. Furthermore, the average degree of any subset of nodes in the 2nd component is 0 in expectation. However, using concentration bounds (details omitted) one can show that it is likely that there will exist a node u in the second component with positive degree $\kappa\sqrt{n}$ and negative degree $\kappa'\sqrt{n}$ with $\kappa > \kappa'$, and therefore positive total degree. Only the use of a $C < 1$ will improve the peeling ordering; e.g., in the extreme case where $C = 0$ the nodes of the second component will be removed first.

Rule-of-Thumb. In practice, given that each run of the algorithm takes linear time, we can afford to run the algorithm for a bunch of C values and return the densest subgraph among the outputs produced by each run, instead of using one value for C. This strategy is applied in Sect. 4.

Algorithm 3: Heuristic-Peeling

Input: $G, C \in (0, +\infty)$
$n \leftarrow |V|, H_n \leftarrow G$ **for** $i \leftarrow n$ to 2 **do**
  | Let v be the vertex of G_i of minimum degree, i.e.,
  | $d(v) = Cdeg^+(v) - deg^-(v)$ (break ties arbitrarily) $H_{i-1} \leftarrow H_i \backslash v$
end
return H_j $that$ $achieves$ $maximum$ $average$ $degree$ $among$ H_is, $i = 1, \ldots, n$.

Shifting the Negative Weights. Finally, for the sake of completeness, we mention that the perhaps natural idea of shifting all the weights by the most negative weight in the graph, in order to obtain non-negative weights, and apply the exact polynomial time algorithm on the weight-shifted graph may perform arbitrarily bad. To see why, consider a graph that consists of three components, a triangle with positive weights equal to 1, an edge with a large negative weight $-\Delta < 0$, and a large clique with small negative weight $-\epsilon < 0$. In this graph, the densest subgraph is the positive triangle, but by shifting the weights by $+\Delta$, there exists values for ϵ, Δ such that the densest subgraph in the weight-shifted graph is the negative clique. Also experimentally, this heuristic performs extremely poorly.

4   Experimental Results

4.1   Experimental Setup

Datasets. All the datasets we have used in our experiments are publicly available, and are described in Table 2. We use four protein-protein interaction uncertain graphs, *Biogrid, Collins, Gavin, Krogan* that have been used in prior biological studies (e.g., [9,14,21]) and are available at [2]. The set of nodes represents proteins and the probability of the edge is equal to the existence probability of the interaction. Another uncertain graph, available at [4], is created from the TMDB movie database as follows. The set of nodes corresponds to actors, and the probability of the edge is equal to the probability that these two actors co-star in a movie. Specifically, for actors u, v, the probability $p(u, v)$ is equal to the Jaccard coefficient $J(M_u, M_v) = \frac{|M_u \cap M_v|}{|M_u \cup M_v|}$, where M_u, M_v are the sets of movies that u, v have co-starred. We choose weights to represent a function of the popularity of the movies, i.e., a score assigned to each movie by TMDB (1 is the lowest score in our collected dataset). Intuitively, these scores reflect the reward of a potential collaboration between two actors. While there are many ways to set the weight of an edge for two actors (e.g. average popularity), we focus on the most popular movies they have co-starred in. The main rationale behind this choice is that the majority of actors play in movies whose majority popularity is 1, i.e., the lowest possible. For a pair of actors $\{u, v\}$, let $s_0 \geq \ldots \geq s_{k-1}$ where $k = \min(|M_u \cap M_v|, 5)$ be the popularity scores of movies they have co-starred in. We set $w(u, v) = \sum_{j=0}^{k-1} \frac{s_j}{2^j}$, i.e., a discounted sum of popularities, focusing more on the most popular movies the two actors have co-starred in.

Finally, we used an open-source twitter API crawler to monitor twitter traffic between February 1st and February 14th, 2018 [25]. We provided detailed information about each daily graph. Here, the number of edges is a five dimensional vector, whose coordinates correspond to the number of follows, mentions, retweets, quotes, and replies respectively. We will make the Twitter datasets available upon proper anonymization. The datasets we use are overall small, and medium sized, therefore our proposed algorithm for a fixed C value, requires few seconds or few minutes for the largest graphs.

Table 2. Datasets used in our experiments. The number of vertices n and edges m is recorded for each graph. The datasets annotated by ⊙ have been created by us, and are publicly available. For details, see Sect. 4.1.

Name	n	m
▨ Biogrid	5 640	59 748
▨ Collins	1 622	9 074
▨ Gavin	1 855	7 669
▨ Krogan core	2 708	7 123
▨ Krogan extended	3 672	14 317
⊙ TMDB	160 784	883 842
⊙ Twitter (Feb. 1)	621 617	(902 834, 387 597, 222 253, 30 018, 63 062)
⊙ Twitter (Feb. 2)	706 104	(1 002 265, 388 669, 218 901, 29 621, 64 282)
⊙ Twitter (Feb. 3)	651 109	(1 010 002, 373 889, 218 717, 27 805, 59 503)
⊙ Twitter (Feb. 4)	528 594	(865 019, 435 536, 269 750, 32 584, 71 802)
⊙ Twitter (Feb. 5)	631 697	(999 961, 396 223, 233 464, 30 937, 66 968)
⊙ Twitter (Feb. 6)	732 852	(941 353, 407 834, 239 486, 31 853, 67 374)
⊙ Twitter (Feb. 7)	742 566	(1 129 011, 406 852, 236 121, 30 815, 68 093)

Unfortunately, due to space constraints we present a representative sample of our findings. The interested reader can find an extended version of this paper online [3].

Machine Specs and Code. The experiments were performed on a single machine, with an Intel Xeon CPU at 2.83 GHz, 6144KB cache size, and 50 GB of main memory. The code is written in Python, and available at https://github.com/negativedsd.

4.2 Risk-Averse DSD

We perform two risk averse DSD experiments. First, for various fixed pairs of (λ_1, λ_2) values, we range the parameter B (reminder: B is the multiplicative factor of $w^-(S)$, see Controlling the risk in practice, Sect. 3.1) to control the trade-off between expected average reward and average risk. A typical outcome of our algorithm on the set of uncertain graphs we have tested it on for $\lambda_1 = \lambda_2 = 1$, and $C = 1$ is summarized in Table 3. As B increases, we tolerate less risk, but the expected average reward drops as well.

In our second experiment we test the effect of rest of the parameters. We fix $B = 1$, and then we perform the following procedure. For each dataset, we fix a pair of (λ_1, λ_2) values and run our proposed algorithm using 7 values of C. The C value 0.5 always resulted in trivial results that would skew a lot the plots so it is omitted. Specifically, for $C = 0.5$ for all three pairs of λ values we use, we obtain (almost) the whole graph as output of the peeling process. The three pairs of λ values we use are $(\lambda_1, \lambda_2) \in \{(0.5, 1), (1, 1), (2, 1)\}$. Our results are shown

Table 3. Exploring the effect of risk tolerance parameter B on the *gavin* dataset. For details, see Sect. 4.2.

B	Average exp. reward	Average risk	$|S^*|$
0.25	0.18	0.09	6
1	0.17	0.08	10
2	0.13	0.06	31

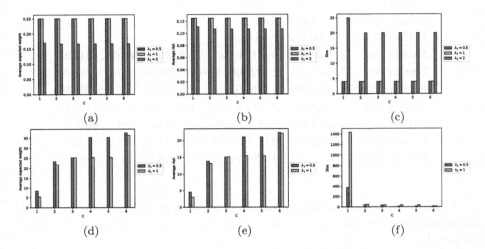

(a)   (b)   (c)

(d)   (e)   (f)

Fig. 2. Risk averse DSD results for Biogrid (a) average expected weight, (b) average risk, (c) output size, and for TMDB (d) average expected weight, (e) average risk, (f) output size. For details, see Sect. 4.2.

in Fig. 2. For the TMDB graph, the last pair of λ values results in obtaining the whole graph as the optimal solution, so we omit it from Figs. 2(d), (e), and (f). We include these two datasets as they show that the change in the C value in principle does not affect risk aversion (Fig. 2(b)), but it could happen due to the different peeling orderings it produces that the output will be associated with different risk (Fig. 2(d)). We also observe that as we increase λ_1 the size of the output increases. This agrees with the insights we provide in Sect. 3; namely, we reward larger sets of nodes.

4.3   Mining Twitter Using DSD-Exclusion Queries

We test our DSD exclusion query primitive on the Twitter daily data. We present results that we obtain for different pairs of graphs induced by different types of interactions, for $C = 1$. For each such pair, we perform all possible non-trivial exclusion queries:

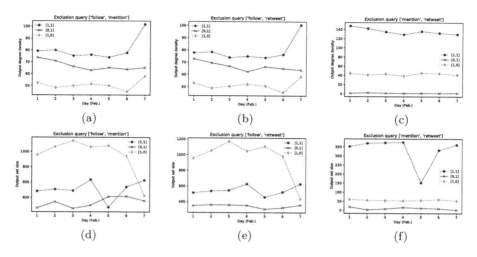

Fig. 3. Degree density (1st row), and output size (2nd row) for three exclusion queries per each pair of interaction types over the period of the first week of February 2018. (a), (d) Follow and mention. (b), (e) Follow and retweet. (c), (f) Mention and retweet.

- Every type of interaction is allowed (query denoted as $[1,1]$).
- One of the two interaction types is excluded (queries denoted as $[1,0]$, and $[0,1]$ for excluding the first and second type of interactions respectively).

Figure 3 shows for each pair of interactions the degree density (1st row), and the output size (2nd row). Interestingly, observe that in Fig. 3(c) the exclusion query $[0,1]$ that excludes mentions and allows retweets results in density close to 0. This is because the Twitter API considers every retweet as a mention. By excluding mentions, we exclude all retweets. The density is not exactly zero, due to some small noise in the crawled mentions, i.e., there exist a few retweets that have not been included in the mentions. We have performed more exclusion queries that involve more types of interactions. For instance, by looking into *reply, quote, retweet* interactions, we find the following results for two queries on February 1st, 2018.

- When we allow all types we find a subset of 351 nodes, whose retweet density is 72.6, reply density 3.86, and quote density 1.08. We observe this difference since the retweet layer of interactions is much denser than the other two.
- When we exclude the retweets, but allow quotes and replies, we find a set of 30 nodes whose reply degree density is 15.46, and quote degree density 0.066.

Effect of C, and W. As we discussed earlier, ranging W, from small values to $+\infty$ quantifies how much we care about excluding the undesired edge types. Table 4 shows what we observe typically on all experiments we have performed.

Specifically, we perform an exclusion query $[1, 0]$ on the *retweet, reply* interactions. We denote by S^* the output of Algorithm 3. By inspecting the last column $\rho_{\text{reply}}(S^*)$ of the table, we observe that even when we set the weight of each reply interaction to -1 (soft query), our algorithm outputs a set S^* with very few replies, for all $C \in \{\frac{1}{10}, 1, 10\}$ values we use. When W is set to the very large value $200\,000$ (hard query), $\rho_{\text{reply}}(S^*)$ becomes 0 but we also observe a drop in the degree density of the retweets. For instance for $C = 1$, $\rho_{\text{retweet}}(S^*)$ drops from 72.70 to 30.38.

Table 4. Exploring the effect of the negative weight $-W$ on the excluded edge types for various C values. For details, see Sect. 4.3.

C	W	$|S^*|$	$\rho_{\text{retweet}}(S^*)$	$\rho_{\text{reply}}(S^*)$
0.1	1	296	63.44	−0.75
	5	99	45.67	−0.01
	200 000	200	30.37	0
1	1	346	72.70	−2.75
	5	319	68.70	−1.29
	200 000	200	30.38	0
10	1	351	73.10	−3.31
	5	351	73.10	−3.31
	200 000	200	30.37	0

5   Open Problems

In this work we have initiated a formal study of DSD with negative weights. Understanding better the complexity of the problem remains open. For example, we provided sufficient conditions under which the problem is poly-time solvable. Developing an approximation or bi-criteria approximation algorithms for risk averse DSD that aims to maximize the expected reward subject to bounds on the risk is also an interesting open problem. Finally, and more broadly, designing risk-averse, efficient graph mining algorithms is an interesting direction.

References

1. Max-cut with negative weight edges by Peter Shor. https://cstheory.stackexchange.com/questions/2312/max-cut-with-negative-weight-edges
2. http://www.paccanarolab.org/static_content/clusterone/cl1_datasets.zip
3. Submitted to ECML-PKDD 2019. https://lastinggems.files.wordpress.com/2019/04/neg-dsd.pdf
4. TMDB uncertain graph. https://drive.google.com/open?id=1C69MndtfSoUflP-keBa0mbiC9FZD6xbpN

5. Bollobás, B., Janson, S., Riordan, O.: The phase transition in inhomogeneous random graphs. Random Struct. Algorithms **31**(1), 3–122 (2007)
6. Bonchi, F., Gullo, F., Kaltenbrunner, A., Volkovich, Y.: Core decomposition of uncertain graphs. In: Proceedings of the 20th ACM SIGKDD Conference, pp. 1316–1325. ACM (2014)
7. Cadena, J., Vullikanti, A.K., Aggarwal, C.C.: On dense subgraphs in signed network streams. In: 2016 IEEE 16th International Conference on Data Mining (ICDM), pp. 51–60. IEEE (2016)
8. Charikar, M.: Greedy approximation algorithms for finding dense components in a graph. In: Jansen, K., Khuller, S. (eds.) APPROX 2000. LNCS, vol. 1913, pp. 84–95. Springer, Heidelberg (2000). https://doi.org/10.1007/3-540-44436-X_10
9. Collins, S.R., et al.: Toward a comprehensive atlas of the physical interactome of *Saccharomyces cerevisiae*. Mol. Cell. Proteomics **6**(3), 439–450 (2007)
10. Dalvi, N.N., Suciu, D.: Efficient query evaluation on probabilistic databases. VLDB J. **16**(4), 523–544 (2007)
11. Galimberti, E., Bonchi, F., Gullo, F.: Core decomposition and densest subgraph in multilayer networks. In: Proceedings of the 2017 ACM on Conference on Information and Knowledge Management, pp. 1807–1816. ACM (2017)
12. Galimberti, E., Bonchi, F., Gullo, F., Lanciano, T.: Core decomposition in multilayer networks: theory, algorithms, and applications. arXiv preprint arXiv:1812.08712 (2018)
13. Gallo, G., Grigoriadis, M.D., Tarjan, R.E.: A fast parametric maximum flow algorithm and applications. J. Comput. **18**(1), 30–55 (1989)
14. Gavin, A.-C., et al.: Proteome survey reveals modularity of the yeast cell machinery. Nature **440**(7084), 631 (2006)
15. Gionis, A., Tsourakakis, C.E.: Dense subgraph discovery: KDD 2015 tutorial. In: Proceedings of the 21th ACM SIGKDD International Conference on Knowledge Discovery and Data Mining, pp. 2313–2314. ACM (2015)
16. Goldberg, A.V.: Finding a maximum density subgraph. Technical report, University of California at Berkeley (1984)
17. He, X., Kempe, D.: Robust influence maximization. In: Proceedings of the 22nd ACM SIGKDD International Conference on Knowledge Discovery and Data Mining, KDD 2016, pp. 885–894. ACM, New York (2016)
18. Jin, R., Liu, L., Aggarwal, C.C.: Discovering highly reliable subgraphs in uncertain graphs. In: Proceedings of KDD 2011, pp. 992–1000 (2011)
19. Kempe, D., Kleinberg, J., Tardos, É.: Maximizing the spread of influence through a social network. In: Proceedings of KDD 2003, pp. 137–146. ACM (2003)
20. Khuller, S., Saha, B.: On finding dense subgraphs. In: Albers, S., Marchetti-Spaccamela, A., Matias, Y., Nikoletseas, S., Thomas, W. (eds.) ICALP 2009, Part I. LNCS, vol. 5555, pp. 597–608. Springer, Heidelberg (2009). https://doi.org/10.1007/978-3-642-02927-1_50
21. Krogan, N.J., et al.: Global landscape of protein complexes in the yeast *Saccharomyces cerevisiae*. Nature **440**(7084), 637 (2006)
22. Liu, L., Jin, R., Aggarwal, C., Shen, Y.: Reliable clustering on uncertain graphs. In: Proceedings of ICDM 2012, pp. 459–468. IEEE (2012)
23. Miyauchi, A., Takeda, A.: Robust densest subgraph discovery. In: 2018 IEEE International Conference on Data Mining (ICDM), pp. 1188–1193. IEEE (2018)
24. Parchas, P., Gullo, F., Papadias, D., Bonchi, F.: The pursuit of a good possible world: extracting representative instances of uncertain graphs. In: Proceedings SIGMOD 2014, pp. 967–978 (2014)

25. Pratikakis, P.: twAwler: a lightweight Twitter crawler. arXiv preprint arXiv:1804.07748 (2018)
26. Ravi, R., Goemans, M.X.: The constrained minimum spanning tree problem. In: Karlsson, R., Lingas, A. (eds.) SWAT 1996. LNCS, vol. 1097, pp. 66–75. Springer, Heidelberg (1996). https://doi.org/10.1007/3-540-61422-2_121
27. Roth, A.E., Sönmez, T., Ünver, M.U.: Kidney exchange. Q. J. Econ. **119**(2), 457–488 (2004)
28. Serra, J., Arcos, J.L.: An empirical evaluation of similarity measures for time series classification. Knowl.-Based Syst. **67**, 305–314 (2014)
29. Tsourakakis, C.E.: The k-clique densest subgraph problem. In: 24th International World Wide Web Conference (WWW) (2015)
30. Tsourakakis, C.E., Bonchi, F., Gionis, A., Gullo, F., Tsiarli, M.: Denser than the densest subgraph: extracting optimal quasi-cliques with quality guarantees. In: Proceedings of the 19th ACM SIGKDD International Conference on Knowledge Discovery and Data Mining (2013)
31. Tsourakakis, C.E., Sekar, S., Lam, J., Yang, L.: Risk-averse matchings over uncertain graph databases. arXiv preprint arXiv:1801.03190 (2018)
32. Zou, Z.: Polynomial-time algorithm for finding densest subgraphs in uncertain graphs. In: Proceedings of MLG Workshop (2013)

Node Representation Learning
for Directed Graphs

Megha Khosla$^{(\boxtimes)}$, Jurek Leonhardt, Wolfgang Nejdl, and Avishek Anand

L3S Research Center, Hannover, Germany
{khosla,leonhardt,nejdl,anand}@l3s.de

Abstract. We propose a novel approach for learning node representations in directed graphs, which maintains separate views or embedding spaces for the two distinct node roles induced by the directionality of the edges. We argue that the previous approaches either fail to encode the edge directionality or their encodings cannot be generalized across tasks. With our simple *alternating random walk* strategy, we generate role specific vertex neighborhoods and train node embeddings in their corresponding source/target roles while fully exploiting the semantics of directed graphs. We also unearth the limitations of evaluations on directed graphs in previous works and propose a clear strategy for evaluating link prediction and graph reconstruction in directed graphs. We conduct extensive experiments to showcase our effectiveness on several real-world datasets on link prediction, node classification and graph reconstruction tasks. We show that the embeddings from our approach are indeed robust, generalizable and well performing across multiple kinds of tasks and graphs. We show that we consistently outperform all baselines for node classification task. In addition to providing a theoretical interpretation of our method we also show that we are considerably more robust than the other directed graph approaches.

Keywords: Directed graphs · Node representations · Link prediction · Graph reconstruction · Node classification

1 Introduction

Unsupervised representation learning of nodes in a graph refers to dimensionality reduction techniques where nodes are embedded in a continuous space and have dense representations. Such node embeddings have proven valuable as representations and features for a wide variety of prediction and social network analysis tasks such as link prediction [14], recommendations [25], vertex label assignment, graph generation [7] etc.

However most of the recent node embedding methods have been focused on undirected graphs with limited attention to the directed setting. Often valuable

Electronic supplementary material The online version of this chapter (https://doi.org/10.1007/978-3-030-46150-8_24) contains supplementary material, which is available to authorized users.

U. Brefeld et al. (Eds.): ECML PKDD 2019, LNAI 11906, pp. 395–411, 2020.
https://doi.org/10.1007/978-3-030-46150-8_24

knowledge is encoded in directed graph representations of real-world phenomena where an edge not only suggests relationships between entities, but the directionality is often representative of important asymmetric semantic information. Prime examples are follower networks, interaction networks, web graphs, and citation networks among others.

Most of the approaches in this regime [8, 19, 22] focus on the goal of preserving neighborhood structure of nodes when embedding one space into another, but suffer from some key limitations when representing directed graphs. First, most of these node embedding techniques operate on a single embedding space and distances in this space are considered to be symmetric. Consequently, even though some of the approaches claim to be applicable for directed graphs, they do not respect the **asymmetric roles** of the vertices in the directed graph. For example, in predicting links in an incomplete web graph or an evolving social network graph, it is more likely that a directed link exists from a less popular node, say Max Smith, to a more popular node, say an authoritative node Elon Musk, than the other way around. Algorithms employing single representations for nodes might be able to predict a link between Elon Musk and Max Smith but cannot predict the direction.

Secondly, approaches like APP [26] overcome the first limitation by using two embedding spaces but are unable to differentiate between directed neighborhoods where these neighborhoods can be distinguished based on reachability. For example, for a given node v there exists a neighborhood which is reachable from v and there exists another type of neighborhood to which v is reachable. More acutely, many nodes with zero outdegree and low indegree might not be sampled because of the training instance generation strategy from its random walk following only outgoing edges. This renders such approaches **not to be robust**, a desirable and important property for unsupervised representations, for several real-world graphs.

Finally, works like HOPE [17] rely on stricter definitions of neighborhoods dictated by proximity measures like Katz [9], Rooted PageRank etc. and cannot be generalized to a variety of tasks. In addition, they do not scale to very large graphs due to their reliance on matrix decomposition techniques. Moreover, the accuracy guarantees of HOPE rely on low rank assumption of the input data. Though not completely untrue for real world data, *singular value decomposition* (SVD) operations used in matrix factorization methods are known to be sensitive even for the case of a single outlier [2]. We later empirically demonstrate in our experiments that HOPE can not be easily adapted for the node classification task as it is linked to a particular proximity matrix.

We argue that the utility and strength of unsupervised node representations is in their (1) robustness across graphs and (2) flexibility and generalization to multiple tasks and propose a simple yet robust model for learning node representations in directed graphs.

Our Contribution. We propose a robust and generalizable approach for learning **N**ode **E**mbeddings **R**especting **D**irectionality (NERD) for directed and (un)–weighted graphs. NERD aims at learning representations that maximize the likelihood of preserving node neighborhoods. But unlike the previous methods, it identifies the existence of **two** different types of node neighborhoods; one in its source role and the other in its target role. We propose an *alternating random walk* strategy to sample such node neighborhoods while preserving their respective role information. Our alternating walk strategy is inspired from SALSA [13] which is a stochastic variation of the HITS [11] algorithm and also identifies two types of important nodes in a directed network: *hubs* and *authorities*. Roughly speaking, the paths generated with our alternating random walks alternate between hubs (source nodes) and authorities (target nodes), thereby sampling both neighboring hubs and authorities with respect to an input node. From a theoretical perspective we derive an equivalence for NERD's optimization in a matrix factorization framework. In addition, we also unearth the limitations of earlier works in the evaluation of models on directed graphs and propose new evaluation strategies for Link Prediction and Graph Reconstruction tasks in directed graphs. Finally we perform exhaustive experimental evaluation that validates the robustness and generalizability of our method.

2 Related Work

Traditionally, undirected graphs have been the main use case for graph embedding methods. Manifold learning techniques [3], for instance, embed nodes of the graph while preserving the local affinity reflected by the edges. Chen et al. [6] explore the directed links of the graph using random walks, and propose an embedding while preserving the local affinity defined by directed edges. Perrault-Joncas et al. [20] and Mousazadeh et al. [16] learn the embedding vectors based on Laplacian type operators and preserve the asymmetry property of edges in a vector field.

Advances in language modeling and unsupervised feature learning in text inspired their adaptations [4,8,19,22,23] to learn node embeddings where the main idea is to relate nodes which can reach other similar nodes via random walks. DeepWalk [19], for instance, samples truncated random walks from the graph, thus treating *walks* as equivalent of sentences, and then samples node-context pairs from a sliding window to train a *Skip-Gram* model [15]. Node2vec [8], on the other hand, uses a *biased* random walk procedure to explore diverse neighborhoods. LINE [22] which preserves first and second order proximities among the node representations can also be interpreted as embedding nodes closer appearing in random walk of length 1. VERSE [23] learns a single embedding matrix while encoding similarities between vertices sampled as first and last vertex in a PageRank style random walk.

Other works [5,10,18,24] investigate deep learning approaches for learning node representations. Like most of the other methods, they also use a single representation for a node, hence ignoring the asymmetric node roles. Other downsides of these deep learning approaches are the computationally expensive optimization and elaborate parameter tuning resulting in very complex models.

Asymmetry Preserving Approaches. To the best of our knowledge, there are only two works [17,26] which learn and use two embedding spaces for nodes, one representing its embedding in the source role and the other in the target role. Note that [1] does not preserve asymmetry for the nodes, which is the main theme of this work (more comparisons and discussions on this method can be found in the Appendix). HOPE [17] preserves the asymmetric role information of the nodes by approximating high-order proximity measures like Katz measure, Rooted PageRank etc. Basically they propose to decompose the similarity matrices given by these measures and use the two decompositions as representations of the nodes. HOPE cannot be easily generalized as it is tied to a particular measure. APP [26] proposes a random walk based method to encode rooted PageRank proximity. Specifically, it uses directed random walks with restarts to generate training pairs. Unlike other DeepWalk style random walk based methods, APP does not discard the learnt context matrix, on the other hand it uses it as a second (target) representation of the node. However, the random walk employed sometimes is unable to capture the global structure of the graph. Consider a directed graph with a prominent hub and authority structure where many authority nodes have no outgoing links. In such a case any directed random walk from a source node will halt after a few number of steps, irrespective of the stopping criteria. In contrast our alternating random walks also effectively sample low out-degree vertices in their target roles, thereby exploiting the complete topological information of a directed graph.

3   The NERD Model

Given a directed graph $G = (V, E)$ we aim to learn d-dimensional ($d << |V|$) representations, Φ_s and Φ_t, such that the similarities between vertices in their respective source and target roles are preserved. We argue that two vertices can be similar to each other in three ways: (i) both nodes in source roles (both pointing to similar authorities) (ii) both the nodes in target roles (for example both are neighbors of similar hubs) (iii) nodes in source-target roles (hub pointing to a authority). We extract such similar nodes via our *alternating random walk* strategy which alternates between vertices in opposite roles. For every vertex two embedding vectors are learnt via a single layer neural model encoding its similarities to other vertices in source and target roles. Alternatively, NERD can be interpreted as optimizing first order proximities in three types of *computational graphs* it extracts from the original graph via alternating random walks. We elaborate on this alternate view while explaining our learning framework in Sect. 3.2.

Notations. We first introduce the notations that would also be followed in the rest of the paper unless stated otherwise. Let $G = (V, E)$ be a directed weighted graph with N nodes and M edges. Let $w(e)$ denote the weight of edge e and $vol(G) = \sum_e w(e)$. For any vertex $v \in V$ let $d^{out}(v)$ denote the total outdegree of v, i.e. the sum of weights of the outgoing edges from v. Similarly $d^{in}(v)$ denotes the total indegree of v. For unweighted graphs, we assume the weight of each edge to be 1. Let $\Phi_s(v)$ and $\Phi_t(v)$ represent the respective embedding vectors for any node $v \in V$ in its role as source and target respectively. Let P^{in} and P^{out} denote the input and output degree distributions of G respectively. Specifically $P^{in}(v) = d^{in}(v)/vol(G)$ and $P^{out}(v) = d^{out}(v)/vol(G)$. We remark that the terms *vertex* and *node* are used interchangeably in this work.

3.1   Alternating Walks

We propose two alternating walks which alternate between source and target vertices and are referred to as *source* and *target* walks respectively. To understand the intuition behind these walks, consider a directed graph $G = (V, \boldsymbol{E})$ with N nodes. Now construct a copy of each of these N nodes and call this set V_c. Construct an undirected bipartite graph $G' = (V \cup V_c, E')$ such that for vertices $u, v \in V$ and $v_c \in V_c$, where v_c is a copy of vertex v, there is an edge $(u, v_c) \in E'$ if and only if $(u, v) \in \boldsymbol{E}$. In the directed graph G the adjacency matrix A is generally asymmetric, however, with our construction we obtain a symmetric adjacency matrix $\mathcal{A}$ for bipartite graph G'.

$$\mathcal{A} = \begin{pmatrix} 0 & A \\ A^T & 0 \end{pmatrix}. \tag{1}$$

A walk on this undirected bipartite G' starting from a vertex in V will now encounter source nodes in the odd time step and target nodes in the even time step. We call such a walk an *alternating* walk. Formally source and target alternating walks are defined as follows.

Definition 1. The Source Walk. Given a directed graph, we define *source-walk* of length k as a list of nodes $v_1, v_2, ..., v_{k+1}$ such that there exists edge (v_i, v_{i+1}) if i is odd and edge (v_{i+1}, v_i) if i is even: $v_1 \to v_2 \leftarrow v_3 \to \cdots$

Definition 2. The Target Walk. A *target walk* of length k, starting with an in-edge, from node v_1 to node v_{k+1} in a directed network is a list of nodes $v_1, v_2, ..., v_{k+1}$ such that there exists edge (v_{i+1}, v_i) if i is odd and edge (v_i, v_{i+1}) if i is even: $v_1 \leftarrow v_2 \to v_3 \leftarrow \cdots$

We now define the alternating random walk which we use to sample the respective neighborhoods of vertices in 3 types of NERD's computational graphs.

Alternating Random Walks. To generate an alternating random walk we first sample the input node for the source/target walks from the indegree/outdegree distribution of G. We then simulate source/target random walks of length ℓ. Let c_i denote the i-th node in the alternating random walk starting with node u. Then

$$\Pr(c_i = v' | c_{i-1} = v) = \begin{cases} \frac{1}{d^{out}(v)} \cdot w(v, v'), & \text{if } (v, v') \in \boldsymbol{E} \\ \frac{1}{d^{in}(v)} \cdot w(v', v), & \text{if } (v', v) \in \boldsymbol{E} \, . \\ 0, & \text{otherwise} \end{cases}$$

All nodes in a source/target walk in their respective roles constitute a neighborhood set for the input (the walk starts at the input node) node.

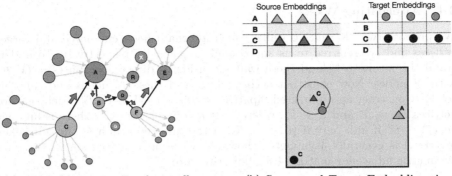

(a) NERD Alternating Random walks

(b) Source and Target Embeddings in NERD

Fig. 1. NERD performing a source walk with input vertex C on an example graph. Node C is the input node. Nodes C, B and F are in source roles and nodes A, D and E are in target roles. Nodes A, D, E and B, F constitute the target and source neighborhood of source node C. In Figure (b), we show two embedding representations for nodes in their source and target roles. Nodes C and A will be embedded closer in their source-target roles whereas will be far away in source-source or target-target roles.

3.2   Learning Framework Using Computation Graphs

As already mentioned NERD can be intuitively understood as optimizing first order proximity (embedding vertices sharing an edge closer) in 3 types of computation graphs that it extracts from G via alternating walks. In particular NERD operates on (i) directed source-target graphs (G_{st}) in which a directed edge exists between nodes of opposite roles (ii) source-source graphs (G_s) in which an undirected edge between nodes represents the similarity between two nodes in their source roles (iii) target-target graphs (G_t) in which an undirected edge between nodes represents the similarity between two nodes in their target roles. For example corresponding to a source walk say $v_1 \rightarrow v_2 \leftarrow v_3 \rightarrow \cdots$, (v_1, v_2) form an edge in G_{st}, (v_1, v_3) form an edge in G_s. For a node/neighbor pair u, v in roles r_1 and r_2 respectively in any of the computation graphs, we are interested in finding representations $\Phi_{r_1}(u)$ and $\Phi_{r_2}(v)$ in their respective roles such that the following objective is maximized.

$$\mathcal{O}(u, v) = \log \sigma(\Phi_{r_1}(u) \cdot \Phi_{r_2}(v)) + \kappa \mathbb{E}_{v' \sim P_{r_2}^n(v')}(\log \sigma(-\Phi_{r_1}(u) \cdot \Phi_{r_2}(v')), \quad (2)$$

where $\sigma(x) = \frac{1}{1+\exp(-x)}$ and $P_{r_2}^n(v')$ is the indegree or outdegree noise distribution and κ is the number of negative examples. We set $P_{r_2}^n(v') = \frac{d^{3/4}(v)}{\sum_{v \in V} d^{3/4}(v)}$, where d is the indegree (if r_2 is the target role) or outdegree (if r_2 is the source role) of vertex v. We optimize Eq. (2) using Asynchronous Stochastic Gradient Descent [21].

Figure 1 shows a toy example depicting the working of NERD. The pseudocode for NERD is stated in Algorithm 1. NERD performs a total of γ walks each walk being source walk or target walk with probability 0.5. The procedure for training a source or target walk is stated in Algorithm 2. The first vertex of the walk is the input vertex whose proximity is optimized (using negative samples) with respect to its neighbors in the opposite role (in line 14) and in the same role (in line 16). The joint training with respect to neighbors of same role can be controlled by a binary parameter JOINT.

Algorithm 1. NERD

Require: graph $G(V, \boldsymbol{E}_w)$, number of nodes to be sampled of each type n, embedding size d, number of walks γ, number of negative samples κ, JOINT $\in \{0, 1\}$
Ensure: matrix of source representations $\Phi_s \in \mathbb{R}^{|V| \times d}$ and target representations $\Phi_t \in \mathbb{R}^{|V| \times d}$

1: **function** NERD$(G, n, d, \gamma, \kappa)$
2:     Initialize Φ_s and Φ_t
3:     **for** $i = 0 \ldots \gamma$ **do**
4:         **if** (rand() > 0.5) **then**
5:             $s_1 \sim P^{out}$
6:             $W_s = $ SOURCEWALK(s_1)
7:             TRAIN$(W_s, s, \kappa, \text{JOINT})$ ▷ source role s
8:         **else**
9:             $t_1 \sim P^{in}$
10:            $W_t = $ TARGETWALK(t_1)
11:            TRAIN$(W_t, t, \kappa, \text{JOINT})$ ▷ target role t

---

We further derive closed form expression for NERD's optimization in the matrix framework as stated in the following theorem (for proof see Supplementary Material). Note that NERD (non-joint) refers to when the optimization is done only on the source/target graph.

Theorem 1. *For any two vertices i and j, NERD (non-joint) finds source $(\Phi_s(i))$ and target $(\Phi_t(j))$ embedding vectors such that $\Phi_s(i) \cdot \Phi_t(j)$ is the (i, j)th entry of the following matrix*

$$\log(vol(G) \sum_{r \in \{1, 3, \ldots, 2n-1\}} (D^{-1}\mathcal{A})^r D^{-1}) - \log \kappa,$$

where n and κ are as in Algorithm 1 and $\mathcal{A}$ is the adjacency matrix of the bipartite network G' obtained by mapping the given directed network G to G' as defined in (1).

Complexity Analysis. Sampling a vertex based on indegree or outdegree distribution requires constant amortized time by building an alias sampling table upfront. At any time only $2n$ neighbors are stored which is typically a small number as we observed in our experiments. In our experiments we set the total number of walks equal to 800 times the number of vertices. In each optimization

Algorithm 2. Train a source or target walk

```
1: function TRAIN(W, r, κ, JOINT)
2:     u ← W[0]
3:     error = 0
4:     for i = 1, 3, . . . 2n − 1 do
5:         for j = 0 . . . κ do
6:             if (j = 0) then
7:                 v1 = W[i]                    ▷ neigbor in opposite role r′
8:                 v2 = W[i + 1]                ▷ neigbor of same role r
9:                 label = 1
10:            else                             ▷ negative samples
11:                label = 1
12:                v1 ∼ P_{r′}^n
13:                v2 ∼ P_r^n
14:            error+ =UPDATE(Φ_r(u), Φ_{r′}(v1), label)
15:            if (JOINT) then
16:                error+ =UPDATE(Φ_r(u), Φ_r(v2), label)
17:        Φ_r(u) + = error
18:
19: function UPDATE(Φ(u), Φ(v), label)          ▷ //gradient update
20:    g = (label − σ(Φ(u) · Φ(v))) · λ
21:    Φ(v)+ = g ∗ Φ(u)
22:    return g ∗ Φ(v)
```

step we use $\kappa = \{3, 5\}$ negative samples, therefore, complexity of each optimization step is $O(d\kappa)$. As it requires $O(|E|)$ time to read the graph initially, the run time complexity for NERD can be given as $O(nd\kappa N + |E|)$. The space complexity of NERD is $O(|E|)$. As our method is linear (with respect to space and time complexity) in the input size, it is scalable for large graphs.

4   Experiments

In this section we present how we evaluate NERD[1] against several state-of-the-art node embedding algorithms. We use the original implementations of the authors for all the baselines (if available). We also employ parameter tuning whenever possible (parameter settings are detailed in Supplementary Material), otherwise we use the best parameters reported by the authors in their respective papers. We perform comparisons corresponding to three tasks – Link Prediction, Graph Reconstruction and Node classification. In the next section we explain the datasets used in our evaluations.

A brief summary of the characteristics of the datasets (details are links provided in the implementation page) is presented in Table 1. We recall that *reciprocity* in a directed graph equals the proportion of edges for which an edge in

---

[1] We make available our implementation with corresponding data at https://git.l3s. uni-hannover.de/khosla/nerd.

Table 1. Dataset characteristics: number of nodes $|V|$, number of edges $|E|$; number of node labels $|\mathcal{L}|$.

Dataset	Size			Statistics		Details		
	$|V|$	$|E|$	$|\mathcal{L}|$	Diameter	Reciprocity	Labels	Vertex	Edges
Cora	23,166	91,500	79	20	0.051	✓	Papers	Citation
Twitter	465,017	834,797	-	8	0.003	-	People	Follower
Epinion	75,879	508,837	-	15	0.405	-	People	Trust
PubMed	19,718	44,327	3	18	0.0007	✓	Papers	Citation
CoCit	44,034	195,361	15	25	0	✓	Papers	Citation

the opposite direction exists, i.e., that are reciprocated. All the above datasets except PubMed and Cocitation datasets have been collected from [12].

Baselines. We compare the NERD model with several existing node embedding models for link prediction, graph reconstruction and node classification tasks. As baselines we consider methods like APP [26] and HOPE [17] which uses two embedding spaces to embed vertices in their two roles. We also compare against other popular single embedding based methods: DeepWalk [19], LINE [22], Node2vec [8] and VERSE [23]. All these methods are detailed in related work. As NERD is an unsupervised shallow neural method, for fair comparisons, semi-supervised or unsupervised deep models are not considered as baselines.

4.1   Link Prediction

The aim of the link prediction task is to predict missing edges given a network with a fraction of removed edges. A fraction of edges is removed randomly to serve as the *test split* while the residual network can be utilized for training. The test split is balanced with negative edges sampled from random vertex pairs that have no edges between them. We refer to this setting as the *undirected* setting. While removing edges randomly, we make sure that no node is isolated, otherwise the representations corresponding to these nodes can not be learned.

Directed Link Prediction. Since we are interested in not only the existence of the edges between nodes but also the directions of these edges, we consider a slight modification in the test split setting. Note that this is a slight departure from the experimental settings used in previous works where only the presence of an edge was evaluated. We posit that in a directed network the algorithm should also be able to decide the direction of the predicted edge. To achieve this, we allow for negative edges that are complements of the true (positive) edges which exist already in the test split.

We experiment by varying the number of such complement edges created by inverting a fraction of the true edges in the test split. A value of 0 corresponds to the classical undirected graph setting while a value in $(0, 1]$ determines what fraction of positive edges from the test split are inverted at most to create negative examples. It can also happen that an inverted edge is actually an edge in the network, in which case we discard it and pick up some random pair which corresponds to a negative edge. Such a construction of test data is essential to check if the algorithm is also predicting the correct direction of the edge along with the existence of the edge. Please note that we always make sure that in the test set the number of negative examples is equal to the number of positive examples. Embedding dimensions are set to 128 for all models for both settings.

Table 2 presents the ROC-AUC (Area Under the Receiver Operating Characteristic Curve) scores for link prediction for three datasets (missing datasets show similar trends, results not presented because of space constraints). More specifically, given an embedding, the inner product of two node representations normalized by the sigmoid function is employed as the similarity/link-probability measurement for all the algorithms. Fraction 0% correspond to the undirected setting in which the negative edges in the test set are randomly picked. The 50% and 100% corresponds to directed setting in which at most 50% and 100% positive edges of test set are inverted to form negative edges. Please note that if an inverted edge is actually an edge in the network, we discard it and pick up some random pair.

Performance on Cora. VERSE outperforms others for the undirected setting in the Cora dataset. But its performance decreases rapidly in the directed setting where the algorithm is forced to assign a direction to the edge. The performance of the three directed methods (APP, HOPE and NERD) is stable supporting the fact that these methods can correctly predict the edge direction in addition to predicting a link. NERD is the next best (AUC of 0.788) and outperforms HOPE for directed setting with 50% and 100% (AUC of 0.813) test set edge reversal. This means that whenever NERD predicts the presence of an edge it in fact also predicts the edge directionality accurately.

Performance on Twitter. For the Twitter dataset, HOPE outperforms all other methods and is closely followed by NERD for 60–40 split of training-test data. Figure 2 shows the performance of three directed graph methods: APP, HOPE and NERD on 70–30 and 90–10 training-test splits for Twitter respectively. Here we plot the AUC scores by varying the fraction of inverted edges in the test split to construct negative test edges. We omit other methods as all of them have a very low performance. We make several interesting observations here. First, HOPE which performs best for 60–40 split shows a decrease in performance with the increase in training data. We believe that the parameters for HOPE namely the attenuation factor which was tuned for best performance on a smaller amount of training data no longer might not be applicable for larger training data. This renders such a method to be very sensitive to structural changes in the graph. Second, APP's performance improves with increasing training data but is not as stable as NERD and HOPE in the directed setting when the fraction of inverted edges is increased, i.e., it does not always correctly predict the direction of an edge. Third, NERD's performance stays stable and improves on increasing the training data, which confirms our justification that it is more robust to structural changes caused by random addition/removal of edges. Moreover, at 90% training data it is the best performing method and second best but consistent (in predicting edge direction) for other splits. Finally we observe that Twitter has a prominent hub-authority structure with more than 99% vertices with zero out-degree. Using non-alternating directed walks on Twitter hinders APP and other similar random walk methods to fully explore the network structure as much as they could do for Cora.

Performance on Epinions. VERSE shows a high performance on Epinions in undirected setting which is not surprising as Epinions has a high reciprocity with more than 40% of the edges existing in both directions. NERD on the other hand beats the two other directed methods APP and HOPE for both the settings. As the fraction of edge reversals increases, NERD also starts performing better than VERSE. We note that even though NERD does not outperforms all methods on link prediction, it shows more robustness across datasets being the second best performing (when not the best) and is consistent in predicting the right edge direction i.e., its performance does not vary a lot (except in Epinions with high reciprocity) with increasing fraction of positive test edge inversions in the directed setting.

Table 2. Link Prediction Results for directed graphs with (1) random negative edges in test set (2) 50% of the test negative edges created by reversing positive edges (3) when all positive edges are reversed to create negative edges in the test set. The top scores are shown in bold whereas the second best scores are underlined.

Method	Cora			Twitter			Epinion		
	0%	50%	100%	0%	50%	100%	0%	50%	100
DeepWalk	0.836	0.669	0.532	0.536	0.522	0.501	0.538	0.560	0.563
Node2vec	0.840	0.649	0.526	0.500	0.500	0.500	<u>0.930</u>	0.750	0.726
VERSE	**0.875**	0.688	0.500	0.52	0.510	0.501	**0.955**	<u>0.753</u>	<u>0.739</u>
APP	<u>0.865</u>	**0.841**	**0.833**	0.723	0.638	0.555	0.639	0.477	0.455
HOPE	0.784	0.734	0.718	**0.981**	**0.980**	**0.979**	0.807	0.718	0.716
LINE-1+2	0.735	0.619	0.518	0.009	0.255	0.500	0.658	0.622	0.617
LINE-1	0.781	0.644	0.526	0.007	0.007	0.254	0.744	0.677	0.668
LINE-2	0.693	0.598	0.514	0.511	0.507	0.503	0.555	0.544	0.543
NERD	0.795	<u>0.788</u>	<u>0.813</u>	<u>0.969</u>	<u>0.968</u>	<u>0.967</u>	0.906	**0.774**	**0.771**

4.2 Graph Reconstruction

In the graph reconstruction task we evaluate how well the embeddings preserve neighborhood information. There are two separate evaluation regimes for graph

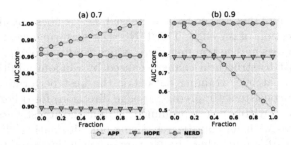

Fig. 2. Link prediction in Twitter. The y-axis shows the AUC scores and the x-axis is the maximum fraction of edges that are inverted in the test split. The models are trained on 70% and 90% of the Twitter edges respectively. The fraction on the x-axis indicates the maximum fraction of inverted positive test edges to create negative test edges. Note that the train-test split is the same over all fractions.

reconstruction in previous works. One line of work [17], that we refer to as *edge-centric* evaluation, relies on sampling random pairs of nodes from the original graphs into their test set. These candidate edges are then ordered according to their similarity in the embedding space. Precision is then computed at different rank depths where the relevant edges are the ones present in the original graph. On the other hand, [23] perform a *node-centric* evaluation where precision is computed on a per-node basis. For a given node v with an outdegree k, embeddings are used to perform a k-nearest neighbor search for v and precision is computed based on how many actual neighbors the k-NN procedure is able to extract.

Directed Graph Reconstruction. We believe that the edge-centric evaluation suffers from sparsity issues typical in real-world networks and even if a large number of node pairs are sampled, the fraction of relevant edges retrieved tends to remain low. More acutely, such an approach does not model the neighborhood reconstruction aspect of graph construction and is rather close to predicting links. We adopt the node-centric evaluation approach where we intend to also compute precision on directed networks with a slight modification. In particular, we propose to compute precision for both outgoing and incoming edges for a given node. This is different from previous evaluation approaches which only considers the reconstruction of adjacency list of a node, i.e., only its outgoing neighbors. Moreover in our proposed evaluation strategy we do not assume the prior knowledge of the indegree or outdegree.

As in Link Prediction, the similarity or the probability of an edge (i, j) is computed as the sigmoid over the dot product of their respective embedding vectors. For HOPE, NERD and APP we use the corresponding source and target vectors respectively. We do not assume the prior knowledge of the indegree or outdegree, rather we compute the precision for $k \in \{1, 2, 5, 10, 100, 200\}$. For a given k we obtain the k-nearest neighbors ranked by sigmoid similarity for each embedding approach. If a node has an outdegree or indegree of zero, we set the precision to be 1 if the sigmoid corresponding to the nearest neighbor is less than 0.51 (recall that $\sigma(\boldsymbol{x} \cdot \boldsymbol{y}) = 0.5$ for $\boldsymbol{x} \cdot \boldsymbol{y} = 0$), otherwise we set it to 0. In other cases, for a given node v and a specific k we compute $P^k_{out}(v)$ and $P^k_{in}(v)$ corresponding to the outgoing and incoming edges as

$$P^k_{out}(v) = \frac{\mathcal{N}^k_{out} \cap N^{out}(v)}{k}, \quad P^k_{in}(v) = \frac{\mathcal{N}^k_{in} \cap N^{in}(v)}{k},$$

where $\mathcal{N}^k_{out}(v)$ and $\mathcal{N}^k_{in}(v)$ are the k nearest outgoing (to whom v has outgoing edges) and incoming (neighbors point to v) neighbors retrieved from the embeddings and $N^{out}(v)$ and $N^{in}(v)$ are the actual outgoing and incoming neighbors of v. We then compute the Micro-F1 score as the harmonic mean of $P^k_{in}(v)$ and $P^k_{out}(v)$. To avoid any zeros in the denominator, we add a very small $\varepsilon = 10^{-5}$ to each precision value before computing the harmonic mean. We finally report the final precision as the average of these harmonic means over the nodes in the test set.

Results. We perform the graph reconstruction task on the Cora, Cocitation and Twitter datasets. In order to create the test set we randomly sample 10% of the nodes for Cora and Cocitation datasets and 1% of Twitter. We plot the final averaged precision corresponding to different values of k in Fig. 3.

For the Cora dataset, NERD clearly outperforms all the other models including HOPE. In particular for $k = 1$, NERD shows an improvement of 63% over HOPE which in some sense is fine tuned for this task.

The trend between NERD and HOPE is reversed for Twitter dataset, where HOPE behaves like an almost exact algorithm. This can be attributed to the low rank of the associated Katz similarity matrix. Note that only 2502 out of more than $400K$ nodes have non-zero outdegree which causes a tremendous drop in the rank of the associated Katz matrix. We recall that HOPE's approximation guarantee relies on the low rank assumption of the associated similarity matrix which seems to be fulfilled quite well in this dataset. The performance of other models in our directed setting clearly shows their inadequacy to reconstruct neighborhoods in directed graphs. For Twitter, we only show plots corresponding to HOPE and NERD as precision corresponding to other methods is close to 10^{-5}.

Again for Cocitation NERD performs the best with an improvement of around 12.5% for $k = 1$ over the second best performing method, HOPE. Once again, NERD exhibited robustness in this task as for Twitter, it is closest to the best performing method. Note that some of the methods like VERSE and APP which were sometimes better performing than NERD in link prediction show a poor performance across all datasets in graph reconstruction task. Note that this task is harder than link prediction as the model not only needs to predict the incoming and outgoing neighbors but also has no prior knowledge of the number of neighbors. Moreover the test set for this task is not balanced in the sense that for each test node the model needs to distinguish between small number of positive edges with a huge number of negative edges, for example for small k.

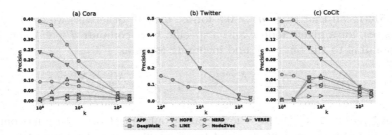

Fig. 3. Graph reconstruction for Cora, Twitter and CoCitation Networks with precision computed on both outgoing and incoming edges. NERD shows an improvement of 63.1% (for $k = 1$) as compared to HOPE in the Cora dataset. The trend is reversed in the Twitter dataset because of the exact nature of HOPE on low-rank Twitter data. For Twitter, all methods except NERD and HOPE have precision close to 10^{-5}, therefore we do not show them in the plots. NERD shows an improvement of 12.5% (for $k = 1$) as compared to HOPE in the CoCit dataset.

4.3   Node Classification

We run experiments for predicting labels in the Cora, CoCitation and PubMed datasets (labels were not available for other two datasets). We report the Micro-F1 and Macro-F1 scores after a 5-fold multi-label classification using one-vs-rest logistic regression. The main aim of this experiment is to show that NERD is generalizable across tasks and also performs well for a task like node classification which is not fine tuned for directed graphs. Unlike APP and HOPE, NERD also performs the best in this task over all the 3 datasets. Other single embedding based methods like DeepWalk and Node2vec also exhibit a good performance for node classification indicating that edge directionality might not be a very important factor for node labels at least for the studied datasets. HOPE which performs very well for link prediction and graph reconstruction tasks shows a poorer performance (Table 3).

As we already pointed out that HOPE is tied to particular proximity matrix and adjusting it for a task becomes much harder and non-intuitive than random walk based methods where hyper parameters can be easily fine-tuned. We also note that for HOPE the similarity between nodes i and j is determined by the effective distance between them which is computed using the Katz measure, penalizing longer distances by an attenuation factor β. The advantage of such a degrading distance measure is that it conserves the adjacency similarity of the graph, which reflects in our experiments on Graph Reconstruction. NERD on the other hand also takes into account how likely i can influence j by taking into account the likelihood of the traversal of various alternating paths between i and j. In other words, NERD constructs the local neighborhood based on how likely this neighborhood can influence the node, which helps the classifier to learn better labels on NERD trained embeddings.

Table 3. Node Classification results in terms of Micro-F1 and Macro-F1. All results are mean of 5-fold cross validations. Each node in Cora has multiple labels, for PubMed and CoCit, there is a single label per node.

Method	PubMed		Cora		CoCit	
	mic.	mac.	mic.	mac.	mic.	mac.
DeepWalk	73.96	71.34	64.98	**51.53**	41.92	30.07
Node2vec	72.36	68.54	65.74	49.12	41.64	28.18
VERSE	71.24	68.68	60.87	45.52	40.17	27.56
APP	69.00	65.20	64.58	47.03	40.34	28.06
HOPE	63.00	54.6	26.23	1.22	16.66	1.91
LINE-1+2	62.29	59.79	54.04	41.83	37.71	26.75
LINE-1	55.65	53.83	62.36	47.19	36.10	25.70
LINE-2	56.81	51.71	51.05	35.37	31.4	20.59
NERD	**76.70**	**74.67**	**67.75**	<u>51.30</u>	**44.84**	**33.49**

5   Conclusion

We presented a novel approach, NERD, for embedding directed graphs while preserving the role semantics of the nodes. We propose an alternating random walk strategy to sample node neighborhoods from a directed graph. The runtime and space complexities of NERD are both linear in the input size, which makes it suitable for large scale directed graphs. In addition to providing advantages of using two embedding representations of nodes in a directed graph, we revisit the previously used evaluation strategies for directed graphs. We chart out a clear evaluation strategy for link prediction and graph reconstruction tasks. We observe in our experiments where we find that a method performing best in one of the tasks might perform the worst in the other task. This beats the whole idea of unsupervised learning which is supposed not to be fine tuned towards a particular task but should be performing well across different tasks. We show that the embeddings from NERD are indeed robust, generalizable and well performing across multiple types of tasks and networks. We have showcased the effectiveness of NERD by employing a shallow neural model to optimize the topology of the extracted computational graphs. In future we will employ deeper models to capture non-linearities while preserving the respective topologies.

Acknowledgements. This work is partially funded by SoBigData (EU's Horizon 2020 grant agreement No. 654024).

References

1. Abu-El-Haija, S., Perozzi, B., Al-Rfou, R.: Learning edge representations via low-rank asymmetric projections. In: CIKM 2017, pp. 1787–1796 (2017)
2. Ammann, L.P.: Robust singular value decompositions: a new approach to projection pursuit. J. Am. Stat. Assoc. **88**(422), 505–514 (1993)
3. Belkin, M., Niyogi, P.: Laplacian eigenmaps and spectral techniques for embedding and clustering. Adv. Neural Inf. Process. Syst. **14**, 585–591 (2002)
4. Cao, S., Lu, W., Xu, Q.: GraRep: learning graph representations with global structural information. In: CIKM 2015, pp. 891–900 (2015)
5. Cao, S., Lu, W., Xu, Q.: Deep neural networks for learning graph representations. In: Proceedings of AAAI, AAAI 2016, pp. 1145–1152 (2016)
6. Chen, M., Yang, Q., Tang, X.: Directed graph embedding. In: IJCAI (2007)
7. Drobyshevskiy, M., Korshunov, A., Turdakov, D.: Learning and scaling directed networks via graph embedding. In: Ceci, M., Hollmén, J., Todorovski, L., Vens, C., Džeroski, S. (eds.) ECML PKDD 2017. LNCS (LNAI), vol. 10534, pp. 634–650. Springer, Cham (2017). https://doi.org/10.1007/978-3-319-71249-9_38
8. Grover, A., Leskovec, J.: Node2vec: scalable feature learning for networks. In: KDD, pp. 855–864 (2016)
9. Katz, L.: A new status index derived from sociometric analysis. Psychometrika **18**(1), 39–43 (1953)
10. Kipf, T.N., Welling, M.: Variational graph auto-encoders. In: NeurIPS Workshop on Bayesian Deep Learning (NeurIPS-16 BDL) (2016)
11. Kleinberg, J.M.: Authoritative sources in a hyperlinked environment. J. ACM **46**(5), 604–632 (1999)
12. Kunegis, J.: KONECT datasets: Koblenz network collection (2015). http://konect.uni-koblenz.de
13. Lempel, R., Moran, S.: SALSA: the stochastic approach for link-structure analysis. ACM Trans. Inf. Syst. (TOIS) **19**(2), 131–160 (2001)
14. Liben-Nowell, D., Kleinberg, J.: The link-prediction problem for social networks. J. Am. Soc. Inf. Sci. Technol. **58**(7), 1019–1031 (2007)
15. Mikolov, T., Sutskever, I., Chen, K., Corrado, G.S., Dean, J.: Distributed representations of words and phrases and their compositionality. In: Proceedings of the 27th Annual Conference on Neural Information Processing Systems 2013, pp. 3111–3119 (2013)
16. Mousazadeh, S., Cohen, I.: Embedding and function extension on directed graph. Sig. Process. **111**(C), 137–149 (2015)
17. Ou, M., Cui, P., Pei, J., Zhang, Z., Zhu, W.: Asymmetric transitivity preserving graph embedding. In: KDD, pp. 1105–1114 (2016)
18. Pan, S., Hu, R., Long, G., Jiang, J., Yao, L., Zhang, C.: Adversarially regularized graph autoencoder for graph embedding. In: IJCAI 2018, pp. 2609–2615 (2018)
19. Perozzi, B., Al-Rfou, R., Skiena, S.: Deepwalk: online learning of social representations. In: Proceedings of SIGKDD, pp. 701–710 (2014)
20. Perrault-Joncas, D.C., Meila, M.: Directed graph embedding: an algorithm based on continuous limits of Laplacian-type operators. In: Advances in Neural Information Processing Systems, pp. 990–998 (2011)
21. Recht, B., Re, C., Wright, S., Niu, F.: Hogwild: a lock-free approach to parallelizing stochastic gradient descent. In: Advances in Neural Information Processing Systems 24, pp. 693–701 (2011)

22. Tang, J., Qu, M., Wang, M., Zhang, M., Yan, J., Mei, Q.: Line: large-scale information network embedding. In: Proceedings of the 24th International Conference on World Wide Web, pp. 1067–1077 (2015)
23. Tsitsulin, A., Mottin, D., Karras, P., Müller, E.: Verse: versatile graph embeddings from similarity measures. In: Proceedings of the 2018 World Wide Web Conference, pp. 539–548 (2018)
24. Wang, D., Cui, P., Zhu, W.: Structural deep network embedding. In: Proceedings of the 22nd ACM SIGKDD International Conference on Knowledge Discovery and Data Mining, KDD 2016, pp. 1225–1234 (2016)
25. Ying, R., He, R., Chen, K., Eksombatchai, P., Hamilton, W.L., Leskovec, J.: Graph convolutional neural networks for web-scale recommender systems. In: KDD, pp. 974–983 (2018)
26. Zhou, C., Liu, Y., Liu, X., Liu, Z., Gao, J.: Scalable graph embedding for asymmetric proximity. In: AAAI Conference on Artificial Intelligence (AAAI 2017) (2017)

Link Prediction via Higher-Order Motif Features

Ghadeer Abuoda[1]([✉]), Gianmarco De Francisci Morales[2],
and Ashraf Aboulnaga[3]

[1] College of Science and Engineering, HBKU, Doha, Qatar
gabuoda@hbku.edu.qa
[2] ISI Foundation, Turin, Italy
gdfm@acm.org
[3] Qatar Computing Research Institute, Doha, Qatar
aaboulnaga@hbku.edu.qa

Abstract. Link prediction requires predicting which new links are likely
to appear in a graph. In this paper, we present an approach for link prediction that relies on higher-order analysis of the graph topology, well
beyond the typical approach which relies on common neighbors. We treat
the link prediction problem as a supervised classification problem, and
we propose a set of features that depend on the patterns or *motifs* that a
pair of nodes occurs in. By using motifs of sizes 3, 4, and 5, our approach
captures a high level of detail about the graph topology. In addition, we
propose two optimizations to construct the classification dataset from the
graph. First, we propose adding negative examples to the graph as an
alternative to the common approach of removing positive ones. Second,
we show that it is important to control for the shortest-path distance
when sampling pairs of nodes to form negative examples, since the difficulty of prediction varies with the distance. We experimentally demonstrate that using our proposed motif features in off-the-shelf classifiers
results in up to 10% points increase in accuracy over prior topology-based
and feature-learning methods.

Keywords: Link prediction · Motifs

1 Introduction

Given a graph $G(V, E)$ at time t_1, the *link prediction* problem requires finding
which edges $\{e \notin E\}$ will appear in the graph at time $t_2 > t_1$ [24]. Predicting
which new connections are likely to be formed is a fundamental primitive in
graph mining, with applications in several domains. In social media, friend and
content recommendations are often modeled as link prediction problems [4]. Link
prediction has also been used to detect credit card fraud in the cybersecurity
domain [24], to predict protein-protein interactions in bioinformatics [5,17], for
shopping and movie recommendation in e-commerce [10], and even to identify
criminals and hidden groups of terrorists based on their activities [6].

© Springer Nature Switzerland AG 2020
U. Brefeld et al. (Eds.): ECML PKDD 2019, LNAI 11906, pp. 412–429, 2020.
https://doi.org/10.1007/978-3-030-46150-8_25

Traditionally, link prediction models rely on topological features of the graph, and on domain-specific attributes of the nodes (usually to induce a similarity function) [7]. Most topological features are based on common neighbors, i.e., they rely on the idea of 'closing triangles' [30]. More advanced approaches such as non-negative matrix factorization (NMF) and graph embeddings have also been tried recently [27,42]. However, traditional topological features that rely on common neighbors, such as the Jaccard index and Adamic/Adar measure [2], have proven to be very strong baselines which are hard to beat [42].

These traditional features are not only effective, but also efficient to compute, as they originate from triadic graph substructures. Fortunately, recent developments in algorithms and systems have improved our ability to efficiently count motifs with more than three nodes [3,41]. Given the outstanding results of traditional topological features, it is natural to look towards more complex features based on motifs for better predictive power [17,32,34]. In this paper, we show that using features based on higher-order motifs with a carefully designed classification dataset significantly improves the accuracy of link prediction models.

The present work focuses only on topological features, as node attribute features are domain- and application-specific, and are orthogonal in scope. As is common practice, we cast the link prediction problem as a binary classification task. We train a machine learning model on a sample of node pairs from the graph, where pairs with an edge between them represent a positive example, and pairs without an edge represent a negative one [12].

When extracting features, two technical issues deserve particular attention: how to generate motif features in a way that is consistent between training and testing, and how to select the negative examples for the dataset. For the first issue, the common practice is to remove a set of existing edges from the graph (the positive test set), and then train the classifier on the remaining edges. Here we propose an alternative based on adding a set of negative examples (non-existing edges) to the graph when extracting the features. In our experiments, this variant consistently outperforms the former in terms of accuracy. For the second issue, we show that distance between nodes in negative examples is an important factor that should be controlled for when creating a dataset (an underappreciated fact in the link prediction literature [44]).

The main contributions of this study are as follows:

- We show that complex topological features based on higher-order motifs are powerful indicators for the link prediction problem in a variety of domains;
- These features improve the accuracy of standard classifiers by up to 10% points over the state-of-the-art;
- We re-examine the common practice of removing existing edges from the graph to create the classification dataset, and propose an alternative based on adding negative examples, which provides better accuracy;
- We detail the effect of the distance of the pair of nodes for negative examples on the classification accuracy.

2   Problem Definition and Preliminaries

Consider graph $G(V, E_{t_1})$ at a given time t_1, where V is the set of nodes in the graph and E_{t_1} is the set of edges that connect the nodes of the graph at that time. Link prediction aims to find which new edges are likely to appear at time $t_2 > t_1$, i.e., to predict the set $\{e : e \notin E_{t_1} \wedge e \in E_{t_2}\}$. We assume G is undirected and unweighted, and the set of nodes V does not change in time.

While the real application of link prediction involves time, very often testing prediction algorithms in these conditions is not straightforward, mostly due to the unavailability of the history of the evolution of the graph structure. Therefore, in most cases, link prediction is cast as a standard binary supervised classification task [6]. In this scenario, each data point corresponds to a pair of nodes (u, v) in a static graph, and the label $L(u, v) = 1$ if $(u, v) \in E$, else $L(u, v) = -1$. The edges in the graph can be used as positive examples, while for negative examples we can sample pairs of nodes in the graph which are not connected by an edge. We call these pairs of nodes *negative edges*.

2.1   Motifs

Motifs are small, connected, non-isomorphic subgraphs which appear in a larger graph [29,38]. Each k-motif represents a topological pattern of interconnection between k nodes in a graph. We denote each motif as '$mk.n$' where k is the number of nodes in the motif and n is an ordinal number which identifies the specific edge pattern in the motif (a list of motifs of sizes 3–5 is available in the extended version of this paper [1]).

Motifs have been shown to be a powerful graph analysis tool in previous work. The motif profile, the frequency distribution of the motifs in a graph, is used as a 'fingerprint' of a graph [28]. Therefore, the usefulness of motifs to capture the macro structure of a graph is well established [43]. However, for our purpose, we are more interested in their ability to capture the micro structure of the graph (i.e., the neighborhood).

Counting k-motifs is an expensive operation, as their number grows exponentially in k. However, thanks to recent advances in both algorithms and systems, we are now able to count k-motifs on graphs with millions of edges for values of k of 5 or more [9,41]. We leverage this capability to capture complex topological features for the link prediction task, and go beyond the simple triangle-based features that have been traditionally used.

3   Motif Features

The features in our model correspond to the number of occurrences of an edge (positive or negative) within different k-motifs. That is, for each example edge in the classification dataset, we enumerate the k-motifs that the edge is part of, and then count the occurrences of each different motif. In this paper, we use 3-, 4-, and 5-motifs. Motifs of even higher order are prohibitively expensive to

			Features					
Graph	Edge	Class	m4.1	m4.2	m4.3	m4.4	m4.5	m4.6
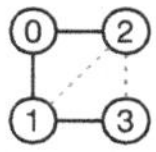	1-2	Positive	1	0	0	0	0	0
	2-3	Negative	1	0	0	0	0	0

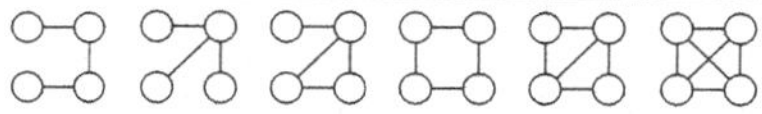

Fig. 1. Motif features when positive examples are removed from the graph (RMV). (Color figure online)

			Features					
Graph	Edge	Class	m4.1	m4.2	m4.3	m4.4	m4.5	m4.6
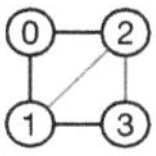	1-2	Positive	2	2	4	0	1	0
	2-3	Negative	4	1	3	1	1	0

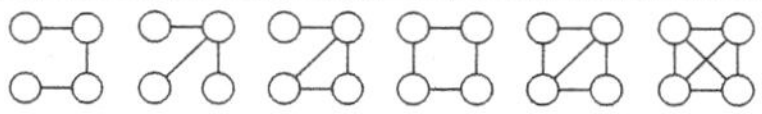

Fig. 2. Motif features when negative examples are inserted into the graph (INS).

compute for large graphs, and we experimentally demonstrate high prediction accuracy with $k \in \{3, 4, 5\}$. There are 2, 6, and 21 motifs for $k = 3, 4$, and 5, respectively, and this is the number of features we generate for each k.

3.1   Equal Treatment of Positive and Negative Examples

It is of paramount importance to treat both positive and negative example edges in the same way with respect to feature extraction, especially when dealing with the test set. To exemplify why this is important, imagine using $k = 3$ and not addressing this issue. The two possible features are then the wedge (or open triangle) and the closed triangle. Positive edges will have a mix of both features, but negative edges will never appear in a closed triangle, by construction. Thus, this way of extracting features leaks information about the class into the features themselves. This leakage is clearly an issue for the test set, but in order for the features to be meaningful, we need to apply the same extraction process to both the training set and the test set.

To solve this issue we have two possible options: (i) remove positive edges from the motif, which we denote RMV, or (ii) insert negative edges into the motif, which we denote INS. The former option corresponds to the traditional way of handling link prediction as a classification task, where a set of (positive) edges are withheld from the model. The latter is a novel way of handling the feature extraction that has not been considered previously. It corresponds to asking the following question: "If this edge was added to the graph, would its neighborhood look like other ones already in the graph?"

In the first method, RMV, we remove the example positive edges from the graph and extract the features by looking at motifs that contain both endpoints of a removed edge. The features for negative edges are computed in a similar manner, by looking at the motifs containing both endpoints of the negative pair. In this case, no modification to the graph is needed for negative edges.

By following this methodology, a number of motifs will never appear as features (e.g., fully connected cliques). In addition, an example edge never contributes to producing the motifs that it is part of. An example for $k = 4$ is shown in Fig. 1. Let green edges be positive examples, red edges be negative examples, and black edges be part of the graph but not in the classification dataset (i.e., not sampled). Additionally, dashed edges are removed from the graph. In this case, positive edge $(1, 2)$ is removed from the graph and negative edge $(2, 3)$ is sampled but not inserted. Removing edge $(1, 2)$ changes the motifs in this neighborhood. For example, motifs m4.2 and m4.3 do not appear even though edge $(1, 2)$ was part of instances of these motifs in the original unmodified graph. After removing edge $(1, 2)$, the only 4-motif that appears is m4.1, which appears once. Since it contains the nodes in edges $(1, 2)$ and $(2, 3)$, both edges have a value 1 for feature m4.1.

In the second method, INS, we insert negative example edges into the graph before extracting and counting motifs. No modification to the graph is needed for positive example edges. After inserting the negative example edges, we count the motifs for positive and negative edges in the same way. All motifs can appear as features, and an example edge contributes to all the motifs it is part of. Figure 2 shows the same example as Fig. 1, but now the negative edge $(2, 3)$ is added to the graph. Each feature of an example edge (positive or negative) corresponds to a motif which includes the edge itself. As an illustration of extracting motif features, consider m4.2 and m4.3 in Fig. 2. Motif m4.2 occurs twice in the graph, $(0, 1)$-$(1, 2)$-$(1, 3)$ and $(0, 2)$-$(1, 2)$-$(2, 3)$. Both occurrences contain edge $(1, 2)$ while only one contains edge $(2, 3)$, so edge $(1, 2)$ has a value 2 for feature m4.2 while edge $(2, 3)$ has a value 1. There are four occurrences of motif m4.3 in the graph, obtained by removing one of the edges $(0, 1)$, $(1, 3)$, $(0, 2)$, or $(2, 3)$. All of these occurrences include edge $(1, 2)$ but only three include edge $(2, 3)$, so edge $(1, 2)$ has a value 4 for feature m4.3 while edge $(2, 3)$ has a value 3.

When using the INS method, we insert all of the negative edges in the graph before doing any feature extraction. Sampling a negative edge in the neighborhood of a positive one changes the extracted features, as shown in Fig. 2. That is, the extracted motifs are not fully independent of the sampling. While this is not desirable, we verify that the occurrence of these cases in practice is very rare, so they do not affect the learning process in any significant way.

3.2   Sampling Negative Edges

Another important question, independent of choosing RMV or INS, is how to sample the edges for the classification dataset. For positive example edges, uniform random sampling is an adequate solution, given the assumption that no edge is easier to predict than another. For negative example edges, however, it is easy to imagine that an edge connecting two nodes in completely different regions of the graph is less likely to occur than one connecting two nodes in the same region. Therefore, the distance between the pair of sampled nodes can play an important role. For this reason, we choose to control for this parameter.

We sample negative edges based on the shortest-path distance between the endpoint nodes. We choose to use a mix of nodes with short distances ($d \in \{2, 3\}$), as these represents the hardest cases. In most of the experiments, we use a 50/50 split between negative example edges at distance 2 and 3. However, we also analyze the effect of the distance on classification accuracy by changing the ratio between these two sub-classes.

When building the classification dataset, we sample an equal number of negative and positive edges. This decision allows us to use simple classification measures, such as accuracy, without the issues that arise due to class imbalance. In a typical graph, most pairs of nodes do not have an edge connecting them, so the negative class would be much larger than the positive class. However, as we are only interested in the relative performance of the features, and because we use off-the-shelf classifiers, we prefer to create a balanced classification dataset.

4 Experimental Evaluation

4.1 Experimental Setup

Datasets. We use three real-world graphs coming from different domains: Amazon, CondMat, and AstroPh. The three graphs are from the Koblenz Network Collection.[1] Table 1a shows basic statistics about these graph datasets.

The first graph represents the co-purchase network of products on Amazon. It is the graph upon which the "customers who bought this also bought that" feature is built. Nodes are products, and an edge between any two nodes shows that the two products have been frequently bought together. The second dataset, CondMat, represents a subset of authorship relations between authors and publications in the arXiv condensed matter physics section. Nodes are authors (first set) or papers (second set). An edge represents that an author has written a given paper. The third and final dataset, AstroPh, is a collaboration graph. In particular, it contains data about scientific collaboration between authors in the arXiv astrophysics section. Each node in the graph represents an author of a paper, and an edge between two authors represents a common publication.

Experimental Settings. For each graph, we extract a classification dataset for which we compute features. We extract a uniform sample of edges from each graph as positive examples. For negative examples, we extract pairs of nodes from the graph which are at distance 2 or 3 hops. Table 1b shows the number of examples chosen from each graph. We extract motif features for example edges

---

[1] http://konect.uni-koblenz.de.

Table 1. Statistics for the graphs and the classification datasets.

Graph	$|V|$	$|E|$	Avg. Deg.	Diameter
Amazon	334 863	925 872	5.530	47
CondMat	22 015	58 595	3.025	36
AstroPh	18 771	198 050	21.102	14

(a) Basic statistics about the graph datasets.

Graph	# Pos. Edges	# Neg. Edges
Amazon	20 000	20 000
CondMat	2000	2000
AstroPh	5000	5000

(b) No. of positive and negative edges sampled for the classification datasets.

by using the Arabesque parallel graph mining framework [41]. We then group by motif, count the occurrences, and finally normalize the counts to create a feature vector which represents the motif distribution of the neighborhood of the edge.[2]

To train the classification models we use the scikit-learn Python library.[3] We train naïve Bayes (NB), logistic regression (LR), decision tree (DT), k-nearest neighbor (KNN), gradient boosted decision tree (GB), and random forest (RF) models. All performance results are computed via 10-fold cross-validation.

Baselines. We use two types of baselines. The first type includes traditional topological features such as triangle closure and paths. We compare our features against common neighbors, Jaccard coefficient, Adamic/Adar measure, Preferential Attachment, rooted PageRank, and Katz index. Of these methods, PageRank and Katz benefit from inserting negative edges in the graph, so we use INS with these two methods.

The second type of baseline includes more complex techniques such as matrix decomposition and deep learning. For matrix decomposition, we use the scores obtained from a non-negative matrix factorization (NMF) trained on the graph with positive edges removed (RMV), as commonly done in the literature [27]. We use the NMF algorithm available in scikit-learn, and use 100 factors for the decomposition. For deep learning, we compare against a recent state-of-the-art graph neural network framework for link prediction called SEAL [45]. SEAL uses subgraph extraction around the example edge to extract latent features, learned via a neural network. This framework has experimentally outperformed other existing deep learning methods such as node2vec and LINE [16,40].

Evaluation Metrics. We evaluate the algorithms via the following metrics:

- Accuracy (ACC): the fraction of examples correctly classified (true positives and true negatives) over the total number of examples (N), $ACC = \frac{TP+TN}{N}$. Given that the classification datasets are balanced, accuracy is a reasonable measure of performance. Better classifiers obtain higher accuracy.
- Area Under the Curve (AUC): the area under the Receiver Operating Characteristic (ROC) curve from the scores produced by the classifiers. It represents the probability that a classifier will rank a random positive example higher than a random negative one. Better classifiers obtain higher AUC.

---

[2] Code available at https://github.com/GhadeerAbuoda/LinkPrediction.

[3] http://scikit-learn.org.

Table 2. Classification performance on Amazon for RMV vs. INS.

RMV

Metric	Classifier	$k=3$	$k=4$	$k=5$	Combined
ACC (%)	NB	57.6	52.4	52.7	52.0
	LR	56.5	59.4	68.0	64.4
	DT	57.6	69.4	70.8	70.6
	KNN	51.5	69.9	71.4	71.0
	GB	58.0	73.3	76.6	76.9
	RF	57.6	71.6	76.3	77.0
AUC	GB	0.58	0.72	0.76	0.76
	RF	0.58	0.72	0.76	0.77
FPR	GB	0.11	0.30	0.26	0.27
	RF	0.11	0.32	0.27	0.27

INS

Metric	Classifier	$k=3$	$k=4$	$k=5$	Combined
ACC (%)	NB	57.7	57.2	52.7	53.6
	LR	62.5	67.7	70.0	67.5
	DT	67.9	66.9	69.6	71.0
	KNN	63.6	66.0	64.0	65.0
	GB	68.2	75.0	76.6	79.4
	RF	68.0	74.8	77.0	79.6
AUC	GB	0.69	0.74	0.76	0.80
	RF	0.68	0.75	0.78	0.80
FPR	GB	0.25	0.25	0.25	0.18
	RF	0.23	0.23	0.21	0.18

- False Positive Rate (FPR): the ratio between the number of negative edges wrongly classified (false positives) and the total number of negative edges, $FPR = \frac{FP}{FP+TN}$. This measure is useful to understand the effect of graph distance of the negative examples. Better classifiers obtain lower FPR.

4.2 Removing Positive Edges vs. Inserting Negative Edges

Table 2 shows the classification results of the two feature extraction methods (RMV and INS, respectively) on the Amazon dataset (the largest one). We report the results for all classifiers when using features based only on motifs of size $k = 3$, size $k = 4$, and size $k = 5$. The last column shows the results when using all three sets of features together in one feature vector (total of 29 features).

By looking at the difference between the two tables, it is clear that INS consistently has higher accuracy than RMV. The difference grows smaller as we add more complex features by increasing k. However, for the two best classifiers (GB and RF), INS still results in approximately 3% points higher accuracy than RMV, even when using the combined features. The simpler classifiers do not seem able to exploit the full predictive power of the motif features.

Table 2 also reports AUC and FPR for the two best classifiers. The AUC and FPR are very similar, and the two classifiers are almost indistinguishable. As expected, the more complex motif features (i.e., larger k) work better, and the combination of all three sets of features is usually the best. For ease of presentation, henceforth we report results only using the RF classifier.

Figure 3 reports the accuracy of RF for both feature extraction methods on all datasets. The results are consistent with what we already observed: INS is consistently better than RMV. Interestingly, INS with just 3-motif features performs better than RMV with combined motif features on CondMat and AstroPh.

We perform a statistical test to compare the classification accuracy of the two methods, INS and RMV. We obtain 100 different samples of the accuracy for each

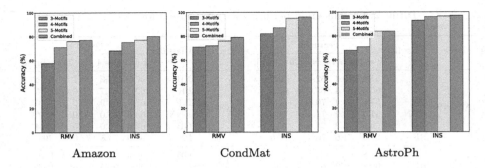

Fig. 3. Classification accuracy of a Random Forest (RF) classifier when using different motif features and different feature extraction methods (RMV vs. INS).

Table 3. Classification performance of a Random Forest (RF) classifier with combined motif features and different feature extraction methods (RMV vs. INS).

Graph	RMV			INS		
	ACC (%)	AUC	FPR	ACC (%)	AUC	FPR
Amazon	77.0	0.77	0.27	79.6	0.80	0.18
CondMat	79.0	0.79	0.04	96.0	0.96	0.04
AstroPh	84.0	0.84	0.30	96.5	0.97	0.02

method by training the RF classifier using different seeds for the pseudo-random number generator. We use Student's t-test to compare the results, and we are able to reject the null hypothesis that the two methods have the same average performance at the $p = 0.05$ significance level. We conclude that the accuracy of the RF classifier with INS feature extraction is better than the one with RMV, and the difference is statistically significant. We return to the reason why the INS feature extraction method is superior in Sect. 4.4.

More complex motif features perform better, with the combination of all motif sizes outperforming each individual size. The latter result might seem surprising, as one would expect the 5-motif features to supersede the smaller ones. Nevertheless, consider that 5-motif features do not encode positional information, i.e., we do not know in which part of the 5-motif the edge appears. Smaller features can supplement this information to the 5-motif features.

Finally, Table 3 reports ACC, AUC, and FPR for RF on all datasets for the two different feature extraction methods when using the combined motif features. The mix of RF, combined motif features, and INS feature extraction is the one that performs consistently on top. Therefore, we use it when comparing our proposal with baseline methods in the following section.

Table 4. Accuracy of the RF classifier (%) with combined motif features (INS) vs. baseline classifiers.

Features	Amazon	CondMat	AstroPh
Common Neighbors	64.6	78.6	81.2
Jaccard Coefficient	61.7	81.1	85.2
Adamic/Adar	61.5	74.7	75.0
Preferential Attachment	55.0	61.2	64.2
Rooted PageRank	53.2	62.0	65.0
Katz Index	60.0	55.0	59.0
Topological Combined	73.0	86.9	87.0
NMF	52.0	54.0	53.5
NMF + Topological Combined	73.0	85.9	89.0
SEAL	69.0	81.3	80.3
SEAL + node2vec Embeddings	62.8	77.2	82.0
Motif Combined (INS)	**79.6**	**96.0**	**96.5**

4.3   Comparison with Baselines

To compare against the baseline topological features proposed in prior work, we train a RF on each of these features, and one on the combination of all of the features. The upper part of Table 4 reports the accuracy of these classifiers. For comparison, the accuracy of the RF classifier trained on the combined motif features extracted via INS is reported in the last row of the table. The first four rows of the table show simple neighborhood-based topological features. The next two rows show path-dependent topological features. For rooted PageRank, we use the standard value for the damping parameter $\alpha = 0.85$. For the Katz index, we optimize the value of the β parameter and we report the highest accuracy obtained (for $\beta = 0.1$). The accuracy of the topological features is in the range 55–85%. Combining all topological features into one feature vector results in the best accuracy in all cases. This is expected since each of these features captures different information about the graph and a powerful classifier such as RF is able to exploit all of this information. Thus, the Topological Combined row in Table 4 can be viewed as the best possible accuracy with current state-of-the-art topological features. However, the motif features achieve much higher accuracy. Specifically, they are 7 to 10% points better in accuracy, which is significant given that advanced features extracted via graph embeddings and deep learning reportedly struggle to beat the traditional topological features [42].

Next, we turn our attention to feature learning methods that allow the model to determine by itself which features are important for link prediction. As mentioned earlier, we focus on two popular approaches: non-negative matrix factorization (NMF) and deep learning. Interestingly, the NMF approach [27] is not very competitive, as shown in Table 4. We hypothesize that the method requires more parameter optimization (e.g., tuning the number of factors used and the regularization parameters). In any case, the gap between NMF and straightforward topological features is quite large, which is quite disappointing. Moreover, adding the NMF features to the topological ones does not improve accuracy by much (only the AstroPh dataset sees some improvement).

Finally, we compare our model with SEAL [45], a recent link prediction framework which uses deep learning (graph neural networks). We test the framework with its default hyperparameters. Interestingly, SEAL only achieves around 70% accuracy on Amazon and 80% accuracy on the other two datasets. SEAL learns on one- or two-hop subgraphs extracted around the tested edge, which is somewhat equivalent to looking into common neighbors. However, the accuracy achieved by SEAL is lower than with the combined topological features.

We also test combining the subgraph features with node representations learned via node2vec [16], as suggested by the authors of SEAL. The accuracy with the node2vec embeddings does not improve on average, and actually drops for two of the datasets. One interpretation of these results is that the node2vec embeddings might actually introduce noise in the node representations, by looking too far into the neighborhoods of the example edges (e.g., the length of the random walks may not be appropriately tuned).

Thus, the overall takeaway from Table 4 is that RF with motif features is more accurate than all the baselines, both traditional topological-based ones and more recent NMF and deep learning ones.

Feature Importance. We analyze the motif features that are most predictive for the classification task. Figure 4 shows the relative importance of the features as inferred by the RF classifier. In most cases the distribution of feature importance is quite skewed, with a few features constituting the backbone of the predictive model. The most predictive feature is always a 5-motif one, which is another indication of the predictive power of deeper structural features. However, it changes from dataset to dataset, and might be domain specific.

Overall, these results prove the predictive power of higher-order motif-based features for link formation. The rest of the experimental section is devoted to two more questions related to motif feature extraction and negative edge sampling. First, we shed some insight about why INS performs better than RMV. Second, we show the importance of choosing the right negative examples, an important factor which has been mostly overlooked in the literature thus far.

4.4 Motif Distribution: RMV vs. INS

Let us now look at the reason why INS outperforms RMV for feature extraction. Consider that both feature extraction methods change the original motifs of the graph, as they alter the graph structure during feature extraction. One hypothesis is that the method which alters the structure the least is better, as the motif patterns it learns are also the closest to the ones found in the original graph. To test this hypothesis, we compute the motif distribution in the original graph and in the modified graphs resulting from the modifications done by RMV and INS (i.e., with a fraction of edges removed or added). We compute the distance

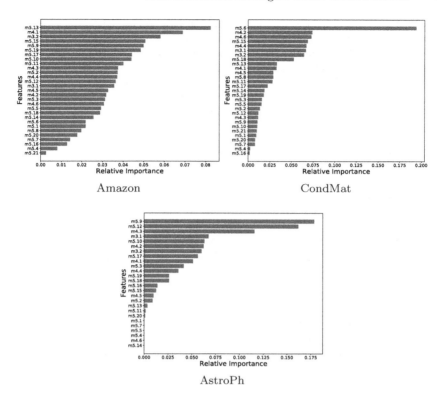

Fig. 4. Feature importance across the three datasets, as inferred from the Random Forest model. In all three datasets the most important feature is a 5-motif, however the specific motif varies by dataset.

between the motif distribution for $k = 3$ and $k = 4$ in the original graph, and the ones obtained by RMV and INS. We use two different distance functions to perform the comparison: Earth Mover's Distance (EMD), and Kullback-Leibler Divergence (KLD). Table 5 reports the results. If our hypothesis is correct, then INS should have a smaller distance than RMV. This is indeed the case for two out of three graphs, for both distance functions, which gives us confidence that our hypothesis is a step in the right direction. However, AstroPh behaves differently, with RMV having a smaller distance than INS. Therefore, we cannot draw a definitive conclusion, and further study is necessary to fully understand the difference between these two feature extraction methods.

4.5   Effect of Distance on Negative Edges

In this experiment we explore the effect of the distance between the node pairs that constitute the negative examples on the accuracy of the classifier. For each graph, we create different classification datasets by varying the composition of

Table 5. Earth Mover's Distance (EMD) and KL Divergence (KLD) between the distribution of motifs in the original graph and the one obtained by each feature extraction method, RMV and INS. A smaller distance indicates that the feature extraction method is more faithful to the original graph.

Graph	EMD		KLD	
	RMV	INS	RMV	INS
Amazon	0.119	0.011	0.007	0.001
CondMat	1.106	0.161	0.533	0.012
AstroPh	0.050	0.529	0.001	0.066

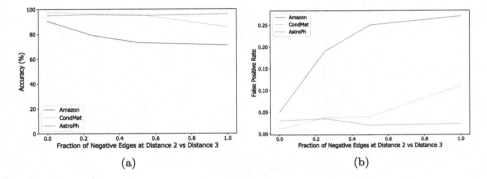

(a)   (b)

Fig. 5. Classification accuracy and false positive rate as a function of the fraction of negative examples at distance 2 (vs. distance 3).

the negative class: from containing only negative edges at distance 3 to containing only negative edges at distance 2. We use the fraction of negative edges of the sub-class at distance 2 as the independent variable in the plots (the rest of the edges are at distance 3). We keep the total number of examples fixed to maintain the balance between positive and negative classes.

Figure 5a shows the classification accuracy for each setting. For both Amazon and ContMat, the edges at distance 2 are harder to classify correctly, which produces a significant decline in the accuracy as we increase the fraction of edges at distance 2. Conversely, the accuracy on AstroPh does not seem affected. The same pattern can be seen in Fig. 5b, which reports the false positive rate. The figure explains the cause of the decrease in accuracy: as we decrease the average distance of the negative examples, the classifier produces more false positives. The higher the fraction of negative examples at distance 2, the higher the rate of misclassification for the negative class.

5   Related Work

There are two main branches of research that are relevant to the current work: graph motifs and link prediction.

Graph Motifs. Motifs are patterns of connectivity that occur significantly more frequently in the given graph than expected by chance alone [43]. Graph motifs have numerous applications, for example, they have been used to classify graphs into "superfamilies" [37], and they have been used in combination with machine learning to determine the most appropriate model for a given real-world network [39]. Palla et al. [31] also show that 4-cliques reveal community structure in word associations and protein-protein interaction graphs. In several social media analysis studies [18,19], graph motif detection and enumeration are used to characterize graph properties statistically.

The significance of motifs is typically assessed statistically by comparing the distribution of subgraphs in an observed graph with the one found in a randomized graph. One of the important reasons why graphs in the real world have more motif structure than the randomized version is that real-world graphs are constrained by particular types of growth rules, which in turn depend on the specific nature of the graph. In this paper, we aim at leveraging this property to learn which specific motifs are predictive of link presence.

Link Prediction. Prior work on link prediction can generally be classified into three broad categories: unsupervised methods, supervised methods, and feature learning methods. Link prediction methods can also be orthogonally classified by the type of information they rely on: node properties or structural properties (including motifs).

In most unsupervised methods, a heuristic is used to rank node pairs in the graph, with a higher rank indicating a higher likelihood of a link existing between the node pair [13,26]. The heuristic is typically a similarity measure, and can be based on application-specific node attributes or on the graph topology.

While node attributes can achieve a high degree of accuracy, they are domain- and application-specific, and cannot be easily generalized. In contrast, features based on graph topology are more general and directly applicable to any graph.

Topological features that are used in unsupervised link prediction are typically related to local (neighborhood) or global (path) properties of the graph. Neighborhood-based features capture the intuition that a link is likely to exist between a pair of nodes if they have many common neighbors. The simplest neighborhood-based feature is to count common neighbors [30]. More advanced features include some form of regularization of the count, such as the Jaccard coefficient of the two sets of neighbors, the Adamic/Adar index [2], which discounts the contribution of high-degree nodes, and preferential attachment [8], which gives a higher likelihood to links between high degree vertices.

Conversely, path-based features look at the global graph structure. A representative path-based feature is the Katz index [20], which counts the number of paths between two nodes, giving a higher weight to shorter paths. Other methods such as hitting time, commute time, and rooted PageRank use random walks on the graph to derive the similarity of two nodes. Global similarity indices typically provide better predictions than local indices, but are more expensive to compute, especially in large graphs. For a detailed survey of unsupervised link prediction methods, see references [15] and [25]. Several studies indicate that unsupervised methods are fundamentally unable to cope with dynamics, imbalance, and other complexities of real-world graphs [6,25]. However, similarity indices can easily be used by supervised methods as features for a machine learning model.

In supervised methods, link prediction is usually cast as a binary classification problem. The label indicates the presence or absence of a link between a node pair. The predictor features are metrics computed from the graph structure or node attributes which describe the given pair [6,23,24,35].

A key challenge for supervised link prediction is designing an effective set of features for the task. Some works use simple topological features such as the number of common neighbors and the Adamic/Adar index [12], while others use more complex features [11]. For detailed surveys on supervised link prediction methods, please refer to [6,14,24].

Some prior work has used motif-like features for link prediction problems. For example, Hulovatyy et al. [17] use features extracted from graphlets for link prediction. Theirs is an unsupervised method that uses a different type of feature extraction compared to our approach. Graphlet-based features are also used in [32] for link prediction. However, the focus of that paper is link prediction in temporally evolving graphs, while we focus on static graphs.

A more sophisticated approach to link prediction is to allow the model to learn by itself which latent features are important for the link prediction task. Feature learning methods such as matrix factorization, graph embedding, or deep learning examine the graph topology to learn a representation that can be used in machine learning tasks.

Matrix factorization models the graph as an $N \times N$ matrix, and then predicts a link by using matrix decomposition. For example, Menon and Elkan [27] consider link prediction as a matrix completion problem and solve it using a non-negative matrix factorization (NMF) method. The basic idea is to let the model learn latent features from the topological structure of a partially observed graph, and then use the model to approximate the unobserved part of the graph. Higher-order network embeddings [33,34] use a motif-based matrix formulation to learn a representation of the graph that can be used for link prediction.

Deep learning is another very popular form of feature learning. In particular, graph convolutional networks (GCNs) have recently emerged as a powerful tool for representation learning on graphs [21]. Lee et al. [22] propose a GCN technique that uses motif information to improve accuracy in classification tasks. GCNs have also been successfully used for link prediction [36,45]. For example, SEAL [45] is a framework which fits a graph neural network to small subgraphs around the example edges in the dataset. By doing so, it learns latent features in the neighborhood structure of the graph which indicate the presence or absence of a link. Therefore, it is very similar in spirit to the current work. In this paper, we compare with NMF and SEAL as examples from the class of representation learning techniques, and we show that our method outperforms these more complex methods.

6   Conclusion

We presented a new approach for link prediction in undirected graphs that relies on using the distribution of k-motifs that a pair of nodes appears in to predict whether a link exists between these two nodes. We pointed out two issues related to the task that were not adequately addressed by prior work. First, it is important to treat positive and negative example edges in the same way. Prior approaches achieve this by removing positive example edges from the graph, and we showed that an alternative (and better) way is to insert negative example edges in the graph. Second, when sampling pairs of nodes to find negative example edges, the shortest-path distance between the sampled nodes affects prediction accuracy, with shorter distances increasing the difficulty of the problem. Thus, it is important to control for this parameter when building the classification dataset. Finally, we showed that, by using off-the-shelf classifiers, our motif features achieve substantial improvement in prediction accuracy compared to prior methods based on topological features or feature learning.

References

1. Abuoda, G., De Francisci Morales, G., Aboulnaga, A.: Link prediction via higher-order motif features. arXiv preprint arXiv:1902.06679 (2019)
2. Adamic, L.A., Adar, E.: Friends and neighbors on the web. Soc. Netw. **25**(3), 211–230 (2003)
3. Ahmed, N.K., Neville, J., Rossi, R.A., Duffield, N.: Efficient graphlet counting for large networks. In: ICDM, pp. 1–10 (2015)
4. Aiello, L.M., Barrat, A., Schifanella, R., Cattuto, C., Markines, B., Menczer, F.: Friendship prediction and homophily in social media. TWEB **6**(2), 9 (2012)
5. Airoldi, E.M., Blei, D.M., Fienberg, S.E., Xing, E.P., Jaakkola, T.: Mixed membership stochastic block models for relational data with application to protein-protein interactions. In: International Biometrics Society Annual Meeting, vol. 15 (2006)
6. Al Hasan, M., Chaoji, V., Salem, S., Zaki, M.: Link prediction using supervised learning. In: Workshop on Link Analysis, Counter-Terrorism and Security (2006)
7. Al Hasan, M., Zaki, M.J.: A survey of link prediction in social networks. In: Aggarwal, C. (ed.) Social Network Data Analytics, pp. 243–275. Springer, Boston (2011). https://doi.org/10.1007/978-1-4419-8462-3_9
8. Barabási, A.L.: Scale-free networks: a decade and beyond. Science **325**(5939), 412–413 (2009)
9. Bressan, M., Chierichetti, F., Kumar, R., Leucci, S., Panconesi, A.: Counting graphlets: space vs. time. In: WSDM, pp. 557–566 (2017)
10. Chen, H., Li, X., Huang, Z.: Link prediction approach to collaborative filtering. In: JCDL, pp. 141–142 (2005)
11. Cukierski, W., Hamner, B., Yang, B.: Graph-based features for supervised link prediction. In: IJCNN (2011)
12. Fire, M., Tenenboim, L., Lesser, O., Puzis, R., Rokach, L., Elovici, Y.: Link prediction in social networks using computationally efficient topological features. In: Proceedings of the International Conference on Privacy, Security, Risk and Trust (PASSAT) (2011)

13. Folino, F., Pizzuti, C.: Link prediction approaches for disease networks. In: Proceedings of the International Conference on Information Technology in Bio and Medical Informatics (2012)
14. Gao, F., Musial, K., Cooper, C., Tsoka, S.: Link prediction methods and their accuracy for different social networks and network metrics. Sci. Program. **2015**, 1 (2015)
15. Getoor, L., Diehl, C.P.: Link mining: a survey. SIGKDD Explor. Newsl. **7**(2), 3–12 (2005)
16. Grover, A., Leskovec, J.: node2vec: scalable feature learning for networks. In: KDD (2016)
17. Hulovatyy, Y., Solava, R.W., Milenković, T.: Revealing missing parts of the interactome via link prediction. PLOS ONE (2014)
18. Juszczyszyn, K., Kazienko, P., Musiał, K.: Local topology of social network based on motif analysis. In: Lovrek, I., Howlett, R.J., Jain, L.C. (eds.) KES 2008. LNCS (LNAI), vol. 5178, pp. 97–105. Springer, Heidelberg (2008). https://doi.org/10.1007/978-3-540-85565-1_13
19. Juszczyszyn, K., Musial, K., Budka, M.: Link prediction based on subgraph evolution in dynamic social networks. In: SocialCom (2011)
20. Katz, L.: A new status index derived from sociometric analysis. Psychometrika **18**(1), 39–43 (1953)
21. Kipf, T.N., Welling, M.: Semi-supervised classification with graph convolutional networks. arXiv preprint arXiv:1609.02907 (2016)
22. Lee, J.B., Rossi, R.A., Kong, X., Kim, S., Koh, E., Rao, A.: Higher-order graph convolutional networks. arXiv preprint arXiv:1809.07697 (2018)
23. Leskovec, J., Huttenlocher, D., Kleinberg, J.: Predicting positive and negative links in online social networks. In: WWW (2010)
24. Liben-Nowell, D., Kleinberg, J.: The link-prediction problem for social networks. J. Assoc. Inf. Sci. Technol. **58**(7), 1019–1031 (2007)
25. Lichtenwalter, R.N., Lussier, J.T., Chawla, N.V.: New perspectives and methods in link prediction. In: KDD, pp. 243–252 (2010)
26. Lu, L., Zhou, T.: Link prediction in complex networks: a survey. arXiv preprint arXiv:1010.0725 (2010)
27. Menon, A.K., Elkan, C.: Link prediction via matrix factorization. In: Gunopulos, D., Hofmann, T., Malerba, D., Vazirgiannis, M. (eds.) ECML PKDD 2011. LNCS (LNAI), vol. 6912, pp. 437–452. Springer, Heidelberg (2011). https://doi.org/10.1007/978-3-642-23783-6_28
28. Milo, R., et al.: Superfamilies of evolved and designed networks. Science **303**(5663), 1538–1542 (2004)
29. Milo, R., Shen-Orr, S., Itzkovitz, S., Kashtan, N., Chklovskii, D., Alon, U.: Network motifs: simple building blocks of complex networks. Science **298**(5594), 824–827 (2002)
30. Newman, M.E.: Clustering and preferential attachment in growing networks. Phys. Rev. E **64**(2), 025102 (2001)
31. Palla, G., Derényi, I., Farkas, I., Vicsek, T.: Uncovering the overlapping community structure of complex networks in nature and society. Nature **435**(7043), 814 (2005)
32. Rahman, M., Hasan, M.A.: Link prediction in dynamic networks using graphlet. In: Frasconi, P., Landwehr, N., Manco, G., Vreeken, J. (eds.) ECML PKDD 2016. LNCS (LNAI), vol. 9851, pp. 394–409. Springer, Cham (2016). https://doi.org/10.1007/978-3-319-46128-1_25
33. Rossi, R.A., Ahmed, N.K., Koh, E.: Higher-order network representation learning. In: Companion Proceedings of the Web Conference (WWW), pp. 3–4 (2018)

34. Rossi, R.A., Ahmed, N.K., Koh, E., Kim, S., Rao, A., Yadkori, Y.A.: HONE: higher-order network embeddings. arXiv preprint arXiv:1801.09303 (2018)

35. Sa, H.R., Prudencio, R.B.: Supervised learning for link prediction in weighted networks. In: Proceedings International Workshop on Web and Text Intelligence (2010)

36. Schlichtkrull, M., Kipf, T.N., Bloem, P., van den Berg, R., Titov, I., Welling, M.: Modeling relational data with graph convolutional networks. In: Gangemi, A., et al. (eds.) ESWC 2018. LNCS, vol. 10843, pp. 593–607. Springer, Cham (2018). https://doi.org/10.1007/978-3-319-93417-4_38

37. Schneider, D.S., Hudson, K.L., Lin, T.Y., Anderson, K.V.: Dominant and recessive mutations define functional domains of Toll, a transmembrane protein required for dorsal-ventral polarity in the Drosophila embryo. Genes Dev. 5(5), 797–807 (1991)

38. Shen-Orr, S.S., Milo, R., Mangan, S., Alon, U.: Network motifs in the transcriptional regulation network of Escherichia coli. Nat. Genet. 31(1), 64 (2002)

39. Soutoglou, E., Talianidis, I.: Coordination of PIC assembly and chromatin remodeling during differentiation-induced gene activation. Science 295(5561), 1901–1904 (2002)

40. Tang, J., Qu, M., Wang, M., Zhang, M., Yan, J., Mei, Q.: LINE: large-scale information network embedding. In: WWW, pp. 1067–1077 (2015)

41. Teixeira, C.H., Fonseca, A.J., Serafini, M., Siganos, G., Zaki, M.J., Aboulnaga, A.: Arabesque: a system for distributed graph mining. In: SOSP, pp. 425–440 (2015)

42. Tsitsulin, A., Mottin, D., Karras, P., Müller, E.: VERSE: versatile graph embeddings from similarity measures. In: WWW (2018)

43. Vazquez, A., Dobrin, R., Sergi, D., Eckmann, J.P., Oltvai, Z., Barabási, A.L.: The topological relationship between the large-scale attributes and local interaction patterns of complex networks. Proc. Natl. Acad. Sci. 101(52), 17940–17945 (2004)

44. Yang, Y., Lichtenwalter, R.N., Chawla, N.V.: Evaluating link prediction methods. Knowl. Inf. Syst. 45(3), 751–782 (2014). https://doi.org/10.1007/s10115-014-0789-0

45. Zhang, M., Chen, Y.: Link prediction based on graph neural networks. In: NeurIPS, pp. 5171–5181 (2018)

SoRecGAT: Leveraging Graph Attention Mechanism for Top-N Social Recommendation

M. Vijaikumar$^{(\boxtimes)}$, Shirish Shevade, and M. N. Murty

Department of Computer Science and Automation, Indian Institute of Science,
Bangalore, India
{vijaikumar,shirish,mnm}@iisc.ac.in

Abstract. Social recommendation systems typically combine extra information like a social network with the user-item interaction network in order to alleviate data sparsity issues. This also helps in making more accurate and personalized recommendations. However, most of the existing systems work under the assumption that all socially connected users have equal influence on each other in a social network, which is not true in practice. Further, estimating the quantum of influence that exists among entities in a user-item interaction network is essential when only implicit ratings are available. This has been ignored even in many recent state-of-the-art models such as SAMN (Social Attentional Memory Network) and DeepSoR (Deep neural network model on Social Relations). Many a time, capturing a complex relationship between the entities (users/items) is essential to boost the performance of a recommendation system. We address these limitations by proposing a novel neural network model, SoRecGAT, which employs multi-head and multi-layer graph attention mechanism. The attention mechanism helps the model learn the influence of entities on each other more accurately. The proposed model also takes care of heterogeneity among the entities seamlessly. SoRecGAT is a general approach and we also validate its suitability when information in the form of a network of co-purchased items is available. Empirical results on eight real-world datasets demonstrate that the proposed model outperforms state-of-the-art models.

Keywords: Social recommendation · Graph attention mechanism

1 Introduction

In the last few years, collaborative filtering (CF) has been successful in building powerful recommendation systems. Given a partially filled implicit rating matrix (for example, a matrix representing likes or clicks), the idea of a top-N recommendation system is to come up with the highly probable list of items that a user may like in future. A common and popular approach is to use a latent factor model to learn low dimensional latent representations for entities (users

© Springer Nature Switzerland AG 2020
U. Brefeld et al. (Eds.): ECML PKDD 2019, LNAI 11906, pp. 430–446, 2020.
https://doi.org/10.1007/978-3-030-46150-8_26

and items) and use the similarity between the entities to predict the unknown ratings. Matrix factorization (MF) [11,17,22] remains one of the successful baselines in such tasks. In practice, however, a user typically interacts with a very small set of available items. This results in data sparsity issues which is a big challenging factor in designing better recommendation systems.

The recent explosive growth in online services and mobile technologies have provided tons of useful information. For example, Yelp[1] has friendship connections amongst users, Amazon[2] has co-purchased network associated with products or Epinion[3] has trust relationships associated with users. Crucially, *social networks*[4] associated with users and items play a pivotal role in recommending products and services to the end users. That is, users are typically influenced by social neighbours in a social network. Therefore, one expects social neighbours to have similar opinions regarding products. By the same argument, co-purchased items are expected to have a strong influence on each other. Thus, social connections associated with users and/or items can be effectively leveraged to alleviate data sparsity issues that exist in traditional recommendation systems to boost their performance.

There have been some works that leverage matrix factorization techniques for social recommendation [8,10,15,31]. While [8] models both implicit and explicit influence of trust, [15] introduces the concept of a social regularizer to represent the social constraints on recommendation systems. These approaches either treat all social relations equally [8,10,31] or make use of a predefined similarity function [15]. Either case may result in the performance degradation of the recommendation system as users with strong ties are more likely to have similar preferences than those with weak ties [25]. Some recently proposed neural network based models which utilize external social networks [5,21] also have the same drawback. Further, in the applications where only implicit ratings are available, it is important to learn the quantum of influence that the different entities have on each other. This would help in getting better latent representations of the entities and better performance of the recommendation system.

A few attempts have been made [3,32] to learn the influence of entities in a network by employing an attention mechanism for recommendations. In particular, Chen *et al.* [3] presented a social attentional memory network which utilizes an attention-based memory module to learn the relation vectors for user-friend pairs. This is combined with the friend level attention mechanism to measure the influence strength among users' friends. Further, [32] proposed ATRank which models heterogeneous user behaviour using an attention model and captures the interaction between users using self-attention. However, the key challenges here are to design a unified model that exploits the influence of entities from both

---

[1] www.yelp.com.

[2] www.amazon.com.

[3] www.epinion.com.

[4] Throughout this paper, we refer to a user-user network (or connection) or a co-purchased item network (or connection) as a social network (or connection).

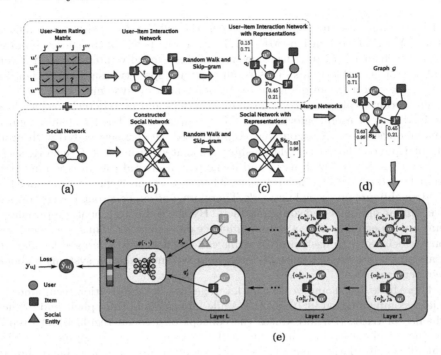

Fig. 1. The illustration of SoRecGAT recommendation setting. The transformations from a user-item rating matrix and a social network (a) to a graph with learned node representations (d) are illustrated via steps (b) and (c). The graph in (d) serves as an input to SoRecGAT (e) which employs a multi-layer and multi-head attention mechanism, and gives final user(u) and item(j) representations p'_u and q'_j and user-item pair representation ϕ_{uj} for (u, j). This ϕ_{uj} is used for predicting rating $\hat{y}_{uj}$. (Best viewed in colour.)

user-item interaction network and social network together, and to capture the complex relationships that exist among entities across networks.

Contributions. Motivated by the success of Graph Attention Networks (GAT) [26], we propose SoRecGAT – a Graph ATtention based framework for top-N Social Recommendation problem. The proposed framework is illustrated in Fig. 1. We represent the user-item interaction network as a graph with nodes representing users and items, and edges representing interactions among them. We assume that no attribute information is available for the nodes, and initial representations (or embeddings) are learned using random walk and skip-gram techniques. We propose a simple approach by which a social network associated with the users or items can seamlessly be incorporated into this graph. The novelty of our approach lies in handling heterogeneous networks (for example, a social network with a user-item interaction network) for a personalised recommendation. Specifically, we propose to obtain the heterogeneous graph node representations in a unified space, which is essential in assigning weights to neighbouring nodes. These node representations are learned using multi-head and multi-layer attention mechanism. The attention mechanism helps in capturing complex relationships among entities in both user-item interaction network and social networks, collectively. Further, the final node representations are used for predicting the ratings. We conduct extensive experiments on eight real-world datasets – four from Amazon and four from Yelp. Experimental results demonstrate the effectiveness of SoRecGAT over state-of-the-art models.

2   The Proposed Model

Problem Formulation. We represent a user-item interaction network and a social network combinedly as a graph $\mathcal{G}(\mathcal{V}, \mathcal{E})$ where $\mathcal{V}$ represents the set of users, items and social entities[5], and $\mathcal{E}$ represents the set of edges present in the graph. We consider the implicit rating setting where the rating between user u and item j is given as

$$y_{uj} = \begin{cases} 1, \text{ if } (u,j) \in \Omega \\ 0, \text{ otherwise} \end{cases}$$

where $\Omega = \{(u,j) : \text{user } u \text{ interacts with item } j\}$. Given $\mathcal{G}(\mathcal{V}, \mathcal{E})$, our goal in this work is to design a model which gives a top-N ranked list of items for each user.

2.1   SoRecGAT

In this section, we explain the proposed model – SoRecGAT, illustrated in Fig. 1. As shown in the figure, a user-item rating matrix can be converted to a graph whose node features (representations) (Fig. 1(c)) can be found (Sect. 2.3). A social network (e.g. a friendship network) is first converted to a bi-partite graph (Fig. 1(b)) by connecting users to "social entities", where each social entity corresponds to a user. Thus, if user $u1$ is connected to user $u2$, then, this would correspond to two edges $(u1, e2)$ and $(u2, e1)$ in Fig. 1(b), where $e1$ and $e2$ are the social entities associated with users $u1$ and $u2$, respectively. The introduction of social entities helps fuse the user-item interaction network and social network to get a combined graph (Fig. 1(d)) with node representations. This proposed idea also helps in combining multiple networks which share entities. In addition, network-specific features (side information) for the nodes can be seamlessly incorporated. A multi-head attention mechanism is then applied layerwise on this graph to predict the rating of a user-item pair. This is explained below.

Let $p_u \in \mathbb{R}^{d_p}$, $q_j \in \mathbb{R}^{d_q}$ and $s_k \in \mathbb{R}^{d_s}$ denote the features of user u, item j and social entity k respectively. Note that the feature dimensions of different entities in a given heterogeneous network can be different. Let N_p, N_q and N_s denote the number of users, items and social entities respectively. We denote the user, item and social entity features compactly as $\mathbf{p}, \mathbf{q}$ and $\mathbf{s}$ respectively, where $\mathbf{p} = (p_1, p_2, ..., p_{N_p})$, $\mathbf{q} = (q_1, q_2, ..., q_{N_q})$, and $\mathbf{s} = (s_1, s_2, ..., s_{N_s})$. The sets of

---

[5] Users/items present in a social network.

neighbours of user u in the user-item interaction network and the social network are denoted by $\mathcal{N}_u^I$ and $\mathcal{N}_u^S$ respectively.

SoRecGAT contains multiple layers, and at every layer, a new set of hidden representations for the nodes $\mathbf{p}' = (p_1', p_2', ..., p_{N_p}')$, $p_u \in \mathbb{R}^{d'}$, $\mathbf{q}' = (q_1', q_2', ..., q_{N_q}')$, $q_j \in \mathbb{R}^{d'}$, and $\mathbf{s}' = (s_1', s_2', ..., s_{N_s}')$, $s_k \in \mathbb{R}^{d'}$ are obtained from the output of previous layers. It is essential to learn multiple levels of representations due to the complex nature of the relationship that exists among entities. Further, the influence of different neighbours on a given node need not be equal. Accounting for these, we explain how hidden representations are obtained in one layer. The same procedure is repeated in the other layers.

If $f(\cdot, \cdot)$ denotes an attention function, then the importance of item j's features to user u can be calculated as

$$\bar{\alpha}_{uj} = f(W_p p_u, W_q q_j), \tag{1}$$

and that of social entity k's (in a social network) features to the same user u is given by

$$\bar{\alpha}_{uk} = f(W_p p_u, W_s s_k), \tag{2}$$

where $W_p \in \mathbb{R}^{d' \times d_p}, W_q \in \mathbb{R}^{d' \times d_q}$ and $W_s \in \mathbb{R}^{d' \times d_s}$ are the weight matrices respectively for users, items and social entities. Due to different types of entities present in a network, it is important to have different weight matrices. These matrices also act as projection matrices for entities with different types and they project the representations of users, items and social entities into a unified space. The function $f(\cdot, \cdot)$ can be a feedforward neural network. In this work, we use a single layer feedforward neural network, parametrized by trainable parameter c. That is,

$$\begin{aligned} f(W_p p_u, W_q q_j) &= a(c^T[W_p p_u \| W_q q_j]), \\ f(W_p p_u, W_q s_k) &= a(c^T[W_p p_u \| W_s s_k]), \end{aligned} \tag{3}$$

where $a(\cdot)$ denotes an activation function and $\|$ denotes concatenation operation. Normalized positive attention weights of item j on user u can be calculated as

$$\alpha_{uj} = \mathrm{softmax}\,(\bar{\alpha}_{uj})$$
$$= \frac{\exp(\bar{\alpha}_{uj})}{\sum_{j' \in \mathcal{N}_u^I} \exp(\bar{\alpha}_{uj'}) + \sum_{k' \in \mathcal{N}_u^S} \exp(\bar{\alpha}_{uk'}) + \exp(\bar{\alpha}_{uu})}$$
$$\text{and } \bar{\alpha}_{uj} = f(W_p p_u, W_q q_j), \bar{\alpha}_{uk} = f(W_p p_u, W_s s_k), \bar{\alpha}_{uu} = f(W_p p_u, W_p p_u), \tag{4}$$

where $\bar{\alpha}_{uj}$ and α_{uj} represent unnormalized and normalized attention weights of item j on user u. The normalized attention coefficients are then used to compute a linear combination of the features of neighbouring nodes to get a new representation of a given node. For example, a representation of user u at the current layer is calculated as

$$p_u' = a(\sum_{j \in \mathcal{N}_u^I} \alpha_{uj}^h W_q^h q_j + \sum_{k \in \mathcal{N}_u^S} \alpha_{uk}^h W_s^h s_k + \alpha_{uu}^h W_p^h p_u). \tag{5}$$

To exploit complex relationships that exist among entities, we employ multi-head attention mechanism. In particular, using H independent attention heads, the representation for user u can be obtained as

$$p'_u = \|_{h=1}^{H} a(\sum_{j \in \mathcal{N}_u^I} \alpha_{uj}^h W_q^h q_j + \sum_{k \in \mathcal{N}_u^S} \alpha_{uk}^h W_s^h s_k + \alpha_{uu}^h W_p^h p_u). \qquad (6)$$

Similarly, one can obtain features representations of items, $\mathbf{q}'$. The final rating of user u on item j can be obtained as

$$\hat{y}_{uj} = \sigma(w \cdot \phi_{uj}), \quad \text{where} \quad \phi_{uj} = g(p'_u, q'_j), \qquad (7)$$

where $\sigma(\cdot)$ is the sigmoid function defined as $\sigma(z) = \frac{1}{1+e^{-z}}$ and w denotes weight vector. Here, $g(\cdot, \cdot)$ is a function which constructs the representation for user-item interaction ϕ_{uj} for (u, j) from p'_u and q'_j. One can use a feedforward neural network for $g(\cdot, \cdot)$. In our experiments, we use $g(p'_u, q'_j) = p'_u \odot q'_j$, where $\odot$ denotes element-wise multiplication.

Note that, as mentioned earlier, it is easy to incorporate the side information of the nodes (for example, gender, age and country for users; and keywords and category for items) in the proposed model. Let user u (with the associated social entity e) be involved in a user-item interaction network and a social network. Let x_u^p and x_e^s denote the side information associated with these nodes. This information may be directly available in the dataset. Then the new representations of the user and social entity nodes can be $p_u \| x_u^p$ and $s_e \| x_e^s$ respectively. Thus, side information, if available, can be easily used in the proposed approach.

2.2   Loss Function

Some commonly used loss functions for the implicit rating setting are cross-entropy (l_{ce}) [9] and pairwise loss (l_{pair}) [22] functions, which can be defined for a user-item pair (u, j) as

$$l_{ce}(y_{uj}, \hat{y}_{uj}) = -y_{uj} \ln(\hat{y}_{uj}) - (1 - y_{uj}) \ln(1 - \hat{y}_{uj}),$$
$$l_{pair}(\hat{y}_{ujj'}) = -\ln(\sigma(\hat{y}_{uj} - \hat{y}_{uj'})), \quad \text{where} \ (u, j) \in \Omega \ \text{and} \ (u, j') \notin \Omega. \qquad (8)$$

In this work, we use cross-entropy loss with negative sampling strategy [16] for training the model. For all the training interactions, the loss function is defined as follows:

$$\min_{\mathcal{W}} \quad \mathcal{L}(\mathcal{W}) = - \sum_{(u,j) \in \mathcal{D}} y_{uj} \ln \hat{y}_{uj} + (1 - y_{uj}) \ln(1 - \hat{y}_{uj}) + \lambda \, \mathcal{R}(\mathcal{W}), \qquad (9)$$

where $\mathcal{R}(\cdot)$ is a regularizer, λ is a non-negative hyperparameter, and $\mathcal{W}$ denotes all the model parameters. Here, $\mathcal{D} = \mathcal{D}^+ \cup \mathcal{D}_{samp}^-$ where $\mathcal{D}^+ := \{(u, j) \in \Omega\}$ and $\mathcal{D}_{samp}^- \subset \{(u, j') \notin \Omega\}$, obtained using negative sampling.

Algorithm 1: SoRecGAT

Input: graph $\mathcal{G}(\mathcal{V}, \mathcal{E})$, epochs T, number of layers L, minibatch size m

1   Initialize $\mathcal{W}$

2   obtain $\mathbf{p}, \mathbf{q}, \mathbf{s}$ from user-item interaction network and social network based on
    equations (10)-(12) **while** $t < T$ **and** *not converged* **do**

3 | $\mathcal{O} \leftarrow$ Shuffle$(\mathbf{p}, \mathbf{q}, \mathbf{s})$

4 | **for** *each minibatch of* $(\bar{\mathbf{p}}, \bar{\mathbf{q}}, \bar{\mathbf{s}}) = (p_i, q_i, s_i)_{i=1}^m \subseteq \mathcal{O}$ **do**

5 | | $\mathcal{W} \leftarrow$ GATEmbedding$(\bar{\mathbf{p}}, \bar{\mathbf{q}}, \bar{\mathbf{s}}, \mathcal{W}, L)$

6   **return**

Algorithm 2: GATEMBEDDING learns weights for attention layers

---

Input: $\mathbf{p}, \mathbf{q}, \mathbf{s}$, network weights $\mathcal{W}$, number of layers L
Output: $\mathcal{W}^{new}$

1   **for** $l = 1 \rightarrow L - 1$ **do**

2 | compute $\mathbf{p}', \mathbf{q}', \mathbf{s}'$ from $\mathbf{p}, \mathbf{q}, \mathbf{s}$ and $\mathcal{W}$ based on equations (3)-(6)

3 | $(\mathbf{p}, \mathbf{q}, \mathbf{s}) \leftarrow (\mathbf{p}', \mathbf{q}', \mathbf{s}')$

4   compute $\hat{\mathbf{y}}$ based on equation (7)

5   $\mathcal{W}^{new} \leftarrow \mathcal{W}^{old} - \eta \frac{\partial \mathcal{L}(\mathcal{W})}{\partial \mathcal{W}}$ $//\eta$ is a learning rate

6   **return** $\mathcal{W}^{new}$

2.3   Node Features

Initial embeddings of graph nodes, before using multi-head attention layers, are obtained using skip-gram technique [16]. Node sequences for a given graph $\mathcal{G}$ are first generated by random walks [4,18]. Treating these sequences as sentences, the skip-gram technique is used to construct graph node embeddings. For a given graph $G(\mathcal{V}, \mathcal{E})$ with entities belonging to the same type, the objective of the skip-gram technique is to maximize the probability of predicting the context node c of a given node v as

$$\max_{\mathbf{x}} \prod_{v \in \mathcal{V}} \prod_{c \in \mathcal{C}(v)} Pr(c|v), \quad \text{where } Pr(c|v) = \frac{e^{x_c \cdot x_v}}{\sum_{c' \in \mathcal{V}} e^{x_{c'} \cdot x_v}}. \tag{10}$$

Here, $\mathcal{C}(v)$ denotes the context of node v, $\mathbf{x} = (x_1, x_2, \ldots, x_{|\mathcal{V}|})$, and x_v represents the embedding of node v. These embeddings are learnt by solving the above optimization problem. In our setting, we have two networks: a user-item interaction network and a user-social_entity social network. The node embeddings for these networks are constructed separately. Note that, this procedure reflects meta-path based node embedding construction for *user-item* and *user-social_entity* meta-paths. Considering heterogeneity among entities has been shown to improve performance over ignoring the types and taking them as homogeneous entities [4].

To reduce the computational cost involved in computing $Pr(c|v)$ (Eq. (10)), we adopt the negative sampling strategy [16] as follows:

$$\ln Pr(c|v) = \ln \sigma(x_c \cdot x_v) + \sum_{m=1}^{M} \mathbb{E}_{c' \sim P_n(c')}[\ln \sigma(x_v \cdot x_{c'})]. \tag{11}$$

where M denotes number of negative samples. Hence, the loss function corresponding to skip-gram model is defined as follows:

$$\min_{\mathbf{x}} \; \mathcal{L}_{rw}(\mathbf{x}) = -\sum_{v \in \mathcal{V}} \sum_{c \in \mathcal{C}(v)} \ln \sigma(x_c \cdot x_v) - \sum_{m=1}^{M} \mathbb{E}_{c' \sim P_n(c')}[\ln \sigma(x_v \cdot x_{c'})]. \tag{12}$$

The complete training procedure for learning the parameters $\mathcal{W}$ for SoRec-GAT is given in Algorithms 1 and 2. During training, we maintain the whole graph structure in a sparse adjacency matrix. In our model, attention weight parameters are shared across all the edges in the graph. Unlike other graph neural network approaches, due to the shared attention weight parameters, we do not operate on embeddings of all the nodes at every mini-batch iteration. Instead, we operate only on the embeddings of the corresponding mini-batch nodes and their neighbours. We randomly select a mini-batch of user-item interactions, that is, the corresponding users and items based on their interactions in the training set. During mini-batch training the gradient propagation happens only to the respective nodes and their neighbours.

In the next section, we will discuss our experimental results.

3   Experiments

To demonstrate the effectiveness of the proposed model, in view of the following research questions, we conduct several experiments:

RQ1 Does our proposed model – SoRecGAT perform better than state-of-the-art social recommendation models? Does influence learning provide an advantage when only the user-item rating matrix is available?

RQ2 What is the effect of various sparsity levels of the training set on the performance of the proposed model?

RQ3 Employing the multi-head attention mechanism helpful for improving the performance of SoRecGAT?

We address these questions after discussing experimental settings.

3.1   Experimental Settings

Datasets. We conduct experiments on eight datasets: four from **Amazon**[6] – an e-commerce recommendation system for products ranging from books, movie

---

[6] http://jmcauley.ucsd.edu/data/amazon.

DVDs to cloth items, and **Yelp**[7] – a user review platform on local businesses ranging from restaurants, hotels to real estates. Amazon dataset contains co-purchased information for the items which we use as the item-social network. Similarly, Yelp dataset contains friendship connections which we use as the user-social network. Datasets contain ratings on the scale, [1–5]. We do the following preprocessing as done in [9,19]: (1) Ratings having value more than 3 are retained and treated as positive interactions (rating value 1 is assigned to them); (2) Those users and items who have at least five ratings associated with them are retained; and (3) Social connections between entities $e1 \rightarrow e2$ for which either $e1$ or $e2$ is a part of user-item interaction network are retained. The details of the datasets are given in Table 1.

Table 1. Dataset statistics.

Dataset		# users	# items	# ratings	# social entities	# social connections
Amazon	Music	2412	1923	33237	6769	129848
	Movie	9498	4786	156633	5835	85495
	CD	7878	7247	137610	18687	485526
	Book	10041	6477	143805	16711	264283
Yelp	Art	3071	1122	31438	7203	458322
	Food	12615	4222	151394	13053	819044
	Hotel	11040	3925	128130	14432	893278
	Restaurant	13877	2233	158384	16702	1076506

Evaluation Procedure. For evaluating the performance of the models, we closely follow [9] and adopt the well-known *leave-one-out* procedure. That is, one item for each user from the dataset is held-out for validation and test purpose respectively and the remaining items are used for training the model. Since it is too time-consuming to rank all the items for each user during the evaluation time, following [9], we randomly sample 50 non-interacted items for each user along with the held-out item to construct validation and test set. Likewise, we randomly extract five such sets. Mean and standard deviation of the models on the test set with respect to best validation set performance is reported as the final result.

Metric. We use two widely adopted ranking metrics – HitRatio@N (HR@N) and normalized discounted cumulative gain (NDCG@N) for comparing the performance of different models [9,19]. While HR@N measures the existence of the items a user has interacted with, NDCG@N emphasizes the position of the same item from the predicted top-N ranked list.

---

[7] https://www.yelp.com/dataset/challenge.

Comparison with Different Models. To evaluate the performance in rating-only and social recommendation setting, we compare SoRecGAT with the following four groups of models. They are: rating-only models based on (i) matrix factorization and (ii) neural networks; and social recommendation models based on (iii) matrix factorization and (iv) neural networks. We select representatives for each group and detail them below:

- **SAMN** [3] is a state-of-the-art model for top-N social recommendation setting. It contains two components. The first component – attention-based memory module learns aspect-level differences among friends, whereas the second component – friend-level attention module learns influence strength of his friends.
- **DeepSoR** [5] follows the two-stage procedure. In the first stage, it obtains user representations from social networks by leveraging random walks. It extends PMF (Probabilistic Matrix Factorization) [17] for social recommendation in the second stage. The representations obtained from the first stage are used as regularizers for users.
- **SBPR** [31] is a state-of-the-model for the top-N recommendation setting. It extends BPR for the social recommendation.
- **TrustSVD** [8] extends the MF based model [11] to social recommendation. It jointly factorizes both social network and user-item rating matrices to learn richer representations.
- **NeuMF** [9] is a recently proposed state-of-the-art model for rating-only setting. It fuses multi-layer perceptron with matrix factorization model in order to exploit both deep and wide representations.
- **GMF** is a generalization of matrix factorization and proposed as a part of NeuMF [9].
- **BPR** [22] is a standard baseline for top-N ranking setting. It optimizes the pairwise loss function during training.
- **MF** [11] is a standard and widely adopted baseline for collaborative filtering.
- **RecGAT** is a special case of our model which uses only user-item interaction network.

Note that, SAMN and DeepSoR are neural network models, and SBPR and TrustSVD are matrix factorization models for social recommendation. In addition, NeuMF is based on a neural network model, and MF, GMF and BPR are matrix factorization models for the rating-only setting.

Parameter Setting and Reproducibility. We use Python, Tensorflow 1.12 for our implementation. Our implementation is available at https://github.com/mvijaikumar/SoRecGAT.

We use the dropout regularizer and adopt RMSProp [7] with mini-batch for optimization. The number of layers, number of heads per layer and number of activation functions per head are sensitive hyperparameters for RecGAT and SoRecGAT. Hyperparameters are tuned using the validation set. From the validation set performance, the number of layers are set to two for RecGAT, SoRecGAT, DeepSoR and NeuMF. Further, for SoRecGAT, the batch size is set

Table 2. Performance of different models on four real-world datasets – Music, CD, Movie, Book from **Amazon**. Social recommendation models are separated from rating-only models. The best overall scores are indicated in boldface, while the best scores among rating-only models are highlighted by asterisk (*). We conduct paired t-test and the improvements using SoRecGAT are statistically significant with $p < 0.01$.

Model	Music		CD	
	HR@5	NDCG@5	HR@5	NDCG@5
MF	0.6482 ± 0.0158	0.4844 ± 0.0107	0.6779 ± 0.0039	0.5198 ± 0.0032
BPR	0.6555 ± 0.0102	0.4855 ± 0.0082	0.6901 ± 0.0052	0.5340 ± 0.0054
GMF	0.6835 ± 0.0106	0.5163 ± 0.0109	0.7163 ± 0.0061	0.5609 ± 0.0056
NeuMF	0.6854 ± 0.0084	0.5182 ± 0.0095	0.7251 ± 0.0030	0.5776 ± 0.0036
RecGAT (ours)	0.7104 ± 0.0116*	0.5416 ± 0.0098*	0.7504 ± 0.0065*	0.6019 ± 0.0047*
SBPR	0.6646 ± 0.0122	0.4914 ± 0.0092	0.6985 ± 0.0047	0.5485 ± 0.0062
TrustSVD	0.6712 ± 0.0113	0.5015 ± 0.0087	0.7043 ± 0.0072	0.5713 ± 0.0049
DeepSoR	0.6759 ± 0.0082	0.5130 ± 0.0084	0.7373 ± 0.0026	0.5841 ± 0.0036
SAMN	0.6795 ± 0.0080	0.5008 ± 0.0046	0.7245 ± 0.0061	0.5695 ± 0.0042
SoRecGAT (ours)	**0.7333 ± 0.0029**	**0.5582 ± 0.0129**	**0.7796 ± 0.0023**	**0.6225 ± 0.0033**
	Movie		Book	
MF	0.5370 ± 0.0021	0.3799 ± 0.0027	0.7193 ± 0.0008	0.5614 ± 0.0014
BPR	0.5401 ± 0.0047	0.3843 ± 0.0042	0.7144 ± 0.0042	0.5626 ± 0.0021
GMF	0.5590 ± 0.0023	0.4006 ± 0.0012	0.7397 ± 0.0038	0.5931 ± 0.0027
NeuMF	0.5607 ± 0.0053	0.4022 ± 0.0037	0.7457 ± 0.0035	0.5965 ± 0.0033
RecGAT (ours)	0.5815 ± 0.0018*	0.4243 ± 0.0015*	0.7734 ± 0.0012*	0.6241 ± 0.0017*
SBPR	0.5493 ± 0.0034	0.3918 ± 0.0021	0.7217 ± 0.0029	0.5998 ± 0.0018
TrustSVD	0.5531 ± 0.0065	0.3973 ± 0.0032	0.7265 ±0.0032	0.5910 ± 0.0024
DeepSoR	0.5610 ± 0.0042	0.4079 ± 0.0035	0.7478 ± 0.0009	0.5964 ± 0.0024
SAMN	0.5621 ± 0.0065	0.4107 ± 0.0033	0.7405 ± 0.0041	0.5937 ± 0.0021
SoRecGAT (ours)	**0.5888 ± 0.0043**	**0.4306 ± 0.0019**	**0.7805 ± 0.0014**	**0.6297 ± 0.0011**

to 1024, the number of heads for layers are set to [8,6] for Food dataset and [12,6] for other datasets the number of activation functions per head is set to 32 in the first layer and 96 for Movie, Book and CD, 48 for Hotel and 64 for other datasets in the second layer, the dropout ratio is set to 0.2 for Art and Book datasets and 0.5 for other datasets, learning rate is set to 0.0004 for Music, 0.0001 for Art and 0.00008 for other datasets. We use LeakyRELU as the activation function in Eq. (3) and exponential linear unit (ELU) as the activation function in other places. Further, we tune l_2-regularization values for SBPR, TrustSVD, DeepSoR, SAMN from {0.005, 0.01, 0.05, 0.1, 0.5, 1, 1.5} and the number of factors for MF, GMF, BPR, SBPR, TrustSVD, DeepSoR and SAMN from {16, 32, 64, 80, 128}, respectively. We use early stopping criterion with the maximum number of epochs for training set to 60.

3.2   Results and Discussion

Overall Performance (**RQ1**). Tables 2 and 3 detail the performance of our models and the other comparison models on eight datasets from Amazon and

Table 3. Performance of different models on four real-world datasets – Art, Hotel, Food and Restaurant from **Yelp**. Social recommendation models are separated from rating-only models. The best overall scores are indicated in boldface, while the best scores among rating-only models are highlighted by asterisk (*). We conduct paired t-test and the improvements using SoRecGAT are statistically significant with $p < 0.01$.

Model	Art		Hotel	
	HR@5	NDCG@5	HR@5	NDCG@5
MF	0.7111 ± 0.0063	0.5124 ± 0.0091	0.8147 ± 0.0006	0.6127 ± 0.0015
BPR	0.7051 ± 0.0057	0.5123 ± 0.0027	0.7994 ± 0.0028	0.6009 ± 0.0025
GMF	0.7235 ± 0.0065	0.5319 ± 0.0068	0.8350 ± 0.0024	0.6359 ± 0.0018
NeuMF	0.7204 ± 0.0083	0.5314 ± 0.0059	0.8313 ± 0.0022	0.6364 ± 0.0017
RecGAT (ours)	0.7371 ± 0.0048*	0.5370 ± 0.0036*	0.8462 ± 0.0044*	0.6454 ± 0.0032*
SBPR	0.7284 ± 0.0062	0.5334 ± 0.0046	0.8332 ± 0.0037	0.6318 ± 0.0026
TrustSVD	0.7310 ± 0.0056	0.5391 ± 0.0032	0.8382 ± 0.0027	0.6353 ± 0.0019
DeepSoR	0.7322 ± 0.0065	0.5363 ± 0.0047	0.8357 ± 0.0040	0.6364 ± 0.0023
SAMN	0.7345 ± 0.0104	0.5374 ± 0.0067	0.8292 ± 0.0025	0.6215 ± 0.0033
SoRecGAT (ours)	**0.7460 ± 0.0051**	**0.5407 ± 0.0038**	**0.8506 ± 0.0039**	**0.6546 ± 0.0035**
	Food		Restaurant	
MF	0.8087 ± 0.0022	0.6086 ± 0.0025	0.7744 ± 0.0017	0.5649 ± 0.0025
BPR	0.7862 ± 0.0027	0.5895 ± 0.0025	0.7536 ± 0.0034	0.5499 ± 0.0023
GMF	0.8285 ± 0.0024	0.6314 ± 0.0015	0.7925 ± 0.0037	0.5881 ± 0.0022
NeuMF	0.8387 ± 0.0038	0.6403 ± 0.0032	0.7945 ± 0.0044	0.5896 ± 0.0034*
RecGAT (ours)	0.8420 ± 0.0016*	0.6442 ± 0.0012*	0.7961 ± 0.0031*	0.5860 ± 0.0029
SBPR	0.8295 ± 0.0028	0.6277 ± 0.0019	0.7904 ± 0.0041	0.5811 ± 0.0028
TrustSVD	0.8380 ± 0.0034	0.6390 ± 0.0024	0.7946 ± 0.0038	0.5874 ± 0.0027
DeepSoR	0.8294 ± 0.0022	0.6333 ± 0.0023	0.7963 ± 0.0025	0.5937 ± 0.0031
SAMN	0.8218 ± 0.0032	0.6119 ± 0.0016	0.7777 ± 0.0034	0.5658 ± 0.0029
SoRecGAT (ours)	**0.8471 ± 0.0074**	**0.6515 ± 0.0017**	**0.8038 ± 0.0042**	**0.5972 ± 0.0033**

Yelp. Learning influence strength among entities in both user-item interaction network and social network is crucial. To understand this phenomenon, we study two cases here – without social network (RecGAT) and with social network (SoRecGAT). RecGAT achieves better performance consistently across the datasets as compared to the rating-only alternatives – MF, BPR, GMF and NeuMF. From this, we observe that when only implicit ratings are available, understanding the influence of users and items on each other is essential. Rec-GAT achieves this by utilizing the multi-head attention mechanism layerwise.

SoRecGAT performs better than both rating-only and other social recommendation models. Note that DeepSoR and SAMN are neural network models. Further, SAMN leverages attention-based memory network and friend-level attention mechanism to learn the influence strength of users from the social network. However, the above procedure is insufficient when we are given access to only implicit ratings. This is because the users may not have an equal opinion on all the items they interact within a system. In contrast, SoRecGAT accounts for this by integrating both user-item interaction network and social network together, and captures the influence strength in an end-to-end fashion using

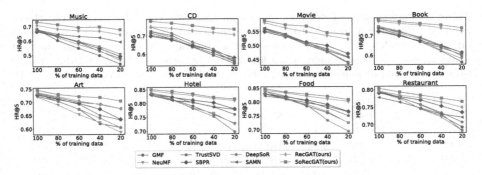

Fig. 2. Performance (**HR@5**) comparison of different models with respect to different sparsity levels on the datasets: Music, CD, Movie, Book, Art, Hotel, Food and Restaurant. Here, we report the mean value obtained from five different experiments for each sparsity level.

graph attention mechanism. Also note that, in SoRecGAT, the representations of any entity in the graph is obtained from all its neighbours irrespective of its entity type. This provides a more unified framework than DeepSoR and SAMN.

Performance of Models with Respect to Different Sparsity Levels (RQ2). To investigate the effectiveness of our models under various sparsity levels, we do the following. We start from the full training set and randomly remove 20% ratings at each step. We continue this until only 20% of the ratings are left in the training set. We repeat this for five different experiments for each sparsity level, and report the mean value. Figures 2 and 3 show the detailed comparison using the metrics HR@5 and NDCG@5, respectively.

As can be seen from Figs. 2 and 3, RecGAT and SoRecGAT consistently perform better than the other models across different datasets, and their performance does not deteriorate drastically as the sparsity level increases. This is particularly evident for Amazon datasets ((a), (b), (c) and (d) in Figs. 2 and 3). This shows that RecGAT and SoRecGAT are more robust to the situations where data are extremely sparse. From this, we can conclude that learning influence strength among entities in the user-item interaction network and social network by our approach helps in alleviating data sparsity issues.

Effect of Multi-head Attention for Obtaining Influence (RQ3). Here, we study the advantage of employing multiple attention heads in layers. We keep two layers, and vary the number of attention heads from [2,1] to [20,10] in the respective layers. The performance of SoRecGAT, in terms of HR@5 and NDCG@5, is depicted in Fig. 4 for Music and Art datasets. From this figure, it is clear that the performance improves, as we increase the number of attention heads. However, in our experiments, we notice that the performance starts deteriorating once the number of attention heads exceeds [12,6] as this results in overfitting. We thus observe that each attention head provides different complementary knowledge

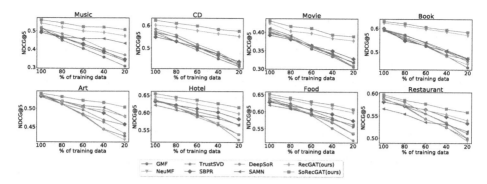

Fig. 3. Performance (**NDCG@5**) comparison of different models with respect to different sparsity levels on the datasets: Music, CD, Movie, Book, Art, Hotel, Food and Restaurant. Here, we report the mean value obtained from five different experiments for each sparsity level.

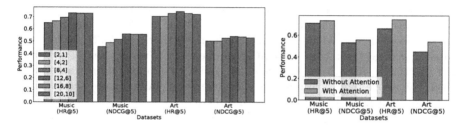

Fig. 4. Performance of SoRecGAT with respect to different number of attention heads in the layers on Music and Art datasets.

Fig. 5. Performance of the proposed architecture without and with attention mechanism on Music and Art datasets.

about the relationship that exists among entities, which boosts the overall performance of SoRecGAT.

Effect of Attention Mechanism. Here, we study the effect of attention mechanism in our graph networks. We use the same architecture (two layers with the number of heads set to [12,6], the number of activation functions set to 32 and 64 respectively in the first and second layers, and the dropout set to 0.5 for Music and 0.2 for Art) without and with attention mechanism on Music and Art datasets. The performance is shown in Fig. 5 for the two datasets. From this figure, we can observe that attention mechanism in the proposed approach improve the performance.

4   Related Work

In the literature of recommendation systems, early successful models are mostly based on matrix factorization techniques [11,17,22]. In particular, [2,22] are proposed for top-N recommendation framework where only implicit ratings are available. Despite being simple, MF models act as strong baselines among collaborative filtering techniques. Owing to its rich representation capability [7,12], a surge of neural networks and deep learning models have been proposed for recommendation systems recently [9,13,28–30]. In contrast to MF, these models replace the simple dot product between latent representation of users and items with neural networks. Further, He *et al.* [9] proposed NeuMF that marries multi-layer perceptron with generalized matrix factorization model to get the best of both MF and neural network world. Nevertheless, these aforementioned models suffer from data sparsity issues.

Exploiting social connections along with the user-item ratings have been shown to greatly improve the performance of recommendation systems over traditional models that use only ratings [1,8,10,14,15,25]. Most existing works on social recommendation extend matrix factorization techniques to incorporate social network information into the recommendation system framework. For instance, SocialMF [10] considers social influence by trust propagation mechanism; SoReg [15] incorporates social connections as regularizers to user representations learned from user-item ratings; and TrustSVD [8] extends SVD++ model [11] to trust and social recommendation. Further, [19,20,31] have been proposed specifically for top-N social recommendation tasks. Neural network models [5,21] also have been proposed for social recommendation framework. However, the above models assume that there exists equal influence across users in the social network, which is not true in practice.

Our work is related to [6,23,27,29] in terms of using graph framework, and [3,24,32] in terms of using attention mechanism for the top-N recommendation setting. However, inspired by GAT [26], we employ multiple levels of attention mechanism to account for complex relationships that exist among entities. Further, in contrast to GAT which is proposed for node classifications in graphs, our model is proposed for top-N recommendation setting and the objective function is designed to predict future links between the users and items. Thus, here, the social network helps in fine-tuning the user and item representations.

Furthermore, the models [23,24,27] are proposed for session-based social recommendations which require temporal information and [32] requires context information in addition to user-item interaction network and social network. In particular, Wu *et al.* [27] proposed SR-GNN that models session sequences as graph structured data. Further, they employ graph neural networks to capture complex transitions of items. Fan *et al.* [6] proposed GraphRec for social recommendation to jointly model interactions and opinions in the user-item graph. In [29], a graph neural network algorithm called PinSage was proposed. PinSage employs low latency random walks and localized graph convolution operations to learn rich representations for nodes. The model [23] uses graph attention mechanism for learning the influence of users in a social network. In contrast, our model is more general and unified than [23], and the former learns influence from both the social network and user-item interaction network, collectively.

5 Conclusion

In this paper, we presented a novel graph attention-based model, SoRecGAT, for top-N social recommendation. More importantly, our model integrates social network with user-item interaction network and learns the complex relationships among entities by multi-head and multi-layer attention mechanism. We conducted extensive experiments on eight real-world datasets, and demonstrated the effectiveness of the proposed model over state-of-the-art models under various settings. Further, the proposed model has an advantage of using network-specific side information, if available of nodes. Our model is more general and it can be used for recommendations with any number of external networks. In future, we plan to extend these ideas to a multimedia recommendation system where data come from different modalities such as audios, images and videos.

References

1. Abbasi, M.A., Tang, J., Liu, H.: Trust-aware recommender systems. In: Machine Learning Book on Computational Trust. Chapman & Hall/CRC Press (2014)
2. Balakrishnan, S., Chopra, S.: Collaborative ranking. In: WSDM, pp. 143–152. ACM (2012)
3. Chen, C., Zhang, M., Liu, Y., Ma, S.: Social attentional memory network: modeling aspect-and friend-level differences in recommendation. In: WSDM, pp. 177–185. ACM (2019)
4. Dong, Y., Chawla, N.V., Swami, A.: metapath2vec: scalable representation learning for heterogeneous networks. In: SIGKDD, pp. 135–144. ACM (2017)
5. Fan, W., Li, Q., Cheng, M.: Deep modeling of social relations for recommendation. In: AAAI (2018)
6. Fan, W., et al.: Graph neural networks for social recommendation. In: WWW, pp. 417–426 (2019)
7. Goodfellow, I., Bengio, Y., Courville, A., Bengio, Y.: Deep Learning, vol. 1. MIT Press, Cambridge (2016)
8. Guo, G., Zhang, J., Yorke-Smith, N.: TrustSVD: collaborative filtering with both the explicit and implicit influence of user trust and of item ratings. In: AAAI, vol. 15, pp. 123–125 (2015)
9. He, X., Liao, L., Zhang, H., Nie, L., Hu, X., Chua, T.S.: Neural collaborative filtering. In: WWW, pp. 173–182 (2017)
10. Jamali, M., Ester, M.: A matrix factorization technique with trust propagation for recommendation in social networks. In: RecSys, pp. 135–142. ACM (2010)
11. Koren, Y., Bell, R., Volinsky, C.: Matrix factorization techniques for recommender systems. Computer 8, 30–37 (2009)
12. LeCun, Y., Bengio, Y., Hinton, G.: Deep learning. Nature 521(7553), 436 (2015)
13. Li, X., She, J.: Collaborative variational autoencoder for recommender systems. In: SIGKDD, pp. 305–314. ACM (2017)
14. Ma, H., Yang, H., Lyu, M.R., King, I.: SoRec: social recommendation using probabilistic matrix factorization. In: CIKM, pp. 931–940. ACM (2008)
15. Ma, H., Zhou, D., Liu, C., Lyu, M.R., King, I.: Recommender systems with social regularization. In: WSDM, pp. 287–296. ACM (2011)

16. Mikolov, T., Sutskever, I., Chen, K., Corrado, G.S., Dean, J.: Distributed representations of words and phrases and their compositionality. In: Advances in Neural Information Processing Systems, pp. 3111–3119 (2013)
17. Mnih, A., Salakhutdinov, R.R.: Probabilistic matrix factorization. In: Advances in Neural Information Processing Systems, pp. 1257–1264 (2008)
18. Perozzi, B., Al-Rfou, R., Skiena, S.: DeepWalk: online learning of social representations. In: SIGKDD, pp. 701–710. ACM (2014)
19. Rafailidis, D., Crestani, F.: Joint collaborative ranking with social relationships in top-N recommendation. In: CIKM, pp. 1393–1402. ACM (2016)
20. Rafailidis, D., Crestani, F.: Learning to rank with trust and distrust in recommender systems. In: RecSys, pp. 5–13. ACM (2017)
21. Rafailidis, D., Crestani, F.: Recommendation with social relationships via deep learning. In: SIGIR, pp. 151–158. ACM (2017)
22. Rendle, S., Freudenthaler, C., Gantner, Z., Schmidt-Thieme, L.: BPR: Bayesian personalized ranking from implicit feedback. In: Proceedings of the Twenty-Fifth Conference on Uncertainty in Artificial Intelligence, pp. 452–461. AUAI Press (2009)
23. Song, W., Xiao, Z., Wang, Y., Charlin, L., Zhang, M., Tang, J.: Session-based social recommendation via dynamic graph attention networks. In: WSDM, pp. 555–563. ACM (2019)
24. Sun, P., Wu, L., Wang, M.: Attentive recurrent social recommendation. In: SIGIR, pp. 185–194. ACM (2018)
25. Tang, J., Hu, X., Liu, H.: Social recommendation: a review. Soc. Netw. Anal. Min. 3(4), 1113–1133 (2013). https://doi.org/10.1007/s13278-013-0141-9
26. Veličković, P., Cucurull, G., Casanova, A., Romero, A., Liò, P., Bengio, Y.: Graph attention networks. In: International Conference on Learning Representations (2018)
27. Wu, S., Tang, Y., Zhu, Y., Wang, L., Xie, X., Tan, T.: Session-based recommendation with graph neural networks. In: AAAI (2019)
28. Xue, H.J., Dai, X., Zhang, J., Huang, S., Chen, J.: Deep matrix factorization models for recommender systems. In: IJCAI, pp. 3203–3209 (2017)
29. Ying, R., He, R., Chen, K., Eksombatchai, P., Hamilton, W.L., Leskovec, J.: Graph convolutional neural networks for web-scale recommender systems. In: SIGKDD, pp. 974–983. ACM (2018)
30. Zhang, S., Yao, L., Sun, A., Tay, Y.: Deep learning based recommender system: a survey and new perspectives. ACM Comput. Surv. (CSUR) 52(1), 5 (2019)
31. Zhao, T., McAuley, J., King, I.: Leveraging social connections to improve personalized ranking for collaborative filtering. In: CIKM, pp. 261–270. ACM (2014)
32. Zhou, C., et al.: ATRank: an attention-based user behavior modeling framework for recommendation. In: AAAI (2018)

Graph Signal Processing for Directed Graphs Based on the Hermitian Laplacian

Satoshi Furutani[1($\boxtimes$)], Toshiki Shibahara[1], Mitsuaki Akiyama[1],
Kunio Hato[1], and Masaki Aida[2]

[1] NTT Secure Platform Laboratories, Tokyo, Japan
{satoshi.furutani.ek,toshiki.shibahara.de,kunio.hato.gm}@hco.ntt.co.jp,
akiyama@ieee.org
[2] Tokyo Metropolitan University, Tokyo, Japan
aida@tmu.ac.jp

Abstract. Graph signal processing is a useful tool for representing, analyzing, and processing the signal lying on a graph, and has attracted
attention in several fields including data mining and machine learning.
A key to construct the graph signal processing is the graph Fourier transform, which is defined by using eigenvectors of the graph Laplacian of
an undirected graph. The orthonormality of eigenvectors gives the graph
Fourier transform algebraically desirable properties, and thus the graph
signal processing for undirected graphs has been well developed. However, since eigenvectors of the graph Laplacian of a directed graph are
generally not orthonormal, it is difficult to simply extend the graph signal
processing to directed graphs. In this paper, we present a general framework for extending the graph signal processing to directed graphs. To this
end, we introduce the Hermitian Laplacian which is a complex matrix
obtained from an extension of the graph Laplacian. The Hermitian Laplacian is defined so as to preserve the edge directionality and Hermitian
property and enables the graph signal processing to be straightforwardly
extended to directed graphs. Furthermore, the Hermitian Laplacian guarantees some desirable properties, such as non-negative real eigenvalues
and the unitarity of the Fourier transform. Finally, experimental results
for representation learning and signal denoising of/on directed graphs
show the effectiveness of our framework.

Keywords: Graph signal processing · Graph Laplacian · Directed
graph

1 Introduction

Graph signal processing has attracted attention in several fields since it is useful
for representing, analyzing, and processing the *graph signal*, which is the signal
defined on the nodes of a graph. Graph signal processing aims to extend the classical signal processing for signals on a Euclidean structure, e.g., time series and
image signals, to signals on any graphs (i.e., both undirected and directed graphs).

© Springer Nature Switzerland AG 2020
U. Brefeld et al. (Eds.): ECML PKDD 2019, LNAI 11906, pp. 447–463, 2020.
https://doi.org/10.1007/978-3-030-46150-8_27

The basic concepts of graph signal processing have already been introduced, such as graph filtering [18,19,23], graph sampling [4,32] and graph-based transforms [13,24,29]. Along with theoretical development, graph signal processing has facilitated advances in data mining, such as community mining [33], shape classification [16], feature learning [35], and representation learning [8]. Furthermore, it is a fundamental theory for generalizing machine learning algorithms for data with an underlying Euclidean or grid-like structure to graph structures, e.g., semi-supervised learning [1,11] and deep neural networks [3,6].

Fourier transform of graph signal, called *graph Fourier transform*, plays a key role in constructing the graph signal processing. The basic approach to define the graph Fourier transform is based on eigenvectors of the graph Laplacian [13,29]. This approach applies to undirected graphs and constructs the Fourier basis as the eigenvector of the graph Laplacian. Because of its orthonormality, the resulting Fourier transform is unitary, and thus the inner product is preserved. Furthermore, since this transform is considered as the natural extension of classical Fourier transform, the Fourier basis is easy to interpret. Specifically, the Fourier basis corresponding to low frequency varies slowly, whereas that corresponding to high frequency varies intensively. However, since eigenvectors of the graph Laplacian of a directed graph are generally not orthonormal, we cannot straightforwardly extend the graph Fourier transform to directed graphs.

The alternative approach to define the graph Fourier transform is based on the Jordan decomposition of the adjacency matrix [23,24]. This approach constructs the Fourier basis by using generalized eigenvectors of the adjacency matrix. This is motivated by the fact that the adjacency matrix of a directed ring graph can be regarded as the shift operator for discrete signals [21]; shift operator is the basis of all shift-invariant linear filtering. Since any square matrices can be decomposed as Jordan form, this approach is applicable to both undirected and directed graphs. However, it has some unsolved critical issues. First, since the Fourier basis based on the Jordan decomposition is not orthonormal, the resulting transform is not unitary. Second, the Fourier basis corresponding to low frequency does not necessarily vary slowly and vice-versa [31]. Third, eigenvalues of the adjacency matrix of a directed graph will take complex values. The complex eigenvalues lead to a large error in the approximated filter responses [22]. Finally, the numerical computation of the Jordan decomposition often incurs numerical instabilities even for medium-sized matrices [12].

A few unique approaches have recently been proposed to extend the graph Fourier transform to directed graphs. Sevi *et al.* [26,27] proposed a framework for constructing the harmonic analysis (i.e., Fourier and wavelet transform) on directed graphs based on the Dirichlet energy of eigenfunctions of a random walk operator. This approach constructs the Fourier basis by using the eigenfunction of the random walk Laplacian [5] of a directed graph. However, this approach is applicable only to strongly connected directed graphs and does not guarantee the orthonormality of the Fourier basis. Another approach is to construct the Fourier basis by solving the non-convex optimization problems under some constraints. Sardellitti *et al.* [25] proposed a method for constructing the Fourier basis as the solution of the minimization problem of Lovász extension of the graph cut under the orthonormality constraints. Lovász extension is a lossless convex relaxation of the graph cut and is read as a smoothness measure of a graph signal. Then, Shafipour *et al.* [28] designed the Fourier basis as the solution of the non-convex orthonormality constrained optimization problems such that frequencies have a desirable property, i.e., frequencies associated with the Fourier bases are evenly spread over the entire frequency domain. Although these methods can construct Fourier bases that have desirable properties, the solutions (Fourier bases) may fall into a local minimum and can vary each time depending on the solving method and/or initial conditions. Moreover, the Fourier bases do not completely preserve the information about an underlying graph structure. Namely, it is difficult to reconstruct the graph structure from Fourier bases and frequencies.

In this paper, we present a general framework for extending the graph signal processing to directed graphs based on the Hermitian Laplacian. The Hermitian Laplacian is defined so as to preserve both the Hermitian property and edge directionality by encoding the edge direction into the argument (phase) in the complex plane. Thanks to the Hermitian property, we can always choose eigenvectors of a Hermitian Laplacian as orthonormal bases. This orthonormality enables the basic concepts of the graph signal processing for undirected graphs to be straightforwardly generalized to that for directed graphs. Furthermore, the Hermitian property guarantees some desirable properties for constructing the graph signal processing, such as non-negative real eigenvalues and the unitarity of the Fourier transform. Finally, we provide experimental results for representation learning and signal denoising of/on directed graphs as application examples of our framework.

2 Preliminaries

2.1 Graph Laplacian and Graph Signals

Let $G = (V, E)$ be an undirected graph without self-loops and multiple edges, where V is the set of N nodes and $E \subset V \times V$ is the set of edges in G. The adjacency matrix $\boldsymbol{A} = [A_{ij}] \in \mathbb{R}^{N \times N}$ is defined as $A_{ij} = w_{ij}$ if $(i, j) \in E$ and $A_{ij} = 0$ otherwise. Here w_{ij} is the real positive weight of edge (i, j), and $w_{ij} = w_{ji}$ in an undirected graph. The degree of each node is $d_i := \sum_{j=1}^{N} w_{ij}$ and the degree matrix is defined as $\boldsymbol{D} := \mathrm{diag}(d_1, \ldots, d_N)$. The graph Laplacian is defined as $\boldsymbol{L} := \boldsymbol{D} - \boldsymbol{A}$.

For connected graphs, $\boldsymbol{L}$ is a non-negative definite matrix and its minimum eigenvalue is 0. Therefore we sort its eigenvalues in ascending order as $0 = \lambda_0 < \lambda_1 \leq \cdots \leq \lambda_{N-1}$, and we choose the orthonormal eigenvector $\boldsymbol{v}_\mu$ associated with eigenvalue λ_μ such that $\langle \boldsymbol{v}_\mu, \boldsymbol{v}_\nu \rangle = \delta_{\mu\nu}$, where $\delta_{\mu\nu}$ is Kronecker's delta. Then, since $\boldsymbol{L}$ of an undirected graph G is real symmetric, $\boldsymbol{L}$ can be decomposed as $\boldsymbol{L} = \boldsymbol{V}\boldsymbol{\Lambda}\boldsymbol{V}^*$, where $\boldsymbol{V} := (\boldsymbol{v}_0, \ldots, \boldsymbol{v}_{N-1})$ is the orthonormal matrix, $\boldsymbol{\Lambda} = \mathrm{diag}(\lambda_0, \ldots, \lambda_{N-1})$ is the diagonal matrix, and $*$ is the adjoint (conjugate transpose). Note that, for undirected graphs, $\boldsymbol{V}^* = \boldsymbol{V}^T$ since $\boldsymbol{V}$ is real.

The graph signal $f : V \to \mathbb{R}^N$ can be represented as a N dimensional vector whose i-th entry $f(i)$ is the signal value at node $i \in V$.

2.2   Graph Signal Processing

In this subsection, we briefly introduce the Laplacian-based graph signal processing [13,29] through comparison with classical signal processing.

Graph Fourier Transform. The classical Fourier transform is defined by the inner product of signal $f(t)$ with the Fourier basis $e^{i\omega t}$ as

$$\hat{f}(\omega) := \langle f, e^{i\omega t}\rangle = \int_{\mathbb{R}} f(t)\, e^{-i\omega t}\, \mathrm{d}t.$$

This means Fourier transform is the expansion of a function f by the Fourier basis that is the eigenfunction of the one-dimensional Laplace operator; $-\triangle e^{i\omega t} = -\frac{\partial^2}{\partial t^2} e^{i\omega t} = \omega^2 e^{i\omega t}$.

Analogously, for undirected graphs, the graph Fourier transform of graph signal $f \in \mathbb{R}^N$ is defined by the eigenvectors of graph Laplacian L as

$$\hat{f}(\lambda_\mu) := \langle f, v_\mu\rangle = \sum_{i=1}^{N} f(i)\, v_\mu^*(i), \tag{1}$$

$$\hat{f} := V^* f, \tag{2}$$

and inverse graph Fourier transform is defined as $f := V\hat{f}$.

In classical Fourier analysis, the eigenvalue ω^2 can be interpreted as frequency: the eigenfunction $e^{i\omega t}$ varies slowly for small ω but intensively for large ω. In the graph setting, the eigenvalues and eigenvectors of graph Laplacian also act identically. For connected graphs, the eigenvector v_0 associated with zero eigenvalue λ_0 is constant; $v_0(i) = 1/\sqrt{N}$ for all i. Then, the eigenvector associated with small eigenvalue varies slowly across the graph. In other words, if two nodes are connected, the corresponding entries of the eigenvector have similar values. This fact is confirmed by the following equation:

$$\lambda_\mu = v_\mu^T L v_\mu = \sum_{(i,j)\in E} w_{ij}\, (v_\mu(i) - v_\mu(j))^2, \tag{3}$$

which is instantly derived from $\Lambda = V^* L V$. Hereinafter, the property that small and large eigenvalues correspond to low and high frequencies, respectively, is referred to as *frequency ordering*.

Spectral Graph Filtering. In classical signal processing, filtering is the process that removes some unwanted components from an input signal f_{in}. Let h

be the filter in the time domain. The filtering is defined by the convolution of f_{in} and h as

$$f_{\text{out}}(t) := \int_{-\infty}^{\infty} f_{\text{in}}(\tau)\, h(t-\tau)\, \mathrm{d}\tau. \tag{4}$$

Taking the Fourier transform of (4), we derive

$$\hat{f}_{\text{out}}(\omega) = \hat{f}_{\text{in}}(\omega)\, \hat{h}(\omega), \tag{5}$$

so-called *convolution theorem*.

We can generalize (5) to define spectral graph filtering as

$$\hat{f}_{\text{out}}(\lambda_\mu) = \hat{f}_{\text{in}}(\lambda_\mu)\, \hat{h}(\lambda_\mu), \tag{6}$$

or, equivalently, we have

$$f_{\text{out}}(i) = \sum_{\mu=0}^{N-1} \hat{f}_{\text{in}}(\lambda_\mu)\, \hat{h}(\lambda_\mu)\, v_\mu(i). \tag{7}$$

We can also write (7) by matrix form as

$$\boldsymbol{f}_{\text{out}} := \boldsymbol{V}\hat{\boldsymbol{H}}\boldsymbol{V}^*\boldsymbol{f}_{\text{in}}, \tag{8}$$

where $\hat{\boldsymbol{H}} := \operatorname{diag}(\hat{h}(\lambda_0), \ldots, \hat{h}(\lambda_{N-1}))$ and $\hat{h}(\lambda)$ is the filter kernel function defined on $[0, \lambda_{N-1}]$.

Spectral Graph Wavelet Transform. Spectral graph wavelet transform is defined by using the Fourier basis previously defined. The construction of wavelets is based on band-pass or low-pass filters in the frequency domain, generated by modulating a unique filter kernel $\hat{g}(s\,\cdot)$ defined on $[0, \lambda_{N-1}]$. The wavelet at scale $s(>0)$ and node i is defined as

$$\boldsymbol{\psi}_{s,i} := \boldsymbol{V}\hat{\boldsymbol{G}}_s\boldsymbol{V}^*\boldsymbol{\delta}_i, \tag{9}$$

where $\hat{\boldsymbol{G}}_s := \operatorname{diag}(\hat{g}(s\lambda_0), \ldots, \hat{g}(s\lambda_{N-1}))$ and $\boldsymbol{\delta}_i$ is the vector whose i-th entry is 1 and others are 0. Then, given any signal $\boldsymbol{f} \in \mathbb{R}^N$, the wavelet coefficient is defined as

$$W_f(s, i) := \langle \boldsymbol{f}, \boldsymbol{\psi}_{s,i} \rangle = \boldsymbol{\psi}_{s,i}^* \boldsymbol{f}.$$

3 Graph Signal Processing for Directed Graphs Based on the Hermitian Laplacian

Obviously, if the graph Laplacian of a directed graph has orthonormal eigenvectors, we can naturally extend the graph signal processing to directed graphs. However, since the graph Laplacian of a directed graph is asymmetric, its eigenvectors are generally not orthonormal. To overcome this non-orthonormality issue, we introduce the Hermitian Laplacian which is a complex matrix obtained from an extension of the graph Laplacian. The Hermitian Laplacian is defined so as to preserve the edge directionality and Hermitian property and enables the graph signal processing to be straightforwardly extended to directed graphs.

3.1   Hermitian Laplacian on Directed Graphs

Hermitian Laplacian. Here we consider a directed graph $\mathcal{G} = (\mathcal{V}, \mathcal{E})$ where $\mathcal{V}$ is the set of N nodes and $\mathcal{E}$ is the set of directed edges such that for each $i, j \in \mathcal{V}$ ordered tuple $(i, j) \in \mathcal{E}$ assigns a directed edge from node i to j. The weighted adjacency matrix $\mathbf{A} = [\mathcal{A}_{ij}] \in \mathbb{R}^{N \times N}$ is defined as $\mathcal{A}_{ij} = w_{ij}$ if $(i, j) \in \mathcal{E}$ and $\mathcal{A}_{ij} = 0$ otherwise. Note that, for a given directed graph, we can uniquely determine the corresponding undirected graph $\mathcal{G}^{(s)} = (\mathcal{V}, \mathcal{E}^{(s)})$ by ignoring the directionality of edges. The (symmetrized) adjacency matrix $\mathbf{A}^{(s)} = [w_{ij}^{(s)}]$ of $\mathcal{G}^{(s)}$ is defined as $w_{ij}^{(s)} := \frac{1}{2}(w_{ij} + w_{ji})$.

As is well known, a Hermitian matrix $\mathbf{H} \in \mathbb{C}^{N \times N}$ is a complex square matrix that is equal to its own adjoint matrix; $\mathbf{H} = \mathbf{H}^*$. The significant properties of Hermitian matrices are as follows:

- The sum of any two Hermitian matrices is Hermitian.
- All eigenvalues of a Hermitian matrix are real.
- A Hermitian matrix has linearly independent eigenvectors. Moreover, N eigenvectors can always be chosen as orthonormal bases of $\mathbb{C}^N$.
- Any Hermitian matrix $\mathbf{H}$ can be decomposed as $\mathbf{H} = \mathbf{U}\mathbf{\Lambda}\mathbf{U}^*$ where $\mathbf{U}$ is a unitary matrix whose columns are its eigenvectors, and $\mathbf{\Lambda}$ is a diagonal matrix of its eigenvalues.

The above properties of a Hermitian matrix, especially the orthonormality of its eigenvectors, motivate us to define the graph Laplacian of a directed graph as a Hermitian matrix. For this purpose, we consider the edge directionality and node connectivity separately, and encode the edge direction into the argument (phase) in the complex plane.

Let us define the function $\gamma : \mathcal{V} \times \mathcal{V} \to U(1)$ such that

$$\gamma(i, j) = \overline{\gamma(j, i)}, \tag{10}$$

where $U(1)$ is the unitary group of degree 1. One of the simplest expressions of γ is

$$\gamma_q(i, j) := \gamma(i, j; q) = e^{i2\pi q(w_{ij} - w_{ji})}, \tag{11}$$

where $q \in [0, 1)$ is a rotation parameter. As shown in Fig. 1, $\gamma_q(i, j)$ encodes the direction of (i, j) into the phase in the complex plane.

By using (11), the Hermitian Laplacian is defined as

$$\mathcal{L}_q := \mathbf{D} - \mathbf{\Gamma}_q \odot \mathbf{A}^{(s)}, \tag{12}$$

where $\mathbf{D}$ is the degree matrix of $\mathcal{G}^{(s)}$, $\mathbf{\Gamma}_q$ is a Hermitian matrix whose (i, j) component is $\gamma_q(i, j)$, and $\odot$ is Hadamar product. Since $\mathbf{\Gamma}_q \odot \mathbf{A}^{(s)}$ is Hermitian, $\mathcal{L}_q$ is Hermitian. In addition, the degree normalized version of $\mathcal{L}_q$, which is given by $\mathcal{N}_q := \mathbf{D}^{-1/2}\mathcal{L}_q\mathbf{D}^{-1/2}$, is also Hermitian.

In the context of quantum physics, the Hermitian Laplacian can be interpreted as the operator that describes the phenomenology of a free charged particle on a graph, which is subject to the action of a magnetic field. Therefore,

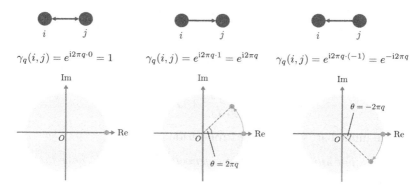

$$\gamma_q(i,j) = e^{i2\pi q \cdot 0} = 1 \qquad \gamma_q(i,j) = e^{i2\pi q \cdot 1} = e^{i2\pi q} \qquad \gamma_q(i,j) = e^{i2\pi q \cdot (-1)} = e^{-i2\pi q}$$

Fig. 1. γ encodes the edge direction into the phase in the complex plane

it is called *magnetic Laplacian* [2,7,14,34]. Due to this physical context, the parameter q is named *electric charge*. Some applications of the magnetic Laplacian for directed graphs have been proposed, e.g., visualization [9], community detection [10], and characterization [17].

Spectral Properties. Let us look at the spectral properties of the Hermitian Laplacian via relationship with the ordinary graph Laplacian. We denote the eigenvalues of the Hermitian Laplacian $\mathcal{L}_q$ in ascending order as $\lambda'_0 \le \cdots \le \lambda'_{N-1}$, and choose the eigenvector $\boldsymbol{u}_\mu$ associated with λ'_μ as the orthonormal eigenbasis. As it is clear from (11), if $\mathcal{G}$ is undirected or $q = 0$, the Hermitian Laplacian $\mathcal{L}_q$ is equivalent to an ordinary graph Laplacian $\boldsymbol{L}$ since $\gamma_q(i,j) = 1$ for all $(i,j) \in \mathcal{V} \times \mathcal{V}$. Thus, for small q, the spectrum of the Hermitian Laplacian is expected to be analogous to the spectrum of the graph Laplacian, such as the presence of a zero eigenvalue and frequency ordering.

We first consider Kato's inequality [15] for the Hermitian Laplacian to look at the relationship between the smallest eigenvalue of $\mathcal{L}_q$ and $\boldsymbol{L}$.

Proposition 1. *For any signal $\boldsymbol{f} \in \mathbb{C}^N$, the following inequality holds:*

$$\langle |\boldsymbol{f}|, \boldsymbol{L}|\boldsymbol{f}| \rangle \le \mathrm{Re}\left[\langle \boldsymbol{f}, \mathcal{L}_q \boldsymbol{f} \rangle \right], \tag{13}$$

where $|\boldsymbol{f}|$ is the real vector whose i-th entry is $|f(i)|$.

Proof. By explicit calculation, we obtain

$$\langle |\boldsymbol{f}|, \boldsymbol{L}|\boldsymbol{f}| \rangle - \mathrm{Re}\left[\langle \boldsymbol{f}, \mathcal{L}_q \boldsymbol{f} \rangle \right]$$

$$= \sum_{i,j=1}^{N} w_{ij}^{(s)} \left(|f(i)|^2 - |f(i)||f(j)| \right) - \mathrm{Re}\left[\sum_{i,j=1}^{N} w_{ij}^{(s)} \left(|f(i)|^2 - \gamma_q(i,j)\, \overline{f(i)}\, f(j) \right) \right]$$

$$= \sum_{i,j=1}^{N} w_{ij}^{(s)} \left(\mathrm{Re}\left[\gamma_q(i,j)\, \overline{f(i)}\, f(j) \right] - |f(i)||f(j)| \right) \le 0,$$

since $\mathrm{Re}\left[\overline{f(i)}\,f(j)\right] \leq |f(i)||f(j)|$ and $|\gamma_q(i,j)| = 1$ for any q. $\square$

Recall that the smallest eigenvalue of the Hermitian Laplacian $\mathcal{L}_q$ is computed as

$$\lambda_0' = \inf\left\{\frac{\langle \boldsymbol{f}, \mathcal{L}_q \boldsymbol{f}\rangle}{\langle \boldsymbol{f}, \boldsymbol{f}\rangle} \mid \langle \boldsymbol{f}, \boldsymbol{f}\rangle \neq 0\right\},$$

we have the immediate corollary of Proposition 1.

Corollary 1. *For any q, the smallest eigenvalue of $\boldsymbol{L}$ and $\mathcal{L}_q$ have the following relationship:*

$$0 = \lambda_0 \leq \lambda_0'. \tag{14}$$

This suggests that the Hermitian Laplacian has non-negative real eigenvalues.

Next, to measure the smoothness of eigenvectors of $\mathcal{L}_q$, we introduce the total variation. We define the total variation of signal $\boldsymbol{f} \in \mathbb{C}^N$ on a graph $\mathcal{G}$ as

$$\mathrm{TV}(\boldsymbol{f}) := \sum_{(i,j)\in\mathcal{E}} |f(i) - f(j)|^2. \tag{15}$$

As it is clear from (15), $\mathrm{TV}(\boldsymbol{f})$ is small (large) if any two adjacent signals on $\mathcal{G}$ take similar (dissimilar) values, respectively. Therefore, we find that (15) measures the smoothness of signals over a graph. Figure 2 shows an example of eigenvalues and total variations of eigenvectors of the Hermitian Laplacian $\mathcal{L}_q$ on a random directed graph with 50 nodes. From this figure, one can find that $\mathcal{L}_q$ satisfies the frequency ordering and has a nearly zero eigenvalue for small q but not for large q because of a larger contribution from the imaginary part.

3.2   Graph Signal Processing for Directed Graphs

In this subsection, we explain the graph signal processing for directed graphs based on the Hermitian Laplacian. As described in Sect. 2.2, the graph Laplacian of an undirected graph has a zero eigenvalue and satisfies the frequency ordering. These properties are useful for understanding the physical meaning of the Fourier basis. Therefore, for extending graph signal processing to directed graphs, the Hermitian Laplacian should also satisfy these properties. For this purpose, we first describe the condition of the rotation parameter q so that $\mathcal{L}_q$ satisfies these properties. Then, we define the graph Fourier transform and some other concepts of graph signal processing on directed graphs.

Selection of q. The choice of the rotation parameter q influences the graph Fourier transform. However, there is not an established method to select it. We here propose an expedient method to select q for graph signal processing. Let ϵ be the tolerance of the smallest eigenvalue λ_0' of the Hermitian Laplacian $\mathcal{L}_q$ $(q > 0)$ of an unweighted directed graph $\mathcal{G}$, that is $0 \leq \lambda_0' \leq \epsilon$. Then, let us denote the

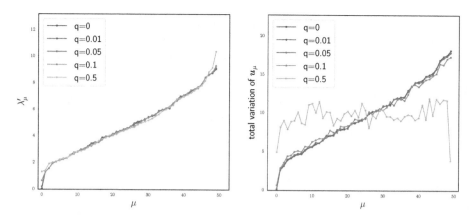

Fig. 2. Spectral properties of the Hermitian Laplacian of a random directed graph with 50 nodes; average degree $\langle d \rangle = 5$.

eigenvalue and associated eigenvector of the symmetrized Laplacian $\boldsymbol{L}^{(s)}$ ($= \mathcal{L}_0$) of $\mathcal{G}^{(s)}$ as $\lambda_\mu^{(s)}$ and $\boldsymbol{u}_\mu^{(s)}$, respectively. According to eigenvalue perturbation theory [20], for small q, the eigenvalue λ'_μ of $\mathcal{L}_q$ is approximated as

$$\lambda'_\mu \simeq \lambda_\mu^{(s)} + \langle \boldsymbol{u}_\mu^{(s)}, \boldsymbol{\Delta}_q \boldsymbol{u}_\mu^{(s)} \rangle, \tag{16}$$

where $\boldsymbol{\Delta}_q := \mathcal{L}_q - \boldsymbol{L}^{(s)}$. Thus, the smallest eigenvalue of $\mathcal{L}_q$ is

$$\lambda'_0 \simeq \lambda_0^{(s)} + \langle \boldsymbol{u}_0^{(s)}, \boldsymbol{\Delta}_q \boldsymbol{u}_0^{(s)} \rangle = \frac{1}{N} \sum_{(i,j) \in \mathcal{E}^{(s)}} (\boldsymbol{\Delta}_q)_{ij},$$

$$\leq \frac{1}{2N} |\mathcal{E}| (2 - e^{i2\pi q} - e^{-i2\pi q}) = \frac{\langle d \rangle}{2} (1 - \cos(2\pi q)),$$

where $\langle d \rangle = \frac{2|\mathcal{E}|}{N}$ is the average in- or out-degree of $\mathcal{G}$. Therefore, by solving the inequality $\lambda'_0 \leq \frac{\langle d \rangle}{2}(1 - \cos(2\pi q)) \leq \epsilon$, we obtain

$$0 \leq q \leq \frac{\cos^{-1}(1 - 2\epsilon/\langle d \rangle)}{2\pi}. \tag{17}$$

Thus, one can choose q depending only on the average degree $\langle d \rangle$ and the tolerance ϵ of the smallest eigenvalue λ'_0.

Graph Fourier Transform on Directed Graphs. Next, we define the graph Fourier transform on directed graphs. Since $\mathcal{L}_q$ is Hermitian, the Hermitian Laplacian can be represented as $\mathcal{L}_q = \boldsymbol{U} \boldsymbol{\Lambda}' \boldsymbol{U}^*$, where $\boldsymbol{U} = (\boldsymbol{u}_0, \dots, \boldsymbol{u}_{N-1})$ and $\boldsymbol{\Lambda}' = \mathrm{diag}(\lambda'_0, \dots, \lambda'_{N-1})$. The graph Fourier transform of the graph signal $\boldsymbol{f} \in \mathbb{R}^N$ on a directed graph can be straightforwardly defined by replacing $\boldsymbol{V}$ of (2) with $\boldsymbol{U}$ as follows:

$$\hat{\boldsymbol{f}} := \boldsymbol{U}^* \boldsymbol{f}, \tag{18}$$

where $\hat{f} \in \mathbb{C}^N$ is generally a complex valued vector. Note that, since U is orthonormal, this definition (18) of graph Fourier transform holds *Parseval's identity*. In other words, for any graph signal $f \in \mathbb{R}^N$, its Fourier transform $\hat{f}$ preserves the inner product; $\langle f, f \rangle = \langle \hat{f}, \hat{f} \rangle$. This means the Fourier transform is unitary.

In the same way, we can easily extend the concepts of the Laplacian-based graph signal processing on undirected graphs to directed graphs. For example, the spectral graph filtering and spectral graph wavelet on a directed graph are respectively defined as

$$f_{\text{out}} := U\hat{H}U^* f_{\text{in}}, \tag{19}$$

and

$$\psi_{s,i} := U\hat{G}_s U^* \delta_i. \tag{20}$$

4   Experiments and Results

In this section, we provide experimental results of representation learning and signal denoising of/on a directed graph as application examples of graph signal processing based on the Hermitian Laplacian. In each experiment, we set the parameter q of Hermitian Laplacian $\mathcal{L}_q$ to $q = 0.02$; our results are not sensitive to small changes in q.

4.1   Representation Learning for Synthetic Graph

We first consider the representation learning of a synthetic directed graph. GraphWave [8] is the representation learning method using the graph signal processing. The embedding function of GraphWave is designed such that structurally similar nodes are embedded close together by leveraging diffusion patterns of each node. We provide an overview of GraphWave below.

For a given graph Laplacian $L = V \Lambda V^T$ of an undirected graph, we here denote the spectral graph wavelet at scale s and node i as $\psi_i(s)$ and its j-th entry as $\psi_{ij}(s)$. If the filter kernel $\hat{g}(s\lambda)$ is heat kernel $\hat{g}(s\lambda) = e^{-s\lambda}$, one can find that the wavelet $\psi_i(s)$ is equal to the solution of the diffusion equation $\frac{d}{ds}\psi(s) = -L\psi(s)$ with the initial value $\psi(0) = \delta_i$, since

$$\psi_i(s) = V\hat{G}_s V^T \delta_i = V e^{-s\Lambda} V^T \delta_i, = e^{-sV\Lambda V^T} \delta_i = e^{-sL} \delta_i. \tag{21}$$

Given the embedding parameters, $t \in \{t_1, \ldots, t_d\}$ and $s \in \{s_1, \ldots, s_m\}$, the embedding function $\chi_i : V \to \mathbb{R}^{2dm}$ is defined as follows:

$$\chi_i = [\text{Re}(\phi_i(s,t)), \ \text{Im}(\phi_i(s,t))]_{t \in \{t_1,\ldots,t_d\}, s \in \{s_1,\ldots,s_m\}}, \tag{22}$$

where $\phi_i(s,t) := \frac{1}{N} \sum_{j=1}^{N} e^{it\,\psi_{ij}(s)}$ is the characteristic function that completely characterizes behavior and properties of the probability distribution. If two nodes are structurally similar within their local graph topology, these diffusion patterns are similar. Therefore, these characteristic functions are also similar, and thus structurally similar nodes are embedded close together. Note that, since eigenvectors of the digraph Laplacian $\mathcal{L} := \mathcal{D} - \mathcal{A}$ are not orthonormal, GraphWave is generally not applicable to directed graphs. However, if the filter kernel is a heat kernel, GraphWave can be made applicable to directed graphs by replacing L of (21) with $\mathcal{L}$, that is $\psi_i(s) = e^{-s\mathcal{L}}\delta_i$.

We evaluate the effectiveness of our framework based on the embedding results by GraphWave for the synthetic directed graph shown in Fig. 3. We set the filter kernel to $\hat{g}(s\lambda) = e^{-s\lambda}$. For comparison, we calculate the embeddings in three ways:

(a) GraphWave based on the symmetrized Laplacian $L^{(s)}$, i.e., ignoring the edge directionality. In this setting, we can directly apply GraphWave to learn embedding.

(b) GraphWave based on the digraph Laplacian $\mathcal{L}$. Since we now assume the heat kernel, we can apply GraphWave to the directed graph as previously mentioned.

(c) GraphWave based on the Hermitian Laplacian $\mathcal{L}_q$, i.e., calculating the wavelet by (20).

To make our evaluation fair, we use the same parameters for each experiment; $s \in \{2.0, 2.1, \ldots, 20.0\}$ and $t \in \{1, 2, \ldots, 10\}$.

Figure 4 shows the results of two-dimensional principal component analysis (PCA) projection of the $\mathbb{R}^{2dm}$ dimensional vector calculated by GraphWave. First, Fig. 4(a) shows that red and blue nodes with the same depth are embedded into the same point without distinction because edge directionality is ignored. Then, Fig. 4(b) reveals that although the edge directionality is considered, sink nodes (nodes with zero out-degree) are embedded into the same point. Specifically, node 13 and nodes 14–17, which are not structurally similar, are embedded into the same point. This is because the characteristic function $\phi_k(s, t)$ is equal for each sink node k, since $^{\forall s}\psi_k(s) = \psi_k(0) = \delta_k$. Finally, Fig. 4(c) shows the GraphWave based on the Hermitian Laplacian succeeds at learning embedding while considering edge directionality and distinction of sink nodes. Specifically, our framework can distinguish not only red and blue nodes with same depth but also sink nodes (i.e., node 13 and nodes 14–17).

4.2   Signal Denoising for Graph of Contiguous United States

Next we consider the signal denoising on a directed graph. In this experiment, we use the directed graph that represents the contiguous United States, excluding Alaska and Hawaii which are not connected by land with the other states. A directed edge between states is assigned based on latitudes; from lower to higher. Then, we consider the average annual temperature of each state as the graph

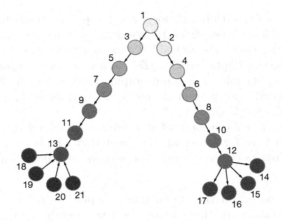

Fig. 3. Synthetic graph.

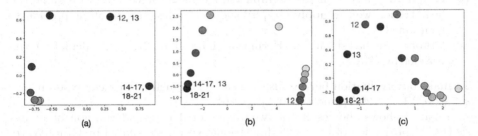

Fig. 4. Two-dimensional PCA projection of embedding as learned by GraphWave based on the symmetrized Laplacian (a), digraph Laplacian (b) and Hermitian Laplacian (c).

signal[1]. In general, the states closer to the equator, i.e., with lower latitude, have higher average temperatures. Thus, assigning directed edges based on state latitudes may be justified to capture the temperature flow. The same settings were used in [28]. Figure 5 shows the temperature signals over the directed contiguous US graph.

To verify the effectiveness of the graph signal processing based on the Hermitian Laplacian, we conduct an experiment to recover original temperature signals from noisy measurements on both the undirected and directed contiguous US graph. Noisy measurements are generated as $g := f + \eta$, where f is the original signals and η is the noise vector whose each entry $\eta(i)$ independently follows the Gaussian distribution with the mean $\mu = 0$ and standard deviation $\sigma = 10$.

---

[1] Latitude and temperature data are respectively obtained from following web sites: https://inkplant.com/code/state-latitudes-longitudes and https://www.currentresults.com/Weather/US/average-annual-state-temperatures.php.

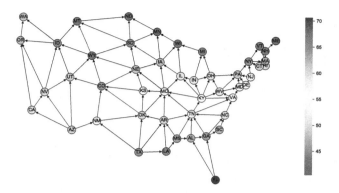

Fig. 5. Graph signal of the average temperature in Fahrenheit for the directed contiguous US.

Then, we use a low-pass filter kernel

$$\hat{h}(\lambda) = \frac{1}{1 + c\lambda}, \tag{23}$$

where $c \, (> 0)$ is the parameter of this kernel [29]. The recovered (denoised) signal $\tilde{f}$ can be calculated as

$$\tilde{f} = U\hat{H}U^*g, \tag{24}$$

where $\hat{H} := \mathrm{diag}(\hat{h}(\lambda_0), \ldots, \hat{h}(\lambda_{N-1}))$. In this experiment, we set the kernel parameter to $c = 2$. Note that although we here use (23) as low-pass filter kernel, one can choose the other filter kernel, such as [30].

Figure 6 shows an example of the original, noisy and denoised temperature signals on the undirected and directed contiguous US graph. Here, Fig. 6(f) illustrates the real part of each signal, $\mathrm{Re}[\tilde{f}(i)]$, since the denoised signals calculated by (24) are generally complex values. From Fig. 6, one can find that the denoised signals on the undirected graph are comparatively smooth in the entire graph, whereas those on the directed graph are comparatively uneven.

To quantitatively evaluate the denoising performance, we consider the denoising error of each state i, which is calculated as $e(i) := |\mathrm{Re}[\tilde{f}(i)] - f(i)|$. Figure 7 shows the average denoising error $\langle e(i) \rangle$ of each state i over the 100 simulations of independent noise. This figure suggests that the denoising performance in the directed case is equal to or slightly superior to that in the undirected case; especially the signal of peripheral nodes, i.e., the nodes with low or high latitudes, such as FL, TX, LA, MN, MT and ND. In the undirected graph, each denoised signal is simply averaged over its adjacent node signals without considering the edge directionality. This leads denoised signals to be smooth in the entire graph. Therefore, the denoising error will be low in the region where the

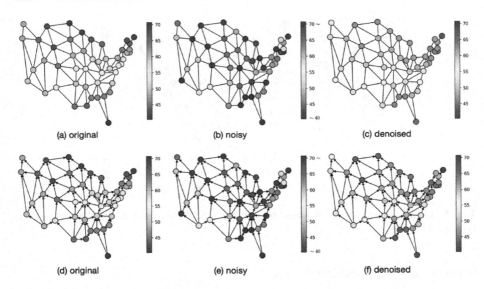

(a) original   (b) noisy   (c) denoised

(d) original   (e) noisy   (f) denoised

Fig. 6. Original, noisy and denoised temperature signals on undirected (upper panel) and directed (lower panel) contiguous US graph. To equalize colorbar scales for each panel, we set lower limit to $\min_i(f(i)) = 40.4$ and upper limit to $\max_i(f(i)) = 70.7$ in (b) and (e).

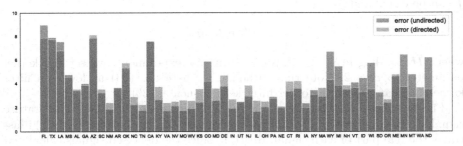

Fig. 7. Semi-transparent bar charts of average denoising error of each state over 100 simulations (in ascending order of state latitudes). The averages of $\langle e(i) \rangle$ in the directed and undirected cases are 3.7719 and 3.8723, respectively.

original signals are smooth but high in the region where they are not. On the other hand, in the directed graph, each denoised signal is averaged over its adjacent node signals while considering the edge directionality. Therefore, it seems that denoised signals capture the temperature flow of original signals without excessive smoothing.

5   Conclusions and Future Work

We have presented a general framework for extending graph signal processing to directed graphs based on the Hermitian Laplacian. The Hermitian Laplacian on a directed graph is defined so as to preserve both the Hermitian property and edge directionality by encoding the edge direction into the phase in the complex plane. The Hermitian property enables the graph signal processing to be straightforwardly generalized to directed graphs and guarantees some desirable properties, such as the non-negative real eigenvalues and the unitarity of the Fourier transform. Based on the Hermitian Laplacian, we have extended the basic concepts of the Laplacian-based graph signal processing on undirected graphs (e.g., graph Fourier transform, spectral graph filtering, and spectral graph wavelet) to directed graphs. Finally, we have shown the effectiveness of our framework through two experiments; representation learning and signal denoising of/on a directed graph. Future work includes theoretically analyzing spectral properties of Hermitian Laplacians (e.g., relation between the rotation parameter q and its eigenvectors), evaluating our framework by larger and complex graphs, and developing other applications of our framework.

References

1. Anis, A., El Gamal, A., Avestimehr, S., Ortega, A.: Asymptotic justification of bandlimited interpolation of graph signals for semi-supervised learning. In: 2015 IEEE International Conference on Acoustics, Speech and Signal Processing (ICASSP), pp. 5461–5465. IEEE (2015)
2. Berkolaiko, G.: Nodal count of graph eigenfunctions via magnetic perturbation. Anal. PDE **6**(5), 1213–1233 (2013)
3. Bronstein, M.M., Bruna, J., LeCun, Y., Szlam, A., Vandergheynst, P.: Geometric deep learning: going beyond Euclidean data. IEEE Signal Process. Mag. **34**(4), 18–42 (2017)
4. Chen, S., Varma, R., Sandryhaila, A., Kovačević, J.: Discrete signal processing on graphs: sampling theory. IEEE Trans. Signal Process. **63**(24), 6510–6523 (2015)
5. Chung, F.: Laplacians and the cheeger inequality for directed graphs. Ann. Comb. **9**(1), 1–19 (2005). https://doi.org/10.1007/s00026-005-0237-z
6. Defferrard, M., Bresson, X., Vandergheynst, P.: Convolutional neural networks on graphs with fast localized spectral filtering. In: Advances in Neural Information Processing Systems, pp. 3844–3852 (2016)
7. Dodziuk, J., Mathai, V.: Kato's inequality and asymptotic spectral properties for discrete magnetic Laplacians. In: Contemporary Mathematics, vol. 398, pp. 69–81 (2006)
8. Donnat, C., Zitnik, M., Hallac, D., Leskovec, J.: Spectral graph wavelets for structural role similarity in networks. arXiv preprint arXiv:1710.10321 (2017)
9. Fanuel, M., Alaíz, C.M., Fernández, Á., Suykens, J.A.: Magnetic eigenmaps for the visualization of directed networks. Appl. Comput. Harmonic Anal. **44**(1), 189–199 (2018)

10. Fanuel, M., Alaíz, C.M., Suykens, J.A.: Magnetic eigenmaps for community detection in directed networks. Phys. Rev. E **95**(2), 022302 (2017)
11. Gadde, A., Anis, A., Ortega, A.: Active semi-supervised learning using sampling theory for graph signals. In: ACM SIGKDD International Conference on Knowledge Discovery and Data Mining, pp. 492–501 (2014)
12. Golub, G.H., Wilkinson, J.H.: Ill-conditioned eigensystems and the computation of the Jordan canonical form. SIAM Rev. **18**(4), 578–619 (1976)
13. Hammond, D.K., Vandergheynst, P., Gribonval, R.: Wavelets on graphs via spectral graph theory. Appl. Comput. Harmonic Anal. **30**(2), 129–150 (2011)
14. Higuchi, Y., Shirai, T.: A remark on the spectrum of magnetic Laplacian on a graph. Yokohama Math. J. **47** (1999)
15. Kato, T.: Schrödinger operators with singular potentials. Israel J. Math. **13**(1–2), 135–148 (1972). https://doi.org/10.1007/BF02760233
16. Masoumi, M., Hamza, A.B.: Shape classification using spectral graph wavelets. Appl. Intell. **47**(4), 1256–1269 (2017). https://doi.org/10.1007/s10489-017-0955-7
17. Messias, B., Costa, L.d.F.: Characterization and space embedding of directed graphs trough magnetic Laplacians. arXiv preprint arXiv:1812.02160 (2018)
18. Narang, S.K., Ortega, A.: Perfect reconstruction two-channel wavelet filter banks for graph structured data. IEEE Trans. Signal Process. **60**(6), 2786–2799 (2012)
19. Narang, S.K., Ortega, A.: Compact support biorthogonal wavelet filterbanks for arbitrary undirected graphs. IEEE Trans. Signal Process. **61**(19), 4673–4685 (2013)
20. Ngo, K.V.: An approach of eigenvalue perturbation theory. Appl. Numer. Anal. Comput. Math. **2**(1), 108–125 (2005)
21. Puschel, M., Moura, J.M.: Algebraic signal processing theory: foundation and 1-D time. IEEE Trans. Signal Process. **56**(8), 3572–3585 (2008)
22. Sakiyama, A., Namiki, T., Tanaka, Y.: Design of polynomial approximated filters for signals on directed graphs. In: 2017 IEEE Global Conference on Signal and Information Processing (GlobalSIP), pp. 633–637. IEEE (2017)
23. Sandryhaila, A., Moura, J.M.: Discrete signal processing on graphs. IEEE Trans. Signal Process. **61**(7), 1644–1656 (2013)
24. Sandryhaila, A., Moura, J.M.: Discrete signal processing on graphs: frequency analysis. IEEE Trans. Signal Process. **62**(12), 3042–3054 (2014)
25. Sardellitti, S., Barbarossa, S., Di Lorenzo, P.: On the graph Fourier transform for directed graphs. IEEE J. Sel. Top. Sig. Process. **11**(6), 796–811 (2017)
26. Sevi, H., Rilling, G., Borgnat, P.: Multiresolution analysis of functions on directed networks. In: Wavelets and Sparsity XVII, vol. 10394, p. 103941Q. International Society for Optics and Photonics (2017)
27. Sevi, H., Rilling, G., Borgnat, P.: Harmonic analysis on directed graphs and applications: from Fourier analysis to wavelets. arXiv preprint arXiv:1811.11636 (2018)
28. Shafipour, R., Khodabakhsh, A., Mateos, G., Nikolova, E.: A directed graph Fourier transform with spread frequency components. arXiv preprint arXiv:1804.03000 (2018)
29. Shuman, D.I., Narang, S.K., Frossard, P., Ortega, A., Vandergheynst, P.: The emerging field of signal processing on graphs: extending high-dimensional data analysis to networks and other irregular domains. IEEE Signal Process. Mag. **30**(3), 83–98 (2013)
30. Shuman, D.I., Ricaud, B., Vandergheynst, P.: Vertex-frequency analysis on graphs. Appl. Comput. Harmonic Anal. **40**(2), 260–291 (2016)

31. Singh, R., Chakraborty, A., Manoj, B.: Graph Fourier transform based on directed Laplacian. In: 2016 International Conference on Signal Processing and Communications (SPCOM), pp. 1–5. IEEE (2016)
32. Tanaka, Y.: Spectral domain sampling of graph signals. IEEE Trans. Signal Process. **66**(14), 3752–3767 (2018)
33. Tremblay, N., Borgnat, P.: Graph wavelets for multiscale community mining. IEEE Trans. Signal Process. **62**(20), 5227–5239 (2014)
34. de Verdière, Y.C.: Magnetic interpretation of the nodal defect on graphs. Anal. PDE **6**(5), 1235–1242 (2013)
35. Verma, S., Zhang, Z.L.: Hunt for the unique, stable, sparse and fast feature learning on graphs. In: Advances in Neural Information Processing Systems, pp. 88–98 (2017)

Learning Aligned-Spatial Graph Convolutional Networks for Graph Classification

Lu Bai[1], Yuhang Jiao[1], Lixin Cui[1(✉)], and Edwin R. Hancock[2]

[1] Central University of Finance and Economics, Beijing, China
{bailucs,cuilixin}@cufe.edu.cn
[2] Department of Computer Science, University of York, York, UK

Abstract. In this paper, we develop a novel Aligned-Spatial Graph Convolutional Network (ASGCN) model to learn effective features for graph classification. Our idea is to transform arbitrary-sized graphs into fixed-sized aligned grid structures, and define a new spatial graph convolution operation associated with the grid structures. We show that the proposed ASGCN model not only reduces the problems of information loss and imprecise information representation arising in existing spatially-based Graph Convolutional Network (GCN) models, but also bridges the theoretical gap between traditional Convolutional Neural Network (CNN) models and spatially-based GCN models. Moreover, the proposed ASGCN model can adaptively discriminate the importance between specified vertices during the process of spatial graph convolution, explaining the effectiveness of the proposed model. Experiments on standard graph datasets demonstrate the effectiveness of the proposed model.

Keywords: Graph Convolutional Networks · Graph classification

1 Introduction

Graph-based representations are powerful tools to analyze structured data that are described in terms of pairwise relationships between components [5,27]. One common challenge arising in the analysis of graph-based data is how to learn effective graph representations. Due to the recent successes of deep learning networks in machine learning, there is increasing interest to generalize deep Convolutional Neural Networks (CNN) [16] into the graph domain. These deep learning networks on graphs are the so-called Graph Convolutional Networks (GCN) [15], and have proven to be an effective way to extract highly meaningful statistical features for graph classification [9].

Generally speaking, most existing state-of-the-art GCN approaches can be divided into two main categories with GCN models based on (a) spectral and (b) spatial strategies. Specifically, approaches based on the spectral strategy define the convolution operation based on spectral graph theory [8,12,19]. By

© Springer Nature Switzerland AG 2020
U. Brefeld et al. (Eds.): ECML PKDD 2019, LNAI 11906, pp. 464–482, 2020.
https://doi.org/10.1007/978-3-030-46150-8_28

transforming the graph into the spectral domain through the eigenvectors of the Laplacian matrix, these methods perform the filter operation by multiplying the graph by a series of filter coefficients. Unfortunately, most spectral-based approaches cannot be performed on graphs with different size numbers of vertices and Fourier bases. Thus, these approaches demand the same-sized graph structures and are usually employed for vertex classification tasks. On the other hand, approaches based on the spatial strategy are not restricted to the same-sized graph structures. These approaches generalize the graph convolution operation to the spatial structure of a graph by directly defining an operation on neighboring vertices [1,10,24]. For example, Duvenaud et al. [10] have proposed a spatially-based GCN model by defining a spatial graph convolution operation on the 1-layer neighboring vertices to simulate the traditional circular fingerprint. Atwood and Towsley [1] have proposed a spatially-based GCN model by performing spatial graph convolution operations on different layers of neighboring vertices rooted at a vertex. Although these spatially-based GCN models can be directly applied to real-world graph classification problems, they still need to further transform the multi-scale features learned from graph convolution layers into the fixed-sized representations, so that the standard classifiers can directly read the representations for classifications. One way to achieve this is to directly sum up the learned local-level vertex features from the graph convolution operation as global-level graph features through a SumPooling layer. Since it is difficult to learn rich local vertex topological information from the global features, these spatially-based GCN methods associated with SumPooling have relatively poor performance on graph classification.

To overcome the shortcoming of existing spatially-based GCN models, Zhang et al. [28] have developed a novel spatially-based Deep Graph Convolutional Neural Network (DGCNN) model to preserve more vertex information. Specifically, they propose a new SortPooling layer to transform the extracted vertex features of unordered vertices from the spatial graph convolution layers into a fixed-sized local-level vertex grid structure. This is done by sequentially preserving a specified number of vertices with prior orders. With the fixed-sized grid structures of graphs to hand, a traditional CNN model followed by a Softmax layer can be directly employed for graph classification. Although this spatially-based DGCNN model focuses more on local-level vertex features and outperforms state-of-the-art GCN models on graph classification tasks, this method tends to sort the vertex order based on each individual graph. Thus, it cannot accurately reflect the topological correspondence information between graph structures. Moreover, this model also leads to significant information loss, since some vertices associated with lower ranking may be discarded. In summary, developing effective methods to learn graph representations still remains a significant challenge.

In this paper, we propose a novel Aligned-Spatial Graph Convolutional Network (ASGCN) model for graph classification problems. One key innovation of the proposed ASGCN model is that of transitively aligning vertices between graphs. That is, given three vertices v, w and x from three different sample graphs, if v and x are aligned, and w and x are aligned, the proposed model can guarantee that v and w are also aligned. More specifically, the proposed model employs the transitive alignment procedure to transform arbitrary-sized graphs into fixed-sized aligned grid structures with consistent vertex orders, guaranteeing that the vertices on the same spatial position are also transitively aligned to each other in terms of the topological structures. The conceptual framework of the proposed ASGCN model is shown in Fig. 1. Specifically, the main contributions are threefold.

First, we develop a new transitive matching method to map different arbitrary-sized graphs into fixed-sized aligned vertex grid structures. We show that the grid structures not only establish reliable vertex correspondence information between graphs, but also minimize the loss of structural information from the original graphs.

Second, we develop a novel spatially-based graph convolution network model, i.e., the ASGCN model, for graph classification. More specifically, we propose a new spatial graph convolution operation associated with the aligned vertex grid structures as well as their associated adjacency matrices, to extract multi-scale local-level vertex features. We show that the proposed convolution operation not only reduces the problems of information loss and imprecise information representation arising in existing spatially-based GCN models associated with SortPooling or SumPooling, but also theoretically relates to the classical convolution operation on standard grid structures. Thus, the proposed ASGCN model bridges the theoretical gap between traditional CNN models and spatially-based GCN models, and can adaptively discriminate the importance between specified vertices during the process of the spatial graph convolution operation. Furthermore, since our spatial graph convolution operation does not change the original spatial sequence of vertices, the proposed ASGCN model utilizes the traditional CNN to further learn graph features. In this way, we provide an end-to-end deep learning architecture that integrates the graph representation learning into both the spatial graph convolutional layer and the traditional convolution layer for graph classification.

Third, we empirically evaluate the performance of the proposed ASGCN model on graph classification tasks. Experiments on benchmarks demonstrate the effectiveness of the proposed method, when compared to state-of-the-art methods.

2 Related Works of Spatially-Based GCN Models

In this section, we briefly review state-of-the art spatially-based GCN models in the literature. More specifically, we introduce the associated spatial graph convolution operation of the existing spatially-based Deep Graph Convolutional Neural Network (DGCNN) model [28]. To commence, consider a sample graph G with n vertices, $X = (x_1, x_2, ..., x_n) \in \mathbb{R}^{n \times c}$ is the collection of n vertex feature vectors of G in c dimensions, and $A \in \mathbb{R}^{n \times n}$ is the vertex adjacency matrix (A can be a weighted adjacency matrix). The spatial graph convolution operation

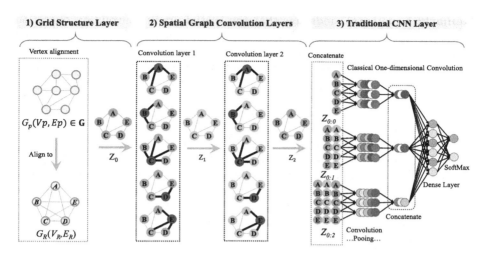

Fig. 1. The architecture of the proposed ASGCN model. An input graph $G_p(V_p, E_p) \in$ **G** of arbitrary size is first aligned to the prototype graph $G_R(V_R, E_R)$. Then, G_p is mapped into a fixed-sized aligned vertex grid structure, where the vertex orders follow that of G_R. The grid structure of G_p is passed through multiple spatial graph convolution layers to extract multi-scale vertex features, where the vertex information is propagated between specified vertices associated with the adjacency matrix. Since the graph convolution layers preserve the original vertex orders of the input grid structure, the concatenated vertex features through the graph convolution layers form a new vertex grid structure for G_p. This vertex grid structure is then passed to a traditional CNN layer for classifications. Note that, vertex features are visualized as different colors (Color figure online).

of the DGCNN model takes the following form

$$Z = \mathrm{f}(\tilde{D}^{-1}\tilde{A}XW), \tag{1}$$

where $\tilde{A} = A + I$ is the adjacency matrix of graph G with added self-loops, $\tilde{D}$ is the degree matrix of $\tilde{A}$ with $\tilde{A}_{i,i} = \sum_j \tilde{A}_{i,j}$, $W \in \mathbb{R}^{c \times c'}$ is the matrix of trainable graph convolution parameters, f is a nonlinear activation function, and $Z \in \mathbb{R}^{n \times c'}$ is the output of the convolution operation.

For the spatial graph convolution operation defined by Eq. (1), the process XW first maps the c-dimensional features of each vertex into a set of new c'-dimensional features. Here, the filter weights W are shared by all vertices. Moreover, $\tilde{A}Y$ ($Y := XW$) propagates the feature information of each vertex to its neighboring vertices as well as the vertex itself. The i-th row $(\tilde{A}Y)_{i,:}$ represents the extracted features of the i-th vertex, and corresponds to the summation or aggregation of $Y_{i,:}$ itself and $Y_{j,:}$ from the neighboring vertices of the i-th vertex. Multiplying by the inverse of $\tilde{D}$ (i.e., $\tilde{D}^{-1}$) can be seen as the process of normalizing and assigning equal weights between the i-th vertex and each of its neighbours.

Remark: Equation (1) indicates that the spatial graph convolution operation of the DGCNN model cannot discriminate the importance between specified vertices in the convolution operation process. This is because the required filter weights of W are shared by each vertex, i.e., the feature transformations of the vertices are all based on the same trainable function. Thus, the DGCNN model cannot directly influence the aggregation process of the vertex features. In fact, this problem also arises in other spatially-based GCN models, e.g., the Neural Graph Fingerprint Network (NGFN) model [10], the Diffusion Convolution Neural Network (DCNN) model [1], etc. Since the associated spatial graph convolution operations of these models also take the similar form with that of the DGCNN model, i.e., the trainable parameters of their spatial graph convolution operations are also shared by each vertex. This drawback influences the effectiveness of the existing spatially-based GCN models for graph classification. In this paper, we aim to propose a new spatially-based GCN model to overcome the above problems.   □

3   Constructing Aligned Grid Structures for Arbitrary Graphs

Although, spatially-based GCN models are not restricted to the same graph structure, and can thus be applied for graph classification tasks. These methods still require to further transform the extracted multi-scale features from graph convolution layers into the fixed-sized characteristics, so that the standard classifiers (e.g., the traditional convolutional neural network followed by a Softmax layer) can be directly employed for classifications. In this section, we develop a new transitive matching method to map different graphs of arbitrary sizes into fixed-sized aligned grid structures. Moreover, we show that the proposed grid structure not only integrates precise structural correspondence information but also minimizes the loss of structural information.

3.1   Identifying Transitive Alignment Information Between Graphs

We introduce a new graph matching method to transitively align graph vertices. We first designate a family of prototype representations that encapsulate the principle characteristics over all vectorial vertex representations in a set of graphs $\mathbf{G}$. Assume there are n vertices from all graphs in $\mathbf{G}$, and their associated K-dimensional vectorial representations are $\mathbf{R}^K = \{R_1^K, R_2^K, \ldots, R_n^K\}$. We utilize k-means [25] to locate M centroids over $\mathbf{R}^K$, by minimizing the objective function

$$\arg\min_{\Omega} \sum_{j=1}^{M} \sum_{R_i^K \in c_j} \|R_i^K - \mu_j^K\|^2, \tag{2}$$

$\Omega = (c_1, c_2, \ldots, c_M)$ represents M clusters, and μ_j^K is the mean of the vertex representations belonging to the j-th cluster c_j.

Let $\mathbf{G} = \{G_1, \cdots, G_p, \cdots, G_N\}$ be the graph sample set. For each sample graph $G_p(V_p, E_p) \in \mathbf{G}$ and each vertex $v_i \in V_p$ associated with its K-dimensional vectorial representation $\mathrm{R}_{p;i}^K$, we commence by identifying a set of K-dimensional prototype representations as $\mathbf{PR}^K = \{\mu_1^K, \ldots, \mu_j^K, \ldots, \mu_M^K\}$ for the graph set $\mathbf{G}$. We align the vectorial vertex representations of each graph G_p to the family of prototype representations in $\mathbf{PR}^K$. The alignment procedure is similar to that introduced in [6] for point matching in a pattern space, and we compute a K-level affinity matrix in terms of the Euclidean distances between the two sets of points, i.e.,

$$A_p^K(i, j) = \|\mathrm{R}_{p;i}^K - \mu_j^K\|_2. \tag{3}$$

where A_p^K is a $|V_p| \times M$ matrix, and each element $A_p^K(i, j)$ represents the distance between the vectrial representation $\mathrm{R}_{p;i}^K$ of $v \in V_p$ and the j-th prototype representation $\mu_j^K \in \mathbf{PR}^K$. If $A_p^K(i, j)$ is the smallest element in row i, we say that the vertex v_i is aligned to the j-th prototype representation. Note that for each graph there may be two or more vertices aligned to the same prototype representation. We record the correspondence information using the K-level correspondence matrix $C_p^K \in \{0, 1\}^{|V_p| \times M}$

$$C_p^K(i, j) = \begin{cases} 1 \text{ if } A_p^K(i, j) \text{ is the smallest in row } i \\ 0 \text{ otherwise.} \end{cases} \tag{4}$$

For each pair of graphs $G_p \in \mathbf{G}$ and $G_q \in \mathbf{G}$, if their vertices v_p and v_q are aligned to the same prototype representation μ_j^K, we say that v_p and v_q are also aligned. Thus, we identify the transitive correspondence information between all graphs in $\mathbf{G}$, by aligning their vertices to a common set of prototype representations.

Remark: The alignment process is equivalent to assigning the vectorial representation $\mathrm{R}_{p;i}^K$ of each vertex $v_i \in V_p$ to the mean μ_j^K of the cluster c_j. Thus, the proposed alignment procedure can be seen as an optimization process that gradually minimizes the inner-vertex-cluster sum of squares over the vertices of all graphs through k-means, and can establish reliable vertex correspondence information over all graphs. $\qquad\qquad\square$

3.2 Aligned Grid Structures of Graphs

We employ the transitive correspondence information to map arbitrary-sized graphs into fixed-sized aligned grid structures. Assume $G_p(V_p, E_p, \tilde{A}_p)$ is a sample graph from the graph set $\mathbf{G}$, with V_p representing the vertex set, E_p representing the edge set, and $\tilde{A}_p$ representing the vertex adjacency matrix with added self-loops (i.e., $\tilde{A} = A + I$, where A is the original adjacency matrix with no self-loops and I is the identity matrix). Let $X_p \in \mathbb{R}^{n \times c}$ be the collection of n ($n = |V_p|$) vertex feature vectors of G_p in c dimensions. Note that, the row of X_p follows the same vertex order of $\tilde{A}_p$. If G_p are vertex attributed graphs,

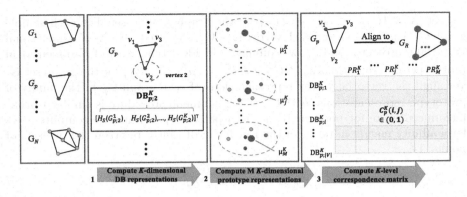

Fig. 2. The procedure of computing the correspondence matrix. Given a set of graphs, for each graph G_p: (1) we compute the K-dimensional depth-based (DB) representation $DB_{p;v}^K$ rooted at each vertex (e.g., vertex 2) as the K-dimensional vectorial vertex representation, where each element $H_s(G_{p;2}^K)$ represents the Shannon entropy of the K-layer expansion subgraph rooted at vertex v_2 of G_p [2]; (2) we identify a family of K-dimensional prototype representations $\mathbf{PR}^K = \{\mu_1^K, \ldots, \mu_j^K, \ldots, \mu_M^K\}$ using k-means on the K-dimensional DB representations of all graphs; (3) we align the K-dimensional DB representations to the K-dimensional prototype representations and compute a K-level correspondence matrix C_p^K.

X_p can be the one-hot encoding matrix of the vertex labels. For un-attributed graphs, we use the vertex degree as the vertex label.

For each graph G_p, we utilize the proposed transitive vertex matching method to compute the K-level vertex correspondence matrix C_p^K that records the correspondence information between the K-dimensional vectorial vertex representations of G_p and the K-dimensional prototype representations in $\mathbf{PR}^K = \{\mu_1^K, \ldots, \mu_j^K, \ldots, \mu_M^K\}$. With C_p^K to hand, we compute the K-level aligned vertex feature matrix for G_p as

$$\bar{X}_p^K = (C_p^K)^T X_p, \tag{5}$$

where $\bar{X}_p^K \in \mathbb{R}^{M \times c}$ and each row of $\bar{X}_p^K$ represents the feature of a corresponding aligned vertex. Moreover, we also compute the associated K-level aligned vertex adjacency matrix for G_p as

$$\bar{A}_p^K = (C_p^K)^T (\tilde{A}_p)(C_p^K), \tag{6}$$

where $\bar{A}_p^K \in \mathbb{R}^{M \times M}$. Both $\bar{X}_p^K$ and $\bar{A}_p^K$ are indexed by the corresponding prototypes in $\mathbf{PR}^K$. Since $\bar{X}_p^K$ and $\bar{A}_p^K$ are computed from the original vertex feature matrix X_p and the original adjacency matrix $\tilde{A}_p$, respectively, by mapping the original feature and adjacency information of each vertex $v_p \in V_p$ to that of the new aligned vertices, $\bar{X}_p^K$ and $\bar{A}_p^K$ encapsulate the original feature and structural information of G_p. Note that, according to Eq. 4 each prototype may be aligned by more than one vertex from V_p, thus $\bar{A}_p^K$ may be a weighted adjacency matrix.

In order to construct the fixed-sized aligned grid structure for each graph $G_p \in \mathbf{G}$, we need to sort the vertices to determine their spatial orders. Since the vertices of each graph are all aligned to the same prototype representations, we sort the vertices of each graph by reordering the prototype representations. To this end, we construct a prototype graph $G_R(V_R, E_R)$ that captures the pairwise similarity between the K-dimensional prototype representations in $\mathbf{PR}^K$, with each vertex $v_j \in V_R$ representing the prototype representation $\mu_j^K \in \mathbf{PR}^K$ and each edge $(v_j, v_k) \in E_R$ representing the similarity between $\mu_j^K \in \mathbf{PR}^K$ and $\mu_k^K \in \mathbf{PR}^K$. The similarity between two vertices of G_R is computed as

$$s(\mu_j^K, \mu_k^K) = \exp(-\frac{\|\mu_j^K - \mu_k^K\|_2}{K}). \tag{7}$$

The degree of each prototype representation μ_j^K is $D_R(\mu_j^K) = \sum_{k=1}^{M} s(\mu_j^K, \mu_k^K)$. We propose to sort the K-dimensional prototype representations in $\mathbf{PR}^K$ according to their degree $D_R(\mu_j^K)$. Then, we rearrange $\bar{X}_p^K$ and $\bar{A}_p^K$ accordingly.

To construct reliable grid structures for graphs, in this work we employ the depth-based (DB) representations as the vectorial vertex representations to compute the required K-level vertex correspondence matrix C_p^K. The DB representation of each vertex is defined by measuring the entropies on a family of k-layer expansion subgraphs rooted at the vertex [3], where the parameter k varies from 1 to K. It is shown that such a K-dimensional DB representation encapsulates rich entropy content flow from each local vertex to the global graph structure, as a function of depth. The process of computing the correspondence matrix C_p^K associated with depth-based representations is shown in Fig. 2. When we vary the number of layers K from 1 to L (i.e., $K \leq L$), we compute the final **aligned vertex grid structure** for each graph $G_p \in \mathbf{G}$ as

$$\bar{X}_p = \sum_{K=1}^{L} \frac{\bar{X}_p^K}{L}, \tag{8}$$

and the associated **aligned grid vertex adjacency matrix** as

$$\bar{A}_p = \sum_{K=1}^{L} \frac{\bar{A}_p^K}{L}, \tag{9}$$

where $\bar{X}_p \in \mathbb{R}^{M \times c}$, $\bar{A}_p \in \mathbb{R}^{M \times M}$, the i-th row of $\bar{X}_p$ corresponds to the feature vector of the i-th aligned grid vertex, and the i-row and j-column element of $\bar{A}_p$ corresponds to the adjacency information between the i-th and j-th aligned grid vertices.

Remark: Equation (8) and Eq. (9) indicate that they can transform the original graph $G_p \in \mathbf{G}$ with arbitrary number of vertices $|V_p|$ into a new aligned grid graph structure with the same number of vertices, where $\bar{X}_p$ is the corresponding aligned grid vertex feature matrix and $\bar{A}_p$ is the corresponding aligned grid vertex adjacency matrix. Since both $\widehat{X}_p$ and $\bar{A}_p$ are mapped from the original graph

G_p, they not only reflect reliable structure correspondence information between G_p and the remaining graphs in graph set $\mathbf{G}$ but also encapsulate more original feature and structural information of G_p. $\qquad\qquad\qquad\qquad\square$

4   The Aligned-Spatial Graph Convolutional Network Model

In this section, we propose a new spatially-based GCN model, namely the Aligned-Spatial Graph Convolutional Network (ASGCN) model. The core stage of a spatially-based GCN model is the associated graph convolution operation that extracts multi-scale features for each vertex based on the original features of its neighboring vertices as well as itself. As we have stated, most existing spatially-based GCN models perform the convolution operation by first applying a trainable parameter matrix to map the original feature of each vertex in c dimensions to that in c' dimensions, and then averaging the vertex features of specified vertices [1,10,24,28]. Since the trainable parameter matrix is shared by all vertices, these models cannot discriminate the importance of different vertices and have inferior ability to aggregate vertex features. To overcome the shortcoming, in this section we first propose a new spatial graph convolution operation associated with aligned grid structures of graphs. Unlike existing methods, the trainable parameters of the proposed convolution operation can directly influence the aggregation of the aligned grid vertex features, thus the proposed convolution operation can discriminate the importance between specified aligned grid vertices. Finally, we introduce the architecture of the ASGCN model associated with the proposed convolution operation.

4.1   The Proposed Spatial Graph Convolution Operation

In this subsection, we propose a new spatial graph convolution operation to further extract multi-scale features of graphs, by propagating features between aligned grid vertices. Specifically, given a sample graph $G(V, E)$ with its aligned vertex grid structure $\bar{X} \in \mathbb{R}^{M \times c}$ and the associated aligned grid vertex adjacency matrix $\bar{A} \in \mathbb{R}^{M \times M}$, the proposed spatial graph convolution operation takes the following form

$$Z^h = \text{Relu}(\bar{D}^{-1}\bar{A} \sum_{j=1}^{c} (\bar{X} \odot W^h)_{:,j}), \qquad (10)$$

where Relu is the rectified linear units function (i.e., a nonlinear activation function), $W^h \in \mathbb{R}^{M \times c}$ is the trainable graph convolution parameter matrix of the h-th convolution filter with the filter size $M \times 1$ and the channel number c, $\odot$ represents the element-wise Hadamard product, $\bar{D}$ is the degree matrix of $\bar{A}$, and $Z^h \in \mathbb{R}^{M \times 1}$ is the output activation matrix. Note that, since the aligned grid vertex adjacency matrix $\bar{A}$ is computed based on the original vertex adjacency matrix with added self-loop information, the degree matrix also encapsulates the self-loop information from $\bar{A}$.

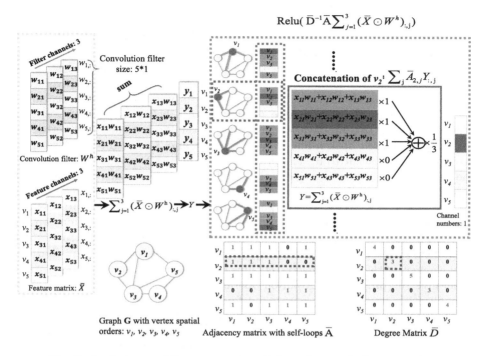

Fig. 3. An instance of the proposed spatial graph convolution operation.

An instance of the proposed spatial graph convolution operation defined by Eq. (10) is shown in Fig. 3. Specifically, the proposed convolution operation consists of four steps. **In the first step**, the procedure $\sum_{j=1}^{c} (\bar{X} \odot W^h)_{:,j}$ commences by computing the element-wise Hadamard product between $\bar{X}$ and W^h, and then summing the channels of $\bar{X} \odot W^h$ (i.e., summing the columns of $\bar{X} \odot W^h$). Figure 3 exhibits this process. Assume $\bar{X}$ is the collection of 5 aligned grid vertex feature vectors in the 3 dimensions (i.e., 3 feature channels), W^h is the h-th convolution filter with the filter size 5×1 and the channel number 3. The resulting $\sum_{j=1}^{3} (\bar{X} \odot W^h)_{:,j}$ first assigns the feature vector $x_{i,:}$ of each i-th aligned grid vertex a different weighted vector $w_{i,:}$, and then sums the channels of each weighted feature vector. Thus, for the first step, $\sum_{j=1}^{c} (\bar{X} \odot W^h)_{:,j}$ can be seen as a new weighted aligned vertex grid structure with 1 vertex feature channel. **The second step** $\bar{A}Y$, where $Y := \sum_{j=1}^{c} (\bar{X} \odot W^h)_{:,j}$, propagates the weighted feature information between each aligned grid vertex as well as its neighboring aligned grid vertices. Specifically, each i-th row $(\bar{A}Y)_{i,:}$ of $\bar{A}Y$ equals to $\sum_{j} \bar{A}_{i,j}Y_{:,j}$, and can be seen as the aggregated feature vector of the i-th aligned grid vertex by summing its original weighted feature vector as well as all the original weighted feature vectors of the j-th aligned grid vertex that is adjacent to it. Note that, since the first step has assigned each i-th aligned grid vertex a different weighted vector $w_{i,:}$, this aggregation procedure is similar to performing a standard fixed-sized convolution filter on a standard grid structure, where the filter first assigns different weighted vectors to the features of each grid element as well as its neighboring grid elements and then aggregates (i.e., sum) the weighted features as the new feature for each grid element. This indicates that the trainable parameter matrix W^h of the proposed convolution operation can directly influence the aggregation process of the vertex features, i.e., it can adaptively discriminate the importance between specified vertices. Figure 3 exhibits this propagation process. For the 2-nd aligned grid vertex v_2 (marked by the red broken-line frame), the 1-st and 3-rd aligned grid vertices v_1 and v_3 are adjacent to it. The process of computing $\sum_j \bar{A}_{2,j} Y_{:,j}$ (marked by the red real-line frame) aggregates the weighted feature vectors of aligned grid vertex v_2 as well as its neighboring aligned grid vertices v_1 and v_3 as the new feature vector of v_2. The vertices participating in this aggregation process are indicated by the 2-nd row of $\bar{A}$ (marked by the purple broken-line frame on $\bar{A}$) that encapsulates the aligned grid vertex adjacent information. **The third step** normalizes each i-th row of $\bar{A}Y$ by multiplying $\bar{D}_{i,i}^{-1}$, where $\bar{D}_{i,i}$ is the i-th diagonal element of the degree matrix $\bar{D}$. This process can guarantee a fixed feature scale after the proposed convolution operation. Specifically, Fig. 3 exhibits this normalization process. The aggregated feature of the 2-nd aligned grid vertex (marked by the red real-line frame) is multiplied by 3^{-1}, where 3 is the 3-rd diagonal element of $\bar{D}$ (marked by the purple broken-line frame on $\bar{D}$). **The last step** employs the Relu activation function and outputs the result.

Note that, since the proposed spatial graph convolution operation only extracts new features for the aligned grid vertex and does not change the vertex orders, the output Z^h is still an aligned vertex grid structure with the same vertex order of $\bar{X}$.

4.2   The Architecture of the Proposed ASGCN Model

In this subsection, we introduce the architecture of the proposed ASGCN Model. Figure 1 has shown the overview of the ASGCN model. Specifically, the architecture is composed of three sequential stages, i.e., (1) the grid structure construction and input layer, (2) the spatial graph convolution layer, and (3) the traditional CNN and Softmax layers.

The Grid Structure Construction and Input Layer: For the proposed ASGCN model, we commence by employing the transitive matching method defined earlier to map each graph $G \in \mathbf{G}$ of arbitrary sizes into the fixed-sized aligned grid structure, including the aligned vertex grid structure $\bar{X}$ and the associated aligned grid vertex adjacency matrix $\bar{A}$. We then input the grid structures to the proposed ASGCN model.

The Spatial Graph Convolutional Layer: For each graph G, to extract multi-scale features of the aligned grid vertices, we stack multiple graph convolution layers associated with the proposed spatial graph convolution operation defined by Eq. (10) as

$$Z_t^h = \text{Relu}(\bar{D}^{-1}\bar{A} \sum_{j=1}^{H_{t-1}} (Z_{t-1} \odot W_t^h)_{:,j}), \tag{11}$$

where Z_0 is the input aligned vertex grid structure $\bar{X}$, H_{t-1} is the number of convolution filters in graph convolution layer $t - 1$, $Z_{t-1} \in \mathbb{R}^{M \times H_{t-1}}$ is the concatenated output of all H_{t-1} convolution filters in layer $t - 1$, Z_t^h is the output of the h-th convolution filter in layer t, and $W_t^h \in \mathbb{R}^{M \times H_{t-1}}$ is the trainable parameter matrix of the h-th convolution filter in layer t with the filter size $M \times 1$ and the channel number H_{t-1}.

The Traditional CNN Layer: After each t-th spatial graph convolution layer, we horizontally concatenate the output Z_t associated with the outputs of the previous 1 to $t-1$ spatial graph convolutional layers as well as the original input Z_0 as $Z_{0:t}$, i.e., $Z_{0:t} = [Z_0, Z_1, \ldots, Z_t]$ and $Z_{0:t} \in \mathbb{R}^{M \times (c + \sum_{z=1}^t H_t)}$. As a result, for the concatenated output $Z_{0:t}$, each of its row can be seen as the new multi-scale features for the corresponding aligned grid vertex. Since $Z_{0:t}$ is still an aligned vertex grid structure, one can directly utilize the traditional CNN on the grid structure. Specifically, Fig. 1 exhibits the architecture of the traditional CNN layers associated with each $Z_{0:t}$. Here, each concatenated vertex grid structure $Z_{0:t}$ is seen as a $M \times 1$ (in Fig. 1 $M = 5$) vertex grid structure and each vertex is represented by a $(c + \sum_{z=1}^t H_t)$-dimensional feature, i.e., the channel of each grid vertex is $c + \sum_{z=1}^t H_t$. Then, we add a one-dimension convolution layer. The convolution operation can be performed by sliding a fixed-sized filter of size $k \times 1$ (in Fig. 1 $k = 3$) over the spatially neighboring vertices. After this, several AvgPooling layers and remaining one-dimensional convolutional layers can be added to learn the local patterns on the aligned grid vertex sequence. Finally, when we vary t from 0 to T (in Fig. 1 $T = 2$), we will obtain $T + 1$ extracted pattern representations. We concatenate the extracted patterns of each $Z_{0:t}$ and add a fully-connected layer followed by a Softmax layer.

4.3   Discussions of the Proposed ASGCN

Comparing to existing state-of-the-art spatially-based GCN models, the proposed ASGCN model has a number of advantages.

First, in order to transform the extracted multi-scale features from the graph convolution layers into fixed-sized representations, both the Neural Graph Fingerprint Network (NGFN) model [10] and the Diffusion Convolution Neural Network (DCNN) model [1] sum up the extracted local-level vertex features as global-level graph features through a SumPooling layer. Although the fixed-sized features can be directly read by a classifier for classifications, it is difficult to capture local topological information residing on the local vertices through the global-level graph features. By contrast, the proposed ASGCN model focuses more on extracting local-level aligned grid vertex features through the proposed spatial graph convolution operation on the aligned grid structures of graphs.

Thus, the proposed ASGCN model can encapsulate richer local structural information than the NGFN and DCNN models associated with SumPooling.

Second, similar to the proposed ASGCN model, both the PATCHY-SAN based Graph Convolution Neural Network (PSGCNN) model [17] and the Deep Graph Convolution Neural Network (DGCNN) model [28] also need to form fixed-sized vertex grid structures for arbitrary-sized graphs. To achieve this, these models rearrange the vertex order of each graph structure, and preserve a specified number of vertices with higher ranks. Although, unify the number of vertices for different graphs, the discarded vertices may lead to significant information loss. By contrast, the associated aligned grid structures of the proposed ASGCN model can encapsulate all the original vertex features from the original graphs, thus the proposed ASGCN model constrains the shortcoming of information loss arising in the PSGCNN and DGCNN models. On the other hand, both the PSGCNN and DGCNN models tend to sort the vertices of each graph based on the local structural descriptor, ignoring consistent vertex correspondence information between different graphs. By contrast, the associated aligned grid structure of the proposed ASGCN model is constructed through a transitive vertex alignment procedure. As a result, only the proposed ASGCN model can encapsulate the structural correspondence information between any pair of graph structures, i.e., the vertices on the same spatial position are also transitively aligned to each other.

Finally, as we have stated in Sect. 4.1, the spatial graph convolution operation of the proposed ASGCN model is similar to performing standard fixed-sized convolution filters on standard grid structures. To further reveal this property, we explain the convolution process one step further associated with Fig. 3. For the sample graph G shown in Fig. 3, assume it has 5 vertices following the fixed spatial vertex orders (positions) v_1, v_2, v_3, v_4 and v_5, $\bar{X}$ is the collection of its vertex feature vectors with 3 feature channels, and W^h is the h-th convolution filter with the filter size 5×1 and the channel number 3. Specifically, the procedure marked by the blue broken-line frame of Fig. 3 indicates that performing the proposed spatial graph convolution operation on the aligned vertex grid structure $\bar{X}$ can be seen as respectively performing the same 5×1-sized convolution filter W^h on five 5×1-sized local-level neighborhood vertex grid structures included in the green broken-line frame. Here, each neighborhood vertex grid structure only encapsulates the original feature vectors of a root vertex as well as its adjacent vertices from G, and all the vertices follow their original vertex spatial positions in G. For the non-adjacent vertices, we assign dummy vertices (marked by the grey block) on the corresponding spatial positions of the neighborhood vertex grid structures, i.e., the elements of their feature vectors are all 0. Since the five neighborhood vertex grid structures are arranged by the spatial orders of their root vertices from G, the vertically concatenation of these neighborhood vertex grid structures can be seen as a 25×1-sized global-level grid structure $\bar{X}_G$ of G. We observe that the process of the proposed spatial convolution operation on $\bar{X}$ is equivalent to sliding the 5×1 fixed-sized convolution filter W^h over $\bar{X}_G$ with 5-stride, i.e., this process is equivalent to sliding a standard classical convolution filter on standard grid structures. As a result, the spatial graph convolution operation of the proposed ASGCN model is theoretically related to the classical convolution operation on standard grid structures, bridging the theoretical gap between the traditional CNN models and the spatially-based GCN models. Furthermore, since the convolution filter W^h of the proposed ASGCN model is related to the classical convolution operation, it assigns each vertex a different weighted parameter. Thus, the proposed ASGCN model can adaptively discriminate the importance between specified vertices during the convolution operation. By contrast, as stated in Sect. 2, the existing spatial graph convolution operation of the DGCNN model only maps each vertex feature vector in c dimensions to that in c' dimensions, and all the vertices share the same trainable parameters. As a result, the DGCNN model has less ability to discriminate the importance of different vertices during the convolution operation.

5 Experiments

In this section, we compare the performance of the proposed ASGCN model to both state-of-the-art graph kernels and deep learning methods on graph classification problems based on seven standard graph datasets. These datasets are abstracted from bioinformatics and social networks. Detailed statistics of these datasets are shown in Table 1.

Table 1. Information of the graph datasets

Datasets	MUTAG	PROTEINS	D&D	ENZYMES	IMDB-B	IMDB-M	RED-B
Max # vertices	28	620	5748	126	136	89	3783
Mean # vertices	17.93	39.06	284.30	32.63	19.77	13.00	429.61
# graphs	188	1113	1178	600	1000	1500	2000
# vertex labels	7	61	82	3	–	–	–
# classes	2	2	2	6	2	3	2
Description	Bioinformatics	Bioinformatics	Bioinformatics	Bioinformatics	Social	Social	Social

Experimental Setup: We compare the performance of the proposed ASGCN model on graph classification problems with (a) six alternative state-of-the-art graph kernels and (b) seven alternative state-of-the-art deep learning methods for graphs. Specifically, the graph kernels include (1) the Jensen-Tsallis q-difference kernel (JTQK) with $q = 2$ [4], (2) the Weisfeiler-Lehman subtree kernel (WLSK) [21], (3) the shortest path graph kernel (SPGK) [7], (4) the shortest path kernel based on core variants (CORE SP) [18], (5) the random walk graph kernel (RWGK) [14], and (6) the graphlet count kernel (GK) [20]. The deep learning methods include (1) the deep graph convolutional neural network (DGCNN) [28], (2) the PATCHY-SAN based convolutional neural network for graphs (PSGCN) [17], (3) the diffusion convolutional neural network

(DCNN) [1], (4) the deep graphlet kernel (DGK) [26], (5) the graph capsule convolutional neural network (GCCNN) [23], (6) the anonymous walk embeddings based on feature driven (AWE) [13], and (7) the edge-conditioned convolutional network (ECC) [22].

Table 2. Classification accuracy (In % ± Standard Error) for comparisons.

Datasets	MUTAG	PROTEINS	D&D	ENZYMES	IMDB-B	IMDB-M	RED-B
ASGCN	**89.70** ± 0.85	**76.50** ± 0.59	**80.40** ± 0.95	50.61 ± 1.01	**73.86** ± 0.92	50.86 ± .85	90.60 ± 0.24
JTQK	85.50 ± 0.55	72.86 ± 0.41	79.89 ± 0.32	**56.41** ± 0.42	72.45 ± 0.81	50.33 ± 0.49	77.60 ± 0.35
WLSK	82.88 ± 0.57	73.52 ± 0.43	79.78 ± 0.36	52.75 ± 0.44	71.88 ± 0.77	49.50 ± 0.49	76.56 ± 0.30
SPGK	83.38 ± 0.81	75.10 ± 0.50	78.45 ± 0.26	29.00 ± 0.48	71.26 ± 1.04	**51.33** ± 0.57	84.20 ± 0.70
CORE SP	88.29 ± 1.55	–	77.30 ± 0.80	41.20 ± 1.21	72.62 ± 0.59	49.43 ± 0.42	**90.84** ± 0.14
GK	81.66 ± 2.11	71.67 ± 0.55	78.45 ± 0.26	24.87 ± 0.22	65.87 ± 0.98	45.42 ± 0.87	77.34 ± 0.18
RWGK	80.77 ± 0.72	74.20 ± 0.40	71.70 ± 0.47	22.37 ± 0.35	67.94 ± 0.77	46.72 ± 0.30	72.73 ± 0.39
Datasets	MUTAG	PROTEINS	D&D	ENZYMES	IMDB-B	IMDB-M	RED-B
ASGCN	**89.70** ± 0.85	**76.50** ± 0.59	**80.40** ± 0.95	50.61 ± 1.01	**73.86** ± 0.92	50.86 ± .85	**90.60** ± 0.24
DGCNN	85.83 ± 1.66	75.54 ± 0.94	79.37 ± 0.94	51.00 ± 7.29	70.03 ± 0.86	47.83 ± 0.85	76.02 ± 1.73
PSGCNN	88.95 ± 4.37	75.00 ± 2.51	76.27 ± 2.64	–	71.00 ± 2.29	45.23 ± 2.84	86.30 ± 1.58
DCNN	66.98	61.29 ± 1.60	58.09 ± 0.53	42.44 ± 1.76	49.06 ± 1.37	33.49 ± 1.42	–
GCCNN	–	76.40 ± 4.71	77.62 ± 4.99	**61.83** ± 5.39	71.69 ± 3.40	48.50 ± 4.10	87.61 ± 2.51
DGK	82.66 ± 1.45	71.68 ± 0.50	78.50 ± 0.22	53.40 ± .90	66.96 ± 0.56	44.55 ± 0.52	78.30 ± 0.30
AWE	87.87 ± 9.76	–	71.51 ± 4.02	35.77 ± 5.93	73.13 ± 3.28	**51.58** ± 4.66	82.97 ± 2.86
ECC	76.11	–	72.54	45.67	–	–	–

For the evaluation, we employ the same network structure for the proposed ASGCN model on all graph datasets. Specifically, we set the number of the prototype representations as $M = 64$, the number of the proposed spatial graph convolution layers as 5, and the number of the spatial graph convolutions in each layer as 32. Based on Fig. 1 and Sect. 4.2, we will get 6 concatenated outputs after the graph convolution layers, we utilize a traditional CNN layer with the architecture as C32-P2-C32-P2-C32-F128 to further learn the extracted patterns, where Ck denotes a traditional convolutional layer with k channels, Pk denotes a classical AvgPooling layer of size and stride k, and FCk denotes a fully-connected layer consisting of k hidden units. The filter size and stride of each Ck are all 5 and 1. With the six sets of extracted patterns after the CNN layers to hand, we concatenate and input them into a new fully-connected layer followed by a Softmax layer with a dropout rate of 0.5. We use the rectified linear units (ReLU) in either the graph convolution or the traditional convolution layer. The learning rate of proposed model is 0.00005 for all datasets. The only hyperparameter we optimized is the number of epochs and the batch size for the mini-batch gradient decent algorithm. To optimize the proposed ASGCN model, we use the Stochastic Gradient Descent with the Adam updating rules. Finally, note that, our model needs to construct the prototype representations to identify the transitive vertex alignment information over all graphs. In this evaluation we propose to compute the prototype representations from both the training and testing graphs. Thus, our model is an instance of transductive learning [11], where all graphs are used to compute the prototype representations but the class labels of the testing graphs are not used during the training process. For our model, we perform 10-fold cross-validation to compute the classification accuracies, with nine folds for training and one fold for testing. For each dataset, we repeat the experiment 10 times and report the average classification accuracies and standard errors in Table 2.

For the alternative graph kernels, we follow the parameter setting from their original papers. We perform 10-fold cross-validation using the LIBSVM implementation of C-Support Vector Machines (C-SVM) and we compute the classification accuracies. We perform cross-validation on the training data to select the optimal parameters for each kernel and fold. We repeat the experiment 10 times for each kernel and dataset and we report the average classification accuracies and standard errors in Table 2. Note that for some kernels we directly report the best results from the original corresponding papers, since the evaluation of these kernels followed the same setting of ours. For the alternative deep learning methods, we report the best results for the PSGCNN, DCNN, DGK models from their original papers, since these methods followed the same setting of the proposed model. For the AWE model, we report the classification accuracies of the feature-driven AWE, since the author have stated that this kind of AWE model can achieve competitive performance on label dataset. Finally, note that the PSGCNN and ECC models can leverage additional edge features, most of the graph datasets and the alternative methods do not leverage edge features. Thus, we do not report the results associated with edge features in the evaluation. The classification accuracies and standard errors for each deep learning method are also shown in Table 2.

Experimental Results and Discussions: Table 2 indicates that the proposed ASGCN model can significantly outperform either the remaining graph kernel methods or the remaining deep learning methods for graph classification. Specifically, compared with the alternative graph kernel methods, only the accuracies on the ENZYMES, IMDB-M and RED-B datasets are not the best for the proposed model. However, the proposed model is still competitive on the IMDB-M and RED-B datasets. On the other hand, compared with the alternative deep learning methods, only the accuracies on the ENZYMES and IMDB-M datasets are not the best for the proposed model. But the proposed model is still competitive on the IMDB-M dataset.

Overall, the reasons for the effectiveness are fourfold. First, the C-SVM classifier associated with graph kernels are instances of shallow learning methods [29]. By contrast, the proposed model can provide an end-to-end deep learning architecture, and thus better learn graph characteristics. Second, as we have discussed earlier, most deep learning based graph convolution methods cannot integrate the correspondence information between graphs into the learning architecture. Especially, the PSGCNN and DGCNN models need to reorder the vertices and some vertices may be discarded, leading to information loss. By contrast, the associated aligned vertex grid structures can preserve more information of each original graph, reducing the problem of information loss. Third, unlike the proposed model, the DCNN model needs to sum up the extracted local-level vertex features as global-level graph features. By contrast, the proposed model can learn richer multi-scale local-level vertex features. The experiments demonstrate the effectiveness of the proposed model. Finally, as instances of spatially-based GCN models, the trainable parameters of the DGCNN and CNN models are shared for each vertex. Thus, these models cannot directly influence the aggregation process of the vertex features. By contrast, the required graph convolution operation of the proposed model is theoretically related to the classical convolution operation on standard grid structures and can adaptively discriminate the importance between specified vertices.

6   Conclusions

In this paper, we have developed a new spatially-based GCN model, namely the Aligned-Spatial Graph Convolutional Network (ASGCN) model, to learn effective features for graph classification. This model is based on transforming the arbitrary-sized graphs into fixed-sized aligned grid structures, and performing a new developed spatial graph convolution operation on the grid structures. Unlike most existing spatially-based GCN models, the proposed ASGCN model can adaptively discriminate the importance between specified vertices during the process of the spatial graph convolution operation, explaining the effectiveness of the proposed model. Experiments on standard graph datasets demonstrate the effectiveness of the proposed model.

Acknowledgments. This work is supported by the National Natural Science Foundation of China (Grant no. 61602535, 61976235 and 61503422), the Open Projects Program of National Laboratory of Pattern Recognition (NLPR), the program for innovation research in Central University of Finance and Economics, and the Youth Talent Development Support Program by Central University of Finance and Economics, No. QYP1908. Corresponding Author: Lixin Cui, Email: cuilixin@cufe.edu.cn. The data/code will be available at https://github.com/baiuoy/ASGCN_ECML-PKDD2019.

References

1. Atwood, J., Towsley, D.: Diffusion-convolutional neural networks. In: Proceedings of NIPS, pp. 1993–2001 (2016)
2. Bai, L., Cui, L., Rossi, L., Xu, L., Hancock, E.: Local-global nested graph kernels using nested complexity traces. Pattern Recogn. Lett. (2019, to appear)
3. Bai, L., Hancock, E.R.: Depth-based complexity traces of graphs. Pattern Recogn. **47**(3), 1172–1186 (2014)
4. Bai, L., Rossi, L., Bunke, H., Hancock, E.R.: Attributed graph kernels using the jensen-tsallis q-differences. In: Calders, T., Esposito, F., Hüllermeier, E., Meo, R. (eds.) ECML PKDD 2014. LNCS (LNAI), vol. 8724, pp. 99–114. Springer, Heidelberg (2014). https://doi.org/10.1007/978-3-662-44848-9_7

5. Bai, L., Rossi, L., Cui, L., Cheng, J., Wang, Y., Hancock, E.R.: A quantum-inspired similarity measure for the analysis of complete weighted graphs. IEEE Trans. Cybern. (2019, to appear)

6. Bai, L., Rossi, L., Zhang, Z., Hancock, E.R.: An aligned subtree kernel for weighted graphs. In: Proceedings of ICML (2015)

7. Borgwardt, K.M., Kriegel, H.P.: Shortest-path kernels on graphs. In: Proceedings of the IEEE International Conference on Data Mining, pp. 74–81 (2005)

8. Bruna, J., Zaremba, W., Szlam, A., LeCun, Y.: Spectral networks and locally connected networks on graphs. CoRR abs/1312.6203 (2013)

9. Defferrard, M., Bresson, X., Vandergheynst, P.: Convolutional neural networks on graphs with fast localized spectral filtering. In: Proceedings of NIPS, pp. 3837–3845 (2016)

10. Duvenaud, D.K., et al.: Convolutional networks on graphs for learning molecular fingerprints. In: Proceedings of NIPS, pp. 2224–2232 (2015)

11. Gammerman, A., Azoury, K.S., Vapnik, V.: Learning by transduction. In: Proceedings of UAI, pp. 148–155 (1998)

12. Henaff, M., Bruna, J., LeCun, Y.: Deep convolutional networks on graph-structured data. CoRR abs/1506.05163 (2015). http://arxiv.org/abs/1506.05163

13. Ivanov, S., Burnaev, E.: Anonymous walk embeddings. In: Proceedings of ICML, pp. 2191–2200 (2018)

14. Kashima, H., Tsuda, K., Inokuchi, A.: Marginalized kernels between labeled graphs. In: Proceedings of ICML, pp. 321–328 (2003)

15. Kipf, T.N., Welling, M.: Semi-supervised classification with graph convolutional networks. CoRR abs/1609.02907 (2016). http://arxiv.org/abs/1609.02907

16. Krizhevsky, A., Sutskever, I., Hinton, G.E.: Imagenet classification with deep convolutional neural networks. Commun. ACM 60(6), 84–90 (2017)

17. Niepert, M., Ahmed, M., Kutzkov, K.: Learning convolutional neural networks for graphs. In: Proceedings of ICML, pp. 2014–2023 (2016)

18. Nikolentzos, G., Meladianos, P., Limnios, S., Vazirgiannis, M.: A degeneracy framework for graph similarity. In: Proceedings of IJCAI, pp. 2595–2601 (2018)

19. Rippel, O., Snoek, J., Adams, R.P.: Spectral representations for convolutional neural networks. In: Proceddings of NIPS, pp. 2449–2457 (2015)

20. Shervashidze, N., Vishwanathan, S., Petri, T., Mehlhorn, K., Borgwardt, K.M.: Efficient graphlet kernels for large graph comparison. J. Mach. Learn. Res. 5, 488–495 (2009)

21. Shervashidze, N., Schweitzer, P., van Leeuwen, E.J., Mehlhorn, K., Borgwardt, K.M.: Weisfeiler-lehman graph kernels. J. Mach. Learn. Res. 1, 1–48 (2010)

22. Simonovsky, M., Komodakis, N.: Dynamic edge-conditioned filters in convolutional neural networks on graphs. In: Proceedings of CVPR, pp. 29–38 (2017)

23. Verma, S., Zhang, Z.: Graph capsule convolutional neural networks. CoRR abs/1805.08090 (2018). http://arxiv.org/abs/1805.08090

24. Vialatte, J., Gripon, V., Mercier, G.: Generalizing the convolution operator to extend CNNs to irregular domains. CoRR abs/1606.01166 (2016). http://arxiv.org/abs/1606.01166

25. Witten, I.H., Frank, E., Hall, M.A.: Data Mining: Practical Machine Learning Tools and Techniques. Morgan Kaufmann, San Francisco (2011)

26. Yanardag, P., Vishwanathan, S.V.N.: Deep graph kernels. In: Proceedings of the 21th ACM SIGKDD International Conference on Knowledge Discovery and Data Mining, Sydney, NSW, Australia, 10–13 August 2015, pp. 1365–1374 (2015)

27. Zambon, D., Alippi, C., Livi, L.: Concept drift and anomaly detection in graph streams. IEEE Trans. Neural Netw. Learning Syst. 29(11), 5592–5605 (2018)

28. Zhang, M., Cui, Z., Neumann, M., Chen, Y.: An end-to-end deep learning architecture for graph classification. In: Proceedings of AAAI (2018)
29. Zhang, S., Liu, C., Yao, K., Gong, Y.: Deep neural support vector machines for speech recognition. In: Proceedings of ICASSP, pp. 4275–4279 (2015)

NODE2BITS: Compact Time- and Attribute-Aware Node Representations for User Stitching

Di Jin[1(✉)], Mark Heimann[1], Ryan A. Rossi[2], and Danai Koutra[1]

[1] University of Michigan, Ann Arbor, USA
dijin@umich.edu
[2] Adobe Research, San Jose, USA

Abstract. Identity stitching, the task of identifying and matching various online references (*e.g.*, sessions over different devices and timespans) to the same user in real-world web services, is crucial for personalization and recommendations. However, traditional user stitching approaches, such as grouping or blocking, require pairwise comparisons between a massive number of user activities, thus posing both computational and storage challenges. Recent works, which are often application-specific, heuristically seek to reduce the amount of comparisons, but they suffer from low precision and recall. To solve the problem in an application-independent way, we take a heterogeneous network-based approach in which users (nodes) interact with content (*e.g.*, sessions, websites), and may have attributes (*e.g.*, location). We propose NODE2BITS, an efficient framework that represents multi-dimensional features of node contexts with binary hashcodes. NODE2BITS leverages *feature-based temporal* walks to encapsulate short- and long-term interactions between nodes in heterogeneous web networks, and adopts SimHash to obtain compact, binary representations and avoid the quadratic complexity for similarity search. Extensive experiments on large-scale real networks show that NODE2BITS outperforms traditional techniques and existing works that generate real-valued embeddings by up to 5.16% in $F1$ score on user stitching, while taking only up to 1.56% as much storage.

1 Introduction

Personalization and recommendations increase user satisfaction by providing relevant experiences and handling the online information overload in news, web search, entertainment, and more. Accurately modeling user behavior and preferences over time are at the core of personalization. However, tracking user activity online is challenging as users interact with tens of internet-enabled devices from different locations daily, leading to fragmented user profiles. Without unified profiles, the observed user data are sparse, non-representative of the population, and insufficient for accurate predictions that drive business success.

In this work, we tackle the problem of *identity or user stitching*, which aims to identify and group together logged-in and anonymous sessions that correspond to the *same* user despite taking place across different channels, platforms, devices and browsers [30]. This problem is a form of entity or identity resolution [2,13],

© Springer Nature Switzerland AG 2020
U. Brefeld et al. (Eds.): ECML PKDD 2019, LNAI 11906, pp. 483–506, 2020.
https://doi.org/10.1007/978-3-030-46150-8_29

also known as entity linking, record linkage, and duplicate detection [2, 6, 21]. Unlike entity resolution where textual information per user (*e.g.*, name, address) is available, identity stitching relies solely on user interactions with online content and web metadata. Although cookies can help stitch several different sessions of the same user, many users have multiple cookies (*e.g.*, a cookie for each device or web browser) [8], and most cookies expire after a short time, and therefore cannot help to stitch users over time. Similarly, IP addresses change across locations resulting in fragmentation or even erroneous stitching between users who have the same IP address at different times (e.g., airports). Meanwhile, fingerprinting approaches [12] capture user similarity based on device or browser configurations, not on behavioral patterns that remain consistent across devices or browsers. On the other hand, exhaustive solutions for entity resolution require quadratic number of comparisons between all pairs of entities, which is computationally intractable for large-scale web services. This can be partially handled via the heuristic of blocking [24], which groups similar entity descriptions into blocks, and only compares entities within the same block.

To overcome these challenges and better tailor to the user stitching setup, our solution is based on the idea that the same user accesses *similar content* across platforms and has *similar behavior* over time. We model the user interactions with different content and platforms over time in a dynamic heterogeneous network, where user stitching maps to the identification of *nodes* that correspond to the same real-world entity. Motivated by the success of node representation learning, we aim to find embeddings of time-evolving 'user profiles' over this rich network of interactions. For large-scale graphs, however, the customary dense node representations for each node can often impose a formidable memory requirement, on par with that of the original (sparse) adjacency matrices [19]. Thus, to efficiently find *sparse* binary representations and link entities based on similar activity while avoiding the pairwise comparison of all user profiles, we solve the following problem:

Problem 1 (Temporal, Hash-based Node Embeddings). *Given a graph $G(V, E)$, the goal of hash-based network embedding is to learn a function $\chi : V \to \{0,1\}^d$ such that the derived binary d-dimensional embeddings (1) preserve similarities in interactions in G, (2) are space-efficient, and (3) accurately capture temporal information and the heterogeneity of the underlying network.*

We introduce a *general* framework called NODE2BITS that captures temporally-valid interactions between nodes in a network, and constructs the contexts based on topological features and (optional) side information of entities involved in the interaction. These

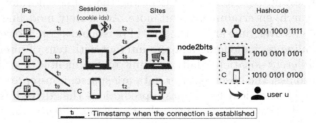

Fig. 1. NODE2BITS overview. NODE2BITS encodes the temporal, heterogeneous information of each node into binary hashcodes for efficient user stitching.

feature-based contexts are then turned into histograms that incorporate node type information at different *temporal distances*, and are mapped to binary hash-codes through SimHash [5]. Thanks to locality sensitive hashing [17], the hash-codes, which are time-, attribute- and structure-aware, preserve the similarities in temporal interaction patterns in the network, and achieve both space and computational efficiency for similarity search. Given these sparse, hash-based embeddings of all entities, we then cast user stitching as a supervised binary classification task or a hashing-based unsupervised task. As an example, in Fig. 1, devices B and C are associated with identical IPs and similar online sales websites visited afterwards, thus they are encoded similarly and could correspond to the same user.

Our contributions are:

- **Embedding-based Formulation:** Going beyond traditional blocking techniques, we formulate the problem of user stitching as the problem of finding temporal, hash-based embeddings in heterogeneous networks such that they maintain *similarities between user interactions over time*.
- **Space-efficient Embeddings:** We propose NODE2BITS, a practical, intuitive, and fast framework that generates *compact, binary embeddings* suitable for user stitching. Our method combines random walk-based sampling of contexts, their feature-based histogram representations, and locality sensitive hashing to preserve the heterogeneous equivalency of contexts over time.
- **Extensive Empirical Analysis:** Our experiments on real-world networks show that NODE2BITS outputs a space-efficient binary representation which uses between $63\times$ and $339\times$ less space than the baselines while achieving comparable or better performance in user stitching tasks. Moreover, NODE2BITS is scalable for large real-world temporal and heterogeneous networks.

For reproducibility, the code is at https://github.com/GemsLab/node2bits.

2   Preliminaries and Definitions

Before we introduce NODE2BITS, we discuss two key concepts that our method is based on: our dynamic heterogeneous network model, and temporal random walks. We give the main symbols and their definitions in Table 1.

2.1   Dynamic Heterogeneous Network Model

As we mentioned above, we model the user interactions with content, websites, devices etc. as a heterogeneous network, which is formally defined as:

Definition 1 (HETEROGENEOUS NETWORK). *A heterogeneous network $G = (V, E, \psi, \xi)$ is comprised of (i) a nodeset V and edgeset E, (ii) a mapping $\psi : V \to \mathcal{T}_V$ of nodes to their types, and (iii) a mapping $\xi : E \to \mathcal{T}_E$ to edge types.*

Table 1. Summary of major symbols and their definitions.

Symbol	Definition
$G(V, E, \xi, \psi)$	(un)directed and (un)weighted heterogeneous network with nodeset V, edgeset E, a mapping ξ from nodes to node types, and an edge mapping ψ, resp.
$\|V\| = N, \|E\| = M$	number of nodes and edges in G
$\mathcal{T}_V, \|\mathcal{T}_V\|; \mathcal{T}_E, \|\mathcal{T}_E\|$	set of node/edge types in the heterogeneous graph and its size, resp.
$\mathbf{F}$	$N \times \|\mathcal{F}\|$ feature matrix including node attributes and derived features
$f_{ij}, f_{(j)}$	$(i,j)^{th}$ element of $\mathbf{F}$ and index of its jth feature, resp.
$\mathcal{W}$	set of random walks
$(\mathbf{w}_L)_{L \in \mathbb{N}}, \mathbf{w}_L[u]$	sequence of nodes in a random walk of length L, and the index of node u, resp.
L	the maximum length of a random walk
Δt	'temporal distance' in $\mathcal{W}$ based on temporally ordered edge transitions
$\mathcal{C}_u^{\Delta t}, \mathcal{C}_u^{\Delta t}\|f$	context of node u at distance Δt, and feature-based context, resp.
$g_i : \mathcal{C} \to \{0,1\}$	i^{th} LSH function that hashes a node context into a binary value
$K^{\Delta t}, K$	embedding dimension at distance Δt, and output dimension $K = \sum_{\Delta t=1}^{MAX} K^{\Delta t}$
$\mathbf{h}(\mathcal{S}), \mathbf{h}(\mathcal{S}\|\cdot)$	unconditional and conditional b-bin histogram of values in enclosed set $\mathcal{S}$, resp.
$\mathbf{Z}$	$N \times K$ output binary embeddings or hashcodes

Many graph types are special cases of heterogeneous networks: (**1**) homogeneous graphs have $\|\mathcal{T}_V\| = \|\mathcal{T}_E\| = 1$ type; (**2**) k-partite graphs consist of $\|\mathcal{T}_V\| = k$ and $\|\mathcal{T}_E\| = k - 1$ types; (**3**) signed networks have $\|\mathcal{T}_V\| = 1$ and $\|\mathcal{T}_E\| = 2$ types; and (**4**) labeled graphs have a single label per node/edge.

Most real networks capture evolving processes (e.g., communication, browsing activity) and thus change over time. Instead of approximating a dynamic network as a sequence of lossy discrete static snapshots $G_1, \ldots, G_T$, we model the *temporal interactions* in a *lossless* fashion as a *continuous-time dynamic network* [23].

Definition 2 (CONTINUOUS-TIME DYNAMIC NETWORK). *A continuous-time dynamic, heterogeneous network $G = (V, E_\tau, \psi, \xi, \tau)$ is a heterogeneous network with E_τ temporal edges between vertices V, where $\tau : E \to \mathbb{R}^+$ is a function that maps each edge to a corresponding timestamp.*

2.2 Temporal Random Walks

A walk on a graph is a sequence of nodes where each pair of successive nodes are connected by an edge. Popular network embedding methods generate walks using randomized procedures [14,25] to construct a corpus of node IDs or node context. In continuous-time dynamic networks, a *temporally valid* walk is defined as a sequence of nodes connected by edges with non-decreasing timestamps (*e.g.*, representing the order that user-content interactions occurred) and they were first used for embeddings in [23].

Definition 3 (TEMPORAL WALK). *A temporal walk of length L from v_1 to v_L in graph $G = (V, E, \psi, \xi)$ is a sequence of vertices $\langle v_1, v_2, \cdots, v_L \rangle$ such that $\langle v_i, v_{i+1} \rangle \in E_\tau$ for $1 \leq i < L$, and the timestamps are in valid temporal order: $\tau(v_i, v_{i+1}) \leq \tau(v_{i+1}, v_{i+2})$ for $1 \leq i < (L - 1)$.*

3   NODE2BITS: Hash-Based Embedding Framework

Motivated by the task of user stitching, we aim to develop NODE2BITS to compactly describe each node/entity in the context of *realistic interactions* (Problem 1). Accordingly, NODE2BITS is required to: (**R1**) support heterogeneous networks where the nodes and edges can be of any arbitrary type (*e.g.*, a user, web page, IP, tag, spatial location); (**R2**) preserve the temporal validity of the events and interactions in the data; (**R3**) scale in runtime to large networks with millions of nodes/edges; and (**R4**) scale in memory requirements with space-efficient yet powerful *binary* embeddings that capture ID-independent similarities. Next we detail the three main steps of NODE2BITS: (Sect. 3.1) Sampling temporal random walks and defining temporal contexts; (Sect. 3.2) Constructing temporal contexts based on multi-dimensional features; (Sect. 3.3) Aggregating and hashing contexts into sparse embeddings. We give the overview of NODE2BITS in Fig. 2 and Algorithm 1.

3.1   Temporal Random Walk Sampling

The first step of NODE2BITS is to capture interactions in a node's context, which is important for the user stitching task: instead of simple interactions corresponding to pairwise edges, it samples more complex interaction sequences via random walks. But unlike many existing representation learning approaches [14,25], our method samples *realistic* interactions in the order that they happen via L-step *temporal* random walks (Definition 3 [23]), thus satisfying requirement **R2**.

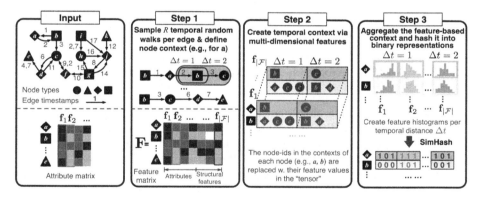

Fig. 2. NODE2BITS workflow. Given a graph and its attribute matrix (optional), NODE2BITS (1) samples *temporal* random walks to obtain sequences that respect time, derives contexts at different temporal distances (temporal contexts of a and b are derived from the walk $\{b, a, b, c\}$, as well as the feature matrix **F**; (2) creates temporal contexts based on multi-dimensional features in **F**; and (3) aggregates them into feature-based histograms to obtain sparse, binary, similarity-preserving embeddings via SimHash. (Color figure online)

NODE2BITS defines the *temporal context* $C_u^{\Delta t}$ of node u at temporal distance Δt as the *collection of entities* that are at Δt-hops away from node u in the sampled random walks. Formally:

$$C_u^{\Delta t} = \{v \; : \; |\mathbf{w}_L[v] - \mathbf{w}_L[u]| = \Delta t, \; \forall \mathbf{w}_L \in \mathcal{W}\}, \tag{1}$$

where $\mathbf{w}_L[\cdot]$ is the index of the corresponding node in the random walk $(\mathbf{w}_L)_{L \in \mathbb{N}}$. For example, in Fig. 2 (Step 1) the context of node a at temporal distance 2 is $C_a^{\Delta t=2} = \{c\}$ (highlighted in red). Depending on the temporal context that we want to capture, Δt can vary up to a MAX distance. Intuitively, small values of temporal distance capture more *direct* interactions and similarities between entities. In static graphs, Δt simply corresponds to the distance between nodes in the sampled sequences, without capturing any temporal information.

Temporal Locality. The context that is defined above does not explicitly incorporate the *time elapsed* between consecutively sampled interactions. However, when modeling temporal user interactions, it is important to distinguish between short-term and long-term transitions. Inspired by [23], NODE2BITS accounts for the *closeness* or *locality* between consecutive contexts (*i.e.*, $C_u^{\Delta t}$ and $C_u^{\Delta t+1}$) through different biased temporal walk policies. For example, in the short-term policy, the transition probability from node u to v is given as the softmax function:

$$P[v|u] = \frac{\exp\left(-\tau(u,v)/d\right)}{\sum_{i \in \Gamma_\tau(u)} \exp\left(-\tau(u,i)/d\right)} \tag{2}$$

where $\tau()$ maps an edge to its timestamp, $d = \max_{e \in E_\tau} \tau(e) - \min_{e \in E_\tau} \tau(e)$ is the total duration of all timestamps, and $\Gamma_\tau(u)$ is the set of temporal neighbors reached from node u through temporally valid edges. Similarly, in the long-term policy, the transition probability from node u to v is given as in Eq. (2) but with positive signs in the numerator and denominator.

3.2   Temporal Context Based on Multi-dimensional Features

The context in Eq. (1) depends on the node identities (IDs). However, in a multi-platform environment, a single entity may have multiple node IDs, thus contributing to seemingly different contexts. To generate ID-independent contexts that are appropriate for user stitching, we make the temporal contexts attribute- or feature-aware (**R1**), by building on the assumption that corresponding or similar entities have similar features. Formally, we assume that a network may have a set of input node attributes (*e.g.*, IP address, device type), as well as a set of derived topological features (*e.g.*, degree, PageRank), all of which are stored in a $N \times |\mathcal{F}|$ feature matrix $\mathbf{F}$ (Fig. 2, Step 1). We then generalize our random walks to not only respect time (**R2**) [23], but also capture this feature information using the notion of attributed/feature-based walks proposed in [1]:

Definition 4 (FEATURE-BASED TEMPORAL WALK). *A feature-based temporal walk of length L from node v_1 to v_L in graph G is defined as a sequence of feature values corresponding to the sequence of vertices in a valid temporal walk*

(Definition 3). For the jth feature $f_{(j)}$, the corresponding feature-based temporal walk is

$$\langle w_{L,f_{(j)}} \rangle_{L \in \mathbb{N}} = \langle f_{v_1,j}, f_{v_2,j}, \ldots, f_{v_L,j} \rangle, \tag{3}$$

where $f_{v_i,j}$ is the value of the jth feature for node v_i, stored in matrix $\mathbf{F}$.

Our definition is general as it allows walks to obey time while each node may have a d-dimensional vector of input attribute values and/or derived structural features, which can be discrete or real-valued [1].

Temporally-Valid, Multi-dimensional Feature Contexts. NODE2BITS extends the previously generated temporal contexts to incorporate node features and remove the dependency on node IDs. Following the definition of feature-based temporal walks, given $|\mathcal{F}|$ features, our method generates $|\mathcal{F}|$-dimensional contexts per node u and temporal distance Δt by replacing the node IDs in Eq. (1) with their corresponding feature values (Fig. 2, Step 2). Formally, the temporally-valid, multi-dimensional feature contexts are defined as:

$$\mathcal{C}_u^{\Delta t} | f_{(j)} = \{ f_{v,j} \; : \; \forall v \in \mathcal{C}_u^{\Delta t} \} \; \forall \text{ feature } f_{(j)} \in \mathcal{F}, \tag{4}$$

where $f_{v,j}$ is the value of the jth feature for node v.

3.3   Feature-Based Context Aggregation and Hashing

The key insight in user stitching is that each user interacts with similarly 'typed' entities through similar relations over time: for example, in online-sales logs, a user likely browses similar types of goods in logged-in and anonymous sessions; and in online social networks, accounts sharing near-identical interaction patterns, such as replies or shares, are potentially from the same person. Based on this insight, NODE2BITS augments the previously generated temporal, multi-dimensional feature contexts with node types (and implicitly the corresponding relations or edge types), which is a key property of heterogeneous networks (**R1**). It subsequently aggregates them and derives similarity-preserving and space-efficient, binary entity representations (**R4**) via locality sensitive hashing.

Context Aggregation. Unlike existing works that aggregate contextual features into a single value such as mean or maximum [15,29], NODE2BITS aggregates them into *less lossy* representations: *histograms* tailored to heterogeneous networks by distinguishing between node types (**R1**). Specifically, it models the transitional dependency across node and relation types by further conditioning the derived contexts in Eq. (4) on the node types $p_i \in \mathcal{T}_V$ (*i.e.*, each temporal context consists of the features of only one node type). We denote the temporal contexts conditioned on both features and node types as $\mathcal{C}_u^{\Delta t} | f, p$. The final histogram representation of node u at temporal distance Δt consists of the concatenation of the histograms over the conditional contexts at Δt (Fig. 2, Step 3):

$$\mathbf{h}(\mathcal{C}_u^{\Delta t}) = [\mathrm{h}(\mathcal{C}_u^{\Delta t} \mid f_{(1)}, p_1), \mathrm{h}(\mathcal{C}_u^{\Delta t} \mid f_{(2)}, p_1), \dots, \mathrm{h}(\mathcal{C}_u^{\Delta t} \mid f_{(|\mathcal{F}|)}, p_{|\mathcal{T}_V|})]. \qquad (5)$$

In this representation, the features are binned logarithmically to account for the often skewed distributions of structural features (*e.g.* degree). We note that the histograms can be further extended to edge types as shown in [19], for example by distinguishing pairs of nodes that are connected by multiple types of edges.

Similarity-Preserving Representations via Hashing. Locality sensitive hashing (LSH) has been widely used for searching nearest neighbors in large-scale data mining [26]. In this work, we adopt SimHash [5] to obtain similarity-preserving and space-efficient representations (**R4**) for all the entities in the heterogeneous network based on their aggregated time-, attribute-, and node type-aware contexts given by Eq. (5).

Given a node-specific histogram $\mathbf{h}(\mathcal{C}_u^{\Delta t}) \in \mathbb{R}^d$ (with dimensionality $d = |\mathcal{F}||\mathcal{T}_V| \cdot b$, and b being the number of logarithmic bins for the features), SimHash generates a $K^{\Delta t}$-dimensional[1] binary hashcode or sketch $\mathbf{z}_u^{\Delta t}$ by projecting the histogram to $K^{\Delta t}$ random hyperplanes $\mathbf{r}_i \in \mathbb{R}^d$ as follows:

$$g_i(\,\mathbf{h}(\mathcal{C}_u^{\Delta t})\,) = \mathrm{sign}\left(\mathbf{h}(\mathcal{C}_u^{\Delta t}) \cdot \mathbf{r}_i\right) \qquad (6)$$

In practice, the hyperplanes do not need to be chosen uniformly at random from a multivariate normal distribution, but it suffices to choose them uniformly from $\{-1, 1\}^d$. The important property of locality sensitive hashing that guarantees that the similarities in the histogram space (which captures the temporal interactions between entities in G) are maintained is the following: for the SimHash family, the probability that a hash function agrees for two different vectors is equal to their cosine similarity. More formally, for two nodes u and v:

$$P(\,g_i(\mathbf{h}(\mathcal{C}_u^{\Delta t})) = g_i(\mathbf{h}(\mathcal{C}_v^{\Delta t}))\,) = 1 - \frac{\cos^{-1}\frac{\mathbf{h}(\mathcal{C}_u^{\Delta t}) \cdot \mathbf{h}(\mathcal{C}_v^{\Delta t})}{|\mathbf{h}(\mathcal{C}_u^{\Delta t})||\mathbf{h}(\mathcal{C}_v^{\Delta t})|}}{180}. \qquad (7)$$

In other words, the cosine similarity between nodes u and v in the context-space is projected to the sketch-space and can be measured by the cardinality of matching between $\mathbf{z}_u^{\Delta t}$ and $\mathbf{z}_v^{\Delta t}$, where $\mathbf{z}_\bullet^{\Delta t} = [g_1(\,\mathbf{h}(\mathcal{C}_\bullet^{\Delta t})\,), g_2(\,\mathbf{h}(\mathcal{C}_\bullet^{\Delta t}), \dots, g_{K^{\Delta t}}(\,\mathbf{h}(\mathcal{C}_\bullet^{\Delta t})]$.

For each node u in G, the final binary representation is obtained by concatenating the hashcodes for contexts at different temporal distances Δt, resulting in a K-dimensional vector (since $K = \sum_{\Delta t=1}^{\mathrm{MAX}} K^{\Delta t}$):

$$\mathbf{z}_u = [\mathbf{z}_u^{\Delta t=1} \;\; \mathbf{z}_u^{\Delta t=2} \;\; \dots \;\; \mathbf{z}_u^{\Delta t=\mathrm{MAX}}] \qquad (8)$$

where we replace the -1 bits with 0s to achieve a more space-efficient representation (**R4**). An example is shown in the second half of Step 3 in Fig. 2, where the

---

[1] We assume that the length of each sketch at distance Δt is given as $K^{\Delta t} = \frac{K}{\mathrm{MAX}}$.

Algorithm 1. NODE2BITS Framework

Require: (un)directed heterogeneous graph $G(V, E, \psi, \xi)$, # random walks R per edge, max
walk length L, max temporal distance MAX, embedding dimensionality $K^{\Delta t}$ at dist. Δt

1 For each edge e, perform R temporal walks based on the short- or long-term policy (§ 3.1)
2 Obtain temporal contexts $\mathcal{C}_u^{\Delta t}$ for each node u at temporal distances $\Delta t \leq$ MAX via Eq. (1)
3 Construct feature matrix **F** with node attributes (if avail.) and topological features (§ 3.2)
4 Derive feature-based temporal contexts $\mathcal{C}_u^{\Delta t}|f_{(j)}$ by replacing $v \in \mathcal{C}_u^{\Delta t}$ with the feature
   value $f_{v,j}$, as shown in Eq. (4)
5 **for each** temporal distance $\Delta t = 1,\dots,$MAX and node $u \in V$ **do**
6 | Obtain u's final histogram $\mathbf{h}(\mathcal{C}_u^{\Delta t})$ over its contexts using Eq. (5)
7 | Obtain a $K^{\Delta t}$-dim, sparse, binary hashcode $z_u^{\Delta t}$ based on (modified) SimHash (§ 3.3)
8 Obtain the binary N2B embeddings $\mathbf{z}_u$ of all nodes across temporal distances Δt via Eq. (8)
9 Perform (un)supervised user stitching via binary classification or hashing (§ 4.1, 4.3)

---

blue shades denote histograms and sketches for contexts in temporal distance
$\Delta t = 1$, and red shades correspond to $\Delta t = 2$. Thus, the K-dimensional representation for each node, $\mathbf{z}_u \in \{0,1\}^K$, captures the similarities between time-,
feature- and node type-aware histograms across multiple temporal distances Δt.
The similarity between two nodes' histograms can be quickly estimated as the
proportion of common bits in their binary representations $\mathbf{z}_\bullet$.

Given these representations, we can perform user stitching by casting the
problem as supervised binary classification or an unsupervised task based on
the output of hashing (Eq. (8)), which we discuss in Sect. 4.1. Putting everything
together, we give the pseudocode of NODE2BITS in Algorithm 1 and its detailed
version (for reproducibility) in Appendix A. The runtime computational complexity of NODE2BITS is $\mathcal{O}(MRL + NK)$, which is linear to the number of edges
when $M \gg N$ as K is relatively small (**R3**). The output space complexity is
$\mathcal{O}(NK)$-bit. NODE2BITS requires even less storage if the binary vectors are represented in the sparse format (see Sect. 4.4 for empirical results). We provide
detailed runtime complexity and space analysis in Appendix B.

4   Experiments

We perform extensive experiments on real-world heterogeneous networks to
answer the following questions: (**Q1**) Is NODE2BITS effective in the user stitching
task, and how does it compare to traditional stitching and embedding methods?
(Sects. 4.2 and 4.3) (**Q2**) Does NODE2BITS have low space requirements, and is it
more space-efficient than the baselines? (Sect. 4.4) (**Q3**) Is NODE2BITS scalable?
(Sect. 4.5).

4.1 Experimental Setup

We ran our analysis on Mac OS platform with 2.5 GHz Intel Core i7, 16 GB RAM.

Data. We use five real-world heterogeneous networks from the Network Repository [28], as well as a real, proprietary user stitching dataset, 'Company X' web logs. The latter data form a temporal heterogeneous network consisting of web sessions of user devices and their IP addresses. High degree nodes representing anomalous behavior (*e.g.*, bots or public WiFi hotspots) are filtered out. Our framework is also capable of modeling domain-specific

Table 2. Network statistics and properties for our six real-world datasets. 'D': directed; 'W': weighted; 'H': heterogeneous; 'T': temporal network.

Data	Nodes	Edges	$|T_V|$	D	W	H	T
citeseer	4460	2892	2		✓	✓	
yahoo	100,058	1,057,050	2	✓	✓	✓	
bitcoin	3,783	24,186	1	✓	✓		✓
digg	283,183	6,473,708	2			✓	✓
wiki	1,140,149	7,833,140	1	✓			✓
comp-X	5,500,802	5,291,270	2	✓	✓	✓	✓

features, such as user-agent strings and geolocation [20], if this is available. Even without them, however, it achieves strong performance. We give the statistics of all the networks in Table 2, and additional details in Appendix C.

Task Setup. With the exception of Sect. 4.3, we cast the user stitching task as a binary classification problem, where for each pair of nodes we aim to predict whether they correspond to the same entity (*i.e.*, we should stitch them). We use logistic regression with regularization strength 1.0 and stopping criterion 10^{-4}.

For the real user stitching data, we use the held-out, ground-truth information to evaluate our method. For the five real-world networks without known user pairs, we introduce user replicas following a similar procedure to [2]: we sample 5% of the nodes with degrees larger than average, introduce a replica u' for each sampled node u, and distribute the original edges between u and u'. Specifically, each edge remains connected to u with probability p_1, otherwise it connects to the replica node u'. Additionally, each edge that is incident to u has probability p_2 to also connect to u'. Unless otherwise specified, we use $p_1 = 0.6$ and $p_2 = 0.3$.

Given the positive replica pairs, we sample an equal number of negative pairs uniformly at random and include these in the training and testing sets. Comp-X, the dataset with ground-truth replicas, also has pre-defined approximately 50/50 training-testing splits that we use. Afterwards, embeddings are derived for each node pair by concatenation: $[\mathbf{z}(u), \mathbf{z}(u')]$. Using these node pair embeddings, we learn a logistic regression (LR) model and use it to predict the node pairs that should be stitched in the held-out test set. These are the nodes that correspond to the same entity. We measure the predictive performance of all the methods in terms of AUC, accuracy and $F1$ score.

Baselines. We compare to various methods that target different network types:

- **Homogeneous networks**: *Static* – **(1)** Spectral embeddings or SE [33], **(2)** LINE [32], **(3)** DeepWalk or DW [25], **(4)** node2vec or n2vec [14], **(5)** struc2vec or s2vec [27], and **(6)** DNGR [4]. *Temporal–* **(7)** CTDNE [23].
- **Heterogeneous networks**: **(8)** Common neighbors (CN) [2], **(9)** metapath2vec or m2vec [10], and **(10)** AspEm [31].

The baselines are configured to achieve the best performance, for $K = 128$-dimensional embeddings, according to the respective papers. For reproducibility, we describe the settings in Appendix D.

NODE2BITS **Setup & Variants.** Similar to the baselines, NODE2BITS performs $R = 10$ walks per edge, with length up to $L = 20$, and we set the max temporal distance MAX $= 3$. We justify these decisions in Appendix E.2. On the largest dataset, Comp-X, we use a maximum walk length $L = 5$ and temporal distance MAX $= 2$. While various node attributes can be given as input to NODE2BITS, for consistency we derive and use the total, in-/out-degree of each node in $\mathbf{F}$.

We experiment with different variants of NODE2BITS (or N2B for short): (1) **NODE2BITS-0** applies to static networks; (2) **NODE2BITS-SH** uses the short-term tactic in the random walks (Sect. 3.1); (3) **NODE2BITS-LN** uses the long-term tactic; and (4) **NODE2BITS-U** targets unsupervised user stitching, which most baselines cannot handle (except for CN). To explore our method's performance in unsupervised settings (Sect. 4.3), we directly 'cluster' the LSH-based, binary node representations $\mathbf{z}_u$ generated by NODE2BITS-0. The idea is that nodes that hash to the same 'bucket' likely map to the same entity and should be stitched. To map entities to buckets we use the banding technique [26]: per band—one per representation $\mathbf{z}^{\Delta t}$ at temporal distance Δt—we apply AND-construction on the output of bit sampling, and then OR-construction across the bands.

4.2   Accuracy in Supervised User Stitching

We start by evaluating the predictive performance of NODE2BITS for supervised user stitching on both static and temporal networks.

Static Networks. Here we evaluate the effectiveness of multi-dimensional feature contexts. Since static networks lack temporal information, NODE2BITS performs random walks similarly to existing works to collect nodes in structural contexts. The main difference lies in representing diverse feature histograms. We run NODE2BITS against both homogeneous and heterogeneous baselines as shown in Table 3, and observe that it performs the best in most evaluation metrics on both graphs. NODE2BITS outperforms existing random-walk based methods as expected: node IDs in the contexts is distorted by the replicas generated, thus feature-based methods should prevail. This is also validated by the results

Table 3. Entity resolution results for *static* networks. Our method outperforms all the baselines. — OOT = Out Of Time (6 h); OOM = Out Of Memory (16 GB). The asterisk * denotes statistically significant improvement over the best baseline at $p < 0.05$ in a two-sided t-test.

	Metric	CN	SE	LINE	DW	n2vec	s2vec	DNGR	m2vec	AspEm	N2B-0
citeseer	AUC	0.9141	0.4846	0.5481	0.5614	0.6188	0.9344	0.5015	0.5546	0.5049	0.9480*
	ACC	0.9141	0.5045	0.5372	0.5579	0.6211	0.8936	0.4688	0.5357	0.5223	0.9196*
	F1	0.9137	0.5028	0.5371	0.5547	0.6159	0.8926	0.4682	0.5348	0.5222	0.9192*
yahoo	AUC	0.6851	0.5378	0.8050	0.7640	0.7636			0.8233	0.4938	0.8088
	ACC	0.6851	0.4760	0.7771	0.7117	0.7233	OOT	OOM	0.7827	0.5018	0.8010
	F1	0.6505	0.4375	0.7764	0.7117	0.7231			0.7823	0.5018	0.7987

for struc2vec, which captures the equivalency of structural feature sequences in embeddings. metapath2vec and LINE achieve promising result on yahoo but not on citeseer, as the latter is an undirected bipartite graph, node distributions of the 2-order contexts explored by LINE are highly correlated and indistinguishable for stitching. On the contrary, CN (common-neighbors) yields promising result on citeseer but not yahoo. This is likely due to the graph structure, which we explain in more detail in Sect. 4.3. We encountered out-of-memory errors for DNGR due to the algorithmic complexity and out-of-time-limit for struc2vec.

CONCLUSION 1. *On static graphs,* NODE2BITS *achieves comparable performance in AUC, and slightly better F1 score with 0.60%–2.10% improvement over baselines in the stitching task.*

Temporal Networks. Table 4 depicts the stitching performance of NODE2BITS using both the short- and long-term tactics against the same set of baselines used in static graphs as well as CTDNE, an embedding framework designed for temporal graphs. We exclude metapath2vec, as metapaths are not meaningful in homogeneous networks, and the method ran out of time for the heterogeneous networks. We observe that NODE2BITS-SH outperforms NODE2BITS-LN in most cases, which is reasonable because NODE2BITS-LN derives shorter contexts constrained by temporal-order. We also justify the effectiveness of temporal random walk by comparing it with both NODE2BITS-0 and static baselines where we only make use of the graph structures without specifying edge timestamps. We observe that NODE2BITS-0 is the best-performing method for the digg dataset and Comp-X over the temporal variants of NODE2BITS. The reason behind this is that there is a tradeoff in constraining temporal walks to respect time: we more accurately model realistic sequences of events at the cost of restricting the possible context. On these particular temporal graphs, walks may already be limited in length by the bipartite structure, so the latter cost becomes more appreciable. Nevertheless, both static and dynamic versions of NODE2BITS almost always outperform other baselines. In particular, across all datasets, NODE2BITS-SH still outperforms the temporal baseline, CTDNE in all cases, which further demonstrates the effectiveness of multi-feature aggregation.

Table 4. Entity resolution results for *temporal* networks: strong performance for NODE2BITS variants. — OOT = Out Of Time (6 h); OOM = Out Of Memory (16 GB); * denotes statistically significant improvement over the best baseline at $p < 0.05$ in a two-sided t-test.

	Metric	CN	SE	LINE	DW	n2vec	s2vec	DNGR	AspEm	CTDNE	N2B-0	N2B-SH	N2B-LN
bitcoin	AUC	0.7474	0.5828	0.6071	0.6306	0.6462	0.8025	0.5909	0.5344	0.6987	0.7584	0.7609	0.7380
	ACC	0.7174	0.5842	0.5842	0.6158	0.6158	0.7263	0.5526	0.5316	0.6000	0.7211	0.7268	0.6737
	F1	0.7001	0.5728	0.5828	0.6158	0.6157	0.7263	0.5525	0.5315	0.5964	0.7209	0.7271	0.6735
digg	AUC	0.6217	0.5171	0.7878	0.7398	0.7445			0.5105	0.6967	0.8185*	0.7611	0.7587
	ACC	0.6217	0.5152	0.7694	0.6971	0.7013	OOT	OOM	0.5088	0.5915	0.7982*	0.7418	0.7444
	F1	0.5585	0.3770	0.7683	0.6960	0.7003			0.5088	0.5884	0.7958*	0.7411	0.7433
wiki	AUC	0.6997		0.7854					0.5374	0.7707	0.8230	0.8259*	0.8214
	ACC	0.6997	OOT	0.7132	OOM	OOM	OOT	OOM	0.5141	0.6488	0.7145	0.7510*	0.7103
	F1	0.6699		0.7129					0.5141	0.6398	0.7088	0.7476*	0.7067
comp-X	AUC	0.5970		0.5000					0.5213		0.8095*	0.7496	0.7525
	ACC	0.5970	OOM	0.6757	OOM	OOM	OOT	OOM	0.5103	OOM	0.8414*	0.7959	0.7975
	F1	0.5189		0.4032					0.5103		0.8154*	0.7581	0.7606

NODE2BITS variants outperform the static methods in nearly all cases except the bitcoin dataset where NODE2BITS-SH achieves lower AUC than struc2vec but higher ACC and $F1$-score. This is because NODE2BITS loses some information when representing the node contexts as binary vectors comparing with real-value representation. However, we consider this loss mild as NODE2BITS still outperforms all the other static baselines. In addition, struc2vec ran out of time on the larger datasets while NODE2BITS achieves promising performance efficiently with 3.90%–5.16% improvement in AUC and 3.58%–4.87% improvement in $F1$ score than the best baseline method. At the same time, our approach uses much less information than the static methods, since the length of the temporal walks are typically shorter than random walks that do not have to respect time.

CONCLUSION 2. *Dynamic and static variants of* NODE2BITS *outperform the other baselines by up to 5.2% in AUC and 4.9% in $F1$ score. Between the two dynamic variants, the short-term tactic performs better than the long-term one.*

Restricting the Output Space Requirements. To evaluate the performance of stitching with explicit storage requirement, we hash the real-value embeddings given by baselines into binary and achieve output storage to be consistent with NODE2BITS. We observe that NODE2BITS still achieves the best performance (refer to Table 6 in Appendix E.1 for more details).

4.3   Accuracy in Unsupervised User Stitching

As mentioned in Sect. 4.1, NODE2BITS can naturally perform unsupervised user stitching by leveraging the generated node representations as hashcodes. Only nodes mapped to the same 'buckets' are candidates for stitching together. This process allows us to stitch entities without involving quadratic comparisons between all pairs of nodes in the graph. Similarly, CN outputs a set of nodes

Table 5. Unsupervised stitching performance between CN and NODE2BITS

Metric	citeseer		yahoo		bitcoin		digg		wiki	
	CN	N2B-U	CN	N2B-U	CN	N2B-U	CN	N2B-U	CN	N2B-U
ACC	0.9141	0.8661	0.6851	0.7553	0.7474	0.7684	0.6217	0.7157	0.6997	0.7350
F1	0.9137	0.8660	0.6505	0.7518	0.7301	0.7663	0.5585	0.7074	0.6699	0.7349

sharing a certain amount of neighbors as the candidates to be stitched together. We evaluate the quality of hashing given by NODE2BITS-U against CN, and make use of the candidates to predict the testing set of node pairs given by following the same setup in Sect. 4.2 in an unsupervised scheme.

Based on the results in Table 5, we observe that NODE2BITS-U outperforms CN on every dataset other than citeseer. The reason is that in this "author contributes to paper" dataset, author references appearing in the same set of papers have high probability to correspond to the same researcher in reality. Therefore the assumption made by CN suits well this scenario, whereas NODE2BITS hashes nodes with similar features in the context instead of those with similar neighbor identities (IDs). For datasets with less strict cross-type relationship, NODE2BITS achieves 2.81%–15.12% improvement in accuracy ACC and 4.96%–26.66% improvement in $F1$ score (including digg, another bipartite graph with inner connected components of the same node types).

CONCLUSION 3. *The unsupervised variant of* NODE2BITS, NODE2BITS-U, *outperforms CN on most graphs.*

4.4 Output Storage Efficiency

Next we evaluate space efficiency of our proposed method over baselines that output node embeddings. Instead of real-value matrices, the binary hashcodes generated by NODE2BITS can be stored in the sparse format so presumably it should take trivial storage. We visualize the storage requirements in Fig. 3 and provide detailed storage usage in Table 7 in Appendix E.3.

CONCLUSION 4. *Compared to the other methods,* NODE2BITS *uses between 63× and 339× less space (while always achieving comparable or better stitching performance as shown in* Sect. 4.2).

4.5 Scalability

To evaluate the scalability, we report the runtime of applying NODE2BITS to obtain node representations for the datasets shown in Table 2 versus their numbers of edges. We note that NODE2BITS-SH runs only on temporal networks, i.e., a subset of the datasets. We also visualize the runtime of node2vec as reference, as it is designed for large graphs and is implemented in the same language

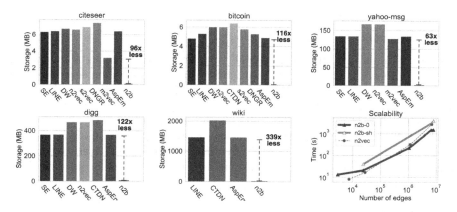

Fig. 3. First 5 plots: output storage in MB for all the methods that completed successfully in five datasets. NODE2BITS is also shown to be scalable for large graphs.

(Python). Based on the last subplot in Fig. 3, we observe that NODE2BITS scales similarly as node2vec with less runtime space as node2vec ran out of memory on the largest dataset (wiki). As shown in Appendix B, the worst-case time complexity is linear in the edges. We give the exact runtimes in Table 8 in the Appendix E.3.

5   Related Work

Entity Resolution (the general problem under which user stitching falls) has been widely studied and applied in different domains such as databases and information retrieval [9,13]. Traditional methods that are based on distances can be broadly categorized into (1) pairwise-ER [7], which independently decide which pairs are same entity based on a distance threshold, and (2) clustering [8], which links nodes in the same cluster. However, these methods are computationally expensive and do not scale to large datasets. Other techniques range from supervised classification [30] to probabilistic soft logic [20] or fingerprinting [12] using side information (*e.g.*, user-agent strings, other web browser features, geolocation). These methods tend to be problem- or even data-specific. On the contrary, our method is general by modeling the data with a heterogeneous, dynamic network that uses both node features (optional) *and* graph structure.

Node embeddings aim to preserve a notion of node similarity into low-dimensional vector space. Most general methods [14,25,32] and the state-of-the-art for heterogeneous or dynamic networks [10,23], define node similarity based on co-occurrence or proximity in the original network (Appendix F). However, in the user stitching problem, it is possible that corresponding entities may not connect to the same entities, resulting in lower proximity-based similarity. Embeddings preserving *structural identity* [1,11,16,18,19,22,27] overcome this drawback. NODE2BITS additionally handles various graph settings (heterogeneous, dynamic) at greater space efficiency thanks to hashing.

Locality sensitivity hashing (LSH) was first introduced as a randomized hashing framework for efficient approximate nearest neighbor search in high dimensional space [17]. It specifies a family of hash functions, $\mathcal{H}$, that maps similar items to the same bucket identified through hash codes with higher probability than dissimilar items [26]. LSH families for different distances have been widely studied, such as SimHash for cosine distance [5], min-hash for Jaccard similarity [3], and more (Appendix F). In our work, we leverage LSH to construct similarity-preserving and space-efficient node representations for user stitching.

6   Conclusion

We have proposed a hash-based network representation learning framework for identity stitching called NODE2BITS. It is both time- and attribute-aware, while also deriving space-efficient sparse binary embeddings of nodes in large temporal heterogeneous networks. NODE2BITS uses the notion of feature-based temporal walks to capture the temporal and feature-based information in the data. Feature-based temporal walks are a generalization of walks that obey time while also incorporating features (as opposed to node IDs). Using these walks, NODE2BITS generates contexts/sequences of temporally valid feature values. Experiments on real-world networks demonstrate the utility of NODE2BITS as it outputs space-efficient embeddings that use orders of magnitude less space compared to the baseline methods while achieving better performance in user stitching. An important practical consideration in the application of our work to user stitching is the balance of greater personalization with user privacy.

Acknowledgements. This material is based upon work supported by the National Science Foundation under Grant No. IIS 1845491, Army Young Investigator Award No. W911NF1810397, an Adobe Digital Experience and an Amazon research faculty award. Any opinions, findings, and conclusions or recommendations expressed in this material are those of the author(s) and do not necessarily reflect the views of the NSF or other funding parties.

Appendix

A   Detailed Algorithm

In Sect. 3 we gave the overview of our proposed method, NODE2BITS. For reproducibility, here we also provide its more detailed pseudocode.

Algorithm 2. NODE2BITS framework in detail

Require:

(un)directed heterogeneous graph $G(V, E, \psi, \xi)$,

number of random walks R per edge, max walk length L,

max temporal distance MAX,

embedding dimensionality $K^{\Delta t}$ at temporal dist. Δt (output dim. $K = \sum_{\Delta t=1}^{MAX} K^{\Delta t}$)

1: Construct $N \times |\mathcal{F}|$ feature matrix $\mathbf{F}$ ▷ Matrix with node attributes and derived features
2: $\mathcal{C}_u^{\Delta t} \leftarrow \emptyset,\ \forall u \in V,\ \Delta t \in [1, \ldots, MAX]$ ▷ Context of u: nodes at temporal distance Δt
3: **for** edge e and walk $= 1, \ldots, R$ **do** ▷ Perform R feature-based temporal rand. walks per edge
4:    $\langle w_L \rangle_{L \in \mathbb{N}} \leftarrow$ up to L-step temporal walk starting from edge e based on tactic ▷ Dfn. 3
5:    $\mathcal{C}_u^{\Delta t} \leftarrow$ update the context of nodes $u \in \langle w_L \rangle_{L \in \mathbb{N}}$ and all temporal distances Δt
6:    **for** $j = 1, \ldots, |\mathcal{F}|$ **do**   ▷ Iterate over all the features in matrix $\mathbf{F}$
7:      ▷ Generate the feature-based context by replacing $v \in \mathcal{C}_u^{\Delta t}$ with the $f_{v,j}$.
8:      ▷ Equivalent to context generation after a feature-based temporal walk (Dfn. 4).
9:      $\mathcal{C}_u^{\Delta t} | f_{(j)} \leftarrow$ update the feature-based context of $u \in \langle w_L \rangle_{L \in \mathbb{N}}$
10:
11: **for** $\Delta t = 1, \ldots, MAX$ **do**
12:    Generate $K^{\Delta t}$ random hyperplanes
13:    **for each** node $u \in V$ **do**   ▷ For each node, summarize its context with
14:      **for each** node $v \in \mathcal{C}_u^{\Delta t}$ **do**   ▷ a histogram per feature and node type.
15:        $\mathbf{h}(\mathcal{C}_u^{\Delta t}) = \text{concatenate}[\mathbf{h}(\mathcal{C}_u^{\Delta t} \mid f_{(1)}, p_1), \ldots, \mathbf{h}(\mathcal{C}_u^{\Delta t} \mid f_{(|\mathcal{F}|)}, p_{|\mathcal{T}_V|})]$ ▷ (Eq. (4))
16:      ▷ Obtain a sparse, binary hashcode per node based on (modified) SimHash.
17:      $z_u^{\Delta t} \leftarrow$ SimHash of node histogram $\mathbf{h}(\mathcal{C}_u^{\Delta t})$ at distance Δt
18:    $\mathbf{Z}^{\Delta t} \leftarrow N \times K^{\Delta t}$ matrix with each node's SimHash code per row
19: **return** Sparse node representation $\mathbf{Z} = \text{concatenate}[\mathbf{Z}^1, \ldots, \mathbf{Z}^{MAX}]$

B   Complexity Analysis

Time Complexity. The runtime complexity of NODE2BITS includes deriving (1) the set of R temporal random walks of length up to L, which is $\mathcal{O}(MRL)$ in the worst case; (2) the feature values of nodes in the walks from step (1); and (3) hashing the feature values of nodes in the context through random projection, which is $\mathcal{O}(NK)$. Thus, the total runtime complexity is $\mathcal{O}(MRL + NK)$, which is linear to the number of edges when $M \gg N$ as K is relatively small (**R3**).

Runtime Space Complexity. The space required in the runtime consists three parts: (1) the set of temporal random walks (represented as vectors) per edge with complexity $\mathcal{O}(MRL)$, (2) the histograms of feature contexts $N|\mathcal{F}||\mathcal{T}_V|$, and (3) the set of randomly-generated hyperplanes NK. Therefore, the total runtime space complexity is $\mathcal{O}(MRL + N(|\mathcal{F}||\mathcal{T}_V| + K))$.

Output Space Complexity. The output space complexity of NODE2BITS is $\mathcal{O}(NK)$-bit. The space required to store binary vectors is guaranteed to be $32\times$ less than vectors represented with real-value floats (4 bytes) with the same dimension. In practice, NODE2BITS requires even less storage if the binary vectors are represented in the sparse format (see Sect. 4.4 for empirical results).

C   Data Description

Below we provide a more detailed description of the network datasets that we use in our experiments (Table 2).

- **citeseer**: CiteSeerX is an undirected, heterogeneous network that contains the bipartite relations between authors and papers they contributed.
- **yahoo**: Yahoo! Messenger Logs is a heterogeneous network capturing message exchanges between users at different locations (node attribute).
- **bitcoin**: soc-bitcoinA is a who-trusts-whom network on the Bitcoin Alpha platform. The directed edges indicate user ratings.
- **digg**: This heterogeneous network consists of users voting stories that they like and forming friendships with other users.
- **wiki**: wiki-talk is a temporal homogeneous network capturing Wikipedia users editing each other's Talk page over time.
- **comp-X**: A temporal heterogeneous network is derived from a company's web logs and consists of web sessions of users and their IPs. In the stitching task, we predict the web session IDs that correspond to the same user.

D   Configuration of Baselines

As we mentioned in Sect. 4.1, we configured all the baselines to achieve the best performance according to the respective papers. For all the baselines that are based on random walks (*i.e.*, node2vec, struc2vec, DeepWalk, metapath2vec, CTDNE), we set the number of walks to 20 and the maximum walk length to $L = 20$. For node2vec, we perform grid search over $p, q \in \{0.25, 0.50, 1, 2, 4\}$ as mentioned in [14] and report the best performance. For metapath2vec, we adopt the recommended meta-path "Type 1-Type 2-Type 1" (*e.g.*, type 1 = author; type 2 = publication). In DNGR, we set the random surfing probability $\alpha = 0.98$ and use a 3-layer neural network model where the hidden layer has 1024 nodes. We use 2nd-LINE to incorporate 2nd-order proximity in the graph. For all the embedding methods, we set the embedding dimension to $K = 128$. Unlike those, CN outputs clusters, each of which corresponds to one entity.

E   Additional Empirical Analysis

E.1   Justification of Hashing

In this experiment we hash the outputs given by baseline embedding methods using SimHash [5] and then perform stitching on two temporal graphs to study their performance under the constraint of storage comparable to NODE2BITS. Based on Table 6, we observe fluctuation in the stitching performance of baseline methods, for example, almost all baselines got degenerated scores in all metrics on the bitcoin dataset, especially for struc2vec. On the other hand, however, node2vec, LINE and CTDNE got slight increased scores on yahoo dataset, which

Table 6. Justification of hashing

	Metric	SC*	LINE*	DW*	n2vec*	CTDNE	s2vec*	AspEm	N2B-0	N2B-SH	N2B-LN
bitcoin	**AUC**	0.5160	0.5807	0.5904	0.6265	0.6652	0.7703	0.5212	0.7584	0.7754	0.7380
	ACC	0.5158	0.5421	0.5632	0.5895	0.6632	0.7105	0.5211	0.7211	0.7368	0.6737
	F1	0.3757	0.5415	0.5611	0.5893	0.6608	0.7087	0.3334	0.7209	0.7361	0.6735
digg	**AUC**	0.5001	0.7909	0.7607	0.7599	0.7203		0.5000	0.8185	0.7611	0.7587
	ACC	0.5001	0.7751	0.7039	0.7030	0.6357	OOT	0.5000	0.7982	0.7418	0.7444
	F1	0.3338	0.7746	0.7039	0.7030	0.6228		0.3332	0.7958	0.7411	0.7433

is likely due to the fact that the small real-values are amplified when hashed into binary for logistic regression binary classification. It is also possibly due to the graph structure. We leave further discussion in the future work, but nevertheless, NODE2BITS outperforms these baselines in all cases. This empirical experiment demonstrates that NODE2BITS effectively preserves context information in the binary hashcodes.

E.2   Sensitivity Analysis

We also perform sensitivity analysis of the hyperparameters used in this work on the bitcoin dataset. Particularly, we perform grid analysis by varying (1) max temporal distances, (2) the number of temporal walks per edge and (3) the length of walks. The results are given in Fig. 4. Figure 4a indicates that when MAX = 3, NODE2BITS achieves the best performance. This implies that although it is potentially beneficial to incorporate nodes in temporally distant contexts, it will also incorporate information that is less relevant. Therefore, we set MAX = 3 by default for the experiments in this work. Figure 4b and c imply that the performance of NODE2BITS is not significantly affected by the number of walks performed or the length of these temporal walks. This is reasonable because NODE2BITS leverages these temporal walks to collect node features into the context and normalizes their occurrences in the histograms. Thus, adding

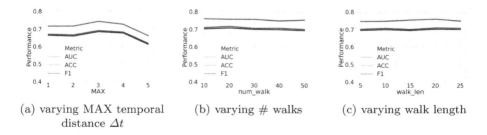

(a) varying MAX temporal distance Δt (b) varying # walks   (c) varying walk length

Fig. 4. Sensitivity Analysis on bitcoin dataset. NODE2BITS achieves highest scores in AUC, ACC and F-1 score when MAX = 3. Increasing the numbers of walks or increasing their lengths do not significantly affect the performance of NODE2BITS.

more nodes in the ordered temporal contexts does not provide extra useful information. We empirically set the number of walks per edge to be 10 and the lengths to be 20 in the experiments of this work.

E.3   Output Storage and Runtime in Detail

We report detailed output storage in Table 7 and the time elapsed when running all methods in Table 8. It can be seen that the node-wise sparse binary vectors generated by NODE2BITS take trivial amount of storage compared to the other methods, while its runtime is comparable to node2vec. NODE2BITS finished running on all datasets while most baselines fail to finish within the time limit on the large datasets, digg and wiki.

Table 7. Space required to store the output in MB. node2bits requires 63×–339× less space than other embedding methods. '–' indicates that the method does not apply to that dataset, or encounters errors such as out-of-memory or out-of-time.

datasets	SC	LINE	DW	n2v	CTDNE	s2vec	DNGR	m2vec	AspEm	N2B
citeseer	6.3	6.4	6.7	6.6	–	6.9	7.4	3.2	6.4	0.033
yahoo	134.4	134.3	167.8	167.6	–	–	–	127.7	134.3	2.1
bitcoin	4.8	5.3	6.0	6.0	6.4	5.8	5.3	–	4.9	0.041
digg	369.1	370.0	469.8	469.8	486.6	–	–	–	369.3	2.9
wiki	–	1430	–	–	1980	–	–	–	1430	4.2

Table 8. Comparison between NODE2BITS and baselines in terms of runtime (in seconds). Note the runtime of dynamic NODE2BITS (short-term) for the *temporal* networks is shown in parentheses.

	citeseer	yahoo	bitcoin	digg	wiki
SC	23.72	766.42	4.80	8091.09	1
LINE*	144.94	223.87	134.48	227.28	415.00
DW*	8.90	209.72	16.99	2115.86	–
n2v*	7.99	222.14	15.91	2751.91	–
CTDNE	–	–	13.25	2227.66	4217.19
s2vec*	325.38	–	897.2	–	–
DNGR	128.63	–	97.09	–	–
m2vec	125.98	–	–	–	–
AspEm	0.62	4.70	0.71	15.318	386.24
CN	0.58	19.59	0.70	63.95	109.11
N2B	13.15	221.84	20.52 (39.97)	1507.95 (3062.13)	1537.24 (3997.85)

F   Additional Related Work

In this section we provide additional related work, complementing our discussion in Sect. 5.

Node Embeddings. Here we give some more details about proximity-based methods, which we employ in our experiments. DeepWalk [25] and node2vec [14] leverage vanilla and 2-order random walk, respectively, to explore the identities of the neighborhood; LINE [32] can be seen as a special case of DeepWalk by setting the context to be 1 [45]; metapath2vec [10] relies on predefined meta-schema to perform random walk in heterogeneous networks. In the field of temporal network embedding, most approaches [37,51] approximate the dynamic network as discrete static snapshots overtime, which does not apply to user stitching tasks as sessions corresponding to the same user could occur in multiple timespans. CTDNE [23] first explores temporal proximity by learning temporally valid embeddings based on a corpus of temporal random walks. Another related field is hashing-based embedding, for example, node2hash [34] proposes to hash the pairwise node proximity derived from random walk into low-dimensional hash-code as the embeddings. Due to the quadratic complexity in computing the pairwise proximity between nodes, node2hash does not apply to large-scale networks. One limitation of these methods is that training a skip-gram architecture on the entire corpus sampled by random walks can be memory-intensive. A further limitation of these approaches, as well as existing deep architectures [15,49] is that for nodes to have similar embeddings, they must be in close proximity (e.g. neighbors or nodes with several common neighbors) in the network. This is not necessarily the case for user stitching, where corresponding entities may exhibit similar behavior (resulting in similar local topologies) but not connect to the same entities.

Compared with proximity-based methods, embedding works exploring structural equivalence or similarity [1,11,16,18,19,22,27,46] are more suitable to handle user stitching. Representative examples include the following: struc2vec [27], xNetMf [16], and EMBER [18] define similarity in terms of degree sequences in node-centric subgraphs; DeepGL [29] learns deep relational functions applied to degree, triangle counts and other graph invariants in an inductive scheme. Role2vec [1] proposes a framework that inductively learns structural similarity by introducing attributed random walk atop relational operators, while MultiLENS [19] summarizes node embeddings obtained by recursive application of relational operators. CCTN [22] embeds and clusters nodes in a network that are not only well-connected but also share similar behavioral patterns (*e.g.*, similar patterns in the degree or other structural properties over time).

Locality Sensitivity Hashing (LSH). More recently, LSH functions that are robust to distortion [35]; require less storage of the hash codes [41,50]; generate codewords with balanced amounts of items [39] or compute hash functions efficiently [38,40,42,48] have attracted much attention. LSH has been used in a variety of data mining applications, including network alignment [36], network inference [47], anomaly detection [44], and more. In addition, there are also works devoted to learning to hash [35] where the main idea is to learn hash codes through an optimization objective function, or intelligently probe multiple adjacent code words that are likely to contain query results in a hash table for similarity search [43]. But these methods do not apply to large-scale graphs directly.

References

1. Ahmed, N.K., et al.: Learning role-based graph embeddings. In: StarAI workshop at IJCAI (2018)
2. Bhattacharya, I., Getoor, L.: Collective entity resolution in relational data. TKDD **1**(1), 1–36 (2007)
3. Broder, A.Z., Glassman, S.C., Manasse, M.S., Zweig, G.: Syntactic clustering of the web. Compu. Netw. ISDN Syst. **29**(8), 1157–1166 (1997)
4. Cao, S., Lu, W., Xu, Q.: Deep neural networks for learning graph representations. In: AAAI, pp. 1145–1152 (2016)
5. Charikar, M.S.: Similarity estimation techniques from rounding algorithms. In: STOC, pp. 380–388 (2002)
6. Christen, P.: Concepts and Techniques for Record Linkage, Entity Resolution, and Duplicate Detection. Springer, Heidelberg (2012)
7. Cohen, W.W., Richman, J.: Learning to match and cluster large high-dimensional data sets for data integration. In: KDD, pp. 475–480 (2002)
8. Dasgupta, A., Gurevich, M., Zhang, L., Tseng, B., Thomas, A.O.: Overcoming browser cookie churn with clustering. In: WSDM, pp. 83–92 (2012)
9. Dong, X.L., Naumann, F.: Data fusion: resolving data conflicts for integration. VLDB **2**(2), 1654–1655 (2009)
10. Dong, Y., Chawla, N.V., Swami, A.: metapath2vec: scalable representation learning for heterogeneous networks. In: KDD, pp. 135–144 (2017)
11. Donnat, C., Zitnik, M., Hallac, D., Leskovec, J.: Learning structural node embeddings via diffusion wavelets. In: KDD, pp. 1320–1329 (2018)
12. Eckersley, P.: How unique is your web browser? In: Atallah, M.J., Hopper, N.J. (eds.) PETS 2010. LNCS, vol. 6205, pp. 1–18. Springer, Heidelberg (2010). https://doi.org/10.1007/978-3-642-14527-8_1
13. Getoor, L., Machanavajjhala, A.: Entity resolution for big data. In: KDD, pp. 1527–1527 (2013)
14. Grover, A., Leskovec, J.: node2vec: scalable feature learning for networks. In: KDD, pp. 855–864 (2016)
15. Hamilton, W., Ying, Z., Leskovec, J.: Inductive representation learning on large graphs. In: NeurIPS, pp. 1024–1034 (2017)
16. Heimann, M., Shen, H., Safavi, T., Koutra, D.: Regal: representation learning-based graph alignment. In: CIKM, pp. 117–126 (2018)
17. Indyk, P., Motwani, R.: Approximate nearest neighbors: towards removing the curse of dimensionality. In: STOC, pp. 604–613 (1998)
18. Jin, D., et al.: Smart roles: inferring professional roles in email networks. In: KDD (2019)
19. Jin, D., Rossi, R.A., Koh, E., Kim, S., Rao, A., Koutra, D.: Latent network summarization: bridging network embedding and summarization. In: KDD (2019)

20. Kim, S., Kini, N., Pujara, J., Koh, E., Getoor, L.: Probabilistic visitor stitching on cross-device web logs. In: WWW, pp. 1581–1589 (2017)
21. Kolb, L., Thor, A., Rahm, E.: Dedoop: efficient deduplication with Hadoop. VLDB **5**(12), 1878–1881 (2012)
22. Liu, Y., Zhu, L., Szekely, P., Galstyan, A., Koutra, D.: Coupled clustering of time-series and networks. In: SDM (2019)
23. Nguyen, G.H., Lee, J.B., Rossi, R.A., Ahmed, N.K., Koh, E., Kim, S.: Continuous-time dynamic network embeddings. In: WWW BigNet (2018)
24. Papadakis, G., Svirsky, J., Gal, A., Palpanas, T.: Comparative analysis of approximate blocking techniques for entity resolution. VLDB **9**(9), 684–695 (2016)
25. Perozzi, B., Al-Rfou, R., Skiena, S.: DeepWalk: online learning of social representations. In: KDD (2014)
26. Rajaraman, A., Leskovec, J., Ullman, J.D.: Mining Massive Datasets (2014)
27. Ribeiro, L.F., Saverese, P.H., Figueiredo, D.R.: struc2vec: learning node representations from structural identity. In: KDD, pp. 385–394 (2017)
28. Rossi, R.A., Ahmed, N.K.: The network data repository with interactive graph analytics and visualization. In: AAAI (2015). http://networkrepository.com
29. Rossi, R.A., Zhou, R., Ahmed, N.K.: Deep inductive network representation learning. In: WWW, pp. 953–960 (2018)
30. Saha Roy, R., Sinha, R., Chhaya, N., Saini, S.: Probabilistic deduplication of anonymous web traffic. In: WWW, pp. 103–104 (2015)
31. Shi, Y., Gui, H., Zhu, Q., Kaplan, L., Han, J.: AspEm: embedding learning by aspects in heterogeneous information networks. In: SDM, pp. 144–152. SIAM (2018)
32. Tang, J., Qu, M., Wang, M., Zhang, M., Yan, J., Mei, Q.: LINE: large-scale information network embedding. In: WWW (2015)
33. Von Luxburg, U.: A tutorial on spectral clustering. Stat. Comput. **17**(4), 395–416 (2007)
34. Wang, Q., Wang, S., Gong, M., Wu, Y.: Feature hashing for network representation learning. In: IJCAI, pp. 2812–2818 (2018)

Additional References

35. Aghazadeh, A., Lan, A., Shrivastava, A., Baraniuk, R.: RHash: robust hashing via l-norm distortion. In: IJCAI, pp. 1386–1394 (2017)
36. Heimann, M., Lee, W., Pan, S., Chen, K.-Y., Koutra, D.: HashAlign: hash-based alignment of multiple graphs. In: Phung, D., Tseng, V.S., Webb, G.I., Ho, B., Ganji, M., Rashidi, L. (eds.) PAKDD 2018. LNCS (LNAI), vol. 10939, pp. 726–739. Springer, Cham (2018). https://doi.org/10.1007/978-3-319-93040-4_57
37. Hisano, R.: Semi-supervised graph embedding approach to dynamic link prediction. In: Cornelius, S., Coronges, K., Gonçalves, B., Sinatra, R., Vespignani, A. (eds.) CompleNet 2018. SPC, pp. 109–121. Springer, Cham (2018). https://doi.org/10.1007/978-3-319-73198-8_10
38. Ji, J., Li, J., Yan, S., Tian, Q., Zhang, B.: Min-max hash for Jaccard similarity. In: ICDM, pp. 301–309 (2013)
39. Kang, B., Jung, K.: Robust and efficient locality sensitive hashing for nearest neighbor search in large data sets. In: NeurIPS BigLearn Workshop, pp. 1–8 (2012)
40. Li, P., Hastie, T.J., Church, K.W.: Very sparse random projections. In: KDD, pp. 287–296 (2006)

41. Li, P., König, A.C.: Theory and applications of b-bit minwise hashing. Comm. ACM **54**(8), 101–109 (2011)
42. Li, P., Owen, A., Zhang, C.H.: One permutation hashing. In: NeurIPS, pp. 3113–3121 (2012)
43. Lv, Q., Josephson, W., Wang, Z., Charikar, M., Li, K.: Multi-probe LSH: efficient indexing for high-dimensional similarity search. In: VLDB, pp. 950–961 (2007)
44. Manzoor, E., Milajerdi, S.M., Akoglu, L.: Fast memory-efficient anomaly detection in streaming heterogeneous graphs. In: KDD, pp. 1035–1044 (2016)
45. Qiu, J., Dong, Y., Ma, H., Li, J., Wang, K., Tang, J.: Network embedding as matrix factorization: Unifying DeepWalk, LINE, PTE, and node2vec. In: WSDM, pp. 459–467 (2018)
46. Rossi, R.A., Ahmed, N.K.: Role discovery in networks. TKDE **27**(4), 1112–1131 (2015)
47. Safavi, T., Sripada, C., Koutra, D.: Scalable hashing-based network discovery. In: ICDM, pp. 405–414, November 2017
48. Shrivastava, A., Li, P.: Densifying one permutation hashing via rotation for fast near neighbor search. In: ICML, pp. 557–565 (2014)
49. Wang, D., Cui, P., Zhu, W.: Structural deep network embedding. In: KDD, pp. 1225–1234 (2016)
50. Weiss, Y., Torralba, A., Fergus, R.: Spectral hashing. In: NeurIPS, pp. 1753–1760 (2009)
51. Zhu, L., Guo, D., Yin, J., Ver Steeg, G., Galstyan, A.: Scalable temporal latent space inference for link prediction in dynamic social networks. IEEE TKDE **28**(10), 2765–2777 (2016)

A Soft Affiliation Graph Model for Scalable Overlapping Community Detection

Nishma Laitonjam[(✉)], Wěipéng Huáng, and Neil J. Hurley

Insight Centre for Data Analytics, University College Dublin, Dublin, Ireland
{nishma.laitonjam,weipeng.huang,neil.hurley}@insight-centre.org

Abstract. We propose an overlapping community model based on the Affiliation Graph Model (AGM), that exhibits the pluralistic homophily property that the probability of a link between nodes increases with increasing number of shared communities. We take inspiration from the Mixed Membership Stochastic Blockmodel (MMSB), in proposing an edgewise community affiliation. This allows decoupling of community affiliations between nodes, opening the way to scalable inference. We show that our model corresponds to an AGM with soft community affiliations and develop a scalable algorithm based on a Stochastic Gradient Riemannian Langevin Dynamics (SGRLD) sampler. Empirical results show that the model can scale to network sizes that are beyond the capabilities of MCMC samplers of the standard AGM. We achieve comparable performance in terms of accuracy and run-time efficiency to scalable MMSB samplers.

1 Introduction

Designing a scalable Markov Chain Monte Carlo (MCMC) inference for a Bayesian model is challenging due to the sequential nature of the mechanism, especially when the model parameters are huge in number and the dataset is large. Probabilistic graphical models define how the observed data is generated and often involve a large number of random variables. A case in point is the modelling of network data, where the datasets of interest nowadays scale to millions of nodes and a typical problem of interest is the extraction of community structure from the network. Many heuristic methods and probabilistic models have been proposed for this problem. In this paper, we focus on the extraction of overlapping community structure. Considering that any subset of the nodes could constitute such an overlapping community, we have *a-priori*, 2^N candidate communities, where N is the number of nodes in the network.

The Affiliation graph model (AGM) [22] is a probabilistic graphical model of overlapping community structures in networks. It proposes a likelihood that exhibits the *pluralistic homophily* property, meaning that the probability of a

Electronic supplementary material The online version of this chapter (https://doi.org/10.1007/978-3-030-46150-8_30) contains supplementary material, which is available to authorized users.

© Springer Nature Switzerland AG 2020
U. Brefeld et al. (Eds.): ECML PKDD 2019, LNAI 11906, pp. 507–523, 2020.
https://doi.org/10.1007/978-3-030-46150-8_30

link between nodes increases with increasing number of shared communities. This property has been observed in the ground truth communities of real world data [22]. The heuristic algorithm proposed in [23] maximises the likelihood through a Non-negative Matrix Factorization (NMF) step and is a good benchmark for community-finding at scale. However, we are interested in developing MCMC algorithms that can sample from the true posterior distribution of the communities. A number of works have examined MCMC inference on models based on the AGM likelihood. For instance, using a Gamma process prior, [25] develop a non-parametric model which is sampled through Gibbs sampling and apply it to networks with the number of nodes and the number of edges below 10^4. The Infinite Multiple Membership Relational model (IMRM) [15] finds general overlapping block structure and reduces to the AGM likelihood when constrained to only within-block interactions. IMRM scales to networks of around 10^5 edges, on which it takes around 70 h for 2,500 iterations.

Another network model of block structure in networks is the Mixed Membership Stochastic Blockmodel (MMSB) [2] and its variant, the assortative-Mixed Membership Stochastic Blockmodel (a-MMSB), that models overlapping communities in the sense that nodes have mixed affiliations to multiple communities. However, the a-MMSB does not exhibit pluralistic homophily because the probability of an edge between two nodes does not increase with the total number of communities that they share. In contrast to the AGM, scalable inference techniques for the MMSB have been proposed in the state-of-the-art, for example, through the use of Stochastic Variational Inference (SVI) [9] and Stochastic Gradient-MCMC (SG-MCMC) [13], that achieve scalability by considering only a mini-batch of the dataset in each update step. Our contribution in this paper, is to propose a new variant of the AGM, which we call the *Soft* AGM (S-AGM), that is inspired by the a-MMSB but maintains the pluralistic homophily property of the AGM. Our model is amenable to the same inference strategies that have proven capable of scaling the MMSB to big network problems. In particular, in this paper, we will discuss how we have developed a SG-MCMC for the *Soft* AGM. Along with the advantage of using a mini-batch in each iteration, the SG-MCMC algorithm is highly parallelizable. We have developed it on **Tensorflow** and achieved tractable inference, beyond the capabilities of other MCMC samplers of the AGM, with networks of 10^5 edges converging within 2 h on a 2.2 GHz Intel Core i7 processor.

The paper is structured as follows. In Sect. 2, we present the generative model of the S-AGM and show how, by collapsing the edge-wise community affiliation parameters, it may be interpreted as an AGM model with soft community affiliations. In Sect. 4, we discuss how to apply a Stochastic Gradient Riemannian Langevin Dynamics sampler to the model parameters, and derive the required gradients. In Sect. 5, we present some experimental results. Finally, we discuss the comparison of the resultant communities with ground truth communities and the merits of our model in comparison to the AGM.

2   Model

Consider an unweighted graph of $N > 0$ nodes, with adjacency matrix $A = \{a_{ij}\}$. Let the training set node pairs, E, be partitioned into the non-link pairs, $E_{NL} = \{(i,j)|a_{ij} = 0\}$ and the link pairs $E_L = \{(i,j)|a_{ij} = 1\}$, such that $E = E_{NL} \cup E_L$. We seek overlapping community structure with $K > 0$ communities. The Affiliation Graph Model (AGM) provides a generative model for networks with latent overlapping community structure, where the likelihood of the network is given by

$$p(A|\Theta) = \prod_{i=1}^{N} \prod_{j>i}^{N} p_{ij}^{a_{ij}} (1 - p_{ij})^{1-a_{ij}} \tag{1}$$

with $\Theta = \{Z = \{z_{ik}\}, \pi\}$ and $p_{ij} = 1 - (1 - \pi_\epsilon) \prod_{k=1}^{K} (1 - \pi_k)^{z_{ik}z_{jk}}$, such that $z_{ik} = 1$ whenever node i is a member of community k, $p(z_{ik}|w_k) \sim \text{Bernoulli}(w_k)$. The community edge density parameters are $\pi_k \sim \text{Beta}(\eta_{k0}, \eta_{k1})$ and π_ϵ is a fixed background edge density. That the model exhibits *pluralistic homophily*, can most easily be observed by noting that, if all the community densities π were equal, then the probability that an edge (i,j) does not exist is proportional to $(1-\pi)^{\sum_k z_{ik}z_{jk}}$ i.e. $(1-\pi)^{s(i,j)}$, where $s(i,j) = \sum_k z_{ik}z_{jk}$ is the number of shared communities. One challenge for Bayesian inference from this model is that the conditional probabilities of the communities assignments $Z = \{z_{ik}\}$ given the network are all inter-dependent and thus require sequential Gibbs sampler.

Motivated to develop a more scalable model that maintains pluralistic homophily, we take inspiration from the assortative Mixed Membership Stochastic Blockmodel (a-MMSB) and propose the *Soft* AGM (S-AGM) as follows: consider that, associated with each node i of the network and each community k, there is a soft community affiliation value, $w_{ik} \in [0,1]$. Now, for all possible interactions between nodes, i and j, each node draws a set of community membership assignments, $z_{ijk} \sim \text{Bernoulli}(w_{ik})$ and $z_{jik} \sim \text{Bernoulli}(w_{jk})$, and the interaction occurs with probability depending on the number of shared communities that are drawn:

$$p_{ij} = 1 - (1 - \pi_\epsilon) \prod_{k=1}^{K} (1 - \pi_k)^{z_{ijk}z_{jik}} . \tag{2}$$

Note that in the S-AGM, each community affiliation is drawn independently from a Bernoulli distribution, so that multiple simultaneous affiliations are allowed and the existence of an edge depends on the overlap of the multiple affiliations between node pairs. In contrast, in the a-MMSB, for each interaction, a *single* community affiliation z_{ijk} is drawn from $\text{Cat}(\mathbf{w}_i)$, where $\sum_k w_{ik} = 1$ and hence $\sum_k z_{ijk} = 1$. The existence of an edge is dependent on whether the single community drawn by node i coincides with that drawn by node j i.e. whether or not $z_{ijk}z_{jik} = 1$ is true. There is therefore no notion of multiple affiliations contributing to an interaction and hence the a-MMSB fails to model pluralistic affiliation.

From a scalability point-of-view, drawing the set of community affiliations independently for each interaction, has the effect of de-coupling the $Z = \{z_{ijk}\}$, so that their conditional probabilities given the network (given in Sect. 3), can be updated in parallel.

The generative process model of S-AGM is given in Algorithm 1. Note that a separate parameter α_k is drawn for each community, modelling that each community may have a different node density.

Algorithm 1. Generative process model

1: **for** $k = 1 : K$ **do**
2:     $\pi_k \sim \text{Beta}(\eta_{k0}, \eta_{k1})$
3: **for** $k = 1 : K$ **do**
4:     $\alpha_k \sim \text{Gamma}(\beta_0, \beta_1)$
5:     **for** $i = 1 : N$ **do**
6:         $w_{ik} \sim \text{Beta}(\alpha_k, 1)$
7: **for** $i = 1 : (N - 1)$ **do**
8:     **for** $j = (i + 1) : N$ **do**
9:         **for** $k = 1 : K$ **do**
10:             $z_{ijk} \sim \text{Bernoulli}(w_{ik})$
11:             $z_{jik} \sim \text{Bernoulli}(w_{jk})$
12:         $p_{ij} = 1 - (1 - \pi_\epsilon) \prod_{k=1}^{K} (1 - \pi_k)^{z_{ijk} z_{jik}}$
13:         $a_{ij} \sim \text{Bernoulli}(p_{ij})$

In fact it is possible to marginalise $p(A, Z, W, \alpha, \pi | \eta, \beta)$, with respect to Z. In Supplementary Material, we show the following lemma,

Lemma 1. *Collapsing* Z: $P(A|W, \pi) = \sum_Z P(A, Z|W, \pi)$ *is given by Eq. (1) with* $\Theta = \{W = \{w_{ik}\}, \pi\}$ *and* $p_{ij} = \rho_{ij}(W, \pi) \triangleq 1 - (1 - \pi_\epsilon) \prod_{k=1}^{K} (1 - \pi_k w_{ik} w_{jk})$.

In this form, we explicitly observe that the S-AGM corresponds to the AGM when w_{ik} are restricted to $\{0, 1\}$. The model may also be compared with the Gamma Process Edge Partition Model (GP-EPM), proposed in [25], in which w_{ik} are drawn from a Gamma distribution and $p_{ij} = 1 - (1 - \pi_\epsilon) \prod_{k=1}^{K} (1 - \pi_k)^{w_{ik} w_{jk}}$. Note that aside from the difference in the form of the edge-connection probability, in the S-AGM, the w_{ik} are restricted to the probability simplex $[0, 1]$, while any positive affiliation weight is allowed in the GP-EPM.

3   MCMC on the Non-collapsed Model

We firstly consider a simple inference strategy on the non-collapsed model and compare the results obtained from S-AGM with those obtained from AGM and a-MMSB. It may be verified that the posterior distribution of α is a Gamma distribution. A Gibbs sampling of the components of α can be carried out independently in parallel. In particular,

$$\alpha_k | w_{\cdot k} \sim \text{Gamma}\left(N + \beta_0, \beta_1 - \sum_i \log(w_{ik})\right). \tag{3}$$

Similarly, we use Gibbs sampling of W with

$$w_{ik} | \alpha_k, Z \sim \text{Beta}(\alpha_k + \sum_{j \neq i} z_{ijk}, 1 + \sum_{j \neq i} (1 - z_{ijk})).$$

The community assignment for each training pair (i, j), i.e. $z_{ij\cdot}$ and $z_{ji\cdot}$ can be sampled in parallel. In particular for each community k, Gibbs sampling is used with

$$z_{ijk}, z_{jik} | Z \setminus \{z_{ijk}, z_{jik}\}, A, W, \pi$$
$$\propto w_{ik}^{z_{ijk}} w_{jk}^{z_{jik}} (1 - w_{ik})^{1 - z_{ijk}} (1 - w_{jk})^{1 - z_{jik}} p_{ij}^{a_{ij}} (1 - p_{ij})^{1 - a_{ij}},$$

where p_{ij}, is given by Eq. (2). As the posterior distribution of π is not in the form of a standard distribution, we use Hamiltonian Monte Carlo (HMC) MCMC to sample from π.

4   Scalable MCMC for the Model

The soft community assignments, W, are the output of most interest from the model. We consider ways to obtain scalable inference with Z collapsed i.e. we seek the posterior distribution, $p(W, \pi, \alpha | A, \eta, \beta)$. The MCMC algorithm iterates updating local parameters (W) and global parameters (π and α). In the case of W and π, we consider sampling strategies that can efficiently explore the sample space.

The Metropolis Adjusted Langevin Algorithm (MALA) [19] is a Metropolis Hastings algorithm with a proposal distribution $q(\theta^* | \theta)$ of the form

$$\theta^* = \theta + \frac{\epsilon}{2}\left(\nabla_\theta \log p(\theta) + \sum_{i=1}^{N} \nabla_\theta p(x_i | \theta)\right) + \xi$$

where ϵ is a fixed step size and $\xi \sim N(0, \epsilon I)$. In [8], it is suggested that MALA can be improved for ill-conditioned problems by introducing an appropriate Riemann manifold pre-conditioner $G(\theta)$, so that the proposal distribution becomes

$$\theta^* = \theta + \frac{\epsilon}{2}\mu(\theta) + G^{-1/2}\xi,$$

where, for an M-dimensional θ, the jth component of $\mu(\theta)$ is given by,

$$\mu(\theta)_j = \left(G^{-1}\nabla_\theta \log p(\theta | X)\right)_j - 2\sum_{k=1}^{M}\left(G^{-1}\frac{dG}{d\theta_k}G^{-1}\right)_{jk} + \sum_{k=1}^{M} G_{jk}^{-1} \text{Tr}\left(G^{-1}\frac{dG}{d\theta_k}\right).$$

In [21], the expensive Metropolis correction step is not adopted. Instead, a mini-batch of the dataset D_t is sampled from X for each iteration and an unbiased but noisy estimate of the gradient is used: $\sum_{i=1}^{N} \nabla_\theta p(x_i|\theta) \approx \frac{N}{|D_t|} \sum_{x_i \in D_t} \nabla_\theta p(x_i|\theta)$ with a variable step-size ϵ_t. Convergence to the true posterior is guaranteed as long as decaying step sizes satisfy $\sum_{t=1}^{\infty} \epsilon_t = \infty$ and $\sum_{t=1}^{\infty} \epsilon_t^2 < \infty$. When applied with a Riemann manifold pre-conditioner, this method is referred to as Stochastic Gradient Riemannian Langevin Dynamics (SGRLD).

We follow [18] to develop an SGRLD algorithm for sampling π and W for the S-AGM. In particular, as these parameters are restricted to $[0, 1]$, it is necessary to re-parameterize so that the update step yields valid proposals in the parameter range. We adopt the expanded mean re-parameterization with mirroring strategy for Dirichlet parameters which is recommended in [18]. In this case, the preconditioner is chosen as $G^{-1} = \text{diag}(\theta)$, and the last two terms of $\mu(\theta)_j$ evaluate to 2 and −1 respectively.

4.1   Sampling π and W

We re-parameterize $\pi_k = \frac{\pi'_{k0}}{\pi'_{k0} + \pi'_{k1}}$, where for $m \in \{0, 1\}$, $\pi'_{km} \sim \text{Gamma}(\eta_{km}, 1)$. The SGRLD update equations for π', taking absolute value to maintain the proposal in the range $\pi'^*_{km} > 0$, becomes

$$\pi'^*_{km} = \left| \pi'_{km} + \frac{\epsilon_t}{2} \mu(\pi'_{km}) + (\pi'_{km})^{1/2} \xi_{km} \right|, \tag{4}$$

with $\xi_{km} \sim N(0, \epsilon_t)$. Then, for a mini-batch of node pairs $\mathcal{E}^t$, we obtain

$$\mu(\pi'_{km}) = \eta_{km} - \pi'_{km} + s(\mathcal{E}^t) \sum_{(i,j) \in \mathcal{E}^t} g^a_{ij}(\pi'_{km}), \tag{5}$$

where $g^a_{ij}(\pi'_{km}) \triangleq \frac{\partial}{\partial \pi'_{km}} \log p(a_{ij}|\pi', w_{i\cdot}, w_{j\cdot})$ and $s(.)$, discussed below, appropriately scales the mini-batch gradient estimate.

For each node i, we re-parameterize $w_{ik} = \frac{w'_{ik0}}{w'_{ik0} + w'_{ik1}}$ where for $m \in \{0, 1\}$, $w'_{ikm} \sim \text{Gamma}(\gamma_{km}, 1)$, $\gamma_{k0} = \alpha_k$ and $\gamma_{k1} = 1$. We perform an SGRLD update for w'_{ik} as follows:

$$w'^*_{ikm} = \left| w'_{ikm} + \frac{\epsilon}{2} \mu(w'_{ikm}) + (w'_{ikm})^{1/2} \xi_{ikm} \right|, \tag{6}$$

where $\xi_{ikm} \sim N(0, \epsilon_t)$ and for a mini-batch of nodes $\mathcal{V}^t_i$,

$$\mu(w'_{ikm}) = \gamma_{km} - w'_{ikm} + \frac{N}{|\mathcal{V}^t_i|} \sum_{j \in \mathcal{V}^t_i} g^a_{ij}(w'_{ikm}), \tag{7}$$

where $g^a_{ij}(w'_{ikm}) \triangleq \frac{\partial}{\partial w'_{ikm}} \log p(a_{ij}|\pi, w'_{i\cdot}, w'_{j\cdot})$. Full expressions for $g^a_{ij}(\pi'_{km})$ and $g^a_{ij}(w'_{ikm})$ are given in the Supplementary Material.

4.2   Mini-batch Selection

We follow the stratified random node sampling strategy which is shown to give the best gains in convergence speed for variational inference on an MMSB model in [9]. All the node pairs incident with each node i are partitioned into u sets, $\mathcal{N}_{il} \subset E_{\mathrm{NL}}$, $l = 1, \ldots, u$ of non-link pairs and one set, $\mathcal{L}_i \subseteq E_{\mathrm{L}}$, of the link pairs. Note that each node pair occurs within these sets exactly $c = 2$ times. To select the mini-batch $\mathcal{E}^t$, firstly a node i is selected at random, and then with probability $1/2$, either the link set is chosen or, otherwise, one of the non-link sets is chosen with probability $1/u$. Let $s(\mathcal{E}^t) = Nu$ if $\mathcal{E}^t = \mathcal{N}_{il}$ for some l and $s(\mathcal{E}^t) = N$ if $\mathcal{E}^t = \mathcal{L}_i$. In the Supplementary Material, we show that this choice of scaling results in an unbiased estimate of the true gradient. To update w'_{ikm}, for each node i in mini-batch $\mathcal{E}^t$ we sample a fixed number of nodes at random to form the mini-batch $\mathcal{V}_i^t$.

The pseudo-code for the full MCMC algorithm is given in Algorithm 2. All the for loops in Algorithm 2 are parallelizable.

Algorithm 2. MCMC for the S-AGM using SGRLD

1: Sample a mini-batch $\mathcal{E}^t$ of node pairs.
2: **for** Each node i in $\mathcal{E}^t$ **do**
3:     Sample a mini-batch of nodes $\mathcal{V}_i^t$.
4:     **for** $k = 1 : K$ **do**   ▷ utilizing the sampled $\mathcal{V}_i^t$
5:         Update w_{ik} according to Equations (6) and (7).
6: **for** $k = 1 : K$ **do**   ▷ utilizing the sampled $\mathcal{E}^t$
7:     Update π_k according to Equations (4) and (5).
8: **for** $k = 1 : K$ **do**
9:     Update α_k according to Equation (3).

---

5   Experimental Results

We initially developed a proof-of-concept `Matlab` code[1] both for the uncollapsed S-AGM model and for the SG-MCMC algorithm. To take advantage of the parallelizability of the collapsed model, we then implemented the SG-MCMC algorithm using `Tensorflow` [1] and ran it on a GPU.

Throughout the experiments we have chosen $\eta_{k0} = 5$, $\eta_{k1} = 1$ as the hyperparameters for the community edge probability incorporating the prior information that a community consists of strongly connected nodes. For the hyperparameters of α_k, we have chosen $\beta_0 = \beta_1 = 1$. We have initialized the probability of a node belonging to a community for S-AGM and a-MMSB to be $1/K$ which also satisfies the condition that $\sum_k 1/K = 1$ for the membership vector of the a-MMSB. The edge probabilities for each community are initialized by drawing from the prior, $\mathrm{Beta}(\eta_{k0}, \eta_{k1})$ for all models.

---

[1]   https://github.com/nishma-laitonjam/S-AGM.

To compare different community assignments we use the overlapping Normalised Mutual Information (NMI) [11]. To compare the convergence of the MCMC chain, we use area under the Receiver Operating Characteristics curve (AUC-ROC) to predict missing links of hold-out test set, T. We also use perplexity defined as the exponential of the negative average predictive log likelihood on the hold-out test set [9], i.e. $\text{perp}(T|\pi, W) = \exp\left(-\frac{\sum_{(i,j)\in T} \log p(a_{ij}|\pi, w_{i\cdot}, w_{j\cdot})}{|T|}\right)$. For small datasets, the change in log likelihood of the training dataset is also used to check for convergence.

5.1   Networks Generated by AGM

To observe whether S-AGM can recover the network structure of the AGM, we compare the two models applied to networks generated from the AGM. For this experiment, we run the SGRLD batch algorithm for S-AGM in Matlab and compare it to a Matlab implementation for AGM that uses Gibbs sampling along with HMC. We use these implementations to examine the run-time advantages of the batch SGRLD algorithm over Gibbs and HMC.

Specifically, networks with two communities are generated using the generative process of AGM, i.e set $K = 2$ and edges between nodes i and j are generated with probability $p_{ij} = 1 - (1 - \pi_\epsilon)\prod_k(1 - \pi_k)^{z_{ik}z_{jk}}$. A community assignment Z is chosen such that in each network, 20% of the nodes belong to the overlapping region of the two communities and 40% of the nodes belong to each community only. The network size is $n = 100$. For Fig. 1, we fix $\pi_k = 0.8 \,\forall k$ and vary the background edge probability π_ϵ. For Fig. 2, we fix $\pi_\epsilon = 0.00005$ and vary π_k. When fitting the models, we fix $\pi_\epsilon = 0.00005$ in all cases, so that the first experiment tests the ability of the algorithm to recover the network with different levels of background noise.

The similarity of the resultant communities with the ground truth communities is reported as NMI. The step size of SGRLD is decreased using, $\epsilon_t = a(1 + \frac{t}{b})^{-c}$ where a is the initial value, t is the iteration number, and $c \in (0.5, 1]$ is the learning rate. Following [18], we have chosen $b = 1,000$ and $c = 0.55$. For these networks, we find $a = 0.01$ performs well for sampling both π and $w_{i\cdot}$. Since S-AGM reports the community assignment of a node as a soft assignment, we use a threshold to convert to a hard assignment before computing NMI. After burn-in of 500 iterations, 500 samples are collected, and the average result of 5 random runs is reported. From Fig. 1, we can see that S-AGM with 0.5 as threshold is more tolerant to background noise than AGM. When there is no noise i.e. when $\pi_\epsilon = 0.00005$, both S-AGM and AGM are able to recover the ground truth network. As noise increases, S-AGM performs better to recover the ground truth communities as the noise is reflected in the inferred model only as a small positive probability of belonging to the other community. Thus S-AGM has higher NMI compared to AGM. From Fig. 2, when we change the within-community edge probability with fixed $\pi_\epsilon = 0.00005$, both S-AGM with 0.3 as threshold and AGM, gives similar NMI recovering the ground truth community well when the within-community edge probability is greater than or equal to 0.4.

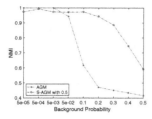

Fig. 1. NMI vs π_ϵ

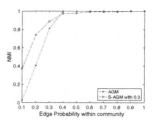

Fig. 2. NMI vs π_k

To compare the runtime between AGM and S-AGM, we generate networks with $k = 2$, $\pi_k = 0.8$ $\forall k$ and $\pi_\epsilon = 0.00005$ but of different sizes n ranging from 100 to 1,000 in a step-size of 100. After burn in of 500 iterations, 500 samples are collected, and the average AUC-ROC score of 5 random runs on Intel core i5, 4 cores is reported in Fig. 4.

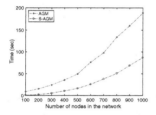

Fig. 3. Time vs n

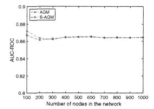

Fig. 4. AUC-ROC vs n

From Fig. 3, we can see that the batch SGRLD for S-AGM performs better than MCMC for AGM, while both give a similar AUC-ROC score. The scalability of the SGLRD for large n, using mini-batch and GPU, is explored in Sect. 5.3.

5.2   Comparing S-AGM with AGM and a-MMSB

In this section, first we show that both AGM and S-AGM exhibit pluralistic homophily. We then compare the performance of S-AGM with AGM and a-MMSB in terms of convergence of the log likelihood on the training dataset and predicting missing links on the hold-out dataset which is comprised of 20% of the node pairs in the dataset, chosen at random. For these experiments we use 3 small networks i.e. Football [17], NIPS234 [14] and Protein230 [3]. We use uncollapsed MCMC for all models with the `Matlab` code. We set the number of communities as $K = 5, 10, 15, 20$, and plot number of shared communities per node pair, i.e. $\sum_k z_{ijk} z_{jik}$ for S-AGM and $\sum_k z_{ik} z_{jk}$ for AGM, against edge probability. (As noted in Sect. 2, in the case of a-MMSB, as $\sum_k z_{ijk} z_{jik} \in \{0, 1\}$ always, there is no direct notion of pluralstic homophily in that model).

Figure 5 shows a clear increase in edge probability with increasing number of shared communities in both the AGM and S-AGM models. These plots are obtained from a single run, for various K.

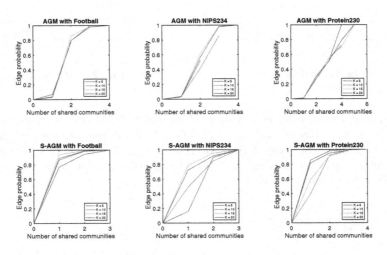

Fig. 5. Pluralistic homophily by AGM and S-AGM

Table 1 shows the average AUC under ROC curve for predicting missing links, taken over 5 random runs where, in each run, 2,500 samples are collected after burn-in of 2,500 iterations. We can see that the AUC-ROC score is very similar for the 3 models with AGM performing best for NIPS234. It may be observed from Fig. 6, that the log likelihood for AGM is highest compared to the other two models. The perplexity is computed after every 100 iterations and the trace plots from a single run are shown in Fig. 7. Again, there is little difference between the three models, even though from Fig. 6 the convergence is slower for non-collapsed S-AGM due to the larger number of parameters to learn.

Comparison with Ground Truth Communities. With the availability of ground truth communities for the Football network, we are able to compare the communities generated by S-AGM with these communities. The Football network contains the network of American football games between Division IA colleges during regular season, Fall 2000. There are 115 teams that are grouped into 11 conferences along with 8 independent teams that are not required to schedule each other for competition, like colleges within conferences must do [6]. We have used the Fruchterman-Reingold algorithm [7,20] to plot the community structure found by S-AGM alongside the ground truth communities in Fig. 8. The 8 independent teams are the black nodes in the ground truth. For the S-AGM plot, the pie-chart at each node indicates its relative membership of each found community.

Table 1. AUC-ROC

Network		Football				NIPS234				Protein230			
K		5	10	15	20	5	10	15	20	5	10	15	20
AUC-ROC	AGM	0.7097 ± 0.028	0.8055 ± 0.043	0.8316 ± 0.016	0.8240 ± 0.015	0.8280 ± 0.019	**0.9266 ± 0.009**	**0.9481 ± 0.008**	**0.9511 ± 0.008**	0.9088 ± 0.017	0.9237 ± 0.015	0.9236 ± 0.015	**0.9290 ± 0.013**
	a-MMSB	**0.8242 ± 0.020**	**0.8637 ± 0.015**	**0.8587 ± 0.016**	**0.8615 ± 0.015**	**0.8855 ± 0.011**	0.9121 ± 0.011	0.9274 ± 0.021	0.9359 ± 0.012	0.8867 ± 0.022	0.8872 ± 0.015	0.8875 ± 0.019	0.8850 ± 0.019
	S-AGM	0.7889 ± 0.017	0.8426 ± 0.021	0.8403 ± 0.017	0.8430 ± 0.017	0.8654 ± 0.028	0.9039 ± 0.016	0.9080 ± 0.021	0.9039 ± 0.0215	**0.9236 ± 0.014**	**0.9296 ± 0.009**	**0.9305 ± 0.010**	0.9287 ± 0.010

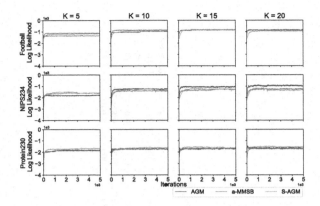

Fig. 6. Trace plot of log likelihood of training data

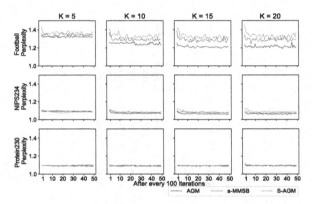

Fig. 7. Trace plot of perplexity of test data

Conferences teams play more intra-conference games than inter-conference games, thus forming a clear community structure, while the 8 independent teams play with other teams as frequently as among themselves. The S-AGM recovers the 11 conferences well when $K = 15$. Three out of 15 found communities are empty. Games between teams from different conferences are not uniform. Rather, geographically close teams tend to play each other more often [10]. This pattern is captured in the overlapping structure identified by S-AGM, where each conference team belongs to a single dominant community, but has some small probability of belonging to another conference, proportional to its distance to teams within that conference.

In Fig. 8, we focus on Western Michigan and Buffalo, two Mid American conference teams, as well as Louisiana Tech, an independent team. Clearly, Louisiana Tech has no clear community assignment, rather, it can be considered as a part of multiple conferences. It plays more games with teams in the West Atlantic conference (dark yellow) and the Southeastern conference (maroon). While Western

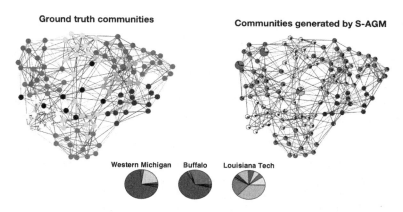

Fig. 8. Communities for Football network. (Color figure online)

Michigan and Buffalo have very strong affiliation to their own conference, due to the geographical proximity, Western Michigan plays more with teams in the Big Ten conference (Iowa and Wisconsin) while Buffallo plays more games with teams in the Big East conference (Syracuse and Rutgers).

Such overlapping structure where a node belongs to multiple communities with a different degree of overlap cannot be captured by the AGM model. In AGM a node either belongs fully to the community or not. For the Football network, with $K = 15$, AGM generates one community that contains all nodes to capture the inter-community edges and other communities as the sub-communities to capture the intra-community edges corresponding to the ground truth communities. Thus the community structure generated by the AGM doesn't provide the information that even though a team belongs to a conference, the team also plays with other teams of different conferences with different frequencies.

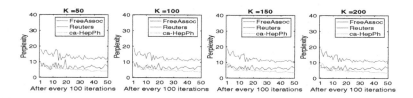

Fig. 9. Trace plot of perplexity of test data for various K

5.3   Larger Problems

For experiments on larger problems, we use the FreeAssoc network [16] (10,468 nodes and 61,677 edges), the Reuters network [4] (13,314 nodes and 148,038 edges) and the ca-HepPh network [12] (12,008 nodes and 118,489 edges) and run the mini-batch SGRLD algorithm for these networks. Taking advantage of the parallelizability of the algorithm, it is implemented on `Tensorflow` and run on a 2.2 GHz Intel Core i7 processor. To overcome the memory problem for larger networks, especially to run with GPUs, we store the network outside the limited GPU memory. Mini-batch samples are stored in the `tf.records Tensorflow` binary storage format. This speeds up the process of passing the mini-batch for each iteration to the GPUs. Thus, first the mini-batch of every 100 iterations is sampled and stored in a `tf.records` structure and one `tf.records` is read in every 100 iterations using an initializable iterator. For gradient computation, we implemented the analytical form directly, rather than using Tensorflow's gradient function. We take $K = 50$, $L = N/u = 1,000$ and $|\mathcal{V}^t| = 1,000$.

The step size of SGRLD is decreased similar to Sect. 5.1 and for these networks, we find $a = 0.001$ performs well for sampling both π and w_i. for these networks. To check the performance for these experiments, a test set consisting of 50% edges and 50% non-edges is chosen at random. The size of the test set is taken as 10% of the edges in the graph. The convergence of the perplexity for the test set is given in Fig. 9. Table 2 shows the runtime in hours for 5,000 iterations and average AUC-ROC scores for 2,500 samples collected after a burn-in of 2,500 iterations. Along with Fig. 9, we can see that the performance of S-AGM does not decrease as K grows, which is also observed in SG-MCMC of a-MMSB [13].

Table 2. AUC-ROC scores of test data and runtime (hrs) for various K

K	AUC-ROC				Runtime (hrs)			
	50	100	150	200	50	100	150	200
FreeAssoc	0.8989	0.9064	0.9041	0.9086	0.6434	1.0844	1.4563	1.8031
Reuters	0.9441	0.9455	0.9472	0.9472	0.6646	1.0725	1.5141	1.8709
ca-HepPh	0.9346	0.9480	0.9503	0.9470	0.6582	1.0815	1.4886	1.8637

Effect of Mini-batch Size. For this experiment, we vary the mini-batch size for the ca-HepPh network with $L = |\mathcal{V}^t| \in \{1000, 500, 100, 5\}$ respectively and study the effect of change in mini-batch size with $K = 50$. In SGRLD, the mini-batch size is a hyperparameter. The convergence speed greatly depends on the mini-batch size though the process with any mini-batch size will finally converge when the MCMC chain is run infinitely. With larger mini batch size, per iteration time is comparatively longer and hence the convergence runtime is also slow. Whereas with very small mini-batch size, only very few w will be updated per iteration and the process will achieve poor predictive performance for missing links due to the larger variance of the stochastic gradient. Shown in Fig. 10, the mini-batch size $L = |\mathcal{V}^t| = 500$ for ca-HepPh obtains the best predictive performance of missing links within 30 min. Although SGRLD with large mini-batch size is faster with no metropolis acceptance step, a better choice of mini-batch size with low variance in stochastic gradient also helps in speeding up the convergence.

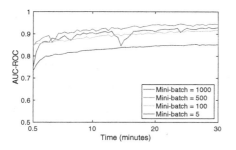 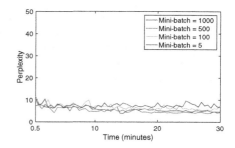

Fig. 10. Trace plot of AUC-ROC score and perplexity of test data for ca-HepPh

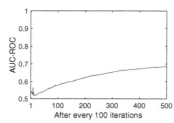 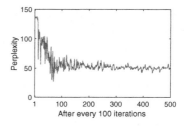

Fig. 11. Trace plot of AUC-ROC score and perplexity of test data for com-dblp

Tensorflow on GPU. To demonstrate the scalability of the inference algorithm, we run the `Tensorflow` code using the com-dblp network [24] which has more than 1 million edges. The experiment is carried out on a machine equipping with an AMD Ryzen 7 Eight-Core Processor at 2.2 GHz, Nvidia GTX TitanX with 12 GB memory, and 64 GB RAM. For this experiment, we consider $K = 2048$, $L = 4096$ and $|\mathcal{V}^t| = 32$. With the same initialization as the above experiments, except for a which is taken as $a = 0.0001$ here, the algorithm is run for $50,000$ iterations and takes 11.5 h. The convergence of perplexity and AUC-ROC score on the test set is given in Fig. 11. From the experiment we can see that S-AGM achieves similar runtime scalability as a-MMSB when implemented with GPU [5].

6   Conclusion and Future Work

In this paper we have developed a new overlapping community model (Soft-AGM) that exhibits pluralistic homophily. Overlapping communities are modelled as soft node to community assignments, which, if constrained to be hard, would result in the Soft AGM likelihood reducing to the standard AGM likelihood. A highly parallelizable and scalable MCMC algorithm for inference based on a stochastic gradient sampler is developed for the model, allowing the inference to be carried out on networks that are well beyond the size of networks tackled by previous MCMC samplers applied to the AGM. In particular, a

Tensorflow implementation has been used to run the model on a network with 10^6 edges. As future work, we would like to implement the algorithm on a HPC infrastructure to find community structure on very large networks, such as "Friendster", "LiveJournal" and so on. We will also consider to make the model non-parametric, allowing the number of non-empty communities to be learned.

Acknowledgments. This project has been funded by Science Foundation Ireland under Grant No. SFI/12/RC/2289.

References

1. Abadi, M., et al.: TensorFlow: Large-scale machine learning on heterogeneous systems (2015). https://www.tensorflow.org/
2. Airoldi, E.M., Blei, D.M., Fienberg, S.E., Xing, E.P.: Mixed membership stochastic blockmodels. J. Mach. Learn. Res. **9**(Sep), 1981–2014 (2008)
3. Butland, G., et al.: Interaction network containing conserved and essential protein complexes in escherichia coli. Nature **433**(7025), 531 (2005)
4. Corman, S.R., Kuhn, T., McPhee, R.D., Dooley, K.J.: Studying complex discursive systems. Centering resonance analysis of communication. Hum. Commun. Res. **28**(2), 157–206 (2002)
5. El-Helw, I., Hofman, R., Bal, H.E.: Towards fast overlapping community detection. In: 2016 16th IEEE/ACM International Symposium on Cluster, Cloud and Grid Computing (CCGrid), pp. 175–178. IEEE (2016)
6. Evans, T.S.: Clique graphs and overlapping communities. J. Stat. Mech: Theory Exp. **2010**(12), P12037 (2010)
7. Fruchterman, T.M., Reingold, E.M.: Graph drawing by force-directed placement. Software Pract. Exper. **21**(11), 1129–1164 (1991)
8. Girolami, M., Calderhead, B.: Riemann manifold Langevin and Hamiltonian Monte Carlo methods. J. Roy. Stat. Soc. B (Stat. Methodol.) **73**(2), 123–214 (2011)
9. Gopalan, P.K., Gerrish, S., Freedman, M., Blei, D.M., Mimno, D.M.: Scalable inference of overlapping communities. In: Advances in Neural Information Processing Systems, pp. 2249–2257 (2012)
10. Gschwind, T., Irnich, S., Furini, F., et al.: Social network analysis and community detection by decomposing a graph into relaxed cliques. Technical report (2015)
11. Lancichinetti, A., Fortunato, S., Kertesz, J.: Detecting the overlapping and hierarchical community structure in complex networks. New J. Phys. **11**(3), 033015 (2009)
12. Leskovec, J., Kleinberg, J., Faloutsos, C.: Graph evolution: densification and shrinking diameters. ACM Trans. Knowl. Discovery Data (TKDD) **1**(1), 2 (2007)
13. Li, W., Ahn, S., Welling, M.: Scalable MCMC for mixed membership stochastic blockmodels. In: Artificial Intelligence and Statistics, pp. 723–731 (2016)
14. Miller, K., Jordan, M.I., Griffiths, T.L.: Nonparametric latent feature models for link prediction. In: Advances in neural information processing systems, pp. 1276–1284 (2009)
15. Mørup, M., Schmidt, M.N., Hansen, L.K.: Infinite multiple membership relational modeling for complex networks. In: 2011 IEEE International Workshop on Machine Learning for Signal Processing (MLSP), pp. 1–6. IEEE (2011)
16. Nelson, D.L., McEvoy, C.L., Schreiber, T.A.: The University of South Florida free association, rhyme, and word fragment norms. Behav. Res. Methods Instrum. Comput. **36**(3), 402–407 (2004)

17. Newman, M.E.: The structure and function of complex networks. SIAM Rev. **45**(2), 167–256 (2003)
18. Patterson, S., Teh, Y.W.: Stochastic gradient Riemannian Langevin dynamics on the probability simplex. In: Advances in Neural Information Processing Systems, pp. 3102–3110 (2013)
19. Roberts, G.O., Rosenthal, J.S.: Optimal scaling of discrete approximations to Langevin diffusions. J. Roy. Stat. Soc. B (Stat. Methodol.) **60**(1), 255–268 (1998)
20. Traud, A.L., Frost, C., Mucha, P.J., Porter, M.A.: Visualization of communities in networks. Chaos Interdisc. J. Nonlinear Sci. **19**(4), 041104 (2009)
21. Welling, M., Teh, Y.W.: Bayesian learning via stochastic gradient Langevin dynamics. In: Proceedings of the 28th International Conference on Machine Learning (ICML-11), pp. 681–688 (2011)
22. Yang, J., Leskovec, J.: Community-affiliation graph model for overlapping network community detection. In: 2012 IEEE 12th International Conference on Data Mining (ICDM), pp. 1170–1175. IEEE (2012)
23. Yang, J., Leskovec, J.: Overlapping community detection at scale: a nonnegative matrix factorization approach. In: Proceedings of the Sixth ACM International Conference on Web Search and Data Mining, pp. 587–596. ACM (2013)
24. Yang, J., Leskovec, J.: Defining and evaluating network communities based on ground-truth. Knowl. Inf. Syst. **42**(1), 181–213 (2013). https://doi.org/10.1007/s10115-013-0693-z
25. Zhou, M.: Infinite edge partition models for overlapping community detection and link prediction. In: Artificial Intelligence and Statistics (AISTATS), pp. 1135–1143 (2015)

Node Classification for Signed Social Networks Using Diffuse Interface Methods

Pedro Mercado[1](✉), Jessica Bosch[2], and Martin Stoll[3]

[1] Department of Computer Science, University of Tübingen, Tübingen, Germany
pedro-eduardo.mercado-lopez@uni-tuebingen.de
[2] Department of Computer Science, The University of British Columbia,
Vancouver, Canada
[3] Faculty of Mathematics, Technische Universität Chemnitz,
Chemnitz, Germany

Abstract. Signed networks contain both positive and negative kinds of interactions like friendship and enmity. The task of node classification in non-signed graphs has proven to be beneficial in many real world applications, yet extensions to signed networks remain largely unexplored. In this paper we introduce the first analysis of node classification in signed social networks via diffuse interface methods based on the Ginzburg-Landau functional together with different extensions of the graph Laplacian to signed networks. We show that blending the information from both positive and negative interactions leads to performance improvement in real signed social networks, consistently outperforming the current state of the art.

1 Introduction

Signed graphs are graphs with both positive and negative edges, where positive edges encode relationships like friendship and trust, and negative edges encode conflictive and enmity interactions. Recently, signed graphs have received an increasing amount of attention due to its capability to encode interactions that are not covered by unsigned graphs or multilayer graphs [40,47,51,53,58], which mainly encode interactions based on similarity and trust.

While the analysis of unsigned graphs follows a long-standing and well established tradition [5,39,44], the analysis of signed graphs can be traced back to [10,29], in the context of social balance theory, further generalized in [16] by introducing the concept of a k-balance signed graph: a signed graph is k-balanced if the set of nodes can be partitioned into k disjoint sets such that inside the sets there are only positive relationships, and between different sets only negative relationships. A related concept is constrained clustering [2], where must-links and cannot-links are constraints indicating if certain pairs of nodes should be assigned to the same or different clusters.

Recent developments of signed graphs have been guided by the concept of k-balance, leading to a diverse paradigm of applications, including: clustering

© Springer Nature Switzerland AG 2020
U. Brefeld et al. (Eds.): ECML PKDD 2019, LNAI 11906, pp. 524–540, 2020.
https://doi.org/10.1007/978-3-030-46150-8_31

[12, 14, 15, 19, 31, 34, 41, 42, 46], edge prediction [22, 33, 35], node embeddings [17, 30, 54, 56], node ranking [13, 48], node classification [49], and many more. See [23, 50] for a recent survey on the topic. One task that remains largely unexplored is the task of node classification in signed networks.

The problem of node classification in graphs is a semi-supervised learning problem where the goal is to improve classification performance by taking into account both labeled and unlabeled observations [11, 60], being a particular case graph-based semi-supervised learning.

The task of graph-based classification methods on unsigned graphs is a fundamental problem with many application areas [3, 57, 59]. A technique that has recently been proposed with very promising results utilizes techniques known from partial differential equations in materials science and combines these with graph based quantities (cf. [5]). In particular, the authors in [5] use diffuse interface methods that are derived from the Ginzburg–Landau energy [1, 6, 26, 52]. These methods have been used in image inpainting where a damaged region of an image has to be restored given information about the undamaged image parts. In the context of node classification in graphs, the undamaged part of an image corresponds to labeled nodes, whereas the damaged part corresponds to unlabeled nodes to be classified based on the information of the underlying graph structure of the image and available labeled nodes. With this analogy, one can readily use results from [4] for the classification problem on graphs. While the materials science problems are typically posed in an infinite-dimensional setup, the corresponding problem in the graph-based classification problem uses the graph Laplacian. This technique has shown great potential and has recently been extended to different setups [7, 24, 43].

Our contributions are as follows: we study the problem of node classification in signed graphs by developing a natural extension of diffuse interface schemes of Bertozzi and Flenner [5], based on different signed graph Laplacians. To the best of our knowledge this is the first study of node classification in signed networks using diffuse interface schemes. A main challenge when considering the application of diffuse interface methods to signed networks is the availability of several competing signed graph Laplacians and how the method's performance depends on the chosen signed graph Laplacian, hence we present a thorough comparison of our extension based on existing signed graph Laplacians. Further, we show the effectivity of our approach against state of the art approaches by performing extensive experiments on real world signed social networks.

The paper is structured as follows. We first introduce the tools needed from graphs and how they are extended to signed networks. We study the properties of several different signed Laplacians. We then introduce a diffuse interface technique in their classical setup and illustrate how signed Laplacians can be used within the diffuse interface approach. This is then followed by numerical experiments in real world signed networks.

Reproducibility: Our code is available at https://github.com/melopeo/GL.

2   Graph Information and Signed Networks

We now introduce the Laplacian for unsigned graphs followed by particular versions used for signed graphs.

2.1   Laplacians for Unsigned Graphs

In this section we introduce several graph Laplacians, which are the main tools for our work. Let $G = (V, W)$ be an undirected graph with node set $V = \{v_1, \ldots, v_n\}$ of size $n = |V|$ and adjacency matrix $W \in \mathbb{R}^{n \times n}$ with non-negative weights, i.e., $w_{ij} \geq 0$.

In the case where a graph presents an assortative configuration, i.e. edge weights of the adjacency matrix W represent similarities (the larger the value of w_{ij} the larger the similarity of nodes the v_i and v_j), then the Laplacian matrix is a suitable option for graph analysis, as the eigenvectors corresponding to the k-smallest eigenvalues convey an embedding into $\mathbb{R}^k$ such that similar nodes are close to each other [39]. The Laplacian matrix and its normalized version are defined as:

$$L = D - W, \qquad L_{\text{sym}} = D^{-1/2} L D^{-1/2}$$

where $D \in \mathbb{R}^{n \times n}$ is a diagonal matrix with $D_{ii} = \sum_{i=1}^{n} w_{ij}$. Observe that L_{sym} can be further simplified to $L_{\text{sym}} = I - D^{-1/2} W D^{-1/2}$. Both Laplacians L and L_{sym} are symmetric positive semi-definite, and the multiplicity of the eigenvalue zero is equal to the number of connected components in the graph G.

For the case where a graph presents a dissasortative configuration, i.e. edges represent dissimilarity (the larger the value of w_{ij} the more dissimilar are the nodes v_i and v_j), then the signless Laplacian is a suitable option, as the eigenvectors corresponding to the k-smallest eigenvalues provide an embedding into $\mathbb{R}^k$ such that dissimilar nodes are close to each other [18, 37, 41]. The signless Laplacian matrix and its normalized version are defined as:

$$Q = D + W, \qquad Q_{\text{sym}} = D^{-1/2} Q D^{-1/2}$$

Observe that Q_{sym} can be further simplified to $Q_{\text{sym}} = I + D^{-1/2} W D^{-1/2}$. Both Laplacians Q and Q_{sym} are symmetric positive semi-definite, with smallest eigenvalue equal to zero if and only if there is a bipartite component in G.

We are now ready to introduce the corresponding Laplacians for the case where both positive and negative edges are present, to later study its application to node classification in signed graphs.

2.2   Laplacians for Signed Graphs

We are now ready to present different signed graph Laplacians. We give a special emphasis on the particular notion of a cluster that each signed Laplacian aims to identify. This is of utmost importance, since this will influence the classification performance of our proposed method.

Signed graphs are useful for the representation of positive and negative interactions between a fixed set of entities. We define a signed graph to be a pair $G^{\pm} = (G^+, G^-)$ where $G^+ = (V, W^+)$ and $G^- = (V, W^-)$ contain positive and negative interactions respectively, between the same set of nodes V, with symmetric adjacency matrices W^+ and W^-. For the case where a single adjacency matrix W contains both positive and negative edges, one can obtain the signed adjacency matrices by the relation $W_{ij}^+ = \max(0, W_{ij})$ and $W_{ij}^- = -\min(0, W_{ij})$.

Notation: We denote the positive, negative and absolute degree diagonal matrices as $D_{ii}^+ = \sum_{j=1}^n W_{ij}^+$, $D_{ii}^- = \sum_{j=1}^n W_{ij}^-$ and $\bar{D} = D^+ + D^-$; the Laplacian and normalized Laplacian of positive edges as $L^+ = D^+ - W^+$, and $L_{\text{sym}}^+ = (D^+)^{-1/2}L^+(D^+)^{-1/2}$; and for negative edges $L^- = D^- - W^-$, and $L_{\text{sym}}^- = (D^-)^{-1/2}L^-(D^-)^{-1/2}$, together with the signless Laplacian for negative edges $Q^- = D^- + W^-$, and $Q_{\text{sym}}^- = (D^-)^{-1/2}Q^-(D^-)^{-1/2}$.

A fundamental task in the context of signed graphs is to find a partition of the set of nodes V such that inside the clusters there are mainly positive edges, and between different clusters there are mainly negative edges. This intuition corresponds to the concept of k-balance of a signed graph, which can be traced back to [16]: *A signed graph is **k-balanced** if the set of vertices can be partitioned into k sets such that within the subsets there are only positive edges, and between them only negative.*

Based on the concept of k-balance of a signed graph, several extensions of the graph Laplacian to signed graphs have been proposed, each of them aiming to bring a k-dimensional embedding of the set of nodes V through the eigenvectors corresponding to the k-smallest eigenvalues, such that positive edges keep nodes close to each other, and negative edges push nodes apart.

Examples of extensions of the graph Laplacian to signed graphs are the signed ratio Laplacian and its normalized version [34], defined as

$$L_{SR} = \bar{D} - W, \qquad L_{SN} = I - \bar{D}^{-1/2}W\bar{D}^{-1/2}$$

Both Laplacians are positive semidefinite. Moreover, they have a direct relationship to the concept of 2-balance of a graph, as their smallest eigenvalue is equal to zero if and only if the corresponding signed graph is 2-balanced. Hence, the magnitude of the smallest eigenvalue tells us how far a signed graph is to be 2-balanced. In [34] it is further observed that the quadratic form $x^T L_{SR} x$ is related to the discrete signed ratio cut optimization problem:

$$\min_{C \subset V} \left(2\text{cut}^+(C, \overline{C}) + \text{assoc}^-(C) + \text{assoc}^-(\overline{C}) \right) \left(\frac{1}{|C|} + \frac{1}{|\overline{C}|} \right)$$

where $\overline{C} = V \backslash C$, $\text{cut}^+(C, \overline{C}) = \sum_{i \in C, j \in \overline{C}} W_{ij}^+$ counts the number of positive edges between clusters, and $\text{assoc}^-(C) = \sum_{i \in C, j \in C} W_{ij}^-$ counts the number of negative edges inside cluster C (similarly for $\text{assoc}^-(\overline{C})$). Therefore we can see that the first term counts the number of edges that keeps the graph away from being 2-balanced, while the second term enforces a partition where both sets are of the same size.

Inspired by the signed ratio cut, the balance ratio Laplacian and its normalized version are defined as follows [12]:

$$L_{BR} = D^+ - W^+ + W^-, \qquad L_{BN} = \bar{D}^{-1/2} L_{BR} \bar{D}^{-1/2},$$

Observe that these Laplacians need not be positive semi-definite, i.e. they potentially have negative eigenvalues. Further, the eigenvectors corresponding to the smallest eigenvalues of L_{BR} are inspired by the following discrete optimization problem:

$$\min_{C \subset V} \left(\frac{\text{cut}^+(C, \overline{C}) + \text{assoc}^-(C)}{|C|} + \frac{\text{cut}^+(C, \overline{C}) + \text{assoc}^-(\overline{C})}{|\overline{C}|} \right)$$

A further proposed approach, based on the optimization of some sort of ratio of positive over negative edges (and hence denoted SPONGE) is expressed through the following generalized eigenvalue problem and its normalized version [14]:

$$(L^+ + D^-)v = \lambda(L^- + D^+)v, \qquad (L^+_{\text{sym}} + I)v = \lambda(L^-_{\text{sym}} + I)v$$

which in turn are inspired by the following discrete optimization problem

$$\min_{C \subset V} \left(\frac{\text{cut}^+(C, \overline{C}) + \text{vol}^-(C)}{\text{cut}^-(C, \overline{C}) + \text{vol}^+(C)} \right)$$

where $\text{vol}^+(C) = \sum_{i \in C} d_i^+$ and $\text{vol}^-(C) = \sum_{i \in C} d_i^-$. Observe that the normalized version corresponds to the eigenpairs of $L_{\text{SP}} := (L^-_{\text{sym}} + I)^{-1}(L^+_{\text{sym}} + I)$. Finally, based on the observation that the signed ratio Laplacian can be expressed as the sum of the Laplacian and signless Laplacian of positive and negative edges, i.e. $L_{SR} = L^+ + Q^-$, in [41] the arithmetic and geometric mean of Laplacians are introduced:

$$L_{AM} = L^+_{\text{sym}} + Q^-_{\text{sym}}, \qquad L_{GM} = L^+_{\text{sym}} \# Q^-_{\text{sym}}.$$

Observe that different clusters are obtained from different signed Laplacians. This becomes clear as different clusters are obtained as solutions from the related discrete optimization problems above described. In the following sections we will see that different signed Laplacians induce different classification performances in the context of graph-based semi-supervised learning on signed graphs.

3   Diffuse Interface Methods

Diffuse interface methods haven proven to be useful in the field of materials science [1,6,9,20,25] with applications to phase separation, biomembrane simulation [55], image inpainting [4,8] and beyond. In [5] it is shown that diffuse interface methods provide a novel perspective to the task of graph-based semi-supervised learning. These methods are commonly based on the minimization of the Ginzburg-Landau (**GL**) functional, which itself relies on a suitable graph Laplacian. Let $S \in \mathbb{R}^{n \times n}$ be a positive semi-definite matrix. We define the **GL** functional for graph-based semi-supervised learning as follows:

$$E_S(u) := \frac{\varepsilon}{2} u^T S u + \frac{1}{4\varepsilon} \sum_{i=1}^{n} (u_i^2 - 1)^2 + \sum_{i=1}^{n} \frac{\omega_i}{2} (f_i - u_i)^2, \tag{1}$$

where f_i contains the class labels of previously annotated nodes.

Observe that this definition of the GL functional for graphs depends on a given positive semi-definite matrix S. For the case of non-signed graphs a natural choice is the graph Laplacian (e.g. $S = L_{\text{sym}}$), which yields the setting presented in [5, 24, 43]. In the setting of signed graphs considered in this paper one can utilize only the information encoded by positive edges (e.g. $S = L_{\text{sym}}^+$), only negative edges (e.g. $S = Q_{\text{sym}}^-$), or both for which a positive semi-definite signed Laplacian that blends the information encoded by both positive and negative edges is a suitable choice (e.g. $S = L_{\text{SR}}, L_{\text{SN}}, L_{\text{SP}}$, or L_{AM}).

Moreover, each element of the GL functional plays a particular role:

1. $\frac{\varepsilon}{2} u^T S u$ induces smoothness and brings clustering information of the signed graph. Different choices of S convey information about different clustering assumptions, as observed in Sect. 2.2,
2. $\frac{1}{4\varepsilon} \sum_{i=1}^{n} (u_i^2 - 1)^2$ has minimizers with entries in $+1$ and -1, hence for the case of two classes it induces a minimizer u whose entries indicate the class assignment of unlabeled nodes,
3. $\sum_{i=1}^{n} \frac{\omega_i}{2} (f_i - u_i)^2$ is a fitting term to labeled nodes given *a priori*, where $\omega_i = 0$ for unlabeled nodes and $\omega_i = w_0$ for labeled nodes, with w_0 large enough (see Sect. 4 for an analysis on w_0.)
4. The interface parameter $\varepsilon > 0$ allows to control the trade-off between the first and second terms: large values of ε make the clustering information provided by the matrix S more relevant, whereas small values of ε give more weight to vectors whose entries correspond to class assignments of unlabeled nodes (see Sect. 4 for an analysis on ε.)

Before briefly discussing the minimization of the GL functional $E_S(u)$, note that the matrix S needs to be positive semi-definite, as otherwise the $E_S(u)$ becomes unbounded below. This discards signed Laplacians like the balance ratio/normalized Laplacian introduced in Sect. 2.2. The minimization of the GL functional $E_S(u)$ in the L^2 function space sense can be done through a gradient descent leading to a modified Allen-Cahn equation. We employ a convexity splitting scheme (see [4, 7, 8, 21, 27, 38, 45]), where the trick is to split $E_S(u)$ into a difference of convex functions:

$$E_S(u) = E_1(u) - E_2(u)$$

with

$$E_1(u) = \frac{\varepsilon}{2} u^T S u + \frac{c}{2} u^T u,$$

$$E_2(u) = \frac{c}{2} u^T u - \frac{1}{4\varepsilon} \sum_{i=1}^{n} (u_i^2 - 1)^2 - \sum_{i=1}^{n} \frac{\omega_i}{2} (f_i - u_i)^2$$

where E_1 and E_2 are convex if $c \geq \omega_0 + \frac{1}{\varepsilon}$; (see e.g. [7]). Proceeding with an implicit Euler scheme for E_1 and explicit treatment for E_2, leads to the following scheme:

$$\frac{u^{(t+1)} - u^{(t)}}{\tau} = -\nabla E_1(u^{(t+1)}) + \nabla E_2(u^{(t)})$$

where $(\nabla E_1(u))_i = \frac{\partial E_1}{\partial u_i}(u)$ and $(\nabla E_2(u))_i = \frac{\partial E_2}{\partial u_i}(u)$ with $i = 1, \ldots, n$, and $u^{(t+1)}$ (resp. $u^{(t)}$) is the evaluation of u at the current (resp. previous) time-point. This further leads to the following

$$\frac{u^{(t+1)} - u^{(t)}}{\tau} + \varepsilon S u^{(t+1)} + c u^{(t+1)} = c u^{(t)} - \frac{1}{\varepsilon} \nabla \psi(u^{(t)}) + \nabla \varphi(u^{(t)}).$$

where $\psi(u) = \sum_{i=1}^{n} (u_i^2 - 1)^2$ and $\varphi(u) = \sum_{i=1}^{n} \frac{\omega_i}{2} (f_i - u_i)^2$.
Let (λ_l, ϕ_l), $l = 1, \ldots, n$, be the eigenpairs of S. By projecting terms of the previous equation onto the space generated by eigenvectors $\phi_1, \ldots, \phi_n$, we obtain

$$\frac{a_l - \bar{a}_l}{\tau} + \varepsilon \lambda_l a_l + c a_l = -\frac{1}{\varepsilon} \bar{b}_l + c \bar{a}_l + \bar{d}_l \quad \text{for } l = 1, \ldots, n \qquad (2)$$

where scalars $\{(a_l, \bar{a}_l, \bar{b}_l, \bar{d}_l)\}_{l=1}^{n}$ are such that $u^{(t+1)} = \sum_{l=1}^{n} a_l \phi_l$, $u^{(t)} = \sum_{l=1}^{n} \bar{a}_l \phi_l$, $\left([\phi_1, \ldots, \phi_n]^T \nabla \psi \left(\sum_{l=1}^{n} \bar{a}_l \phi_l \right) \right)_l = \bar{b}_l$, $\left([\phi_1, \ldots, \phi_n]^T \nabla \varphi \left(f - \sum_{l=1}^{n} \bar{a}_l \phi_l \right) \right)_l = \bar{d}_l$. Equivalently, we can write this as

$$(1 + \varepsilon \tau \lambda_l + c \tau) a_l = -\frac{\tau}{\varepsilon} \bar{b}_l + (1 + c \tau) \bar{a}_l + \tau \bar{d}_l \quad \text{for } l = 1, \ldots, n \qquad (3)$$

where the update is calculated as $u^{(t+1)} = \sum_{l=1}^{n} a_l \phi_l$. Once either convergence or the maximum of iterations is achieved, the estimated label of node v_i is equal to $\text{sign}(u_i)$. The extension to more than two classes is briefly introduced in the appendix of this paper. Finally, note that the eigenvectors corresponding to the smallest eigenvalues of a given Laplacian are the most informative, hence the projection above mentioned can be done with just a small amount of eigenvectors. This will be further studied in the next section.

4   Experiments

In our experiments we denote by **GL**(S) our approached based on the Ginzburg-Landau functional defined in Eq. 1. For the case of signed graphs we consider

$\mathbf{GL}(L_{\mathrm{SN}}), \mathbf{GL}(L_{\mathrm{SP}})$, and $\mathbf{GL}(L_{\mathrm{AM}})$. To better understand the information relevance of different kind of interactions we further evaluate our method based only on positive or negative edges, i.e. $\mathbf{GL}(L_{\mathrm{sym}}^{+})$ and $\mathbf{GL}(Q_{\mathrm{sym}}^{-})$, respectively.

We compare with different kinds of approaches to the task of node classification: First, we consider transductive methods designed for unsigned graphs and apply them only to positive edges, namely: local-global propagation of labels (**LGC**) [57], Tikhonov-based regularization (**TK**) [3], and Label Propagation with harmonic functions (**HF**) [59].

We further consider two methods explicitly designed for the current task: **DBG** [28] based on a convex optimization problem adapted for negative edges, and **NCSSN** [49] a matrix factorization approach tailored for social signed networks.

Parameter Setting. The parameters of our method are set as follows, unless otherwise stated: the fidelity parameter $\omega_0 = 10^3$, the interface parameter $\varepsilon = 10^{-1}$, the convexity parameter $c = \frac{3}{\varepsilon} + \omega_0$, time step-size $dt = 10^{-1}$, maximum number of iterations 2000, stopping tolerance 10^{-6}. Parameters of state of the art approaches are set as follows: for LGC we set $\alpha = 0.99$ following [57], for TK we set $\gamma = 0.001$ following [3], for DBG we set $\lambda_1 = \lambda_2 = 1$, and for NCSSN we set $(\lambda = 10^{-2}, \alpha = 1, \beta = 0.5, \gamma = 0.5)$ following [49]. We do not perform cross validation in our experimental setting due to the large execution time in some of the benchmark methods here considered. Hence, in all experiments we report the *average classification accuracy* out of 10 runs, where for each run we take a different sample of labeled nodes of same size.

Table 1. Dataset statistics of largest connected components of G^+, G^- and $G^\pm$.

	Wikipedia RfA			Wikipedia Elections			Wikipedia Editor		
	G^+	G^-	$G^\pm$	G^+	G^-	$G^\pm$	G^+	G^-	$G^\pm$
# nodes	3024	3124	3470	1997	2040	2325	17647	14685	20198
+ nodes	55.2%	42.8%	48.1%	61.3%	47.1%	52.6%	38.5%	33.5%	36.8%
# edges	204035	189343	215013	107650	101598	111466	620174	304498	694436
+ edges	100%	0%	78.2%	100%	0%	77.6%	100%	0%	77.3%

4.1 Datasets

We consider three different real world networks: wikipedia-RfA [36], wikipedia-Elec [36], and Wikipedia-Editor [56]. Wikipedia-RfA and Wikipedia-Elec are datasets of editors of Wikipedia that request to become administrators, where any Wikipedia member may give a supporting, neutral or opposing vote. From these votes we build a signed network for each dataset, where a positive (resp. negative) edge indicates a supporting (resp. negative) vote by a user and the corresponding candidate. The label of each node in these networks is given by the output of the corresponding request: positive (resp. negative) if the editor is chosen (resp. rejected) to become an administrator.

Wikipedia-Editor is extracted from the UMD Wikipedia dataset [32]. The dataset is composed of vandals and benign editors of Wikipedia. There is a positive (resp. negative) edge between users if their co-edits belong to the same (resp. different) categories. Each node is labeled as either benign (positive) or vandal (negative).

In the following experiments we take the largest connected component of either G^+, G^- or $G^\pm$, depending on the method in turn: for LGC, TK, HF, and $\mathbf{GL}(L_{\mathrm{sym}}^+)$ we take the largest connected component of G^+, for $\mathbf{GL}(Q_{\mathrm{sym}}^-)$ we take the largest connected component of G^-, and for the remaining methods we take the largest connected component of $G^\pm$.

In Table 1 we show statistics of the corresponding largest connected components of each dataset: all datasets present a larger proportion of positive edges than of negative edges in the corresponding signed network $G^\pm$, i.e. at least 77.3% of edges are positive in all datasets. Further, the distribution of positive and negative node labels is balanced, except for Wikipedia-Editor where the class of positive labels is between 33.5% and 38.5% of nodes.

Table 2. Average classification accuracy with different amounts of labeled nodes. Our method $\mathbf{GL}(L_{\mathrm{SN}})$ and $\mathbf{GL}(L_{\mathrm{AM}})$ performs best among transductive methods for signed graphs, and outperforms all methods in two out of three datasets.

Labeled nodes	Wikipedia RfA				Wikipedia Elections				Wikipedia Editor			
	1%	5%	10%	15%	1%	5%	10%	15%	1%	5%	10%	15%
LGC(L^+)	0.554	0.553	0.553	0.553	0.614	0.614	0.613	0.613	0.786	0.839	0.851	0.857
TK(L^+)	0.676	0.697	0.681	0.660	0.734	0.763	0.742	0.723	0.732	0.761	0.779	0.791
HF(L^+)	0.557	0.587	0.606	0.619	0.616	0.623	0.637	0.644	0.639	**0.848**	**0.854**	**0.858**
$\mathbf{GL}(L_{\mathrm{sym}}^+)$	0.577	0.564	0.570	0.584	0.608	0.622	0.626	0.614	0.819	0.759	0.696	0.667
DGB	0.614	0.681	0.688	0.650	0.648	0.602	0.644	0.609	0.692	0.714	0.721	0.727
NCSSN	0.763	0.756	0.745	0.734	0.697	0.726	0.735	0.776	0.491	0.533	0.559	0.570
$\mathbf{GL}(Q_{\mathrm{sym}}^-)$	0.788	0.800	0.804	0.804	0.713	0.765	0.764	0.766	0.739	0.760	0.765	0.770
$\mathbf{GL}(L_{\mathrm{SP}})$	0.753	0.761	0.763	0.765	0.789	0.793	0.797	0.798	0.748	0.774	0.779	0.779
$\mathbf{GL}(L_{\mathrm{SN}})$	0.681	0.752	0.759	0.764	0.806	0.842	0.851	0.852	**0.831**	0.841	0.846	0.847
$\mathbf{GL}(L_{\mathrm{AM}})$	**0.845**	**0.847**	**0.848**	**0.849**	**0.879**	**0.885**	**0.887**	**0.887**	0.787	0.807	0.814	0.817

4.2   Comparison of Classification Performance

In Table 2 we first compare our method $\mathbf{GL}(S)$ with competing approaches when the amount of labeled nodes is fixed to 1%, 5%, 10% and 15%. We can see that among methods for signed graphs, our approach with $\mathbf{GL}(L_{\mathrm{SN}})$ and $\mathbf{GL}(L_{\mathrm{AM}})$ performs best. Moreover, in two out of three datasets our methods based on signed graphs present the best performance, whereas for the dataset Wikipedia-Editor the unsigned graph method HF performs best. Yet, we can observe that the performance gap with our method $\mathbf{GL}(L_{\mathrm{SN}})$ is of at most one percent. Overall we can see that the classification accuracy is higher when the signed graph is taken, in comparison to the case where only either positive or negative edges are considered. This suggests that merging the information encoded by both positive and negative edges leads to further improvements.

In the next section we evaluate the effect on classification performance of different amounts of labeled nodes.

4.3   Effect of the Number of Labeled Nodes

We now study how the classification accuracy of our method is affected by the amount of labeled nodes. For our method we fix the number of eigenvectors to $N_e \in \{20, 40, 60, 80, 100\}$ for Wikipedia-RfA and Wikipedia-Elec, and $N_e \in \{200, 400, 600, 800, 1000\}$ for Wikipedia-Editor. Given N_e, we evaluate our method with different proportions of labeled nodes, going from 1% to 25% of the number of nodes $|V|$.

The corresponding average classification accuracy is shown in Fig. 1. As expected, we can observe that the classification accuracy increases with larger amounts of labeled nodes. Further, we can observe that this effect is more pronounced when larger amounts of eigenvectors N_e are taken, i.e. the smallest classification accuracy increment is observed when the number of eigenvectors N_e is

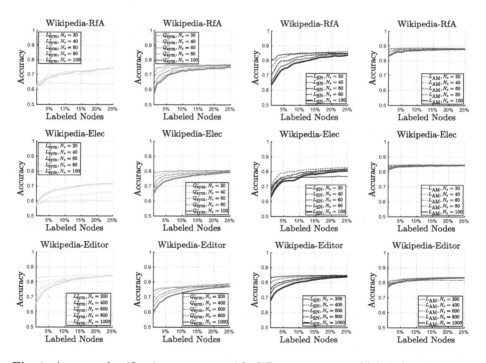

Fig. 1. Average classification accuracy with different amounts of labeled nodes given a fixed number of eigenvectors. Each row presents classification accuracy of dataset Wikipedia-RfA, Wikipedia-Elec, and Wikipedia-Editor. Each column presents classification accuracy of $\mathbf{GL}(L_{\mathrm{sym}}^{+})$, $\mathbf{GL}(Q_{\mathrm{sym}}^{-})$, $\mathbf{GL}(L_{SN})$, and $\mathbf{GL}(L_{AM})$.

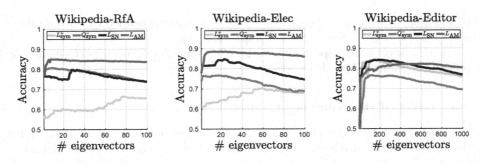

Fig. 2. Average classification accuracy with 5% labeled nodes and different amounts of eigenvectors. Average accuracy is computed out of 10 runs. Our method based on Laplacians L_{SN} and L_{AM} consistently presents the best classification performance.

20 for Wikipedia-RfA and Wikipedia-Elec and 100 eigenvectors for Wikipedia-Editor. Further, we can observe that overall our method based on $\mathbf{GL}(L_{SN})$ and $\mathbf{GL}(L_{AM})$ performs best, suggesting that blending the information coming from both positive and negative edges is beneficial for the task of node classification.

While our method based on signed Laplacians $\mathbf{GL}(L_{SN})$ and $\mathbf{GL}(L_{AM})$ overall presents the best performance, we can observe that they present a slightly difference when it comes to its sensibility to the amount of labeled nodes. In particular, we can observe how the increment on classification accuracy $\mathbf{GL}(L_{SN})$ is rather clear, whereas with $\mathbf{GL}(L_{AM})$ the increment is smaller. Yet, $\mathbf{GL}(L_{AM})$ systematically presents a better classification accuracy when the amount of labeled nodes is limited.

4.4   Effect of the Number of Eigenvectors

We now study how the performance of our method is affected by the number of eigenvectors given through different Laplacians. We fix the amount of labeled nodes to 5% and consider different amounts of given eigenvectors. For datasets Wikipedia-RfA and Wikipedia-Elec we set the number of given eigenvectors N_e in the range $N_e = 1, \ldots, 100$ and for Wikipedia-Editor in the range $N_e = 1, 10, \ldots, 1000$.

The average classification accuracy is shown in Fig. 2. For Wikipedia-RfA and Wikipedia-Elec we can see that the classification accuracy of our method based on $\mathbf{GL}(Q^-_{\text{sym}})$ outperforms our method based on the Laplacian $\mathbf{GL}(L^+_{\text{sym}})$ by a meaningful margin, suggesting that for the task of node classification negative edges are more informative than positive edges. Further, we can see that $\mathbf{GL}(L_{AM})$ consistently shows the highest classification accuracy indicating that taking into account the information coming from both positive and negative edges is beneficial for classification performance.

For the case of Wikipedia-Editor the previous distinctions are not clear anymore. For instance, we can see that the performance of our method based on the Laplacian $\mathbf{GL}(L^+_{\text{sym}})$ outperforms the case with $\mathbf{GL}(Q^-_{\text{sym}})$. Moreover, the information coming from positive edges presents a more prominent performance, being competitive to our method based on the Laplacian $\mathbf{GL}(L_{\mathrm{SN}})$ when the number of eigenvectors is relatively small, whereas the case with the arithmetic mean Laplacian $\mathbf{GL}(L_{\mathrm{AM}})$ presents a larger classification accuracy for larger amounts of eigenvectors. Finally, we can see that in general our method first presents an improvement in classification accuracy, reaches a maximum and then decreases with the amount of given eigenvectors.

4.5 Joint Effect of the Number of Eigenvectors and Labeled Nodes

We now study the joint effect of the number of eigenvectors and the amount of labeled nodes in the classification performance of our method based on $\mathbf{GL}(L_{\mathrm{SN}})$. We let the number of eigenvectors $N_e \in \{10, 20, \ldots, 100\}$ for datasets Wikipedia-RfA and Wikipedia-Elec and $N_e \in \{100, 200, \ldots, 1000\}$ for dataset Wikipedia-Editor. Further, we let the amount of labeled nodes to go from 1% to 25%. The corresponding results are shown in Fig. 3, where we confirm that the classification accuracy consistently increases with larger amounts of labeled nodes. Finally, we can notice that the classification accuracy first increases with the amount of eigenvectors, it reaches a maximum, and then slightly decreases. To better appreciate the performance of our method under various settings, we present the difference between the lowest and largest average classification accuracy in the bottom table of Fig. 3. We can see that the increments go from 25.13% to 36.54%.

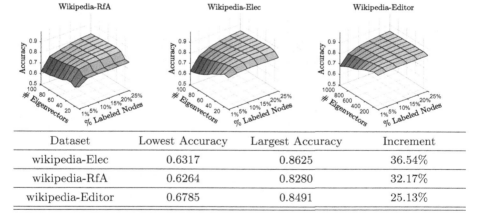

Dataset	Lowest Accuracy	Largest Accuracy	Increment
wikipedia-Elec	0.6317	0.8625	36.54%
wikipedia-RfA	0.6264	0.8280	32.17%
wikipedia-Editor	0.6785	0.8491	25.13%

Fig. 3. Top: Average classification accuracy of our method with $\mathbf{GL}(L_{SN})$ under different number of eigenvectors and different amounts of labeled nodes. Bottom: Lowest and largest average classification accuracy of $\mathbf{GL}(L_{\mathrm{SN}})$ per dataset.

4.6   Joint Effect of Fidelity (ω_0) and Interface (ε) Parameters

We now study the effect of fidelity (ω_0) and interface (ε) parameters on the classification accuracy of our method based on $\mathbf{GL}(L_{SN})$. We fix the number of eigenvectors to $N_e = 20$, and let the amount of labeled nodes to go from 1% to 15%. Further, we set the fidelity parameter ω_0 to take values in $\{10^0, 10^1, \ldots, 10^5\}$ and the interface parameter ε to take values in $\{10^{-5}, 10^{-4}, \ldots, 10^4, 10^5\}$. The results are shown in Fig. 4. We present the following observations:

First: we can see that the larger the amount of labeled nodes, the smaller is the effect of parameters (ω_0, ε). In particular, we can observe that when the amount of labeled nodes is at least 10% of the number of nodes, then the parameter effect of (ω_0, ε) is small, in the sense that the classification accuracy remains high.

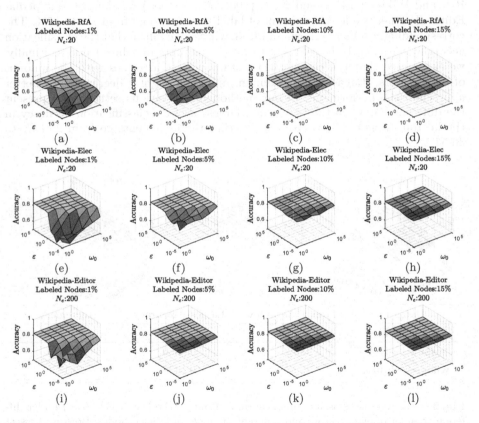

Fig. 4. Average classification accuracy of our method based on $\mathbf{GL}(L_{SN})$ with different values of fidelity (ω_0) and interface (ε). Columns (from left to right): amount of labeled nodes: $1\%, 5\%, 10\%, 15\%$. Rows (from top to bottom): classification accuracy on datasets Wikipedia-RfA, Wikipedia-Elec, and Wikipedia-Editor.

Second: we can see that there is a relationship between the fidelity parameter ω_0 and the interface parameter ε describing a *safe region*, in the sense that the classification accuracy is not strongly affected by the lack of large amounts of labeled nodes. In particular, we can observe that this region corresponds to the cases where the interface parameter ε is larger than the fidelity parameter ω_0, i.e. $\varepsilon(k_1) > \omega_0(k_2)$ where $\varepsilon(k_1) = 10^{k_1}$ and $\omega_0(k_2) = 10^{k_2}$, with $k_1 \in \{10^0, 10^1, \ldots, 10^5\}$ and $k_2 \in \{10^{-5}, 10^{-4}, \ldots, 10^4, 10^5\}$. This can be well observed through a slightly triangular region particularly present for the case where the amount of labeled nodes is 1% on all datasets, which is depicted in Fig. 4a, e, and i.

5 Conclusion

We have illustrated that the semi-supervised task of node classification in signed networks can be performed via a natural extension of diffuse interface methods by taking into account suitable signed graph Laplacians. We have shown that different signed Laplacians provide different classification performances under real world signed networks. In particular, we have observed that negative edges provide a relevant amount of information, leading to an improvement in classification performance when compared to the unsigned case. As future work the task of non-smooth potentials can be considered, together with more diverse functions of matrices that would yield different kinds of information merging of both positive and negative edges.

References

1. Allen, S.M., Cahn, J.W.: A microscopic theory for antiphase boundary motion and its application to antiphase domain coarsening. Acta Metall. **27**(6), 1085–1095 (1979)
2. Basu, S., Davidson, I., Wagstaff, K.: Constrained Clustering: Advances in Algorithms, Theory, and Applications. CRC Press, Boca Raton (2008)
3. Belkin, M., Matveeva, I., Niyogi, P.: Regularization and semi-supervised learning on large graphs. In: Shawe-Taylor, J., Singer, Y. (eds.) COLT 2004. LNCS (LNAI), vol. 3120, pp. 624–638. Springer, Heidelberg (2004). https://doi.org/10.1007/978-3-540-27819-1_43
4. Bertozzi, A.L., Esedoḡlu, S., Gillette, A.: Inpainting of binary images using the Cahn-Hilliard equation. IEEE Trans. Image Process. **16**(1), 285–291 (2007)
5. Bertozzi, A.L., Flenner, A.: Diffuse interface models on graphs for classification of high dimensional data. Multiscale Model. Simul. **10**(3), 1090–1118 (2012)
6. Blowey, J.F., Elliott, C.M.: Curvature dependent phase boundary motion and parabolic double obstacle problems. In: Ni, W.M., Peletier, L.A., Vazquez, J.L. (eds.) Degenerate Diffusions. The IMA Volumes in Mathematics and its Applications, vol. 47, pp. 19–60. Springer, New York (1993). https://doi.org/10.1007/978-1-4612-0885-3_2
7. Bosch, J., Klamt, S., Stoll, M.: Generalizing diffuse interface methods on graphs: nonsmooth potentials and hypergraphs. SIAM J. Appl. Math. **78**(3), 1350–1377 (2018)

8. Bosch, J., Kay, D., Stoll, M., Wathen, A.J.: Fast solvers for Cahn-Hilliard inpainting. SIAM J. Imaging Sci. **7**(1), 67–97 (2014)
9. Cahn, J.W., Hilliard, J.E.: Free energy of a nonuniform system. I. Interfacial free energy. J. Chem. Phys. **28**(2), 258–267 (1958)
10. Cartwright, D., Harary, F.: Structural balance: a generalization of Heider's theory. Psychol. Rev. **63**(5), 277–293 (1956)
11. Chapelle, O., Schlkopf, B., Zien, A.: Semi-Supervised Learning. The MIT Press, Cambridge (2010)
12. Chiang, K., Whang, J., Dhillon, I.: Scalable clustering of signed networks using balance normalized cut, pp. 615–624. CIKM (2012)
13. Chung, F., Tsiatas, A., Xu, W.: Dirichlet PageRank and ranking algorithms based on trust and distrust. Internet Math. **9**(1), 113–134 (2013)
14. Cucuringu, M., Davies, P., Glielmo, A., Tyagi, H.: SPONGE: a generalized eigenproblem for clustering signed networks. AISTATS (2019)
15. Cucuringu, M., Pizzoferrato, A., van Gennip, Y.: An MBO scheme for clustering and semi-supervised clustering of signed networks. CoRR abs/1901.03091 (2019)
16. Davis, J.A.: Clustering and structural balance in graphs. Human Relat. **20**, 181–187 (1967)
17. Derr, T., Ma, Y., Tang, J.: Signed graph convolutional networks. In: ICDM (2018)
18. Desai, M., Rao, V.: A characterization of the smallest eigenvalue of a graph. J. Graph Theory **18**(2), 181–194 (1994)
19. Doreian, P., Mrvar, A.: Partitioning signed social networks. Soc. Netw. **31**(1), 1–11 (2009)
20. Elliott, C.M., Stinner, B.: Modeling and computation of two phase geometric biomembranes using surface finite elements. J. Comput. Phys. **229**(18), 6585–6612 (2010)
21. Eyre, D.J.: Unconditionally gradient stable time marching the Cahn-Hilliard equation. In: MRS Proceedings (1998)
22. Falher, G.L., Cesa-Bianchi, N., Gentile, C., Vitale, F.: On the troll-trust model for edge sign prediction in social networks. In: AISTATS (2017)
23. Gallier, J.: Spectral theory of unsigned and signed graphs. Applications to graph clustering: a survey. arXiv preprint arXiv:1601.04692 (2016)
24. Garcia-Cardona, C., Merkurjev, E., Bertozzi, A.L., Flenner, A., Percus, A.G.: Multiclass data segmentation using diffuse interface methods on graphs. IEEE Trans. Pattern Anal. Mach. Intell. **36**(8), 1600–1613 (2014)
25. Garcke, H., Nestler, B., Stinner, B., Wendler, F.: Allen-Cahn systems with volume constraints. Math. Models Methods Appl. Sci. **18**(8), 1347–1381 (2008)
26. Garcke, H., Nestler, B., Stoth, B.: A multi phase field concept: numerical simulations of moving phasee boundaries and multiple junctions. SIAM J. Appl. Math. **60**, 295–315 (1999)
27. van Gennip, Y., Guillen, N., Osting, B., Bertozzi, A.L.: Mean curvature, threshold dynamics, and phase field theory on finite graphs. Milan J. Math. **82**(1), 3–65 (2014)
28. Goldberg, A.B., Zhu, X., Wright, S.: Dissimilarity in graph-based semi-supervised classification. In: AISTATS (2007)
29. Harary, F.: On the notion of balance of a signed graph. Michigan Math. J. **2**, 143–146 (1953)
30. Kim, J., Park, H., Lee, J.E., Kang, U.: Side: representation learning in signed directed networks. In: WWW (2018)
31. Kirkley, A., Cantwell, G.T., Newman, M.E.J.: Balance in signed networks. Phys. Rev. E **99**, (2019)

32. Kumar, S., Spezzano, F., Subrahmanian, V.: VEWS: a Wikipedia vandal early warning system. In: KDD. ACM (2015)
33. Kumar, S., Spezzano, F., Subrahmanian, V., Faloutsos, C.: Edge weight prediction in weighted signed networks. In: ICDM (2016)
34. Kunegis, J., Schmidt, S., Lommatzsch, A., Lerner, J., Luca, E., Albayrak, S.: Spectral analysis of signed graphs for clustering, prediction and visualization. In: ICDM, pp. 559–570 (2010)
35. Leskovec, J., Huttenlocher, D., Kleinberg, J.: Predicting positive and negative links in online social networks. In: WWW, pp. 641–650 (2010)
36. Leskovec, J., Krevl, A.: SNAP Datasets: Stanford Large Network Dataset Collection, June 2014. http://snap.stanford.edu/data
37. Liu, S.: Multi-way dual cheeger constants and spectral bounds of graphs. Adv. Math. **268**, 306–338 (2015)
38. Luo, X., Bertozzi, A.L.: Convergence analysis of the graph Allen-Cahn scheme. Technical report, UCLA (2016)
39. Luxburg, U.: A tutorial on spectral clustering. Stat. Comput. **17**(4), 395–416 (2007)
40. Mercado, P., Gautier, A., Tudisco, F., Hein, M.: The power mean Laplacian for multilayer graph clustering. In: AISTATS (2018)
41. Mercado, P., Tudisco, F., Hein, M.: Clustering signed networks with the geometric mean of Laplacians. In: NIPS (2016)
42. Mercado, P., Tudisco, F., Hein, M.: Spectral clustering of signed graphs via matrix power means. In: ICML (2019)
43. Merkurjev, E., Garcia-Cardona, C., Bertozzi, A.L., Flenner, A., Percus, A.G.: Diffuse interface methods for multiclass segmentation of high-dimensional data. Appl. Math. Lett. **33**, 29–34 (2014)
44. Newman, M.E.J.: Modularity and community structure in networks. Proc. Nat. Acad. Sci. **103**(23), 8577–8582 (2006)
45. Schönlieb, C.B., Bertozzi, A.L.: Unconditionally stable schemes for higher order inpainting. Commun. Math. Sci **9**(2), 413–457 (2011)
46. Sedoc, J., Gallier, J., Foster, D., Ungar, L.: Semantic word clusters using signed spectral clustering. In: ACL (2017)
47. Serafino, F., Pio, G., Ceci, M.: Ensemble learning for multi-type classification in heterogeneous networks. In: IEEE TKDE (2018)
48. Shahriari, M., Jalili, M.: Ranking nodes in signed social networks. Soc. Netw. Anal. Min. **4**(1), 172 (2014)
49. Tang, J., Aggarwal, C., Liu, H.: Node classification in signed social networks. In: SDM (2016)
50. Tang, J., Chang, Y., Aggarwal, C., Liu, H.: A survey of signed network mining in social media. ACM Comput. Surv. **49**(3), 42:1–42:37 (2016)
51. Tang, W., Lu, Z., Dhillon, I.S.: Clustering with multiple graphs. In: ICDM (2009)
52. Taylor, J.E., Cahn, J.W.: Linking anisotropic sharp and diffuse surface motion laws via gradient flows. J. Stat. Phys. **77**(1–2), 183–197 (1994)
53. Tudisco, F., Mercado, P., Hein, M.: Community detection in networks via nonlinear modularity eigenvectors. SIAM J. Appl. Math. **78**(5), 2393–2419 (2018)
54. Wang, S., Tang, J., Aggarwal, C., Chang, Y., Liu, H.: Signed network embedding in social media. In: SDM (2017)
55. Wang, X., Du, Q.: Modelling and simulations of multi-component lipid membranes and open membranes via diffuse interface approaches. J. Math. Biol. **56**(3), 347–371 (2008)

56. Yuan, S., Wu, X., Xiang, Y.: SNE: signed network embedding. In: Kim, J., Shim, K., Cao, L., Lee, J.-G., Lin, X., Moon, Y.-S. (eds.) PAKDD 2017. LNCS (LNAI), vol. 10235, pp. 183–195. Springer, Cham (2017). https://doi.org/10.1007/978-3-319-57529-2_15
57. Zhou, D., Bousquet, O., Lal, T.N., Weston, J., Schölkopf, B.: Learning with local and global consistency. In: NIPS (2003)
58. Zhou, D., Burges, C.J.: Spectral clustering and transductive learning with multiple views. In: ICML (2007)
59. Zhu, X., Ghahramani, Z., Lafferty, J.: Semi-supervised learning using Gaussian fields and harmonic functions. In: ICML (2003)
60. Zhu, X., Goldberg, A.B.: Introduction to semi-supervised learning. Synth. Lect. Artif. Intell. Mach. Learn. 3(1), 1–30 (2009)

Triangle Completion Time Prediction Using Time-Conserving Embedding

Vachik S. Dave$^{(\boxtimes)}$ and Mohammad Al Hasan

Indiana University Purdue University Indianapolis, Indianapolis, IN, USA
vsdave@iupui.edu, alhasan@cs.iupui.edu

Abstract. A triangle is an important building block of social networks, so the study of triangle formation in a network is critical for better understanding of the dynamics of such networks. Existing works in this area mainly focus on triangle counting, or generating synthetic networks by matching the prevalence of triangles in real-life networks. While these efforts increase our understanding of triangle's role in a network, they have limited practical utility. In this work we undertake an interesting problem relating to triangle formation in a network, which is, to predict the time by which the third link of a triangle appears in a network. Since the third link completes a triangle, we name this task as **T**riangle **C**ompletion **T**ime **P**rediction (*TCTP*). Solution to *TCTP* problem is valuable for real-life link recommendation in social/e-commerce networks, also it provides vital information for dynamic network analysis and community generation study.

An efficient and robust framework (*GraNiTE*) is proposed for solving the *TCTP* problem. *GraNiTE* uses neural networks based approach for learning a representation vector of a triangle completing edge, which is a concatenation of two representation vectors: first one is learnt from graphlet based local topology around that edge and the second one is learnt from time-preserving embedding of the constituting vertices of that edge. A comparison of the proposed solution with several baseline methods shows that the mean absolute error (MAE) of the proposed method is at least one-forth of that of the best baseline method.

Keywords: Time prediction · Embedding method · Edge centric graphlets

1 Introduction

It is a known fact that the prevalence of triangles in social networks is much higher than their prevalence in a random network. It is caused predominantly by the social phenomenon that friends of friends are typically friends themselves. A large number of triangles in social networks is also due to the "small-world network" property [23], which suggests that in an evolving social network, new links are formed between nodes that have short distance between themselves. Leskovec et al. [17] have found that depending on the kinds of networks, 30 to

© Springer Nature Switzerland AG 2020
U. Brefeld et al. (Eds.): ECML PKDD 2019, LNAI 11906, pp. 541–557, 2020.
https://doi.org/10.1007/978-3-030-46150-8_32

60 percent of new links in a network are created between vertices which are only two-hops apart, i.e., each of these links is the third edge of a new triangle in the network. High prevalence of triangles is also observed in directed networks, such as, trust networks, and follow-follower networks—social balance theory [1] can be attributed for such as observation.

There exist a number of works which study triangle statistics and their distribution in social networks. The majority among these works are focused on triangle counting; for a list of such works, see the survey [14] and the references therein. A few other works investigate how different network models perform in generating synthetic networks whose clustering coefficients match

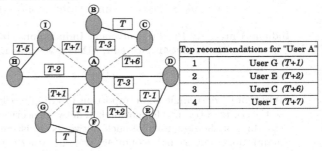

Fig. 1. Simple illustration of the utility of *TCTP* problem for providing improved friend recommendation. In this figure, user *A* is associated with 4 triangles, whose predicted completion times are noted as label on the triangles' final edges (red dotted lines). The link recommendation order for *A* at a time *T*, based on the earliest triangle completion time, is shown in the table on the right. (Color figure online)

with those of real-life social networks [20]. Huang et al. [16] have analyzed the triad closure patterns and provided a graphical model to predict triad closing operation. Durak et al. [11] have studied the variance of degree values among the nodes forming a triangle in networks arising from different domains. These works are useful for discovering the local network context in which triangles appear, but they do not tell us whether local context can be used to predict when a triangle will appear. In this work, we fill this void by building a prediction model which uses local context of a network to predict *when a triangle will appear?* One of the similar time prediction problem in directed networks i.e. reciprocal link time prediction (RLTP), is studied and solved by Dave et al. [5,6], where they used existing survival analysis models with socially motivated topological features. However, never designed features that incorporate time information. Also the proposed model utilizes the ordering and difference between the edge creation times in an innovative way, which significantly boost the accuracy of triangle completion time prediction.

The knowledge of triangle completion time is practically useful. For instance, given that the majority of new links in a network complete a triangle, the knowledge—whether a link will complete a triangle in a short time—can be used to improve the performance of a link prediction model [15]. Specifically, by utilizing this knowledge, a link prediction model can assign a different prior probability of link formation when such links would complete a triangle in near future. Besides, link creation time is more informative than a value denoting the chance of link formation. Say, an online social network platform wants to recommend a friend; it is much better for the platform if it recommends a member who is likely to accept the friend request in a day or two than recommending another who may accept the friend request after a week or few weeks (as illustrated in the Fig. 1). In the e-commerce domain, a common product recommendation criterion is recommending an associated item (say, $item_2$) of an item (say, $item_1$) that a user u has already purchased. Considering a user-item network, in which $item_1 - item_2$ is a triangle's first edge, $item_1 - u$ is the triangle's second edge, the *TCTP* task can be used to determine the best time interval for recommending the user u the $item_2$, whose purchase will complete the $u - item_1 - item_2$ triangle. Given the high prevalence of triangle in real-life networks, the knowledge of triangle completion time can also improve the solution of various other network tasks that use triangles, such as, community structure generation [2], designing network generation models [17], and generating link recommendation [9].

In this work, we propose a novel framework called *GraNiTE*[1] for solving the *Triangle Completion Time Prediction* (*TCTP*) task. *GraNiTE* is a network embedding based model, which first obtains latent representation vectors for the triangle completing edges; the vectors are then fed into a traditional regression model for predicting the time for the completion of a triangle. The main novelty of *GraNiTE* is the design of an edge representation vector learning model, which embeds edges with similar triangle completion time in close proximity in the latent space. Obtaining such embedding is a difficult task because the creation time of an edge depends on both local neighborhood around the edge and the time of the past activities of incident nodes. So, existing network embedding models [7,8,12] which utilize the neighborhood context of a node for learning its representation vector cannot solve the *TCTP* problem accurately. Likewise, existing network embedding models for dynamic networks [3,18,25,26] are also ineffective for predicting the triangle completion time, because such embedding models dynamically encode network growth patterns, not the edge creation time.

To achieve the desired embedding, *GraNiTE* develops a novel supervised approach which uses local graphlet frequencies and the edge creation time. The local graphlet frequencies around an edge is used to obtain a part of the embedding vector, which yields a time-ordering embedding. Also, the edge creation time of a pair of edges is used for learning the remaining part of the embedding vector, which yields a time-preserving embedding. Combination of these two brings edges with similar triangle completion time in close proximity of each other in the embedding space. Both the vectors are learned by using a supervised deep learning setup. Through experiments[2] on five real-world datasets, we show that *GraNiTE* reduces the mean absolute error (MAE) to one-forth of the MAE value of the best competing method while solving the *TCTP* problem.

---

[1] *GraNiTE* is an anagram of the bold letters in **Gra**phlet and **N**ode based **Ti**me-conserving **E**mbedding.

[2] Code and data for the experiments are available at https://github.com/Vachik-Dave/GraNiTE_solving_triangle_completion_time_prediction.

The rest of the paper is organized as follows. In Sect. 2, we define the *TCTP* problem formally. In Sect. 3, we show some interesting observation relating to triangle completion time on five real-world datasets. The *GraNiTE* framework is discussed in Sect. 4. In Sect. 5, we present experimental results which validate the effectiveness of our model over a collection of baseline models. Section 6 concludes the work.

2 Problem Statement

2.1 Notations

Throughout this paper, scalars are denoted by lowercase letters (e.g., n). Vectors are represented by boldface lowercase letters (e.g., $\mathbf{x}$). Bold uppercase letters (e.g., $\mathbf{X}$) denote matrices, the ith row of a matrix $\mathbf{X}$ is denoted as $\mathbf{x}_i$ and j^{th} element of the vector $\mathbf{x}_i$ is represented as x_i^j. $\|\mathbf{X}\|_F$ is the Frobenius norm of matrix $\mathbf{X}$. Calligraphic uppercase letter (e.g., $\mathcal{X}$) is used to denote a set and $|\mathcal{X}|$ is used to denote the cardinality of the set $\mathcal{X}$.

2.2 Problem Formulation

Given, a time-stamped network $G = (\mathcal{V}, \mathcal{E}, \mathcal{T})$, where $\mathcal{V}$ is a set of vertices, $\mathcal{E}$ is a set of edges and $\mathcal{T}$ is a set of time-stamps. There also exists a mapping function $\tau : \mathcal{E} \rightarrow \mathcal{T}$, which maps each edge $e = (u, v) \in \mathcal{E}$ to a time-stamp value, $\tau(e) = t_{uv} \in \mathcal{T}$ denoting the creation time of the edge e. A triangle formed by the vertices $a, b, c \in \mathcal{V}$ and the edges $(a, b), (a, c), (b, c) \in \mathcal{E}$ is represented as Δ_{abc}. If exactly one of the three edges of a triangle is missing, we call it an open triple. Say, among the three edges above, (a, b) is missing, then the open triple is denoted as Λ_{ab}^c. We use Δ for the set of all triangles in a graph.

Given an open triple Λ_{uv}^w, the objective of *TCTP* is to predict the time-stamp (t_{uv}) of the missing edge (u, v), whose presence would have formed the triangle Δ_{uvw}. But, predicting the future edge creation time from training data is difficult as the time values of training data are from the past. So we make the prediction variable an invariant of the absolute time value by considering the interval time from a reference time value for each triangle, where reference time for a triangle is the time-stamp of the second edge in creation time order. For example, for the open triple Λ_{uv}^w the reference time is the latter of the time-stamps t_{wu} and t_{wv}. Thus the interval time (target variable) that we want to predict is the time difference between t_{uv} and the reference time, which is $\max(t_{wu}, t_{wv})$. The interval time is denoted by I_{uvw}; mathematically, $I_{uvw} = t_{uv} - \max(t_{wu}, t_{wv})$. Then the predicted time for the missing edge creation is $t_{uv} = I_{uvw} + max(t_{wu}, t_{wv})$.

Predicting the interval time from a triangle specific reference time incurs a problem, when a single edge completes multiple (say k) open triples, we call such an edge a k-triangle edge. For such a k-triangle edge, ambiguity arises regarding the choice of triples (out of k triples), whose second edge should be used for the reference time—for each of the reference time, a different prediction can be obtained. We solve this problem by using a weighted aggregation approach, a detailed discussion of this is available in Sect. 4.4 "Interval time prediction".

3   Dataset Study

The problem of predicting triangle completion time has not been addressed in any earlier works, so before embarking on the discussion of our prediction method, we like to present some observations on the triangle completion time in five real-world datasets.

Among these datasets, Bit-coinOTC[3] is a trust network of Bitcoin users, Facebook[4] and Digg-friend (See footnote 4) are online friendship networks, Epinion (See footnote 4) is an online trust network and DBLP (See footnote 4) is a co-authorship network.

Table 1. Statistics of datasets (* $\mathcal{T}$ in years for DBLP)

Datasets	$|\mathcal{V}|$	$|\mathcal{E}|$	$|\mathcal{T}|$ (days)	$|\Delta|$
BitcoinOTC	5,881	35,592	1,903	33,493
Facebook	61,096	614,797	869	1,756,259
Epinion	131,580	711,210	944	4,910,076
DBLP	1,240,921	5,068,544	23*	11,552,002
Digg-friend	279,374	1,546,540	1,432	14,224,759

Overall information, such as the number of vertices ($|\mathcal{V}|$), edges ($|\mathcal{E}|$), time-stamps ($|\mathcal{T}|$) and triangles ($|\Delta|$) for these datasets are provided in Table 1. Note that, we pre-process these graphs to remove duplicate edges and edges without valid time-stamps, which leads to removal of disconnected nodes.

3.1   Study of Triangle Generation Rate

As network grows over time, so do the number of edges and the number of triangles. In this study our objective is to determine whether there is a temporal correlation between the growth of edges and the growth of triangles in a network. To observe this behavior, we plot the number of new edges (green line) and the number of new triangles (blue line) (y-axis) over different time values (x-axis); Fig. 2 depicts five plots, one for each dataset. The ratio of newly created triangle count to newly created link count is also shown (red line).

Trend in the plots is similar; as time passes, the number of triangles and the number of links created at each time stamp steadily increase (except Epinion dataset), which represents the fact that the network is growing. Interestingly, triangle to link ratio also increases with time. This happens because as a network gets more dense, the probability that a new edge will complete one or more triangles increases. This trend is more pronounced in Digg-friend and DBLP networks. Especially, in Digg-friend network, each link contributes around 20 triangles during the last few time-stamps. On the other hand, for BitcoinOTC, Facebook and Epinion datasets, the triangle to link ratio increases slowly.

---

[3] http://snap.stanford.edu/data/.
[4] http://konect.uni-koblenz.de/.

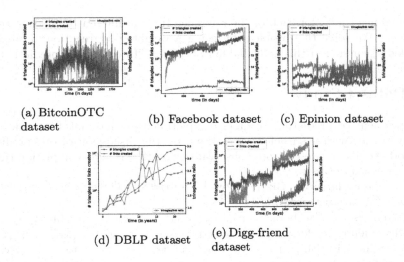

(a) BitcoinOTC dataset (b) Facebook dataset (c) Epinion dataset

(d) DBLP dataset (e) Digg-friend dataset

Fig. 2. Frequency of new edges (green line) and new triangles (blue line) created over time. Ratio of newly created triangle to the newly created link frequency is shown in red line. Y-axis labels on the left show frequency of triangles and link, and the y-axis labels on right show the triangle to link ratio value. (Color figure online)

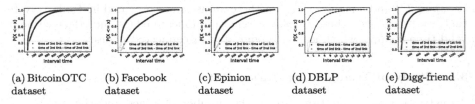

(a) BitcoinOTC dataset (b) Facebook dataset (c) Epinion dataset (d) DBLP dataset (e) Digg-friend dataset

Fig. 3. Plots of cumulative distribution function (CDF) for interval times (Color figure online)

For Facebook dataset, after slow and steady increase, we observe a sudden hike in all three values around day 570. After investigation, we discovered that, it is a consequence of a newly introduced recommendation feature by "Facebook" in 2008. This feature, exploits common friends information which leads to create many links completing multiple open triples.

3.2 Interval Time Analysis

For solving $TCTP$, we predict interval time between the triangle completing edge and the second edge in time order. In this study, we investigate the distribution of the interval time by plotting the cumulative distribution function (CDF) of the interval time for all the datasets (blue lines in the plots in Fig. 3). For comparison, these plots also show the interval time between triangle completing edge and the first edge (red lines).

From Fig. 3, we observe that for all real-world datasets the interval time between the third link and the second link creation follows a distribution from exponential family; which means most of the third links are created very soon after the generation of the second link. This observation agrees with the social balance theory [1]. As per this theory, triangles and individual links are balanced structures while an open triple is an imbalanced structure. All real-world networks (such as social networks) try to create a balanced structure by closing an open triple as soon as possible; which is validated in Fig. 3 as the red curve quickly reaches to 1.0 compared to the ascent of the blue curve.

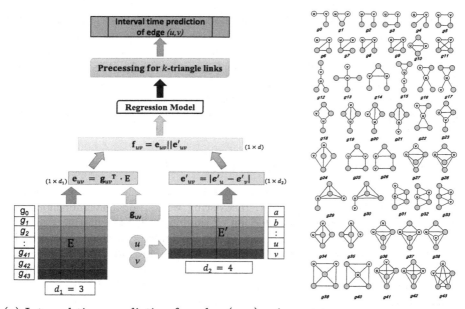

(a) Interval time prediction for edge (u, v) using Proposed *GraNiTE*.

(b) Local graphlets for given edge (u, v)

Fig. 4. Proposed *GraNiTE* and local graphlets

4   *GraNiTE* Framework

GraNiTE framework first obtains a latent representation vector for an edge such that edges with similar interval time have latent vectors which are in close proximity. Such a vector for an edge is learned in a supervised fashion via two kinds of edge embeddings: first, a graphlet-based edge embedding, which embeds the local graphlets into embedding space such that their embedding vectors capture the information of edge ordering based on the interval time. So, we call the edge representation obtained from the graphlet-based embedding method *time-ordering embedding*. Second, a node-based edge embedding that learns node embedding such that proximity of a pair of nodes preserves the interval time of the triangle completing edge. We call the node-based edge embedding *time-preserving embedding*. Concatenation of these two vectors gives the final edge representation vector, which is used to predict a unique creation time for a given edge.

The overall architecture of *GraNiTE* is shown in Fig. 4a. Here nodes u, v and local graphlet frequency vector of edge (u, v) are inputs to the *GraNiTE*. $\mathbf{E}$ and $\mathbf{E}'$ are graphlet embedding and node embedding matrices, respectively. For an edge (u, v), corresponding time-ordering embedding $\mathbf{e}_{uv} \in \mathbb{R}^{d_1}$ and time-preserving embedding $\mathbf{e}'_{uv} \in \mathbb{R}^{d_2}$ are concatenated to generate final feature vector $\mathbf{f}_{uv} = \mathbf{e}_{uv} || \mathbf{e}'_{uv} \in \mathbb{R}^{d(=d_1+d_2)}$. This feature vector $\mathbf{f}_{uv}$ is fed to a regression model that predicts interval time for (u, v). Lastly, we process the regression model output to return a unique interval time for (u, v), in case this edge completes multiple triangles. In the following subsections, we describe graphlet-based time-ordering embedding and node-based time-preserving embedding.

4.1 Graphlet-Based Time-Ordering Embedding

In a real world network, local neighborhood of a vertex is highly influential for a new link created at that vertex. In existing works, local neighborhood of a vertex is captured through a collection of random walks originating from that vertex [19], or by first-level and second level neighbors of that node [21]. For finding local neighborhood around an edge we can aggregate the local neighborhood of its incident vertices. A better way to capture edge neighborhood is to use local graphlets (up to a given size), which provide comprehensive information of local neighborhood of an edge [4]. For an edge (u, v), a graphical structure that includes nodes u, v and a subset of direct neighbors of u and/or v is called a local graphlet for the edge (u, v). Then, a vector containing the frequencies of (u, v)'s local graphlets is a quantitative measure of the local neighborhood of this edge. In Fig. 4b, we show all local graphlets of an edge (u, v) up to size-5, which we use in our time-ordering embedding task. To calculate frequencies of these local graphlets, we use E-CLoG algorithm [4], which is very fast and parallelizable algorithm because graphlet counting process is independent for each edge. After counting frequencies of all 44 graphlets[5], we generate normalized graphlet frequency (NGF), which is an input to our supervised embedding model.

---

[5] Note that, by strict definition of local graphlet, $g3$ and $g7$ are not local, but we compute their frequencies anyway because these are popular 4-size graphlets.

Graphlet frequencies mimic edge features which are highly informative to capture the local neighborhood of an edge. For instance, the frequency of g_1 is the common neighbor count between u and v, frequency of g_5 is the number of 2-length paths, and frequency of g_{43} is the number of five-size cliques involving both u and v. These features can be used for predicting link probability between the vertex pair u and v. However, these features are not much useful when predicting the interval time of an edge. So, we learn embedding vector for each of the local graphlets, such that edge representation built from these vectors captures the ordering among the edges

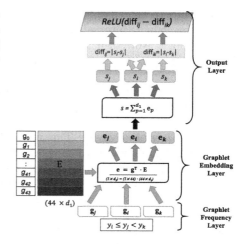

Fig. 5. Learning of the graphlet embedding matrix using three data instances.

based on their interval times, so that they are effective for solving the *TCTP* problem. In the following subsection graphlet embedding model is discussed.

Learning Model. The embedding model has three layers: graphlet frequency layer, graphlet embedding layer and output layer. As shown in the Fig. 5, graphlet frequency layer takes input, graphlet embedding layer calculates edge embedding for the given set of edges using graphlet embedding matrix and graphlet frequencies, and the output layer calculates our loss function for the embedding, which we optimize by using adaptive gradient descent. The loss function implements the time-ordering objective. Given, three triangle completing edges i, j and k and their interval times, y_i, y_j, and y_k, such that $y_i \leq y_j \leq y_k$, our loss function enforces that the distance between the edge representation vectors of i and j is smaller than the distance between the edge representation vectors of i and k. Thus, the edges which have similar interval time are being brought in a close proximity in the embedding space.

Training data for this learning model is the normalized graphlet frequencies (NGF) of all training instances (triangle completing edges with known interval values), which are represented as $\mathbf{G} \in \mathbb{R}^{m \times g_n}$, where m is the number of training instances and g_n is equal to 44 representing different types of local graphlets. Each row of matrix $\mathbf{G}$ is an NGF for a single training instance i.e. if i^{th} element corresponds to the edge (u, v), $\mathbf{g}_i$ ($= \mathbf{g}_{uv}$) is its normalized graphlet frequency. The target values (interval time) of m training instances are represented as vector $\mathbf{y} \in \mathbb{R}^m$. Now, the layers of the embedding model (Fig. 5) are explained below:

Graphlet Frequency Layer: In input layer we feed triples of three sampled data instances i, j and k, such that $y_i \leq y_j \leq y_k$ with their NGF i.e. $\mathbf{g}_i$ $\mathbf{g}_j$, and $\mathbf{g}_k$.

Graphlet Embedding Layer: This model learns embedding vectors for each local graphlets, represented with the embedding matrix $\mathbf{E} \in \mathbb{R}^{g_n \times d_1}$, where d_1 is the (user-defined) embedding dimension. For any data instance i in training data $\mathbf{G}$, corresponding time-ordering edge representation $\mathbf{e}_i \in \mathbb{R}^{d_1}$ is obtained by vector to matrix multiplication i.e. $\mathbf{e}_i = \mathbf{g}_i^T \cdot \mathbf{E}$. In the embedding layer, for input data instances i, j and k, we calculate three time-ordering embedding vectors $\mathbf{e}_i$, $\mathbf{e}_j$ and $\mathbf{e}_k$ using this vector-matrix multiplication.

Output Layer: This layer implements our loss function. For this, first we calculate the score of each edge representation using vector addition i.e. for $\mathbf{e}_i$ the score is $s_i = \Sigma_{p=1}^{d_1} e_i^p$. After that, we pass the score difference between instances i and j (diff_{ij}) and the score difference between i and k (diff_{ik}) to an activation function. The activation function in this layer is ReLU, whose output we minimize. The objective function after regularizing the graphlet embedding matrix is as below:

$$\mathscr{O}_g = \min_{\mathbf{E}} \sum_{\forall (i,j,k) \in T_{ijk}} ReLU(\text{diff}_{ij} - \text{diff}_{ik}) + \lambda_g \cdot \|\mathbf{E}\|_F^2 \qquad (1)$$

where, $\text{diff}_{ij} = |s_i - s_j|$, λ_g is a regularization constant and T_{ijk} is a training batch of three qualified edge instances from training data.

4.2 Time-Preserving Node Embedding

This embedding method learns a set of node representation vectors such that the interval time of an edge is proportional to the l_1 norm of incident node vectors. If an edge has higher interval time, the incident node vectors are pushed farther, if the edge have short interval time, the incident node vectors are close to each other in latent space. Thus, by taking the l_1 norm of node-pairs, we can obtain an embedding vector of an edge which is interval time-preserving and is useful for solving the *TCTP* problem. As depicted in the Fig. 6, this embedding method is composed of three layers: input layer, node & edge embedding layer, and time preserving output layer. Functionality of each layer is discussed below:

Input Layer: For this embedding method, input includes two edges, say (u, v) and (x, y) with their interval times, y_{uv} and y_{xy}. The selection of these two edges is based on the criterion that $y_{uv} > y_{xy}$.

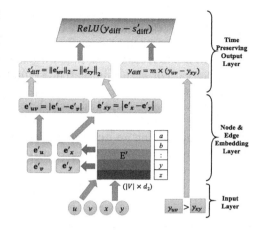

Fig. 6. Learning of the node embedding matrix using two edges (node-pairs).

Node & Edge Embedding Layer: In this layer, we learn embedding matrix $\mathbf{E}' \in \mathbb{R}^{|\mathcal{V}| \times d_2}$, where d_2 is (user-defined) embedding dimension. From the embedding matrix $\mathbf{E}'$, we find node embedding for a set of 4 nodes incident to the edges (u, v) and (x, y). For any node u, node embedding vector is $\mathbf{e}'_u \in \mathbb{R}^{d_2}$ i.e. u^{th} element of matrix $\mathbf{E}'$. From the node embedding vectors $\mathbf{e}'_u$ and $\mathbf{e}'_v$, we calculate corresponding time-preserving edge embedding vector for (u, v). The time-preserving edge embedding is defined as l_1-distance between the node embedding vectors, i.e. $\mathbf{e}'_{uv} = |\mathbf{e}'_u - \mathbf{e}'_v| \in \mathbb{R}^{d_2}$.

Time-Preserving Output Layer: The objective of this embedding is to preserve the interval time information into embedding matrix, such that time-preserving edge vectors are proportional to their interval time. For that, we calculate an edge score using l_2-norm of an edge embedding, i.e. (u, v) edge score $s'_{uv} = \|\mathbf{e}'_{uv}\|_2$. We design the loss function such that edge score difference $s'_{\text{diff}} = s'_{uv} - s'_{xy}$ between edges (u, v) and (x, y) is proportional to their interval time difference $y_{uv} - y_{xy}$. The objective function of the embedding is

$$\mathcal{O}_n = \min_{\mathbf{E}'} \sum_{\forall (u,v),(x,y) \in T_{uv,xy}} ReLU(y_{\text{diff}} - s'_{\text{diff}}) + \lambda_n \cdot \|\mathbf{E}'\|_F^2 \qquad (2)$$

where, $y_{\text{diff}} = m \times (y_{uv} - y_{xy})$, λ_n is a regularization constant, $T_{uv,xy}$ is a training batch of edge pairs, and m is a scale factor.

4.3   Model Inference and Optimization

We use mini-batch adaptive gradient decent (AdaGrad) to optimize the objective functions (Eqs. 1 and 2) of both embedding methods. Mini-batch AdaGrad is a modified mini-batch gradient decent approach, where learning rate of each dimension is different based on gradient values of all previous iterations [10]. This independent adaption of learning rate for each dimension is especially well suited for graphlet embedding method as graphlet frequency vector is mostly a sparse vector which generates sparse edge embedding vectors. For time-preserving node embedding, independent learning rate helps to learn the embedding vectors more efficiently such that two node can maintain its proximity in embedding space proportional to interval time.

For mini-batch AdaGrad, first we generate training batch, say T, from training instances. For each mini-batch, we uniformly choose training instances that satisfy the desired constrains: for graphlet embedding, a training instance consists of three edges i, j and k, for which $y_i \leq y_j \leq y_k$ and for time-preserving node embedding, a training instance is an edge pair, $i = (u, v)$ and $j = (x, y)$, such that, $y_i \leq y_j$. During an iteration, AdaGrad updates each embedding vector, say **e**, corresponding to all samples from training batch using following equation:

$$e_i^{t+1} = e_i^t - \alpha_i^t \times \frac{\partial \mathscr{O}}{\partial e_i^t} \tag{3}$$

where, e_i^t is an ith element of vector **e** at iteration t. Here we can see that at each iteration t, AdaGrad updates embedding vectors using different learning rates α_i^t for each dimension.

For time complexity analysis, given a training batch T, the total cost of calculating gradients of objective functions ($\mathscr{O}_g$ and $\mathscr{O}_n$) depends on the dimension of embedding vector i.e. $\Theta(d_i)$, $d_i \in \{d_1, d_2\}$. Similarly, calculating learning rate and updating embedding vector also costs $\Theta(d_i)$. In graphlet embedding, we need to perform vector to matrix multiplication, which costs $\Theta(44 \times d_1)$. Hence, total cost of the both embedding methods is $\Theta(44 \times d_1 + d_2) = \Theta(d_1 + d_2)$. As time complexity is linear to embedding dimensions, both embedding methods are very fast in learning embedding vectors even for large networks.

4.4   Interval Time Prediction

We learn both time-ordering graphlet embedding matrix and time-preserving node embedding matrix from training instances. We generate edge representation for test instances from these embedding matrices, as shown in Fig. 4a. This edge representation is fed to a traditional regression model (we have used Support Vector Regression) which predicts an interval time. However, predicting the interval time of a k-triangle link poses a challenge, as any regression model predicts multiple (k) creation times for such an edge. The simplest approach to overcome this issue is to assign the mean of k predictions as the final predicted value for the k-triangle link. But, as we know mean is highly sensitive to outliers especially for the small number of samples (mostly $k \in [2, 20]$), so using a mean value does not yield the best result. From the discussion in Sect. 3.2, we know that triangle interval time follows exponential distribution. Hence we use exponential decay $W(I_{uvw}) = w_0 \cdot \exp(-\lambda \cdot I_{uvw})$ as a weight of each prediction, where λ is a decay constant and w_0 is an initial value. We calculate weighted mean which serves as a final prediction value for a k-triangle link.

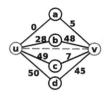

Fig. 7. (u, v) as 4-triangle link

In Fig. 7, we show a toy graph with creation time of each link and (u, v) is a 4-triangle link. Let's assume our model predicts 4 interval times $(40, 3, 1, 1)$ corresponding to four open triples $(\Lambda_{uv}^a, \Lambda_{uv}^b, \Lambda_{uv}^c, \Lambda_{uv}^d)$ respectively. Hence, we have 4 predicted creation times i.e. $(5 + 40 = 45, 51, 50, 51)$ for link (u, v). So, the final prediction for the edge (u, v) is calculated by using the equation below:

$$\widehat{t_{uv}} = \frac{W(40) \times 45 + W(3) \times 51 + W(1) \times 50 + W(1) \times 51}{W(40) + W(3) + W(1) + W(1)}$$

5 Experiments and Results

We conduct experiments to show the superior performance of the proposed *GraNiTE* in solving the *TCTP* problem. No existing works solve the *TCTP* problem, so we build baseline methods from two approaches described as below:

The first approach uses features generated directly from the network topology.

1. **Topo. Feat.** (Topological features) This method uses traditional topological features such as common neighbor count, Jaccard coefficient, preferential attachment, adamic-adar, Katz measure with five different β values $\{0.1, 0.05, 0.01, 0.005, 0.001\}$. These features are well-known for solving the link prediction task [15]. We generate topological features for an edge (last edge of triangle) from the snapshot of the network when the second link of the triangle appears; triangle interval time is also computed from that temporal snapshot.
2. **Graphlet Feat.** In this method we use local graphlet frequencies of an edge (last edge of triangle) as a feature set for the time prediction task. These graphlet frequencies are also calculated from the temporal snapshot of the network as mentioned previously in Topo. Feat.

The second approach uses well known network embedding approaches.

3. **LINE** [21]: LINE embeds the network into a latent space by leveraging both first-order and second-order proximity of each node.
4. **Node2vec** [12]: Node2vec utilizes Skip-Gram based language model to analyze the truncated biased random walks on the graph.
5. **GraphSAGE** [13]: It presents an inductive representation learning framework that learns a function and generates embeddings by sampling and aggregating features from a node's local neighborhood.
6. **AROPE** [24]: AROPE is a matrix decomposition based embedding approach, which preserves different higher-order proximity for different input graphs and it provides global optimal solution for a given order.
7. **VERSE** [22]: It is a versatile node embedding method that preserves specific node similarity measure(s) and also captures global structural information.

5.1   Experiment Settings

For this experiment, we divide the time-stamps of each dataset into three chronologically ordered partitions with the assumption that initial partition is network growing period, which spans from the beginning up to 50% of total time-stamps. The second partition, which spans from 50% to 70% of the total time-stamps, is the train period, and finally, from 70% till the end is the test period. We select the edges completing triangles during the train period as training instances and the edges completing triangles during the test period as test instances. We also retain 5% of test instances for parameter tuning. Note that, this experiment setting is not suitable for dynamic network embedding methods, so we cannot compare with them.

There are a few user defined parameters in the proposed *GraNiTE*. For both embedding approaches, we fix the embedding dimensions as 50, i.e. $d_1 = d_2 = 50$. Hence, final embedding dimension is $d = 100$ as discussed in Sect. 4 "*GraNiTE* Framework". Similarly, regularization rates for both embedding methods are set as $\lambda_g = \lambda_n = 1e - 5$. Initial learning rate for AdaGrad optimization is set as 0.1. The training batch size is 100 and the number of epochs is set to 50. For time preserving node embedding, the scale factor is set to 0.01 i.e. $m = 0.01$. Additionally, for predicting time of k-triangle links, decay constant (λ) and initial weight (w_0) are set to 1.0 for calculating exponential decay weights. Lastly, we use support vector regression (SVR) with linear kernel and penalty $C = 1.0$ as a regression method for *GraNiTE* and for all competing methods. For fair comparison, SVR is identically configured for all methods.

For all competing embedding methods the embedding dimensions are set as 100, same size of our feature vector ($d = 100$). We grid search the different tuning parameters to find the best performance of these embedding methods. We select learning rate from set $\{0.0001, 0.001, 0.01, 0.1\}$ for all methods. For Node2vec, we select walk bias factors p and q from $\{0.1, 0.5, 1.0\}$ and number of walks per node is selected from $\{5, 10, 15, 20\}$. For AROPE, the order of proximity is selected from set $\{1, 2, 3, 4, 5\}$. For VERSE, we select personalized pagerank parameter α from set $\{0.1, 0.5, 0.9\}$.

5.2   Comparison Results

We evaluate the models using mean absolute error (MAE) over two groups of interval times: 1-month (≤ 30 days) and 2-months (31 to 60 days) for all datasets, except DBLP, for which the two intervals are 0–2 years and 3–7 years. Instances that have higher than 60 days of interval time are outlier instances, hence they are excluded. Besides, for real-life social network applications, predicting an interval value beyond two months is probably not very interesting. Within 60 days, we show results in two groups: 1-month, and 2-month, because some of the competing methods work well for one group, but not the other.

Comparison results for all five datasets are shown in Table 2, where each column represents a prediction method. Rows are grouped into five, one for each dataset; each dataset group has three rows: small interval ($\leq 30d$), large interval

Table 2. Comparison experiment results using MAE for interval times in 1st (≤ 30 *days*) and 2nd-month (31–60 *days*). [for DBLP dataset: 0–2 years and 3–7 years]. For *GraNiTE*, % improvement over the best competing method (underlined) is shown in brackets.

Dataset		Topo. Feat.	Graphlet Feat.	LINE	Node2vec	GraphSAGE	AROPE	VERSE	GraNiTE
Bitcoin-OTC	$\leq$ 30d	17.22	17.7	**8.86**	26.68	11.99	28.62	25.81	9.08 (-2.48%)
	31–60d	21.92	18.29	34.03	**16.55**	28.84	21.59	20.56	19.95 (-20.54%)
	Avg.	19.57	<u>17.995</u>	21.445	21.615	20.415	25.105	23.185	**14.515** (19.34%)
Facebook	$\leq$ 30d	7.78	7.93	8.36	7.95	8.37	7.93	<u>7.98</u>	**5.64** (27.51%)
	31–60d	32.04	<u>30.9</u>	31.98	32.87	31.96	32.55	32.73	**13.65** (55.83%)
	Avg.	19.91	19.415	20.17	20.41	<u>20.165</u>	20.24	20.355	**9.645** (50.32%)
Epinion	$\leq$ 30d	15.88	14.31	<u>12.52</u>	17.09	13.79	14.3	19.85	**3.28** (73.8%)
	31–60d	22.02	24.82	25.18	20.17	23.45	23.22	<u>17.9</u>	**5.36** (70.06%)
	Avg.	18.95	19.565	18.85	18.63	<u>18.62</u>	18.76	18.875	**4.32** (76.8%)
DBLP	$\leq$ 30d	0.526	<u>0.525</u>	0.527	0.527	0.526	0.526	0.5267	**0.449** (14.48%)
	31–60d	3.623	<u>3.618</u>	3.624	3.623	3.623	3.624	3.623	**0.969** (73.22%)
	Avg.	2.0745	<u>2.0715</u>	2.0755	2.075	2.0745	2.075	2.0748	**0.709** (65.77%)
Digg-friends	$\leq$ 30d	6.75	6.25	6.03	7.73	<u>5.95</u>	7.37	6.95	**2.13** (64.2%)
	31–60d	41.06	37.34	38.77	<u>32.66</u>	38.85	34.34	34.75	**9.76** (70.12%)
	Avg.	23.905	21.795	22.4	<u>20.195</u>	22.4	20.855	20.85	**5.945** (70.56%)

(30–60*d*) and Average (Avg.) over these two intervals. Results of our proposed method (*GraNiTE*) is shown in the last column; besides MAE, in this column we also show the percentage of improvement of *GraNiTE* over the best of the competing methods(underlined). The best results in each row is shown in bold font.

We can observe from the table that the proposed *GraNiTE* performs the best for all the datasets considering the average. The improvements over the competing methods, at a minimum, 19.34% for the BitcoinOTC dataset, and, to the maximum, 76.8% for the Epinion dataset. If we consider short and long intervals ($\leq 30d$ and 30–60*d*) independently, *GraNiTE* performs the best in all datasets, except BitcoinOTC dataset. However, notice that for BitcoinOTC dataset, although Node2vec performs the best for large interval times, for small interval times its performance is extremely poor (almost thrice MAE compared to *GraNiTE*). Similarly, LINE performs the best for small interval times and incurs huge error for large interval times. Only *GraNiTE* shows consistently good results for both small and large interval ranges over all the datasets.

Another observation is that, for all datasets, results of large interval times (31–60 days) is worse than the results of small interval time (≤ 30 days). For competing methods, these values are sometimes very poor that it is meaningless for practical use. For instance, for Epinion, each of the competing methods have an MAE around 20 or more for large interval, whereas *GraNiTE* has an MAE value of 5.36 only. Likewise, for Digg-friends, each of the competing methods have an MAE more than 32, but *GraNiTE*'s average MAE is merely 5.95. Overall, for both intervals over all the datasets, *GraNiTE*shows significantly (t-test with p-value $\ll 0.01$) lower MAE than the second best method. The main reason for poor performance of competing methods is that, those methods can capture the local and/or global structural information of nodes/edges but fail to capture temporal information. While for *GraNiTE*, the graphlet embedding method is able to translate the patterns of local neighborhood into time-ordering edge vector; at the same time, time preserving node embedding method is able to capture the interval time information into node embedding vector. Both of the features help to enhance the performance of *GraNiTE*.

6   Conclusion

In this paper, we propose a novel problem of triangle completion time prediction (*TCTP*) and provide an effective and robust framework *GraNiTE* to solve this problem by using graphlet based time-ordering embedding and time-preserving node embedding methods. Through experiments on five real-world datasets, we show the superiority of our proposed method compared to baseline methods which use known graph topological features, graphlet frequency features or popular and state-of-art network embedding approaches. To the best of our knowledge, we are the first to formulate the *TCTP* problem and to propose a novel framework for solving this problem.

References

1. Antal, T., Krapivsky, P., Redner, S.: Social balance on networks: the dynamics of friendship and enmity. Physica D **224**, 130–136 (2006)
2. Bianconi, G., Darst, R.K., Iacovacci, J., Fortunato, S.: Triadic closure as a basic generating mechanism of communities in complex networks. Phys. Rev. E **90**(4), 042806 (2014)
3. Bonner, S., Brennan, J., Kureshi, I., Theodoropoulos, G., McGough, A.S., Obara, B.: Temporal graph offset reconstruction: towards temporally robust graph representation learning. In: IEEE Big Data, pp. 3737–3746 (2018)
4. Dave, V.S., Ahmed, N.K., Hasan, M.A.: E-clog: counting edge-centric local graphlets. In: IEEE Intternational Conference on Big Data, pp. 586–595, December 2017
5. Dave, V.S., Al Hasan, M., Reddy, C.K.: How fast will you get a response? Predicting interval time for reciprocal link creation. In: Eleventh International AAAI Conference on Web and Social Media, ICWSM 2017 (2017)
6. Dave, V.S., Hasan, M.A., Zhang, B., Reddy, C.K.: Predicting *interval time* for reciprocal link creation using survival analysis. Soc. Netw. Anal. Min. **8**(1), 1–20 (2018). https://doi.org/10.1007/s13278-018-0494-1
7. Dave, V.S., Zhang, B., Al Hasan, M., AlJadda, K., Korayem, M.: A combined representation learning approach for better job and skill recommendation. In: ACM International Conference on Information and Knowledge Management, CIKM 2018, pp. 1997–2005 (2018)
8. Dave, V.S., Zhang, B., Chen, P.Y., Hasan, M.A.: Neural-brane: neural Bayesian personalized ranking for attributed network embedding. Data Sci. Eng. (2019)
9. Dong, Y., et al.: Link prediction and recommendation across heterogeneous social networks. In: IEEE International Conference on Data Mining, pp. 181–190 (2012)

10. Duchi, J., Hazan, E., Singer, Y.: Adaptive subgradient methods for online learning and stochastic optimization. J. Mach. Learn. Res. **12**, 2121–2159 (2011)
11. Durak, N., Pinar, A., Kolda, T.G., Seshadhri, C.: Degree relations of triangles in real-world networks and graph models. In: ACM International Conference on Information and Knowledge Management, pp. 1712–1716 (2012)
12. Grover, A., Leskovec, J.: Node2vec: scalable feature learning for networks. In: KDD 2016, pp. 855–864 (2016)
13. Hamilton, W., Ying, Z., Leskovec, J.: Inductive representation learning on large graphs. In: Advances in Neural Information Processing Systems (NIPS), vol. 30, pp. 1024–1034 (2017)
14. Hasan, M.A., Dave, V.: Triangle counting in large networks: a review. Wiley Interdisc. Rev. Data Min. Knowl. Discov. **8**(2), e1226 (2018)
15. Hasan, M.A., Zaki, M.J.: A survey of link prediction in social networks. In: Aggarwal, C. (ed.) Social Network Data Analytics, pp. 243–275. Springer, Boston (2011). https://doi.org/10.1007/978-1-4419-8462-3_9
16. Huang, H., Tang, J., Liu, L., Luo, J., Fu, X.: Triadic closure pattern analysis and prediction in social networks. IEEE Trans. Knowl. Data Eng. **27**(12), 3374–3389 (2015)
17. Leskovec, J., Backstrom, L., Kumar, R., Tomkins, A.: Microscopic evolution of social networks. In: KDD 2008, pp. 462–470 (2008)
18. Nguyen, G.H., Lee, J.B., Rossi, R.A., Ahmed, N.K., Koh, E., Kim, S.: Continuous-time dynamic network embeddings. In: Companion of the Web Conference 2018, pp. 969–976 (2018)
19. Perozzi, B., Al-Rfou, R., Skiena, S.: DeepWalk: online learning of social representations. In: KDD 2014, pp. 701–710 (2014)
20. Sala, A., Cao, L., Wilson, C., Zablit, R., Zheng, H., Zhao, B.Y.: Measurement-calibrated graph models for social network experiments. In: ACM International Conference on World Wide Web, pp. 861–870 (2010)
21. Tang, J., Qu, M., Wang, M., Zhang, M., Yan, J., Mei, Q.: Line: large-scale information network embedding. In: International Conference on World Wide Web, pp. 1067–1077 (2015)
22. Tsitsulin, A., Mottin, D., Karras, P., Müller, E.: Verse: versatile graph embeddings from similarity measures. In: The World Wide Web Conference, pp. 539–548 (2018)
23. Watts, D.J., Strogatz, S.H.: Collective dynamics of small-world networks. Nature **393**(6684), 440 (1998)
24. Zhang, Z., Cui, P., Wang, X., Pei, J., Yao, X., Zhu, W.: Arbitrary-order proximity preserved network embedding. In: KDD 2018, pp. 2778–2786 (2018)
25. Zhou, L., Yang, Y., Ren, X., Wu, F., Zhuang, Y.: Dynamic network embedding by modeling triadic closure process. In: Conference on Artificial Intelligence (2018)
26. Zuo, Y., Liu, G., Lin, H., Guo, J., Hu, X., Wu, J.: Embedding temporal network via neighborhood formation. In: ACM SIGKDD International Conference on Knowledge Discovery & Data Mining, pp. 2857–2866 (2018)

Decision Trees, Interpretability, and Causality

Adjustment Criteria for Recovering Causal Effects from Missing Data

Mojdeh Saadati$^{(\boxtimes)}$ and Jin Tian

Department of Computer Science, Iowa State University,
2434 Osborn Dr, Ames, IA 50011, USA
{msaadati,jtian}@iastate.edu

Abstract. Confounding bias, missing data, and selection bias are three common obstacles to valid causal inference in the data sciences. Covariate adjustment is the most pervasive technique for recovering casual effects from confounding bias. In this paper we introduce a covariate adjustment formulation for controlling confounding bias in the presence of missing-not-at-random data and develop a necessary and sufficient condition for recovering causal effects using the adjustment. We also introduce an adjustment formulation for controlling both confounding and selection biases in the presence of missing data and develop a necessary and sufficient condition for valid adjustment. Furthermore, we present an algorithm that lists all valid adjustment sets and an algorithm that finds a valid adjustment set containing the minimum number of variables, which are useful for researchers interested in selecting adjustment sets with desired properties.

Keywords: Missing data · Missing not at random · Causal effect · Adjustment · Selection bias

1 Introduction

Discovering causal relationships from observational data has been an important task in empirical sciences, for example, assessing the effect of a drug on curing diabetes, a fertilizer on growing agricultural products, and an advertisement on the success of a political party. One major challenge to estimating the effect of a treatment on an outcome from observational data is the existence of *confounding bias* - i.e., the lack of control on the effect of spurious variables on the outcome. This issue is formally addressed as the *identifiability problem* in [13], which concerns with computing the effect of a set of treatment variables ($\mathbf{X}$) on a set of outcome variables ($\mathbf{Y}$), denoted by $P(\mathbf{y} \mid do(\mathbf{x}))$, given observed probability distribution $P(\mathbf{V})$ and a causal graph G, where $P(\mathbf{V})$ corresponds to the observational data and G is a directed acyclic graph (DAG) representing qualitative causal relationship assumptions between variables in the domain. The effect $P(\mathbf{y} \mid do(\mathbf{x}))$ may not be equal to its probabilistic counterpart $P(\mathbf{y} \mid \mathbf{x})$ due to the existence of variables, called *covariates*, that affect both the treatments

© Springer Nature Switzerland AG 2020
U. Brefeld et al. (Eds.): ECML PKDD 2019, LNAI 11906, pp. 561–577, 2020.
https://doi.org/10.1007/978-3-030-46150-8_33

and outcomes, and the difference is known as confounding bias. For example, Fig. 1(a) shows a causal graph where variable Z is a covariate for estimating the effect of X on Y.

Confounding bias problem has been studied extensively in the field. In principle the identifiability problem can be solved using a set of causal inference rules called *do-calculus* [12], and complete identification algorithms have been developed [5,19,23]. In practice, however, the most widely used method for controlling the confounding bias is the "adjustment formula" $P(\mathbf{y} \mid do(\mathbf{x})) = \sum_{\mathbf{z}} P(\mathbf{y} \mid \mathbf{x}, \mathbf{Z} = \mathbf{z})P(\mathbf{Z} = \mathbf{z})$, which dictates that the causal effect $P(\mathbf{y} \mid do(\mathbf{x}))$ can be computed by *controlling* for a set of covariates $\mathbf{Z}$. Pearl provided a back-door criterion under which a set $\mathbf{Z}$ makes the adjustment formula hold [12].

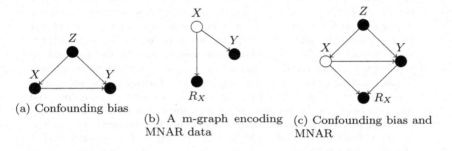

(a) Confounding bias

(b) A m-graph encoding MNAR data

(c) Confounding bias and MNAR

Fig. 1. Examples for confounding bias and MNAR

Another major challenge to valid causal inference is the missing data problem, which occurs when some variable values are missing from observed data. Missing data is a common problem in empirical sciences. Indeed there is a large literature on dealing with missing data in diverse disciplines including statistics, economics, social sciences, and machine learning. To analyze data with missing values, it is imperative to understand the mechanisms that lead to missing data. The seminal work by Rubin [15] classifies missing data mechanisms into three categories: *missing completely at random (MCAR)*, *missing at random (MAR)*, and *missing not at random (MNAR)*. Roughly speaking, the mechanism is MCAR if whether variable values are missing is completely independent of the values of variables in the data set; the mechanism is MAR when missingness is independent of the missing values given the observed values; and the mechanism is MNAR if it is neither MCAR nor MAR. For example, assume that in a study of the effect of family income (FI) and parent's education level (PE) on the quality of child's education (CE), some respondents chose not to reveal their child's education quality for various reasons. Figure 2 shows causal graphs representing the three missing data mechanisms where R_{CE} is an indicator variable such that $R_{CE} = 0$ if the CE value is missing and $R_{CE} = 1$ otherwise. In these graphs solid circles represent always-observed variables and hollow circles represent variables that could have missing values. The model in Fig. 2(a) is MCAR, e.g., respondents decide to reveal the child's education quality based on coin-flips. The model in Fig. 2(b) is MAR, where respondents with higher family income have a higher chance of revealing the child's education quality; however whether the CE values are missing is independent of the actual values of CE given the FI value. The model in Fig. 2(c) is MNAR, where respondents with higher child's education quality have a higher chance of revealing it, i.e., whether the CE values are missing depends on the actual values of CE.

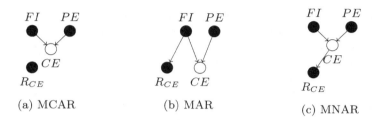

$$FI \quad PE \qquad\qquad FI \quad PE \qquad\qquad FI \quad PE$$

$$CE \qquad\qquad\qquad\qquad\qquad\qquad CE$$

$$R_{CE} \qquad\qquad R_{CE} \quad CE \qquad\qquad R_{CE}$$

(a) MCAR   (b) MAR   (c) MNAR

Fig. 2. Three types of missing data mechanisms

It is known that when the data is MAR, the underlying distribution is estimable from observed data with missing values. Then a causal effect is estimable if it is identifiable from the observed distribution [10]. However, if the data is MNAR, whether a probabilistic distribution or a causal effect is estimable from missing data depends closely on both the query and the exact missing data mechanisms. For example, in the MNAR model in Fig. 1(b), $P(X)$ cannot be estimated consistently even if infinite amount of data are collected, while $P(y|do(x)) = P(y|x) = P(y|x, R_X = 1)$ is estimable from missing data. On the other hand, in the MNAR model in Fig. 1(c), $P(y|do(x))$ is not estimable. In the MNAR model in Fig. 2(c), neither $P(CE)$ nor $P(CE \mid do(FI))$ can be estimated from observed data with missing values.

Various techniques have been developed to deal with missing data in statistical inference, e.g., listwise deletion [7], which requires data to be MCAR to obtain unbiased estimates, and multiple imputation [16], which requires MAR. Most of the work in machine learning makes MAR assumption and use maximum likelihood based methods (e.g. EM algorithms) [6], with a few work explicitly incorporates missing data mechanism into the model [6,8,9].

The use of graphical models called *m-graphs* for inference with missing data was more recent [11]. M-graphs provide a general framework for inference with arbitrary types of missing data mechanisms including MNAR. Sufficient conditions for determining whether probabilistic queries (e.g., $P(\mathbf{y} \mid \mathbf{x})$ or $P(\mathbf{x}, \mathbf{y})$) are estimable from missing data are provided in [10,11]. General algorithms for identifying the joint distribution have been developed in [18,22].

The problem of identifying causal effects $P(\mathbf{y} \mid do(\mathbf{x}))$ from missing data in the causal graphical model settings has not been well studied. To the best of our knowledge the only results are the sufficient conditions given in [10]. The goal of this paper is to provide general conditions under which the causal effects can be identified from missing data using the covariate adjustment formula – the most pervasive method in practice for causal effect estimation under confounding bias.

We will also extend our results to cope with another common obstacles to valid causal inference - *selection bias*. Selection bias may happen due to preferential exclusion of part of the population from sampling. To illustrate, consider a study of the effect of diet on blood sugar. If individuals that are healthy and consume less sugar than average population are less likely to participate in the study, then the data gathered is not a faithful representation of the population and biased results will be produced. This bias cannot be removed by sampling more examples or controlling for confounding bias. Note that, in some sense, selection bias could be considered as a very special case of missing data mechanisms, where values of all of the variables are either all observed or all missing simultaneously. Missing data problem allows much richer missingness patterns such that in any particular observation, some of the variables could be observed and others could be missing. Missing data is modeled by introducing individual missingness indicators for each variable (such that $R_X = 0$ if X value is missing), while selection bias is typically modeled by introducing a single selection indicator variable (S) representing whether a unit is included in the sample or not (that is, if $S = 0$ then values of all variables are missing).

Identifying causal effects from selection bias has been studied in the literature [1, 2]. Adjustment formulas for recovering causal effects under selection bias have been introduced and complete graphical criteria have been developed [3, 4]. However these results are not applicable to the missing data problems which have much richer missingness patterns than could be modeled by selection bias. To the best of our knowledge, using adjustment for causal effect identification when the observed data suffers from missing values or both selection bias and missing values has not been studied in the causal graphical model settings. In this paper we will provide a characterization for these tasks.

Specifically, the contributions of this paper are:

1. We introduce a covariate adjustment formulation for recovering causal effects from missing data, and provide a necessary and sufficient graphical condition for when a set of covariates are valid for adjustment.
2. We introduce a covariate adjustment formulation for causal effects identification when the observed data suffer from both selection bias and missing values, and provide a necessary and sufficient graphical condition for the validity of a set of covariates for adjustment.
3. We develop an algorithm that lists *all* valid adjustment sets in polynomial delay time, and an algorithm that finds a valid adjustment set containing the minimum number of variables. The algorithms are useful for scientists to select adjustment sets with desired properties (e.g. low measurement cost).

The proofs are presented in the Appendix in [17] due to the space constraints.

2   Definitions and Related Work

Each variable will be represented with a capital letter (X) and its realized value with the small letter (x). We will use bold letters $(\mathbf{X})$ to denote sets of variables.

Structural Causal Models. The systematic analysis of confounding bias, missing data mechanisms, and selection bias requires a formal language where the characterization of the underlying data-generating model can be encoded explicitly. We use the language of Structural Causal Models (SCM) [13]. In SCMs, performing an action/intervention of setting $\mathbf{X}=\mathbf{x}$ is represented through the do-operator, $do(\mathbf{X}=\mathbf{x})$, which induces an experimental distribution $P(\mathbf{y}|do(\mathbf{x}))$, known as the causal effect of $\mathbf{X}$ on $\mathbf{Y}$. We will use do-calculus to derive causal expressions from other causal quantities. For a detailed discussion of SCMs and do-calculus, we refer readers to [13].

Each SCM M has a causal graph G associated to it, with directed arrows encoding direct causal relationships and dashed-bidirected arrows encoding the existence of an unobserved common causes. We use typical graph-theoretic terminology $Pa(\mathbf{C}), Ch(\mathbf{C}), De(\mathbf{C}), An(\mathbf{C})$ representing the union of $\mathbf{C}$ and respectively the parents, children, descendants, and ancestors of $\mathbf{C}$. We use $G_{\overline{\mathbf{C}_1}\underline{\mathbf{C}_2}}$ to denote the graph resulting from deleting all incoming edges to $\mathbf{C}_1$ and all outgoing edges from $\mathbf{C}_2$ in G. The expression $(\mathbf{X} \perp\!\!\!\perp \mathbf{Y} \mid \mathbf{Z})_G$ denotes that $\mathbf{X}$ is d-separated from $\mathbf{Y}$ given $\mathbf{Z}$ in the corresponding causal graph G [13] (subscript may be omitted).

Missing Data and M-Graphs. To deal with missing data, we use *m-graphs* introduced in [11] to represent both the data generation model and the missing data mechanisms. M-graphs enhance the causal graph G by introducing a set $\mathbf{R}$ of binary missingness indicator variables. We will also partition the set of observable variables $\mathbf{V}$ into $\mathbf{V}_o$ and $\mathbf{V}_m$ such that $\mathbf{V}_o$ is the set of variables that will be observed in all data cases and $\mathbf{V}_m$ is the set of variables that are missing in some data cases and observed in other cases. Every variable $V_i \in \mathbf{V}_m$ is associated with a variable $R_{V_i} \in \mathbf{R}$ such that, in any observed data case, $R_{V_i} = 0$ if the value of corresponding V_i is missing and $R_{V_i} = 1$ if V_i is observed. We assume that $\mathbf{R}$ variables may not be parents of variables in $\mathbf{V}$, since $\mathbf{R}$ variables are missingness indicator variables and we assume that the data generation process over $\mathbf{V}$ variables does not depend on the missingness mechanisms. For any set $\mathbf{C} \subseteq \mathbf{V}_m$, let $\mathbf{R}_{\mathbf{C}}$ represent the set of $\mathbf{R}$ variables corresponding to variables in $\mathbf{C}$. See Fig. 2 for examples of m-graphs, in which we use solid circles to represent always observed variables in $\mathbf{V}_o$ and $\mathbf{R}$, and hollow circles to represent partially observed variables in $\mathbf{V}_m$.

Causal Effect Identification by Adjustment. Covariate adjustment is the most widely used technique for identifying causal effects from observational data. Formally,

Definition 1 (Adjustment Formula [13]**).** *Given a causal graph G over a set of variables* V, *a set* Z *is called* covariate adjustment *(or adjustment for short) for estimating the causal effect of* X *on* Y, *if, for any distribution* $P(V)$ *compatible with G, it holds that*

$$P(y \mid do(x)) = \sum_{z} P(y \mid x, z) P(z). \tag{1}$$

Pearl developed the celebrated "Backdoor Criterion" to determine whether a set is admissible for adjustment [12] given in the following:

Definition 2 (Backdoor Criterion). *A set of variables* Z *satisfies the backdoor criterion relative to a pair of variables* (X, Y) *in a causal graph G if:*

(a) No node in Z *is a descendant of* X.
(b) Z *blocks every path between* X *and* Y *that contains an arrow into* X.

Complete graphical conditions have been derived for determining whether a set is admissible for adjustment [14, 20, 24] as follows.

Definition 3 (Proper Causal Path). *A proper causal path from a node* $X \in$ X *to a node* $Y \in$ Y *is a causal path (i.e., a directed path) which does not intersect* X *except at the beginning of the path.*

Definition 4 (Adjustment Criterion [20]**).** *A set of variables* Z *satisfies the adjustment criterion relative to a pair of variables* (X, Y) *in a causal graph G if:*

(a) No element of Z *is a descendant in* $G_{\overline{X}}$ *of any* $W \notin X$ *which lies on a proper causal path from* X *to* Y.
(b) All non-causal paths between X *and* Y *in G are blocked by* Z.

A set Z is an admissible adjustment for estimating the causal effect of X on Y by the adjustment formula if and only if it satisfies the adjustment criterion.

3   Adjustment for Recovering Causal Effects from Missing Data

In this section we address the task of recovering a causal effect $P(y \mid do(x))$ from missing data given a m-graph G over observed variables $V = V_o \cup V_m$ and missingness indicators R. The main difference with the well studied identifiability problem [13], where we attempt to identify $P(y \mid do(x))$ from the joint distribution $P(V)$, lies in that, given data corrupted by missing values, $P(V)$ itself may not be recoverable. Instead, a distribution like $P(V_o, V_m, R = 1)$ is assumed to be estimable from observed data cases in which all variables in V are observed (i.e., complete data cases). In general, in the context of missing data, the probability distributions in the form of $P(V_o, W, R_W = 1)$ for any $W \subseteq V_m$, called *manifest distributions*, are assumed to be estimable from observed data cases in which all variables in $\mathbf{W}$ are observed (values of variables in $\mathbf{V}_m \setminus \mathbf{W}$ are possibly missing). The problem of recovering probabilistic queries from the manifest distributions has been studied in [10,11,18,22].

We will extend the adjustment formula for identifying causal effects to the context of missing data based on the following observation which is stated in Theorem 1 in [11]:

Lemma 1. *For any* $\mathbf{W}_o, \mathbf{Z}_o \in \mathbf{V}_o$ *and* $\mathbf{W}_m, \mathbf{Z}_m \in \mathbf{V}_m$, $P(\mathbf{W}_o, \mathbf{W}_m \mid \mathbf{Z}_o, \mathbf{Z}_m, \mathbf{R}_{\mathbf{W}_m \cup \mathbf{Z}_m} = 1)$ *is recoverable.*

Formally, we introduce the adjustment formula for recovering causal effects from missing data by extending Eq. (1) as follows.

Definition 5 (M-Adjustment Formula). *Given a m-graph G over observed variables* $\mathbf{V} = \mathbf{V}_o \cup \mathbf{V}_m$ *and missingness indicators* $\mathbf{R}$, *a set* $\mathbf{Z} \subseteq \mathbf{V}$ *is called a m-adjustment (adjustment under missing data) set for estimating the causal effect of* $\mathbf{X}$ *on* $\mathbf{Y}$, *if, for every model compatible with G, it holds that*

$$P(\mathbf{y} \mid do(\mathbf{x})) = \sum_z P(\mathbf{y} \mid \mathbf{x}, \mathbf{z}, \mathbf{R_W} = 1)P(\mathbf{z} \mid \mathbf{R_W} = 1), \qquad (2)$$

where $\mathbf{W} = \mathbf{V}_m \cap (\mathbf{X} \cup \mathbf{Y} \cup \mathbf{Z})$.

In the above formulation, we allow that the treatments $\mathbf{X}$, outcomes $\mathbf{Y}$, and covariates $\mathbf{Z}$ all could contain $\mathbf{V}_m$ variables that have missing values. Both terms on the right-hand-side of Eq. (2) are recoverable based on Lemma 1. Therefore the causal effect $P(\mathbf{y} \mid do(\mathbf{x}))$ is recoverable if it can be expressed in the form of m-adjustment.

We look for conditions under which a set $\mathbf{Z}$ is admissible as m-adjustment. Intuitively, we can start with the adjustment formula (1), consider an adjustment set as a candidate m-adjustment set, and then check for needed conditional independence relations. Based on this intuition, we obtain a straightforward sufficient condition for a set $\mathbf{Z}$ to be a m-adjustment set as follows.

Proposition 1. *A set $\mathbf{Z}$ is a m-adjustment set for estimating the causal effect of* $\mathbf{X}$ *on* $\mathbf{Y}$ *if, letting* $\mathbf{W} = \mathbf{V}_m \cap (\mathbf{X} \cup \mathbf{Y} \cup \mathbf{Z})$,

(a) $\mathbf{Z}$ *satisfies the adjustment criterion (Definition 4),*
(b) $\mathbf{R_W}$ *is d-separated from* $\mathbf{Y}$ *given* $\mathbf{X}, \mathbf{Z}$, *i.e.,* $(\mathbf{Y} \perp\!\!\!\perp \mathbf{R_W} \mid \mathbf{X}, \mathbf{Z})$, *and*
(c) $\mathbf{Z}$ *is d-separated from* $\mathbf{R_W}$, *i.e.,* $(\mathbf{Z} \perp\!\!\!\perp \mathbf{R_W})$.

Proof. Condition (a) makes sure that the causal effect can be identified in terms of the adjustment formula Eq. (1). Then given Conditions (b) and (c), Eq. (1) is equal to Eq. (2).

However this straightforward criterion in Proposition 1 is not necessary. To witness, consider the set $\{V_{m1}, V_{m2}\}$ in Fig. 3 which satisfies the back-door criterion but not the conditions in Proposition 1 because V_{m2} is not d-separated from R_2. Still, it can be shown that $\{V_{m1}, V_{m2}\}$ is a m-adjustment set (e.g. by do-calculus derivation).

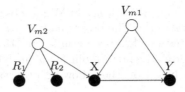

Fig. 3. In this m-graph V_{m2} is not d-separated from R_2. However, $\{V_{m2}, V_{m1}\}$ is an admissible m-adjustment set.

Next we introduce a complete criterion to determine whether a covariate set is admissible as m-adjustment to recover causal effects from missing data, extending the existing work on adjustment [3,4,14,20,24].

Definition 6 (M-Adjustment Criterion). *Given a m-graph G over observed variables $\boldsymbol{V} = \boldsymbol{V_o} \cup \boldsymbol{V_m}$ and missingness indicators $\boldsymbol{R}$, and disjoint sets of variables $\boldsymbol{X}, \boldsymbol{Y}, \boldsymbol{Z} \subseteq \boldsymbol{V}$, letting $\boldsymbol{W} = \boldsymbol{V_m} \cap (\boldsymbol{X} \cup \boldsymbol{Y} \cup \boldsymbol{Z})$, $\boldsymbol{Z}$ satisfies the m-adjustment criterion relative to the pair $(\boldsymbol{X}, \boldsymbol{Y})$ if*

(a) *No element of $\boldsymbol{Z}$ is a descendant in $G_{\overline{\boldsymbol{X}}}$ of any $W \notin \boldsymbol{X}$ which lies on a proper causal path from $\boldsymbol{X}$ to $\boldsymbol{Y}$.*
(b) *All non-causal paths between $\boldsymbol{X}$ and $\boldsymbol{Y}$ in G are blocked by $\boldsymbol{Z}$ and $\boldsymbol{R_W}$.*
(c) *$\boldsymbol{R_W}$ is d-separated from $\boldsymbol{Y}$ given $\boldsymbol{X}$ under the intervention of do($\boldsymbol{x}$), i.e., $(\boldsymbol{Y} \perp\!\!\!\perp \boldsymbol{R_W} \mid \boldsymbol{X})_{G_{\overline{\boldsymbol{X}}}}$.*
(d) *Every $X \in \boldsymbol{X}$ is either a non-ancestor of $\boldsymbol{R_W}$ or it is d-separated from $\boldsymbol{Y}$ in $G_{\underline{X}}$, i.e., $\forall X \in \boldsymbol{X} \cap An(\boldsymbol{R_W}), (X \perp\!\!\!\perp \boldsymbol{Y})_{G_{\underline{X}}}$.*

Theorem 1 (M-Adjustment). *A set $\boldsymbol{Z}$ is a m-adjustment set for recovering causal effect of $\boldsymbol{X}$ on $\boldsymbol{Y}$ by the m-adjustment formula in Definition 5 if and only if it satisfies the m-adjustment criterion in Definition 6.*

Conditions (a) and (b) in Definition 6 echo the adjustment criterion in Definition 4, and it can be shown that if $\boldsymbol{Z}$ satisfies the m-adjustment criterion then it satisfies the adjustment criterion (using the fact that no variables in $\boldsymbol{R}$ can be parents of variables in $\boldsymbol{V}$). In other words, we only need to look for m-adjustment sets from admissible adjustment sets.

As an example consider Fig. 3. Both $\{V_{m1}\}$ and $\{V_{m1}, V_{m2}\}$ satisfy the m-adjustment criterion (and the adjustment criterion too). According to Theorem 1, $P(y \mid do(x))$ can be recovered from missing data by m-adjustment as

$$P(y \mid do(x)) = \sum_{v_{m1}} p(y \mid x, v_{m1}, R_1 = 1) P(v_{m1} \mid R_1 = 1), \tag{3}$$

$$= \sum_{v_{m1}, v_{m2}} P(y \mid x, v_{m1}, v_{m2}, R_1 = 1, R_2 = 1) P(v_{m1}, v_{m2} \mid R_1 = 1, R_2 = 1). \tag{4}$$

4   Listing M-Adjustment Sets

In the previous section we provided a criterion under which a set of variables
Z is an admissible m-adjustment set for recovering a causal effect. It is natural
to ask how to find an admissible set. In reality, it is common that more than
one set of variables are admissible. In such situations it is possible that some
m-adjustment sets might be preferable over others based on various aspects such
as feasibility, difficulty, and cost of collecting variables. Next we first present an
algorithm that systematically lists all m-adjustment sets and then present an
algorithm that finds a minimum m-adjustment set. These algorithms provide
flexibility for researchers to choose their preferred adjustment set based on their
needs and assumptions.

4.1   Listing All Admissible Sets

It turns out in general there may exist exponential number of m-adjustment sets.
To illustrate, we look for possible m-adjustment sets in the m-graph in Fig. 4 for
recovering the causal effect $P(y \mid do(x))$ (this graph is adapted from a graph
in [4]). A valid m-adjustment set **Z** needs to close all the k non-causal paths
from X to Y. **Z** must contain at least one variable in $\{V_{i1}, V_{i2}, V_{i3}\}$ for each
$i = 1, \ldots, k$. Therefore, to close each path, there are 7 possible **Z** sets, and for k
paths, we have total 7^k **Z** sets as potential m-adjustment sets. For each of them,
Conditions (c) and (d) in Definition 6 are satisfied because $(\mathbf{R} \perp\!\!\!\perp Y \mid X)_{G_{\overline{X}}}$ and
X is not an ancestor of any **R** variables. We obtain that there are at least 7^k
number of m-adjustment sets.

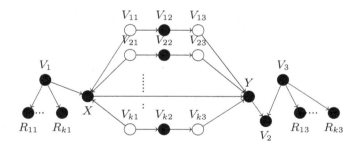

Fig. 4. An example of exponential number of m-adjustment sets

The above example demonstrates that any algorithm that lists all m-
adjustment sets will be exponential time complexity. To deal with this issue,
we will provide an algorithm with polynomial delay complexity [21]. Polynomial
delay algorithms require polynomial time to generate the first output (or indicate failure) and the time between any two consecutive outputs is polynomial as
well.

To facilitate the construction of a listing algorithm, we introduce a graph transformation called *Proper Backdoor Graph* originally introduced in [24].

Definition 7 (Proper Backdoor Graph [24]). *Let G be a causal graph, and X, Y be disjoint subsets of variables. The proper backdoor graph, denoted as $G_{X,Y}^{pbd}$, is obtained from G by removing the first edge of every proper causal path from X to Y.*

Next we present an alternative equivalent formulation of the m-adjustment criterion in Definition 6 that will be useful in constructing a listing algorithm.

Definition 8 (M-Adjustment Criterion, Math. Version). *Given a m-graph G over observed variables $V = V_o \cup V_m$ and missingness indicators R, and disjoint sets of variables X, Y, $Z \subseteq V$, letting $W = V_m \cap (X \cup Y \cup Z)$, Z satisfies the m-adjustment criterion relative to the pair (X, Y) if*

(a) $Z \cap Dpcp(X, Y) = \phi$
(b) $(Y \perp\!\!\!\perp X \mid Z, R_W)_{G_{X,Y}^{pbd}}$
(c) $(Y \perp\!\!\!\perp R_W \mid X)_{G_{\overline{X}}}$
(d) $((X \cap An(R_W)) \perp\!\!\!\perp Y)_{G_X}$

where $D_{pcp}(X, Y) = De((De(X)_{G_{\overline{X}}} \setminus X) \cap An(Y)_{G_{\overline{X}}})$.

In Definition 8, $D_{pcp}(X, Y)$, originally introduced in [24], represents the set of descendants of those variables in a proper causal path from X to Y.

Proposition 2. *Definition 8 and Definition 6 are equivalent.*

Finally to help understanding the logic of the listing algorithm we introduce a definition originally introduced in [4]:

Definition 9 (Family of Separators [4]). *For disjoint sets of variables X, Y, E, and $I \subseteq E$, a family of separators is defined as follows:*

$$Z_{G(X,Y)}\langle I, E \rangle := \{ Z \mid (X \perp\!\!\!\perp Y \mid Z)_G \text{ and } I \subseteq Z \subseteq E \}, \qquad (5)$$

which represents the set of all sets that d-separate X and Y and encompass all variables in set I but do not have any variables outside E.

Algorithm 1 presents the function ListMAdj that lists all the m-adjustment sets in a given m-graph G for recovering the causal effect of $\mathbf{X}$ on $\mathbf{Y}$. We note that the algorithm uses an external function FindSep described in [24] (not presented in this paper). FindSep(G, $\mathbf{X}$, $\mathbf{Y}$, $\mathbf{I}$, $\mathbf{E}$) will return a set in $Z_{G(\mathbf{X},\mathbf{Y})}\langle \mathbf{I}, \mathbf{E} \rangle$ if such a set exists; otherwise it returns $\perp$ representing failure.

Algorithm 1: Listing all the m-adjustment sets

1 Function $ListMAdj$ $(G, \boldsymbol{X}, \boldsymbol{Y}, \boldsymbol{V}_o, \boldsymbol{V}_m, \boldsymbol{R})$
2 $\quad$ $G_{\boldsymbol{X}, \boldsymbol{Y}}^{pbd} \leftarrow$ compute proper back-door graph G
3 $\quad$ $\boldsymbol{E} \leftarrow (\boldsymbol{V}_o \cup \boldsymbol{V}_m \cup \boldsymbol{R}) \setminus \{\boldsymbol{X} \cup \boldsymbol{Y} \cup D_{pcp}(\boldsymbol{X}, \boldsymbol{Y})\}$.
4 $\quad$ ListSepConditions$(G_{\boldsymbol{X}, \boldsymbol{Y}}^{pbd}, \boldsymbol{X}, \boldsymbol{Y}, \boldsymbol{R}, \boldsymbol{V}_o, \boldsymbol{V}_m, \boldsymbol{I} = \{\boldsymbol{R}_{\boldsymbol{X} \cap \boldsymbol{V}_m} \cup \boldsymbol{R}_{\boldsymbol{Y} \cap \boldsymbol{V}_m}\}, \boldsymbol{E})$
5 Function $ListSepConditions$ $(G, \boldsymbol{X}, \boldsymbol{Y}, \boldsymbol{R}, \boldsymbol{V}_o, \boldsymbol{V}_m, \boldsymbol{I}, \boldsymbol{E})$
6 $\quad$ **if** $(\boldsymbol{Y} \perp\!\!\!\perp \boldsymbol{R}_I \mid \boldsymbol{X})_{G_{\overline{\boldsymbol{X}}}}$ and $((\boldsymbol{X} \cap An(\boldsymbol{R}_I)) \perp\!\!\!\perp \boldsymbol{Y})_{G_{\underline{\boldsymbol{X}}}}$ and
       $\quad\quad$ $FindSep(G, \boldsymbol{X}, \boldsymbol{Y}, \boldsymbol{I}, \boldsymbol{E}) \neq \perp$ **then**
7 $\quad\quad$ **if** $\boldsymbol{I} = \boldsymbol{E}$ **then**
8 $\quad\quad\quad$ Output$(\boldsymbol{I} \setminus \boldsymbol{R})$
9 $\quad\quad$ **else**
10 $\quad\quad\quad$ W $\leftarrow$ arbitrary variable from $\boldsymbol{E} \setminus (\boldsymbol{I} \cup \boldsymbol{R})$
11 $\quad\quad\quad$ **if** $W \in \boldsymbol{V}_o$ **then**
12 $\quad\quad\quad\quad$ ListSepConditions$(G, \boldsymbol{X}, \boldsymbol{Y}, \boldsymbol{R}, \boldsymbol{V}_o, \boldsymbol{V}_m, \boldsymbol{I} \cup \{W\}, \boldsymbol{E})$
13 $\quad\quad\quad\quad$ ListSepConditions$(G, \boldsymbol{X}, \boldsymbol{Y}, \boldsymbol{R}, \boldsymbol{V}_o, \boldsymbol{V}_m, \boldsymbol{I}, \boldsymbol{E} \setminus \{W\})$
14 $\quad\quad\quad$ **if** $W \in \boldsymbol{V}_m$ and $R_W \in \boldsymbol{E}$ **then**
15 $\quad\quad\quad\quad$ ListSepConditions$(G, \boldsymbol{X}, \boldsymbol{Y}, \boldsymbol{R}, \boldsymbol{V}_o, \boldsymbol{V}_m, \boldsymbol{I} \cup \{W, R_W\}, \boldsymbol{E})$
16 $\quad\quad\quad\quad$ ListSepConditions$(G, \boldsymbol{X}, \boldsymbol{Y}, \boldsymbol{R}, \boldsymbol{V}_o, \boldsymbol{V}_m, \boldsymbol{I}, \boldsymbol{E} \setminus \{W, R_W\})$

Function ListMAdj works by first excluding all variables lying in the proper causal paths from consideration (Line 3) and then calling the function List-SepConditions (Line 4) to return all the m-adjustment sets. The function of ListSepConditions is summarized in the following proposition:

Proposition 3 (Correctness of ListSepCondition). *Given a m-graph G and sets of disjoint variables $\boldsymbol{X}$, $\boldsymbol{Y}$, $\boldsymbol{E}$, and $\boldsymbol{I} \subseteq \boldsymbol{E}$, ListSepConditions lists all sets $\boldsymbol{Z}$ such that:*

$$\boldsymbol{Z} \in \{\boldsymbol{Z} \mid (\boldsymbol{X} \perp\!\!\!\perp \boldsymbol{Y} \mid \boldsymbol{Z}, \boldsymbol{R}_Z, \boldsymbol{R}_{\boldsymbol{X} \cap \boldsymbol{V}_m}, \boldsymbol{R}_{\boldsymbol{Y} \cap \boldsymbol{V}_m})_{G_{\boldsymbol{X}, \boldsymbol{Y}}^{pbd}} \,\&\, (\boldsymbol{Y} \perp\!\!\!\perp \boldsymbol{R}_Z \mid \boldsymbol{X})_{G_{\overline{\boldsymbol{X}}}} \,\&$$
$$((\boldsymbol{X} \cap An(\boldsymbol{R}_Z)) \perp\!\!\!\perp \boldsymbol{Y})_{G_{\underline{\boldsymbol{X}}}} \,\&\, \boldsymbol{I} \subseteq \boldsymbol{Z} \subseteq \boldsymbol{E}\} \text{ where } \boldsymbol{R}_Z \text{ is a shorthand for } \boldsymbol{R}_{\boldsymbol{Z} \cap \boldsymbol{V}_m}.$$

ListSepConditions, by considering both including and not including each variable, recursively generates all subsets of $\boldsymbol{V}$ and for each generated set examines whether the conditions (b), (c), and (d) in Definition 8 hold or not. If those conditions were satisfied, the algorithm will return that candidate set as a m-adjustment set. ListSepConditions generates each potential set by taking advantage of back-tracking algorithm and at each recursion for a variable $W \in \boldsymbol{V}$ examines two cases of having W in candidate set or not. If $W \in \boldsymbol{V}_o$, then the algorithm examines having and not having this variable in the m-adjustment set and continues to decide about the rest of the variables in next recursion. If $W \in \boldsymbol{V}_m$, then the algorithm includes both W and R_W in the candidate m-adjustment set. Therefore, the algorithm considers both cases of having W, R_W and not having them in the candidate set. ListSepConditions, at the beginning of each recursion (Line 7), examines whether the candidate m-adjustment set so far satisfies the conditions (b), (c), (d) in Definition 8 or not. If any of them is not satisfied, the recursion stops for that candidate set. The function FindSep examines the existence of a set containing all variables in $\boldsymbol{I}$ and not having any of $\mathbf{V} \setminus \mathbf{E}$ that d-separates $\mathbf{X}$ from $\mathbf{Y}$. If this set does not exist FindSep returns $\perp$. ListSepConditions utilizes FindSep in order to check the satisfaction of condition (b) in Definition 8 for the candidate set. Since the graph G given to FindSep is a proper back-door graph, all paths between $\mathbf{X}$ and $\mathbf{Y}$ in this graph is non-causal. Therefore, if a set separates $\mathbf{X}$ and $\mathbf{Y}$ in G^{pbd}, this set blocks all non-causal paths from $\mathbf{X}$ to $\mathbf{Y}$ in G.

The following theorem states that ListMAdj lists all the m-adjustment sets in a given m-graph G for recovering the causal effect of $\mathbf{X}$ on $\mathbf{Y}$.

Theorem 2 (Correctness of ListMAdj). *Given a m-graph G and disjoint sets of variables $\mathbf{X}$ and $\mathbf{Y}$, ListMAdj returns all the sets that satisfy the m-adjustment criterion relative to $(\mathbf{X}, \mathbf{Y})$.*

The following results state that Algorithm 1 is polynomial delay.

Proposition 4 (Time Complexity of ListSepConditions). *ListSepConditions has a time complexity of $O(n(n+m))$ polynomial delay where n and m are the number of variables and edges in the given graph G respectively.*

Theorem 3 (Time Complexity of ListMAdj). *ListMAdj returns all the m-adjustment sets with $O(n(n+m))$ polynomial delay where n and m are the number of variables and edges in the given graph G respectively.*

4.2 Finding a Minimum M-Adjustment Set

The problem of finding a m-adjustment set with minimum number of variables is important in practice. Using a small adjustment set can reduce the computational time. The cost of measuring more variables might be another reason researchers may be interested in finding a minimum adjustment set. Next we present an algorithm that for a given graph G and disjoint sets $\mathbf{X}$ and $\mathbf{Y}$ returns a m-adjustment set with the minimum number of variables.

Algorithm 2: Find minimum size m-adjustment set

1 **Function** *FindMinAdjSet(G, $\mathbf{X}$, $\mathbf{Y}$, $\mathbf{V}_o$, $\mathbf{V}_m$, $\mathbf{R}$)*
2      $G' \leftarrow$ compute proper back-door graph $G^{pbd}_{X,Y}$
3      $\mathbf{E} \leftarrow (\mathbf{V}_o \cup \mathbf{V}_m) \setminus \{\mathbf{X} \cup \mathbf{Y} \cup D_{pcp}(\mathbf{X}, \mathbf{Y})\}$.
4      $\mathbf{E}' \leftarrow \{E \in \mathbf{E} \mid E \in \mathbf{V}_o \text{ or } E \in \mathbf{V}_m \text{ and } (\mathbf{R}_E \perp \mathbf{Y} \mid \mathbf{X})_{G'_{\underline{X}}}\}$
5      $\mathbf{E}'' \leftarrow \{E \in \mathbf{E}' \mid \mathbf{E} \in \mathbf{V}_o \text{ or } E \in \mathbf{V}_m \text{ and } (\mathbf{X} \cap An(\mathbf{R_E}) \perp \mathbf{Y})_{G'_{\underline{X}}}\}$
6      $\mathbf{W} \leftarrow 1$ for all variables
7      $\mathbf{I} \leftarrow$ empty set
8      $\mathbf{N} \leftarrow$ FindMinCostSep(G', $\mathbf{X}$, $\mathbf{Y}$, $\mathbf{I}$, $\mathbf{E}''$, $\mathbf{W}$)
9   return $\mathbf{N} \cup \mathbf{R}_N$

Function FindMinAdjSet takes a m-graph G as input and returns a m-adjustment set with minimum number of variables. The function works by first removing all variables that violate Conditions (a), (c), and (d) in the m-adjustment criterion Definition 8 in lines 2 to 5, and then calling an external function FinMinCostSep given in [24] which returns a minimum weight separator. FindMinAdjSet sets all the weights for each variable to be 1 to get a set with minimum size.

Theorem 4 (Correctness of FindMinAdjSet). *Given a m-graph G and disjoint sets of variables X, and Y, FindMinAdjSet returns a m-adjustment set relative to (X, Y) with the minimum number of variables.*

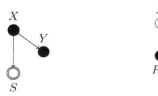

ID	X	R_X	Y	S
1	1	1	0	1
2	0	1	1	1
3	NA	NA	NA	0
4	NA	0	1	1
5	NA	NA	NA	0

(a) Selection bias

(b) MNAR model with selection bias

(c) An example data set compatible with the model in Fig. 5(b)

Fig. 5. Examples of selection bias and MNAR

Theorem 5 (Time Complexity of FindMinAdjSet). *FindMinAdjSet has a time complexity of $O(n^3)$.*

5 Adjustment from Both Selection Bias and Missing Data

In Sects. 3 and 4 we have addressed the task of recovering causal effects by adjustment from missing data. In practice another common issue that data scientists face in estimating causal effects is selection bias. Selection bias can be modeled by introducing a binary indicator variable S such that $S = 1$ if a unit is included in the sample, and $S = 0$ otherwise [2]. Graphically selection bias is modeled by a special hollow node S (drawn round with double border) that is pointed to by every variable in V that affects the process by which an unit is included in the data. In Fig. 5(a), for example, selection is affected by the treatment variable X.

In the context of selection bias, the observed distribution is $P(V \mid S = 1)$, collected under selection bias, instead of $P(V)$. The goal of inference is to recover the causal effect $P(y \mid do(x))$ from $P(V \mid S = 1)$. The use of adjustment for recovering causal effects in this setting has been studied and complete adjustment conditions have been developed in [3,4].

What if the observed data suffers from both selection bias and missing values? In the model in Fig. 5(b), for example, whether a unit is included in the sample depends on the value of the outcome Y. If a unit is included in the sample, the values of treatment X could be missing depending on the actual X values. Figure 5(c) shows an example data set compatible with the model in Fig. 5(b) illustrating the difference between selection bias and missing data. To the best of our knowledge, causal inference under this setting has not been formally studied.

In this section, we will characterize the use of adjustment for causal effect identification when the observed data suffers from both selection bias and missing values. First we introduce an adjustment formula called *MS-adjustment* for recovering causal effect under both missing data and selection bias. Then we provide a complete condition under which a set $\mathbf{Z}$ is valid as MS-adjustment set.

Definition 10 (MS-Adjustment Formula). *Given a m-graph G over observed variables $\mathbf{V} = \mathbf{V}_o \cup \mathbf{V}_m$ and missingness indicators $\mathbf{R}$ augmented with a selection bias indicator S, a set $\mathbf{Z} \subseteq \mathbf{V}$ is called a ms-adjustment (adjustment under missing data and selection bias) set for estimating the causal effect of $\mathbf{X}$ on $\mathbf{Y}$, if for every model compatible with G it holds that*

$$P(\mathbf{y} \mid do(\mathbf{x})) = \sum_z P(\mathbf{y} \mid \mathbf{x}, \mathbf{z}, \mathbf{R_W} = 1, S = 1)P(\mathbf{z} \mid \mathbf{R_W} = 1, S = 1), \quad (6)$$

where $\mathbf{W} = \mathbf{V}_m \cap (\mathbf{X} \cup \mathbf{Y} \cup \mathbf{Z})$.

Both terms on the right-hand-side of Eq. (6) are recoverable from selection biased data in which all variables in $\mathbf{X} \cup \mathbf{Y} \cup \mathbf{Z}$ are observed. Therefore the causal effect $P(\mathbf{y} \mid do(\mathbf{x}))$ is recoverable if it can be expressed in the form of ms-adjustment.

Next we provide a complete criterion to determine whether a set $\mathbf{Z}$ is an admissible ms-adjustment.

Definition 11 (MS-Adjustment Criterion). *Given a m-graph G over observed variables $\mathbf{V} = \mathbf{V}_o \cup \mathbf{V}_m$ and missingness indicators $\mathbf{R}$ augmented with a selection bias indicator S, and disjoint sets of variables $\mathbf{X}, \mathbf{Y}, \mathbf{Z}$, letting $\mathbf{W} = \mathbf{V}_m \cap (\mathbf{X} \cup \mathbf{Y} \cup \mathbf{Z})$, $\mathbf{Z}$ satisfies the ms-adjustment criterion relative to the pair $(\mathbf{X}, \mathbf{Y})$ if*

(a) *No element of $\mathbf{Z}$ is a descendant in $G_{\overline{X}}$ of any $W \notin \mathbf{X}$ which lies on a proper causal path from $\mathbf{X}$ to $\mathbf{Y}$.*

(b) *All non-causal paths between $\mathbf{X}$ and $\mathbf{Y}$ in G are blocked by $\mathbf{Z}$, $\mathbf{R_W}$, and S.*

(c) *$\mathbf{R_W}$ and S are d-separated from $\mathbf{Y}$ given $\mathbf{X}$ under the intervention of $do(\mathbf{x})$. i.e., $(\mathbf{Y} \perp\!\!\!\perp (\mathbf{R_W} \cup S) \mid \mathbf{X})_{G_{\overline{X}}}$*

(d) *Every $X \in \mathbf{X}$ is either a non-ancestor of $\{\mathbf{R_W}, S\}$ or it is d-separated from $\mathbf{Y}$ in $G_{\underline{X}}$. i.e., $\forall X \in \mathbf{X} \cap An(\mathbf{R_W} \cup S), (X \perp\!\!\!\perp \mathbf{Y})_{G_{\underline{X}}}$.*

Theorem 6 (MS-Adjustment). *A set $\mathbf{Z}$ is a ms-adjustment set for recovering causal effect of $\mathbf{X}$ on $\mathbf{Y}$ by the ms-adjustment formula in Definition 10 if and only if it satisfies the ms-adjustment criterion in Definition 11.*

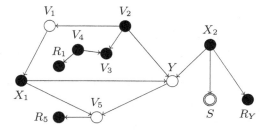

Fig. 6. An example for recovering causal effect under both selection bias and MNAR data

To demonstrate the application of Theorem 6, consider the causal graph in Fig. 6 where V_1, V_5, Y may have missing values and the selection S depends on the values of X_2. To recover the causal effect of $\{X_1, X_2\}$ on variable Y, V_1 satisfies the ms-adjustment criterion. We obtain $P(y \mid do(x_1, x_2)) = \sum_{V_1} P(y \mid x_1, x_2, V_1, S = 1, R_y = 1, R_1 = 1)P(V_1 \mid S = 1, R_y = 1, R_1 = 1)$.

We note that the two algorithms given in Sect. 4, for listing all m-adjustment sets and finding a minimum size m-adjustment set, can be extended to list all ms-adjustment sets and find a minimum ms-adjustment set with minor modifications.

6   Conclusion

In this paper we introduce a m-adjustment formula for recovering causal effect in the presence of MNAR data and provide a necessary and sufficient graphical condition - m-adjustment criterion for when a set of covariates are valid m-adjustment. We introduce a ms-adjustment formulation for causal effects identification in the presence of both selection bias and MNAR data and provide a necessary and sufficient graphical condition - ms-adjustment criterion for when a set of covariates are valid ms-adjustment. We develop an algorithm that lists all valid m-adjustment or ms-adjustment sets in polynomial delay time, and an algorithm that finds a valid m-adjustment or ms-adjustment set containing the minimum number of variables. The algorithms are useful for data scientists to select adjustment sets with desired properties (e.g. low measurement cost). Adjustment is the most used tool for estimating causal effect in the data sciences. The results in this paper should help to alleviate the problem of missing data and selection bias in a broad range of data-intensive applications.

Acknowledgements. This research was partially supported by NSF grant IIS-1704352 and ONR grant N000141712140.

References

1. Bareinboim, E., Tian, J.: Recovering causal effects from selection bias. In: Proceedings of the Twenty-Ninth AAAI Conference on Artificial Intelligence, pp. 3475–3481 (2015)
2. Bareinboim, E., Tian, J., Pearl, J.: Recovering from selection bias in causal and statistical inference. In: Proceeding of the Twenty-Eighth AAAI Conference on Artificial Intelligence, pp. 2410–2416 (2014)
3. Correa, J.D., Bareinboim, E.: Causal effect identification by adjustment under confounding and selection biases. In: Proceedings of the Thirty-First AAAI Conference on Artificial Intelligence, pp. 3740–3746 (2017)
4. Correa, J.D., Tian, J., Bareinboim, E.: Generalized adjustment under confounding and selection biases. In: Thirty-Second AAAI Conference on Artificial Intelligence, pp. 6335–6342 (2018)
5. Huang, Y., Valtorta, M.: Identifiability in causal Bayesian networks: a sound and complete algorithm. In: Proceedings of the 21st National Conference on Artificial Intelligence, vol. 2, pp. 1149–1154 (2006)
6. Koller, D., Friedman, N., Bach, F.: Probabilistic Graphical Models: Principles and Techniques. MIT Press, Cambridge (2009)
7. Little, R.J.A., Rubin, D.B.: Statistical Analysis with Missing Data. Wiley, Hoboken (1986)
8. Marlin, B.M., Zemel, R.S., Roweis, S.T., Slaney, M.: Collaborative filtering and the missing at random assumption. In: Proceedings of the Twenty-Third Conference on Uncertainty in Artificial Intelligence, pp. 267–275 (2007)
9. Marlin, B.M., Zemel, R.S., Roweis, S.T., Slaney, M.: Recommender systems, missing data and statistical model estimation. In: Proceedings of the 22nd International Joint Conference on Artificial Intelligence, pp. 2686–2691 (2011)
10. Mohan, K., Pearl, J.: Graphical models for recovering probabilistic and causal queries from missing data. In: Advances in Neural Information Processing Systems, pp. 1520–1528 (2014)
11. Mohan, K., Pearl, J., Tian, J.: Graphical models for inference with missing data. In: Advances in Neural Information Processing Systems, pp. 1277–1285 (2013)
12. Pearl, J.: Causal diagrams for empirical research. Biometrika $82(4)$, 669–688 (1995)
13. Pearl, J.: Causality: Models, Reasoning and Inference, 2nd edn. Cambridge University Press, Cambridge (2009)
14. Perkovic, E., Textor, J., Kalisch, M., Maathuis, M.H.: Complete graphical characterization and construction of adjustment sets in markov equivalence classes of ancestral graphs. J. Mach. Learn. Res. $18(1)$, 8132–8193 (2017)
15. Rubin, D.: Inference and missing data. Biometrika $63(3)$, 581–592 (1976)
16. Rubin, D.B.: Multiple imputations in sample surveys-a phenomenological Bayesian approach to nonresponse. In: Proceedings of the Survey Research Methods Section of the American Statistical Association, vol. 1, pp. 20–34 (1978)
17. Saadati, M., Tian, J.: Adjustment criteria for recovering causal effects from missing data. Technical report, Department of Computer Science, Iowa State University (2019). arXiv:1907.01654
18. Shpitser, I., Mohan, K., Pearl, J.: Missing data as a causal and probabilistic problem. In: Proceedings of the Thirty-First Conference on Uncertainty in Artificial Intelligence, pp. 802–811 (2015)
19. Shpitser, I., Pearl, J.: Identification of joint interventional distributions in recursive semi-Markovian causal models. In: Proceedings of the National Conference on Artificial Intelligence, vol. 21, p. 1219 (2006)

20. Shpitser, I., VanderWeele, T., Robins, J.M.: On the validity of covariate adjustment for estimating causal effects. In: Proceedings of the Twenty-Sixth Conference on Uncertainty in Artificial Intelligence, pp. 527–536 (2010)
21. Takata, K.: Space-optimal, backtracking algorithms to list the minimal vertex separators of a graph. Discrete Appl. Math. **158**(15), 1660–1667 (2010)
22. Tian, J.: Recovering probability distributions from missing data. In: Proceedings of the Ninth Asian Conference on Machine Learning, vol. PMLR 77 (2017)
23. Tian, J., Pearl, J.: A general identification condition for causal effects. In: Eighteenth National Conference on Artificial Intelligence, pp. 567–573 (2002)
24. van der Zander, B., Liśkiewicz, M., Textor, J.: Constructing separators and adjustment sets in ancestral graphs. In: Proceedings of the Thirtieth Conference on Uncertainty in Artificial Intelligence, pp. 907–916 (2014)

An Algorithm for Reducing the Number of Distinct Branching Conditions in a Decision Forest

Atsuyoshi Nakamura$^{(\boxtimes)}$ (iD) and Kento Sakurada

Hokkaido University, Kita 14, Nishi 9 Kita-ku, Sapporo 060-0814, Japan
{atsu,k_sakurada}@ist.hokudai.ac.jp

Abstract. Given a decision forest, we study a problem of reducing the number of its distinct branching conditions without changing each tree's structure while keeping classification performance. A decision forest with a smaller number of distinct branching conditions can not only have a smaller description length but also be implemented by hardware more efficiently. To force the modified decision forest to keep classification performance, we consider a condition that the decision paths at each branching node do not change for $100\sigma\%$ of the given feature vectors passing through the node for a given $0 \leq \sigma < 1$. Under this condition, we propose an algorithm that minimizes the number of distinct branching conditions by sharing the same condition among multiple branching nodes. According to our experimental results using 13 datasets in UCI machine learning repository, our algorithm succeeded more than 90% reduction on the number of distinct branching conditions for random forests learned from 3 datasets without degrading classification performance. 90% condition reduction was also observed for 7 other datasets within 0.17 degradation of prediction accuracy from the original prediction accuracy at least 0.673.

Keywords: Decision forest · Algorithm · Simplification

1 Introduction

A decision tree is a popular classifier not only for its classification performance but also for its high interpretability. As base classifiers of an ensemble classifier, decision trees are also preferred due to its usability such as being able to calculate feature importance. Therefore, several decision-tree-based ensemble classifiers such as random forests [3], extremely randomized trees [8] and gradient boosted regression trees [7] have been developed so far.

Various researches have been done to obtain more useful decision trees and forests, and one of them is their simplification such as pruning [9,10]. Simplification of decision trees and forests is important not only as a countermeasure for overfitting but also as enhancement measures of interpretability and prediction time-and-space complexities.

© Springer Nature Switzerland AG 2020
U. Brefeld et al. (Eds.): ECML PKDD 2019, LNAI 11906, pp. 578–589, 2020.
https://doi.org/10.1007/978-3-030-46150-8_34

Simplification methods developed so far for a decision forest, reduce the number of branching nodes or trees. Here, however, we proposed an algorithm that reduces the number of distinct branching conditions without changing the structure of each tree in a given forest. So, the number of branching nodes does not change but multiple nodes become to share the same branching condition by applying our algorithm.

This research is motivated by the recent development of hardware implementation of a random forest for fast inference. Implementation using FPGA has been successful in accelerating the inference process of a random forest [1,12]. In the system proposed in [1], all the branching conditions are processed by fast comparators in parallel, then their binary outputs are used to parallelly evaluate which leaf is reached through a boolean net. The decrease of the number of distinct branching conditions reduces the number of comparators needed for this implementation.

In this paper, we first formalize our simplification problem as the problem of minimizing the number of distinct branching conditions in a decision forest by sharing conditions under the restriction that, given a set of feature vectors D_L and $0 \leq \sigma < 1$, at each branching node in each component tree, paths of at most $100\sigma\%$ of the vectors $\mathbf{x} \in D_L$ passing through the node, can be changed. Assume that all the features are numerical and all the branching conditions are expressed as $x_i \leq \theta_i$ for ith component x_i of a feature vector $\mathbf{x}$ and a fixed threshold θ_i. Under the above restriction, the range in which θ_i can take a value becomes some interval $[\ell_i, u_i)$, and the above problem can be reduced to the problem of obtaining a minimum set that intersects all the given intervals, which are defined for each feature. We propose Algorithm Min_IntSet for this reduced problem and prove its correctness. We also develop Algorithm Min_DBN for our original problem using Min_IntSet to solve the reduced problem for each feature.

Effectiveness of our algorithm Min_DBN is demonstrated for the random forests that are learned from 13 datasets in UCI machine learning repository [6]. Without prediction performance degradation, Min_DBN with $\sigma = 0$ succeeds to reduce the number of distinct branching conditions at least 48.9% for all the datasets but RNA-Seq PANCAN dataset, which has more than 30 times larger number of features than the number of its train instances. For hapmass and magic datasets, which have the two largest number of instances, more than 90% condition reduction is achieved by running Min_DBN with $\sigma = 0$. All the datasets except RNA-Seq PANCAN, iris and blood datasets, whose vectors of the last two datasets are composed of only four features, achieves more than 90% condition reduction by allowing larger rate of path change ($\sigma = 0.1, 0.2, 0.3$) within about 0.17 prediction accuracy decrease from the original prediction accuracy, which is at least 0.673.

2   Problem Setting

Consider a d-dimensional real feature space $X = \mathbb{R}^d$ and a finite class-label space $C = \{1, \ldots, \ell\}$. A *classifier* $f : X \to C$ is a function that assigns some label

$c \in C$ to an arbitrary input feature vector $\mathbf{x} = (x_1, ..., x_d) \in \mathbb{R}^d$. A *decision tree* T is a kind of classifier that decides the class label assignment c of an input $\mathbf{x}$ by starting from the root node, repeatedly choosing a child node at each internal node depending on the branching condition attached to the node, and assigning label c that is labeled at the reached leaf node. Here, we assume that each internal node has just two child nodes and the attached branching condition is in the form of $x_i \leq \theta_i$. For a given feature vector $\mathbf{x}$, the left child node is chosen at a node if its branching condition $x_i \leq \theta_i$ is satisfied in the class label assignment process using a decision tree. Otherwise, the right child node is chosen. The $\mathbf{x}$'s *path in a decision tree* T is the path from the root node to the reached leaf node in the class label assignment process. We let a pair (i, θ_i) of a feature id i and a threshold θ_i denote the branching condition $x_i \leq \theta_i$. A set of decision trees is called a *decision forest*.

We consider the following problem.

Problem 1 *(Problem of minimizing the number of distinct branching conditions in a decision forest).* For a given decision forest $\{T_1, ...T_m\}$, a given set of feature vectors $\{\mathbf{x}_1, ..., \mathbf{x}_n\}$ and a given path-changeable rate $0 \leq \sigma < 1$, minimize the number of distinct branching conditions (i, θ_i) by changing the values of some θ_i without changing more than $100\sigma\%$ of feature vectors' paths passing through each node of each decision tree T_i $(i = 1, \ldots, m)$.

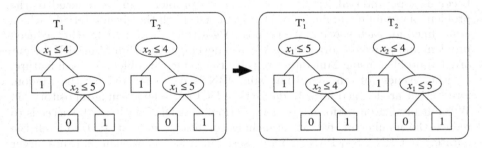

Fig. 1. The number of distinct branching conditions $(1,4), (1,5), (2,4), (2,5)$ in decision forest $\{T_1, T_2\}$ can be reduced to $(1,5), (2,4)$ by changing conditions $(1,4)$ and $(2,5)$ in T_1 to $(1,5)$ and $(2,4)$, respectively, without changing the path of any feature vector in $\{(1,1), (2,7), (7,2), (8,8)\}$.

Example 1. Consider Problem 1 for a decision forest $\{T_1, T_2\}$ in Fig. 1, a feature vector set $\{(1,1), (2,7), (7,2), (8,8)\}$, and a path-changeable rate $\sigma = 0$. The distinct branching conditions (i, θ_i) in decision forest $\{T_1, T_2\}$ are the following four:

$$(i, \theta_i) = (1,4), (1,5), (2,4), (2,5).$$

The branching conditions $(1,4)$ and $(2,5)$ in T_1 can be changed to $(1,5)$ and $(2,4)$, respectively, without changing the path of any feature vector in the given set $\{(1,1),(2,7),(7,2),(8,8)\}$. Decision tree T_1' in Fig. 1 is the one that is made from T_1 by this branching-condition change. Decision forest $\{T_1', T_2\}$ has two distinct conditions $(1,5),(2,4)$, which is a solution of Problem 1.

Remark 1. Decision forest $\{T_1, T_2\}$ in Fig. 1 can be outputted by a decision forest learner with training samples $((x_1, x_2), y) = ((1,1),1),((2,7),0),((7,2),0),$ $((8,8),1)$. Assume that two sets of bootstrap samples are $D_1 = \{((1,1),1),$ $((7,2),0),((8,8),1)\}$ and $D_2 = \{((1,1),1),((2,7),0),((8,8),1)\}$, and all the features are sampled for both the sets. In the implementation that the middle points of adjacent feature values are used as threshold candidates for branching conditions, CART algorithm can output T_1 for D_1 and T_2 for D_2. Decision tree T_1' in Fig. 1 has the same Gini Impurity as T_1 at each corresponding branching node for the set of samples D_1.

3   Problem of Minimum Set Intersecting All the Given Intervals

For a given path-changeable rate $0 \le \sigma < 1$, at each branching node with condition (i, θ_i), the range in which θ_i can take a value without changing more than $100\sigma\%$ of given feature vectors' paths passing through the node, becomes interval $[\ell_i, u_i)$. So, the problem of minimizing the number of distinct branching conditions in a decision forest can be solved by finding clusters of conditions (i, θ_i) whose changeable intervals have a common value for each feature i. Thus, solving Problem 1 can be reduced to solving the following problem for each feature i.

Problem 2 (Problem of Minimum Set Intersecting All the Given Intervals). For a given set of intervals $\{[\ell_1, u_1), \ldots, [\ell_n, u_n)\}$, find a minimum set that intersects all the intervals $[\ell_j, u_j)$ $(j = 1, \ldots, n)$.

We propose Min_IntSet (Algorithm 1) as an algorithm for Problem 2. The algorithm is very simple. First, it sorts the given set of intervals $\{[\ell_1, u_1), \ldots, [\ell_n, u_n)\}$ by lower bound ℓ_i in ascending order (Line 1). For the obtained sorted list $([\ell_{i_1}, u_{i_1}), \ldots, [\ell_{i_n}, u_{i_n}))$, starting from $k = 1$ and $b_1 = 1$, the algorithm finds the kth point s_k by calculating the maximal prefix $([\ell_{i_{b_k}}, u_{i_{b_k}}), \ldots, [\ell_{i_{j-1}}, u_{i_{j-1}}))$ of the list $([\ell_{i_{b_k}}, u_{i_{b_k}}), \ldots, [\ell_{i_n}, u_{i_n}))$ that contain non-empty intersection

$$\bigcap_{h=b_k}^{j-1} [\ell_{i_h}, u_{i_h}) = [\ell_{i_{j-1}}, \min_{h=b_k,\ldots,j-1} u_{i_h}),$$

and t_k is updated such that $t_k = \min_{h=b_k,\ldots,j-1} u_{i_h}$ holds (Line 9). The algorithm can know the maximality of the prefix $([\ell_{i_{b_k}}, u_{i_{b_k}}), \ldots, [\ell_{i_{j-1}}, u_{i_{j-1}}))$ by checking the condition $\ell_{i_j} \ge t_k$ which means that the intersection $[\ell_{i_j}, t_k)$ is empty (Line 4). After finding the maximal prefix with non-empty intersection $[\ell_{i_{j-1}}, t_k)$,

---

Algorithm 1. Min_IntSet

Input: $\{[\ell_i, u_i] | i \in I\}$: Non-empty set of intervals
Output: $\{s_1, ..., s_k\}$: Minimum set satisfying $\{s_1, ..., s_k\} \cap [\ell_i, u_i) \neq \emptyset$ $(i = 1, ..., n)$
$\qquad \{I_1, ..I_k\} : I_j = \{i \in I | s_j \in [\ell_i, u_i)\}$ $(j = 1, ..., k)$

1: $[\ell_{i_1}, u_{i_1}), ..., [\ell_{i_n}, u_{i_n})$ ← list sorted by the values of ℓ_i in ascending order.
2: $k \leftarrow 1, t_1 \leftarrow u_{i_1}, b_1 \leftarrow 1$
3: **for** $j = 2$ to n **do**
4: $\quad$ **if** $\ell_{i_j} \geq t_k$ **then**
5: $\qquad s_k \leftarrow \frac{\ell_{i_{j-1}} + t_k}{2}$
6: $\qquad I_k \leftarrow \{i_{b_k}, ..., i_{j-1}\}$
7: $\qquad k \leftarrow k + 1, t_k \leftarrow u_{i_j}, b_k \leftarrow j$
8: $\quad$ **else if** $u_{i_j} < t_k$ **then**
9: $\qquad t_k \leftarrow u_{i_j}$
10: $\quad$ **end if**
11: **end for**
12: $s_k \leftarrow \frac{\ell_{i_n} + t_k}{2}, I_k \leftarrow \{i_{b_k}, ..., i_n\}$
13: **return** $\{s_1, ..., s_k\}, \{I_1, .., I_k\}$

---

the middle point of the interval is set to s_k (Line 5) and repeat the same procedure for the updated k and b_k (Line 8).

The following theorem holds for Algorithm Min_IntSet.

Theorem 1. *For a given set of intervals* $\{[\ell_1, u_1], ..., [\ell_n, u_n]\}$, *the set* $\{s_1, ..., s_k\}$ *outputted by Algorithm Min_IntSet is a minimum set that intersects all the intervals* $[\ell_j, u_j)$ $(j = 1, ..., n)$.

Proof. We prove the theorem by mathematical induction in the number of intervals n. For $n = 1$, for-sentence between Line 3 and 11 is not executed. At Line 12, s_1 is set as

$$s_1 = \frac{\ell_{i_1} + u_{i_1}}{2}$$

because $t_1 = u_{i_1}$, and at Line 13 Min_IntSet outputs $\{s_1\}$, which is trivially a minimum set that intersects all the interval in the given set $\{[\ell_1, u_1)\}$.

Consider the case with $n = k + 1$. When if-sentence at Line 4 never holds, $\ell_{i_j} \leq \ell_{i_n} < t_1$ holds for all $j = 1, ..., n$ and Line 8–9 ensures $t_1 \leq u_{i_j}$ for all $j = 1, ..., n$. Thus, $[\ell_{i_n}, t_1)$ is contained by all the intervals and the set that is composed of its middle point s_1 only is trivially a minimum set that intersects all the intervals in the given set $\{[\ell_1, u_1), ..., [\ell_n, u_n)\}$.

When if-sentence at Line 4 holds at least once, s_1 is set as

$$s_1 = \frac{\ell_{i_{j-1}} + t_1}{2},$$

and the rest for-loop is executed for j from $j + 1$ to n given $k = 2$, $t_2 = u_{i_j}$, and $b_2 = j$. It is easy to check that $s_2, ..., s_k$ calculated in the rest part are the same as those outputted by

$$\text{Min\_IntSet}(\{[\ell_{i_j}, u_{i_j}), ..., [\ell_{i_n}, u_{i_n})\}).$$

The condition of if-sentence at Line 4 ensures that the intersection $[\ell_{i_{j-1}}, t_1)$ of $[\ell_{i_1}, u_{i_1}), \ldots, [\ell_{i_{j-1}}, u_{i_{j-1}})$ does not intersect the rest intervals $[\ell_{i_j}, u_{i_j}), \ldots, [\ell_{i_n}, u_{i_n})$. So, any minimum set that intersects all the intervals, must contain at least one value that is at most t_1. Any value s_1 in $[\ell_{i_{j-1}}, t_1)$ can minimize the set of the rest intervals that does not contain s_1. In fact, s_1 is set to the middle point of $[\ell_{i_{j-1}}, t_1)$, so the rest set of intervals is minimized. The set of the rest points $s_2, \ldots, s_k$ calculated by Min_IntSet is the same as the set outputted by $Min\_IntSet(\{[\ell_{i_j}, u_{i_j}), \ldots, [\ell_{i_n}, u_{i_n})\})$, so the minimum set intersecting all the intervals in $\{[\ell_{i_j}, u_{i_j}), \ldots, [\ell_{i_n}, u_{i_n})\}$ can be obtained using inductive assumption. Thus, Min_IntSet outputs a minimum set that intersects all the given intervals in the case with $n = k + 1$. □

The time complexity of Algorithm Min_IntSet is $O(n \log n)$ for the number of intervals n due to the bottleneck of sorting. Its space complexity is trivially $O(n)$.

4 Algorithm for Minimizing the Number of Distinct Branching Conditions

Min_DBN (Algorithm 2) is an algorithm for the problem of minimizing the number of distinct branching conditions in a decision forest. The algorithm uses Algorithm Min_IntSet for each feature $i = 1, \ldots, d$ to find a minimum set of branching thresholds that can share the same value without changing $100\sigma\%$ of paths of given feature vectors passing through each node of each tree in a given decision forest.

Algorithm 2. Min_DBN

Input: $\{\mathbf{x}_1, \ldots, \mathbf{x}_n\}$: Set of feature vectors
   $\{T_1, \ldots, T_m\}$: decision forest
   σ : path-changeable rate $(0 \leq \sigma < 1)$
1: $L_i \leftarrow \emptyset$ for $i = 1, \ldots, d$
2: **for** $j = 1$ to m **do**
3:    **for each** branching node $N_{j,h}$ in T_j **do**
4:      $(i, \theta_i) \leftarrow$ branching condition attached to $N_{j,h}$
5:      $[\ell_{j,h}, u_{j,h}] \leftarrow$ the range of values that θ_i can take without changing
              more than $100\sigma\%$ of paths of $\mathbf{x}_1, \ldots, \mathbf{x}_n$ passing through $N_{j,h}$ in T_j
6:      $L_i \leftarrow L_i \cup \{[\ell_{j,h}, u_{j,h}]\}$
7:    **end for**
8: **end for**
9: **for** $i = 1$ to d **do**
10:    $\{s_1, \ldots, s_k\}, \{I_1, \ldots, I_k\} \leftarrow$ Min_IntSet(L_i)
11:    **for** $g = 1$ to k **do**
12:      **for each** $(j, h) \in I_g$ **do**
13:        Replace the branching condition (i, θ_i) attached to node $N_{j,h}$ with (i, s_g).
14:      **end for**
15:    **end for**
16: **end for**

For the branching condition (i, θ_i) attached to each branching node $N_{j,h}$ of decision tree T_j in a given decision forest $\{T_1, \ldots, T_m\}$, Algorithm Min_DBN calculates the range of values $[\ell_{j,h}, u_{j,h})$ that θ_i can take without changing $100\sigma\%$ of paths of a given feature vectors $\mathbf{x}_1, \ldots, \mathbf{x}_n$ passing through $N_{j,h}$ in T_j (Line 2–8), and adds the range (interval) to L_i, which is initially set to $\emptyset$ (Line 1). Then, by running Min_IntSet for each L_i $(i = 1, \ldots, d)$, Min_DBN obtains its output $\{s_1, \ldots, s_k\}$ (Line 10), and the branching condition (i, θ_i) of node $N_{j,h}$ with $s_g \in [\ell_{j,h}, u_{j,h})$ is replaced with (i, s_g) (Line 11–15).

Note that, for node $N_{j,h}$ with branching condition (i, θ_i) in decision tree T_j, the interval $[\ell_{j,h}, u_{j,h})$ in which threshold θ_i can take a value without changing more than $100\sigma\%$ of paths of feature vectors $\mathbf{x}_1, \ldots, \mathbf{x}_n$ passing through $N_{j,h}$ in T_j, is expressed as

$$\ell_{j,h} = \inf_{\ell}\{\ell \mid |\{\mathbf{x}_f \in X_{j,h} \mid \ell < x_{f,i} \le \theta_i\}| \le \sigma|X_{j,h}|\} \text{ and}$$

$$u_{j,h} = \sup_{u}\{u \mid |\{\mathbf{x}_f \in X_{j,h} \mid \theta_i < x_{f,i} \le u\}| \le \sigma|X_{j,h}|\},$$

where

$$X_{j,h} = \{\mathbf{x}_f | \text{The path of } \mathbf{x}_f \text{ in } T_j \text{ passes through node } N_{j,h}\},$$

and $|S|$ for set S denotes the number of elements in S.

Let us analyze time and space complexities of Min_DBN. Let N denote the number of nodes in a given decision forest. For each branching node $N_{j,h}$, Min_DBN needs $O(|X_{j,h}| \log(\sigma|X_{j,h}| + 1)) \le O(n \log(\sigma n + 1))$ time for calculating $\ell_{j,h}$ and $u_{j,h}$ using size-$(\sigma|X_{j,h}| + 1)$ heap. Min_IntSet(L_i) for all $i = 1, \ldots, d$ totally consumes at most $O(N \log N)$ time. Considering that $O(d)$ time is needed additionally, time complexity of Min_DBN is $O(N(n \log(\sigma n + 1) + \log N) + d)$. Space complexity of Min_DBN is $O(dn + N)$ because space linear in the sizes of given feature vectors and decision forest are enough to run Min_DBN.

5   Experiments

We show the results of the experiments that demonstrate the effectiveness of Algorithm Min_DBN.

5.1   Settings

We used 13 numerical-feature datasets registered in UCI machine learning repository [6], whose numbers of instances, features and distinct class labels are shown in Table 1. In the table, datasets are sorted in the order of the number of instances. The largest one is hepmass dataset that has 7 million instances. The dataset with the largest number of features is RNA-Seq PANCAN whose number of features is more than 20 thousands. Note that the number of features is larger than the number of instances only for this dataset. The number of distinct class

Table 1. Dataset used in our experiments

Dataset	#instance	#feature	#class	Reference
Iris	150	4	3	Iris [6]
Parkinsons	195	22	2	Parkinsons [11]
Breast cancer	569	30	2	Breast Cancer Wisconsin (Diagnostic) [6]
Blood	748	4	2	Blood Transfusion Service Center [13]
RNA-Seq PANCAN	801	20531	5	gene expression cancer RNA-Seq [4]
Winequality red	1599	11	11	Wine Quality [5]
Winequality white	4898	11	11	Wine Quality [5]
Waveform	5000	40	3	Waveform Database Generator (Version 2) [6]
Robot	5456	24	4	Wall-Following Robot Navigation [6]
Musk	6598	166	2	Musk (Version 2) [6]
Epileptic seizure	11500	178	5	Epileptic Seizure Recognition [2]
Magic	19020	10	2	MAGIC Gamma Telescope [6]
Hepmass	7000000	28	2	HEPMASS (train) [6]

labels are not so large for all the dataset we used, and winequality datasets have the largest number of distinct labels (11 distinct labels).

Decision forests used in the experiments are random forest classifiers [3] which are outputted by the fit method of the sklearn.ensemble.RandomForestClassifier class[1] for the input of each dataset. The parameters of the classifier were set to defaults except the number of trees (n_estimators), the number of jobs to run in parallel (n_jobs) and and the seed used by the random number generator (random_state): n_estimators = 100, n_jobs = −1 (which means the same as the number of processors) and random_state = 1. Note that parameter random_state was fixed in order to ensure that the same decision forest is generated for the same training dataset. Also note that the number of randomly selected features used for branching conditions of each decision tree was set to $\sqrt{d}$ as default value. Each dataset was split into training and test datasets using function sklearn.model_selection.train_test_split, and the training dataset only is fed to the fit method of the classifier. The non-default option parameters for train_test_split are the proportions of the dataset to include in the test (test_size) and the train (train_size) splits, and the seed used the random number generator (random_state): test_size = 0.2, train_size = 0.8 and random_state = 0, ..., 9. Note that 10 different pairs of train and test datasets were generated for each dataset by setting different values to random_state parameter. For each pair of train and test datasets (D_L, D_P), a random forest RF was learned using D_L, and Min_DBN with parameter σ was run for the RF to obtain RF_σ in which the number of distinct branching conditions was minimized. Accuracies of RF and RF_σ for D_P were checked for the labels predicted by the predict method of the classifier. We conducted this procedure for 10 train-test splits of each dataset and obtained the number of distinct branching conditions and

---

[1] https://scikit-learn.org/stable/modules/generated/sklearn.ensemble.RandomForest Classifier.html.

the accuracy averaged over 10 runs for each dataset and each random forest in $\{RF\} \cup \{RF_\sigma \mid \sigma = 0.0, 0.1, 0.2, 0.3\}$.

5.2 Results

The number of distinct branching conditions and prediction accuracy for each original decision forest and those with reduced distinct branching conditions are shown in Table 2. In the table, *reduction rate of the number of distinct branching conditions*, which is defined as

$$1 - \frac{\#(\text{distinct branching conditions in } RF_\sigma)}{\#(\text{distinct branching conditions in } RF)},$$

and *prediction accuracy decrease*, which is defined as

$$(\text{accuracy of } RF) - (\text{accuracy of } RF_\sigma) \quad \text{for the test dataset}$$

are also shown for original decision forest RF and decision forests RF_σ that are outputted by Algorithm Min_DBN for the input decision forest RF and path-changeable-rate σ.

Under the condition that the path of any given feature vector in each decision tree must be the same as that in the original tree ($\sigma = 0$), the reduction rate on the number of distinct branching conditions is at least 48.9% for all the datasets but RNA-Seq PANCAN dataset. The number of features is more than 30 times lager than the number of training instances in RNA-Seq PANCAN dataset, and number of distinct features in the original decision tree is less than 1/10 of the number of features, so the number of appearing branching conditions for each feature might be small, which makes condition-sharing difficult. The reduction rate exceeds 90% for magic and hepmass datasets, and especially it reaches 99% for hepmass dataset. Note that the prediction accuracy decrease is between -0.004 and 0.007 for all the datasets, so no degradation of prediction performance was observed.

There is a tradeoff between reduction rate and prediction accuracy decrease, that is, larger reduction rate causes larger prediction accuracy decrease, and it can be to some extent controllable by path-changeable rate σ. By using larger σ, reduction rate can be increased but prediction accuracy decrease is also increased. 90% reduction rate is achieved by waveform dataset with 0.3% prediction accuracy decrease (PAD), by parkinsons and breast cancer datasets with 5–7% PAD, by musk and epileptic seizure datasets with about 11% PAD, by winequality and robot datasets with 14–17% PAD. Note that the minimum prediction accuracy of the original random forests among the 13 datasets is 67.3%. The reduction rate cannot reach 90% for iris, blood and RNA-Seq PANCAN datasets even using $\sigma = 0.3$. Iris and blood datasets have only four features, which causes a small number of distinct branching conditions even for original decision forest: 168.3 and 154.2 distinct branching conditions for iris and blood datasets, respectively, in 100 decision trees. Considering comparison to the number of trees, such relatively small number of distinct branching conditions seems to be difficult to reduce.

Table 2. Number of distinct branching conditions and prediction accuracy of original random forest classifier and those outputted by Min_DBN

| | Original | Outputted by Min_DBN | | | |
		$\sigma = 0.0$	$\sigma = 0.1$	$\sigma = 0.2$	$\sigma = 0.3$
Dataset	#(distinct conditions)(95% confidence interval) reduction rate of #(distinct conditions) prediction accuracy(95% confidence interval) prediction accuracy decrease				
Iris	168.3(±6.5)	53.1(±2.1)	46.0(±2.3)	37.8(±2.4)	31.1(±2.1)
	0	0.684	0.727	0.775	0.815
	0.943(±0.044)	0.937(±0.043)	0.917(±0.038)	0.857(±0.058)	0.833(±0.059)
	0	0.007	0.027	0.087	0.11
Parkinsons	1005.5(±33.9)	398.0(±13.4)	176.9(±6.5)	105.9(±1.8)	77.7(±2.5)
	0	0.604	0.824	0.895	0.923
	0.89(±0.031)	0.885(±0.029)	0.854(±0.036)	0.846(±0.032)	0.841(±0.031)
	0	0.005	0.036	0.044	0.049
Breast cancer	1389.8(±54.7)	572.0(±15.2)	210.7(±7.3)	130.8(±4.7)	98.5(±2.9)
	0	0.588	0.848	0.906	0.929
	0.961(±0.015)	0.958(±0.015)	0.911(±0.028)	0.891(±0.03)	0.86(±0.026)
	0	0.003	0.05	0.069	0.101
Blood	154.2(±5.8)	78.5(±2.7)	71.0(±3.4)	62.7(±3.0)	58.5(±2.6)
	0	0.491	0.54	0.593	0.621
	0.761(±0.018)	0.765(±0.015)	0.755(±0.014)	0.75(±0.012)	0.743(±0.014)
	0	−0.004	0.006	0.011	0.018
RNA-Seq PANCAN	1938.5(±24.1)	1851.5(±21.7)	1664.2(±23.9)	1641.0(±23.7)	1633.8(±22.9)
	0	0.045	0.142	0.153	0.157
	0.998(±0.003)	0.998(±0.003)	0.996(±0.004)	0.994(±0.004)	0.99(±0.003)
	0	0.0	0.001	0.003	0.007
Winequality red	4066.2(±25.4)	873.8(±8.7)	583.7(±7.3)	424.8(±5.2)	340.0(±5.2)
	0	0.785	0.856	0.896	0.916
	0.68(±0.01)	0.684(±0.008)	0.626(±0.015)	0.566(±0.009)	0.524(±0.016)
	0	−0.003	0.054	0.114	0.156
Winequality white	7194.9(±48.3)	1358.2(±12.3)	871.7(±5.8)	661.8(±6.6)	559.9(±10.3)
	0	0.811	0.879	0.908	0.922
	0.673(±0.012)	0.673(±0.011)	0.583(±0.017)	0.5(±0.012)	0.443(±0.011)
	0	0.0	0.09	0.173	0.23
Waveform	32232.4(±140.8)	5774.0(±26.3)	1233.6(±12.0)	646.2(±7.8)	471.8(±6.6)
	0	0.821	0.962	0.98	0.985
	0.849(±0.004)	0.847(±0.006)	0.846(±0.009)	0.838(±0.009)	0.824(±0.01)
	0	0.002	0.003	0.011	0.025
Robot	9337.7(±171.0)	2966.1(±51.7)	986.9(±18.3)	579.1(±11.4)	396.1(±10.3)
	0	0.682	0.894	0.938	0.958
	0.994(±0.002)	0.994(±0.002)	0.91(±0.009)	0.853(±0.009)	0.854(±0.014)
	0	0.0	0.084	0.141	0.14
Musk	12306.9(±141.4)	6288.6(±66.1)	2700.7(±26.6)	1617.5(±25.3)	1125.2(±20.3)
	0	0.489	0.781	0.869	0.909
	0.977(±0.004)	0.977(±0.004)	0.935(±0.008)	0.885(±0.01)	0.867(±0.008)
	0	0.0	0.042	0.092	0.11

Table 2. (*continued*)

Dataset	Original	Outputted by Min_DBN			
		$\sigma = 0.0$	$\sigma = 0.1$	$\sigma = 0.2$	$\sigma = 0.3$
Dataset		#(distinct conditions)(95% confidence interval)			
		reduction rate of #(distinct conditions)			
		prediction accuracy(95% confidence interval)			
		prediction accuracy decrease			
Epileptic	75492.5(±131.4)	23540.7(±61.0)	6857.6(±29.0)	3746.4(±21.1)	2738.8(±13.7)
seizure	0	0.688	0.909	0.95	0.964
	0.696(±0.009)	0.695(±0.008)	0.587(±0.006)	0.441(±0.008)	0.304(±0.008)
	0	0.001	0.109	0.256	0.392
Magic	110441.9(±526.1)	9535.3(±34.1)	2440.7(±24.7)	1352.1(±10.2)	985.6(±8.2)
	0	0.914	0.978	0.988	0.991
	0.877(±0.003)	0.877(±0.003)	0.8(±0.005)	0.595(±0.008)	0.426(±0.007)
	0	0.0	0.077	0.282	0.451
Hepmass	45125069.6(±8951.8)	431851.6(±263.1)	57199.1(±60.1)	29626.6(±83.4)	21704.1(±63.8)
	0	0.99	0.999	0.999	1.0
	0.821(±0.0)	0.821(±0.0)	0.809(±0.0)	0.773(±0.001)	0.684(±0.003)
	0	0.0	0.011	0.048	0.137

6   Conclusions and Future Work

We formalized a novel simplification problem of a decision forest, proposed an algorithm for the problem and demonstrated its effectiveness on reduction rate of the number of distinct branching conditions for the random forests that were trained using 13 datasets in UCI machine learning repository. Hardware implementation for checking effectiveness of the proposed algorithm on inference efficiency is planned for our next step.

Practically better problem formalization may exist. It might be better to restrict the rate of path changes not at each branching node but at each whole tree. Furthermore, important thing is not the rate of path changes but the rate of reached leaf label changes, so its control might be more preferred. There are a tradeoff between the number of distinct branching conditions and prediction accuracy. So, formalization with restriction directly on one of them might be more useful. As our future work, we would like to pursue better formalizations of the problem, develop their algorithms and analyze their complexity.

Acknowledgments. We thank Assoc. Prof. Ichigaku Takigawa and Assoc. Prof. Shinya Takamaeda-Yamazaki of Hokkaido University for helpful comments to improve this research. We also thank Prof. Hiroki Arimura of Hokkaido University and Prof. Masato Motomura of Tokyo Institute of Technology for their support and encouragement. This work was supported by JST CREST Grant Number JPMJCR18K3, Japan.

References

1. Amato, F., Barbareschi, M., Casola, V., Mazzeo, A.: An FPGA-based smart classifier for decision support systems. In: Zavoral, F., Jung, J., Badica, C. (eds.) Intelligent Distributed Computing VII. SCI, vol. 511, pp. 289–299. Springer, Cham (2014). https://doi.org/10.1007/978-3-319-01571-2_34

2. Andrzejak, R., Lehnertz, K., Rieke, C., Mormann, F., David, P., Elger, C.E.: Indications of nonlinear deterministic and finite dimensional structures in time series of brain electrical activity: dependence on recording region and brain state. Phys. Rev. E **64**, 061907 (2001)

3. Breiman, L.: Random forests. Mach. Learn. **45**(1), 5–32 (2001). https://doi.org/10.1023/A:1010933404324

4. Weinstein, J.N., et al.: The cancer genome atlas pan-cancer analysis project. Nat. Genet. **45**(10), 1113–1120 (2013). Cancer Genome Atlas Research Network

5. Cortez, P., Cerdeira, A., Almeida, F., Matos, T., Reis, J.: Modeling wine preferences by data mining from physicochemical properties. Decis. Support Syst. **47**(4), 547–553 (2009)

6. Dua, D., Taniskidou, E.K.: UCI machine learning repository (2017). http://archive.ics.uci.edu/ml

7. Friedman, J.H.: Greedy function approximation: a gradient boosting machine. Ann. Stat. **29**, 1189–1232 (2000)

8. Geurts, P., Ernst, D., Wehenkel, L.: Extremely randomized trees. Mach. Learn. **63**(1), 3–42 (2006). https://doi.org/10.1007/s10994-006-6226-1

9. Hastie, T., Tibshirani, R., Friedman, J.: The Elements of Statistical Learning. SSS. Springer, New York (2009). https://doi.org/10.1007/978-0-387-84858-7

10. Kulkarni, V.Y., Sinha, P.K.: Pruning of random forest classifiers: a survey and future directions. In: 2012 International Conference on Data Science Engineering (ICDSE), pp. 64–68 (2012)

11. Little, M.A., McSharry, P.E., Roberts, S.J., Costello, D.A., Moroz, I.M.: Exploiting nonlinear recurrence and fractal scaling properties for voice disorder detection. BioMed. Eng. OnLine **6**, 23 (2007). https://doi.org/10.1186/1475-925X-6-23

12. Van Essen, B., Macaraeg, C., Gokhale, M., Prenger, R.: Accelerating a random forest classifier: multi-core, GP-GPU, or FPGA? In: Proceedings of the 2012 IEEE 20th International Symposium on Field-Programmable Custom Computing Machines, pp. 232–239 (2012)

13. Yeh, I.C., Yang, K.J., Ting, T.M.: Knowledge discovery on RFM model using Bernoulli sequence. Expert Syst. Appl. **36**(3), 5866–5871 (2009)

Fast Gradient Boosting Decision Trees
with Bit-Level Data Structures

Laurens Devos[✉], Wannes Meert, and Jesse Davis

Department of Computer Science, KU Leuven, Leuven, Belgium
{laurens.devos,wannes.meert,jesse.davis}@cs.kuleuven.be

Abstract. A gradient boosting decision tree model is a powerful machine learning method that iteratively constructs decision trees to form an additive ensemble model. The method uses the gradient of the loss function to improve the model at each iteration step. Inspired by the database literature, we exploit bitset and bitslice data structures in order to improve the run time efficiency of learning the trees. We can use these structures in two ways. First, they can represent the input data itself. Second, they can store the discretized gradient values used by the learning algorithm to construct the trees in the boosting model. Using these bit-level data structures reduces the problem of finding the best split, which involves counting of instances and summing gradient values, to counting one-bits in bit strings. Modern CPUs can efficiently count one-bits using AVX2 SIMD instructions. Empirically, our proposed improvements can result in speed-ups of 2 to up to 10 times on datasets with a large number of categorical features without sacrificing predictive performance.

Keywords: Gradient boosting · Decision tree · Bitset · Bitslice

1 Introduction

Gradient boosting decision trees (GBDTs) are a powerful and theoretically elegant machine learning method that constructs an additive ensemble of trees. GBDT methods employ an iterative procedure, where the gradient of the loss function guides learning a new tree such that adding the new tree to the model improves its predictive performance. GBDTs are widely used in practice due the availability of high quality and performant systems such as XGBoost [3], LightGBM [7] and CatBoost [10]. These have been successfully applied to many real-world datasets, and cope particularly well with heterogeneous and noisy data.

This paper explores how to more efficiently learn gradient boosting decision tree models without sacrificing accuracy. When learning a GBDT model, the vast majority of time is spent evaluating candidate splits when learning a single tree. This involves counting instances and summing gradients. State-of-the-art GBDT implementations use full 32- or 64-bit integers or floats to represent the data and the gradients. We propose the BitBoost algorithm which represents

© Springer Nature Switzerland AG 2020
U. Brefeld et al. (Eds.): ECML PKDD 2019, LNAI 11906, pp. 590–606, 2020.
https://doi.org/10.1007/978-3-030-46150-8_35

the data and gradients using bitsets and bitslices, two data structures originating from database literature. This allows BitBoost to exploit the bit-level
parallelism enabled by modern CPUs. However, these data structures impose
strict limitations on how and which numbers can be expressed. This necessitates
adapting three operations in the standard GBDT learning algorithm: summing
gradients, performing (in)equality checks, and counting. Empirically, BitBoost
achieves competitive predictive performance while reducing the runtime by a
large margin. Moreover, BitBoost is a publicly available package.[1]

2   Background and Related Work

2.1   Gradient Boosting

Schapire [12] proposed the theoretical idea of boosting, which was implemented
in practice by AdaBoost [5,13]. This idea was generalized by the generic *gradient
boosting* algorithm, which works with any differentiable loss function [6,9]. Given
N input instances $\{(\mathbf{x}_i, y_i)\}_{i=1}^{N}$ and a differentiable loss function $\mathcal{L}$, gradient boosting models iteratively improve the predictions of y from $\mathbf{x}$ with respect to $\mathcal{L}$ by
adding new weak learners that improve upon the previous ones, forming an addi-
tive ensemble model. The additive nature of the model can be expressed by:

$$F_0(\mathbf{x}) = c, \qquad F_m(\mathbf{x}) = F_{m-1}(\mathbf{x}) + h_{\theta,m}(\mathbf{x}), \tag{1}$$

where m is the iteration count, c is an initial guess that minimizes $\mathcal{L}$, and $h_{\theta,m}(\mathbf{x})$
is some weak learner parametrized by θ such as a linear model or a decision tree.

  In this paper, we focus on *gradient boosting decision trees* or *GBDTs*, which
are summarized in Algorithm 1. Gradient boosting systems minimize $\mathcal{L}$ by gradually taking steps in the direction of the negative gradient, just as numerical
gradient-descent methods do. In GBDTs, such a step is a single tree constructed
to fit the negative gradients. One can use a least-squares approach to find a tree
$h_{\theta^*,m}$ that tries to achieve this goal:

$$\theta^* = \arg\min_{\theta} \sum_{i=1}^{N} [-g_m(\mathbf{x}_i, y_i) - h_{\theta,m}(\mathbf{x}_i)]^2, \tag{2}$$

where $g_m(\mathbf{x}, y) = \partial_{\hat{y}}\mathcal{L}(y, \hat{y})|_{\hat{y}=F_{m-1}(\mathbf{x})}$ is the gradient of the loss function $\mathcal{L}$.

$F_0(\mathbf{x}) = \arg\min_c \sum_{i=1}^{N} \mathcal{L}(y_i, c)$
for $m \leftarrow 1$ *to* M **do**
  $\quad g_{m,i} = \partial_{\hat{y}}\mathcal{L}(y_i, \hat{y})\,|_{\hat{y}=F_{m-1}(\mathbf{x}_i)}$
  $\quad h_{\theta,m}$ = a tree that optimizes Equation 2
  $\quad F_m(\mathbf{x}) = F_{m-1}(\mathbf{x}) + \rho_m\, h_{\theta,m}(\mathbf{x})$
end

Algorithm 1: The gradient boosting algorithm.

---

[1] BitBoost is hosted on GitHub: https://github.com/laudv/bitboost.

In practice, each individual tree is typically built in a greedy top-down manner: the tree learning algorithm loops over all internal nodes in a depth-first order starting at the root, and splits each node according to the best split condition. The best split condition is found by identifying the feature with the best split candidate. For example, the best split candidate for a numerical feature is a value s that partitions the instance set – the data instances that sort to the current node – into a left and right subset according to the condition $x < s$ with maximal gain, with x the feature value. Gain is defined as the difference in the model's loss before and after the split.

Competitive gradient boosting systems use a histogram-based approach to generate a limited number of split candidates (e.g., 256). This means that for each feature, the learner iterates over all remaining instances in the instance set of the node to be split, and fills a histogram by collecting statistics about the instances that go left given a split condition. The statistics include, depending on the system, the sums of the first and optionally the second gradient, and usually also an instance count. The aggregated statistics contain all the necessary information to calculate the best split out of the (limited number of) candidate splits. The complexity of this approach is $\mathcal{O}(F \cdot (n + S))$, with n the instance set size, S the histogram size, and F the feature count.

We will compare our finding with three such competitive systems. XGBoost [3] was introduced in 2016 and improved the scalability of learning by introducing sparsity-aware split finding, a novel parallel architecture, and the ability to take on out-of-core learning. LightGBM [7] was presented one year later and proposed a new gradient weighted sampling technique (GOSS), and a technique to reduce the number features by combining features that have no non-zero values for the same instance (EFB). Lastly, CatBoost [10] improved the accuracy of learning from high-cardinality categorical data by identifying the problem of *prediction shift* and resolving it with a new method called *ordered boosting*. All these systems are efficient, complete, and open-source libraries.

2.2   Bitsets and Bitslices

Bitsets and bitslices are two data structures that originated in the database literature [2,11]. We wish to utilize these structures in the gradient boosting algorithm with the goal of improving learning times.

A *bitset* is a simple yet effective bit-level data structure used to represent a set of items. A bitset is a string of bits of length N. The ith bit is 1 if the ith item is present in the set and 0 if it is not.

A *bitslice* is a data structure used to represent a sequence of unsigned integers. In a typical array of integers, all bits of an individual number are stored consecutively: $x_1, x_2, \ldots, x_N$, where each x_i is made up of B bits $x_i^B \cdots x_i^2 x_i^1$, with x_i^B the most significant bit (MSB) and x_i^1 is the least significant bit (LSB).

A bitslice transposes this structure; instead of consecutively storing all bits of a single number, it groups bits with the same significance:

$$\underbrace{x_1^B x_2^B \cdots x_N^B}_{\text{MSBs}}, \quad \ldots, \quad x_1^2 x_2^2 \cdots x_N^2, \quad \underbrace{x_1^1 x_2^1 \cdots x_N^1}_{\text{LSBs}},$$

There are two main advantages of using bitslices for small integers. First, bitslices can efficiently store integers smaller than the minimally addressable unit – a single byte or 8 bits on modern systems – because of its transposed storage format. For example, naively storing 1000 3-bit integers requires 1000 bytes of storage. A bitslice only needs $3 \times 125 = 375$ bytes. Second, elements in a bitslice can be efficiently summed. To sum up values in a bitslice, one adds up the contributions of each bit group, optionally masking values with a bitset:

$$\sum_{b=1}^{B} 2^{b-1} \times \texttt{CountOnebits}(x_1^b x_2^b \cdots x_N^b \ \wedge \ \underbrace{s_1 s_2 \cdots s_N}_{\text{bitset mask}}) \tag{3}$$

The `CountOneBits` operation, also known as the population count or *popcount* operation, counts the number of one-bits in a bit string. This can be done very efficiently using the vectorized Harley Seal algorithm [8], taking advantage of AVX2 SIMD instructions operating on 32-byte wide registers.

3   BitBoost Algorithm

When learning a decision tree, the central subroutine is selecting which feature to split on in a node. This entails evaluating the gain of all potential variable-value splits and selecting the one with the highest gain. As in Eq. 2, a single tree fits the negative gradients g_i of $\mathcal{L}$ using least-squares. A split's gain is defined as the difference in the tree's squared loss before and after the split. Splitting a parent node p into a left and a right child l and r results in the following gain:

$$\text{gain}(p, l, r) = \sum_{i \in I_p} (-g_i + \Sigma_p/|I_p|)^2 - \sum_{i \in I_l} (-g_i + \Sigma_l/|I_l|)^2 - \sum_{i \in I_r} (-g_i + \Sigma_r/|I_r|)^2$$

$$= -\Sigma_p^2/|I_p| + \Sigma_l^2/|I_l| + \Sigma_r^2/|I_r|, \tag{4}$$

where I_* gives the set of instances that are sorted by the tree to node $*$ and $\Sigma_* = \sum_{i \in I_*} g_i$ is the sum of the gradients for node $*$. In other words, computing the gain of a split requires three operations:

1. *summing* the gradients in both leaves;
2. *performing (in)equality* checks to partition the node's instance sets based on the split condition being evaluated; and
3. *counting* the number of examples in each node's instance set.

Current implementations use 32- or 64-bit integers or floats to represent the gradients, data, and example IDs in instance sets. Hence, the relevant quantities in Eq. 4 are all computed using standard mathematical or logical operations.

Our hypothesis is that employing native data types uses more precision than is necessary to represent each of these quantities. That is, by possibly making some approximations, we can much more compactly represent the gradients, data, and instance sets using bitslice and bitset data structures. The primary advantage of the bit-level representations is speed: we can train a tree much faster by exploiting systems-level optimizations. First, we exploit instruction-level parallelism to very efficiently compute the relevant statistics used in Eq. 4. Second, by representing the data and instance sets using bitsets, important operations such as partitioning the data at a node can be translated to vectorized bitwise logical operations, which are much faster to perform than comparison operators on floats or integers.

3.1   Representing the Gradients Using Bitslices

When learning a GBDT model, each instance is associated with a real-valued gradient value, which is updated after each iteration in the boosting process. Existing gradient boosting systems typically use 32-bit, or even 64-bit floats to represent these gradients. However, the individual trees tend to be shallow to combat over-fitting. Consequently, rather than precisely partitioning data instances into fine-grained subsets, a tree loosely groups instances with similar gradient values. Intuitively, a gradient value represents an instance's *optimization need*, which is a measure of how much an instance requires a prediction update, and the trees categorize instances according to this need.

Based on this observation, our insight is that storing the precise gradient values may be superfluous, and it may be possible to represent these values using fewer bits without affecting the categorization of the data instances. Therefore, *we explore discretizing the gradient values and storing the values in a bitslice*. A bitslice of width k can represent values $0, \ldots, 2^k - 1$. To map the gradient values to the values that can be represented by the bitslice, the outer bounds $b_{\min}$ and $b_{\max}$, corresponding to the bitslice values 0 and $2^k - 1$ respectively, need to be chosen first. Then, gradient values g can be mapped to bitslice values using a simple linear transformation:

$$g \leftarrow \text{round}\left(\frac{\min(b_{\max}, \max(b_{\min}, g)) - b_{\min}}{b_{\max} - b_{\min}} \right). \tag{5}$$

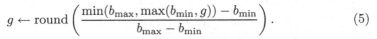

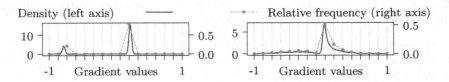

Fig. 1. Gradient value densities and the relative frequency of the 4-bit discretized values of the first and the last iterations. The values were produced by an unbalanced (1/5 positive) binary classification problem using binary log-loss. The gray vertical dotted lines indicate which 16 values can be represented with the 4-bit discretization.

The gradient values are thus mapped to a set of 2^k linearly spaced points. An example of this can be seen in Fig. 1.

Hence, the key question is how to select the boundaries for the discretization. This is loss-function dependent, and we consider five of the most commonly used loss functions:

- *Least absolute deviation (LAD)*: This loss function is widely used in practice due its better handling of outliers compared to least-squares. The LAD is:

$$\mathcal{L}_1(F(\mathbf{x}), y) = |y - F(\mathbf{x})|, \tag{6}$$

  and its gradients are either -1, indicating that an estimation for a particular instance should increase, or 1, indicating that an estimation should decrease. This information can be expressed with a single bit in a bitslice of width 1, yet existing systems use a full float to represent this.
- *Least-squared loss*: The gradient values do not have naturally defined boundaries, and the magnitude of the extreme values depends on the targets of the regression problem. Interestingly, choosing boundary values on the gradients of the least-squared loss makes it equivalent to Huber loss. For that reason, we look at Huber loss for inspiration when choosing boundaries.
- *Huber loss*: Huber loss is often used instead of squared-loss to combine the faster convergence of least-squared loss with the resilience to outliers of LAD. It has a single parameter δ:

$$\mathcal{L}_{H,\delta}(F(\mathbf{x}), y) = \begin{cases} \frac{1}{2}(y - F(\mathbf{x}))^2 & \text{if } |y - F(\mathbf{x})| \leq \delta, \\ \delta(|y - F(\mathbf{x})| - \frac{1}{2}\delta) & \text{otherwise.} \end{cases} \tag{7}$$

  The boundaries of the gradient values are naturally defined by the parameter δ: $b_{\min} = -\delta$, the most negative gradient values, and $b_{\max} = \delta$, the most positive gradient value. The value of δ is often taken to be the α quantile of the residuals at iteration m, i.e., $\delta_m = \text{quantile}_\alpha\{|y_i - F_{m-1}(\mathbf{x}_i)|\}$ [6].
- *Binary log-loss*: Given labels y_i in $\{-1, 1\}$, binary log-loss is used for binary classification problems and is defined as:

$$\mathcal{L}_{\log}(F(\mathbf{x}), y) = \log(1 + \exp(-2yF(\mathbf{x}))). \tag{8}$$

  This function's gradient values are naturally confined to $[-2, 2]$, so we choose the boundary values accordingly. However, we have found that choosing more *aggressive* boundaries (e.g., $-1.25, 1.25$) can speed up convergence.
- *Hinge loss*: Like binary log-loss, hinge loss is used for binary classification problems. It is defined as:

$$\mathcal{L}_{\text{hinge}}(F(\mathbf{x}), y) = \max(0, 1 - y\, F(\mathbf{x})). \tag{9}$$

  The possible (sub-)gradient values are -1, 0, and 1.

3.2   Representing the Data Using Bitsets

The standard way to represent the data in GBDT implementations is to use arrays of integers or floats. In contrast, we propose encoding the data using bitsets. How this is done depends on the feature. We distinguish among three feature types: low-cardinality categorical, high-cardinality categorical, and numerical features. To differentiate between low-cardinality and high-cardinality categorical features, we define an upper limit K on a feature's cardinality. A good value of K is dataset specific, but we typically choose K between 8 and 32.

Low-Cardinality Categorical Features. We use a one-hot encoding scheme: given a feature f with r possible values $v_0, \ldots, v_r$, we create r length-N bitsets. The ith position of the kth bitset is set to one if the ith value of f equals v_k. The resulting bitsets can be used to evaluate all possible equality splits: for any equality split $f = v_j$, we compute the instance set of the left subtree by applying the logical AND to the current instance set and bitset j (see Fig. 2, right).

High-Cardinality Features. This requires more work as considering all possible equality splits has two main downsides. First, creating a bitset for each value would negate both the space and computational efficiency of using this representation. Second, because we consider binary trees, splitting based on an equality against a single attribute-value would tend to result in an unbalanced partition of the instance set, which may reduce the quality of the trees. Therefore, we pre-process these features and group together feature values with similar mean gradient statistics and construct one bitset per group. The mean gradient statistic s_j of a categorical value v_j is defined as the summed gradient values g_i for all instances i that have value v_j. Then, we compute K quantiles q_k of s_j and use these to partition the categorical feature values. A bitset is generated for each quantile q_k. The kth bitset has a one for each instance i that has value v_j and $s_j < q_k$. Because the gradient values change at every iteration, we repeat this grouping procedure every t iterations of the boosting procedure, where t is a user-defined parameter. We refer to this parameter t as the *pre-processing rate*. We found that a value of 20 is a reasonable default.

Numerical Features. We treat these in an analogous manner as the high-cardinality categorical features. We estimate K weighted quantiles q_k using the absolute gradient values as weights. We use the quantiles as ordered split candidates, and generate K bitsets such that bitset k has a one in the ith position if instance i's value is less than q_k. Like in the high-cardinality case, we perform this transformation and reconstruct the bitsets every t iterations of the boosting procedure, where t is the pre-processing rate.

3.3   Representing an Instance Set Using a Bitset

The instance set I_p of a node p in a tree contains the training data instances that satisfy the split conditions on the path to node p from the root. In existing

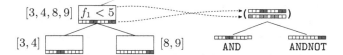

Fig. 2. An illustration of instance lists versus instance bitsets. The dataset comprises 10 instances indexed by $0, 1, \ldots, 9$. Values of feature f_1 are $2, 8, 5, \underline{4}, \underline{3}, 6, 1, 2, \underline{6}, \underline{8}$. The bitset representations of the instance sets are indicated below the node boxes, dark squares are 1s, others are 0s. The instance list $[3, 4, 8, 9]$ using 64-bit integers requires 256 bits, whereas the bitset representation uses only 10 bits.

systems, these instance sets are stored as an array of indexes into the input data, i.e., they are *instance lists*. We introduce the use of *instance bitsets* for this purpose. An instance bitset represents the instance set by having a 1 for instances that are in the instance set, and a zero for others. Figure 2 illustrates the difference on the left.

We have to contend with one subtlety when using a bitset to represent the instance set: the length of the bitset is always N, which is the number of training examples. This is problematic when partitioning the data at each node. Assuming a perfectly balanced tree, the size of an instance set halves at each level of the tree. The length of the bitset remains fixed, but the number of zeros, which represent examples not filtered to the node in question, in the bitset increases. Constructing all nodes of a tree at depth d requires passing over 2^d length-N bitsets, for a total cost of $\mathcal{O}(2^d N)$. In contrast, when using a list-based representation of the instance set, the length of the list halves at each level of the tree. Hence, constructing all nodes at depth d has a total cost of $\mathcal{O}(N)$. Computationally, it is much faster to process a bitset than the list-based representation, even if the list is much shorter than the bitset. The trade-off is that we have to process more bitsets. As the tree gets deeper, the number of bitsets and the fact that each one's length is equal to the number of training examples will eventually make this representation slower than using a list-based representation.

Fortunately, we can exploit the fact that as the depth of the tree increases, the bitsets become progressively sparser by applying a compression scheme to the bitsets. Many compression schemes exist for bitsets, such as CONCISE [4] and Roaring Bitmaps [1], but most of these schemes are optimized for the general use-case. We have a specific use case and wish to optimize for speed more than for storage efficiency. Therefore, we apply the following simple compression scheme.

We view each bitset as a series of 32-bit blocks. An uncompressed bitset consists of a single array of 32-bit blocks which explicitly stores all blocks in the bitset. A compressed bitset comprises two arrays: IDENTIFIERS, which stores sorted 32-bit identifiers of the non-zero blocks, and BLOCKS, which stores the bit-values of the non-zero 32-bit blocks. For any block i in the bitset, either there exists a j such that IDENTIFIERS$(j) = i$ and the bits of the ith block are BLOCKS(j), or the ith block consists of zero-bits. There are two main reasons why we choose 32-bit blocks: (1) 64-bit blocks are too unlikely to be all-zero, and (2) it is hard to efficiently integrate smaller 8- or 16-bit blocks into the CountOneBits routine, which heavily relies on SIMD vectorization.

When constructing a tree, after having split a node, we compare the ratio of the number of zero blocks and total number of blocks with a configurable threshold. If the threshold is exceeded, the instance set of the child node is compressed. The threshold determines how aggressively compression is applied.

3.4   Finding the Best Split

Algorithm 2 shows our split finding algorithm based on bitsets and bitslices. As is also the case in XGBoost, LightGBM, and CatBoost, it only considers binary splits. Analogous to the classical histogram-based version, it loops over all features f and initializes a new histogram H_f with bins for each candidate split. The main difference is the inner for-loop. The classical algorithm loops over all instances in the instance set individually, and accumulates the gradient values and instance counts in the histogram bins. In contrast, our algorithm loops over the split candidates which are the bitset representations we generated (see Subsect. 3.2). In the body of the loop, the statistics required to evaluate the gain are computed: the sum of the discretized gradients Σ_l of the instances going left is computed using Eq. 3, and the number of instances $|I_l|$ going left is computed using the fast CountOneBits procedure.

Input: Instance set I_p and gradient sum Σ_p of node p, and gradient bitslice G.
for *all features f* **do**

> H_f = InitializeNewHist(f)
> **for** *all candidate splits s of f with accompanying bitset B_s* **do**
>
>> Σ_l = BitsliceSum($G, B_s \wedge I_p$)   /* Equation 3 */
>> $|I_l|$ = CountOneBits($B_s \wedge I_p$)
>> $H_f[s] = (\Sigma_l, |I_l|)$ /* Store relevant statistics of s in H_f */
>
> **end**

end

Find split s^* with maximum gain in all H_f by evaluating $\frac{\Sigma_l^2}{|I_l|} + \frac{(\Sigma_p - \Sigma_l)^2}{|I_p| - |I_l|} - \frac{\Sigma_p^2}{|I_p|}$.
return $(s^*, B_{s^*}, \Sigma_{l^*}, \Sigma_p - \Sigma_{l^*})$

Algorithm 2: Bit-level split finding.

The nested loops fill the histogram H_f for each feature f. Once all histograms are constructed, the best split s^* is determined by comparing the gain of each split. Because we only consider binary splits, we use the property that $I_r = I_p - I_l$, and thus $|I_r| = |I_p| - |I_l|$, and $\Sigma_r = \Sigma_p - \Sigma_l$.

For each feature and each feature split candidate, we perform the BitsliceSum and CountOneBits operations which are linear in the number of instances. The complexity of the classical algorithm does not include the number of split candidates. This discrepancy is mitigated in two ways. First, the CountOneBits operation, which also forms the basis for BitsliceSum, is much faster than iterating over the instances individually. Second, we only consider a small number of candidate splits by pre-processing the numerical and high-cardinality categorical features. Note that the classical algorithm does not benefit from a small number of candidate splits, as it can fill the histograms from Algorithm 2 in a single pass over the data.

3.5   Overview of the BitBoost Algorithm

Algorithm 1 gave an overview of the generic boosting algorithm. It minimizes the loss function $\mathcal{L}$ by iteratively constructing trees that update the predictions in the direction of the negative gradient. Bitboost adds three additional steps to this algorithm. First, the bitsets for the low-cardinality categorical features are generated once at the start of the learning process and reused thereafter. Second, at the beginning of each iteration the gradients are discretized using a certain number of *discretization bits* and stored in a bitslice. Third, every t iterations, the data bitsets of the high-cardinality categorical and numerical features are regenerated. The parameter t expresses the *pre-processing rate*.

Input: Gradient bitslice G
stack $= \{(I_1, \sum_{i=1}^{N} g_i)\}$ /* Root node; I_1 is all-ones instance bitset */
while *popping* (I_p, Σ_p) *from* stack *succeeds* **do**
   if *p is at maximum depth* **then**
      ChooseLeafValue(p)
   else
      $(s^*, B_{s^*}, \Sigma_l, \Sigma_r) = $ FindBestSplit(I_p, Σ_p, G)   /* Algorithm 2 */
      $I_l = I_p \wedge B_{s^*}$ and $I_r = I_p \wedge \neg B_{s^*}$ /* Instance sets of children */
      Apply compression to I_l and/or I_r if threshold exceeded.
      Push(stack, (I_r, Σ_r)) and Push(stack, (I_l, Σ_l))
   endif
end

Algorithm 3: BitBoost tree construction algorithm.

The individual trees are built in a standard, greedy, top-down manner, as shown in Algorithm 3. The algorithm maintains a stack of nodes to split, which initially only contains the root node. These nodes are split by the best split condition, which is found using Algorithm 2, and the instance sets of the children are generated using simple logical operations. Compression is applied before child nodes are pushed onto the stack when the ratio of zero blocks over the total number of blocks exceeds the configurable threshold.

Leaf nodes hold the final prediction values. To pick the best leaf values, as ChooseLeafValue does in Algorithm 3, we use the same strategy as Friedman [6]. For LAD, we use the median gradient value of the instances in the instance set. For least-squares, the values $\Sigma_p/|I_p|$ would be optimal *if the gradient values g_i were exact*. This is not the case, so we recompute the mean using the exact gradients. We refer to Friedman's work for the Huber loss and binary log-loss.

4   Experiments

First, we empirically benchmark BitBoost against state-of-the-art systems. Second, we analyze the effect of the four BitBoost-specific parameters on performance.

4.1   Comparison with State-of-the-Art Systems

In this first experiment we compare our system, BitBoost, to three state-of-the-art systems: XGBoost, CatBoost and LightGBM.

Datasets and Tasks. We show results for four benchmark datasets that have different characteristics: (1) *Allstate*,[2] an insurance dataset containing 188k instances, each with 116 categorical and 14 continuous features. (2) *Bin-MNIST*,[3], a binary derivative of the famous MNIST dataset of 70k handwritten digits. We converted its 784 features into black and white pixels and predict if a number is less than 5. This dataset represents BitBoost's best case scenario, as all features are binary. (3) *Covertype*,[4] a forestry dataset with 581k instances, each with 44 categorical and 10 continuous features. We consider two classification tasks: for $CovType_1$, we predict lodgepole-pine versus all (balanced, 48.8% positive); for $CovType_2$, we predict broadleaf trees versus rest (unbalanced, 2.1% positive). (4) *YouTube*,[5] a dataset with YouTube videos that are trending over a period of time. Numerical features are log-transformed, date and time features are converted into numerical features, and textual features are converted into 373 bag-of-word features (e.g. title and description). This results in a dataset with 121k instances, each with 399 features. We predict the 10-log-transformed view count, i.e., we predict whether a video gets thousands, millions, or billions of views. We use 5-fold cross validation, and average times and accuracies over all folds.

Settings. Most of the parameters are shared across the four systems and only a few of them are system-specific: (1) *Loss function*, we use binary log-loss and hinge loss for classification, and least-squares, Huber loss and LAD for regression. Not all systems support all loss functions: XGBoost does not support Huber loss or LAD. CatBoost does not support Huber loss or hinge loss. LightGBM does not support hinge loss. (2) *Learning rate* is a constant factor that scales the predictions of individual trees to distribute learning over multiple trees. We choose a single learning rate per problem and use the same value for all systems. (3) *Maximum tree depth* limits the depth of the individual trees. We use depth 5 for Allstate, 6 for Covertype and Bin-MNIST, and 9 for YouTube. (4) *Bagging fraction* defines the fraction of instances we use for individual trees. By applying

---

[2] https://www.kaggle.com/c/allstate-claims-severity.
[3] http://yann.lecun.com/exdb/mnist.
[4] https://archive.ics.uci.edu/ml/datasets/covertype.
[5] https://www.kaggle.com/datasnaek/youtube-new.

bagging, better generalizing models are build faster. (5) *Feature fraction* defines the fraction of features we use per tree. CatBoost only supports feature selection per tree level. (6) *Minimum split gain* reduces over-fitting by avoiding splits that are not promising. We use a value of 10^{-5} for all systems. (7) *Maximum cardinality K* sets the maximum cardinality of low-cardinality categorical features (BitBoost only). (8) *Pre-processing rate t* sets the rate at which we execute the pre-processing procedure. This is used to avoid pre-processing numerical and high-cardinality features at each iteration (BitBoost only).

For XGBoost, we use the histogram tree method since it is faster; for Light-GBM, we use the GBDT boosting type; and for CatBoost we use the plain boosting type. We disable XGBoost's and LightGBM's support for sparse features to avoid unrelated differences between the systems. To measure the efficiency of the tree learning algorithms rather than the multi-threading capabilities of the systems, we disable multi-threading and run all experiments on a single core.

Parameter sets were chosen per dataset based on the performance on a validation set and the reported accuracies were evaluated on a separate test set. We provide results for two different parameter sets for BitBoost. BitBoost_A aims to achieve the best possible accuracies, whereas BitBoost_S prioritizes speed. The number of discretization bits, i.e., the precision with which we discretize the gradients, is chosen depending on the problem. Binary log-loss tends to require at least 4 or 8 bits. Hinge loss requires only 2 bits, but is less accurate. We use 4 or 8 bits for least-squares, 2 or 4 for Huber loss. Both least-squares and Huber behave like LAD when using a single bit, the only difference being the lack of resilience to outliers for least-squares. More extensive results and the specific parameter values can be found in the BitBoost repository.

Table 1. Comparison of BitBoost with three state-of-the-art systems. Time is in seconds. Loss is expressed in binary error for classification and mean absolute error (MAE) for regression. The BitBoost_A row shows the results when choosing accuracy over speed. The BitBoost_S row shows the results when choosing speed over accuracy, staying within reasonable accuracy boundaries.

	Allstate		Covtype$_1$		Covtype$_2$		Bin-MNIST		YouTube	
	Time	Loss	Time	Loss	Time	Loss	Time	Loss	Time	Loss
BitBoost$_A$	4.8	1159	17.1	12.0	10.7	0.79	4.5	2.78	14.3	0.07
BitBoost$_S$	1.0	1194	5.4	14.9	7.2	1.02	1.9	3.52	2.5	0.12
LightGBM	12.3	1156	24.1	11.9	21.0	0.71	24.8	2.86	35.0	0.07
XGBoost	11.5	1157	37.0	10.8	35.3	0.63	24.7	2.66	24.9	0.07
CatBoost	82.6	1167	58.1	13.1	52.9	0.91	16.5	3.23	33.6	0.11

Results. Table 1 shows a comparison of the training times and accuracies. On the Allstate dataset, we perform two to over ten times faster than LightGBM and XGBoost, while still achieving accuracies that are comparable to the state of the art. The results for the Covertype dataset show that BitBoost can also handle numerical and high-cardinality features effectively. The Bin-MNIST dataset illustrates that BitBoost is able to construct competitively accurate models using only 20% of the time, and, when giving up some accuracy, can achieve speed-ups of a factor 10. The YouTube dataset requires deeper trees because of its sparse bag-of-word features only splitting off small chunks of instances. The results show that BitBoost also performs well in this case.

In general, BitBoost is able to effectively explore the trade-off between accuracy and speed. Besides the usual parameters like bagging fraction and feature sampling fraction, BitBoost provides one main additional parameter unavailable in other systems: *the number of discretization bits*. This parameter controls the precision at which BitBoost operates, and together with a suitable loss function like LAD or hinge loss, enables trading accuracy for speed in a novel way.

4.2 Effect of the Number of Bits Used to Discretize the Gradient

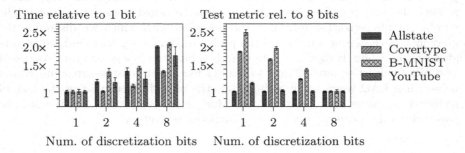

Fig. 3. The effect of the width of bitslice used to discretize the gradient on the model construction time (left) and the performance metric (right). The run times are relative to the fastest option (i.e., one-bit discretization), meaning higher is slower. The performance metric values are relative to the best performing option (i.e., eight-bit discretization), meaning higher is less accurate.

The number of discretization bits used in the bitslice that stores the gradient values will affect BitBoost's performance. Figure 3 shows the effect of using 1, 2, 4 and 8 bits on run time and predictive performance. The trade-off is clear: using fewer bits decreases the training time, but using more bits improves the predictive performance. Bin-MNIST has the largest effect in terms of run time because it only contains binary features. Hence, there is no work associated with repeatedly converting high-cardinality or real-valued features into bitsets, meaning that the extra computational demand arising from the bigger bitslice has a larger percentage effect on the run time. Note that Allstate's accuracy is unaffected. This is due to the use of LAD loss whose gradient values can be stored with a single bit. We used Huber loss for YouTube, which was able to guide the optimization process effectively using only 2 bits.

4.3   Effect of the Low-Cardinality Boundary K

The parameter K determines which categorical features are considered to be low-cardinality. It will affect run time as higher values of K require considering more split candidates. However, smaller values of K also introduce overhead in terms of the pre-processing needed to cope with high-cardinality attributes, that is, grouping together similar values for an attribute and generating the associated bitsets. K may also affect predictive performance in two ways: (1) some high-categorical features may have more natural groupings of values than others, and (2) it controls the number of split candidates considered for numerical features.

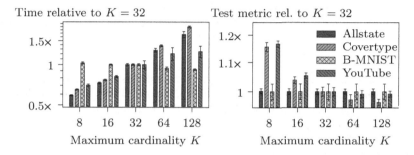

Fig. 4. The effect of K on the run time times relative to $K = 32$ (left); and the accuracies, also relative to $K = 32$ (right).

Figure 4 shows the effect of varying K on the run time and predictive performance. As K increases, so does the run time, indicating that the extra effort associated with considering more split candidates is more costly than the additional pre-processing necessary to group together similar feature values. Interestingly, the value of K seems to have little effect on the predictive performance for the Allstate dataset, meaning that considering *more fine-grained splits* does not produce better results. The Covertype and YouTube datasets seem to benefit from a higher K value, but the increase in accuracy diminishes for values larger than 32. As the Bin-MNIST dataset only has binary features and does not require any pre-processing, the run time and predictive performance is unaffected by K. In terms of accuracy, a good value of K is likely to be problem specific.

4.4   Effect of Compressing the Instance Bitset on Run Time

Compressing the instance bitset affects run time and involves a trade-off. Always compressing will introduce unnecessary overhead at shallow levels of the tree where there is little sparsity in the instance bitsets. Conversely, never compressing will adversely affect run time when the tree is deeper. To quantify its effect, we measure model construction time as a function of the compression threshold.

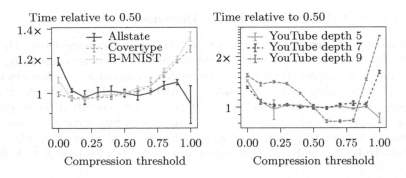

Fig. 5. The model construction time as a function of the compression threshold, which varies from 0.0 (always apply compression) to 1.0 (never apply compression). The time is relative to a threshold of 0.5, which was used in all experiments.

Figure 5 plots the run times for compression thresholds ranging from 0.0 (always apply compression) to 1.0 (never apply compression). The trade-off is clearly visible for Covertype and Bin-MNIST (left). Allstate only considers trees of depth 5, which causes instance sets to be more dense on average, making compression less effective. This is confirmed by the results for YouTube that are plotted for different tree depths (right). Shallower trees do not benefit from compression, whereas deeper trees with sparser instance sets do.

4.5   Effect of Pre-processing Rate

BitBoost reconverts high-cardinality and continuous features into bitmaps every t iterations. Figure 6 shows how the model construction time and predictive performance vary as a function of t on the Covertype, Allstate and YouTube

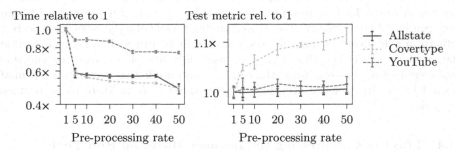

Fig. 6. The effect of the pre-processing rate t on model construction time (left) and predictive performance (right). The results are shown relative to $t = 1$.

datasets. Bin-MNIST is not included as it has neither high-cardinality nor continuous features and thus requires no pre-processing. As expected, run time drops as t increases. Interestingly, it plateaus for values of $t \geq 10$. For Allstate and YouTube, predictive performance is unaffected by this parameter. However, performance slightly degrades for the Covertype dataset for higher values of t.

5 Conclusion

We have introduced BitBoost, a novel way of integrating the bitset and bitslice data structures into the gradient boosting decision tree algorithm. These data structure can benefit from bit-level optimizations in modern CPUs to speed up the computation. However, bitslices cannot be used as is in existing gradient boosting decision trees. BitBoost discretizes the gradients such that it has only a limited effect on the predictive performance. The combination of using a bitslice to store the gradient values and representing the data and the instance sets as bitsets reduces the core problem of learning a single tree to summing masked gradients, which can be solved very efficiently. We have empirically shown that this approach can speed up model construction 2 to 10 times compared to state-of-the-art systems without harming predictive performance.

Acknowledgments. LD is supported by the KU Leuven Research Fund (C14/17/070), WM by VLAIO-SBO grant HYMOP (150033), and JD by KU Leuven Research Fund (C14/17/07, C32/17/036), Research Foundation - Flanders (EOS No. 30992574, G0D8819N) and VLAIO-SBO grant HYMOP (150033).

References

1. Chambi, S., Lemire, D., Kaser, O., Godin, R.: Better bitmap performance with roaring bitmaps. Softw. Pract. Exp. **46**(5), 709–719 (2016)
2. Chan, C.Y., Ioannidis, Y.E.: Bitmap index design and evaluation. In: ACM SIGMOD Record, vol. 27, pp. 355–366. ACM (1998)
3. Chen, T., Guestrin, C.: XGBoost: a scalable tree boosting system. In: Proceedings of ACM SIGKDD, pp. 785–794 (2016)
4. Colantonio, A., Pietro, R.D.: Concise: compressed 'n' composable integer set. Inf. Process. Lett. **110**(16), 644–650 (2010)
5. Freund, Y., Schapire, R.E.: A decision-theoretic generalization of on-line learning and an application to boosting. J. Comput. Syst. Sci. **55**(1), 119–139 (1997)
6. Friedman, J.H.: Greedy function approximation: a gradient boosting machine. Ann. Stat. **29**(5), 1189–1232 (2001)
7. Ke, G., et al.: LightGBM: a highly efficient gradient boosting decision tree. In: Advances in Neural Information Processing Systems, vol. 30, pp. 3146–3154 (2017)
8. Kurz, N., Muła, W., Lemire, D.: Faster population counts using AVX2 instructions. Comput. J. **61**(1), 111–120 (2017)
9. Mason, L., Baxter, J., Bartlett, P.L., Frean, M.R.: Boosting algorithms as gradient descent. In: Advances in Neural Information Processing Systems, pp. 512–518 (2000)

10. Prokhorenkova, L., Gusev, G., Vorobev, A., Dorogush, A.V., Gulin, A.: CatBoost: unbiased boosting with categorical features. In: Advances in Neural Information Processing Systems, vol. 31, pp. 6638–6648 (2018)
11. Rinfret, D., O'Neil, P., O'Neil, E.: Bit-sliced index arithmetic. In: ACM SIGMOD Record, vol. 30, pp. 47–57. ACM (2001)
12. Schapire, R.E.: The strength of weak learnability. Mach. Learn. **5**(2), 197–227 (1990)
13. Schapire, R.E., Freund, Y., Bartlett, P., Lee, W.S.: Boosting the margin: a new explanation for the effectiveness of voting methods. Ann. Stat. **26**(5), 1651–1686 (1998)

Shrinkage Estimators for Uplift Regression

Krzysztof Rudaś[1,2(✉)] and Szymon Jaroszewicz[2]

[1] Warsaw University of Technology, Warsaw, Poland
krzysztof.rudas@ipipan.waw.pl
[2] Institute of Computer Science, Polish Academy of Sciences, Warsaw, Poland

Abstract. Uplift modeling is an approach to machine learning which allows for predicting the net effect of an action (with respect to not taking the action). To achieve this, the training population is divided into two parts: the treatment group, which is subjected to the action, and the control group, on which the action is not taken. Our task is to construct a model which will predict the difference between outcomes in the treatment and control groups conditional on individual objects' features. When the group assignment is random, the model admits a causal interpretation. When we assume linear responses in both groups, the simplest way of estimating the net effect of the action on an individual is to build two separate linear ordinary least squares (OLS) regressions on the treatment and control groups and compute the difference between their predictions. In classical linear models improvements in accuracy can be achieved through the use of so called shrinkage estimators such as the well known James-Stein estimator, which has a provably lower mean squared error than the OLS estimator. In this paper we investigate the use of shrinkage estimators in the uplift modeling problem. Unfortunately direct generalization of the James-Stein estimator does not lead to improved predictions, nor does shrinking treatment and control models separately. Therefore, we propose a new uplift shrinkage method where estimators in the treatment and control groups are shrunk jointly so as to minimize the error in the predicted net effect of the action. We prove that the proposed estimator does indeed improve on the double regression estimator.

1 Introduction

Selecting observations which should become targets for an action, such as a marketing campaign or a medical treatment, is a problem of growing importance in machine learning. Typically, the first step is to predict the effect of the action (response) using a model built on a sample of individuals subjected to the action. A new observation is classified as suitable for the action if the predicted response

---

Electronic supplementary material The online version of this chapter (https://doi.org/10.1007/978-3-030-46150-8_36) contains supplementary material, which is available to authorized users.

U. Brefeld et al. (Eds.): ECML PKDD 2019, LNAI 11906, pp. 607–623, 2020.
https://doi.org/10.1007/978-3-030-46150-8_36

is above a certain threshold. Unfortunately this approach is not correct because the response that would have been observed had the action not been taken is ignored.

To clarify the problem, let us give a simple example. Suppose that we are owners of a shop which sells chocolate bars. In order to increase the sales of this product we give discounts to customers. Consider two cases. The first customer would have spent \$100 on chocolate after receiving the discount and \$95 in a situation when it was not given to him. The second one will spend \$50 and \$10, respectively. When we base our predictions only on a sample of customers subjected to the action (i.e. given the discount), we will prefer the first customer, but when we compare the amounts of money spent in cases of receiving and not receiving the discount, we will be disposed to send it to the second customer.

Clearly, the proper way to select targets for an action is to consider the difference between y^T, the response in case the individual is subjected to the action (treated) and y^C, the response when the individual is not subjected to the action (control). Unfortunately these two pieces of information are never available to us simultaneously. Once we send the discount we cannot 'unsend' it. This is known as the Fundamental Problem of Causal Inference [28].

Uplift modeling offers a solution to this problem based on dividing the population into two parts: treatment: subjected to the action and control on which the action is not taken. This second group is used as background thanks to which it is possible to partition the treatment response into a sum of two terms. The first is the response, which would have been observed if the treated objects were, instead, in the control group. The second is the additional effect observed only in the treatment group: the effect of the action. Based on this partition it is possible to construct a model predicting the desired difference between responses in the treatment and control groups [22].

Let us now introduce the notation used throughout the paper. We begin by describing the classical ordinary least squares regression. Only facts needed in the remaining part of the paper are given, full exposition can be found e.g. in [2]. We will assume that the predictor variables are arranged in an $n \times p$ matrix X and the responses are given in an n-dimensional vector y. We assume that y is related to X through a linear equation

$$y = X\beta + \varepsilon,$$

where β is an unknown coefficient vector and ε is a random noise vector with the usual assumptions that $\mathrm{E}\,\varepsilon_i = 0$, $\mathrm{Var}\,\varepsilon_i = \sigma^2$ and the components of ε are independent of each other. Moreover, we will make the assumption that the matrix X is fixed, which is frequently made in regression literature [2]. Our goal is to find an estimator of β which, on new test data X_{test}, y_{test}, achieves the lowest possible *mean squared error*

$$MSE(\hat{\beta}) = \mathrm{E}\,\|y_{test} - X_{test}\hat{\beta}\|^2, \tag{1}$$

where $\hat{\beta}$ is some estimator of β, and the expectation is taken over ε_{test} and $\hat{\beta}$. The most popular estimator is the Ordinary Least Squares (OLS) estimator obtained by minimizing the training set MSE $\|y - X\hat{\beta}\|^2$, given by

$$\hat{\beta} = (X'X)^{-1}X'y, \tag{2}$$

where $'$ denotes matrix transpose. In the rest of the paper $\hat{\beta}$ without additional subscripts will always denote the OLS estimator. It is well known that $\hat{\beta}$ is unbiased, $\mathrm{E}\,\hat{\beta} = \beta$, and its covariance matrix is $\sigma^2(X'X)^{-1}$ [2].

Let us now move to the case of regression in uplift modeling which is based on two training sets: treatment and control. We will adopt the convention that quantities related to the treatment group are denoted with superscript T, quantities related to the control group with a superscript C, and quantities related to the uplift itself with superscript U. Thus, in our context we will have two training sets X^T, y^T and X^C, y^C. Additionally denote $X = [X^{T'}|X^{C'}]'$, $y = [y^{T'}|y^{C'}]'$, i.e. the dataset obtained by concatenating treatment and control data records.

In this paper we will make an assumption (frequently made in statistical literature when linear models are considered), that responses in both groups are linear:

$$y^C = X^C\beta^C + \varepsilon^C,$$
$$y^T = X^T\beta^T + \varepsilon^T = X^T\beta^C + X^T\beta^U + \varepsilon^T.$$

The additional effect observed in the treatment group, $X^T\beta^U$, is the quantity of interest and our goal, therefore, is to find an estimator of β^U. The easiest way to obtain such an estimator is to construct separate Ordinary Least Squares (OLS) estimators of β^T and β^C on treatment and control groups respectively, and to calculate the difference between them:

$$\hat{\beta}_d^U = \hat{\beta}^T - \hat{\beta}^C. \tag{3}$$

This estimator is called the *double regression estimator* [9]. It is easy to show that the estimator is an unbiased estimator of β^U [9].

In classical regression analysis there are several ways of lowering the predictive error of the ordinary least squares model by reducing its variance at the expense of introducing bias [2]. One class of such estimators are *shrinkage estimators* which scale the ordinary least squares estimate $\hat{\beta}$ by a factor $\alpha < 1$. The best known of such estimators is the James-Stein estimator [27]. Another choice is a class of shrinkage estimators based on minimizing predictive MSE [19].

The goal of this paper is to find shrinkage estimators for uplift regression, whose accuracy is better than that of the double regression estimator. We may shrink the treatment and control coefficients separately obtaining the following general form of uplift shrinkage estimator

$$\hat{\beta}_{\alpha^T,\alpha^C}^U = \alpha^T\hat{\beta}^T - \alpha^C\hat{\beta}^C.$$

with an appropriate choice of α^T and α^C.

We introduce two types of such estimators, the first following the James-Stein approach, the second the MSE minimization approach. For each type we again introduce to sub-types: one in which treatment and control shrinkage factors α^T and α^C are found independently of each other (these are essentially double shrinkage models) and another which in shrinkage factors are estimated jointly in order to produce the best possible estimates of β^U. We demonstrate experimentally that MSE minimization based shrinkage with joint optimization of α^T and α^C gives the best uplift shrinkage estimator. We also formally prove that under certain assumptions it dominates the double regression estimator $\hat{\beta}_d^U$.

1.1   Literature Overview

We will now review the literature on uplift modeling. Literature related to shrinkage estimators will be discussed in Sect. 2.

Uplift modeling is a part of broader field of causal discovery and we will begin by positioning it within this field. The goal of causal discovery is not predicting future outcomes, but, instead, modeling the effects of interventions which directly change the values of some variables [20]. One can distinguish two general approaches to causal discovery: one based on purely observational data [20,26] and another one, in which the action being analyzed has actively been applied to a subgroup of the individuals.

Only the second approach is relevant to this paper. Large amount of related research has been conducted in the social sciences. However, their main research focus is on the cases where treatment assignment is nonrandom or biased [5,7]. Examples of methods used are propensity score matching or weighting by inverse probability of treatment [5,7]. Unfortunately, the success of those method depends on untestable assumptions such as 'no unmeasured confounders'. Only random treatment assignment guarantees that the causal effect is correctly identified. Most of those methods use double regression and do not try to improve the estimator itself. Uplift modeling differs from those methods since it is focused on obtaining the best possible estimate of an action's effect based on a randomized trial.

Most uplift modeling publications concern the problem of classification. The first published methods were based on decision trees [22,24]. They used modified splitting criteria to maximize difference in responses between the two groups. Similar methods have been devised under the name of estimating heterogenous treatment effects [1,8]. Later works extend these methods to ensembles of trees [4,25]. Work on linear uplift models includes approaches based on class variable transformation [10,11,15] used with logistic regression and approaches based on Support Vector Machines [13,14,29]. These methods can be used only with classification problems. Uplift regression methods were proposed in [9]. The paper also contained a theoretical analysis comparing several regression models.

The paper is organized as follows. In Sect. 2 we discuss shrinkage estimators used in classical linear regression. In Sect. 3 we derive four uplift shrinkage estimators and prove that, under certain assumptions, one of them dominates the double regression model. In Sect. 4 we evaluate the proposed estimators on two real-life datasets and conclude in Sect. 5.

2   Shrinkage Estimators for Linear Regression

We now present a short review of shrinkage estimators for classical ordinary least squares models which is sufficient for understanding the results in Sect. 3.

2.1   James-Stein Estimator

The famous James-Stein estimator has been presented in early 60s [27]. The authors proved that it allows for obtaining estimates with lower mean squared error than maximum likelihood based methods, which came as a shock to the statistical community. More specifically, let $Z \sim N(\mu, I)$ be a p-dimensional random vector whose mean μ is to be estimated based on a single sample z. The best unbiased estimator is $\hat{\mu} = z$. However, it can be proven [27] that the estimator

$$\hat{\mu}_{JS1} = \left(1 - \frac{(p-2)}{||\hat{\mu}||^2}\right)\hat{\mu} \tag{4}$$

has a lower mean squared error $\mathrm{E}\,||\hat{\mu}_{JS1} - \mu||^2 \leq \mathrm{E}\,||\hat{\mu} - \mu||^2$. The biggest gain is achieved for $\mu = 0$ and decreases when the norm of μ becomes large. To mitigate this effect, a modified shrinkage estimator was proposed by Efron [18]:

$$\hat{\mu}_{JS2} = \left(1 - \frac{(p-3)}{||\hat{\mu} - \overline{\hat{\mu}}||^2}\right)(\hat{\mu} - \overline{\hat{\mu}}) + \overline{\hat{\mu}}, \tag{5}$$

where $\overline{\hat{\mu}} = (\frac{1}{n}\sum_{i=1}^{p}\hat{\mu}_i)(1, \dots, 1)'$ is a column vector with each coordinate equal to the mean of $\hat{\mu}$'s coordinates.

The James-Stein estimator can be directly applied to the OLS estimator of regression coefficients $\hat{\beta}$, after taking into account their covariance matrix $\sigma^2(X'X)^{-1}$ [3, Chapter 7]:

$$\hat{\beta}_{JS1} = \left(1 - \frac{(p-2)}{\hat{\beta}'(\sigma^2(X'X)^{-1})^{-1}\hat{\beta}}\right)\hat{\beta}. \tag{6}$$

If σ^2 is unknown, we can substitute the usual estimate $\hat{\sigma}^2 = \frac{r'r}{n-p}$, where r is the vector of residuals. It can be shown that $\hat{\beta}_{JS1}$ has smaller predictive error than the standard OLS estimator [3, Chapter 7]. Adapting the trick given in Eq. 5 we get yet another estimator

$$\hat{\beta}_{JS2} = \left(1 - \frac{(p-3)}{(\hat{\beta} - \overline{\hat{\beta}})'(\sigma^2(X'X)^{-1})^{-1}(\hat{\beta} - \overline{\hat{\beta}})}\right)(\hat{\beta} - \overline{\hat{\beta}}) + \overline{\hat{\beta}}, \tag{7}$$

where $\overline{\hat{\beta}}$ is defined analogously to $\overline{\hat{\mu}}$ above. This form will be used to obtain a shrinked uplift regression estimator.

2.2   Shrinkage Estimators Based on Optimizing Predictive MSE

In [19] Ohtani gives an overview of another family of shrinkage estimators which improve on the OLS estimator. Their form is similar to the James-Stein estimator, but the shrinkage parameter is now obtained by minimizing the predictive mean squared error. Such estimators were first described in [6]. In our paper we use the following shrinkage factor proposed in [23]

$$\alpha = \frac{\beta'(X'X)\beta}{\beta'(X'X)\beta + \sigma^2}. \tag{8}$$

Notice that it depends on the unknown true coefficient vector β and error variance σ^2. Using the standard practice [19] of substituting OLS estimates $\hat{\beta}$ and $\hat{\sigma^2} = \frac{r'r}{n-p}$ (where r is the residual vector) we obtain an operational estimator

$$\hat{\beta}_{SMSE} = \frac{\hat{\beta}'(X'X)\hat{\beta}}{\hat{\beta}'(X'X)\hat{\beta} + \frac{r'r}{n-p}} \hat{\beta}, \tag{9}$$

where $SMSE$ stands for **S**hrinkage based on minimizing **MSE**. In [12] the MSE of this estimator was computed and sufficient conditions for it to dominate the OLS estimator were provided.

3   Shrinkage Estimators for Uplift Regression

In this section we present the main contribution of this paper: shrinkage estimators for uplift regression. We begin by deriving James-Stein style estimators and later derive versions based on minimizing predictive MSE.

3.1   James-Stein Uplift Estimators

The most obvious approach to obtaining a shrinked uplift estimator is to use two separate James-Stein estimators in Eq. 3, in place of OLS estimators $\hat{\beta}^T$ and $\hat{\beta}^C$. We obtain the following uplift shrinkage estimator

$$\hat{\beta}_{JSd}^U = \hat{\beta}_{JS2}^T - \hat{\beta}_{JS2}^C. \tag{10}$$

The d in the subscript indicates a 'double' model. This approach is fairly trivial and one is bound to ask whether it is possible to obtain a better estimator by directly shrinking the estimator $\hat{\beta}_d^U$ given by Eq. 3. To this end we need to estimate the variance of $\hat{\beta}_d^U$ and apply it to Eq. 7.

We note that $\hat{\beta}_d^U$ is the difference of two independent random vectors, so the variance of $\hat{\beta}_d^U$ is the sum of variances of $\hat{\beta}^T$ and $\hat{\beta}^C$

$$\text{Var}\,\hat{\beta}_d^U = \sigma^{T2}(X^{T'}X^T)^{-1} + \sigma^{C2}(X^{C'}X^C)^{-1}.$$

Substituting the usual estimators of σ^{T^2} and σ^{C^2} in the expression above and using it in Eq. 7 we obtain following estimator:

$$\hat{\beta}_{JS}^U = \frac{(p-3)}{(\hat{\beta}_d^U - \overline{\hat{\beta}_d^U})'V^{-1}(\hat{\beta}_d^U - \overline{\hat{\beta}_d^U})}(\hat{\beta}_d^U - \overline{\hat{\beta}_d^U}) + \overline{\hat{\beta}_d^U}, \qquad (11)$$

where $V = \frac{r^{T'}r^T}{n^T - p}(X^{T'}X^T)^{-1} + \frac{r^{C'}r^C}{n^C - p}(X^{C'}X^C)^{-1}$, r^T, r^C are OLS residuals in, respectively, treatment and control groups, and $\overline{\hat{\beta}_d^U} = (\frac{1}{n}\sum_{i=1}^p(\hat{\beta}_d^U)_i)(1,\dots,1)'$.

3.2   MSE Minimizing Uplift Estimators

We may also adapt the MSE-minimizing variant of shrinkage estimators [19] to the uplift modeling problem. The first approach is to use the shrinkage estimator given in Eq. 9 separately for β^T and β^C and construct a double uplift estimator:

$$\hat{\beta}_{SMSEd}^U = \hat{\beta}_{SMSE}^T - \hat{\beta}_{SMSE}^C. \qquad (12)$$

The d in the subscript indicates a 'double' model.

Another possibility is to estimate α^T, α^C jointly such that the mean squared prediction error is minimized. This is an entirely new method and the main contribution of this paper. Recall from Sect. 1 that the general shrinked double uplift estimator is

$$\hat{\beta}_{\alpha^T,\alpha^C}^U = \alpha^T(X^{T'}X^T)^{-1}X^{T'}y^T - \alpha^C(X^{C'}X^C)^{-1}X^{C'}y^C,$$

where α^T and α^C are the shrinkage factors. Since there is no explicit value of 'uplift response' which can be observed we will define the analogue of the MSE as $E\|X_{test}\beta^U - X_{test}\hat{\beta}_{\alpha^T,\alpha^C}^U\|^2$ where β^U is the true parameter vector, X_{test} is some test data, and the expectation is taken over $\hat{\beta}_{\alpha^T,\alpha^C}^U$. We have

$$E\|X_{test}\beta^U - X_{test}\hat{\beta}_{\alpha^T,\alpha^C}^U\|^2$$
$$= E\,\mathrm{Tr}\left\{(\beta^U - \hat{\beta}_{\alpha^T,\alpha^C}^U)'X_{test}'X_{test}(\beta^U - \hat{\beta}_{\alpha^T,\alpha^C}^U)\right\}$$
$$= E\,\mathrm{Tr}\left\{(X_{test}'X_{test})(\beta^U - \hat{\beta}_{\alpha^T,\alpha^C}^U)(\beta^U - \hat{\beta}_{\alpha^T,\alpha^C}^U)'\right\}$$
$$= \mathrm{Tr}\left\{(X_{test}'X_{test})\left(\mathrm{Var}\,\hat{\beta}_{\alpha^T,\alpha^C}^U + (\beta^U - E\,\hat{\beta}_{\alpha^T,\alpha^C}^U)(\beta^U - E\,\hat{\beta}_{\alpha^T,\alpha^C}^U)'\right)\right\}$$
$$= (E\,\hat{\beta}_{\alpha^T,\alpha^C}^U - \beta^U)'(X_{test}'X_{test})(E\,\hat{\beta}_{\alpha^T,\alpha^C}^U - \beta^U)$$
$$+ \mathrm{Tr}\left\{(X_{test}'X_{test})\left((\alpha^T)^2\,\mathrm{Var}\,\hat{\beta}^T + (\alpha^C)^2\,\mathrm{Var}\,\hat{\beta}^C\right)\right\}, \qquad (13)$$

where $E\,\hat{\beta}_{\alpha^T,\alpha^C}^U = \alpha^T\beta^T - \alpha^C\beta^C$, the second equality is obtained by changing the multiplication order within the trace, and the third follows from the bias-variance decomposition. Variance of $\hat{\beta}_{\alpha^T,\alpha^C}^U$ can be decomposed since it is the sum of two independent components. Differentiating with respect to α^T and equating to zero we get

$$0 = 2\alpha^T \beta^{T'}(X'_{test}X_{test})\beta^T - 2\alpha^C \beta^{T'}(X'_{test}X_{test})\beta^C$$
$$- 2\beta^{T'}(X'_{test}X_{test})\beta^U + 2\alpha^T \operatorname{Tr}((X'_{test}X_{test})\operatorname{Var}(\hat{\beta}^T)).$$

Analogously for α^C we obtain

$$0 = 2\alpha^C \beta^{C'}(X'_{test}X_{test})\beta^C - 2\alpha^T \beta^{T'}(X'_{test}X_{test})\beta^C$$
$$+ 2\beta^{C'}(X'_{test}X_{test})\beta^U + 2\alpha^C \operatorname{Tr}((X'_{test}X_{test})\operatorname{Var}(\hat{\beta}^C)).$$

Denote $W = X'_{test}X_{test}$. We can write the above system of equations for α^T and α^C in matrix form

$$\begin{bmatrix} \beta^{T'}W\beta^T + \operatorname{Tr}(W\operatorname{Var}(\hat{\beta}^T)) & -\beta^{T'}W\beta^C \\ -\beta^{C'}W\beta^T & \beta^{C'}W\beta^C + \operatorname{Tr}(W\operatorname{Var}(\hat{\beta}^C)) \end{bmatrix} \begin{bmatrix} \alpha^T \\ \alpha^C \end{bmatrix} = \begin{bmatrix} \beta^{T'}W\beta^U \\ -\beta^{C'}W\beta^U \end{bmatrix}.$$

Unfortunately we don't know true values of β^T and β^C so we have to replace them with their OLS estimators. Moreover, we cannot also use the test dataset while constructing the estimator. Therefore, in accordance with the fixed X assumption (see Sect. 1) we take $X_{test} = X$. Finally, we denote $V^T = (\hat{\sigma}^T)^2(X'X)(X^{T'}X^T)^{-1}$ and $V^C = (\hat{\sigma}^C)^2(X'X)(X^{C'}X^C)^{-1}$ to obtain an operational system of equations

$$\begin{bmatrix} \hat{\beta}^{T'}X'X\hat{\beta}^T + \operatorname{Tr}V^T & -\hat{\beta}^{T'}X'X\hat{\beta}^C \\ -\hat{\beta}^{C'}X'X\hat{\beta}^T & \hat{\beta}^{C'}X'X\hat{\beta}^C + \operatorname{Tr}V^C \end{bmatrix} \begin{bmatrix} \hat{\alpha}^T \\ \hat{\alpha}^C \end{bmatrix} = \begin{bmatrix} \hat{\beta}^{T'}X'X\hat{\beta}^U_d \\ -\hat{\beta}^{C'}X'X\hat{\beta}^U_d \end{bmatrix}. \quad (14)$$

Finally we are ready to define our shrinkage uplift regression estimator:

Definition 1. *Assume that $\hat{\beta}^T$ and $\hat{\beta}^C$ are OLS regression estimators built respectively on the treatment and control groups. Denote by $\hat{\alpha}^T$ and $\hat{\alpha}^C$ the solutions to the system of Eq. 14. Then the estimator*

$$\hat{\beta}^U_{SMSE} = \hat{\alpha}^T \hat{\beta}^T - \hat{\alpha}^C \hat{\beta}^C$$

is called the uplift MSE-minimizing estimator.

Because the unknown values of β^T, β^C, σ^T, σ^C have been replaced with their estimators, we have no guarantee that $\hat{\beta}^U_{SMSE}$ minimizes the predictive mean squared error. However, under additional assumptions we are able to prove the following theorem.

Theorem 1. *Assume that the matrices X^T and X^C are orthogonal, i.e. $X^{T'}X^T = X^{C'}X^C = I$. Assume further, that the error vectors ε^T, ε^C are independent and normally distributed as $N(0, I)$, i.e. assume that $\sigma^T = \sigma^C = 1$. Then for $p \geqslant 6$*

$$\operatorname{E}\|X\beta^U - X\hat{\beta}^U_{SMSE}\|^2 \leqslant \operatorname{E}\|X\beta^U - X\hat{\beta}^U_d\|^2.$$

The proof of the theorem can be found in the Appendix. Additionally the supplementary material contains a symbolic computation script verifying the more technical sections of the proof.

The theorem says that under orthogonal design the uplift MSE-minimizing estimator given in Definition 1 has a lower expected prediction error than the double estimator given in Eq. 3. The requirement for an orthogonal design is restrictive but we were not able to prove the theorem in a more general setting. Even with this assumption, the proof is long and fairly technical. For more general settings we resort to experimental verification in Sect. 4.

4   Experiments

In this section we present an experimental evaluation of the proposed shrinkage estimators. Before presenting the results we will describe two real life datasets used in the study, as well as the testing methodology we adopted.

4.1   Descriptions of Datasets

The first dataset we consider is the well known Lalonde dataset [21] describing the effects of a job training program which addressed a population of low skilled adults. A randomly selected sample of the population was invited to take part in a job training program. Their income in the third year *after* randomization is the target variable. Our goal is to build a model predicting whether the program will be effective for a given individual. There are a total of 185 treatment records and 260 controls.

The second dataset we use is the IHDP dataset [16]. The dataset describes the results of a program whose target groups were low birth weight infants. A randomly selected subset of them received additional support such as home visits and access to a child development center. We want to identify infants for whose IQ (the target variable used in the study) increased *because* of the intervention program. There are 377 treatment and 608 control cases.

4.2   Methodology

The biggest problem in evaluating uplift models is that we never observe y_i^T and y_i^C simultaneously and, thus, do not know the true value of the quantity we want to predict $y_i^T - y_i^C$. Therefore we are forced to make the comparison on larger groups. Here we will estimate the so called Average Treatment Effect on the Treated (ATT) [5,7] using two methods: one based on predictions of a model with coefficients $\hat{\beta}^U$, the other based on true outcomes using a so called difference-in-means estimator [5]. Both quantities are given, respectively, by the following equations

$$ATT_{model}(\hat{\beta}^U) = \frac{1}{n^T} \sum_{i=1}^{n^T} X_i \hat{\beta}^U, \qquad ATT_{means} = \frac{1}{n^T} \sum_{i=1}^{n^T} y_i^T - \frac{1}{n^C} \sum_{i=1}^{n^C} y_i^C.$$

The difference-in-means estimator will play the role of ground truth. We define the absolute error in ATT estimation of a model with coefficients $\hat{\beta}^U$ as

$$ErrATT(\hat{\beta}^U) = |ATT_{model}(\hat{\beta}^U) - ATT_{means}|.$$

Model comparison will be based on their ErrATTs.

Each dataset was split into a training and testing part. Splitting was done separately in the treatment and control groups, 70% of cases assigned to the training set and the remaining cases to the test set. We repeat this procedure 1000 times and aggregate the results. To compare estimators $\hat{\beta}_1^U$ and $\hat{\beta}_2^U$ we will compute the difference $ErrATT(\hat{\beta}_1^U) - ErrATT(\hat{\beta}_2^U)$ for each simulation and display the differences using box plots in order to better visualize how often an by what margin each model is better. We found this approach to give more meaningful results than simply comparing mean prediction errors.

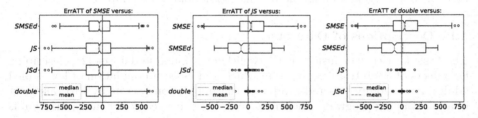

Fig. 1. Differences between errors in ATT estimation for pairs of models for the Lalonde dataset. Each boxplot summarizes the distribution of differences for a pair of models over 1000 train/test splits. For example, the first chart compares the proposed uplift MSE-minimizing shrinkage estimator $\hat{\beta}_{SMSE}^U$ against all other estimators. The mean/median lines on the negative side indicate the model in figure title performs better

4.3   Results

Our experiments involve five different estimators: the double regression estimator $\hat{\beta}_d^U$ given in Eq. 3, two double shrinkage estimators: the double James-Stein estimator $\hat{\beta}_{JSd}^U$ and the double MSE minimizing shrinkage estimator $\hat{\beta}_{SMSE}^U$ given, respectively, in Eqs. 10 and 12, and finally the two direct uplift shrinkage estimators: $\hat{\beta}_{JS}^U$ given in Eq. 11 and $\hat{\beta}_{SMSEd}^U$ given in Definition 1. In the figures the estimators are denoted with just their subscripts, e.g. $SMSEd$ instead of $\hat{\beta}_{SMSEd}^U$, except for $\hat{\beta}_d^U$ denoted by *double* for easier readability.

Results on the Lalonde dataset are shown in Fig. 1. The first chart on the figure compares the proposed uplift MSE-minimizing estimator will all remaining estimators. It can be seen that the estimator outperforms all others: the original double regression and all three other shrinkage estimators. The improvement can be seen both in the mean and in the median of differences between $ErrATT$'s which are negative. The difference is not huge, but it is consistent, so there is little argument for not using the shrinkage estimator. Moreover, the results are statistically significant (notches in the box plot denote a confidence interval for the median).

The second chart shows the performance of another proposed estimator, the James-Stein version of uplift estimator $\hat{\beta}_{JS}^{U}$. Here, a different story can be seen. The performance is practically identical to that of the classical double regression and double James-Stein estimator; the boxplots have in fact collapsed at zero. There is an improvement in the median of error difference over $\hat{\beta}_{SMSEd}^{U}$ but it disappears when one looks at the mean: one cannot expect practical gains from using this estimator.

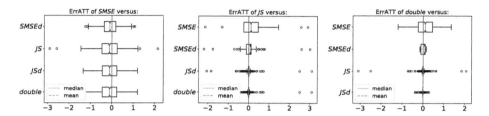

Fig. 2. Differences between errors in ATT estimation for pairs of models for the IHDP dataset. Each boxplot summarizes the distribution of differences for a pair of models over 1000 train/test splits. For example, the first chart compares the proposed uplift MSE-minimizing shrinkage estimator $\hat{\beta}_{SMSE}^{U}$ against all other estimators. The mean/median lines on the negative side indicate the model in figure title performs better

The two remaining double shrinked estimators performed similarly and charts comparing them to all other models are not shown. For completeness we compare the unshrinked double regression with all shrinkage estimator in the third chart of Fig. 1. It can be seen that only the estimator given in Definition 1 dominates it.

The results for the IHDP dataset are shown in Fig. 2. All conclusions drawn from the Lalonde dataset are essentially replicated also on IHDP, giving the results more credibility.

5   Conclusions and Future Work

We have proposed four different shrinkage estimators for uplift regression problem. One of them successfully and consistently reduced prediction error on two real life datasets. The estimator was different from others in that it jointly optimized the treatment and control shrinkage factors such that good uplift predictions are obtained.

The three other estimators did not bring improvement over the classical double regression model. One concludes, that simply applying shrinkage to treatment and control models separately is not enough to obtain a good uplift shrinkage estimator. Neither is applying the James-Stein approach directly the estimated uplift coefficients as is done in the $\hat{\beta}^U_{JS}$ estimator.

Future work will address the problem of adapting shrinkage methods to other uplift regression estimators such as those proposed in [9]. The task is challenging since the finite sample variance of those estimators is not known.

A   Proof of Theorem 1

Since large parts of the proof require lengthy derivations, the supplementary material contains a Python script which verifies certain equations symbolically using the Sympy [17] package.

From assumptions we have $X^{T'}X^T = X^{C'}X^C = I$, implying $X'X = 2I$. Taking this into account we can simplify the system of Eq. (14) to

$$
\begin{bmatrix} \hat{\beta}^{T'}\hat{\beta}^T + p & -\hat{\beta}^{T'}\hat{\beta}^C \\ -\hat{\beta}^{C'}\hat{\beta}^T & \hat{\beta}^{C'}\hat{\beta}^C + p \end{bmatrix} \begin{bmatrix} \hat{\alpha}^T \\ \hat{\alpha}^C \end{bmatrix} = \begin{bmatrix} \hat{\beta}^{T'}\hat{\beta}^U \\ -\hat{\beta}^{C'}\hat{\beta}^U \end{bmatrix}. \tag{15}
$$

Denote $b^{TT} = \hat{\beta}^{T'}\hat{\beta}^T$, $b^{CC} = \hat{\beta}^{C'}\hat{\beta}^C$ and $b^{TC} = \hat{\beta}^{T'}\hat{\beta}^C$. Denoting further $A = \begin{bmatrix} b^{TT} + p & -b^{TC} \\ -b^{TC} & b^{CC} + p \end{bmatrix}$ and $B = \begin{bmatrix} b^{TT} - b^{TC} \\ b^{CC} - b^{TC} \end{bmatrix}$ the system of equations simplifies further to:

$$
A \begin{bmatrix} \hat{\alpha}^T \\ \hat{\alpha}^C \end{bmatrix} = B. \tag{16}
$$

As a result, denoting $K = \frac{1}{(b^{TT}+p)(b^{CC}+p)-(b^{TC})^2}$, we obtain:

$$
\begin{bmatrix} \hat{\alpha}^T \\ \hat{\alpha}^C \end{bmatrix} = A^{-1}B = K \begin{bmatrix} b^{CC} + p & b^{TC} \\ b^{TC} & b^{TT} + p \end{bmatrix} \begin{bmatrix} b^{TT} - b^{TC} \\ b^{CC} - b^{TC} \end{bmatrix}.
$$

Equivalently we can write the parameters (verified in the supplementary material) as

$$
\hat{\alpha}^T = K \left(b^{CC}b^{TT} - (b^{TC})^2 + pb^{TT} - pb^{TC} \right) = 1 - pK \left(b^{CC} + b^{TC} + p \right)
$$
$$
\hat{\alpha}^C = K \left(b^{CC}b^{TT} - (b^{TC})^2 + pb^{CC} - pb^{TC} \right) = 1 - pK \left(b^{TT} + b^{TC} + p \right) \tag{17}
$$

The predictive MSE of the double model is

$$
\mathrm{E}(\hat{\beta}^U_d - \beta^U)'(\hat{\beta}^U_d - \beta^U) = 2p. \tag{18}
$$

To see this, note that the estimator is unbiased and, under the assumptions of the theorem, $\mathrm{Var}\,\hat{\beta}^T = \mathrm{Var}\,\hat{\beta}^C = I$. Apply the trace in (13) to get the result.

Now we will calculate the predictive MSE of new shrinked and prove that it is less than $2p$. It is easy to see that

$$\mathrm{E}(\hat{\beta}^U_{SMSE} - \beta^U)'(\hat{\beta}^U_{SMSE} - \beta^U) = \mathrm{E}(\hat{\beta}^U_{SMSE} - \hat{\beta}^U_d)'(\hat{\beta}^U_{SMSE} - \hat{\beta}^U_d)$$
$$- \mathrm{E}(\hat{\beta}^U_d - \beta^U)'(\hat{\beta}^U_d - \beta^U) + 2\,\mathrm{E}(\hat{\beta}^U_{SMSE} - \beta^U)'(\hat{\beta}^U_d - \beta^U). \qquad (19)$$

Denote:

$$\hat{\beta}^T_s = p\left(b^{CC} + b^{TC} + p\right)\hat{\beta}^T,$$
$$\hat{\beta}^C_s = p\left(b^{TT} + b^{TC} + p\right)\hat{\beta}^C.$$

Then the first term of (19) is (verified in the supplementary material)

$$\mathrm{E}(\hat{\beta}^U_{SMSE} - \hat{\beta}^U_d)'(\hat{\beta}^U_{SMSE} - \hat{\beta}^U_d)$$
$$= \mathrm{E}((\hat{\alpha}^T - 1)\hat{\beta}^T - (\hat{\alpha}^C - 1)\hat{\beta}^C)'((\hat{\alpha}^T - 1)\hat{\beta}^T - (\hat{\alpha}^C - 1)\hat{\beta}^C)$$
$$= K^2\,\mathrm{E}\left(\hat{\beta}^T_s - \hat{\beta}^C_s\right)'\left(\hat{\beta}^T_s - \hat{\beta}^C_s\right) \qquad (20)$$
$$= K^2\,\mathrm{E}\left(p^4(b^{TT} - 2b^{TC} + b^{CC})\right.$$
$$\left. + p^2\left(b^{TT}b^{CC} - b^{TC2}\right)\left((b^{TT} + 2b^{TC} + b^{CC}) + 4p\right)\right). \qquad (21)$$

Now we will concentrate on third term of (19):

$$2\,\mathrm{E}(\hat{\beta}^U_{SMSE} - \beta^U)'(\hat{\beta}^U_d - \beta^U) = 2\,\mathrm{E}(\hat{\alpha}^T\hat{\beta}^T - \beta^T)'(\hat{\beta}^T - \beta^T) \qquad (22)$$
$$+ 2\,\mathrm{E}(\hat{\alpha}^C\hat{\beta}^C - \beta^C)'(\hat{\beta}^C - \beta^C) \qquad (23)$$
$$- 2\,\mathrm{E}(\hat{\alpha}^T\hat{\beta}^T - \beta^T)'(\hat{\beta}^C - \beta^C) - 2\,\mathrm{E}(\hat{\alpha}^C\hat{\beta}^C - \beta^C)'(\hat{\beta}^T - \beta^T). \qquad (24)$$

We will first look at $2\,\mathrm{E}(\hat{\alpha}^T\hat{\beta}^T - \beta^T)'(\hat{\beta}^T - \beta^T)$ following the classical proof for James-Stein estimator

$$2\,\mathrm{E}(\hat{\beta}^T - \beta^T)'(\hat{\alpha}^T\hat{\beta}^T - \beta^T) = 2\sum_{i=1}^{p}\mathrm{E}(\hat{\beta}^T_i - \beta^T_i)(\hat{\alpha}^T\hat{\beta}^T_i - \beta^T_i)$$

$$= 2\sum_{i=1}^{p}\int..\int(\hat{\beta}^T_i - \beta^T_i)(\hat{\alpha}^T\hat{\beta}^T_i - \beta^T_i)f(\hat{\beta}^T)d\hat{\beta}^T_i, d\hat{\beta}^T_1...d\hat{\beta}^T_p$$

where $f(\hat{\beta}^T)$ is density function of distribution of $\hat{\beta}^T$, which, by assumptions is multivariate normal $N(\beta^T, I)$. Using integration by parts (derivatives calculated w.r.t. $\hat{\beta}_i$) with

$$u = \hat{\alpha}^T\hat{\beta}^T_i - \beta^T_i \qquad\qquad dv = (\hat{\beta}^T_i - \beta^T_i)\frac{\exp\left(-\frac{1}{2}\sum_{j=1}^{p}\left(\hat{\beta}^T_j - \beta^T_j\right)^2\right)}{2\pi^{\frac{p}{2}}}d\hat{\beta}^T_i$$

$$du = \frac{d}{d\hat{\beta}^T_i}(\hat{\alpha}^T\hat{\beta}^T_i - \beta^T_i)d\hat{\beta}^T_i \qquad v = -\frac{\exp\left(-\frac{1}{2}\sum_{j=1}^{p}\left(\hat{\beta}^T_j - \beta^T_j\right)^2\right)}{2\pi^{\frac{p}{2}}}$$

we obtain:

$$\int \cdots \int (\hat{\beta}_i^T - \beta_i^T)(\hat{\alpha}^T \hat{\beta}_i^T - \beta_i^T) f(\hat{\beta}^T) d\hat{\beta}_i^T d\hat{\beta}_1^T ... d\hat{\beta}_p^T$$

$$= \int \cdots \int (\hat{\beta}_i^T - \beta_i^T)(\hat{\alpha}^T \hat{\beta}_i^T - \beta_i^T) \frac{1}{2\pi^{\frac{p}{2}}} \exp\left(-\frac{1}{2} \sum_{j=1}^{p} \left(\hat{\beta}_j^T - \beta_j^T\right)^2\right) d\hat{\beta}_i^T d\hat{\beta}_1^T ... d\hat{\beta}_p^T$$

$$= \left[\int \cdots \int - \left(\hat{\alpha}^T \hat{\beta}_i^T - \beta_i^T\right) \frac{\exp\left(-\frac{1}{2} \sum_{j=1}^{p} \left(\hat{\beta}_j^T - \beta_j^T\right)^2\right)}{2\pi^{\frac{p}{2}}} \right]_{-\infty}^{\infty} d\hat{\beta}_1^T ... d\hat{\beta}_p^T$$

$$+ \int \cdots \int \frac{d}{d\hat{\beta}_i^T}(\hat{\alpha}^T \hat{\beta}_i^T - \beta_i^T) \frac{\exp\left(-\frac{1}{2} \sum_{j=1}^{p} \left(\hat{\beta}_j^T - \beta_j^T\right)^2\right)}{2\pi^{\frac{p}{2}}} d\hat{\beta}_i^T d\hat{\beta}_1^T ... d\hat{\beta}_p^T.$$

First term in last expression is 0, due to exponential decrease of normal density. Finally we obtain:

$$= \int \cdots \int f(\hat{\beta}^T) \frac{d}{d\hat{\beta}_i^T}(\hat{\alpha}^T \hat{\beta}_i^T - \beta_i^T) d\hat{\beta}_i^T d\hat{\beta}_1^T ... d\hat{\beta}_p^T.$$

Repeating the above process for $i = 1, \ldots, p$ we get

$$2\,\mathrm{E}(\hat{\alpha^T}\hat{\beta}^T - \beta^T)'(\hat{\beta}^T - \beta^T) = 2\,\mathrm{E}\sum_{i=1}^{p} \frac{d}{d\hat{\beta}_i^T}(\hat{\alpha}^T \hat{\beta}_i^T - \beta_i^T) = 2p\hat{\alpha}^T + 2\hat{\beta}^{T'}\frac{d\hat{\alpha}^T}{d\hat{\beta}^T}.$$

For the third term of (24) we obtain:

$$2\,\mathrm{E}(\hat{\alpha^T}\hat{\beta}^T - \beta^T)'(\hat{\beta}^C - \beta^C) = 2\,\mathrm{E}\sum_{i=1}^{p} \frac{d}{d\hat{\beta}_i^C}(\hat{\alpha}^T \hat{\beta}_i^T - \beta_i^T) = 2\hat{\beta}^{T'}\frac{d\hat{\alpha}^T}{d\hat{\beta}^C},$$

where the last factor is the vector derivative of a scalar. The remaining two terms are analogous. Combining the expressions and using the chain rule we obtain:

$$\mathrm{E}(\hat{\alpha^T}\hat{\beta}^T - \beta^T)'(\hat{\beta}^T - \beta^T) - \mathrm{E}(\hat{\alpha}^C\hat{\beta}^C - \beta^C)'(\hat{\beta}^T - \beta^T)$$

$$= [p \mid 0] \begin{bmatrix} \hat{\alpha}^T \\ \hat{\alpha}^C \end{bmatrix} + [\hat{\beta}^{T'} \mid -\hat{\beta}^{C'}] \begin{bmatrix} \frac{d\hat{\alpha}^T}{d\hat{\beta}^T} \\ \frac{d\hat{\alpha}^C}{d\hat{\beta}^T} \end{bmatrix}$$

$$= [p \mid 0] \begin{bmatrix} \hat{\alpha}^T \\ \hat{\alpha}^C \end{bmatrix} + [\hat{\beta}^{T'} \mid -\hat{\beta}^{C'}] \begin{bmatrix} \frac{d\hat{\alpha}^T}{db^{TT}}\frac{db^{TT}}{d\hat{\beta}^T} + \frac{d\hat{\alpha}^T}{db^{TC}}\frac{db^{TC}}{d\hat{\beta}^T} + \frac{d\hat{\alpha}^T}{db^{CC}}\frac{db^{CC}}{d\hat{\beta}^T} \\ \frac{d\hat{\alpha}^C}{db^{TT}}\frac{db^{TT}}{d\hat{\beta}^T} + \frac{d\hat{\alpha}^C}{b^{TC}}\frac{db^{TC}}{d\hat{\beta}^T} + \frac{d\hat{\alpha}^C}{db^{CC}}\frac{db^{CC}}{d\hat{\beta}^T} \end{bmatrix}$$

$$= [p \mid 0] \begin{bmatrix} \hat{\alpha}^T \\ \hat{\alpha}^C \end{bmatrix} + 2[b^{TT} \mid -b^{TC}] \begin{bmatrix} \frac{d\hat{\alpha}^T}{db^{TT}} \\ \frac{d\hat{\alpha}^C}{db^{TT}} \end{bmatrix} + [b^{TC} \mid -b^{CC}] \begin{bmatrix} \frac{d\hat{\alpha}^T}{db^{TC}} \\ \frac{d\hat{\alpha}^C}{db^{TC}} \end{bmatrix}$$

$$= [p \mid 0] A^{-1}B + 2[b^{TT} \mid -b^{TC}] \frac{dA^{-1}B}{db^{TT}} + [b^{TC} \mid -b^{CC}] \frac{dA^{-1}B}{db^{TC}}. \tag{25}$$

Analogously we obtain:

$$\mathrm{E}(\hat{\alpha}^C\hat{\beta}^C - \beta^C)'(\hat{\beta}^C - \beta^C) - \mathrm{E}(\hat{\alpha}^T\hat{\beta}^T - \beta^T)'(\hat{\beta}^C - \beta^C)$$

$$= [0 \mid p]\, A^{-1}B + 2\left[-b^{TC} \mid b^{CC}\right]\frac{dA^{-1}B}{d\,b^{CC}} + \left[-b^{TT} \mid b^{TC}\right]\frac{dA^{-1}B}{d\,b^{TC}}. \tag{26}$$

Combining (25) and (26) we obtain (verified in the supplementary material):

$$2\,\mathrm{E}(\hat{\beta}^U_{SMSE} - \beta^U)'(\hat{\beta}^U_d - \beta^U) = 2\left[p \mid p\right]A^{-1}B$$

$$- 2K\begin{bmatrix} 3b^{TT}b^{CC} - 3\left(b^{TC}\right)^2 + 2b^{TT}p + b^{CC}p - b^{TC}p \\ 3b^{TT}b^{CC} - 3\left(b^{TC}\right)^2 + 2b^{CC}p + b^{TT}p - b^{TC}p \end{bmatrix}\left(A^{-1}B - 1\right) \tag{27}$$

$$= 2p(\hat{\alpha}^T + \hat{\alpha}^C) - 2(2\hat{\alpha}^T + 1)\hat{\alpha}^T - 2(2\hat{\alpha}^C + 1)\hat{\alpha}^C - 4Kp^2$$

$$= 4p + 2(p-3)(\hat{\alpha}^T - 1 + \hat{\alpha}^C - 1) - 4Kp^2 - 4(\hat{\alpha}^T - 1)^2 - 4(\hat{\alpha}^C - 1)^2, \tag{28}$$

where $\mathbf{1} = (1,1)'$. Now we have calculated each term of (19). Now we will combine (28) and (18).

$$2\,\mathrm{E}(\hat{\beta}^U_{SMSE} - \beta^U)'(\hat{\beta}^U_d - \beta^U) - \mathrm{E}(\hat{\beta}^U_d - \beta^U)'(\hat{\beta}^U_d - \beta^U)$$

$$= 2p - \mathrm{E}\,K^2\left(\frac{1}{K}\left(2p(p-3)\left(b^{TT} + 2b^{TC} + b^{CC}\right) - 4p^2(p-2)\right)\right.$$

$$\left. - 4\left(\left(pb^{TT} + pb^{TC} + p^2\right)^2 + \left(pb^{CC} + pb^{TC} + p^2\right)^2\right)\right). \tag{29}$$

Combining further (29) with (21) we obtain the following expression for (19) (verified in the supplementary material):

$$\mathrm{E}(\hat{\beta}^U_{SMSE} - \beta^U)'(\hat{\beta}^U_{SMSE} - \beta^U) = 2p - \tag{30}$$

$$\mathrm{E}\,K^2\Big(p(p-6)(b^{TT} + 2b^{TC} + b^{CC})\left(b^{TT}b^{CC} - b^{TC2}\right) \tag{31}$$

$$+ 2p^2(p-3)(b^{TT} + 2b^{TC} + b^{CC})\left(b^{TT} + b^{CC}\right) \tag{32}$$

$$+ 2p^3(p-3)(b^{TT} + 2b^{TC} + b^{CC}) \tag{33}$$

$$- 8p^2\left(b^{TT}b^{CC} - b^{TC2}\right) \tag{34}$$

$$+ 4p^3(p-2)\left(b^{TT} + b^{CC} + p\right) \tag{35}$$

$$+ 4p^2\left(b^{TT} + b^{TC} + p\right)^2 + 4p^2\left(b^{CC} + b^{TC} + p\right)^2 \tag{36}$$

$$- p^4(b^{TT} - 2b^{TC} + b^{CC})\Big). \tag{37}$$

We see that (31) is greater than or equal to 0 when $p \geqslant 6$ and (33) when $p \geqslant 3$. Now combining (35) and (37) for $p \geqslant 4$ we get:

$$4p^3(p-2)\left(b^{TT} + b^{CC} + p\right) - p^4(b^{TT} - 2b^{TC} + b^{CC})$$

$$= 2p^3(p-4)\left(b^{TT} + b^{CC} + p\right) + 2p^4\left(b^{TT} + b^{CC} + p\right) - p^4(b^{TT} - 2b^{TC} + b^{CC})$$

$$\geqslant 2p^3(p-4)\left(b^{TT}+b^{CC}+p\right)+2p^4\left(b^{TT}+b^{CC}+p\right)-2p^4(b^{TT}+b^{CC})$$
$$= 2p^3(p-4)\left(b^{TT}+b^{CC}+p\right)+2p^5 > 0,$$

where the first inequality follows from $b^{TT}-2b^{TC}+b^{CC}\leqslant 2(b^{TT}+b^{CC})$.

Now, combining (32), (34) and (36), we obtain (verified in the supplementary material):

$$-K^2\left(2p^2(p-3)(b^{TT}+2b^{TC}+b^{CC})\left(b^{TT}+b^{CC}\right)-8p^2(b^{TT}b^{CC}-b^{TC^2})\right.$$
$$\left.+4p^2\left(b^{TT}+b^{TC}+p\right)^2+4p^2\left(b^{CC}+b^{TC}+p\right)^2\right)$$

$$= K^2\left(-2p^2(p-5)(b^{TT}+2b^{TC}+b^{CC})\left(b^{TT}+b^{CC}\right)\right. \tag{38}$$

$$-\left(8p^2(b^{TT}+b^{TC})^2+8p^2(b^{CC}+b^{TC})^2\right) \tag{39}$$

$$\left.-\left(8p^3(b^{TT}+2b^{TC}+b^{CC})+p\right)\right) \tag{40}$$

We can observe that (39) and (40) are always non positive and (38) is negative when $p > 5$. So the whole expression above is also negative when $p > 5$. So, the only positive term in (30)–(37) is $2p$ proving that predictive error of the shrinked estimator is lower than that of double regression (equal to $2p$) for $p \geqslant 6$.

References

1. Athey, S., Imbens, G.: Recursive partitioning for heterogeneous causal effects. Proc. Nat. Acad. Sci. **113**(27), 7353–7360 (2016)
2. Heumann, C., Nittner, T., Rao, C.R., Scheid, S., Toutenburg, H.: Linear Models: Least Squares and Alternatives. Springer, New York (2013). https://doi.org/10.1007/978-1-4899-0024-1
3. Efron, B., Hastie, T.: Computer Age Statistical Inference: Algorithms, Evidence, and Data Science, 1st edn. Cambridge University Press, New York (2016)
4. Guelman, L., Guillén, M., Pérez-Marín, A.M.: Random forests for uplift modeling: an insurance customer retention case. In: Engemann, K.J., Gil-Lafuente, A.M., Merigó, J.M. (eds.) MS 2012. LNBIP, vol. 115, pp. 123–133. Springer, Heidelberg (2012). https://doi.org/10.1007/978-3-642-30433-0_13
5. Imbens, G.W., Rubin, D.B.: Causal Inference for Statistics, Social, and Biomedical Sciences: An Introduction. Cambridge University Press, New York (2015)
6. Theil, H.: Principles of Econometrics. John Wiley, New York (1971)
7. Robins, J.M., Hernán, M.A.: Causal Inference. Chapman & Hall/CRC, Boca Raton (2018)
8. Hill, J.L.: Bayesian nonparametric modeling for causal inference. J. Comput. Graph. Stat. **20**(1), 217–240 (2011)
9. Rudaś, K., Jaroszewicz, S.: Linear regression for uplift modeling. Data Min. Knowl. Disc. **32**(5), 1275–1305 (2018). https://doi.org/10.1007/s10618-018-0576-8
10. Jaśkowski, M., Jaroszewicz, S.: Uplift modeling for clinical trial data. In: ICML 2012 Workshop on Machine Learning for Clinical Data Analysis, Edinburgh, June 2012

11. Kane, K., Lo, V.S.Y., Zheng, J.: Mining for the truly responsive customers and prospects using true-lift modeling: comparison of new and existing methods. J. Mark. Anal. **2**(4), 218–238 (2014)
12. Ohtani, K.: Exact small sample properties of an operational variant of the minimum mean squared error estimator. Commun. Stat. Theory Methods **25**(6), 1223–1231 (1996)
13. Kuusisto, F., Santos Costa, V., Nassif, H., Burnside, E., Page, D., Shavlik, J.: Support vector machines for differential prediction. In: ECML-PKDD (2014)
14. Zaniewicz, L., Jaroszewicz, S.: l_p-support vector machines for uplift modeling. Knowl. Inf. Syst. **53**(1), 269–296 (2017)
15. Lai, L.Y.-T.: Influential marketing: a new direct marketing strategy addressing the existence of voluntary buyers. Master's thesis, Simon Fraser University (2006)
16. Brooks-Gunn, J., Liaw, F., Klebanov, P.: Effects of early intervention on cognitive function of low birth weight preterm infants. J. Pediatr. **120**, 350–359 (1991)
17. Meurer, A., et al.: SymPy: symbolic computing in Python. Peer J. Comput. Sci. **3**, e103 (2017)
18. Efron, B., Morris, C.: Stein's paradox in statistics. Sci. Am. **236**(5), 119–127 (1977)
19. Namba, A., Ohtani, K.: MSE performance of the weighted average estimators consisting of shrinkage estimators. Commun. Stat. Theory Methods **47**(5), 1204–1214 (2018)
20. Pearl, J.: Causality. Cambridge University Press, Cambridge (2009)
21. Lalonde, R.: Evaluating the econometric evaluations of training programs. Am. Econ. Rev. **76**, 604–620 (1986)
22. Radcliffe, N.J., Surry, P.D.: Real-world uplift modelling with significance-based uplift trees. Portrait Technical report TR-2011-1, Stochastic Solutions (2011)
23. Farebrother, R.W.: The minimum mean square error linear estimator and ridge regression. Technometrics **17**(1), 127–128 (1975)
24. Rzepakowski, P., Jaroszewicz, S.: Decision trees for uplift modeling with single and multipletreatments. Knowl. Inf. Syst. **32**(2), 303–327 (2011)
25. Sołtys, M., Jaroszewicz, S., Rzepakowski, P.: Ensemble methods for uplift modeling. Data Min. Knowl. Discov. **29**(6), 1–29 (2014). online first
26. Spirtes, P., Glymour, C., Scheines, R.: Causation, Prediction, and Search. MIT Press, Cambridge (2001)
27. James, W., Stein, C.: Estimation with quadratic loss. In: Proceedings of Fourth Berkeley Symposium on Mathematical Statistics and Probability, vol. 1, pp. 361–379 (1961)
28. Holland, P.W.: Statistics and causal inference. J. Am. Stat. Assoc. **81**(396), 945–960 (1986)
29. Zaniewicz, L., Jaroszewicz, S.: Support vector machines for uplift modeling. In: The First IEEE ICDM Workshop on Causal Discovery (CD 2013), Dallas, December 2013

Strings and Streams

String Sanitization: A Combinatorial Approach

Giulia Bernardini[1], Huiping Chen[2], Alessio Conte[3], Roberto Grossi[3,4],
Grigorios Loukides[2(✉)], Nadia Pisanti[3,4], Solon P. Pissis[4,5],
and Giovanna Rosone[3]

[1] Department of Informatics, Systems and Communication,
University of Milano-Bicocca, Milan, Italy
`giulia.bernardini@unimib.it`
[2] Department of Informatics, King's College London, London, UK
{`huiping.chen,grigorios.loukides`}`@kcl.ac.uk`
[3] Department of Computer Science, University of Pisa, Pisa, Italy
{`conte,grossi,pisanti`}`@di.unipi.it, giovanna.rosone@unipi.it`
[4] ERABLE Team, Inria, Lyon, France
[5] CWI, Amsterdam, The Netherlands
`solon.pissis@cwi.nl`

Abstract. String data are often disseminated to support applications
such as location-based service provision or DNA sequence analysis. This
dissemination, however, may expose sensitive patterns that model confidential knowledge (*e.g.,* trips to mental health clinics from a string representing a user's location history). In this paper, we consider the problem
of sanitizing a string by concealing the occurrences of sensitive patterns,
while maintaining data utility. First, we propose a time-optimal algorithm, TFS-ALGO, to construct the shortest string preserving the order
of appearance and the frequency of all non-sensitive patterns. Such a
string allows accurately performing tasks based on the sequential nature
and pattern frequencies of the string. Second, we propose a time-optimal
algorithm, PFS-ALGO, which preserves a partial order of appearance
of non-sensitive patterns but produces a much shorter string that can
be analyzed more efficiently. The strings produced by either of these
algorithms may reveal the location of sensitive patterns. In response,
we propose a heuristic, MCSR-ALGO, which replaces letters in these
strings with carefully selected letters, so that sensitive patterns are not
reinstated and occurrences of spurious patterns are prevented. We implemented our sanitization approach that applies TFS-ALGO, PFS-ALGO
and then MCSR-ALGO and experimentally show that it is effective and
efficient.

1 Introduction

A large number of applications, in domains ranging from transportation to web
analytics and bioinformatics feature data modeled as *strings*, *i.e.,* sequences of
letters over some finite alphabet. For instance, a string may represent the history

© Springer Nature Switzerland AG 2020
U. Brefeld et al. (Eds.): ECML PKDD 2019, LNAI 11906, pp. 627–644, 2020.
https://doi.org/10.1007/978-3-030-46150-8_37

of visited locations of one or more individuals, with each letter corresponding to a location. Similarly, it may represent the history of search query terms of one or more web users, with letters corresponding to query terms, or a medically important part of the DNA sequence of a patient, with letters corresponding to DNA bases. Analyzing such strings is key in applications including location-based service provision, product recommendation, and DNA sequence analysis. Therefore, such strings are often disseminated beyond the party that has collected them. For example, location-based service providers often outsource their data to data analytics companies who perform tasks such as similarity evaluation between strings [14], and retailers outsource their data to marketing agencies who perform tasks such as mining frequent patterns from the strings [15].

However, disseminating a string intact may result in the exposure of confidential knowledge, such as trips to mental health clinics in transportation data [20], query terms revealing political beliefs or sexual orientation of individuals in web data [17], or diseases associated with certain parts of DNA data [16]. Thus, it may be necessary to sanitize a string prior to its dissemination, so that confidential knowledge is not exposed. At the same time, it is important to preserve the utility of the sanitized string, so that data protection does not outweigh the benefits of disseminating the string to the party that disseminates or analyzes the string, or to the society at large. For example, a retailer should still be able to obtain actionable knowledge in the form of frequent patterns from the marketing agency who analyzed their outsourced data; and researchers should still be able to perform analyses such as identifying significant patterns in DNA sequences.

Our Model and Setting. Motivated by the discussion above, we introduce the following model which we call *Combinatorial String Dissemination* (CSD). In CSD, a party has a string W that it seeks to disseminate, while satisfying a set of *constraints* and a set of desirable *properties*. For instance, the constraints aim to capture privacy requirements and the properties aim to capture data utility considerations (*e.g.,* posed by some other party based on applications). To satisfy both, W must be transformed to a string X by applying a sequence of edit operations. The computational task is to determine this sequence of edit operations so that X satisfies the desirable properties subject to the constraints.

Under the CSD model, we consider a specific setting in which the sanitized string X must satisfy the following constraint **C1**: for an integer $k > 0$, no given length-k substring (also called pattern) modeling confidential knowledge should occur in X. We call each such length-k substring a *sensitive pattern*. We aim at finding the shortest possible string X satisfying the following desired properties: (**P1**) the order of appearance of all other length-k substrings (*non-sensitive patterns*) is the same in W and in X; and (**P2**) the frequency of these length-k substrings is the same in W and in X. The problem of constructing X in this setting is referred to as TFS (Total order, Frequency, Sanitization). Clearly, substrings of arbitrary lengths can be hidden from X by setting k equal to the length of the shortest substring we wish to hide, and then setting, for each of these substrings, any length-k substring as sensitive.

Our setting is motivated by real-world applications involving string dissemination. In these applications, a *data custodian* disseminates the sanitized version
X of a string W to a *data recipient*, for the purpose of analysis (*e.g.*, mining).
W contains confidential information that the data custodian needs to hide, so
that it does not occur in X. Such information is specified by the data custodian based on domain expertise, as in [1,4,11,15]. At the same time, the data
recipient specifies **P1** and **P2** that X must satisfy in order to be useful. These
properties map directly to common data utility considerations in string analysis.
By satisfying **P1**, X allows tasks based on the sequential nature of the string,
such as blockwise q-gram distance computation [12], to be performed accurately.
By satisfying **P2**, X allows computing the frequency of length-k substrings [19]
and hence mining frequent length-k substrings with no utility loss. We require
that X has minimal length so that it does not contain redundant information.
For instance, the string which is constructed by concatenating all non-sensitive
length-k substrings in W and separating them with a special letter that does not
occur in W, satisfies **P1** and **P2** but is not the shortest possible. Such a string
X will have a negative impact on the efficiency of any subsequent analysis tasks
to be performed on it.

Note, existing works for sequential data sanitization (*e.g.*, [4,11,13,15,22])
or anonymization (*e.g.*, [2,5,7]) cannot be applied to our setting (see Sect. 7).

Our Contributions. We define the TFS problem for string sanitization and a
variant of it, referred to as PFS (Partial order, Frequency, Sanitization), which
aims at producing an even shorter string Y by relaxing **P1** of TFS. Our algorithms for TFS and PFS construct strings X and Y using a separator letter #,
which is not contained in the alphabet of W. This prevents occurrences of sensitive patterns in X or Y. The algorithms repeat proper substrings of sensitive
patterns so that the frequency of non-sensitive patterns overlapping with sensitive ones does not change. For X, we give a deterministic construction which
may be easily reversible (*i.e.*, it may enable a data recipient to construct W
from X), because the occurrences of # reveal the exact location of sensitive patterns. For Y, we give a construction which breaks several ties arbitrarily, thus
being less easily reversible. We further address the reversibility issue by defining
the MCSR (Minimum-Cost Separators Replacement) problem and designing an
algorithm for dealing with it. In MCSR, we seek to replace all separators, so that
the location of sensitive patterns is not revealed, while preserving data utility.
We make the following specific contributions:

1. We design an algorithm for solving the TFS problem in $\mathcal{O}(kn)$ time, where
   n is the length of W. In fact we prove that $\mathcal{O}(kn)$ time is worst-case optimal
   by showing that the length of X is in $\Theta(kn)$ in the worst case. The output
   of the algorithm is a string X consisting of a sequence of substrings over the
   alphabet of W separated by # (see Example 1 below). An important feature
   of our algorithm, which is useful in the efficient construction of Y discussed
   next, is that it can be implemented to produce an $\mathcal{O}(n)$-sized representation
   of X with respect to W in $\mathcal{O}(n)$ time. See Sect. 3.

Example 1. Let $W = $ aabaaaababbbaab, $k = 4$, and the set of sensitive patterns be {aaaa, baaa, bbaa}. The string $X = $ aabaa#aaababbba#baab consists of three substrings over the alphabet {a, b} separated by #. Note that no sensitive pattern occurs in X, while all non-sensitive substrings of length 4 have the same frequency in W and in X (*e.g.*, aaba appears twice) and appear in the same order in W and in X (*e.g.*, babb precedes abbb). Also, note that any shorter string than X would either create sensitive patterns or change the frequencies (*e.g.*, removing the last letter of X creates a string in which baab no longer appears).   □

2. We define the PFS problem relaxing **P1** of TFS to produce shorter strings that are more efficient to analyze. Instead of a *total order* (**P1**), we require a *partial order* ($\Pi1$) that preserves the order of appearance only for sequences of successive non-sensitive length-k substrings that overlap by $k - 1$ letters. This makes sense because the order of two successive non-sensitive length-k substrings with no length-$(k - 1)$ overlap has anyway been "interrupted" (by a sensitive pattern). We exploit this observation to shorten the string further. Specifically, we design an algorithm that solves PFS in the optimal $\mathcal{O}(n+|Y|)$ time, where $|Y|$ is the length of Y, using the $\mathcal{O}(n)$-sized representation of X. See Sect. 4.

Example 2 (Cont'd from Example 1). Recall that $W = $ aabaaaababbbaab. A string Y is aaababbba#aabaab. The order of babb and abbb is preserved in Y since they are successive, non-sensitive, and with an overlap of $k - 1 = 3$ letters. The order of abaa and aaab, which are successive and non-sensitive, is not preserved since they do not have an overlap of $k - 1 = 3$ letters.   □

3. We define the MCSR problem, which seeks to produce a string Z, by deleting or replacing all separators in Y with letters from the alphabet of W so that: no sensitive patterns are reinstated in Z; occurrences of spurious patterns that may not be mined from W but can be mined from Z, for a given support threshold, are prevented; the distortion incurred by the replacements in Z is bounded. The first requirement is to preserve privacy and the next two to preserve data utility. We show that MCSR is NP-hard and propose a heuristic to attack it. See Sect. 5.

4. We implemented our combinatorial approach for sanitizing a string W (*i.e.*, all aforementioned algorithms implementing the pipeline $W \to X \to Y \to Z$) and show its effectiveness and efficiency on real and synthetic data. See Sect. 6.

2 Preliminaries, Problem Statements, and Main Results

Preliminaries. Let $T = T[0]T[1] \ldots T[n-1]$ be a *string* of length $|T| = n$ over a finite ordered alphabet Σ of size $|\Sigma| = \sigma$. By Σ^* we denote the set of all strings over Σ. By Σ^k we denote the set of all length-k strings over Σ. For two positions i and j on T, we denote by $T[i \mathinner{.\,.} j] = T[i] \ldots T[j]$ the *substring* of T that starts at position i and ends at position j of T. By ε we denote the *empty string* of length 0. A *prefix* of T is a substring of the form $T[0 \mathinner{\ldotp\ldotp} j]$, and a *suffix* of T is a substring of the form $T[i \mathinner{\ldotp\ldotp} n - 1]$. A *proper* prefix (suffix) of a string is not equal to the string itself. By $\mathrm{Freq}_V(U)$ we denote the number of occurrences of string U in string V. Given two strings U and V we say that U has a *suffix-prefix overlap* of length $\ell > 0$ with V if and only if the length-ℓ suffix of U is equal to the length-ℓ prefix of V, i.e., $U[|U| - \ell \mathinner{\ldotp\ldotp} |U| - 1] = V[0 \mathinner{\ldotp\ldotp} \ell - 1]$.

We fix a string W of length n over an alphabet $\Sigma = \{1, \ldots, n^{\mathcal{O}(1)}\}$ and an integer $0 < k < n$. We refer to a length-k string or a *pattern* interchangeably. An occurrence of a pattern is uniquely represented by its starting position. Let $\mathcal{S}$ be a set of positions over $\{0, \ldots, n - k\}$ with the following closure property: for every $i \in \mathcal{S}$, if there exists j such that $W[j \mathinner{\ldotp\ldotp} j + k - 1] = W[i \mathinner{\ldotp\ldotp} i + k - 1]$, then $j \in \mathcal{S}$. That is, if an occurrence of a pattern is in $\mathcal{S}$ all its occurrences are in $\mathcal{S}$. A substring $W[i \mathinner{\ldotp\ldotp} i + k - 1]$ of W is called *sensitive* if and only if $i \in \mathcal{S}$. $\mathcal{S}$ is thus the set of occurrences of sensitive patterns. The difference set $\mathcal{I} = \{0, \ldots, n - k\} \setminus \mathcal{S}$ is the set of occurrences of *non-sensitive* patterns.

For any string U, we denote by $\mathcal{I}_U$ the set of occurrences of non-sensitive length-k strings over Σ. (We have that $\mathcal{I}_W = \mathcal{I}$.) We call an occurrence i the *t-predecessor* of another occurrence j in $\mathcal{I}_U$ if and only if i is the largest element in $\mathcal{I}_U$ that is less than j. This relation induces a *strict total order* on the occurrences in $\mathcal{I}_U$. We call i the *p-predecessor* of j in $\mathcal{I}_U$ if and only if i is the t-predecessor of j in $\mathcal{I}_U$ *and* $U[i \mathinner{\ldotp\ldotp} i + k - 1]$ has a suffix-prefix overlap of length $k - 1$ with $U[j \mathinner{\ldotp\ldotp} j + k - 1]$. This relation induces a *strict partial order* on the occurrences in $\mathcal{I}_U$. We call a subset $\mathcal{J}$ of $\mathcal{I}_U$ a *t-chain* (resp., *p-chain*) if for all elements in $\mathcal{J}$ except the minimum one, their t-predecessor (resp., p-predecessor) is also in $\mathcal{J}$. For two strings U and V, chains $\mathcal{J}_U$ and $\mathcal{J}_V$ are *equivalent*, denoted by $\mathcal{J}_U \equiv \mathcal{J}_V$, if and only if $|\mathcal{J}_U| = |\mathcal{J}_V|$ and $U[u \mathinner{\ldotp\ldotp} u + k - 1] = V[v \mathinner{\ldotp\ldotp} v + k - 1]$, where u is the jth smallest element of $\mathcal{J}_U$ and v is the jth smallest of $\mathcal{J}_V$, for all $j \le |\mathcal{J}_U|$.

Problem Statements and Main Results

Problem 1 (TFS). *Given W, k, $\mathcal{S}$, and $\mathcal{I}$ construct the* shortest *string X:*

C1 *X does not contain any sensitive pattern.*
P1 *$\mathcal{I}_W \equiv \mathcal{I}_X$, i.e., the t-chains $\mathcal{I}_W$ and $\mathcal{I}_X$ are equivalent.*
P2 *$\mathrm{Freq}_X(U) = \mathrm{Freq}_W(U)$, for all $U \in \Sigma^k \setminus \{W[i \mathinner{\ldotp\ldotp} i + k - 1] : i \in \mathcal{S}\}$.*

TFS requires constructing the shortest string X in which all sensitive patterns from W are concealed (**C1**), while preserving the order (**P1**) and the frequency (**P2**) of all non-sensitive patterns. Our first result is the following.

Theorem 1. *Let W be a string of length n over $\Sigma = \{1, \ldots, n^{\mathcal{O}(1)}\}$. Given $k < n$ and $\mathcal{S}$, TFS-ALGO solves Problem 1 in $\mathcal{O}(kn)$ time, which is worst-case optimal. An $\mathcal{O}(n)$-sized representation of X can be built in $\mathcal{O}(n)$ time.*

P1 implies **P2**, but **P1** is a strong assumption that may result in long output strings that are inefficient to analyze. We thus relax **P1** to require that the order of appearance remains the same only for sequences of successive non-sensitive length-k substrings that also overlap by $k - 1$ letters (p-chains).

Problem 2 (PFS). *Given W, k, $\mathcal{S}$, and $\mathcal{I}$ construct a* shortest *string Y:*

C1 Y *does not contain any sensitive pattern.*
Π1 *There exists an injective function f from the p-chains of $\mathcal{I}_W$ to the p-chains of $\mathcal{I}_Y$ such that $f(\mathcal{J}_W) \equiv \mathcal{J}_W$ for any p-chain $\mathcal{J}_W$ of $\mathcal{I}_W$.*
P2 $Freq_Y(U) = Freq_W(U)$, *for all $U \in \Sigma^k \setminus \{W[i\mathinner{.\,.}i+k-1] : i \in \mathcal{S}\}$.*

Our second result, which builds on Theorem 1, is the following.

Theorem 2. *Let W be a string of length n over $\Sigma = \{1, \ldots, n^{\mathcal{O}(1)}\}$. Given $k < n$ and $\mathcal{S}$, PFS-ALGO solves Problem 2 in the optimal $\mathcal{O}(n + |Y|)$ time.*

To arrive at Theorems 1 and 2, we use a special letter (separator) $\# \notin \Sigma$ when required. However, the occurrences of $\#$ may reveal the locations of sensitive patterns. We thus seek to delete or replace the occurrences of $\#$ in Y with letters from Σ. The new string Z should not reinstate any sensitive pattern. Given an integer threshold $\tau > 0$, we call pattern $U \in \Sigma^k$ a τ-*ghost* in Z if and only if $Freq_W(U) < \tau$ but $Freq_Z(U) \geq \tau$. Moreover, we seek to prevent τ-*ghost occurrences* in Z by also bounding the total *weight* of the *letter choices* we make to replace the occurrences of $\#$. This is the MCSR problem. We show that already a restricted version of the MCSR problem, namely, the version when $k = 1$, is NP-hard via the *Multiple Choice Knapsack* (MCK) problem [18].

Theorem 3. *The* MCSR *problem is NP-hard.*

Based on this connection, we propose a non-trivial heuristic algorithm to attack the MCSR problem for the general case of an arbitrary k.

3   TFS-ALGO

We convert string W into a string X over alphabet $\Sigma \cup \{\#\}$, $\# \notin \Sigma$, by reading the letters of W, from left to right, and appending them to X while enforcing the following two rules:

R1: When the last letter of a sensitive substring U is read from W, we append $\#$ to X (essentially replacing this last letter of U with $\#$). Then, we append the succeeding non-sensitive substring (in the t-predecessor order) after $\#$.
R2: When the $k - 1$ letters before $\#$ are the same as the $k - 1$ letters after $\#$, we remove $\#$ and the $k - 1$ succeeding letters (inspect Fig. 1).

R1 prevents U from occurring in X, and **R2** reduces the length of X (*i.e.*, allows to protect sensitive patterns with fewer extra letters). Both rules leave unchanged the order and frequencies of non-sensitive patterns. It is crucial to observe that applying the idea behind **R2** on more than $k - 1$ letters would decrease the frequency of some pattern, while applying it on fewer than $k - 1$ letters would create new patterns. Thus, we need to consider just **R2** *as-is*.

Let C be an array of size n that stores the occurrences of sensitive and non-sensitive patterns: $C[i] = 1$ if $i \in \mathcal{S}$ and $C[i] = 0$ if $i \in \mathcal{I}$. For technical reasons we set the last $k - 1$ values in C equal to $C[n - k]$; *i.e.*, $C[n - k + 1] := \ldots :=$

$$W = \overline{\text{aab}}\underline{\overline{\text{aaaa}}}\overline{\text{bab}}\underline{\overline{\text{bbaab}}}$$

$$\tilde{X} = \overline{\text{aabaaa}}\#\underline{\overline{\text{aaaba}}}\#\overline{\text{babb}}\#\underline{\overline{\text{bbbaab}}}$$

$$X = \overline{\text{aab}}\underline{\overline{\text{aaaba}}}\#\overline{\text{babb}}\#\underline{\overline{\text{bbbaab}}}$$

Fig. 1. Sensitive patterns are overlined in red; non-sensitive are under- or over-lined in blue; $\tilde{X}$ is obtained by applying **R1**; and X by applying **R1** and **R2**. In green we highlight an overlap of $k - 1 = 3$ letters. Note that substring $\mathtt{aaaababbb}$, whose length is greater than k, is also not occurring in X. (Color figure online)

$C[n - 1] := C[n - k]$. Note that C is constructible from $\mathcal{S}$ in $\mathcal{O}(n)$ time. Given C and $k < n$, TFS-ALGO efficiently constructs X by implementing **R1** and **R2** concurrently as opposed to implementing **R1** and then **R2** (see the proof of Lemma 1 for details of the workings of TFS-ALGO and Fig. 1 for an example). We next show that string X enjoys several properties.

Lemma 1. *Let W be a string of length n over Σ. Given $k < n$ and array C, TFS-ALGO constructs the shortest string X such that the following hold:*

1. *There exists no $W[i \mathinner{.\,.} i + k - 1]$ with $C[i] = 1$ occurring in X (**C1**).*
2. *$\mathcal{I}_W \equiv \mathcal{I}_X$, i.e., the order of substrings $W[i \mathinner{.\,.} i + k - 1]$, for all i such that $C[i] = 0$, is the same in W and in X; conversely, the order of all substrings $U \in \Sigma^k$ of X is the same in X and in W (**P1**).*
3. *$Freq_X(U) = Freq_W(U)$, for all $U \in \Sigma^k \setminus \{W[i \mathinner{.\,.} i + k - 1] : C[i] = 1\}$ (**P2**).*
4. *The occurrences of letter $\#$ in X are at most $\lfloor \frac{n-k+1}{2} \rfloor$ and they are at least k positions apart (**P3**).*
5. *$0 \le |X| \le \lceil \frac{n-k+1}{2} \rceil \cdot k + \lfloor \frac{n-k+1}{2} \rfloor$ and these bounds are tight (**P4**).*

Proof. Proofs of **C1** and **P1**–**P4** can be found in [3]. We prove here that X has minimal length. Let X_j be the prefix of string X obtained by processing $W[0 \mathinner{.\,.} j]$. Let $j_{\min} = \min\{i \mid C[i] = 0\} + k - 1$. We will proceed by induction on j, claiming that X_j is the shortest string such that **C1** and **P1**–**P4** hold for $W[0 \mathinner{.\,.} j]$, $\forall j_{\min} \le j \le |W| - 1$. We call such a string *optimal*.

Base case: $j = j_{\min}$. By Lines 3–4 of TFS-ALGO, X_j is equal to the first non-sensitive length-k substring of W, and it is clearly the shortest string such that **C1** and **P1**–**P4** hold for $W[0 \mathinner{.\,.} j]$.

Inductive hypothesis and step: X_{j-1} is optimal for $j > j_{\min}$. If $C[j - k] = C[j - k + 1] = 0$, $X_j = X_{j-1}W[j]$ and this is clearly optimal. If $C[j - k + 1] = 1$, $X_j = X_{j-1}$ thus still optimal. Finally, if $C[j - k] = 1$ and $C[j - k + 1] = 0$ we have two subcases: if $W[f \mathinner{.\,.} f + k - 2] = W[j - k + 1 \mathinner{.\,.} j - 1]$ then $X_j = X_{j-1}W[j]$, and once again X_j is evidently optimal. Otherwise, $X_j = X_{j-1}\#W[j - k + 1 \mathinner{.\,.} j]$. Suppose by contradiction that there exists a shorter X'_j such that **C1** and **P1**–**P4** still hold: either drop $\#$ or append less than k letters after $\#$. If we appended

---

TFS-ALGO($W \in \Sigma^n, C, k, \# \notin \Sigma$)

---

1 $X \leftarrow \varepsilon; j \leftarrow |W|; \ell \leftarrow 0;$

2 $j \leftarrow \min\{i|C[i] = 0\}; /* \ j$ is the leftmost pos of a non-sens. pattern */

3 **if** $j + k - 1 < |W|$ **then**   /* Append the first non-sens. pattern to X */

4    $X[0..k-1] \leftarrow W[j..j+k-1]; j \leftarrow j+k; \ell \leftarrow \ell+k;$

5 **while** $j < |W|$ **do**   /* Examine two consecutive patterns */

6    $p \leftarrow j - k; c \leftarrow p + 1;$

7   **if** $C[p] = C[c] = 0$ **then**   /* If both are non-sens., append the last letter of the rightmost one to X */

8      $X[\ell] \leftarrow W[j]; \ell \leftarrow \ell+1; j \leftarrow j+1;$

9   **if** $C[p] = 0 \wedge C[c] = 1$ **then**   /* If the rightmost is sens., mark it and advance j */

10     $f \leftarrow c; j \leftarrow j+1;$

11   **if** $C[p] = C[c] = 1$ **then** $j \leftarrow j+1;$ /* If both are sens., advance j */

12   **if** $C[p] = 1 \wedge C[c] = 0$ **then**   /* If the leftmost is sens. and the rightmost is not */

13   **if** $W[c..c+k-2] = W[f..f+k-2]$ **then**   /* If the last marked sens. pattern and the current non-sens. overlap by $k-1$, append the last letter of the latter to X */

14       $X[\ell] \leftarrow W[j]; \ell \leftarrow \ell+1; j \leftarrow j+1;$

15   **else**   /* Else append $\#$ and the current non-sensitive pattern to X */

16       $X[\ell] \leftarrow \#; \ell \leftarrow \ell+1;$

17       $X[\ell..\ell+k-1] \leftarrow W[j-k+1..j]; \ell \leftarrow \ell+k; j \leftarrow j+1;$

18 **report** X

---

less than k letters after $\#$, since TFS-ALGO will not read $W[j]$ ever again, **P2**–**P3** would be violated, as an occurrence of $W[j - k + 1..j]$ would be missed. Without $\#$, the last k letters of $X_{j-1}W[j - k + 1]$ would violate either **C1** or **P1** and **P2** (since we suppose $W[f..f + k - 2] \neq W[j - k + 1..j - 1]$). Then X_j is optimal. $\square$

Theorem 1. *Let W be a string of length n over $\Sigma = \{1, \ldots, n^{\mathcal{O}(1)}\}$. Given $k < n$ and $\mathcal{S}$, TFS-ALGO solves Problem 1 in $\mathcal{O}(kn)$ time, which is worst-case optimal. An $\mathcal{O}(n)$-sized representation of X can be built in $\mathcal{O}(n)$ time.*

Proof. For the first part inspect TFS-ALGO. Lines 2–4 can be realized in $\mathcal{O}(n)$ time. The *while* loop in Line 5 is executed no more than n times, and every operation inside the loop takes $\mathcal{O}(1)$ time except for Line 13 and Line 17 which take $\mathcal{O}(k)$ time. Correctness and optimality follow directly from Lemma 1 (**P4**).

For the second part, we assume that X is represented by W and a sequence of pointers $[i, j]$ to W interleaved (if necessary) by occurrences of $\#$. In Line 17, we can use an interval $[i, j]$ to represent the length-k substring of W added to X. In all other lines (Lines 4, 8 and 14) we can use $[i, i]$ as one letter is added to X per one letter of W. By Lemma 1 we can have at most $\lfloor \frac{n-k+1}{2} \rfloor$ occurrences of letter #. The check at Line 13 can be implemented in constant time after linear-time pre-processing of W for longest common extension queries [9]. All other operations take in total linear time in n. Thus there exists an $\mathcal{O}(n)$-sized representation of X and it is constructible in $\mathcal{O}(n)$ time.   □

4 PFS-ALGO

Lemma 1 tells us that X is the shortest string satisfying constraint **C1** and properties **P1**–**P4**. If we were to drop **P1** and employ the partial order $\varPi 1$ (see Problem 2), the length of $X = X_1 \# \ldots \# X_N$ would not always be minimal: if a *permutation* of the strings $X_1, \ldots, X_N$ contains pairs X_i, X_j with a suffix-prefix overlap of length $\ell = k - 1$, we may further apply **R2**, obtaining a shorter string while still satisfying $\varPi 1$.

We propose PFS-ALGO to find such a permutation efficiently constructing a shorter string Y from W. The crux of our algorithm is an efficient method to solve a variant of the classic NP-complete *Shortest Common Superstring* (SCS) problem [10]. Specifically our algorithm: (I) Computes string X using Theorem 1. (II) Constructs a collection $\mathcal{B}'$ of strings, each of two symbols (two identifiers) and in a one-to-one correspondence with the elements of $\mathcal{B} = \{X_1, \ldots, X_N\}$: the first (resp., second) symbol of the ith element of $\mathcal{B}'$ is a unique identifier of the string corresponding to the length-ℓ prefix (resp., suffix) of the ith element of $\mathcal{B}$. (III) Computes a shortest string containing every element in $\mathcal{B}'$ as a distinct substring. (IV) Constructs Y by mapping back each element to its distinct substring in $\mathcal{B}$. If there are multiple possible shortest strings, one is selected arbitrarily.

Example 3 (Illustration of the workings of PFS-ALGO*).* Let $\ell = k - 1 = 3$ and

$$X = \texttt{aabbc\#bccaab\#bbca\#aaabac\#aabcbbc}.$$

The collection $\mathcal{B}$ is $\texttt{aabbc, bccaab, bbca, aaabac, aabcbbc}$, and the collection $\mathcal{B}'$ is $24, 62, 45, 13, 24$ (id of prefix · id of suffix). A shortest string containing all elements of $\mathcal{B}'$ as distinct substrings is: $13 \cdot 24 \cdot 6245$ (obtained by permuting the original string as $13, 24, 62, 24, 45$ then applying **R2** twice). This shortest string is mapped back to the solution $Y = \texttt{aaabac\#aabbc\#bccaabcbbca}$. For example, 13 is mapped back to $\texttt{aaabac}$. Note, Y contains two occurrences of # and has length 24, while X contains 4 occurrences of # and has length 32.   □

We now present the details of PFS-ALGO. We first introduce the *Fixed-Overlap Shortest String with Multiplicities* (FO-SSM) problem: Given a *collection* $\mathcal{B}$ of strings $B_1, \ldots, B_{|\mathcal{B}|}$ and an integer ℓ, with $|B_i| > \ell$, for all $1 \leq i \leq |\mathcal{B}|$, FO-SSM seeks to find a shortest string containing each element of $\mathcal{B}$ as a distinct substring using the following operations on any pair of strings B_i, B_j:

1. $\texttt{concat}(B_i, B_j) = B_i \cdot B_j$;
2. $\ell\texttt{-merge}(B_i, B_j) = B_i[0 .. |B_i| - 1 - \ell] B_j[0 .. |B_j| - 1] = B_i[0 .. |B_i| - 1 - \ell] \cdot B_j$.

Any solution to FO-SSM with $\ell := k - 1$ and $\mathcal{B} := X_1, \ldots, X_N$ implies a solution to the PFS problem, because $|X_i| > k - 1$ for all i's (see Lemma 1, **P3**)

The FO-SSM problem is a variant of the SCS problem. In the SCS problem, we are given a *set* of strings and we are asked to compute the shortest common superstring of the elements of this set. The SCS problem is known to be NP-Complete, even for binary strings [10]. However, if all strings are of length two, the SCS problem admits a linear-time solution [10]. We exploit this crucial detail positively to show a linear-time solution to the FO-SSM problem in Lemma 3. In order to arrive to this result, we first adapt the SCS linear-time solution of [10] to our needs (see Lemma 2) and plug this solution to Lemma 3.

Lemma 2. *Let $\mathcal{Q}$ be a collection of q strings, each of length two, over an alphabet $\Sigma = \{1, \ldots, (2q)^{\mathcal{O}(1)}\}$. We can compute a shortest string containing every element of $\mathcal{Q}$ as a distinct substring in $\mathcal{O}(q)$ time.*

Proof. We sort the elements of $\mathcal{Q}$ lexicographically in $\mathcal{O}(q)$ time using radixsort. We also replace every letter in these strings with their *lexicographic rank* from $\{1, \ldots, 2q\}$ in $\mathcal{O}(q)$ time using radixsort. In $\mathcal{O}(q)$ time we construct the de Bruijn multigraph G of these strings [6]. Within the same time complexity, we find all nodes v in G with in-degree, denoted by $\mathrm{IN}(v)$, smaller than out-degree, denoted by $\mathrm{OUT}(v)$. We perform the following two steps:

Step 1: While there exists a node v in G with $\mathrm{IN}(v) < \mathrm{OUT}(v)$, we start an arbitrary path (with possibly repeated nodes) from v, traverse consecutive edges and delete them. Each time we delete an edge, we update the in- and out-degree of the affected nodes. We stop traversing edges when a node v' with $\mathrm{OUT}(v') = 0$ is reached: whenever $\mathrm{IN}(v') = \mathrm{OUT}(v') = 0$, we also delete v' from G. Then, we add the traversed path $p = v \ldots v'$ to a set $\mathcal{P}$ of paths. The path can contain the same node v more than once. If G is empty we halt. Proceeding this way, there are no two elements p_1 and p_2 in $\mathcal{P}$ such that p_1 starts with v and p_2 ends with v; thus this path decomposition is minimal. If G is not empty at the end, by construction, it consists of only cycles.

Step 2: While G is not empty, we perform the following. If there exists a cycle c that *intersects* with any path p in $\mathcal{P}$ we splice c with p, update p with the result of splicing, and delete c from G. This operation can be efficiently implemented by maintaining an array A of size $2q$ of linked lists over the paths in $\mathcal{P}$: $A[\alpha]$ stores a list of pointers to all occurrences of letter α in the elements of $\mathcal{P}$. Thus in constant time per node of c we check if any such path p exists in $\mathcal{P}$ and splice the two in this case. If no such path exists in $\mathcal{P}$, we add to $\mathcal{P}$ any of the path-linearizations of the cycle, and delete the cycle from G. After each change to $\mathcal{P}$, we update A and delete every node u with $\mathrm{IN}(u) = \mathrm{OUT}(u) = 0$ from G.

The correctness of this algorithm follows from the fact that $\mathcal{P}$ is a minimal path decomposition of G. Thus any concatenation of paths in $\mathcal{P}$ represents a shortest string containing all elements in $\mathcal{Q}$ as distinct substrings.   □

Omitted proofs of Lemmas 3 and 4 can be found in [3].

Lemma 3. *Let $\mathcal{B}$ be a collection of strings over an alphabet $\Sigma = \{1, \ldots, ||\mathcal{B}||^{\mathcal{O}(1)}\}$. Given an integer ℓ, the FO-SSM problem for $\mathcal{B}$ can be solved in $\mathcal{O}(||\mathcal{B}||)$ time.*

Thus, PFS-ALGO applies Lemma 3 on $\mathcal{B} := X_1, \ldots, X_N$ with $\ell := k - 1$ (recall that $X_1 \# \ldots \# X_N = X$). Note that each time the `concat` operation is performed, it also places the letter $\#$ in between the two strings.

Lemma 4. *Let W be a string of length n over an alphabet Σ. Given $k < n$ and array C, PFS-ALGO constructs a shortest string Y with **C1**, $\Pi 1$, and **P2-P4**.*

Theorem 2. *Let W be a string of length n over $\Sigma = \{1, \ldots, n^{\mathcal{O}(1)}\}$. Given $k < n$ and $\mathcal{S}$, PFS-ALGO solves Problem 2 in the optimal $\mathcal{O}(n + |Y|)$ time.*

Proof. We compute the $\mathcal{O}(n)$-sized representation of string X with respect to W described in the proof of Theorem 1. This can be done in $\mathcal{O}(n)$ time. If $X \in \Sigma^*$, then we construct and return $Y := X$ in time $\mathcal{O}(|Y|)$ from the representation. If $X \in (\Sigma \cup \{\#\})^*$, implying $|Y| \leq |X|$, we compute the LCP data structure of string W in $\mathcal{O}(n)$ time [9]; and implement Lemma 3 in $\mathcal{O}(n)$ time by avoiding to read string X explicitly: we rather rename $X_1, \ldots, X_N$ to a collection of two-letter strings by employing the LCP information of W directly. We then construct and report Y in time $\mathcal{O}(|Y|)$. Correctness follows directly from Lemma 4.   □

5   The MCSR Problem and MCSR-ALGO

The strings X and Y, constructed by TFS-ALGO and PFS-ALGO, respectively, may contain the separator $\#$, which reveals information about the location of the sensitive patterns in W. Specifically, a malicious data recipient can go to the position of a $\#$ in X and "undo" Rule **R1** that has been applied by TFS-ALGO, removing $\#$ and the $k - 1$ letters after $\#$ from X. The result will be an occurrence of the sensitive pattern. For example, applying this process to the first $\#$ in X shown in Fig. 1, results in recovering the sensitive pattern abab. A similar attack is possible on the string Y produced by PFS-ALGO, although it is hampered by the fact that substrings within two consecutive $\#$s in X often swap places in Y.

To address this issue, we seek to construct a new string Z, in which $\#$s are either deleted or replaced by letters from Σ. To preserve privacy, we require separator replacements not to reinstate sensitive patterns. To preserve data utility, we favor separator replacements that have a small cost in terms of occurrences of τ-ghosts (patterns with frequency less than τ in W and at least τ in Z) and incur a bounded level of distortion in Z, as defined below. This is the MCSR problem, a restricted version of which is presented in Problem 3. The restricted version is referred to as $\text{MCSR}_{k=1}$ and differs from MCSR in that it uses $k = 1$ for the pattern length instead of an arbitrary value $k > 0$. $\text{MCSR}_{k=1}$ is presented next for simplicity and because it is used in the proof of Lemma 5 (see [3] for the proof). Lemma 5 implies Theorem 3.

Problem 3 (MCSR$_{k=1}$). *Given a string Y over an alphabet $\Sigma \cup \{\#\}$ with $\delta > 0$ occurrences of letter $\#$, and parameters τ and θ, construct a new string Z by substituting the δ occurrences of $\#$ in Y with letters from Σ, such that:*

$$(\mathrm{I}) \quad \sum_{\substack{i:Y[i]=\#,\ Freq_Y(Z[i])<\tau \\ Freq_Z(Z[i])\geq\tau}} Ghost(i, Z[i]) \text{ is minimum, and (II)} \sum_{i:Y[i]=\#} Sub(i, Z[i]) \leq \theta.$$

The cost of τ-ghosts is captured by a function *Ghost*. This function assigns a cost to an occurrence of a τ-ghost, which is caused by a separator replacement at position i, and is specified based on domain knowledge. For example, with a cost equal to 1 for each gained occurrence of each τ-ghost, we penalize more heavily a τ-ghost with frequency much below τ in Y and the penalty increases with the number of gained occurrences. Moreover, we may want to penalize positions towards the end of a temporally ordered string, to avoid spurious patterns that would be deemed important in applications based on time-decaying models [8].

The replacement distortion is captured by a function *Sub* which assigns a weight to a letter that could replace a $\#$ and is specified based on domain knowledge. The maximum allowable replacement distortion is θ. Small weights favor the replacement of separators with desirable letters (*e.g.*, letters that reinstate non-sensitive frequent patterns) and letters that reinstate sensitive patterns are assigned a weight larger than θ that prohibits them from replacing a $\#$. Similarly, weights larger than θ are assigned to letters which would lead to implausible patterns [13] if they replaced $\#$s.

Lemma 5. *The MCSR$_{k=1}$ problem is NP-hard.*

Theorem 3. *The MCSR problem is NP-hard.*

MCSR-ALGO. Our MCSR-ALGO is a non-trivial heuristic that exploits the connection of the MCSR and MCK [18] problems and works by:

(I) Constructing the set of all candidate τ-ghost patterns (*i.e.*, length-k strings over Σ with frequency below τ in Y that can have frequency at least τ in Z).

(II) Creating an instance of MCK from an instance of MCSR. For this, we map the ith occurrence of $\#$ to a class C_i in MCK and each possible replacement of the occurrence with a letter j to a different item in C_i. Specifically, we consider all possible replacements with letters in Σ and also a replacement with the empty string, which models deleting (instead of replacing) the ith occurrence of $\#$. In addition, we set the costs and weights that are input to MCK as follows. The cost for replacing the ith occurrence of $\#$ with the letter j is set to the sum of the Ghost function for all candidate τ-ghost patterns when the ith occurrence of $\#$ is replaced by j. That is, we make the worst-case assumption that the replacement forces all candidate τ-ghosts to become τ-ghosts in Z. The weight for replacing the ith occurrence of $\#$ with letter j is set to $Sub(i, j)$.

(III) Solving the instance of MCK and translating the solution back to a (possibly suboptimal) solution of the MCSR problem. For this, we replace the ith occurrence of # with the letter corresponding to the element chosen by the MCK algorithm from class C_i, and similarly for each other occurrence of #. If the instance has no solution (*i.e.*, no possible replacement can hide the sensitive patterns), MCSR-ALGO reports that Z cannot be constructed and terminates.

Lemma 6 below states the running time of MCSR-ALGO (see [3] for the proof on an efficient implementation of this algorithm).

Lemma 6. MCSR-ALGO *runs in* $\mathcal{O}(|Y| + k\delta\sigma + \mathcal{T}(\delta, \sigma))$ *time, where* $\mathcal{T}(\delta, \sigma)$ *is the running time of the MCK algorithm for δ classes with $\sigma + 1$ elements each.*

6 Experimental Evaluation

We evaluate our approach, referred to as TPM, in terms of *data utility* and *efficiency*. Given a string W over Σ, TPM sanitizes W by applying TFS-ALGO, PFS-ALGO, and then MCSR-ALGO, which uses the $\mathcal{O}(\delta\sigma\theta)$-time algorithm of [18] for solving the MCK instances. The final output is a string Z over Σ.

Experimental Setup and Data. We do not compare TPM against existing methods, because they are not alternatives to our approach (see Sect. 7). Instead, we compared against a greedy baseline referred to as BA.

BA initializes its output string Z_{BA} to W and then considers each sensitive pattern R in Z_{BA}, from left to right. For each R, it replaces the letter r of R that has the largest frequency in Z_{BA} with another letter r' that is not contained in R and has the smallest frequency in Z_{BA}, breaking all ties arbitrarily. If no such r' exists, r is replaced by # to ensure that a solution is produced (even if it may reveal the location of a sensitive pattern). Each replacement removes the occurrence of R and aims to prevent τ-ghost occurrences by selecting an r' that will not substantially increase the frequency of patterns overlapping with R.

Table 1. Characteristics of datasets and values used (default values are in bold).

Dataset	Data domain	Length n	Alphabet size $|\Sigma|$	# sensitive patterns	# sensitive positions $|\mathcal{S}|$	Pattern length k
OLD	Movement	85,563	100	[30, 240] (**60**)	[600, 6103]	[3, 7] (**4**)
TRU	Transportation	5,763	100	[30, 120] (**10**)	[324, 2410]	[2, 5] (**4**)
MSN	Web	4,698,764	17	[30, 120] (**60**)	[6030, 320480]	[3, 8] (**4**)
DNA	Genomic	4,641,652	4	[25, 500] (**100**)	[163, 3488]	[5, 15] (**13**)
SYN	Synthetic	20,000,000	10	[10, 1000] (**1000**)	[10724, 20171]	[3, 6] (**6**)

We considered the following publicly available datasets used in [1,11,13,15]: Oldenburg (OLD), Trucks (TRU), MSNBC (MSN), the complete genome of

Escherichia coli (DNA), and synthetic data (uniformly random strings, the largest of which is referred to as SYN). See Table 1 for the characteristics of these datasets and the parameter values used in experiments, unless stated otherwise.

The sensitive patterns were selected randomly among the frequent length-k substrings at minimum support τ following [11, 13, 15]. We used the fairly low values $\tau = 10$, $\tau = 20$, $\tau = 200$, and $\tau = 20$ for TRU, OLD, MSN, and DNA, respectively, to have a wider selection of sensitive patterns. We also used a uniform cost of 1 for every occurrence of each τ-ghost, a weight of 1 (resp., ∞) for each letter replacement that does not (resp., does) create a sensitive pattern, and we further set $\theta = \delta$. This setup treats all candidate τ-ghost patterns and all candidate letters for replacement uniformly, to facilitate a fair comparison with BA which cannot distinguish between τ-ghost candidates or favor specific letters.

To capture the utility of sanitized data, we used the *(frequency) distortion* measure $\sum_U (\mathrm{Freq}_W(U) - \mathrm{Freq}_Z(U))^2$, where $U \in \Sigma^k$ is a non-sensitive pattern. The distortion measure quantifies changes in the frequency of non-sensitive patterns with low values suggesting that Z remains useful for tasks based on pattern frequency (*e.g.*, identifying motifs corresponding to functional or conserved DNA [19]). We also measured the number of τ-ghost and τ-lost patterns in Z following [11, 13, 15], where a pattern U is τ-*lost* in Z if and only if $\mathrm{Freq}_W(U) \geq \tau$ but $\mathrm{Freq}_Z(U) < \tau$. That is, τ-lost patterns model knowledge that can no longer be mined from Z but could be mined from W, whereas τ-ghost patterns model knowledge that can be mined from Z but not from W. A small number of τ-lost/ghost patterns suggests that frequent pattern mining can be accurately performed on Z [11, 13, 15]. Unlike BA, by design TPM *does not* incur any τ-lost pattern, as TFS-ALGO and PFS-ALGO preserve frequencies of nonsensitive patterns, and MCSR-ALGO can only increase pattern frequencies.

All experiments ran on an Intel Xeon E5-2640 at 2.66 GHz with 16 GB RAM. Our source code, written in C++, is available at https://bitbucket.org/stringsanitization. The results have been averaged over 10 runs.

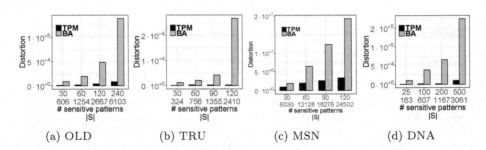

(a) OLD   (b) TRU   (c) MSN   (d) DNA

Fig. 2. Distortion vs. number of sensitive patterns and their total number $|\mathcal{S}|$ of occurrences in W (first two lines on the X axis).

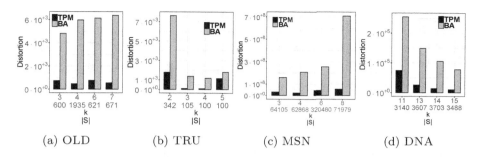

Fig. 3. Distortion vs. length of sensitive patterns k (and $|\mathcal{S}|$).

Data Utility. We first demonstrate that TPM incurs *very low distortion*, which implies high utility for tasks based on the frequency of patterns (*e.g.*, [19]). Figure 2 shows that, for varying number of sensitive patterns, TPM incurred on average 18.4 (and up to 95) times lower distortion than BA over all experiments. Also, Fig. 2 shows that TPM remains effective even in challenging settings, with many sensitive patterns (*e.g.*, the last point in Fig. 2b where about 42% of the positions in W are sensitive). Figure 3 shows that, for varying k, TPM caused on average 7.6 (and up to 14) times lower distortion than BA over all experiments.

Next, we demonstrate that TPM permits *accurate frequent pattern mining*: Fig. 4 shows that TPM led to no τ-lost or τ-ghost patterns for the TRU and MSN datasets. This implies no utility loss for mining frequent length-k substrings with threshold τ. In all other cases, the number of τ-ghosts was on average 6 (and up to 12) times smaller than the total number of τ-lost and τ-ghost patterns for BA. BA performed poorly (*e.g.*, up to 44% of frequent patterns became τ-lost for TRU and 27% for DNA). Figure 5 shows that, for varying k, TPM led to on average 5.8 (and up to 19) times fewer τ-lost/ghost patterns than BA. BA performed poorly (*e.g.*, up to 98% of frequent patterns became τ-lost for DNA).

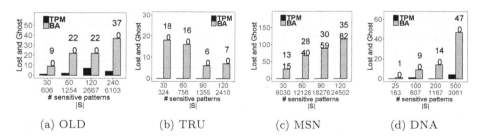

Fig. 4. Total number of τ-lost and τ-ghost patterns vs. number of sensitive patterns (and $|\mathcal{S}|$). $\frac{x}{y}$ on the top of each bar for BA denotes x τ-lost and y τ-ghost patterns.

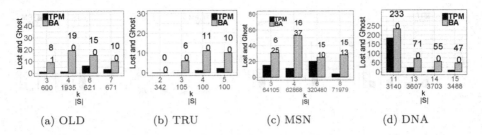

(a) OLD   (b) TRU   (c) MSN   (d) DNA

Fig. 5. Total number of τ-lost and τ-ghost patterns vs. length of sensitive patterns k (and $|\mathcal{S}|$). $\frac{x}{y}$ on the top of each bar for BA denotes x τ-lost and y τ-ghost patterns.

We also demonstrate that PFS-ALGO reduces the length of the output string X of TFS-ALGO substantially, creating a string Y that contains *less redundant information* and allows for more efficient analysis. Figure 6a shows the length of X and of Y and their difference for $k = 5$. Y was much shorter than X and its length decreased with the number of sensitive patterns, since more substrings had a suffix-prefix overlap of length $k - 1 = 4$ and were removed (see Sect. 4). Interestingly, the length of Y was close to that of W (the string before sanitization). A larger k led to less substantial length reduction as shown in Fig. 6b (but still few thousand letters were removed), since it is less likely for long substrings of sensitive patterns to have an overlap and be removed.

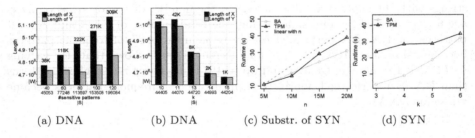

(a) DNA   (b) DNA   (c) Substr. of SYN   (d) SYN

Fig. 6. Length of X and Y (output of TFS-ALGO and PFS-ALGO, resp.) for varying: (a) number of sensitive patterns (and $|\mathcal{S}|$), (b) length of sensitive patterns k (and $|\mathcal{S}|$). On the top of each pair of bars we plot $|X| - |Y|$. Runtime on synthetic data for varying: (c) length n of string and (d) length k of sensitive patterns. Note that $|Y| = |Z|$.

Efficiency. We finally measured the runtime of TPM using prefixes of the synthetic string SYN whose length n is 20 million letters. Figure 6c (resp., Fig. 6d) shows that TPM scaled linearly with n (resp., k), as predicted by our analysis in Sect. 5 (TPM takes $\mathcal{O}(n + |Y| + k\delta\sigma + \delta\sigma\theta) = \mathcal{O}(kn + k\delta\sigma + \delta\sigma\theta)$ time, since the algorithm of [18] was used for MCK instances). In addition, TPM is efficient, with a runtime similar to that of BA and less than 40 s for SYN.

7 Related Work

Data sanitization (*a.k.a.* knowledge hiding) aims at concealing patterns modeling confidential knowledge by limiting their frequency, so that they are not easily mined from the data. Existing methods are applied to: (I) a *collection* of set-valued data (transactions) [21] or spatiotemporal data (trajectories) [1]; (II) a *collection* of sequences [11,13]; or (III) a *single* sequence [4,15,22]. Yet, none of these methods follows our CSD setting: Methods in category I are not applicable to string data, and those in categories II and III do not have guarantees on privacy-related constraints [22] or on utility-related properties [4,11,13,15]. Specifically, unlike our approach, [22] cannot guarantee that all sensitive patterns are concealed (constraint **C1**), while [4,11,13,15] do not guarantee the satisfaction of utility properties (*e.g.*, $\Pi 1$ and **P2**).

Anonymization aims to prevent the disclosure of individuals' identity and/or information that individuals are not willing to be associated with [2]. Anonymization works (*e.g.*, [2,5,7]) are thus not alternatives to our work (see [3] for details).

8 Conclusion

In this paper, we introduced the Combinatorial String Dissemination model. The focus of this model is on *guaranteeing* privacy-utility trade-offs (*e.g.*, **C1** *vs.* $\Pi 1$ and **P2**). We defined a problem (TFS) which seeks to produce the shortest string that preserves the order of appearance and the frequency of all non-sensitive patterns; and a variant (PFS) that preserves a partial order and the frequency of the non-sensitive patterns but produces a shorter string. We developed two time-optimal algorithms, TFS-ALGO and PFS-ALGO, for the problem and its variant, respectively. We also developed MCSR-ALGO, a heuristic that prevents the disclosure of the location of sensitive patterns from the outputs of TFS-ALGO and PFS-ALGO. Our experiments show that sanitizing a string by TFS-ALGO, PFS-ALGO and then MCSR-ALGO is effective and efficient.

Acknowledgments. HC is supported by a CSC scholarship. GR and NP are partially supported by MIUR-SIR project CMACBioSeq grant n. RBSI146R5L. We acknowledge the use of the Rosalind HPC cluster hosted by King's College London.

References

1. Abul, O., Bonchi, F., Giannotti, F.: Hiding sequential and spatiotemporal patterns. TKDE **22**(12), 1709–1723 (2010)
2. Aggarwal, C.C., Yu, P.S.: A framework for condensation-based anonymization of string data. DMKD **16**(3), 251–275 (2008)
3. Bernardini, G., et al.: String sanitization: a combinatorial approach. CoRR abs/1906.11030 (2019)
4. Bonomi, L., Fan, L., Jin, H.: An information-theoretic approach to individual sequential data sanitization. In: WSDM, pp. 337–346 (2016)

5. Bonomi, L., Xiong, L.: A two-phase algorithm for mining sequential patterns with differential privacy. In: CIKM, pp. 269–278 (2013)
6. Cazaux, B., Lecroq, T., Rivals, E.: Linking indexing data structures to de Bruijn graphs: construction and update. J. Comput. Syst. Sci. **104**, 165–183 (2016)
7. Chen, R., Acs, G., Castelluccia, C.: Differentially private sequential data publication via variable-length n-grams. In: CCS, pp. 638–649 (2012)
8. Cormode, G., Korn, F., Tirthapura, S.: Exponentially decayed aggregates on data streams. In: ICDE, pp. 1379–1381 (2008)
9. Crochemore, M., Hancart, C., Lecroq, T.: Algorithms on Strings. Cambridge University Press, Cambridge (2007)
10. Gallant, J., Maier, D., Storer, J.A.: On finding minimal length superstrings. J. Comput. Syst. Sci. **20**(1), 50–58 (1980)
11. Gkoulalas-Divanis, A., Loukides, G.: Revisiting sequential pattern hiding to enhance utility. In: KDD, pp. 1316–1324 (2011)
12. Grossi, R., et al.: Circular sequence comparison: algorithms and applications. AMB **11**, 12 (2016)
13. Gwadera, R., Gkoulalas-Divanis, A., Loukides, G.: Permutation-based sequential pattern hiding. In: ICDM, pp. 241–250 (2013)
14. Liu, A., Zhengy, K., Liz, L., Liu, G., Zhao, L., Zhou, X.: Efficient secure similarity computation on encrypted trajectory data. In: ICDE, pp. 66–77 (2015)
15. Loukides, G., Gwadera, R.: Optimal event sequence sanitization. In: SDM, pp. 775–783 (2015)
16. Malin, B., Sweeney, L.: Determining the identifiability of DNA database entries. In: AMIA, pp. 537–541 (2000)
17. Narayanan, A., Shmatikov, V.: Robust de-anonymization of large sparse datasets. In: S&P, pp. 111–125 (2008)
18. Pissinger, D.: A minimal algorithm for the multiple-choice Knapsack problem. Eur. J. Oper. Res. **83**(2), 394–410 (1995)
19. Pissis, S.P.: MoTeX-II: structured MoTif eXtraction from large-scale datasets. BMC Bioinform. **15**, 235 (2014)
20. Theodorakopoulos, G., Shokri, R., Troncoso, C., Hubaux, J., Boudec, J.L.: Prolonging the hide-and-seek game: optimal trajectory privacy for location-based services. In: WPES, pp. 73–82 (2014)
21. Verykios, V.S., Elmagarmid, A.K., Bertino, E., Saygin, Y., Dasseni, E.: Association rule hiding. TKDE **16**(4), 434–447 (2004)
22. Wang, D., He, Y., Rundensteiner, E., Naughton, J.F.: Utility-maximizing event stream suppression. In: SIGMOD, pp. 589–600 (2013)

Online Linear Models for Edge Computing

Hadar Sivan[1]([⊠]), Moshe Gabel[2], and Assaf Schuster[1]

[1] Technion - Israel Institute of Technology, 3200 Haifa, Israel
{hadarsivan,assaf}@cs.technion.ac.il
[2] University of Toronto, Toronto, Canada
mgabel@cs.toronto.edu

Abstract. Maintaining an accurate trained model on an infinite data stream is challenging due to concept drifts that render a learned model inaccurate. Updating the model periodically can be expensive, and so traditional approaches for computationally limited devices involve a variation of online or incremental learning, which tend to be less robust.

The advent of heterogeneous architectures and Internet-connected devices gives rise to a new opportunity. A weak processor can call upon a stronger processor or a cloud server to perform a complete batch training pass once a concept drift is detected – trading power or network bandwidth for increased accuracy.

We capitalize on this opportunity in two steps. We first develop a computationally efficient bound for changes in any linear model with convex, differentiable loss. We then propose a sliding window-based algorithm that uses a small number of batch model computations to maintain an accurate model of the data stream. It uses the bound to continuously evaluate the difference between the parameters of the existing model and a hypothetical optimal model, triggering computation only as needed.

Empirical evaluation on real and synthetic datasets shows that our proposed algorithm adapts well to concept drifts and provides a better tradeoff between the number of model computations and model accuracy than classic concept drift detectors. When predicting changes in electricity prices, for example, we achieve 6% better accuracy than the popular EDDM, using only 20 model computations.

1 Introduction

Consider a computationally limited device like a wireless sensor or a router that receives an infinite stream of (occasionally) labeled samples, and applies machine learning to perform tasks such as gesture recognition or network attack detection, or employs it as part of a mobile healthcare application [12,20]. Classic offline learning algorithms assume a fixed distribution of the data to make some guarantees about the accuracy of learned model. However, this is not always the case in data streams, where the underlying distribution may change over time.

© Springer Nature Switzerland AG 2020
U. Brefeld et al. (Eds.): ECML PKDD 2019, LNAI 11906, pp. 645–661, 2020.
https://doi.org/10.1007/978-3-030-46150-8_38

This is known as a *concept drift*. To maintain an accurate model, the device has to update the model whenever the concept changes, a computationally expensive task.

Concept drift has been widely studied. Algorithms designed for learning from data streams with concept drifts rely on two main strategies. *Incremental learning algorithms* [7,24,27,31,32] adapt to the new concept implicitly by updating the model periodically. They incrementally update the model using only the previous model and a single new sample from the stream rather than an entire batch of samples. However, for stochastic gradient descent, which is a popular learning method for incremental algorithms, the convergence rate is approximately linearly dependent on the condition number of the problem [6, p. 467]. Concept drifts such as changes in variable scaling or covariance structure can increase this condition number, causing slower adaptation to the new concept (since incremental algorithms process one sample at a time). Conversely, algorithms based on either *sliding windows* or *adaptive windows* use a batch of recent samples to compute the current model [3,30]. Such algorithms are more immune to outliers since multiple samples are used simultaneously. They also explicitly forget irrelevant samples, as the computed model is based only on samples that appear in a recent window. Despite these advantages, sliding window algorithms are less computationally efficient than incremental algorithms. As such, they are difficult to use in settings with low-powered devices such as those used in edge computing and IoT (Internet of Things) [20,29].

Connected devices in edge computing and IoT settings present a new opportunity to tradeoff communication or battery power for better accuracy. These often have limited computational power, but are connected to stronger machines. Smart cities, for example, are composed of many weak sensors which use a cloud server to perform learning tasks [2]. Thus, weak edge devices can occasionally call on stronger machines for heavy computational tasks such as batch learning.

However, many weak devices could flood the network and overwhelm the cloud. This gives rise to a tradeoff between accuracy and the network overhead (or required computations). A similar tradeoff exists in *heterogeneous architectures*, which incorporate power-efficient weak processors and power-hungry strong processors on the same device. These are common in edge computing settings where client or edge devices are often battery-powered [19]. The weak processor can wake the strong processor to perform computationally intensive tasks such as recomputing the model, but with higher power consumption. Algorithms must therefore be carefully designed to minimize model recomputations by efficiently detecting when they are necessary.

Our Contributions. We present DRUiD (for **D**rift detecto**R** from bo**U**nded **D**istance): a novel sliding window algorithm designed for learning from data streams in edge computing and IoT settings. DRUiD is suitable for any linear model with convex differentiable loss, while supporting both classification and regression tasks.

We develop a bound that estimates the difference between the last batch-computed model and the hypothetical model that could be computed from the current position of the sliding window. While most other algorithms monitor the error rate of the model to detect concept drifts, DRUiD monitors changes to the model coefficients. By only recomputing models as needed, DRUiD reduces the number of model recomputations while maintaining high accuracy. We also show that our new bound is tighter than bounds in previous work [23] by recasting the mathematical proof of the bounds from prior work in simpler, geometric terms. Our reanalysis also points to a limitation on using previous bounds to infer the class predictions of the hypothetical model.

Evaluated on synthetic and real-world data sets, DRUiD provides more accurate predictions than other online learning methods. It also provides more accurate predictions than an equivalent method using previous bounds. For example, when predicting change in electricity price, DRUiD achieves 6% higher accuracy over existing work while recomputing only 20 times (roughly 0.04% of the stream length), or 2.5% higher accuracy with only 10 recomputations.

2   Related Work

We divide existing work on concept drift into algorithms which focus on accurately detecting concept changes, and incremental algorithms that implicitly adapt the learned model to the new concept.

Concept Drift Detection. DDM by Gama et al. [13] monitors the classifier error rate by assuming that it decreases as the number of examples increases. If the error rate increases significantly the data is considered to have undergone concept drift. Similarly, EDDM by Baena-García et al. [1] detects concept drifts by monitoring the number of correct predictions between two consecutive classification errors.

Some adaptive algorithms also rely on sliding windows. FLORA2 by Widmer and Kubat [30] adjusts the window size to maintain model accuracy above a user-defined accuracy threshold. Harel et al. [15] use an adaptive sliding window to detect concept drifts: each window is split several times to different train and test sets, and the models built from each partition are expected to have similar accuracy. Otherwise, a concept drift is likely to have occurred. Multiple model computations make this approach unsuitable for systems with limited computational resources. Klinkenberg [18] suggests monitoring the values of three performance indicators – accuracy, recall and precision. If a concept drift is detected, the window is decreased to its minimal size, which is equal to one batch size. Klinkenberg and Joachims [17] presented an approach that selects an SVM window size such that the estimated generalization error on new examples is minimized. Such approaches require batch computation whenever the window is adjusted, or even to set its size in the first place, making them impractical when computational power is limited. ADWIN by Bifet and Gavaldà [3] adapts the window size by monitoring the difference in the mean value of the samples for every potential split of the window, and shrinking the window if this difference is too large. It is designed for one-dimensional samples and requires that the feature values be within a known range.

Our algorithm resembles concept drift detectors in that it considers both the features and the labels when detecting concept drifts. However, unlike most concept drift detectors, which only monitor the predictions of the model, we can monitor changes to the model coefficients. As we show in our evaluation, this results in superior tradeoff of model computation and accuracy.

DILSQ by Gabel et al. [10] is a distributed sliding window algorithm that triggers model recomputation when the Euclidean distance between models is too large. Though similar to DRUiD in that respect, DILSQ focuses on reducing the network overhead using geometric monitoring techniques [11, 28], rather than trading accuracy, and is limited to least squares regression models.

Incremental Learning. These algorithms can implicitly adapt to concept drifts. One such example is SGD, which applies first-order updates to the model [31]. Other incremental algorithms use second-order optimization, such as AROW by Crammer et al. [7] and NAROW by Orabona and Crammer [24]. Although not explicitly designed for concept drift detection, they may be adapted for this task. Our proposed algorithm can use any incremental learner internally when a concept drift is suspected, then use batch learning from the sliding window once enough samples from the new concept have been obtained.

3   Problem Definition and Notations

Consider a stream of data, where only some of the samples are labeled. The labeled data arrives as tuples $\{x_i, y_i\}$, while $y_i \in \{-1, 1\}$ for classification problems or $y_i \in \mathbb{R}$ for regression problems. Unlabeled samples have $y_i = null$.

We focus on sliding windows with a fixed or time-based window size. When a new labeled sample arrives, the window is updated – older samples in the window are removed and the new sample is added. We define W to be the sliding window at time t, and let $\mathcal{D}$ be the set of indices of labeled samples inside W.

Let $f(x, \beta) = x^T \beta$ be a linear function and let the loss function $\ell(\cdot, \cdot)$ be a differentiable and convex function with respect to the second argument. The model β_t^* is the optimal solution for the following optimization problem:

$$\beta_t^* = \arg\min_{\beta \in \mathbb{R}^d} C \sum_{i \in \mathcal{D}} \ell(y_i, f(x_i, \beta)) + \frac{1}{2}\|\beta\|^2, \quad C > 0. \tag{1}$$

Given an objective function of the form $a \sum_{i \in \mathcal{D}} \ell(y_i, f(x_i, \beta)) + b\|\beta\|^2$, choosing $C = \frac{a}{2b}$ will bring it to the standard form (1).

The optimization problem could be classification or regression, where for classification the linear classifier is $\hat{y} = \text{sgn}(f(x, \beta_t^*))$ while for regression the linear model is $\hat{y} = f(x, \beta_t^*)$.

For simplicity, we define a compact notation for the loss function for a specific sample. Let $\ell_i := \ell(y_i, f(x_i, \beta))$ be the loss with respect to sample $\{x_i, y_i\}$. Then $\nabla \ell_i(\beta^*)$ is the gradient of ℓ_i with respect to β at the point β^*.

This work focuses on the problem of maintaining high model accuracy over a stream of data with concept drift. The naïve approach would be to compute a new optimal solution β_t^* for every window update, which is infeasible if the computational power is limited. Instead, we aim to understand when concept drift occurs and to compute a new model only then.

4 Bounding Model Differences

Consider two sliding windows, W_1 and W_2, where W_1 is the sliding window at some previous time t_1 and W_2 is the window at current time t_{current}. If the concept we are trying to model has not changed, we expect the two models computed from two windows to be similar. For example, the Euclidean distance between the models is expected to be small. When the concept has changed, the opposite is expected.

We first develop a bound that estimates the difference between the last computed model and the model based on the current sliding window, without actually computing it. In Sect. 4.3 we propose algorithm that uses this bound to monitor that difference: it computes a new model only when the estimated difference is large.

4.1 Bound the Distance Between Models

Let β_1 and β_2 be the models trained on the labeled samples in the windows W_1 and W_2. We define the difference between two models as the Euclidean distance between the two model vectors: $\|\beta_1^* - \beta_2^*\|$. We propose a bound for this distance that can be computed without knowing β_2^*. Monitoring this bound over the stream helps the algorithms detect changes in the concept, thus preventing unnecessary computations while maintaining accurate models.

Theorem 1. *Let P be an optimization problem over a window W with sample indices $\mathcal{D}$, of the standard form (1):*

$$P : \beta_p^* = \arg \min_{\beta \in \mathbb{R}^d} C_p \sum_{i \in \mathcal{D}} \ell_i + \frac{1}{2}\|\beta\|^2,$$

with its associated constant C_P. Let β_1^* be the optimal solution of P_1 over previous window W_1 containing the labeled samples with indices $\mathcal{D}_1$, let β_2^* be the solution of P_2 over current window W_2 containing labeled samples $\mathcal{D}_2$, let C_1 be the associated constant of P_1 and let C_2 be the associated constant of P_2. Let $\mathcal{D}_\mathcal{A}$ be the set of indices of labeled samples added in W_2: $\mathcal{D}_\mathcal{A} = \mathcal{D}_2 \backslash \mathcal{D}_1$. Similarly, let $\mathcal{D}_\mathcal{R}$ be the set of indices of samples removed in W_2: $\mathcal{D}_\mathcal{R} = \mathcal{D}_1 \backslash \mathcal{D}_2$. Finally, let Δg be

$$\Delta g := \sum_{i \in \mathcal{D}_\mathcal{A}} \nabla \ell_i(\beta_1^*) - \sum_{i \in \mathcal{D}_\mathcal{R}} \nabla \ell_i(\beta_1^*).$$

Then the distance between β_1^* and β_2^* is bounded by: $\|\beta_1^* - \beta_2^*\| \leq 2\|r\|$, where

$$r = \frac{1}{2}\left(\beta_1^* - \frac{C_2}{C_1}\beta_1^* + C_2 \Delta g\right). \tag{2}$$

Table 1. Objective functions, losses, and associated bound parameter r.

Model	Objective function	Loss	r
L_2-reg LR	$\min\limits_{\beta} C \sum\limits_i \log\left(1 + \exp(-y_i x_i^T \beta)\right) + \frac{1}{2}\|\beta\|^2$	$\log\left(1 + \exp(-y_i x_i^T \beta)\right)$	$\frac{C}{2}\Delta g$
L_2-reg SVM	$\min\limits_{\beta} C \sum\limits_i \left(\max\{0, 1 - y_i x_i^T \beta\}\right)^2 + \frac{1}{2}\|\beta\|^2$	$\left(\max\{0, 1 - y_i x_i^T \beta\}\right)^2$	$\frac{C}{2}\Delta g$
Ridge Reg.	$\min\limits_{\beta} \sum\limits_i \left(y_i - x_i^T \beta\right)^2 + \alpha\|\beta\|^2$	$\left(y_i - x_i^T \beta\right)^2$	$\frac{1}{4\alpha}\Delta g$

Theorem 1 bounds the difference between computed models for any convex differentiable loss given the difference of their training sets. For example, we can apply Theorem 1 to L_2-regularized logistic regression, as defined in Liblinear [9], $C_1 = C_2 = C$. Assigning this in (2) gives $r = \frac{C}{2}\Delta g$. For L_2-regularized MSE loss, the constants C_1 and C_2 depend on the number of samples in the windows, and thus may differ if the size of the windows W_1 and W_2 is different. Table 1 lists r for several important optimization problems.

Proof. The proof of Theorem 1 proceeds in three steps: (i) use the convexity of the objective function to get a sphere that contains β_2^*; (ii) use the convexity of the objective function again to express the sphere's radius as a function of Δg; and (iii) bound the distance between β_1^* and β_2^* using geometric arguments.

(i) Sphere Shape Around β_2^*: This step adapts the proof in [23] to the canonical form and simplifies it. Recall that β_2^* is the optimal solution of (1), so according to the first-order optimality condition [6], $C_2 \sum_{i \in \mathcal{D}_2} \nabla \ell_i(\beta_2^*) + \beta_2^* = 0$. This could be written as

$$\beta_2^* = -C_2 \sum_{i \in \mathcal{D}_2} \nabla \ell_i(\beta_2^*). \tag{3}$$

ℓ_i is convex and differentiable, and therefore its gradient is monotonic non-decreasing (see Lemma 1 in [8] for the proof of this feature of convex function):

$$(\nabla \ell_i(\beta_2^*) - \nabla \ell_i(\beta_1^*))^T (\beta_2^* - \beta_1^*) \geq 0. \tag{4}$$

By summing (4) over all $i \in \mathcal{D}_2$, opening brackets and rearranging the inequality, we obtain:

$$\sum_{i \in \mathcal{D}_2} \nabla \ell_i(\beta_2^*)^T (\beta_2^* - \beta_1^*) \geq \sum_{i \in \mathcal{D}_2} \nabla \ell_i(\beta_1^*)^T (\beta_2^* - \beta_1^*). \tag{5}$$

Multiplying both sides of (5) with C_2 ($C_2 > 0$), and using (3), gives

$$\beta_2^{*T}(\beta_2^* - \beta_1^*) + C_2 \sum_{i \in \mathcal{D}_2} \nabla \ell_i(\beta_1^*)^T (\beta_2^* - \beta_1^*) \leq 0. \tag{6}$$

Denote $r := \frac{1}{2}\left(\beta_1^* + C_2 \sum_{i \in \mathcal{D}_2} \nabla \ell_i(\beta_1^*)\right)$, and observe that we can write:
$\beta_1^* - r = \frac{1}{2}\left(\beta_1^* - C_2 \sum_{i \in \mathcal{D}_2} \nabla \ell_i(\beta_1^*)\right)$. Completing the square of (6), we have:

$$\|\beta_2^* - (\beta_1^* - r)\|^2 = \underbrace{\beta_2^{*T}(\beta_2^* - \beta_1^*) + C_2 \sum_{i \in \mathcal{D}_2} \nabla \ell_i(\beta_1^*)^T (\beta_2^* - \beta_1^*)}_{\leq 0, \text{ due to } (6)} + \|r\|^2.$$

Then from (6) we have $\|\beta_2^* - (\beta_1^* - r)\|^2 \leq \|r\|^2$. Denoting $m := \beta_1^* - r$, we can rewrite it as: $\beta_2^* \in \Omega$, where $\Omega := \left\{\beta \,\middle|\, \|\beta - m\|^2 \leq \|r\|^2\right\}$. Thus the new optimal solution β_2^* is within a sphere Ω with center m and radius vector r.

(ii) Express the Radius Vector as a Function of Δg: β_1^* is the optimal solution of (1). Then by the first-order optimality condition: $C_1 \sum_{i \in \mathcal{D}_1} \nabla \ell_i(\beta_1^*) + \beta_1^* = 0$. This implies $\sum_{i \in \mathcal{D}_1} \nabla \ell_i(\beta_1^*) = -\frac{\beta_1^*}{C_1}$. From the fact that $\mathcal{D}_2 = \mathcal{D}_1 + \mathcal{D}_{\mathcal{A}} - \mathcal{D}_{\mathcal{R}}$, and the definition of Δg:

$$\sum_{i \in \mathcal{D}_2} \nabla \ell_i(\beta_1^*) = \sum_{i \in \mathcal{D}_1} \nabla \ell_i(\beta_1^*) + \underbrace{\sum_{i \in \mathcal{D}_{\mathcal{A}}} \nabla \ell_i(\beta_1^*) - \sum_{i \in \mathcal{D}_{\mathcal{R}}} \nabla \ell_i(\beta_1^*)}_{\triangleq \Delta g} = -\frac{\beta_1^*}{C_1} + \Delta g.$$

Substituting this into the definition of r above, we obtain (2).

(iii) Upper Bounds to $\|\beta_1^* - \beta_2^*\|$: We observe that both β_1^* and β_2^* are inside or on the surface of the sphere Ω. For β_1^* this follows since Ω is centered at $m = \beta_1^* - r$ with radius vector r. For β_2^* this property is obtained from the definition of Ω.

This implies that the maximum distance between β_1^* and β_2^* is obtained when β_1^*, β_2^* are on the surface of the sphere at two opposite sides of the sphere's diameter, which has length $2\|r\|$, yielding the upper bound in Theorem 1. $\square$

Improved Tightness. The bound in Theorem 1 is tighter than the previous bound [23, Corollary 2] by a factor of $\sqrt{d}$, and in fact does not depend on the number of attributes d. The proof is technical and omitted for space reasons. The intuition is that [23] relies on summing d bounds on the coefficients of $\beta_1^* - \beta_2^*$.

Tikhonov Regularization. We can extend our approach to Tikhonov Regularization with an invertible Tikhonov matrix A [6]. The objective function remains convex with respect to the weights, and the canonical form (1) changes to: $\beta^* = \arg\min_{\beta \in \mathbb{R}^d} C \sum_{i \in \mathcal{D}} \ell_i + \frac{1}{2}\|A\beta\|^2$. By the first-order optimality condition, $C_2 \sum_{i \in \mathcal{D}} \nabla \ell_i(\beta^*) + A^T A \beta^* = 0$. Repeating the steps for the proof of Theorem 1 starting from (3), we obtain: $r = \frac{1}{2}\left(\beta_1^* - \frac{C_2}{C_1}\beta_1^* + C_2(A^T A)^{-1}\Delta g\right)$. The only change to r is the addition of $(A^T A)^{-1}$ before Δg.

4.2   Bounding the Predictions of the New Model

To compare to previous work [23], we describe an alternative measure for the difference between two models: the difference in the prediction of the two models for a given sample. We describe upper and lower bounds for the prediction of β_2^* for a new sample. As before, we can compute these bounds without computing β_2^*, using the predictions from β_1^*.

Using the observation from Sect. 4.1 that β_2^* is within a sphere Ω with center m and radius vector r, we can obtain lower and upper bounds on applying β_2^* to a new sample x:

Lemma 1. *Let β_1^*, β_2^* and r be as in Theorem 1, and let x be a sample. Then the upper and lower bounds on the prediction of β_2^* for x are:*

$$L(x^T \beta_2^*) := \min_{\beta \in \Omega} x^T \beta = x^T \beta_1^* - x^T r - \|x\| \|r\| \tag{7a}$$

$$U(x^T \beta_2^*) := \max_{\beta \in \Omega} x^T \beta = x^T \beta_1^* - x^T r + \|x\| \|r\| . \tag{7b}$$

The proof follows by applying Theorem 1, then expressing β as $m + u$, where m is the center of the sphere Ω, u is parallel to x, and $\|u\| = \|r\|$. See Okumura et al. [23] for an alternative derivation of these bounds in a different form.

Lemma 1 could be used for concept drift detection in classification problems: if the upper and lower bounds (7) agree on the sign, then the classification of β_2^* is known [23]. The frequency of the disagreement between the bounds could be another indication for the quality of β_1^*; as the deviation of the current model from the older model increases due to concept drift, we expect more frequent sign disagreement as well.

However, it turns out that the bounds only agree on the class of a new sample when β_1^* and β_2^* also agree. Since both β_1^* and β_2^* are inside or on the surface of the sphere Ω, then from the definition of $L(x^T \beta_2^*)$ and $U(x^T \beta_2^*)$ we have that $L(x^T \beta_2^*) \leq x^T \beta_1^*, x^T \beta_2^* \leq U(x^T \beta_2^*)$. Hence, if $\text{sgn}\left(x^T \beta_1^*\right) \neq \text{sgn}\left(x^T \beta_2^*\right)$, then necessarily $\text{sgn}\left(L(x^T \beta_2^*)\right) \neq \text{sgn}\left(U(x^T \beta_2^*)\right)$.

The above implies that if the class of a sample is different under β_1^* and β_2^*, it cannot be determined from the bounds (7), and instead the bounds disagree on the sign (this limitation also applies to the bounds from [23]). Moreover, it is still possible that the bounds disagree even if the classifiers do agree on the classification. Therefore, this method for evaluating the quality of β_1^* is more sensitive to the data distribution than the bound in Sect. 4.1.

4.3   The DRUiD Algorithm

DRUiD is a sliding window algorithm suitable for both classification and regression problems. For every new sample that arrives, DRUiD: (a) computes β_1^*'s prediction of the new sample and updates the sliding window; (b) bounds the difference $\|\beta_1^* - \beta_2^*\|$ using Theorem 1; and (c) if the difference is too large, recomputes β_1^* from the current window. Algorithm 1 shows how DRUiD handles new samples. We describe DRUiD in detail below.

Algorithm 1. DRUiD

---

initialization: $\beta_{\text{cur}} \leftarrow \beta_1^*$, $n_{\mathcal{A}} \leftarrow 0$, $n_{\mathcal{R}} \leftarrow 0$, $\Delta g \leftarrow \mathbf{0}$, $numWarnings \leftarrow 0$

procedure HANDLENEWLABELEDSAMPLE($\{x_i, y_i\}$)

    Let $\{x_r, y_r\}$ be the oldest sample in the sliding window W

    Update sliding window W and count of added (removed) samples $n_{\mathcal{A}}$ $(n_{\mathcal{R}})$

    $\Delta g \leftarrow \Delta g + \nabla \ell_i(\beta_1^*) - \nabla \ell_r(\beta_1^*)$

    $\beta_{\text{cur}} \leftarrow$ incrementalUpdate($\beta_{\text{cur}}, \{x_i, y_i\}$)

    if $n_{\mathcal{A}} < N$ **then**

        Collect $\|\Delta g\|$ for fitting

    else

        if $n_{\mathcal{A}} = N$ **then**

            Fit χ_d to collected $\|\Delta g\|$ and choose T_α such that $\Pr\left[\|\Delta g\| \leq T_\alpha\right] > \alpha$

        if $\|\Delta g\| > T_\alpha$ **then** $numWarnings \leftarrow numWarnings + 1$

        else $numWarnings \leftarrow 0$

        if $numWarnings > T_N$ **then**

            Train on window W: $\beta_1^* \leftarrow$ batchTrain(W)

            Reset window: $\beta_{\text{cur}} \leftarrow \beta_1^*$, $n_{\mathcal{A}} \leftarrow 0$, $\Delta g \leftarrow \mathbf{0}$

procedure PREDICT(x)

    if $numWarnings = 0$ **then return** $\beta_1^{*T} x$

    else return $\beta_{\text{cur}}^T x$

As long as the bound indicates that β_1^* and β_2^* are similar, DRUiD uses the last computed model β_1^* for prediction; however, it also maintains an incrementally updated model β_{cur}. If the bound indicates that the concept is changing, DRUiD switches to the incrementally updated model β_{cur}. Finally, once enough labeled samples from the new concept are available, DRUiD recomputes β_1^* using a full batch learning pass.

DRUiD detects concept drifts by monitoring changes in $\|r\|$ from Theorem 1. When new labeled samples arrive, DRUiD updates Δg and the sliding window (since r is a linear function of Δg, monitoring changes in Δg is equivalent to monitoring changes in r); it also fits a χ_d distribution to $\|\Delta g\|$, where degrees of freedom d is the number of attributes of the data. Once enough new samples have arrived to accurately estimate the distribution parameters of $\|\Delta g\|$, DRUiD tests for potential concept drifts (we denote this constant N and set it to the window size in our evaluation). We use a simple one-tailed test[1]: a potential concept drift occurs whenever $\|\Delta g\|$ is above a user-determined α percentile of the fitted χ_d distribution, denoted as T_α: $\Pr\left[\|\Delta g\| \leq T_\alpha\right] > \alpha$.

Even when a potential concept drift is detected, DRUiD does not immediately recompute the model. Instead, it waits until $\|\Delta g\|$ is above the threshold T_α for T_N times in a row (we set T_N to the window size). This not only guarantees the batch learner a sufficiently large sample from the new concept, but also

---

[1] We caution against ascribing such tests too much meaning. If values of Δg are i.i.d. Gaussians, then $\|\Delta g\| \sim \chi_d$. However, as with similar tests in the literature, in practice the elements are seldom i.i.d. Gaussians and even successive Δg are often not independent. Our evaluation in Sect. 5 explores a range of thresholds.

helps reduce false positives caused by outliers. To maintain high accuracy while collecting enough samples for batch learning, DRUiD switches to using β_{cur} for predictions instead of β_1^*. The model β_{cur} is initialized to β_1^* after batch recomputation and is incrementally updated for each new labeled sample, for example using an SGD update step [31]. However, it is only used after the first potential concept drift is detected, and only until enough samples are collected.

5   Evaluation

We evaluate DRUiD on real-world and synthetic datasets.

We consider batch model computation as a heavy operation which requires waking up the stronger processor (in heterogeneous architectures) or communication with a remote server (in connected devices). An effective edge-computing algorithm is able to tradeoff a small number of model computations for additional accuracy. To provide a point of comparison to other concept drift detection algorithms, we also consider drift detection events as model computation.

We use *tradeoff curves* to evaluate performance and compare algorithms. For every configuration of algorithm parameters, we plot a point with the resulting accuracy as the Y coordinate and the number of computations as the X coordinate. This builds a curve that shows how the algorithm behaves as we change its parameters. Practitioners can then choose a suitable operating point based on how many batch model computations they are willing to accept.

5.1   Experimental Setup

We compare DRUiD to several baseline algorithms. Since we are interested in linear models, the baselines were chosen accordingly.

- **Sliding Window** is a non-adaptive, periodic sliding window algorithm, as in the original FLORA [30]. A period parameter determines how often batch model recomputation is performed: every labeled example, every two labeled examples, and so on. The implementation of the algorithm uses Liblinear [9] logistic regression with L_2 regularization.
- **Incremental SGD** uses an SGD-based [31] first-order method update to the model. We use the SGDClassifier implementation in sklearn [25], with logistic regression loss. A full batch model is computed only once to obtain the initial model.
- **DDM** by Gama et al. [13] and **EDDM** by Baena-García et al. [1] are two popular concept drift detectors that can use batch mode or incremental base learners. They monitor the base learner accuracy and decide when to update models. We implemented batch and incremental modes for both algorithms using the Tornado framework [26].
- **PredSign**: to compare to existing bounds on model predictions [23], we describe an algorithm that uses the signs of the classification bounds from Sect. 4.2 to decide when a model should be recomputed. As with DRUiD, we

update Δg and the sliding window when labeled samples arrive. Unlabeled sample are first evaluated using the bounds U and L. When the bounds U and L have different sign, this could indicate a concept drift. Once the number of samples for which the U and L bounds disagree on the sign exceeds a user-defined threshold T_D, PredSign recomputes the model β_1^*.

– **ADWIN** [3] is a concept drift detector for batch or incremental base learners. We used the implementation in scikit-multiflow [21]: every time a concept drift is detected, we compute a new model from the samples in the adaptive window. ADWIN's performance across all experiments was equivalent or inferior to DDM's and EDDM's, and is therefore not included in the figures.

We mainly focus on L_2 regularized logistic regression (Table 1). The fraction of labeled examples is set to 10%: every 10th sample of the stream is considered labeled while the other samples are treated as unlabeled (their labels are only used for evaluation, not training). For the labeled examples, we use prequential evaluation: we first use the samples to test the model and only then to train it [14]. We set a window size of 2000 samples (i.e., 200 labels per window), and use the first 2000 samples from the stream to tune the learning rates and regularization parameters. Results using different window sizes were fairly similar, but this size resulted in best performance for the EDDM and DDM baselines.

The tradeoff curve for each algorithm is created by running it on the data with different parameters. For DDM, we set drift levels $\alpha \in [0.01, 30]$. The warning level β was set according to the drift level – if $\alpha > 1$, then $\beta = \alpha - 1$; otherwise $\beta = \alpha$. For EDDM, we set warning levels $\alpha \in [0.1, 0.99999]$. The drift level β was set according to the warning level – if the $\alpha > 0.05$, then $\beta = \alpha - 0.05$; otherwise $\beta = \alpha$. We ran PredSign with threshold $T_D \in [60, 50000]$. For DRUiD, we set α values $\in [0.01, 0.9999999]$. For ADWIN, we set δ values $\in [0.0001, 0.9999999]$. Finally, the period parameter for Sliding Window was set between 60 to 30000.

5.2   Electricity Pricing Dataset

The **ELEC2** dataset described by Harris et al. [16] contains 45,312 instances from Australian New South Wales Electricity, using 8 input attributes recorded every half an hour for two years. The classification task is to predict a rise ($y_i = +1$) or a fall ($y_i = -1$) in the price of electricity. We used the commonly available MOA [4] version of the dataset without the date, day, and time attributes.

Figure 1a compares the performance of the different algorithms on the ELEC2 dataset. Every point in the graph represents one run of an algorithm on the entire stream with a specific value of the algorithm's meta-parameter – the closer to the top-left corner, the better. Connecting the points creates a curve that describes the tradeoff between computation and accuracy.

Overall, the accuracy of sliding window algorithms that use batch learning (Sliding Window, PredSign and DRUiD) is superior to that of the incremental learning algorithms (Incremental SGD, DDM and EDDM).

DRUiD gives the best tradeoff of model computations to accuracy: at every point, it offers the highest accuracy with the fewest model computations. For

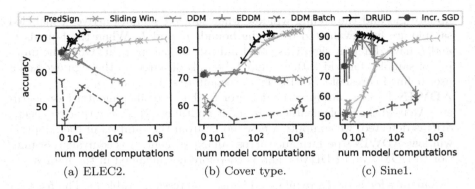

Fig. 1. The tradeoff between accuracy and number of model computations in ELEC2, Forest Covertype, and Sine1 datasets, for different parameter configurations of each algorithm (EDDM Batch performance is similar to DDM Batch). Vertical lines in Sine1 show standard deviation over 5 experiments. The optimal number of model computations is 10, since this dataset has 10 concepts. In all cases DRUiD achieves a better tradeoff, showing equal or superior accuracy at lower computational cost than all other algorithms across a large range of configurations.

example, DRUiD achieves 70% accuracy using 10 batch model computations throughout the entire stream (0.02% of stream size), while Sliding Window and PredSign need two orders of magnitude more computation to reach similar accuracy. DDM, EDDM and Incremental SGD are unable to achieve such accuracy on this dataset, despite careful tuning efforts.

Though PredSign is able to match the performance of the sliding window algorithm, DRUiD offers a superior computation-accuracy tradeoff. Bounding the model difference (Sect. 4.1) results in fewer false concept drift detections than the approach in [23], which bounds the model prediction (Sect. 4.2).

Surprisingly, the accuracy of DDM and EDDM drops even when we use more model computations. Digging deeper, we saw that DDM and EDDM switch too soon to a new model without sufficient training. A thorough parameter sweep using a fine grid, including the parameter values recommended by the authors, shows that for most configurations DDM and EDDM do not detect any concept drifts in this data and simply use the initial model from the first window – it is the optimal point for these algorithms on this dataset. The few configurations that cause DDM and EDDM to detect drifts end up performing poorly as they switch to a new model too soon, without sufficient training samples.

DDM and EDDM perform poorly in batch mode on all tested datasets, since across all test configurations they yield few samples between the warning and drift threshold, resulting in low accuracy models built from few samples.[2]

---

[2] As far as we can tell, this is consistent with practice: the implementations of DDM and EDDM that we found use incremental base learners [4,22,26].

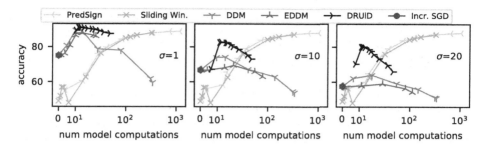

Fig. 2. Tradeoff curves for the Sine1+ dataset with different scale values (σ). The accuracy on the incremental based algorithms drops where the scale is larger.

5.3 Forest Covertype

The **Forest Covertype** dataset contains the forest cover type for $30 \times 30\,\text{m}$ cells obtained from US Forest Service data [5]. It includes 581,012 samples with 54 attributes each that are divided into 7 classes. To convert the problem to a binary classification problem, we set the label y_i to $+1$ for class number 2, the Lodgepole Pine cover type, and -1 for the rest of the classes (this results in near equal number of positive and negative examples).

Figure 1b shows the computation-accuracy tradeoff for this dataset. Sliding window algorithms give more accurate results than the incremental algorithms, except for the extreme case where the number of model computations is close to zero. DRUiD shows the best accuracy with the least model computations.

5.4 Sine1+

The **Sine1+** artificial dataset is based on the Sine1 artificial dataset presented in [1,13], but extended to more than 2 attributes and to allow non-uniform scales. It contains 9 abrupt concept drifts, each with 10,000 samples (hence the optimal number of model computations is 10). The dataset has $d \geq 2$ attributes: x_1 is uniformly distributed in $[0, \sigma]$, where $\sigma \geq 1$ sets its scale compared to other attributes $x_2, ..., x_d$ which are uniformly distributed in $[0, 1]$. In the first concept, points that lie below the curve $x_d = sin\left(\frac{(x_1/\sigma) + \sum_{i=2}^{d-1} x_i}{d-1}\right)$ are classified as $+1$ and the rest are classified as -1. After the concept drift, the classification is reversed. Note that for $d = 2, \sigma = 1$ we get the original Sine1 dataset, with the separating line $x_2 = sin(x_1)$.

Figure 1c shows the computation-accuracy tradeoff for the original Sine1 dataset ($d = 2$ and $\sigma = 1$). Every point in the graph is the average of 5 runs with different random seeds (for every seed, all algorithms see the same data), and the vertical lines are the standard deviation error bars.

DRUiD detects all concept drifts even when set to very low sensitivity levels (high α), so the number of model computations does not go below 10. It maintains high accuracy and a small number of model computations for all α values.

For almost every number of model computations, PredSign accuracy is higher than Sliding Window. This is because PredSign can change the timing of its model computations, which is not possible in Sliding Window.

Figure 2 shows the computation-accuracy tradeoff for $d = 2$ and different σ values. As we explain below, DRUiD's batch mode computation maintains high accuracy even as the problem becomes increasingly ill-conditioned.

Conversely, incremental algorithms are sensitive to non-uniform attribute scales. Figure 3 shows the effect of scale on convergence in the Sine1+ dataset. The top figures show the accuracy over time of Incremental SGD, DDM, and DRUiD between two consecutive concept drifts (EDDM behaves similarly to DDM). As σ increases, the convergence time of the incremental based algorithms also grows, as expected [6, p. 467]. The bottom figures show the contour lines of the L_2-regularized logistic regression objective functions for different σ values (the loss surface). As σ increases, the shape of the loss surface becomes more elliptic, with a higher condition number and slower convergence for gradient descent methods. For higher condition number, the batch based algorithms require more iterations of gradient descent to converge on recomputation of a new model. However, this recomputation is performed on the strong processor or cloud server, with no effect on the accuracy. The effect of σ does not depend on the number of attributes. Using $d = 50$ attributes yields similar results to only 2: larger σ values reduce the accuracy of incremental algorithms, even though σ only affects x_1 (figures omitted due to lack of space).

Feature normalization or other preconditioning is not always possible in streams that have concept drifts, since the distribution of the attributes is not

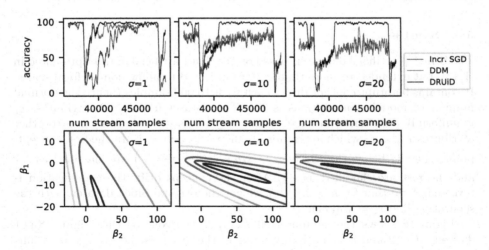

Fig. 3. Effect of different σ values on Sine1+. Top: accuracy over time between two concept drifts. Bottom: the contour lines of the L_2-regularized logistic regression objective functions. The optimization problem becomes increasingly ill-conditioned when the scale σ increases, so Incremental SGD recover more slowly after a concept drift.

known and can change unexpectedly. Algorithms that use batch learning are better suited for ill-conditioned streams than relying solely on incremental learning.

5.5   Ridge Regression

We evaluate DRUiD performance on an artificial regression task, and compare it to Incremental SGD and Sliding Window (PredSign, DDM, and EDDM only support classification). We generate 10 concepts, each with a different true model β_{true} with 2 coefficients drawn from a standard normal distribution. For each epoch concept we generate 10,000 samples, where each sample x has 2 attributes drawn from a standard normal distribution. As with Sine1+, one of the attributes is then expanded by a factor of $\sigma \geq 1$. Each label is $y = x^T \beta_{true} + \epsilon$, where ϵ is random Gaussian noise: $\epsilon \sim N(0, 1)$.

As in the Sine1+ dataset, non-uniform scaling increases the condition number of the problem. The computation and accuracy tradeoff follow similar trends as in classification (figures omitted due to lack of space). For a well-conditioned problem, the incremental algorithm and DRUiD achieve the same RMSE as the best periodic algorithm (albeit with far fewer model computations). However, when the condition number increases, DRUiD achieves a better tradeoff than the incremental algorithm, since the batch learning convergence rate does not affect the accuracy along the stream.

6   Conclusions

DRUiD is an online algorithm for data streams with concept drifts, designed for edge computing systems. It improves accuracy with minimal cost by running batch computations of new data only when the model changes. DRUiD relies on an improved bound for the difference between two linear models with convex differentiable loss. Evaluation on real and synthetic data shows that DRUiD provides a better tradeoff between model computation and accuracy than traditional concept drift detectors, and that its batch-based computation is better suited for ill-conditioned problems than methods based on incremental learning.

References

1. Baena-García, M., Campo-Ávila, J., Fidalgo-Merino, R., Bifet, A., Gavald, R., Morales-Bueno, R.: Early drift detection method. In: Fourth International Workshop on Knowledge Discovery from Data Streams (2006)
2. Prahlada Rao, B.B., Saluja, P., Sharma, N., Mittal, A., Sharma, S.: Cloud computing for Internet of Things & sensing based applications. In: ICST (2012)
3. Bifet, A., Gavaldà, R.: Learning from time-changing data with adaptive windowing. In: SIAM 2007 (2007)
4. Bifet, A., Holmes, G., Kirkby, R., Pfahringer, B.: MOA: massive online analysis. JMLR **11**, 1601–1604 (2010)

5. Blackard, J.A., Dean, D.J.: Comparative accuracies of artificial neural networks and discriminant analysis in predicting forest cover types from cartographic variables. Comput. Electron. Agric. **24**, 131–151 (1999)
6. Boyd, S., Vandenberghe, L.: Convex Optimization. Cambridge University Press, Cambridge (2004)
7. Crammer, K., Kulesza, A., Dredze, M.: Adaptive regularization of weight vectors. Mach. Learn. **91**(2), 155–187 (2013)
8. Dunn, J.: Convexity, monotonicity, and gradient processes in Hilbert space. J. Math. Anal. Appl. **53**, 145–158 (1976)
9. Fan, R.E., Chang, K.W., Hsieh, C.J., Wang, X.R., Lin, C.J.: LIBLINEAR: a library for large linear classification. J. Mach. Learn. Res. **9**, 1871–1874 (2008)
10. Gabel, M., Keren, D., Schuster, A.: Monitoring least squares models of distributed streams. In: KDD 2015 (2015)
11. Gabel, M., Keren, D., Schuster, A.: Anarchists, unite: practical entropy approximation for distributed streams. In: KDD 2017 (2017)
12. Gama, J.: A survey on learning from data streams: current and future trends. Prog. Artif. Intell. **1**(1), 45–55 (2012)
13. Gama, J., Medas, P., Castillo, G., Rodrigues, P.: Learning with drift detection. In: Bazzan, A.L.C., Labidi, S. (eds.) SBIA 2004. LNCS (LNAI), vol. 3171, pp. 286–295. Springer, Heidelberg (2004). https://doi.org/10.1007/978-3-540-28645-5_29
14. Gama, J., Sebastião, R., Rodrigues, P.P.: On evaluating stream learning algorithms. Mach. Learn. **90**(3), 317–346 (2012). https://doi.org/10.1007/s10994-012-5320-9
15. Harel, M., Crammer, K., El-Yaniv, R., Mannor, S.: Concept drift detection through resampling. In: ICML 2014 (2014)
16. Harries, M., South Wales, N.: Splice-2 Comparative Evaluation: Electricity Pricing, August 1999
17. Klinkenberg, R., Joachims, T.: Detecting concept drift with support vector machines. In: ICML 2000 (2000)
18. Klinkenberg, R., Renz, I.: Adaptive information filtering: learning drifting concepts. In: FGML 1998 (1998)
19. Liaqat, D., et al.: Sidewinder: an energy efficient and developer friendly heterogeneous architecture for continuous mobile sensing. In: ASPLOS 2016 (2016)
20. Mahdavinejad, M.S., Rezvan, M., Barekatain, M., Adibi, P., Barnaghi, P., Sheth, A.P.: Machine learning for Internet of Things data analysis: a survey. Digit. Commun. Netw. **4**(3), 161–175 (2018)
21. Montiel, J., Read, J., Bifet, A., Abdessalem, T.: Scikit-multiflow: a multi-output streaming framework. JMLR **19**(72), 1–5 (2018)
22. Nishida, K.: Learning and detecting concept drift. Ph.D. thesis, Hokkaido University (2008)
23. Okumura, S., Suzuki, Y., Takeuchi, I.: Quick sensitivity analysis for incremental data modification and its application to leave-one-out CV in linear classification problems. In: KDD 2015 (2015)
24. Orabona, F., Crammer, K.: New adaptive algorithms for online classification. In: NIPS 2010 (2010)
25. Pedregosa, F., et al.: Scikit-learn: machine learning in Python. JMLR **12**, 2825–2830 (2011)
26. Pesaranghader, A., Viktor, H.L., Paquet, E.: A framework for classification in data streams using multi-strategy learning. In: Calders, T., Ceci, M., Malerba, D. (eds.) DS 2016. LNCS (LNAI), vol. 9956, pp. 341–355. Springer, Cham (2016). https://doi.org/10.1007/978-3-319-46307-0_22

27. Read, J.: Concept-drifting data streams are time series; the case for continuous adaptation. CoRR abs/1810.02266 (2018)
28. Sharfman, I., Schuster, A., Keren, D.: Shape sensitive geometric monitoring. In: PODS 2008 (2008)
29. Shi, W., Cao, J., Zhang, Q., Li, Y., Xu, L.: Edge computing: vision and challenges. IEEE Internet Things J. **3**(5), 637–646 (2016)
30. Widmer, G., Kubat, M.: Learning in the presence of concept drift and hidden contexts. Mach. Learn. **23**(1), 69–101 (1996)
31. Xu, W.: Towards optimal one pass large scale learning with averaged stochastic gradient descent. CoRR abs/1107.2490 (2011)
32. Zinkevich, M.: Online convex programming and generalized infinitesimal gradient ascent. In: ICML 2003 (2003)

Fast Likelihood-Based Change Point Detection

Nikolaj Tatti[⊠]

HIIT, University of Helsinki, Helsinki, Finland
nikolaj.tatti@helsinki.fi

Abstract. Change point detection plays a fundamental role in many real-world applications, where the goal is to analyze and monitor the behaviour of a data stream. In this paper, we study change detection in binary streams. To this end, we use a likelihood ratio between two models as a measure for indicating change. The first model is a single bernoulli variable while the second model divides the stored data in two segments, and models each segment with its own bernoulli variable. Finding the optimal split can be done in $\mathcal{O}(n)$ time, where n is the number of entries since the last change point. This is too expensive for large n. To combat this we propose an approximation scheme that yields $(1 - \epsilon)$ approximation in $\mathcal{O}(\epsilon^{-1} \log^2 n)$ time. The speed-up consists of several steps: First we reduce the number of possible candidates by adopting a known result from segmentation problems. We then show that for fixed bernoulli parameters we can find the optimal change point in logarithmic time. Finally, we show how to construct a candidate list of size $\mathcal{O}(\epsilon^{-1} \log n)$ for model parameters. We demonstrate empirically the approximation quality and the running time of our algorithm, showing that we can gain a significant speed-up with a minimal average loss in optimality.

1 Introduction

Many real-world applications involve in monitoring and analyzing a constant stream of data. A fundamental task in such applications is to monitor whether a change has occurred. For example, the goal may be monitoring the performance of a classifier over time, and triggering retraining if the quality degrades too much. We can also use change point detection techniques to detect anomalous behavior in the data stream. As the data flow may be significant, it is important to develop efficient algorithms.

In this paper we study detecting change in a stream of binary numbers, that is, we are interested in detecting whether the underlying distribution has recently changed significantly. To test the change we will use a standard likelihood ratio statistic. Namely, assume that we have already observed n samples from the last time we have observed change. In our first model, we fit a single bernoulli

Electronic supplementary material The online version of this chapter (https://doi.org/10.1007/978-3-030-46150-8_39) contains supplementary material, which is available to authorized users.

U. Brefeld et al. (Eds.): ECML PKDD 2019, LNAI 11906, pp. 662–677, 2020.
https://doi.org/10.1007/978-3-030-46150-8_39

variable to these samples. In our second model, we split these samples in two halves, say at point i, and fit two bernoulli variables to these halves. Once this is done we compare the likelihood ratio of the models. If the ratio is large enough, then we deem that change has occurred.

In our setting, index i is not fixed. Instead we are looking for the index that yields the largest likelihood. This can be done naively in $\mathcal{O}(n)$ time by testing each candidate. This may be too slow, especially if n is large enough and we do not have the resources before a new sample arrives. Our main technical contribution is to show how we can achieve $(1 - \epsilon)$ approximate of the optimal i in $\mathcal{O}(\epsilon^{-1} \log^2 n)$ time.

To achieve this we will first reduce the number of candidates for the optimal index i. We say that index j is a *border* if each interval ending at $j - 1$ has a smaller proportion of 1s that any interval that starts at j. A known result states that the optimal change point will be among border indices. Using border indices already reduces the search time greatly in practice, with theoretical running time being $\mathcal{O}(n^{2/3})$.

To obtain even smaller bounds we show that we can find the optimal index among the border indices for *fixed* model parameters, that is, the parameters for the two bernoulli variables, in $\mathcal{O}(\log n)$ time. We then construct a list of $\mathcal{O}(\epsilon^{-1} \log n)$ candidates for these parameters. Moreover, this list will contain model parameters that are close enough to the optimal parameters, so testing them yields $(1 - \epsilon)$ approximation guarantee in $\mathcal{O}(\epsilon^{-1} \log^2 n)$ time.

The remaining paper is organized as follows. In Sect. 2 we introduce preliminary notation and define the problem. In Sect. 3 we introduce border points. We present our main technical contribution in Sects. 4 and 5: first we show how to find optimal index for fixed model parameters, and then show how to select candidates for these parameters. We present related work in Sect. 6 and empirical evaluation in Sect. 7. Finally, we conclude with discussion in Sect. 8.

2   Preliminaries and Problem Definition

Assume a sequence of n binary numbers $S = s_1, \ldots, s_n$. Here s_1 is either the beginning of the stream or the last time we detected a change. Our goal is to determine whether a change has happened in S. More specifically, we consider two statistical models: The first model M_1 assumes that S is generated with a single bernoulli variable. The second model M_2 assumes that there is an index i, a change point, such that $s_1, \ldots, s_{i-1}$ is generated by one bernoulli variable and $s_i, \ldots, s_n$ is generated by another bernoulli variable.

Given a sequence S we will fit M_1 and M_2 and compare the log-likelihoods. Note that the model M_2 depends on the change point i, so we need to select i that maximizes the likelihood of M_2. If the ratio is large enough, then we can determine that change has occurred.

To make the above discussion more formal, let us introduce some notation. Given two integers a and b, and real number between 0 and 1, we denote the log-likelihood of a bernoulli variable by

$$\ell(a, b; p) = a \log p + b \log(1 - p).$$

For a fixed a and b, the log-likelihood is at its maximum if $p = a/(a+b)$. In such a case, we will often drop p from the notation and simply write $\ell(a, b)$.

We have the following optimization problem.

Problem 1 (CHANGE). Given a sequence $S = s_1, \ldots, s_n$, find an index i s.t.

$$\ell(a_1, b_1) + \ell(a_2, b_2) - \ell(a, b)$$

is maximized, where

$$a_1 = \sum_{j=1}^{i-1} s_i, \quad b_1 = i - 1 - a_1, \quad a_2 = \sum_{j=i}^{k} s_i, \quad b_2 = k - i - a_2,$$

$$a = a_1 + a_2, \text{ and } b = b_1 + b_2.$$

Note that CHANGE can be solved in $\mathcal{O}(n)$ time by simply iterating over all possible values for i. Such running time may be too slow, especially in a streaming setting when new points arrive constantly, and our goal is to determine whether change has occurred in real time. The main contribution of this paper is to show how to compute $(1 - \epsilon)$ estimate of CHANGE in $\mathcal{O}(\epsilon^{-1} \log^2 n)$ time. This algorithm requires additional data structures that we will review in the next section. As our main application is to search change points in a stream, these structures need to be maintained over a stream. Luckily, there is an amortized constant-time algorithm for maintaining the needed structure, as demonstrated in the next section.

Once we have solved CHANGE, we compare the obtained score against the threshold σ. Note that M_2 will always have a larger likelihood than M_1. In this paper, we will use BIC to adjust for the additional model complexity of M_2. The model M_2 has three parameters while the model M_1 has 1 parameter. This leads to a BIC penalty of $(3 - 1)/2 \log n = \log n$. In practice, we need to be more conservative when selecting M_2 due to the multiple hypothesis testing problem. Hence, we will use $\sigma = \tau + \log n$ as the threshold. Here, τ is a user parameter; we will provide some guidelines in selecting τ during the experimental evaluation in Sect. 7.

When change occurs at point i we have two options: we can either discard the current window and start from scratch, or we can drop only the first i elements. In this paper we will use the former approach since the latter approach requires additional maintenance which may impact overall computational complexity.

3   Reducing Number of Candidates

Our first step for a faster change point discovery is to reduce the number of possible change points. To this end, we define a variant of CHANGE, where we require that the second parameter in M_2 is larger than the first.

Problem 2 (CHANGEINC). Given a sequence $S = s_1, \ldots, s_n$, find an index i s.t.

$$\ell(a_1, b_1) + \ell(a_2, b_2) - \ell(a, b)$$

is maximized, where

$$a_1 = \sum_{j=1}^{i-1} s_i, \ b_1 = i - 1 - a_1, \quad a_2 = \sum_{j=i}^{k} s_i, \ b_2 = k - i - a_2,$$

$$a = a_1 + a_2, \text{ and } b = b_1 + b_2$$

with $a_1/(a_1 + b_1) \leq a_2/(a_2 + b_2)$.

From now on, we will focus on solving CHANGEINC. This problem is meaningful by itself, for example, if the goal is to detect a deterioration in a classifier, that is, sudden increase in entries being equal to 1. However, we can also use CHANGEINC to solve CHANGE. This is done by defining a flipped sequence $S' = s'_1, \ldots, s'_n$, where $s'_i = 1 - s_i$. Then the solution for CHANGE is either the solution of CHANGEINC(S) or the solution of CHANGEINC(S').

Next we show that we can limit ourselves to *border* indices when solving CHANGEINC.

Definition 1. *Assume a sequence of binary numbers $S = (s_i)_{i=1}^n$. We say that index j is a* border *index if there are no indices x, y with $x < j < y$ such that*

$$\frac{1}{j-x} \sum_{i=x}^{j-1} s_i \geq \frac{1}{y-j} \sum_{i=j}^{y-1} s_i.$$

In other words, j is a border index if and only if the average of any interval ending at $j - 1$ is smaller than the average of any interval starting at j.

Proposition 1. *There is a border index i that solves* CHANGEINC.

The proposition follows from a variant of Theorem 1 in [19]. For the sake of completeness we provide a direct proof in Appendix in supplementary material.

We address the issue of maintaining border indices at the end of this section.

The proposition permits us to ignore all indices that are not borders. That is, we can group the sequence entries in blocks, each block starting with a border index. We can then search for i using these blocks instead of using the original sequence.

It is easy to see that these blocks have the following property: the proportion of 1s in the next block is always larger. This key feature will play a crucial role in the next two sections as it allows us to use binary search techniques and reduce the computational complexity. Let us restate the original problem so that we can use this feature. First, let us define what is a block sequence.

Definition 2. *Let $B = \langle (u_i, v_i) \rangle_{i=1}^k$ be a sequence of k pairs of non-negative integers with $u_i + v_i > 0$. We say that B is* block sequence *if $\frac{u_{i+1}}{u_{i+1}+v_{i+1}} > \frac{u_i}{u_i+v_i}$.*

We obtain a block sequence B from a binary sequence S by grouping the entries between border points: the counter u_i indicates the number of 1s while the counter v_i indicates the number of 0s.

Our goal is to use block sequences to solve CHANGEINC. First, we need some additional notation.

Definition 3. *Given a block sequence B, we define $B[i;j] = (a,b)$, where $a = \sum_{k=i}^{j} u_k$ and $b = \sum_{k=i}^{j} v_k$. If $i > j$, then $a = b = 0$. Moreover, we will write*

$$av(i,j;B) = \frac{a}{a+b}.$$

If B is known from the context, we will write $av(i,j)$.

Definition 4. *Given a block sequence B, we define the score of a change point i to be*

$$q(i;B) = \ell(a_1,b_1) + \ell(a_2,b_2) - \ell(a,b), \tag{1}$$

where $(a_1,b_1) = B[1;i-1]$, $(a_2,b_2) = B[i;k]$, and $a = a_1 + a_2$ and $b = b_1 + b_2$.

Note that $\ell(a,b)$ is a constant but it is useful to keep since $q(i;B)$ is a log-likelihood ratio between two models, and this formulation allows us to estimate the objective in Sect. 5.

*Problem 3 (*CHANGEBLOCK*).* Given a block sequence B find a change point i that maximizes $q(i;B)$.

We can solve CHANGEINC by maintaining a block sequence induced by the border points, and solving CHANGEBLOCK. Naively, we can simply compute $q(i;B)$ for each index in $\mathcal{O}(|B|)$ time. If the distribution is static, then $|B|$ will be small in practice. However, if there is a concept drift, that is, there are more 1s in the sequence towards the end of sequence, then $|B|$ may increase significantly. Calders et al. [8] argued that when dealing with binary sequences of length n, the number of blocks $|B| \in \mathcal{O}(n^{2/3})$. In the following two sections we will show how to solve CHANGEBLOCK faster.

However, we also need to maintain the block sequence as new entries arrive. Luckily, there is an efficient update algorithm, see [8] for example. Assume that we have already observed n entries, and we have a block sequence of k blocks B induced by the border points. Assume a new entry s_{n+1}. We add $(k+1)$th block (u_{k+1}, v_{k+1}) to B, where $u_{k+1} = [s_{n+1} = 1]$ and $v_{k+1} = [s_{n+1} = 0]$. We then check whether $av(k+1, k+1) \leq av(k,k)$, that is, whether the average of the last block is smaller than or equal to the average of the second last block. If it is, then we merge the blocks and repeat the test. This algorithm maintains the border points correctly and runs in amortized $\mathcal{O}(1)$ time.

It is worth mentioning that the border indices are also connected to isotonic regression (see [16], for example). Namely, if one would fit isotonic regression to the sequence S, then the border points are the points where the fitted curve changes its value. In fact, the update algorithm corresponds to the pool adjacent violators (PAVA) algorithm, a method used to solve isotonic regression [16].

4   Finding Optimal Change Point for Fixed Parameters

In this section we show that if the model parameters are known and fixed, then we can find the optimal change point in logarithmic time.

First, let us extend the definition of $q(\cdot)$ to handle fixed parameters.

Definition 5. *Given a block sequence B, an index i, and two parameters p_1 and p_2, we define*

$$q(i; p_1, p_2, B) = \ell(a_1, b_1; p_1) + \ell(a_2, b_2; p_2) - \ell(a, b),$$

where $(a_1, b_1) = B[1; i-1]$, $(a_2, b_2) = B[i; k]$, and $a = a_1 + a_2$ and $b = b_1 + b_2$.

We can now define the optimization problem for fixed parameters.

Problem 4. Given a block sequence B, two parameters $0 \leq p_1 < p_2 \leq 1$, find i maximizing $q(i; p_1, p_2, B)$.

Let i^* be the solution for Problem 4. It turns out that we can construct a sequence of numbers, referred as d_j below, such that $d_j > 0$ if and only if $j < i^*$. This allows us to use binary search to find i^*.

Proposition 2. *Assume a block sequence $B = \langle (u_j, v_j) \rangle$ and two parameters $0 \leq p_1 < p_2 \leq 1$. Define*

$$d_j = \ell(u_j, v_j, p_1) - \ell(u_j, v_j, p_2).$$

Then there is an index i such that $d_j > 0$ if and only if $j < i$. Moreover, index i solves Problem 4.

Proof. Let us first show the existence of i. Let $t_j = u_j + v_j$, and write $X = \log p_1 - \log p_2$ and $Y = \log(1 - p_1) - \log(1 - p_2)$. Then

$$\frac{d_j}{t_j} = \frac{u_j}{t_j}X + \frac{v_j}{t_j}Y = \frac{u_j}{t_j}X + Y - \frac{u_j}{t_j}Y = \frac{u_j}{t_j}(X - Y) + Y.$$

Since B is a block sequence, the fraction u_j/t_j is increasing. Since $X < 0$ and $Y > 0$, we have $X - Y < 0$, so d_j/t_j is decreasing. Since d_j and d_j/t_j have the same sign, there is an index i satisfying the condition of the statement.

To prove the optimality of i, first note that

$$d_j = q(j + 1; p_1, p_2, B) - q(j; p_1, p_2, B).$$

Let i^* be a solution for Problem 4. If $i < i^*$. Then

$$q(i^*; p_1, p_2, B) - q(i; p_1, p_2, B) = \sum_{j=i}^{i^*-1} d_j \leq 0,$$

proving the optimality of i. The case for $i > i^*$ is similar. $\square$

Proposition 2 implies that we can use binary search to solve Problem 4 in $\mathcal{O}(\log |B|) \in \mathcal{O}(\log n)$ time. We refer to this algorithm as FINDSEGMENT(p_1, p_2, B).

5 Selecting Model Parameters

We have shown that if we know the optimal p_1 and p_2, then we can use binary search as described in the previous section to find the change point. Our main idea is to test several candidates for p_1 and p_2 such that one of the candidates will be close to the optimal parameters yielding an approximation guarantee.

Assume that we are given a block sequence B and select a change point i. Let $(a_1, b_1) = B[1; i-1]$, $(a_2, b_2) = B[i; k]$, $a = a_1 + a_2$, $b = b_1 + b_2$ be the counts. We can rewrite objective given in Eq. 1 as

$$
\begin{aligned}
q(i; B) &= \ell(a_1, b_1) + \ell(a_2, b_2) - \ell(a, b) \\
&= (\ell(a_1, b_1, p_1) - \ell(a_1, b_1, q)) + (\ell(a_2, b_2, p_2) - \ell(a_2, b_2, q)),
\end{aligned}
\tag{2}
$$

where the model parameters are $p_1 = a_1/(a_1 + b_1)$, $p_2 = a_2/(a_2 + b_2)$, and $q = a/(a + b)$.

The score as written in Eq. 2 is split in two parts, the first part depends on p_1 and the second part depends on p_2. We will first focus solely on estimating the second part. First, let us show how much we can vary p_2 while still maintaining a good log-likelihood ratio.

Proposition 3. *Assume $a, b > 0$, and let $p = a/(a + b)$. Assume $0 < q \le p$. Assume also $\epsilon > 0$. Define $h(x) = \ell(a, b; x) - \ell(a, b; q)$. Assume r such that*

$$
\log q + (1 - \epsilon)(\log p - \log q) \le \log r \le \log p.
\tag{3}
$$

Then $h(r) \ge (1 - \epsilon)h(p)$.

Proof. Define $f(u) = h(\exp u)$. We claim that f is concave. To prove the claim, note that the derivative of f is equal to

$$
f'(u) = a - b\frac{\exp u}{1 - \exp u}.
$$

Hence, f' is decreasing for $u < 0$, which proves the concavity of f.

Define $c = \frac{\log r - \log q}{\log p - \log q}$. Equation 3 implies that $1 - \epsilon \le c$. The concavity of $f(u)$ and the fact that $h(q) = 0$ imply that

$$
h(r) = f(\log r) \ge f(\log q) + c\,[f(\log p) - f(\log q)] = ch(p) \ge (1 - \epsilon)h(p),
$$

which proves the proposition.   □

We can use the proposition in the following manner. Assume a block sequence B with k entries. Let i^* be the optimal change point and p_1^* and p_2^* be the corresponding optimal parameters. First, let

$$
P = \{av(i, k) \mid i = 1, \ldots, k\}
$$

be the set of candidate model parameters. We know that the optimal model parameter $p_2^* \in P$. Instead of testing every $p \in P$, we will construct an index set C, and define $R = \{av(i,k) \mid i \in C\}$, such that for each $p \in P$ there is $r \in R$ such that Eq. 3 holds. Proposition 3 states that testing the parameters in R yields a $(1 - \epsilon)$ approximation of the second part of the right-hand side in Eq. 2.

We wish to keep the set C small, so to generate C, we will start with $i = 1$ and set $C = \{i\}$. We then look how many values of P we can estimate with $av(i,k)$, that is, we look for the smallest index for which Eq. 3 does not hold. We set this index to i, add it to C, and repeat the process. We will refer to this procedure as FINDCANDS(B, ϵ). The detailed pseudo-code for FINDCANDS is given in Algorithm 1.

Algorithm 1: FINDCANDS(B, ϵ), given a block sequence B of k entries and an estimation requirement $\epsilon > 0$, constructs a candidate index set C that is used to estimate the model parameter p_2.

---

1 $C \leftarrow \{1\}$; $i \leftarrow 1$; $q \leftarrow av(1,k)$;
2 **while** $i < k$ **do**
3 $\quad$ $\rho \leftarrow (\log av(i,k) - \log q)/(1 - \epsilon)$;
4 $\quad$ $i \leftarrow$ smallest index j s.t. $\log av(j,k) - \log q > \rho$, or k if j does not exist;
5 $\quad$ add i to C;
6 **return** C;

Proposition 4. *Assume a block sequence B with k entries, and let $\epsilon > 0$. Set $P = \{av(i,k) \mid i = 1, \ldots, k\}$. Let $C = $ FINDCANDS(B, ϵ), and let $R = \{av(i,k) \mid i \in C\}$. Then for each $p \in P$ there is $r \in R$ such that Eq. 3 holds.*

Proof. Let $p \in P \setminus R$. This is only possible if there is a smaller value $r \in R$ such that $(1 - \epsilon)(\log p - \log q) < \log r - \log q$ holds. $\qquad \square$

Finding the next index i in FINDCANDS can be done with a binary search in $\mathcal{O}(\log |B|)$ time. Thus, FINDCANDS runs in $\mathcal{O}(|C| \log n)$ time. Next result shows that $|C| \in \mathcal{O}(\epsilon^{-1} \log n)$, which brings the computational complexity of FINDCANDS to $\mathcal{O}(\epsilon^{-1} \log^2 n)$.

Proposition 5. *Assume a block sequence B with k entries generated from a binary sequence S with n entries, and let $\epsilon > 0$. Let $P = \{av(i,k) \mid i = 1, \ldots, k\}$. Assume an increasing sequence $R = (r_i) \subseteq P$. Let $q = av(1,k)$. If*

$$\log q + (1 - \epsilon)(\log r_i - \log q) > \log r_{i-1}, \tag{4}$$

then $|R| \in \mathcal{O}\left(\frac{\log n}{\epsilon}\right)$.

Proof. We can rewrite Eq. 4 as $(1 - \epsilon)(\log r_i - \log q) > \log r_{i-1} - \log q$ which automatically implies that

$$(1 - \epsilon)^i (\log r_{i+2} - \log q) > \log r_2 - \log q.$$

To lower-bound the right-hand side, let us write $r_2 = x/y$ and $q = u/v$, where x, y, u, and v are integers with $y, v \leq n$. Note that $r_2 > q$, otherwise we violate Eq. 4 when $i = 2$. Hence, we have $xv \geq uy + 1$. Then

$$\log r_2 - \log q = \log xv - \log uy \geq \log(uy + 1) - \log uy = \log(1 + \frac{1}{uy})$$

$$\geq \log(1 + \frac{1}{n^2}) \geq \frac{n^{-2}}{1 + n^{-2}} = \frac{1}{1 + n^2}.$$

We can also upper-bound the left-hand side with

$$\log r_{i+2} - \log q \leq \log 1 - \log u/v = \log v/u \leq \log n.$$

Combining the three previous inequalities leads to

$$\log n \geq \log r_{i+2} - \log q > \frac{\log r_2 - \log q}{(1 - \epsilon)^i} \geq \frac{1}{(1 - \epsilon)^i} \frac{1}{1 + n^2}.$$

Solving for i,

$$i \leq \frac{\log(1 + n^2) + \log\log n}{\log \frac{1}{1-\epsilon}} \leq \frac{\log(1 + n^2) + \log\log n}{\epsilon} \in \mathcal{O}\left(\frac{\log n}{\epsilon}\right),$$

completes the proof.   □

We can now approximate p_2^*. Our next step is to show how to find similar value for p_1^*. Note that we cannot use the previous results immediately because we assumed that $p \geq q$ in Proposition 3. However, we can fix this by simply switching the labels in S.

Proposition 6. *Assume $a, b > 0$, and let $p = a/(a+b)$. Assume q with $0 < p \leq q$. Assume also $\epsilon > 0$. Define $h(x) = \ell(a, b; x) - \ell(a, b; q)$. Assume r such that*

$$\log(1 - q) + (1 - \epsilon)(\log(1 - p) - \log(1 - q)) \leq \log(1 - r) \leq \log(1 - p). \quad (5)$$

Then $h(r) \geq (1 - \epsilon)h(p)$.

Proof. Set $a' = b$, $b' = a$, $q' = 1 - q$, and $r' = 1 - r$. The proposition follows immediately from Proposition 3 when applied to these variables.   □

Proposition 6 leads to an algorithm, similar to FINDCANDS, for generating candidates for p_1^*. We refer to this algorithm as FINDCANDS$'$, see Algorithm 2.

Assume that we have computed two sets of candidate indices C_1 and C_2; the first set is meant to be used to estimate p_1^*, while the second set is meant to be used to estimate p_2^*. The final step is to determine what combinations of parameters should we check. A naive approach would be to test every possible combination. This leads to $\mathcal{O}(|C_1||C_2|)$ tests.

However, since p_1^* and p_2^* are induced by the same change point i^*, we can design a more efficient approach that leads to only $\mathcal{O}(|C_1| + |C_2|)$ tests.

Algorithm 2: FINDCANDS$'(B, \epsilon)$, given a block sequence B of k entries and an estimation requirement $\epsilon > 0$, constructs a candidate index set C that is used to estimate the model parameter p_1.

---

1 $C \leftarrow \{k\}$; $i \leftarrow k$; $q \leftarrow av(1, k)$;
2 **while** $i > 1$ **do**
3 $\quad$ $\rho \leftarrow (\log(1 - av(1, i-1)) - \log(1 - q))/(1 - \epsilon)$;
4 $\quad$ $i \leftarrow$ largest index j s.t. $\log(1 - av(1, j-1)) - \log(1 - q) > \rho$, or 1 if j does not exist;
5 $\quad$ add i to C;
6 **return** C;

In order to do so, first we combine both candidate sets, $C = C_1 \cup C_2$. For each index $c_i \in C$, we compute the score $q(c_i; B)$. Also, if there are blocks between c_{i-1} and c_i that are not included in C, that is, $c_{i-1} + 1 < c_i$, we set $p_1 = av(1, c_i - 1)$ and $p_2 = av(c_{i-1}, k)$, compute the optimal change point $j = $ FINDSEGMENT(p_1, p_2, B), and test $q(j, B)$. When all tests are done, we return the index that yielded the best score. We refer to this algorithm as FINDCHANGE(B, ϵ), and present the pseudo-code in Algorithm 3.

Proposition 7. FINDCHANGE(B, ϵ) *yields* $(1 - \epsilon)$ *approximation guarantee.*

Proof. Let i^* be the optimal value with the corresponding parameters p_1^* and p_2^*. Let C_1, C_2 and C be the sets as defined in Algorithm 3. If $i^* \in C$, then we are done. Assume that $i^* \notin C$. Then there are $c_{j-1} < i^* < c_j$, since $1, k \in C$. Let $r_2 = av(c_{j-1}, k)$. Then r_2 and p_2^* satisfy Eq. 3 by definition of C_2. Let $r_1 = av(1, c_j - 1)$. Then r_1 and p_1^* satisfy Eq. 5 by definition of C_1. Let i be the optimal change point for r_1 and r_2, that is, $i = $ FINDSEGMENT(r_1, r_2, B).

Propositions 3 and 6 together with Eq. 2 imply that

$$q(i; B) \geq q(i; r_1, r_2, B) \geq q(i^*; r_1, r_2, B) \geq (1 - \epsilon)q(i^*; B).$$

This completes the proof. $\qquad\qquad\qquad\qquad\qquad\qquad\qquad\qquad\qquad\qquad$ □

We complete this section with computational complexity analysis. The two calls of FINDCANDS require $\mathcal{O}(\epsilon^{-1} \log^2 n)$ time. The list C has $\mathcal{O}(\epsilon^{-1} \log n)$ entries, and a single call of FINDSEGMENT for each $c \in C$ requires $\mathcal{O}(\log n)$ time. Consequently, the running time for FINDCHANGE is $\mathcal{O}(\epsilon^{-1} \log^2 n)$.

6   Related Work

Many techniques have been proposed for change detection in a stream setting. We will highlight some of these techniques. For a fuller picture, we refer the reader to a survey by Aminikhanghahi and Cook [2], and a book by Basseville and Nikiforov [5].

Algorithm 3: FINDCHANGE(B, ϵ), yields $(1 - \epsilon)$ approximation guarantee for CHANGEBLOCK.

---

1 $C_2 \leftarrow$ FINDCANDS(B, ϵ);
2 $C_1 \leftarrow$ FINDCANDS$'(B, \epsilon)$;
3 $C \leftarrow C_1 \cup C_2$;
4 **foreach** $c_j \in C$ **do**
5   test $q(c_j; B)$;
6   **if** $c_{j-1} + 1 < c_j$ **then**
7 $r_1 \leftarrow av(1, c_j - 1)$;
8 $r_2 \leftarrow av(c_{j-1}, k)$;
9 $i \leftarrow$ FINDSEGMENT(r_1, r_2, B);
10   test $q(i; B)$;
11   **return** index i^* having the best score $q(i; B)$ among the tested indices;

A standard approach for change point detection is to split the stored data in two segments, and compare the two segments; if the segments are different, then a change has happened. Bifet and Gavalda [7] proposed an adaptive sliding window approach: if the current window contains a split such that the averages of the two portions are different enough, then the older portion is dropped from the window. Nishida and Yamauchi [17] compared the accuracy of recent samples against the overall accuracy using a statistical test. Kifer et al. [15] proposed a family of distances between distributions and analyzed them in the context of change point detection. Instead of modeling segments explicitly, Kawahara and Sugiyama [14] proposed estimating density ratio directly. Dries and Rückert [9] studied transformations a multivariate stream into a univariate stream to aid change point detection. Harel et al. [13] detected change by comparing the loss in a test segment against a similar loss in a permuted sequence.

Instead of explicitly modeling the change point, Ross et al. [18] used exponential decay to compare the performance of recent samples against the overall performance. Baena-Garcia et al. [10], Gama et al. [4] proposed a detecting change by comparing current average and standard deviation against the smallest observed average and standard deviation. Also avoiding an explicit split, a Bayesian approach for modeling the time since last change point was proposed by Adams and MacKay [1].

An offline version of change point detection is called *segmentation*. Here we are given a sequence of entries and a budget k. The goal is divide a sequence into k minimizing some cost function. If the global objective is a sum of individual segment costs, then the problem can be solved with a classic dynamic program approach [6] in $\mathcal{O}(n^2 k)$ time. As this may be too slow speed-up techniques yielding approximation guarantees have been proposed [11, 20, 21]. If the cost function is based on one-parameter log-linear models, it is possible to speed-up the segmentation problem significantly in practice [19], even though the worst-case running time remains $\mathcal{O}(n^2 k)$. Guha and Shim [12] showed that if the objective is the maximum of the individual segment costs, then we can compute the exact solution using only $\mathcal{O}(k^2 \log^2 n)$ evaluations of the individual segment costs.

7   Experimental Evaluation

For our experiments, we focus on analyzing the effect of the approximation guarantee ϵ, as well as the parameter τ.[1,2] Here we will use synthetic sequences. In addition, we present a small case study using network traffic data.

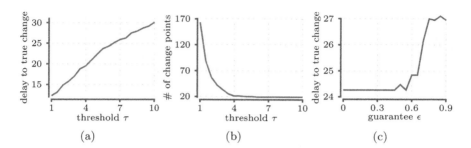

(a)   (b)   (c)

Fig. 1. Change point detection statistics as a function of threshold parameter τ and approximation guarantee ϵ *Step* data: (a) average delay for discovering a true change point ($\epsilon = 0$), (b) number of discovered change points ($\epsilon = 0$), and (c) average delay for discovering a true change point ($\tau = 6$). Note that in *Step* there are 19 true change points. For $\tau = 0.5$, the algorithm had average delay of 1.42 to a true change point but reported 46 366 change points (these values are omitted due to scaling issues).

Synthetic Sequences: We generated 3 synthetic sequences, each of length 200 000. For simplicity we will write $Bern(p)$ to mean a bernoulli random variable with probability of 1 being p. The first sequence, named *Ind*, consists of 200 000 samples from $Bern(1/2)$, that is, fair coin flips. The second sequence, named *Step*, consists of 10 000 samples from $Bern(1/4)$ followed by 10 000 samples from $Bern(3/4)$, repeated 10 times. The third sequence, named *Slope*, includes 10 segments, each segment consists of 10 000 samples from $Bern(p)$, where p increases linearly from $1/4$ to $3/4$, followed by 10 000 samples from $Bern(p)$, where p decreases linearly from $3/4$ to $1/4$. In addition, we generated 10 sequences, collectively named *Hill*. The length of the sequences varies from 100 000 to 1 000 000 with increments of 100 000. Each sequence consists of samples from $Bern(p)$, where p increases linearly from $1/4$ to $3/4$.

Results: We start by studying the effect of the threshold parameter τ. Here, we used *Step* sequence; this sequence has 19 true change points. In Fig. 1a, we show the average delay of discovering the true change point, that is, how many entries are needed, on average, before a change is discovered after each true change. In Fig. 1b, we also show how many change points we discovered: ideally we should find only 19 points. In both experiments we set $\epsilon = 0$. We see from the results

---

[1] Recall that we say that change occurs if it is larger than $\sigma = \tau + \log n$.
[2] The implementation is available at https://version.helsinki.fi/dacs/.

674   N. Tatti

that the delay grows linearly with τ, whereas the number of false change points is significant for small values of τ but drop quickly as τ grows. For $\tau = 6$ we detected the ideal 19 change points. We will use this value for the rest of the experiments.

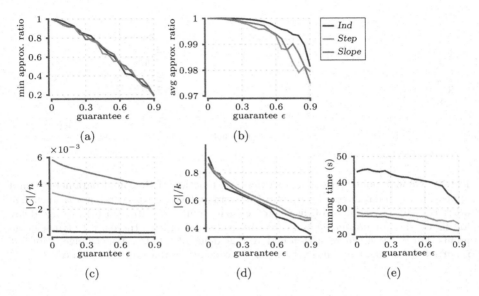

Fig. 2. Performance metrics as a function of approximation guarantee ϵ on synthetic data. Y-axes are as follows: (a) minimum of ratio $\text{FINDCHANGE}(B, \epsilon)/OPT$, (b) average of ratio $\text{FINDCHANGE}(B, \epsilon)/OPT$, (c) number of candidates tested/window size (note that y-axis is scaled), (d) number of candidates tested/number of blocks, and (e) running time in seconds.

Our next step is to study the quality of the results as a function of ϵ on synthetic data. Here we measure the ratio of the scores $g = \text{FINDCHANGE}(B, \epsilon)$ and $OPT = \text{FINDCHANGE}(B, 1)$, that is, the score of the solution to CHANGE. Note we include all tests, not just the ones that resulted in declaring a change. Figure 2a shows the smallest ratio that we encountered as a function of ϵ, and Fig. 2b shows the average ratio as a function of ϵ. We see in Fig. 2a that the worst case behaves linearly as a function of ϵ. As guaranteed by Proposition 7, the worst case ratio stays above $(1 - \epsilon)$. While the worst-case is relatively close to its theoretical boundary, the average case, shown in Fig. 2b, performs significantly better with average ratio being above 0.97 even for $\epsilon = 0.9$. The effect of ϵ on the actual change point detection is demonstrated in Fig. 1c. Since, we may miss the optimal value, the detector becomes more conservative, which increases the delay for discovering true change. However, the increase is moderate (only about 10%) even for $\epsilon = 0.9$.

Our next step is to study speed-up in running time. Figure 2c shows the number of tests performed compared to n, the number of entries from the last change point as a function of ϵ. We see from the results that there is significant speed-up when compared to the naive $\mathcal{O}(n)$ approach; the number of needed tests is reduced by 2–3 orders of magnitude. The main reason for this reduction is due to the border points. Reduction due to using FINDCANDS is shown in Fig. 2d. Here we see that the number of candidates reduces linearly as a function of ϵ, reducing the number of candidates roughly by $1/2$ for the larger values of ϵ. The running times (in seconds) are given in Fig. 2e. As expected, the running times are decreasing as a function of ϵ.

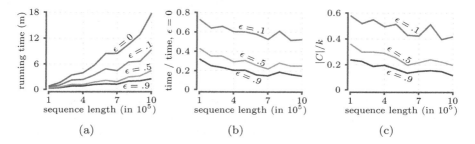

Fig. 3. Computational metrics as a function of sequence length for *Hill* sequences: (a) running time in minutes, (b) running time/running time for $\epsilon = 0$, and (c) number of candidates tested/number of blocks. Note that $\epsilon = 0$ is equivalent of testing every border index.

While the main reason for speed-up comes from using border indices, there are scenarios where using FINDCANDS becomes significant. This happens when the number of border indices increases. We illustrate this effect with *Hill* sequences, shown in Fig. 3. Here, for the sake of illustration, we increased the threshold τ for change point detection so that at no point we detect change. Having many entries with slowly increasing probability of 1 yields many border points, which is seen as a fast increase in running time for $\epsilon = 0$. Moreover, the ratio of candidates tested by FINDCANDS against the number of blocks, as well as the running time, decreases as the sequence increases in size.

Use Case with Traffic Data: We applied our change detection algorithm on traffic data, *network2*, collected by Amit et al. [3]. This data contains observed connections between many hosts over several weeks, grouped in 10 min periods. We only used data collected during 24.12–29.12 as the surrounding time periods contain a strong hourly artifact. We then transformed the collected data into a binary sequence by setting 1 if the connection was related to SSL, and 0 otherwise. The sequence contains 282 754 entries grouped in 743 periods of 10 min. Our algorithm ($\epsilon = 0$, $\tau = 6$) found 12 change points, shown in Fig. 4.

These patterns show short bursts of non-SSL connections. One exception is the change after the index 300, where the previously high SSL activity is resolved to a normal behavior.

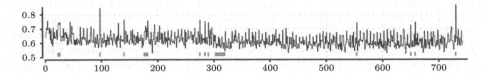

Fig. 4. Proportion of non-SSL connections in *Network2* traffic data over time, in 10 min periods. The bars indicate the change points: the end of the bar indicates when change was discovered and the beginning of the bar indicate the optimal split.

8   Conclusions

In this paper we presented a change point detection approach for binary streams based on finding a split in a current window optimizing a likelihood ratio. Finding the optimal split needs $\mathcal{O}(n)$ time, so in order for this approach to be practical, we introduced an approximation scheme that yields $(1 - \epsilon)$ approximation in $\mathcal{O}(\epsilon^{-1} \log^2 n)$. The scheme is implemented by using border points, an idea adopted from segmentation of log-linear models, and then further reducing the candidates by ignoring indices that border similar blocks.

Most of the time the number of borders will be small, and the additional pruning is only required when the number of borders start to increase. This suggests that a hybrid approach is sensible: we will iterate over borders if there are only few of them, and switch to approximation technique only when the number of borders increase.

We should point that even though the running time is poly-logarithmic, the space requirement is at worst $\mathcal{O}(n^{2/3})$. This can be rectified by simply removing older border points but such removal may lead to a suboptimal answer. An interesting direction for a future work is to study how to reduce the space complexity without sacrificing the approximation guarantee.

In this paper, we focused only on binary streams. Same concept has the potential to work also on other type of data types, such as integers or real-values. The bottleneck here is Proposition 5 as it relies on the fact that the underlying stream is binary. We will leave adopting these results to other data types as a future work.

References

1. Adams, R.P., MacKay, D.J.: Bayesian online changepoint detection. Technical report, University of Cambridge, Cambridge, UK (2007)

2. Aminikhanghahi, S., Cook, D.J.: A survey of methods for time series change point detection. Knowl. Inf. Syst. **51**(2), 339–367 (2016). https://doi.org/10.1007/s10115-016-0987-z

3. Amit, I., Matherly, J., Hewlett, W., Xu, Z., Meshi, Y., Weinberger, Y.: Machine learning in cyber-security—problems, challenges and data sets. In: The AAAI-19 Workshop on Engineering Dependable and Secure Machine Learning Systems (2019)

4. Baena-Garcia, M., Campo-Avila, J.D., Fidalgo, R., Bifet, A., Gavalda, R., Morales-Bueno, R.: Early drift detection method. In: 4th International Workshop on Knowledge Discovery from Data Streams (2006)

5. Basseville, M., Nikiforov, I.V.: Detection of Abrupt Changes – Theory and Application. Prentice-Hall, Upper Saddle River (1993)

6. Bellman, R.: On the approximation of curves by line segments using dynamic programming. Commun. ACM **4**(6), 284–284 (1961)

7. Bifet, A., Gavalda, R.: Learning from time-changing data with adaptive windowing. In: SIAM International Conference on Data Mining, pp. 443–448 (2007)

8. Calders, T., Dexters, N., Goethals, B.: Mining frequent items in a stream using flexible windows. Intell. Data Anal. **12**(3), 293–304 (2008)

9. Dries, A., Rückert, U.: Adaptive concept drift detection. Stat. Anal. Data Min. **2**(5–6), 311–327 (2009)

10. Gama, J., Medas, P., Castillo, G., Rodrigues, P.: Learning with drift detection. In: SBIA Brazilian Symposium on Artificial Intelligence, pp. 286–295 (2004)

11. Guha, S., Koudas, N., Shim, K.: Approximation and streaming algorithms for histogram construction problems. ACM Trans. Database Syst. **31**(1), 396–438 (2006)

12. Guha, S., Shim, K.: A note on linear time algorithms for maximum error histograms. IEEE Trans. Knowl. Data Eng. **19**(7), 993–997 (2007)

13. Harel, M., Mannor, S., El-Yaniv, R., Crammer, K.: Concept drift detection through resampling. In: Proceedings of of the 31st International Conference on Machine Learning, ICML, pp. 1009–1017 (2014)

14. Kawahara, Y., Sugiyama, M.: Sequential change-point detection based on direct density-ratio estimation. Stat. Anal. Data Min. **5**, 114–127 (2012)

15. Kifer, D., Ben-David, S., Gehrke, J.: Detecting change in data streams. In: Proceedings of the 13th International Conference on Very Large Data Bases, VLDB, pp. 180–191 (2004)

16. de Leeuw, J., Hornik, K., Mair, P.: Isotone optimization in R: pool-adjacent-violators algorithm (PAVA) and active set methods. J. Stat. Softw. **32**(5), 1–24 (2009)

17. Nishida, K., Yamauchi, K.: Detecting concept drift using statistical testing. In: Proceedings of the 10th International Conference on Discovery Science, pp. 264–269 (2007)

18. Ross, G.J., Adams, N.M., Tasoulis, D.K., Hand, D.J.: Exponentially weighted moving average charts for detecting concept drift. Pattern Recogn. Lett. **33**(2), 191–198 (2012)

19. Tatti, N.: Fast sequence segmentation using log-linear models. Data Min. Knowl. Disc. **27**(3), 421–441 (2013)

20. Tatti, N.: Strongly polynomial efficient approximation scheme for segmentation. Inf. Process. Lett. **142**, 1–8 (2019). https://doi.org/10.1016/j.ipl.2018.09.007

21. Terzi, E., Tsaparas, P.: Efficient algorithms for sequence segmentation. In: Proceedings of the 6th SIAM International Conference on Data Mining (SDM), pp. 316–327 (2006)

A Drift-Based Dynamic Ensemble Members Selection Using Clustering for Time Series Forecasting

Amal Saadallah[✉], Florian Priebe, and Katharina Morik

Artificial Intelligence Group, Department of Computer Science, TU Dortmund,
Dortmund, Germany
{amal.saadallah,florian.priebe,katharina.morik}@tu-dortmund.de

Abstract. Both complex and evolving nature of time series structure
make forecasting among one of the most important and challenging tasks
in time series analysis. Typical methods for forecasting are designed to
model time-evolving dependencies between data observations. However,
it is generally accepted that none of them is universally valid for every
application. Therefore, methods for learning heterogeneous ensembles by
combining a diverse set of forecasts together appear as a promising solution to tackle this task. Hitherto, in classical ML literature, ensemble
techniques such as stacking, cascading and voting are mostly restricted
to operate in a static manner. To deal with changes in the relative performance of models as well as changes in the data distribution, we propose
a drift-aware meta-learning approach for adaptively selecting and combining forecasting models. Our assumption is that different forecasting
models have different areas of expertise and a varying relative performance. Our method ensures dynamic selection of initial ensemble base
models candidates through a performance drift detection mechanism.
Since diversity is a fundamental component in ensemble methods, we
propose a second stage selection with clustering that is computed after
each drift detection. Predictions of final selected models are combined
into a single prediction. An exhaustive empirical testing of the method
was performed, evaluating both generalization error and scalability of
the approach using time series from several real world domains. Empirical results show the competitiveness of the method in comparison to
state-of-the-art approaches for combining forecasters.

Keywords: Model clustering · Dynamic ensemble · Meta-learning ·
Drift-detection

1 Introduction

Time series forecasting is one of the most challenging tasks in time series analysis
due to the dynamic behavior of this data type, which may involve non-stationary
and complex processes [6,18,28]. Forecasting has considerably attracted the

© Springer Nature Switzerland AG 2020
U. Brefeld et al. (Eds.): ECML PKDD 2019, LNAI 11906, pp. 678–694, 2020.
https://doi.org/10.1007/978-3-030-46150-8_40

attention of both academic and industrial communities and has always been one of the principal steps in real-time decision-making and planning across various applications such as traffic prediction, weather forecasts, stock market prices prediction [18].

Several machine learning methods have been successfully applied to time series forecasting either by dealing with the data as an ordered sequence of observation in an offline or a streaming fashion, or by using an embedding of the time series to reformulate the forecasting task as a regression task [6]. However, it is generally accepted that none of the ML methods is universally valid for every task, in particular for forecasting. Therefore, one reasonable solution is to combine the opinion of a diverse set of models using an ensemble method. Ensembles consist of a collection of several models (i.e., experts) that are combined together to address the same defined task [22]. Ensemble construction can be divided into three main stages: (i) base model generation, where n multiple possible hypotheses are formulated to model a given phenomenon; (ii) model pruning, where only a subset of $m < n$ hypotheses is kept and (iii) model integration, where these hypotheses are combined together in one single model.

Most of the existing methods for ensemble learning on time series are focusing on optimizing the last stage [6,22,28]. Combination strategies can be grouped into three main families [30]. The first family relies on voting approaches using majority or (weighted) average votes to decide for the final output (e.g. bagging [3]). The second main family englobes methods relying on cascading strategy, where base models outputs are iteratively included once at a time, as new features in the training set. The third group is based on the stacking paradigm [33]. Using stacking, most often a meta-learning approach is employed to combine the available forecasts. This method implicitly learns an adequate combination by modelling inter-dependencies between models.

Another key point in learning ensemble for time series data is to be able to cope the time-evolving nature of data. This can be achieved by building dynamic ensemble selection frameworks through adaptive ensemble constructions on different levels (i.e. base models selection, base models/ensemble parameters adaption, blind/informed retraining).

In this paper, we propose a dynamic ensemble selection framework that operates on two main ensemble construction stages: pruning and integration. Given a pool of candidate base models, the first stage of the framework is motivated by the fact that due to the time-evolving nature of the data structure, base models performance changes over time. This performance is also subject to concept-drifts, when considering the relation between the output predictions of base models and the target time series. A drift detection mechanism is employed to exclude models whose performance becomes significantly poor compared to the remaining models and to identify the top base models in terms of performance. Performance is assessed in this context using a custom measure based on the Pearson's correlation (i.e. commonly used to deal with time series data [27]) between base models forecasts and the target time series on a sliding window validation set. After each drift detection, the top base models are identified.

Since diversity is a fundamental component in ensemble methods [4], we propose a second stage selection through clustering model outputs. Clusters and top base models are updated after each drift detection. At each cluster computation, the models that belong to the cluster representatives are selected. Finally, the outputs of the selected models are combined together using a voting strategy based on a sliding-window weighted average. Our framework is denoted in the rest of the paper, **DEMSC**: Drift-based Ensemble Member Selection using Clustering. DEMSC is illustrated in Fig. 1.

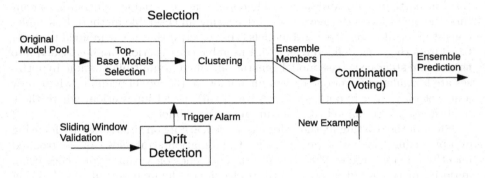

Fig. 1. Components of our method DEMSC

We validate our framework using 16-real world time series data sets. Different variations of our method have been carried out to assess the impact of each stage (i.e. component) by changing the clustering method or the combination rules (i.e. for example, using stacking nstead of voting). Empirical results suggest that our method outperforms traditional state-of-art methods for ensemble learning and other metalearning approaches such as stacking [33] and bagging [3] and is competitive with adaptive approaches for dynamic ensemble selection [6]. We note that all experiments are fully reproducible. Both code and datasets are publicly available in this repository.[1]

The main contributions of this paper are as follows:

- A drift-based dynamic selection ensemble framework is introduced. Opposingly to existing dynamic ensemble selection methods which rely on continuous updates (i.e. blindly at each time instant or periodically), our selection is automatically and adaptively performed in an **informed manner** based on models performance drift detection mechanism.
- An online clustering approach in combination with a pre-selection is applied for model selection. The model selection is triggered by the drift detection mechanism.
- The framework is devised to work in an automated fashion, in the sense that a sliding-window validation set is used for the drift inspection. The data from

---

[1] https://github.com/AmalSd/DEMSC.

the validation set is used as input for the clustering. The clustering method also optimizes the number of clusters.

– A comparative empirical study with S.o.A ensemble methods and different variations of our framework, including a discussion about their implications in terms of predictive performance and computational resources, is conducted.

In the remainder of this paper, we describe the proposed approach, after discussing related work. Then, we present an exhaustive experimental evaluation of its efficiency and scalability. Finally, the last section concludes the paper.

2   Related Works

Ensembles for time series forecasting have always attracted the attention of the machine learning community [18,26]. More precisely, methods for dynamically combining models outputs, using both windowing strategies [26,28] and metalearning approaches [6,7] have particularly intrigued the interest of the community over the last few years. In this section, we briefly describe the state-of-the-art methods within these approaches. We list their characteristics and limitations and we highlight our contributions.

Combination in an ensemble can be made using the average of the available base models' outputs. This was commonly applied not only in forecasting [8], but also in regression [22]. Simple averages can be enhanced by the use of model selection before aggregation, this approach is known as trimmed means [21]. To deal with time-evolving data, one of the most successful approaches is to compute weighted averages over a time-sliding window, by setting up the weights to be proportional to some performance measures [26,28]. A forgetting mechanism can be employed to the time window to increase the impact of recent observations (i.e most recent performance of the predictive models).

Our method uses the weighted sliding-window average for the combination of the base models' predictions to produce the final forecast value. However, we have tested different variations of our method by replacing this combination strategy with metalearning. More details are provided in Sect. 3.

Metalearning as a way for modeling the learning process of a learning algorithm, can be exploited in both pruning and combination stages. Most of existing works followed this approach to learn models combination (i.e. integration) rules given the set of model forecasts [15,30,33].

Furthermore, combination can be performed dynamically so that its rules are changing over time. A popular approach for dynamically combining experts is to apply multiple regression on the output of the experts. For example, Gaillard and Goude [15] use Ridge regression to adaptively estimate the weights that are assigned to the base-learners. Another recent approach which has successfully exploited metalearning based on arbitrating [6], which was originally introduced for the combination of classifiers. Arbitrated Dynamic Ensemble (ADE) [7] uses meta-learning for estimating each candidates errors and selects members based on the estimated errors. ADE uses Random Forest as meta-learner. For each candidate, a separate meta-model is trained. The selected members are combined with a convex combination. Each candidate weight is based on the estimated errors combined with a softmax. The weights are additionally adapted to take diversity between ensemble members into account.

Our framework exploits metalearning in the pruning stage where a dynamic clustering of base models is performed. Only the cluster representatives are selected to take part in the integration phase. The idea of model clustering was introduced in [28] to cluster a pool of base models into main families to enhance diversity. However, in [28] the clustering was performed offline and kept static in the online phase. Only cluster representatives changed over time in [28]. Oppositely, in our framework, model clusters are recomputed each time dependencies between base models and the target series change significantly in the current sliding-window validation set. This **informed** ability is a key point in our method and to the best of our knowledge this is the first approach to perform dynamic ensemble selection adaptively following a drift in models performance detection mechanism. Oppositely, most of existing methods for dynamic selection keep the learned meta-model static (i.e. no meta-learner retraining is performed) in the testing phase and only few works state the advantage of performing periodic retraining in a blind manner [7] (i.e. just setting up a fixed period for the meta-learner retraining).

3   Methodology

This Section introduces **DEMSC** and its three basic components: (i) First, we describe the drift-based pre-selection step to get the top base models in terms of performance; (ii) The second stage consists of first clustering the top base models and select one representative model for each cluster; (iii) Finally, each selected model's output is combined in a weighted average where the weights are inversely proportional to the model recent loss.

3.1   Problem Formulation

A time series X is a temporal sequence of values $X = \{x_1, x_2, \cdots, x_t\}$, where x_i is the value of X at time i. Typical solution for time series forecasting include traditional univariate time series analysis models, such as the popular Box-Jenkins ARIMA family of methods [2] or exponential smoothing methods [20]. Typical regression models can be applied in the context of forecasting by using a time delay embedding which maps a set of target observations to a K-dimensional feature space corresponding to the K past lagged values of each observation [6].

Denote with $P_M = \{M_1, M_2, \cdots, M_N\}$ the pool of trained base forecasting models. Let $\hat{x} = (\hat{x}_{M_1}, \hat{x}_{M_2}, \cdots, \hat{x}_{M_N})$ be the vector of forecast values of X at time instant $t + 1$ (i.e. x_{t+1}) by each of the base model in P_M. The goal of the dynamic selection is identifying which $\hat{x}_{M_i}$ values should be integrated in the weighted average.

To do so, a two-staged selection procedure is devised. The first stage is a pre-selection stage which aims to keep only accurate model forecasts using a model performance drift detection. This stage discards models with poor performance whose forecasts inclusion in the ensemble would deteriorate the forecasting accuracy. This deterioration is more perceptible using simple average for integration and can be covered to some extent using a weighting strategy. The second stage aims to enhance diversity aspect with the use of clustering.

3.2   A Drift-Based Model Pre-selection

The drift-based time series selection was first applied in [28] in the context of spatio-temporal features selection to be the input of a multivariate autoregressive model. Similarly, we can treat the set of base models forecasts as a set of explanatory variables or causes to our target time series. To do so, dependencies between the set of base model forecasts and target time series can be continuously computed and monitored over a sliding-window validation set. Suppose we want to compute the prediction for time instant $t + 1$, the validation sliding-window of size W over X is defined by the sequence $X_{W,t} = \{x_{t-W+1}, x_{t-W+2}, \cdots, x_t\}$. Let $\hat{X}_{W,t}^{M_i} = \{\hat{x}_{t-W+1}^{M_i}, \hat{x}_{t-W+2}^{M_i}, \cdots, \hat{x}_t^{M_i}\}$ be the predicted sequence of values by the model M_i on $X_{W,t}$, where $M_i \in P_M$.

A subset K of highly correlated models with the target, denoted "top-base" models, are selected using a sliding-window similarity measure computed on $X_{W,t}$. K is a user-defined hyperparameter. Hereby, we propose to use a custom measure based on the Pearson's correlation - commonly used to deal with time series data [27]-denoted as SRC - Scaled Root Correlation and defined as:

$$corr(\hat{X}_{W,t}^{M_i}, X_{W,t}) = \frac{\tau - \frac{\sum_{j=1}^{W} \hat{x}_{t-W+j}^{M_i} \sum_{j=1}^{W} x_{t-W+j}}{W}}{\sqrt{\sum_{j=1}^{W} (\hat{x}_{t-W+j}^{M_i})^2 - \frac{(\sum_{j=1}^{W} \hat{x}_{t-W+j}^{M_i})^2}{W}} \sqrt{\sum_{j=1}^{W} (x_{t-W+j})^2 - \frac{(\sum_{j=1}^{W} x_{t-W+j})^2}{W}}} \tag{1}$$

$$SRC(\hat{X}_{W,t}^{M_i}, X_{W,t}) = \sqrt{\frac{1 - corr(\hat{X}_W^{M_i}, X_W)}{2}} \in [0, 1] \tag{2}$$

where $\tau = \sum_{j=1}^{W} \hat{x}_{t-W+j}^{M_i} x_{t-W+j}$. Naturally, with time-evolving data, dependencies change over time and follow non-stationary concepts. Stationarity in this context can be formulated as follow:

Definition 1 (Weak stationary Dependencies). *Let $C_t \in \mathbb{R}^{N \times N}$ be a resulting symmetric similarity matrix between the base models and the target time series over W (i.e. derived from the above similarity metric), where $N = |P_M|$ and c_t be a vector containing all the elements in C_t where $c_{j,t} \geq c_{j-1,t}, \forall j \in \{1 \ldots N^2\}$. Let μ denote the minimum SRC coefficient of P_M at the initial instant of its generation t_i. The dependence structure is said to be weakly stationary if the true mean of Δc_t is 0:*

$$\Delta c_t = |c_{1,t} - \mu| \tag{3}$$

Following this definition, we can assume that the distance between the two most dissimilar random processes within the same pool of models sets its boundary under a form of a logical *diameter*. If this boundary diverges in a significant way over time, a drift is assumed to take place. We propose to detect the validity of such assumption using the well-known Hoeffding Bound [19], which states that after W independent observations of a real-value random variable with range R, its true mean has not diverged if the sample mean is contained within $\pm \epsilon_F$:

$$\epsilon_F = \sqrt{\frac{R^2 \ln(1/\delta)}{2W}} \tag{4}$$

with a probability of $1 - \delta$ (a user-defined hyperparameter). Once the condition of the *weak stationary dependencies* presented in Definition 1 is violated, an alarm is triggered, the top base models using C_t are updated. Afterwards, the dependency monitoring process is continued by sliding the time window for the next prediction and the reference *diameter* μ is reset by setting $t_i = t$.

3.3 Model Clustering

One of the most important aspects for successful ensembles is diversity [4,7, 28]. Typically, this diversity is initially reflected in the distinctive patterns of each base learner's inductive bias derived from the different hypothesis on which each base learner is built to model the input data and its dependence structure. Surprisingly, the enforcement and evaluation of diversity on ensembles for time series data is still a quite unexplored topic-especially for forecasting problems [23, 28]. However, the expected error decomposition for ensemble schemata [4,31] in general helps to get an intuition about the importance of diversity. More precisely, the expected error can be decomposed into *bias*, *variance* and *covariance*.

In DEMSC, we propose a second-stage selection that tries to ensure such diversity through *clustering*. Predictions of K top-base models on the time sequence $X_{W,t}$, are considered as W-dimensional vector features to cluster the models. To compute clusters for time series, several techniques are proposed in literature such as K-means and hierarchical clustering [1]. However, one of the main issues presented by time series clustering is the choice of similarity/distance measure as most of typical distance measures such as the Euclidean distance do not take dependence structures of time series data into account [1]. To overcome this issue, we used an improper maximum likelihood estimator based clustering method (IMLEC) [9], which is based on a multivariate Gaussian model where parameters are estimated using Expectation Maximization algorithm [25].

This method has the advantage over Euclidean Distance (ED)-based clustering methods by contributing to the reduction of the covariance term of the ensemble error and thus to the reduction of the overall error. For instance, ED-based clustering methods like K-Means, do not take into account the covariance of the data. If we consider two candidate time series that have dependence over a high number of components of their W-dimensional feature space (i.e. high covariance is assumed to take place), the probability of attributing them to the same cluster by fitting the adequate parameters of the Gaussian mixture to the data is higher than simply using an ED-based method, which would probably assign them to different clusters based on their closeness to the current cluster centres. As a results, models belonging to different clusters have more likely low covariance. Therefore, the final step in the selection consists of selecting one representative model for each cluster. We simply select the closest model to each cluster center.

3.4   Model Combination

The final selected base-models are integrated using a sliding-window weighted average [26,28]. Let P_{M^f} be the pool of final selected base models to take part in the ensemble for the prediction of time instant $t + 1$ and $\hat{x}_{j,t+1}$ the output of model M_j in time instant $t + 1$. The final prediction is obtained by:

$$\hat{x}_{t+1} = \sum_{j=1}^{|P_{M^f}|} \frac{\left[\left(1 - \chi_{j,t}\right)\hat{x}_{j,t+1}\right]}{\sum_{j=1}^{|P_{M^f}|}\left(1 - \chi_{j,t}\right)} : \chi_{j,t} \in [0, 1], \forall j, t \tag{5}$$

where $\chi_{j,t}$ is a normalized version of the recent loss of the model M_j on $[t - W + 1, t]$ on the random process which computation is given by an evaluation metric of interest (i.e Normalized Root Mean Square Error (NRMSE) in our case).

This methodology was exhaustively tested over data collected from 16 real-world datasets. Further details are provided in the following Section.

4   Experiments

In this section, we present the experiments carried out to validate DEMSC and to answer the following research questions:

Q1: How is the performance of DEMSC compared to the state-of-the-art methods for time series forecasting tasks and to existing dynamic ensemble selection approaches?

Q2: What is the advantage of the performance drift detection mechanism, which triggers the ensemble members pre-selection, in terms of accuracy?

Q3: What is the impact of clustering and how does the IMLEC-clustering perform compared to commonly used clustering strategies for time series data?

Q4: What is the impact of different combination strategies on the performance?

Q5: Is there an advantage in terms of computational resources if the ensemble members selection is done in an **informed** fashion (i.e. only triggered by the drift detection alarm)?

4.1   Experimental Setup

The methods used in the experiments were evaluated using RMSE. In each experiment, the time series data was split to 75% for training, and 25% for testing. The results are compared using the non-parametric Wilcoxon Signed Rank test. We used 16 real-world time series shown in Table 1 for our experiments. An embedding dimension of 5 was used for all the time series.

Table 1. List of datasets used for the experiments.

ID	Time series	Data source	Data characteristics
1	Water consumption	Oporto city [7]	Daily obs. Jan, 2012–Oct, 2016
2	Temperature	Bike sharing [7]	
3	Feeling temperature		Hourly values from Jan. 1, 2011
4	Humidity		to Mar. 01, 2011
5	Windspeed		
6	Registered users		
7	Total bike rentals		
8	Global horizontal radiation	Solar radiation	Hourly values Feb. 16,
9	Direct normal radiation	monitoring [7]	2016–May 5, 2016
10	Diffuse horizontal radiation		
11	Vatnsdalsa	River flow [7]	Daily observations from Jan. 1,
12	Jokulsa Eystri		1972 to Dec. 31, 1974
13	Chill temperature	Weather data [29]	Hourly observations from Apr.
14	Total cloud cover		25, 2016 to Aug. 25, 2016
15	Wind speed		
16	Precipitation		

4.2 Ensemble Setup and Baselines

There is no forecasting method that performs best on every time series. For our candidate pool, we inconstantly used and tested different families of models:

GBM Gradient Boosting Machine [12];   **GP** Gaussian Process [32]

SVR Support Vector Regression [11];   **RFR** Random Forest [3]

PPR Projection Pursuit Regr. [13];   **MARS** MARS [14];

PCMR [24] Principal Component Regr.   **DT** Decision Tree Regr.;

PLS [24] Partial Least Squares Regr.   **MLP** [17] Multilayer Perceptron

Different parameter settings for the models, generate a pool of 30 candidate models, that we will use for the ensemble methods. We can see in Fig. 2, that the forecasting methods have a high variance as their performance changes across the different time series.

There is no clear best performing model. This motivates the dynamic combination of different forecasting models to an ensemble.

DEMSC has a number of hyperparameters that are summarized in Table 2. For IMLEC-clustering, we used the R-package of the authors of [9]. The maximum number of cluster is a user-defined parameter. However, it can be automatically reduced by removing outliers and noisy data that cannot be fitted to any cluster.

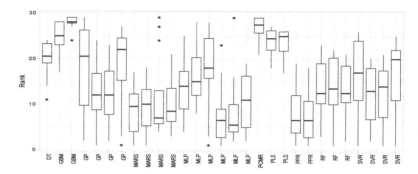

Fig. 2. Distribution of rank of the base models across the 16 time series (similar models names in the x-axis have different parameters)

Table 2. Hyperparameter of DEMSC and their chosen values for the experiments.

Parameter	Value
Number of top base models	Half of candidate pool
Maximum number of clusters	Half of top base models
Hoeffding-bound δ	0.95
Size of sliding window W	A user-defined hyperparameter

We compare the performance of DEMSC against the following approaches:

RF [3]: Random Forest uses bagging to create an ensemble of regression trees.

GBM [12]: Gradient boosting machine that uses boosting to create an ensemble of regression trees.

SE [8]: A static ensemble that averages the performance of all base learners using arithmetic mean.

SWE [26]: A linear combination of the base learners predictions. The weights are based upon recent performance over a time sliding-window.

ARIMA [2]: ARIMA model for time series forecasting.

EWA [16]: Forecasting combination with exponential weighted averages.

FS [16]: The fixed share approach from Herbster and Warmuth, which is designed for tracking the best expert across a time series.

OGD [16]: An approach based on online gradient descent that provides theoretical loss bound guarantees.

MLPOL [16]: A polynomially weighted average forecast combination.

Stacking [33]: An approach for ensembles using Random Forest as metalearner.

DETS [5]: An advanced version of SWE, selecting a subset of members based on recent errors and uses a smoothing function on the average of recent errors for weighting.

ADE [6]: Uses a Random Forest for estimating each candidates errors and selects member based on the estimated errors. Weighting is also based on the estimated errors combined with a softmax. Weights are additionally adapted to take diversity between ensemble members into account.

We also compare DEMSC with some variants of itself. All of these variants except one, use the sliding window ensemble for combining the ensemble members predictions.

DEMSC-NoSel: Same as our method but without the Top-Base Models selection. Clusters are updated periodically.

Top-Base Models: Only the pre-selection of the Top-Base models based on correlation (no clustering is applied afterwards)

DEMSC-kMeans: The clustering method is replaced with K-Mean with ED distance (K is tuned using the average silhouette method).

DEMSC-DTW: The clustering method is replaced with dynamic time warping clustering.

DEMSC-stacking: The stacking variant differs from our method only in the combination step. Instead of a sliding window ensemble, a stacking approach is used in this variant (**PLS** is used as metalearner).

4.3   Results

Table 3 presents the average ranks and their deviation for all methods. For the paired comparison, we compare our method DEMSC against each of the other methods. We counted wins and losses for each dataset using the RMSE scores. We use the non-parametric Wilcoxon Signed Rank test to compute significant wins and losses, which are presented in parenthesis (i.e. the significance level = 0:05). Figure 3 presents the distribution of ranks across the different time series for all methods.

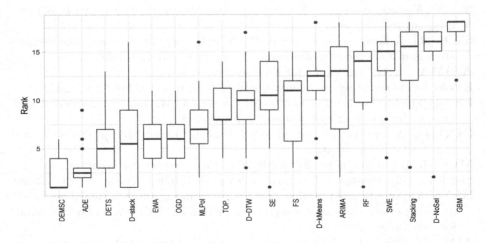

Fig. 3. Distribution of the ranks of ensemble methods across the different time series, D is used as abbreviation for DEMSC

Table 3. Paired comparison between DEMSC and different baseline methods for 16 time series. The rank column presents the average rank achieved by each model and the standard deviation of the rank across the different time series. A rank of 1 means the model was the best performing on all time series.

Method	Our method		
	Losses	Wins	Avg. rank
RF	1(0)	15(13)	12.2 ± 3.7
GBM	0(0)	16(16)	17.0 ± 2.0
SE	1(0)	15(13)	10.4 ± 3.6
SWE	0(0)	16(14)	13.8 ± 3.5
ARIMA	1(1)	15(11)	11.5 ± 5.1
EWA	1(0)	15(12)	6.3 ± 2.6
FS	1(0)	15(13)	9.5 ± 3.6
OGD	1(0)	15(12)	6.3 ± 2.5
MLPOL	2(1)	14(10)	7.2 ± 3.5
Stacking	1(1)	15(14)	13.9 ± 3.8
ADE	7(7)	7(3)	3.1 ± 2.0
DETS	4(4)	7(4)	5.4 ± 2.8
DEMSC-NoSel	0(0)	16(14)	13.9 ± 4.7
Top-Base Models	1(0)	15(14)	9.2 ± 2.9
DEMSC-kMeans	0(0)	16(16)	11.7 ± 3.1
DEMSC-DTW	1(0)	15(14)	9.6 ± 3.5
DEMSC-stacking	5(2)	9(6)	5.7 ± 4.3
DEMSC	–	–	2.3 ± 1.7

DEMSC has advantages over the compared methods except for ADE. The approaches for combining individual forecasters, which are SE, SWE, OGD, FS, EWA and MLPOL, show a big difference in the average rank compared to DEMSC. ARIMA, a state-of-the-art method for forecasting, has a big difference in the average rank as well. Common ensemble methods like RF, GBM, OGD and Stacking, compare poorly to all methods specialized for combining forecasters. The two competitive approaches to our method are ADE and DETS, with DETS having a higher average rank but performing well in the pairwise comparison. ADE is competitive to DEMSC and have a higher average rank, but it is comparable to DEMSC in terms of wins and losses. Looking at the distribution of ranks in Fig. 3, we see that ADE has some clear outliers, while being robust in the other cases. DEMSC is within the range of the first 4 ranks and has a median of 1 with no clear outliers.

To further investigate the differences in the average ranks, we use the post-hoc Bonferroni-Dunn test [10] to compute critical differences. We present the critical differences between the methods relative to each other in Fig. 4. Adding to the results of Table 3, we note critical differences between DEMSC and most of the other methods, with the exceptions of ADE, DETS, EWA, ODG and MLPOL. We already discussed the comparable performance of DEMSC and ADE. Both methods share the critical differences to other methods. Regarding research question **Q1**, our results show that DEMSC is competitive with ADE and outperforms other combination approaches for time series forecasting. The average rank of DEMSC is better than ADE, but we do not see the main advantage of our method in the performance but more in the complexity and computational requirements, which we will discuss later.

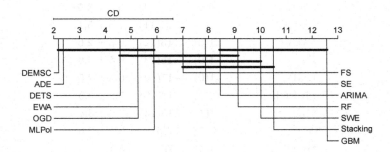

Fig. 4. Critical difference diagram for the post-hoc Bonferroni-Dunn test, comparing DEMSC with the other baseline ensemble methods.

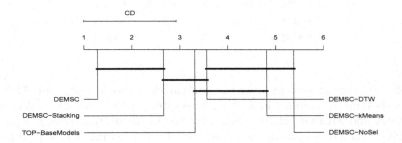

Fig. 5. Critical difference diagram for the post-hoc Bonferroni-Dunn test, comparing DEMSC against variants of our method.

Comparing DEMSC to different variants of our method, we see a clear advantage in using all the presented components. The results are the worst, if we only use clustering for selection (DEMSC-NoSel). The pre-selection is needed to ensure that the clustering uses the set of the most accurate models. Using only the top-Base Models, gives a useful performance, but we show that it can be further improved using clustering. Comparing the three different clustering methods (DEMSC-kMeans, DEMSC-DTW, DEMSC(IMLEC)) we can see the clear advantage of the IMLEC-clustering. Using a time warping clustering gives a slight improvement over K-means, but both of them do not improve the pre-selection. Using IMLEC-clustering improves the performance drastically. This can be explained partially by enhancing the diversity aspect discussed in Sect. 3. We see that the combination part of our method has a small impact. Both variants using IMLEC-clustering, with either sliding window ensemble or stacking for the combination, have a clear advantage over the other clustering variants (see question **Q3**). We present in Fig. 5 the critical differences of the methods regarding the average rank. The only variant, where the difference in average rank to DEMSC is not critically different is the stacking variant (DEMSC-stacking). The stacking variant's average rank is higher. This answers the research question **Q4** regarding the impact of each component of the method.

We can also answer research question **Q2**, asking about the impact of using a drift detection to trigger the member selection. Performance wise, we see that our method performs on the same level or even slightly better than the best state-of-the-art approach. The motivation for using a drift detection is to update the ensemble only when necessary. This should result in faster predictions and less computational requirements (see question **Q5**). We see in Table 4 that the average runtime of ADE is more than twice as long as the runtime of our method. The high deviation of the runtime of our method is due to the different datasets, that have more or less drifts detected.

Table 4. Empirical runtime comparison between DMESC and the most competitive state-of-the-art method (ADE).

Method	Avg. runtime in sec.
DEMSC	66.39 ± 26.4
ADE	156.97 ± 18.3

4.4 Discussion

We presented results that empirically show that DEMSC has performance advantages compared to other ensemble methods for forecasting and is competitive with the most recent state-of-the-art approaches for dynamically combining forecasting methods.

We show that our method, using a combination of clustering and a performance based pre-selection, is able to perform on a high level. The pre-selection assures that only accurate models are used in the ensemble. The clustering groups similar models based on their predictions. We then select clusters representatives. This leads to an ensemble with accurate and diverse members, which has been theoretically shown to be required for an ensemble to outperform it's members. Neither of the parts can reach state-of-the-art performance on its own, but the combination makes them very powerful.

The usage of drift detection enables our method to construct a new ensemble given changes in the nature of the dependencies between base-models and the target time series. If there is no change, then there is also no need to construct a new ensemble. Therefore, the drift detection reduces the computations.

DEMSC method and the complex meta-learning approach ADE perform on the same level. To reach same performance, we only need pre-selection and clustering, triggered by a drift detection. Compared to ADE, which needs to train a meta-model for each candidate, our method is computationally cheaper. For the experiments a prediction with ADE needed on average twice as long as our method.

5 Final Remarks

This paper introduces DEMSC: a novel, practically useful dynamic ensemble members selection framework for time series forecasting. DEMSC uses a two-staged selection procedure which on the one hand enhances accuracy by performing informed selection of base learners at test time based on a base models performance drift detection mechanism and diversity on the other hand through an online clustering approach. An exhaustive empirical evaluation, including 16 real-world datasets and multiple comparison algorithms shows the advantages of DEMSC. As a future work, we aim to add a drift-informed procedure for retraining the base-learners.

Acknowledgments. This work is supported by the Deutsche Forschungsgemeinschaft (DFG) within the Collaborative Research Center SFB 876 and the Federal Ministry of Education and Research of Germany as part of the competence center for machine learning ML2R (01S18038A).

References

1. Aghabozorgi, S., Shirkhorshidi, A.S., Wah, T.Y.: Time-series clustering–a decade review. Inf. Syst. **53**, 16–38 (2015)
2. Box, G.E., Jenkins, G.M., Reinsel, G.C., Ljung, G.M.: Time Series Analysis: Forecasting and Control. Wiley, San Francisco (2015)
3. Breiman, L.: Bagging predictors. Mach. Learn. **24**(2), 123–140 (1996)
4. Brown, G., Wyatt, J.L., Tiňo, P.: Managing diversity in regression ensembles. J. Mach. Learn. Res. **6**(2), 1621–1650 (2005)
5. Cerqueira, V., Torgo, L., Oliveira, M., Pfahringer, B.: Dynamic and heterogeneous ensembles for time series forecasting. In: IEEE International Conference on Data Science and Advanced Analytics (DSAA), pp. 242–251. IEEE (2017)
6. Cerqueira, V., Torgo, L., Pinto, F., Soares, C.: Arbitrated ensemble for time series forecasting. In: Ceci, M., Hollmén, J., Todorovski, L., Vens, C., Džeroski, S. (eds.) ECML PKDD 2017. LNCS (LNAI), vol. 10535, pp. 478–494. Springer, Cham (2017). https://doi.org/10.1007/978-3-319-71246-8_29
7. Cerqueira, V., Torgo, L., Pinto, F., Soares, C.: Arbitrage of forecasting experts. Mach. Learn. **108**(6), 913–944 (2018). https://doi.org/10.1007/s10994-018-05774-y
8. Clemen, R.T., Winkler, R.L.: Combining economic forecasts. J. Bus. Econ. Stat. **4**(1), 39–46 (1986)

9. Coretto, P., Hennig, C.: Robust improper maximum likelihood: tuning, computation, and a comparison with other methods for robust gaussian clustering. J. Am. Stat. Assoc. **111**(516), 1648–1659 (2016)
10. Demšar, J.: Statistical comparisons of classifiers over multiple data sets. J. Mach. Learn. Res. **7**, 1–30 (2006)
11. Drucker, H., Burges, C.J., Kaufman, L., Smola, A.J., Vapnik, V.: Support vector regression machines. In: Advances in Neural Information Processing Systems, pp. 155–161 (1997)
12. Friedman, J.H.: Greedy function approximation: a gradient boosting machine. Ann. Stat. **29**, 1189–1232 (2001)
13. Friedman, J.H., Stuetzle, W.: Projection pursuit regression. J. Am. Stat. Assoc. **76**(376), 817–823 (1981)
14. Friedman, J.H., et al.: Multivariate adaptive regression splines. Ann. Stat. **19**(1), 1–67 (1991)
15. Gaillard, P., Goude, Y.: Forecasting electricity consumption by aggregating experts; how to design a good set of experts. In: Antoniadis, A., Poggi, J.-M., Brossat, X. (eds.) Modeling and Stochastic Learning for Forecasting in High Dimensions. LNS, vol. 217, pp. 95–115. Springer, Cham (2015). https://doi.org/10.1007/978-3-319-18732-7_6
16. Gaillard, P., Goude, Y.: opera: Online Prediction by Expert Aggregation (2016). https://CRAN.R-project.org/package=opera. r package version 1.0
17. Goodfellow, I., Bengio, Y., Courville, A.: Deep Learning. MIT Press (2016). http://www.deeplearningbook.org
18. Gooijer, J.G.D., Hyndman, R.J.: 25 years of time series forecasting. Int. J. Forecast. **22**(3), 443–473 (2006)
19. Hoeffding, W.: Probability inequalities for sums of bounded random variables. In: Fisher, N.I., Sen, P.K. (eds.) The Collected Works of Wassily Hoeffding, pp. 409–426. Springer, New York (1994). https://doi.org/10.1007/978-1-4612-0865-5_26
20. Hyndman, R.J., Koehler, A.B., Snyder, R.D., Grose, S.: A state space framework for automatic forecasting using exponential smoothing methods. Int. J. Forecast. **18**(3), 439–454 (2002)
21. Jose, V.R.R., Winkler, R.L.: Simple robust averages of forecasts: some empirical results. Int. J. Forecast. **24**(1), 163–169 (2008)
22. Khiari, J., Moreira-Matias, L., Shaker, A., Ženko, B., Džeroski, S.: MetaBags: bagged meta-decision trees for regression. In: Berlingerio, M., Bonchi, F., Gärtner, T., Hurley, N., Ifrim, G. (eds.) ECML PKDD 2018. LNCS (LNAI), vol. 11051, pp. 637–652. Springer, Cham (2019). https://doi.org/10.1007/978-3-030-10925-7_39
23. Krawczyk, B., Minku, L.L., Gama, J., Stefanowski, J., Woźniak, M.: Ensemble learning for data stream analysis: a survey. Inf. Fusion **37**, 132–156 (2017)
24. Mevik, B.H., Wehrens, R., Liland, K.H.: PLS: Partial Least Squares and Principal Component Regression (2018). https://CRAN.R-project.org/package=pls
25. Moon, T.K.: The expectation-maximization algorithm. IEEE Signal Process. Mag. **13**(6), 47–60 (1996)
26. Moreira-Matias, L., Gama, J., Ferreira, M., Mendes-Moreira, J., Damas, L.: Predicting taxi-passenger demand using streaming data. IEEE Trans. Intell. Transp. Syst. **14**(3), 1393–1402 (2013)
27. Rodrigues, P.P., Gama, J., Pedroso, J.: Hierarchical clustering of time-series data streams. IEEE Trans. Knowl. Data Eng. **20**(5), 615–627 (2008)
28. Saadallah, A., Moreira-Matias, L., Sousa, R., Khiari, J., Jenelius, E., Gama, J.: Bright-drift-aware demand predictions for taxi networks. IEEE Trans. Knowl. Data Eng. **32**, 234–245 (2018)

29. Stoffel, T., Andreas, A.: NREL solar radiation research laboratory (SRRL): Baseline measurement system (BMS); Golden, Colorado (data), July 1981
30. Todorovski, L., Džeroski, S.: Combining classifiers with meta decision trees. Mach. Learn. **50**(3), 223–249 (2003)
31. Ueda, N., Nakano, R.: Generalization error of ensemble estimators. In: 1996 IEEE International Conference on Neural Networks, no. xi, pp. 90–95 (1996)
32. Williams, C.K., Rasmussen, C.E.: Gaussian Processes for Machine Learning, vol. 2. MIT Press, Cambridge (2006)
33. Wolpert, D.H.: Stacked generalization. Neural Netw. **5**(2), 241–259 (1992)

Privacy and Security

A Differentially Private Kernel Two-Sample Test

Anant Raj[1] , Ho Chung Leon Law[2(✉)] , Dino Sejdinovic[2] ,
and Mijung Park[1]

[1] Max Planck Institute for Intelligent Systems, Tübingen, Germany
{anant.raj,mijung.park}@tuebingen.mpg.de
[2] Department of Statistics, University of Oxford, Oxford, UK
{ho.law,dino.sejdinovic}@stats.ox.ac.uk

Abstract. Kernel two-sample testing is a useful statistical tool in determining whether data samples arise from different distributions without imposing any parametric assumptions on those distributions. However, raw data samples can expose sensitive information about individuals who participate in scientific studies, which makes the current tests vulnerable to privacy breaches. Hence, we design a new framework for kernel two-sample testing conforming to differential privacy constraints, in order to guarantee the privacy of subjects in the data. Unlike existing differentially private parametric tests that simply add noise to data, kernel-based testing imposes a challenge due to a complex dependence of test statistics on the raw data, as these statistics correspond to estimators of distances between representations of probability measures in Hilbert spaces. Our approach considers finite dimensional approximations to those representations. As a result, a simple chi-squared test is obtained, where a test statistic depends on a mean and covariance of empirical differences between the samples, which we perturb for a privacy guarantee. We investigate the utility of our framework in two realistic settings and conclude that our method requires only a relatively modest increase in sample size to achieve a similar level of power to the non-private tests in both settings.

Keywords: Differential privacy · Kernel two-sample test

1 Introduction

Several recent works suggest that it is possible to identify subjects that have participated in scientific studies based on publicly available aggregate statistics (cf. [20, 23] among many others). The *differential privacy* formalism [8] provides a way to quantify the amount of information on whether or not a single individual's data is included (or modified) in the data and also provides rigorous privacy guarantees in the presence of *arbitrary side information*.

A. Raj and H. C. L. Law—Equal contribution.

© Springer Nature Switzerland AG 2020
U. Brefeld et al. (Eds.): ECML PKDD 2019, LNAI 11906, pp. 697–724, 2020.
https://doi.org/10.1007/978-3-030-46150-8_41

An important tool in statistical inference is *two-sample testing*, in which samples from two probability distributions are compared in order to test the null hypothesis that the two underlying distributions are identical against the general alternative that they are different. In this paper, we focus on the non-parametric, *kernel-based* two-sample testing approach and investigate the utility of this framework in a differentially private setting. The kernel-based two-sample testing was introduced by Gretton et al. [15,16] who considers an estimator of maximum mean discrepancy (MMD) [3], the distance between embeddings of probability measures in a reproducing kernel Hilbert space (RKHS) (See [26] for a recent review), as a test statistic for the nonparametric two-sample problem.

Many existing differentially private testing methods are based on categorical data, i.e. counts [12,13,28], in which case a natural way to achieve privacy is simply adding noise to these counts. However, when we consider a more general input space $\mathcal{X}$ for testing, the amount of noise needed to privatise the data essentially becomes the order of diameter of the input space (explained in Appendix D). For spaces such as $\mathbb{R}^d$, the level of noise that needs to be added can destroy the utility of the data as well as that of the test.

Here we take an alternative approach and privatise only the quantities that are required for the test. In particular, for the two-sample testing, we only require the empirical kernel embedding $\frac{1}{N} \sum_i k(\mathbf{x}_i, \cdot)$ corresponding to a dataset, where $\mathbf{x}_i \in \mathcal{X}$ and k is some positive definite kernel. Now, as the kernel embedding lives in $\mathcal{H}_k$, a space of functions, a natural way to protect them is to add Gaussian process noise as suggested in [19] (discussed in Appendix C.1). Although sufficient for situations where the functions themselves are of interest, embeddings impaired by a Gaussian process does not lie in the same RKHS [30], and hence one cannot estimate the RKHS distances between such noisy embeddings. Alternatively, one could consider adding noise to an estimator of MMD [16]. However, asymptotic null distributions of these estimators are data dependent and the test thresholds are typically computed by permutation testing or by eigendecomposing centred kernel matrices of the data [17]. In this case neither of these approaches is available in a differentially private setting as they both require further access to data.

Contribution. In this paper, we build a differentially private two-sample testing framework, by considering *analytic representations* of probability measures [6,22], aimed at large scale testing scenarios. Through this formulation, we are able to obtain a test statistic that is based on means and covariances of feature vectors of the data. This suggests that privatisation of summary statistics of the data is sufficient to make the testing differential private, implying a reduction of level of noise needed versus adding to the data directly (as summary statistics are less sensitive to individual changes). Further, we show that while the asymptotic distribution under the null hypothesis of the test statistic does not depend on the data, unlike the non-private case, using the asymptotic null distribution to compute p-values can lead to grossly miscalibrated Type I control. Hence, we propose a remedy for this problem, and give approximations of the finite-sample null distributions, yielding good Type I error control and power-privacy tradeoffs experimentally in Sect. 6.

Related Work. To the best of our knowledge, this paper is the *first* to propose a two sample test in a differential private setting. Although, there are various differentially private hypothesis test in the literature, most of these revolve around categorical data [12,13,28] on chi-squared tests. This is very different to our work, which considers the problem of identifying whether two distributions are equal to each other. Further, while there are several works that connect kernel methods with differential privacy, including [2,19,21], none of these attempts to make the kernel-based two sample testing procedure private. It is also important to emphasise that in a hypothesis testing, it is not sufficient to make the test statistic differentially private, as one has to carefully construct the distribution under the null hypothesis in a differential private manner, taking into account the level of noise added.

Motivation and Setting. We now present the two privacy scenarios that we consider and motivate their usage. In the first scenario, we assume there is a trusted curator and also an untrusted tester, in which we want to protect data from. In this setting, the trusted curator has access to the two datasets and computes the mean and covariance of the empirical differences between the feature vectors. The curator can protect the data in two different ways: (1) perturb mean and covariance separately and release them; or (2) compute the statistic without perturbations and add noise to it directly. The tester can now take these perturbed quantities and performs the test at a desired significance level. Here, we separate the entities of tester and curator, as sometimes a decision whether to reject or not is of interest, for example one can imagine that the tester may require the test-statistic/p-values for multiple hypothesis testing corrections. In the second scenario, we assume that there are two data-owners, each having one dataset each, and a tester. In this case, as no party trust each other, each data-owner has to perturb their own mean and covariance of the feature vectors and release them to the tester. Under these two settings, we will exploit various differentially private mechanisms and empirically study the utility of the proposed framework. We start by providing a brief background on kernels, differential privacy and the two privacy settings we consider in this paper in Sect. 2. We derive essential tools for the proposed test in Sect. 3 and in Sect. 4, and describe approximations to finite-sample null distributions in Sect. 5. Finally, we illustrate the effectiveness of our algorithm in Sect. 6.

2   Background

2.1   Mean Embedding and Smooth Characteristic Function Tests

First introduced by [6] and then extended and further analyzed by [22], these two tests are the state-of-the-art kernel based testing approaches applicable to large datasets. Here, we will focus on the approach by [22], and in particular on the mean embedding (ME) and on a characterisation approach based on the smooth characteristic function (SCF). Assume that we observe samples $\{\mathbf{x}_i\}_{i=1}^n \sim P$ and $\{\mathbf{y}_i\}_{i=1}^n \sim Q$, where P and Q are some probability measures on $\mathbb{R}^D$. Now our goal is to test the null hypothesis $\mathbf{H}_0 : P = Q$ against all alternatives. Both ME and SCF tests consider finite-dimensional feature representations of the empirical measures P_n and Q_n corresponding to the samples $\{\mathbf{x}_i\}_{i=1}^n \sim P$ and $\{\mathbf{y}_i\}_{i=1}^n \sim Q$ respectively. The ME test considers feature representation given by $\phi_{P_n} = \frac{1}{n}\sum_{i=1}^n [k(\mathbf{x}_i, T_1), \cdots, k(\mathbf{x}_i, T_J)] \in \mathbb{R}^J$, for a given set of test locations $\{T_j\}_{j=1}^J$, i.e. it evaluates the kernel mean embedding $\frac{1}{n}\sum_{i=1}^n k(\mathbf{x}_i, \cdot)$ of P_n at those locations. We write $\mathbf{w}_n = \phi_{P_n} - \phi_{Q_n}$ to be the difference of the feature vectors of the empirical measures P_n and Q_n. If we write

$$\mathbf{z}_i = \Big[k(\mathbf{x}_i, T_1) - k(\mathbf{y}_i, T_1), \cdots, k(\mathbf{x}_i, T_J) - k(\mathbf{y}_i, T_J)\Big],$$

then $\mathbf{w}_n = \frac{1}{n}\sum_{i=1}^n \mathbf{z}_i$. We also define the empirical covariance matrix $\Sigma_n = \frac{1}{n-1}\sum_{i=1}^n (\mathbf{z}_i - \mathbf{w}_n)(\mathbf{z}_i - \mathbf{w}_n)^\top$. The final statistic is given by

$$s_n = n\, \mathbf{w}_n^\top (\Sigma_n + \gamma_n I)^{-1}\mathbf{w}_n, \tag{1}$$

where, as [22] suggest, a regularization term $\gamma_n I$ is added onto the empirical covariance matrix for numerical stability. This regularization parameter will also play an important role in analyzing sensitivity of this statistic in a differentially private setting. Following [22, Theorem 2], one should take $\gamma_n \to 0$ as $n \to \infty$, and in particular, γ_n should decrease at a rate of $\mathcal{O}(n^{-1/4})$. The SCF setting uses the statistic of the same form, but considers features based on empirical characteristic functions [27]. Thus, it suffices to set $\mathbf{z}_i \in \mathbb{R}^J$ to

$$\mathbf{z}_i = \Big[g(\mathbf{x}_i)\cos(\mathbf{x}_i^\top T_j) - g(\mathbf{y}_i)\cos(\mathbf{y}_i^\top T_j),$$

$$g(\mathbf{x}_i)\sin(\mathbf{x}_i^\top T_j) - g(\mathbf{y}_i)\sin(\mathbf{y}_i^\top T_j)\Big]_{j=1}^J,$$

where $\{T_j\}_{j=1}^{J/2}$ is a given set of frequencies, and g is a given function which has an effect of smoothing the characteristic function estimates (cf. [6] for derivation). The test then proceeds in the same way as the ME version. For both cases, the distribution of the test statistic (1) under the null hypothesis $\mathbf{H}_0 : P = Q$ converges to a chi-squared distribution with J degrees of freedom. This follows from a central limit theorem argument whereby $\sqrt{n}\mathbf{w}_n$ converges in law to a zero-mean multivariate normal distribution $\mathcal{N}(0, \Sigma)$ where $\Sigma = \mathbb{E}[\mathbf{z}\mathbf{z}^\top]$, while $\Sigma_n + \gamma_n I \to \Sigma$ in probability.

While [6] uses random distribution features (i.e. test locations/frequencies $\{T_j\}_j$ are sampled randomly from a predefined distribution), [22] selects test locations/frequencies $\{T_j\}_j$ which maximize the test power, yielding interpretable differences between the distributions under consideration. Throughout the paper, we assume that we use bounded kernels in the ME test (e.g. Gaussian and Laplace Kernel), in particular $k(\mathbf{x}, \mathbf{y}) \leq \kappa/2, \;\; \forall \mathbf{x}, \mathbf{y}$, and that the weighting function in the SCF test is also bounded: $h(\mathbf{x}) \leq \kappa/2$ Hence, $||\mathbf{z}_i||_2 \leq \kappa\sqrt{J}$ in both cases, for any $i \in [1, n]$.

2.2 Differential Privacy

Given an algorithm $\mathcal{M}$ and neighbouring datasets $\mathcal{D}$, $\mathcal{D}'$ differing by a single entry, the *privacy loss* of an outcome o is

$$L^{(o)} = \log \frac{Pr(\mathcal{M}_{(\mathcal{D})} = o)}{Pr(\mathcal{M}_{(\mathcal{D}')} = o)}. \tag{2}$$

The mechanism $\mathcal{M}$ is called ϵ-DP if and only if $|L^{(o)}| \leq \epsilon, \forall o, \mathcal{D}, \mathcal{D}'$. A weaker version of the above is (ϵ, δ)-DP, if and only if $|L^{(o)}| \leq \epsilon$, with probability at least $1 - \delta$. The definition states that a single individual's participation in the data do not change the output probabilities by much, hence this limits the amount of information that the algorithm reveals about any one individual.

A differentially private algorithm is designed by adding noise to the algorithms' outputs. Suppose a deterministic function $h : \mathcal{D} \mapsto \mathbb{R}^p$ computed on sensitive data $\mathcal{D}$ outputs a p-dimensional vector quantity. In order to make h private, we can add noise in function h, where the level of noise is calibrated to the *global sensitivity* GS_h [7], defined by the maximum difference in terms of L_2-norm $||h(\mathcal{D}) - h(\mathcal{D}')||_2$, for neighboring $\mathcal{D}$ and $\mathcal{D}'$ (i.e. differ by one data sample). In the case of Gaussian mechanism (Theorem 3.22 in [9]), the output is perturbed by

$$\tilde{h}(\mathcal{D}) = h(\mathcal{D}) + \mathcal{N}(0, GS_h^2 \sigma^2 \mathbf{I}_p)$$

The perturbed function $\tilde{h}(\mathcal{D})$ is then (ϵ, δ)-DP, where $\sigma \geq \sqrt{2\log(1.25/\delta)}/\epsilon$, for $\epsilon \in (0, 1)$ (See the proof of Theorem 3.22 in [9] why σ has such a form). When constructing our tests, we will use two important properties of differential privacy. The composability theorem [7] tells us that the strength of privacy guarantee degrades with repeated use of DP-algorithms. In particular, when two differentially private subroutines are combined, where each one guarantees (ϵ_1, δ_1)-DP and (ϵ_2, δ_2)-DP respectively by adding independent noise, the parameters are simply composed by $(\epsilon_1 + \epsilon_2, \delta_1 + \delta_2)$. Furthermore, post-processing invariance [7] tells us that the composition of any arbitrary data-independent mapping with an (ϵ, δ)-DP algorithm is also (ϵ, δ)-DP. Here below in the next section, we discuss the two privacy settings which we are considering for our study in this paper.

2.3 Privacy Settings

We consider the two different privacy settings as shown in Fig. 1:

(A) Trusted-Curator (TC) Setting. There is a trusted entity called curator that handles datasets and outputs the private test statistic, either in terms of perturbed $\tilde{\mathbf{w}}_n$ and $\tilde{\boldsymbol{\Sigma}}_n$, or in terms of perturbed test statistic $\tilde{s}_n$. An untrusted tester performs a chi-square test given these quantities.

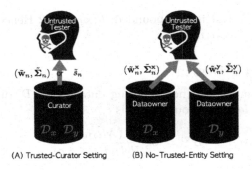

Fig. 1. Two privacy settings. **(A)** A trusted curator releases a private test statistic or private mean and covariance of empirical differences between the features. **(B)** Data owners release private feature means and covariances calculated from their samples. In both cases, an untrusted tester performs a test using the private quantities.

(B) No-Trusted-Entity (NTE) Setting. Each data owner outputs private mean and covariance of the feature vectors computed on their own dataset, meaning that the owner of dataset $\mathcal{D}_x$ outputs $\tilde{\mathbf{w}}_n^x$ and $\tilde{\mathbf{\Sigma}}_n^x$ and the owner of dataset $\mathcal{D}_y$ outputs $\tilde{\mathbf{w}}_n^y$ and $\tilde{\mathbf{\Sigma}}_n^y$. An untrusted tester performs a chi-squared test given these quantities.

It is worth noting that the NTE setting is different from the typical two-party model considered in the differential privacy literature. In the two-party model, it is typically assumed that Alice owns a dataset $\mathcal{D}_x$ and Bob owns a dataset $\mathcal{D}_y$, and they wish to compute some functionality $f(\mathcal{D}_x, \mathcal{D}_y)$ in a differentially private manner. In this case, the interest is to obtain a two-sided ϵ-differentially private protocol for f, i.e., each party's view of the protocol should be a differentially private function of the other party's input. For instance, the probability of Alice's views conditioned on $\mathcal{D}_y$ and $\mathcal{D}_{y'}$ should be e^ϵ multiplicatively close to each other, where $\mathcal{D}_y$ and $\mathcal{D}_{y'}$ are adjacent datasets [14,25]. On the other hand, in our NTE setting, we are not considering a joint function that takes two datasets. Rather, we consider a function (statistics) which each data-owner computes given their own dataset independent of the dataset that the other party has. We would like to analyze how the performance of the test run by an untrusted third party using those separately released DP statistics from each party degrades with the level of DP guarantees.

3 Trusted-Curator Setting

In this setting, a trusted curator releases either a private test statistic or private mean and covariance which a tester can use to perform a chi-square test. Given a total privacy budget (ϵ, δ), when we perturb mean and covariance separately, we spend (ϵ_1, δ_1) for mean perturbation and (ϵ_2, δ_2) for covariance perturbation, such that $\epsilon = \epsilon_1 + \epsilon_2$ and $\delta = \delta_1 + \delta_2$.

3.1   Perturbing Mean and Covariance

Mean Perturbation. We obtain a private mean by adding Gaussian noise based on the analytic Gaussian mechanism recently proposed in [1]. The main reason for using this Gaussian mechanism over the original [9] is that it provides a DP guarantee with smaller noise.

For $\mathbf{w}_n : \mathcal{D} \to \mathbb{R}^J$ that has the global L2-sensitivity $GS_2(\mathbf{w}_n)$, the analytic Gaussian mechanism produces $\tilde{\mathbf{w}}_n(\mathcal{D}) = \mathbf{w}_n(\mathcal{D}) + \mathbf{n}$, where $\mathbf{n} \sim \mathcal{N}(\mathbf{0}_J, \sigma_{\mathbf{n}}^2 \mathbf{I}_{J \times J})$. Then $\tilde{\mathbf{w}}_n(\mathcal{D})$ is (ϵ_1, δ_1)-differentially private mean vector if $\sigma_{\mathbf{n}}$ follows the regime in Theorem 9 of [9], here implicitly $\sigma_{\mathbf{n}}$ depends on $GS_2(\mathbf{w}_n), \epsilon_1$ and δ_1. Assuming an entry difference between two parts of datasets $\mathcal{D} = (\mathcal{D}_x, \mathcal{D}_y)$ and $\mathcal{D}' = (\mathcal{D}'_x, \mathcal{D}'_y)$ the global sensitivity is simply

$$GS_2(\mathbf{w}_n) = \max_{\mathcal{D}, \mathcal{D}'} \| \mathbf{w}_n(\mathcal{D}) - \mathbf{w}_n(\mathcal{D}') \|_2$$
$$= \max_{\mathbf{z}_i, \mathbf{z}'_i} \frac{1}{n} \| \mathbf{z}_i - \mathbf{z}'_i \|_2 \leq \frac{\kappa \sqrt{J}}{n}. \tag{3}$$

where $\mathbf{z}_i$ is as the corresponding feature maps defined in Sect. 2.

Covariance Perturbation. To obtain a private covariance, we consider [10] which utilises Gaussian noise. Here since the covariance matrix is given by $\boldsymbol{\Sigma}_n = \boldsymbol{\Lambda} - \frac{n}{n-1} \mathbf{w}_n \mathbf{w}_n^\top$, where $\boldsymbol{\Lambda} = \frac{1}{n-1} \sum_{i=1}^n \mathbf{z}_i \mathbf{z}_i^\top$, we can simply privatize the covariance by simply perturbing the 2nd-moment matrix $\boldsymbol{\Lambda}$ and using the private mean $\tilde{\mathbf{w}}_n$, i.e., $\tilde{\boldsymbol{\Sigma}}_n = \tilde{\boldsymbol{\Lambda}} - \frac{n}{n-1} \tilde{\mathbf{w}}_n \tilde{\mathbf{w}}_n^\top$. To construct the 2nd-moment matrix $\tilde{\boldsymbol{\Lambda}}$ that is (ϵ_2, δ_2)-differentially private, we use $\tilde{\boldsymbol{\Lambda}} = \boldsymbol{\Lambda} + \boldsymbol{\Psi}$, where $\boldsymbol{\Psi}$ is obtained as follows:

1. Sample from $\boldsymbol{\eta} \sim \mathcal{N}(0, \beta^2 \mathbf{I}_{J(J+1)/2})$, where β is a function of global sensitivity $GS(\boldsymbol{\Lambda}), \epsilon_2, \delta_2$, outlined in Theorem 4 in the appendix.
2. Construct an upper triangular matrix (including diagonal) with entries from $\boldsymbol{\eta}$.
3. Copy the upper part to the lower part so that resulting matrix $\boldsymbol{\Psi}$ becomes symmetric.

Now using the composability theorem [7] gives us that $\tilde{\boldsymbol{\Sigma}}_n$ is (ϵ, δ)-differentially private.

3.2   Perturbing Test Statistic

The trusted-curator can also release a differentially private statistic, to do this we use the analytic Gaussian mechanism as before, perturbing the statistic by adding Gaussian noise. To use the mechanism, we need to calculate the global sensitivity needed of the test statistic $s_n = \mathbf{w}_n^\top (\boldsymbol{\Sigma}_n + \gamma_n I)^{-1} \mathbf{w}_n$, which we provide in this Theorem (proof in Appendix B):

Theorem 1. *Given the definitions of* $\mathbf{w}_n$ *and* $\boldsymbol{\Lambda}_n$, *and the L2-norm bound on* $\mathbf{z}_i$'s, *the global sensitivity* $GS_2(s_n)$ *of the test statistic* s_n *is* $\frac{4\kappa^2 J\sqrt{J}}{n\gamma_n}\left(1 + \frac{\kappa^2 J}{n-1}\right)$, *where* γ_n *is a regularization parameter, which we set to be smaller than the smallest eigenvalue of* $\boldsymbol{\Lambda}$.

4   No-Trusted-Entity Setting

In this setting, the two samples $\{\mathbf{x}_i\}_{i=1}^{n_\mathbf{x}} \sim P$ and $\{\mathbf{y}_j\}_{j=1}^{n_\mathbf{y}} \sim Q$ reside with different data owners each of which wish to protect their samples in a differentially private manner. Note that in this context we allow the size of each sample to be different. The data owners first need to agree on the given kernel k as well as on the test locations $\{T_j\}_{j=1}^{J}$. We denote now $\mathbf{z}_i^\mathbf{x} = \left[k(\mathbf{x}_i, T_1), \cdots, k(\mathbf{x}_i, T_J)\right]^\top$ in the case of the ME test or $\mathbf{z}_i^\mathbf{x} = \left[h(\mathbf{x}_i)\cos(\mathbf{x}_i^\top T_j), h(\mathbf{x}_i)\sin(\mathbf{x}_i^\top T_j)\right]_{j=1}^{J}$ in the case of the SCF test. Also, we denote

$$\mathbf{w}_{n_\mathbf{x}}^\mathbf{x} = \frac{1}{n_\mathbf{x}}\sum_{i=1}^{n}\mathbf{z}_i^\mathbf{x} \qquad \boldsymbol{\Sigma}_{n_\mathbf{x}}^\mathbf{x} = \frac{1}{n_\mathbf{x}-1}\sum_{i=1}^{n_\mathbf{x}}(\mathbf{z}_i^\mathbf{x} - \mathbf{w}_{n_\mathbf{x}}^\mathbf{x})(\mathbf{z}_i^\mathbf{x} - \mathbf{w}_{n_\mathbf{x}}^\mathbf{x})^\top$$

and similarly for the sample $\{\mathbf{y}_j\}_{j=1}^{n_\mathbf{y}} \sim Q$. The respective means and covariances $\mathbf{w}_{n_\mathbf{x}}^\mathbf{x}, \boldsymbol{\Sigma}_{n_\mathbf{x}}^\mathbf{x}$ and $\mathbf{w}_{n_\mathbf{y}}^\mathbf{y}, \boldsymbol{\Sigma}_{n_\mathbf{y}}^\mathbf{y}$ are computed by their data owners, which then impair them independently with noise according to the sensitivity analysis described in Sect. 3.1. As a result we obtain differentially private means and covariances $\tilde{\mathbf{w}}_{n_\mathbf{x}}^\mathbf{x}$, $\tilde{\boldsymbol{\Sigma}}_{n_\mathbf{x}}^\mathbf{x}$ and $\tilde{\mathbf{w}}_{n_\mathbf{y}}^\mathbf{y}, \tilde{\boldsymbol{\Sigma}}_{n_\mathbf{y}}^\mathbf{y}$ at their respective users. All these quantities are then released to the tester whose role is to compute the test statistic and the corresponding p-value. In particular, the tester uses the statistic given by

$$\tilde{s}_{n_\mathbf{x},n_\mathbf{y}} = \frac{n_\mathbf{x}n_\mathbf{y}}{n_\mathbf{x}+n_\mathbf{y}}(\tilde{\mathbf{w}}_{n_\mathbf{x}}^\mathbf{x} - \tilde{\mathbf{w}}_{n_\mathbf{y}}^\mathbf{y})^\top(\tilde{\boldsymbol{\Sigma}}_{n_\mathbf{x},n_\mathbf{y}} + \gamma_n I)^{-1}(\tilde{\mathbf{w}}_{n_\mathbf{x}}^\mathbf{x} - \tilde{\mathbf{w}}_{n_\mathbf{y}}^\mathbf{y}),$$

where $\tilde{\boldsymbol{\Sigma}}_{n_\mathbf{x},n_\mathbf{y}} = \frac{(n_\mathbf{x}-1)\tilde{\boldsymbol{\Sigma}}_{n_\mathbf{x}}^\mathbf{x}+(n_\mathbf{y}-1)\tilde{\boldsymbol{\Sigma}}_{n_\mathbf{y}}^\mathbf{y}}{n_\mathbf{x}+n_\mathbf{y}-2}$ is the pooled covariance estimate.

5   Analysis of Null Distributions

In the previous sections, we discussed necessary tools to make the kernel two sample tests private in two different settings by considering sensitivity analysis of quantities of interest.[1] In this section, we consider the distributions of the test statistics under the null hypothesis $P = Q$ for each of the two settings.

---

[1] See Appendix C.3 and C.2 for other possible approaches.

5.1 Trusted-Curator Setting: Perturbed Mean and Covariance

In this scheme, noise is added both to the mean vector $\mathbf{w}_n$ and to the covariance matrix $\boldsymbol{\Sigma}_n$ (by dividing the privacy budget between these two quantities). Let us denote the perturbed mean by $\tilde{\mathbf{w}}_n$ and perturbed covariance with $\tilde{\boldsymbol{\Sigma}}_n$. The noisy version of the test statistic $\tilde{s}_n$ is then given by

$$\tilde{s}_n = n\tilde{\mathbf{w}}_n^\top (\tilde{\boldsymbol{\Sigma}}_n + \gamma_n I)^{-1}\tilde{\mathbf{w}}_n \tag{4}$$

where γ_n is a regularization parameter just like in the non-private statistic (1). We show below that the asymptotic null distribution (as sample size $n \to \infty$) of this private test statistic is in fact identical to that of the non-private test statistic. Intuitively, this is to be expected: as the number of samples increases, the contribution to the aggregate statistics of any individual observation diminishes, and the variance of the added noise goes to zero.

Theorem 2. *Assuming the Gaussian noise for $\tilde{\mathbf{w}}_n$ with the sensitivity bound in (3) and the perturbation mechanism introduced in Sect. 3.1 for $\tilde{\boldsymbol{\Sigma}}_n$, $\tilde{s}_n$ and s_n converge to the same limit in distribution, as $n \to \infty$. Also, under the alternate, $\tilde{s}_n = s_n(1 + \epsilon)$ and ϵ goes down as $\mathcal{O}(n^{-1+\gamma})$.*

Proof is provided in Appendix F. We here assume that under the alternate the relation $\mathbf{w}_n^\top \boldsymbol{\Sigma}^{-1}\mathbf{w}_n \geq \mathcal{O}(n^{-\gamma})$ for $\gamma < 1$ holds. Based on the Theorem, it is tempting to ignore the additive noise and rely on the asymptotic null distribution. However, as demonstrated in Sect. 6, such tests have a *grossly mis-calibrated Type I error*, hence we propose a non-asymptotic regime in order to improve approximations of the null distribution when computing the test threshold.

In particular, let's start by recalling that we previously relied on $\sqrt{n}\mathbf{w}_n$ converging to a zero-mean multivariate normal distribution $\mathcal{N}(0, \boldsymbol{\Sigma})$, with $\boldsymbol{\Sigma} = \mathbb{E}[\mathbf{z}\mathbf{z}^\top]$ [6]. In the private setting, we will also approximate the distribution of $\sqrt{n}\tilde{\mathbf{w}}_n$ with a multivariate normal, but consider explicit non-asymptotic covariances which appear in the test statistic. Namely, the covariance of $\sqrt{n}\tilde{\mathbf{w}}_n$ is $\boldsymbol{\Sigma} + n\sigma_{\mathbf{n}}^2 I$ and its mean is 0, so we will approximate its distribution by $\mathcal{N}(0, \boldsymbol{\Sigma} + n\sigma_{\mathbf{n}}^2 I)$. The test statistic can be understood as a squared norm of the vector $\sqrt{n} \left(\tilde{\boldsymbol{\Sigma}}_n + \gamma_n I\right)^{-1/2} \tilde{\mathbf{w}}_n$. Under the normal approximation to $\sqrt{n}\tilde{\mathbf{w}}_n$ and by treating $\tilde{\boldsymbol{\Sigma}}_n$ as fixed (note that this is a quantity released to the tester), $\sqrt{n} \left(\tilde{\boldsymbol{\Sigma}}_n + \gamma_n I\right)^{-1/2} \tilde{\mathbf{w}}_n$ is another multivariate normal, i.e. $\mathcal{N}(0, \mathbf{C})$, where

$$\mathbf{C} = (\tilde{\boldsymbol{\Sigma}}_n + \gamma_n I)^{-1/2}(\boldsymbol{\Sigma} + n\sigma_{\mathbf{n}}^2 I)(\tilde{\boldsymbol{\Sigma}}_n + \gamma_n I)^{-1/2}.$$

The overall statistic thus follows a distribution given by a weighted sum $\sum_{j=1}^J \lambda_j \chi_j^2$ of independent chi-squared distributed random variables, with the weights λ_j given by the eigenvalues of $\mathbf{C}$. Note that this approximation to the null distribution depends on a *non-private* true covariance $\boldsymbol{\Sigma}$. While that is clearly not available to the tester, we propose to simply replace this quantity with the privatized empirical covariance, i.e. $\tilde{\boldsymbol{\Sigma}}_n$, so that the tester approximates the null distribution with $\sum_{j=1}^{J} \tilde{\lambda}_j \chi_j^2$, where $\tilde{\lambda}_j$ are the eigenvalues of

$$\tilde{\mathbf{C}} = (\tilde{\boldsymbol{\Sigma}}_n + \gamma_n I)^{-1} (\tilde{\boldsymbol{\Sigma}}_n + n\sigma_{\mathbf{n}}^2 I),$$

i.e. $\tilde{\lambda}_j = \frac{\tau_j + n\sigma_{\mathbf{n}}^2}{\tau_j + \gamma_n}$, where $\{\tau_j\}$ are the eigenvalues of $\tilde{\boldsymbol{\Sigma}}_n$ (note that $\tilde{\lambda}_j \to 1$ as $n \to \infty$ recovering back the asymptotic null). This approach, while a heuristic, gives a correct Type I control, good power performance and is differentially private. This is unlike the approach which relies on the asymptotic null distribution and ignores the presence of privatizing noise. We demonstrate this empirically in Sect. 6.

5.2 Trusted-Curator Setting: Perturbed Test Statistic

In this section, we will consider how directly perturbing the test statistic impacts the null distribution. To achieve private test statistics, we showed that we can simply add Gaussian noise[2] using the Gaussian mechanism, described in Sect. 3.2. Similarly to Theorem 2, we have a similar theorem below, which says that the perturbed statistic then has the same asymptotic null distribution as the original statistic.

Theorem 3. *Using the noise variance $\sigma_\eta^2(\epsilon, \delta, n)$ defined by the upper bound in Theorem 1, $\tilde{s}_n$ and s_n converge to the same limit in distribution, as $n \to \infty$. More specifically, the error between s_n and $\tilde{s}_n$ goes down approximately at the rate of $\mathcal{O}(n^{-1/2})$.*

The proof follows immediately from $\sigma_\eta(\epsilon, \delta, n) \to 0$, as $n \to \infty$. The specific order of convergence directly comes after applying the Chebysev inequality since the variance σ^2 is of the order of $\mathcal{O}(n^{-1})$. As in the case of perturbed mean and covariance, we consider approximating the null distribution with the sum of the chi-squared with J degrees of freedom and a normal $\mathcal{N}(0, \sigma_\eta^2(\epsilon, \delta, n))$, i.e., the distribution of the true statistic is approximated with its asymptotic version, whereas we use exact non-asymptotic distribution of the added noise. The test threshold can then easily be computed by a Monte Carlo test which repeatedly simulates the sum of these two random variables. It is important to note that since $\sigma_\eta^2(\epsilon, \delta, n)$ is *independent of the data* (Appendix B), an untrusted tester can simulate the approximate null distribution without compromising privacy.

5.3 No-Trusted-Entity Setting

Similarly as in Sect. 5.1, as $n_{\mathbf{x}}, n_{\mathbf{y}} \to \infty$ such that $n_{\mathbf{x}}/n_{\mathbf{y}} \to \rho \in (0, 1)$, asymptotic null distribution of this test statistic remains unchanged as in the non-private setting, i.e. it is the chi-squared distribution with J degrees of freedom. However, by again considering the non-asymptotic case and applying a

---

[2] While this may produce negative privatized test statistics, the test threshold is appropriately adjusted for this. See Appendix C.2 and C.3 for alternative approaches for privatizing the test statistic.

chi-squared approximation, we get improved power and type I control. In particular, the test statistic is close to a weighted sum $\sum_{j=1}^{J} \lambda_j \chi_j^2$ of independent chi-square distributed random variables, with the weights λ_j given by the eigenvalues of

$$\mathbf{C} = \frac{n_\mathbf{x} n_\mathbf{y}}{n_\mathbf{x} + n_\mathbf{y}} (\tilde{\mathbf{\Sigma}}_{n_\mathbf{x},n_\mathbf{y}} + \gamma_n I)^{-1/2} (\mathbf{\Sigma}^\mathbf{x}/n_\mathbf{x} + \mathbf{\Sigma}^\mathbf{y}/n_\mathbf{y} + (\sigma_{n_\mathbf{x}}^2 + \sigma_{n_\mathbf{y}}^2)I)(\tilde{\mathbf{\Sigma}}_{n_\mathbf{x},n_\mathbf{y}} + \gamma_n I)^{-1/2}$$

where $\mathbf{\Sigma}^\mathbf{x}$ and $\mathbf{\Sigma}^\mathbf{y}$ are the true covariances within each of the samples, $\sigma_{n_\mathbf{x}}^2$ and $\sigma_{n_\mathbf{y}}^2$ are the variances of the noise added to the mean vectors $\mathbf{w}_{n_\mathbf{x}}$ and $\mathbf{w}_{n_\mathbf{y}}$, respectively. While $\mathbf{\Sigma}^\mathbf{x}$ and $\mathbf{\Sigma}^\mathbf{y}$ are clearly not available to the tester, the tester can replace them with their privatized empirical versions $\tilde{\mathbf{\Sigma}}_{n_\mathbf{x}}^\mathbf{x}$ and $\tilde{\mathbf{\Sigma}}_{n_\mathbf{y}}^\mathbf{y}$ and compute eigenvalues $\tilde{\lambda}_j$ of

$$\tilde{\mathbf{C}} = \frac{n_\mathbf{x} n_\mathbf{y}}{n_\mathbf{x} + n_\mathbf{y}} (\tilde{\mathbf{\Sigma}}_{n_\mathbf{x},n_\mathbf{y}} + \gamma_n I)^{-1/2} (\tilde{\mathbf{\Sigma}}_{n_\mathbf{x}}^\mathbf{x}/n_\mathbf{x} + \tilde{\mathbf{\Sigma}}_{n_\mathbf{y}}^\mathbf{y}/n_\mathbf{y} + (\sigma_{n_\mathbf{x}}^2 + \sigma_{n_\mathbf{y}}^2)I)(\tilde{\mathbf{\Sigma}}_{n_\mathbf{x},n_\mathbf{y}} + \gamma_n I)^{-1/2}$$

Note that this is a differentially private quantity. Similarly as in the trusted-curator setting, we demonstrate that this corrected approximation to the null distribution leads to significant improvements in power and Type I control.

6   Experiments

Here we demonstrate the effectiveness of our private kernel two-sample test[3] on both synthetic and real problems, for testing $\mathbf{H_0} : P = Q$. The total sample size is denoted by N and the number of test set samples by n. We set the significance level to $\alpha = 0.01$. Unless specified otherwise use the isotropic Gaussian kernel with a bandwidth θ and fix the number of test locations to $J = 5$. Under the trusted-curator (TC) setting, we use 20% of the samples N as an independent training set to optimize the test locations and θ using gradient descent as in [22]. Under the no-trusted-entity (NTE) setting, we randomly sample J locations and calculate the median heuristic bandwidth [18].

For all our experiments, we average them over 500 runs, where each run repeats the simulation or randomly samples without replacement from the data set. We then report the empirical estimate of $\mathcal{P}(\tilde{s}_n > T_\alpha)$, computed by proportion of times the statistic $\tilde{s}_n$ is greater than the T_α, where T_α is the test threshold provided by the corresponding approximation to the null distribution. Regularization parameter $\gamma = \gamma_n$ is fixed to 0.001 for TC under perturbed test statistics (TCS), with the choice of this investigated in Fig. 7. In the trusted-curator mean covariance perturbation (TCMC) and NTE, given the privacy budget of (ϵ, δ), we use $(0.5\epsilon, 0.5\delta)$ to perturb the mean and covariance seperately. We compare these to its non-private counterpart ME and SCF, as there are no available appropriate baseline to compare against. We will also demonstrate the importance of using an approximated finite-null distribution versus the asymptotic null distribution. More details and experiments can be found in Appendix E.

---

[3] Code is available at https://github.com/hcllaw/private_tst.

6.1   Synthetic Data

We demonstrate our tests on 4 separate synthetic problems, namely, Same Gaussian (SG), Gaussian mean difference (GMD), Gaussian variance difference (GVD) and Blobs, with the specifications of P and Q summarized in Table 1. The same experimental setup was used in [22]. For the Blobs dataset, we use the SCF approach as the baseline, and also the basis for our algorithms, since [6,22] showed that SCF outperforms the ME test here (Fig. 2).

Table 1. Synthetic problems (Null hypothesis $\mathbf{H_0}$ holds only for SG). Gaussian Mixtures in $\mathbb{R}^2$, also studied in [6,18,22].

Data	P	Q
SG	$\mathcal{N}(0, I_{50})$	$\mathcal{N}(0, I_{50})$
GMD	$\mathcal{N}(0, I_{100})$	$\mathcal{N}((1, 0, \dots, 0)^\top, I_{100})$
GVD	$\mathcal{N}(0, I_{50})$	$\mathcal{N}(0, diag(2, 1, \dots, 1))$

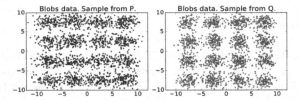

Fig. 2. Blobs data sampled from **P** on the left and from **Q** in the right.

Varying Privacy Level ϵ. We now fix the test sample size n to be 10 000, and vary ϵ between 0 and 5 with a fixed $\delta = 1e - 5$. The results are shown in the top row of Fig. 4. For SG dataset, where $\mathbf{H_0} : P = Q$ is true, we can see that if one simply applies the asymptotic null distribution of a χ^2 on top, we will obtain a massively inflated type I error. This is however not the case for TCMC, TCS and NTE, where the type I error is approximately controlled at the right level, this is shown more clearly in Fig. 5 in the Appendix. In GMD, GVD and Blobs dataset, the null hypothesis does not hold, and we see that our algorithms indeed discover this difference. As expected we observe a trade-off between privacy level and power, for increasing privacy (decreasing ϵ), we have less power. These experiments also reveals the order of performance of these algorithms, i.e. TCS > TCMC > NTE. This is not surprising, as for TCMC and NTE, we are pertubing the mean and covariance separately, rather than the statistic directly which is the direct quantity we want to protect. The power analysis for the SVD and Blobs dataset also reveal the interesting nature of sampling versus optimisation in our two settings. In the SVD dataset, we observe

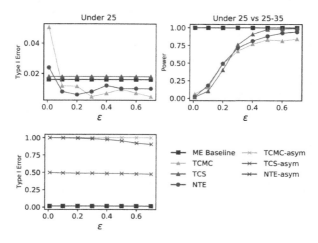

Fig. 3. Type I error for the under25 only test, Power for the under25 vs 25to35 test over 500 runs, with $n = 2500, \delta = 1e^{-5}$. *-asym represents using the asymptotic χ^2 null distribution.

that NTE performs better than TCS and TCMC, however if we use the same test locations and bandwidth of NTE for TCS and TCMC, the order of performance is as we expect, better for sampling over optimization. However, in the Blobs dataset, we observe that NTE has little or no power, because this dataset is sensitive to the choice of test frequency locations, highlighting the importance of optimisation in this case.

Varying Test Sample Size n. We now fix $\epsilon = 2.5$, $\delta = 1.0^{-5}$ and vary n from 1000 to 15 000. The results are shown in the bottom row of Fig. 4. The results for the SG dataset further reinforce the importance of not simply using the asymptotic null distribution, as even at very large sample size, the type I error is still inflated when naively computing the test threshold form a chi-squared distribution. This is not the case for TCMC, TCS and NTE, where the type I error is approximately controlled at the correct level for all sample sizes, as shown in Fig. 5 in the Appendix.

6.2 Real Data: Celebrity Age Data

We now demonstrate our tests on a real life celebrity age dataset [29], containing 397 949 images of 19 545 celebrities and their corresponding age labels. Here, we will follow the preprocessing of [24], where images from the same celebrity are placed into the same bag, and the bag label is calculated as the mean age of that celebrity's images and use this to construct two datasets, under25 and 25to35. Here the under25 dataset is the images where the corresponding celebrity's bag label is < 25, and the 25to35 dataset is the images corresponding to the celebrity's bag label that is between 25 and 35. The dataset under25 contains

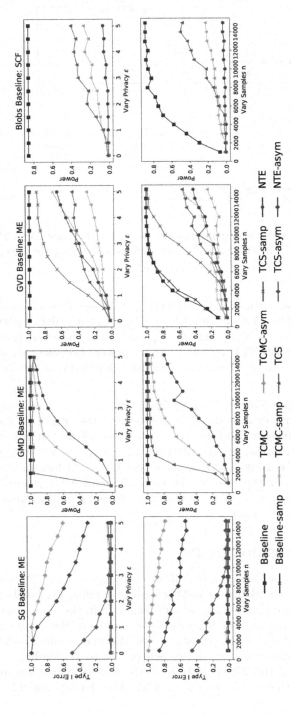

Fig. 4. Type I error for the SG dataset, Power for the GMD, GVD, Blobs dataset over 500 runs, with $\delta = 1e^{-5}$. **Top:** Varying ϵ with $n = 10000$. **Bottom:** Varying n with $\epsilon = 2.5$. Here *-asym represents using the asymptotic χ^2 null distribution, while *-samp represents sampling locations and using the median heuristic bandwidth.

58095 images, and the dataset 25to35 contains 126415 images. For this experiment, we will focus on using the ME version of the test and consider the kernel

$$k(\mathbf{x}, \mathbf{y}) = \exp \left(-\frac{||\varphi(\mathbf{x}) - \varphi(\mathbf{y})||^2}{2\theta^2} \right)$$

where $\varphi(x) : \mathbb{R}^{256 \times 256} \to \mathbb{R}^{4096}$ is the feature map learnt by the CNN in [29], mapping the image in the original pixel space to the last layer. For our experiment, we take $N = 3125$, and use 20% of the data for sampling test locations, and calculation of the median heuristic bandwidth. Note here we do not perform optimization, due to the large dimension of the feature map φ. We now perform two tests, for one test we compare samples from under25 only (i.e. $H_0 : P = Q$ holds), and the other we compares samples from under25 to samples from 25to35 (i.e. $\mathbf{H_0} : P = Q$ does not hold). The results are shown in Fig. 3 for ϵ from 0.1 to 0.7. We observe that in the under25 only test, the TCMC, TCS and NTE all achieve the correct Type I error rate, this is unlike their counterpart that uses the χ^2 asymptotic null distribution. In the under25 vs 25to35 two sample test, we see that our algorithms can achieve a high power (with little samples) at a high level of privacy, protecting the original images from malicious intent.

7 Conclusion

While kernel-based hypothesis testing provides flexible statistical tools for data analysis, its utility in differentially private settings is not well understood. We investigated differentially private kernel-based two-sample testing procedures, by making use of the sensitivity bounds on the quantities used in the test statistics. While asymptotic null distributions for the modified procedures remain unchanged, ignoring additive noise can lead to an inflated number of false positives. Thus, we propose new approximations of the null distributions under the private regime which give improved Type I control and good power-privacy tradeoffs, as demonstrated in extensive numerical evaluations.

Appendix

A Covariance Perturbation

Theorem 4 (Modified Analyze Gauss). *Draw Gaussian random variables* $\boldsymbol{\eta} \sim \mathcal{N}(0, \beta^2 \mathbf{I}_{J(J+1)/2})$ *where* $\beta = \frac{\kappa^2 J \sqrt{2 \log(1.25/\delta_2)}}{(n-1)\epsilon_2}$. *Using* $\boldsymbol{\eta}$, *we construct a upper triangular matrix (including diagonal), then copy the upper part to the lower part so that the resulting matrix* $\mathbf{D}$ *becomes symmetric. The perturbed matrix* $\tilde{\boldsymbol{\Lambda}} = \boldsymbol{\Lambda} + \mathbf{D}$ *is* (ϵ_2, δ_2)-*differentially private*[4].

---

[4] To ensure $\tilde{\boldsymbol{\Lambda}}$ to be positive semi-definite, we project any negative sigular values to a small positive value (e.g., 0.01).

The proof is the same as the proof for Algorithm 1 in [10] with the exception that the global sensitivity of $\mathbf{\Lambda}$ is

$$GS(\mathbf{\Lambda}) = \max_{\mathcal{D},\mathcal{D}'} \|\mathbf{\Lambda}(\mathcal{D}) - \mathbf{\Lambda}(\mathcal{D}')\|_F = \max_{\mathbf{v},\mathbf{v}'} \|\mathbf{v}\mathbf{v}^\top - \mathbf{v}'\mathbf{v}'^\top\|_F \le \frac{\kappa^2 J}{n-1}, \quad (5)$$

where $\mathbf{v}$ is the single entry differing in $\mathcal{D}$ and $\mathcal{D}'$, and $\|\mathbf{v}\|_2 \le \frac{\kappa\sqrt{J}}{\sqrt{n-1}}$.

B Sensitivity of $\mathbf{w}_n^\top \left(\mathbf{\Sigma}_n + \gamma_n \mathbf{I}\right)^{-1} \mathbf{w}_n$

We first introduce a few notations, which we will use for the sensitivity analysis.

- We split $\mathbf{w}_n = \mathbf{m} + \frac{1}{\sqrt{n}}\mathbf{v}$, where $\mathbf{m} = \frac{1}{n}\sum_{i=1}^{n-1} \mathbf{z}_i$ and $\mathbf{v} = \frac{1}{\sqrt{n}}\mathbf{z}_n$.
- Similarly, we split $\mathbf{\Lambda} = \mathbf{M}^\top\mathbf{M} + \frac{n}{n-1}\mathbf{v}\mathbf{v}^\top + \gamma_n \mathbf{I}$, where $\mathbf{M}^\top\mathbf{M} = \frac{1}{n-1}\sum_{i=1}^{n-1}\mathbf{z}_i\mathbf{z}_i^\top$, we denote $\mathbf{M}_{\gamma_n} = \mathbf{M}^\top\mathbf{M} + \gamma_n \mathbf{I}$, where $\gamma_n > 0$
- We put a dash for the quantities run on the neighbouring dataset $\mathcal{D}'$, i.e., the mean vector is $\mathbf{w}_n'$, the 2nd-moment matrix is $\mathbf{\Lambda}'$ (including a regularization term of $\gamma_n \mathbf{I}$). Here, $\mathbf{w}_n = \mathbf{m} + \frac{1}{\sqrt{n}}\mathbf{v}'$, $\mathbf{v}' = \frac{1}{\sqrt{n}}\mathbf{z}_n'$, and $\mathbf{\Lambda}' = \mathbf{M}^\top\mathbf{M} + \frac{n}{n-1}\mathbf{v}'\mathbf{v}'^\top + \gamma_n \mathbf{I} = \mathbf{M}_{\gamma_n} + \frac{n}{n-1}\mathbf{v}'\mathbf{v}'^\top$. Similarly, the covariance given the dataset $\mathcal{D}$ is $\mathbf{\Sigma} = \mathbf{\Lambda} - \frac{n}{n-1}\mathbf{w}_n\mathbf{w}_n^\top$ and the covariance given the dataset $\mathcal{D}'$ is $\mathbf{\Sigma}' = \mathbf{\Lambda}' - \frac{n}{n-1}\mathbf{w}_n\mathbf{w}_n^\top$.
- Note that $\mathbf{\Lambda}$ and $\mathbf{M}_{\gamma_n}$ is positive definite, and hence invertible and have positive eigenvalues, we let eigen-vectors of $\mathbf{M}_{\gamma_n}$ are denoted by $\mathbf{u}_1, \cdots, \mathbf{u}_J$ and the corresponding eigenvalues by $\mu_1, \cdots, \mu_J$. We also define the eigenvectors such that $\mathbf{Q}$ is orthogonal. Here $\mathbf{Q}$ has columns given by the eigenvectors.

The L2-sensitivity of test statistic is derived using a few inequalities that are listed below:

$$GS_2(s_n) = \max_{\mathcal{D},\mathcal{D}'} \left| s_n(\mathcal{D}) - s_n(\mathcal{D}') \right|, \quad (6)$$

$$= n \max_{\mathbf{v},\mathbf{v}'} \left| \mathbf{w}_n^\top \mathbf{\Sigma}^{-1}\mathbf{w}_n - \mathbf{w}_n^\top \mathbf{\Sigma}'^{-1}\mathbf{w}_n \right| \quad (7)$$

$$= n \max_{\mathbf{v},\mathbf{v}'} \left| \mathbf{w}_n^\top (\mathbf{\Lambda} - \frac{n}{n-1}\mathbf{w}_n\mathbf{w}_n^\top)^{-1}\mathbf{w}_n - \mathbf{w}_n^\top (\mathbf{\Lambda}' - \frac{n}{n-1}\mathbf{w}_n\mathbf{w}_n^\top)^{-1}\mathbf{w}_n \right|, \quad (8)$$

$$\le 2n \max_{\mathbf{v},\mathbf{v}'} \left| \mathbf{w}_n^\top \mathbf{\Lambda}^{-1}\mathbf{w}_n - \mathbf{w}_n^\top \mathbf{\Lambda}'^{-1}\mathbf{w}_n \right|, \text{ due to inequality I} \quad (9)$$

$$\le 2n \max_{\mathbf{v},\mathbf{v}'} \left(\left| \mathbf{w}_n'^\top (\mathbf{\Lambda}^{-1} - \mathbf{\Lambda}'^{-1})\mathbf{w}_n' \right| + \left| \mathbf{w}_n^\top \mathbf{\Lambda}^{-1}\mathbf{w}_n - \mathbf{w}_n'^\top \mathbf{\Lambda}^{-1}\mathbf{w}_n' \right| \right), \quad (10)$$

$$\le 2n \max_{\mathbf{v},\mathbf{v}'} \|\mathbf{w}_n\|_2^2 \|\mathbf{\Lambda}^{-1} - \mathbf{\Lambda}'^{-1}\|_F + \frac{4\kappa^2 J}{n}\frac{\sqrt{J}}{\mu_{min}(\mathbf{\Lambda})}, \text{Cauchy Schwarz and IV,} \quad (11)$$

$$\le \frac{2\kappa^2 J}{n} \max_{\mathbf{v},\mathbf{v}'} \|\mathbf{\Lambda}^{-1} - \mathbf{\Lambda}'^{-1}\|_F + \frac{4\kappa^2 J}{n}\frac{\sqrt{J}}{\mu_{min}(\mathbf{\Lambda})}, \text{ since } \|\mathbf{w}_n\|_2^2 \le \frac{1}{n^2}\kappa^2 J, \quad (12)$$

$$\leq \frac{4\kappa^2 J\sqrt{J}B^2}{(n-1)\|\mu_{min}(\mathbf{M}_{\gamma_n})\|} + \frac{4\kappa^2 J}{n}\frac{\sqrt{J}}{\mu_{min}(\mathbf{\Lambda})}, \text{ due to inequality III.} \tag{13}$$

$$\leq \frac{4\kappa^2 J\sqrt{J}B^2}{(n-1)\gamma_n} + \frac{4\kappa^2 J}{n}\frac{\sqrt{J}}{\gamma_n} \tag{14}$$

$$= \frac{4\kappa^2 J\sqrt{J}}{n\gamma_n}\left(1 + \frac{\kappa^2 J}{n-1}\right) \tag{15}$$

Here, the regularization parameter λ_n is the lower bound on the minimum singular values of the matrices $\mathbf{\Lambda}$ and $\mathbf{M}_\lambda$.

Hence the final sensiitvity of the data can be upper bound by $\frac{4\kappa^2 J\sqrt{J}}{n\gamma_n}\left(1 + \frac{\kappa^2 J}{n-1}\right)$.

The inequalities we used are given by

- I: Due to the Sherman–Morrison formula, we can re-write

$$\mathbf{w}_n{}^\top\left(\mathbf{\Lambda} - \frac{n}{n-1}\mathbf{w}_n\mathbf{w}_n{}^\top\right)^{-1}\mathbf{w}_n = \mathbf{w}_n{}^\top\mathbf{\Lambda}^{-1}\mathbf{w}_n + \frac{\frac{n}{n-1}(\mathbf{w}_n{}^\top\mathbf{\Lambda}^{-1}\mathbf{w}_n)^2}{1 + \frac{n}{n-1}\mathbf{w}_n{}^\top\mathbf{\Lambda}^{-1}\mathbf{w}_n}. \tag{16}$$

Now, we can bound

$$\left|\mathbf{w}_n{}^\top\left(\mathbf{\Lambda} - \frac{n}{n-1}\mathbf{w}_n\mathbf{w}_n{}^\top\right)^{-1}\mathbf{w}_n - \mathbf{w}_n{}^\top\left(\mathbf{\Lambda}' - \frac{n}{n-1}\mathbf{w}_n\mathbf{w}_n{}^\top\right)^{-1}\mathbf{w}_n\right|$$

$$\leq |\mathbf{w}_n{}^\top\mathbf{\Lambda}^{-1}\mathbf{w}_n - \mathbf{w}_n{}^\top\mathbf{\Lambda}'^{-1}\mathbf{w}_n| + \left|\frac{\frac{n}{n-1}(\mathbf{w}_n{}^\top\mathbf{\Lambda}^{-1}\mathbf{w}_n)^2}{1 + \frac{n}{n-1}\mathbf{w}_n{}^\top\mathbf{\Lambda}^{-1}\mathbf{w}_n} - \frac{\frac{n}{n-1}(\mathbf{w}_n{}^\top\mathbf{\Lambda}'^{-1}\mathbf{w}_n)^2}{1 + \frac{n}{n-1}\mathbf{w}_n'{}^\top\mathbf{\Lambda}'^{-1}\mathbf{w}_n'}\right|,$$

$$\leq 2|\mathbf{w}_n{}^\top\mathbf{\Lambda}^{-1}\mathbf{w}_n - \mathbf{w}_n{}^\top\mathbf{\Lambda}'^{-1}\mathbf{w}_n|, \tag{17}$$

where the last line is due to $\mathbf{w}_n{}^\top\mathbf{\Lambda}^{-1}\mathbf{w}_n \geq \frac{(\mathbf{w}_n{}^\top\mathbf{\Lambda}^{-1}\mathbf{w}_n)^2}{1+\mathbf{w}_n{}^\top\mathbf{\Lambda}^{-1}\mathbf{w}_n} \geq 0$, and $\mathbf{w}_n{}^\top\mathbf{\Lambda}'^{-1}\mathbf{w}_n \geq \frac{(\mathbf{w}_n'{}^\top\mathbf{\Lambda}'^{-1}\mathbf{w}_n')^2}{1+\mathbf{w}_n'{}^\top\mathbf{\Lambda}'^{-1}\mathbf{w}_n'} \geq 0$. Let $a = \mathbf{w}_n{}^\top\mathbf{\Lambda}^{-1}\mathbf{w}_n$ and $b = \mathbf{w}_n'{}^\top\mathbf{\Lambda}'^{-1}\mathbf{w}_n'$, then:

$$A = \left|\frac{a^2}{1+a} - \frac{b^2}{1+b}\right| = \left|\frac{a^2 - b^2 + a^2 b - b^2 a}{(1+a)(1+b)}\right| = \left|\frac{(a-b)(a+b) + (a-b)ab}{(1+a)(1+b)}\right|$$

$$= \left|\frac{(a-b)[(a+b)+ab]}{(1+a)(1+b)}\right|$$

and then we have that:

$$A = \left|\frac{(a-b)[(1+a)(1+b)-1]}{(1+a)(1+b)}\right| \leq |a-b|$$

Hence, $\left|\frac{\frac{n}{n-1}(\mathbf{w}_n{}^\top\mathbf{\Lambda}^{-1}\mathbf{w}_n)^2}{1+\frac{n}{n-1}\mathbf{w}_n{}^\top\mathbf{\Lambda}^{-1}\mathbf{w}_n} - \frac{\frac{n}{n-1}(\mathbf{w}_n{}^\top\mathbf{\Lambda}'^{-1}\mathbf{w}_n)^2}{1+\frac{n}{n-1}\mathbf{w}_n'{}^\top\mathbf{\Lambda}'^{-1}\mathbf{w}_n'}\right| \leq \left(\frac{n}{n-1}\right)\left(\frac{n-1}{n}\right)|\mathbf{w}_n{}^\top\mathbf{\Lambda}^{-1}\mathbf{w}_n - \mathbf{w}_n{}^\top\mathbf{\Lambda}'^{-1}\mathbf{w}_n|$

- II: For a positive semi-definite $\mathbf{\Sigma}$, $0 \leq \mathbf{m}^\top\mathbf{\Sigma}\mathbf{m} \leq \|\mathbf{m}\|_2^2\|\mathbf{\Sigma}\|_F$, where $\|\mathbf{\Sigma}\|_F$ is the Frobenius norm.

– III: We here will denote $\tilde{\mathbf{v}} = \sqrt{\frac{n}{n-1}}\mathbf{v}$ and $\tilde{\mathbf{v}}' = \sqrt{\frac{n}{n-1}}\mathbf{v}'$. Due to the Sherman–Morrison formula,

$$\mathbf{\Lambda}^{-1} = (\mathbf{M}_{\gamma_n})^{-1} - (\mathbf{M}_{\gamma_n})^{-1}\frac{\tilde{\mathbf{v}}\tilde{\mathbf{v}}^\top}{1 + \tilde{\mathbf{v}}^\top(\mathbf{M}_{\gamma_n})^{-1}\tilde{\mathbf{v}}}(\mathbf{M}_{\gamma_n})^{-1}. \tag{18}$$

For any eigenvectors $\mathbf{u}_j, \mathbf{u}_k$ of $\mathbf{M}^\top\mathbf{M}$, we have

$$\mathbf{u}_j{}^\top(\mathbf{\Lambda}^{-1} - \mathbf{\Lambda}'^{-1})\mathbf{u}_k = \mu_j^{-1}\mu_k^{-1}\left(\frac{(\mathbf{u}_j{}^\top\tilde{\mathbf{v}})(\tilde{\mathbf{v}}^\top\mathbf{u}_k)}{1 + \tilde{\mathbf{v}}^\top(\mathbf{M}_{\gamma_n})^{-1}\tilde{\mathbf{v}}} - \frac{(\mathbf{u}_j{}^\top\tilde{\mathbf{v}}')(\tilde{\mathbf{v}}'^\top\mathbf{u}_k)}{1 + \tilde{\mathbf{v}}'^\top(\mathbf{M}_{\gamma_n})^{-1}\tilde{\mathbf{v}}'}\right), \tag{19}$$

where μ_j, μ_k are corresponding eigenvalues. Now, we rewrite the Frobenius norm as (since it is invariant under any orthogonal matrix, so we take the one formed by the eigenvectors from $M^\top M$ with this property):

$$\|(\mathbf{\Lambda}^{-1} - \mathbf{\Lambda}'^{-1})\|_F^2 = \|Q(\mathbf{\Lambda}^{-1} - \mathbf{\Lambda}'^{-1})Q^\top\|_F^2,$$

$$= \sum_{j,k}^J \left(\mathbf{u}_j{}^\top(\mathbf{\Lambda}^{-1} - \mathbf{\Lambda}'^{-1})\mathbf{u}_k\right)^2,$$

$$\leq \frac{2}{(1 + \tilde{\mathbf{v}}^\top(\mathbf{M}_{\gamma_n})^{-1}\tilde{\mathbf{v}})^2}\sum_{j,k}^J \frac{(\mathbf{u}_j{}^\top\tilde{\mathbf{v}})^2(\tilde{\mathbf{v}}^\top\mathbf{u}_k)^2}{\mu_j^2\mu_k^2}$$

$$+ \frac{2}{(1 + \tilde{\mathbf{v}}'^\top(\mathbf{M}_{\gamma_n})^{-1}\tilde{\mathbf{v}}')^2}\sum_{j,k}^J \frac{(\mathbf{u}_j{}^\top\tilde{\mathbf{v}}')^2(\tilde{\mathbf{v}}'^\top\mathbf{u}_k)^2}{\mu_j^2\mu_k^2}, \tag{20}$$

$$[\text{due to } \|a - b\|_2^2 \leq 2\|a\|_2^2 + 2\|b\|_2^2],$$

$$\leq \frac{2}{(\tilde{\mathbf{v}}^\top(\mathbf{M}_{\gamma_n})^{-1}\tilde{\mathbf{v}})^2}\sum_{j,k}^J \frac{(\mathbf{u}_j{}^\top\tilde{\mathbf{v}})^2(\tilde{\mathbf{v}}^\top\mathbf{u}_k)^2}{\mu_j^2\mu_k^2}$$

$$+ \frac{2}{(\tilde{\mathbf{v}}'^\top(\mathbf{M}_{\gamma_n})^{-1}\tilde{\mathbf{v}}')^2}\sum_{j,k}^J \frac{(\mathbf{u}_j{}^\top\tilde{\mathbf{v}}')^2(\tilde{\mathbf{v}}'^\top\mathbf{u}_k)^2}{\mu_j^2\mu_k^2}, \tag{21}$$

$$\leq \frac{\mu_{min}(\mathbf{M}_{\gamma_n})^2}{B^4 J}\sum_{j,k}^J \frac{2((\mathbf{u}_j{}^\top\tilde{\mathbf{v}})^2(\tilde{\mathbf{v}}^\top\mathbf{u}_k)^2 + (\mathbf{u}_j{}^\top\tilde{\mathbf{v}}')^2(\tilde{\mathbf{v}}'^\top\mathbf{u}_k)^2)}{\mu_j^2\mu_k^2} \tag{22}$$

$$\leq \frac{(n-1)^2\mu_{min}(\mathbf{M}_{\gamma_n})^2}{n^2 B^4 J}\sum_{j,k}^J \frac{2((\mathbf{u}_j{}^\top\tilde{\mathbf{v}})^2(\tilde{\mathbf{v}}^\top\mathbf{u}_k)^2 + (\mathbf{u}_j{}^\top\tilde{\mathbf{v}}')^2(\tilde{\mathbf{v}}'^\top\mathbf{u}_k)^2)}{\mu_{min}(\mathbf{M}_{\gamma_n})^4} \tag{23}$$

$$\leq \frac{(n-1)^2 2J}{n^2\mu_{min}(\mathbf{M}_{\gamma_n})^2 B^4}(\|\tilde{\mathbf{v}}\|_2^8 + \|\tilde{\mathbf{v}}'\|_2^8), \tag{24}$$

$$\leq \left(\frac{n}{n-1}\right)^2\frac{4J}{\mu_{min}(\mathbf{M}_{\gamma_n})^2}B^4, \tag{25}$$

Note that we can get Eq. 25 by noticing that:

$$\tilde{\mathbf{v}}^\top(\mathbf{M}_{\gamma_n})^{-1}\tilde{\mathbf{v}} \leq \|\tilde{\mathbf{v}}\|_2^2\|(\mathbf{M}_{\gamma_n})^{-1}\|_F \leq \left(\frac{n}{n-1}\right)B^2\sqrt{\frac{1}{\mu_1^2(\mathbf{M}_{\gamma_n})} + \cdots + \frac{1}{\mu_{min}^2(\mathbf{M}_{\gamma_n})}}$$

$$\leq \left(\frac{n}{n-1}\right)\frac{B^2\sqrt{J}}{\mu_{min}(\mathbf{M}_{\gamma_n})}$$

– IV:

$$\max_{\mathbf{v},\mathbf{v}'} \left| \mathbf{w}_n^\top \boldsymbol{\Lambda}^{-1} \mathbf{w}_n - {\mathbf{w}_n'}^\top \boldsymbol{\Lambda}'^{-1} \mathbf{w}_n' \right| \leq \max_{\mathbf{v},\mathbf{v}'} \left[\left| {\mathbf{w}_n'}^\top \boldsymbol{\Lambda}^{-1} \mathbf{w}_n' - {\mathbf{w}_n'}^\top \boldsymbol{\Lambda}'^{-1} \mathbf{w}_n' \right| \right.$$

$$\left. + \left| \mathbf{w}_n^\top \boldsymbol{\Lambda}^{-1} \mathbf{w}_n - {\mathbf{w}_n'}^\top \boldsymbol{\Lambda}^{-1} \mathbf{w}_n' \right| \right]$$

We write $\mathbf{w}_n^\top \boldsymbol{\Lambda}^{-1} \mathbf{w}_n = \left(\boldsymbol{\Lambda}^{-1/2} \mathbf{w}_n \right)^\top \left(\boldsymbol{\Lambda}^{-1/2} \mathbf{w}_n \right)$ and similarly ${\mathbf{w}_n'}^\top \boldsymbol{\Lambda}^{-1} \mathbf{w}_n' = \left(\boldsymbol{\Lambda}^{-1/2} \mathbf{w}_n' \right)^\top \left(\boldsymbol{\Lambda}^{-1/2} \mathbf{w}_n' \right)$.

$$\left| \mathbf{w}_n^\top \boldsymbol{\Lambda}^{-1} \mathbf{w}_n - {\mathbf{w}_n'}^\top \boldsymbol{\Lambda}^{-1} \mathbf{w}_n' \right| = \left| \left(\boldsymbol{\Lambda}^{-1/2} \mathbf{w}_n \right)^\top \left(\boldsymbol{\Lambda}^{-1/2} \mathbf{w}_n \right) - \left(\boldsymbol{\Lambda}^{-1/2} \mathbf{w}_n' \right)^\top \left(\boldsymbol{\Lambda}^{-1/2} \mathbf{w}_n' \right) \right|$$

$$= \left| \left(\boldsymbol{\Lambda}^{-1/2} \mathbf{w}_n + \boldsymbol{\Lambda}^{-1/2} \mathbf{w}_n' \right)^\top \left(\boldsymbol{\Lambda}^{-1/2} \mathbf{w}_n - \boldsymbol{\Lambda}^{-1/2} \mathbf{w}_n' \right) \right|$$

$$= \left| \left(\boldsymbol{\Lambda}^{-1/2} \left(\mathbf{w}_n + \mathbf{w}_n' \right) \right)^\top \left(\boldsymbol{\Lambda}^{-1/2} \left(\mathbf{w}_n - \mathbf{w}_n' \right) \right) \right|$$

$$\leq \left\| \boldsymbol{\Lambda}^{-1/2} \left(\mathbf{w}_n + \mathbf{w}_n' \right) \right\|_2 \left\| \boldsymbol{\Lambda}^{-1/2} \left(\mathbf{w}_n - \mathbf{w}_n' \right) \right\|_2$$

$$\leq \left\| \boldsymbol{\Lambda}^{-1/2} \left(\mathbf{w}_n + \mathbf{w}_n' \right) \right\|_2 \frac{\kappa \sqrt{J}}{n} \left\| \boldsymbol{\Lambda}^{-1} \right\|_F^{1/2} \text{ using equality (II)}$$

$$\leq \frac{2\kappa^2 J}{n^2} \left\| \boldsymbol{\Lambda}^{-1} \right\|_F,$$

$$= \frac{2\kappa^2 J}{n^2} \sqrt{\frac{1}{\mu_1^2(\boldsymbol{\Lambda})} + \cdots + \frac{1}{\mu_{min}^2(\boldsymbol{\Lambda})}},$$

$$\leq \frac{2\kappa^2 J}{n^2} \frac{\sqrt{J}}{\mu_{min}(\boldsymbol{\Lambda})}.$$

where the last equality comes from that $\boldsymbol{\Lambda}$ is real and symmetric.

C   Other Possible Ways to Make the Test Private

C.1   Perturbing the Kernel Mean in RKHS

In [4], the authors proposed a new way to make the solution of the regularized risk minimization differentially private by injecting the noise in objective itself. That is :

$$f_{priv} = \arg\min \left(J(f, \boldsymbol{x}) + \frac{1}{n} \boldsymbol{b}^\top f \right)$$

However, it is not an easy task to add perturbation in functional spaces. The authors in [19] proposes to add a sample path from Gaussian processes into the function to make it private.

Lemma 1 (Proposition 7 [19]). *Let G be a sample path of a Gaussian process having mean zero and covariance function k. Let K denote the Gram matrix i.e. $K = [k(\boldsymbol{x}_i, \boldsymbol{x}_j)]_{i,j=1}^n$. Let $\{f_D : D \in \mathcal{D}\}$ be a family of functions indexed by databases. Then the release of :*

$$\tilde{f}_D = f_D + \frac{\Delta c(\beta)}{\alpha} G$$

is (α, β)-differentially private (with respect to the cylinder σ-field F) where Δ is the upper bound on

$$\sup_{D \sim D'} \sup_{n \in \mathbb{N}} \sup_{x_1, \dots, x_n} \sqrt{(\mathbf{f}_D - \mathbf{f}_{D'})^\top K^{-1} (\mathbf{f}_D - \mathbf{f}_{D'})} \tag{26}$$

and $c(\beta) \geq \sqrt{2 \log \frac{2}{\beta}}$.

Now, we consider the optimization problem given for MMD and inject noise in the objective itself. The optimization problem then becomes:

$$\begin{aligned}
d_{priv}(p, q) &= \sup_{f \in \mathcal{H}, \, \|f\|_{\mathcal{H}} \leq 1} \left[\mathbb{E}_{\boldsymbol{x} \sim p}[f(\boldsymbol{x})] - \mathbb{E}_{\boldsymbol{x} \sim q}[f(\boldsymbol{x})] + \left\langle f, g(\Delta, \beta, \alpha) G \right\rangle \right] \\
&= \sup_{f \in \mathcal{H}, \, \|f\|_{\mathcal{H}} \leq 1} \left[\left\langle f, \mu_p - \mu_q \right\rangle + \left\langle f, g(\Delta, \beta, \alpha) G \right\rangle \right] \\
&= \sup_{f \in \mathcal{H}, \, \|f\|_{\mathcal{H}} \leq 1} \left[\left\langle f, \mu_p - \mu_q + g(\Delta, \beta, \alpha) G \right\rangle \right] \\
&= \| \mu_p - \mu_q + g(\Delta, \beta, \alpha) G \|_{\mathcal{H}}
\end{aligned}$$

In the similar way, one get the empirical version of the perturbed MMD distance just by replacing the true expectation with the empirical one. The problem with a construction above where embedding is injected with a Gaussian process sample path with the same kernel k is that the result will not be in the corresponding RKHS $\mathcal{H}_k$ for infinite-dimensional spaces (these are well known results known as Kallianpur's 0/1 laws), and thus MMD cannot be computed, i.e. while f_D is in the RKHS, $\tilde{f}_D$ need not be. This has for example been considered in Bayesian models for kernel embeddings [11], where an alternative kernel construction using convolution is given by:

$$r(x, x') = \int k(x, y) k(y, x') \nu(dy), \tag{27}$$

where ν is a finite measure. Such smoother kernel r ensures that the sample path from a $GP(0, r)$ will be in the RKHS $\mathcal{H}_k$.

The key property in [19] is Prop. 8, which shows that for any $h \in \mathcal{H}_k$ and for any finite collection of points $\mathbf{x} = (x_1, \dots, x_n)$:

$$\mathbf{h}^\top K^{-1} \mathbf{h} \leq \|h\|_{\mathcal{H}_k}^2.$$

which implies that we only require $\sup_{D \sim D'} \|f_D - f_{D'}\|_{\mathcal{H}_k} \leq \Delta$ to hold to upper bound (26). However, in nonparametric contexts like MMD, one usually considers permutation testing approaches. But this is not possible in the case of private testing as one would need to release the samples from the null distribution.

C.2   Adding χ^2-noise to the Test Statistics

Since the unperturbed test statistics follows the χ^2 distribution under the null, hence it is again natural to think to add noise sampled from the chi-square distribution to the test statistics s_n. The probability density function for chi-square distribution with $k-$degree of freedom is given as:

$$f(x, k) = \begin{cases} \dfrac{x^{\frac{k}{2}-1} \exp(-\frac{x}{2})}{2^{\frac{k}{2}} \Gamma(\frac{k}{2})}, & \text{if } x \geq 0. \\ 0, & \text{otherwise.} \end{cases}$$

For $k = 2$, we simply have $f(x) = \frac{\exp(-\frac{x}{2})}{2}$, $if\ x \geq 0$. As we have been given $s_n = n\mathbf{w}_n \mathbf{\Sigma}_n^{-1}\mathbf{w}_n$ which essentially depends on $\mathbf{z}_i\ \forall i \in [n]$. Now, we define s_n' which differs from s_n at only one sample *i.e.* s_n' depends on $\mathbf{z}_1, \cdots \mathbf{z}_{i'}, \cdots \mathbf{z}_n$. We denote $\Delta = s_n - s_n'$. The privacy guarantee is to bound the following term:

$$\frac{p(s_n + x = s_n + x_0)}{p(s_n + x = s_n + x_0)} = \frac{p(x = x_0)}{p(x = s_n' - s_n + x_0)} \tag{28}$$

$$= \frac{\exp\left(-\frac{x_0}{2}\right)}{\exp\left(-\frac{s_n' - s_n + x_0}{2}\right)} = \exp\left(-\frac{s_n - s_n'}{2}\right) \leq \exp\left(\frac{GS_2}{2}\right) \tag{29}$$

Hence, we get the final privacy guarantee by Eq. (29). But the problem to this approach that since the support for chi-square distributions are limited to positive real numbers. Hence the distribution in the numerator and denominator in the Eq. (29) might have different support which essentially makes the privacy analysis almost impossible in the vicinity of zero and beyond. Hence, to hold Eq. (29), x_0 must be greater than $s_n - s_n'$ for all two neighbouring dataset which essentially implies $x_0 > GS_2(s_n)$. Hence, we get no privacy guarantee at all when the test statistics lies very close to zero.

However, proposing alternate null distribution is simple in this case. As sum of two chi-square random variable is still a chi-square with increased degree of freedom. Let X_1 and X_2 denote 2 independent random variables that follow these chi-square distributions :

$$X_1 \sim \chi^2(r_1) \quad \text{and} \quad X_2 \sim \chi^2(r_2)$$

then $Y = (X_1 + X_2) \sim \chi^2(r_1 + r_2)$. Hence, the perturbed statistics will follow chi-square random variable with $J + 2$ degree of freedom.

C.3   Adding Noise to $\mathbf{\Sigma}_n^{-1/2}\mathbf{w}_n$

One might also achieve the goal to make test statistics private by adding Gaussian noise in the quantity $\sqrt{n}\mathbf{\Sigma}_n^{-1/2}\mathbf{w}_n$ and finally taking the 2$-$norm of the perturbed quantity. As we have done the sentitivity analysis of $\mathbf{w}_n^{\top}\mathbf{\Sigma}_n^{-1}\mathbf{w}_n$ in the Theorem 1, the sensitivity analysis of $\sqrt{n}\mathbf{\Sigma}_n^{-1/2}\mathbf{w}_n$ can be done in very similar way. Again from the application of slutsky's theorem, we can see that asymptotically the perturbed test statistics will converge to the true one. However, similar to Sect. 5, we approximate it with the other null distribution which shows more power experimentally under the noise as well. Suppose we have to add the noise $\boldsymbol{\eta} \sim \mathcal{N}(0, \sigma^2(\epsilon, \delta_n))$ in the $\boldsymbol{\Sigma}_n^{-1/2}\mathbf{w}_n$ to make the statistics s_n private. The noisy statistics is then can be written as

$$\tilde{s}_n = \sqrt{n}\left(\boldsymbol{\Sigma}_n^{-1/2}\mathbf{w}_n + \boldsymbol{\eta}\right)^\top \sqrt{n}\left(\boldsymbol{\Sigma}_n^{-1/2}\mathbf{w}_n + \boldsymbol{\eta}\right)$$

Eventually, $\tilde{s}_n$ can be written as the following: $\tilde{s}_n = \left(\widetilde{\boldsymbol{\Sigma}_n^{-1/2}\mathbf{w}_n}\right)^\top \mathbf{A}$ $\left(\widetilde{\boldsymbol{\Sigma}_n^{-1/2}\mathbf{w}_n}\right)$ where

$$\widetilde{\boldsymbol{\Sigma}_n^{-1/2}\mathbf{w}_n} = \begin{pmatrix} \sqrt{n}\boldsymbol{\Sigma}_n^{-1/2}\mathbf{w}_n \\ \sqrt{n}\frac{\boldsymbol{\eta}}{\sigma(\epsilon, \delta_n)} \end{pmatrix} \tag{30}$$

$\widetilde{\boldsymbol{\Sigma}_n^{-1/2}\mathbf{w}_n}$ is a $2J$ dimensional vector. The corresponding covariance matrix $\hat{\boldsymbol{\Sigma}}_n$ is an identity matrix $\mathbf{I}_{2J}$ of dimension $2J \times 2J$. Hence, under the null $\widetilde{\boldsymbol{\Sigma}_n^{-1/2}\mathbf{w}_n} \sim \mathcal{N}(0, \mathbf{I}_{2J})$. We define one more matrix which we call as $\mathbf{A}$ which is

$$\mathbf{A} = \begin{bmatrix} \mathbf{I}_J & \mathbf{V} \\ \mathbf{V} & \mathbf{V}^2 \end{bmatrix} \text{ where } \mathbf{V} = \text{Diag}(\sigma(\epsilon, \delta_n)) \tag{31}$$

By definition matrix A is a symmetric matrix which essentially means that there exist a matrix $\mathbf{H}$ such that $\mathbf{H}^\top \mathbf{A}\mathbf{H} = diag(\lambda_1, \lambda_2 \cdots \lambda_r)$ where $\mathbf{H}^\top \mathbf{H} = \mathbf{H}\mathbf{H}^\top = \mathbf{I}_J$. Now if we consider a random variable $\mathbf{N}_2 \sim \mathcal{N}(0, \mathbf{I}_2 J)$ and $\mathbf{N}_1 = \mathbf{H}\mathbf{N}_2$ then following holds asymptotically:

$$\left(\widetilde{\boldsymbol{\Sigma}_n^{-1/2}\mathbf{w}_n}\right)^\top \mathbf{A} \left(\widetilde{\boldsymbol{\Sigma}_n^{-1/2}\mathbf{w}_n}\right) \sim (\mathbf{N}_2)^\top \mathbf{A} (\mathbf{N}_2) \sim (\mathbf{H}\mathbf{N}_2)^\top \mathbf{A} (\mathbf{H}\mathbf{N}_2) \sim \sum_{i=1}^r \lambda_i \chi_1^{2,i}$$

As a short remark, we would like to mention that the in this approach the weights for the weighted sum of χ^2-random variable are not directly dependent on the data which is essentially a good thing from the privacy point of view. Sensitivity of $\boldsymbol{\Sigma}_n^{-1/2}\mathbf{w}_n$ can be computed in a similar way as in Theorem 1.

D Perturbed Samples Interpretation of Private Mean and Co-variance

In order to define differential privacy, we need to define two neighbouring dataset $\mathcal{D}$ and $\mathcal{D}'$. Let us consider some class of databases $\mathcal{D}^N$ where each datset differ with another at just one data point. Let us also assume that each database carries n data points of dimension d each. Now if we privately want to release data then we consider a function $f : \mathcal{D}^N \to \mathbb{R}^{nd}$ which simply takes all n data points of the database and vertically stack them in one large vector of dimension nd. It is not hard to see now that:

$$GS_2(f) = \sup_{\mathcal{D}, \mathcal{D}'} \|f(\mathcal{D}) - f(\mathcal{D}')\|_2 \approx \mathcal{O}(diam(\mathcal{X})) \tag{32}$$

where $diam(\mathcal{X})$ denotes the input space. Since the sensitive is way too high (of the order of diameter of input space), the utility of the data is reduced by a huge amount after adding noise in it.

Here below now we discuss the perturbed sample interpretation of private mean and co-variance. That is to anylyze what level of noise added directly on samples itself would follow the same distribution as private mean. From Lemma 2, we see that the variance of the noise come out to be much more tractable in private mean case than adding noise directly to samples.

Lemma 2. *Let us assume that $\sqrt{n}\tilde{\mathbf{w}}_n = \sqrt{n}\mathbf{w}_n + \eta$ where $\eta \sim \mathcal{N}(0, \frac{c}{n})$ for any positive constant c, $\sqrt{n}\mathbf{w}_n = \frac{1}{\sqrt{n}}\sum_{i=1}^{n} \mathbf{z}_i$ and $\mathbf{z}_i$s are i.i.d samples. Then $\sqrt{n}\mathbf{w}_n \to \frac{1}{\sqrt{n}}\sum_{i=1}^{n} \tilde{\mathbf{z}}_i$ where $\tilde{\mathbf{z}}_i = \mathbf{z}_i + \zeta$ and $\zeta \sim \mathcal{N}(0, \sigma_p^2)$ if $\sigma_p^2 = \frac{c}{n}$*

Proof. It is easier to see that $\mathbb{E}\left[\sqrt{n}\tilde{\mathbf{w}}_n\right] = \sqrt{n}\mathbf{w}_n = \mathbb{E}\left[\frac{1}{\sqrt{n}}\sum_{i=1}^{n} \tilde{\mathbf{z}}_i\right]$. Now, we try to analyze the variance of both the term.

$$\frac{c}{n} = n\frac{\sigma_p^2}{n}$$

Hence, $\sigma_p^2 = \frac{c}{n}$

Now similar to Lemma 2, we want to translate the noise added in the covariance matrix to the sample case. The empirical covaraince matrix $\boldsymbol{\Sigma}_n = \frac{1}{n-1}\sum_{i=1}^{n}(\mathbf{z}_i - \mathbf{w}_n)(\mathbf{z}_i - \mathbf{w}_n)^\top$. For now, if we say $(\mathbf{z}_i - \mathbf{w}_n) = \hat{\mathbf{z}}_i$, then $\boldsymbol{\Sigma}_n = \sum_{i=1}^{n} \frac{\hat{\mathbf{z}}_i}{\sqrt{n-1}}\frac{\hat{\mathbf{z}}_i}{\sqrt{n-1}}^\top$. Now, adding a Gaussian noise in each $\hat{\mathbf{z}}_i$ results in the following:

$$\hat{\boldsymbol{\Sigma}}_n = \sum_{i=1}^{n}\left(\frac{\hat{\mathbf{z}}_i}{\sqrt{n-1}} + \eta_i\right)\left(\frac{\hat{\mathbf{z}}_i}{\sqrt{n-1}} + \eta_i\right)^\top \qquad \text{where } \eta_i \sim \mathcal{N}(0, \sigma^2(\epsilon, \delta_n))$$

$$= \sum_{i=1}^{n}\left(\frac{\hat{\mathbf{z}}_i}{\sqrt{n-1}}\frac{\hat{\mathbf{z}}_i}{\sqrt{n-1}}^\top + \frac{\hat{\mathbf{z}}_i}{\sqrt{n-1}}\eta_i^\top + \eta_i\frac{\hat{\mathbf{z}}_i}{\sqrt{n-1}}^\top + \eta_i\eta_i^\top\right)$$

As can be seen by the above equations, we have similar terms like adding wishart noise in the covariance matrix with 2 extra cross terms. Hence instead of using the matrix $\tilde{\boldsymbol{\Sigma}}_n$, one can use $\hat{\boldsymbol{\Sigma}}_n$ for $\boldsymbol{\Sigma}_n$ to compute the weights for the null distribution *i.e.* weighted sum of chi-square in Sect. 5.1.

E   Additional Experimental Details

We see that indeed the Type I error is approximately controlled at the required level for TCMC, TCS and NTE algorithm, for both versions of the test, as shown in Fig. 5, note that here we allow some leeway due to multiple testing. Again, we emphasis that using the asymptotic χ^2 distribution naively would provide inflated Type I error as shown in Fig. 6.

In Fig. 7, we show the effect of the regularisation parameter γ_n on the TCS algorithm performance in terms of Type I error and power on the SG, GMD and GVD datasets. For simplicity, we take $\gamma_n = \gamma$ here, rather then let it depend on the sample size n. From the results, we can see that if the γ to be too small, we will inject too much noise, and hence we will lose power. Note that any $\gamma > 0$ will provide us differential privacy, however if we choose it to be too large, our null distribution will now be mis-calibrated, hurting performance. Hence, there is a trade off between calibration of the null distribution and also the level of noise you need to add.

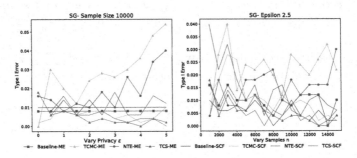

Fig. 5. Type I Error for the SG Dataset, with baselines ME and SCF, $\delta = 1e-5$. **Left:** Vary ϵ, fix $n = 10000$ **Left:** Vary n, fix $\epsilon = 2.5$

F   Proof of Theorem 5.1

Proof. The variance $\sigma_\mathbf{n}^2$ of the zero-mean noise term $\mathbf{n}$ added to the mean vector $\mathbf{w}_n$ is of the order $\mathcal{O}(\frac{1}{n^2})$. Hence the variance of $\sqrt{n}\mathbf{n}$ is of the order $\mathcal{O}(\frac{1}{n})$. According to Slutsky's theorem, $\sqrt{n}\tilde{\mathbf{w}}_n$ and $\sqrt{n}\mathbf{w}_n$ thus converge to the same limit in distribution, which under the null hypothesis is $\mathcal{N}(0, \Sigma)$, with $\Sigma = \mathbb{E}\left[\mathbf{z}\mathbf{z}^\top\right]$. Similarly, the eigenvalues of the covariance matrix corresponding to the Wishart noise to be added in Σ_n are also of the order $\mathcal{O}(\frac{1}{n})$ which implies that $\tilde{\Sigma}_n + \gamma_n I$ and $\Sigma_n + \gamma_n I$ converge to the same limit, i.e. Σ. Therefore, $\tilde{s}_n$ converges in distribution to the same limit as the non-private test statistic, i.e. a chi-squared random variable with J degrees of freedom. We also assume that $\tilde{\Sigma}^{-1}$ and Σ is bounded above by a constant c. If under the alternate we have $\mathbf{w}^\top\Sigma^{-1}\mathbf{w} \geq \mathcal{O}(n^{-\gamma})$ for $\gamma < 1$ which is also related to smallest local departure detectable [16]. Then, we consider the following:

$$\tilde{s}_n = \tilde{s}_n - s_n + s_n$$
$$= s_n \left(1 + \frac{\tilde{s}_n - s_n}{s_n}\right) = s_n \left(1 + \frac{\tilde{\mathbf{w}}_n^\top \tilde{\Sigma}_n^{-1} \tilde{\mathbf{w}}_n - \mathbf{w}_n^\top \Sigma_n^{-1} \mathbf{w}_n}{\mathbf{w}_n^\top \Sigma^{-1} \mathbf{w}_n}\right)$$

We consider the following term:

$$\tilde{\mathbf{w}}_n^\top \tilde{\boldsymbol{\Sigma}}_n^{-1} \tilde{\mathbf{w}}_n - \mathbf{w}_n^\top \boldsymbol{\Sigma}_n^{-1} \mathbf{w}_n = (\tilde{\mathbf{w}}_n - \mathbf{w}_n)^\top \tilde{\boldsymbol{\Sigma}}_n^{-1} (\tilde{\mathbf{w}}_n + \mathbf{w}_n) + \mathbf{w}_n^\top \left(\tilde{\boldsymbol{\Sigma}}_n^{-1} - \boldsymbol{\Sigma}_n^{-1} \right) \mathbf{w}_n$$

$$= (\tilde{\mathbf{w}}_n - \mathbf{w}_n)^\top \tilde{\boldsymbol{\Sigma}}_n^{-1} (\tilde{\mathbf{w}}_n + \mathbf{w}_n) + \mathbf{w}_n^\top \tilde{\boldsymbol{\Sigma}}_n^{-1} \left(\boldsymbol{\Sigma}_n - \tilde{\boldsymbol{\Sigma}}_n \right) \boldsymbol{\Sigma}_n^{-1} \mathbf{w}_n$$

$$\leq \underbrace{\|\tilde{\mathbf{w}}_n - \mathbf{w}_n\| \|\tilde{\boldsymbol{\Sigma}}_n^{-1}\| \|\tilde{\mathbf{w}}_n + \mathbf{w}_n\|}_{:=\text{term 1}} + \underbrace{n \|\boldsymbol{\Sigma}_n^{-1} \mathbf{w}_n\| \|\tilde{\boldsymbol{\Sigma}}_n^{-1} \mathbf{w}_n\| \|\boldsymbol{\Sigma}_n - \tilde{\boldsymbol{\Sigma}}_n\|}_{:=\text{term 2}}$$

Let us consdier the term 1 first.

$$\|\tilde{\mathbf{w}}_n - \mathbf{w}_n\| \|\tilde{\boldsymbol{\Sigma}}_n^{-1}\| \|\tilde{\mathbf{w}}_n + \mathbf{w}_n\| \leq c\kappa^2 \|\tilde{\mathbf{w}}_n - \mathbf{w}_n\|^2$$

Again since variance σ^2 for $\tilde{\mathbf{w}}_n$ is of the order of $\mathcal{O}(n^{-2})$, hence by chebyshev inequality [5] term 1 goes down at the rate $\mathcal{O}(n^{-1})$. Similarly, we consider the term 2.

$$\|\boldsymbol{\Sigma}_n^{-1} \mathbf{w}\| \|\tilde{\boldsymbol{\Sigma}}_n^{-1} \mathbf{w}\| \|\boldsymbol{\Sigma}_n - \tilde{\boldsymbol{\Sigma}}_n\| \leq c^2 \kappa^2 \|\boldsymbol{\Sigma}_n - \tilde{\boldsymbol{\Sigma}}_n\|$$

Now,

$$\|\boldsymbol{\Sigma}_n - \tilde{\boldsymbol{\Sigma}}_n\| = n \|\boldsymbol{\Lambda}_n - \tilde{\boldsymbol{\Lambda}}_n + \frac{n}{n-1} \tilde{\mathbf{w}}_n \tilde{\mathbf{w}}_n^\top - \frac{n}{n-1} \mathbf{w}_n \mathbf{w}_n^\top \|$$

$$\leq \underbrace{\|\boldsymbol{\Lambda}_n - \tilde{\boldsymbol{\Lambda}}_n\|}_{:=\text{term 21}} + \underbrace{\frac{n}{n-1} \|\tilde{\mathbf{w}}_n \tilde{\mathbf{w}}_n^\top - \mathbf{w}_n \mathbf{w}_n^\top\|}_{:=\text{term 22}}$$

Using the same arguement as before, for a fixed J, term 21 will go down as $\mathcal{O}(n^{-2})$ and term 22 will go down as $\mathcal{O}(n^{-1})$. Hence, under the alternate and assumption mentioned in the proof $\tilde{s}_n = s_n(1 + \epsilon)$ where ϵ goes down with rate $\mathcal{O}(n^{-1+\gamma})$ (Fig. 8).

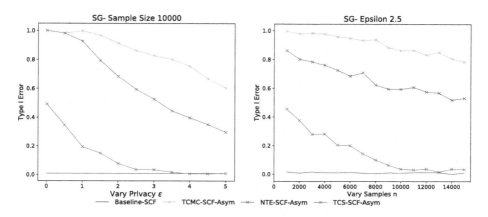

Fig. 6. Type I error for the SCF versions of the test, using the asymptotic χ^2 distribution as the null distribution.

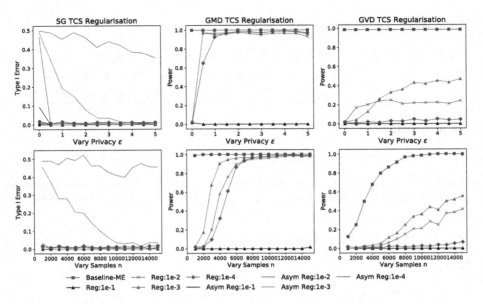

Fig. 7. Type I error for the SG dataset, Power for the GMD, GVD dataset over 500 runs, with $\delta = 1e-5$ for the TCS algorithm with different regularisations. **Top:** Varying ϵ with $n = 10000$. **Bottom:** Varying n with $\epsilon = 2.5$. Here Asym * represents using the asymptotic χ^2 null distribution.

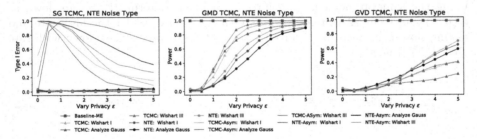

Fig. 8. Type I error for the SG dataset, Power for the GMD, GVD dataset over 500 runs, with $\delta = 1e-5$ for the TCMC and NTE algorithm with different covariance pertubation methods. Here, we vary privacy level ϵ with test samples $n = 10000$. Here we *-Asym represents using the asymptotic χ^2 null distribution.

References

1. Balle, B., Wang, Y.-X.: Improving the gaussian mechanism for differential privacy: analytical calibration and optimal denoising (2018)
2. Balog, M., Tolstikhin, I., Schölkopf, B.: Differentially private database release via kernel mean embeddings (2017). arXiv:1710.01641
3. Borgwardt, K.M., Gretton, A., Rasch, M.J., Kriegel, H.-P., Schölkopf, B., Smola, A.J.: Integrating structured biological data by kernel maximum mean discrepancy. Bioinformatics **22**(14), e49–e57 (2006)

4. Chaudhuri, K., Monteleoni, C., Sarwate, A.D.: Differentially private empirical risk minimization. JMLR **12**, 1069–1109 (2011)
5. Chen, X.: A new generalization of Chebyshev inequality for random vectors. arXiv preprint arXiv:0707.0805 (2007)
6. Chwialkowski, K.P., Ramdas, A., Sejdinovic, D., Gretton, A.: Fast two-sample testing with analytic representations of probability measures. In: NIPS, pp. 1981–1989 (2015)
7. Dwork, C., Kenthapadi, K., McSherry, F., Mironov, I., Naor, M.: Our data, ourselves: privacy via distributed noise generation. In: Vaudenay, S. (ed.) EUROCRYPT 2006. LNCS, vol. 4004, pp. 486–503. Springer, Heidelberg (2006). https://doi.org/10.1007/11761679_29
8. Dwork, C., McSherry, F., Nissim, K., Smith, A.: Calibrating noise to sensitivity in private data analysis. In: Halevi, S., Rabin, T. (eds.) TCC 2006. LNCS, vol. 3876, pp. 265–284. Springer, Heidelberg (2006). https://doi.org/10.1007/11681878_14
9. Dwork, C., Roth, A.: The algorithmic foundations of differential privacy. Found. Trends Theor. Comput. Sci. **9**, 211–407 (2014)
10. Dwork, C., Talwar, K., Thakurta, A., Zhang, L.: Analyze Gauss: optimal bounds for privacy-preserving principal component analysis. In: Symposium on Theory of Computing, STOC 2014, pp. 11–20 (2014)
11. Flaxman, S., Sejdinovic, D., Cunningham, J.P., Filippi, S.: Bayesian learning of kernel embeddings. In: UAI, pp. 182–191 (2016)
12. Gaboardi, M., Lim, H.W., Rogers, R., Vadhan, S.P.: Differentially private chi-squared hypothesis testing: goodness of fit and independence testing. In: ICML, vol. 48, ICML 2016, pp. 2111–2120 (2016)
13. Gaboardi, M., Rogers, R.M.: Local private hypothesis testing: Chi-square tests. CoRR, abs/1709.07155 (2017)
14. Goyal, V., Khurana, D., Mironov, I., Pandey, O., Sahai, A.: Do distributed differentially-private protocols require oblivious transfer?. In: ICALP, pp. 29:1–29:15 (2016)
15. Gretton, A., Borgwardt, K.M., Rasch, M., Schölkopf, B., Smola, A.J.: A kernel method for the two-sample-problem. In: Schölkopf, B., Platt, J.C., Hoffman, T. (eds.) NIPS, pp. 513–520. MIT Press (2007)
16. Gretton, A., Borgwardt, K.M., Rasch, M.J., Schölkopf, B., Smola, A.: A kernel two-sample test. JMLR **13**(1), 723–773 (2012)
17. Gretton, A., Fukumizu, K., Harchaoui, Z., Sriperumbudur, B.K.: A fast, consistent kernel two-sample test. In: NIPS, pp. 673–681 (2009)
18. Gretton, A., et al.:. Optimal kernel choice for large-scale two-sample tests. In: NIPS (2012)
19. Hall, R., Rinaldo, A., Wasserman, L.: Differential privacy for functions and functional data. JMLR **14**, 703–727 (2013)
20. Homer, N.: Resolving individuals contributing trace amounts of DNA to highly complex mixtures using high-density SNP genotyping microarrays. PLoS Genet. **4**(8), 1–9 (2008)
21. Jain, P., Thakurta, A.: Differentially private learning with kernels. In: Proceedings of the 30th International Conference on Machine Learning, ICML 2013, Atlanta, GA, USA, 16–21 June 2013, pp. 118–126, July 2013
22. Jitkrittum, W., Szabó, Z., Chwialkowski, K., Gretton, A.: Interpretable distribution features with maximum testing power. In: NIPS (2016)
23. Johnson, A., Shmatikov,V.: Privacy-preserving data exploration in genome-wide association studies. In: ACM SIGKDD 2013 (2013)

24. Law, H.C.L., Sutherland, D.J., Sejdinovic, D., Flaxman, S.: Bayesian approaches to distribution regression. In: UAI (2017)
25. McGregor, A., Mironov, I., Pitassi, T., Reingold, O., Talwar, K., Vadhan, S.: The limits of two-party differential privacy. In: IEEE, October 2010
26. Muandet, K., Fukumizu, K., Sriperumbudur, B., Schölkopf, B.: Kernel mean embedding of distributions: a review and beyond. Found. Trends® Mach. Learn. 10(1–2), 1–141 (2017)
27. Rahimi, A., Recht, B.: Random features for large-scale kernel machines. In: Advances in Neural Information Processing Systems, pp. 1177–1184 (2008)
28. Rogers, R., Kifer, D.: A new class of private chi-square hypothesis tests. In: Artificial Intelligence and Statistics, pp. 991–1000 (2017)
29. Rothe, R., Timofte, R., Van Gool, L.: Deep expectation of real and apparent age from a single image without facial landmarks. Int. J. Comput. Vision 126(2), 144–157 (2016). https://doi.org/10.1007/s11263-016-0940-3
30. Wahba, G.: Spline Models for Observational Data. Society for Industrial and Applied Mathematics (1990)

Learning to Signal in the Goldilocks Zone: Improving Adversary Compliance in Security Games

Sarah Cooney[1]([⊠]), Kai Wang[1], Elizabeth Bondi[1], Thanh Nguyen[2],
Phebe Vayanos[1], Hailey Winetrobe[1], Edward A. Cranford[3],
Cleotilde Gonzalez[3], Christian Lebiere[3], and Milind Tambe[1]

[1] University of Southern California, Los Angeles, CA 90089, USA
{cooneys,wang319,bondi,phebe.vayanos,hwinetro,tambe}@usc.edu
[2] University of Oregon, Eugene, OR 97403, USA
thanhhng@cs.uoregon.edu
[3] Carnegie Mellon University, Pittsburgh, PA 15289, USA
{cranford,coty,cl}@cmu.edu

Abstract. Many real-world security scenarios can be modeled via a game-theoretic framework known as a security game in which there is a defender trying to protect potential targets from an attacker. Recent work in security games has shown that deceptive signaling by the defender can convince an attacker to withdraw his attack. For instance, a warning message to commuters indicating speed enforcement is in progress ahead might lead to them driving more slowly, even if it turns out no enforcement is in progress. However, the results of this work are limited by the unrealistic assumption that the attackers will behave with perfect rationality, meaning they always choose an action that gives them the best expected reward. We address the problem of training boundedly rational (human) attackers to comply with signals via repeated interaction with signaling without incurring a loss to the defender, and offer the four following contributions: (i) We learn new decision tree and neural network-based models of attacker compliance with signaling. (ii) Based on these machine learning models of a boundedly rational attacker's response to signaling, we develop a theory of signaling in the *Goldilocks zone*, a balance of signaling and deception that increases attacker compliance and improves defender utility. (iii) We present game-theoretic algorithms to solve for signaling schemes based on the learned models of attacker compliance with signaling. (iv) We conduct extensive human subject experiments using an online game. The game simulates the scenario of an inside attacker trying to steal sensitive information from company computers, and results show that our algorithms based on learned models of attacker behavior lead to better attacker compliance and improved defender utility compared to the state-of-the-art algorithm for rational attackers with signaling.

Keywords: Security · Stackelberg games · Behavioral modeling and learning · Bounded rationality · Signaling · Deception

© Springer Nature Switzerland AG 2020
U. Brefeld et al. (Eds.): ECML PKDD 2019, LNAI 11906, pp. 725–740, 2020.
https://doi.org/10.1007/978-3-030-46150-8_42

1   Introduction

Imagine a highway on which many commuters with a tendency to speed travel each day. Suppose the police have a limited amount of time to patrol this highway, but still want to stop people from speeding. One solution is to use deceptive signals, or warnings. For example, a sign noting that speed enforcement is in progress ahead could be used, even if this is not actually the case. It is easy to imagine that if this sign were displayed very often with no real police patrols, the commuters would quickly realize and continue speeding. However, if the commuters knew there was a good chance of actually being stopped and issued a ticket, they would probably slow down. The question is how often can the police display the sign deceptively (without enforcing speed) and still cause the commuters to slow down?

This is the question answered by Xu et al. with their framework for deceptive signaling in Stackelberg Security Games (SSGs) [30]. SSGs model the interaction between an attacker and a defender (in our example, the commuters and the police), and have successfully helped security agencies worldwide optimize the use of limited security resources to mitigate attacks across domains from protecting ports and flights, to mitigating the poaching of endangered animals [2,13,21,26,28]. (We use the term attack broadly to refer to any unwanted behavior or illegal activity, such as speeding.) With the addition of signaling, Xu et al.'s framework allows the defender to strategically reveal information about her defensive strategy to the attacker [30]. On seeing a signal (e.g., a warning that speed enforcement is in effect), a compliant attacker will withdraw his attack to the defender's benefit. The main advantage of signaling is the ability to deter attacks using deception, instead of deploying scarce or costly defensive resources.

This signaling framework was shown in simulation to improve the defender utility against a *perfectly rational* attacker (who always takes the action with the *best* utility for him) compared to the traditional SSG model. Unfortunately, real-world attackers are almost always boundedly rational (*not* always selecting the action with the best utility). Therefore, we focus on finding methods to improve the compliance rates of boundedly rational attackers, who may not comply even if it is rational to do so, but instead learn to react via repeated interactions with signals. This framework could be used to deter boundedly rational attackers in a variety of real-world settings where attackers might repeatedly interact with signals. For instance, speeding commuters, fare evaders on public transit [17], opportunistic criminals looking for chances to strike [34], or cyber-attackers repeatedly probing a system [18].

In order to increase the compliance of boundedly rational attackers, we focus on the frequency of signaling, or deciding how often to signal, and use machine learning models and optimization to learn the overall number of warnings to show, as showing too many warnings can cause attackers to simply ignore them. A key result of this paper is the discovery of a *Goldilocks zone* for signaling—a careful balance of signaling and deception that considers underlying characteristics of individual targets—via the use of machine learning models of attacker behavior, which leads to an increase in human attacker compliance and an improvement of defender utility. Our main contributions are as follows: (i) We learn new models of attacker compliance with regard to signaling based on decision trees and neural networks. (ii) Utilizing insights from these learned models we propose a theory of signaling in the *Goldilocks zone*, a balance of signaling and deception that increases the compliance of boundedly rational adversaries while mitigating losses to the defender. (iii) We present game-theoretic algorithms to solve for signaling schemes based on the learned models. (iv) Using an online game based on the scenario of an inside attacker, we conduct extensive human subject experiments, which show that against boundedly rational subjects, our new modeling-based signaling algorithms outperform the state-of-the-art algorithm designed for perfectly rational attackers.

2 Related Work

Two key game-theoretic frameworks, which have been studied and applied extensively, are SSGs, which model interactions between a defender and an attacker [1,14,29], and signaling games, which model an interaction between two parties in which one party (the sender) reveals some hidden information to the other (the receiver), with the goal of influencing his behavior [22,25]. With the growing interest in the use of deception for security, particularly in the cyber realm [7], game theory researchers have also begun incorporating deception into the security and signaling game frameworks [10,19,36]. Recent work has combined the security and signaling game frameworks with deception, such that the defender strategically reveals (possibly deceptive) information about her defensive strategy to the attacker in hopes of causing him to withdraw his attack [12,31].

However, previous work in game-theoretic frameworks with deception has not investigated human behavior in response to deception, but has instead assumed all respondents are perfectly rational. This is a major limitation to translating these frameworks for use in the real world. In contrast, we focus on this combined signaling-security game framework with boundedly rational attackers who need to be trained to comply with signaling, which has not previously been considered.

There is extensive work modeling the behavior of boundedly rational attackers in classic SSGs without signaling. Early models relied on specific assumptions about attacker behavior [24], using functional forms based on these assumptions such as quantal response [20,32] or prospect theory [33]. More recent work has turned to machine learning models, which use real-world data and do not rely on specific assumptions about attacker behavior [15,35]. Two methods that have been used to predict the behavior of humans in game-theoretic settings are decision trees, which have been used to predict the actions of poachers in Green Security Games [13], and neural networks, which have recently been used to predict the distribution of actions for a player in normal-form, simultaneous move games [11]. We use both of these models, but in contrast to previous work, we are the first to address human behavior *with regard to signaling in a SSG*.

3   Background

In a SSG, there is a set of targets $T = \{t_1, t_2, \ldots, t_n\}$ which the defender protects by allocating $K < n$ resources over them. A *pure* defense strategy is an allocation of the resources, with a *mixed* strategy being a randomization over these pure strategies. Without scheduling constraints, a *mixed* strategy can be equivalently represented as marginal coverage probabilities over the targets, denoted $\mathbf{z} = \{z_t\}$, with $z_t \in [0, 1]$, and $\sum_t z_t = K$, where z_t is the

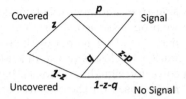

Fig. 1. The signaling scheme for a target t.

probability of protecting target t [14]. The attacker is aware of $\mathbf{z}$ (but not the pure strategy) and chooses a target t to attack accordingly. If the defender is protecting t, the attacker incurs a penalty of $U_a^c(t) < 0$ and the defender is rewarded with $U_d^c(t) \geq 0$. If t is unprotected, the attacker gets a reward of $U_a^u(t) > 0$ and the defender gets a penalty of $U_d^u(t) < 0$. Xu et al. [30] introduced a two-stage SSG with a signaling scheme, allowing the defender to influence the attacker's decision making to her benefit by exploiting the fact that the attacker is unaware of the pure strategy at any given time. A round of the two-stage game plays out as follows:

1. The defender allocates her resources, covering a random subset of the targets based on her mixed strategy $\mathbf{z}$.
2. Aware of the defender's mixed strategy, the attacker chooses a target, t, to attack accordingly.
3. The defender sends a (possibly deceptive) signal to the attacker regarding the current protection status of t.
4. Based on the information given in the signal, the attacker chooses to either (1) continue attacking or (2) withdraw his attack yielding payoffs of zero for both players.

The first stage (steps 1 & 2) is identical to the classic SSG. The second stage (steps 3 & 4) introduces signaling. We can formalize a signaling scheme as follows:

Definition 1 (Signaling Scheme [30]**).** *Given* (t, z_t) *and a signal* σ*, a signaling scheme regarding* t *consists of probabilities* (p_t, q_t) *with* $0 \leq p_t \leq z_t$ *and* $0 \leq q_t \leq 1 - z_t$*, such that* p_t *and* q_t *are the probabilities of showing* σ *given that* t *is currently covered and uncovered, respectively.*

Figure 1 visualizes a signaling scheme for a target t, where z_t is the coverage probability, p_t [q_t] is the probability of signaling given t is covered [uncovered]. A signaling scheme tells the defender how often to warn the attacker broken down into the cases (1) when the warning is true (p_t) and (2) when it is false (q_t). For instance, with probability $(1 - z_t)$, t is not protected by a defensive resource. In this case, we will send a deceptive signal telling the attacker t is protected with probability $\frac{q_t}{1-z_t}$. Intuitively, it is the optimal combination of bluffing and truth telling to ensure the attacker always believes the bluff. The goal is to bluff as much as possible while maintaining this belief.

4 Signaling Schemes for Boundedly Rational Attackers

While previous work focused on a perfectly rational attacker [30], we devise a signaling scheme that increases the compliance of (human) boundedly rational attackers. We let x_t [y_t] be the probability the adversary attacks the chosen target t given a signal is shown [no signal is shown]. For a perfectly rational attacker [30], $x_t = 0$ and $y_t = 1$. As we show in Sect. 7, humans do not behave in such a deterministic manner, so our goal is to find a signaling scheme (p_t and q_t) that provides the most benefit to the defender, despite human behavior. We measure benefit by the expected utility of the defender, defined as follows, where g_t is the probability that the attacker selects t, term (i) is the expected defender utility given no signal is shown, and term (ii) is the expected defender utility otherwise. In each term, we sum up the total expected utility for target t, which has defender reward $U_d^c(t)$ and penalty $U_d^u(t)$:

$$U^d = \sum_t g_t [\underbrace{y_t(z_t - p_t)U_d^c(t) + y_t(1 - z_t - q_t)U_d^u(t)}_{(i)} + \underbrace{x_t p_t U_d^c(t) + x_t q_t U_d^u(t)}_{(ii)}]$$

In the signaling scheme proposed by Xu et al. [30] (hereafter referred to as the peSSE algorithm), term (ii) is always equal to zero (i.e. $x_t = 0$), which is the optimal solution for a perfectly rational attacker. It is the maximum amount of signaling that can be shown and still cause the attacker to withdraw anytime he sees a signal. Further, under the peSSE scheme, the defender only employs deception when a signal is shown. When no signal is shown, it is *always* true that the given target is uncovered (i.e. $z_t - p_t = 0$), and the attacker will succeed. We refer to this type of scheme, as a *1-way* deceptive signaling scheme.

As we show in Sect. 7, in the presence of a boundedly rational attacker, using a signaling scheme, even one designed for perfectly rational attackers, improves defender utility when compared to the traditional SSG framework. We also show that boundedly rational attackers display a training effect via experience with signals. As they experience signals and the consequences of attacking, they become more compliant—attacking less frequently as time goes on. However, under the peSSE scheme, this decrease in attack probability is both gradual and small in magnitude. Therefore, we seek a way to both increase the overall rate of compliance and to speed up the training process without incurring additional loss to the defender. The natural starting point based on insights from literature on using warnings to deter risky cyber behavior [16], is to adjust the false positive (deception) rate. We used a regression tree to learn the probability of attack given a signal (x_t), based on features of each target, including the rate of deception. However, in order to handle instances in which there is no signal—a sure loss to the defender—the optimization process suggested more signaling. We will show this led to the defender being worse off than under the peSSE scheme.

Given these results, we hypothesized that the overall frequency of signaling, not just the deception rate, also has an impact on attacker behavior. In particular, that a high frequency of signaling was causing the attacker to become desensitized and less compliant. Therefore, we propose a new scheme which we call a

2-way deceptive signaling scheme, which lowers the overall frequency of showing a signal without changing the deception rate, and introduces uncertainty for the attacker when no signal is shown. As shown in Sect. 7, 2-way signaling schemes result in faster training of the attacker, an overall increase in compliance, and better expected utility for the defender against boundedly rational attackers. In a 2-way signaling scheme, we decrease p_t and q_t proportionally to reduce the frequency of signaling, while adding uncertainty about the protection status of t when no signal is shown. We formally define the new scheme as follows:

Definition 2 (2-Way Signaling Scheme). *Let $\mathbf{f}$ be a vector such that $\mathbf{f} \in \mathbb{R}^{|T|}$ and $f_t \in [0, 1]$ for all $t \in T$. Then,*

$$(i)\ p_t = f_t z_t \qquad\qquad (ii)\ q_t = -p_t U_a^c(t)/U_a^u(t)$$

In equation (ii), we ensure that the expected value when a signal is shown is equal to zero for all targets. This keeps the deception rate consistent with the **peSSE** scheme, allowing us to focus on the effect of signaling frequency without confounding the effect of changes in deception rate. Intuitively, f_t is the proportion of signals shown compared to the **peSSE** strategy. For example, if $f_t = 0.5$, we show half as many signals as the **peSSE** strategy.

We can visualize 2-way signaling in relation to the **peSSE** scheme by looking at the feasible region of (p, q) in the optimization used to solve for the **peSSE** scheme (Fig. 2). Figure 2 gives the intuition for part two of the following theorem (its proof is in the appendix)[1]:

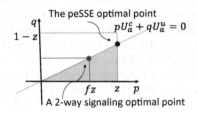

Fig. 2. The (p, q)-feasible regions for the **peSSE** and 2-way signaling schemes.

Theorem 1. *Given a 2-way deception scheme with $f_t \in (0, 1) \ \forall\ t$, if the attacker is perfectly rational, then:*

*(i) The attacker's expected utility per target will be equal to his expected utility under the **peSSE** signaling scheme.*

*(ii) The defender's expected utility per target will be worse than hers under the **peSSE** signaling scheme.*

Two-way signaling makes the signaling scheme sub-optimal for the defender against a perfectly rational attacker, but as we show in Sect. 7, it improves her utility against boundedly rational attackers. The question is *how to choose the correct value of f_t?*

As a baseline, we uniformly reduce the signaling frequency on all targets ($f_t = 0.75, \forall t$), and show that this leads to faster training of subjects, an improvement in the end compliance rate, and an improvement in expected utility for the defender. However, we hypothesize that we can do better by exploiting

---

[1] Link: https://www.dropbox.com/s/uum5tpnb4h1gmym/ECML_Supplement.pdf?dl =0.

the boundedly rational attackers' differing preferences over the targets [20, 23]. We consider learned models of attacker behavior with regard to signaling to determine optimal frequencies of signaling across targets, leading us to find the *Goldilocks zone* for signaling for each target (Sect. 6.3), which outperforms the baseline's uniform reduction of signaling.

5   Learning Models of Attacker Compliance

Recent work has shown machine learning models of human behavior to outperform classic statistically-based behavioral models such as SUQR [9]. Therefore, to model the attacker's response to signaling, we chose two machine learning methods: (i) a decision tree (DT), which has shown recent success in applications to patrol planning to stop

Table 1. Accuracy of attacker models

Round	Model	Accuracy	Precision	Recall
Round 1:	DT	0.711	0.714	0.986
	NN	0.783	0.783	1.0
Round 2:	DT	0.725	0.727	0.995
	NN	0.720	0.731	0.973
Round 3:	DT	0.690	0.705	0.944
	NN	0.683	0.744	0.822
Round 4:	DT	0.654	0.660	0.935
	NN	0.623	0.680	0.786

poachers [8]; and (ii) a neural network (NN), which is generally considered the state-of-the-art in predictive modeling.

We compiled a data set of 17,786 instances on which subjects saw a signal, from three different experiments—peSSE, deception-based, and 2-way signaling baseline (see Sect. 7.1). The features of each data point were the attacker reward and penalty ($U_a^u(t)$ & $U_a^c(t)$), the coverage probability (z_t), and the signaling frequency ($p_t + q_t$), for the attacker's target selection t. We predicted the subject's action ($1 =$ Attack, $0 =$ Withdraw). In order to account for the fact that the level of experience with signals so far has an impact on subject behavior, we separated the data by round, resulting in four data sets with 4448, 4475, 4229, and 4634 instances, respectively. We trained DT and NN models on each round separately. The DT model was trained in R using the `rpart` library, which utilizes the CART algorithm to create classification trees [27]. The complexity parameter (CP) was set to 0.003 to avoid over-fitting. The NN was built in Python using the Keras[2] library. The network was composed of two hidden layers with 50 and 100 nodes, respectively. For training, a weighted categorical crossentropy loss function was used, where the "attack" class (1) was weighted by 0.4 and the "withdraw" class (0) was weighted by 0.6 due to class imbalance. The Nesterov Adam optimizer was used with Glorot normal initialization. The number of nodes, optimizer, and initialization were determined using randomized search hyperparameter optimization from scikit-learn[3]. This was repeated for multiple weights, and the best combination on the validation set was used. Table 1 shows the precision, recall, and mean accuracy on 100 random 80/20 splits of the data.

---

[2] https://keras.io.
[3] https://scikit-learn.org/stable/.

Despite similar accuracy, the models have different strengths. The DT model can give more insight into the features that are most important for increasing compliance. In fact, rpart gives an importance value to each variable, and consistent with our hypothesis, frequency is the most important feature. However, the DT model has a more coarse-grained set of predicted attack probabilities. The NN model is a black-box when it comes to explaining the importance of different features, but gives more fine-grained predictions of attack probability. In the following, we propose new game-theoretic algorithms to find the corresponding optimal signaling scheme for the defender based on both models. As we show in Sect. 7, both methods outperform the peSSE algorithm, with the NN method only slightly outperforming the DT scheme. Thus, practitioners can choose a method based on the trade-off between performance and explainability best suited to their application.

6   Using Learned Models of Behavior to Compute a Signaling Scheme

Using the DT and NN models of attacker compliance, our goal is to compute a signaling scheme that maximizes defender expected utility as expressed in Sect. 4. Evidence from initial experiments show that when there is no signal participants always attack, so we simplify the computation, letting $y_t = 1.0$, and encode the probability of attack given a signal (x_t) as a function of the models' predictions. We focus only on finding the signaling probabilities (p_t, q_t), setting the coverage (z_t) using the algorithm given in [30] and using experimental data to set the selection probabilities (g_t).

6.1   Decision Tree Based Signaling Scheme

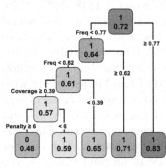

Our goal is to determine what signaling frequency to set in order to maximize the defender's expected utility, where the attacker's response to signaling is given by a DT. For example, Fig. 3, where each node lists the predicted action ($0 = $ No Attack, $1 = $ Attack) and the percentage of attacks ($1's$) at the node (x_t). We will use a mixed-integer linear program (MILP) to find the optimal frequencies. Here we introduce general techniques for building a MILP from the DT model. (The full MILP based on Fig. 3 is in the appendix.)

Fig. 3. The DT modeling the probability of attack given a signal for Round 2 of the Insider Attack Game.

We begin by linearizing the expression of defender utility introduced in Sect. 4, which requires introducing two additional variables, $m_t = x_t q_t$ and $n_t = x_t p_t$:

$$U^d = \sum_t g_t[(z_t - p_t)U_d^c(t) + (1 - z_t - q_t)U_d^u(t) + n_t U_d^c(t) + m_t U_d^u(t)]$$

Each branch splits the data on one of four features—attacker reward (U_a^u), attacker penalty (U_a^c), and coverage probability (z_t), and signaling frequency ($p_t + q_t$). We define binary variables to represent the frequency branches. For each branch on frequency of α, we define a binary variable b_t such that $b_t = 1$ if $p_t + q_t \geq \alpha$ and $b_t = 0$ otherwise. This is enforced by the following constraints, where $M, \epsilon > 0$ are a large and small constants, respectively:

$$\alpha - (1 - b_t)M \leq p_t + q_t \leq \alpha + b_t M - \epsilon$$

For each leaf, we define constraints that enforce that the correct predicted value is substituted for (x_t), constraining the values of m_t and n_t. For example, the constraints on m_t associated with the fourth leaf in Fig. 3 are as follows:

$$0.71q_t - b_t M - (1 - c_t)M \leq m_t \leq 0.71q_t + b_t M + (1 - c_t)M$$

where b_t and c_t are the binary variables associated with branching on frequency $= 0.77$ and $= 0.62$, respectively. These constraints enforce that $x_t = 0.71$, meaning $m_t = 0.71q_t$, when $b_t = 0$ and $c_t = 1$, which is equivalent to frequency $\in [0.62, 0.77)$.

6.2 Neural Network Based Signaling Scheme

To optimize over the black-box NN model, we optimize over a piece-wise linear (PWL) approximation of the predictions using the technique described in [8]. We let f_t define frequency ($p_t + q_t$) according to Definition 2, and introduce the constraint, $p_t = f_t z_t \ \forall \ t \in T$.

Then, we let $\chi_t(f_t)$ be the black-box function predicting attack probability given a signal (x_t), according to the static features z_t, $U_a^c(t)$, and $U_a^u(t)$, taking f_t as an argument. We build a data set (D_χ) of sample predictions at m levels of f_t for each of the T targets, defined by z_t, U_a^u, and U_a^c. Using D_χ, we construct the PWL approximation, representing any value $f_t \in [0, 1]$ and it's prediction $\chi(f_t)$, as a convex combination of its nearest neighbors in the data set for t. Let $B \in D_\chi$ be the break points of the PWL function. We define sets of weights $\lambda_{t,i}$ such that they belong to a *Specially Ordered Set of Type 2*—a set of variables in which at most two can be non-zero, and the non-zero variables must be consecutive. We can then approximate $\chi_t(f_t)$ as a convex combination of (X_t, λ_t) as $\bar{\chi}_t(f_t) = \sum_i \lambda_{t,i}\chi_t(B_{t,i})$. We replace x_t with this expression to formulate defender utility:

$$U^d = \sum_t g_t[y_t(z_t - p_t)U_d^c(t) + y_t(1 - z_t - q_t)U_d^u(t) \tag{1}$$
$$+ \ (\sum_i \lambda_{t,i}\bar{\chi}_t(B_{t,i}))p_t U_d^c(t) + (\sum_i \lambda_{t,i}\bar{\chi}_t(B_{t,i}))q_t U_d^u(t)]$$

6.3 Signaling in the Goldilocks Zone

We now show empirically that using a learned model of attacker behavior *should* improve on a scheme that uniformly reduces signaling frequency on all targets. First, we show there is an expression which can be used to compute the optimal value of f_t for each target individually.

Theorem 2. *Finding an optimal* NN-*based signaling scheme is equivalent to minimizing* $f_t(y_t - \bar{\chi}(f_t))(U_d^c(t)U_a^u(t) - U_d^u(t)U_a^c(t))$ *for each* $t \in T$ *individually, where* $\bar{\chi}(f_t)$ *is the piecewise-linear version of* $\chi(f_t)$. *Specifically, if* $U_d^c(t)U_a^u(t) - U_d^u(t)U_a^c(t) < 0[> 0]$, *it is equivalent to maximizing [minimizing]* $f_t(y_t - \bar{\chi}(f_t))$ *for all* $t \in T$.

In our experimental setting, the utilities satisfy $U_d^c(t)U_a^u(t) - U_d^u(t)U_a^c(t) < 0$, and since the attacker empirically always attacks when no signal is presented ($y_t = 1$), we have the following simplified corollary following from Theorem 2:

Corollary 1. *The optimal* NN-*based solution coincides with* **peSSE** *when* $f_t(1 - \chi(f_t))$ *is monotonically increasing for all* t.

We refer to the value of f_t given by this computation as the *Goldilocks zone* for each target. To give a better intuition about finding the *Goldilocks zone*, we visualize the trend of the function described in Theorem 2, $f_t(1 - \chi(f_t))$, using the DT's and NN's predictions of $\chi(f_t)$ (dropping the bar over $\chi(f_t)$ for simplicity and setting $y_t = 1$, per our setup). The graphs in Fig. 4 show a plot of $f_t(1 - \chi(f_t))$ on the y-axis at 20 levels of f_t (x-axis) for two of the targets from round 2 of our experiment. Observe that the relationship between f_t and $f_t(y_t - \chi(f_t))$ is different for the two targets. Notice that for Target 1 (left), the baseline value of $\mathbf{f} = 0.75$ (yellow dot) is sub-optimal in that it signals too little compared to the optimal NN scheme. However, for Target 4 (right), the baseline signals too often compared to the optimal NN solution. Notice that this is also true for the DT scheme. By optimizing over our learned models, we can find the *Goldilocks zone* for signaling for each target. As we show in Sect. 7, the learning-based signaling schemes actually outperform the baseline in practice.

In general, we find that for more conservative, and thus typically less desirable targets, like Target 1 (reward 5/penalty 3), the optimal signaling rate is higher, with f_t tending toward 1. With more risky, but more appealing, targets such as Target 4 (reward 8/penalty 9),

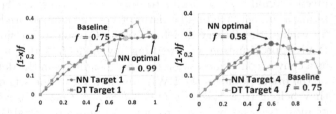

Fig. 4. The relationship between f_t & $(1 - x_t)f_t$ given by the NN and DT for targets 1 (left) and 4 (right) in round 2 of the insider attack game. For some targets, the baseline signaling frequency is too low [high]. (Color figure online)

the *Goldilocks zone* is lower, with f_t tending toward 0.5. A table of the values of f_t for all of the targets under the evaluated signaling schemes can be found in the appendix.

7   Experiments and Results

To evaluate the signaling schemes, we recruited human subjects from Amazon Mechanical Turk to play an online game based on the inside attacker scenario described in [4]. Before starting the game, subjects were given instructions about how it worked, took a short quiz on the instructions, and played a practice round of 5 trials, allowing them to get a sense for the game. Subjects played four rounds of 25 trials each. To study how the subjects' behavior changed with repeated exposure to signaling, the four rounds were played in a fixed order. Each round had six targets (computers) with a different coverage and payoff structure (see Table 1 in [4], as well as the online appendix). After selecting a target t, with probability $(p_t + q_t)$, the subject is shown a warning message. Given a warning and the probability it is false, the subjects then decided whether or not to attack. For consistency, the subjects were also given the choice to attack or withdraw even when no signal was shown. Screenshots of the game interface and details about the participant pool and payment structure can be found in the appendix.

7.1 Evaluated Algorithms

We compare the solution quality of the signaling schemes given by the following algorithms: (i) *no-signaling algorithm*—the defender plays according to the SSE (equivalently, $f_t = 0 \; \forall \; t$); (ii) peSSE—the optimal signaling scheme for a perfectly rational attacker [30] (equivalently, $f_t = 1 \; \forall \; t$); (iii) *2-way signaling baseline*—we set $f_t = 0.75 \; \forall \; t$; (iv) DT *based algorithm*; (v) NN *based algorithm*; and (vi) *deception-based algorithm*.

Evaluation Criteria. We evaluate the algorithms with regard to the average defender expected utility, which is defined for each trial as follows:

$$\frac{1}{N} \sum_{i=1}^{m} A_i [(-1)(1 - z_t)]$$

where A_i is the action take by the attacker at round i ($A_i = 1$ being attack and $A_i = 0$ being withdraw), N is the number of participants, and m is the number of trials. We report $p-$values for a 2-tailed t-test comparing mean expected defender utility per trial. The net score was computed across rounds (e.g., earning 20 points in round 1 and -10 points in round 2 would result in a net score of 10), so we report statistics at both the round and aggregate levels.

7.2 Human Subject Results

Signaling Works. Figure 5 (top) shows the average defender expected utility (y-axis) for each round of the insider attack game. It shows that there is significant benefit ($p < 0.01$) to the defender when using signaling against boundedly rational attackers compared to using no signaling, even when using the peSSE algorithm, designed for perfectly rational attackers. This is also true at the aggregate level ($p < 0.01$) (Fig. 5 (bottom)).

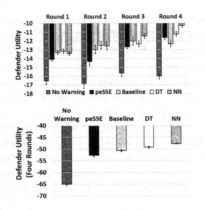

Fig. 5. Comparison of average expected defender utility at the round (top) and aggregate (bottom) levels

Signaling Frequency Matters. At the aggregate level, all three 2-way signaling schemes outperformed the peSSE algorithm at $p < 0.01$ (Fig. 5 (bottom)). As we hypothesized, reducing the frequency of signaling improves performance against boundedly rational attackers.

Learning-Based Schemes Perform Best. As can be seen in Fig. 5, the signaling algorithms based on learned models of attacker behavior performed the best, outperforming both the peSSE and 2-way baseline schemes. The DT scheme outperformed the peSSE in rounds 1 ($p < 0.01$), 2 ($p < 0.01$), and 4 ($p < 0.08$) with no significant difference in round 3. It outperformed the baseline in rounds 2 ($p < 0.03$) and 4 ($p < 0.01$), with no significant difference in utility in rounds 1 and 3. The NN-based algorithm outperformed peSSE in all rounds ($p < 0.01$). It also outperformed the baseline in rounds 2 ($p < 0.08$), 3 and 4 (both $p < 0.01$), with no significant difference in round 1.

The Goldilocks Zone for Signaling. A key finding of our experiments is that using learned models of subject behavior to find the proper signaling frequency (the *Goldilocks zone*) increases its impact, which aligns with our theoretical results (Sect. 6.3). Figure 6 (left), shows the average percent of trials in each round on which subjects saw a signal across the four signaling algorithms. The baseline algorithm signals the least and also achieves almost the best compliance (Fig. 6 (right), the average rate of attack given a signal). The DT and NN based algorithms have middling signaling frequencies on average, and also middling levels of compliance, raising the question: *How do they outperform the baseline scheme?*

Although the baseline achieves high rates of compliance in the signaling case, we did not achieve compliance in the no-signaling case with any of the algorithms. (The average attack rate on instances of no-signal was upwards of 96% across all conditions.) As Fig. 6 (middle) shows, the baseline has a much higher rate of no-signal instances, which are almost always attacked, resulting in high losses for the defender. The DT and NN schemes give up some compliance in the case of a signal by signaling in a more middling range, but make up for this loss by having less no signal instances. In general, lowering the signaling frequency can increase compliance with regard to signals, but must be carefully balanced so that instances in which no signal is shown do not offset the gain to the defender.

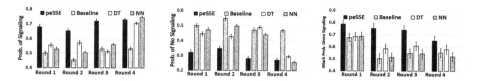

Fig. 6. The balance between lowering signaling probability, to increase compliance, and allowing many instances with no signal. (left) Probability of Showing a Signal. (middle) Probability of Showing No Signal. (right) Probability of Attack Given a Signal.

The learning based approaches do not just find a uniform frequency of signaling somewhere between $f_t = 0.75$ and $f_t = 1$. As mentioned in Sect. 6.3, the NN-based algorithm tends to increase the rate of signaling on less desirable targets, while decreasing it on more popular targets. This varied signaling frequency tuned to the features of each target is what causes the middling range of frequency on average, and also what allows the model-based algorithms to outperform the baseline, by performing better at the target level. Additional discussion of the performance of individual targets can be found in the appendix.

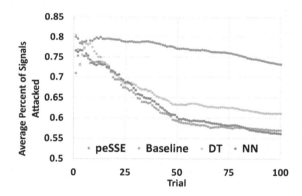

Fig. 7. The average percent of signals attacked (y-axis) up to the current trial (x-axis).

Exploiting the Training Effect. Boundedly rational subjects adjust their response to signaling given repeated exposure to signals and the consequences of attacking. The y-axis of Fig. 7 shows the average percent of signals attacked up to the current trial, which is given on the x-axis. It shows that initially subjects behave in a very exploratory manner, attacking frequently. However, as time passes they become more compliant. In rounds 1–3, the average rate of signaling of the NN signaling scheme falls between the peSSE and baseline algorithms, but in round 4 the NN signaling scheme is equal to the peSSE scheme (see Fig. 6 (right)). Yet, the defender's expected utility is significantly better than in the peSSE experiment. As expected, using 2-way signaling in rounds 1–3 leads to an increased rate of compliance by the final round, as well as a sharp and early drop in attack probability over the course of the first two rounds, compared to the peSSE scheme. Boosting the level of signaling in the fourth round exploits this improved compliance rate, taking advantage of the benefit of signaling to increase the defender's expected utility. We see a similar effect with the DT algorithm. However, this effect is not exploited by the baseline algorithm, which uniformly reduces signaling in all four rounds, and actually performs significantly worse than the peSSE scheme in round 4 (see Fig. 5), even though the level of compliance with signaling is much lower.

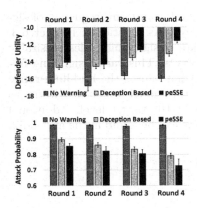

Fig. 8. Average expected defender utility (top) and attack probability (bottom) between the deception-based, peSSE, and no-signaling schemes.

Only Learning the Deception Rate Does Not Work. As discussed in Sect. 4, we compared peSSE with a regression tree-based algorithm that learned the optimal deception rate, but *ignored signaling frequency.* This method led to significantly lower defender expected utility ($p < 0.01$) (Fig. 8) and significantly higher attack probability ($p < 0.06$) (Fig. 8), as by not accounting for the frequency of signaling, it signals too much, causing subjects to become desensitized and non-compliant.

8   Conclusions and Future Work

We have shown that using machine learning to model an attacker's response to deceptive signaling leads to an optimal signaling scheme to deter boundedly rational attackers. We present decision tree- and neural network-based signaling schemes to find the *Goldilocks zone* for signaling. We show via human subject experiments that learning-based signaling schemes improve defender performance, and that these schemes lead humans to become more compliant over repeated interaction. Whereas our results are based on the Mechanical Turk population and game setting, further testing should use realistic simulation with expert participants [6] or even occur "in the wild" [5]. Personalized signaling schemes [3] and defending against adversary manipulation of the system should also be studied.

Acknowledgments. This research was sponsored by the Army Research Office and accomplished under MURI Grant Number W911NF-17-1-0370.

References

1. An, B., Tambe, M., Ordonez, F., Shieh, E., Kiekintveld, C.: Refinement of strong Stackelberg equilibria in security games. In: Twenty-Fifth AAAI (2011)

2. Basilico, N., Gatti, N.: Strategic guard placement for optimal response to alarms in security games. In: Proceedings of the 2014 AAMAS, pp. 1481–1482 (2014)
3. Cranford, E.A., Gonzalez, C., Aggarwal, P., Cooney, S., Tambe, M., Lebiere, C.: towards personalized deceptive signaling for cyber defense using cognitive models. In: Proceedings of the Proceedings of the 17th ICCM (2019, in press)
4. Cranford, E.A., Lebiere, C., Gonzalez, C., Cooney, S., Vayanos, P., Tambe, M.: Learning about cyber deception through simulations: predictions of human decision making with deceptive signals in Stackelberg Security Games. In: CogSci 2018, pp. 25–28 (2018)
5. Delle Fave, F.M., et al.: Security games in the field: an initial study on a transit system. In: Proceedings of the 2014 AAMAS, pp. 1363–1364 (2014)
6. Ferguson-Walter, K., et al.: The Tularosa study: an experimental design and implementation to quantify the effectiveness of cyber deception. In: Proceedings of the 52nd Hawaii International Conference on System Sciences (2019)
7. Fraunholz, D., et al.: Demystifying deception technology: a survey. arXiv preprint arXiv:1804.06196 (2018)
8. Gholami, S., et al.: Adversary models account for imperfect crime data: forecasting and planning against real-world poachers (2018)
9. Gholami, S., Yadav, A., Tran-Thanh, L., Dilkina, B., Tambe, M.: Don't put all your strategies in one basket: playing green security games with imperfect prior knowledge. In: Proceedings of the 18th AAMAS, pp. 395–403 (2019)
10. Guo, Q., An, B., Bosanský, B., Kiekintveld, C.: Comparing strategic secrecy and Stackelberg commitment in security games. In: IJCAI, pp. 3691–3699 (2017)
11. Hartford, J.S., Wright, J.R., Leyton-Brown, K.: Deep learning for predicting human strategic behavior. In: NIPS, pp. 2424–2432 (2016)
12. He, X., Islam, M.M., Jin, R., Dai, H.: Foresighted deception in dynamic security games. In: 2017 IEEE ICC, pp. 1–6 (2017)
13. Kar, D., et al.: Cloudy with a chance of poaching: adversary behavior modeling and forecasting with real-world poaching data. In: Proceedings of the 16th AAMAS, pp. 159–167 (2017)
14. Korzhyk, D., Conitzer, V., Parr, R.: Complexity of computing optimal Stackelberg strategies in security resource allocation games. In: Twenty-Fourth AAAI (2010)
15. Kraus, S.: Predicting human decision-making: from prediction to action. In: Proceedings of the 6th HAI, p. 1. ACM (2018)
16. Krol, K., Moroz, M., Sasse, M.A.: Don't work. can't work? Why it's time to rethink security warnings. In: Risk and Security of Internet and Systems (CRiSIS), 2012, pp. 1–8. IEEE (2012)
17. Luber, S., Yin, Z., Delle Fave, F.M., Jiang, A.X., Tambe, M., Sullivan, J.P.: Game-theoretic patrol strategies for transit systems: the trusts system and its mobile app. In: AAMAS, pp. 1377–1378. Citeseer (2013)
18. Maimon, D., Alper, M., Sobesto, B., Cukier, M.: Restrictive deterrent effects of a warning banner in an attacked computer system. Criminology **52**(1), 33–59 (2014)
19. Nguyen, T.H., Wang, Y., Sinha, A., Wellman, M.P.: Deception in finitely repeated security games. In: 33th AAAI (2019)
20. Nguyen, T.H., Yang, R., Azaria, A., Kraus, S., Tambe, M.: Analyzing the effectiveness of adversary modeling in security games. In: AAAI (2013)
21. Okamoto, S., Hazon, N., Sycara, K.: Solving non-zero sum multiagent network flow security games with attack costs. In: Proceedings of the 11th AAMAS-Volume 2, pp. 879–888 (2012)
22. Pawlick, J., Zhu, Q.: Deception by design: evidence-based signaling games for network defense. arXiv preprint arXiv:1503.05458 (2015)

23. Pita, J., Jain, M., Ordóñez, F., Tambe, M., Kraus, S., Magori-Cohen, R.: Effective solutions for real-world Stackelberg games: when agents must deal with human uncertainties. In: Proceedings of the 8th AAMAS-Volume 1, pp. 369–376 (2009)

24. Smith, S.W.: Security and cognitive bias: exploring the role of the mind. IEEE Secur. Priv. **10**(5), 75–78 (2012)

25. Sobel, J.: Signaling games. In: Meyers, R.A. (ed.) Encyclopedia of Complexity and Systems Science, vol. 19, pp. 8125–8139. Springer, Heidelberg (2009). https://doi.org/10.1007/978-3-642-27737-5

26. Tambe, M.: Security and Game Theory: Algorithms, Deployed Systems, Lessons Learned. Cambridge University Press, Cambridge (2011)

27. Timofeev, R.: Classification and Regression Trees (Cart) Theory and Applications. Humboldt University, Berlin (2004)

28. Wang, B., Zhang, Y., Zhou, Z.-H., Zhong, S.: On repeated stackelberg security game with the cooperative human behavior model for wildlife protection. Appl. Intell. **49**(3), 1002–1015 (2018). https://doi.org/10.1007/s10489-018-1307-y

29. Wilczyński, A., Jakóbik, A., Kołodziej, J.: Stackelberg security games: models, applications and computational aspects. J. Telecommun. Inf. Technol. **2016**, 70–79 (2016)

30. Xu, H., Rabinovich, Z., Dughmi, S., Tambe, M.: Exploring information asymmetry in two-stage security games. In: AAAI, pp. 1057–1063 (2015)

31. Xu, H., Wang, K., Vayanos, P., Tambe, M.: Strategic coordination of human patrollers and mobile sensors with signaling for security games. In: Thirty-Second AAAI (2018)

32. Yang, R., Kiekintveld, C., Ordonez, F., Tambe, M., John, R.: Improving resource allocation strategy against human adversaries in security games. In: Twenty-Second IJCAI (2011)

33. Yang, R., Kiekintveld, C., OrdóñEz, F., Tambe, M., John, R.: Improving resource allocation strategies against human adversaries in security games: an extended study. Artif. Intell. **195**, 440–469 (2013)

34. Zhang, C., Jiang, A.X., Short, M.B., Brantingham, P.J., Tambe, M.: Defending against opportunistic criminals: new game-theoretic frameworks and algorithms. In: Poovendran, R., Saad, W. (eds.) GameSec 2014. LNCS, vol. 8840, pp. 3–22. Springer, Cham (2014). https://doi.org/10.1007/978-3-319-12601-2_1

35. Zhang, C., Sinha, A., Tambe, M.: Keeping pace with criminals: designing patrol allocation against adaptive opportunistic criminals. In: Proceedings of the 2015 AAMAS, pp. 1351–1359 (2015)

36. Zhuang, J., Bier, V.M., Alagoz, O.: Modeling secrecy and deception in a multiple-period attacker-defender signaling game. Eur. J. Oper. Res. **203**(2), 409–418 (2010)

Optimization

A Stochastic Quasi-Newton Method with Nesterov's Accelerated Gradient

S. Indrapriyadarsini[1], Shahrzad Mahboubi[2], Hiroshi Ninomiya[2], and Hideki Asai[1(✉)]

[1] Shizuoka University, Hamamatsu, Shizuoka Prefecture, Japan
{s.indrapriyadarsini.17,asai.hideki}@shizuoka.ac.jp
[2] Shonan Institute of Technology, Fujisawa, Kanagawa Prefecture, Japan
18T2012@sit.shonan-it.ac.jp, ninomiya@info.shonan-it.ac.jp

Abstract. Incorporating second order curvature information in gradient based methods have shown to improve convergence drastically despite its computational intensity. In this paper, we propose a stochastic (online) quasi-Newton method with Nesterov's accelerated gradient in both its full and limited memory forms for solving large scale non-convex optimization problems in neural networks. The performance of the proposed algorithm is evaluated in Tensorflow on benchmark classification and regression problems. The results show improved performance compared to the classical second order oBFGS and oLBFGS methods and popular first order stochastic methods such as SGD and Adam. The performance with different momentum rates and batch sizes have also been illustrated.

Keywords: Neural networks · Stochastic method · Online training · Nesterov's accelerated gradient · Quasi-Newton method · Limited memory · Tensorflow

1 Introduction

Neural networks have shown to be effective in innumerous real-world applications. Most of these applications require large neural network models with massive amounts of training data to achieve good accuracies and low errors. Neural network optimization poses several challenges such as ill-conditioning, vanishing and exploding gradients, choice of hyperparameters, etc. Thus choice of the optimization algorithm employed on the neural network model plays an important role. It is expected that the neural network training imposes relatively lower computational and memory demands, in which case a full-batch approach is not suitable. Thus, in large scale optimization problems, a stochastic approach is more desirable. Stochastic optimization algorithms use a small subset of data (mini-batch) in its evaluations of the objective function. These methods are particularly of relevance in examples of a continuous stream of data, where the partial data is to be modelled as it arrives. Since the stochastic or online methods operate on small subsamples of the data and its gradients, they significantly reduce the computational and memory requirements.

© Springer Nature Switzerland AG 2020
U. Brefeld et al. (Eds.): ECML PKDD 2019, LNAI 11906, pp. 743–760, 2020.
https://doi.org/10.1007/978-3-030-46150-8_43

1.1   Related Works

Gradient based algorithms are popularly used in training neural network models. These algorithms can be broadly classified into first order and second order methods [1]. Several works have been devoted to stochastic first-order methods such as stochastic gradient descent (SGD) [2,3] and its variance-reduced forms [4–6], AdaGrad [7], RMSprop [8] and Adam [9]. First order methods are popular due to its simplicity and optimal complexity. However, incorporating the second order curvature information have shown to improve convergence. But one of the major drawbacks in second order methods is its need for high computational and memory resources. Thus several approximations have been proposed under Newton [10,11] and quasi-Newton [12] methods in order to make use of the second order information while keeping the computational load minimal.

Unlike the first order methods, getting quasi-Newton methods to work in a stochastic setting is challenging and has been an active area of research. The oBFGS method [13] is one of the early stable stochastic quasi-Newton methods, in which the gradients are computed twice using the same sub-sample, to ensure stability and scalability. Recently there has been a surge of interest in designing efficient stochastic second order variants which are better suited for large scale problems. [14] proposed a regularized stochastic BFGS method (RES) that modifies the proximity condition of BFGS. [15] further analyzed the global convergence properties of stochastic BFGS and proposed an online L-BFGS method. [16] proposed a stochastic limited memory BFGS (SQN) through sub-sampled Hessian vector products. [17] proposed a general framework for stochastic quasi-Newton methods that assume noisy gradient information through first order oracle (SFO) and extended it to a stochastic damped L-BFGS method (SdLBFGS). This was further modified in [18] by reinitializing the Hessian matrix at each iteration to improve convergence and normalizing the search direction to improve stability. There are also several other studies on stochastic quasi-Newton methods with variance reduction [19–21], sub-sampling [11,22] and block updates [23]. Most of these methods have been proposed for solving convex optimization problems, but training of neural networks for non-convex problems have not been mentioned in their scopes. The focus of this paper is on training neural networks for non-convex problems with methods similar to that of the oBFGS in [13] and RES [14,15], as they are stochastic extensions of the classical quasi-Newton method. Thus, the other sophisticated algorithms [11,16–23] are excluded from comparison in this paper and will be studied in future works.

In this paper, we introduce a novel stochastic quasi-Newton method that is accelerated using Nesterov's accelerated gradient. Acceleration of quasi-Newton method with Nesterov's accelerated gradient have shown to improve convergence [24,25]. The proposed algorithm is a stochastic extension of the accelerated methods in [24,25] with changes similar to the oBFGS method. The proposed method is also discussed both in its full and limited memory forms. The performance of the proposed methods are evaluated on benchmark classification and regression problems and compared with the conventional SGD, Adam and o(L)BFGS methods.

2   Background

$$\min_{\mathbf{w} \in \mathbb{R}^d} E(\mathbf{w}) = \frac{1}{b} \sum_{p \in X} E_p(\mathbf{w}), \tag{1}$$

Training in neural networks is an iterative process in which the parameters are updated in order to minimize an objective function. Given a mini-batch $X \subseteq T_r$ with samples $(x_p, d_p)_{p \in X}$ drawn at random from the training set T_r and error function $E_p(\mathbf{w}; x_p, d_p)$ parameterized by a vector $\mathbf{w} \in \mathbb{R}^d$, the objective function is defined as in (1) where $b = |X|$, is the batch size. In full batch, $X = T_r$ and $b = n$ where $n = |T_r|$. In gradient based methods, the objective function $E(\mathbf{w})$ under consideration is minimized by the iterative formula (2) where k is the iteration count and $\mathbf{v}_{k+1}$ is the update vector, which is defined for each gradient algorithm.

$$\mathbf{w}_{k+1} = \mathbf{w}_k + \mathbf{v}_{k+1}. \tag{2}$$

In the following sections, we briefly discuss the full-batch BFGS quasi-Newton method and full-batch Nesterov's Accelerated quasi-Newton method in its full and limited memory forms. We further extend to briefly discuss a stochastic BFGS method.

Algorithm 1. BFGS Method

Require: ε and k_{max}
Initialize: $\mathbf{w}_k \in \mathbb{R}^d$ and $\mathbf{H}_k = \mathbf{I}$.
1: $k \leftarrow 1$
2: Calculate $\nabla E(\mathbf{w}_k)$
3: **while** $||E(\mathbf{w}_k)|| > \varepsilon$ and $k < k_{max}$ **do**
4:      $\mathbf{g}_k \leftarrow -\mathbf{H}_k \nabla E(\mathbf{w}_k)$
5:      Determine α_k by line search
6:      $\mathbf{v}_{k+1} \leftarrow \alpha_k \mathbf{g}_k$
7:      $\mathbf{w}_{k+1} \leftarrow \mathbf{w}_k + \mathbf{v}_{k+1}$
8:      Calculate $\nabla E(\mathbf{w}_{k+1})$
9:      Update $\mathbf{H}_{k+1}$ using (4)
10:      $k \leftarrow k + 1$
11: **end while**

Algorithm 2. NAQ Method

Require: $0 < \mu < 1$, ε and k_{max}
Initialize: $\mathbf{w}_k \in \mathbb{R}^d$, $\mathbf{H}_k = \mathbf{I}$ and $\mathbf{v}_k = 0$.
1: $k \leftarrow 1$
2: **while** $||E(\mathbf{w}_k)|| > \varepsilon$ and $k < k_{max}$ **do**
3:      Calculate $\nabla E(\mathbf{w}_k + \mu \mathbf{v}_k)$
4:      $\hat{\mathbf{g}}_k \leftarrow -\hat{\mathbf{H}}_k \nabla E(\mathbf{w}_k + \mu \mathbf{v}_k)$
5:      Determine α_k by line search
6:      $\mathbf{v}_{k+1} \leftarrow \mu \mathbf{v}_k + \alpha_k \hat{\mathbf{g}}_k$
7:      $\mathbf{w}_{k+1} \leftarrow \mathbf{w}_k + \mathbf{v}_{k+1}$
8:      Calculate $\nabla E(\mathbf{w}_{k+1})$
9:      Update $\hat{\mathbf{H}}_k$ using (9)
10:      $k \leftarrow k + 1$
11: **end while**

2.1   BFGS Quasi-Newton Method

Quasi-Newton methods utilize the gradient of the objective function to achieve superlinear or quadratic convergence. The Broyden-Fletcher-Goldfarb-Shanon (BFGS) algorithm is one of the most popular quasi-Newton methods for unconstrained optimization. The update vector of the quasi-Newton method is given as

$$\mathbf{v}_{k+1} = \alpha_k \mathbf{g}_k, \tag{3}$$

where $\mathbf{g}_k = -\mathbf{H}_k \nabla E(\mathbf{w}_k)$ is the search direction. The hessian matrix $\mathbf{H}_k$ is symmetric positive definite and is iteratively approximated by the following BFGS formula [26].

$$\mathbf{H}_{k+1} = (\mathbf{I} - \mathbf{s}_k \mathbf{y}_k^T / \mathbf{y}_k^T \mathbf{s}_k) \mathbf{H}_k (\mathbf{I} - \mathbf{y}_k \mathbf{s}_k^T / \mathbf{y}_k^T \mathbf{s}_k) + \mathbf{s}_k \mathbf{s}_k^T / \mathbf{y}_k^T \mathbf{s}_k, \qquad (4)$$

where $\mathbf{I}$ denotes identity matrix,

$$\mathbf{s}_k = \mathbf{w}_{k+1} - \mathbf{w}_k \quad \text{and} \quad \mathbf{y}_k = \nabla E(\mathbf{w}_{k+1}) - \nabla E(\mathbf{w}_k). \qquad (5)$$

The BFGS quasi-Newton algorithm is shown in Algorithm 1.

Limited Memory BFGS (LBFGS): LBFGS is a variant of the BFGS quasi-Newton method, designed for solving large-scale optimization problems. As the scale of the neural network model increases, the $O(d^2)$ cost of storing and updating the Hessian matrix $\mathbf{H}_k$ is expensive [13]. In the limited memory version, the Hessian matrix is defined by applying m BFGS updates using only the last m curvature pairs $\{\mathbf{s}_k, \mathbf{y}_k\}$. As a result, the computational cost is significantly reduced and the storage cost is down to $O(md)$ where d is the number of parameters and m is the memory size.

2.2   Nesterov's Accelerated Quasi-Newton Method

Several modifications have been proposed to the quasi-Newton method to obtain stronger convergence. The Nesterov's Accelerated Quasi-Newton (NAQ) [24] method achieves faster convergence compared to the standard quasi-Newton methods by quadratic approximation of the objective function at $\mathbf{w}_k + \mu \mathbf{v}_k$ and by incorporating the Nesterov's accelerated gradient $\nabla E(\mathbf{w}_k + \mu \mathbf{v}_k)$ in its Hessian update. The derivation of NAQ is briefly discussed as follows.

Let $\Delta \mathbf{w}$ be the vector $\Delta \mathbf{w} = \mathbf{w} - (\mathbf{w}_k + \mu \mathbf{v}_k)$. The quadratic approximation of the objective function at $\mathbf{w}_k + \mu \mathbf{v}_k$ is defined as,

$$E(\mathbf{w}) \simeq E(\mathbf{w}_k + \mu \mathbf{v}_k) + \nabla E(\mathbf{w}_k + \mu \mathbf{v}_k)^T \Delta \mathbf{w} + \frac{1}{2} \Delta \mathbf{w}^T \nabla^2 E(\mathbf{w}_k + \mu \mathbf{v}_k) \Delta \mathbf{w}. \qquad (6)$$

The minimizer of this quadratic function is explicitly given by

$$\Delta \mathbf{w} = -\nabla^2 E(\mathbf{w}_k + \mu \mathbf{v}_k)^{-1} \nabla E(\mathbf{w}_k + \mu \mathbf{v}_k). \qquad (7)$$

Therefore the new iterate is defined as

$$\mathbf{w}_{k+1} = (\mathbf{w}_k + \mu \mathbf{v}_k) - \nabla^2 E(\mathbf{w}_k + \mu \mathbf{v}_k)^{-1} \nabla E(\mathbf{w}_k + \mu \mathbf{v}_k). \qquad (8)$$

This iteration is considered as Newton method with the momentum term $\mu \mathbf{v}_k$. The inverse of Hessian $\nabla^2 E(\mathbf{w}_k + \mu \mathbf{v}_k)$ is approximated by the matrix $\hat{\mathbf{H}}_{k+1}$ using the update Eq. (9)

$$\hat{\mathbf{H}}_{k+1} = (\mathbf{I} - \mathbf{p}_k \mathbf{q}_k^T / \mathbf{q}_k^T \mathbf{p}_k) \hat{\mathbf{H}}_k (\mathbf{I} - \mathbf{q}_k \mathbf{p}_k^T / \mathbf{q}_k^T \mathbf{p}_k) + \mathbf{p}_k \mathbf{p}_k^T / \mathbf{q}_k^T \mathbf{p}_k, \qquad (9)$$

Algorithm 3. Direction Update

Require: current gradient $\nabla E(\theta_k)$, memory size m, curvature pair $(\sigma_{k-i}, \ \gamma_{k-i})$
$\forall i = 1, 2, ..., min(k-1, m)$ where σ_k is the difference of current and previous weight
vector and γ_k is the difference of current and previous gradient vector
1: $\eta_k = -\nabla E(\theta_k)$
2: **for** $i := 1, 2, ..., min(m, k-1)$ **do**
3:     $\beta_i = (\sigma_{k-i}^T \eta_k)/(\sigma_{k-i}^T \gamma_{k-i})$
4:     $\eta_k = \eta_k - \beta_i \gamma_{k-i}$
5: **end for**
6: **if** $k > 1$ **then**
7:     $\eta_k = \eta_k(\sigma_k^T \gamma_k/\gamma_k^T \gamma_k)$
8: **end if**
9: **for** $i : k - min(m, (k-1)), ..., k-1, k$ **do**
10:     $\tau = (\gamma_i^T \eta_k)/(\gamma_i^T \sigma_i)$
11:     $\eta_k = \eta_k - (\beta_i - \tau)\sigma_i$
12: **end for**
13: **return** η_k

---

where

$$\mathbf{p}_k = \mathbf{w}_{k+1} - (\mathbf{w}_k + \mu\mathbf{v}_k) \ \text{ and } \ \mathbf{q}_k = \nabla E(\mathbf{w}_{k+1}) - \nabla E(\mathbf{w}_k + \mu\mathbf{v}_k). \tag{10}$$

(9) is derived from the secant condition $\mathbf{q}_k = (\hat{\mathbf{H}}_{k+1})^{-1}\mathbf{p}_k$ and the rank-2 updating formula [24]. It is proved that the Hessian matrix $\hat{\mathbf{H}}_{k+1}$ updated by (9) is a positive definite symmetric matrix given $\hat{\mathbf{H}}_k$ is initialized to identity matrix [24]. Therefore, the update vector of NAQ can be written as:

$$\mathbf{v}_{k+1} = \mu\mathbf{v}_k + \alpha_k \hat{\mathbf{g}}_k, \tag{11}$$

where $\hat{\mathbf{g}}_k = -\hat{\mathbf{H}}_k \nabla E(\mathbf{w}_k + \mu\mathbf{v}_k)$ is the search direction. The NAQ algorithm is given in Algorithm 2. Note that the gradient is computed twice in one iteration. This increases the computational cost compared to the BFGS quasi-Newton method. However, due to acceleration by the momentum and Nesterov's gradient term, NAQ is faster in convergence compared to BFGS.

Limited Memory NAQ (LNAQ). Similar to LBFGS method, LNAQ [25] is the limited memory variant of NAQ that uses the last m curvature pairs $\{\mathbf{p}_k, \mathbf{q}_k\}$. In the limited-memory form note that the curvature pairs that are used incorporate the momemtum and Nesterov's accelerated gradient term, thus accelerating LBFGS. Implementation of LNAQ algorithm can be realized by omitting steps 4 and 9 of Algorithm 2 and determining the search direction $\hat{\mathbf{g}}_k$ using the two-loop recursion [26] shown in Algorithm 3. The last m vectors of $\mathbf{p}_k$ and $\mathbf{q}_k$ are stored and used in the direction update.

2.3   Stochastic BFGS Quasi-Newton Method (oBFGS)

The online BFGS method proposed by Schraudolph et al. in [13] is a fast and scalable stochastic quasi-Newton method suitable for convex functions. The changes proposed to the BFGS method in [13] to work well in a stochastic setting are discussed as follows. The line search is replaced with a gain schedule such as

$$\alpha_k = \tau/(\tau + k) \cdot \alpha_0, \tag{12}$$

where $\alpha_0, \tau > 0$ provided the Hessian matrix is positive definite, thus restricting to convex optimization problems. Since line search is eliminated, the first parameter update is scaled by a small value. Further, to improve the performance of oBFGS, the step size is divided by an analytically determined constant c. An important modification is the computation of $\mathbf{y}_k$, the difference of the last two gradients is computed on the same sub-sample X_k [13,14] as given below,

$$\mathbf{y}_k = \nabla E(\mathbf{w}_{k+1}, X_k) - \nabla E(\mathbf{w}_k, X_k). \tag{13}$$

This however doubles the cost of gradient computation per iteration but is shown to outperform natural gradient descent for all batch sizes [13]. The oBFGS algorithm is shown in Algorithm 4. In this paper, we introduce direction normalization as shown in step 5, details of which are discussed in the next section.

Stochastic Limited Memory BFGS (oLBFGS). [13] further extends the oBFGS method to limited memory form by determining the search direction $\mathbf{g}_k$ using the two-loop recursion (Algorithm 3). The Hessian update is omitted and instead the last m curvature pairs $\mathbf{s}_k$ and $\mathbf{y}_k$ are stored. This brings down the computation complexity to $2bd + 6md$ where b is the batch size, d is the number of parameters, and m is the memory size. To improve the performance by averaging sampling noise step 7 of Algorithm 3 is replaced by (14) where σ_k is $\mathbf{s}_k$ and γ_k is $\mathbf{y}_k$.

$$\eta_k = \begin{cases} \epsilon\eta_k & \text{if } k = 1, \\ \dfrac{\eta_k}{\min(k, m)} \displaystyle\sum_{i=1}^{\min(k,m)} \dfrac{\sigma_{k-i}^{\mathrm{T}}\gamma_{k-i}}{\gamma_{k-i}^{\mathrm{T}}\gamma_{k-i}} & \text{otherwise.} \end{cases} \tag{14}$$

3   Proposed Algorithm - oNAQ and oLNAQ

The oBFGS method proposed in [13] computes the gradient of a sub-sample mini-batch X_k twice in one iteration. This is comparable with the inherent nature of NAQ which also computes the gradient twice in one iteration. Thus by applying suitable modifications to the original NAQ algorithm, we achieve a stochastic version of the Nesterov's Accelerated Quasi-Newton method. The proposed modifications for a stochastic NAQ method is discussed below in its full and limited memory forms.

3.1 Stochastic NAQ (oNAQ)

The NAQ algorithm computes two gradients, $\nabla E(\mathbf{w}_k + \mu\mathbf{v}_k)$ and $\nabla E(\mathbf{w}_{k+1})$ to calculate $\mathbf{q}_k$ as shown in (10). On the other hand, the oBFGS method proposed in [13] computes the gradient $\nabla E(\mathbf{w}_k, X_k)$ and $\nabla E(\mathbf{w}_{k+1}, X_k)$ to calculate $\mathbf{y}_k$ as shown in (13). Therefore, oNAQ can be realised by changing steps 3 and 8 of Algorithm 2 to calculate $\nabla E(\mathbf{w}_k + \mu\mathbf{v}_k, X_k)$ and $\nabla E(\mathbf{w}_{k+1}, X_k)$. Thus in oNAQ, the $\mathbf{q}_k$ vector is given by (15) where $\lambda\mathbf{p}_k$ is used to guarantee numerical stability [27–29].

$$\mathbf{q}_k = \nabla E(\mathbf{w}_{k+1}, X_k) - \nabla E(\mathbf{w}_k + \mu\mathbf{v}_k, X_k) + \lambda\mathbf{p}_k, \tag{15}$$

Further, unlike in full batch methods, the updates in stochastic methods have high variance resulting in the objective function to fluctuate heavily. This is due to the updates being performed based on small sub-samples of data. This can be seen more prominently in case of the limited memory version where the updates are based only on m recent curvature pairs. Thus in order to improve the stability of the algorithm, we introduce direction normalization as

$$\hat{\mathbf{g}}_k = \hat{\mathbf{g}}_k / \|\hat{\mathbf{g}}_k\|_2, \tag{16}$$

where $\|\hat{\mathbf{g}}_k\|_2$ is the l_2 norm of the search direction $\hat{\mathbf{g}}_k$. Normalizing the search direction at each iteration ensures that the algorithm does not move too far away from the current objective [18]. Figure 1 illustrates the effect of direction normalization on oBFGS and the proposed oNAQ method. The solid lines indicate the moving average. As seen from the figure, direction normalization improves the performance of both oBFGS and oNAQ. Therefore, in this paper we include direction normalization for oBFGS also.

The next proposed modification is with respect to the step size. In full batch methods, the step size or the learning rate is usually determined by line search methods satisfying either Armijo or Wolfe conditions. However, in stochastic methods, line searches are not quite effective since search conditions apply global validity. This cannot be assumed when using small local sub-samples [13]. Several studies show that line search methods does not necessarily ensure global convergence and have proposed methods that eliminate line search [27–29]. Moreover, determining step size using line search methods involves additional function computations until the search conditions such as the Armijo or Wolfe condition is satisfied. Hence we determine the step size using a simple learning rate schedule. Common learning rate schedules are polynomial decays and exponential decay functions. In this paper, we determine the step size using a polynomial decay schedule [30]

$$\alpha_k = \alpha_0 / \sqrt{k}, \tag{17}$$

where α_0 is usually set to 1. If the step size is too large, which is the case in the initial iterations, the learning can become unstable. This is stabilized by direction normalization. A comparison of common learning rate schedules are illustrated in Fig. 2.

The proposed stochastic NAQ algorithm is shown in Algorithm 5. Note that the gradient is computed twice in one iteration, thus making the computational cost same as that of the stochastic BFGS (oBFGS) proposed in [13].

Algorithm 4. oBFGS Method

Require: minibatch X_k, k_{max} and $\lambda \geq 0$,

Initialize: $\mathbf{w}_k \in \mathbb{R}^d$, $\mathbf{H}_k = \epsilon\mathbf{I}$ and $\mathbf{v}_k = 0$

1: $k \leftarrow 1$
2: **while** $k < k_{max}$ **do**
3:      $\nabla\mathbf{E}_1 \leftarrow \nabla E(\mathbf{w}_k, X_k)$
4:      $\mathbf{g}_k \leftarrow -\mathbf{H}_k\nabla E(\mathbf{w}_k, X_k)$
5:      $\mathbf{g}_k = \mathbf{g}_k/\|\mathbf{g}_k\|_2$
6:      Determine α_k using (12)
7:      $\mathbf{v}_{k+1} \leftarrow \alpha_k\mathbf{g}_k$
8:      $\mathbf{w}_{k+1} \leftarrow \mathbf{w}_k + \mathbf{v}_{k+1}$
9:      $\nabla\mathbf{E}_2 \leftarrow \nabla E(\mathbf{w}_{k+1}, X_k)$
10:     $\mathbf{s}_k \leftarrow \mathbf{w}_{k+1} - \mathbf{w}_k$
11:     $\mathbf{y}_k \leftarrow \nabla\mathbf{E}_2 - \nabla\mathbf{E}_1 + \lambda\mathbf{s}_k$
12:     Update $\mathbf{H}_k$ using (4)
13:     $k \leftarrow k + 1$
14: **end while**

Algorithm 5. Proposed oNAQ Method

Require: minibatch X_k, $0 < \mu < 1$ and k_{max}

Initialize: $\mathbf{w}_k \in \mathbb{R}^d$, $\hat{\mathbf{H}}_k = \epsilon\mathbf{I}$ and $\mathbf{v}_k = 0$

1: $k \leftarrow 1$
2: **while** $k < k_{max}$ **do**
3:      $\nabla\mathbf{E}_1 \leftarrow \nabla E(\mathbf{w}_k + \mu\mathbf{v}_k, X_k)$
4:      $\hat{\mathbf{g}}_k \leftarrow -\hat{\mathbf{H}}_k\nabla E(\mathbf{w}_k + \mu\mathbf{v}_k, X_k)$
5:      $\hat{\mathbf{g}}_k = \hat{\mathbf{g}}_k/\|\hat{\mathbf{g}}_k\|_2$
6:      Determine α_k using (17)
7:      $\mathbf{v}_{k+1} \leftarrow \mu\mathbf{v}_k + \alpha_k\hat{\mathbf{g}}_k$
8:      $\mathbf{w}_{k+1} \leftarrow \mathbf{w}_k + \mathbf{v}_{k+1}$
9:      $\nabla\mathbf{E}_2 \leftarrow \nabla E(\mathbf{w}_{k+1}, X_k)$
10:     $\mathbf{p}_k \leftarrow \mathbf{w}_{k+1} - (\mathbf{w}_k + \mu\mathbf{v}_k)$
11:     $\mathbf{q}_k \leftarrow \nabla\mathbf{E}_2 - \nabla\mathbf{E}_1 + \lambda\mathbf{p}_k$
12:     Update $\hat{\mathbf{H}}_k$ using (9)
13:     $k \leftarrow k + 1$
14: **end while**

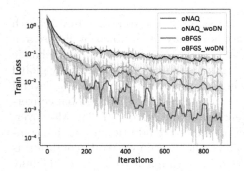
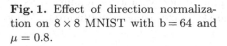

Fig. 1. Effect of direction normalization on 8×8 MNIST with b $= 64$ and $\mu = 0.8$.

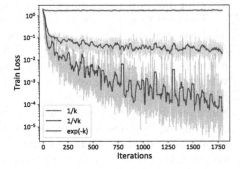

Fig. 2. Comparison of α_k schedules on 8×8 MNIST with b $= 64$ and $\mu = 0.8$.

3.2   Stochastic Limited-Memory NAQ (oLNAQ)

Stochastic LNAQ can be realized by making modifications to Algorithm 5 similar to LNAQ. The search direction $\hat{\mathbf{g}}_k$ in step 4 is determined by Algorithm 3.

oLNAQ like LNAQ uses the last m curvature pairs $\{\mathbf{p}_k, \mathbf{q}_k\}$ to estimate the Hessian matrix instead of storing and computing on a $d \times d$ matrix. Therefore, the implementation of oLNAQ does not require initializing or updating the Hessian matrix. Hence step 12 of Algorithm 5 is replaced by storing the last m curvature pairs $\{\mathbf{p}_k, \mathbf{q}_k\}$. Finally, in order to average out the sampling noise in the last m steps, we replace step 7 of Algorithm 3 by Eq. (14) where σ_k is $\mathbf{p}_k$ and γ_k is $\mathbf{q}_k$. Note that an additional $2md$ evaluations are required to compute (14). However the overall computation cost of oLNAQ is much lesser than that of oNAQ and the same as oLBFGS.

4   Simulation Results

We illustrate the performance of the proposed stochastic methods oNAQ and oLNAQ on four benchmark datasets - two classification and two regression problems. For the classification problem we use the 8×8 MNIST and 28×28 MNIST datasets and for the regression problem we use the Wine Quality [31] and CASP [32] datasets. We evaluate the performance of the classification tasks on a multi-layer neural network (MLNN) and a simple convolution neural network (CNN). The algorithms oNAQ, oBFGS, oLNAQ and oLBFGS are implemented in Tensorflow using the ScipyOptimizerInterface class. Details of the simulation are given in Table 1.

4.1   Multi-layer Neural Networks - Classification Problem

We evaluate the performance of the proposed algorithms for classification of handwritten digits using the 8×8 MNIST [33] and 28×28 MNIST dataset [34]. We consider a simple MLNN with two hidden layers. ReLU activation function and softmax cross-entropy loss function is used. Each layer except the output layer is batch normalized.

Table 1. Details of the simulation - MLNN.

	8×8 MNIST	28×28 MNIST	Wine quality	CASP
Task	Classification	Classification	Regression	Regression
Input	8×8	28×28	11	9
MLNN structure	64-20-10-10	784-100-50-10	11-10-4-1	9-10-6-1
Parameters (d)	1,620	84,060	169	173
Train set	1,198	55,000	3,918	36,584
Test set	599	10,000	980	9,146
Classes/output	10	10	1	1
Momentum (μ)	0.8	0.85	0.95	0.95
Batch size (b)	64	64/128	32/64	64/128
Memory (m)	4	4	4	4

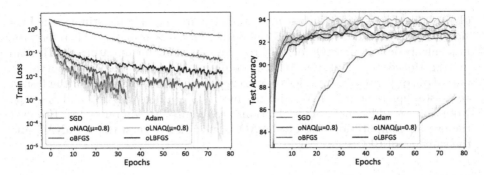

Fig. 3. Comparison of train loss and test accuracy versus number of epochs required for convergence of 8×8 MNIST data with a maximum of 80 epochs.

Results on 8×8 MNIST Dataset: We evaluate the performance of oNAQ and oLNAQ on a reduced version of the MNIST dataset in which each sample is an 8×8 image representing a handwritten digit [33]. Figure 3 shows the number of epochs required to converge to a train loss of $<10^{-3}$ and its corresponding test accuracy for a batch size $b = 64$. The maximum number of epochs is set to 80. As seen from the figure, it is clear that oNAQ and oLNAQ require fewer epochs compared to oBFGS, oLBFGS, Adam and SGD. In terms of computation time, o(L)BFGS and o(L)NAQ require longer time compared to the first order methods. This is due to the Hessian computation and twice gradient calculation. Further, the oBFGS and oNAQ per iteration time difference compared to first order methods is much larger than that of the limited memory algorithms with memory $m = 4$. This can be seen from Fig. 4 which shows the comparison of train loss and test accuracy versus time for 80 epochs. It can be observed that for the same time, the second order methods perform significantly better compared to the first order methods, thus confirming that the extra time taken by the second order methods does not adversely affect its performance. Thus, in the subsequent sections we compare the train loss and test accuracy versus time to evaluate the performance of the proposed method.

Results on 28×28 MNIST Dataset: Next, we evaluate the performance of the proposed algorithm on the standard 28×28 pixel MNIST dataset [34]. Due to system constraints and large number of parameters, we illustrate the performance of only the limited memory methods. Figure 5 shows the results of oLNAQ on the 28×28 MNIST dataset for batch size $b = 64$ and $b = 128$. The results indicate that oLNAQ clearly outperforms oLBFGS and SGD for even small batch sizes. On comparing with Adam, oLNAQ is in close competition with Adam for small batch sizes such as $b = 64$ and performs better for larger batch sizes such as $b = 128$.

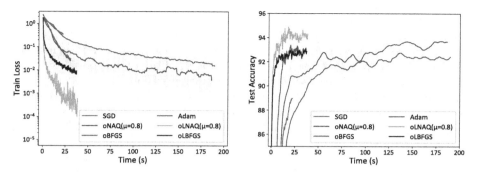

Fig. 4. Comparison of train loss and test accuracy over time on 8×8 MNIST (80 epochs).

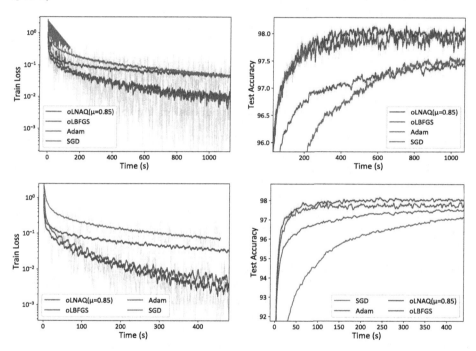

Fig. 5. Results on 28×28 MNIST for $b = 64$ (top) and $b = 128$ (bottom).

4.2   Convolution Neural Network - Classification Task

We study the performance of the proposed algorithm on a simple convolution neural network (CNN) with two convolution layers followed by a fully connected layer. We use sigmoid activation functions and softmax cross-entropy error function. We evaluate the performance of oNAQ using the 8×8 MNIST dataset with a batch size of 64 and $\mu = 0.8$ and number of parameters $d = 778$. The

CNN architecture comprises of two convolution layers of 3 and 5 5×5 filters respectively, each followed by 2×2 max pooling layer with stride 2. The convolution layers are followed by a fully connected layer with 10 hidden neurons. Figure 6 shows the CNN results of 8×8 MNIST. Calculation of the gradient twice per iteration increases the time per iteration when compared to the first order methods. However this is compensated well since the overall performance of the algorithm is much better compared to Adam and SGD. Also the number of epochs required to converge to low error and high accuracies is much lesser than the other algorithms. In other words, the same accuracy or error can be achieved with lesser amount of training data. Further, we evaluate the performance of oLNAQ using the 28×28 MNIST dataset with batch size $b = 128, m = 4$ and $d = 260,068$. The CNN architecture is similar to that as described above except that the fully connected layer has 100 hidden neurons. Figure 7 shows the results of oLNAQ on the simple CNN. The CNN results show similar performance as that of the results on multi-layer neural network where oLNAQ outperforms SGD and oBFGS. Comparing with Adam, oLNAQ is much faster in the first few epochs and becomes closely competitive to Adam as the number of epochs increases.

4.3   Multi-layer Neural Network - Regression Problem

We further extend to study the performance of the proposed stochastic methods on regression problems. For this task, we choose two benchmark datasets - prediction of white wine quality [31] and CASP [32] dataset. We evaluate the performance of oNAQ and oLNAQ on multi-layer neural network as shown in Table 1. Sigmoid activation function and mean squared error (MSE) function is used. Each layer except the output layer is batch normalized. Both datasets were z-normalized to have zero mean and unit variance.

Results on Wine Quality Dataset. We evaluate the performance of oNAQ and oLNAQ on the Wine Quality [31] dataset to predict the quality of the white wine on a scale of 3 to 9 based on 11 physiochemical test values. We split the dataset in 80–20% for train and test set. For the regression problems, oNAQ with smaller values of momemtum $\mu = 0.8$ and $\mu = 0.85$ show similar performance as that of oBFGS. Larger values of momentum resulted in better performance. Hence we choose a value of $\mu = 0.95$ which shows faster convergence compared to the other methods. Further comparing the performance for different batch sizes, we observe that for smaller batch sizes such as $b = 32$, oNAQ is close in performance with Adam and oLNAQ is initially fast and gradually becomes close to Adam. For bigger batch sizes such as $b = 64$, oNAQ and oLNAQ are faster in convergence initially. Over time, oLNAQ continues to result in lower error while oNAQ gradually becomes close to Adam. Figure 8 shows the root mean squared error (RMSE) versus time for batch sizes $b = 32$ and $b = 64$.

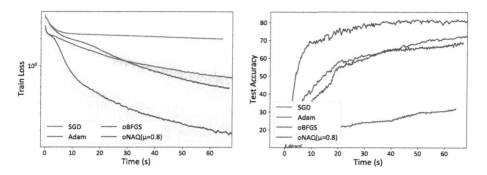

Fig. 6. Convolution Neural Network results on 8×8 MNIST with $b = 64$.

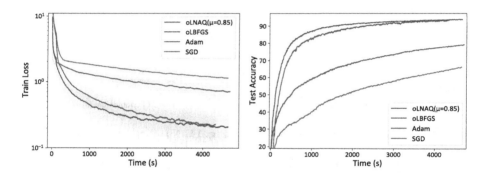

Fig. 7. CNN results on 28×28 MNIST with $b = 128$.

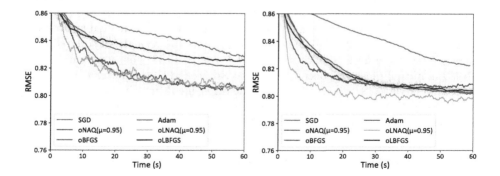

Fig. 8. Results of Wine Quality Dataset for $b = 32$ (left) and $b = 64$ (right).

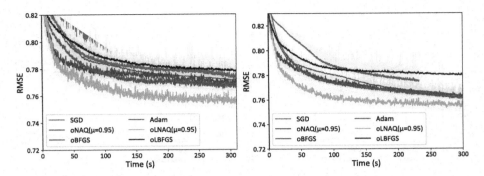

Fig. 9. Results of CASP Dataset for batch size $b = 64$ (left) and $b = 128$ (right).

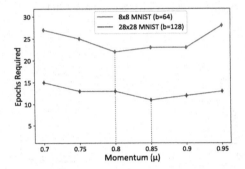

Fig. 10. No. of epochs required to converge for different values of μ with $m = 4$ for oLNAQ classification problems.

Fig. 11. No. of epochs required to converge for different values of μ with $m = 4$ for oLNAQ regression problems.

Results on CASP Dataset. The next regression problem under consideration is the CASP (Critical Assessment of protein Structure Prediction) dataset from [32]. It gives the physicochemical properties of protein tertiary structure. We split the dataset in 80–20% for train and test set. Similar to the wine quality problem, a momentum of $\mu = 0.95$ was fixed. Figure 9 shows the root mean squared error (RMSE) versus time for batch sizes $b = 64$ and $b = 128$. For both batch sizes, oNAQ in initially fast and becomes close to Adam and shows better performance compared to oBFGS and oLBFGS. On the other hand, we observe that oLNAQ consistently shows decrease in error and outperforms the other algorithms for both batch sizes.

4.4 Discussions on Choice of Parameters

The momentum term μ is a hyperparameter with a value in the range $0 < \mu < 1$ and is usually chosen closer to 1 [24,35]. The performance for different values of the momentum term have been studied for all the four problem sets in this paper.

Table 2. Summary of computational cost and storage.

	Algorithm	Computational cost	Storage
Full batch	BFGS	$nd + d^2 + \zeta nd$	d^2
	NAQ	$2nd + d^2 + \zeta nd$	d^2
	LBFGS	$nd + 4md + 2d + \zeta nd$	$2md$
	LNAQ	$2nd + 4md + 2d + \zeta nd$	$2md$
Online	oBFGS	$2bd + d^2$	d^2
	oNAQ	$2bd + d^2$	d^2
	oLBFGS	$2bd + 6md$	$2md$
	oLNAQ	$2bd + 6md$	$2md$

Figure 10 and Fig. 11 show the number of epochs required for convergence for different values of μ for the classification and regression datasets respectively. For the limited memory schemes, a memory size of $m = 4$ showed optimum results for all the four problem datasets with different batch sizes. Larger memory sizes also show good performance. However considering computational efficiency, memory size is usually maintained smaller than the batch size. Since the computation cost is $2bd + 6md$, if $b \approx m$ the computation cost would increase to $8bd$. Hence a smaller memory is desired. Memory sizes less than $m = 4$ does not perform well for small batch sizes and hence $m = 4$ was chosen.

4.5 Computation and Storage Cost

The summary of the computational cost and storage for full batch and stochastic (online) methods are illustrated in Table 2. The cost of function and gradient evaluations can be considered to be nd, where n is the number of training samples involved and d is the number of parameters. The Nesterov's Accelerated quasi-Newton (NAQ) method computes the gradient twice per iteration compared to the BFGS quasi-Newton method which computes the gradient only once per iteration. Thus NAQ has an additional nd computation cost. In both BFGS and NAQ algorithms, the step length is determined by line search methods which involves ζ function evaluations until the search condition is satisfied. In the limited memory forms the Hessian update is approximated using the two-loop recursion scheme, which requires $4md + 2d$ multiplications. In the stochastic setting, both oBFGS and oNAQ compute the gradient twice per iteration, making the computational cost the same in both. Both methods do not use line search and due to smaller number of training samples (minibatch) in each iteration, the computational cost is smaller compared to full batch. Further, in stochastic limited memory methods, an additional $2md$ evaluations are required to compute the search direction as given (14). In stochastic methods the computational complexity is reduced significantly due to smaller batch sizes ($b < n$).

5   Conclusion

In this paper we have introduced a stochastic quasi-Newton method with Nesterov's accelerated gradient. The proposed algorithm is shown to be efficient compared to the state of the art algorithms such Adam and classical quasi-Newton methods. From the results presented above, we can conclude that the proposed o(L)NAQ methods clearly outperforms the conventional o(L)BFGS methods with both having the same computation and storage costs. However the computation time taken by oBFGS and oNAQ are much higher compared to the first order methods due to Hessian computation. On the other hand, we observe that the per iteration computation of Adam, oLBFGS and oLNAQ are comparable. By tuning the momentum parameter μ, oLNAQ is seen to perform better and faster compared to Adam. Hence we can conclude that with an appropriate value of μ, oLNAQ can achieve better results. Further, the limited memory form of the proposed algorithm can efficiently reduce the memory requirements and computational cost while incorporating second order curvature information. Another observation is that the proposed oNAQ and oLNAQ methods significantly accelerates the training especially in the first few epochs when compared to both, first order Adam and second order o(L)BFGS method. Several studies propose pretrained models. oNAQ and oLNAQ can possibly be suitable for pretraining. Also, the computational speeds of oNAQ could be improved further by approximations which we leave for future work. Further studying the performance of the proposed algorithm on bigger problem sets, including that of convex problems and on popular NN architectures such as AlexNet, LeNet and ResNet could test the limits of the algorithm. Furthermore, theoretical analysis of the convergence properties of the proposed algorithms will also be studied in future works.

References

1. Haykin, S.: Neural Networks and Learning Machines, 3rd edn. Pearson Prentice Hall, Upper Saddle River (2009)
2. Bottou, L., Cun, Y.L.: Large scale online learning. In: Advances in Neural Information Processing Systems, pp. 217–224 (2004)
3. Bottou, L.: Large-scale machine learning with stochastic gradient descent. In: Lechevallier, Y., Saporta, G. (eds.) Proceedings of COMPSTAT' 2010. Physica-Verlag HD (2010). https://doi.org/10.1007/978-3-7908-2604-3_16
4. Robbins, H., Monro, S.: A stochastic approximation method. Ann. Math. Stat. **22**, 400–407 (1951)
5. Peng, X., Li, L., Wang, F.Y.: Accelerating minibatch stochastic gradient descent using typicality sampling. arXiv preprint arXiv:1903.04192 (2019)
6. Johnson, R., Zhang, T.: Accelerating stochastic gradient descent using predictive variance reduction. In: Advances in Neural Information Processing Systems, pp. 315–323 (2013)
7. Duchi, J., Hazan, E., Singer, Y.: Adaptive subgradient methods for online learning and stochastic optimization. J. Mach. Learn. Res. **12**(Jul), 2121–2159 (2011)

8. Tieleman, T., Hinton, G.: Lecture 6.5-RMSprop, Coursera: neural networks for machine learning. University of Toronto, Technical Report (2012)
9. Kingma, D.P., Ba, J.: Adam: a method for stochastic optimization. arXiv preprint arXiv:1412.6980 (2014)
10. Martens, J.: Deep learning via Hessian-free optimization. ICML **27**, 735–742 (2010)
11. Roosta-Khorasani, F., Mahoney, M.W.: Sub-sampled newton methods I: globally convergent algorithms. arXiv preprint arXiv:1601.04737 (2016)
12. Dennis Jr., J.E., Moré, J.J.: Quasi-Newton methods, motivation and theory. SIAM Rev. **19**(1), 46–89 (1977)
13. Schraudolph, N.N., Yu, J., Günter, S.: A stochastic quasi-Newton method for online convex optimization. In: Artificial Intelligence and Statistics, pp. 436–443 (2007)
14. Mokhtari, A., Ribeiro, A.: RES: regularized stochastic BFGS algorithm. IEEE Trans. Signal Process. **62**(23), 6089–6104 (2014)
15. Mokhtari, A., Ribeiro, A.: Global convergence of online limited memory BFGS. J. Mach. Learn. Res. **16**(1), 3151–3181 (2015)
16. Byrd, R.H., Hansen, S.L., Nocedal, J., Singer, Y.: A stochastic quasi-Newton method for large-scale optimization. SIAM J. Optim. **26**(2), 1008–1031 (2016)
17. Wang, X., Ma, S., Goldfarb, D., Liu, W.: Stochastic quasi-Newton methods for nonconvex stochastic optimization. SIAM J. Optim. **27**(2), 927–956 (2017)
18. Li, Y., Liu, H.: Implementation of stochastic quasi-Newton's method in PyTorch. arXiv preprint arXiv:1805.02338 (2018)
19. Lucchi, A., McWilliams, B., Hofmann, T.: A variance reduced stochastic Newton method. arXiv preprint arXiv:1503.08316 (2015)
20. Moritz, P., Nishihara, R., Jordan, M.: A linearly-convergent stochastic l-BFGS algorithm. In: Artificial Intelligence and Statistics, pp. 249–258 (2016)
21. Bollapragada, R., Mudigere, D., Nocedal, J., Shi, H.J.M., Tang, P.T.P.: A progressive batching l-BFGS method for machine learning. arXiv preprint arXiv:1802.05374 (2018)
22. Byrd, R.H., Chin, G.M., Neveitt, W., Nocedal, J.: On the use of stochastic Hessian information in optimization methods for machine learning. SIAM J. Optim. **21**(3), 977–995 (2011)
23. Gower, R., Goldfarb, D., Richtárik, P.: Stochastic block BFGS: squeezing more curvature out of data. In: International Conference on Machine Learning, pp. 1869–1878 (2016)
24. Ninomiya, H.: A novel quasi-Newton-based optimization for neural network training incorporating Nesterov's accelerated gradient. Nonlinear Theory Appl. IEICE **8**(4), 289–301 (2017)
25. Mahboubi, S., Ninomiya, H.: A novel training algorithm based on limited-memory quasi-Newton method with Nesterov's accelerated gradient in neural networks and its application to highly-nonlinear modeling of microwave circuit. IARIA Int. J. Adv. Softw. **11**(3–4), 323–334 (2018)
26. Nocedal, J., Wright, S.J.: Numerical Optimization. Springer Series in Operations Research, 2nd edn. Springer, New York (2006). https://doi.org/10.1007/978-0-387-40065-5
27. Zhang, L.: A globally convergent BFGS method for nonconvex minimization without line searches. Optim. Methods Softw. **20**(6), 737–747 (2005)
28. Dai, Y.H.: Convergence properties of the BFGS algoritm. SIAM J. Optim. **13**(3), 693–701 (2002)

29. Indrapriyadarsini, S., Mahboubi, S., Ninomiya, H., Asai, H.: Implementation of a modified Nesterov's accelerated quasi-Newton method on Tensorflow. In: 2018 17th IEEE International Conference on Machine Learning and Applications (ICMLA), pp. 1147–1154. IEEE (2018)
30. Zinkevich, M.: Online convex programming and generalized infinitesimal gradient ascent. In: Proceedings of the 20th International Conference on Machine Learning (ICML 2003), pp. 928–936 (2003)
31. Cortez, P., Cerdeira, A., Almeida, F., Matos, T., Reis, J.: Modeling wine preferences by data mining from physicochemical properties. Decis. Support Syst. **47**(4), 547–553 (2009). https://archive.ics.uci.edu/ml/datasets/wine+quality
32. Rana, P.: Physicochemical properties of protein tertiary structure data set. UCI Machine Learning Repository (2013). https://archive.ics.uci.edu/ml/datasets/Physicochemical+Properties+of+Protein+Tertiary+Structure
33. Alpaydin, E., Kaynak, C.: Optical recognition of handwritten digits data set. UCI Machine Learning Repository (1998). https://archive.ics.uci.edu/ml/datasets/optical+recognition+of+handwritten+digits
34. LeCun, Y., Cortes, C., Burges, C.: MNIST handwritten digit database. AT&T Labs. http://yann.lecun.com/exdb/mnist (2010)
35. Sutskever, I., Martens, J., Dahl, G.E., Hinton, G.E.: On the importance of initialization and momentum in deep learning. In: ICML, vol. 28, no. 3, pp. 1139–1147 (2013)

Correction to: Heavy-Tailed Kernels Reveal a Finer Cluster Structure in t-SNE Visualisations

Dmitry Kobak, George Linderman, Stefan Steinerberger,
Yuval Kluger, and Philipp Berens

Correction to:
**Chapter "Heavy-Tailed Kernels Reveal a Finer Cluster
Structure in t-SNE Visualisations" in: U. Brefeld et al. (Eds.):**
Machine Learning and Knowledge Discovery in Databases,
LNAI 11906, https://doi.org/10.1007/978-3-030-46150-8_8

The chapter was inadvertently published without the supplementary file. The supplementary file and its ESM Hint have been added to the chapter.

The updated version of this chapter can be found at
https://doi.org/10.1007/978-3-030-46150-8_8

Author Index

Printed in the United States
By Bookmasters